WEATHER
(U. S. Weather Bureau Forecast)
Eastern Pennsylvania: Mostly Cloudy And Mild Tuesday Followed By Rain West Portion In Late Afternoon And Most Of Area At Night; Showers Wednesday Morning Followed By Clearing And Colder.

Intelligencer Journal.

The Leading Newspaper in the Garden Spot of America, Home Owned for Home Folks Since 1794

Y0-BNC-827

TONIGHT
And Every Night
Monday Through Friday*
INTELL RADIO EDITIONS
6:15 P. M. and 11:10 P. M. ON WGAL (1490)
* SUNDAYS 11:10 P. M. ONLY

154th Year.—No. 127. | Lancaster City Zone Population, Official Figures of Audit Bureau of Circulations 112,897 | LANCASTER, PA., TUESDAY MORNING, NOVEMBER 11, 1947. | CITY | TWENTY-TWO PAGES. 25c PER WEEK—5c Per Copy

PLAN $2,250,000 GENERAL HOSPITAL

Record $2,756,400 In Yule Savings To Be Distributed Here

Total To Be Given Depositors By Dec. 1 Exceeds 1946 Sum By Over Half Million; More Than 38,000 Depositors In 33 Banks

Christmas savings checks totalling more than $2,756,400 will be mailed between Thanksgiving and December 1 to approximately 38,184 depositors in Lancaster city and county, according to announcements made Monday by bank officials. This will be the largest sum ever distributed in this form of savings since the plan was put into effect many years ago.

The total exceeded by about $578,039 the fund last year when the total distribution was in the vicinity of $2,178,361, then a record high. The total of 38,184 depositors this year is about 3,920 in excess of the 34,264 depositors of 1946.

The size of the average check this year will also show an increase over preceding years, bank officials pointed out. This year the average per depositor is $72.18, compared with the average of $63.57 of 1946.

Nationally, the amount to be distributed runs close to $747,000,000 with about 9,500,000 Christmas Club members to share in the distribution. The total distribution is 17.6 per cent ahead of last year and represents an all-time high for the 37 years of Christmas Club operation.

In a recent nation-wide survey of the uses to which the funds will be put by the recipients, it was indicated that Christmas purchases will claim 38 per cent of the savings, while permanent savings will be increased by 30 per cent of the total of $747,000,000. Insurance premiums will claim 8 per cent of the savings, debt retirement 3 per cent, year-end bills 11 per cent, taxes 7 per

Turn To Page 8 For More Of SAVINGS

U. S. AND SOVIET AGREE ON PLAN FOR PALESTINE

America Accepts Russian Compromise At UN; British Position Doubtful

Lake Success — (AP) — The United States and Russia, with a rare show of unity, agreed late Monday on a Soviet compromise plan for enforcement of the proposed partition of Palestine.

The plan was sent on immediately to the United Nations Assembly's subcommittee considering proposals for cutting up the Holy Land into sovereign Arab and Jewish countries.

SEES EARLY VOTE

Dr. Herbert V. Evatt of Australia, chairman of the Assembly's 57-nation Special Palestine Committee, predicted a vote would be taken on the partition plan within four days.

British sources received the announcement of U. S.-Soviet agreement on the new plan without comment except to say Britain's position had been stated by Colonial Secretary Arthur Creech-Jones when he told the full Palestine Committee Sept. 26:

"If the Assembly should recommend a policy which is not acceptable to the Jews and Arabs, the United Kingdom government would not feel able to implement it."

A spokesman for the Jewish Agency for Palestine said "We are pleased" over the U. S.-Soviet agreement and "believe" it will assure a two-thirds majority vote in the Assembly."

Arab representatives had no immediate comment.

The new plan calls for termination of the British mandate over Palestine May 1, 1948, and the creation of independent Arab and Jewish nations not later than July 1, 1948.

Russia previously had proposed termination of the mandate Jan. 1, while the U. S. had specified a date not later than July 1.

Takes Stand

Howard Hughes (above), Hollywood airplane and movie man, listens to a question while testifying before the Senate War Investigating committee in Washington.

HUGHES CLAIMS GENERAL SOUGHT $200,000 LOAN

Millionaire Testifies Meyers Was Negotiating Plane Contract At Time

Washington —(AP)— Millionaire planemaker Howard Hughes said Monday Maj. Gen. Bennett E. Meyers sought unsuccessfully to get Hughes to lend him $200,000 for a $10,000,000 bond-buying deal at a time when the general was negotiating a wartime contract with him.

Further Hughes told Senators on the War Investigating Committee, Meyers wanted Hughes to guarantee him against losing money on the bond transaction.

The plane builder denied previous testimony by Meyers that Hughes offered him, during the war, a postwar job in which he could name his own salary.

"I wasn't looking for a general manager after the war," Hughes told the committee, "because I had sense enough to know they'd be a dime a dozen then."

HAS MEYERS SNORTING

Meyers, seated nearby, snorted angrily as Hughes told his story. The planemaker said it was his recollection that the proposed bond deal involved the buying of $10,000,000 of Liberty Bonds on margin.

He said Meyers proposed that, with the $200,000 covering two margin points on the bond purchase, Hughes would guarantee to put up $100,000 for each additional point they declined.

Hughes said his refusal to lend the $200,000 "resulted in a complete breach of friendship between me and Benny Meyers" but that Meyers apparently approved a Hughes contract for photo reconnaissance planes anyhow.

Treasury officials said Hughes must have been using the term

Turn To Page 8 For More Of HUGHES

AID COST FOR 19 MONTHS PUT AT $8 BILLIONS

Marshall Urges 'Risks' Upon Congress To Help 'Prostrate' Europe

Washington— (AP) —Secretary of State Marshall solemnly urged Congress Monday to take the "real risks" of helping "prostrate" Europe at a cost of $8,097,000,000 in the next 19 months — and more billions later.

Marshall told members of the Senate and House Foreign Affairs Committees the need "is real and it is urgent" for:

"Speedy" action on an emergency fund of $597,000,000 to enable France, Italy and Austria to "survive" through March 31.

Another $7,500,000,000 for the following 15 months to start a "world recovery program" in 16 Western European nations. Over four years the cost might soar to $16,000,000,000 or $20,000,000,000, he said.

He spoke just a week before Congress meets in a special session to tackle European aid and domestic inflation. Some key members of the Senate and House Committees quickly chorused a measure of approval of the general ideas Marshall offered. But they said they want all the facts.

Rep. Eaton (R-NJ), chairman of the House Foreign Affairs Committee, told reporters that plans are to introduce an emergency bill next Monday and have it ready for the House by Wednesday.

"We hope to get it to the floor the middle of next week, but we can't guarantee that," he said.

Marshall made it clear that only opposition can be expected from Russia, even though the program "menaces no one," and "pursues no sinister purpose."

He said:

"We can act for our own good

Turn To Page 8 For More Of AID

Flag From Brother's Coffin

Willis Bauman, brother of Pfc. Leroy Bauman, who was killed in action in Europe, accepts the flag from his brother's coffin as last rites for the war hero were held Monday in Gettysburg National Cemetery. Presentation of the flag was made by a technical sergeant of the U. S. Army Ground Forces, which was in charge of the ceremony. Left of Bauman is another brother, Elam. Pfc. Bauman was the son of Mr. and Mrs. Isaac Bauman, Reinholds R1, formerly of Martindale.

TO ASK PUBLIC FOR $1,500,000 IN MAY DRIVE

Construction Of New Lancaster General Hospital To Begin In Spring

Work on the construction of new hospital facilities at the Lancaster General Hospital, will be started next Spring and will cost an estimated $2,250,000, it was revealed by John Carter, president of the Board of Directors, following a meeting held Monday night.

The decision to go ahead with the construction was contained in an announcement that a campaign will be conducted next May to raise $1,500,000, the sum necessary for building needs and debt reduction.

Carter, in announcing the campaign said:

"For a number of months the Board of Directors of the Lancaster General Hospital has been pushing forward plans for expansion of hospital facilities.

"These plans are now sufficiently advanced to show that the total cost of the new building program will be $2,250,000.

"Building funds now available approximate $1,000,000 leaving $1,250,000 still to be raised for building needs.

"In addition to this $1,250,000 the hospital needs $160,000 to retire the outstanding debt which is due in 1948, $60,000 for charity work, and $30,000 for maintenance and replacement of equipment, bringing the total sum needed to one and one-half million dollars.

"It was the considered judgment of the Board that the program adopted tonight is the most economic way for the community to meet its hospital needs immediately and in the future."

WAR POSTPONED ACTION

The building fund of $1,000,000 now available was gathered in a

Turn To Page 8 For More Of HOSPITAL

CASH DONATIONS FOR 'TRAIN' FOODS NEAR $5,000 MARK

Drive To Furnish Loaded Cars For Friendship Train In Home Stretch

As Lancaster's drive to provide foodstuffs for the "Friendship Train" started down the home stretch, cash donations started to keep pace with contributions of wheat, flour, sugar, dried beans and peas and evaporated milk.

With shipments of food being centralized at downtown warehouses for the start of packing on Wednesday, Roy M. Pleam, treasurer of the local drive, announced that $4,464 had been sent in by individuals and church and civic groups by Monday evening.

This total was boosted considerably by the persons who stopped in at the downtown headquarters on the first floor at 8 W. King St. On Monday a total of $582.37 was received by volunteer workers staffing the downtown agency. This amount was four times greater than collections on any previous day.

"The treasurer's report and the comments of committee chairmen in county boroughs and towns are indications of how things are starting to snow ball as we enter the final stages of the drive, but we must continue our all-out efforts during the next two days in order to make a good showing here," was the comment of Clair R. McCollough, local chairman of the "Friendship Train" committee.

He stressed that actual totals of contributions in churches this past Sunday were still unknown and that much depended on the response from religious organizations and from the various schools in the county.

SCHOOL CHILDREN ACTIVE

School children in all sections of the county arrived at large high schools and one-room schools bear-

Turn To Page 8 For More Of TRAIN

UAW Calls For Non-Red Pledges; Reuther Favored

Atlantic City, N. J.—(AP)—President Walter Reuther of the CIO United Auto Workers was endorsed for another term by CIO President Philip Murray Monday and the union convention then backed Reuther on a key issue of signing non-Communist affidavits.

The delegates, by at least a two to one margin on a standing vote, decided to direct all national UAW officers to sign the affidavits so that the union can carry bargaining and unfair labor cases to the National Labor Relations Board under the Taft-Hartley Act.

Murray's hearty endorsement virtually assured Reuther of no major opposition for the presidency. Combined with the convention floor victory, it boosted

Turn To Page 8 For More Of UAW

Truman Reports Greek Military Picture Darker

Washington—(AP)—President Truman said Monday that American aid has kept Greece "still free," but that the overall military picture has darkened because of support thrown to Communist-led guerrillas by Greece's northern neighbors.

In his first report to Congress on the $400,000,000 Greek-Turkish aid program, Mr. Truman made these points:

1. There are no U.S. combat troops in Greece.

2. To restore order, "reliance must be placed" on creation of a United Nations Commission "which can effectively seal the Greek border against assistance to the guerrillas from Greece's northern neighbors" — Yugosla-

Turn To Page 8 For More Of TRUMAN

2 MORE COUNTIANS LAID TO REST IN WAR HERO GRAVES

Pfc. Leroy Bauman, Pfc. Earl Hable Interred With Military Rites

Military rites for two more Lancaster county war dead were held Monday in Lancaster and Gettysburg, with local veterans organizations paying final tribute to two heroes.

Laid to rest were Pfc. Leroy Bauman, son of Mr. and Mrs. Isaac Bauman, Reinholds R1, formerly of Martindale, and Pfc. Earl "Pete" Hable, son of Mr. and Mrs. Earl Hable, 617 S. Lime St.

Pfc. Bauman was among the three returned war dead buried with full military honors at 3 p. m. Monday at Gettysburg National Cemetery. The dead were escorted to the cemetery by an hour guard of soldiers and separate services were held at each graveside, including prayers by Gettysburg pastors, firing of a final salute and blowing of taps.

FAMILIES GET FLAGS

Flags which draped the coffins were presented to members of the heroes' families by servicemen in charge of the ceremonies. Isaac Bauman received the flag from his son's casket.

Officiating clergyman was the Rev. Floyd A. Carroll, pastor of the Gettysburg Methodist Church, and

Turn To Page 8 For More Of FUNERALS

NEW DEMOCRATIC SOCIETY PLANS TO RECRUIT IN PENNA.

Mrs. Horting On Board Of Group Headed By John S. Rice

Harrisburg—(AP)—The Democratic Society of Pennsylvania, a new organization quietly organized by Democratic leaders, laid plans Monday to carry an organization drive for members in all counties of Pennsylvania.

Chartered as a non-profit organization, the Society is headed by John S. Rice, of Gettysburg, unsuccessful candidate for Governor last year, with Philip Matthews, of Carlisle, acting as executive director.

"It was established to promote Democratic ideals and give the public a better idea of what the party stands for," explained Democratic State Chairman J. Warren Mickle. "It is assisting the Democratic State Committee."

He said the dues for membership are $10 annually and any registered Democrat is eligible to join, adding the funds will be used to disseminate "general information" about the Democratic party.

Asked if the Society was set up with a view to the crucial 1948 Presidential election campaign, Mickle said "it is a permanent organization, for 1948 and the years after that too."

NAME MRS. HORTING

In addition to Rice and Matthews, members of the board of directors include Mayor David Lawrence of Pittsburgh; U. S. Sen. Francis J. Myers, of Philadelphia; State Trea-

Turn To Page 8 For More Of DEMOCRATS

LOCAL PCA GROUP ORGANIZED MONDAY WITH 50 MEMBERS

Praise Liberal, Progressive Policies Of Henry Wallace At Meeting

A Lancaster County chapter of the Progressive Citizens of America was organized Monday night at a meeting held at the Hotel Brunswick during which the "liberal and progressive policies" of Henry Wallace, former vice-president and ex-Secretary of Commerce, were extolled to the 50 persons present.

The fledgling organization, which boasts of 60 members in the city and surrounding county towns, mapped out an elaborate plan of action and a vigorous drive for members.

MEMBERSHIP AIMS

Irwin Giffen, who presided at the meeting, highlighted the membership aims of the chapter with these words:

"If we can sign up 1,500 to 2,000 liberal Democrats we can swing the Democratic party in Lancaster county to progressive views. As far as the Republicans go, that is a different story, their preponderant registration raises a problem."

The local chapter, formed about a nucleus of seven, who joined the PCA at a recent mass meeting in Philadelphia, at which Wallace spoke, plans an organization locally which will reach down to ward levels.

TO ELECT OFFICERS

Local officers will be elected by

Turn To Page 8 For More Of PCA

"We Lead All The Rest" FARM CORNER

By The Farm Editor

GOVT. WOULD BUY LOW-PRODUCTIVE HENS FOR STORAGE

Offers Farmers Plan To Save 30,000,000 Bushels Of Grain

Washington —(AP)— The government Monday offered to buy up hens which don't lay eggs and put them into "deep freeze" for later use. The move is designed to save upwards of 30,000,000 bushels of grain for Europe in the next 11 months.

Simultaneously, Chairman Charles Luckman of the Citizens Food Committee called on the nation's milling industries to volunteer their help in the overall grain-saving program.

Luckman notified 23 major milling concerns that he will call them to Washington shortly and ask a "definite proposal" for the saving of grain. Originally he set Thursday as the day, but later postponed it until further notice to avoid conflict with an Agriculture Department meeting on farm conservation in which several of the millers will take part.

The government's offer to buy low-productive hens from farmers is expected to encourage poultry men to cull at least 40,000,000 more hens from their flocks by Jan. 1 than they would normally eliminate.

The hens will be killed, frozen and stored for resale to consumers, the armed services, and possible export markets next year when supplies of poultry

Turn To Page 17 For More Of FARM CORNER

Weather Calendar

COMPARATIVE TEMPERATURES

Station	High	Low
Water Works	52	29
Ephrata	53	39
Last Year (Ephrata)	66	36
Official High for Year, August 14	96	
Official Low for Year, Feb. 4	6	
Character of Day		Clear

SUN
Rises 6:43 a. m. Sets 4:52 p. m.

MOON
Sets 5:15 p. m. New Moon Nov. 12

STARS
Morning—Mars, Saturn.
Evening—Venus, Jupiter.

NEARBY FORECASTS
(U. S. Weather Bureau)
Maryland—Mostly cloudy and mild Tuesday with rain West portion in afternoon and in entire state Tuesday night; showers Wednesday morning followed by clearing and cooler in afternoon.
Delaware and New Jersey—Cloudy and mild Tuesday; rain and continued mild Tuesday night, showers Wednesday morning followed by clearing and cooler in afternoon and night.

Inspecting Food Donations At Manor Township School

A. Norman Ranck, supervising principal of the Manor Township schools, helps a number of township schoolboys arrange two tables full of food collected at the Hambrights Consolidated School for the "Friendship Train". The boys, left to right, are: Jerry Eckman, nine; Harry Kauffman, seven; Andy Funk, seven; Amos Funk, eight; Phil ip Barton, ten; and Donald Urey, twelve. (Intell Photo)

NEARLY 10,000 FAIL TO CAST BALLOT ON WAR MEMORIAL

Nearly 10,000 city and county residents who went to the polls last Tuesday sidestepped casting a ballot on the controversial $2,000,000 bond issue for a community center as a war memorial.

This estimate was made on the basis of the official count of the vote cast, which was completed Monday. The official figures will not be announced until the clerks have had time to check and tabulate the results.

Unofficial figures show the war memorial bond issue lost by a vote of 22,919 to 7,857.

George H. Carpenter defeated A. E. McCollough, Jr. for the minority county commissioner post by 609 votes.

WHACKY WANT-ADS

Whimsical Want-Ads occasionally pop up in the nation's newspapers providing unexpected mirth. Here's another one of a national collection:

Positively no more baptizing in my pasture. Twice in the last 2 months my gate has been left open by Christian people, and before I chase my heifers all over the country again, all the sinners can go to purgatory.

Many heifers leave the pastures of Lancaster county farms BUT they usually leave because a Lancaster Newspapers Want-Ad sold them.

Mr. Clyde Fellenbaum found it easy to sell a 4-day-old heifer for $30.00 through this Want-Ad:

HEIFER CALF, Pure Bred. Phone 175-J-12 Lititz.

For PROVEN RESULTS like this phone 5252 and ask for an Ad-Taker.

Today Is MEATLESS TUESDAY

Vicious Great Dane Takes Over Baggage Car On Crack PRR Train

St. Louis—(AP)—A huge Great Dane, apparently vicious from fright and hunger, ruled a baggage car on a Pennsylvania train all the way from Indianapolis to St. Louis Monday.

During the 240-mile trip, the black dog defied all attempts at baggage removal at four stops and was the reason for the train, the crack Jeffersonian, arriving here an hour and a half late.

When the dog was taken aboard at Richmond, Ind., the baggage handlers found the only available crate too small for the 115-pound animal. Instead its long leash was anchored under the crate.

BIG TERRITORY

The leash gave the dog quite a sphere of influence, as the baggagemen discovered at Indianapolis. The train was held up for 30 minutes there as the unwilling passenger then in an ugly mood, snapped and growled at efforts to unfie its leash. The dog was supposed to have gotten off at Indianapolis — but it didn't. Nor did any of the luggage in range of its leash.

Finally the baggagemen slammed the car door and said: "Let

Turn To Page 8 For More Of DOG

WEATHER
(U. S. Weather Bureau Forecast)
Eastern Pennsylvania—Cloudy And Somewhat Warmer With Occasional Light Rain Friday; Mostly Cloudy, Windy And Much Colder With Snow Flurries In Mountains Friday Night; Saturday Partly Cloudy, Colder And Rather Windy.

Intelligencer Journal.

The Leading Newspaper in the Garden Spot of America, Home Owned for Home Folks Since 1794

TONIGHT
And Every Night
Monday Through Friday*
INTELL RADIO EDITIONS
6:15 P. M. and 11:10 P. M. ON WGAL (1490)
* SUNDAYS 11:10 P. M. ONLY

154th Year.—No. 177. Lancaster City Zone Population, Official Figures of Audit Bureau of Circulations 112,897 LANCASTER, PA., FRIDAY MORNING, JANUARY 9, 1948. CITY THIRTY-SIX PAGES. 25c PER WEEK—5c Per Copy

TAFT WARNS OF "TOTALITARIANISM"

New St. Joseph's Hospital Plans Revealed

$96,615,000 Value Placed On Lancaster County Farm Lands

Rural Homes In Best Condition In History, With Most Needing Only Minor Repairs, Report Based On Bureau Of Census Surveys Indicates

Farm property in Lancaster County is now worth more than $96,615,000, and rural homes here and throughout the State are in the best condition in history, according to a report just released by the Tile Council of America.

Ninety per cent of farm dwellings in Pennsylvania an, the Northeastern states are in excellent condition or need only such minor repairs as painting or general maintenance, the report revealed. Only 73.3 per cent were in good repair in 1940. The report was based on Bureau of the Census surveys.

"The rise in farm incomes and property values since 1940 has been accompanied by a great increase in the number of rural homes equipped with such modern conveniences as electric lights, baths and showers and running water," said F. B. Ortman, chairman of the Council's residential construction committee.

Electricity, for instance, has gone into tens of thousands of rural dwellings in this state and others in the Northeastern area since 1940, Ortman noted. More than 85 per cent of such farm homes now have electric lights, in contrast to 63.9 per cent in 1940.

More than 64 per cent of rural dwellings in the Northeastern region today have running water, and 43.5 per cent have private baths. In 1940, 46.1 per cent had running water and only 29.5 per cent private baths.

LANCASTER COUNTY HIGHWAY DEATHS

1

Since Jan. 1, 1948

Same Date—1947—0

COUNTY GIRL, 16, DIES OF INJURIES AFTER AUTO CRASH

Violet Elaine Wenger First Traffic Accident Victim Of Year Here

Miss Violet Elaine Wenger, sixteen, daughter of Mr. and Mrs. H. Maurice Wenger, Old Philadelphia pike, died at 11:40 a. m. Thursday at the Lancaster General Hospital, where she was admitted on Sunday after the automobile in which she was a passenger was involved in a collision on "Death Highway" the Lincoln Highway, east.

The girl, a member of the junior class of the East Lampeter Township High School, was the first highway accident victim in Lancaster county this year. Death was caused by a fractured skull, Dr. C. P. Stahr, deputy coroner, said.

Violet Wenger

Miss Wenger was one of three teen-agers riding in an automobile operated by Donald Kautzman, seventeen, 817 N. Queen Street, according to State Police, who investigated. Kautzman also is a patient at the hospital. His condition was described as good Thursday night.

John E. Coulter, seventeen, Bird-in-Hand, a passenger in the same vehicle with Miss Wenger, was reported in a semi-conscious condition Thursday at the Lancaster General Hospital.

According to State Policeman Charles Simmons, who investigated the accident, the Kautzman vehicle was traveling west, four miles east of the city on Route 30, when it suddenly skidded on a patch of ice and slid into the east

Turn To Page 14 For More Of GIRL

"We Lead All The Rest"

FARM CORNER

By The Farm Editor

COUNTY WILL ENTER APPLES AND HOLSTEINS IN STATE FARM SHOW

County-wide "Garden Spot" entries of apples and Holstein dairy cattle are already assured for the Pennsylvania State Farm Show which opens a five-day exhibit at Harrisburg Monday morning.

In addition to exhibits by individuals, members of the Lancaster County Fruit Growers' Association are arranging a "Lancaster Association" display of apples, and members of the Lancaster County Holstein Breeders' Association have also entered a "County Herd" display in the state-wide competition.

Among the junior exhibits going to Harrisburg will be 40 head of baby beeves—20 Aberdeen Angus and 20 Herefords—and 18 pens of fat lambs, which will be shown by members of the Red Rose 4-H Club of Lancaster County.

Six members of the Lancaster County 4-H Holstein Dairy Club will combine their animals to make up a "Lancaster County Herd" display in the 4-H classes of dairy cattle.

A local chorus of 24 voices will participate in the rural talent festival to be held in the large arena of the Farm Show building Tuesday evening.

Officials again pointed out that exhibits in the general premium list will be transported to Harrisburg free of charge to county residents on Saturday. A truck will leave from the Lancaster postoffice building at 9 a. m., carrying show

Turn To Page 31 For More Of FARM CORNER

Weather Calendar

COMPARATIVE TEMPERATURES

Station	High	Low
Water Works	35	14
Ephrata	35	18
Last Year (Ephrata)	40	33
Official High for Year, January 5		38
Official Low for Year, January 8		18
Character of Day	Partly Cloudy	

SUN
Rises—7:26 a. m. Sets—4:56 p. m.

MOON
Sets—6:22 p. m. New Moon, Jan. 11

STARS
Morning—Mars, Jupiter, Saturn.
Evening—Venus.

NEARBY FORECASTS
(U. S. Weather Bureau)

Maryland: Cloudy and somewhat warmer with scattered light showers Friday; clearing windy and considerably colder except snow flurries in mountains Friday night; Saturday partly cloudy, colder and rather windy.

Delaware and New Jersey: Cloudy and somewhat warmer with occasional light rain Friday; clearing windy and considerably colder Friday night; Saturday partly cloudy colder and rather windy.

PROPOSE UNIT FOR CARE OF MENTALLY ILL

Campaign For Additional Funds To Precede Actual Construction

Plans for the future St. Joseph's Hospital were revealed here Thursday evening at the annual dinner meeting of the hospital's medical staff and advisory board.

The new unit is envisioned as an imposing nine-story structure, of which one important feature will be the provision for "scientific, humane and personal care of mentally ill patients."

In a description of the proposed structure, designed to face on Walnut Street, and continue along College Avenue to the present building, Samuel E. Dyke, chairman of the New Building Committee, told the combined meeting that in planning the new building special emphasis has been placed on clinics, physiotherapy, X-ray, mentally ill and contagious diseases.

The meeting also included the election of Advisory Board officers, of which Bernard M. Zimmerman was re-elected president, and a talk on "The Future of St. Joseph's Hospital" by the Most Rev. George L. Leech, D.D., J.C.D., Bishop of the Diocese of Harrisburg.

Dr. C. Howard Witmer, medical director of the hospital, was toastmaster at the annual affair and introduced Bishop Leech and Mr. Dyke as well as Mr. Zimmerman who discussed "Historical Aspects of the Hospital," and Dr. John L. Atlee, whose topic was "The Hospital and the Community."

It is unofficially believed that

Turn To Page 14 For More Of HOSPITAL

Architect's Drawing Of Proposed St. Joseph's Hospital

The future St. Joseph's Hospital is shown above in an architect's drawing. Facing on Walnut Street, the building is planned to continue along College Avenue (at left of picture) to the present building (far left) to which it will be connected by underground passages. The nine-story structure depicted above calls for exterior walls of face brick with stone trim, and its construction will make it fireproof and modern in every respect. Building may begin within two years.

TRUMAN PLANS LAMBASTED IN AIR ADDRESS

Declares President's Program Would Put Government In 'Santa Claus' Role

Taft Text On Page 26

Washington — (AP) — Senator Taft (R-Ohio) lambasted President Truman's program Thursday night as one which would put the federal government in the role of "Santa Claus" and lead to "national bankruptcy."

Everything that Mr. Truman proposed in his tate of the Union message of Wednesday is not bad, said Taft, but:

"Taken together, they add up to national bankruptcy.

"Taken together they will add up to a totalitarian state."

Taft, head of the Republican Policy Committee in the Senate and a candidate for the 1948 Republican Presidential nomination, gave his "reply to Truman" in a speech for the ABC network.

The speech was confined largely to domestic issues, and Taft struck particularly at Mr. Truman's proposal of a $40 income tax cut for each taxpayer and dependent, with the $3,200,000,000 revenue loss therefrom to be made up by boosting taxes on corporations.

Taft recalled that twice last year Mr. Truman vetoed tax cut bills and now, in an election year, has come forward with a proposal to lift income taxes from millions of people.

CHARGES POLITICS

"It looks to me like playing politics with your money," he said.

"In this picture the federal government comes forward again as Santa Calus himself, with a rich present for every special group in the United States. x x x If anyone has expressed a desire in a letter to Santa Claus, that desire is to be promptly fulfilled."

Taft criticized Mr. Truman for urging high corporation taxes at the same time he urged business to make a $50,000,000,000 expansion in the next few years.

"How," he asked, "does the President expect business to make this great investment of 50 billion dollars if taxes take away the profits and make it unprofitable for new money to go into business?"

ON RAISING STANDARDS

Of Mr. Truman's proposals for raising American standards over the next decade, Taft commented tartly:

"A ten-year Truman plan would leave about as much freedom in this country as Stalin's five-year plan has left in Russia."

He had sharp words, too, for the President's call for universal military training and his request for a national health program, saying:

"It (the President's message) asks again the power to draft a million two hundred thousand boys a year out of their homes and schools and trades and professions into military training.

SOCIALIZEL MEDICINE

"It asks again for power to socialize and nationalize medicine."

Of the $40 income tax cut plan of the President, Taft said it is

Turn To Page 14 For More Of TAFT

General Hospital's Need To Expand Supported By Survey

The Lancaster General Hospital is not large enough to serve adequately all who apply for care, in the opinion of 84 out of each 100 persons who have so far replied in the poll of public opinion regarding the hospital and its services. This was reported Thursday by John H. Carter, president of the hospital's board of directors, following the first analysis of returns from questionnaires mailed last week by a community relations committee of the board to several thousand city and county residents of the hospital's service area.

"These early results in the survey," said Carter, "indicate general public understanding of the fact that the hospital is seriously overcrowded. This has become a problem of primary concern for the board of trustees and the staff."

Pointing out that needed expansion of the hospital's facilities had been held up for four years, first by wartime building restrictions and then by shortages of labor and materials, Carter disclosed that in that short period admissions had gone up by 3,231 or 44 per cent and births had increased by 998 or 69 per cent.

"Faced with unprecedented demands for modern, specialized medical, surgical and nursing services available only in hospitals," Carter said, "we have placed extra beds in private rooms and in wards to expand patient capacity. Every sunporch in the hospital has been

Turn To Page 14 For More Of SURVEY

GUNS BLAZE IN PALESTINE FIGHT, 16 LIVES CLAIMED

Jerusalem —(AP)— Gunfire blazed across Jerusalem's ancient hills Thursday as bitter communal fighting elsewhere in the Holy Land claimed 16 lives—eight Jews, five Arabs, a British policeman and a Pole.

Thousands of bullets crashed and ricocheted into grey stone buildings and rocky hillsides in the confused three cornered fighting in southern Jerusalem among Arabs, Jews and British soldiers and police.

Despite the amount of ammunition expended — ammunition which sells for 48 cents a round in the black markets of the old

Turn To Page 14 For More Of PALESTINE

DRIVER CHARGED WITH ACCOSTING GIRL POSTS FORFEIT FOR HEARING

A twenty-nine-year-old Ephrata man was arrested by city police Thursday and charged with disorderly conduct after, police said, he attempted to pick up a seventeen-year-old city girl while driving an automobile Wednesday night.

The man, Harold Sensenig, posted a forfeit of $16.55 for a police court hearing before Alderman David F. Rose and was released.

Police said the man was traced by a license number clue furnished by the girl who, according to police, was molested by Sensenig as she was walking in the vicinity of Fulton and Franklin Streets around 7:30 p. m. Sensenig attempted to persuade her to enter the vehicle, police said, but she refused and notified police.

After questioning by city detectives the disorderly conduct charge was filed and Sensenig posted the forfeit for the hearing Friday (today).

WGAL IS GRANTED TELEVISION PERMIT FOR STATION HERE

Hope To Go On Air Late This Year Or Early Next Year

Washington —(AP)— The Federal Communications Commission Thursday announced a grant to WGAL, Inc., for a new commercial television station at Lancaster, Pa.

Clair R. McCollough, president of WGAL, Inc., said Thursday night that he is hopeful that the new television station will get on the air late in 1948 or early in 1949.

Preliminary commitments have been made for the necessary equipment, Mr. McCollough said.

Charge Board At Washington Boro Barred Public

Stanley Mason, a spokesman for a group of Washington Boro residents, said Thursday night that a delegation of residents, with a petition asking that the borough schools either be improved and modernized or closed and consolidated with the adjacent districts of either Columbia, Millersville or Manor township, was denied entrance to a meeting of the Washington Boro School Board Wednesday night.

The petition bearing 225 signatures or approximately two-thirds of the taxpayers in Washington Boro, was drafted recently on the advice of Dr. A. P. Mylin, county superintendent of schools, Mason said. The community has two schools, primary and secondary.

The president of the board, J. S. Wertz, said Thursday although the regular date for the meeting is the first Wednesday of the month, the Wednesday session, held at his home, was an "executive" meeting closed to the public, and called to decide on a new tax collector to succeed the late Robert Irwin. No decision was reached on filling the office, although he admitted that other business was transacted.

At present, the residents of the community, according to Mason, are unable to state what steps they will next take. Mason said that according to Dr. Mylin, the petition drawn up by the citizens must

Turn To Page 14 For More Of WASHINGTON BORO

85,000-Pound Explosives Shipment Seized On Farm

Wall Township, N. J. — (AP) — A shipment of 85,000 pounds of explosives was seized late Thursday on a farm here by State Police and later a truck arriving from the Seneca Government War Surplus Depot at Romulus, N. Y., was seized near a warehouse in Asbury Park.

The explosives taken on the farm, Monmouth County Prosecutor J. Victor Carton said, came from the depot at Romulus and he added he was "fairly certain" they were "tied up with" a shipment of 77 crates containing 65,000 pounds of TNT which was seized Saturday on an American export line pier in Jersey City.

The truck was taken near a warehouse Carton said was owned by Charles Lowy of Asbury Park, who, he said, also owned the farm.

Carton said the explosives were army surplus demolition blocks which had been sold at the government surplus depot in Romulus, N. Y., and were consigned to the Foundry Associates, Inc., 41 East 42nd St., New York City.

He identified two of the men arrested as Charles Lowy of Asbury Park, owner of the farm and of a local trucking company, and Harry

Turn To Page 6 For More Of EXPLOSIVES

2 QUARRYVILLE R1 MEN SENTENCED IN MD. ROBBERY CASE

Two twenty-three-year-old Quarryville R1 men were sentenced to five years in the Maryland State Reformatory for Males Thursday as the result of an armed holdup of a Conowingo, Md., taproom proprietor which netted the pair $94 in cash December 3.

The men, Gerald Hake and Robert Rush, were sentenced in the Cecil County Circuit Court, Elkton, Md., Thursday, by Judge Floyd D. Kintner, after they admitted the holdup.

Police said the pair was taken into custody three days after they stole an automobile in Quarryville, owned by John Armstrong, New Providence R1, drove to the

Turn To Page 14 For More Of QUARRYVILLE

CTC BUS DRIVER PROSECUTED BY POLICE

A driver for the Conestoga Transportation Co. was among five motorists prosecuted by city police for motor code violations Thursday.

The bus driver, Frank Wright, thirty-five, 518 E. Fulton St., was charged with reckless driving as the result of an accident at Race and Marietta Avenues at 4:20 p. m. Wednesday. Police said Wright driving a Landisville bus of the CTC, attempted to overtake an automobile driven East on Marietta Avenue. As he pulled abreast the auto, driven by H. Marie Wiley, fifty-three, 25 Spencer Ave., police said, the woman began to execute a left turn and the bus collided with the car.

Also prosecuted, police, were: William Dusel, 621 First St., charged with operating a motor vehicle without registration plates; Raymond F. Weaver, 216 S. West End Ave., ignoring a red traffic signal; Walter Posey, Lancaster R6, driving too fast for conditions; and Victor Groff, Jr., 436 Poplar St., ignoring a stop sign.

S. Lancaster School Bus Drivers To Hold Safety Clinic Monday

A safety conference for Southern Lancaster County School District school bus drivers—the first meeting of its kind ever held in this county—will be held at 7:30 p. m., Monday, in the library of the Southern Lancaster County Joint High School, Quarryville. V. L. Schreiber, principal of the school, who will serve as chairman, Thursday night extended an invitation to school bus drivers from other regions to attend.

Theme for the conference will be "Better and Safer Transportation for School Children." The session is sponsored by the divisions of consolidation and transportation, highway safety education and public service institute, of the State Department of Public Instruction. Also participating in the program will be the Lancaster Automobile Club and the Pennsylvania State Police.

The program will begin at 7:30 p. m. when registration for the bus drivers from the Southern Lancas-

Turn To Page 6 For More Of SAFETY

Florin Native, One Of Oldest Vets Of 28th Div., Dies In VA Hospital

Elmer Schlegelmilch, seventy-one-year-old veteran of World War I, died Thursday morning at the Veterans' Administration Hospital at Lebanon. Schlegelmilch, who had been undergoing treatment for years as a result of being gassed while in service, was a native of Florin.

The Lancaster countian, one of the oldest members of the famed 28th Division, served through World War I and saw active duty with the Division in the combat areas at the Argonne and Chateau Thierry. It was for service in the latter area that he was awarded the Distinguished Service Cross.

Schlegelmilch

Schlegelmilch enlisted in the National Guard in 1915 and went into active service with the division, serving as a first duty sergeant with Companies B and C, 109th Machine Gun Battalion. During his tour of duty his son, Frank, served as bugler in the same outfit. He was honorably discharged from service on May 5, 1919.

WED 50 YEARS

He underwent treatment in many service hospitals and just last November 14, he celebrated his golden wedding anniversary while a patient at the Butler, Pa., hos-

Turn To Page 14 For More Of VETERAN

Football Season Arrives As Practice Begins For City And County High Schools

Ephrata Has 80 For Opening; 35 Report At Lititz

Football material turned out some 115 strong at two county high schools — 80 at Ephrata and 35 at Lititz—for the opening of practice Monday. In addition, 90 other county gridders began drills in special training camps, 55 at Elizabethtown High's camp at Pine Grove Furnace and 35 at Columbia High's camp at French Creek.

Head coach George Male at Ephrata, reported, however, that his 80 varsity and jay-vee candidates would have to be cut because equipment is available for only 60 players. Eight lettermen were included in the huge turnout.

Light drills began at 9 a. m. The workout included calisthenics, kicking, passing, and signals practice. The afternoon session opened with more calisthenics and was followed by a dummy scrimmage

Although he lost 12 boys from last year's Conference of the Roses championship team, Male stated that in size he has a "bigger team than ever." He added that the team is much "bigger than usual." Supporting Male's claim to a big team are the Givler twins, Leon and Lloyd, both six feet, five inches tall. Leon is an end and Lloyd plays tackle.

Also back from last season are Guards Ken Royer and Les Hoover end Richard Wills, and backs Don Howett, Gerald Matt, and Robert Lesher. Male explained that one and a half hour practice sessions would be held daily in the morning and afternoon.

T-FORMATION FOR LITITZ

A new coach, Bernard Rider, was on hand to greet the Lititz gridders. The first thing he did was to announce to his boys that Lititz would use the T-formation this season, the first time in the school's history. Rider had three sets of backfields running plays from the T in the afternoon drill.

Rider said the reason he installed the T-formation was because Lititz has no heavy backs, but has plenty of fast backfield material. Mike Burcin assisted Rider in the opening days workouts. Assistants Earl Reist and Harry Zavacky were not on hand.

Calisthenics and light drills were held in the morning, with signal drills and the running of plays against a dummy line featuring the afternoon practice. Thirteen of the candidates are back from last year, including the hefty Frederick brothers, Earl and Harold, both of whom tip the scales over the 200-pound mark.

Others are: Hen Hershey, Dubs Haldeman, Glenn Roth, Roy Steif, Don Brenner, Gary Hanna, Harold Keppley, Gil Hess, John Steffy, Wendell Hower, and Richard Oberlin. Practices will be held twice daily.

CATHOLIC COACH MEETS GRIDDERS AT FIRST WORKOUT—Catholic High's coach Larry Berger, kneeling right front, talks with five of his football candidates at the first practice Monday on the Rossmere gridiron. Left to right around the coach are: Buck Hohenwarter, Moe Harnish, Fat Schleger, Phil Fittipaldi, and John Painter. (Intell Sports Photo.)

THROUGH THE TIRES IN AFTERNOON DRILL—After 60 boys took physical exams and received their equipment Monday morning at McCaskey High, Coach Woody Sponaugle sent the grid prospects through a light conditioning workout in the afternoon. Leading the way through the tires, above, is Halfback Jerry Wagner, one of the 14 Red and Black lettermen back this fall. (Intell Sports Photo.)

MEET THE COACHES—Coach Woody Sponaugle, getting out on the field to run his McCaskey High School football candidates through their first workout Monday, had an assistant, replete with moleskins, on hand to help him. You guessed it, it was none other than Woody's eight-year-old son, Woody, Jr., who spent a busy afternoon catching footballs for dad. (Intell Sports Photo)

60 At First McCaskey Drills; Catholic Gets 41 Candidates

More than 100 city high school boys turned out for the opening of football practice at McCaskey and Catholic Monday. Sixty reported to head coach Woody Sponaugle at McCaskey, and 41 others journeyed to chief mentor Larry Berger at Catholic. Thirty more are expected at McCaskey this Tuesday.

Physical examinations were taken and equipment was issued to the three-score McCaskey candidate Monday morning. In the afternoon, the gridders went through light limbering up drills.

Fourteen lettermen form the basis for the Tornado eleven, which, Sponaugle reported, "looks like one of the heaviest teams ever at McCaskey." He added that the boys "look in good shape."

Back from last year with letters are: Ed Heidig and Art Johnson, ends; Dick Sourwine, Dwight Kauffman and Merv Kreider, tackles; Russ Schelling and Bill Anderson, guards; Jim Smithgall and Sam Marshall, centers; and Jerry Wagner, Frank Millhouse, Jack Gunzenhauser, John Hohenadel, and George Myers, backs.

Sponaugle stated that he will use the single wing formation right and left this season. "In the last two seasons we've won 16 out of 18 games and averaged 27 points per game, so I'm not going to change for our nine games this season," Woody commented.

McCaskey will be competing in the new Central Pennsy Conference, and will be fighting for a league trophy and the Edward "Snaps" Emmanuel memorial trophy, also.

Individual fundamentals will be stressed the rest of this week, with no scrimmage. Drills will be held from 9:30 to 11 a. m. and from 2:30 to 4:30 p. m. daily. The squad will be divided later in this week, with Cliff Hartman taking charge of the jay-vees. Boyd Sponaugle will work with the linemen, and Woody will coach the backs and ends.

Out on the Rossmere gridiron, Berger, along with his assistants Russ Gilbert and Gus Muehleisen, took the Crusaders through preliminary loosening up exercises in preparation for heavier work. From calisthenics, the gridders will work into signal drills and blocking and tackling workouts.

Berger has 10 veterans back from last year's team — William Fittipaldi, John Painter, Charles Schleger, Buck Hohenwarter, Tom Floyd, Moe Harnish, James Burger, Gene Weiser, Gene Costarella, and Dick Leinaweaver. Last year's entire backfield is gone, and Gene Butz will not be able to play because of injuries sustained last season.

Although his team looks heavier, Berger said that he will have trouble filling the backfield. The Purple and Gold will use the single wing again this fall. Two promising backfield candidates are John Roeser and Rod O'Day from last year's jay-vee team.

Burger explained that he may switch Moe Harnish to the backfield. Other leading prospects up from the jay-vees are Tom Long, Tom Kingree, Harry Hutchinson, and Ken Wiegend. Next week the players will go into blocking and tackling with the dummies.

RONNIE STUART'S NO-HITTER GIVES GRANDVIEW FLAG

Ronnie Stuart, Grandview star mound performer, effectively settled the question of the regular season championship in the Manheim Twp. Midget League Monday evening as he toseed a no-hit, norun performance at Eden and led his mates to an 11-0 victory.

Friday evening Stuart limited Eden to 1 hit as Grandview copped the victory and deadlocked the race for first place, necessitating Monday evening's playoff.

Eden	ab	r	h	o	a	Grandview	ab	r	h	o	a
Char's 3b	1	0	0	1	1	Druc'd 1b	4	2	2	6	0
Leay'n 2b	1	0	0	0	2	Krick 2b	3	2	0	1	1
M'n p ss	2	0	0	0	5	Gerh't rf	3	2	1	0	0
J. S'e c p	2	0	0	1	0	Resh 3b	2	3	1	2	2
Wil'ms lf	2	0	0	0	0	Forrey c	3	1	3	5	0
Shull 1b	2	0	0	10	0	Stuart p	4	0	1	1	2
L'h ss p c	2	0	0	1	2	Wilson ss	3	0	0	0	1
M. S'e rf	2	0	0	1	0	Miller cf	2	0	0	0	0
B. M'y cf	2	0	0	1	0	Pfautz lf	3	1	3	0	0
Totals	16	0	0	15	10	Totals	27	11	11	15	6

GRANDVIEW	340 22	—11
EDEN	000 00	— 0

Errors—Leayman 2, Morgan, Forrey, Stuart. Three base hits—Resh, Forrey. Two base hit—Druckenbrod. Sacrifices—Krick, Forrey. Stolen bases—Stuart 2, Charles 2, Pfautz 2, Resh 2, Miller. Double play—Resh to Krick to Druckenbrod. Base on balls—Off Morgan 1, Leh 1, F. Shipe 1, Stuart 11. Struck out—By Morgan 1, Stuart 6. Hit by pitcher—By Stuart (Charles). Passed balls—Forrey 2, Shipe 2, Leh 2. Winning pitcher—Stuart. Losing pitcher — Morgan. Umpires—Lerbscher and Sneath. Time of game—1:30.

Tuesday's Local Sports Lineup

BASEBALL

INTERSTATE LEAGUE
Lancaster Roses vs. Hagerstown at Stumpf Field, 8:15 p. m.

JUNIOR CITY-COUNTY LEAGUE
(First Round Championship Playoffs)
West Lampeter at Tri-Town, 6 p. m. (First of a three-game series).

CITY-COUNTY LEAGUE
Rothsville vs. Armstrong at F. & M., 6:15 p. m.

EXHIBITION
City Legion League All-Stars vs. Lebanon Legion All-Stars at F. & M., 6:15 p. m.

SOFTBALL

CITY-COUNTY LEAGUE
Maples vs. El Capitan.
Letort vs. Hoak's.
(Both games at Maple Grove, first starting 7 p. m.)

LANCASTER COUNTY LEAGUE
Lititz at Mount Joy.
Elizabethtown at Manheim.

Atlantic City Entries

1ST—$2,500, clmg., 4 y. o. and up, 6 f.: aCol. Steve 124, Saguaro 124, Crys-Doll 115, Ascertain 124, aBoy Angler 119, Liquid Lunch 112, Peacock Lady 119, Belle Cole 109, Black Tempest 112, Court Ace 116, Ardent Miss 114, Pansy Brigade 111, Bee Twenty Nine 111, Wind Whither 111, One Sun 119, Kitty Kilts 117. a-Edw. Strauss-Kel-Brand Stable.

2ND—$3,000, 2 y. o., 6 f.: Cuban Bill 120, Skydue 117, Omaha Jr. 115, aGallant Jake 120, Polly's Delay 120, Seconomy 120, Fuglers 119, Custody 120, Lark Boy 116, aBinky B. 120, Petes Playmate 120, Dutel 120, Lady Airy 110, Happy Victor 120, Royal Scot 120. a-W. Y. Goldsborough-H. L. Straus entry.

3RD—$2,500, 3 y. o. and up, 6 f.: Miss Fighter 108, Play Neddie 113, Graymar Lassie 111, The Bean 108, Roy C. 104, Wee Jimmie 113.

4TH—$3,600, 3 y. o., 6 f.: In Suspense 112, Heliotrope 107, Starry Cant 110, Denagee 112, Flag of Truce 106, Hasty Phil 117, Night Count 112, Pied Piper 117, Camel Town 112, River Play 119, Mr. Chap 117, Grand Surprise 117, Twenty Knots 104, Smart Start 103.

5TH—$3,500, 4 y. o. and up, 6 f.: Nowadays 118, Tony's Find 113, New Moon 124, Ariel Song 116, Tourelay 110, Lanlast 116, Uncle Doc 118, Cock Feather 110, Ginargie 116, Shako 107.

6TH—$3,500, 4 y. o. and up, 1 1-16 mi.: Sir Helix 116, True Dream 115, David T. 110, Riar Black 116, Wary Flight 121, Hearth Mouse 110, Travancore 115, Svengali 119.

7TH—$3,500, clmg., 4 y. o. and up, 1 1-16 mi.: Bold Regard 117, Mirbriar 117, Pegasus 117, Cab Sir 119, Return Call 117, Broad Daylight 112, Cross Bayou 112, Pine Lake 112.

8TH—$2,500, clmg., 4 y. o. and up, 1⅛ mi.: Puritan 116, Limehouse 122, Sunstorm 119, I'll Be Back 111, Comic Ann 111, Darten 116, Halgas 119, Rex Romanus 111, Gremlin 114, Dove Shoot 116, Black Brat 111, Felt Hat 116, That's Pretty 116, Cherokee V. 116, Outsider 116, Bellclapper 109.

Atlantic City Results

1ST—$2,500, clmg., 4 y. o. and up, 6 f.:

Winks Forty (Mora)	$6.60	$3.50	$2.70
Star Time (Gilbert)		3.60	2.70
Right Hand (Boston)			3.40

Time: 1.14 1-5. Scratched—Damion's Maid, Serinidad.

2ND—$2,500, clmg., 3 y. o., 6 f.:

Capt. Bernard (McTague)	$95.00	$40.30	$28.30
Loutey (Wahler)		8.20	6.20
Vitesse (Polk)			9.80

Time: 1.14. Scratched—Desert Isle, Opening Day.

DAILY DOUBLE—(Winks Forty and Capt. Bernard) Paid $335.10.

3RD—$2,500, 3 y. o., 1 1-16 mi.:

Chance Had (Schmidl)	$18.90	$8.80	$5.50
Demi-Z (Stout)		4.40	3.30
Sun Gay (Roberts)			5.80

Time: 1.49 1-5. No scratches.

4TH—$3,500, 2 y. o., 6 f.:

Mr. Ace (Moon)	$9.60	$6.10	$3.80
First Nighter (Basile)		3.90	3.10
Slamish (Stout)			4.60

Time: 1.13 4-5. Scratched—Miss Jersey, Kashmir, Bovard, Royal Pigeon.

5TH—$4,000, 3 y. o. and up, 1 1-16 mi.:

Rampart (Stout)	$4.00	$3.10	$2.60
Galamilk (Polk)		5.80	3.90
Miss War (Gilbert)			5.10

Time: 1.47 2-5. No scratches.

6TH—$3,500, 4 y. o. and up, 6 f.:

Big Pop (Caffarella)	$12.20	$7.60	$4.50
Fact Finder (Strange)		5.00	4.00
Laran (Kirk)			3.70

Time: 1.13 1-5. No scratches.

7TH—$2,500, 4 y. o. and up, 1⅛ mi.:

Diah (Hacker)	$45.30	$22.10	$11.00
Value Mark (Turner)		4.90	3.50
Payable (Polk)			4.00

Time: 1.57 2-5. Scratched—Little Action, Memory Boss, Karakel, Ann San, Karanette, Dunde.

8TH—$3,000, 3 y. o. and up, 1⅛ mi.:

Jellico (Buttler)	$14.40	$6.40	$4.10
Grand Destiny (Caffarella)		6.80	4.40
The Demander (Balzaretti)			3.30

Time: 1.55 3-5. Scratched — Tutelo, Grian, Dorada, Sandy Trail.

WILLIE PEP PUTS TITLE UP FRIDAY

New York—(AP)—Willie Pep, the busy featherweight champion from Hartford, Conn., puts his title on the block against Jock Leslie, hard-hitting contender from Flint, Mich., in a 15-rounder in Flint's Atwood Stadium Friday night.

The Connecticut champion, in good shape again after being injured in an airplane accident last winter, is being guaranteed $25,000 for the title shot. Leslie will get 70 per cent of the net receipts after Pep collects his share.

Another champion, welterweight King Ray (Sugar) Robinson of New York, will see action during the week but his crown won't be in danger. The Sugar Man fights Sammy Secree of Pittsburgh in an over-the-weight 10-rounder at Akron, O., Thursday night.

Sto-Mac Tigers Trip Short Sox, 10 To 4

The Sto-Mac Tigers had two big innings, the first and second, Monday evening in which they scored eight runs to take a big lead they never relinquished and went on to defeat the Short Sox, 10-4, in a Manheim Township Midget-Midget League baseball game.

Sto-Mac Tigers	ab	r	h	o	a	Short Sox	ab	r	h	o	a
B. W'r ss	3	2	1	1	1	D. S's 3b	3	0	0	0	0
T. H'e c	4	2	2	9	0	R. T'd cf	2	0	2	0	0
J. D'e lf	4	2	2	0	0	J. G'f 2b	3	1	2	0	0
D. G'y 3b	3	3	3	0	0	J. W'y p	2	0	0	1	2
R. S'r rf	3	0	1	0	0	T. G'f c	3	1	0	5	0
G. P'n 2b	2	1	1	2	1	J. C'e ss	3	0	0	0	0
L. D'l cf	3	0	0	0	0	R. N'e rf	2	1	1	0	0
Wilson p	3	0	1	0	12	J. H'n lf	2	0	0	0	0
M'C'y 1b	3	0	0	3	0	T. B't 1b	2	0	0	8	0
York 1b	0	0	0	0	0	J. G'f p	0	0	0	0	2
D. H'e cf	0	0	0	0	0	Cons'e 2b	0	0	0	0	0
						Way ss	0	0	0	0	0
						J. Fry cf	2	1	1	1	0
						Brosey 3b	0	0	0	0	0
						Brought p	0	0	0	0	0
						Shiff't lf	0	0	0	0	0
Totals	28	10	11	15	14	Totals	24	4	6	15	4

STO-MAC	440 20	—10
SHORT SOX	003 10	— 4

Error—J. Way. Home run—Gockley. Three base hit—Duke. Two base hits—Gockley, T. Hinkle, Stover. Base on balls—Off Wilson 3, Groff 2, Way 1. Struck out—By Wilson 9, Way 2, Groff 2.

The Army Athletic Association has loaned the motion picture company producing "Army Black and Gold" the entire file of West Point films on Glenn Davis and Doc Blanchard.

Batting Leaders Hold Fast In Both Leagues

New York —(AP)— The Philadelphia Phillies are going nowhere in the National League pennant race but Harry Walker in his first year with the tailenders, is well on his way to bringing the batting championship to the Quaker City as a consolation prize.

Collecting 12 hits in 31 times at bat during the week ended Sunday, the Philly flychaser pulled his average up three points to .347 and increased his margin over the runner-up, Augie Galan of Cincinnati, to 25 points. Last week Walker Cooper of New York was second with .325 but the Giants' catcher faded to third on a .316 mark as Galan moved up with .322.

Fourth and sixth places were taken over by newcomers, Pete Reiser of Brooklyn and Ralph Kiner of Pittsburgh. Reiser got the necessary 250 times at bat and moved into fourth place with .315 while Kiner flashed a .310 mark. Frankie Gustine of Pittsburgh is fifth with .312.

Besides advancing into the list of top batsmen, Kiner poled out a bushel of homers during the week. His tremendous clouting soared him into second place in the home run chase, with 35 to 36 for New York's Johnny Mize, and advanced him into a tie for second place in the runs batted in department with 91 to 97 for Mize. Willard Marshall of the Giants also had 91 RBIS.

Other department leaders include: Mize, 103 runs; Frankie Baumholtz, Cincinnati, 144 hits; Holmes, 26 doubles; Harry Walker, 13 triples; Jackie Robinson, Brooklyn, 20 stolen bases; Ewell Blackwell, Cincinnati, 159 strikeouts and a 19-5 record.

Chicago —(AP)— Despite a seven-point slump last week, manager-shortstop Lou Boudreau of Cleveland Monday clung to the American League batting leadership, but faced a threat from Luke Appling, 38-year-old Chicago White Sox shortstop, who was only four points behind.

Boudreau held the top with .333, while Appling, seeking his third League batting crown, surged seven points last week to a runner-up mark of .329.

KELL TUMBLES 13 POINTS

Meanwhile, third sacker George Kell of Detroit, who last week shared the lead with Boudreau at .340, collected only six hits in 33 trips, to tumble 13 points to fifth spot with .327.

Tied for third place a point behind Appling with .328 were Joe Di Maggio of New York and Ted Williams of Boston, the latter climbing 12 points during the week.

Boston's Bobby Doerr was the only new leader in the specialized departments, wresting the runs-batted-in lead from team-mate Williams with 78.

Williams, however, continued to set the pace in home runs with 25 and runs scored with 88. Johnny Pesky, Boston, was tops in hits with 139, while Boudreau led in doubles with 35; Mickey Vernon of Washington was ahead in triples with 11; and Bob Dillinger, St. Louis, continued as the pace-setter in stolen bases with 29.

Vic Raschi of New York maintained the percentage lead in pitching with .857 on a 6-1 record, followed by his Yankee team-mate Frank Shea, with 11-4. Bob Feller of Cleveland kept his strike-out lead with 149.

READING "9" AGAIN IN LEGION FINALS

Reading, Pa. —(AP)— Reading's Keystone Juniors blanked Olyphant, 7-0, Monday, behind Lefty Reedy's two-hit pitching to win the Eastern Pennsylvania American Legion Junior Baseball title before more than 3,500 spectators at George Field.

It was the tenth eastern title for the Gregg Post tossers who will meet the western champion in Forbes Field, Pittsburgh, on Thursday, Friday and Saturday for the championship.

Reedy struck out 18 batters to zoom his total to 183 as he was posting his 11th straight victory. The Keys scored twice in the first, four times in the second and once in the eighth and will be questing their sixth state diadem when they invade Pittsburgh.

The United States Trotting Association has published a trotting and pacing guide listing the leading drivers and best races of standardbreds.

Softball

Lehigh Clinches Western Title; Grace Wins In Church Playoff

Lehigh clinched the Western Division title in the City Industrial League and Grace Lutheran took the opening game in the championship finals of the City Church League in the top softball games of the day here Monday evening.

Berks were the victims of the Lehigh victory by a narrow 8-7 margin. Lehigh tallied all their runs between the second and fourth frames and stood off a Berks rally in the sixth to win.

Free-hititng marked the Church League game with Grace collecting 10 blows to whip St. Paul's Reformed, 12-9. The second game of the three-game series will be played Wednesday on the Edward Hand diamond.

CHURCH LEAGUE

ST. PAUL'S R.	000 041 4—9	8	2
GRACE LUTH.	430 500 x—12	10	6

Batteries: St. Paul's Ref.—Geyer and Holland; Grace Luth.—Starr and W. Slaugh.

CITY INDUSTRIAL LEAGUE

BERKS	230 002 0—7	9	0
LEHIGH	033 200 x—8	10	3

Ganse and Fuller; Miller and E. Shindle.

LIBERTY	020 000 001—3	11	0
FIDELITY	110 000 000—2	11	0

Rathvon and Plantholt; Kreiner and Storm.

Kennel Club Members Win At Ohio Show

Two local members of the Lancaster Kennel Club, Mrs. W. R. Calaway of East Berlin and Mrs. Paul M. Hess, Conestoga, Pa. came through with victories in the All Breed Open Show at Salem, Ohio Sunday.

Mrs. W. R. Calaway's Doberman Pinscher, "Cal's Colonel V. Wilfocal" won honors in its class and Mrs. Hess took first place in the Open Class with a black and tan cocker spaniel, "Conestoga Cicero."

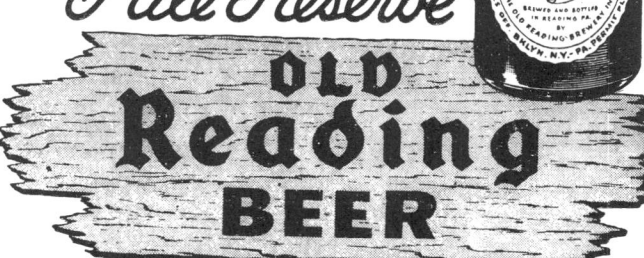

Teachers-In-Training Find There's Lots To Learn

COMMUTING STUDENT-TEACHERS arrive at Millersville State Teachers College by bus on this typical morning, and here's the girl the camera will follow through a day's schooling—Miss Helen Flinchbaugh, of 520 N. Mary St., Lancaster, about to step down out of the doorway.

EVERYBODY LEARNS at Millersville Boro School, for Helen's 8:45 a. m. third-grade class is part of her education as a teacher, while the youngsters are getting the benefit of the latest instructional techniques which she picks up in her college classes and conferences with her faculty advisors.

TIME OUT from teaching and learning will be spent at the campus soda fountain (above) or, on nice days, brushing up on assignments by the lake. In photo at left, Helen shares a bench with Miss Kathryn Davies, left, and Paul Burector.

SEVEN TO GO FOR CENTENNIAL, Millersville is proud of its title as Pennsylvania's first normal school, as announced to the world in signs recently placed by Pennsylvania Museum and Historical Commission.

SCHOOL DAYS can go all the way from kindergarten to college between classes for students at MSTC, who teach while they learn. One day in the life of a typical Millersville student, illustrated on this page, may help the thousands who will visit local schools during Education Week, starting Monday, to appreciate background of today's school teacher.

HOCKEY, NOT HOOKEY—Sports are part of a teacher's education, for many will be called upon to coach when they leave MSTC and take school jobs. Here Helen, at left, a member of the hockey team, is taking a "bully" with Elmira Eckert, East Petersburg, at right; background, Mary Workman, East Petersburg, and Irene Sload, Charles Road.

DAY'S END, STILL DISHING IT OUT—Since a teacher is expected to take an important place in any community's social life, Helen and her friends are on hand for college functions such as the President's Reception. This job takes plenty of punch. (Photos by Prof. George Anderson.)

Winter Party

SET TO GO—Winter parties at the Carl Reynolds' place below Quarryville may start anytime on a Sunday afternoon with a scene like this, with Mrs. Ernest Miller of Homeville getting lots of help donning skis at the hilltop. (She went downhill on her own.)

WOODEN SHOE-SHINE—Waxing skis by the fireplace gives the experts that last-minute polish that a good stem-turn may need, while the novices know they can always stop with a flop. Here Carl Reynolds, Jr., imparts the right finish as Miss Norma Anne Reese takes a final warm-up against the outdoors cold.

POGO-STICK TECHNIQUE sends Henry Reynolds, twelve, off to a flying start on the long hill that slants down towards the picturesque gorge of the Octoraro's West Branch.

SMOOTH SLEDDING—Off on a double-decker belly-bumper ride go Miss Ethel McClure and John Storb. It's a quarter-mile trip, with a stop advised this side of the swimming pool.

HUMAN AVALANCHE in the making is William Fisher, about to take a fast spill. "Track!" means "Gangway!" on the slope, but this audience will see the maneuver known as a "Purzelbaum," ski-talk for somersault.

SNOWFALLS ARE FUN if you get the drift with a pair of hickory-sticks on your feet, **or if you can be the lucky man in the sandwich between a pretty girl and a sled.** Many a Lancaster **Summer home makes the seasonal shift from swim-suits to ski-pants with a cold-weather bonus of zest.** So the Sunday News **takes you herewith to a real Winter Party as staged by Mr. and Mrs.** Carl Reynolds, of **Quarryville, in the snowy wonderland of the Octoraro hills. Their house, headquarters for the final rites of Groundhog Day, also is the rallying-point for congenial friends from eight to the eighties on many a Sunday afternoon when the snow lies deep on the hill. Spare skis and sleds will take you for a friendly ride—and so will the onlookers when you fall off. When sunset gilds and greys the slopes, there's always a pair of blazing open fires in the old stone house among the pines, an appetizing tableful of food, and square-dance melodies to make it the end of a perfect day.**

"JUST LIKE OLD TIMES" chortles "Uncle Harry" Miller, eighty-seven, as he gives Mrs. Ernest Fauth an old-fashioned bounce on his lap to indicate that the indoor-sport portion of the Winter party is underway.

THE HEARTH IS THE HEART of the party, and the Reynolds keep two of them blazing to greet the skiers and coasters. Bill Fisher throws another log on the fire, abetted by Jean Trimble and Barbara Smith.

HOT-DOGS HOWL when the hungry guests drift in out of the snow after a hard day's sport. Everybody brings something—potato salad, rolls, frankfurters, chips, cookies, cake, pretzels—and the hosts chip in such items as a vast kettle of steaming baked beans, gallons of hot coffee, and mountains of ice cream topped with frozen peaches.

SWING YOUR PARTNERS!—It's a Gelandesprung without the skis when, after the outside fun and the inside feed, the record-player sounds off with a square dance with the signals interpreted by Carl Reynolds himself, (center rear), who describes just what the dancers must do to "dig for the clam" or "dive for the oyster."

"And very early in the morning the first day of the week they came unto the sepulchre at the rising of the sun."—Mark 16:2.

Early Easter

"I AM THE RESURRECTION AND THE LIFE"—Easter's meaning of ever-returning Spring is interpreted again today in traditional dawn services at churches urban and rural. Spirit of Easter morning is caught in the sunlight upon this typical country house of worship, with its old trees, its peaceful churchyard, its curving stone wall at St. Luke's Lutheran Church near Bridgeville in York County.

EARLIEST EASTER IN EIGHT YEARS had a warming preparatory in the first week of Spring which coincided with Holy Week and brought out the first flowers and blossoms in a symbolic renewal of the holiday's perpetual promise. Early-morning worship on this early Easter serves to remind of the scene at the Holy Sepulchre which represented the true dawn of the Christian Era two milleniums ago. Favorite of the Easter flowers banked around hundreds of altars this morning are the lilies, repeating the message that "the Winter is past . . . the flowers appear on the earth . . ." Admiring blooms above is Joan Ranck, Leola RD.

WE ALL "BECOME AS LITTLE CHILDREN" AT EASTER-NEST TIME—For the first year since before the war, egg-hunts again developed into a widespread feature of the Easter season here, as chocolate rabbits and eggs, and jelly-beans, and all the other traditional sweets of the holiday made their appearance in unrationed plenty. Pupils of Miss Downey's Kindergarten gathered around to compare baskets, above, after their Easter-week celebration at 950 Columbia Ave.

EVERY DAY IS EASTER at the busy egg warehouses in this area, which handle some of the tremendous output of Lancaster County hens—some 22 million dozen eggs a year. Miss Nelda Keller of Ephrata RI, displays some New York-bound eggs among layer-on-layer of filled crates at Ephrata warehouse.

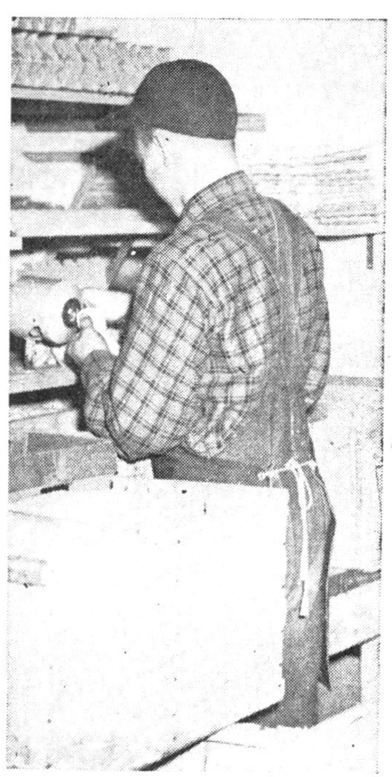

THREE-SECOND EGG—Candling is the process by which egg dealers make sure you'll get a good egg for breakfast. David Steinmetz uses an electric "candle."

EARLY IN THE MORNING OUR SONG SHALL RISE TO THEE — Pre-Easter sunrise service by Student Christian Association at Millersville State Teachers College awoke echoes of old hymns across the morning stillness of the campus lake. This morning many groups of early-risers were up before dawn to join in similar services in many parts of the city and county.

Ewell Equals World's 100-Meter Mark, Wins Olympic Post

'round the town

Moyer Still Belting the Ball. Good News for Ephrata Teams. Other Bits of Sports 'Info'.

by GEORGE KIRCHNER

STRICTLY ON THE CUFF . . . His many friends here will be pleased to learn that Bob Moyer, former first sacker for our Red Roses, is pasting that apple in the Southern Association . . . Bob's now with the Little Rock, Ark. Travelers and is currently hitting around the .320 mark . . . Mr. and Mrs. C. Nelson Charles and Mr. and Mrs. Harold Saylor of East Petersburg, were down that way recently and brought back copies of the Little Rock paper which had Moyer's picture smack in the center of the sports page, along with a rave notice in which they give Bobby credit for the Travelers' string of 11 wins in their last 17 games . . . Nice going, Robert, keep it up . . . And thanks, people, for turning the clippings over to this bureau.

Good news for the teams in Ephrata . . . They're now using the new War Memorial Field for all of their home games and it's quite a nice setup . . . Both the Ephrata Junior Legion as well as the Ephrata Senior Legion team will play there . . .

LOU Ruchser, who was just signed to play first base for the Roses, is a product of the Brooklyn sandlots . . . In fact, he still calls Brooklyn his home town . . . Played with Montreal for a spell last year and was then sent to Nashua in the New England League . . . Looked good enough there to warrant a trial with Mobile of the Southern Association . . . Business complications at his home in Watertown, N. Y., caused catcher Johnny Thackston to leave the Roses . . . Whether he'll be back is questionable . . . Until he makes up his mind, Lou Libhart, the Marietta boy, is helping out with the reserve backstopping.

There'll be quite a few fight fans from our town who will be in Philly on Monday night to see the Beau Jack-Ike Williams lightweight title fight at Shibe Park . . . Count Wally Erisman, a dyed-in-the-wool ringster, among them . . . After all what's a trip to Philly to a guy who made two to New York and wound up seeing such a dull heavyweight title fight? . . . At least, that's the way Erisman is looking at it . . .

BUILDING trouble in Wildwood has prevented Benny Volk and Roxy Forgione from getting their pro wrestling and boxing program underway at Wildwood . . . Speaking of that seashore resort, Harry (Cheesie) Kirchner and his side-kick, Joe Kirk are summering down there, just as they did last year . . . Woody Sponaugle, the F and M coach, is taking his mind off football during the Summer months by playing golf when he's not painting his house . . . The latest reports say that Montreal has sent Joe Tepsic, the Penn State star, to Newport News, Va. of the Piedmont League . . . Because he has such great possibilities, local fans would like to see Tepsic snap out of his slump and go on . . .

Pete Flick doesn't have to worry about his spare time . . . When he isn't working, he's coaching a team in the American Legion Junior League, as well as coaching both

(See Page 11 — Round the Town)

Lancaster's Olympic Star Started Winning Early

Above, Barney Ewell with some of the trophies he won before graduating from McCaskey High School in June, 1937. Left, the same Ewell, 11 years later, winning the 100-meter sprint in 10.2 and gaining a place on Uncle Sam's Olympic team.

City Sprinter Upsets Patton, Ties Mark of 10.2 in Final Trials

(Special to The New Era)

EVANSTON, Ill., July 10—Ten years of dreaming and hoping during which time the Olympic flame burned bright in his breast were rewarded here last night when Barney Ewell, thirty-one-year-old sprint wonder from Lancaster, Pa., blazed his way to victory in the 100-meters of the final Olympic tryouts in Dyche Stadium.

With this victory under his belt, Ewell now heads for the Olympic Games in London as the No. 1 100-meter sprinter on the United States team.

Ol' Barney equaled the world 100-meter record of 10.2 with a breath-taking burst of speed that astounded a crowd of 20,000 and dealt a stunning defeat, first of the year, to Mel Patton, the six-foot 145-pound wonder sprinter from the University of Southern California.

Ewell beat Patton by a yard, with Harrison (Bones) Dillard of Baldwin-Wallace, the world's best hurdler and as swift on the flat as he is over the sticks, third. Eddie Conwell, former NYU star, was fourth.

The Lancastrian, who won his first preliminary heat in a time of 10.5, shaved three-tenths of a second off his time in the final to equal the 10.2 mark established by Jesse Owens of Ohio State in 1936 and equalled by Hal Davis, of Southern California, in 1941.

WITH THIS VICTORY in his possession and a place on the U. S. team assured, Barney was still aiming at another today as the Trials wind up.

His immediate goal is the 200-meter event, and the blaze of speed which he displayed in winning the 100 last night indicated that today's longer race could be one of the real highlights of the trials.

AS FAR AS THE fans are concerned, they'll long remember last night's spectacular dash.

The field of six, who made the final after two semi-final heats, got off raggedly without any false starts. Conwell, the bullet starter and indoor AAU champion, was off on top, with Ewell, Mathis and Dillard close behind. Patton, no world-beater off the mark, went off poorly. Campbell, on the pole, was virtually left at the post.

Ewell collared Conwell at thirty yards. At fifty, Barney, Conwell and Mathis were bunched shoulder to shoulder in adjacent lanes with Dillard a foot behind and Patton two yards back in fifth place.

HALFWAY UP THE track, Ol' Barney exploded, running as he never has run before. He made every stride a winning one and hit the tape a clear winner. Patton, in the outside lane, came on with great space-eating strides. Ten yards from home he was shut out, this Navy veteran of twenty-three, who set a world 100-yard record of 9.3 seconds this Spring, but his magnificent closing drive brought him into second place, nipping Dillard.

Ewell, who won the AAU 100-meter title last Saturday, has been winning titles for a dozen years. He won his National Junior 100 meters as a schoolboy in 1936 and his first National Senior AAU title as a Penn State Freshman in 1939. In three varsity years, he scored an unprecedented IC4-A triple, taking the 100, 220 and broad jump for three straight years.

ELEVEN EVENTS, with the first three finishers in each winning an Olympic berth, are scheduled and a crowd of nearly 35,000 is expected to turn out.

Half of the team has now been determined. Ewell, Patton and Dillard gained a place by their 1-2-3 finish in the 100-meters. Ed Conwell of Jersey City, a close fourth, will probably be included also to round out the 400 meter relay team.

NINETEEN TEAM members were decided plus 15 who had previously qualified in separately conducted trials in the 10,000 meter walk, 10,000 meter run, 50,000 meter walk, the marathon and decathlon.

In today's 11 finals, 33 more will win places. The schedule includes the 800 meter run, 3,000 meter steeplechase, 110 meter hurdles, 200 meter dash, 1500 meter run, 400 meter run, pole vault, broad jump, shot put, hop-step-jump and discus throw.

HERE ARE THE other team members selected in the tryouts last night, listed in the order of their finish with the winning performance:

5,000 METER RUN—Curtis Stone, Philadelphia, Pa.; Jerry Thompson, Texas; Clarence Robinson,' Brigham Young, 14:40.7.

400 METER HURDLES — Roy Cochran, Los Angeles Athletic Club; Richard Ault, Missouri; Jeff Kirk, Penn, 51.7 seconds.

HIGH JUMP — Verne McGrew, Rice; George Stanich, Los Angeles Athletic Club; Dwight Eddleman, Illinois, 6 feet 8¼ inches.

JAVELIN THROW—Martin Biles, San Francisco Olympic Club; Robert Likins, San Jose, Cal.; Steve Seymour, Los Angeles Athletic Club, 225 feet 9 inches.

HAMMER THROW — Bob Bennett, Apponaug, R. I.; Henry Dreyer, New York Athletic Club; Sam Felton, Harvard, 177 feet 8½ inches.

Ewell's Friends Surprised by His Win in Shorter Race

Barney Ewell's blazing victory in the 100-meter finals, which earned him a place on the U. S. Olympic team, came as pleasant news to his many friends here . . . but a consensus of opinion revealed that it surprised the majority.

Not that they didn't figure Barney to land a berth on the team, for many had him down as a third place finisher in the 100, but more particularly they had counted on his winning in the 200 meters or longer distance.

John Sturgis, one of Barney's close friends, said, for instance, that Barney told him just before he left for Evanston that he figured his best race would be over the longer distance.

AND THAT'S the way it was with most of the trackmen in this area. They figured that Barney, who in his pre-war days had shown signs of duplicating Jesse Owens' great sprint feats, had passed his peak in the shorter races, but was still good enough for the longer jaunts.

Abe Herr, the man who actually gave Ewell his start when Barney was a pupil at the Edward Hand —(then East Junior High)— School apparently wasn't figuring it that way. He evidently foresaw big things for his protege, so he took no chances and went to the Trials, accompanied by his son, Abram, Jr. and Charley Frey, former F and M athlete.

They were on hand in Northwestern's Dyche Stadium last night as Ewell blazed his way to victory in the world-equalling record time of 10.2. If Barney didn't have any other rooters among the 20,000 at the Trials he at least had these three guys pulling for him as he outsprinted the favored Mel Patton all the way to the wire.

WITH THIS VICTORY to post to his credit, Barney has a chance to climax a brilliant running career that began when he was in knee pants in Junior High. As a Junior High runner, Ewell was the fastest thing in the State, but that was only the beginning.

He went through McCaskey as the State champion sprinter and from there to Penn State where he carried on in equally brilliant fashion. In between his college races, Ewell managed to make most of the big amateur meets, so that he soon became one of the country's top-notch sprinters.

THE WAR TOOK him out of big-time competition, but Barney managed to squeeze in a few of the bigger events while soldiering in this country and thus he was able to preserve his record. Consequently, he was regarded among the leading contestants in these Olympic Trials.

One of Barney's handicaps in recent years has been his lack of time to practice. He had to sandwich his drills in between his hours of work at a local plant and this meant that he was working out at F and M long after the college athletes had gone home for supper.

EVERYONE CONNECTED with track knew that this was asking too much and Ewell wasn't blinded to the seriousness of the situation, either. Finally, he decided to devote more time to his running in a last effort to make the grade and a fund was started here to help support his family.

With these worries off his mind, Barney got down to the serious business of training and the results of this work were shown in his great race last night.

MAYOR DALE E. CARY sounded the reaction of local fans when he said "I was certainly delighted to hear that Barney has come through and we're all pleased that Lancaster is going to be represented in the Olympics. I know he'll have the town with him."

And that's the way Ewell's many friends here felt about it. In fact, the first reaction to the news indicated that there probably would be a welcoming committee on hand to greet him when he comes home from the trials.

Iannicelli Fails in Javelin Throw

If Barney Ewell's victory in the 100 meters of the Olympic Trials gave the folks here something to cheer about, there was one sad note sounded in last night's events.

Bill Iannicelli, Franklin and Marshall College's great athlete, failed to qualify in the javelin throw.

Martin Biles, of the San Francisco Olympic club, won the event with a heave of 225 feet, nine inches.

However, there was some good news for F and M. Steve Seymour—(he was Seymour Cohen when he was a student here) who used to toss the spear for the Diplomats, finished second to Biles and qualified for the trip to London. Seymour now represents the Los Angeles Athletic Club.

Ann Curtis Sets Record in Swimming

DETROIT, July 10.— (AP) —Ann Curtis, San Francisco star, bettered Olympic record time in winning her heat in the 400-meter free style in 5 minutes 25.9 seconds today in preliminaries of the final trials for places on the U. S. Olympic team.

Miss Curtis, who holds American records at distances from 100 yards to 880 yards in the free style, staged a one-girl runaway to lead qualifiers for berths in final trials in the 400 here tomorrow.

Her time was a half second under the Olympic record of 5:26.4 set in 1936 at Berlin by Rita Mastenbroek of Holland.

Miss Curtis already had qualified here in the 100 meters and is a cinch to swim in the two events under American colors in London.

AMERICAN chances in swimming and diving at the 1948 Olympic Games hinge on the rise of new boy and girl wonders, a pair of 17-year-old stars stood ready today to fill the bill.

They are slender Jimmy McLane, Akron, Ohio, free style swimming sensation now attending Andover Academy — and heading for Yale—and pretty Zoe Ann Olsen, Oakland, Calif., springboard diver who is a senior in high school. Pool-side galleries were abuzz with their achievements today as the final American Olympic tank trials went into the third and semi-final day.

McLANE OUTSPED Hawaiian Bill Smith, veteran Ohio State University free-styler, for a three-length triumph in the 400-meter event yesterday and was rated a sure thing to head the 1,500-meter parade as well on Sunday's wind-up program here.

Miss Olsen, coached by her father, topped the 3-meter feminine diving events where America's 1-2 finishers in the 1936 Berlin Olympics failed to qualify for the 1948 team.

McLANE'S TIME in the 400 was four minutes 45.6 seconds, barely a second above Jack Medica's Olympic record, but it wasn't good enough for the U. S. Olympic swim coach, Robert J. H. Kiphuth, of Yale.

Full "Tummies" Clean Sheets for Olympic Athletes

LONDON, July 10 — (AP) — The 5,000 Olympic competitors will sleep between crisp sheets and run on full tummies, the British promised today.

Stanley J. Briault, housing and catering manager for the British Olympic Organizing Committee, assured the 61 competing Nations that their favorite sons would get good care in belt-tightened Britain.

"We are fully operational," Briault declared. He pointed out that two Olympic villages—Richmond Park and Uxbridge—are open and teams are arriving daily.

"My staff is strained to the limit, working long hours seven days a week. I don't anticipate many complaints on food. Most of the vanguard is highly delighted with our fare."

ABOUT 40 NATIONS are supplying part of their own food to supplement British menus, which are based on heavy industrial workers rations.

Chinese athletes brought their own oiled bamboo shoots, Hungary brought 20,000 lemons and the United States is bringing 5,000 steaks.

Mexico wanted to send 600 live fowls, but the Ministry of Agriculture saved their lives, Briault said. There are too many rules about inspection.

Russia Frowns on "Our Kids"

Charges U. S., Western Europe Counting on Youngsters to Win in Olympic Games

By Eddy Gilmore

MOSCOW, July 10— (AP) —The United States and Western European Nations were accused by a Russian newspaper today of "exploiting children" in the coming Olympics games.

Russia is not competing in the Olympics.

The Moscow News said:

"Exploitation of children is widely practiced in the United States and Western Europe.

"Jimmy McLane, the American 'Olympic hope' is a 16-year-old lad. (McLane, now seventeen, is one of three Americans who qualified yesterday for the 400 meter event in swimming. He is from Akron, Ohio.) According to the French Newspaper record, Australia will be represented at the Olympic games by a 13-year-old, Marjorie Mackaway, and England by 14-year-old Eleanor Gordon and 15-year-old John Wadrope.

"The National teams of many Western European countries will evidently likewise include children whose sport careers are doomed to be crippled before they get a chance to mature."

THE NEWSPAPER pointed out that exploitation of child athletes was impossible by law in the USSR.

While the Olympics are going on in England the USSR is going to see one of its greatest Summer sports seasons. But it will be a season in which juveniles are forbidden to enter races or other events against adults.

Sports authorities here estimate at least 2,000,000 youngsters, 14 to 18 years old, will take part in official sporting events.

Tennis, swimming, football (soccer), basketball, gymnastics and track hold the Summer sports spotlight.

Wm. Grove Races

Williams Grove, Pa. — Drivers competing in the AAA big car auto races this Saturday afternoon on the half-mile Williams Grove Speedway will face a grueling 50-lap grind in the feature race, 20 laps more than the usual length of the feature race.

A's Still Eying Pennant Cash

Mackmen Refuse to Fold, Dog Cleveland's Footsteps

By The Associated Press

HALF way through the pennant race, the amazing Philadelphia Athletics continue to dog the footsteps of the front-running Cleveland Indians.

Instead of folding their pennant ambitions and settling for an expected comfortable berth on the fringe of the first division, Connie Mack's underrated A's insist on eyeing that World Series cash. Every day it becomes tougher to say they're wrong.

ONCE AGAIN the Cleveland Tribe has to line up a friendly array of percentage points to protect its shrinking American League lead. The A's have won three more than the Indians but they've also lost three more. Consequently they remain 10 points back with exactly half of the 154-game schedule still ahead.

They did it the hard way last night, coming from behind twice to outlast the slugging Boston Red Sox 8-7.

LONG BEFORE THIS final result had been posted, the A's knew that Cleveland had been thumped by St. Louis, 5-3, a seventh loss for Bob Lemon who has won 12 games.

Satchel Paige, famous Negro pitcher, made his big league debut on relief for Cleveland, working two shutout innings in which he allowed two singles and struck out one batter.

NEW YORK ALSO moved up on the Tribe by a 9-0 romp over Washington. Eddie Lopat lived up to his rep as a "hot weather" pitcher with a four-hit shutout.

Detroit copped its fifth in a row, downing Chicago, 4-2. Freddie Hutchinson earned his fifth win with a six-hit effort, losing a shutout in the ninth when Aaron Robinson homered with one on.

SHORTLY AFTER learning that second baseman Eddie Stanky would be out of action with a broken right ankle until mid-September the Boston Braves overwhelmed Philadelphia, 13-2. Aided by this 14-hit assault, Johnny Sain became the first National Leaguer to cop 11 games.

The Braves opened up a 3½ game lead on the Pittsburgh Pirates who bowed to Chicago, 2-1, in the Majors' only day game.

REX BARNEY of Brooklyn reeled off his second winning effort in succession, taming New York with four hits, 10-3, before 50,819 customers in the Polo Grounds. This was the largest National League crowd of the year. The Dodgers regained fifth place, only a half game behind the Giants.

Errors by Danny Litwhiler and

Ruth Reported "Up and About"

NEW YORK, July 10 —(AP)— Babe Ruth is reported "up and about most of the time" at Memorial Hospital. An attendant said yesterday that Ruth has improved steadily since entering the hospital June 24. He is receiving radiation treatments.

Red Stallcup enabled St. Louis to trim Cincinnati, 6-4, on a pair of unearned runs in the eighth. Musial singled and came home when Litwhiler, subbing at third base, threw Enos Slaughter's bunt into the right field bull pen. Slaughter scored on Stallcup's boot. Musial hammered his 20th homer in the fourth with a man on base.

Bill Nicholson's 11th homer of the year with Andy Pafko on base in the sixth provided Chicago's 2-1 margin over Pittsburgh's Elmer Riddle.

Tomorrow's Sports

BASEBALL

INTERSTATE LEAGUE
Hagerstown vs. Lancaster Roses, Stumpf Field (2 games, 1st starting at 1:45 p. m.)

CITY-COUNTY LEAGUE
Lanc. Legion at Elizabethtown.
Millersville at Mountville.
Maytown at Bird-in-Hand.

GREATER COUNTY LEAGUE
Holtwood at Marietta.
Bainbridge at Quarryville.
Lititz at Chestnut Hill.
Manheim at Strasburg.

EASTERN COUNTY LEAGUE
Terre Hill at Reamstown.
Schoeneck at Brownstown.
Bowmansville at New Holland.
Denver at Ephrata.

SOUTHERN END LEAGUE
Quarryville at Kirkwood.
New Holland at Smithville.
Strasburg at Fulton.
Georgetown at Marticville.

JUNIOR CITY-COUNTY LEAGUE
Columbia at Reinholds.

Lanco Midget Loop

Manheim	ab	r	h	o	a	Elizabethtown	ab	r	h	o	a
J.Sh'k 3b	4	2	2	0	3	Haw'ne rf	3	0	1	0	0
W.Ro'r 2b	3	0	1	0	0	Seitz c	3	0	1	4	1
Wei'n 2b	2	2	0	0	0	Ru'f'd 2b	2	1	0	3	0
Adair ss	4	2	1	1	1	Goodl g lf	1	1	1	2	0
C.Hen'y	4	2	1	4	0	Miller 3b	2	1	1	1	2
B.Cas'l 1b	3	2	1	5	0	Bein'r cf	1	0	1	0	0
M.Gi'h rf	3	1	1	1	0	Shenk cf	1	1	0	0	0
Ham'r lf	3	0	0	3	0	Parrett 1b	2	0	0	5	0
D.Sh'k cf	3	0	0	1	0	Warfel 1b	1	0	0	1	0
Miller p	2	0	2	0	4	Haines ss	1	0	0	0	3
						Haw'e ss	1	0	1	0	0
						Acorn p	2	0	0	3	2
Totals	30	11	8	15	9	Totals	20	4	5	15	11

MANHEIM .... 105 41—11
ELIZABETHTOWN .... 010 30— 4

Three base hit—J. Shank. Two base hit—Beinhauer. Base on balls—Off Miller 4, Acorn 1. Struck out—By Miller 1, Acorn 3. Umpires—Wanamaker, Evans.

The STANDINGS

NATIONAL LEAGUE

Teams	W.	L.	Pct.	G.B.
Boston	44	31	.587	..
Pittsburgh	39	33	.542	3½
St. Louis	39	34	.534	4
New York	35	36	.493	7
Brooklyn	34	36	.486	7½
Philadelphia	36	40	.474	8½
Cincinnati	35	40	.467	9
Chicago	31	43	.419	12½

AMERICAN LEAGUE

Teams	W.	L.	Pct.	G.B.
Cleveland	44	27	.620	..
Philadelphia	47	30	.610	
New York	43	31	.581	2½
Boston	37	34	.521	7
Detroit	37	37	.500	8½
Washington	33	41	.446	12½
St. Louis	27	44	.380	17
Chicago	23	47	.329	20½

INTERSTATE LEAGUE

Teams	W.	L.	Pct.	G.B.
Wilmington	39	27	.591	..
Trenton	40	28	.588	..
York	36	29	.554	2½
Allentown	34	29	.540	3½
Harrisburg	38	33	.535	3½
Sunbury	34	37	.479	7½
Lancaster	31	40	.437	10½
Hagerstown	20	49	.290	20½

YESTERDAY'S RESULTS

NATIONAL LEAGUE
Boston 13, Philadelphia 2.
Brooklyn 10, New York 3.
St. Louis 6, Cincinnati 4.
Chicago 2, Pittsburgh 1.

AMERICAN LEAGUE
New York 9, Washington 0.
Philadelphia 8, Boston 7.
Detroit 4, Chicago 2.
St. Louis 5, Cleveland 3.

INTERSTATE LEAGUE
Allentown 8, Lancaster 5.
Trenton 6, Wilmington 0.
Harrisburg 4, Sunbury 3.
Hagerstown 9, York 5.

INTERNATIONAL LEAGUE
Toronto 7, Rochester 6.
Jersey City 7, Syracuse 1.
Baltimore 1, Newark 0.
Buffalo 15, Montreal 9.

AMERICAN ASSOCIATION
Toledo 9, Indianapolis 4
Columbus 9, Louisville 8
Only games scheduled.

EASTERN LEAGUE
Wilkes-Barre 3, Elmira 2, 10 innings
Binghamton 10, Hartford 4
Utica 5, Albany 2
Scranton 7, Williamsport 4

TONIGHT'S GAMES

INTERSTATE LEAGUE
Hagerstown at Lancaster.
York at Allentown.
Sunbury at Wilmington.
Harrisburg at Trenton.

NATIONAL LEAGUE
Philadelphia at Boston
Cincinnati at St. Louis

TOMORROW'S SCHEDULE

American League—St. Louis at Cleveland (2), New York at Washington, Boston at Philadelphia (2), Chicago at Detroit.

National League—Brooklyn at New York, Philadelphia at Boston, Pittsburgh at Chicago, Cincinnati at St. Louis.

MAJOR LEAGUE LEADERS

By The Associated Press

AMERICAN LEAGUE
Batting—Williams, Boston .388
Runs Batted In—DiMaggio, New York 74
Runs—Williams, Boston 66
Hits—Williams, Boston 102
Doubles—Williams, Boston 21
Triples—DiMaggio, New York 10
Home Runs—Keltner, Cleveland 20
Stolen Bases—Coan, Washington 13
Strikeouts—Brissie, Philadelphia 77
Pitching—Fowler, Philadelphia 7-1 .875

NATIONAL LEAGUE
Batting—Musial, St. Louis .412
Runs Batted In—Sauer, Cincinnati 64
Runs—Musial, St. Louis 65
Hits—Musial, St. Louis 120
Doubles—Robinson, Brooklyn 20
Triples—Hopp, Pittsburgh 10
Home Runs—Sauer, Cincinnati 24
Stolen Bases—Ashburn, Philadelphia 21
Strikeouts—Branca, Brooklyn 82
Pitching—Post, New York 8-2 .800

FOP, Rangers, Christiana 9's Win Loop Frays

Pounding out five runs in the fifth inning and adding four more in the sixth, the F.O.P. nine routed the Optimists, 12 to 1, last night in a City Junior Legion baseball tilt at McCaskey High School.

In County Legion competition, Christiana pushed across two runs in the sixth inning on three hits and a walk to break a scoreless deadlock with Ephrata at the Christiana diamond. Luke Willard on the mound for Christiana limited the Ephrata nine to two hits, one in the third inning and the second in the fourth inning.

Willard accounted for twelve Ephrata batters via the strikeout rout and maintained perfect control with no free tickets granted to the opposing batters. Bill Hyman was on the mound for the Ephrata squad.

Optimists	ab	r	h	o	a	F.O.P.	ab	r	h	o	a
Gra'm c	3	0	1	7	1	R.Mil'r p	3	4	1	0	3
Wilson ss	3	1	1	0	0	Sharpe rf	3	1	0	1	0
Ehr'rt lf	4	0	1	1	0	Forrest cf	3	2	2	6	0
Green p	3	0	1	0	3	G.My's cf	4	2	1	1	0
Ganse 1b	3	0	0	7	0	Matr'i 1b	2	1	0	9	1
Ream 3b	2	0	0	1	0	J.Mil'r 3b	3	1	0	1	3
Ziegler 2b	2	0	1	1	3	Duss'r ss	4	1	1	0	1
Myers rf	3	0	1	0	0	Keg'ls 2b	2	0	0	1	0
Dela'y cf	2	0	1	1	0	Pic'l 2b lf	3	0	0	2	1
						Wecker lf	2	0	0	0	0
Totals	25	1	7	18	7	Totals	29	12	5	21	9

OPTIMISTS .... 000 000 1— 1
F.O.P. .... 201 054 x—12

Errors—Ganse, Forrest, Ream, J. Miller, Green, Ziegler, Matroni. Home runs—G. Myers. Two base hits—Dussinger, R. Miller, Wilson. Base on balls—Off Green 5, R. Miller 3. Struck out—By Green 6, R. Miller. Umpires—Rosenburg, Ganzl. Time of game—2:00.

Ephrata	ab	r	h	o	a	Christiana	ab	r	h	o	a
Brill 1b	2	0	0	5	0	Har'n 2b	3	0	0	0	2
Win'h 2b	3	0	0	2	1	Fieles 1b	3	1	1	6	0
Fry'r rf	3	0	1	0	0	Steel ss	3	0	2	1	0
Kilhe'r 3b	3	0	0	1	1	Hilton 3b	3	1	0	1	0
Reich cf	3	0	1	2	0	Morg'h rf	2	0	2	1	0
Loose ss	2	0	0	2	3	Yost c	3	0	1	11	2
Zim'n lf	3	0	0	0	0	A.Wil'd lf	3	0	0	0	0
Gerh't c	2	0	0	5	0	L.Wil'd p	3	0	0	0	2
Hyman p	2	0	0	0	0	Baker cf	2	0	1	1	0
Royer 1b	1	0	0	1	0						
Totals	24	0	2	18	5	Totals	25	2	7	21	6

EPHRATA .... 000 000 0—0
CHRISTIANA .... 000 002 x—2

Errors—L. Willard. Base on balls—Off Hyman 1. Struck out—By Hyman 5, L. Willard 12. Umpires—Fieles, Waidley. Time of game—1:30.

CIO	ab	r	h	o	a	Rangers	ab	r	h	o	a
Eck't ss	5	2	4	1	2	Rohrer 2b	2	2	0	0	2
Wagner p	4	2	1	0	1	Rutter lf	4	2	1	2	0
Daum 3b	4	0	2	0	2	Flick p	4	2	2	0	4
Reinf'd 1b	5	0	1	4	0	Evans c	2	0	1	2	1
Smith'l c	3	2	1	12	0	Kr'der 1b	2	0	2	10	1
Min'ch lf	4	0	0	0	0	Stock'r rf	4	0	0	0	0
Hart'n 2b	3	1	1	0	1	Blan'r ss	3	1	1	4	1
Kamm rf	4	1	1	0	0	McF'ls cf	3	2	1	2	0
Chris'n cf	3	1	0	1	0	Jones 3b	3	2	2	1	3
						Finger p	0	1	0	0	0
Totals	34	9	11	18	6	Totals	27	12	10	21	12

CIO .... 111 112 2— 9
RANGERS .... 004 008 x—12

Errors—Blankenmeyer, Evans, Jones, Finger, Minnich. Three base hits—Eckert, Kreider, Daum, McFalls. Two base hits—Evans, Eckert, Rutter, Kreider. Sacrifices—Minnich, Hartman. Base on balls—Off Flick 2, Wagner 5, Finger 2. Struck out—By Flick 3, Wagner 8, Finger 3. Hits—Off Flick in 5 innings 8; off Finger in 2 innings 3. Hit by pitcher—Wagner (Rohrer); Finger (Christman, Daum). Winning pitcher—Finger. Losing pitcher—Wagner. Umpires—Keays, Dunkle. Time of game—2:15.

Here's \$2½ Million Chunk Of New Construction

BREAK GROUND FOR APARTMENTS—Ground was broken this week for a three-story, 24-apartment building on the Long Home property, Race Ave. Arrow points to site of the building, where water and sewer lines have been dug. Income from the building will help finance the home's operation. Court has released \$200,000 of trust funds to finance construction. Home building is in upper center of air view.

MILLION DOLLAR OFFICES—New addition to Armstrong Cork Company's General Administration building is well underway on W. Liberty St. Expected to cost \$1,000,000, the addition will give the firm 30 percent more office space, an auditorium and a display room. It's biggest of local projects, should be complete early next year. New warehouse at floor plant is also underway.

COPS' QUARTERS—Masonry work nears completion on Lancaster's new \$300,000 State Police Barracks, Lincoln Highway East, near Highway Dept. garage. Work on the structure is expected to be finished early in 1949. Barracks will feature 15 dormitory rooms, 30-car garage, radio and teletype facilities. Quarters are now at 434 E. King St.

COMMUNITY HOSPITAL—Ephrata Community Hospital, a modern \$500,000 structure, is approximately half completed. Financed by the community, the hilltop building is due for completion sometime next Spring and will greatly increase facilities of the institution.

THE BUILDING BOOM which has swept the United States since the end of World War II is materializing in Lancaster County in the form of new industrial, civic, school, residential, business and office structures, as well as hundreds of private homes. Despite comparative shortages of some materials and fluctuating prices, many structures planned before materials were available have advanced into the actual building stage. Heavy construction projects pictured on this page will represent some two and one-half million dollars worth of steel, concrete, brick, lumber and labor by the time they are completed. There are many more, not shown.

HIGH SCHOOL GRANDSTAND—Most of the concrete foundation for new grandstand at McCaskey High School is completed. Located at the East side of the school's stadium, the new grandstand will increase seating capacity from the present 2,600 to 7,100. Cost is \$90,000.

)WN STORE—The steel skeleton of the H. L. Green Company's new \$200,000 store and office build- ge and N. Queen Sts. takes shape as it grows skyward. Digging foundation through solid rock delayed ccupancy is expected in late December or early January.

TRADE SCHOOL SHOPS—New shop building (arrow at left) at Thaddeus Stevens Trade School, started las Fall, is "under roof." Being erected by State Department of Public Instruction, the \$150,000 structure will enable the school to add three new trades to its curriculum. Main building, with tower, at right of center.

Indian Girl Will Try To Reach N. Y. Despite 'Jim Crow'

Flagstaff, Ariz., Oct. 2 —(AP)— Florence Iva Begay, seventeen, a Navajo Indian, said today she will make another attempt to' reach New York and Sarah Lawrence College where she has a $2,000 scholarship.

But this time she will go "way around Texas," she said.

Miss Begay, who is planning to become a doctor that she may work among her people, returned to her home here rather than ride in a "Jim Crow" bus.

When her bus reached Amarillo. Texas. Miss Begay said, she was ordered to sit in the rear section, reserved for non-whites.

Ex-Sheriff Ends Life In Fulton Co.

McConnellsburg, Pa., Oct. 2—(AP) —Former Fulton County sheriff Roy Sipes, seventy, died today of a bullet wound in his head which coroner E. H. MacKinley said was self-inflicted.

Sipes was found in the basement of his home here yesterday and was taken to the Everett Hospital where he died 24 hours later. MacKinley said Sipes had been depressed recently.

WGAL

N B C • 1490 Kc. • Mutual
AND
WGAL • FM • 101.3 Mc.

SUNDAY, OCTOBER 3, 1948

7:00 AM—United Press News
7:05—Sunday Musicale
7:40—Weather Report
7:45—Tempos of Today
8:00—NBC World News
8:05—George Crooks, Organist
8:30—String Ensemble
9:00—Dolly Madison News
9:15—Story to Order
9:30—Cameo of Music
9:45—Melody Time
10:00—Radio Bible Class
10:30—AMVETS Installation
11:00—Calvary Church
12:00—Treasure Chest
12:15 PM—United Press News
12:30—Guest Star
12:45—Meet the Band
1:00—Miss Helen Fogg, Interview
1:15—Accent on Melody
1:30—Your Pleasure Parade
2:00—First Piano Quartet
2:30—Concert Master
3:00—AMVETS Installation
3:30—One Man's Family
4:00—The Quiz Kids
4:30—Guy Lombardo Show
5:00—The Shadow
5:30—RCA Victor Show
6:00—Red Kain, Commentary
6:15—Kay Lorraine Show
6:30—Favorite Story
7:00—Jack Benny
7:30—Phil Harris—Alice Faye
8:00—Charlie McCarthy
8:30—Fred Allen
9:00—Manhattan Merry-Go-Round
8:30—American Album of Familiar Music
10:00—Take It or Leave It
10:30—Horace Heidt
11:00—United Press News & Sports
11:10—Intell Radio Edition
11:15—What America Is Playing
11:30—Dave Garroway
12:00—NBC News
12:05 AM—The Mr. Smith Show
12:30—News—Sign Off —Adv.

WLAN

ABC • 1390kc ★ FM • 96.9mc

SUNDAY — OCT. 3

7:00 AM—Wake Up Smiling
8:00—The Calvary Hour
8:30—The Lutheran Hour
9:00—Pentecostal Echoes
9:30—Voice of Prophecy
10:00—Old-Fashioned Revival Hour
11:00—F. & M. Seminary Group
12:00—In Search of Gold
12:15 PM—Foreign Reporters
12:30—Happy Clarks—Wright's Bakery
12:45—Say It with Music—Filbey
1:00—Sam Pettengill
1:15—Christian Business Men
1:29—FM Sign On
1:30—The Comic Weekly Man
2:00—This Week Around the World
2:30—Mr. President
3:00—Marine Story
3:15—American Almanac
3:30—Sunday Serenade
4:00—Radio Gospel Hour
5:00—Quiet, Please!
5:30—Counterspy
6:00—Drew Pearson, News
6:15—Monday Morning Headlines
6:30—Guest Star
6:45—Adventures of Red Feather Man
7:00—Go for the House
7:30—Carnegie Hall, Rise Stevens
8:00—Stop the Music
9:00—Walter Winchell
9:15—Louella Parsons
9:30—Theatre Guild, U. S. Steel, Marlene Dietrich and Walter Pidgeon in "The Letter"
10:30—Proudly We Hail
11:00—News of Tomorrow
11:15—Vera Massey Sings
11:30—Hotel Ambassador Orchestra
12:00—Sign Off —Adv.

NETWORK KEY STATIONS

Morning

9:00—WNBC, World News; WOR News, H Hennessy; WCBS, World News; WJZ, Sunday Men's Page
9:15—WNBC, Sunday Comics; WCBS E Power Biggs, Organ Recital; WOR, Little Robin Morgan
9:30—WOR, Radio Chapel; WJZ, Coast to Coast on a Bus, News
9:45—WCBS, Trinity Choir; WNBC Male Quartet
10:00—WNBC, National Radio Pulpit; WJZ, Message of Israel; WCBS, Church of the Air; WOR, News, H. Gladstone
10:15—WOR, Wise Handyman
10:30—WNBC, Children's Hour; WJZ Southernaires; WOR, A. L. Alexander; WCBS, Church of the Air
10:45—WOR, Let's Go
11:00—WOR, News; WCBS, News, H K Smith; WJZ, The Fitzgeralds; WNBC, Children's Hour
11:15—WOR, Brunch with Dorothy and Dick; WCBS, Newsmaker
11:30—WNBC, News, C. F. McCarthy; WJZ, Hour of Faith; WCBS, Salt Lake City—Tabernacle Choir
11:45—WNBC, Bob Houston, songs

Afternoon

12:00—WOR, The Show Shop; WJZ, News, G. C. Putnam; WCBS, Invitation to Learn; WNBC, Tex and Jinx
12:30—WNBC, Eternal Light; WOR, News, Melvin Elliott; WJZ, Piano Playhouse; WCBS, Peoples Platform
12:45—WOR, M Rettenberg, Piano
1:00—WNBC, America United; WCBS, Joseph C. Harsch; WJZ, Sam Pettengill; WOR, William L. Shirer
1:15—WJZ, Edward Weeks; WOR, John B. Kennedy
1:30—WNBC, Author Meets Critics; WJZ, National Vespers; WCBS, Tell It Again; WOR, Music Box
2:00—WNBC, The Hungry Dollar; WJZ, This Week Around the World; WOR, Babe Ruth Symphony; WCBS, Festival of Song
2:30 — WNBC, University Theater; WCBS, You Are There; WOR, News, H. Hennessy; WJZ, Mr. President, Drama
2:45—WOR, Periscope
3:00—WCBS, C.B.S. Symphony Orch.; WOR, Michael O'Duffy; WJZ, Harrison Woods
3:30—WNBC, One Man's Family, WOR, Juvenile Jury Quiz; WJZ, Treasury Band Show
4:00—WNBC, The Quiz Kids; WOR House of Mystery; WJZ, Cal Tinney
4:30—WJZ, Favorite Story; WNBC News, Living—1948; WCBS, Skyway to Stars; WOR, Detective Mysteries
5:00—WOR, The Shadow; WJZ, Quiet Please; WCBS, Robert E. Lewis Show; WNBC, Jane Pickens Show
5:30—WOR, Quick as a Flash; WJZ, David Harding; WCBS, Variety; WNBC, Robert Merrill

Evening

6:00—WNBC, The Catholic Hour; WOR Roy Rogers Show; WJZ, Drew Pearson; WCBS, Family Hour
6:15—WNBC, News, Gardiner
6:30—WOR, Nick Carter, Drama; WJZ Greatest Story Ever Told, Drama; WCBS, Percy Faith Orch.; WNBC, Adventures of Ozzie and Harriet, Comedy
7:00—WNBC, Jack Benny Show; WOR, Sherlock Holmes; WJZ, Go For the House, Quiz; WCBS, Gene Autry Show
7:30—WNBC, Phil Harris and Alice Faye, Comedy; WOR, Behind Front Page, Gabriel Heatter; WCBS My Favorite Husband; WJZ, Carnegie Hall
8:00—WNBC, Charlie McCarthy, Don Ameche; WJZ, Stop the Music; WOR, A. L. Alexander's Mediation Board; WCBS, Adventures of Sam Spade
8:30—WNBC, Fred Allen; WCBS, The Man Called X; WOR, News, Melvin Elliott
8:45—WOR, Robert S. Allen
9:00—WNBC, Thomas L. Thomas, Marian McManus; WOR, Secret Missions; WJZ, Walter Winchell; WCBS One Sunday Afternoon
9:15—WJZ, Louella Parsons
9:30—WCBS, Our Miss Brooks; WNBC, Donald Dame, Tenor; WOR, Jimmie Fidler; WJZ, Theatre Guild: The Letter
10:00—WNBC, Take It Or Leave It; WOR, Hobby Lobby; WCBS, Lum 'N' Abner
10:30—WNBC, Horace Heidt Show; WCBS, Strike It Rich, Quiz; WJZ, Jimmie Fidler; WOR, Pat Hollis, Songs
10:45—WJZ, Sidney Walton; WOR, The Handyman
11:00—WNBC, News, Bob Trout; WJZ, News; WOR, News, Melvin Elliott; WCBS, News, G. Bancroft
11:15—WOR, News; WNBC, News, C. Utley; WCBS, U.N. in Action; WJZ, Jacques Fray Show
11:30—WNBC, Chicago Round Table; WOR, Noro Morale's Orch.; WJZ, Del Courtney Orch.; WCBS, Buddy Monero's Orch.
12:00—WNBC, News, Beasley Smith's Orch.; WOR, News, Shandor Orch.; WJZ, News, Midnight Music Shop; WCBS, News, Tex Beneke's Orch.

Annie Gets Gun For 1,000th Time Thursday

By ROBERT GARLAND

New York—(INS)—As of this coming Thursday, Broadway's Annie Oakley will have gone and got her Remington for one thousand consecutive afternoons and evenings at the Imperial. As of today, Miss Oakley's gun-gettin' times add up to nine hundred and ninety-five. On any showshop's well-kept tally card, that is a notable number of occasions. Yet I am not surprised at its great figure.

For, nine hundred and ninety-five performances ago—the date would be May 16, 1946: the newspaper would be the New York Journal-American — I put my name to a rave review in which there were no "ifs" or "buts" or even "maybes" to mar the fine effect of a thoroughly off-the-deep-end notice, "Annie Get Your Gun" could have blown it up outside its handsome playhouse.

Which, as a matter of fact, is exactly what it did!

Now, in the October of 1948, after two years, five months and four days, it still is there to entice the potential customer who, by some curious, almost unheard-of, mischance has not been informed that the Irving Berlin-Herbert and Dorothy Fields musical-comedy is the best of its kind in town. Last week I saw it for the twelfth time and found it still pretty near perfection.

Albanian Cabinet Army Head Shuffled

London, Oct. 2—(AP)—Radio Tirana said tonight Albanian Premier Enver Hoxha has reshuffled his cabinet and appointed a new army chief of staff.

The bare announcement of the cabinet and army shakeup gave no clue as to the significance of the move. The tiny Soviet satellite has been quarreling with neighboring Yugoslavia since the Cominform denounced Marshal Tito.

Mj. Gen. Mehmet Sheh was transferred from his post as communications minister and appointed chief of staff of the national army.

WEATHER
(U. S. Weather Bureau Forecast)
Eastern Pennsylvania: Warm And Windy Followed By Showers And Scattered Thunderstorms Saturday Afternoon And Night. Colder Saturday Night. Sunday Rather Cloudy And Colder.

Intelligencer Journal.

The Leading Newspaper in the Garden Spot of America, Home Owned for Home Folks Since 1794

The Next Intell Radio Edition will be on the air at 11:10 P. M. Sunday on WGAL (1490)

55th Year.—No. 123. | Lancaster City Zone Population, Official Figures of Audit Bureau of Circulations 112,897 | LANCASTER, PA., SATURDAY MORNING, NOVEMBER 6, 1948. | CITY | TWENTY-TWO PAGES. | 30c PER WEEK—5c Per Copy

COMMUNITY LEADERS OFFER IDEAS ON MOST VITAL NEEDS OF CITY

"What Lancaster Needs Most" Is Subject Of 5 Speakers At American Legion Forum

Five community leaders who took part in a forum Friday night on "What Lancaster Needs Most," are shown with the moderator prior to the meeting in the home of Lancaster Post 34, American Legion, sponsors of the forum. Left to right, they are: Col. J. Hale Steinman, Lancaster newspaper publisher; C. W. Mayser, professor emeritus, who served as athletic director at Franklin and Marshall college for 25 years; Miss Sara Ann Stauffer, who served with the American Red Cross overseas during World War II; Col. Frederick S. Foltz, who served in World War II; Francis D. Rineer, City Commissioner of streets and public improvements, and the Rev. Harvey W. Swanson, Post 34 public affairs committee chairman, who served as moderator. (Intell Photo)

LIST HOUSING

By-Pass, Leadership, Civic Auditorium Cited By Panel As Required

TEXTS ON PAGE 18

Low-cost housing, a by-pass, leadership and a civic auditorium were cited Friday evening by five community leaders as "What Lancaster Needs Most," at a forum sponsored by Lancaster Post 34, American Legion.

The five members of the panel and what they said "Lancaster Needs Most," are as follows:

Miss Sara Ann Stauffer, who served with the American Red Cross overseas during World War II, called for low-cost housing; Francis D. Rineer, City Commissioner of streets and public improvements, called for a by-pass; Col. Frederick S. Foltz, who served in World War II, called for better leadership by increasing the boundaries of the city; Prof. C. W. Mayser, emeritus, who served as athletic director at Franklin and Marshall College for 25 years, called for a civic auditorium; and Col. J. Hale Steinman, Lancaster newspaper publisher, called for leadership—several kinds.

PUBLIC DISCUSSION

The Rev. Harvey W. Swanson, Post 34 public affairs committee chairman, served as moderator. Following the addresses by members of the panel, the Rev. Mr. Swanson turned the meeting into a public discussion.

In his introductory remarks the Rev. Mr. Swanson said, "Our purpose here tonight is not to throw brickbats at Lancaster, but to meet with the hope that out of this will

Turn To Page 4 For More Of FORUM

HARDSHIP SEEN IN FAILURE OF CHEST DRIVE

Visiting Nurse Association Expected To Be Hard Hit By Shortage

Failure of the annual Community Chest campaign to attain its goal of $424,991 may cause a great deal of hardship to the Visiting Nurses' Association, one of the 18 Red Feather agencies benefiting from the local drive, it was announced Friday.

Miss Vesta M. Miller, director of the Visiting Nurses' Association, 134 N. Lime St., said Friday "We don't know just how much the failure of the Community Chest campaign to attain its goal will have on our organization, but we are hoping for the best."

In discussing what she termed an under-maned staff, the VNA director said that under present conditions her organization is unable to meet the public's greatly increased demand for public nursing service.

"We now have 14 nurses, including a parochial school nurse and myself as director, on our staff. Five nurses are located at various points throughout the county, which leaves a staff of seven nurses to handle calls in the city of Lancaster," Miss Miller said.

The VNA director said it would be possible to add an additional nurse to the staff at this time, but since the Community Chest campaign failed to reach its goal, it is only a question of how long the budget would permit the increased costs of another nurse.

"Formerly our nurses averaged seven calls per day," Miss Miller said, "but now they average as high as nine or 10 calls each day."

VNA nurses in many sections of Pennsylvania work only a five-day week, Miss Miller said. "Our nurses in Lancaster County have been working a five-and-one-half day week for quite some time,

Turn To Page 4 For More Of VNA

FARM CORNER

"We Lead All The Rest"
By The Farm Editor

FARM IN LEXINGTON BRINGS $14,000.04

The 12-acre farm located in Lexington, Warwick Twp., offered at sale Friday afternoon by Katie E. Musser, was sold to Leroy S. Shirk, Elizabeth Township, for $14,000.04. Henry J. Snavely was the auctioneer.

SHOW STEER BRINGS $5 A POUND

Pittsburgh —(AP)— The grand champion steer of the 1948 Pittsburgh Junior Livestock Show sold at auction for $5 a pound, to equal the previous high figure paid a year ago.

The 1,085-pound purebred Angus brought its owner, fourteen-year-old John L. Tait of Mercer, RD4, a check for $5,425. The grand champion Southdown lamb, owned by Arthur Baxter, Jackson Center, brought $3 a pound.

Both champions were Four-H Club projects, as were about two-thirds of the 330 beeves and 131 lambs in the show.

The steers weighed a total of 318,630 pounds and sold for $124,322.55, an average of about 39.02 cents a pound. The lambs weighed

Turn To Page 4 For More Of FARM CORNER

Weather Calendar

COMPARATIVE TEMPERATURES

Station	High	Low
Water Works	70	51
Ephrata	70	59
Last Year (Ephrata)	59	47
Official High for Year Aug. 27		100
Official Low for Year Jan. 3		—3
Character of Day		Cloudy

SUN
Rises—6:38 a. m. Sets—4:57 p. m.

MOON
Sets—9:21 p. m. First Quarter, Nov. 8

STARS
Morning—Venus, Saturn
Evening—Mars, Jupiter

NEARBY FORECASTS
(U. S. Weather Bureau)

New Jersey and Delaware—Warm and windy followed by showers and scattered thunderstorms Saturday afternoon and night. Sunday rather cloudy and considerably cooler.

Maryland—Warm and windy with showers and scattered thunderstorms West portion spreading into East portion Saturday afternoon. Showers Saturday night with cooler in Central and West portions. Sunday partly cloudy and cooler.

EXTENDED FORECAST
(U. S. Weather Bureau)

Extended weather forecast for the period from Friday through Wednesday follows:

Eastern Pennsylvania and Middle Atlantic States: Rain Saturday and showers likely Sunday; rain again about Wednesday; total precipitation one-half to one inch; temperature will average four or five degrees above normal; cooler Sunday and warmer Wednesday.

Slaying Victim

New York — (AP Wirephoto) — A man identified as Colin Cameron MacKellar (above), general sales manager of the Dominion Textile Company, Ltd., was found slain Friday in his 19th floor suite in the Waldorf-Astoria hotel.

WALDORF'S GUEST SLAYING CHARGED TO SALESMAN, 19

New York Police Obtain Confession In Less Than Twelve Hours

New York —(AP)— A Canadian businessman was found beaten to death in the fashionable Waldorf Astoria Hotel Friday and less than 12 hours later police said they had a confession from a nineteen-year-old salesman.

Assistant District Attorney George Monaghan said Friday night the salesman, Ralph Edmund Barrows, had admitted "full participation" in the fatal beating of Cameron MacKellar, fifty-six-year-old textile company official.

Barrows, six feet tall, dark-haired and well-dressed, was being held at a police station for further questioning.

Monaghan said there was "no question" that police had the right man and that police were preparing to take a written statement from Barrows.

Police said Barrows was traced by a match-book cover found on the floor of MacKellar's suite.

The match-book listed the name and address of a tavern. Later Barrows was found in the tavern, police said.

Police advanced no motive for the crime immediately.

A pair of highball glasses and some setups for whisky drinks were slender clues left police for a possible solution to the "Murder at the Waldorf."

The glasses and the setups indicated that MacKeller, general sales manager of the Dominion Textile Co., Ltd., of Montreal, had had company in his room.

He was found lying on the floor of the living room of the apartment, leased to him through the Canadian Club of which he was a non-resident member. He was fully clad but the pockets of his

Turn To Page 4 For More Of WALDORF

FIRST STEP TAKEN IN PLANNING 1949 SOAP BOX DERBY

The first step in planning an all-American soap box derby for 1949 was completed this week.

A letter from national derby headquarters in Detroit addressed to Carl B. Slabach, local derby chairman, announced that Lancaster has again been selected to sponsor an authorized soap box derby in 1949 through the Lancaster New Era, Intelligencer Journal and Sunday News. The cooperation and enthusiasm displayed by the many persons who contributed to the success of this year's Derby prompted the consideration for another Derby-Day event.

The management of Lancaster Newspapers announced the acceptance and signing of the agreement with the Chevrolet Motor Division of General Motors Corporation, co-sponsors of the event. This action was taken in behalf of the boys of Lancaster city and county for the purpose of encouraging craftsmanship and sportsmanship and further to provide entertainment for youth and grown-ups as well.

New derby rule books are expected to arrive the latter part of December. No date has been set for the 1949 race.

PAPER CUTS GALLUP

Peoria, Ill. —(AP)— The Peoria Journal Friday cancelled the Gallup poll, a regular feature of the paper for at least 15 years, because, the editor said, readers "would not have faith in any Gallup poll findings from now on."

N. ATLANTIC TREATY DRAFT DUE NEXT WEEK

Hope To Hand Alliance Plans To Congress In January

Paris—(AP) — The Brussels Alliance will begin next week the outline and perhaps the actual draft of a proposed North Atlantic pact with Canada and the United States, British and French sources said Friday night. The object is to have the treaty ready to submit to Congress in January.

The report came as John Foster Dulles, Republican member of the U. S. delegation, told the UN Assembly's Political Committee that "our strength is not for ourselves alone. x x x It is our purpose so to unite and strengthen the forces of freedom that they will not have to fear."

This development followed the disclosure that the United States already has re-equipped three French divisions in Germany from surplus material. The Russian-licensed press in Berlin termed this action the implementation of a new "Truman doctrine for France", a reference to American military aid for Greece and Turkey to prevent the spread of Communism.

High American, British and French commanders in Germany will confer this week-end with Field Marshal Lord Montgomery, Chief Military Planner of the Brussels Alliance, to map strategic plans for European defense, dispatches from Frankfurt reported.

This will take place at Hannover, residence of the British military Governor of Germany, even before the representatives of Britain, France, Belgium, the Netherlands and Luxembourg gather in London next week to discuss the projected North Atlantic Pact.

The Frankfurt dispatches ex-

Turn To Page 4 For More Of ALLIANCE

Announce Drive For St. Joseph's Hospital Funds

Bernard M. Zimmerman, president of St. Joseph's Hospital advisory board, announced Friday a campaign to raise $1,500,000 for the hospital will open Nov. 15. Funds will be used to help finance an all-new 300-bed hospital building to be erected at Walnut Street and College Avenue.

The present building, according to tentative plans, will be retained as a nurses' home, living space for the Sisters, classrooms for student nurses and storage space.

SERIOUS NEED

"The need for the new hospital has become more and more serious in the past few years," Zimmerman explained, pointing out that not only is the present building inadequate for proper service, but population increases here have brought about a shortage of 411 general hospital beds.

Even with construction of planned additions to other local hospitals, there still will be a shortage of 261 beds, of which the new St. Joseph's will supply 70, Zimmerman said.

The opening rally of the county-wide drive for funds will be held Nov. 14 at Moose Hall when the Most Rev. George L. Leech, D.D., J.C.D., Bishop of Harrisburg, will be the principal speaker.

Seven major operating units are planned in the new hospital. St. Joseph's now has an operation schedule of a dozen surgeries every day and often elective

Turn To Page 4 For More Of HOSPITAL

BUS SERVICE ON NINE CITY LINES TO BE REDUCED

Changes To Be Made In Schedules November 22, CTC Announces

Nine city bus lines will be affected by changes in bus service announced Friday by Lewis W. McFarland, general manager of the Conestoga Transportation Company.

The changes for all nine lines involved, call for reduction in service, commencing Monday, Nov. 22. In addition, it was announced that three county bus lines will be re-shuffled.

CITY CHANGES

Changes in city lines, as announced by McFarland, are as follows:

College Avenue, Duke Street, Sixth Ward and Rossmere lines will lose one regular bus at 6 p. m. daily, except on Fridays. All four lines will lose one regular bus all day on Sundays.

Watch Factory, East Belt, Pearl Street, Elm Avenue and Race Avenue lines will lose one regular bus each at 9 p. m. daily, with the exception of Fridays. These five lines also will lose one bus all day on Sundays.

The new changes, it was pointed out, means there will be no Watch Factory bus in operation after 9 p. m. on Monday through

Turn To Page 4 For More Of BUS

SAFETY PIN TAKEN FROM GIRL'S THROAT

Sixteen - months - old Darlene Davis, daughter of Mr. and Mrs. Harry Davis, Kinzer R1, had a safety pin removed from her throat at the University of Pennsylvania Hospital Friday.

Hospital officials described the removal as routine and said the little girl was getting along fine and would be home within a few days.

The child was first treated at St. Joseph's Hospital, where her parents told authorities she had taken the pin, which was about an inch in length, from a curtain in their home. She was conveyed to Philadelphia Friday morning.

Roaring Welcome Accorded President In Washington

Washington—(AP)—The Capitol proudly poured forth its people and its plaudits Friday in roaring acclaim of a returning President who wouldn't be beaten.

From the north portico of the White House he will occupy for four more years, Harry S. Truman responded simply and humbly:

"I thank you from the bottom of my heart."

He looked across swarms of people on the White House lawn, crammed along broad Pennsylvania Avenue and overflowing Lafayette Park. His warm smile disappeared for a moment. He remarked gravely:

"I shall look forward to the help and cooperation of all the people, because we are faced with great issues now which I think we can bring to a successful conclusion."

Sharing the tumultuous welcome, as he shared the triumph of Tuesday's election, was Senator Alben W. Barkley of Kentucky, the next Vice President.

But mostly Washington and the folks of nearby Maryland and Virginia turned out to thrust out a friendly hand to the man who almost alone carried the Democratic banner to an upset victory.

750,000 PRESENT

Three quarters of a million strong the little people and big men of government and the diplomatic corps shrieked out their welcome to the Chief Executive.

With Barkley by his side, sitting on the folded top of a long, black car, Mr. Truman paraded slowly along the historic Pennsylvania Avenue route from Union Station to the White House. His hat and grin were going strong.

All the motorcycle police in Washington, an even 100, formed the honor guard ahead. Fire trucks swung 100-foot extension ladders across the avenue in tremendous,

Turn To Page 4 For More Of TRUMAN

'Phantom' Killer Role Revealed In Suicide's Note

Fayetteville, Ark. —(AP)— A University of Arkansas Freshman ended his life here Friday and later a note was found in his room in which he admitted to committing two "double murders" at Texarkana. In 1946, a wave of unsolved slayings in the Texarkana area—there were five in all—were attributed to a "phantom" killer.

Sheriff Bruce Crider of Washington county said the student was H. B. (Dooty) Tennison, seventeen, a member of a widely known Texarkana, Ark., family.

NOTE IN STRONGBOX

He said the youth took poison. A poem found on a dresser said that if the puzzle it contained could be solved, it would disclose how to open a strong box in Tennison's room. Authorities, instead broke up the strong box by force. The note was inside.

Sheriff Crider said the note read:

"Why did I take my own life? You may be asking that question? Well, when you committed two double murders you would too. Yes, I did kill Betty Jo Booker and Paul Martin in the city park that night, and kill Mr. Starks (Virgil Starks) and tried to get Mrs. Starks."

Miss Booker, fifteen, and young

Turn To Page 4 For More Of PHANTOM

HOSPITAL REPORTS 3 NEW POLIO CASES

Three more infantile paralysis cases were reported at Lancaster General Hospital polio unit Friday, making the 1948 total in Lancaster County thirty.

New victims are Lynne Sharpless, twenty-one-months-old daughter of Mr. and Mrs. William Sharpless, 623 First St.; John Stadel, seventeen, son of A. F. Stadel, East Petersburg, and Norman Edward Connelly, two, son of Mr. and Mrs. Norman Connelly, 35 Logan Ave., Manheim.

The hospital said Friday night the new cases were mild and that all were in satisfactory condition.

The Sharpless child was admitted to the hospital Nov. 2. John Stadel and the Connelly child were admitted Nov. 4.

This year's total of thirty is twenty-five more than were reported during 1947.

One death from the disease has been reported during this year.

President's Lead Is Now Approaching Two Million Votes

Washington — (AP) — With the count still incomplete, the vote for President Friday night stood:

Truman	23,079,060.
Dewey	21,094,756
Wallace	1,094,877
Thurmond	925,226
Total	46,193,919

The total includes votes from 126,576 of the nation's 135,864 precincts. This will be augmented by the remaining precinct count plus the vote for minor party candidates which usually requires weeks to tabulate.

STATE ACCEPTS NEW HOLLAND PIKE

The recently completed New Holland Pike has been made a part of the Pennsylvania Highway system, it was announced Friday by C. W. Good, contractor.

Mr. Good explained that the only stretch of the road still waiting state approval was accepted Friday. Last week the section of the pike from Lancaster to the Conestoga Creek was taken over by the State, and on Friday the remainder of the construction work was approved.

BOY VICTIM OF SEX KILLER FOUND IN CHICAGO SEWER

Youth's Mother Dies Suddenly After Reporting Him Missing To Police

Chicago—(AP)—The body of a boy, a suspected sex attack victim, was found in a manhole Friday, a few hours after his mother suffered a fatal heart attack while reporting him missing.

Dr. Kearns said the victim apparently was strangled by hand. The killer used such a vicious grip, he said, that a muscle in William's throat was broken.

The victim was 13 year old William Gervais. His body had been dumped into an electrical conduit vault on the South Side that youngsters had been using as a playhouse cave. Although a blood-stained 18-inch bar was found near the body, Dr. Jerry Kearns, coroner's physician, said the youth had been strangled.

His mother, Mrs. Clara Foote, forty-five, a widow, was stricken Thursday night in the Stockyards

Turn To Page 4 For More Of VICTIM

STOCK PRICES DROP IN BROADEST MARKET

New York — (AP) — Stock prices dropped drastically Friday in the broadest market on record.

Brokers said it was a renewal of the post-election plunge fed by Wall Street fears of restrictive legislation affecting business.

Total market value of all shares on the New York Stock Exchange has gone down nearly $5,000,000,000 since the re-election of President Truman.

Friday's declines were $1 to more than $8 a share with extreme losses going to $14. Most of the selling was at prices around $2 to $7 below Thursday night's closing quotations.

Hazleton Woman Found Dead On Bus At Station

Mrs. Clara E. Gantert, sixty-seven, 640 McKinley St., Hazleton, was found dead on a Greyhound bus when it arrived in Lancaster at 6:05 p. m. Friday for a 10-minute stop-over.

Dr. Charles P. Stahr, deputy coroner, said death was due to acute heart failure, with diabetes as a contributing cause. He said he learned the woman got on the bus at Harrisburg to make a trip to Coatesville, where she was to attend a GAR meeting. He said she apparently died about half-way between Harrisburg and Lancaster.

A son, William J. Gantert, who lives at 1008 Wheatland Ave., was notified of his mother's death after city police contacted Hazleton in order to determine the woman's home and relatives. Police were then told she had a son in Lancaster, who did not know she was scheduled to pass through the city.

The woman was discovered to be dead by Charles Emery, 4253 N. Marshall St., Philadelphia, the driver of the bus. He told police the bus passengers got off for the 10-

Turn To Page 4 For More Of WOMAN

Armistice Day Parade Sunday To Honor Dead Of World Wars

More than 20 bands and a long list of social, fraternal and military organizations will march in the six divisions in the annual Armistice Day parade here Sunday afternoon, which honors the dead of both World Wars.

Gen. Daniel B. Strickler will be parade marshal, and Col. K. L. Shirk will be chief of staff. Division aides will be John Kiehl, Joseph Lamonica, Charles Burie, William Stengle, Lambert J. Sullenberger and Daniel W. Shaub.

The chief marshal and his staff will review the parade from their position at South Ann and South

Turn To Page 4 For More Of PARADE

PARADE ROUTE

The Armistice Day parade, scheduled to move at 2 p. m. Sunday from Duke and Lemon Streets, will follow this route: South on Duke Street to East King Street, East on King Street to Ann Street, and South on Ann Street to Riverview Burial Park, where services will be held at the American Legion plot.

Game Protectors Warn Hunters On Violations Of Safety Zones

State Game Protectors Friday night issued a warning to hunters shooting game near the outskirts of the city and in built-up sections after one city woman was struck by a shotgun pellet Friday afternoon and other persons made complaints.

State Game Protector John H. Haverstick reported Friday night that Mrs. Robert Flinchbaugh, 827 E. Orange St., was struck by a pellet as she was waiting in her automobile for her children to come out of the Wickersham School. He said his office had also received complaints of shooting near the city and that four hunters had already been fined $25 on field receipts for shooting in the rear of the 300 block of N. Broad St.

Mrs. Flinchbaugh reported to city police at 12:05 p. m. Friday that a

Turn To Page 4 For More Of HUNTERS

High Spots For Tonight's Traditional Tour Of Displays

STIEGEL TOWN GLAZED FOR CHRISTMAS—One of the county's most elaborately holiday-lighted towns is Manheim, whose wide square is a blaze of Christmas garlands centering in a big community tree. Illuminated, incidentally, are boro's new parking meters.

TWO-STORY PUTZ—Famous around the county are the outdoor displays which Chester Bixler, Lititz R4, confects on his porch. This manger scene is framed in lighted trees.

LIGHT FROM A SINGLE STAR just 1,948 years ago has kindled a flame in millions of hearts to be reflected in the brilliance of Christmas displays on front lawns and porches, in public squares, churches and places of business. Touring the country on the first Sunday night after Christmas to see the outdoor yule displays is a tradition with many Lancastrians, and they'll find that this year's lighting effects show new originality and color in addition to a depth of feeling for the spirit of the holiday. Several contests have spurred home-owners to new efforts. In the city area, home decoration prizes were offered by the Junior Chamber of Commerce, and in Lancaster Township the Wheatland Lions Club sponsors a contest. Displays shown on this page, in addition to such "regulars" as that on the grounds of Hamilton Watch Co., will attract many visitors on tonight's family trips.

BETHLEHEM IN LANCASTER—This 32-foot painting of the Nativity has been attracting attention at the DeHaven used car lot, S. Prince St.

BRIGHTEST BLOCK—Pre-Christmas snow reflects brilliant display of holiday and community spirit of those who dwell in this row of houses in 800 block of Fremont St., Lancaster.

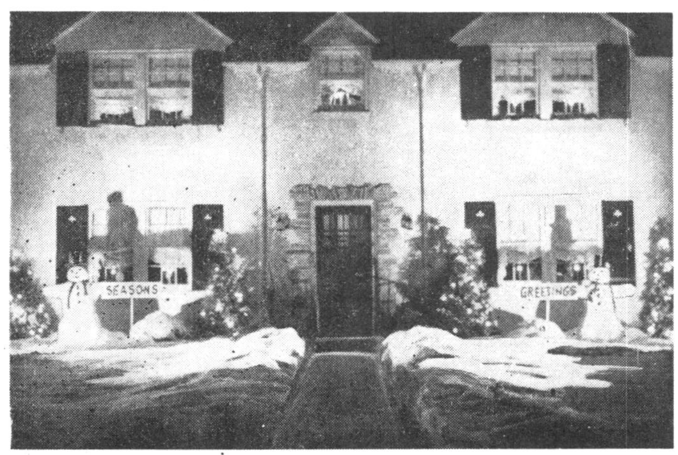

SNOW-MEN SNOWED IN—Top-hatted snow-men hold an original greeting in front of home of Mr. and Mrs. Jack Lausch, Blossom Hill Manor.

FIREMEN'S FANCY—Christmas lights outline the Eden fire house.

TRAVELERS' SHRINE—Huge painting of the wise men following the star brings home Christmas message to all who pass through Lancaster PRR Station.

WEATHER
(U. S. Weather Bureau Forecast)
Eastern Pennsylvania: Increasing Cloudiness And Moderately Cold Saturday. Not So Cold Saturday Night. Sunday Occasional Rain Possibly Beginning Late Saturday Night.

Intelligencer Journal.

The Leading Newspaper in the Garden Spot of America, Home Owned for Home Folks Since 1794

The Next Intell Radio Edition will be on the air at 11:10 P. M. Sunday on WGAL (1490)

155th Year.—No. 182. Lancaster City Zone Population, Official Figures of Audit Bureau of Circulations 112,897 LANCASTER, PA., SATURDAY MORNING, JANUARY 15, 1949. CITY SIXTEEN PAGES. 30c PER WEEK—5c Per Copy

TIGHTER ESPIONAGE LAWS PROPOSED

Gov. Duff Asks For Larger State Police Force

Lancaster County Residents Sweep Awards At Show

Red Rose Exhibitors Reap Record 820 Rewards Running Through Range Of Classes; Champion 4-H Baby Beef Brings $1.40 Pound Record Price

By M. M. RESSLER
Intell Farm Editor

Harrisburg—Leaving the last roundup as the State Farm Show closed its doors Friday evening, exhibitors returned to Lancaster County with the king's share of the booty—a new all-time record of 820 prize awards to Garden Spot farmers, their wives and children. Their score at the 1948 Farm Show was 559 awards.

Local farm folk either showed more or better products, or both, this year than last to account for the new record. Farm women did better this year than ever before with displays of food, clothing and home improvements. The 4-H youths of the county also stepped up their winnings.

580,000 ATTEND

Climaxing Friday's closing program of the five-day agrarian classic which attracted 580,000 persons, was the sale of the grand champion 4-H Baby beef for $1.40 a pound, equalling the all-time record price set last year.

Rugh Brothers, Bolivar, paid $1.519 for "Midnight," the 1085-pound steer exhibited by 17-year-old Jay Nissley, Manheim R3, and Jay said he is going to use the money to help buy an automobile for the family.

Reserve grand champion, also an Angus, shown by Ray Buss, Easton R3, was purchased for 67 1-2 cents a pound by the Economy Meat Market, of York. Last year's reserve champ sold for 85 1-2 cents

Harry Samuelson representing the Economy Meat Market, of York, paid 96 cents a pound for

Turn To Page 4 For More Of FARM SHOW

"We Lead All The Rest"

FARM CORNER

By The Farm Editor

$1.28 PER BUSHEL PAID FOR CORN AT COUNTY SALE

Corn sold for $1.28 per bushel and tobacco lath at $3 a hundred at the sale of farm equipment and household goods of Daniel W. Smith, near New Providence Thursday afternoon.

A cow was sold for $172.50, a pair of mules brought $62 and lamps brought from $3 to $4 each. Parke Shaub was the auctioneer.

MEAT MORE PLENTIFUL

Washington —(AP)— Choice beef steaks and roasts will be more plentiful the rest of the Winter and the coming Spring than last year.

This was indicated by an Agriculture Department report Thursday that livestock farmers have a record number of cattle being fattened on grain nd other concentrated feeds for the slaughter market. In general, cattle fattened on grain make better quality beef than those fed on grass.

But the supply of medium and lower quality beef is expected to

Turn To Page 4 For More Of FARM CORNER

Weather Calendar

COMPARATIVE TEMPERATURES

Station	High	Low
Water Works	45	25
Ephrata	45	30
Last Year (Ephrata)	30	19
Official High for Year, Jan. 9		59
Official Low for Year, Jan. 3		22
Character of Day		Partly Cloudy

SUN
Rises 7:24 a. m. Sets 5:03 p. m.

MOON
Rises 5:57 p. m. Last Quarter, Jan. 21

STARS
Morning—Venus, Jupiter, Saturn.
Evening—Mars.

NEARBY FORECASTS
(U. S. Weather Bureau)

Delaware and New Jersey: Partly cloudy and moderately cold Saturday. Increasing cloudiness and not as cold Saturday night, Sunday occasional light rain and milder.

Maryland: Increasing cloudiness and little colder Saturday. Sunday occasional rain and milder with rain probably beginning in West portion Saturday night.

EXTENDED FORECAST
(U. S. Weather Bureau)

Extended forecast for period Friday through Wednesday:

Eastern Pennsylvania, Eastern New York and Mid-Atlantic States: Temperature will average near normal in Eastern New York and three to five degrees above normal in Middle Atlantic States; moderately cold in Eastern New York Saturday; moderate temperature elsewhere followed by colder Sunday and Monday and rising trend Tuesday and Wednesday; rain totaling around one-half inch for the period in South portion and one-quarter inch in North portion.

LOCAL COURTS UPHELD IN TAX DEDUCTION CASE

Employers Must Deduct Delinquent Per Capita School Levy From Pay

The Superior Court of Pennsylvania in an opinion handed down Friday upheld a decision of the Lancaster County courts requiring the employer to deduct delinquent head taxes from employes wages at the request of the tax collector.

Judge Joseph B. Wissler handed down here last May 28, an opinion in which judgment was denied William Hartman, who contested deduction of $10.50 tax money from his pay at the Columbia Malleable Castings Corporation, Columbia. A motion for an appeal also was denied.

At that time Hartman was seeking reversal of a previous ruling which upheld both the constitutionality and principle of the tax deduction requested by the Borough of Columbia. Hartman then appealed to the Superior Court.

The State Court's decision affirmed that of the local Common Pleas Court in the test case for approximately 700 other Columbia employes at the plant who have also had delinquent head taxes deducted from their wages.

The question involved concerned the taking of both the husband and wife's delinquent taxes for Columbia school district from the husband's wages upon the request of the borough's tax collector. The test case was started here Aug. 19, 1947.

LOCAL COURT UPHELD

The judgment of Judge Oliver S. Schaeffer was also affirmed by the Superior Court in the case of Alice Smith, of Columbia, vs. the State Mutual Benefit Society, which

Turn To Page 4 For More Of COURT

CLOUDINESS FORECAST FOR COUNTY TODAY

The Weatherman said Friday evening there would be considerable cloudiness Saturday (today), accompanied with moderately cold temperatures. Sunday, he said, may bring occasional rain, possibly beginning late Saturday night.

Strong, cold winds, more closely associated with March than January, swept across Lancaster County Friday as pedestrians battled to keep their hats in place.

Temperatures Friday ranged from a high of 45 degrees at the official weather station in Ephrata to a low of 25 degrees at the City Water Works.

Polio Victim Now Plays Basketball

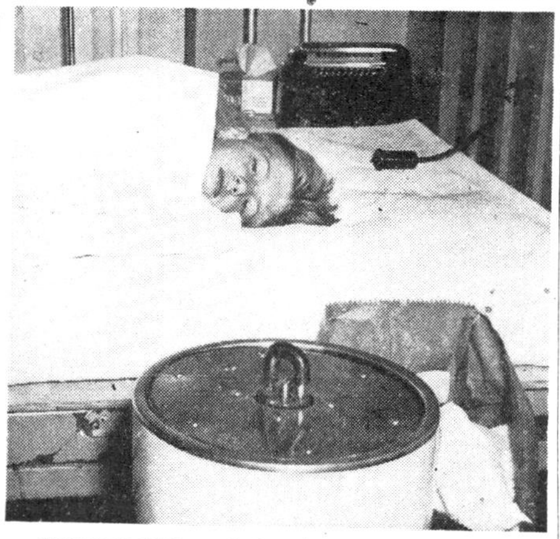

Eleven-year-old George Greiner, Jr., son of Mr. and Mrs. George Greiner, Sr., Neffsville, had only remote visions of getting back on the basketball court when he was confined to a bed in Lancaster General Hospital last October (above), stricken with dreaded polio. However, through the aid of funds from the March of Dimes campaign, he was provided with the best of everything in his struggle to again lead a normal life. Now, the youth (pictured at the left) is back on the basketball court leading a normal life.

March Of Dimes Helps Youth To Gain Victory Over Polio

Stricken with dreaded poliomyelitis last October, eleven-year-old George Greiner, Jr., son of Mr. and Mrs. George H. Greiner, Sr., of Neffsville, is back on the basketball court once again, following a gallant battle against the crippling disease.

A pupil at the John Henry Neff school, the lad was admitted to the Lancaster General Hospital as a polia patient Oct. 16. He responded quickly to the Kenny treatment, hot packs and muscular resuscitation, much to the joy of his worried parents.

Showing undaunted courage for a child, George battled the odds of the dreaded disease which had affected him in the throat and shoulder muscles.

George evidently won his struggle to again be a normal American "kid" as he was discharged from the hospital on Nov. 8, returning to his normal school routine severla weeks later.

Mr. and Mrs. Greiner, frantic when they first learned of their only child's plight, attribute most of their son's speedy victory over polio to the "dimes and dollars Lancastrians contributed for the battle against poliomyletis during various local campaigns."

Pointing to the Lancaster Chapter for Infantile Paralysis as its best friend during the crisis, the family related their son received the best in doctors, nurses, care, equipment and training, because people had contributed to March of Dimes campaigns.

Christian C. Rudy, general chairman for the local March of Dimes Campaign, Friday cited the case of the Neffsville youth as typical of the thousands of cases across the nation where money contributed to the cause eases the minds of anxious parents and at the same time provides the best

Turn To Page 4 For More Of POLIO

Low Pa. Tunnels May Keep 'Merci' Train From City

More than a thousand gifts from French people of all walks of life had to be turned down Friday as France's "Thank You Train" sailed from Le Havre, France, because there was no more room in the boxcars.

The train, composed of 49 cars of gifts from the people of France in gratitude for the "Friendship Train", are aboard the cargo ship Magellan bound for New York. "Merci America" is emblazoned in capital letters on a huge canvas sign on the side of the ship.

There was a possibility Friday evening as the ship was America bound that the entire section of the gratitude train might not pass through Lancaster as originally planned.

Officials explained that some sections of the train might not pass through many low tunnels in Pennsylvania because the "40 and 8" World War I boxcars must be mounted on American flat cars in order to comply with Interstate Commerce Commission safety rules.

Final information regarding the train's eventual visit to Pennsyl-

Turn To Page 4 For More Of 'MERCI' TRAIN

FIREMEN RESPOND TO TWO FIRE CALLS

City firemen were called out twice Friday night to answer fire calls.

At 8:14 p. m. sparks coming from the chimney of a building at 25 W. Chestnut Street caused a fire scare. Chief Harry E. Miller said firemen responded but their services were not required. Members of the Lancaster Little Theater Group holding try outs in the second floor of the building were undisturbed by the alarm.

A hedge fence in the back yard at the home of Nelson Derr, 340 Beaver St., was slightly burned by a rubbish fire at 5:32 p. m. Friday, the chief said.

Bulletin

TIENTSIN REPORTED OCCUPIED BY REDS

Shanghai —(Saturday) —(AP)— Reports reaching here today said Chinese Communists have occupied Tientsin.

(The source of the reports was not given in this brief dispatch.)

These accounts said Red soldiers moved through the streets, firing their rifles into the air, and shouting for the Nationalists troops to come out of hiding and surrender.

PROPOSES 400 BE ADDED TO ROAD PATROL

Cost Of Adding Officers Put At $4,000,000 In Next 2 Years

Harrisburg — (AP) — Gov. James H. Duff Friday called for legislation to provide 400 more State Police to patrol Pennsylvania highways.

Acting on a recommendation of Col. C. M. Wilhelm, State Police Commissioner, the Governor announced it will be sent to the legislature for action. It would cost $4,000,000 in the next two years.

Duff said that at present there are 1,600 State Policemen but only about 70 per cent are available for traffic duty on shifts.

"That means that at any one time of day, somewhat less than 500 men are assigned to patrolling some 41,000 miles of highways, an impossible task where highway safety is concerned," he said in a statement.

"Surveys of traffic accidents have shown that where State Policemen assigned to traffic duties are concentrated in one area the accident rate shows a sharp decline. When this concentration of traffic supervision is eased, the aacident rate immediately increases."

The Governor said that his Highway Safety Advisory Committee last week reported 5,555 highway deaths in 1948, an increase of three over the previous year.

"It would seem that if we are to continue our program of looking toward the conservation of human lives on the highways of the Commonwealth we must provide more adequate police protection for those lives," he added.

At the same time, Duff noted that $10,000,000 of the $15,000,000 spent for State Police operations in the current two years came from the State Motor Fund and added:

"It would further seem that the cost of this additional manpower

Turn To Page 4 For More Of STATE POLICE

JEWS, EGYPTIANS TAKE FIRST STEP TO ASSURE PEACE

Both Sides Pledge No Offensive During Present Armistice Conference

Rhodes —(AP)— Jews and Egyptians took their first definite step toward peace Friday by agreeing to keep their military forces in check while negotiations for an armistice are on.

At their second formal session, lasting 15 minutes, the delegates approved the text of a conference preamble which pledged each side to start no new military offensives and to respect the national security of the other while the armistice conference is in progress.

EXPLOSIVE AGENDA

The point on no military offensives was No. 1 in an explosive-laden agenda which the representatives of Israel and Egypt had

Turn To Page 4 For More Of PALESTINE

PRISON GATES SWING OPEN FOR WOMAN, 34, EXPECTING CHILD

Harrisburg, Pa. — (AP) — Gov. James H. Duff and two state agencies cut red tape Friday so a baby might be born outside prison.

The Governor and the Pardon Board commuted the manslaughter sentence of Mrs. Clara Shipcuskie Yeager, thirty-four, an expectant mother, of Northumberland County, making her eligible for parole.

Then the State Parole Board promptly granted Mrs. Yeager a parole.

Mrs. Yeager was convicted in Northumberland County of manslaughter in the fatal stabbing of Clem Koveleskie after a quarrel in his apartment in May, 1945. She was held in jail, however, for 16 months before trial due to the absence of a material witness.

After her conviction late in 1946, she was released on bond pending action on a motion for a new trial. That motion subsequently was denied and she began the jail term last July 12.

While at liberty on bond, she and Claude Yeager were married. Her attorney told the Pardon Board at a hearing last December the baby was expected in February.

RACE RIOTS FLARE IN SOUTH AFRICA, LEAVE 50 DEAD

Property Damage Put At $1,000,000; Military Called To Subdue Rioters

Durban, Union of South Africa (Saturday) —(AP)— At least 50 natives and Indians have been killed in a two-day race riot which has injured more than 300. No Europeans (whites) are know to have been injured.

For the first time in the history of South Africa the Army, Navy and Air Force were called out to help police restore order. Damage was estimated at $1,000,000.

The riots started Thursday when a young native boy was injured by an Indian market stallholder (push-cart peddler). He was taken to a hospital with severe headwounds and rumors spreading like wild-fire said that he had been killed.

Natives started attacking Indians indiscriminately: thousands of them ran amok and whole families of Indians were slain in their homes.

When the armed forces got the situation under control in the center of the city, the orgy of killing and sacking spread to the suburbs.

CHANTING BATTLE CRIES

Chanting African battle cries, the natives swept out to the sparse-

Turn To Page 4 For More Of RIOTS

Clark Also Asks Wire-Tapping To Insure Security

ATTY. GENL. TOM CLARK

Attorney General Would Drop Statute Of Limitations In Spy Cases

Washington— (AP) — Attorney General Clark Friday night formally proposed a broad-scale tightening of the espionage laws and asked that wire-tapping be legalized "in the interest of national security."

Clark said he had sent a bill embodying his proposals to Speaker of the House Sam Rayburn (D-Texas) and Senator McCarran (D-Nev), chairman of the Senate Judiciary Committee.

High among his recommendations was a plan for eliminating the statute of limitations so far as espionage cases are concerned.

The bill sent to Capital Hill would provide that a person accused of violating these statutes might be indicted at any time after the offense.

As the law now stands, the indictment must be returned within three years, if the offense occurred in peacetime.

Clark also asked that the laws be changed to cover the passing on of information relating to the national defense "which could be used to the injury of the United States or to the advantage of any foreign nation."

The present law simply covers the dissemination of information "with intent or reason to believe it is to be used to the injury of the United States."

Other proposals include a ban

Turn To Page 4 For More Of ESPIONAGE

'LEAK' IN EXPORT QUOTA FOR FATS SOUGHT BY U. S.

Extra Allocation Revealed; Advance Tip Sent Some Prices Up Temporarily

Washington— (AP) —The Agriculture Department hunted for a "leak" Friday night as it announced an extra export allocation of food fats and oils for the current quarter.

It said that 109,000,000 pounds of lard, cottonseed oil, soy beans, soy bean oil, and peanuts had been approved for overseas shipments in the January-March period. This is in addition to regular allocations previously announced.

Department officials meanwhile sought to track down the origin of reports which tipped off traders last week to the government's plans. At that time word was circulated that the government was preparing to grant supplementary export allocations of 107,000,000 pounds of the fats and oils—just 2,000,000 shy of the actual figure.

On the heels of this report, prices of some fats and oils went up temporarily.

Officials said a probe was being made by the compliance and investigation branch of the department's production and marketing administration.

SECRET QUOTAS SET

Export allocation plans are kept strictly secret to prevent speculation on the commodity markets which would alter the price ranges. They are determined by the Agriculture and Commerce Departments with advice from representatives of the State and Defense Departments.

The countries which will receive the extra quotas and the type of procurement will be announced Monday.

720 GREEKS KILLED

Paris —(AP)— Greek government forces lost 720 men killed or wounded in Friday's fighting around Naoussa, a communique from Communist chieftain Markos Vafiades said Friday night.

New Find Slows Cancer's Growth In Rabbit Cells

Washington—(AP)—Discovery of a human urine substance that slows the growth of rabbit cancer cells in a test tube and alleviates anemia in rats was reported Friday.

Biochemists Earl R. Norris and John J. Majnarich of the University of Washington, Seattle, who made the report, offered no statement as to whether the discovery had implications for the attack on human cancer and anemia.

They described their finding in "Science," weekly journal of the American Association for the Advancement of Science.

They have tentatively named the substance "vitamin B-14" although they said its origin and function is probably more that of a "hormone" than a vitamin. (A hormone is a kind of chemical messenger—a substance that is formed in one part of the body, but stimulates activity in another part. A vitamin is a nutrition substance.)

IDENTIFY 2 PARTS

The material, isolated from urine, is a brownish crystalline substance. The researchers have identified ni-

Turn To Page 4 For More Of CANCER

Mrs. Horting To Lead Inaugural Invasion

Mrs. Ruth Grigg Horting, vice chairman of the State Democratic Committee, will head the Lancaster County delegation to Washington for the inauguration of President Truman next Thursday.

Mrs. Horting, who will be accompanied by her husband, John F. Horting, well-known business man, will be one of the Democratic representatives of the State of Pennsylvania at all the important functions in Washington next week.

OTHERS GOING

Other prominent Democratic leaders who will be in Washington are Mr. and Mrs. C. E. Eaby, Ephrata; A. H. Fritz, Quarryville, and A. E. McCollough, Jr., Lancaster.

Eaby is a member of the Democratic State Committee and his wife was a presidential elector in 1948. Fritz is a former chairman of the Democratic Committee and McCollough is the present chairman.

Mr. and Mrs. Horting will leave for Washington Tuesday. At noon that day Mrs. Horting will attend a luncheon for National Committee Women and State vice-chairman to be held at the Women's National Democratic Club.

On Wednesday evening Mr. and Mrs. Horting will attend the presidential electors dinner to be held at the Mayflower Hotel. Mr. and

Turn To Page 4 For More Of DEMOCRATS

INAUGURATION BUS DEADLINE IS TODAY

Mrs. George H. Carpenter, head of a committee from the Women's Democratic Club, said that Saturday noon (today) is the deadline for making reservations on the chartered bus for the Truman inauguration Thursday.

There are still some vacant seats on the bus, and persons interested should call her at 2-0437.

The deadline for making reservations on the inaugural special, a crack train being sponsored by the Central Democratic Club of Harrisburg, is Monday noon, Mrs. Carpenter said.

Number Of Persons Losing Jobs Shows Gain In Certain U. S. Areas

New York—(AP)—The number of people losing their jobs is increasing across the country. Some areas are affected more than others.

While disturbing to the individuals and communities concerned, federal and state government experts say there is no cause for alarm. For the country as a whole there are only 2,000,000 unemployed, an unusually low figure, and the number of employed is nearly 60,00,000, hovering around all-time records for this season of the year.

But there are more workers out of jobs today than at this time a year ago. An Associated Press survey in nearly a score of principal

Turn To Page 4 For More Of JOBS

SOME WORK LAYOFFS ARE REPORTED HERE

Some economic dislocation has been reported in Lancaster County, where groups of employes have been laid off for indefinite periods.

The Lancaster Office of the Pennsylvania State Employment Service has opened temporary offices at Columbia and Ephrata to assist workers to apply for unemployment compensation.

Some of the lay-offs already have remedied themselves with workers returning to their jobs. This is especially true in the textile field.

Lancaster is Smallest City in U. S. With TV

TELEVISION SECTION

DAILY INTELLIGENCER JOURNAL, LANCASTER, PA., TUESDAY, MAY 3, 1949—13

Television Has Come of Age in 1949

WGAL-TV Promises Top Entertainment

Wednesday, June 1, will be TV-Day in Lancaster, when WGAL-TV will begin formal operation.

On that day one of the greatest scientific advances in the long history of man will be brought to the people of Lancaster and surrounding areas as television becomes a reality to thousands of families.

This achievement of combining sight with sound has opened a new era of broadcasting entertainment, education and information to the home. Lancaster will be one of the comparative handful of cities in the United States to enjoy its benefits and pleasures, joining only 36 other cities in the country which now have television stations.

VARIED PROGRAMS

When WGAL-TV begins regularly scheduled program operation on June 1, local televiewers will have an additional advantage in that the station will be a multiple network outlet. Programs from the National Broadcasting Company, and the Columbia Broadcasting System will be available on Channel 4. Combining the best network service with carefully planned local programming assures the WGAL-TV audience a variety of shows that will run the gamut from puppets to opera, from comedians to cooking schools, from prize fights to forums.

Programs in television break down into two broad classifications. The first covers remote broadcasts — the programs that originate outside of the studios. The second pertains to the day-to-day program fare which originates in the studios of the networks and the local station.

WGAL-TV will present a program schedule that will combine top-ranking remote broadcasts such as boxing bouts and spot news reports, with highly rated variety, comedy and musical shows originating in studios. And those entertainment features will be well balanced with local and national forums on public issues, educational features and public service broadcasts for organizations such as the Red Cross, Community Chest, schools, and similar groups.

Many viewers believe that spot news provides television's most dramatic and effective program source. The combination of network remote pick-ups from all parts of the country and reports of local news will give Channel 4 viewers a front-room seat to witness history in the making. The fact that this new art makes an eye-witness of the person at home increases immeasurably the dramatic impact of any news event.

NEWEST EQUIPMENT

To bring this exciting program fare to its local audience WGAL-TV will employ skilled personnel and the latest and most modern equipment. As a matter of fact, WGAL-TV will have some equipment not used by any other station because it is the latest television outlet to be placed in operation in the country. With only a few exceptions, RCA equipment has been installed throughout, from a small slide projector to the main transmitter. This equipment has been supplemented by a GE projector and a Projectall — an ultramodern projector of amazing flexibility.

One of the newest and most unique pieces of equipment to be built especially for Television, the Projectall is made with four apertures, permitting the projection of four different visual units through a series of mirrors into one telecast picture. This will make it possible to project as one picture the correct time, the weather forecast, news bulletins and station identification. WGAL-TV is one of the very few television stations in the country to have this piece of modern equipment.

Other new equipment installed in the local station includes two RCA film cameras, two studio cameras, high fidelity turntables, and an elaborate monitoring system.

During the past several weeks each piece of equipment has been subjected to the most rigid tests. The technical staff from WGAL-TV and consulting engineers from RCA have been checking every one of the literally thousands of parts, connections and miles of special wiring. Part of this elaborate checking includes the broadcast of a test pattern, a minutely accurate geometrical design which enables television service men to make careful installation of receivers in homes to assure viewers of the best possible picture reception. Also, the test pattern has been used by WGAL-TV to establish its coverage pattern, a necessary preliminary to the inauguration of regular program service on June 1.

In addition to these technical tests, the operating and production staff members have also been given a thorough schooling in methods and techniques of using the equipment.

TV TIME

Present plans call for WGAL-TV to be in operation from 5 o'clock in the afternoon until 10:30 or 11:00 o'clock at night, seven days a week. This schedule will probably be maintained during the Summer months. However, it is hoped that by Fall a combination of local and network programming will enable the station to increase its program service to include afternoon operation.

The establishment of WGAL-TV places Lancaster in a very select class of cities in the country where progressive and able leadership have made it possible to give the public the benefits of this new and powerful means of communication. As it has with WGAL and WGAL-FM, public service programming will play a major role in the operation of WGAL-TV. The station is aware of its responsibility and challenging opportunity to serve the public.

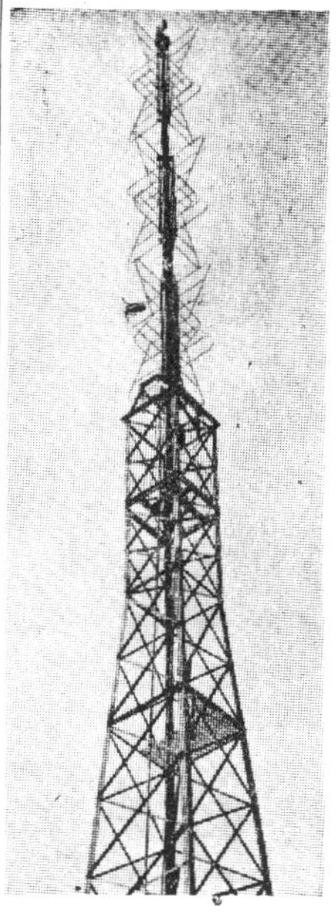

WGAL-TV antenna, mounted on top of steel tower will send programs from studio to your receiver.

PROGRAM DIRECTOR and control operators watch WGAL-TV test pattern on monitoring equipment in control room. Also shown are two station identification announcements, the one at the far left showing the top of the monument in Center Square, the next depicting a Conestoga wagon. All TV program pictures will be monitored on this equipment before going to the main transmitter to be telecast.

BRINGING A TELECAST FROM THE STUDIO TO YOU REQUIRES THE EFFORTS OF MANY TRAINED TECHNICIANS

TRAINED CAMERAMAN takes an angle shot with one of WGAL-TV's new studio cameras. Mounted on a tripod, a camera of this type can be moved easily to any point in the studios, permitting flexibility in programming. The headset and phone which the operator is wearing keeps him in direct contact with engineers and program director.

FAMILIAR SIGHT. Two factory-trained technicians install a television antenna atop a home. Outdoor antennas insure the set owner's receiving a strong, clear signal within the service area of a station.

Daytime Television Shows Are Attracting Countless Listeners

When Don McNeill and "The Breakfast Club", one of the most popular morning network radio programs, were recently televised simultaneously with their regular radio broadcast, it is probable that a great many housewives in the New York, Philadelphia, Baltimore and Washington areas left their breakfast dishes unwashed so that they could see as well as hear this telecast.

This immediately brings up some interesting questions. Will daytime television foment a revolution as well as an evolution in the home? Are television programs going to be so interesting that they will distract housewives from their chores and students from their schoolbooks, and perhaps even keep wandering husbands close to home and fireside?

Since most electrical - appliance manufacturers build radio and radio-phonographs as well as television receivers, the question of how much time people do spend, and will spend, in television viewing as against radio listening is more than ivory-tower speculation.

Recent surveys indicate that the average "television family" spends about three hours a day watching programs. Multiply three by the seven days of the week, and you'll find that viewers have their sets in use about two-thirds of the time that telecasts are actually on the air. Of course, this is a much higher percentage of operating time than surveys of radio listening have shown in recent years.

Part of the higher percentage may be attributed to the novelty of television. But many believe that, as this novelty wears off, television programs will continue to improve, along with broadcasting techniques and home receivers themselves, so that "sets-turned-on" for television will continue to represent an impressive statistic in researchers' surveys.

Television industrialists believe that in the immediate future the ratio between television-viewing and radio-listening in the relatively few television cities will continue to grow in favor of television even though in the daytime few programs have yet been developed that will assure a large audience, except for sports and after-school telecasts appealing primarily to children.

A notable example of the latter is Bob Smith and his "Howdy-Doody" show originating in New York. This program, when a "give-away" button was offered, drew nearly 100,000 letters from eager children in seven states and the District of Columbia.

One man has remarked that on "Howdy-Doody" days his children eat supper in the living room; moreover, television has disrupted the schedule for their evening baths, which now must wait until after the program is off the air. All in all, however, every television-owning parent we know regards video as a blessing in helping both to entertain and educate active children.

As time goes on, it is probable that many of the popular daytime radio programs will be broadcast and telecast simultaneously by the networks. The trend toward these "simulcasts" of radio and television network shows is already apparent with such programs as "We, The People", "America's Town Meeting" and others being televised and broadcast by radio simultaneously. Feature motion pictures, many of them made especially for television, will be telecast during the day, with repeat showings in the evenings to entertain those too busy to watch them in daylight. The television networks are now assigning their best creative minds to develop new daytime shows, ranging from video soap opera to audience participation and how-to-do-it programs.

Four Room "House" is Home of Popular Manhattan TV Show

One of the new wonders of New York City is a typical suburban home situated in the heart of Manhattan on 106th Street between Park and Lexington Avenues. The location, a good deal higher than street level, is ideal, yet the residents only occupy the house on week-ends when they invite practically all their friends to see them. Although it is only a four room house, and was just completed on February 27th the callers already number many thousands.

Most of these friends who have come to visit the house, generally on Sundays, have returned every week. Once inside a visitor finds himself in a spacious hall complete with staircase. Through the large archway, to the right is the living room, with its built-in bookcases and a picture of "Uncle Tiffany" hanging over the fireplace. "Uncle Tiffany" is supposed to leave the couple some money and until he decides definitely the picture remains in this place of honor. In the meantime on the back of his portrait, the lady of the house has done a modernistic painting which she calls "Monday," because, "It's busy, blue and a little bent."

Separated from the living room by double doors is the personal study of the master of the house. Since most of the four by six foot area is occupied by a huge desk and chair, the owner finds himself rather crowded at times. Yet, despite his difficulties, he refuses to admit that "his room" was once a closet.

Probably the room most envied by apartment-dwelling New Yorkers, is the kitchen. While everyone else in the city struggles with 2 x 4 cooking facilities this house has a full size modern kitchen. Like many a house that has been built since the war, this one can be converted and added onto at anytime. And like many a woman, the housewife is constantly making radical conversions. Most of the activity occurs on Saturday night when she decides to get things set for their Sunday company. During the past few weeks the bedroom alone has at various times been turned into a sitting room, a basement, a playroom and even a patio.

One object that the owners would like to remove from their front yard has presented an insurmountable problem. It is the set of steel doors leading into their lawn. The doors are the entrance to the second floor of NBC's television studios where 61 Sycamore Circle is located. Actually this house is the setting for the new television show starring Paul and Grace Hartman which is seen over NBC's television network every Sunday evening. And the people who visit the Hartmans are actual viewers who watch them solve their household problems every Sunday night via their television sets.

Aside from the doors, their home is just like a regular house minus the exterior walls. The doorways are all extra large so that the television cameras can move from room to room and in and out the front door. The cameras, of course, can also go completely around the house in either direction. This makes it possible, for example, for one camera to show Grace in the kitchen while through the door, Paul is seen greeting guests at the front entrance. Action going on in three different rooms can thus be picked up at will by the producer. This set, built strictly for television and adapted to the cameras is lived in by the Hartmans more than their own home on Long Island.

TV Adds to, Changes America's Vocabulary

Time was when a flicker was a bird and a mosaic belonged in a museum. No longer. They have become part of TV-lingo.

To the next generation a "flicker" will probably mean what it does now to the television technician . . . the objectional variation of the light value of a picture. And a mosaic? A specially constructed light-sensitive screen located in the picture-pickup tube.

A "ghost image" has no connection with Halloween. It's merely a shadow or echo picture on the television screen, usually caused by the reception of a reflected and delayed wave along with the direct wave.

How about a "blacker-than-black region?" It's not what you may think. It's that portion of the demodulated signal which is above the amplitude necessary to prevent the electron beam from reaching the screen. Figure that one out!

The "back level?" . . . not part of a chair, but the amplitude of the modulation signal corresponding to the scanning of a black area in the transmitted picture.

Finally, we have "raster". It's definition, believe it or not is a "field" . . . but not the kind we plow. This field is simply another name for one set of scanning lines in a frame.

TV Seen Raising Living Standards Thru Information to Consumers

Paralleling the advent and development of virtually every major invention during the past century, the living standards of American families have moved up a corresponding notch, and the process is again working in the rapid spread of television. This is the broad social size-up of the new industrial giant by Benjamin Abrams, president of Emerson Radio & Phonograph Corporation and a pioneer in television production and promotion.

"While bringing animate entertainment, visual education and endless on-the-spot picturizations of events into the home," Mr. Abrams stated, "television is carrying graphic and moving information on countless goods and services which are designed to improve living conditions, consequently increasing industrial and other production which results in more employment and more wages to make additional purchases possible. This is free enterprise at work and it is the process which has given Americans the highest living standards in the world.

"Before the war," Mr. Abrams said, "television broadcasting was done on an experimental scale only. The channels allocated by the Federal Communications Commission for this purpose were granted with the understanding that no paid commercial advertising was to be included in the programs and it would not have greatly mattered had the ruling been otherwise. Not enough television sets were in use to constitute a profitable audience for the advertiser and with no supporting revenue to pay for entertainment, the broadcasters were hard put to it to finance interesting programs. By the same token, the absence of such attractions left little incentive to the public to buy receivers. This was the impasse, but it was gradually broken down by the faith of broadcasters who spent their own money on good programs until the public began to learn what television really has in store and began buying receivers in earnest.

"Today, with licenses being granted all over the country by the FCC, with well engineered sets available for satisfactory reception, and rapidly increasing numbers of programs on the air, the issue in millions of homes is no longer one of whether a television set is to be purchased. In the television-serviced localities, the question is merely what set is to be chosen and when it will be delivered. In non-serviced areas, it is merely a matter of waiting until stations can be erected. How rapidly that development is taking place is indicated by the fact that in 1947 there were only eighteen operating stations and today there are 57 television broadcasting stations in operation in 31 cities, with 62 stations in construction, and 126 additional license applications filed with the FCC. With the establishment of more cable and relay systems, the spread will gradually cover the entire country."

Mr. Abrams stated that in his opinion, provided basic materials are available, the production of television receivers in 1949 might well top two million units of all types, representing a business amounting to close to 1 1-2 billion dollars. He feels that his prediction is warranted by such factors as the rapid increase in stations, the establishment of cable and relay facilities, enlarged audiences and improved programs, and the wider experience of television set manufacturers.

Production of TV Sets May Double in 1949

Production for the television industry will be more than doubled in 1949 with an estimated 2,000,000 television units being produced as against 800,000 for 1948, says Ross D. Siraqusa, president of the Admiral Corporation.

It is predicted that the end of 1949 will find 3,000,000 sets in operation, and 10,000,000 by the end of 1952. These estimates are based on reports from the fewer than 25 television set makers now accounting for 98 per cent of this country's total production of video units.

If these figures are to be reached, the television industry promises to represent an expenditure of $5,000,000,000 within the next few years, and will thus be America's fastest growing post-war industry. In 1947, video's first full year, it did a greater dollar volume of business than the auto industry after ten years.

Because of rapid expansion, it is difficult to compile accurately total employment figures for television. However, it is generally agreed that within the next decade many hundreds of thousands of persons will have found employment in all phases of television, ranging from production of programs to the manufacture of receivers, distribution and sales.

Gyroscope and Ram-Jet May Aid Air Defense
See Joseph Alsop—Editorial Page

LANCASTER NEW ERA

The Weather
U. S. Weather Bureau Forecast: Scattered Showers

73rd Year—No. 22,360 | Lancaster City Zone Population, Official Figures of Audit Bureau of Circulations 112,897 | LANCASTER, PA., SATURDAY, JUNE 18, 1949 | CITY EDITION | 14 PAGES | 30c PER WEEK—5c Per Copy

1,100 Attend Dedication of Airport

MORE N. QUEEN BUS CHANGES DUE MONDAY

Paving will Start on 2nd Block if Weather Permits Next Week

Rebuilding of the second block of N. Queen St. — from Orange to Chestnut Sts. — will start Monday — if weather permits.

To make way for the construction, city officials announced today, all bus stops in the second block of N. Queen St. will be moved into the first block of N. Queen.

IN ADDITION, most buses that were moved away due to street work will renew their stops in the first block of N. Queen. However, two, Pearl St. and Watch Factory lines, will continue to stop on W. King St. and at the YMCA on W. Orange St., continuing to omit the first block of N. Queen.

This means, officials said, that the emergency stops on W. King will be abolished for all but Pearl St. and Watch Factory.

The stops in the first block of N. Queen will be between Grant and Orange Sts. and in front of the Fulton Bank Building. There will be none in front of the Woolworth building, which is being torn down..

THE FIRST BLOCK of N. Queen St. from Penn Square to Orange is completed except a narrow strip along the east side of the street.

If weather conditions clear during the night, the final seal coat to the east curb line will be applied tomorrow. If weather conditions do not clear then the final operation will be delayed until next week.

WORKMEN WILL start tearing up the second block of N. Queen St. on the east side. Traffic will use the west side of the street during operations. Once the east side is completed, operations will be transferred to the other half of the block.

Working forces are now well organized and city engineers hope to complete the entire project in another week or 10 days if weather conditions are favorable.

Except for the very narrow strip along the first block between Penn Square and Orange St., N. Queen St. will be open for two lanes of traffic over the week-end.

POLICE HAVE CLOSED Grant St. from Queen to Christian and Christian from Grant to King Sts. because of building operations on the McCrory and Woolworth sites.

The two blocks of streets are being used to accomodate trucks carrying materials to and from the two building operations.

Deplores Parking Space Lack after Trips on Highways

PRINCETON, N. J., June 18 —(AP)—We have a beautiful highway system in America, but no place to park when we get where we're going.

That's the analysis of Prof. Philip Kissam, member of the Department of Civil Engineering at Princeton University. Kissam said State Highway commissions are organized to build highways between towns. The result, he said, is that "we have a beautiful highway system and no terminal facilities." He said this situation exists practically everywhere in the United States.

"Recent traffic surveys have shown that the greatest number of vehicle miles are extended not on the great highway system but within a few miles of the center of each town," Kissam said.

To remedy the snarl, Kissam urged "free ways" — roads on which a car can travel about 50 miles an hour with additional lanes so motorists can slow down and move off the roads.

The Weather

LOCAL FORECAST. EASTERN PENNSYLVANIA and WESTERN PENNSYLVANIA and NEW JERSEY: Rather cloudy with a few widely scattered showers tonight and Sunday; some drizzle likely late tonight.

TODAY'S TEMP.	
1 AM—69	
2 AM—68	
3 AM—68	
4 AM—68	
5 AM—69	
6 AM—69	
7 AM—69	
8 AM—70	
9 AM—71	
10 AM—73	
11 AM—72	
Noon—72	
1 PM—76	
2 PM—81	
YESTERDAY	
3 PM—81	
4 PM—81	
5 PM—80	
6 PM—78	
7 PM—76	
8 PM—74	
9 PM—73	
10 PM—71	
11 PM—70	
12 PM—69	

Comparative Temperatures	High Yester-day	Low Last Night
Wat. Wks.	81	67
Ephrata	83	68
High for year	93	
Low for year	1	

Humidity
8 AM—100
10 AM—100
Noon—91
2 PM—90

Sun Rose 5:34 AM
Sun Sets 8:35 PM

Moon Rises at 1:16 AM
Last Quarter, June 18
New Moon June 26

Morning Stars
Mars, Jupiter
Evening Stars
Saturn, Venus

Today's New Era

17 Are Feared Dead in W. Va. Flash Floods

By The Associated Press

Harsh extremes in weather dotted the country today — bringing attendant death and destruction. Seventeen dead were feared in the Potomac-Shenandoah Valley areas of West Virginia and Virginia.

There were rain-hungry and rain-soaked areas, a few small tornadoes, hail, wind and electrical storms. In Montana, snowplows were in operation.

The northeastern states sweltered in hot and humid weather. The continued lack of heavy rains further endangered crops and threatened serious forest fires.

IN THE HEART of West Virginia's Eastern Panhandle flash floods forced thousands to flee their homes. Unconfirmed reports said twelve persons lost their lives in the floods in the valley area near Petersburg, W. Va. Seven persons were missing in Bridgewater, Va. Five were said to be dead at Moorefield, W. Va. Entire communities were isolated.

Officials expressed fear for the safety of tourists who invaded the area for the opening of the bass fishing season today.

POLICE SAID THERE was 4 1-2 inches of rain in 24 hours. New rains dispelled hope of immediate abatement of the flood waters.

Among the missing were state police Cpl. A. M. Hurst, and his son. Hurst's home on the river bank near Petersburg, W. Va., was swept away during the night.

Hurst's wife and daughter were located this morning in Rowlesburg, after first being reported missing.

A rescue team of firemen reported setting out to pick up three men marooned on Kellers Island, near Moorefield. Before the stranded trio could be saved, the rescuers said, darkness settled over the island and water soon slipped over it.

The marooned group was not heard from thereafter.

A TELEPHONE operator said two others were seen floating on a

(See Page 10 — WEATHER)

ALABAMA FIGHTS 'HOODED' ORDERS

Senate Votes to Outlaw Masks in Public

MONTGOMERY, Ala., June 18.—(AP)—The Alabama Senate voted 23 to 3 to outlaw masks in public after Gov. James E. Folsom launched a legal campaign yesterday against all "hooded" orders.

Folsom said he had requested Atty. Gen. Albert Carmichael to bring legal proceedings against all "hooded" organizations in Alabama.

Folsom said he was sending papers of incorporation of one of the groups to the Attorney General. He did not name the organization, but said he understood the Federated Ku Klux Klan is incorporated in Jefferson (Birmingham) County.

IN BIRMINGHAM, the head of Federated Ku Klux Klans, Inc., said the organization would fight any effort to revoke its charter.

Dr. E. P. Pruitt, a physician and chairman of the Klan board of governors, said:

"We have not violated any law. We are going to fight for our rights."

THE FEDERATED Klan's charter asserts the organization is a "social, fraternal, religious, elee-

(See Page 10 — ALABAMA)

Find Man's Body Beside Tracks

The body of a man was found beside the Pennsylvania railroad tracks near Washington Borough at 5 a. m. today.

Cards and papers in the man's pockets bore the name Theodore Joseph Pillate, 8 E. Third St., New York City. Sgt. Joseph Duersmith and Pvt. Golden, of the State Police, said some of the papers, bearing the name were issued by the Veterans' Administration of New York.

Dr. J. P. Taylor, Columbia, deputy coroner, said the man is about 38 years old. He was practically decapitated and both arms were severed. Dr. Taylor said it is possible that the man was stealing a ride on a freight train and fell beneath the wheels.

More Showers Help Local Drought Conditions

More rain today helped local drought conditions.

Heavy showers fell this morning and drizzles followed up to noon. The mercury was in the low 80's this afternoon, but the humidity was high.

The forecast called for rather cloudy with widely-scattered showers tonight and tomorrow. Farm officials said the sporadic showers that have fallen during the last two days would give farmlands a "new lease on life" but steady rain for a day or two is needed to help the crops.

New Era Photo

Miss Ruth Shafer, Philadelphia, girl tower operator, flashes signals as she controls air traffic at the airport from the control tower. Red and green beams are flashed to the planes overhead.

New Era Photo

Mayor Cary welcomes State Commerce Secretary Theodore Roosevelt, III, to Lancaster preceding Hamilton Club luncheon. Left to right, Ralph W. Cummings, luncheon host; Mayor Cary, William Anderson, director of the State Aeronautics Commission; Secretary Roosevelt, and Col. J. Hale Steinman, dedication chairman.

CZECH PRELATE LEAVES PALACE

Tests Police Intent by Trip to Monastery

PRAGUE, June 18—(AP)—Catholic Archbishop Josef Beran emerged tonight from his palace where he has been under secret police surveillance the last four days. He left to participate in religious services at Strahov Monastery.

Catholics by the scores entered the monastery as the Archbishop drove up with other priests.

Many doubtless came to hear whether he would make any new pronouncement against the Communist government in the continuing church-state feud.

A CLOSE FRIEND of Beran had predicted earlier in the day that the prelate would test the intentions of watchful police by leaving his residence.

The Archbishop told the crowd packing the monastery:

"I come to you and swear to you that I will never sign an agreement that violates the laws of the church."

His emergence tonight made it appear certain he plans tomorrow to lead the procession and Corpus Christi services in St. Vitus cathedral.

A confidant who had seen Beran under police watch in the palace said government pressure so angered him that he wanted to tell the world the true situation of the state's anti-church campaign.

Despite secret police guards at the entrances and telephone switchboard of the palace this friend said he has been in communication with the Roman Catholic prelate.

He quoted Archbishop Beran as saying:

"Now I am angry. I plead with you to tell someone in authority that things that have been written are true.

"I intend to try to leave the palace late today to go to Strahovsky Cloister (this is the huge monastery high on a hill above Prague) and preach there."

THIS WORD came out despite a close guard put on the palace.

His friends, including those in the diplomatic corps, have been turned away.

Newsmen have been denied access to the Archbishop.

Bond Sales Hit $996,083, 69 P.C. of County Quota

A total of $996,083 worth of E bonds have been sold in Lancaster County so far during the Opportunity Savings Bond drive, Milton H. Ranck, county chairman, announced today.

Ranck pointed out that this is 69 per cent of the county's quota of $1,426,907. The drive now is two-thirds over, Ranck said.

The State-wide sales average to date was listed as 76 per cent.

4 DIE AS PLANE HITS MOUNTAIN

Air Force Trainer Trying Middletown Landing

NEW CUMBERLAND, June 18.—(AP)—An Air Force training plane crashed into Cumberland mountain today killing all four occupants of the craft.

At Cleveland, Col. Charles A. Bassett, commanding officer of the 2240 Air Force Reserve Training unit at Municipal Airport identified the victims as:

Lieut. Roy D. Lenser, twenty-four, Cleveland.

Lieut. William S. Shaffer, twenty-eight, Hudson, Ohio.

Pfc. George Christian, nineteen, Middleport, Pa.

Pfc. Leonard Novak, nineteen, Pippston, Pa.

COLONEL BASSETT said the two lieutenants were pilots on a routine training flight and that the two privates first class were on their way home on week-end passes.

Lieut. Arthur Lloyd, public relations officer at the nearby Middletown Air Force Base, said the craft was a twin-motor, five-passenger T-11. He said it crashed, burned and exploded about 150 yards from the summit of the tree-covered 1,000-foot mountain two miles southwest of here.

THE AREA WAS shrouded in a heavy mist at the time of the crash and Lloyd said he believed the plane was attempting to land at the Middletown Air Force field.

The bodies, all badly burned, were removed from the wreckage and taken to the Middletown base.

Lloyd said the plane took off from Cleveland and was flying a west-east course.

Democratic Trend Higher, Analysis by Roper Shows

By Elmo Roper

Over six months have passed since President Truman scored his upset victory over Governor Dewey.

What actually took place when a little over half the eligible voters went to the polls last November 2? Which half went? Who stayed home? What really happened?

That question is still important for at least two reasons: (1) An analysis of the last election reveals significant and important shifts in voting habits on the part of the American people between 1944 and 1948 — shifts which may well foreshadow a new and important trend in politics; and (2) in all the explanations of why the polls failed to predict the last election, none have taken the trouble to examine the facts of what actually did happen in the voting places across the nation.

An analysis of what happened at the polls might throw a good deal of light on what happened to the polls.

EVER SINCE November 2, statisticians and analysts in my organization have been examining the election results ward by ward and county by county in key areas of the country. This report presents our first findings on this post-election analysis. During the course of this study, great difficulties were encountered in obtaining election figures — difficulties I think it worth while to mention.

We are a full fifty years out of date in our election fact-finding facilities. Today in this country there is no single governmental agency which collects election results at the ward or precinct level. As a result of the chaotic state of our fact-gathering facilities in this country in the field of election statistics, we have had to obtain information from individual Boards of Elections scattered over the land.

And in many cities it is no mean feat to obtain the facts of what

(See Page 10 — ROPER)

AIRPORT AMONG TOP 11 IN STATE

Contribution to Progress, Roosevelt Says

The new Lancaster Municipal Airport is a "material contribution" to the commercial progress of Pennsylvania, State Commerce Secretary Theodore Roosevelt III said here today.

Roosevelt was guest of honor at a pre-dedication luncheon at the Hamilton Club. He also attended the dedication ceremony at the airport.

AS A RESULT of the enlargement program, Roosevelt says the local airport now ranks in the top 11 airports of the State.

The others he listed as Philadelphia, Pittsburgh, Erie, Johnstown, Altoona, Harrisburg, Williamsport, Scranton-Wilkes-Barre, Allentown-Bethlehem-Easton, and Reading.

Seventeen persons attended the luncheon, at which Ralph W. Cummings, this city, was host. Cummings is an executive assistant in the State Commerce Department.

CUMMINGS LISTED the other guests as: William Anderson, director of the State Aeronautics Commission; John Macfarlane, State airport inspector; Col. J. Hale Steinman, general chairman of the local dedication; Mayor Cary, State Sen. G. Graybill Diehm, State Secretary of Property and Supplies Chester M. Woolworth.

Dr. H. M. J. Klein, dedication speaker; E. George Siedle, secretary of the Airport Commission; Dr. Theodore A. Distler, president of Franklin and Marshall College; John H. Carter, editor of the New Era.

Hess E. Fritz, president, and Walter C. Miller, secretary, Manufacturers' Association; William Price, president of the Traffic Club; Richard N. Bomberger, chairman of the dedication executive committee; and Frederic S. Klein, a member of the executive committee.

Millville Mayor Guilty of $22,142 Tax Evasion

CAMDEN, N. J., June 18—(AP)—A Federal Court jury found Simon M. Cherivtch, 35-year-old mayor of Millville, guilty of evading income tax payemnts of $22,142 for the years 1944 and 1945.

The jury of seven women and five men deliberated three hours before reaching its verdict yesterday. Cherivtch, an automobile dealer who assumed the office of mayor last month, received the verdict calmly.

7 New Polio Cases Add to Epidemic in Texas City

SAN ANGELO, Texas, June 18—(AP)—Seven new polio cases are in hospitals today bringing to 74 the number under treatment in this West Texas city. It is the worst infantile paralysis epidemic in the history of this city of 42,000 persons.

The disease resurged just as San Angelo got $40,000 for its polio war chest—and just as the epidemic had shown signs of easing off.

Sneezing Boy Quits After 37-Day Siege

LONDON, June 18 —(AP)— The sneezing boy finally has quit sneezing.

Fourteen-year-old Michael Hipisley, whose 37-day siege of uncontrollable achoos attracted world-wide attention, was reported cured today by a London Nursing Home. Just how the sneezes, averaging one every three seconds, were stopped remained a mystery. So also did Michael's present whereabouts.

Airport Authority Needed, Siedle Says at Dedication

Non-Political Group Necessary to Assure Future Success of $2 Million Field, Pioneer Backer States

If the Lancaster Municipal Airport is to be built up as a growing business, it should have an Airport Authority to manage it.

A full-time, non-political Authority is necessary to insure progressive and efficient operation, said E. George Siedle, secretary of the Municipal Airport Commission, the body which now runs the airport.

Siedle spoke during the dedication ceremonies after he was cited for his work over two decades in helping to secure a modern airport for Lancaster.

SIEDLE SAID an authority is needed to assure continuity of airport management without breaks during changes in political administration, and for long-range planning.

The airport presently is managed by a five-man commission, consisting of two representatives of the city government, two from the county government, and a public representative.

Members are Mayor Cary, chairman; County Commissioners G. Graybill Diehm and Harry R. Metzler and City Commissioner H. Clifford Kreisle, and Siedle, as secretary and public representative.

An authority presumably would be composed of private citizens with full-time responsibility for managing the airport, regardless of change in political offices. It also would hold power to finance the airport through bond issues, etc.

SIEDLE DECLARED:

"We have here a plant which has cost in excess of two million dollars — a plant which needs not

(See Page 10 — AUTHORITY)

Sunday's Program Starts at 10 a. m.; Showers Forecast

Scattered showers are promised for the all-day air show tomorrow, concluding event of Lancaster's Airport Dedication Week-end.

The early forecast had called for fair weather tomorrow but later today the weatherman changed the predictions.

Tomorrow's program will be held regardless of the weather, officials said. But it is expected that rain would curtail some of the events.

The complete schedule:

10 a. m.—Two-hour model airplane demonstration by Lancaster Model Airplane Club.

1 p. m.—Air National Guard exhibition, with F-47 Thunderbolts.

1:30 p. m.—Navy pilots' exhibition, F6F Wildcats.

2 p. m.—Acrobatics by Bevo Howard, international stunt champion.

2:40-3:15 p. m.—Arrival and departure of TWA airliners.

3:15 p. m.—Crop-dusting exhibition by Christian Stoltzfus.

3:30 p. m.—Helicopter exhibition by William Johnson.

4 p. m.—Aerial acrobatics by Dave Long and his Midget Mustang.

4:30 p. m.—Parachute jump by Pat Patterson.

5 p. m.—Exhibition of "How Not to Fly", by Jesse Jones, of Baltimore, former Municipal Airport manager.

Both today and tomorrow sightseeing trips were scheduled via DC-3 airliners, wheather permitting.

Cab Driver Given Beating

Paul Dornes, twenty-two, 155 E. James St., an employe of the Yellow Cab Co., was dragged from his cab on Chesapeake St. near Marshall, early today, and beaten.

Dornes told police two men engaged his cab at Queen and Chestnut Sts. and ordered him to drive to Chesapeake and Marshall Sts. At the intersection, he said, he was told he was driving in the wrong direction. Dornes said when he turned the cab around he was dragged from his seat by the two men and three others who were waiting on the curb.

Drivers of the taxicab company have been on strike.

2 Ligonier Theaters Reopen after Tax Dispute

LIGONIER, Pa., June 18.—(AP)—People in this little borough are happy again — they can go to the movies six days a week.

Operators of the two theaters who had closed their houses June 1 to protest a 10 per cent amusement tax levied by Council opened for business again yesterday. But they emphasized it was a "trial" and that if business doesn't warrant, they'll only stay open Friday and Saturday nights.

KLEIN HAILS CEREMONY AS CITY EPOCH

Air Tour Planes Delayed by Rain; Program to Continue Tomorrow

Lancaster today dedicated the new and bigger Lancaster Municipal Airport, the city's challenge to the age of air travel.

The actual dedication ceremonies, held at 2 p. m., started at a lull between all-day showers. The skies darkened again after the sun had broken through the clouds briefly.

Long lines of automobiles wended their way to the airport over the Lititz Pike as rainy weather showed signs of clearing. At 2 p.m. the still-increasing crowd was estimated at more than 1,100 persons.

THEY RAPIDLY filled the gay flag-bedecked field, where new white concrete runways have been lengthened to 4,100 feet each — to accommodate airliners and put Lancaster on the commercial airlines of the nation.

A band played martial music.

The celebration continues with an all-day air show tomorrow, slated to be held rain or shine. The weatherman forecast scattered showers tonight and tomorrow.

In the main dedication speech, Dr. H. M. J. Klein, educator and civic leader, hailed the dedication as "one of the epoch-making events in the Greater Lancaster Community of the future."

The airport, he said, is a testimonial to Lancaster's transportation leadership through the years and to the spirit of community cooperation which exists here.

AND, UNVEILING a new airport plaque, Mayor Cary saluted the new airport as "an example of true community enterprise."

Today, he said, the people of Lancaster take possession of a "fine airport which is a real credit to our community and the envy of hundreds of cities even much larger than Lancaster."

The plaque, containing the names of individuals and agencies connected with the airport expansion—completed this Spring — will be installed on the outside wall of the airport administration building.

COL. J. HALE STEINMAN, was chairman of the ceremonies. Dr. Theodore A. Distler was master of ceremonies.

Dr. Distler presented a citation to E. George Siedle, secretary of the Municipal Airport Commission, saluting Siedle for his work in promoting airport development.

Among the officials on the speakers' stand were State Commerce Secretary Theodore Roosevelt III and William Anderson, director of the State Aeronautics Commission.

PRECEDING the dedication ceremony, Miss Mildred Martin, winner of an airport essay contest, christened a silver All American liner "The City of Lancaster."

Spectators milled about the field. Many came prepared for rain. They wore raincoats and carried umbrellas. Special concession stands sold soft drinks and hot dogs.

The first weather crimp hit the plans of the Pennsylvania Air Tour. A group of 300 planes from all parts of the State was scheduled to start arriving here at 10 a. m.

However, the first air tour plane didn't arrive until 11:15 a. m. That contained William C. Anderson, director of the Pennsylvania Aeronautics Board and titular leader of the tour.

He was accompanied by John Macfarlane, chief inspector of State airports.

ANDERSON said he feared most of the toursmen would not arrive until later this afternoon. He estimated additionally that the tour probably will be cut down "to about 75 or 100 planes" because of the

(See Page 10 — AIRPORT)

Latest News

5 Western Foreign Ministers in Accord

Luxembourg, Luxembourg, June 18—(AP)—Foreign ministers of the five Western European Alliance nations reported at the end of a two-day session today they are in complete accord on their role in world affairs.

The ministers from Britain, France and the Benelux countries wound up their current business in a three-hour mid-day meeting.

Hungary Repudiates Yugoslav Pact

Budapest, Hungary, June 18—(AP)—The government declared today Hungary no longer considers her trade pact with Yugoslavia in effect. A note was sent to Marshal Tito's government, which said "the Hungarian government cannot tolerate that Yugoslavia should continually violate the agreement and thus hinder the economic progress of this country."

Girl Scouts Roam Over 86-Acre Camp Opening Season Out-Doors

HQ FOR ADMINISTRATION and infirmary for the Girl Scouts' Camp in Furnace Hills, northern Lancaster County, is Mika House and old stone building renovated when the girls took over the 86-acre site. Girls sleep in tents.

SURROUNDED BY NATURE the girls at the Furnace Hills Camp have access to all manner of botanical studies. Here's a campfire circle with the Brownies. Program includes archery, horseback riding, folk dancing, camp crafts, swimming and a dozen other activities.

***ALL SET FOR SUMMER** Lancaster County's Girl Scouts are winding up the Day Camps and heading for the big Furnace Hills Camp in Clay Twp. Developed in the past three years it is about finished except for future expansion. On the 86 acres the Camp Committee of the Lancaster County Girl Scouts Council has built a dozen new structures and a swimming pool. The Camp's capacity is 75 girls a week. Counselors and administrative staff supervise a program divided into weekly periods, runs from June 26 to Aug. 21. Unit system provides program for Brownies, Scouts and Senior Scouts.*

HORSEBACK TYROS learn riding through arrangement with a nearby Denver riding school. They ride the Horseshoe Trail.

HOLLEY HALL BELL on porch rings calls for dinner or assembly. Mrs. Walter F. Kaufman pulls the rope. She is chairman of the Camp Committee and was active in development of the site.

ON THEIR OWN, older girls prepare for luncheon in unit house. Each unit had own troop cabin and wash house, with running water.

PLENTY OF ROOM for swimming is provided by the forty-by-eighty native red sandstone swimming pool, one of the additions to the camp, developed last year.

MOST POPULAR SPOT is Holley Hall, dining hall, well-equipped kitchen and store room. Here the girls eat most meals and gather for all camp programs.

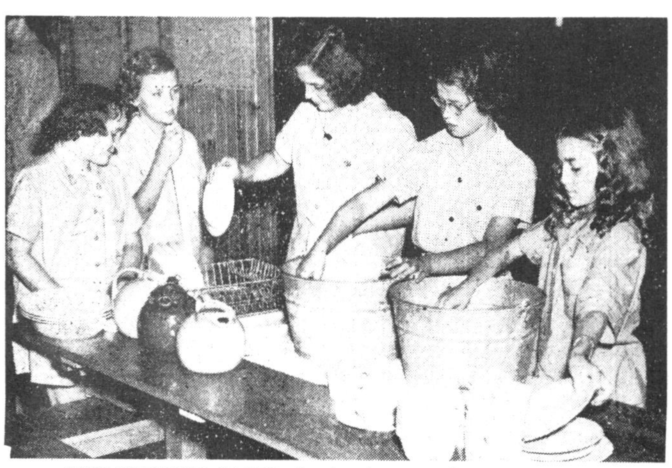

DISH WASHING CAPER—Routine chores are all part of the program. On the job above are Lois Bryson, Barbara Mellinger, Arlene Wyble, Kay Brosey and Marlene Wolf.

HORSESHOE TRAIL, famous local mountain route, is a feature. Hike above is being conducted by John M. Cavanaugh, nature counselor.

UNDER CANVAS gives final touch for the outdoor life. Girls and officials sleep in 21 tents. There are 14 buildings, all but one erected as part of the camp development.

Musser Park is Dedicated, Formally Presented to City

Flag and Flagpole Given by Kiwanis Club also Accepted; Memorial Cost $150,000

Musser Memorial Park was dedicated yesterday as one of the features of Lancaster's Fourth of July program. . .

Speakers paid tribute to the memory of the late Harry M. Musser, manufacturer, who left money for the park; there was a flag-raising and band concert.

The park was presented to the city by Harold Fry, representative of the Musser Trustees. It was accepted by Mayor Cary on behalf of the city.

Fry told the assembled crowd that "I am sure Mr. Musser would have been pleased with the way in which the provisions of his will have been carried out." To which Mayor Cary responded by saying "I am happy to accept this beautiful park on behalf of the community."

THE DEDICATORY address was delivered by former Congressman J. Roland Kinzer. In his address, the former Congressman said:

"It is indeed most fitting and appropriate that we should meet here today—on the anniversary of the freedom and independence of our country—to pay a fitting tribute to the memory of that citizen of our community who actuated by the deepest feelings of patriotism and love of his fellow men — gave so freely of his substance that we, the citizens of this city, may enjoy the beauties of nature, peace and recreation here provided in this park.

"Our city and community have been most fortunate, indeed, in having and developing citizens who, actuated by high ideals and principals of humanitarianism, have provided for and given us parks and places of quiet and peaceful recreation."

THE SPEAKER pointed out that Mr. Musser was not born in Lancaster but that he received his education here and developed an industry which employed 300 persons. He died April 21, 1928, at the age of 52 years. He read a portion of the will which bequeathed the estate to the community and then concluded:

"This park, of which our city takes possession today, is located almost in the center of Lancaster. It is rich in historic association. One-half block south is the building where Franklin college was first established. Just around the corner on Orange St. is the home of that patriot and Colonial diarist Christopher Marshall.

"In the next block of Lime St. to the south, where the Jewish Synagogue is now erected, was the home of Caleb Cope where Major Andre was confined as a British spy. On the northwest corner of Orange and Lime Sts. was located the Edward Shippen home, and across the street from us on the property now occupied by myself, John Wise, the pioneer and martyr in aviation, lived.

"With a community background and historic association such as this—the memory of Harry M. Musser and Elsie Eberly Musser, his wife—will ever be revered by our citizens and residents—with a sense of obligation and deep appreciation for this beautiful park."

THE FLAG AND flagpole was presented to the park by the Lancaster Kiwanis Club. Formal presentation was made by John C. Truxal, president of the club. The flag was raised by D. R. Long, a past president; Earl F. Rebman and Dr. A. E. Kabakjian.

The flag was accepted by Commissioner H. C. Kreisle after which Harry J. Taylor, city clerk, led in singing "The Star Spangled Banner." The band was provided by members of the local Musicians' Union.

Dr. V. W. Dippell, retired member of the F and M faculty, and Commissioner Kreisle, the co-chairmen, introduced the speakers.

The park was opened early this Spring and has been in daily use. It was built at a cost of about $150,000. The remainder of the estate was divided between the General and St. Joseph's Hospitals.

Part of crowd assembled to participate in dedication of Musser Memorial Park. Inset shows former Congressman J. Roland Kinzer delivering dedicatory address.

New Era Photo

Two Divorce Suits Filed Here Saturday

Two suits for divorce were filed here Saturday.

Thelma M. McDonnell, forty-seven, 714 Manor St., is seeking a divorce from Theodore A. McDonnell, forty-six, 441 South Shippen St., on the grounds of indignities. They were married May 24, 1923.

Charles William Houck, Jr., twenty-one, 19 East Farnum St., is seeking a divorce from Eva F. Houck, twenty-two, 416 Manor St., also on the grounds of indignities. They were married March 19, 1949.

Judge Bowman to Help Dedicate Denver Park

DENVER, July 5.—Judge John Bowman will be the guest speaker at the ceremonies of the dedication of the Denver Memorial Park, Sunday. The Pottstown band will present concerts from 2 to 4 p. m. and from 7 to 10 p. m. The ceremonies will be held during the intermission of the afternoon concert.

At 4 p. m. there will be a ball game between Denver and Lititz.

CAPTURED MAN LOOTED 8 PLACES

Trapped By Local School Engineer and Brother

Two brothers, Charles and Kenneth Haus, of 433 East End Ave., teamed up to capture a burglary suspect in the George Washington School, S. Ann St., Sunday morning.

Police said the suspect, Joseph C. Milburn, twenty-three, Lancaster R7, confessed to eight burglaries. He is being held for a hearing before Alderman Wetzel. Detective Al Farkas, the prosecutor, said Milburn admitted breaking into the George Washington School on two occasions, also to entering the Riverside Club April 19, the Sara Jaschik warehouse, Susquehanna St., and the home of Elsie Bowman, Creek Lane, July 1.

Charles Haus, engineer at the Washington School, accompanied by his brother, Kenneth, discovered Milburn inside the building while making a check Sunday and used the ruse of pretending to be armed to hold the suspect until police arrived. When searched, Milburn was found to have an open six-inch jack-knife in his trouser pocket.

Cpl. J. J. Haggerty, of the State Police, today charged Milburn with burglarizing the home of William Homsher, Lancaster R4, of clothing valued at $25 on July 2; stealing a rifle from the home of Lee Brenner, Lancaster R6, and looting a cottage at Rocky Springs Park, owned by James Figari, of a shirt and pair of trousers which he was wearing when arrested.

200 Youngsters Enrolled for Free Swimming Instructions

More than 200 children have registered for the 19th annual free swimming instruction program of the city playgrounds which starts Friday at the Maple Grove Pool, Recreation Association director Grant D. Brandon announced today.

The swimming classes, sponsored jointly by the Lancaster Recreation Association, the Lancaster New Era and Maple Grove Pool, will be held at 9 a. m. each Friday until August 5. "In case of rain," Brandon said, "classes will be extended until five lessons are taught."

CHILDREN who have turned in white cards containing parental permission will be assigned colored cards at city playgrounds tomorrow indicating their swimming class hours. Children who have not yet turned in white cards do not have to miss the first swimming class, Brandon emphasized, if they appear at the pool Friday morning with written parental permission. Swimmers will be divided into four classes — minnows, sunfish, sharks and whales.

Water safety instructors from the Maple Grove Pool are: Daniel S. Templeton, director of the pool; Loise Kinsey, James Bradigan and Bud Morrison. Recreation Association instructors are: Grant D. Brandon, director; Dorothy Shertzer, Orville Snoke and Richard A. Reese, Jr.

Six new handicraft tables arrived at the Recreation Association today and will be distributed to playgrounds where needed.

Prize Winners Among Junior Girls Listed at Camp Andrews

Winners have been announced for the Junior Girls session of Camp Andrews which ended Saturday with a capacity enrollment of 41 campers, five counselors, and three teachers.

The Junior Boys' camp opened Sunday, also at capacity, but openings continue for the Intermediate Boys' camp which will start July 17, according to Harold W. Shaar, camp director.

Cabin No. 2 of the Junior Girls' camp won the highest number of points based on "Morning Inspection," a scavenger hunt, and good work in classes. Led by Counselor Nancy Ambrose, campers in Cabin No. 2 were Patricia Hoffman, Judy Kreider, Elaine Sharp, Judy Bishop, Beck Hostetter, Joyce DeHart, Jean Buckwalter, and Judy Potts.

THE FOLLOWING GIRLS won places in the weekly swimming meet for ten events: Shirley Kreider, Mary Anna Moorhouse, Dianna Kling, Elaine Sharp, Carol Zahm, Joanne Bishop, Judy Zimmerman, Florence Herr, Shelby Sensenderfer, Nancy Mellinger, Joyce DeHart, Barbara Brubaker, Dolores Miller, Joan Weeber, Maryellen Bachman, Mildred Kemper, Judy Krieder, Marian Neely, Kitty Reese, Helen Herr, Edith Stradtman, and Fay Minney.

Counselors for the Junior Girls' camp were Maryellen Bachman, Nancy Ambrose, Mildred Kemper, Claudette Silvius and Ruth Muthard. Teachers for the session were Dr. T. A. Alspach, the Rev. Beatrice Weaver, and Milton May who was also assistant camp director.

2 County Draft Boards to Move Here Tomorrow

Two county draft boards No. 83 and 84 and city draft board No. 85 will move tomorrow morning to the Old Municipal Building, Penn Square.

The three draft boards will occupy offices on the second floor of the building.

York Paper Plant Sold for $52,000 at Auction

YORK, July 5.—The Industrial Litho Company, formerly the York Paper Manufacturing Company bought the paper manufacturing plant in Springettsbury Township along Paper Mill Road for $52,000 at Sheriff's Sale Saturday.

There were no other bids.

NAB 2 DRIVERS AS ZIGZAGGERS

10 Others Arrested for Traffic Violations

Two alleged drunken drivers were included among 12 motorists apprehended by city and State Police over the holiday week-end.

Ralph Waldo Emerson, sixty-five, Kennett Square, charged with zigzagging at Lime and King Sts., was arrested early last evening by Sgt. Robert Swab of city police.

Isaac Doutrich, sixty-one, 33 Chester St., was arrested on zig-zag charges by State policeman Fred Germ after colliding with three cars on the Manheim pike, four miles north of the city, Saturday night. Both drivers will be given hearings before Alderman Wetzel.

CITY POLICE also prosecuted the following for traffic violations: Paul R. Carpenter, 115 E. James St.; Harold G. Herr, Refton; John H. Dieterle, 335 W. King St., and Isaac Kauffman, Paradise R1, reckless driving; James P. Hiltz, 721-1-2 E. Chestnut St., ignoring stop sign; Charles E. Miller, 535 W. Lemon St., driving through red traffic light; Clyde H. Hemperly, Jr., 82 Prangley Ave., and Paul H. Booth, 11 N. Mulberry St., driving too fast for conditions; Lloyd D. Mellinger, Jr., 318 Alley I, Columbia, and Kenneth J. Cash, Jr., Lancaster R6, driving without operator's license.

DAY KAMP BOYS TO TOUR MUSEUM

Award Winners Announced for Second Week

Special events for this week's program of the YMCA Day Kamp include a trip through F and M College Museum and a whittling contest, director Theodore M. Scheckart announced today.

The following award winners were named last week at the close of the second weekly period of the six-week Day Kamp: Lloyd Boose, honor camper; Donald Pattason, honor athlete; Marvin Godman, honor craftsman; and Edward Kraft, honor swimmer.

The following boys qualified for the rating of: Braves; Edward Kraft; Bucks, Gerald Beyer, Lloyd Boose, Clair Garman; Papoose, Raymond Bookefield, David Kreider, Joseph Hatfield, Lewis Wright, Gerald Beyer, William Herr, Leonard Proctor, Kenneth Kramer, Peter Uakeas, Max Walton, Paul Eherle and Ronald Retallak.

Junior chiefs of the winning Blackfeet tribe are Dale Henderson and Glenn Bomberger.

CHARGES WITHDRAWN

Charges of larceny against Robert W. Shank, twenty, Gap, and John Scott, twenty-one, Gap R1, arrested by State Police on Saturday, were withdrawn before Justice of the Peace John B. Weiler, Gap, yesterday when restitution was made and the costs were paid. Mrs. Edna M. Trout, Paradise R1, charged them with the theft of a $250 diamond engagement ring during a visit at her home.

17 Fires Here Over Holiday, Most in Wheat, Grass Fields

Stovepipe Causes $500 Loss in Upper Leacock Twp.; Defective Aerial Bomb Ignites Field Near Lititz

City and county firemen were called to extinguish 17 fires over the week-end, most of them blazes in parched grass and wheat fields caused by the dry conditions.

City firemen answered two alarms today.

Shortly before noon, they were summoned to the apartment of Mr. and Mrs. Charles Kline, in the basement at 222 W. Vine St., but their services were not needed. According to Assistant Chief Frank Deen, Kline had been working about a gas stove and accidentally turned on the gas leading into the oven. Firemen turned off the gas. No one was made ill. Companies 1, 2 and Truck B responded.

At 9:15 a. m., firemen extinguished a slight blaze in a parked auto in the first block of S. Water St. The owner of the car, which bore license 61-338, could not be located. A short circuit in the wiring was blamed for the fire, according to Assistant Chief Deen who responded with Engine Co. 1.

AN ESTIMATED $500 damage was suffered when a defective stovepipe set fire to a washhouse at the home of Christian S. Glick, Upper Leacock Twp. at 9:15 a. m. yesterday. The Leacock, Bareville, and Leola fire companies were called.

At 5:20 p. m., the same three companies where they put out a fire in a wheat field on the farm of Daniel S. Stoltzfus and tenanted by Abram Barton, at Bard's Crossing. Damage was set at $200.

GRASS FIRES included:

Blaze on the property of James Leininger, Denver R1, extinguished at 2 p. m. yesterday by Denver Fire Co.; burning brush near Mt. Vernon Inn, Lincoln Highway East, put out at 4 p. m. by Gap firemen; grass fire on Isaac Huyard farm, near New Holland, extinguished at 3:30 p. m. by New Holland Fire Co.

At Lititz, a defective aerial bomb set fire to a field during a fireworks display. Lititz firemen put out the blaze.

Other fires: City firemen quelled a grass fire in a field in the 700 block of Dauphin St. at 2:26 p. m. yesterday; city firemen also were called for a fire in the automobile of Donald Barnett, 806 N. Shippen St., at Clay and Duke Sts., at 7:15 p. m. yesterday.

AT ELIZABETHTOWN, the Friendship Fire Co. was called at 12:15 a. m. yesterday when high tension wires in the 100 block of N. Market St. burned and fell to the road. Elizabethtown firemen also were called to the Benjamin Burkholder farm, Bainbridge R1, for a grass fire.

Four grass fires were estinguished by Manheim Twp.'s three fire companies Sunday. The Eden company extinguished a dump fire along the Grofftown road and a grass fire at Zook's Corner.

The Southern Manheim Twp. company put out a grass blaze along the Pennsylvania Railroad right-of-way between the Harrisburg and Manheim Pikes. And the Neffsville company put out a grass fire near the rear of the Penn Boiler and Burner Manufacturing Co., Fruitville Pike.

International Photo

Trial Figure Weds

CENTRAL FIGURE in the sensational yacht-death trial, Louise Overell, twenty, is shown with Robert Cannon, a Los Angeles policeman, shortly after their marriage at the First Christian Church in North Hollywood, California. Louise was acquitted in connection with deaths of her parents.

Pollet Or Spahn May Toss First Ball For N.L. All-Stars Tuesday

Boudreau, Southworth Name Choices Today; A.L. Still Favorite

Brooklyn—(AP)—Manager Billy Southworth is expected to start Howie Pollet of St. Louis or Warren Spahn of his own Boston Braves against the favored American Leaguers Tuesday afternoon at 12:30 p. m. (EST) in the 16th annual All-Star baseball game.

Although neither manager will announce his pitching selections until this Monday morning when the batting orders will be made public, Manager Lou Boudreau of the American Leaguers probably will make his starting pick from Virgil Trucks of Detroit, Lou Brissie of Philadelphia, Bob Lemon of Cleveland and Vic Raschi of New York. Trucks, Raschi and Lemon are righthanders.

Trailing 11-4 in the series dating back to 1933, the National League will be a 7 to 5 underdog in its battle to snap a three-game losing streak. Not since 1944 (there was no game in 1945) has the National won. Then it was Southworth who led them to a 7-1 triumph at Pittsburgh.

For the first time in many years, the All-Star squads are coming up to the annual Summer clash with no long list of injured players and no reluctant athletes. Last year there was some talk of applying penalties to players who did not choose to play but no official action was taken. Bobby Feller's "withdrawal" last year at St. Louis promoted the agitation.

With the possible exception of Tommy Henrich of the New York Yankees, who was picked to start in right field on the nation-wide fan vote, everybody is ready for the bell. Henrich injured his knee in a fall into the Washington dugout last weekend and hasn't played since. He is about ready to return to the lineup and might make an appearance.

With the exception of the pitchers, the starting lineup must remain intact for at least three innings. These eight men in each league were picked by the fans on some 4,637 votes.

The Brooklyn fans who never have had an All-Star game will see the Nationals line up with Johnny Mize of New York at first base, Jackie Robinson and Pee Wee Reese, their own second base-shortstop combination, and Eddie Kazak of St. Louis at third. In the outfield will be Ralph Kiner of Pittsburgh, Stan Musial of St. Louis and Willard Marshall of New York. Andy Seminick, the Phils' home run-hitting catcher, will start.

Robinson of Washington at first, Cass Michaels of Chicago at second, Eddie Joost of Philadelphia at short and George Kell of Detroit at third form the American infield. It will be Williams and Dom DiMaggio of Boston and possibly Henrich in the outfield with Birdie Tebbets of Boston behind the plate.

ANOTHER ONE FOR KELLY

Lucerne, Switzerland —(AP)— John B. Kelly, Jr., of the University of Pennsylvania won the two-kilometer skiff race at the International Rowing Regatta here Sunday.

THE LIP WELCOMES NEW HELP—Acquisition of two Negro stars to the New York Giants' roster, first Negro players ever to wear the Giants' uniform, brings a happy smile to the face of Manager Leo Durocher, who is hopeful his new help will give the Giants a boost. The two stars are Henry Thompson, left, infielder from Jersey City, and Monte Irvin, outfielder from same club.

Pirates' 8-Game Win Streak Ends Abruptly As Cubs Take Doubleheader, 8-6 And 9-6

Pittsburgh—(AP)—The Chicago Cubs put a decisive halt to the Pirate eight game win streak Sunday, sweeping both ends of a doubleheader, 8 to 6 and 9 to 6. The nightcap was an abbreviated six inning affair, cut short by Pennsylvania's Sunday curfew law. A disappointed crowd of 29,317 witnessed the Pittsburgh rout.

Phil Cavarretta's hitting sparked the tail-end Cubs in both contests. In the opener, he slammed out two triples and a double off starting pitcher Bob Chesnes and a single off relief pitcher Murry Dickson to drive in five runs.

2 KINER HOMERS

Ralph Kiner smashed out two home runs, the first with Dino Restelli aboard in the third, to run his season total to 23.

The Cubs hopped on Bill Werle for five runs in the first inning of the nightcap. Hank Sauer hit a three-run homer during the onslaught and Frankie Gustine homered with no one aboard. Werle, who lasted only a third of an inning, was charged with the loss.

(First Game)

Chicago	ab	h	o	a	Pittsburgh	ab	h	o	a
Baumht'z cf	5	0	4	0	Castig'ne 3b	5	0	2	3
Jeffcoat cf	0	0	1	0	Hopp 1b	5	0	7	1
Cavar'ta 1b	5	4	7	1	Restelli cf	4	1	7	1
Edwards rf	4	0	2	0	Kiner lf	4	2	1	0
Sauer lf	4	0	3	0	Westlake rf	3	1	0	0
Pafko 3b	3	0	0	1	Fitzgerald c	1	1	2	0
A.Walker c	5	4	7	0	Basgall 2b	3	1	2	6
Gustine 2b	4	1	0	3	Rojek ss	2	0	1	2
Smalley ss	4	0	2	1	Saffell rf	2	1	2	0
Rush p	3	1	0	3	McC'ough c	2	0	2	0
Dubiel p	0	0	1	0	aF. Walker	1	0	0	0
					Bockman 3b	2	0	0	0
					Chesnes p	1	0	0	0
					Dicksom p	3	2	1	0
Totals	37	10	27	9	Totals	38	9	27	13

a-Flied out for McCullough in 6th.

CHICAGO .... 210 200 021—8
PITTSBURGH .... 002 000 031—6

R—Baumholtz, Cavaretta, Edwards, A. Walker, Gustine, Smalley, Rush 2, Restelli, Kiner 2, Fitzgerald, Basgall, Saffell. E — McCullough, Smalley 2, Dickson. RBI—Sauer, A. Walker, Cavaretta 5, Kiner 3, Dickson 3, Gustine. 2B—Cavarretta, Dickson 2, A. Walker, Gustine. 3B—Cavaretta 2. HR—Kiner 2. S—Gustine. DP—Basgall, Rojek and Hopp. Left—Chicago 11, Pittsburgh 11. BB—Chesnes 4, Rush 6, Dickson 3. SO—Chesnes 1, Rush 3, Dickson 1, Dubiel 3. HO—Chesnes 5 in 3 1-3 innings; Dickson 5 in 5 2-3; Rush 5 in 7 1-3; Dubiel 4 in 1 2-3. HBP—by Dickson (Smalley). Winner—Rush (7-10). Loser—Chesnes (4-4). T—2:57.

(Second Game)

Chicago	ab	h	o	a	Pittsburgh	ab	h	o	a
Jeffcoat cf	3	0	2	0	Castig'ne 3b	4	2	1	0
Cavar'ta 1b	3	2	2	0	Hopp 1b	3	0	6	0
Reich rf	3	0	3	0	Restelli cf	4	1	2	0
Sauer lf	3	2	1	0	Kiner lf	1	1	0	0
Pafko 3b	2	1	0	3	Westlake rf	4	2	2	0
Gustine 2b	3	2	8	2	Basgall 2b	2	2	2	1
Owen c	3	1	1	0	Rojek ss	2	1	1	5
Smalley ss	3	1	1	3	cSaffell	1	0	0	0
Chipman p	2	1	0	1	Masi c	4	1	4	0
Lade p	1	0	0	0	Werle p	0	0	0	0
Dubiel p	0	0	0	0	Poat p	1	0	0	1
					aFitzgerald	1	0	0	0
					Casey p	0	0	0	0
					bBockman	1	1	0	0
					Bonham p	0	0	0	0
Totals	26	10	18	9	Totals	28	11	18	7

a-Hit into force play for Poat in 4th.
b-Singled for Casey in 5th.
c-Flied out for Rojek in 6th.

CHICAGO .... 520 020—9
PITTSBURGH .... 200 022—6

(Called end sixth inning, Sunday law.)
R—Cavarretta 2, Reich, Sauer, Pafko 2, Gustine 2, Chipman, Castiglione, Restelli, Kiner 3, Westlake. E—Pafko. RBI—Sauer 3, Gustine 3, Kiner, Rojek 2, Cavarretta 2, Owen, Bockman, Westlake, Basgall. 2B—Pafko, Gustine. HR—Sauer, Gustine, Cavarretta. S—Jeffcoat. DP—Pafko, Gustine and Cavarretta; Smalley, Gustine and Cavarretta; Rojek, Basgall and Hopp. Left—Chicago 3, Pittsburgh 11. BB—Werle 2, Chipman 6, Lade 1. SO—Poat 3, Chipman 1, Bonham 1. HO—Werle 2 in 1-3 inning; Poat 4 in 3 2-3; Casey 3 in 1; Chipman 8 in 4 2-3; Lade 2 in 2-3; Bonham 1 in 1; Dubiel 1 in 2-3. WP—Poat. Winner—Chipman (6-5). Loser—Werle (5-6). U—Barr, Ballanfant and Barlick. T—1:55. A—26,317.

Anglers' Almanac

JULY

Su	Mo	Tu	We	Th	Fr	Sa
					1	2
3	4	5	6	7	8	9
10	11	12	13	14	15	16
17	18	19	20	21	22	23
24	25	26	27	28	29	30
31						

(From Coble's Fisherman's Calendar) KEY—Blacker the fish—better the day for fishing.

SUSQUEHANNA OUTLOOK
(Sunday, July 10)

Columbia: A lot of bass and catties being taken. River low and slightly cloudy.

Safe Harbor Dam: River low. About 300 anglers out. Some bass and catties being taken.

Pequea: River fairly high. Numerous anglers on hand. High boat reported about 10 bass taken.

Holtwood Dam: A few fishermen out. River low and muddy with a few catties being hooked.

Fishing Creek: River clear and at normal height. All boats out with the high reporting 18. One cattie weighed 6 lbs.

Peach Bottom: River normal and a little cloudy. Some catties being taken with few fishermen out. One cattie taken weighed 15 lbs. and measured 31 inches.

WILMINGTON NINE SPLITS TWIN BILL

Wilmington, Del.—(AP)—The Wilmington Blue Rocks remained one and a half games off the pace in the torrid Inter-State League pennant chase by splitting a twin bill Sunday night with Harrisburg's Senators.

(First Game, 7 Innings)

Harrisburg	ab	h	o	a	Wilmington	ab	h	o	a
Malmb'g ss	2	1	1	4	Tesauro lf	2	0	4	0
Carey cf	3	0	0	0	Romello ss	2	1	2	0
Hansen 2b	2	1	3	5	Woods rf	3	0	2	0
Lemon lf	2	0	1	0	Werner c	3	1	5	0
Cox rf	3	0	0	0	Davenp't 1b	3	0	5	0
Carrow 3b	3	0	0	1	Whalen cf	3	1	1	0
Forbes 1b	2	0	9	2	Mathews 3b	2	1	1	2
Naragon c	2	0	4	0	Riley 2b	3	1	1	1
Reilly p	2	0	0	1	Walz p	1	0	0	2
aBobzean	1	0	0	0					
Totals	22	2	18	13	Totals	22	5	21	5

a-Struck out for Reilly in ninth.

HARRISBURG .... 000 000 0—0
WILMINGTON .... 000 010 x—1

R—Riley. E—Carrow. RBI—Romello. S—Mathews, Lemon, Walz. Left—Harrisburg 6, Wilmington 8. BB—Off Walz 4, Reilly 3. SO—By Walz 5, Reilly 4. Winner—Walz (5-7). Loser—Reilly (4-6). U—Woods and Warren. T—1:38.

(Second Game)

Harrisburg	ab	h	o	a	Wilmington	ab	h	o	a
Malmb'g ss	5	1	2	4	Riley 2b	3	1	3	2
Carey cf	6	0	4	0	Romello ss	4	0	3	5
Hansen 2b	6	1	7	4	Werner lf	3	3	1	1
Lemon lf	5	2	2	0	Oswald c	4	1	8	1
Cox rf	3	0	1	0	Whalen cf	5	0	1	0
Carrow 3b	3	1	0	1	Woods rf	5	1	2	0
Forbes 1b	4	1	8	3	Mathews 3b	3	1	2	3
Bannon c	3	3	5	0	Davenp't 1b	3	0	9	2
Piercey p	3	1	1	1	Smullen p	3	0	1	1
aNaragon	0	0	0	0	Brittin p	0	0	0	0
bWood	0	0	0	0	cTesauro	1	0	0	0
Frebel p	1	0	0	0	Olvesen p	0	0	0	0
					Schmidt p	0	0	0	1
Totals	39	10	30	13	Totals	34	7	30	16

a-Walked for Piercy in 8th.
b-Ran for Naragon in 8th.
c-Flied out for Brittin in 9th.

HARRISBURG .... 021 000 010 3—7
WILMINGTON .... 100 200 100 0—4

R—Malmberg, Lemon, Cox, Carrow 3, Forbes, Werner 2, Oswald, Mathews. E—Carrow, Smullen, Mathews, Davenport. RBI—Werner, Bannon, Piercey, Lemon, Oswald, Naragon, Bannon 3, Hansen. 2B—Bannonn. 3B—Malmberg. HR—Werner, Oswald, Mathews. S—Romello, Mathews, Carrow. DP—Malmberg, Hansen and Forbes; Mathews and Davenport. Left—Harrisburg 12; Wilmington 8.

Skeet

(Continued From Page 10)

P. Althouse-C. W. Kulp	189
FIVE-MAN TEAM	
M. D. Waters, J. E. Waters, Jay Groff, Park Althouse, L. W. Englert	479
RESIDENT (CLASS AA)	
L. Ballard	96
J. Gallaky	94
K. Lindberg	94
(CLASS A)	
F. Bonds	96
E. Bentzel	96
Heilman	96
(CLASS B)	
K. Gardner	96
T. Garner	95
C. Hoffman	95
(CLASS C)	
J. Cona	94
A. McLafferty	93
J. Frost	92
(CLASS D)	
A. Cullison	89
A. M. Hefler	89
(CLASS E)	
K. Osterhelat	92
R. Stumpf	88
HIGH OVER ALL (Women)	
Mrs. J. A. Lafore	259
(Non-Resident)	
Frank Vervaet	278
(Resident)	
M. D. Waters	273
JUNIOR CHAMPIONSHIP	
K. Gardner	96
H. Tshudy	86
WOMEN'S CHAMPIONSHIP	
Mrs. J. A. LaFore	91
Mrs. E. P. Linville	86

BASEBALL'S BIG SIX

(By The Associated Press)

LEADING BATSMEN
(3 Leaders Each League)

Player and Club	G	AB	R	H	Pct.
Robinson, Dodgers	78	307	68	111	.362
Kell, Tigers	69	281	50	97	.345
DiMaggio, Red Sox	74	301	65	102	.339
Kiner, Pirates	75	273	55	91	.333
Schoendienst, Cards	75	319	47	106	.332
Williams, Red Sox	79	288	76	94	.326

HOME RUNS

National League		American League	
Kiner, Pirates	23	Stephens, R. Sox	20
Gordon, Giants	16	Williams, R. Sox	20
Musial, Cards	15	Joost, Athletics	18
Sauer, Cubs	15		

RUNS BATTED IN

National League		American League	
Robinson, D'dg's	65	Stephens, R. Sox	86
Hodges, Dodgers	65	Williams, R. Sox	85
Gordon, Giants	56	Wertz, Tigers	79

ONLY 2 MATCHES IN NET TOURNEY; BIG CARD TODAY

Rain washed out all but two of the first round men's singles matches in the Lancaster City and County Closed Tournament Sunday as the Lancaster Tennis Club's eleventh annual tournament got underway.

In Sunday's matches, Dick Young and Ralph Engstrom turned in victories. Young was extended to three sets by Dick Kramer in a gruelling match and finally won out with a 4-6, 8-6, 6-1 verdict. In the second match, Engstrom turned back Pete Honaman, 6-2, 6-4.

Bob Zink, tournament committee chairman reported that all matches postponed Sunday will be played this Monday in addition to the scheduled Monday matches. Zink added that play will probably begin about 4:00 p. m.

Monday's matches:

(MEN'S SINGLES-FIRST ROUND)

D. Gerhart vs. E. Barber
D. Mull vs. E Koth
R. Harnish vs. J. Foreman
A. Belden vs. G. Young
H. Schleeger vs. R. Divett
E. Crider vs. K. Dalby
P. Lowell vs. E. Retew
B. Zink vs. K. Broome
T. Hurst vs. Martin
H. Fellenbaum vs. C. McCue
B. Freiler vs. J. Germer
E. Snyder vs. J. Guiles
E. Frey vs. R. Paden

TIGERS DIVIDE WITH WHITE SOX

Chicago —(AP)— The Detroit Tigers split a doubleheader with the Chicago White Sox by winning the second game, 1-0, after losing the opener, 4-2, before 24,702 persons Sunday.

VICO SUSPENDED 10 DAYS

Chicago — (AP) — Will Harridge, American League president, has suspended George Vico, Detroit first baseman, for 10 days and fined him $100 for throwing his bat into a box seat during an argument with an umpire.

A first inning double by Vic Wertz—one of two hits Randy Gumpert surrendered in pitching his twelfth complete game—followed a base on balls to Pat Mullin to account for the only run of the second game. In the first game Bill Wight limited Detroit to five hits. He won his ninth game as the White Sox gained a 2-1 series edge.

Wertz drove his double to the foot of the right field fence after Mullin walked with two out.

(First Game)

Detroit	ab	h	o	a	Chicago	ab	h	o	a
Campbell 1b	4	2	9	0	Rhawn 3b	4	2	0	3
Kollo'ay 2b	3	0	1	1	Philley rf	4	1	5	1
Kell 3b	4	1	3	1	Appling ss	3	2	1	1
Wertz rf	4	0	0	0	Metk'ch cf	4	1	2	0
Evers lf	4	1	5	0	Michaels 2b	2	0	1	2
Groth cf	3	1	3	0	Kress 1b	3	1	12	0
Lipon ss	3	0	1	1	Souch'ck lf	3	0	3	0
Swift c	4	0	2	2	Wheeler c	4	0	2	0
Newh'ser p	1	0	0	3	Wight p	4	0	1	3
aBerry	1	0	0	0					
Hutchin'n p	0	0	0	1					
bLake	0	0	0	0					
Grissom p	0	0	0	0					
Totals	31	5	24	9	Totals	31	7	27	10

a-Grounded out for Newhouser in 6th.
b-Walked for Hutchinson in 8th.

DETROIT .... 000 000 002—2
CHICAGO .... 200 200 00x—4

R—Kolloway, Kell, Rhawn, Philley, Appling, Metkovich. E—Groth, Lipon. RBI—Kress 2, Appling 2, Evers 2. 2B—Rhawn, Appling, Campbell, Philley, Kell. Left—Detroit 6, Chicago 8. BB—Off Newhouser 3, Wight 4, Hutchinson 1, Grissom 1. SO—By Newhouser 1, Wight 2, Hutchinson 1, Grissom 1. HO—Newhouser 6 in 5 innings; Hutchinson 1 in 2; Grissom 0 in 1. Winner—Wight (9-6). Loser—Newhouser (10-7). U—Rommel, Passarella and Boyer. T—1:50.

(Second Game)

Detroit	ab	h	o	a	Chicago	ab	h	o	a
Campbell 1b	4	1	7	0	Rhawn 3b	3	0	1	1
Kell 3b	3	0	1	3	Philley rf	4	0	5	0
Mullin cf	3	0	1	0	Appling ss	2	1	1	3
Wertz rf	3	1	1	1	aPierretti	0	0	0	0
Wakefield lf	3	0	4	0	Metko'ch cf	4	1	5	0
Evers lf	0	0	1	0	Michaels 2b	3	0	2	0
Robinson c	3	0	5	2	Kress 1b	4	0	10	1
Lipon ss	2	0	3	0	Souch'ck lf	4	1	0	0
Berry 2b	3	0	4	4	Tipton c	3	1	3	1
Houttem'n p	3	0	0	2	Gumpert p	3	0	0	3
Totals	27	2	27	12	Totals	30	4	27	9

a-Ran for Appling in 9th.

DETROIT .... 100 000 000—1
CHICAGO .... 000 000 000—0

R—Mullin. E—None. RBI—Wertz 2B—Wertz. S—Kell. Left—Detroit 4; Chicago 7. BB—Gumpert 4, Houtteman 4. SO—Gumpert 3, Houtteman 5. Winner—Houtteman (6-4). Loser—Gumpert (7-7). U—Passarella, Boyer and Rommel. T—1:54. A—24,72.

Bloomsburg State Teachers College undefeated football team, the only perfect-record team in college football last season, was the only grid aggregation in the history of the college to write a perfect season into the record books.

SPORTS Pages 10, 11, 12

CITY LEGION "9" ON TOP

The Lancaster CIO Jr. American Legion team defeated the Marietta Jr. American Legion in an exhibition game at Marietta Saturday afternoon.

CIO	720 300 0—	12	6	2
Marietta	002 020 0—	4	3	4

Batteries: Clark, Webb and Hartman, Smithgall; Seaman and Roberts.

NBC • 1490 Kc. • Mutual WGAL AND WGAL • FM • 101.3 Mc.

MONDAY, JULY 11, 1949

6:30 AM—United Press News
6:35—Musical Clock
7:00—United Press News
7:05—Musical Clock
7:25—Dolly Madison Musical Clock
7:30—Dolly Madison News
7:40—Weather Report, Old Co. Lehigh
7:45—Musical Clock
8:00—NBC World News Roundup
8:15—New Era Local News
8:20—Music for Listening
8:30—Morning Devotions
8:45—Musical Moments
8:55—Watt and Shand Morning Melodies
9:00—El Capitan Money Man
9:15—Bob Eberly Show
9:30—Good Morning, Neighbor
10:00—Welcome Travelers
10:30—Marriage for Two
10:45—To Be Announced
11:00—Dr. Paul
11:15—We Love and Learn
11:30—Jack Berch Show
11:45—Lora Lawton
12:00—Luncheon Club
12:15 PM—U. P. News, Home Insulation
12:25—New Era Local News
12:30—Garden Spot Farm Journal
12:45—Strictly Off the Record
1:55—Disabled Veterans
2:00—Double or Nothing
2:30—Guest Star
2:45—Three Quarter Time
2:55—United Press News
3:00—Life Can Be Beautiful
3:15—Road of Life
3:30—Pepper Young's Family
3:45—Right to Happiness
4:00—Backstage Wife
4:15—Stella Dallas
4:30—Lorenzo Jones
4:45—Young Widder Brown
5:00—Five O'Clock Special
5:25—Early News and Sports
5:30—Songs of Our Times, Bon Ton
5:45—Songs by Curly Bradley
6:00—World News, Lanc. Lincoln-Mercury
6:10—Intell Radio Edition
6:15—Interlude
6:25—Sports Parade, General Tire
6:30—Music by Guy Lombardo, Brubaker Motors
6:45—Sunoco Three Star Extra
7:00—Chesterfield Supper Club
7:15—News of the World
7:30—Watt & Shand Musical Highlights
8:00—One Man's Family
8:30—Voice of Firestone
9:00—Telephone Hour
9:30—Jane Pickens Show
10:00—Carnation Contented Hour
10:30—Fishing and Hunting Club
10:55—Interlude
11:00—Hager's News and Sports
11:10—Intell Radio Edition
11:15—11:15 Club and NBC News
12:30 AM—News—Sign Off —Adv.

WGAL—TV CHANNEL 4

MONDAY, JULY 11, 1949

10:00 AM—Test Pattern
12:00 Noon—Sign Off
2:00—Test Pattern
5:00—Film Presentation
5:30—Howdy Doody
6:00—World News
6:15—Round Up Time
6:30—Melody Time
6:45—Brandt on Baseball
6:55—New Era News
7:00—Judy Splinters
7:15—Mary Kay and Johnny
7:30—Kaleidoscopic Melodies
7:45—Camel News Caravan
8:00—Chevrolet on Broadway
8:30—The Clock
9:00—Vic and Sade
9:30—The Nature of Things
9:45—The Three Flames
10:00—Meet the Press
10:30—Intell Journal News
10:35—Sign Off —Adv.

WLAN ABC • 1390 kc ★ FM • 96.9mc

MONDAY, JULY 11

6:30 AM—Farm Show—(N. C. Ridge Runners)
6:45—Friendly Ranch
6:55—News
7:00—Wake Up Smiling
7:55—Farmers Bank News
8:00—Martin Agronsky, News
8:15—Wake Up Smiling
9:00—Music and Money
9:15—Breakfast Club
10:00—Home-Makers Club
10:15—Organ Varieties
10:25—Feature News
10:30—Songs by the Stars
10:45—Who's Talking
11:00—Modern Romances
11:30—Dinner Bell
11:45—Galen Drake—Pillsbury
12:00—Listen to This
12:30 PM—N. C. Ridge Runners (Lanc. Sales Co.)
1:00—Man on the Street
1:30—Melody Matinee
1:45—Dick and Ruth Neiman
1:55—Interlude
2:00—Breakfast in Hollywood
2:30—News
2:35—Melody Matinee
3:30—Add A Line
3:59—FM Sign On
4:00—Kyser's College of Fun and Knowledge
4:30—Rhythm By Request
5:00—In Tune With The Times
5:30—Farmers Arcade Market Show
5:45—Ask-It Basket (Miller Coffee)
5:55—CTC News
6:00—Wacker Sports Review—Bob Harnish
6:05—In Tune With the Times
6:30—Susquehanna Mountaineers (Queen Motors)
6:45—Susquehanna Mountaineers (Rocky Springs)
7:00—Don Gardiner, News
7:05—Headline Edition (Duquesne Brewing Co.)
7:15—Elmer Davis, News
7:30—Thro' the Listening Glass
8:00—The Railroad Hour—Lucille Norman & Gordon MacRae in "Salute to Jimmy McHugh"
8:30—It's the Tops
8:45—Henry J. Taylor—News
9:00—Red Rose Hit Parade
9:30—The Harmonaires
9:45—Rendezvous with Song
10:00—Arthur Gaeth
10:15—U. S. Navy Band
10:30—On Trial
11:00—News of Tomorrow
11:15—Ephrata American Legion Express
11:45—Dance Band
12:00—Sign Off —Adv

NETWORK KEY STATIONS

8:00—WNBC, News; Bob Smith Show; WOR, News, P. Robinson; WJZ News, M. Agronsky; WCBS, News Roundup
8:15—WOR, Breakfast With Dorothy and Dick; WCBS, Phil Cook Show WJZ, The Fitzgeralds
8:30—WCBS, Margaret Arlen; WNBC, Jinx Falkenburg
8:55—WJZ, Talk, Dr. J. M. Stitt
9:00—WNBC, News, Peter Roberts; WOR, News, H. Hennessy; WJZ, Breakfast Club; WCBS, Bob Hite News
9:15—WOR, Music Shop; WCBS, This Is New York; WNBC, Ivan Sanderson
9:30—WNBC, Norman Brokenshire WOR, Alfred W. McCann
10:00—WNBC, Fred Waring Show; WOR, News, H. Gladstone; WJZ, My True Story; WCBS, Missus Goes Shopping
10:15—WOR, Martha Deane
10:30—WNBC, Road of Life; WJZ Betty Crocker; WCBS, Arthur Godfrey
10:45—WJZ, Earl Wrightson; WNBC, The Brighter Day
11:00—WNBC, Dr. Paul, Drama; WOR, News; WJZ, Modern Romances, Drama
11:15—WNBC, We Love and Learn, WOR, Health Talk
11:30—WNBC, Jack Berch Show; WOR, Gabriel Heatter; WJZ, Ted Malone
WCBS, Grand Slam Quiz
11:45—WNBC, Lora Lawton; WCBS, Rosemary; WJZ, Rosa Rio
12:00—WJZ, Welcome Travelers; WCBS, Wendy Warren, News; WOR, Kate Smith Speaks; WNBC, News
12:15—WNBC, News; WCBS, Aunt Jenny; WOR, Kate Smith Sings
12:30—WJZ, News; WCBS, Helen Trent; WNBC, Norman Brokenshire
12:45—WCBS, Our Gal Sunday; WOR, News
1:00—WNBC, Mary M. McBride; WOR, Luncheon at Sardi's; WJZ, Party Time; WCBS, Big Sister
1:15—WJZ, Nancy Craig; WCBS, Ma Perkins; WOR, Bill Slater
1:30—WOR, Bill Slater; WCBS, Young Doctor Malone
1:45—WCBS, The Guiding Light; WJZ, Dorothy Dix; WOR, Lanny Ross
2:00—WNBC, Double or Nothing; WOR, Queen For a Day; WJZ, Breakfast in Hollywood; WCBS, Second Mrs. Burton
2:15—WCBS, Perry Mason
2:30—WNBC, Today's Children; WJZ, Bride and Groom; WCBS, This Is Nora Drake; WOR, John Nesbit
2:45—WNBC, Light of the World; WCBS, What Makes You Tick; WOR, Gabriel Heatter
3:00—WNBC, Life Can Be Beautiful; WJZ, Talk Your Way Out of It; WCBS, David Harum; WOR, Tello-Test Quiz
3:15—WNBC, Ma Perkins; WCBS, Hilltop House
3:30—WNBC, Pepper Young Family; WJZ, House Party; WOR, Best Girl; WCBS, Robert Q. Lewis Show
3:45—WNBC, Right to Happiness
4:00—WNBC, Back Stage Wife; WOR, Barbara Welles; WCBS, News and Beat the Clock; WJZ, Kay Kyser's College
4:15—WNBC, Stella Dallas
4:30—WNBC, Lorenzo Jones; WOR, Prince Charming; WJZ, Add A Line; WCBS, Winner Take All
4:45—WNBC, Young Widder Brown; WJZ, Eleanor Roosevelt; WCBS, Treasury Band
5:00—WNBC, When a Girl Marries; WOR, Superman; WJZ, Drama; WCBS, Galen Drake
5:15—WNBC, Portia Faces Life; WOR, Superman
5:30—WNBC, Just Plain Bill; WOR, Captain Midnight; WJZ, Johnny Lujack of Notre Dame; WCBS, Hits and Misses
5:45—WNBC, Front Page Farrell; WOR, Tom Mix, Adventure
6:00—WNBC, News; WOR, News; WJZ, News; WCBS, News
6:15—WNBC, Sports; WJZ, Allen Prescott; WCBS, J. C. Harsch; WOR, On the Century
6:30—WJZ, Don Gardiner; WCBS, Curt Massey Time; WOR, News, Van-Deventer; WNBC, Wayne Howell Show
6:45—WNBC, Three Star Extra; WOR, Stan Lomax; WCBS, C. Collingwood
7:00—WNBC, Supper Club; WOR Fulton Lewis Jr.; WJZ, Head Line Edition; WCBS, Spin and Win
7:15—WNBC, News of the World; WOR, The Answer Man; WJZ, News, Elmer Davis; WCBS, Jack Smith Show
7:30—WNBC, World Playhouse; WOR, Gabriel Heatter; WJZ, The Lone Ranger; WCBS, Club 15
7:45—WNBC, H V. Kaltenborn; WOR, Bill Brandt, Sports; WCBS, Ed R. Murrow
8:00—WNBC, Cavalcade of America; WOR, Western Drama; WJZ, The Railroad Hour; WCBS, Inner Sanctum
8:30—WNBC, Howard Barlow; WOR, Sherlock Holmes; WCBS, Arthur Godfrey
8:45—WNBC, Howard Barlow; WJZ, Henry J. Taylor
8:55—WOR, News
9:00—WNBC, Lee Fairfax; WOR, Periscope News; WCBS, Lux Radio Theatre; WJZ, Consent of the Governed
9:15—WOR, A. L. Alexander; WJZ, R. Norman's Orch.
9:30—WJZ, The Harmonaires; WNBC, Breakfast with Burrows; WOR, Secret Missions
10:00—WNBC, Buddy Clark; WOR, American Forum of the Air; WJZ, News, Arthur Graeth; WCBS, Concert
10:30—WNBC, Radio City Playhouse; WOR, The Symphonette; WJZ, On Trial; WCBS, Bob Hawk Show
11:00—WNBC, News, K Banghart; WOR, News, Vandeventer; WJZ, News; WCBS, News, R. C. Hottelet
11:15—WNBC, Rockabye Dudley; WOR, Herald Tribune News; WJZ, Weather, Joe Hasel; WCBS, Have You Forgotten
11:30—WNBC, Appointment with Music; WOR, Deems Taylor Concert; WJZ, Ray Anthony's Orch.; WCBS, Starlight Salute—Galen Drake

Your Carrier Boy And 500 More Are Headliners At Picnic

EXTRA THRILL for carrier boys at Lancaster Newspapers picnic was jackrabbit ride.

CRUISING DOWN THE CREEK—Paddling instead of peddling papers at the moment were picnicking carrier boys (front to rear) Tony Stammer, Clyde Lawrence, Paul Moser, Gilbert Mann and Jack Givler, all of Lancaster.

***500 CARRIER BOYS FROM FOUR COUNTIES** were guests of the Sunday News, Lancaster New Era and Intelligencer Journal at the annual newspaperboys' picnic at Lancaster's Rocky Springs Park on Tuesday. Everything was on the house, from a luncheon to start off the merriment, to rides on all the breathtakers and swimming in the pool. There were ball games, contests and prizes. Carriers from Lancaster, York, Lebanon and Chester Counties were among those pitching baseballs at the rubber milkbottles and getting enmeshed in the cotton candy.*

IT'S NO PICNIC without the traditional "cotton candy," and so David Carbaugh, of York, heads into a big coneful of the spun-sugar confection while he takes it easy beside a tree.

NEWS PICTURE—Lebanon carriers defied the background sign to stay outside and get shot at by their buddy, Joseph Arnold. In the two-way picture are Warren Light, Harry Boltz, John Stegman, John Dissinger, Charles Kreitz, Harry Felty, and Parke Tooner. They all carry Lancaster Newspapers in Lebanon.

PLENTY OF SNAP is what it takes to be a carrier, and here on the Whip are Donald Schrom and Harold Stambaugh, York, first car; Donald Roseberry and Roland Dinterman, Lancaster, second car; Charles Haberstroh, Donald Kline and Richard Haberstroh, Lancaster, third car.

EEE-YOW!—If the expressions of fun-house explorers Oscar Seager and Jackie Chronister, both of York, seem a little startled, think how you'd feel to come bumping around a dark corner smack into a flashing skeleton backed up by an even more flashing news camera.

CONESTOGA CHOOCHOO—Job as a carrier of the Sunday News, Intelligencer Journal or Lancaster New Era was the only ticket needed to ride the miniature train at Rocky Springs Tuesday. All rides were free to the 500 boys attending, and in addition they got a free lunch.

ACCURACY of the newspaperboy who puts your paper where it ought to be stood these Lancaster City carriers in good stead. Left to right are John Gallagher, Ray Cooper, Don Vollrath and Joe Saam.

HAGER'S & CHARM Magazine Agree:

The American Business Girl is "The Best-dressed Girl in the World"!

Here's some good news for you fashion-wise business girls. The American business girl will be "The Best-Dressed Girl in the World" this Fall, because she has the knack of picking clothes that can go from desk to date with surest confidence. At Hager's, you will see exciting new fashions and fabrics taken straight from the pages of the September issue of Charm, the Magazine for the Business Girl. Best news of all is the down-to-earth price of each outfit, selected by Charm to fit the B.G.'s tastes, needs, and pocketbook.

This Weskit-and-Skirt illustrates how talented designers make the American Business Girl "The Best-Dressed Girl in the World." A soft, fleecy wool tweed, one of this season's newest fabric developments in Winter-green or brown. Misses' sizes. **Weskit, $16.95; Skirt, $16.95; Black Wool Blouse, $12.95.** HAGER'S SPORTS DEPT., Third Floor

A highlight of Hager's showing of desk-and-date ensembles is this checked suit. Made of worsted textured sharkskin, it's featured on the cover of the September issue of Charm. Red and-black, green-and-black, and rust-and-black. Misses sizes. *Pictured above,* **$59.95**

Not only during office hours, but after five, too, the American Business girl is "The Best-Dressed Girl in the World"! This black rayon taffeta date dress has a flattering portrait neckline and jauntily bowed hip pockets. *Pictured below,* **$25.**

HAGER'S APPAREL DEPT., Third Floor

The American Business Girl has the knack of accessorizing a dress so that it can go from desk to date. This wool crepe is a perfect example. With a bright scarf, it's ready for business; with "good" gold jewelry, it's perfect for dinner-and-theater. In black, red and gold. Misses' sizes. *Pictured above,* **$25.00**

HAGER'S APPAREL DEPT., Third Floor

This tweed greatcoat, designed to be worn either belted or full, is one of the reasons why the American Business Girl will be "The Best-Dressed Girl in the World" this Fall. Red-and-black, rust-and-black, and grey-and-black. Misses' sizes. *Pictured right,* **$49.95**

HAGER'S APPAREL DEPT., Third Floor

HAGER'S

New Fall Hours! Open Daily 9:30 A. M. to 5:30 P. M.

SANTA'S ARRIVAL AT WATT & SHAND'S

1. Santa arrived at the Municipal Airport Saturday at 9:30 A. M. after a flight over Lancaster county and was greeted by the four members of the Watt & Shand firm. Reading from left to right they are: John M. Sullivan, William Shand, Charles G. Watt (shaking Santa's hand) and Peter Watt. A large crowd of children was on hand to welcome Santa to Lancaster and the Watt & Shand store.

2. Santa has entered his special car driven by David S. Watt, who met him at the Airport and carried him with his big bag of toys from the airport to the Watt & Shand store in Lancaster. Hundreds of kiddies lined the highways all the way from the Airport to the city to see Santa as he passed by. Santa dropped 120,000 greetings from the sky in his flight over Lancaster city and county.

3. Santa arrives at the Watt & Shand store where thousands of kiddies and their parents await him. Santa is shown in his special car in the foreground waving to the crowd. In front of Santa's car is the white car with the loud speakers that met him at the airport and provided Santa music all the way to the store.

4. Santa, with his big bag of toys is shown at the top of the ladder just before he entered the window to the 4th floor of the Watt & Shand store. It is estimated that 15,000 people were on hand to see this spectacle that thrilled both old and young. The beautiful exterior trim of the store can be seen in the background.

5. This view, taken from Watt & Shand's 4th floor, shows Santa climbing the big fire truck ladder with thousands of upturned faces watching him climb to his Castle on Watt & Shand's 4th floor. Santa spoke over the air on WLAN at the airport, at the fire truck and on his arrival on the 4th floor of the store. The program was carried on the air from 9 to 10:15 A. M.

6. Santa is shown on his throne in his Castle on the 4th floor of the Watt & Shand store greeting the first of the thousands of kiddies who came to greet him at Watt & Shand's. Santa's little helper is shown on the left, who assists Santa in passing out the Christmas books that he gives to each child. Santa will be in his Castle this week 2 to 5 daily; Friday 2 to 5 and 7 to 8:30; Saturday 10 to 12 and 2 to 5 P. M.—Adv.

WEATHER
(U. S. Weather Bureau)
Eastern Pennsylvania: Considerable Cloudiness And Milder, Scattered Showers Northwest Portion Wednesday. Thursday Cloudy With Occasional Rain Turning Colder West And North Portions.

Intelligencer Journal.

The Leading Newspaper in the Garden Spot of America, Home Owned for Home Folks Since 1794

Intelligencer Journal. 155 Years of Newspaper Service 1794 - 1949

156th Year.—No. 161. Lancaster City Zone Population, Official Figures of Audit Bureau of Circulations 112,897 LANCASTER, PA., WEDNESDAY MORNING, DECEMBER 21, 1949. CITY TWENTY-SIX PAGES. 30c PER WEEK—5c Per Copy

WHISKY BUYS MADE BY MINOR IN EVERY CITY BAR, LIQUOR STORE

19-Year-Old Goes Unchallenged On Intell Survey Of 84 Spots

Every State Store, Bar, Cafe, Taproom, Hotel In Lancaster Visited

Whisky was sold to a minor in every public bar in the City of Lancaster licensed by the Pennsylvania Liquor Control Board, as well as the three State liquor stores, a survey just completed by the Intelligencer Journal reveals.

Conclusive proof that, contrary to the Commonwealth's liquor laws, a minor with sufficient funds could ask for and be served whiskey in each of the 81 bars, cafes, taprooms and hotels in this city, was obtained.

And this seemingly shocking fact, as evidenced by the survey results, was accomplished without the minor telling any untruths, or without employing any disguises to mislead bartenders.

Two employes of the Intelligencer Journal — one a minor, nineteen years of age, and the other of legal age — worked a number of nights in making the survey and then reported they had batted a startling 1.000 per cent.

The minor asked for, was served and paid for whisky in each of the 81 licensed public bars. Then, he visited each of the three local State stores, and was sold a pint of whisky in each store.

NOT CHALLENGED

In his travels, the minor was not challenged once about his age.

Results of the survey became more astounding with each night's work. For instance, in at least four local liquor establishments, it was noted by the Intell men that minors apparently are regular customers.

In each of these public bars, waitresses and bartenders referred to the young-looking people by first names and served them readily. It also was noted that the young people were the only customers.

And in only one instance, did the newspapermen see anyone challenged on their age. The same bartender, who a few minutes earlier had served the investigators, challenged two young fellows, who followed them to the bar.

One of the pair did not hesitate to leave the bar, while the second fellow made an attempt to produce papers from his wallet. However, he too decided to leave, and as he did he uttered a string of oaths.

Both then stood outside the doors a few minutes shouting remarks at the bartender. Then, as suddenly as they appeared, they disappeared from in front of the establishment.

Meanwhile, the bartender did not hesitate to serve the minor newspaperman, yet he looked no younger, or older than the two who had been challenged.

Further proof that a minor with enough money can get whisky readily in local public bars—without going to the trouble of telling lies or wearing a hat to appear older — was brought out. In many establishments bartenders asked the minor if he would like a "double shot," or else urged him to have a second round.

SIGNS ON DISPLAY

Several of the public bars had on prominent display, signs declaring that they do not serve minors. In most instances, the signs had been provided as advertisements for certain brands of whisky.

Yet, this nineteen-year-old stepped up to the bar, ordered his drink, paid for it and never once was questioned as to his age.

During their travels, the two Intelligencer Journal employes found many of the public bars comparatively empty. On other occasions, they found large crowds in the bars, many watching television programs.

Twice during the survey, the two Intell men noticed bartenders casting suspicious glances in their direction, but after they had been served whisky. And despite the apparent quizzical glances, no questions ever were asked.

Complete List Of Places In Which Minor Purchased Whisky

Following is the list of public bars licensed by the Pennsylvania Liquor Control Board, and three State stores in the city of Lancaster, in which two Intelligencer Journal employes, one a minor, made purchases of whisky:

Pennsylvania Liquor Control Board Store 603 Manor St.

Pennsylvania Liquor Control Board Store 49 S. Duke St.

Pennsylvania Liquor Control Board Store 252 N. Queen St.

Walter H. Barr
Barrs Grill
211 N. Queen St.

Gideon H., Marian L. Berkebile and Ona L. Berkebile
Lincoln Hotel
32-34 S. Queen St.

Albert B. Bishop
655-657 Manor St.

Bruce A. Boggs Jr. and Jeanne A. Boggs
522 E. King St.

Eva W. Brown
Delmonico Cafe
14 Penn Square

Joseph Brunner
Schiller House Hotel
233 N. Queen St.

Brunswick Hotel of Lancaster Inc.
169-171 N. Queen St.

Andrew K. Bucher
Arcadia Cafe
27 W. Orange St.

Harry W. Buckius
Buckius Cafe
201 W. Orange St.

John Camizzi
Camizzi Hotel
237-243 W. King St.

Joseph Capp
Capps Cafe
750 Rockland St.

Patsy Centini
Patsy's
601 S. Marshall St.

Bruno J. and John A. Coluzzi
Rose Bowl Cafe
337-339 N. Queen St.

John Delaurentis
Red Rose Tap Room
47 S. Queen St.

Lila Kochel Dushl
701 E. Walnut St.

Jean Faranda
Imperial Bar Cafe
172 N. Queen St.

R. Ralph Farmer
The Fulton Bar
637 N. Plum St.

Lawton W. Fleming
Eddy's Tavern
240 W. King St.

Ann E. Forsythe
Glassbrenner's Hotel
402 N. Queen St.

Amos E. Frazer and John I. Sturgis Jr.
458-462 S. Duke St.

Arthur W. Garvin
Garvin's Cafe
28-30 W. Lemon St.

Clarence E. Gerfin
Sparkys Cafe
301 New Dorwart St.

George M. and May E. Graybill
Graybills Grill
463 S. Prince St.

Francis J. Haefner and Richard H. Powl
Town Tavern
403 and 407 N. Mary St.

Albert A. Hall Jr. and William Robert Hall
Halls Cafe
834 N. Plum St.

S. J. Hampilos
The Coronet
155 N. Queen St.

Harry H. and Harry H. Heagy Jr.
Conestoga Cafe
647 E. Chestnut St.

Raymond C. Herr
Fairmount House
402 E. King St.

S. Lester Hess
Hess Hotel
26-28 N. Prince St.

Virginia Hildebrecht and Thedore Robertson
Hildy's Tavern
448 W. Frederick St.

Julia V. Hoenninger
Melrose Hotel
402-408 N. Prince St.

Albert Karch
Fibbers Cafe
476 Poplar St.

Clarence C. Kegel
551 W. King St.

Edward E. Kirchner
Kirchners Hotel
602 W. King St.

Mary C. Kirchner
North Pole Cafe
716-718 N. Queen St.

Martin L. Klingseisen
Seventh Ward Hotel
501 Rockland St.

Henry Koestner and Frances Koestner
561-563 N. Prince St.

John Lermer
Lermers Cafe
552-554 St. Joseph St.

Albert Levin
Al's Cafe
47 W. New St.

Joseph S., James V. Lombardo and D. R. Lombardo
Lombardo's Cafe
226-228 Harrisburg Ave.

Alek Manos and John Rossos
Pelican Bar and Grill
49 W. King St.

Michael Mastros
54-56 E. Vine St.

Roy S. McComsey
McComsey's Cafe
915 N. Plum St.

William L. Melchior
Melchiors Restaurant
323-325 S. Queen St.

Nevin L. and John W. Miller
Obie Miller's
128 W. Strawberry St.

Clyde M. Myles
Myles' Cafe
701 S. Prince St.

Guy A. Neel
Neel's Cafe
220 N. Prince St.

Winfield S. Noden
Noden's Cafe
223 E. King St.

Rose Nuss and Abram L. Hershey Jr.
Washington House
201 Locust St.

Francis X. Penn
Local Inn Cafe
527 N. Christian St.

E. L. Peters
Wheatland Tavern
160-162 N. Queen St.

John W. Reese
Reeses Cafe
103 Locust St.

Margaret E. Roschel
Roschel Cafe
702-706 St. Joseph St.

E. G. Rothweiler and Charles H. Myers
Rothweilers
206-208 W. King St.

Irvin E. Schiding
558 High St.

Paul J. Severino
P. and J. Cafe
339-341 E. King St.

Lester V. Sharp
The Shamrock
312 W. Walnut St.

Richard E. Shaub
Horse Inn
539 E. Chestnut St., rear

H. Daniel Shenk
Shenks Cafe
549 E. Chestnut St.

James L. Shillow
William Penn Hotel
429-431 N. Mulberry St.

William G. Shuffelbottom
401-403 S. Duke St.

Anna M. Smith and Ethel M. Gaenzle
Smith's Cafe
121-123 Dorwart St.

Howard P. Snavely
Snapper's
251 E. Chestnut St.

John Soldner
217-219 W. King St.

James Speros
Jims Cafe
252-254 E. Frederick St.

Charles A. Steinbaecher and Rose Steinbaecher
358 E. Orange St.

William J. Steinbaecher
764-766 High St.

Stevens House Inc.
2 S. Prince St.

Hotel Swan Inc.
101-103 S. Queen St.

Tem Hotel Corp.
Hotel Weber
105-107 E. King St.

Oscar J. and Anna B. Thomas
Little Dutch Cafe
201 W. Walnut St.

Denzil H. Tripple
464-466 Manor St.

The Union Bus Depot of Lancaster Inc.
28-34 E. Chestnut St.

Nick Vekios and Peter Photis
Pittsburgh Restaurant
156 N. Queen St.

George T. Vlassis
Wonder Bar Cafe
302 S. Prince St.

Wiggins Candy and Restaurant Co.
141-143 N. Queen St.

Alvin D. Wolfer
170-172 E. King St.

James N. Yarnall
Hi-Boy Cafe
322 E. King St.

Arthur C. Zercher
659 First St.

George L. Ziegler
502 High St.

Josephine L. Ziegler
Zieglers Restaurant
457-459 New Holland Ave.

Editorial

A SAD, SAD STORY

A MINOR can buy whisky in all of the public licensed bars in Lancaster city, and the State Liquor stores as well, a survey just completed by the Intelligencer Journal shows.

It is a shocking revelation, of course, for it indicates complete disrespect for the law by the State as well as by the public whisky sellers, and without doubt shows a complete breakdown of liquor law enforcement, both on the local and state level.

It is a sad, sad story, too, for it shows the ease with which a teen-ager can obtain a drink of whisky and, in some cases, be encouraged to "have another" or take a "double-shot" by the bar-keeper, intent on ringing up another sale, or a bigger sale.

Reports that the sale of whisky to minors is common in this area prompted the Intelligencer Journal to undertake this survey. Originally it was intended to cover the entire county, including the city. Finally the city alone was agreed upon, but only because of a lack of time.

With the holiday season at hand, the Intelligencer Journal wanted to get the facts before the public in the hope that it could break up this vicious practice because of the potential tragedies that could result.

There seems to be no question in our mind, that if the survey had included the county, the result would have been the same, especially in view of the result in the city, where law enforcement is at least thought to be of a greater potency.

So much for that.

How can it be stopped? That is the question.

Since every boy, over 18, is required by federal law to carry a draft registration card, containing his birth date and a description of him, the answer seems obvious.

Whisky sellers, both state and private, should demand to see draft cards before making sales to any youth.

It is as simple as that.

The cry during prohibition was that prohibition was bad because it resulted in situations, such as this newspaper finds existing today, right here in Lancaster. Liquor interests said then that if prohibition was repealed, the liquor laws would be enforced to the letter and that the evils of prohibition would vanish.

We are not advocating a return to prohibition.

Rather we are calling for observance of the liquor laws to wipe out the evils which resulted from prohibition. And what is more, we should like to have—in fact, we demand—an explanation for the failure of the whisky dispensers to live up to the letter of the law, as they have promised, and for the state and local authorities to explain their laxness in full enforcement of this important statute.

GIRLS USED TO LURE GI'S TO COMMIE PARTY

Senate Committee Hears Testimony Of Subversive Red Activities During War

Washington — (AP) — Girls who had "no morals whatsoever" and who "went to any extremes" were enlisted by the Communist Party during the war to lure American servicemen to Communism, a Senate Committee has been told.

The committee also has testimony, made public Tuesday night by Senator McCarran (D-Nev), that the Communists "have taken over or infiltrated" labor unions in key industries in this country and are in position to call "extensive strikes."

The testimony was given under oath by John J. Huber of Mt. Vernon, N. Y., who told a Senate Judiciary Subcommittee he was an undercover agent for the FBI from 1938 to 1947.

DECLINES COMMENT

The FBI declined to comment on that when the subcommittee, headed by McCarran, put out the first installment of Huber's account last Saturday. The witness testified behind closed doors last September 8 and 9, and again on Oct. 28.

McCarran's group is studying legislation designed to bar the immigration gates to subversive aliens and to get rid of any already in the United States.

Huber said he joined the Communist Party in New York at the FBI's request after he told the agency that some of his fellow workers in the old WPA were Communists. He said he reported to the FBI on Communist activities for nine years, and then ended the undercover work "of my own volition."

When he went before the subcommittee in October, Huber testified that:

"One of the most ambitious plans of the Communist Party to carry on its subversive work

Turn To Page 10 For More Of SUBVERSIVES

"We Lead All The Rest"
FARM CORNER
By The Farm Editor

Two Cigar Leaf Tobacco Shows To Be Held Here

Prize samples, representing the cream of the 1949 crop of Lancaster county tobacco, will be on exhibit at two local cigar leaf tobacco shows to be held in Lancaster on Friday, Dec. 30.

Roundup of the 4-H Tobacco Club will be held in the Bayuk Cigar Co. warehouse, 850 N. Water St., with judging of the entries shown by the youthful tobacco growers of the county scheduled to start at 9 a.m.

The annual Lancaster county tobacco show, open to all growers in the Garden Spot, will be staged Friday afternoon on the fourth floor of the Lancaster County Tobacco Growers' Cooperative Association warehouse, located at 220 N. Water St. The deadline for entries is 1:30 p.m.

B. F. Coon and Edwin O. Schneider, of the local Tobacco Experimental Laboratory staff, near Roseville, are scheduled to speak during a meeting of growers to be held while the tobacco show is being judged.

Coon will give the results of ex-

Turn To Page 22 For More Of FARM CORNER

Weather Calendar

COMPARATIVE TEMPERATURES

Station	High	Low
Water Works	48	28
Ephrata	52	32
Last Year (Ephrata)	39	22
Official High for Year, July 4		101
Official Low for Year, Feb. 3		5
Character of Day		Clear

SUN
Rises—7:22 a. m. Sets—4:42 p. m.

MOON
Sets—6:34 p. m. First Quarter, Dec. 27

STARS
Morning—Mars, Saturn.
Evening—Venus, Jupiter.

NEARBY FORECASTS
(U. S. Weather Bureau)

Maryland: Considerable cloudiness and mild highest 60 to 65 Wednesday. Thursday mostly cloudy and continued mild occasional rain likely.

New Jersey and Delaware: Some cloudiness and milder highest around 60 Wednesday. Thursday mostly cloudy and continued mild with some rain likely.

Chesapeake Bay: Southerly winds increasing and becoming 15 to 25 MPH Wednesday afternoon.

EXTENDED FORECASTS
(U. S. Weather Bureau)

Extended forecast for the period Wednesday through Sunday.

Eastern Pennsylvania, Eastern New York and Mid Atlantic States: Temperatures will average a little above normal with mild weather Wednesday and over the weekend and a cold spell Thursday and Friday: rain Wednesday and possibly again Sunday.

"Mr. Boxoffice" Takes A Bride

Solvang, Calif.—(AP Wirephoto)—Actor Clark Gable, who abdicated "eligibility" throne Tuesday, is shown with his bride, the former Lady Sylvia Ashley, widow of Douglas Fairbanks, Sr., and wedding cake after their marriage at the rustic Alisal guest ranch near here.

Film Star Gable And Widow Of Doug Fairbanks Sr. Wed

Santa Barbara, Calif.—(AP)—Clark Gable, the ideal of millions of women, and Douglas Fairbanks' Sr.'s widow were married Tuesday—each for the fourth time.

Gable, 48, and the former Lady Ashley, 39, were wed at 6:15 p. m. today on a ranch 30 miles north of here, with only a few close friends in attendance.

SURPRISE

It followed by a few hours an elopement which surprised all but a few Hollywood associates. They drove to San Luis Obispo, on the coast north of here, and obtained a license after Gable had passed the required state blood test.

Gable used his own name, as did his bride. But few knew her as Sylvia Stanley Alderley. She is the former Sylvia, wife of Lord Stanley of Alderley. They were divorced 18 months ago.

The ceremony was performed on the Alisal Ranch of Mr. and Mrs. Lynn Gilham, longtime personal friends of Gable.

The Rev. Aage Moller, pastor of the Danish Lutheran Church in nearby Solvang officiated.

In attendance were Lady Stan-

Turn To Page 10 For More Of GABLE

Bulletin

PACKAGE OF DYNAMITE IS FOUND AT UAW HQ

Detroit (Wednesday)—(AP)—An apparent attempt to blow up the headquarters of the CIO United Auto Workers was made Tuesday night.

Police reported that 39 sticks of dynamite, set for explosion, were found on a rear outside stairway of the union's headquarters building.

Fuses had been lighted and then extinguished, police said.

Earlier in the night, police said, there had been "a report" that the building was to be blown up.

Malicious Fires Ignited In City, Police Are Told

Two maliciously ignited fires, one among Christmas cards in an apartment hallway and the other in the basement of the Fulton Theater, are being investigated by city detectives.

Neither caused damage but police said the offenders, presumably young boys, may face prosecution on arson charges if caught.

Detective A. J. Daecher said George C. Crudden, Jr., who lives in an apartment at 102 S. Ann St., reported Tuesday night a fire was started in the hallway of the building.

He told police another resident in the apartment house, William B. Eberts, heard some commotion in the hallway at 6:15 p. m. and investigated to find that someone had started a fire there, using Christmas cards which had just been delivered as fuel.

MAIL LEFT OUT

Eberts extinguished the fire without damage and notified Crudden who reported the act to police. Police explained that during the heavy Christmas mail rush, mail is merely thrown in the hallway instead of placed in the individual mail boxes.

The fire in the basement of the theater was discovered by employes. It was among waste paper which had been taken from a recptacle in the men's wash room.

On Dec. 10 Fire Inspector Walter Snyder of the city department nabbed a sixteen-year-old Lancaster R7 boy as he was preparing to ignite some toilet tissue in the same wash room. He since has been committee to an institution as a result of Juvenile Court action.

TWO CITY MARKETS HAVE YULE SCHEDULE

Special Christmas holiday shopping hours will be observed at two city markets this week-end:

Farmers Arcade Market will open early — 9 o'clock Friday and 10 o'clock Saturday, continuing the remainder of the day.

Central Market, after the usual Friday session, will open at 5:30 a. m. Saturday and run until 3 p. m.

Regular all-day hours will be observed at the Southern Market house Saturday. The usual Saturday morning session will be held at the Fulton Market. The regular Friday hours will be observed at the Northern Market, with no market on Saturday.

UE WITHDRAWS SUIT, DENHAM OUSTER ASKED

Battle For Bargaining Rights For 300,000 Back In Lap Of NLRB

Washington—(AP)—The battle for bargaining rights for 300,000 workers in the electrical manufacturing industry was back in the lap of the National Labor Relations Board Tuesday after these swift developments:

1. The United Electrical Workers (UE), Left Wing union which is fighting to save its representation rights after its ouster by the CIO, withdrew a $100,000 suit against the NLRB and General Counsel Robert N. Denham. But UE President Albert J. Fitzgerald called on President Truman to fire Denham and investigate the board.

2. Denham revised what the UE called a "secret order" to his regional and subregional officers. The original order provided that at forthcoming NLRB hearings to determine whether new collective bargaining elections should be held in the industry, the UE could not introduce certain evidence about the bargaining contracts it has. Under the new ruling, UE can introduce all the evidence it wants about contracts.

Denham indicated he changed the order reluctantly and at the board's insistence. He said he thought it would delay rather than speed the elections to determine which union now represents a majority of workers in such plants as General Electric, Westinghouse, RCA, General Motors and others.

3. The rival International union of Electrical Workers (IUE), set up by the CIO as its new organization in the electrical and radio industry, called the withdrawal of the suit as a setback for the UE.

Federal Judge Charles F. McLaughlin, who had been ready to hear testimony from UE on the union's petition for an injunction

Turn To Page 10 For More Of UE

Charter Presented To IUE Local At RCA Plant Here

There were two important developments Tuesday in the battle raging between the newly-organized International Union of Electrical, Radio and Machine Workers (CIO), and the left-wing United Electrical, Radio and Machine Workers of America (UE). They are:

(1) A group of right-wingers at the local Radio Corporation of America plant were chartered by the new CIO Electrical Workers Union as Local 124, IUE-CIO.

(2) IUE-CIO, it was learned, has deviated from its previous program, and has requested the National Labor Relations Board to hold bargaining agency elections at RCA plants in Camden, N. J., and Pulaski, Va.

Previously, IUE-CIO officials had requested industry-wide bargaining agency elections. The sudden change in plans, it was learned, was decided upon in a move to get both of these RCA plants under the fold of the new CIO union.

A petition for an election at RCA Lancaster, it is understood, will not be presented until after the first of next year. A card signing campaign now is being conducted at the plant.

Bargaining rights at the local RCA

Turn To Page 10 For More Of IUE

Cloudy, Mild And Showers Forecast For Debut Of Winter Here Tonight

Cloudy, mild and scattered showers have been forecast for the debut of Winter at 11:28 p. m. Wednesday (tonight), but U. S. Weather Bureau forecasters cocked an eye toward the Rocky Mountain states where a storm bearing sleet, freezing rain and snow was heading eastward.

The Lancaster area, however, was not expected to have a white Christmas. Colder weather is forecast Thursday and Friday with rain a possibility Christmas Day.

Lancaster basked in clear, mild weather Tuesday, the mercury soaring from a low of 32 at the Ephrata Weather Station to a high of 52 degrees in the afternoon.

A cold wave hit Nebraska and

Turn To Page 10 For More Of WEATHER

MOTORISTS WARNED

Harrisburg —(AP)— The Christmas week-end may be a tragic one unless you motorists are careful.

That's the warning sounded Tuesday by Col. C. M. Wilhelm, State Police commissioner.

"Sudden changes in temperature, unexpected fog and storms, or the carelessness that results from hurrying may cause a break in the traditional family circle at Christmas time," said Wilhelm.

He advised motorists to check all safety equipment before starting out on a trip. Information on road conditions, he said, is available at all state and municipal police stations equipped with police teletypewriters.

OFFICERS NOMINATED BY BUS DRIVER LOCAL

Officers were nominated by Local 1241, Amalgamated Association of Street, Electric Railway and Motor Coach Employes (AFL), during a series of meetings Tuesday.

However, Anthony Flick, union president, said following a second meeting that he was unable to announce the slate because it had not been confirmed.

Officers will be elected during the January meeting.

Crackdown on Slum Owners Urged in Report

Racketeers in Unions Extorted Millions
See Pegler—Editorial Page

LANCASTER NEW ERA

73rd Year—No. 22,526 | Lancaster City Zone Population, Official Figures of Audit Bureau of Circulations 112,897 | LANCASTER, PA., MONDAY, JANUARY 2, 1950 | NOON EDITION | 24 PAGES | 30c PER WEEK—5c Per Copy

The Weather
U. S. Weather Bureau Forecast: Cloudy and Milder

Bare, 36, is Inaugurated As City's Youngest Mayor

Review of 1949

Parking Meters, Television, First Air Service Here

Traffic Becomes Problem with Promise of By-Pass Around City; Building Operations Amount to $8 Million; Doctors, Druggists Set Up 24-Hr. Service

Lancastrians wrapped up another decade in 1949, a year that saw this history-rich city write another chapter in its date book with destiny.

The top news events included such "firsts" as parking meters, television, commercial air service, and the youngest mayor in history.

Hammers and bulldozers were beating out new construction, to the tune of more than eight million dollars and the biggest post-war building year.

And the city became "stick-'em-up" conscious. A wave of burglaries swept stores, restaurants, and jewelry shops.

Politics

KENDIG C. BARE, 36-year-old World War II veteran, was elected mayor as Dr. Dale E. Cary ended a 12-year hitch as the city's chief executive. That was the longest any mayor ever served here.

Running on a platform, "the people have work to be done," Bare easily outdistanced Harry Goodhart, his Democratic foe. Republicans throughout the city and county swatted their customarily high batting average, yielding only a few stolen bases to the Democrats.

As year ended, Lancastrians Daniel B. Strickler and Guy K. Bard emerged in the spotlight for Republican and Democratic Gubernatorial nominations respectively.

Traffic

LIKE THE OLD WOMAN in a shoe, Lancaster had so many cars she didn't know what to do . . .

The curbs sprouted parking meters. The meters weathered first the argument they were no good unless the funds were earmarked for parking lots. Then they broke down and had to get new innards.

A four-lane Harrisburg Pike stretched seven modernistic miles and led the list of completed road jobs. The

(See Page 7—REVIEW)

New Year's Holiday Quiet Here Under Leaden Skies

Lancastrians Relax After Week-End Celebration, Face Ahead to Start of New Decade

Lancaster was closing out the last day of the New Year week-end today and facing ahead to 12 months of 1950 and the start of a new decade.

The holiday weather could be described as dull, at best, with leaden skies, mild temperatures, and intermittent drizzles.

But that didn't faze most Lancastrians who, after a hilarious New Year's Eve, were spending the time indoors with family reunions, parties, or just quiet relaxation, before returning to the work-a-day world.

Today was a legal holiday, with most stores, the postoffice, offices, and banks closed down tight. But there was activity at City Hall and the Courthouse, with a new mayor being inaugurated and city and county officials taking office.

EVEN THE CITY HALL and Courthouse were due for a letdown. The ceremonies ended at noon and then the two government buildings were clamped down tight for the remainder of the day.

The mercury climbed into the [illegible] before noon after sinking to a [illegible] low of 32 degrees. It rained [illegible] and on. The forecast called for more of the same tonight and tomorrow — "cloudy, milder, and fine drizzle."

The leaden skies prevailed over most of the nation. And it rained in most areas.

But it snowed in the Northwest states. And forecasters predicted the snow will move eastward and blanket Minnesota, Wisconsin, and Iowa tomorrow, or Wednesday at the latest.

LANCASTER'S New Year's Eve celebration Saturday night included parties in homes, hotels, and night clubs. Also solemn Watch Night services and mid-night Masses in the churches.

In the matter of weather, the 1949 elements in Lancaster county produced one of the hottest Summers and precipitation that was below normal — 39.29 inches in 1949 compared with the 40.34-inch normal in 1948.

Today's New Era

Cracked Store Window Causes Burglar Scare

City police were summoned when a passerby noticed a cracked window at Bischoff's Jewelry store, 56 N. Prince St., and suspected a burglary shortly after 8 a. m. today.

Detective Frank Matt said the proprietor, A. C. Bischoff, 144 E. Ross St., was summoned and he said the glass had been cracked some time ago.

City Inaugural

3 Ex-Mayors Now Living: 1 Republican, 2 Democrats

JAMES H. ROSS
Mayor 1934-38

SIMON SHISSLER
Mayor 1898-1900

Lancaster now has three living ex-mayors:

Simon Shissler (1898-1900). Shissler is now ninety-three years old and lives at the Elizabethtown Masonic Home. He is a Democrat.

James H. Ross (1934-38). Now a local merchant. Democrat.

Dr. Dale E. Cary (1938-50). Republican.

MAYOR BARE followed tradition by using his own "pet" gavel to pound out order in Council sessions and to call meetings to order.

He first used the gavel at a State DeMolay convention, then when he presided at an organization meeting of the Junior Chamber of Commerce in Lancaster, Sept. 14, 1938 and when he was installed as president of that organization on Sept. 13, 1937.

He used it again at an organization of Association of Draftees on Nov. 20, 1940 in the First Presbyterian chapel and when he was in-

(See Page 21—EX-MAYORS)

Mummers Parade Is Postponed by Rain Until Saturday

PHILADELPHIA Jan. 2—(AP)—Rain and cloudy skies today forced postponement of the traditional Philadelphia Mummers parade.

Parade officials, at a last minute conference decided to hold the gayly costumed march next Saturday in hopes of better weather.

The 7,000 marchers, many carrying their string band instruments, were already to begin strutting up Broad Street when word of the postponement was received.

Billed as one of the biggest and best parades in the 150-year-history of the Mummers, this year's march was carried over until today because Jan. 1 fell on Sunday. Some 500,000 persons had been expected along the route of the parade.

EPHRATA OWLS CLUB IS ROBBED

Safe and $1,500 Taken; Believe Thieves Had Key

The Ephrata Owls' Home, 131 E. Main St., was robbed between 3 and 7 a. m. today by thieves who hauled away a 2,000-pound safe containing an estimated $1,500 in cash.

The burglary was reported by John Zerbe, an employe, shortly after he arrived at the club at 7 a. m. today. Police believe one of the thieves had access to a key since there were no signs of forcible entry.

JACK ROUSEY, who lives with his parents at 22 Lake St., Ephrata, told police he saw three men hurling stones at the arc light near the Owls Home and later observed them with something on a light truck before driving away.

Borough Police Chief Harry Doremus is conducting an investigation and said that a fingerprint expert from State Police at Lancaster had been called to the scene.

Girl Is Stabbed in Restaurant

Mattie G. Jones, twenty-five, 445 Rockland St., suffered stab wounds of the neck and left forearm during an altercation at Murray's Restaurant, 405 S. Duke St., at 10:15 p. m. yesterday.

She was admitted to the General Hospital, where her condition today was reported fair.

Police are holding Katie Sumrall, thirty-three, 324 Locust St., who detectives said admitted stabbing the woman with a small knife during an argument over a wrist watch. Hospital attendants said the stab wound in the neck severed a vein. Twelve sutures were used to close the wounds.

HEALTH DEPT. ASKS CLEANUP IN CITY SLUMS

Landlords would Be given 6 Months Time; Fire, Other Bureau Reports

A crackdown on the owners of some of the worst slum housing in Lancaster was urged today by Dr. Harold K. Hogg, executive secretary of the City Board of Health.

Dr. Hogg recommended that homes with bad sanitary facilities, such as outside toilets not connected with the sewer, "be given six months to meet certain sanitary requirements."

If these requirements are not fulfilled, he added, "we feel that the landlords should not be permitted to rent these homes until the requirements are met."

DR. HOGG'S recommendation was one of the highlights of city department reports to City Council today.

The department of public safety, headed by Commissioner K. L. Shirk, came up with the greatest number of recommendations — a total of 18. They call for, among other things, a new ladder truck for the fire department, a new pumper, a fire drill tower, land for new fire houses, a central fire alarm system, and repairs for all fire houses.

Dr. Hogg reported in a recent inspection the health department found that the city has 400 outside toilets, 97 of which are not connected with city sewers.

A similar enforcement of health laws to clean up slums has been urged by Mayor-elect Kendig C. Bare and by Alfred C. Alspach, chairman of the City Housing Authority.

ON THE SLUM problem, Dr. Hogg said:

"At the past two meetings of the Board of Health we have discussed ways and means of improving our housing situation in Lancaster. The Board of Health feels some action should be taken in slum clearance in the near future. By a house-to-house canvas made by this department, it was found that we have 400 outside toilets.

(See Page 7—HEALTH)

HOLIDAY DEATH TOLL SLACKENS

330 Expected to Die in Traffic; Total Is 180

By the Associated Press

The nation apparently took to heart advice that caution and care would be rewarded in the new year.

Americans bid 1949 farewell and said hello to 1950 by dodging the violence which was to take an estimated 330 lives in traffic slaughter alone.

THE NATIONAL Safety Council, whose figures usually are an accurate forecast, predicted 330 persons would die between 6 p. m. Friday and midnight Monday, (local time) in traffic mishaps. The council set no figure for other deaths.

However, the final day of the extended holiday began with 180 dead in traffic accidents and there seemed little likelihood this figure would zoom to 330. Fires claimed 40 lives, and 61 died in miscellaneous accidents, for a total of 281.

(Sixteen persons were hurt in week-end highway crashes in Lancaster City and County. Only one was hospitalized.)

The Weather

LOCAL FORECAST and EASTERN PENNSYLVANIA, SOUTHERN NEW JERSEY, DELAWARE and MARYLAND: Cloudy, a little milder with occasional rain and some drizzle tonight and Tuesday.

CHESAPEAKE BAY: Gentle winds mostly southerly. Weather cloudy. Occasional rain with some squalls and poor visibility today and tonight.

TODAY TEMP. AT NEW ERA	
1 AM	39
2 AM	39
3 AM	39
4 AM	39
5 AM	38
6 AM	38
7 AM	38
8 AM	38
9 AM	38
10 AM	40
11 AM	41
Noon	42
YESTERDAY	
1 PM	40
2 PM	40
3 PM	40
4 PM	40
5 PM	39
6 PM	39
7 PM	39
8 PM	39
9 PM	38
10 PM	38
11 PM	38
12 PM	38

Comparative Temperature	High Yesterday	Low Last Night
Wat. Wks.	41	32
Ephrata	40	35
High for year		41
Low for year		32

Humidity
8 AM—81
10 AM—82
Noon—85
2 PM—

Sun Rose 7:26 AM
Sun Sets 4:50 PM

Moon Set 6:13 AM
Full Moon Jan. 4

Morning Stars
Mars, Saturn,
Evening Stars
Mercury, Venus, Jupiter

Rainfall here 24-hr. period ending 7:30 AM—.03 in.

New Era Photo

Retiring Mayor Cary (right) administers oath to Mayor Kendig C. Bare.

New Mayor Calls on All to Help Build a Better City

Mayor Kendig C. Bare in his inaugural address today called upon every citizen to shoulder his share of the responsibility in building a better Lancaster.

The opportunity to serve is "an inspiring one" but the task of building for the future "cannot be done alone," Mayor Bare declared.

THE COMPLETE TEXT of the Mayor's inaugural address, only 222 words long, follows:

"Today we accept a new responsibility. We are charged with directing and guiding the destiny of Lancaster for the next four years. Our actions and results in that period will be more important than anything that we may say here today. We recognize that ours is a grave responsibility. We accept it gladly. We will endeavor to serve you well.

'The citizens, as well as the elected officials, have responsibilities. It is not enough merely to vote once or twice a year. Each citizen should not only be interested, but should actively participate in community activities and in government — every day of the year. In the days ahead your community will make demands upon many of you for service on committees, commissions and advisory bodies. We hope that you will respond cheerfully and willingly to that call.

"THE OPPORTUNITY to help build a better and finer Lancaster is an inspiring one. It cannot be done alone. It must be participated in by all of us. We propose to meet our assignment. We hope that each citizen will meet his.

"The people have work to be done. We are here to do that work. The only way to get things done is to do them. With God's help and guidance, and the active interest, participation and support of its citizens, Lancaster will move forward."

Cary in His Farewell Cites Zoning, Better Police Force

Dr. Dale E. Cary today wound up his 12-year term as Mayor of Lancaster with a valedictory address that contained a resounding "thank you" to all the people of Lancaster.

It was a brief accounting to the people of a city who elected him for three successive terms. Again the retiring chief executive summed up his administration as "four years preparing for war, four years of war and four years of post-war adjustments."

He pointed with pride to annexation, a Zoning law and a better Police Department as some of the major accomplishments of his 12 years.

THE TEXT follows:

"The Good Book tells us that we must give an account of our stewardship. Therefore it is appropriate at this time you be given a summary of your government during this administration. Since it has lasted twelve years, some of the happenings will seem like ancient history, particularly to the younger citizen. Yearly reports have been printed in the journals, and I shall endeavor at this time to include only the more important items of progress that were accomplished during this administration.

"Historians will find much to record in world events during the past twelve years. They will write of the political alliances and so-called peace treaties among the various countries of Europe. Then the sudden outbreak of war and a

(See Page 7—CARY)

Girl Pedestrian Is Injured by Car

Mary Bair, twenty, 19 Old Dorwart St., suffered minor injuries of the right leg and left hand when struck by an auto at King and Strawberry Sts., at 6:50 a. m. today. She was treated at the General Hospital.

Robert W. Decker, thirty-two, 34 1-2 N. Queen St., told police he had stopped for a traffic light at King and Manor Sts., and when the lights changed, he started to make a right turn hitting the girl. He told police the atmosphere was hazy. Miss Bair, who was enroute to work at Hotel Brunswick, was wearing a dark raincoat.

Marilyn Maxwell Is Bride of Cafe Owner

SANTA BARBARA, Calif., Jan. 2—(AP)—Marilyn Maxwell, blonde screen lovely, is honeymooning today with Anders McIntyre, Beverly Hills cafe operator.

The twenty-seven-year-old actress and McIntyre, thirty-one, were wed yesterday in a cottage of the Santa Barbara Biltmore. A Presbyterian minister performed the rites.

JUDGE BOWMAN TAKES HIS OATH

Begins His 10-Year Term; New Officials Start Duties

Orphans' Court Judge John L. Bowman took his oath for his first full 10-year term today as other elected county officials officially took office today.

Judge Bowman was administered his oath by Common Pleas Judge Oliver S. Schaeffer in Judge Schaeffer's chambers at the courthouse shortly before noon.

The ceremonies were brief. Slated to attend were U. S. Judge Guy K. Bard, Judge Joseph B. Wissler, Mrs. Bowman, and Miss Dorothy Good, court stenographer.

Judge Bowman was named last Spring to succeed Judge T. Roberts Appel, who retired. He was elected to a full term in November.

CHESTER GOCKLEY, of Murrell, is slated to be elected president of the Lancaster County Board of Prison Inspectors when that body reorganizes at the courthouse at 9:30 a. m. tomorrow.

Other officers slated for re-election under a rotation system: A. B. Becker, Terre Hill, secretary, and Edward Lefever, Conestoga, treasurer.

To be sworn into office are four directors re-elected in November: Mrs. Anna Parker this city; Lefever, Becker, and Raymond Sweigart, Denver. There is one vacancy on the board caused by the recent death of Mrs. Archer Tunis.

OTHER COUNTY officials who assumed office today (they took oaths last week):

County Recorder of Deeds Frank L. Spence, County Controller George W. Howells, Jury Commissioners Miss Bess Gilfillan and Mrs. Esther Groff, and Prison-keeper Walter L. Foust.

Bard Is Being Mentioned for U. S. Appeals Court

PHILADELPHIA, Jan. 2—U. S. District Court Judge Guy K. Bard is being seriously considered for appointment to the U. S. Circuit Court of Appeals for the Philadelphia area, it was reported today.

Judge Bard, who lives at Ephrata RD, Lancaster county, last week rounded out 10 years as a Federal jurist.

He has been prominently mentioned also as a possible candidate for the Democratic nomination for Governor of Pennsylvania.

Donald Yearout Born Just 2 Minutes Late

YAKIMA, Wash., Jan. 2—(AP)—Donald was born at 12:01 a. m. New Year's Day—just two minutes late, it would seem.

He's the son of Mr. and Mrs. Donald D. Yearout of Wapato, Wash.

THREE OTHER OFFICERS ALSO TAKE OATHS

McCartney Sworn in as Police Chief in Brief City Hall Ceremony

Kendig C. Bare, a veteran of World War II, was inaugurated today as the 30th Mayor of Lancaster.

The city's new chief executive, now thirty-six years old, is the youngest man ever to occupy the position in the past 132 years.

Mayor Bare succeeds Dr. Dale E. Cary who today completed his third term — for a total of 12 years. That, too, is a record because it is the longest span of years ever served by any Mayor of Lancaster.

Today's inaugural ceremony, simple and stream-lined marked the start of a new municipal administration.

THE NEW MAYOR, dressed in a blue business suit with striped tie, repeated his oath firmly as it was administered to him by retiring Mayor Cary.

He had his left hand placed on a Bible belonging to Mayor Cary, which Cary has used ever since the time long ago when he taught school.

Nearly 200 persons crammed full the small flower-banked Council Chamber and overflowed into adjoining rooms and the City Hall corridor outside.

IN THE AUDIENCE were the attractive wife of the new mayor, his mother, Mrs. Kendig H. Bare, and his brother, Howard Bare, a local attorney. Also his father-in-law, Dr. Benjamin B. Herr, principal of McCaskey High School.

Also in the audience were Lt.-Gov. Daniel B. Strickler, State Assemblyman Paul G. Murray, and Harry Goodhart, the unsuccessful Democratic candidate for mayor in November.

Before he began his short inaugural address, Mayor Bare extemporaneously paid tribute to Dr. Cary. He said:

"I express along with all the citizens of Lancaster a deep appreciation for the hard work and devoted service Mayor Cary has given to the city of Lancaster.

"Now as you (Dr. Cary) join the ranks of the elder statesmen, I know we can depend upon your advice and counsel in administering the affairs of the city we love."

Mayor Bare swore in the new Council members, Harry A. Schnitzer and John E. Spidle.

Two members of Council, who have two more years to serve, remain to complete the executive branch of the city government. They are: K. L. Shirk and Francis D. Rineer.

RICHARD A. SMITH was sworn in as City Controller to succeed Acting-Controller George Diehl who was named to the position fol-

(See Page 7—INAUGURATION)

Public Protest Ends Loud-Speaker Ads at Grand Central

NEW YORK, Jan. 2—(AP)—Out-squawked by commuters, the new commercial broadcasts at Grand Central terminal will go silent at midnight tonight.

The decision was apparently a total victory for exasperated travelers who condemned the music and advertising programs at a three-day public hearing of the Public Service Commission.

The cancellation was a voluntary move on the part of the terminal, however. The commission will not make its own ruling until after Jan. 10.

Terminal manager E. B. Moorhouse said a "substantial majority" of the passengers favored the programs.

Local, National, World News Are Summarized

Today's New Era has many features summarizing local, national, and world news events for 1949.

They include local news pictures on page seven.

A full page of national and world news pictures on page 11.

The "best stories of 1949" on Page nine.

A "dot and dash" review, page 19.

Famous people of the first half of the 20th century, Page 21.

From Foxhole to Grammar School
See Boyle—Editorial Page

LANCASTER NEW ERA

The Weather
U. S. Weather Bureau Forecast:
Cloudy and Cold

73rd Year—No. 22,559 | Lancaster City Zone Population, Official Figures of Audit Bureau of Circulations 112,897 | LANCASTER, PA., THURSDAY, FEBRUARY 9, 1950 | CITY EDITION | 44 PAGES | 30c PER WEEK—5c Per Copy

Plan $1 Million School Bond Issue

Atom Expert Tells What to Do Should A-Bomb Hit Penn Square

Local Man Says Cellar Would Be Safest Spot

If you got word an enemy plane carrying an A-bomb or an H-bomb was winging toward Lancaster, your best bet for living would be to hurry down the cellar and flop flat on your stomach.

Children playing outdoors might be trained to jump into the nearest street corner sewer opening.

That advice comes from a Lancaster resident who is recognized as one of the top authorities on atom bombs and how they affect human beings.

He is Richard Gerstell, 355 N. West End Ave., former radiological defense adviser in the Office of Civilian Defense Planning and now engaged in more defense work.

In an exclusive interview with the New Era, Gerstell brought home for the first time an idea of how an atom bomb blast might affect a city like Lancaster, its people, and its buildings.

AND HE TOLD what might happen were an A-bomb to be exploded over the middle of Penn Square. It wouldn't be healthy, he admits, to be in the downtown section. But the danger lessens materially as you get farther out, even a half-mile out.

Buildings would be pretty well demolished within a two-mile limit. After that, the damage lessens appreciably.

In his study of atom bomb effects, Gerstell said he started with the idea that A-bombs such as were exploded in World War II would mean the end of mankind.

TODAY, SAYS THE local man, he has frankly changed his mind. He has concluded, Gerstell said, that while the atom bomb comes up to its billing as the most destructive force loosed by mankind, it does not mean liquidation of the human race.

Especially if the proper precautions are taken, he adds.

Gerstell studiously confined his remarks to the World War II style of A-bomb. What American scientists have found out about the more terrible hydrogen bomb is not yet ready for public announcement, he declared.

But he did say this: While the hydrogen bomb has been advertised as 1,000 times more powerful than its ancestor A-bomb, it does not necessarily follow that its effects on people and buildings are 1,000 times greater.

A slim, studious-looking man of thirty-nine with short wiry hair, Gerstell used Lancaster as a guinea pig for his remarks.

The take-to-the-cellar advice comes because Lancaster doesn't have subways or other underground shelters like some of the larger cities, Gerstell points out.

"In fact," he says, "cellars offer as good and in some cases better protection."

IF YOU AREN'T too close to the bomb blast and you can avoid falling timbers and debris, said the bomb expert, a cellar offers you the best protection from such things as flash burns and radiation.

Gerstell lists the dangers from atom bombs in this 1-2-3 order, placing first what he considers the most dangerous:

1. Flying objects. 2. Flash burns. 3. Radiation.

CONTRARY TO popular belief, says Gerstell, there is a very definite limit to the range of the effects of radiation.

Inside the first half mile, he points out, chances for escape are two out of 100. Chances are you would die immediately. If not from

(See Page 34—ATOM BLAST)

New Era Aerial Photo by Edgar M. Sachs

'Total Destruction' Area Would Radiate Half-Mile from Explosion Site

Area within white line on above air view of Lancaster would be area of "total destruction" were an A-bomb to be dropped on Penn Square. It is all within one-half mile radius of Penn Square.

Because of limitations of picture, the boundary is shown only for north and west Lancaster. It extends in the same arc for east and south Lancaster.

SCIENTISTS SAY all buildings in this area would be destroyed, although not necessarily leveled since steel and concrete reinforcement would stand.

While not within these limits, both General and St. Joseph's Hospitals would be knocked out, scientists say, because they sit on knolls.

THE "TOTAL DESTRUCTION" area is bounded on N. Queen St. at a point half-way between Lemon and James Sts.; on E. King St., between Plum and Ann Sts.; on S. Queen St., between Andrew and Hazel; and W. King St., between Mary and Pine.

Other boundary points would be Lemon-Mulberry St. corner; Charlotte and Walnut Sts.; Dorwart and Freemont Sts.; Green and Strawberry Sts.; Pershing Ave. and Green St.; and Lime and Lemon Sts.

AREA OUTSIDE one-half mile circle and within mile would have residential buildings almost destroyed. Only fire-proof and shock-resistant buildings would be immune to any appreciable extent.

One to one and a half miles: Blast damage still extensive to residences. Fire damage extensive in inflammable areas.

ONE AND A HALF to two miles: At Hiroshima, the average limit of heavy structural damage was roughly two miles from point of explosion. The limits of fire damage would roughly coincide with this boundary, except where wind causes wider effects.

Over two miles: Structural damage due to blast and fire is appreciably lessened. The maximum distance of a recorded structural damage at Hiroshima, however, was 4.1 miles.

FLORIN MAN IS HELD FOR MURDER TRIAL

Dr. Schlosser Says He Planned Autopsy Before Bullet Was Found

Forty-two-year-old John Peter Troutwine, Florin junkman, was held without bail for court today on a charge of fatally shooting his neigabor, Harry G. Eichelberger.

He was given a 25-minute hearing before Alderman J. Edward Wetzel. The only witnesses were Dr. David E. Schlosser, deputy coroner, and State Police Sgt. Vernon E. Simpson.

Troutwine sat with folded hands and let out several audible sighs during proceedings. He did not testify.

DR. SCHLOSSER gave his account of what happened between the time Eichelberger's body was found and an autopsy which determined, the next day, that the man had been shot.

The Mt. Joy deputy coroner said he had the autopsy in mind even before a Mt. Joy undertaker, preparing the body for burial, accidentally discovered a .22-calibre rifle bullet in the body.

Previous to the finding of the bullet, Dr. Schlosser testified, he didn't know what was the cause of death, despite an examination of the dead man.

SGT. SIMPSON testified about his investigation. He said Troutwine signed his confession with an "X" since he can't read or write.

Later, he said, the confession was approved by Troutwine when it was read in his presence and the presence of Alderman Wetzel and a representative from the District Attorney's office.

SIMPSON SAID Troutwine told him he shot Eichelberger:

"To scare him so he would not keep me up all day."

Police have quoted Troutwine, who collects and sells junk for a living, as saying Eichelberger knocked on his door the Sunday morning of the shooting day and he fired as Eichelberger entered the house.

THE ELDERLY man did not collapse. Troutwine was quoted as saying, but turned and walked back to his own residence on adjoining Railroad Ave. Several times that day, Troutwine is quoted as saying, he visited his wounded neighbor and said he was sorry for the shooting.

Sgt. Simpson testified that the bullet was found by the undertaker while he was preparing it for embalming.

Sgt. Simpson said .22-calibre rifle bullets were found hidden in a match box under a sofa in Troutwine's two-room shack.

DR. SCHLOSSER said he was called to the Eichelberger home and arrived at 11:45 o'clock that Sunday night.

He and two neighbors, Mr. and Mrs. James Althouse, Sr., who had discovered the body, he said, look-

(See Page 34—MURDER)

Ink Blot Test Given to Gibbs at Prison

The "Rorschach" ink blot test was given to Edward L. Gibbs at the Lancaster County jail yesterday afternoon.

Miss Eleanor Ross, Philadelphia psychologist who gave the examination, declined to comment afterwards. It is one of a battery of tests to determine Gibbs' mental condition.

Results are expected to be presented when he goes on trial next month for the murder of Marian Baker.

Will Written on Gin Rummy Score Sheet Ruled Valid

DES MOINES, Feb. 9.—(AP)—A will written on a gin rummy score sheet during a game and witnessed by two rummy players is valid, a judge has ruled.

District Judge Tom K. Murrow yesterday ruled the will of George Russo, who died Jan. 5, was in proper form.

Testimony disclosed that Russo had talked of making out a will while playing rummy last Oct. 15. He explained he had difficulty writing because of an infirmity.

A friend wrote out the will. Two other members of the foursome witnessed it.

KNIFE-WIELDER STEALS N.Y. BUS

Berserk Man Nabbed After Frightening Scores

NEW YORK, Feb. 9—(AP)—A tall, dark and handsome longshoreman went beserk with a knife in the Times Square area today, frightening scores of persons but hurting none.

This, said police, is what happened after the man who variously gave the names of John Maione and Russo, took over a southbound Broadway bus at 44th Street:

He flashed a knife and turned the driver and a score of passengers out into the rain.

LEAPING INTO the drivers seat, he drove the bus south on Seventh Avenue to 42d Street and maneuvered the big vehicle through 42d Street traffic west to Ninth Avenue. There he jumped out of the bus, leaving its motor running.

Two policemen, who knew nothing about the bus incident, saw him acting suspiciously on Eighth Avenue. When they accosted him, he started to run, shouting he'd kill the policemen and himself, too.

The police pounded after him. One drew a gun and shouted he'd shoot.

The chase led near a crowd emerging from the 42d Street station of the Independent subway. People scattered.

AS THEY SEIZED the man, his kitchen knife clattered to the ground.

AS THE POLICEMEN gained on the man he threatened to kill himself. Then he cried, "if you come any closer, I'll give it to you."

"Drop that knife or I'll shoot you," replied Patrolman Philip J. Kelly.

An instant later the man's kitchen knife clattered to the ground. Kelly and Patrolman Edward Rockowitz seized him.

Gilbert I. Lyons Injured in Fall

Gilbert I. Lyons, fifty, 322 E. Orange St., was admitted to the General Hospital today, suffering from a possible fracture of the back.

Lyons, who is in the insulation business, was examining a job at the Robert Myers gasoline service station, New Holland Ave., yesterday, when a 20-foot ladder, on which he and Joseph Smith, 30 W. Strawberry St., an employe, were standing, slipped.

Lyons, according to hospital attendants, fell about eight feet. Smith, who was above him on the ladder, landed on top of Lyons and was unhurt.

Most Coffee Prices Rise 2 Cents Per Pound Here

Prices on most brands of coffee advanced 2 cents a pound in grocery stores here this week.

The boosts brought coffee prices to their highest level since the pre-Christmas season.

Most of the major vacuum-packed brands are now selling around 86 cents a pound, with caffein-free brands selling as high as 96 cents a pound.

ADDITION TO WICKERSHAM ANNOUNCED

$300,000 Cost Estimate Bond Issue Also to Finance Lafayette

The City School Board is planning a one million dollar bond issue this Summer to pay for:

1. The new $650,000 Lafayette grade school going up at St. Joseph and Pearl Sts.

2. A new $300,000 addition onto the Wickersham grade school, Reservoir St. and Lehigh Ave., slated for construction this Summer.

PLANS FOR the Wickersham addition were announced for the first time today. The addition will include eight new classrooms, an auditorium, two gymnasiums, and a student club and activities room.

It will increase the pupil capacity of Wickersham from 420 to 660 pupils. Architect's plans are slated to be submitted to the School Board at its regular meeting tonight.

If all goes well, it is hoped to have at least the new classrooms ready for the start of the 1950-51 term next September.

Both the new Lafayette building and the Wickersham addition are part of the School Board's five-year modernization program which started in 1947 and is nearing completion.

SLATED PROBABLY for next year is a contemplated addition onto Washington grade school on S. Ann St. The actual size of that addition hinges upon plans for the City Housing Authority's 100-home public project slated for that neighborhood.

Officials said today the cost of the Washington school enlargement may also be included in the proposed bond issue. In that event, it may exceed one million dollars.

VOTER APPROVAL of the new bond issue is not required, pointed out C. Abram Snyder, School Board president. That is so, he said, because State law says the School Board may borrow up to two per cent of the assessed property valuation of 100 million dollars without a referendum.

Any amount exceeding two million dollars must first be okayed by the city voters.

At present, the School Board has a total outstanding debt of $1,447,000. But, of that, $1,115,000 worth of bond issue was approved by the electorate.

Some of these bonds go back to 1924. Others date from 1937-38 when the McCaskey High School was paid for. They will come due between now and 1957.

IT IS PLANNED tentatively that the new 1950 bond issue will be either of 20 or 30-year duration.

Architect Henry Y. Shaub and associate architect H. C. Kreisle submitted some details of the proposed Wickersham addition which

(See Page 34—SCHOOLS)

Thieves Loot 'Gas' Station, Drive Off in Stolen Jeep

Thieves looted the Texaco gasoline service station opposite Maple Grove Park, Lincoln Highway West, last night and then drove off in a stolen Willys jeep, valued at between $800 and $900, according to State Police.

The jeep, owned by Jack F. Tracey, 549 W. Vine St., operator of the station, was parked in a garage adjoining the office. It was painted green with white stripes and bore license 515-BH.

State policeman Rufus Williams said entrance was gained by breaking a rear window. In addition to the jeep, the thieves stole a small portable radio, a jar of nickel bags of peanuts, a U. S. Marine Corps blanket, a box of chocolate bars, two flashlights and other smaller articles.

New Era Photo

At aldermanic hearing (left to right): John P. Troutwine, accused slayer; defense attorney Charles W. Eaby, Jr.; and Dr. David E. Schlosser, deputy coroner.

YMCA WILL OPEN $26,000 DRIVE

Funds To Be Used for Budget Purposes

The Lancaster Young Men's Christian Association will open its annual two-week budget campaign Tuesday. Goal of the campaign is $26,000.

The opening date and the goal of the campaign were announced today by H. Clay Burkholder, newly-elected president of the YMCA.

J. Shober Barr, of the F and M College faculty, has been named general chairman.

BURKHOLDER pointed out that the $26,00 goal is 19 per cent of the local YMCA's total budget. Of the total amount, $1,000 will go to the International YMCA World Youth program, and $300 toward the annual Community Father and Son banquet. The balance—$24,700—will

(See Page 34—Y.M.C.A.)

BORO BUDGETS

'50 Boro Expenses to Range from $3,500 to Half Million

$50,000 Elizabethtown Sewage Addition Biggest Project Listed; Some Taxes to Rise

(Last of two articles on borough budgets)

Borough budgets—which this year here will soar above the $1-million-mark—are anything but standard.

They range all the way from $3,500 to $500,000.

Ephrata's $500,000 budget almost equals the combined expenditures of all other 18 boroughs. The county's smallest budget—$3,500—is proposed by Washington Boro.

NEXT TO EPHRATA'S in size is the budget of Columbia, where officials estimate that approximately $110,000 will be needed to operate the borough government in 1950.

Anticipated receipts, according to Stanley Albright, chairman of the Council's finance committee, "will not run many dollars over expenditures."

An attempt was made to raise the borough's tax rate of 15 mills to take care of debt service, but the move was beaten down in a recent special session of Council. The amusement tax brought in $12,000 last year, but officials were of the belief that the 1950 yield would not be that much. The take on parking meters last year was also $12,000.

CLOSE ON THE HEELS of Columbia in proposed expenditures is

(See Page 39—BOROS)

The Weather

LOCAL FORECAST and EASTERN PENNSYLVANIA: Partly cloudy with a low of 26-32 tonight. Friday generally fair and moderately cold.

MARYLAND: Occasional rain ending by early tonight in the extreme east portion and clearing in the west and general portions. Friday partly cloudy and somewhat colder followed by rain at night.

CHESAPEAKE BAY: Southeast winds veering to south and southwest 15 to 25 miles per hour today and shifting to northwest tonight. Cloudy with rain today ending early tonight followed by clearing. Rather poor visibility today, improving tonight.

TODAY TEMP. AT NEW ERA

1 AM	33
2 AM	34
3 AM	34
4 AM	35
5 AM	35
6 AM	36
7 AM	36
8 AM	39
9 AM	39
10 AM	42
11 AM	44
Noon	45
1 PM	48
2 PM	50

YESTERDAY

3 PM	39
4 PM	40
5 PM	38
6 PM	35
7 PM	33
8 PM	32
9 PM	32
10 PM	32
11 PM	32
12 PM	32

Comparative Temperature

	High Yesterday	Low Last Night
Wat. Wks.	39	27
Ephrata	39	30

High for year 78
Low for year 13

HUMIDITY
8 AM—100
10 AM—100
Noon—100
2 PM—87

Sun Rose 7:05 AM
Sun Sets 5:33 PM

Moon Rose 12:22 AM
Last Quarter Feb. 9th

Morning stars
Mars, Mercury
Venus
Saturn Jupiter

Rainfall here 24-hr. period preceding 7:30 AM today .68 ins. at Ephrata .8 in.

Rain and Mild Here, Snow in Other Areas

Rain and mild temperatures prevailed in Lancaster today while some sections of the state had four inches of snow.

The rain halted, at least temporarily, early this afternoon and the sun came out. The mercury climbed into the 50s from a night low of 27. It will be partly cloudy tonight and fair and moderately cold tomorrow, the weatherman said.

Snow, mixed with freezing rain, fell in central Pennsylvania. Snow fell at Harrisburg, Williamsport, Wilkes-Barre, and Altoona.

Today's New Era

2 ADMIT PART IN ROSE GEM THEFT

3 Others are Sought in $25,000 Jewel Robbery

NEW YORK, Feb. 9.—(AP)—Two men today admitted taking part in the $25,000 jewel robbery of showman Billy Rose's home.

Police commissioner William P. O'Brien, who disclosed the arrests as the climax to a three-State manhunt, said three other men also are being sought in the theft.

Earlier the loot, at first valued at $100,000, was said to include several valuable fur pieces, but O'Brien revealed today that only gems were taken. The jewels belonged to Rose's comely wife, former Olympic swim champion Eleanor Holm.

O'BRIEN SAID one of the men sought for questioning was William Lalamio, twenty-two, a friend of the Roses' Negro butler, James McDonald. He said McDonald and Lalamio had an engagement at the Rose home the night of the robbery.

He identified the two men in custody as Andrew Finnegan, thirty-four, a longshoreman, and Alex (Red) Grenlick, thirty-three, of Astoria, Queens. Both men have long police records, O'Brien said.

Name Is Sought for City Housing Project

The City Housing Authority is looking for a name for the 100-home State-aid project it is planning to build in southeast Lancaster.

State law requires some means of identifying the project, said chairman Alfred C. Alspach.

Authority members will be polled for suggestions as to name at an Authority meeting today, Alspach reported.

EARLY WANT-AD DEADLINE

Due to the increased size of Friday's Intelligencer - Journal the Want-Ad deadline will be 8:00 P. M. for today only, instead of 9:00 o'clock.

Want-Ads received after 8:00 P. M. will be started in Friday's New Era.

Atom Defense Report Urges Dispersal of War Plants

WASHINGTON, Feb. 9—(AP)—The federal government today handed the nation a grim primer in construction problems of the Atomic Age.

It issued a report entitled "damage from Atomic Explosion and Design of Protective Structures," dealing in matter-of-fact language with requirements for building which might have to undergo the tremendous force of a nearby A-bomb blast.

The best advice it could offer builders was to erect important structures as far from strategic areas as possible, or put them underground.

It called for dispersal of potential war plants, and said the most vital industries might have to bury themselves deep in caves and mines.

THE REPORT was prepared by the National Security Resources Board, for use by Civil Defense planners across the nation. It will be distributed by the MSRB to the Governors of all the States.

The report's findings are based on studies made largely in Hiroshima, the first city ever to feel the terrible effect of an atomic explosion. It included no reference to later, more powerful A-bombs, nor did it mention the fearful hydrogen bomb now being developed.

Surveys made in Japan, it said, showed that heavily framed steel and reinforced concrete buildings offered the greatest resistance to atomic blast. Those which offered the weakest showing were shed-type structures with light frames and long, unsupported beams.

AS FOR HOUSING, the report well-constructed frame buildings

(See Page 34—SURVEY)

THOUSANDS OF VALUE-SEEKING FOOD SHOPPERS HAIL FOOD FAIR'S
FOOD FAIR
BUYERS' WEEK!
Open 9 to 9 Thurs. and Sat. 9 to 10 Friday
Opportunity TO BUY NOW for Easter!
SWIFT'S Premium HAMS
—AT A PRE-EASTER SAVING!!
Food Fair Fu' Cut Shank Half
America's Fav rite Ham!
lb 49¢
Famous name quality—small, short shank—generous Food Fair full cuts from 12- to 16-lb. hams—with center slices left on!
FYNE-TASTE Assorted
JELLY EGGS
Colorful, pure, wholesome jelly eggs spice and fruit flavored . . . sealed in cellophane — Buy now for the Kiddies' Easter Baskets.
1-lb cello bag 19¢
Chocolate Covered Cocoanut Cream
EASTER EGGS
Full pound — large, plain dark chocolate-covered cocoanut cream egg packed in a handsome Easter Gift Box!
1-lb egg 29¢
Calif. Green
ASPARAGUS
Tender green spears of California fresh garden Asparagus — Buyers' Week priced to save you money! — in our fresh Produce Dept. None priced higher.
lb 23¢
PSG Tender, Fresh
PORK Shoulder
Fresh Picnic Style shoulders of Pork . . . Cut from young, baby Porkers! . . . Roast or make two meals of it — cook with sauerkraut!
lb 33¢
Lean, Sugar-Cured
SLICED BACON
Serve crisp, lean, sizzling bacon with your Food Fair Eggs for breakfast! Our low price makes it a thrifty buy for your budget!
lb 37¢
For Making Easter Eggs!
XXXX SUGAR
Well known brand—confectioners sugar . . . just what you need to make Easter eggs at home. You'll appreciate the low price.
1-lb box 10¢
STRATFORD FARMS As'td
PRESERVES
Top Quality—Peach, Apricot, Plum and Orange Marmalade in attractive reusable table service jars. Take home several jars at this Low Price.
8-oz jar 10¢
Calif. Crisp Tender
Pascal CELERY
Fresh, Clean! — crisp and green — the kind that snaps when you bite into it. Not stringy or coarse — SAVE money. None priced higher.
stalk 15¢
Our Own "Kitchen-Fresh"
POTATO SALAD
Delicious, creamed style. Made Fresh daily in our own sanitary salad kitchen! Finest ingredients in an old family recipe.
1-lb cont 23¢
ARMOUR'S Star or SWIFT'S Premium
CANNED HAMS
Buy now and put away for Easter! They're Boneless and Cooked—Ready-To-Eat! Sold whole (in the can) at marked weights — 9 to 12-lb avg.
lb 73¢
OVENKIST Salted
CRACKERS
Fresh, Flaky — extra thin square soda crackers. Ideal for the kiddies after-school-snack. A Super-Value!
1-lb box 19¢
Whole Unpeeled
Libby's APRICOTS
Delightful fruit favorite for dessert or salad centers. Libby's famous Quality at a Food Fair Buyers' Week low price!
large No. 2½ can 21¢
Crisp "ICEBERG"
LETTUCE
"Salad Time" calls for plenty of fresh, clean, crisp Iceberg! None Priced Higher!
2 heads 19¢
SNOW CROP Tender
GREEN PEAS
Famous Snow Crop Quality — Tender sweet green peas quick frozen to give you garden-fresh flavor. Regularly priced at 25c —
12-oz pkg 19¢
KRAFT Tasty
VELVEETA
Delightful, piquant cheese flavor! — a favorite everywhere for its fine melting quality in cooking! . . . for salads! . . . for sandwiches! Save!
8-oz pkg 23¢
SAN GEORGIO
MACARONI & SPAGHETTI
2 1-lb boxes 25¢
★ Pussy Cat Food 3 8-oz. cans 22c
★ Keebler Butter Thins 11½-oz. pkg. 25c
★ Keebler Wafers—Cocoanut 12 oz. pkg. 35c
★ 20-Mule Team Borax 2-lb. pkg. 29c
★ Boraxo Hand Cleaner 8-oz. can 17c
CHEF BOYARDEE Spagh. SAUCE
Smooth, hardy sauce — Meat or Mushroom!
2 8-oz. cans 27c
SWANEE Household
PAPER TOWELS
Economy for your kitchen or bathroom! 150 strong, absorbent sheets on each thrifty roll! A Buyers' Week sensation at —
150 sheet roll 10¢
LADY FAIR Plain or Seeded
HEAT 'N EAT ROLLS
Oven fresh rolls for your table in 7 minutes . . . the FIRST moment of FRESHNESS is yours! Serve 'em hot with Food Fair Butter-m-m-m!
pkg of 12 25¢
Large White La.
FRESH SHRIMP
Tender, meaty shrimp from Louisiana . . . these sparkling large beauties are a real treat at a rare low price this weekend . . .
lb 65¢
Fancy Imported Meaty
LOBSTER TAILS
So delicious! So meaty! and so easy to prepare! . . . Enjoy this luxury delicacy at a special Buyers' Week Saving!
lb 85¢
826 Manor Street
W. James & Lancaster
E. Chestnut & Franklin
McCORMICK'S TEA BAGS
The favorite of millions— Blended from the world's finest tea!
Pkg of 25 31¢ Pkg of 50 57c
PHILLIP'S Delicious SOUPS
Vegetable 2 cans 21c
Veg.-Beef 3 cans 29c
Tomato . 3 cans 25c
PARD DOG FOOD
Supplies every food element your dog needs.
2 1-lb Cans 25¢
SWIFT'NING
SWIFT'S SHORTENING
3-lb. can 79c
CRISCO
For lighter cakes, flaky pie crust, for delicious fried foods!
3-lb. can 83c
For Year 'Round Use!
DRIED CORN KEEPS PERFECTLY
COPE'S Evaporated White SWEET CORN 11-oz can 29¢
COPE'S Ready-to-Serve Evap. White SWEET CORN No. 2 can 16¢

McCaskey Fields First Diamond Squad In School History For Opener Today

Manheim Twp. Will Be Initial Test For Coach Hartman's Nine

Intell SPORTS Journal

(Pete Busser)

BASEBALLS filled the air. There was the familiar crack as bat met ball. A group of boys were limbering up their arms on the sidelines as the rest of the squad went through batting drill.

That was the scene we surveyed one cold windy afternoon.

But the sport didn't seem to be in keeping with the weather or vice versa, as we turned up our overcoat collar and walked across the field, in the face of a biting cold wind. The temperature was in the high thirties and I thought to myself that these kids should be playing football rather than baseball.

Inquiring of one of the players along the sideline as to the whereabouts of the coach, we were directed to a figure standing behind the pitching mound.

Turning our gaze that way, we saw a slight, scholarly, bespectacled gentleman, attired in familiar baseball garb, who seemed to bear a slight resemblance to Burt Shotton, pilot of the Brooklyn Dodgers.

* * * *

OUR assignment was a story on his team, but, knowing full well that practice this year has been cut to a minimum, due to the weather, we decided not to bother the coach as he sent his squad through their paces, and to just watch the proceedings.

Well, we got a story without asking the gentleman one question.

One of the players was taking his turn at batting practice. He hit three or four weak grounders to the infielders and on his last attempt the coach told him to check his feet. The boy did and the coach remarked that he was stepping back from the pitch instead of into it. The next couple of pitches were turned into hot, sizzling grounders that the infielders could not handle.

The kid left the batter's box with a big grin of satisfaction on his face.

Next to take his turn was a tall, rangy, righthanded swinger. Two or three long, high, outfield flies convinced us that the kid had power. "Good power," was the comment of the coach. "Now keep your eyes on a level with the pitcher's waist." The next couple of pitches were converted into whistling line drives to the far reaches of the outfield.

And just a little bit more confidence had been added to a kid interested in playing baseball.

Another lad, in attempting to "lay one down," baseball jargon for a bunt or sacrifice, was a little too eager to run and henceforth was hitting the ball so hard that it could be turned into a force play. A few kindly, instructive words from the coach and the lad then bunted the ball in such a way that his sacrifice would have been successful. And many a sacrifice hit has won a ball game.

* * * *

AS PLAYER after player took his turn at batting practice, his faults were corrected. Little items of omission or commission did not escape the watchful eye of the gentleman behind the mound.

We soon got the feeling that here was a man who knew baseball, who loved baseball, who could teach baseball. A man who in his gentle unassuming way could install knowledge and skill of the game of baseball into a group of raw recruits.

But, above all else. Here was a man who could install in young players the one vital thing they need to succeed as players and a team. Confidence. Confidence in their ability. The confidence that comes from seeing errors corrected by an interested man who knows. The confidence that leads to winning base hits and game-saving plays.

That man was McCaskey High School's baseball coach, Mr. Cliff Hartman.

Joe Finger Draws Starting Mound Assignment Against Blue Streaks

McCaskey High School, fielding the first baseball team in the history of the school, inaugurates its 1950 campaign this Thursday with one of the strong contenders in the County High School League, Manheim Twp.

Manheim Twp., 15-1 victors over West Lampeter Tuesday in the opening day action for Section 2 of the County High School League, will be the home team.

Coach Clifford Hartman Wednesday night named Joe Finger, a righthander, for mound duty while Ronnie Owens and Don Mulhatten will be standing by for relief roles.

Coach Paul Wenrich, who sent his leading mound candidate, Buddy Young, against West Lampeter Tuesday, will use either Ronnie Stewart or Charlie Hoffman for the pitching chores.

Hartman reported Wednesday night that cold weather has hampered him considerably this Spring. With only three outdoor drills and a practice game with Manor to go on, the McCaskey mentor is still undecided on his club's strength.

"We are woefully weak in hitting," Hartman reported, "but this may come around when the weather gets warmer. It's a bit difficult for the boys to show any power at the plate right now." On pitching, Hartman reported Finger a pretty good prospect. "He looked good for two innings against Manor," Hartman said. The McCaskey coach said Finger has a good fast ball but he has not permitted any of his pitchers to throw any hooks or curves during this cold spell.

"On paper the club should be fast," Hartman added. "The outfield is exceptionally fast for high school competition and the infield has shown some good fielding ability. Only the hitting appears weak now but that may develop," Hartman stated.

Hartman also stated that illness has hit his club pretty heavily and made his job of analyzing a completely new squad more difficult. His only acquaintance with many of the players was made through the City Junior Legion Baseball program.

For this opening day action with the Blue Streaks Hartman has tentatively assigned John Smithgall to the catching job; Bob Hill at first base; Bob Brubaker at second base; Frank Herr or Howard Keays at shortstop, and Jack Wilson at third base.

In the outfield, Tom Headrick will probably win the starting berth in leftfield, Robert Hershock in centerfield and Nevin Krentz in rightfield.

Keglers' Korner

MERCHANT LEAGUE

High Single—Sam Rosser	256
High Triple—Win Kennard	627
High Team Single—Dombach-Nagle	1068
High Team Triple—Dombach-Nagle	2958

CHRISTIANA MAJOR LEAGUE

High Single—Rocco Valenti	257
High Triple—Rocco Valenti	692
High Team Single—MacIntires	1041
High Team Triple—MacIntires	2972

CHANGE LEAGUE

High Single—Jerry Swartz	194
High Triple—Arlean Richmond	535
High Team Single—Halves	771
High Team Triple—Halves	2219

ENG. SHOPS OFFICE LEAGUE

High Single—Charles Eckman	201
High Triple—Ray Gaul	515
High Team Single—Schedules	933
High Team Triple—Machinists	2585

HOUSE LEAGUE

High Single—Ray Mair	226
High Triple—Geo. Seifert	591
High Team Single—Indians	929
High Team Triple—Indians	2699

MALTA A.B.C. LEAGUE

High Single—Geo. Wiley	212
High Triple—Elvin Slaugh	549
High Team Single—Dukes	861
High Team Triple—Kings	2415

ROSES REMAIN UNDEFEATED IN FIFTH CONTEST

(Special To The Intell)

Vero Beach, Fla.—The Lancaster Red Roses remained undefeated following their fifth Spring exhibition game here Wednesday, playing Asheville of the Tri-State League to a 1-1 tie in seven innings.

The game was called at the conclusion of the seventh inning because of rain, with both Class "B" teams playing on even terms to that point, each collecting four base hits.

Ray Moring, right - handed pitcher stood out offensively and defensively for the Lancaster club. Moring worked the first three innings for the Roses, and blasted a three base hit in the third. Representing the leading run at that point, Moring was thrown out at the plate attempting to stretch the triple into a home run.

John Wilcox took over for Moring in the fourth inning and worked the remainder of the contest, before rain halted activity. Wilcox yielded two Asheville hits, the same number that Moring had given up in the first three frames.

Lancaster's lone run came in the sixth inning when the Roses put together a double by Don Runge and a single by Bob Umstead. Asheville picked off its only tally in the fourth inning at the expense of Wilcox.

NEW PROSPECT

Tony Contini, younger brother of Hal Contini, manager of the Lebanon team of the North Atlantic League, is working out with the Lancaster club, general manager William Cowdrick announced Wednesday.

The younger Contini, a graduate of Lafayette College, will be a candidate for an infield position, Cowdrick revealed, trying out for the short stop or second base post.

Lancaster	000 001 0—1	4	0
Asheville	000 100 0—1	4	1

F&M Golf Team Nips Swarthmore By 5-4 Decision

Franklin and Marshall's golf team opened its 1950 season Wednesday afternoon with a narrow 5 to 4 victory over Swarthmore College.

Playing over the par 71 Rolling Green Country Club course in Philadelphia, the Dips and Garnet split even on the six individual matches, but F&M copped two out of the three best ball decision for the triumph.

Individual winners for F&M were Bill Haines, Don Stouffer and Ben Harry, the three holdovers from last year's team. Haines was low man for F&M with a 76, but medalist honors for the match went to Swarthmore's Tom McCarthy with a 71.

The summaries:

Bill Haines, F&M, defeated Mike Remerenco, 5 and 4.

Tom McCarthy, Swarthmore, defeated Bernie Ebersole, 7 and 6.

(Best ball won by Swarthmore, 4 and 3.)

Don Stauffer, F&M, defeated Norman McAvoy, 5 and 4.

Charles Warden, Swarthmore, defeated Bill Flugelman, 3 and 2.

(Best ball won by F&M, 3 and 1.)

Ben Harry, F&M, defeated Jack Lawrence, 8 and 7.

Nick Meyers, Swarthmore, defeated John MacDonald, 3 and 2.

(Best ball won by F&M, 3 and 2.)

100 BOYS COMPETE IN Y INDOOR MEET

More than one hundred Cadets competed recently in the annual YMCA indoor athletic meet, W. Barnhart, Boys' Physical Director, announced Wednesday.

The meet consisted of five events conducted in two weight divisions. The first, second and third place winners in each division are listed below.

OVER 85 LBS.

Track (2 laps): 1. L. Boose and K. Weaver; 2. C. Krammes and D. Wagner; 3. J. Shank. **Shot Put:** 1. F. Heistand; 2. K. Weaver; 3. F. Longenecker. **High Jump:** 1. T. Eby; 2. L. Boose; 3. C. Krammes and J. Eppley. **Standing Broad:** 1. L. Boose; 2. R. Shirker; 3. B. Boas. **Potato Race:** 1. L. Smith; 2. L. Boose; 3. E. Frailey.

UNDER 85 LBS.

Track (2 laps): 1. B. Dissinger; 2. H. Bear; 3. B. Myers and H. Musselman. **Shot Put:** 1. H. Bear; 2. B. Wegner; 3. D. Kelly. **High Jump:** 1. G. Bear and B. Horn; 2. R. Swab; 3. R. Laudenberger and R. Hartsel. **Standing Broad:** 1. F. Longenecker; 2. J. Hammond; 3. B. Horn. **Potato Race:** 1. H. Bear; 2. R. Barnhart; 3. R. Lewis.

AMERICAN ATHLETE-PREACHER ABROAD—Gil Dodds (left), famous distance runner, who is in Japan on a preaching tour under the auspices of the Pocket Testament League of New York, talks with Sgt. Rollie Rowlands at the Armed Forces radio station in Tokyo.

NCAA Doubles Size Of Post-Season Cage Tournament; "Sanity Code" Under Study

Chicago—(AP)—The National Collegiate Athletic Association decided Wednesday to double the size of its post-season basketball tournament, the final round of which will probably be played elsewhere than Madison Square Garden.

Next year 16 teams instead of eight will be selected under new rules of procedure.

MAY MODIFY CODE

The NCAA Executive Committee also set up machinery that probably will bring recommendations to the 1951 convention in Dallas for modifying the controversial "sanity code" that governs subsidization of college athletes. Sentiment appears to favor softening the code to permit providing board and room in addition to tuition. This would please Southern rebels.

In another major action the NCAA resumed its financial support of the National Collegiate Statistical Bureau which compiles detailed figures in football and basketball. This means stories on the national football leaders, both major and minor, in such fields as rushing, passing, punting, and defensive play will again be available over press service wires.

The decision to change the basketball setup came following howls of protest over this year's selection methods—only one team was chosen from each of the eight national districts of the NCCA. This meant that strong small schools in areas dominated by major conference champions were bypassed.

WORKING OUT METHOD

Arthur Lonborg of Northwestern heads the committee that is working out the new methods of selection. The NCAA press spokesman was asked if this would mean that hereafter two teams would be chosen from each of the eight districts and he replied "not necessarily."

If the two-teams-to-a-district method is rejected, one alternative would be to designate the winners of major conference titles as automatically qualified for the big tournament, plus a few other schools to be selected from among the strong left-overs regardless of district.

The expanded basketball tournament will still be divided into Eastern and Western halves, with the Western finals in Kansas City, and the Eastern finals possibly in New York.

The national finals, pitting the two sectional winners and the two sectional runners up, may go to the University of Minnesota at Minneapolis, whose arena seats 18,000.

Shea, Mole And 2 Others Go To Kansas City From Yanks

St. Petersburg, Fla.—(AP)—The New York Yankees sent four players to their Kansas City farm club for more work Wednesday, with indications the men wouldn't be on hand when the season opens April 18.

They were pitchers Frank Shea, Wally Hood and Paul Hinrichs and first baseman Fenton Mole.

The players have not been assigned to the American Association club but remain on the New York player list, at least momentarily, according to publicity chief Arthur Patterson.

Waivers have been asked on Shea, who won only one game for the World Champions last year and none during his stay at Newark. He is not "farmable."

Patterson said it had not been decided what would be done with the four men, who for the time being will be going through their paces at Kansas City's Lake Wales camp.

Hood and Mole likely will wind up with Kansas City. Waivers, if asked on Hinrichs, can't be withdrawn and he likely would be claimed. He is in the "bonus" category, having received around $40,000 to sign.

Shea, a star in the Yanks' 1947 pennant and World Series winning team has been ineffective ever since. Overweight was blamed in 1948 and a neck ailment last year.

Hinrichs, a divinity student at the Lutheran Seminary at Concordia in St. Louis, Mo., was signed as a free agent last year.

GOOD PROSPECT

Hood, a young righthander, was signed upon graduation from the University of Southern California and is regarded as a good prospect. He divided last season between Newark and Kansas City, winning eight and losing eight games.

Mole, a lefthanded hitting first baseman, has shown flashes of power the last two years but has been inconsistent. He banged 22 homers for Portland of the Coast League in 1948 but dropped to 16 and a .269 batting mark last year at Newark. He has never hit higher than .283 in a complete season since he broke in with Norfolk of the Piedmont League in 1946.

NORKUS STOPS KENNEDY

New York—(AP)—Charley Norkus, hard-hitting 21-year-old Bayonne, N. J., heavyweight, evened accounts with Curt Kennedy Wednesday night by knocking out the Wichita, Kan., fighter in 1:54 of the first round of a scheduled ten at St. Nicholas Arena. Norkus a 2 to 1 underdog, weighed 190½ to Kennedy's 191.

TWO TROPHIES AT STAKE IN COUNTY LIVE BIRD SHOOT

Two trophies will be at stake in the annual Lancaster County White Flyer championship shoot at the New Holland Rod and Gun Club this Saturday at 11 a. m.

One trophy will go the county resident winner and another for the top non-resident entry. Bob Sellers of Silver Springs is the defending titleholder.

The shoot in past years has been held at the Utilities Trap and Skeet Club. Several Utilities gunners will be on hand.

A top list of out-of-county shooters is expected from Lebanon and Berks Counties. Another hot local contender is C. Ralph Binkley of Neffsville, former state champion.

Syracuse—Syracuse University's Archbold Stadium will have 6,000 new steel seats in place in time for this Fall's opener against Rutgers, Sept. 23.

M'CASKEY J-V NET TEAM WINS OPENING MATCH

McCaskey High School's jayvee net team opened its Inter-County Scholastic Tennis League activity with a 5-2 decision over Manheim Twp. Wednesday afternoon on the McCaskey courts.

The Red and Black junior netsters swept three singles and two doubles matches to take the verdict. The contest was also Manheim Township's first taste of 1950 league competition. Both teams had been scheduled for opening day action Monday but were rained out.

Robert Kant and Bernard Baymiller recorded the only Blue Streak victories of the day. Kant matched strokes with John May in a duel that went three sets and was a battle the whole way. The Manheim Twp. No. 1 man took the initial set, 6-2, but May forged back to square the match with a 6-2 verdict in the second set. Kant was extended in the final set before winning, 7-5.

Baymiller, who recorded the other Blue Streak win, took the match in straight sets but was extended in both. The opening set went to Baymiller, 9-7, and the second set by an 8-6 count.

SINGLES

Kant, Manheim Twp., defeated May, 6-2, 2-6, 7-5.

Slothour, McCaskey, defeated Henderson, 6-4, 5-4 (default).

Dommel, McCaskey, defeated Kohler, 4-6, 6-3, 6-1.

Aznavorian, McCaskey, defeated Pfautz, 6-2, 6-0.

Baymiller, Manheim Twp., defeated Sheitzer, 9-7, 8-6.

DOUBLES

May and Kegerreis, McCaskey, defeated Kant and Pfautz, 6-2, 7-5.

Slothour and Dommel, McCaskey, defeated Kohler and Richards, 8-6, 6-2.

CHANDLER, HARRIDGE WILL SPEAK AT MACK TESTIMONIAL DINNER

Philadelphia—(AP)—Baseball Commissioner A. B. Chandler and Will Harridge, president of the American League, will attend the celebration planned in observance of Connie Mack's 50th year as manager of the Philadelphia Athletics.

Chandler and Harridge will attend the anniversary dinner April 20, and will participate in the daylong festivities April 21, William Hollenbach, chairman of the golden jubilee celebration committee, announced Wednesday.

WOMEN'S BOWLING TOURNEY OPENS AT OVERLOOK SUNDAY

The ladies take over the Overlook Bowling Alleys Sunday, April 8th, for the first Women's Flight Tournament, a handicap eliminations event patterned on the men's tourney rolled several months ago.

Only 32 women are in the tournament which will get underway at 6:46 p. m. Some of the top entries are Becky Flemish, Helen Artigini, Polly Wolf, Ginnie Mowrer and Thelma Shirk.

6:45 P. M.

Becky Flemish vs. Irene Grossman.
Naomi Butzer vs. Helen Artigiani.
Ruth Mentzer vs. Molly King.
Ann Severino vs. Polly Wolf.
Lillian Hiemenz vs. Emma Kepner.
Ruth King vs. Lena McConnell.
Helen Winger vs. Helen Davidson.
Louise Lauer vs. Ginnie Mowrer.

8:00 P. M.

Thelma Shirk vs. Norma Chryst.
Anna Mae Mellinger vs. Liz Marabella.
Viola Sauder vs. Erla Witmer.
Ruth Jonas vs. "Tut" Brunner.
Blanche Shelly vs. Flossie Miller.
Blanche Godshall vs. Reba Braner.
Joe Burnett vs. V. Harnish.
Dotty Prentice vs. Mabel Gerhart.

BORDER LEAGUE SIGNS SIX UMPIRES FOR '50

Odgensburg, N. Y. —(AP)— The Border Baseball League announced Wednesday signing of six umpires, including three of last year's staff.

The holdovers are Fred Baindford of Toronto, Hugh J. MacDonald of Lowell, Mass., and Robert C. Shrader of Sayre, Pa.

Newcomers to the Class C circuit are Harry Gardner of Chicago, George (Barney) Barnicle of Fitchburg, Mass., and Theodore Pelletier of Webster, Mass.

Sports
READ 'EM AND WEEP
Results

HOCKEY

AMERICAN LEAGUE

Indianapolis 4, Cleveland 1. (Indianapolis leads 1-0 in final best of seven series.)

BASEBALL

COLLEGIATE

Georgetown 12, Lafayette 6.
Maryland 5, Bucknell 4.

BASKETBALL

NBA

Minneapolis 75, Anderson 50.

SWIMMER ARRIVES — Greta Anderson, Danish swimmer, shows medals she won in 1948 Olympic Games as she arrives at New York International Airport enroute to San Francisco.

Hen Krushinsky Of Presidents '11' Heads Mid Atlantic League Again

Hen Krushinsky, business manager for the Lancaster Presidents, was re-elected president of the Middle Atlantic Football Conference last Sunday at a meeting in Westminster, Md.

C. F. Flurie, of Harrisburg, was named vice-president and Guy Brewer, of Westminster, secretary treasurer. Bucky Nehr, publicity manager for the Lancaster Presidents, reported Wednesday evening.

The conference will function this year with the Harrisburg Bears, Westminster, Hagerstown, Cornwall A.A. and the Presidents meeting twice during the campaign. Cornwall is a new addition to the circuit and Nehr stated Wednesday that the league is seeking a sixth team for action this year.

The Lancaster Presidents copped the league title last year with an undefeated record in league competition. This year, however, the league should be faster due to new additions made to club rosters, Nehr stated. Lancaster is also scheduled to see some new faces in the line-up for the 1950 campaign.

The conference will meet again May 7 at Harrisburg to draw up and approve a schedule for the year.

SPORTS On Pages 18, 19 & 20

"American Look" is Set For 50 Years—Says Adrian

Hollywood Designer Sees 1950 Fashions as Representing Ideal In Styles for Functional Age

By Dorothy Roe

American women have arrived at the ultimate ideal in functional fashion, and will keep essentially the same silhouette for the next 50 years.

So says Adrian, the Hollywood tradition-buster, showing a collection of sleek, slim, pared-down daytime fashions which, he claims, represent the kind of clothes women need and want for the kind of lives they lead. Says he:

"There will be no drastic changes in daytime fashion for the next 50 years . . . The attempt to insinuate violent change in silhouette in modern time died with the 'new look.'

"Skirts for daytime will never be longer than 13 to 14 inches from the floor and maybe a trifle shorter.

"The American women can — for once — feel secure that her trim, square-shouldered suit will be as familiar 50 years from today as it is today."

Adrian bases his predictions on observance of modern life, pointing out:

"Every modern invention for ease or speed underwrites this fact. If a woman travels by air in a rocket plane or is jet-propelled in the future—she never can be cluttered again. The compact space allowed both in traveling and luggage has signed her fashion future more than any ambitious designers with ideas for attracting attention ever can.

"Fashion has become as contemporary as the rest of our life. Switching skirt lengths seasonally or other hysterical fashion changes for daytime can never have any enduring influence again.

"The American influence is the influence of the future."

NOW AND FOREVER . . . The trim, slim American suit, in gray and black wool, for going places.

THE ATOMIC 50'S . . . This is Adrian's idea of the way a woman should look at the mid-century mark, and from then on. At left is his black taffeta and crepe dinner sheath with wing-like drapery; next, his American quilt print chiffon evening gown, called 'Martha's Vineyard', airy, strapless and flattering.

Tips for Teens

Going Home on Time Is Not Being Sissy—It's Smart

By ELINOR WILLIAMS

SEEMS LIKE every high-schooler wants to set a new record as a night owl and never go home until morning.

Why? There's no bore like the one who never knows when it's time to go home. Didn't you know that the cleverest showmen always end their most successful acts at the high point . . . the time when the audience is enjoying it most ("Always leave 'em laughing") and will want to see them again?

It's partly a matter of good psychology. It's better to keep your date eager to see you again than it is to bore him or her with a too-long evening. Fun eventually wears thin and boredom creeps in if you prolong even the biggest date too, too long. So why not be clever and keep a reasonable deadline for going home . . . for popularity as well as for your parents' and health's sake.

A survey of teensters all over the country shows that the average curfew hour for weekday dates is 11 p. m., for Saturday night dates, 12, and for formal proms, 1 A. M.

These hours make sense because they give you time to get some sleep to keep you looking and feeling well . . . able to do things you want to do and have to do. They help you avoid troubles that begin in cars that are parked too long or in not-so-nice places that are sometimes the only ones open to go to later at night.

Boys think more of girls who have a deadline than of those who are allowed to stay out all hours. So going home on time isn't being a sissy. It's smart from every angle.

(For tips on how to look prettier, send a stamped, self-addressed envelope to Elinor Williams at this paper for a free leaflet, "ABC's of Good Grooming.")

New Era Photo

Prize-winners in the Junior Evening Class of the Lancaster Junior Assembly, shown above are, (l. to r.): Sally Clare Feagley, John S. May, Barbara Breneman, Robert Reehling, Dorothy Hartman and Drew Hiestand, Jr.

Prizes Awarded as Junior Assembly Season Ends

Completion of the annual series of dances for the Lancaster Junior Assembly was marked this week with the final meetings of the season and awarding of prizes to winning dancers at concluding parties.

The Assembly groups, in four sections divided according to the ages of the boys and girls, were held on Thursdays from last November throughout the Winter season, in the ballroom of the Stevens House.

The 200 boys and girls were instructed in dance steps as well as ballroom deportment, by Dart Thorne, New York City.

PRIZE WINNERS in the four groups are the following:

Kim Stephenson, Carol Ann Nissley, Frances Alspach, Fred Orr, Jr., Rodger Anderson and William Kinzer, Jr., in the 4:15 p. m. class; Susan Snyder, Linda Stephenson, Marcia Fraim, Susan Schuberth, Edward Dryer and Adrian Colley, 5:15 p. m. class.

Dorothy Hartman, Barbara Breneman, Sally Clare Feagley, Drew Heistand, Robert Reehling and John May, Junior evening class; Beatrice Lou Kittredge, Mary Martha Armstrong, Eric Herr, Ray Miller and William Erb, Senior evening class.

ASSEMBLY committee for this year included:

Mrs. John E. McGrann, Mrs. John S. Mellinger, Mrs. Lathrop Nelson, Mrs. Albert C. Pierson, Mrs. Richard C. Schiedt, Jr. Mrs. Clarence L. Snavely, Mrs. Kenneth R. Stephenson, Mrs. J. Laurence Strickler, Mrs. John P. Woodward, Mrs. John L. Atlee, Jr., Mrs. Louis L. Bentley, Mrs. Joseph M. Breneman, Mrs. W. Hensel Brown Mrs. Victor R. Despard, Jr., Mrs. Harry N. Fackert, Jr., Mrs. Frederick S. Franklin, Mrs. Rufus A. Fulton and Mrs. Louis S. May.

Miss Parrish Is Married to C. A. Erisman

The marriage of Miss Mildred Christine Parrish, daughter of Mr. and Mrs. Edgar Goodloe Parrish, Manassas, Va., to Charles Augustus Erisman, son of Mrs. G. H. Courdier, 926 Buchanan Ave., and the late Charles Erisman, takes place today at 3:30 p. m. in the First Presbyterian Church, with the Rev. Dr. Henry B. Strock, pastor, officiating.

Given in marriage by her father, the bride is attended by Miss Jane Stabley, this city, as maid of honor. The bridesmaids are Mrs. Charles Carneal, sister of the bride, and Mrs. Frank Parrish, sister-in-law of the bride, both of Manassas.

Jack Biggs, this city, is serving as best man, and the ushers are Richard Haydon and Harold Clegg, both of this city.

Reginald Lunt, organist, is playing the traditional wedding music, with Warren Eby as vocal soloist.

A RECEPTION at the Iris Club follows the ceremony. After a wedding trip to Florida the couple will reside at 926 Buchanan Ave.

The bride, a graduate of Randolph-Macon Women's College and Smith College, has been a chemist in the research laboratories of Armstrong Cork Co. The bridegroom, a graduate of Franklin and Marshall College, is employed by McMinn's Industries.

Mr. and Mrs. Walter C. McMinn, Jr., brother-in-law and sister of the bridegroom, entertained at a cocktail party at their home, 1032 Buchanan Ave., and at dinner at the Hamilton Club last evening following the wedding rehearsal.

Their guests included members of the bridal party and guests from Washington and Virignia who are attending the wedding today.

PATRICIA ANNE LICHTY

DeMolay Will Honor Queen at Spring Dance

Miss Patricia Anne Lichty, "Miss DeMolay of 1950", will be honored by Lancaster Chapter, Order of DeMolay, at the annual Spring dance next Friday at the Iris Club.

The DeMolay Queen, eighteen, daughter of Mr. and Mrs. Paul C. Lichty, 123 E. James St., is a freshman at Millersville State Teachers College. She was elected queen at the chapter's annual Christmas ball.

THE PARTY next Friday will be a closed dance with each DeMolay allowed to take one guest couple. The dance will be semi - formal, with corsages banned. Dancing will be from 9 p. m. to midnight.

Decorations will be in a Spring theme and an orchestra will furnish music. Charles Snader is chairman with Eugene Fenninger, ex-officio. Committee members include Stanley Snyder, James Smith, Jack Snader, Robert Mitchell, William Smith.

Russian Booth with Cossacks and 'Bear' Wins 1st Prize at YW

The Russian booth decorated by the Debuteen Club won first prize at the annual Y-Teen World-Wide Bazaar held yesterday at the YWCA.

The Debuteens were dressed in Cossack costumes and decorated their room as a Russian inn with Russian figures placed on either side of the fireplace. One Debuteen was dressed as a Russian bear. The girls sold gingerbread bears dressed in miniature calico costumes. The Debuteens are an 11th grade group.

Second prize went to the T. C. Teens, 10th graders, for their Chinese booth designed as a cave with a huge green dragon coming out of the booth. The booth was made with chicken wire and crepe paper, and the girls served tea and colored nut meats.

LES JEUNNES Filles won third prize for their outdoor Spanish cafe with small tables covered with checkered cloths. The girls wore Spanish costumes and sold barbecues and coffee.

Honorable mention was given to the Suits-Us Club for their German root-beer tavern, decorated as an outdoor beer garden with German signs.

A total of 21 booths representing foreign countries were set up throughout the building. The Holland booth of the Petite Debs was in the front lobby and featured a flower sale.

MEMBERS of the Hang-Out Council provided recorded music during the evening. Dancing was held in the gym following the bazaar. About 300 persons attended.

Dr. and Mrs. Ivan LeFevre and Miss Julia Mowrer were judges. Dawn Giberson and Janice Althouse were co-chairmen.

DOROTHY JANE STEELE

Miss Steele Will Be Wed to C. J. Krall

Mr. and Mrs. John H. Steele, 923 Edgewood Ave., announce the engagement of their daughter, Dorothy Jane, to C. Joseph Krall, son of Mr. and Mrs. Chester Krall, 517 Fourth St.

Miss Steele is a graduate of the class of 1948, Pennsylvania Hospital School of Nursing, Philadelphia, and is employed in the office of Dr. Henry J. Glah.

Mr. Krall is attending Mount St. Mary's College, Emmitsburg, Md. The wedding will take place in the near future.

Grace Price Wed to A. W. Hawthorne

The marriage of Miss Grace L. Price, daughter of Mr. and Mrs. Lloyd S. Price, 428 S. Prince St., and Arthur W. Hawthorne, Jr., son of Mr. and Mrs. Arthur W. Hawthorne, 521 E. Strawberry St., took place today at 10 a. m. in St. Stephen's Lutheran Church. The Rev. Harland D. Fague officiated at the ceremony.

Given in marriage by her father, the bride wore a yellow frosted organdy street length dress with white accessories, and carried an arm bouquet of white rosebuds and snapdragons.

Mrs. Carl Eichelberger, matron of honor, wore a blue frosted organdy street length dress with white accessories and carried a bouquet of mixed flowers.

Albert Beats served as best man. Harry Aukamp played the wedding music. A reception was held at 531 E. Strawberry St., where the couple will reside after a wedding trip to Philadelphia.

The bride is a stenographer at Armstrong Cork Co. and the bridegroom is employed by Oregon Casting Co.

Quadrangle Club Plans Dinner Dance

Quadrangle Club will hold a dinner dance at 7 p. m. April 22 at the Stevens House.

The committee includes: Mrs. William J. Poorbaugh, Mrs. Wallace A. Anderson, Mrs. Harry C Baker, Mrs. Charles W. Northup, and Mrs. Paul J. Keller, president and general chairman.

YOUR FUTURE

Propitious vibrations greet you on this birthday. Allow nothing to mar your happiness in the year ahead. Originality is likely to be most noted in the child born today.

On Sunday, April 16: Some good fortune should eventuate in the year just starting. Born on this date, a child may expect help in any emergencies.

BPW CARD PARTY

The Business and Professional Women's Club will have a card party at 8 p. m. Tuesday in Malta Temple. Prizes will be awarded. Proceeds will benefit the Shelter Home, project of the club this year.

Clubs

Gamma Sigma Chapter

Gamma Sigma Chapter of Beta Sigma Phi Sorority elected Miss Kitty Young president at a meeting this week at the Iris Club.

Also elected were Mrs. Mary Kauffman, vice-president; Miss Kathleen Rutter, treasurer; Miss Allison Lockwood, recording secretary; Mrs. Janet Deardorff, corresponding secretary; Mrs. Tennyson Thomas, extension officer; Gene Miller, City Council representatives, with Mrs. Charlotte Groah as alternate.

Mrs. Nancy Lefever was named a candidate for Queen to be selected at the dance which will be held June 10 by Lancaster and York sororities.

The annual Founders' Day banquet will be held at 7 p.m. Thursday, April 27, in the Green Club room of the YWCA. Mrs. Ann Wendler was in charge of the program on "Prose."

Homemakers

Mrs. Paul Eshelman spoke on "Handcraft in the Home" at a meeting of the Homemakers Club last night at the YWCA. Mrs. Ralph Phillips presided.

Mrs. B. Franklin Herr was appointed chairman of the flower show to be held by members at their next meeting, May 5, at the YWCA. Plans were made for a garden party on June 21 at the home of Mrs. Herr, 1514 Esbenshade Rd., with Mrs. Frazer Cole and Mrs. Harvey Herr as chairmen.

The members will attend a kitchen demonstration on April 19 at 8 p. m. at the Griest Building. A food sale will be held April 21, beginning at 9:30 a. m. at the Garvin Store.

St. Andrew's Mothers

St. Andrew's Mothers Club will meet Monday at 8 p. m. at the church when plans will be made for a Mother and Daughter banquet at the church on May 12 and also for a banquet to be served Farm Women on May 3.

Mrs. Richard I. Stevens will preside and hostesses will be Mrs. Richard Smuck, Mrs. Walter Getz, Mrs. Warren Aument, Mrs. L. B. Habalar and Mrs. Frank Landis.

Village Queen Is Chosen At Calico Dance

Mrs. Lon Haley, Manheim R4, was chosen Village Queen at "Calico Hoe-down" sponsored by the Lancaster Auxiliary to the Osteopathic Hospital last night at Rocky Springs ballroom.

Mrs. Haley, who is a teacher at McKinley School in Rapho Twp., was presented with a number of gifts from local merchants. She told the dancers that square dancing is her hobby and that she square dances five nights a week.

More than 250 persons attended the hoe-down that featured square dancing, Paul Jones, and a cake walk. Special prizes were awarded for the dances and cake walk. Special prizes were awarded for the dances and cake walk. Bill Fink was caller for the square dances.

General chairman of the dance was Mrs. John W. Butts and Mrs. L. M. Yuninger was chairman of the patron tickets. Judges for the queen selection were Richard Marr, Dr. Leroy Lovelidge, and John W. Byer. Mrs. Elwood Swift was chairman of the prize committee.

THE COTILLION CLUB held its last formal dance of the season last night at Wiggins Restaurant with 75 couples attending. Decorations were in a Spring theme with window boxes filled with potted plants centering the tables arranged around the sides of the room.

The annual dinner meeting at which officers for the ensuing year will be elected, will be held May 5 at the Manheim Legion Home. An informal dance will follow the dinner.

THE FINAL SQUARE dance of the season for members of St. James' Episcopal Church was held at the parish house last evening. About 25 persons danced to recorded music. Mrs. John E. Holden was in charge assisted by Miss Marjorie Smith.

AUXILIARY MEETING

The Women's Auxiliary of St. John's Episcopal Church, W. Chestnut and Mulberry Streets, will hold its monthly meeting at 8 p. m. Monday in the parish house. The Rev. Father Alpheus Packard, Holy Cross Mission, will be the speaker.

NURSE TO END COURSE

Miss Evelyn Christen, of Sinking Springs, graduate nurse of the Lancaster General Hospital class of 1947, will complete a six-months' course in orthopaedic nursing at the University of Illinois Research and Educational Hospitals next Thursday.

Miss Green, Daughter Of Admiral, Is Wed

A wedding of local interest took place in San Francisco, Calif., today when Miss Gloria Green, daughter of Rear Admiral and Mrs. Clark Lawrence Green, became the bride of Ensign Warren Flores Brown, USN, in the Star of the Sea Chapel, Treasure Island, Calif.

A reception was held after the ceremoy at 4 p. m. at the home of Adm. and Mrs. Green at Yerba Buena Island, San Francisco. The bride's mother is the daughter of Mrs. Walter Madigan, formerly of Lancaster, now residing in California, and the late Walter Madigan.

Following a wedding trip, the couple will reside in Troy, N. Y.

Weddings

Nauss—Kissinger

Miss Betty Jane Kissinger, daughter of Mr. and Mrs. Thomas Kissinger, 31 W. College Ave., Elizabethtown; and Harvey E. Nauss, son of Mr. and Mrs. Charles Nauss, Bainbridge R1, were married at 2 o'clock this afternoon in the United Brethren Church, Palmyra, by the Rev. Harold Hollingsworth.

Miss Jean Brandt, of Elizabethtown, was maid of honor and George Nauss was best man.

The bride wore a blue suit with white accessories and an orchid corsage. Her attendant wore a pink suit with blue accessories and a corsage of rosebuds.

A reception was held at the home of the bride where the couple will reside. Both are employed by the Lancaster Shoe Co., at Elizabethtown.

Witmer—Hillard

The marriage of Miss June Hillard, daughter of Mr. and Mrs. John S. Hillard, New Holland R2, to Harold K. Witmer, son of Mrs. Esther Witmer, New Holland R2, took place at 7 p. m. yesterday in the home of the bride. The Rev. C. R. Swartz officiated.

Miss Joan Snader, Clifton Heights, Pa., attended her aunt as bridesmaid. Edwin Hillard, Blue Ball, brother of the bride, was best man. Serving as ushers were Mr. Witmer and Roy E. Martin.

Mrs. Witmer is employed by the Enterprise Telephone Co.

Kreider—Campbell

Miss Laura Ella Campbell, daughter of Mrs. Laura E. Campbell, Conestoga R2, and Frank L. Kreider, Jr., son of Mr. and Mrs. Frank L. Kreider, Lancaster R4, were married at 10 a. m. today at Safe Harbor Methodist Church by the Rev. Harold E. Homer. They were attended by Betty Campbell, of Conestoga R2 and Raymond Deater, of Rothsville.

(OTHER WEDDINGS ON PAGE 7)

Emily Post Advises:

Initial of Couple's Last Name Can Be Used to Mark New Silver

How to mark some new silver and linen is the problem of this married couple. The husband writes: "My wife and I are not agreed at all about how some new linen and silver should be marked after fifteen years of marriage. I think it should now be a combination of our initials or else just the last initial. (Mine of course.) She thinks everything should be marked as it was in her original trousseau."

Emily Post

Any silver that exactly matches the old should be marked in the same way. New silver and linen would be marked with your wife's present initials. Or you can use the single initial of your last name.

DEAR MRS. POST: Could you possibly sanction a newspaper invitation to many friends of my parents who are to be invited to their Golden Wedding celebration? Not everyone in this town is to be invited, but far more are welcome than we could possibly send personal invitations to. The half dozen married children are giving the party because we think it is quite an occasion. Our parents are the oldest married couple in the town.

Answer: Unless you are going to include everyone in the town whom they know, a notice in the newspaper will be very impractical because certain people whom they especially would like to see might hesitate to come and others not especially welcome would come. The only possible way that you have of including those you want and no others is to send out the simplest kind of card invitation that you buy at the stationers. Divided among six of you, the envelope addressing should not be a great task.

DEAR MRS. POST: How should I refer to my husband to (1) our grown children, (2) their young children and (3) my daughter-in-law?

Answer: (1) "Your father." (2) "Your grandfather" or "Grampy" or whatever they call him. (3) "Your father-in-law" or "John's father." unless there is an especial name by which she calls him.

Engaged

Mr. and Mrs. Frederick J. Fritsch, 435 Pearl St., announce the engagement of their daughter, Miss Eileen Fritsch, to William F. Carey, son of Mr. and Mrs. Thomas F. Carey, Pittsburgh.

Miss Fritsch is employed in the office of Armstrong Cork Co. and her fiance is employed at the Hamilton Watch Co.

Mr. and Mrs. S. Paul Kiefer, 128 N. Poplar St., Elizabethtown, announce the engagement of their daughter, Marian R., to Lester W. Roland, son of Mr. and Mrs. John D. Roland, Mount Joy R1.

DEMOCRATIC CARD PARTY

The Women's Democratic Club will hold a card party Thursday at 8:15 p. m. in Malta Temple. Committee chairmen are: Mrs. Nellie Bitner, tikets; Mrs. Nanette Foulke, prizes; Mrs. Elizabeth Hess, refreshments; Miss Kathryn Fisher, markers; and Mrs. Ruth Weaver, publiity.

ELECTED ART EDITOR

Priscilla Gerlach, daughter of Dr. and Mrs. George W. Gerlach, 545 N. Duke St., has been elected art editor of the Crestiad newspaper of Cedar Crest College, Allentown, where she is a sophomore.

WEATHER
(U. S. Weather Bureau)
Eastern Pennsylvania: Mostly Sunny With Slowly Rising Temperature Saturday Highest Around 55 In North And 60 In South Portion. Sunday Partly Cloudy And Milder.

Intelligencer Journal.

The Leading Newspaper in the Garden Spot of America, Home Owned for Home Folks Since 1794

Intelligencer Journal. 156 Years of Newspaper Service 1794 - 1950

156th Year.—No. 265. | Lancaster City Zone Population, Official Figures of Audit Bureau of Circulations 112,897 | LANCASTER, PA., SATURDAY MORNING, APRIL 22, 1950. | CITY | TWENTY PAGES. | 30c PER WEEK—5c Per Copy

NATIONAL PHONE STRIKE LOOMS

BACK STAGE

A "now-and-then" Column by "Intell" Editors and Reporters

SHOULD the voters of Lancaster and Chester Counties provide U. S. Rep. Paul B. Dague, guardian of their prestige and welfare in the Halls of Congress, with a press agent?

This startling and bizarre question cropped out the other day during a visit here of one of Congressman Dague's Chester County neighbors.

The visitor was Philip Ragan, producer of documentary films, who lives and has his studio near Malvern, and who as the Democratic candidate, hopes to permanently kill, come November, Mr. Dague's ambition of sitting along the Potomac for his third term.

Of course, the earnest and forthright Mr. Dague has a hurdle to cross before he takes on Mr. Ragan. That is the matter of disposing of S. Gerald Darlington, who is conducting a quiet, but none-the-less industricus campaign to send the Chester County gentlemen to the showers May 16, primary day.

* * *

BUT TO GET back to the question of Mr. Dague and press agents.

During the course of meeting Democratic leaders in Columbia, Ephrata and Lancaster, Mr. Ragan, with the spirit of a true and trained researcher, sought to measure the achievements of Mr. Dague in the minds of Garden Spot residents.

Mr. Ragan was hunting for Mr. Dague's strong points as a Congressman, the types of bills he introduced, his participation in debates, his public utterances on national and international matters as they pertain to Lancaster and Chester Counties.

He drew a perfect blank. Here, as in Chester County, he confided, Mr. Dague's record appears hidden under a bushel basket.

Mr. Ragan felt so badly about the situation that he publicly asked Democratic leaders to please provide him with facts on a half-century of Republican Congressional rule in Lancaster County.

"It's hard to get the facts on my opponent," he declared.

* * *

MR. RAGAN'S appeal was made with a trace of embarrassment. Here was a trained re-

Turn To Page 4 For More Of BACK STAGE

"We Lead All The Rest"

FARM CORNER

By The Farm Editor

NEW BREEDING PLAN UPS EGG PRODUCTION

Harrisburg—Not much more than generation ago the average farmer in Pennsylvania had no eggs to sell during mid-Winter months.

Egg production on most farms then ranged from practically zero to just enough to keep the farm family supplied even from a farm flock of up to 100 birds.

On many Winter mornings eggs for breakfast were as scarce as hen's teeth on some farms.

Then science took a hand in the situation and most Keystone farm flock owners now have eggs for sale the year 'round, totaling more than three billion in each of the past three years, according to the State Department of Agriculture. Today Pennsylvania stands first among all states in farm cash income from eggs.

In 1925 the average farm hen produced about 128 eggs a year. By 1949 production per bird had advanced to 177 eggs per layer, an increase of 38 per cent.

A major factor in this remarkable climb to hen success in nest performance has been a series of cooperative efforts in the improvement of farm flocks for both egg and meat production. Outstanding is the Pennsylvania-United States Poultry Improvement Plan which features the Pennsylvania - United States Record of Performance Program, known by farmers as the R. O. P. breeding program.

Weather Calendar

COMPARATIVE TEMPERATURES

Station	High	Low
Water Works	56	35
Ephrata	55	37
Last Year (Ephrata)	75	39
Official High for Year, April 19	79	
Official Low for Year, Feb. 21	8	
Character of Day	Cloudy	

SUN
Rises—5:17 a. m. Sets—6:48 p. m.

MOON
First Quarter, April 25.

STARS
Morning—Venus, Jupiter.
Evening—Mercury, Saturn, Mars.

NEARBY FORECASTS
(U. S. Weather Bureau)

New Jersey, Delaware and Maryland: Mostly sunny and milder Saturday highest 60 to 65. Sunday fair and mild.

Lower Potomac and Chesapeake Bay: Southwesterly winds 10 to 15 MPH Saturday. Fair weather with good visibility.

EXTENDED FORECAST
(U. S. Weather Bureau)

Extended forecast for period Saturday through Wednesday:

Eastern Pennsylvania, Eastern New York and Mid Atlantic States: Rising trend in temperature, reaching normal values Sunday; cooler Monday night in North portion and rising trend by Wednesday; temperatures averaging normal to two degrees below normal, scattered light showers North portion Sunday night and throughout the area about Wednesday, totaling two-tenths to four-tenths of an inch.

Acheson Accuses Russia Of Trying To Cause Trouble

Secretary Of State Says Situation Is Serious; Capitol Resounds With Hot And Angry Words On Baltic Sea Navy Plane Shooting Incident

Washington—(AP)—Secretary of State Acheson said Friday Soviet Russia is trying to stir up trouble in several critical areas of the world and the situation is serious. But he added that he does not see East and West moving into war.

Even as he spoke out against Russia at a news conference, the Capitol resounded with hot and angry words on the same subject. Demands were raised for strong action by the United States as a result of the Baltic plane shooting incident and Moscow's latest note regarding it.

House Democratic Leader John McCormack (Mass) issued a statement calling the Russian attitude on the Baltic incident "insulting." He declared this country should either recall Ambassador Alan G. Kirk for a "long period of consultation" or completely break off diplomatic relations with the Kremlin.

Chairman Vinson (D-Ga) of the House Armed Services Committee demanded in a speech from the floor that this country "maintain sufficient armed forces to insure Russian respect — otherwise we will race pell mell into another war, a war fomented by our own military weakness."

Vinson spoke just before the House passed, 330 to 0, a resolution calling for decorations for 10 American naval airmen lost in the Baltic area April 8 when Soviet fighters allegedly shot down their unarmed "Privateer" plane. The Senate had previously passed the resolution 66 to 0.

The newest Russian note was delivered to Ambassador Kirk by Soviet Foreign Minister Vishinsky in Moscow Friday. Russia completely rejected the American version of the Baltic incident and also American demands for indemnities.

The United States had told the Kremlin last Tuesday that the only military plane in the Baltic area on April 8 was the unarmed Priva-

Turn To Page 4 For More Of ACHESON

RUSSIAN TRIESTE ACCUSATIONS ARE DENOUNCED BY U.S.

Secretary Acheson Declares Charges Are "Wholly False" Statements And "Nonsense"

Washington —(AP)— Secretary of State Acheson Friday roundly denounced Russia's charges that the United States is violating the Italian peace treaty by maintaining troops at Trieste.

Acheson told his news conference the accusations are a combination of "wholly false" statements and "nonsense." The Secretary's quick rejection of Thursday night's note from Moscow clearly foreshadowed similar emphatic turndowns by France and Britain.

In a prepared statement, Acheson defended the right of Britain and the United States to keep troops in Trieste as "in complete conformity with the obligations of the Italian peace treaty."

DISRUPTION CHARGED

Looking into Moscow's motive, he said Russia is trying "to disrupt efforts to achieve a solution" of the Trieste problem by Italy and Yugoslavia.

Tiny but strategically important, the 430-square-mile area of Trieste lies at the top of the Italian "boot" on the frontier between Italy and Yugoslavia. Formerly Italian, it was taken from that country as a result of the last war.

The Italian peace treaty of 1946 provided that it was to become a free territory. However, the Western Allies could not reach agreement with Russia on a governor. Then, in 1948, the United States, Britain and France proposed giving the area back to Italy. But Russia and Yugoslavia objected.

American and British troops now occupy zone "A," which includes the city of Trieste, while Yugoslav forces occupy zone 'B."

Acheson said any one who has been to Trieste "can plainly see for himself" that Russian claims

Turn To Page 4 For More Of TRIESTE

HEART HAVEN GETTING TELEVISION SET TODAY

Mr. and Mrs. Edward G. Wilson, 859 Grandview Blvd., and their son, Boyd, who recently recovered from rheumatic fever, will present a television set to the Lancaster Heart Haven at ceremonies at 11:30 a. m. Saturday (today).

"Our son found so much recreation and relaxation from television during the six months that he was required to remain in bed that we decided to present a set for the use of the child patients at Heart Haven." Wilson said.

Boyd, who is now an active and healthy youth, helped contribute toward the purchase of the set, his father added.

Fate Of 35 Aboard AF Plane Down In Japan Unknown

Tokyo (Saturday) —(AP)— A U.S. Air Force transport plane carrying 35 persons crashed in a rainstorm southwest of Tokyo Friday night, and the fate of those aboard still is uncertain.

Air Force headquarters said searching aircraft and ground parties had been unable to sight the wreckage hours after the crash. Earlier it was reported erroneously that one ground party had reached the scene.

WRECKAGE LOCATED

The newspaper Asahi said, however, Japanese searchers had located the wreckage but gave no indication of any survivors. The newspaper put the scene near the town of Hirugataka, 17 miles north of Odawara.

The plane, bound to Japan from the Philippines, went down in mountainous, wooded country near Odawara, a seacoast town 52 miles southwest of Tokyo.

Several search parties were working their way through the

Turn To Page 4 For More Of CRASH

Rags To Riches

Baling Paper Proves Profitable With New Twist To An Old Game

A pile of waste paper suddenly turned into a gold mine for a couple of enterprising gents here Friday.

Contained in the pile, according to the story constructed by City Detective Frank P. Matt were a number of blank checks printed for the Northern Bank and Trust Company, a bank that has been out of business for six months.

CASH 3 FOR $35

Within three hours three of the "worthless" checks were worth exactly $35 to the "lucky finders."

Detective Matt said the men, whom he identified as Harry B. Buford, thirty-eight, of Washington, D. C., and Samuel Jungman, alias S. S. Jungman, fifty-four, of St. Paul, Minn., passed all three checks at the Jane Louise Shoppe, 101 W. King St.

He said they got the blank checks while engaged in baling paper at the Water Street Rescue Mission, 214 W. King St.

John Zimnis, manager of the Jane Louise, said one of the men cashed one check for $10 about 10 a. m. Both of them, he said, returned about 1 p. m. and cashed two more for $10 and $15.

His suspicions aroused by the second visit, Zimnis told Detective Matt he sent his wife to the bank, where she learned the checks were worthless.

About 4 p. m. Zimnis related, he saw the men again and gave them two hours to return the money.

That, it developed, was just about two hours too many.

Early Friday evening, Detective Matt learned, the two suspects had packed their belongings and, quite obviously, departed the city.

Preview Of New Movie Interior

(Intell Photo)

This first interior photo of the city's newest motion picture house, the King Theater, in the 400 block of East King St., shows the extent of work already completed as workmen labor on a twenty-four hour basis in an effort to meet next Thursday's deadline, the formal opening day. This photo, taken from the rear of the theater, shows the staggered seating arrangement and workmen preparing the mountings for the very latest in screens, a spun fiber glass screen.

CITY MOVIE HOUSE WILL OFFER MANY NEW INNOVATIONS

'King' Theater To Have Staggered Seating, TV Room, 'Crying Room' For Tots

Work on Lancaster City's newest motion picture house, the ultra-modern King Theater, is being rushed to completion in time for the formal opening next Thursday.

Each fitting and piece of furniture rapidly is being placed in position, as workmen toil on an around-the-clock basis.

Original estimates for construction of the new community theatre placed the cost of the project at about $300,000. However, original estimates are said to have been exceeded.

Larry MacKay, who formerly managed the Arcadia Theatre in Philadelphia has been named manager of Lancaster's new community movie house.

The luxurious theatre, leaves nothing to be desired. In addition to the latest in screen, seating facilities, acoustics, and projection techniques, the theatre also boasts a separate television room, as well as a "crying room" for small children who don't happen to appreciate the presentation.

PLUSH SEATS

Comfortable plush seats are available in the exquisitely decorated TV room, which has been planned to enable the customers to follow the movie as well as the video screen.

Mothers should be pleased with the "crying room" which is

Turn To Page 4 For More Of THEATER

TWO MEN INJURED, ONE SERIOUSLY, IN LITITZ PIKE CRASH

Two city men were injured, one seriously, when an automobile in which they were riding crashed against a utilities pole on Route 501 four miles North of Lititz around 11 p. m. Friday.

Seriously hurt was Harold Priest, twenty-eight, 53 S. Franklin St. He was admitted to Lancaster General Hospital with a severe scalp laceration and possible head injuries. Also admitted to the hospital with a lacerated nose and possible head injuries was Lloyd Hoover forty-six, 318 Reservoir St.

State Policeman Robert Plummer said the men were riding in an automobile operated by Robert Harnish, twenty-four, 454 Poplar St., which ran out of control across Route 501 and struck a pole as he was driving South. The pole, located on the East side of the road was broken off, police said, causing a disruption in telephone facilities in the immediate vicinity.

Dr. Franklin Cassel, Lititz, administered emergency treatment at the scene and summoned the ambulance from the hospital. Harnish was shaken up but suffered no apparent injury, according to police.

Cooke Forces Plan To Set Up Campaign Hdqs. Here

The Jay Cooke for Governor Committee plans to invade Lancaster County, name a campaign chairman and open a vigorous fight on behalf of the Philadelphia banker's candidacy for the gubernatorial nomination.

The decision of the Grundy-Owlett forces to battle State Sen. G. Graybill Diehm, Republican County Chairman, and the Duff-Fine faction, it was learned, was made Friday at a strategy committee meeting held at Philadelphia.

A spokesman at Philadelphia admitted that a move was on foot "to consolidate Cooke forces in Lancaster County."

This source, who declined to be quoted by name, said that he was not authorized to release the name of the Cooke chairman for Lancaster County, "even if one had been picked."

But local Cooke supporters said that three names "were under consideration." They were listed as Walter C. Miller, secretary of the Lancaster County Manufacturers' Association; W. W. Heidelbaugh, and J. Edward Mack, business men.

Miller, these sources said, has top priority for the post, if he wants it. He has not been active in politics for years.

Political observers Friday night saw the luncheon rally of the Duff-Fine ticket here Thursday as the "blow" which ended the "politicians' truce" between the GOP factions in Lancaster County.

Gov. James H. Duff, candidate for the Senate nomination, lashed out against former U. S. Senator Joseph R. Grundy and GOP National Committeeman G. Mason Owlett, and Cooke in his address.

Appearing with the governor at the rally at the Stevens House were Judge John S. Fine, running for the gubernatorial nomination; State Sen. Lloyd H. Wood for lieutenant governor; William S. Livengood, Jr., for secretary of Internal Affairs, and Judge Blair

Turn To Page 4 For More Of COOKE

$493,600 School Budget Proposed In Manheim Twp.

The Manheim Township School board, at its meeting Friday night, approved a tentative budget of $493,600 for 1950-51, an increase of $98,225 over the 1949-50 budget of $395,375.

The budget will be on public display in the office of the Manheim Township High School for a minimum of 20 days, and will come up for final adoption at a meeting of the board May 19, when the tax rate also will be set. At present the property tax is 25 mills, with an additional per capita tax of $5 per person.

Receipts from the property tax are estimated at $240,000, which indicates that the tax rate will remain the same as last year. The total assessment of the township has increased by about a half million dollars, estimated now at $9,757,270, compared with $9,292,335 last year.

This will yield an additional $12,500 to the tax coffers. More township residents also mean more money from the per capita tax, which is anticipated to yield $21,000 this year; compared with $17,000 last year.

The anticipated receipts also include a bond issue of $96,000, which will go toward the estimated expenditure of a total of $136,850 for capital outlay.

The principal item of capital expenditure is for the proposed new addition to the Nathan Schaeffer

Turn To Page 4 For More Of MANHEIM TWP.

REDS ASKED TO RETURN TO 4-POWER RULE IN BERLIN MINUS VETO

Berlin —(AP)— The Western Powers invited the Russians to return Friday night to four-power rule in Berlin but without the veto privilege that wrecked the old machinery.

The American, British and French commandants in a joint news conference told correspondents they "hope" the Soviets go along with a proposal for city-wide elections and then come back to the Kommandatura.

However, the three generals declared, the Russians will have to accept the rules under which the present Kommandatura has functioned for almost a year.

LATTIMORE SCOFFS AT RED CHARGES, DERIDES M'CARTHY

Professor Wisecracks At Senator, Star Witness Louis Budenz At Hearing

Washington —(AP)— Owen Lattimore Friday derided charges that he was a member of a Communist cell and scoffed at Senator McCarthy (R-Wis) as a man whose knowledge is limited to "what he has learned from Charlie Chan movies."

Cited by McCarthy as the No. 1 Soviet spy in the United States, Lattimore turned a torrent of sarcasm on his accusers at a news conference in which he declared:

"As a loyal American citizen who is not and never has been a Communist or anything but an American, I say it is long past time to

Turn To Page 4 For More Of LATTIMORE

PLANT-WIDE VACATION PLANS SET FOR RCA

The first two weeks in July have been set for plant-wide vacations of production workers at the local plant of the Radio Corporation of America.

According to the schedule, third shift employes will stop work at 7 a. m. Friday, June 30, and will resume work at their regularly scheduled time Monday, July 17, 1950.

All other workers will stop at their regularly scheduled time on Friday, June 30, and will resume work Tuesday, July 18.

MERCURY DROPS NEAR FREEZING FOLLOWING SHOWERS AND SNOW

With the temperature at 35 degrees at midnight Friday, weather observers held out a strong possibility of frost by Saturday (this) morning. The cooler weather followed a day of mixed showers, hail and snow flurries Friday.

The weatherman held out the hope for sunny and warmer weather for Saturday (today) but said Sunday would be partly cloudy, albeit mild.

High temperatures Friday were 55 degrees at the official weather station at Ephrata, and 56 at the City Water Works. Low readings were 37 at Ephrata and 35 at the Water Works.

According to the extended forecast, Monday night of next week is to be cooler with rising temperature trends Wednesday. More showers are on the agenda for Wednesday, the forecast says.

MINOR TIEUPS COULD SET OFF BIG WALKOUT

Murray Says CIO Is Solidly Behind Telephone Workers In Fight

New York—(AP)—Scattered walkouts flared along America's vast grid of telephone wires Friday, threatening to blaze into an all-out national phone strike next week.

A CIO official here said the minor walkouts could be the beginning of the national phone strike set for next Wednesday.

In Washington, CIO President Philip Murray told a news conference the multi-million member CIO was solidly behind the angry telephone workers in their wage dispute.

He parried questions about a purported scheme by CIO members to jam struck dial phone equipment with calls until the overworked machinery broke down.

The CIO Communications Workers Union here said walkouts started Friday in Seattle, Wash., Portland, Ore. Tonawanda, N. Y., Fargo, N. D., and other cities. There was no estimate of how many men took part.

The union said a dispute over working conditions of 104 Western Electric Co. employes in South Bend, Ind., touched off the walkouts.

Western Electric is the manufacturing arm of Bell Telephone Co. Some 10,000 Western Electric employes are members of Division 6, CWA-CIO.

Said Ernest Weaver, president of Division 6:

"By all indications the whole 10,000 will be out by Monday. This could be the beginning of a nationwide telephone strike and it will be unless some suitable arrangement is made by the company concerning the South Bend workers."

SET FOR MONDAY

At Niles, Mich., local and regional officials of the division said they, too, understood a general walkout of the 1,000 members was set for Monday unless the South Bend dispute was settled.

However, a CWA spokesman in Washington was inclined to look at the walkouts as a divisional matter and not part of the national tele-

Turn To Page 4 For More Of PHONES

Doctor Questions Infection Theory Of Common Cold

Boston —(AP)— Your own body's air-conditioning and heating system is more responsible than anything else for common colds, the American College of Physicians was told Friday.

This explanation was made by Dr. William J. Kerr, University of California Medical School, San Francisco.

He said your air-conditioning is your nasal passages. They warm the air and remove all dust and impurities. Your heating system is something you inherit, and it keeps your body at even temperature in all kinds of changes.

DIRECT CONDITION

Dr. Kerr reported experiments showing a direct connection between the air-conditioner in the nose and the temperature of your skin. Skins can get cold without a drop in internal temperature. When

Turn To Page 4 For More Of COLDS

Only Make-Believe

Fake Judge For-A-Day Forgiven By Real Jurist He Hoodwinked

Cleveland — (AP) — Burly, six-foot, six-inch Charles T. Ferguson, the fake judge-for-a-day who "tried to be a big shot," was forgiven and set free Friday by the judge he hoodwinked.

In real life a $600-a-month salesman for the Dayton (O.) Rubber Co., Ferguson breezed into the Common Pleas Court of Judge Joseph Silbert last Tuesday and introduced himself as a "presiding circuit court judge from St. Louis."

Judge Silbert introduced him around and even had him sit beside him on the bench during the day's hearing for five accused extortionists.

COMMON PRACTICE

This is a fairly common courtesy extended visiting jurists. Ferguson merely listened gravely from the bench.

That night the 45-year-old Ferguson left town. When his fakery was discovered by a phone call to St. Louis, an alarm was put out for him. Friday, he meekly turned

Turn To Page 4 For More Of JUDGE

Wildwood Ready To Welcome More Guests Than Ever

Wildwood N. J. June 15, 1950—All indications point to another outstanding resort season at Wildwood-by-the-Sea this Summer.

Transportation companies are planning to operate extra sections for the expected heavy travel, while hotel proprietors here say advance reservations and inquiries are being received from all parts of the country.

Wildwood, this season is prepared also to welcome more visitors than ever. Additions have been made to hotels while new apartment houses have been constructed, together with guest homes.

MYRIAD OF PLEASURES

The resort community, situated on an island boardering on the Atlantic Ocean, affords a myriad of advantages and pleasures which has already made it a high place among the most popular resorts in the United States.

The natural advantages which have been developed to the highest degree in comparatively recent years by the founders of the resort are heritages from the time when the Indians of the Lenni-Lenape Tribe made the resort their vacation headquarters centuries ago.

Wildwood is definitely known as a seashore resort which boasts of having an abundance of amusements.

From end to end, the boardwalk is flanked by a series of amusements of various kinds which provide a wide range of choice for visitors.

Several rest pavilions are placed conveniently on the ocean side of the boardwalk. Fitted with comfortable chairs, these pavilions provide ideal surroundings from which to watch the ceaseless flow of the boardwalk promenaders as well as the activity on the beach.

SIGHT-SEEING CARS

An innovation on the boardwalk, introduced for the first time last year, are the sight-seeing cars which provide so popular last Summer. Here a person may ride the car, and view the activity along the beach and boardwalk.

Numerous events are scheduled for the Summer, highlighting the activity with the annual Baby Parade.

The third annual women's eastern States Amateur golf tournament will be held at the Wildwood Golf and Country Club, three days starting June 23. Golfers from all sections of the country enter the tourney. Betty

Turn To Page 43 For More Of WILDWOOD

The blooming mountain laurel is the focal point of interest in this view from the Pocon s.

Stone Harbor Offers Variety In Recreation

Stone Harbor, N.J., June 15, 1950 — Long known as the Seashore at its Best, this friendly, distinctive family resort offers more than ever before in vacation pleasure to both young and old. Its smooth, safe beach along the ocean, its inland waterways and seven picturesque man-made inland basins and its civic and municipally sponsored attractions provide every seashore sport and recreation for all age groups.

Two childrens playgrounds, a recreation center for adults and a number of tennis courts are maintained by the Borough for the use of vacationists. An athletic field is being constructed in the northern end of the resort and will, it is hoped, be completed for use this season.

The resort has recently doubled the size of the municipal fishing

Turn To Page 43 For More Of STONE HARBOR

This lovely water sprite finds the ocean enchanting at Wildwood, N. J.

Laurel Blossom Time Is Running Late In Poconos

Pocono Mountains, Pa., June 15, 1950—The Pocono Mountains, northeastern Pennsylvania's popular year-round resort, are just getting into the full swing of the summer season. The mountain laurel has burst into bloom, the late-opening hotels have thrown their doors wide to oncoming crowds, and Pocono golf courses resound to the "Fore!" of many a foursome.

Covering not more than 1200 square miles, the Poconos attract thousands annually, from sources which are by no means exclusively eastern. The operator of a filling station in Stroudsburg, hub of the Pocono region, annually checks license plates of cars he services. By mid-season, he has wiped dusty windshields from every state in the union, with Canadian provinces thrown in for extra measure. An informal check of a small hotel's parking lot recently revealed that each automobile bore a different registration, no two coming from the same state. "Pennsylvania's Picturesque Playground", as the area is sometimes tagged, would seem to be a playground for the entire nation.

Currently attracting many visitors to the Pocono region, Laurel Blossom Time was set back by a late Spring. Ordinarily running from about June 5th to 25th, the season for the state flower is about a week later this year. With individual hotels holding coronation ceremonies for their own laurel queens, and a whirl of dances at different resorts dedicated to the pink and white blossoms, it seems that the social scene will almost rival Dame

Turn To Page 43 For More Of POCONOS

Over 8,000 See Columbia and Millersville Win Midget Baseball Titles at Stumpf Field *(Story, Other Pictures on Sports Pages)*

New Era Photo

GI Escapes from Korean Reds in a 'Gook' Suit
See Boyle—Editorial Page

LANCASTER NEW ERA

The Weather
U. S. Weather Bureau Forecast: Fair and Cooler

74th Year—No. 22,706 | Lancaster City Zone Population, Official Figures of Audit Bureau of Circulations 112,897 | LANCASTER, PA., WEDNESDAY, AUGUST 2, 1950 | CITY EDITION | 20 PAGES | 30c PER WEEK—5c Per Copy

GI's Recapture Heights Near Chinju

28TH GOING TO INDIANA BASE ABOUT SEPT. 1

Local Units Will Return from Camp Monday; Must Take Physicals

Pennsylvania's 28th Infantry Division intensified its war exercises today at Indiantown Gap in preparation for active federal duty about Sept. 1 at Camp Atterbury, near Edinburg, Ind.

Maj. Gen. Daniel B. Strickler, Lancaster, commanding general of the Keystone National Guard Division, told his troops yesterday that the Summer encampment would end Sunday instead of the following week to allow time for clearing up of civilian affairs.

The call to service was announced by Gov. James H. Duff who said the 30-day waiting period would give Gen. Strickler time to expand the Division to full strength.

LANCASTER COUNTY'S contingent of approximately 700 Guardsmen will return home Monday to wind up their civilian affairs before reporting to Camp Atterbury.

Prior to reporting for federal duty, the division's officers and men will be required to undergo a physical examination. The physicals will follow receipt of the actual induction orders.

The traditional "Governor's Day" ceremony will mark the close of the training period Sunday. Gen. Mark Clark, chief of the Army Field Forces, and the Governor will review the division at the ceremony.

Camp Atterbury is under the Army Field Forces chief's command, Gen. Strickler stated.

"We are ready," the 28th's commander stated when asked to com-

(See Page 12—28TH DIVISION)

Showers Forecast to Reduce Heat and Humidity

Showers and scattered thunderstorms early tonight are expected to reduce the extreme heat and humidity, the U. S. Weather Bureau said today.

Lowest readings tonight should be in the middle 60's, said the cheering forecast, and tomorrow will be fair and less humid, with moderate temperatures.

Low last night was 68, at the City Water Works. The highest temperature yesterday, was 91 at Ephrata. Today's 2 p. m. reading was 80.

Warm and dry weather is in prospect for this area through most of August, according to a 30-day forecast released by the Weather Bureau in Washington. The Bureau said temperatures will be above normal.

The Weather

LOCAL FORECAST and EASTERN PENNSYLVANIA: Showers and scattered thunderstorms early tonight becoming fair and cooler and less humid late tonight. Low tonight 60-66. Thursday fair and less humid with moderate temperature.

SOUTHERN NEW JERSEY and DELAWARE: Considerably cloudiness and a few showers tonight. Thursday, partly cloudy, less humid and moderate temperatures.

MARYLAND: Partly cloudy with a few scattered showers early tonight. Cooler and less humid tonight. Thursday partly cloudy and less humid, cooler east portion.

CHESAPEAKE BAY: Variable winds northwest 15 to 20 miles per hour tonight. Thundersqualls early tonight. Visibility mostly good.

TODAY TEMP. AT NEW ERA

1 AM	76
2 AM	76
3 AM	76
4 AM	74
5 AM	73
6 AM	72
7 AM	72
8 AM	73
9 AM	75
10 AM	77
11 AM	80
Noon	82
1 PM	80
2 PM	80
Yesterday	
3 PM	88
4 PM	88
5 PM	86
6 PM	87
7 PM	86
8 PM	84
9 PM	81
10 PM	80
11 PM	78
12 PM	78

COMPARATIVE TEMPERATURE

	High Yesterday	Low Last Night
Wat. Wks.	88	68
Ephrata	91	71
High for year		95
Low for year		8

HUMIDITY

8 AM	94
10 AM	91
Noon	76
2 PM	83

Sun Rose 6:02 AM
Sun Sets 8:17 PM

Moon Rises 10:39 PM
Last Quarter Aug 5th

Morning Stars Venus, Jupiter.
Evening Stars Saturn, Mars.

New Era Photo

Overturned tractor-trailer truck is shown at right on Lincoln Highway West. At left, repairman is shown at work.

1ST DRAFT TESTS TOMORROW

25 Called; Boards Can't Fill 245 Quota for Aug.

The first contingent of Lancaster County men to take pre-induction physical examinations since the outbreak of the Korean War will go to Harrisburg tomorrow.

The men—numbering 25—are from Draft Board 83, representing the northern part of the county.

They are the first of 245 men that Lancaster County draft boards have been told to furnish for pre-induction physical examinations. But the boards say they will not be able to fill this quota because they have not been able to process questionnaires fast enough.

The State Selective Service headquarters has not set a quota of men for Lancaster who will be inducted. Much will depend upon the percentage of men who can pass the physical examinations.

THE ORIGINAL quota set by the state for the first pre-induction call was 38 from Board 83.

The same board was instructed to send 60 more men to the State capital for physicals on Saturday, but none will leave on that date.

Enough men are registered with the board to fill both calls, but replies to the board's letters have been limited by the number of questionnaires sent the selectees.

The number of questionnaires mailed out has been inadequate because of the lack of clerical help at the board. The staff was cut to

(See Page 16—DRAFT)

City Zoning Board Will Hear 7 Appeals Monday

Seven appeals have been listed to be heard by the Zoning Board of Appeals at its monthly meeting Monday at 4 p. m.

The appeals are described as minor in nature and were filed because the building inspector has ruled that plans do not entirely conform with zoning laws. The appeals follow: Iris Club, 323 N. Duke St.; Norman and Ruth Wenger, 254 E. New St.; Lillian Huber, 722 E. King St.; Marie Doerr, 353 E. Chestnut St.; Lenora B. Bricker, 166 Pearl St.; Friendly Tabernacle, rear 702 S. Duke St. and George and Leah W. Lehman, 249 N. Mulberry St.

Today's New Era

No Hope Now of Defending Europe Against Russ Attack

But U. S. Leaders Believe That Within Reasonable Time France and Britain Could Lead Successful Stand

PARIS, Aug. 2—(AP)—America's leaders have no hope of defending Western Europe from a Russian attack if it comes tomorrow.

But in "X" months—there's a top secret label on the value of "X"—they believe Britain and France can be so strengthened morally and militarily that they could lead a successful stand.

Authoritative sources here who describe that situation say the number of months "X" represents can be shortened if many Europeans are won away from the currently popular attitude of "What's the use?"

That's the view being forcefully argued to the Europeans at North Atlantic pact meetings in London and in man-to-man conferences with officials throughout Western Europe. The Americans make no effort to hide it, though they fight shy of putting their names to it publicly.

THE COMMUNIST ATTACK in Korea and its success have put the razor edge on American awareness of how helpless Europe would be in the face of a full Russian assault. Before, this was understood in a dull and distant way, if at all.

This is the way they now paint the picture:

The Russians, according to British Defense Minister Emanuel Shinwell, could put 175 Army Divisions into the field tomorrow. Western Europe probably could not scrape together 15. While it might not necessarily take 175 divisions to stop 175, it would take a lot more than 15.

AMERICAN REARMAMENT of the Atlantic world is going ahead on

(See Page 12—EUROPE)

Critical Job List to be Announced

WASHINGTON, Aug. 2. —(AP)— The Defense Department is expected to announce within 24 hours policies for deferment from military service of men in critical jobs and industries. The deferment rules would apply both to draftees and reservists.

Government sources said the Commerce Department will release a list of essential industries as a guide, and the Labor Department will issue a rather short list of "critical occupations."

The military establishment, it was reported, will emphasize that the lists are not guarantees of exemption from military service.

It will state, however, that the armed forces intend to use men at their highest skills, whether in military or essential civilian roles, and to prevent any serious manpower drain on vital industrial crafts.

TRUMAN URGES TAX HIKE SPEED

George Predicts Passage of $5 Billion Boost

WASHINGTON, Aug. 2.— (AP) — President Truman sent a new letter to Congress today urging speed in raising taxes $5,000,000,000 to help pay for rebuilding America's defense against Communism.

The letter, addressed to Chairman George (D-Ga), was read to the Senate Finance committee as it began consideration of the tax increases.

Mr. Truman's new communication arrived as demands were made in Congress for an excess profits tax, aimed at profiteering."

SENATOR BREWSTER (R-Me) told reporters the President, in his new letter, did not call for an excess profits levy now. "But he did not close the door on it," Brewster added.

George predicted quick passage of the $5,000,000,000 tax boosting bill, "substantially as submitted" by the President.

SECRETARY OF the Treasury Snyder also asked Congress for speed. Snyder gave notice that another proposal, to increase taxes

(See Page 12—TAXES)

War Scare Buying On Wane In Cincinnati

CINCINNATI, Aug. 2. —(AP)— War scare buying in greater Cincinnati food stores appears to be slowing down to a walk. Consumers are finding the stores well-stocked with merchandise.

A survey of the wholesale grocers and chain stores showed some shortages, but they were due largely to delays in shipping.

Wilbur Korengel, Cincinnati branch manager for the Kroger Co., said the 125 stores in this area have been limited on sugar only, due entirely to delay in shipments.

POWER IS CUT OFF BY TRUCK CRASH

West End Dimmed for 39 Minutes; Driver Unhurt

Hundreds of homes and business places in the West End and adjacent suburban territory were without electric power for 39 minutes early today as the result of a truck accident on the Columbia pike, near the Herr ice pond.

The 2 1-2-ton trailer, driven by John H. Topper, forty-five, New Oxford RD, battered down two poles which crashed onto the highway, tore down 11,000 volt electric lines and then plunged from the north side of the highway and overturned.

Topper crawled from the wreckage with only a minor scratch. He was the first to notify State Police and ask for help.

TRAFFIC ON THE Lincoln Highway was halted for a brief time, but one-way travel was established shortly after the crash.

The truck carried a load of merchandise and was enroute from Philadelphia to York. It was owned by the York Motor Express.

Topper told police his truck plunged from the highway when he tried to get back in his line of traffic after changing his mind about passing an auto ahead of him.

PP AND L OFFICIALS said electric power failed at 6:10 a. m. but was restored to all customers except Maple Grove park by 6:49 a. m. The park got its power back by noon.

The Hamilton Watch Co., gasoline service stations in the West End and hundreds of homes were without electricity.

A spokesman for the PP and L. estimated that about one-eighth of the city, portions of Lancaster Twp. and West Lancaster were affected.

Glasses Lead to Arrest of Thief, Hit-Run Driver

An optometrist's prescription for eye glasses plus the ingenuity of a city detective today led to the arrest of Robert D. Labezius, eighteen, 218 N. Arch St., wanted for the theft of a policeman's motorcycle and a hit and run accident.

Last Friday, the motorcycle of Policeman William Dull, a privately-owned machine, was stolen from a parking lot. A short time after the theft the motorcycle crashed with an automobile driven by Mrs. Glenn H. Horst, East Petersburg, at Lehigh and Franklin St. The rider abandoned the machine and escaped.

The crash hurled a pair of eye glasses into the automobile. By measuring the glasses and identifying the prescription, an optometrist was able to tell police to whom they belonged. This afternoon Labezius was arrested. Police said he confessed.

SENATE GROUP VOTES PRISON FOR HOARDERS

New Control Bill with Wage Ceilings, Rationing Is Up in House

WASHINGTON, Aug. 2. —(AP)— Prison sentences and $10,000 fines for hoarders and blackmarketeers were voted by a Senate Committee today as Congress pressed swiftly toward action on economic mobilization legislation.

A House vote on the administration's requested control powers—plus standby wage and price controls — was possible late in the day but may not come until tomorrow.

Democratic leaders put before the House a substitute for the administration's original allocations and credit control measure. The new bill would give Mr. Truman power to slap ceilings on wages and roll prices back to the levels of the May 24-June 24 period.

The new bill also would allow the President to order rationing.

REPUBLICANS, rallying behind a bill of their own, protested the last-minute introduction of a new administration measure. The GOP bill also would provide for standby wage and price controls.

Rep. Halleck (R-Ind), called the administration move "deplorable." He said it gave the House "no fair chance" to consider the proposals and was "a poor way to legislate."

The plan for crackdown powers on hoarders and black-market operators was approved today by the Senate Banking Committee.

THE COMMITTEE also approved a broad system of credit controls that would apply to all real estate construction after noon tomorrow. These would apply to all privately financed construction and would be administered by the Federal Reserve System.

The committee put off until later in the day a vote on whether Mr.

(eSe Page 12—CONGRESS)

HINT DUPONT TO DEVELOP H-BOMB

AEC and Firm Seeking 200,000-Acre Site

WASHINGTON, Aug. 2 —(AP)— The government today apparently gave the DuPont Company top responsibility for developing the hydrogen bomb.

An Atomic Energy Commission announcement provided that hint.

AEC said only that the big chemical firm has been selected to design, construct and operate new facilities to produce materials for atomic weapons or fuels potentially useful for power purposes.

Company officials at Wilmington said "the project is of vital importance to the security of the United States."

THE AEC SAID the new plants will be of "advanced design and their operation will provide new knowledge that will speed the progress of the atomic energy program."

But commission officials, as usual, shied away from any direct mention of the H-bomb, the new weapon President Truman has ordered for the atomic arsenal.

Where the new plants will be located has not yet been decided. DuPont and government experts have been looking for a site, expected to cover some 200,000 acres.

THE NEW PROJECT is of such importance that AEC said it has set up a special operations office to supervise it. Temporarily located in Washington, it is under the management of Curtis A. Nelson.

Almost simultaneously with the AEC-DuPont announcements, Senator McMahon (D-Conn) said on Capitol Hill he favors an even greater expansion of the nation's A- and H-bomb programs that has been recommended by Mr. Truman.

1st Cavalry Gives Up Kumchon On Central Front; Blazing Villages Mark Battle Line

TOKYO, Thursday, Aug. 3—(AP)—U. S. 24th Division troops recaptured hill positions northeast of Chinju and held on today in a flaming battle 40 miles from the main port of Pusan.

The arching battleline was marked by burning villages all the way from the southern coast to abandoned Kumchon, which blazed, too.

Gen. MacArthur's headquarters said U. S. troops and the North Korean Sixth Division were locked in a grim battle east of Chinju at the western approaches to Pusan.

"No gains by the enemy have been made in this fighting in the last 12 hours," the war summary said. It was released at 12:55 a. m. (9:55 a. m. EST Wednesday.)

For 18 hours or more the battle between tanks, artillery and men raged on the heights just eight miles northeast of Chinju.

ON THE CENTRAL front Kumchon, ablaze and abandoned by the U. S. First Cavalry Division, scorched in ruins as the Reds moved into its outskirts.

Disputed Yongdok, east coast anchor town which has changed hands frequently, was no-man's land.

But the hardest fighting was just north of Chinju, about 40 miles west of Pusan.

Battle weary U. S. 24th Division troops were almost surrounded when they counterattacked. They suffered many casualties and lost some tanks.

ASSOCIATED PRESS Correspondent Hal Boyle who flew over the whole flaming front said the battleline could be followed by a string of flaming villages. Boyle first reported the abandonment of Kumchon.

Help for the doughboys was near. Fighting Marines in force were at a southeastern port only 40 miles from the battlezone. The Marines came equipped with 45-ton tanks, tank-killer bazookas and other weapons new to the Korean war.

AMERICAN PLANES set fire to Kumchon as they had done at Chinju after it fell.

The 24th was almost surrounded by strong Red flanking forces. The Americans had counter-attacked to regain high ground they had lost Tuesday.

The Reds sidestepped them and attacked.

The American hill positions were described as good for defensive fighting.

Red pressure mounted on almost all fronts.

On the front near Kumchon, First Cavalrymen offered stubborn resistance "to each North Korean attack."

The communique said South Koreans were battling for Yongdok on the east coast anchor of the battle line. But the city, once reported in southern hands, belonged to "neither side."

O. H. P. King, Associated Press correspondent in the hills near Chinju, reported both Chinju and the nearby village of Sanchon were

(See Page 12—KOREA)

Situation 'Improving' But 'Still Serious'

WASHINGTON, Aug. 2. —(AP)— Defense Department spokesmen today described the overall Korean situation as "improving."

But briefing officers said the situation is "still serious, and anyone would be foolish to indicate anything else."

They said late military reports clearly indicate the Red Koreans are "throwing everything they have" in the drive for Pusan.

"They have so far failed in this effort," air - Army spokesman said, "because they have not succeeded in preventing the arrival of fresh U. S. troops and equipment."

Scope, Intensity of Air War Will Be Stepped Up

WASHINGTON, Aug. 2.—(AP)—Indications are that the air war in Korea will be stepped up in scope and intensity soon.

The tip-off was the dispatch of two more medium bomber (probably B-29) groups to the Far East. They supplement several units of B-29's ordered out nearly a month ago. Air officers concede that means strategic bombing of a substantial nature instead of the flashes of activity in North Korea thus far.

A full strategic air war is not in prospect, however, because the ultimate source of North Korean arms lies outside its territory.

Arrival of Marine air units, skilled in close ground support tactics, will help on the United Nations' shortened battlefront.

THOSE DEVELOPMENTS will put the Korean air war in better

(See Page 16—AIR WAR)

GI's Faced with Killing All 'Refugees' to Protect Selves

By Don Whitehead

WITH AMERICAN TROOPS IN KOREA, Aug. 2. —(Delayed) —(AP) — The American soldier must harden his heart and coldly shoot down anyone wearing civilian clothes in the combat area — if he is to protect his own life in this war.

The Americans haven't done it yet. The kids from New York and Ohio and Texas and California with Sunday School background have respected people in civilian garb. And too many of them have paid for it with their own lives.

This isn't the orthodox war of North Africa, Sicily, Italy and Europe where generally the recognized rules of warfare were followed. This is guerrilla war, a sneaking, dirty war where the enemy uses every trick in the book to kill Americans.

"REFUGEES" are the big problem. They have been coming through the American lines for days in droves.

Some of them are South Koreans fleeing before the Reds. But among them are the guerrillas who spy out American positions, who slip into the hills as snipers, and who harass the Americans from the rear.

The Army has been trying to solve this problem by creating a so - called "security belt" from which all natives are evacuated in the combat area. Presumably anyone found in this area would be an enemy and treated as a guerrilla. But it hasn't worked that way..

THE REASON IS that the Americans don't have the flinty hearts of killers who have no conscience

(See Page 12—REFUGEES)

Phils Set 'to Shoot Works' at Yankees

SPORTS

Roberts May Start in First Game

Pitcher Teams with Sisler to Beat Brooks in Deciding Contest

PHILADELPHIA, Oct. 2—(AP)—Their first pennant in 35 years safely stowed away, the Philadelphia Phillies today planned to shoot the works against the highly favored New York Yankees in the World Series starting Wednesday.

Unless he has a change of heart, Manager Eddie Sawyer of the Phils will open with Robin Roberts, 4-1 conqueror of the Brooklyn Dodgers yesterday in the game that gave the Whiz Kids the National League flag. Roberts will be opposed by Allie Reynolds in a battle of righthanders.

HAVING CLINCHED the American League pennant last Friday, the well-rested Yankees will rule 2-1 favorites over the tired Phils. Experts figure the Yanks have too much experience, deeper reserve strength and stronger pitching than the youthful Whiz Kids.

Philly manager Sawyer does not appear to be worried about the Yankee prowess.

"We weren't figured to have a chance to beat Brooklyn for the pennant, were we?" he reminded.

"I haven't decided who will pitch the opener," the jubilant 40-year-old candidate for "manager of the year" added. "But I'd say that Roberts is a strong possibility."

"After all, what was good enough for the Dodgers might be good enough for the Yankees."

ROSE-CHEEKED Robin undoubtedly pitched the greatest game of his life. However, he knew he was in a battle with Brooklyn's Don Newcombe. If Dick Sisler hadn't hit that homer with two on in the top of the 10th to snap a 1-1 tie, the game might be going on yet.

The blow by Sisler, son of the immortal George who acts as Brooklyn's head scout, ended Brooklyn's "miracle" finish that for a time threatened to throw the race into another flat-footed last day tie. It gave Roberts his 20th victory of the year after the youngster had made five futile tries for it.

ALTHOUGH ROBERTS yielded but five blows to 11 for Newcombe, he had to summon all his wile and cunning to hold off a Brooklyn bases-loaded threat in the ninth that appeared destined to bring about the Phillies' sixth straight defeat.

A crowd of 35,073, biggest of the year at Ebbets Field, went into hysterics as Cal Abrams led off the last of the ninth with a walk and took second on a single by Pee Wee Reese.

That brought up Duke Snider, the best left-handed hitter on the club. With everyone expecting a bunt, Snider teed off and slashed a line single to center. Abrams attempted to score from second but Richie Ashburn made a one-handed scoop of the ball and threw on the run to the plate. The ball came on a good hop right into Stan Lopata's hands. Abrams didn't have a chance and was tagged standing up.

THEN IT WAS the Phillies turn. Roberts opened with a single to center. Eddie Waitkus blooped another single to center. Ashburn, attempting to sacrifice, bunted into a force play at tihrd. That set the stage for Sisler's game-winning clout.

The Phils drew first blood, tallying in the top of the sixth on three singles after two were out.

The Dodgers tied the score in

(See Page 19—BASEBALL)

AP Wirephoto

Welcoming the Champs Home

Some of the more enthusiastic Phillies fans brought signs to welcome the National League pennant winners when they returned to Philadelphia. This group unfurled this big sign in Pennsylvania Station and gave the returning Phils a hearty welcome.

Pitching Biggest Factor in Phils' Drive to Pennant

By Herb Altschull

PHILADELPHIA, Oct. 2—(AP)—The Philadelphia Phillies took over first place for good in the National League pennant race on July 25 with a letter-perfect demonstration of the way they won the championship.

Two of the Phils' brilliant young pitchers, Bubba Church and Robin Roberts, threw shutouts at the Chicago Cubs, winning 7-0 ad 1-0. neither allowed a walk as the Phils advanced over the St. Louis Cardinals to the league's top rung, a position they never relinquished.

UP TO THAT time, it had been touch and go among the Phils, Cardinals, Brooklyn Dodgers and Boston Braves. The Phillies bounced in and out of first place seven times after May 10, never falling lower than third.

On July 4 traditional midway point of the season, they trailed the Cardinals in second place, but moved back into first on July 7.

They clung to the top spot until July 16, when they dropped to second. But they moved back into first on the 18th. At that point, the Phils lost five straight on a western road trip and slipped into third place on the 20th. But on the 23rd they were back in first, only to fall to second on the 24th.

THEN CAME the twinight doubleheader with the Cubs. The second game of that twin bill was one of the most dramatic games of the year at Shibe Park.

Roberts and the Cubs' Bob Rush matched shutout pitching through eight and one-half innings. With one out in the ninth, manager Eddie Sawyer sent Roberts to bat for himself. Roberts worked Rush for a walk.

At that point, Sawyer removed Roberts for pinch runner Ralph Caballero, Eddie Waitkus pushed Caballero to second on a hit-and-run play. Richie Ashburn poked a Rush pitch to center and Caballero streaked home with the only run.

THERE WERE dramatic moments a-plenty for the Phils in 1950. Most of them came when Jim Konstanty was summoned from the bullpen to pitch. The clever 33-year-old fireman repeatedly halted scoring threats to save games for starting pitchers or win them for himself.

His two finest exhibitions came late in the season in extra inning games. He worked nine full innings of relief against the Pirates in August's 15-inning marathon, allowing five hits and one run—a homer by Ralph Kiner. Jim won that game.

AND, THEN, on Sept. 15, at Shibe Park, Konstanty came along in the ninth inning of a game in which the Phils trailed 5-3. His teammates put him in the ball game with a two-run ninth inning rally. Until the 18th, Konstanty matched shutout innings with the Reds' Herman Wehmeier.

But the peerless reliefer weakened in the 18th and walked three straight batters with one out. Ted Kluszewski who earlier that day had sent Church to the hospital when he lined a hit off the young pitcher's face, bounced a ball past shortstop and two runs scored.

The fighting Phillies socked Wehmeier for two runs in the last of the 18th to tie the game. Blix Donnelly, relieving Konstanty in the 19th, won his first game of the season when the Phils put across the winning counter on two singles, a walk and a drive off the left field wall by Del Ennis.

PITCHING WON the pennant for the Phils, the work of young Roberts and Church as well as Curt Simmons, Russ Meyer and Bob Miller and the superb relief work of Konstanty.

Simmons, a $65,000 bonus lefthander four years ago, achieved the stardom which had eluded him since he came into the majors at 17. He won 17 games for the Phils before he was inducted into the Army in mid-September, the first major leaguer to enter the armed forces in the Korean conflict.

THE PHILS won the pennant with eight regular players. Only briefly did a substitute appear on the scene to replace any of the starting lineup. The infield of Eddie Waitkus, Mike Goliat, Granny Hamner and Willie Jones, the outfield of Dick Sisler, Richie Ashburn and Del Ennis and catcher Andy Seminick were on the job day in and day out. Injuries sidelined Sisler, Waitkus, Ennis and Seminick for brief stretches and young Goliat was spelled on occasion by veteran Jimmy Bloodworth but all of the substitutions were brief.

Only in the last month of the season did injury hamper the Phillies, but by that time they were too far ahead to be seriously affected in the regular season. Sisler suffered a painful wrist injury; reserve outfielder Bill Nicholson was lost to the club because of diabetes; Church was sidelined by the smash off Kluszewski's bat; Miller was out with a pulled muscle . . . and Simmons gone to the army.

Happy Days Are Here Again!

AP Photo

Happy Days are here again for Philadelphia's baseball fans as the Phillies win their first National League pennant in 35 years. Largely responsible for the victory was Dick Sisler, who clouted a tenth inning homer with two men on against Brooklyn yesterday and Dick (No. 8) is being met by a host of mates from the Philadelphia bench.

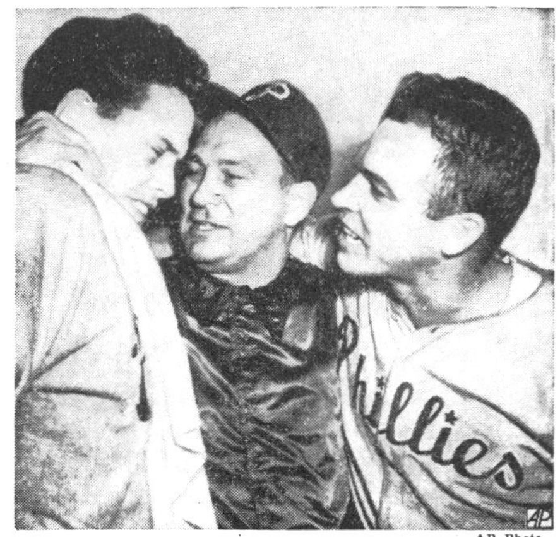

AP Photo

Manager Eddie Sawyer, center, smiles as he hugs winning pitcher, Robin Roberts, left and Dick Sissler in the dressing room after it was all over.

Philadelphia Gives Champs Wild Reception

By Orlo Robertson

PHILADELPHIA, Oct. 2—(AP)—The pent-up emotions of a baseball starved city let loose like a mighty bomb shell as the Philadelphia Phillies returned home with the National League championship—their first in 35 years.

Within a few minutes after the Phillies conquered the Brooklyn Dodgers 4-1 yesterday, the Nation's third largest city became a bedlam. Old and young danced in the streets in hundreds of neighborhood celebrations.

THOUSANDS thronged to central city, tying traffic in a knot around City Hall. But the biggest and loudest of all awaited the conquering heroes at two railroad stations.

Police estimated that upwards of 5,000 gathered at the Pennsylvania Railroad's North Philadelphia station, merely to catch a glimpse of Manager Eddie Sawyer's Whiz Kids as the train made its regular stop.

But the celebration there was only minute to that which greeted Sawyer, owner Bob Carpenter and the players at the 30th Street station. Trainmatser Charles H. Sample estimated the jammed-packed mob at 15,000.

IMPROVISED bands went into action, automobile horns honked, whistles blew and everybody yelled as police made a valiant effort to clear the way through the station to waiting buses.

Dick Sisler, whose home run carried the Phils to their 10-inning victory, relief pitcher Jim Konstanty and third baseman Willie Jones, escaped some of the pushing around, back slapping and kisses by jumping off the train at North Philadelphia and disappearing almost before the crowd recognized them.

CARPENTER AND his wife led the procession, if it could be called that, through the almost hysterical crowd. Then came Del Ennis, taking a beating as never before. He was followed by Sawyer and the Mrs. Robin Roberts, Andy Seminick and the remainder of the team.

Ennis, smiling and turning to greet almost everybody that yelled his name, was a bedraggled young man by the time he got on the bus. Roberts, escorted by two husky policemen, missed some of the tossing about but Seminick didn't as he limped painfully on his injured ankle.

PARENTS HELD babies aloft to see the Whiz Kids. Bobby-soxers gave out with "swooning" shrieks they once reserved for Frank Sinatra. Oldsters who remember Grover Cleveland Alexander when he pitched the Phils to the 1915 pennant strained their necks to get a good look at this bunch of youngsters who refused to quit.

"I never guessed it would be anything like this," gasped Del as he stumbled on the waiting bus.

Roberts, Richie Ashburn, Ken Heintzelman, Eddie Waitkus and the others sat as if they couldn't believe all of this was for them.

OLD TIMERS, including coach Benny Bengough who was with pennant winning New York Yankee teams, agreed they never saw anything like this.

"St. Louis went wild when the Cards won in 1926 but it wasn't equal to this one. I'm surprised we have any ball players left," said baldheaded Benny as he wiped lip-stick from his face. And it wasn't Mrs. Bengough's lip-stick either.

ONCE IN THE comparative safety of the buses, the players had to wait another half-hour before the police could clear a path.

From there to the hotel, where the Phils staged their own private victory party, it was a parade through thousands more.

And even far into night, the fans continued to celebrate with honking of horns and shouts of joy.

The Phillies had returned home with the National League pennant and they wanted the world to know it.

Baseball Crowds Off 15%

Big Leagues Drew 17,226,824 Fans This Year

NEW YORK, Oct. 2—(AP)—Major League baseball drew 17,226,824 fans during the 1950 season, a drop of 15 per cent from 1949 according to an unofficial survey by the Associated Press.

The National League lured 8,025,169 customers and the American 9,201,655 during the campaign which ended yesterday. In 1949 9,484,718 fans patronized National League games and 10,730,647 American League contests for a two-league total of 20,215,365. The National League attendance in 1950 was off 16 per cent and the American 14 per cent.

PHILADELPHIA'S pennant-winning Phillies, Brooklyn, Pittsburgh, St. Louis and New York drew over a million this year. Only Philadelphia and Cincinnati failed to draw a million in 1949.

The American League champion New York Yankees, Detroit, Cleveland and Boston were the only American League clubs to draw more than a million fans this season. The same teams also were the only ones to draw a million in 1949.

Goodman Wins AL Title; Kell 14 Pts. Behind

CHICAGO, Oct. 2 — (AP) — Billy Goodman, brilliant handyman of the Boston Red Sox, is the new American League Batting Champion.

The 24-year-old Concord, N. C., star won his first league batting title on an average of .354 to succeed George Kell, the Detroit Tigers' 1949 batting king.

Goodman, who weighs only 162 pounds, overtook Kell in the final stages of the season, then swept to an easy win. He finished 14 points ahead of Kell, who last season shaded Ted Williams of the Red Sox for top slugging honors.

HIS UNOFFICIAL average is eight points better than that of Stan Musial, big gun of the St. Louis Cardinals who won his fourth National League Batting Title.

Goodman bats left-handed and has played outfield, first, second, short and third for the Red Sox.

On the heels of Kell, who had. 340, were Dom DiMaggio, Boston, .326, and Phil Rizzuto, New York, and Larry Doby, Cleveland, each with .324.

FINAL STANDINGS

NATIONAL LEAGUE

Teams	W.	L.	Pct.	G.B.
Philadelphia	91	63	.591	...
Brooklyn	89	65	.578	2
New York	86	68	.558	5
Boston	83	71	.539	8
St. Louis	78	75	.510	12½
Cincinnati	66	87	.431	24½
Chicago	64	89	.418	26½
Pittsburgh	57	96	.373	33½

AMERICAN LEAGUE

Teams	W.	L.	Pct.	G.B.
New York	98	56	.636	
Detroit	95	59	.617	3
Boston	94	60	.610	4
Cleveland	92	62	.594	6
Washington	67	87	.435	31
Chicago	60	94	.390	38
St. Louis	58	96	.377	40
Philadelphia	52	102	.338	46

YESTERDAY'S RESULTS

NATIONAL LEAGUE

Philadelphia 4, Brooklyn 1 (10 inns.).
Cincinnati 3, Pittsburgh 2 (1st).
Pittsburgh 3, Cincinnati 1 (2nd).
New York 5, Boston 1.
Chicago 3, St. Louis 2 (11 inns).

AMERICAN LEAGUE

Boston 7, New York 3.
Philadelphia 5, Washington 3.
Cleveland 7, Detroit 5.
Chicago 4, St. Louis 3 (1st).
St. Louis 10, Chicago 6 (2nd).

Bill Goodman Stan Musial

Musial Cops NL Bat Title for 4th Time

NEW YORK, Oct. 2—(AP)—Stan Musial, the "Ball Player's Ball Player" of the St. Louis Cardinals, is the National League's batting champion for the fourth time in his illustrious career.

The belting beauty of the Red Birds finished the 1950 season yesterday with an unofficial average of .346 to win the crown by 18 points from Jackie Robinson of Brooklyn, the defending titalist, who wound up at .328.

MUSIAL IS only the third batter in the long history of the League to win more than three batting championships. The other two are Hall of Famers Honus Wagner of Pittsburgh and Rogers Hornsby of the Cards and Boston. Wagner won eight and Hornsby seven including six straight years while with the Cards from 1920 to 1925. The only other player to win as many as three is Paul Waner of Pittsburgh.

Duke Snider, Robinson's teammate, placed third in the batting derby with .321, the first time he has hit over .300 in his Major League career.

Del Ennis of the champion Philadelphia Phillies and Walker Cooper, veteran catcher of the Boston Braves were tied for fifth place at .313.

SPORTS MIRROR

By the Associated Press

TODAY A YEAR AGO — New York defeated Boston, 5-3, to clinch the American League pennant and Brooklyn halted Philadelphia, 9-7, to cement the National League flag.

FIVE YEARS AGO—Mrs. Winifred Reed Landis, widow of baseball Commissioner Landis, renounced his will which left her entire estate of $150,000.

TEN YEARS AGO—The Detroit Tigers beat the Cincinnati Reds, 7-2, in the first game of the World Series.

FIFTEEN YEARS AGO — The Chicago Cubs, behind Lon Warneke, beat the Detroit Tigers, 3-0, in first game of World Series.

Views of Sports

Phils Topple into Series after 12 Days of Losing

by RED SMITH

NEW YORK, Oct. 2—The tallest, steepest, swiftest, dizziest, dare-devil, death-defying dive ever undertaken by a baseball team came off with a rich and fruity climax yesterday when the Phillies toppled headlong into the World Series.

For thirty-five years, the Phillies struggled to win a National League pennant. For the last twelve days they battled mightily to lose one. Then in the tenth inning of the 155th game of their season, all snarled up in a strangling tie with the team that had closed eight laps on them in a fortnight, they were knocked kicking into the championship by the bat of Dick Sisler.

GEORGE SISLER, probably the greatest first baseman who ever lived, whose .400 hitting couldn't get him into a World Series, sat in Ebbets Field and saw his big son slice a three-run homer which shattered the pennant hopes of the Dodgers, whom George now serves.

Sisler's hit won the game, 4 to 1. Minutes earlier, lustrous pitching by Robin Roberts had saved it, after the Dodgers had come within a dozen feet of the victory which would have closed the season in a tie and brought Philadelphia and Brooklyn together for a play-off.

There hasn't been such a finish," said Mr. Warren Brown, the noted Chicago author, "since sporting British officials carried Durando over the line in the 1908 Olympic marathon."

On Sept. 19 the Phillies had the pennant won in every sense save the mathematical one. They were seven and a half games ahead of the Boston Braves, and Erooklyn was third, nine games off the pace. The Dodgers won fourteen of their next seventeen games, the Phillies three of their twelve. So when they showed up yesterday before Ebbets Field's largest gathering of the year, the Phils' lead was exactly one game, with one game to play.

THEY HAD neither won nor lost the championship, but they had qualified handsomely for off-season employment—substituting for the diving horse in Atlantic City.

They had also brought gold pouring in a bright yellow stream into the Brooklyn box office. Instead of leasing out their park for family picnics this week end, the Dodgers sold 58,952 tickets for the last two games, many of them to customers who stood outside the bleacher gates all Saturday night.

By 4 a. m., cars were pulling into parking lots near the field. By 6:30, there were 5,000 or 6,000 persons in line. By 1 p. m. all gates were closed and nobody without a reserved seat ticket was admitted. Cops estimated that 25,000 were turned away. It was bigger than many World Series crowds in Brooklyn, and properly so, for this was bigger than a World Series game, where even the losers gather much loot. The losers of this game got the Winter off.

In spite of everything, the Phillies managed a surface appearance of confidence. Before the game the Philadelphia manager was ask-

(See Page 20—SMITH)

Attention, F & M

Former Dip Player Warns 1950 Team. Other Brief Bits

by GEORGE KIRCHNER

WORD OF WARNING . . . Last week mention was made here concerning the downfall of the 1929 Franklin and Marshall College football team in its Thanksgiving Day battle with Gettysburg.

Today a member of that team comes to the front for the express purpose of warning Woody Sponaugle's boys not to take their coming battle with the Bullets lightly. He is Harry (Hank) Eman and since Hank was one of those '29 F and Mers who fell under that 25 to 0 stinging administered by the Bullets he is, quite naturally, concerned with the outcome of this year's game and, in the hopes that the boys don't take the game lightly and meet with the same disaster as befell the 1929 outfit, Hank passes along these words of advice:

Dear George:

After reading your article on the "1929" team I can't help but write a few lines to remind this year's club of one or two facts pertaining to G-burg.

Your article brings back vivid memories and believe me, I don't want to see another F and M team line up for that Turkey Day kick-off thinking the game is in the old hip pocket.

First of all, Hen Bream is still there and don't ever sell Hen or any G-burg team short. Disregard all other games and remember that the Bullets will be primed for this one.

F and M's 1950 team with a perfect record to date will be a perfect target for Hen and his (sure to be) hepped-up Bullets.

If the rest of the 1929 team were to voice their opinion I know they would join me in saying "Never underrate Hen Bream and his Bullets."

Outcharge them from the first whistle to the last and you can't miss.

Best of luck to Woody and the boys, the whole town is pulling for them.

Hank Eman, '32.

There's only one other thing to add to Hank's letter and that is that all of us sincerely hope that the boys on this year's squad take his advice seriously. They can bet that the Bullets will be coming here prepared to truly shoot the works and a team in that frame of mind must always be considered formidable.

DOTS AND DASHES . . . Our professional Rockets will get a chance to display their wares in Hershey for they've been booked to play the Harrisburg Senators in an exhibition game as the preliminary to the Philadelphia Warriors-New York Knickerbockers NBA contest over there on December 27 . . . Incidentally, the Rockets are still dickering with a couple of the other NBA clubs to come here for exhibitions . . . They play the Warriors at the Grove next Sunday, you know . . . No increase in admission prices, either.

When it comes down to being loyal to the community's teams, Dr. and Mrs. T. M. Thompson of Elizabethtown, can step up and take a bow . . . For 10 years they've been entertaining the scholastic athletes, cheerleaders, bandsmen and friends and relatives and at the latest banquet last week, the good Doc got up and told his audience that "there'll be another of these affairs the third Thursday of next November no matter how you fellows fare on the football field" . . . That's the kind of spirit that goes to make life in the smaller communities the envy of the city kids.

League Seeks Bowlers

The Sacred Heart Bowling League is looking for additional members to join in the current bowling sessions. All persons interested should call Carl Nicklaus, chairman of the loop, either at 2-9356, or 3-9815.

Oklahoma Is Top Team in Nation

Sooners Received 173 First Place Votes; Army 2nd, Ketnucky 3rd

NEW YORK, Nov. 21—(AP)—The University of Oklahoma, knocking on the front door in the weekly Associated Press football poll all season, finally got into the living room today as the Nation's No. 1 team.

Now the question is: Can the rampaging Sooners of coach Bud Wilkinson retain that lofty perch until the end of this unpredictable season, and become the first member of the Big Seven Conference to cop this mythical football crown? Oklahoma was voted the No. 2 team last year when Notre Dame ended the season as the No. 1 club.

Unlike recent years, when a mighty Notre Dame, Michigan or Army team led the poll week after week through the long Fall, Oklahoma is the fifth outfit to hold the No. 1 spot this season.

OKLAHOMA, which blasted Missouri last week 41-7, to run its unbeaten string to 29 straight, replaced Ohio State. The Buckeyes, who lost to Illinois, fell from first to eighth place.

In seven previous polls this Fall, Oklahoma was voted third four times as the Nation's sportswriters and sportscasters put the finger on other teams. The Sooners were rated No. 2 twice, and No. 5 in the first poll Oct. 2.

Wilkinson was almost speechless when advised his team had been voted No. 1 with a total of 2,964 points. This was 526 better than Army.

Oklahoma, voted No. 1 with 2,964 points, polled 173 first place votes, compared with 36 for Army, and 55 for Kentucky, which moved into third for the first time this year. Army, winner over Stanford in the rain and mud, 7-0, received 2,438 points and Kentucky, which walloped helpless North Dakota, 83-0, got 2,346. Kentucky was fifth a week ago.

CALIFORNIA, with 20 first place votes, held its fourth place rating for the second week in a row with 2,188 points. The Golden Bears also overcame San Francisco in the mud, 13-7.

Texas moved from sixth to fifth, as the Longhorns trimmed Texas Christian, 21-7, while Illinois, eighth a week ago, advanced to sixth by defeating Ohio State, 14-7. The Texas victory assured a Cotton Bowl berth as well as the Southwest Conference title.

PRINCETON hung on to seventh place, lashing Yale, 47-12. In ninth and tenth places are Tennessee and Michigan State, which held the same ranking last week.

Army rests now until the Navy game, Dec. 2. Kentucky gets the acid test against Tennessee. California tackles Stanford, Illinois plays Northwestern, Princeton plays Dartmouth, Ohio State meets Michigan. These games are Saturday. Texas plays Texas A. and M. Nov. 30, and L. S. U. Dec. 9. Tennessee has another game after Kentucky, meeting Vanderbilt Dec. 2. Michigan State's schedule is complete.

Maryland, Tex. A-M in President's Tilt

WASHINGTON, Nov. 21 — (AP) — American Legion sponsors of the game were reported ready today to name Maryland and the Texas Aggies as opponents in the President's Cup Football contest to be played at College Park, Md., Dec. 9.

Game officials would not confirm that those two teams had been selected, but said an announcement of the opponents could probably be expected in the afternoon. Unofficially, all signs pointed to the Aggies and Terrapins as contestants in the event to be staged for benefit of the Legion welfare fund.

THE WASHINGTON Post and the Dallas News both said those two teams had been chosen. The Houston Chronicle said they had been invited.

Byrd Stadium, the brand new site of the brand-new contest, is located at the University of Maryland, just outside Washington. President Truman endorced the contest when Legion officials suggested it as a means of raising money for Legion rehabilitation activities.

11 Local Boys on F and M Grid Team

High

Ebersole

Schlager

Lewis

4 Seniors Played Under Sponaugle at McCaskey High

An unprecedented number of Lancaster boys will see action with the Franklin and Marshall football forces Thursday in F and M's 53rd annual Turkey Day classic with Gettysburg on Williamson Field.

Four seniors who are three-year veterans and who played under their present coach Woody Sponaugle as schoolboy gridders at McCaskey High School, wind up their F and M playing days Thursday. They are Co-captain Bobby King, Johnny Hartman, Bobby High and Herbie Galebach. King, High and Galebach are members of the Dip defensive team and Hartman is an offensive end.

Millhouse

The Lancaster juniors playing against Gettysburg for the second time are: Russ Schelling, Bob Hannum, Bernie Ebersole and Bob Lewis.

THE "BABY" members of the squad from Lancaster are Charlie Schlager and Wendell (Moose) Hower, a pair of Sophomores, who have become outstanding linemen in one season.

An eleventh Lancastrian who will not be able to play against the Bullets this year because of a broken leg is Frankie Millhouse, barrel-chested fullback.

Hartman

King

Hannum

Galebach

Schelling

Hower

Manheim Twp. Cagers Open Season Tomorrow

Manheim Township High's basketball team opens its 1950-51 season tomorrow night when they entertain the East Hempfield cagers in an exhibition game.

Following a practice adopted in recent years of opening their cage season the evening prior to Thanksgiving, two games are listed, with the jayvee tilt starting at 7 o'clock and the varsity game at 8:15 o'clock.

Yale May Some Day Play Notre Dame

by RED SMITH

When 'Erman smote 'is bloomin' lyre,
He'd 'eard the losing coaches wail;
Ten years, 'e thought, it might require
To get a winner up at Yale.

NEW YORK, Nov. 21—Shivering in the Yale Bowl last Saturday watching the inauguration of Herman Hickman's Ten-Year Plan for New Haven football, one realized tardily that the athletic authorities up there did more than merely hire a coach when they committed themselves to a decade of listening to the kinfolk yarns and the rhymes of the poet laureate of the Little Smokies.

When 'Erman smote 'is bloomin' lyre and signed a new contract to supervise undergraduate bloodshed through the season of 1960, Yale was not merely giving a vote of confidence to an employee. Yale was stating its football program for the future, and reaffirming its faith in a game which may be in for some very difficult days.

THE TIMING of the announcement of Hickman's reappointment was interesting. A week or ten days before the defeat by Princeton, the Yales had decided they wanted Hickman for the next ten years, at least. The new contract had been drafted and photographs had been made of the ceremony of signing.

At first it was intended to release the news right after the Princeton game, but somebody got the notion, which seems fantastic now, that Yale might bring off a miracle and defeat Princeton. Had that been the case, it would have looked as though Yale was rewarding its coach for a single victory, and that wasn't the point at all.

The contract was Yale's way of stating publicly its satisfaction with the job Hickman has been doing, and declaring the university's determination to continue the rebuilding program as Herman has started it.

In other words, Yale means to climb back, with the old mountaineer leading the way, toward the place it once held in the football scene. This doesn't mean letting down the bars and setting out after national championships. It means developing teams of undergraduates coached to play creditable football with opponents that are representative of the best, academically and athletically.

NOBODY CAN predict now the extent to which college football will be affected by the international situation and the military draft in the next few years. But Yale has made clear its confidence that the best

HERMAN HICKMAN

in athletics will continue to go hand in hand with the best in education, that proper training on the sports field still will have its place in a balanced system of schooling.

It would not be altogether surprising to see the program progress to the point of a football series with Notre Dame, a prospect which genuinely stirs the imagination. This idea is not so outlandish as it might seem at first blush.

Yale is the fountainhead of football, the mother house from which missionaries fanned out to spread the football gospel across the land. Notre Dame football has represented the highest refinement of the modern game. With the immediate future uncertain, Yale, which has contributed so much, would be making a further contribution by joining forces with the best of the present-day crop.

Both are great colleges with a great football traditon. Notre Dame, which did not come East this year, has been missed by its vast following in this area. Always an attractive team, Notre Dame, playing in Yale Bowl, a somewhat hallowed shrine of football, would be the biggest thing since the quilted jersey.

NOT THAT IT would be without precedent. Notre Dame played at Yale in 1914 when Knute Rockne was a pup, and Yale won, 28 to 0. Years later, when somebody asked Rockne where the Notre Dame shift had originated, Rock replied without hesitation:

"Where everything else in football came from—Yale."

This is the first year since the war that the mere name of Notre Dame has not caused athletic directors to awake screaming in the dark. The unbroken record of success which Frank Leahy's teams enjoyed for several seasons, together with the timorous reluctance of other teams to schedule them, created an impression that the squads were composed entirely of critters wiht green heads, fur all over their torsos and arms that hung down to the ground.

IT HAS REQUIRED this season to demonstrate that they are human and vincible. Notre Dame is not exempt from the cycle of famine and plenty which applies to all undergraduate groups. There will be seasons when the Irish will be too strong for Yale, as Princeton is too strong for Yale, and probably for Notre Dame, this year.

But Yale is going to have its cycles, too. Inside the next ten years, Herman's going to produce something besides sonnets, he'll smite something besides 'is bloomin' lyre.

Roses and Dodgers Likely to Continue Agreement

Cowdrick Says Matter Will Be Decided at Florida Meeting; Inter State Re-elects Nugent for Third Straight Term

by GEORGE KIRCHNER

"THERE'S a good possibility that we'll again work with Brooklyn."

That's the way W. D. (Bill) Cowdrick, general manager of the Lancaster Red Roses, summed it up yesterday when he was asked concerning a working agreement for his club for the 1951 Inter State League campaign.

COWDRICK ATTENDED the League's annual Fall meeting in Harrisburg and helped to re-elect Gerald H. Nugent as president for a three-year term at a salary of $3,500 per year, plus $1,000 in expense money.

All of the eight cities that competed last year announced they would be back this season and only the Roses and York were uncertain on working agreements. York split with the Pittsburgh Pirates at the end of last season when the club changed ownership.

BUT LANCASTER'S status was not announced when Branch Rickey resigned as president of the Dodgers to become general manager of the Pirates.

So, yesterday, Cowdrick was asked concerning his plans and his answer was that "there's a good possibility that we will again work with the Dodgers."

"No agreement has been signed," the business manager elaborated, "and probably won't be until the National Association meeting in St. Petersburg next month."

Beyond that the Roses' official would not comment. He said that he had made several trips to Brooklyn, but that the agreement had not been brought up at any of these times.

GEORGE SMITH, was announced as the new owner of the Trenton club, which Smith said, has signed a working agreement with the Philadelphia Athletics.

The 1951 season will see the revival of the League's All-Star game in early July. It will feature teams representing the Eastern and Western sections of the circuit.

THE EAST includes Allentown, Lancaster, Trenton and Wilmington while the West is comprised of Harrisburg, Hagerstown, Sunbury and York.

Site of the game will be the city having the largest total attendance as of July 1.

League fans will be given the opportunity of voting for their favorite players and the votes will be tabulated by the president's office. The team in first place in its respective division as of July 1 will furnish the managers for each all-star team.

A tentative schedule for the 1951 season was also approved. It again calls for 140 games, with each team making four trips around the circuit during the campaign.

The league, he said, will also go to the minor league meetings next month prepared to vote for abolishment of the bonus rule.

Nugent also disclosed the league will reduce its umpire staff from nine to eight men next season.

THE NEXT meeting of the Inter State League will be held sometime in February in Trenton in connection with the annual Inter State League Sportswriters and

(See Page 20—BASEBALL)

When you've got a yen...
for a midnight feed...

Lifelike Dolls Are Big News This Christmas Season

Woman Bitten by Cat, Another Hurt in Fall

Three persons were treated at the General Hospital for minor injuries over the week-end.

Mrs. Melina C. Naolitan,p thirty-five, 423 Manor St., was bitten on a finger of the right hand by a pet cat.

Mrs. Sallie A. Haddon, seventy-seven, 413 E. Strawberry St., lacerated her right eye in a fall in the 500 block of North St.

Elmer Shreiner, fifty-four, 740 S. Broad St., Lititz, injured his right ankle in a fall from a ladder.

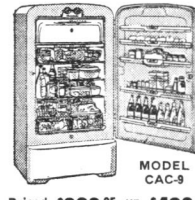

Every Girl Loves A Christmas Doll

It's a toss-up whether it's mother or daughter who looks most longingly at the frothy collection of dolls on display in local stores, for the shelves are loaded with all sorts, from eight-inch baby dolls to a 31-inch number, undoubtedly a giant in toyland.

A new doll with lips that pucker and kiss like a human being's and, according to toy makers, may revolutionize the industry will make its debut under many Christmas trees this holiday season.

This love-me baby supplies the one thing which dolls have lacked until now—the ability to respond to the affection heaped upon them. Dolls of the past have walked, cried, drunk, wet, closed their eyes and moved their heads, but never before could one reciprocate the love of its doting young mother.

The secret of the doll's kiss lies in the working of a plunger mechanism in its back, developed exclusively by the largest doll manufacturers in the world. This mechanism allows the baby to move its tongue, frown, pout, suck its thumb and nurse.

The baby's mobility of expression stems from her magic vinylite skin which feels warm, soft and pliable as any real baby's. Her head and limbs are made of a soft, durable vinylite resin. The cotton stuffed body, equally soft and resilient, contains a realistic voice box to match the facial expressions.

This baby comes nestled in its own pink, beribboned baby blanket, covering its full three-weeks-old size. Its clothes are of the quality and realism of a true baby wardrobe.

OTHERS IN FAMILY

This latest development is the newest member of a famous family of sisters and brothers including a doll whose nylon hair "takes" a sugar and water home permanent; a head-moving ventriloquist doll; a baby who coos and Sparkle Plenty, the cartoon-strip favorite of youngsters from coast to coast.

The majority of this year's dolls are made either from soft, skin-like rubber, plastic (which also feels like the real thing), and some hard rubber. Their cries are realistic wails. Real hair is gradually being replaced with nylon tresses, some of which can be washed, put up in curlers, or given a home permanent innumerable times.

Doll clothes are becoming more and more lifelike—hems are carefully sewn in, snaps and hooks and eyes close all openings, there's even rubber tape in bright red skating panties. Doll dresses hang on their own little hangers and many come complete with dainty lace-trimmed bonnets.

News this year is the Cinderella doll whose bright golden hair is topped with a shining crown and whose dress is of blue satin with silver trim. Her companion piece is Prince Charming, a boy doll dressed in a pink and white costume of the period and who carries the renowned glass slipper.

Another doll wears a ballerina-length dress which is also styled like a dancer's. Her frock is of nylon, as is her hair, which is combed in ballerina fashion. Still another doll to delight little girls comes with her own plastic box of curlers.

Dolls for very young misses are made completely of soft rubber and their fragile appearance belies the rough treatment they can take. Although made of rubber, the facial features are carefully and faithfully reproduced.

Twins, triplets and even quadruplets, tucked into their pink satin and tulle baskets are designed to keep a tiny mother busy.

And these are only a few of the hundreds of dolls on display. There are other, smaller ones dressed in costumes of foreign countries and still others who wear exquisite dresses of organdy, eyelet embroidery and read straw bonnets and roller skates. And these toys range in price from under two to fifty dollars.

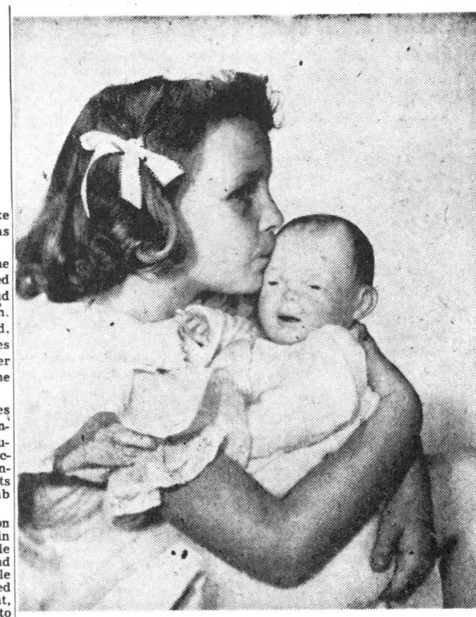

NEWEST DOLL TO COME off the manufacturers assembly line Is closest to the real thing yet made. Plunger mechanism on its back enables the owner to make dolly move its tongue, frown and pout. Head and limbs are made of a pliable vinylite resin.

IN SOME SECTIONS of England, no one will give matches, fire or light to be taken from the house on Christmas Day, believing that trouble would arise.

IN MIDDLE EUROPE if your light goes out on Christmas morning you will see spirits and if you burn Elder on Christmas Eve all witches will be revealed to you.

WHICH IS WHICH?—One of the largest dolls on display this season proves to be quite an armful for three-year old Dorinda Kochel who finds that rocking her doll can become a bit complicated.

SOMETHING FOR SIS—a washable, handmade negligee-nightgown of novelty tricot nylon.

IN SHROPSHIRE and other sections of Europe, no ashes may be thrown out on Christmas Day, for fear that they will be thrown into the face of the Savior.

ENGLISH IMPORT . . . Collectors will love this Farmer's Wife toby.

HENRY

By Carl Anderson

BIG SISTER

By Les Forgrave

BRINGING UP FATHER

Follow Jiggs And Maggie In The Sunday News

By George McManus

ORPHAN ANNIE

By Harold Gray

HARRISBURG TO HAVE RECORD BUDGET FROM CITY SALARY BOOSTS

Harrisburg —(AP)— A budget of $3,063,453 for Harrisburg for 1951, largest in the city's history, was completed Tuesday.

The budget, an increase of $179,162 from the 1950 budget, will be called up for action by city council Sept. 29. A tax-fixing budget increasing the city levy from 14 to 15 mills on the dollar valuation will be up for action at the same time.

The bulk of the increase represented a recent eight and one-third per cent cost-of-living salary increase granted city employes. Departments also were allowed increased appropriations to allow for higher cost of materials.

TOONERVILLE FOLKS

By Fontaine Fox

(Released by The Bell Syndicate, Inc.)

OUT OUR WAY

By J. R. Williams

ANNOUNCEMENT!

Attention those Employees of Local RCA Plant, Department 15, who were affected by the Shut Down because of material shortages caused by the recent storm.

1st SHIFT EMPLOYEES should report at their Regular Schedule Time 7 A. M. Wednesday Morning, Nov. 29.

2nd SHIFT EMPLOYEES should report at their Regular Schedule Time 3 P. M. Wednesday Afternoon, Nov. 29.

3rd SHIFT EMPLOYEES should report at their Regular Schedule Time 11 P. M. Wednesday Night, Nov. 29.

BLAIR HOUSE GETTING PROTECTIVE SCREENS

Washington —(AP)— Workmen Tuesday began placing heavy protective screens on Blair House—home of President Truman while the White House is being repaired.

The screens are described as strong enough to repel some types of missiles, but are not considered bullet proof.

They will be placed on all front windows and some of those in the rear of Blair House and the adjoining Blair Lee House.

GENEVA COLLEGE CLOSED

Beaver Falls, Pa. —(AP)— Geneva College has suspended day and night classes at least until Thursday because of weather conditions.

James McGill, founder, of McGill university, Montreal, Quebec, was born in Scotland and went to Canada in 1770.

BLONDIE

Follow Blondie In The Sunday News

By Chick Young

FRECKLES AND HIS FRIENDS

Follow Freckles In The Sunday News

By Merrill Blosser

ALLEY OOP

Follow Alley Oop In The Sunday News

By V. T. Hamlin

SECRET AGENT X-9

By Mel Graff

WASH TUBBS

By Leslie Turner

DIXIE DUGAN

Follow Dixie Dugan In The Sunday News

By McEvoy and Striebel

MUGGS AND SKEETER

By Wally Bishop

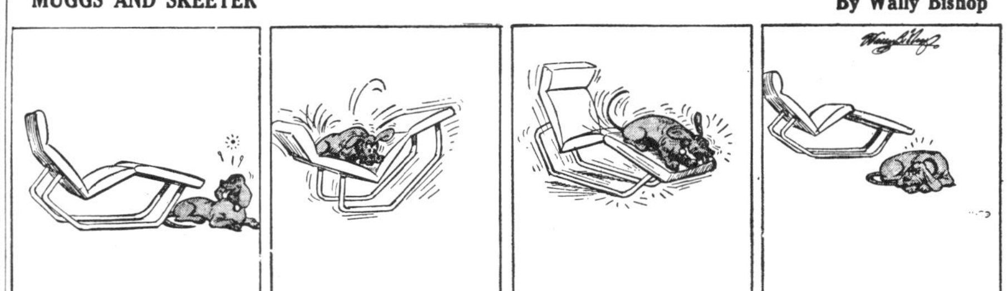

TIPPIE AND "CAP" STUBBS

By Edwina

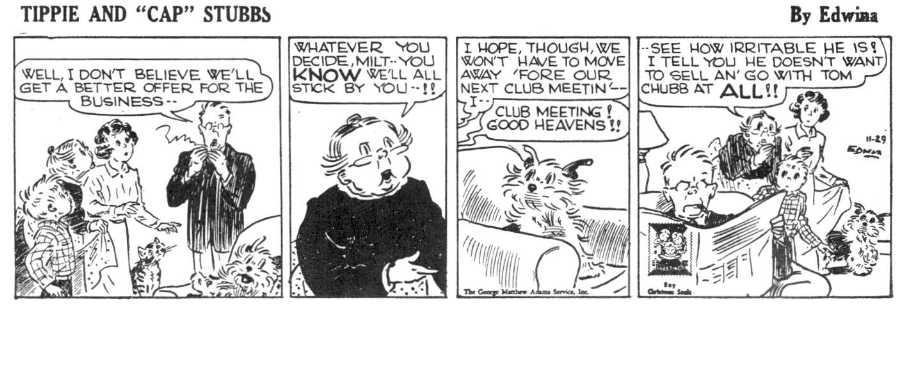

The National Geographic Society says the atmosphere is so thin in Tibet's uplands that rocks get scorching hot in the sun while nearby shaded areas are freezing cold.

The population of Tibet is believed to be decreasing because of the large number of celibate Buddhist monks and the practice of polyandry.

Letters from American Become New Weapon in the Cold War

NEW TROY, Nov. 29.—(NEA)—A man who escaped from a Hungarian prison camp writes back to Hungary every week to a man he despises — to "make him writhe with envy."

The letters describe the ex-prisoner's new life in America, his $99-a-week job, his home, his car, his freedom. But it is not a one-man campaign. These weekly letters are part of America's newest weapon in the Cold War, a written partner to the Voice of America.

"Letters from America," the new weapon, capitalizes on a great American natural resource—people like the ex-Hungarian prisoner and 35,000,000 other first and second generation Americans who have relatives and friends abroad.

Idea Not New One

The tactic of encouraging these people to write to their folks abroad is not a new one. It was employed during the last Italian election, in a successful effort to defeat Communism at the polls.

But, under the sponsorship of the Common Council for American Unity, directed by Read Lewis, the current campaign is the biggest effort in that direction. And it is the first to enlist the support of foreign language newspapers and radio stations throughout America.

The Council publishes a weekly release for these newspapers and radio stations. These messages suggest topics to be mentioned in letters and emphasize the advantages of living under a democracy. The Council translates them into 20 different languages, and says that they finally appear in about 27 languages.

The releases are published regularly in 229 newspapers and broadcast over about 200 foreign language radio stations. The Council estimates that some 8,000,000 people read or hear them each week.

In Simple Terms

Written in simple terms, the messages stress the interest Europeans have in every-day life in America. A Sunday drive in the country, for example, seems commonplace to Americans, but to Europeans it is a fabulous thing. It means the writer has a car, that he is free to drive about as he pleases, that he has leisure and relaxation.,

One release discusses the movies, and urges letter writers to tell European relatives and friends that the films don't show America in "a true light." Other releases talk of labor agreements, American weddings, graduation, the Fourth of July, American culture, vacations, and serious subjects like the Korean War and inflation.

All are designed to suggest topics letter writers might use, bringing in their own personal experiences.

Still other Council releases are signed articles on the meaning of Democracy, written by such people as Bernard Baruch, James B. Carey, the CIO's secretary-treasurer, Eleanor Roosevelt and former Secretary of War Robert Patterson.

A pro-Communist Hungarian paper in New York editorially blasted the "Letters from America" campaign, saying that it would be used by the "Fascist and reactionary" press to make "a tool of propaganda for the Cold War" out of Hungarian-Americans.

Women

Good Resolutions for Parents to Make to Enrich the Home

By Garry Cleveland Myers, Ph.D.

Parents who wish to make some New Year's resolutions might desire to consider some or all of the following:

I'm going to try to be a better wife or husband and do my best to build on the strength of my spouse and often celebrate his or her successes, so that we might grow more companionable and together might provide more family love and security for our children.

Therefore, I shall try to speak less often to my spouse or anybody else about his or her weaknesses, even to think less often of them. I shall endeavor to work upon myself to win the cooperation of my husband or wife in all matters related to the family, especially to the children.

I SHALL TRY to cultivate good physical and emotional health in myself, so as to promote best mental health and happiness in my spouse and my children. Accordingly, I shall, with the help of my husband or wife, aim to regulate my everyday work and life at home in such a way as to avoid as far as possible excessive fatigue and needless nervous strain but enjoy relaxation, so that I may have physical and mental poise and be always a master of my emotions. I shall pray for calm and poise and self-control.

I shall try to control my voice as well as my speech, so as never to speak in loud or shrill tones or utter words which might stir up anger or undue antagonisms in any other member of the family. I won't scold and nag or engage in word-battles in my home.

IN 1951 I SHALL try hard to understand my children, how each one grows and develops, what he can think and do, what his strongest interests and urges are at each stage of his development.

I shall not make fun of my children or laugh at their mistakes or resort to shame and ridicule for punishment. Neither shall I let myself grow angry at their mistakes when they try to learn.

WITH THE HELP of the other parent, I am going to try to guide and discipline my children so skillfully that they will learn to respect the rights and feelings of other persons, learn self-reliance and responsibility; and thus enable them to feel less annoyed at me and me at them.

I am going to try to grow up with my children and treat them as precious persons, have fun with them and enjoy them. I am going to smile and laugh more in 1951 than in any earlier year and thus arouse more smiles and laughter in our family.

By everything I do and say in my family I will try to prove abundant affection for all of them and thus try to win their abiding love and esteem.

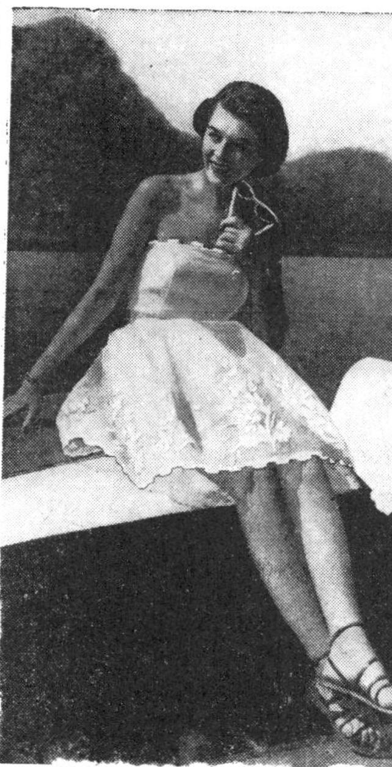

ORGANDIE IN THE SWIM . . . This is a swim suit of white pique with organdie apron appliqued with pique posies.

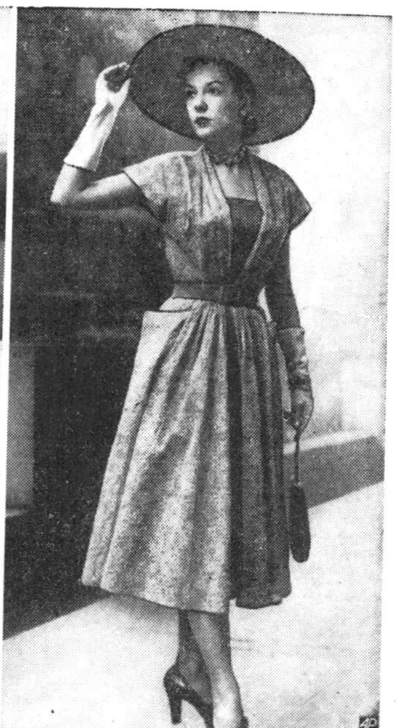

SHEER SWANK . . . Summer town ensemble: taupe and white print organdie coat over a suntop sleeveless dress in taupe linen.

FOUR-WAY OUTFIT . . . This orange organdie blouse and plaid organdie skirt top a swim suit with organdie covered shorts, and an orange wraparound skirt.

AP Photos

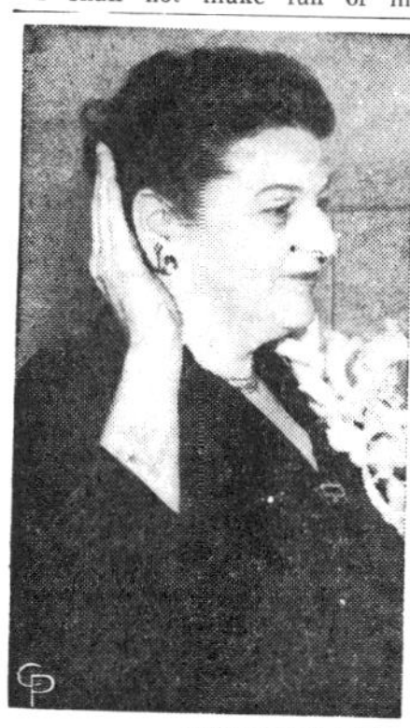

International Photo

Her Honor

Sworn in as the first Democratic woman mayor of Red Bank, N. J., Mrs. Katherine E. White takes the oath of office.

Weddings

Bowman—Wittrig

The marriage of Miss Iola Dorene Wittrig, of Ephrata, daughter of Mr. and Mrs. Amos Wittrig, of Hopedale, Pa., to Silas S. Bowman, son of Mr. and Mrs. Jacob G. Bowman, of Terre Hill, took place on Christmas Day at the home of the bride's parents. The Rev. Ivan J. Kauffman, of the Hopedale Mennonite Church, officiated. Mr. and Mrs. Loren Wittrig, brother and sister-in-law of the bride, were the attendants.

After a wedding trip through the Southern States the couple will reside in Ephrata where the bride is a doctor of chiropractic. She is a graduate of the Palmer School of Chiropractic, Davenport, Iowa.

The bridegroom is employed in the office of the New Holland Concrete Products Co.

Will Wed Jan. 20

Invitations have been issued by Mr. and Mrs. George Dorwart, 544 Ruby St., for the marriage of their daughter, Janet, to William G. Weisser, son of Mr. and Mrs. William B. Weisser, 807 Chestnut St., Columbia.

The ceremony will take place at a Nuptial High Mass at 9:30 a.m. Saturday, Jan. 20, in Sacred Heart Church. The Rev. John J. Kealy, rector, will officiate at the double ring ceremony.

Miss Dorwart, who will be given in marriage by her father, will be attended by Miss Patricia Kleine, city, as maid of honor. Bridesmaids will be Miss Mary Ann Fix and Miss Joan Zeck, both of this city. Winifred Foster, city, cousin of the bride-elect, will be flower girl.

Eugene Weisser will attend his brother as best man. Ushers will be Bernard Weisser, another brother, and Robert Hagen, city.

Music will be provided by the Children's Choir and Miss Mary Louise Danz, vocalist.

Following a reception in the Stevens House the couple will leave on a wedding trip to Florida and Cuba. They will reside with the bridegroom's parents.

Miss Dorwart is employed in the billing department of Armstrong Cork Co., and Mr. Weisser, at the Marietta Transportation Corps Depot.

Dance Will Follow Game at McCaskey

The McCaskey High School social committee will sponsor a dance, "Nouveau Annus Tanze," tonight in the school gymnasium following the McCaskey-John Harris basketball game.

Chaperons will be Dr. and Mrs. B. B. Herr, Mr. and Mrs. Donald Witmer, Mr. and Mrs. Ernest Kilgore, Mr. and Mrs. Ross Myers, Mr. and Mrs. James Neely, Mr. and Mrs. Harry Langford and Mr. and Mrs. Clarence Henderson.

Club Activities

Business Women

The Publications committee, Miss E. Blanche Seyfert chairman, of the Business and Professional Women's Club was in charge of the dinner meeting of the club last night at the Brunswick.

A review of "Eleanor of Aquitane" was given by Mrs. Charles E. Workman, who was introduced by Mrs. Olivia Stoner. Miss Marianne Weicksel sang a solo accompanied by Kathryn Byers Johnstone.

An invitation was received to attend a meeting of the York Club on Monday when the speaker will be Dr. Madeline Holland, of Philadelphia, state president of BPW. The sum of $5 was voted to the Community Council program. Miss Hilda Mowrer presided.

Decorations were Winter gardens, flags and magazine covers. The next meeting will be on Jan. 18 at the Brunswick with the International Relations committee, Miss Eleanor Work, chairman, in charge.

Catholic Daughters

The Catholic Daughters of America, Court Queen of Peace No. 1023, will hold a white elephant party Jan. 18 at 8:15 p. m. in the Knights of Columbus Hall. Mrs. Esther Fisher was named chairman of the committee at a meeting last evening in the K. of C. Hall.

Members of her committee are Mrs. Elizabeth Musser, Mrs. Margaret Schneider, Miss Mary Painter, Miss Mary Paige and Miss Agnes Sauer.

The next meeting will be held Feb. 1 at 8 p. m. in the K of C Hall

Temple Sisterhood

The film, "One God," was shown at the luncheon meeting of the Sisterhood of Temple Shaarai Shomayim yesterday afternoon in Wise Memorial Hall. Dr. Lester Roubey led a discussion which followed the showing. Mrs. Sidney Brener presided.

The luncheon committee included Mrs. Kurt Aronsohn, Mrs. Louis Wascou, Mrs. Samuel Halperin, Mrs. John Hogan, Mrs. Roland Loeb, Mrs. Samuel Slotkin and Mrs. Robert Proler.

Maids of Athens

Miss Lucy Pikolas, Loyal Maid of the Maids of Athens, appointed new committees at a meeting this week in the Greek Community Hall.

They are: Sick and gift, Dorothy Francos, Artemis Samaras; membership, Katherine Macrogeane; publicity, Clara Theros; inter-executive council, Venice Dontis; entertainment, Artemis Samaras, Koula Vasias, Katherine Macrogeane, Rosie Macrides, Christine Pavlides; refreshment, Thalia Patounas, Rosie Macrides, Mary Xakellis; church council, Clara Theros; album, Mary Xakellis, Christine Pavlides; initiation, Venice Dontis, Koula Andreades, Thalia Patounas, Dorothy Francos.

The next meeting will be held Jan. 24.

Beth El Sisterhood

The Sisterhood of Temple Beth El will sponsor a Sweetheart Dinner Dance on Feb. 18. Plans for the dance were made at a meeting of the board last evening at the home of Mrs. Herman Rosman, 960 Helen Ave.

The Sisterhood will be hostess at the Hadassah Sabbath on Jan. 12 at 8 p. m. at the temple. The group also will participate in the installation of the new officers of the temple on Jan. 28 at 8 p. m. at which time Rabbi Paul Rosenfeld will be installed and honored.

A rummage sale is planned for Jan. 13 and 15 at 32 S. Duke St. A card party will be held Monday at 8 p. m. at the home of Mrs. Hyman Mishkin, 945 W. Walnut St. Hostesses will be Mrs. Allen Alboum, Mrs. Jack Bergsman, Mrs. John Hogan and Mrs. F. Weber. Mrs. Benjamin Solsky presided.

A dessert meeting will be held Jan. 10 at 1 p. m. in the temple social rooms. Mrs. Evelyn Webb will speak on "Guiding Your Child."

Farm Women No. 17

A demonstration on remodeling lights in the home, given by a representative of the P P and L Co., featured the meeting of Farm Women's Society No. 17 yesterday at the home of Mrs. Elizabeth Herr, at the Buck. A reading, prepared by Mrs. Sara Stauffer, was given by Mrs. Hazel Mylin.

A kitchen band, composed of ten members, was led by Mrs. Mary Burkins. Mrs. Everett Kreider presided. Co-hostesses were Mrs. Bertha Johnson and Mrs. Pearl Wenger. The next meeting will be on Feb. 1, at 1:30 p. m. at the home of Mrs. Bertha Johnson, Quarryville R1.

La Nobles

The luncheon meeting of the La-Nobles Club yesterday afternoon in Hotel Brunswick was attended by 45 members. Cards followed a business session.

The next meeting will be held Feb. 1 at 12:45 p. m. at the hotel. The business session at 2 p. m. will be followed by cards.

PETUNIA!

Checking the total, I'm sure as can be That someone got gypped — And I think it was me.
FRIDAY SPECIALS

Quite possible, Petunia, when you shop at the busiest times . . . like Friday. The BEST clerks get harried and hurried . . . and mistakes are easy to make. Shop EARLY.

BISHOP-BRACKEN

Couples Club to Have First Dance of Year

The Couples Club will have the first dance of the New Year tomorrow at the Stevens House from 9 to 12 o'clock. About 60 couples are expected to attend. Mr. and Mrs. H. Neff Kehler, of 121 Yale Ave., will entertain 20 couples at a cocktail party at their home prior to the dance.

Women of the Moose Will Banquet Wednesday

The anniversary banquet of the Lancaster Chapter, No. 767, Women of the Moose, will be held Wednesday at 7 p. m. in Moose Home. Deputy Grand Regent Mary Dorwart of the Elizabethtown Chapter, will be guest speaker.

Jane Debus, Columbia, and officers of the local LOOM Lodge No. 299 will be guests. Plans for the banquet were made at a meeting of the chapter this week. The next meeting will be held Jan. 15 at 8 p. m. Chairmen and co-chairmen of committees will meet Jan. 12 at 8 p. m. to plan a food sale.

"Off-Season" Vegetables Are Plentiful Here

The "off-season" vegetables were in heavy supply at local markets today.

Lots of top quality celery was seen on many stands because of the favorable weather during the growing season. Unusually large stalks were available for 10 to 15 cents. Smaller stalks were 25 cents a bunch.

Among the most plentiful commodities were apples, with the largest Stayman Winesap and Delicious varieties at 35 to 40 cents a quarter peck. Persimmons sold for 15 cents a pint and 25 cents a quart.

Onions were 10 and 15 cents a pint, with some extra-large home-grown Bermudas 10 cents.

Many large topped carrots were 10 and 15 cents a quart box. Another substantial vegetable continuing in heavy supply today was sweet potatoes, at the steady low price of 25 cents a quart box.

Iceburg lettuce was scare, at 25 cents.

Beauty Hints

No Matter What the Weather May Be— Take a Wa'k

By Helen Jameson

No matter how busy you are, there is a little side-duty that must not be overlooked. It is the important matter of taking care of yourself, keeping within finger touch of your youth. There is no virtue in self-neglect. Many good women would be better off if they were a little selfish. The mother and wife who takes fastidious care of her family and lets herself go to seed is not doing right by her husband and children. The mama is their pride, or should be.

THIS IS THE SEASON of the year when complexions go wan and grey, and figures are inclined to take on an inch or so at the waistline. No matter what the weather may be, get out and walk. If you stay indoors most of the time, you will feel as if your spirits had mildewed, and your bones as well.

It is worth while to retain youthful lines. When you were a teenager, you were galloping around fast enough. You had gym work in high school and college. Then what happened? You resigned yourself to fate.

IT MAY NOT be convenient or possible for you to skate or ski or attend gym classes, but you can put on your seven league boots and tramp a mile or two. We're so accustomed to having transportation of one kind or another that some women consider it a terrific effort to propel themselves to the nearest letter box.

Walking is an excellent exercise. It keeps the musculature strong and resilient, aids digestion, peps up circulation, puts the pink carnation bloom in the cheeks. But it must be accomplished correctly.

Walk as if you were glad to be alive—chest high, head balanced, spinal column stretched full length. Cultivate a springy step. Let the arms swing easily; don't toddle, clutching your purse under your arm, with your head snuggled down in your coat collar.

New Pin-up Queen Says She Is "Bookish" Type

By Bob Thomas

HOLLYWOOD, Jan. 5 —(AP)— The first new pin-up queen of the war would frankly prefer to curl up with a good book than pose for cheesecake on the beach.

Marilyn Monroe is the girl with the body beautiful that is threatening such pin-up stalwarts as Jane Russell and Betty Grable. This week she received word that she was named "Miss Cheesecake" by the GI editors of Stars and Stripes in Germany.

After a hasty appraisal, I could see that Miss Monroe is well qualified for the honor. She is busty, blonde and beautiful with a creamy complexion and a slinky movement that recalls Jean Harlow. It was therefore unusual to learn that she is more concerned with philosophy books than bathing suits.

"Oh, I don't mind cheesecake," she told me. "I realize it is a necessary thing in the movie business and it comes natural to me. I did a lot of posing for posters and calendars before I got into the movies.

"Also, I'm happy if the boys in the service like my pictures. I have received a lot of mail from Korea and that is very gratifying. I have tried to answer it all personally."

ASIDE FROM the physical aspects, Marilyn doesn't fit the usual starlet pattern at all. She doesn't drink or smoke and she doesn't like night clubs. She'd rather read a book.

Right now she is plowing through a life of Albert Schweitzer, the renowned philosopher-missionary. She is also reading all the works of Antoine de Saint Exupery, the French novelist.

Her ambition? "To be a really good actress," she answered earnestly. Her idols are Vivien Leigh and Olivia DeHavilland.

Marilyn is determined to be a dramatic star, even if she has to be "Miss Cheesecake" at present.

AP Photo

MARILYN MONROE

Community Dance Chaperons Named

The Community Dance Committee of the Lancaster Recreation Association will sponsor a dance in the YWCA gymnasium tomorrow from 8:30 to 11:30 p. m.

The Manor High School representatives, Joanne Schrite and Patsy Brenner, will be in charge. Douglas Thompson will be floor manager.

Prize events will be a snowball dance and prize waltz. Chaperons will be Mr. and Mrs. Michael Wenglasc.

Engaged

Mr. and Mrs. H. Maurice Wenger, Lancaster R4, announce the engagement of their daughter, Arlene, to Ronald B. Mellinger, son of Mr. and Mrs. Clarence B. Mellinger, New Holland. Miss Wenger is a music teacher and also is employed by Hubley Mfg. Co. Mr. Mellinger is employed by New Holland Machine Co.

Mr. and Mrs. Joseph H. Terrell, 650 Martha Ave., announce the engagement of their daughter, Elaine Lee, to Pfc. Lawrence M. Lamborn, son of Mr. and Mrs. Benjamin Lamborn, Cochranville.

Miss Terrell is employed in the office of Hager and Bros. Pfc. Lamborn is stationed at Fort Lee, Va.

Mr. and Mrs. Jacob Maser, Parkesburg R1, announce the engagement of their daughter, Erma, to Aldus L. Myers, Jr., son of Mrs. Beulah A. Myers, Parkesburg R1.

Miss Maser is employed by Sweet-Orr and Co., Inc., Paradise, and Mr. Myers, by Lukenweld Steel Co., Coatesville.

Mr. and Mrs. Carl Probst, Christiana R1, announce the engagement of their daughter, Marian E., to Marlin K. Witwer, son of Mr. and Mrs. David Witwer, Christiana R1. No date has been set for the wedding.

Mr. and Mrs. Harry Frymyer, 295 Eleventh St., Akron, announce the engagement of their daughter, Nancy, to Vernon Weidman, son Mr. and Mrs. Fred Smith, 114 Lincoln Ave., Ephrata. No date has been set for the wedding.

Mr. and Mrs. Howard Worrest, Millersville, announced the engagement of their daughter, Jean, to Wendell Buck, son of Mrs. Grace Buck, Randolph, Vt., and the late Mr. Buck, at a party held at their home recently.

Miss Worrest is a registered medical technician at the Northern Westchester Hospital, Mount Kisco, N. Y. Mr. Buck is an X-ray technician at the same hospital.

Mr. and Mrs. Robert J. Hanna, 38 E. Second Ave., Lititz, announce the engagement of their daughter, Jean to Robert M. Bender, son of Dr. and Mrs. J. Richard Bender, E. Main St., Lititz.

Miss Hanna is employed by the Animal Trap Co. of America and Mr. Bender is a student at the University of Pennsylvania.

Mr. and Mrs. Charles Drescher, 305 N. Second St., Columbia, announce the engagement of their daughter, Dorothy J., to Luther J. Hess, son of Mrs. Myrtle Hess, Florin.

Miss Drescher is employed by the United Throwing Co., Columbia. Mr. Hess is in the Navy stationed at Dahlgren, Va.

Mr. and Mrs. Ira Mellott, Drumore R1, announce the engagement of their daughter, Thelma Ethel, to Jay Stanley Kline, son of Mr. and Mrs. Frank Kline, Jr., Manheim R4.

Mr. Kline is engaged in farming.

ENTERTAINS AT TEA

Mrs. Charles R. Law, of Blossom Hill, entertained the membership committee of the YWCA Newcomers Club at a tea at her home yesterday afternoon. Mrs. Harold Landis presided at the tea table and decorations were in green and white.

WEATHER
(U. S. Weather Bureau)
Eastern Pennsylvania—Partly Cloudy Highest In Middle 20s Saturday. Sunday Considerable Cloudiness And Not So Cold, Some Snow Likely West And North Portions.

Intelligencer Journal.

The Leading Newspaper in the Garden Spot of America, Home Owned for Home Folks Since 1794

Lancaster County Highway Deaths Since Jan. 1, 1951
6
Same Date—1950—4

158th Year.—No. 204. | Lancaster City Zone Population, Official Figures of Audit Bureau of Circulations 112,897 | LANCASTER, PA., SATURDAY MORNING, FEBRUARY 10, 1951. | CITY | EIGHTEEN PAGES. | 30c PER WEEK—5c Per Copy

FLOOD HITS COLUMBIA WATER SUPPLY

ANOTHER VICTIM FOR DEATH HIGHWAY

Bulletin

PATROL ENTERS SEOUL

With The U. S. 25th Division, Korea, (Saturday) — (AP) — A South Korean patrol crossed the Han River today into the outskirts of Seoul and engaged enemy forces in a firefight.

US TROOPS GRAB SEOUL SUBURB, SWEEP TO HAN

Tokyo, (Saturday)—(AP)—U. S. troops today seized industrial Yongdungpo across the Han River from ruined Seoul, swept in force to the river and menaced the old capital's port of Inchon to the West.

An estimated 1,000 Reds, caught between two jaws of a pincer touching the Han on both sides of Seoul, fled across the river under firebomb and machinegun attack by pouncing warplanes.

They were the only enemy troops spotted still south of the Han on the approaches to Seoul. Enemy defenses before the city had vanished. Shells from tanks and howitzers screamed into Seoul.

Off the west coast the U. S. battleship Missouri slammed its 16-inch blockbuster shells into enemy positions around Inchon. Allied forces moving up three miles from Inchon sent a patrol into the port.

A field dispatch said Yongdungpo fell to the U.S. 25th Division without a shot being fired.

NO REARGUARD

An eighth Army spokesman said the enemy had pulled out from positions before Inchon and Seoul without even leaving a rearguard.

The "limited" offensive designed to seek out and destroy the enemy south of the Han, appeared at the start of the 17th day to be the first major victory of the Eighth

Turn To Page 13 For More Of WAR

"We Lead All The Rest"

FARM CORNER

By The Farm Editor

U.S. LOAN RATE OF 15 TO 54 CENTS A POUND FOR TYPE 53 TOBACCO

(Intell Washington Bureau)

Washington — The Department of Agriculture Friday announced a loan schedule ranging from 15 to 54 cents a pound for Pennsylvania and New York Havana seed tobacco, Type 53.

This is the first year in which support has been requested by the growers, the department said, because in the past market prices have exceeded the required support level, applicable under federal legislation.

There is no known Type 53 grown in Lancaster County, it was learned Friday night. However, sources point out that if any is grown here it is for experimental or novelty purposes. The binder type is known in northern counties of the state and New York state.)

The average loan level will be 25.5 cents per pound, assuming a crop of average quality. Prices received by growers for the 1949 crop averaged 22 cents a pound.

The 1950 crop is estimated at 1,510,000 pounds, compared with 1,455,000 in 1949.

Growers may obtain loans by

Turn To Page 4 For More Of FARM CORNER

Weather Calendar

COMPARATIVE TEMPERATURES

Station	High	Low
Water Works	22	6
Ephrata	25	6
Last Year (Ephrata)	30	30
Official High for Year Jan.	20	68
Official Low for Year Feb.	9	6
Character of Day		Clear

WINDS
Calm

SUN
Rises 7:04 a. m. Sets 5:33 p. m.

MOON
Sets 10:33 p. m. First Quarter, Feb. 20

STARS
Morning—Saturn
Evening—Venus, Mars, Jupiter

NEARBY FORECASTS
(U. S. Weather Bureau)

Maryland — Considerable cloudiness highest around 30 Saturday. Sunday partly cloudy and milder.

New Jersey and Delaware—Considerable cloudiness and continued cold Saturday highest near 30. Sunday partly cloudy and milder.

Lower Potomac and Chesapeake Bay—Winds northeast to east 10 to 15 MPH Saturday weather mostly cloudy some light snow likely over lower bay. Visibility fair to good.

EXTENDED FORECAST
(U. S. Weather Bureau)

Extended forecast for the period Saturday through Wednesday.

Eastern Pennsylvania, Eastern New York and Mid-Atlantic States—Temperature will average four to six degrees below normal; quite cold entire period but coldest Monday and Tuesday; some light snow likely Sunday and again about Wednesday.

Home Where 4 Were Burned Once Called Unfit For Habitation

Detectives Want To Know If Law Violated When Family Moved Into Tiny Concrete Block House In Rear Of Rockland Street

The sorry conditions under which some Lancastrians live was underscored Friday in a tragic fire in which a mother and her three children lost their lives.

The fatalities were directly the result of a kerosene stove explosion, according to City Firemen—but the building in which they occurred had been pronounced unfit for human habitation a year ago.

City detectives Friday began an investigation to determine why two families had been permitted to move into quarters which the City Board of Health had characterized as "not in a condition to meet the minimum requirements for human occupancy."

Captain of Detectives John P. Kirchner, in speaking of the investigation, emphasized that the police were not trying to determine the cause of the fire. "We know how that started," he said. "We want to know by what provision the family was permitted to move in. We are trying to determine if an ordinance has been violated.

Joyce Crawford

Mrs. Ida May Crawford, twenty-two, wife of Thomas Crawford, and her children, Joyce, three, Jean, two, and Thomas, Jr., eleven months, died in the early morning blaze which destroyed their temporary home at the rear of 515 Rockland St.

Mrs. Geneva McKinney, twenty-five, who is divorced, and her son, Clarence, two, escaped from the burning building. She told police that she was awakened when she saw flames shooting through the

Turn To Page 9 For More Of FIRE

WHOLESALE PRICES HIT RECORD HIGH DESPITE "FREEZE"

OPS Takes Steps To Prevent Meat Black Markets; Slaughtering Controlled

Washington — (AP) — Wholesale prices reached a new record high this week despite the two - weeks old price "freeze."

Meats, although under ceilings, shot up 3.2 percent. Wholesale prices as a whole rose 0.7 per cent, attaining a peak 16 per cent higher than before the Korean war.

As this was announced Friday, the Office of Price Stabilization took steps to prevent meat black markets by issuing an order controlling all commercial livestock slaughter.

The OPS hope is to keep the nation's meat stocks moving to the housewife at regulated prices. In World War II the grocer's meat counters were empty a large part of the time, while black markets flourished.

The wholesale price index, announced by the Bureau of Labor Statistics for the week ended Feb. 6, was 182.2, compared with 180.9 on Jan. 30. It was the 13th week in a row that a new record had been set.

The week's main increases were in prices of food and farm products, up 1.9 and 1.6 percent

Turn To Page 9 For More Of CONTROLS

CANCER IS FATAL TO BAND LEADER DUCHIN

New York —(AP)— Band leader Eddie Duchin, 41, whose nimble-fingered piano playing delighted millions of dancers, radio listeners and movie fans, died Friday night of cancer.

Only a few hours earlier, the Navy cited him for his World War II service.

He enlisted in the Navy at the age of 33 and served in some of the toughest engagements both in the Atlantic and Pacific.

Duchin studied to be a druggist and worked at a soda fountain as a youth before his great piano playing got him started on a musical career.

His first wife was a wealthy socialite, who died two years after their marriage and six days after the birth of his only son. He later married again.

He died in Memorial Hospital at 7:30 p. m.

J. Shober Barr Will Direct YMCA Drive For $26,000 For Activities

J. Shober Barr, director of athletics at Franklin and Marshall College, Friday was appointed general chairman of the Lancaster YMCA's annual budget campaign.

Goal of this year's campaign—from Feb. 15 to March 1—will be $26,000, H. Clay Burkholder, president of the board of directors, announced. The 1950 "Y" budget goal also was $26,000.

Mr. Barr served as chairman of the organization's annual budget canvass in 1948.

O. L. Hampton, general secretary of the YMCA, will serve as director of the campaign which will be carried on by a corps of 130 volunteer workers.

Leroy B. Breneman and Robert B. Myers will command the Red Division, with Robert A. Preston and John Hollinger heading the Blue Division.

Report meetings have been scheduled for Feb. 22 and March 1.

J. SHOBER BARR

AIRMAN DIES AFTER CRASH ON ROUTE 30

Wenonah, N.J., Man Fatally Hurt As Auto Skids On Ice

"Death Highway," the Lincoln Highway East, which claimed seven lives in automobile crashes last year, took its second victim of 1951 Friday, when Air Force Sgt. Philip C. Ellis, twenty-seven, Wenonah, N. J., died in Lancaster General Hospital.

He died at 6:10 p. m. Friday, four hours after his automobile skidded on ice-glazed Route 30, between Vintage and Leaman Place, crashing broadside with a tractor-semitrailer truck, according to state police.

Dr. H. K. Hogg, acting deputy coroner, said death was immediately due to a fractured skull. An autopsy of the body was dependent on instructions from the Commanding General at Olmstead Air Force Base, Middletown.

State Policemen V. P. Meilly and T. M. Nagle investigated. They reported that Ellis, alone in his car, was driving east, passing an eastbound truck. His car skidded on an icy patch of the highway and spun across into the westbound lane in front of a truck, driven by S. B. Caldwell, forty-six, Washington, Pa., R3. The passenger car was struck on the right side and was a total loss, Officer Nagle said.

The Christiana ambulance, returning from a trip to Lancaster, arrived at the scene shortly after the accident. The unconscious Ellis was taken to Lancaster Gen-

Turn To Page 9 For More Of ACCIDENT

Turnpike Speed Reduction From 70 To 60 Recommended

Harrisburg — (AP) — A new recommendation that the legal speed limit for automobiles be reduced from 70 to 60 miles an hour on the Pennsylvania Turnpike was heard Friday.

It came from the Pennsylvania Turnpike Safety Committee which met with representatives of the Turnpike Commission.

A nine-point program, drawn up by a subcommittee and approved Friday by the committee as a whole, also would limit the speed of heavy trucks on the state's toll road to 45 miles an hour.

The committee represents trucking interests, automobile clubs, bus companies, state police, the U.S. Army, car carriers and the Interstate Commerce Commission.

Earlier this week a bill was introduced in the House of Representatives by Rep. George A. Penglase (D-Philadelphia) to limit automobiles to 60 miles an hour on the Turnpike.

The bill, however, is at variance with the committee's recommended limit of trucks. It would hold trucks to maximums of 10 miles above the rate allowed on other state roads. At present they are allowed to go 20 miles faster.

Gerard Gilbert, Turnpike Commission safety engineer, said the committee's program, designed to aid in accident prevention, would

Turn To Page 9 For More Of TURNPIKE

Siedle Tells CAB Of North-South Air Service Need

Civil Aeronautics Board officials in Washington, D.C., Friday were given a first-hand account of Lancaster's need for North-South air service from the $2,500,000 Municipal Airport.

E. George Siedle, chairman of the Joint Air Facilities Committee of the Chamber of Commerce and Manufacturers' Association, placed Lancaster's case informally before two top CAB officials.

Originally the five-man Air Facilities Committee was scheduled to sit in on the "exploratory conference", but because of a mechanical failure in the airplane which was to transport the group, only Siedle made the trip, via rail.

Following the meeting with James H. Verner, CAB executive director, and Harry Brown, chief examiner, Siedle reported:

"I was told what we are seeking is not hopeless. However, we were told that a real job lies ahead."

Two things must be indicated clearly by Lancaster if it is to obtain the much-desired North-South

Turn To Page 9 For More Of SERVICE

POLICE TO PROSECUTE PROPERTY OWNERS FOR HAZARDOUS SIDEWALKS

Commissioner of Police Fred G. McCartney issued a warning Friday that a ice-covered city pavements must either be cleaned or cindered at once to safeguard pedestrians.

If persons in charge of the neglected properties fail to do this, McCartney said, prosecution will follow under the city ordinance which requires snow to be removed within five hours after it falls.

"We have received many complaints since Wednesday night's snow-fall," McCartney said, "and the calls have been more than justified."

If prosecution results, a fine of from $1 to $50 can be levied.

Ice, Water Over River Banks At Columbia

Ice chokes the Susquehanna River and thrusts against the buildings of the Columbia Lace Mill in this air view taken Friday as the river surged out of its banks behind a big ice jam. The rising waters forced the pumping station to cease operations, threatening the borough's supply of drinking water. (AP Photo)

HOOVER WARNS US NOT TO RISK LAND WAR WITH SOVIET

Former President Proposes Build-Up Of Sea, Air Power Instead

New York —(AP)— Former Republican President Herbert Hoover warned America Friday night to "stop, look and listen" before risking a land war with Soviet Russia. He said such a war "risks the loss of all civilization."

In his second major foreign policy speech in six weeks, Hoover proposed instead that America build up air and sea power and, if the Soviets attack Europe, pour it against Russia "until they have had enough."

In the light of later remarks, Hoover seemed to consider such air and sea power — plus Europe's will to defend itself — as Western civilization's first line of defense.

Hoover spoke to a nationwide au-

Turn To Page 9 For More Of HOOVER

TODAY DEADLINE FOR VOTE REINSTATEMENT

Saturday (today) is the deadline for 10,736 city and county voters whose names were stricken from the registration rolls for failure to vote to be reinstated.

Failure to mail or return in person reinstatement cards Saturday will require re-registration before they can cast a ballot in the 1951 municipal elections.

The names of those removed Feb. 1 were persons who had failed to cast a ballot for two consecutive years.

Registration clerks estimated that up to Friday less than 2,000 persons had returned signed reinstatement cards.

The cards may be mailed or the individuals can call in person at the office in the Court House from 8:30 a. m. to noon Saturday.

Senate Group Stamps OK On Limited 18-Year-Old Draft

Washington—(AP)—Limited authority to draft 18-year-olds, and extension of draft service from 21 to 24 months was voted Friday by the Senate Preparedness Subcommittee.

Further, the committee approved the idea of a modified "foreign legion" proposal, under which up to 125,000 "carefully screened" foreigners could enlist in the U.S. Army during the next five years.

Chairman Lyndon Johnson (D-Texas) said the vote on the 18-year-olds plan in the subcommittee, a branch of the Senate Armed Services Committee, was 7 to 1. Senator Morse (R-Ore) dissented.

Under this plan, draft boards would have to take all available men in the present 19 to 25 age group, before drafting any 18-year-olds. Then, they would have to take first those nearing the age of 19, such as those 18 years and 9 months old.

In voting to extend the draft service from the present 21 months, the Senate group decided to put the total of 24 months not counting leave time.

A serviceman's leave time accumulates at a rate of a month each year. Thus, if he took his leave his service would extend 2 years, 2 months and about a week.

The Pentagon had asked a 27-month minimum service. It also had asked flat permission to draft 18-year-olds.

The legislation now goes to the full 13-member Armed Services Committee headed by chairman

Turn To Page 9 For More Of DRAFT

Air Raid Test Preparations Nearly Complete

Preparations were virtually complete Friday evening for the first full-scale mock air raid on Pennsylvania Saturday (today) since World War II.

The raid, by "enemy" squadrons of planes, won't involve the general public except that you'll hear the wailing of sirens sometime between 2 and 4 p. m.

Civil Defense officials expressed the hope you'll remember the sounds of those sirens and consider what you'd do if the sirens signalled a real enemy attack.

The test will be repeated Sunday.

Meanwhile, the Lancaster County Civil Defense control center was opened Friday. It is on the second floor of the Manufacturers' Association. Chairs and tables were moved in, telephones installed and charts and maps hung in preparation for the week-end tests.

In another development, Col. J. Hale Steinman, county Civil De-

Turn To Page 9 For More Of TESTS

ONLY 1½ DAYS' NORMAL USAGE NOW AVAILABLE

Pumping Station Inundated; Residents Warned To Boil All Water

A severe flash flood struck the river communities of Columbia and Washington Boro Friday, curtailing all operations of the Columbia Pumping Station and inundating virtually all the homes in the low section of Washington Boro. Factories in Columbia were ordered closed at noon, idling about 2,000 workers in order to save the borough's supply of drinking water.

A state of extreme emergency existed late Friday night in Columbia, where officials estimated the water supply will last only until Sunday.

T. H. Kain, superintendent of the Water Works, issued a warning to all Columbia residents to boil their drinking water, since emergency measures are being undertaken.

Water from a nearby creek, Kain said, is being by-passed into the Columbia reservoir after a temporary chlorinating process, and such water should be boiled before drinking it. Only 200 gallons per minute is being obtained by this "by-pass" method, he said, and will not greatly aid the extreme water shortage.

The localized flood, which struck with suddenness early Friday morning, caught most residents of Washington Boro completely unprepared for evacuation. Persons scrambled as best they could to upper floors, lugging household goods with them.

Turn To Page 13 For More Of FLOOD

Trainmen Fined $25,000 For Dec. "Sick" Walkout

By The Associated Press

The Brotherhood of Railroad Trainmen, whose members have just ended a long and costly strike, was fined $25,000 Friday for engaging in a similar "sick" walkout in December.

Federal Judge Michael L. Igoe found the union guilty of contempt of court in a hearing at Chicago.

The union faces similar charges for the second walkout of switchmen which started Jan. 30.

This walkout virtually collapsed Thursday after the Army issued a "work or be fired" edict. All mail and express service has been restored but it will take some time to straighten out the freight tangle.

MASS FORMATION

Judge Igoe ruled that the strikers acted in mass formation, but he discharged 40 individuals also on trial in the case. These included National BRT officers and local

Turn To Page 9 For More Of TRAINMEN

WASHINGTON BORO P. O. FORCED TO MOVE—B. F. Sherick's store—the post office for Washington Boro — which was flooded out Friday is shown above. Water from the ice-jammed river flooded out the first floor of the building, and the post office equipment was moved to higher ground. In the center of the photo, under the ice cream sign, can be seen the top of an auto, caught in the flood waters. (Intell Photo)

Mink Blended

Let-Out Marmot Capes

$125

These Elegant New Capes, Made of Silky Imported Fur, Are The Nearest Resemblance to Mink. They're a Wonderful Value at This Price

Shop Garvin's For Spring Fur Scarfs, Capes, Jackets and Stoles

Convenient Credit Terms Arranged

GARVIN'S—Third Floor *Plus Tax*

Pure Silk Squares & Novelty Ties

To Circle Your Throat . . . To Loop Through a Belt . . . Or Around Your Waist

98c

Choose from a wide variety: tuck-in ascots, stubby ascots, long pleated scarfs, long chiffon print scarfs, long sheer chiffon scarfs . . . plain or hand painted. Also 18" hand-rolled squares, 24" ombre & print squares. 36" chiffon or silk squares. Large assortment of patterns & solid colors.

GARVIN'S—Neckwear Dept.—First Floor

SALE! Salesman's Samples Ass't. Fancy Linens

29c to 14.21

regularly 39c to 18.95

Printed tablecloths in spun rayon, all linen or sailcloth, linen & rayon damask sets, printed towels, scarfs & vanity sets, sheet sets, boxed pillow cases, etc. Many only one of a kind. Because they are samples, they're 25% less than the regular price.

GARVIN'S—Linen Dept.—First Floor

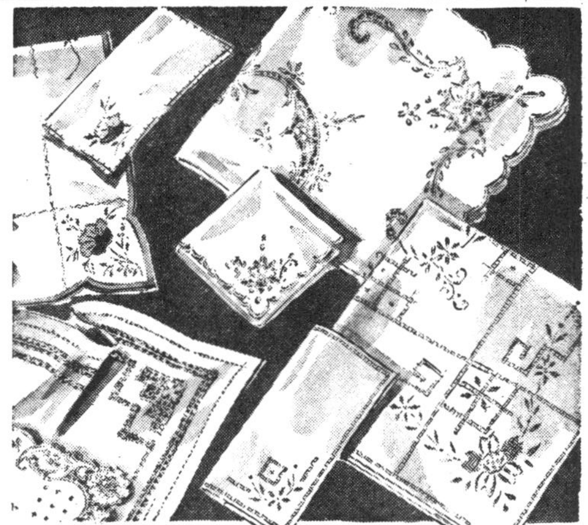

GARVIN'S

"It Works" says Paulette Goddard

How to Lose Weight and Look Lovelier
Now! Lose weight the way Nature intended you to! The Ayds Plan is a quick, easy way with no risk to health. When you take Ayds before meals as directed, you can eat what you want—all you want.

Users report losing up to ten pounds or more with their very first box. You will lose weight with your first box or money back ($2.98).

● "More and more women are finding the Ayds Way really works," says lovely movie star, Paulette Goddard. "It's such an easy, pleasant way to reduce. I recommend it to all my friends!"

GARVIN'S—Candies—First Floor

The Nearest Thing To An Indestructible Shirt

Wings "Super-Fort" White Dress Shirts

With Guaranteed Airplane Cloth Collar & Cuffs

3.95

Gleaming white, high count broadcloth "Super-Fort" shirt . . . carefully tailored. Both collar and cuffs are made of genuine airplane cloth and are both guaranteed for the life of the shirt. Sizes 14 to 17.

GARVIN'S—Men's Shop—First Floor

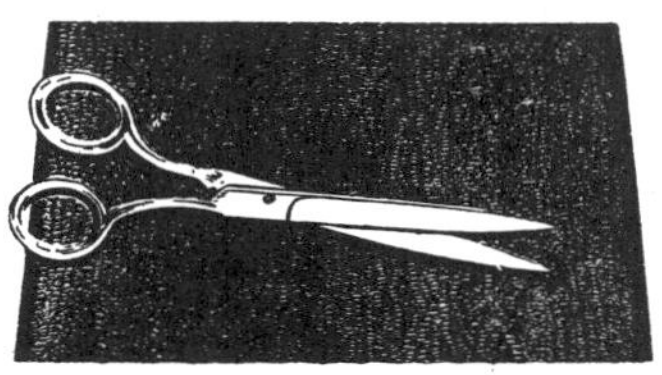

Swank Tidy-Tie Tools

2.50 *Plus Tax*

Pretty sharp—this two-tone Tie Klip! Swank has fashioned a whole kit of them, patterned after familiar and useful tools. Also available in pearl inlay. Come in and pick out one or more to go with your favorite ties. Swank miniatures include: scissors, saw, hammer, spade & axe.

Other Swank Jewelry Items, Cuff Links & Tie Chains *(Plus Tax)* . . . 2.50 to 7.50

GARVIN'S—Men's Shop—First Floor

Proudly Presenting

Silver & Gold

A Smart New Color Combination In Spring Ties

Fashioned by Wembley

$2

Wembley spring ties . . . for the man in her life. Each beautiful pattern in six different spring color combinations.

Other Ties $1 & 1.50

GARVIN'S—Men's Shop—First Floor

Tru-Health Shoulder Braces & Health Belts

Deluxe Wide Health Belts

4.50

Scientifcially designed for large abdomens. For men and women. Comfortably supports abdomen. Controls waist-line. Sizes 30 to 53.

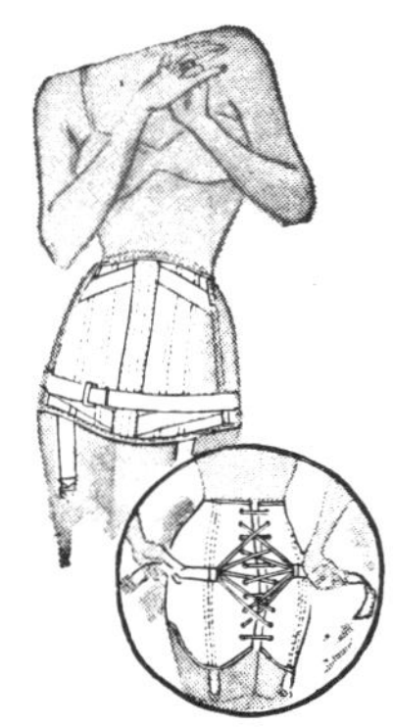

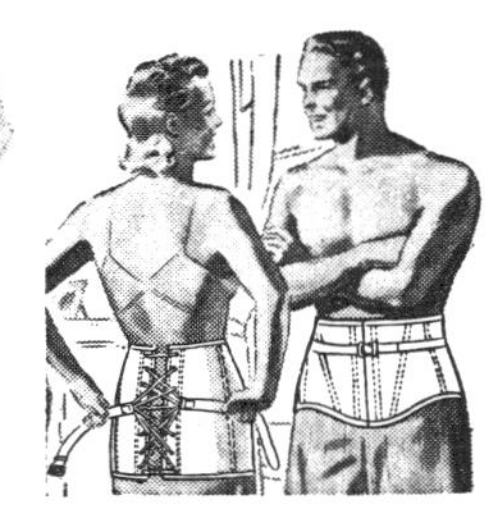

Tru-Health Health Belts

$2

Supports the back. Improves the posture. Reduces the abdomen. Sizes 25 to 47.

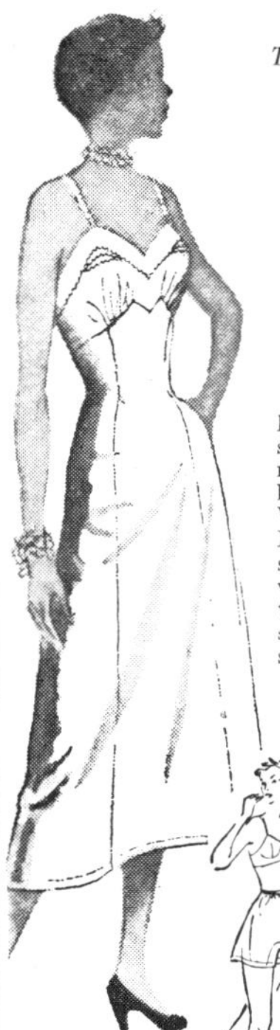

They Look Lovely When You Buy Them . . . Stay Lovely Through Countless Washings

Knitted Nylon Undies

1.95 to 7.95

Knitted nylon jersey slips . . . plain tailored, run proof, two-bar tricot knit, wide hem bottom. White, sizes 34 to 42. Knitted nylon jersey slips trimmed with net, white or pink. Sizes 34 to 42. Knitted nylon jersey briefs, trunks or stepins.

GARVIN'S—Second Floor

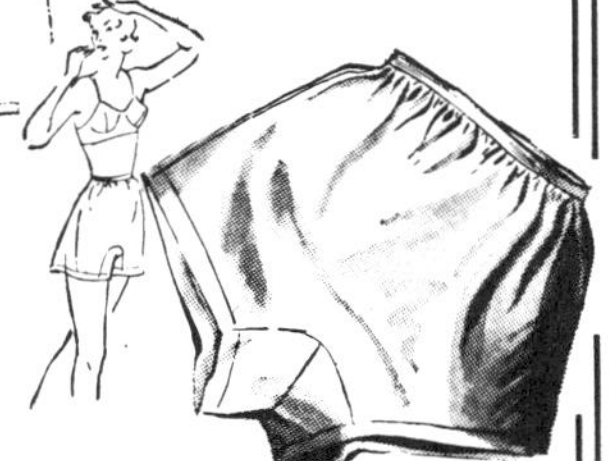

Pick Your Flowers While They're Fresh

49c to 98c

Wonderful assortment, for your hat, suit, coat or dress. Violets, roses, lilies of the valley, pansies, lilacs, gardenias, geraniums, etc. Also flower corsages with pins in assorted dainty styles.

GARVIN'S—First Floor

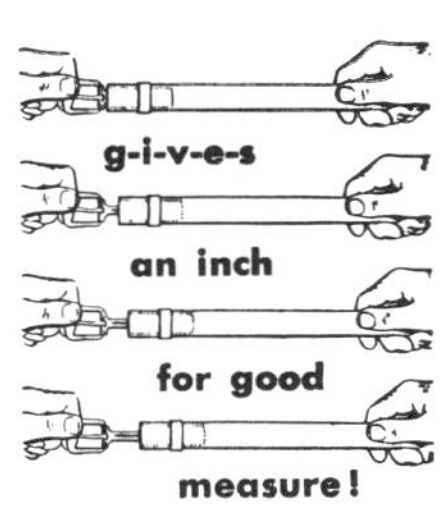

The Belt of the Year by Pioneer

Stretchway

$2 & 2.50

Here at last! A brand new idea in belt comfort — for men of action. Pioneer patented spring action makes Stretchway the true luxury belt! Finely styled in a range of quality leathers. Black, tan, grey or brown. Sizes 30 to 50.

Tru-Health Shoulder Braces

$2

Straightens round shoulders. Supports back. Aids in correct breathing. Helps your posture. For men and women. Sizes 25 to 50.

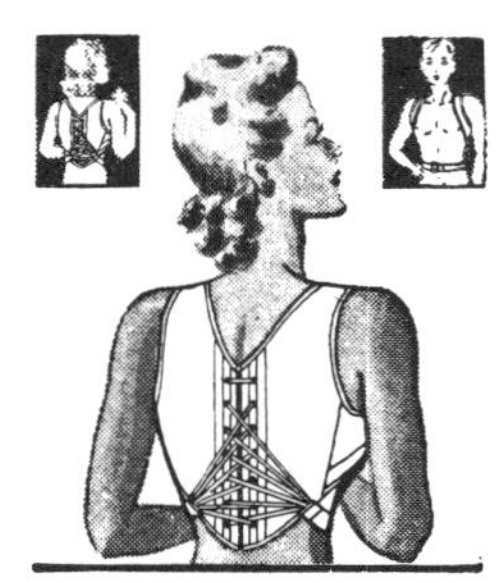

The New Way To Serve Smart Parties

Hasco Lap Trays

With 3 Gold Letter Monograms At No Extra Cost

2.49 Set of 4

Perfect for luncheons, buffets, bridge, dinners, suppers. In plain walnut or mahogany. Also decorated with yellow roses, red roses or puppies. No table crowding or table setting. Guests are more comfortable, parties are peppier, hostesses happier. Size 7½"x16" . . . set of 4 in smart gift pkg.

GARVIN'S—Housewares Dept.—Basement

Mirro-Matic Pressure Cookers
10.95 to 17.95

Hammered Alum. & Chrome Bread Trays . . 1.19 to 3.19

Nut Bowls with Nut Crackers & Picks 3.19

Sandwich Trays . . 1.19 & 3.19

Butter Dishes, 1.89

Candy Dishes, 1.59 & 2.19

Fruit Bowls . . 1.19 & 1.95

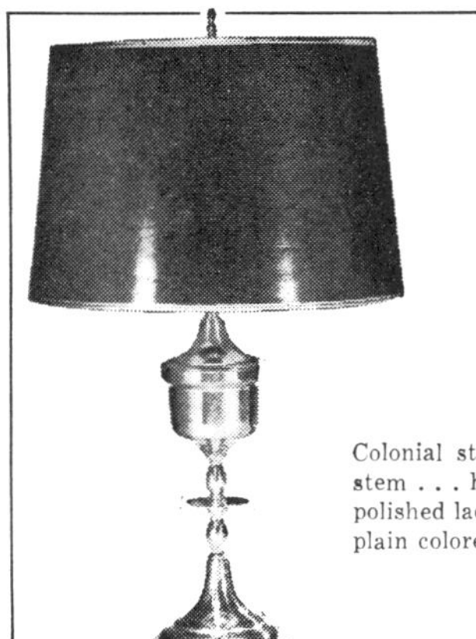

Colonial Styled

Solid Brass Table Lamps

5.95

Colonial styled table lamp with solid brass stem . . . heavily weighted base . . . highly polished lacquered finish. 23 inches high . . . plain colored shades of wine or green.

GARVIN'S—Housefurnishings—Fourth Floor

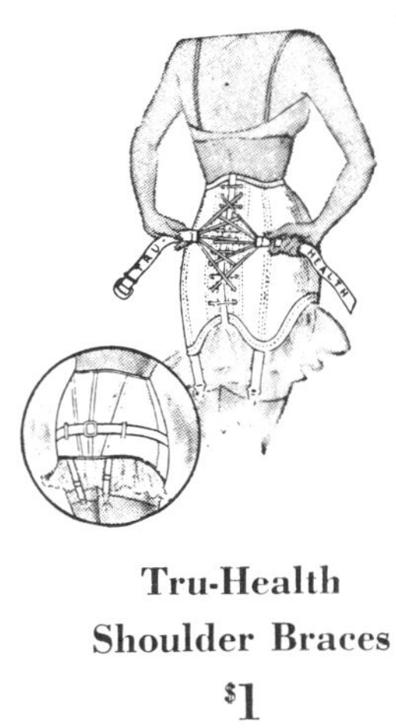

Tru-Health Health Belts

3.50

Fine quality fabric. Flesh color. With supporters. Sizes 25 to 43.

Tru-Health Shoulder Braces

$1

Supports the back. Improves the posture. Reduces the abdomen. Sizes 25 to 47.

GARVIN'S Notions—First Floor

Our Ideas

It's Up to Truman Now

Having published, at some length, an analysis of the Far Eastern situation and our position in it by John S. Knight, readers may be interested in Mr. Knight's appraisal of where we go from here.

For one thing, he says flatly that "with MacArthur gone, it is now up to Truman." He writes:

* * * *

In making up your mind as to our future foreign policy in Asia, these factors should be taken into consideration:

1. Nationalist China, our ally, was treacherously "sold down the river" to Stalin by Roosevelt and Churchill at the Yalta conference.

This "sell-out" was later further implemented by the Truman administration's open encouragement of the Chinese Communists and its indifference to the fate of Formosa and Korea, as became evident in various public utterances made by Secretary of State Dean Acheson.

2. China is now dominated by the Reds, once erroneously called "agrarian reformers" by the late Gen. Joe Stillwell.

They have millions of well-trained troops as against Chiang Kai-shek's mythical army of 600,000" now garrisoned in Formosa, actually some 350,000 or 400,000.

If we become involved in all-out war with Red China, Chiang's army would be useful, but not determinative. Moreover, we would be committed to send arms, supplies and men to Chiang in any projected invasion of the continent.

The hopelessness of any such a land invasion is best typified by this story. Back in the days when China was warring with Japan, an American remarked to a Chinese that he was surprised at the vast number of Chinese who were being killed by the enemy. The Chinese replied: "Japanese kill 10 Chinese, while Chinese kill only one Japanese. Pretty soon, no more Japanese."

* * * *

3. The United States went into Korea under the flag of the United Nations to repel international banditry on the principle of maintaining collective security.

We have won no decisive victory because as William R. Matthews, editor of the Arizona Star says: "We should see by now that most governments, despite expressions of the noblest sentiments, simply will not assume sacrifices in remote disputes where their interests are not apparently involved."

4. Korea is of no strategic military value to us. It is instead a distinct liability. Ultimate victory would find us with a devastated country and more than 25,000,000 helpless, homeless and hungry people on our hands.

* * * *

It would appear, therefore, that having been the victims of bungling diplomacy in the first instance, and of an impossible military commitment in the second, thought should now be given to the advisability of withdrawing our forces from Korea while strengthening our air and naval power along the Japan-Okinawa-Ruyukus-Phillipine defense perimeter.

To the diplomats, this would mean losing face. Such a move might tend also to weaken the determination of European nations to resist Russia on the continent, although in the past their irresolute policy in Korea has been matched by their fear of MacArthur's burning conviction that war is war and you can't achieve victory without hitting the enemy where it hurts.

Since the United States and the United Nations won't win the Korean war under present rules, one alternative is to negotiate a "peace" by some diplomatic gimmick; the other is to withdraw.

* * * *

With MacArthur gone, it is now up to Truman.

As we commented last Thursday, we and the United Nations had better get into high gear with some basic and enduring decisions on foreign policy in the Far East.

Unhappily, nothing that President Truman said in his address of Wednesday night offers much encouragement that either he or his vacillating Secretary of State could recognize a sound foreign policy if it was handed to them on a platter.

Piling Up a Good Record

The general public seems to have little appreciation of one tremendous job being done for UN troops wounded in Korea. That is the swift evacuation of casualties by the Military Air Transport Service (MATS) and other Air Force evacuation units.

True, a number of newspaper and magazine feature articles have been written about MATS. But it goes about its work of life-saving in such quiet, unspectacular fashion that it just doesn't rate daily headlines. Yet, thanks to these huge, long-range flying hospitals, thousands of wounded UN fighters are being hospitalized in Japan and the United States more speedily, more comfortably and more economically than ever before in warfare's tragic history.

During the UN withdrawals in North Korea, when the Chinese Communists, flushed with initial victory, swarmed down from Manchuria, the Fifth Air Force and the Troop Carrier Command flew 14,812 patients from Korea to Japan, in one eight-day period, 3,192 of them within six hours. During the first six months of the Korean war, MATS flew out a total of 15,939 patients, 12,462 of them Korean casualties.

Though the public generally may not be too aware of the MATS' flying hospital service, you can bet that the thousands of casualties who benefited and their families know about it — with deep gratitude.

This Could Be Serious

Boyle

Dexter Embarrassed by Valentino Role

NEW YORK, April 18 —(AP)— A young clergyman's son is perturbed at the task of enacting the life story of the screen's greatest lover—Rudolph Valentino.

"I feel embarrassed," admitted Anthony Dexter.

Hal Boyle

He feels a little worried, too, wondering how middle-aged housewives and their teen-age daughters will react to his portrayal of the all-time film sheik.

The film, "Valentino," produced by Edward Small for Columbia pictures, has been a 13-year project. The studio says Dexter, a 31-year-old stage actor, got the role over 75,000 candidates.

Dexter, the son, grandson, great-grandson and nephew of clergymen, was born in Nebraska and christened Walter Reinhold Alfred Frederick Fleischmann. Figuring that was too much for the average theater marquee, he changed his name to Walter Craig. His producer changed it again to Anthony Dexter after signing him for the Valentino part in 1947.

Elegant Sideburns

In the years since then Dexter spent his time studying Valentino, learning tango dancing, bull whip cracking, fencing, "watching polo and football games and waiting for the writers to finish a script."

This also gave him plenty of time to grow an elegant pair of sideburns. The sideburns, long enough to cover his upper molars, still make him uneasy. People stare at them, just as they would if a 1927 flapper pranced by them.

"Playing the role of a great lover—you've got three strikes against you before you start," said Dexter, a bit morosely. "I am no more like Valentino than you are."

I thought this was rather gracious of him, as I am more often compared to the late Lon Chaney, Sr.

Actually Dexter bears quite a resemblance to Valentino.

"I'm about an inch taller than he was and weigh ten pounds more," he admitted. "But he had black hair and was darker; he had an olive complexion. Also he was a good horseman. I used to do a little calf riding out of chutes back in the Middlewest, but I wouldn't know what to do with an Eastern Saddle."

Valentino Shy, Moody

Valentino died of peritonitis in 1926. Dexter feels the legend has outgrown the man.

"He was a shy, quiet moody type—worried a lot," he said. He was intelligent and had a good head on him. The people who used to work with him say he was straightforward and cooperative. He didn't run around with women. He was a hell of a good mechanic and liked to putter around with motors."

LANCASTER NEW ERA
and EXAMINER
Published every evening except Sunday at 8 West King Street, Lancaster, Pa.
— by —
NEW ERA COMPANY
J. F. Steinman............President
J. H. Carter............Editor
I. Z. Buckwalter............G. Mgr.
Members: Audit Bureau of Circulations
MEMBERS OF THE ASSOCIATED PRESS

TERMS TO SUBSCRIBERS: By carriers 30c per week, $3.90 for 3 months: $7.75 for 6 months; $15.45 per year. By mail on R F D Routes or in towns in Lancaster and adjoining counties where no delivery service is maintained $10.00 per year; $5.50 for 6 months; $2.90 for 3 months; $1.00 for 1 month. By mail outside of Lancaster and adjoining counties $15.45 per year; $7.75 for 6 months; $3.90 for 3 months. $1.30 for 1 month. All mail subscriptions payable in advance.

The Era Hears—

By The New Era Staff

Life in Lancaster . . .

Show business has a new Lancaster sister juggling act that may someday take top billing in entertainment.

For the two little girls — Francine, ten, and Rita, eight, daughters of Mr. and Mrs. Harry Rose — life began on a circus lot. It looks as if they'll spend a lot of their time in the future in the world of greasepaint.

New Era Photo

Francine (right) and Rita Rose.

Although their father, who is a member of the theatrical agency of Cooke and Rose, is maintaining their status, as amateur for the time being, they already have several distinctions:

They're the youngest girl juggling act ever known,' and one of the few in action today. And Francine, who does the juggling with her sister as assistant, is believed to be the only girl juggling on a "rollo."

(A "rollo" consists of a log under a small platform on which the performer stands. As Francine juggles, her feet keep the "rollo" moving from left to right and back again. If you think it's easy, try it.)

Juggling came into Francine's life when she and Rita spent a week's vacation with the Hunt Bros. Circus last Summer. They were the guests of the Colleano Family, top acrobats and jugglers. On their return Francine received parental permission to give up the accordion, at which she was pretty good, and start juggling.

The clubs Francine learned with were given her by Trixie, ice show juggling star, and her father, Oscar Frischkee. Now she can keep four objects in the air at one time. She specializes in hoops, balls and spinning plates, and works on a rolling globe as well as the rollo.

She practices at least two hours a day, every day, voluntarily. Francine's in the fifth grade at Fulton School, and Rita's in the third, and their father feels they're both excellent students.

Rose and his wife are both show business veterans. He had his own circus when the children were born, but he sold the show during the war to enter booking. He wants to see the girls complete their schooling, and then he thinks they'll do okay with their act.

The girls will spend another week this Summer with the Hunt Bros. show. They also will attend the jugglers' convention at Williamsport.

— Gerry Lestz

Out of the Past

25 YEARS AGO

HEADS EDUCATORS—Prof. Paul E. Witmyer, superintendent of Columbia schools, was elected president of the Superintendents' and Principals' Conference of the local Normal School District, comprising Lancaster, York and Lebanon counties.

BOYS' WEEK — Nine civic organizations, including Rotary, Kiwanis, Lions, Exchange, and American Business Clubs, the American Legion, Boy Scouts, YMCA and Playground Association, announced they will sponsor Boys' Week here, May 1 to 8.

10 YEARS AGO

WHEATLAND CELEBRATION — A colorful patriotic ceremony, including music by four outstanding school bands, will be held at Wheatland in celebration of the sesqui-centennial of the birth of James Buchanan, Pennsylvania's only president.

NAZI VICTORY — Col. Charles A. Lindberg, in an address delivered at a rally sponsored by the American First Committee, expressed the opinion that a Nazi victory was an accomplished fact, and that England and France were defeated before they began to fight.

PEGLER ON VACATION

Westbrook Pegler is on a 4-week vacation. His column will be resumed late in May.

Joseph Alsop

Iran Being Gnawed to Death by Red Group

TEHERAN, April 18—There is a very simple measure of the folly of the Iranian ruling class and the flabby short-sightedness of American and British policy here.

This country is being gnawed to death by a headless worm. Nowhere else in the world could the Tudeh party, without any nationally known leader, with only the smallest hard core of true Communists, constitute a serious threat. But as recent events all too clearly testify, the Tudeh party is a serious threat in Iran.

Joseph Alsop

You ask any Iranian who heads the Tudeh, who leads and directs it, and even if he is one of the Tudeh's young intellectual fellow travellers, he replies with a shrug, "the Soviet Embassy."

The whole party financing, estimated at the locally enormous sum of 2,000,000 tomans a month, is openly derived from Soviet sources. Much of the flood of Tudeh literature is printed by a "clandestine" press in the Soviet embassy's huge compound. In short, a more naked operation would be hard to imagine.

Soviet Influence Strong

In addition, the nature of Soviet intentions in Iran was disclosed as bluntly as possible during the Azerbaijan crisis in 1946, when the Tudeh following melted down almost to the hard core alone. Finally the party operates under the handicap of illegality. Although the Partisans of Peace and League to Combat the Anglo-Iranian oil company serve as useful fronts, the fact that the party is theoretically illegal at least causes inconvenience.

In the face of all this, the Tudeh has completely penetrated what passes for a labor movement in Iran. With the memory of Azerbaijan fading, it has made such headway among younger men that 50 per cent of the university students and recent graduates are estimated to be members or fellow travellers.

It possesses its own underground communications net, including a large radio station in Shiraz, and it sends its orders about the country as rapidly as the Iranian government itself. It is able to unleash strikes and severe disorders wherever and whenever it desires, as the last days have shown. And if present conditions continue unchanged, it will go on gaining strength and will almost inevitably win in the end.

Four Causes Cited

There are four causes for this situation.

First, and most important of all, Iran's own leading men, the landlords and merchant-politician-millionaires who control the country, have signally failed to put the national house in order. The wartime occupation swelled the urban proletariat and opened the eyes of the peasant masses to the wretchedness of their lot. But the weak and corrupt postwar governments have utterly failed to combat the misery and hopelessness that daily increases here.

Second, the masters of the Kremlin about a year ago shrewdly changed their whole tone towards Iran, abandoning loud menace for smooth amiability. No longer reminded daily of the danger in the north, the Iranian politicians have been encouraged both to forget their dependence for protection on the West, and to fall out more readily among themselves.

Third, the British long continued to behave here, almost as though this were still the epoch of the Darcy concession. They seemed to think anything and everything could still be "arranged" in the old way until the shock of oil nationalization woke them up.

Fourth and finally, the Americans have made almost every conceivable mistake, arousing great hopes of lavish economic aid which never came; arousing great hopes also of helping the Iranians to escape from their unhappy position between the Russians and British but making no effort to do so; neither working intimately with the British nor developing an independent policy; occasionally intervening to influence local political events but never intervening decisively to produce a real result.

Chaos Was Created

In the chaos thus created, the Tudeh has emerged as the only truly organized and powerful national grouping. Besides the Tudeh, there is only the band of politicians of the National Front, led by Dr. Mussadegh, and their religious fanatic allies, the Fedayan Islam of the Mullah Kashani, one of whose followers murdered Gen. Razmara. The murder of Razmara, as everyone knows, led to the oil nationalization vote. As a result the National Front now dominates the official political scene.

But of these events also, the Tudeh will inherit the benefits. On the one hand, the political assassinations have largely demoralized the run of the mill Iranian politicians. On the other hand, the bitter outburst of anti-foreign feeling has greatly diminished the opportunities for American and British policy to influence the situation. And meanwhile nationalization itself remains as an immense, unsolved problem, to complicate, confuse and violently exaggerate the whole political process.

The likelihood of some sort of eventual explosion is all too plain. Fortunately, American and British influence has not been wholly dissipated. The Shah remains a commanding figure and the Army, still loyal to the Shah, still seems able to control the situation. If bold, clear headed action is taken in Washington, London and Teheran, a disaster here may yet be avoided. But this action must be taken very soon.

James Marlow

MacArthur Day Ideal for Sneak Attack

WASHINGTON, April 18. —(AP)— Washington is a bombardier's dream.

An enemy who wanted to drop an atomic bomb couldn't pick a better time than tomorrow, MacArthur Day, with all the big government brass here.

But, except for MacArthur, tomorrow is like most any other weekday in the capital:

All the key men in the government are bunched together in a really small area: President, Vice President, Cabinet, Congress, Army, Navy, Air Force.

James Marlow

True, all work in separate offices and separate buildings but when the bombs start falling those buildings aren't far apart.

In addition, hundreds of thousands of government workers are concentrated here.

So the brains and records and nerve centers of the government are jammed together in a relatively small area.

Congress has been chewing over the idea that maybe something ought to be done to make Washington a less easy target or, rather, to spread out the government a bit so it wouldn't all be wiped out in one attack.

70 Per Cent Might Get Through

If you think the Air Force could keep enemy bombers away, just remember that the top Air Force people say:

No air-defense system, no matter how perfect nor how well developed, can be relied upon to stop completely a determined enemy attack. Top Air Force officials have estimated as many as 70 per cent of any attacking planes would get through to drop their bombs.

So today the Senate was finally getting around to consideration of a bill that would disperse some government agencies.

There's quite a difference between "disperse" and "decentralize."

Decentralize means transferring federal agencies, or parts of them, to places far removed from the capital because they're the kind that can do their work, in war or peace, far from here.

For example, bureaus in the Agriculture Department, dealing with animals, could be moved to the midwest or somewhere else.

Disperse means moving essential government agencies — very essential to what's being done in Washington — from the heart of Washington to some place outside it but not more than 20 miles away.

For example, it might be possible to disperse some parts of the Treasury Department.

Can't Disperse Congress

But neither the President nor Congress could very well be dispersed. If they were, Washington would hardly be the capital any more.

A subcommittee of the Senate's committee on public works held a lot of hearings on the problem of dispersing some government agencies.

Briefly, if this bill became law this is what would happen:

The government, on land it bought, would put up four big buildings within 20 miles of Washington, in nearby Virginia and Maryland.

Each of the buildings would be big enough for 5,000 workers. And highways would be built by-passing Washington and, by offshoots, leading into it.

These highways would serve several purposes: General traffic which wanted to use the highways to by-pass Washington could do so; there'd be faster and easier travel between Washington and the dispersed agencies; and in event of attack these highways could be used in evacuating some of the Washington population.

Would Cost $107,000,000

The cost of land, buildings, and highways would run about $107,000,000.

This would, of course, have nothing to do with decentralization of the government, since the less essential government agencies could be moved to far-away places where and when room was found for them.

During World War II some agencies were decentralized, taking about 30,000 workers out of crowded Washington. After the war most of them came back.

Whether anything comes of this bill is something else. At least the ice has been broken to make Washington less inviting as a target.

Victor Riesel

Reds' Secret Tactics Inside Labor Bared

CAN you think of any 720 persons — some of whom would have to be women — whom you could mobilize in Michigan for successful seizure of almost half of Henry Ford's huge, and militarily vital, River Rouge plant? Sound fantastic? Yet that's just what the Communists apparently have succeeded in doing in the past few months.

No direct assault, of course. They simply moved into Detroit their top national "agitation-propagandists" (agit-props) and most brilliant organizers from their "Trade Union Commission" in New York. And today the Communists exert great influence over, or control directly, the men who speak for almost 30,000 CIO Ford workers in seven of the sprawling buildings at that famed gargantuan plant, now the hub of an industrial machine with over one billion dollars in war orders.

And there are exactly 720 Communist party members in Michigan today according to an undercover FBI count. So, the next time you hear the professional intellectuals chide you, as though you were a pre-Ice Age fossilized skull, for worrying about what exactly 43,217 U. S. Communist party members can do — remember Ford River Rouge.

I'd like to tell you what these few disciplined thousands are in a position to do right through our industrial-war production life line, right this minute.

Could Cripple Steel Mills

Our security police at this moment are closely watching one man who is in a position to choke off production in giant steel mills, huge blast furnaces and tin plate plants. Again, it may sound fantastic. But, he is a friend of those who believe the recent Communist Peace Crusade is a great boon to humanity. And he can call a strike which would choke off supplies going into, and millions of tons rolling out of, the world's greatest industrial system. Yup — just like that. It might not last long. But, however long it lasted, it would hurt bad.

Our security police know of Communist cells, just a handful of people, gentlemen, who can start, right now, a bitter race riot in one of the giant steel mills not too far out of Chicago.

All this, of course, in addition to what the party can do in and around our atomic energy motor building plants, jet factories, etc., all in the electronic field — not the least vulnerable of which are the Pittsburgh Westinghouse plants and the northeastern General Electric installations.

How do they do it? Well, here's how they did it at Ford River Rouge where they even elected "with overwhelming majorities," the five pro-Commies on trial before the union on charges of "subservience to the Communist party." Here's how they did it despite the fight by Walter Reuther, himself a brilliant strategist.

First, they rehashed for themselves, in specially assigned little Communist party commissions, all grievances found among the plant's 60,000 workers. Then they set their best propaganda writers in New York and Detroit working on a constant flow of leaflets and speeches.

Here Is Their Plan

According to their own special report from the plant itself:

"The central feature of the 'Progressive' campaign (at Ford) was a "Straight From the Shoulder" peace offensive. Tabloids, leaflets and mass meetings explained to the workers that war is not inevitable. Progressives warned that conversion to war production would not bring peace and prosperity. . .

To this were added demands for "pie in the sky." Huge wage increases, lowering of production standards and speeds, special upgrading for Negroes, heavy taxes on industry and lowering of excises on workers, removal of all wartime restrictions which cause layoffs in civilian production, and even control of company rights to produce machines in its other plants.

There were hundreds of other demands, all tailor-made to fit all grievances. And that's exactly what to look for in all industries. Then watch for strike sentiment to be whipped up when the companies don't dish out this "pie in the sky" on red hot platters.

The Unseen Audience

By H. T. Webster

I LIKE YOUR INTEREST IN EDUCATION, BUT DON'T OVER-DO IT. YOU OUGHT TO GET AWAY FROM YOUR STUDIES NOW AND THEN. REMEMBER THAT ALL WORK AND NO PLAY MAKES JACK A DULL BOY
TV, THE NEW AID TO EDUCATION

WEATHER
(U. S. Weather Bureau)
Eastern Pennsylvania: Fair And A Little Warmer Saturday, Highest 80 To 85 Degrees. Sunday Some Cloudiness And Warm With High Humidity.

Intelligencer Journal.

The Leading Newspaper in the Garden Spot of America. Home Owned for Home Folks Since 1794

159th Year.—No. 18. | Lancaster City Zone Population, Official Figures of Audit Bureau of Circulations 112,897 | LANCASTER, PA., SATURDAY MORNING, JULY 7, 1951. | CITY | EIGHTEEN PAGES. | 30c PER WEEK—5c Per Copy

INDIA'S RESISTANCE

Prime Minister Nehru is keeping everyone at arms' length, says J. M. Roberts, Jr., AP news analyst. For more on the Indian situation see today's Editorial Page.

$62,000,000 AIR BASE PROPOSED HERE

Red Envoys Believed Moving Toward Kaesong

Allied Planes Stay Far Away From Road Convoy Will Follow

Communists Allow Themselves Enough Time For Snail's-Pace Progress Down Highway Used By North Korean Invaders At Start Of War

Tokyo, (Saturday) — (AP) — Red negotiators were presumed to be moving south today from Pyongyang in a 10-vehicle convoy, bound for a Sunday meeting at Kaesong with allied representatives to discuss preliminaries for a Korean cease-fire conference.

Several hours after they were scheduled to depart this morning from the North Korean capital, there was no word whether they actually had left.

Allied aircraft are not likely to pick up movement of the Communist convoy. An American Air Force officer said:

"We are staying so far away from that road with our planes that I doubt that we'll get any word on the movement of the convoy. We are even keeping spotter planes out of that territory."

The Communists had allowed themselves sufficient time for almost snail's pace progress down the bomb-pitted Pyongyang - Seoul highway used by North Koreans in invading South Korea at the outset of the 54-weeks-old war.

They were to meet at Kaesong, three miles south of parallel 38, with three allied colonels for preliminary cease-fire talks.

North Koreans captured Kaesong, ancient former capital, at the outset of the invasion June 25, 1950.

Seven days of radio exchanges ended late Friday night with agreement opening the way for a possible stop to the fighting. Sunday's negotiators will try to arrange for higher level talks at Kaesong a few days hence.

THEIR TERMS

By their own terms, the Communists were to start at 5 a.m.

Turn To Page 4 For More Of KOREA

RUSSIA PREPARES TO INVADE IRAN, NEWSMAN REPORTS

Red Soldiers In Tanks, Jeeps Conduct Nightly Forays Across Border

New York — (AP) — American Broadcasting Company correspondent Ray Brock said Friday that the Russian army is "preparing for a fullscale invasion of Iran."

In a report to his New York office from Ankara, Turkey, Brock said "Russian soldiers in tanks and jeeps conduct almost nightly forays across the Azerbaijan border in northern Iran to test Iranian defenses."

Brock quoted an "official U. S. Army observer recently arrived from Tehran" as saying that the "Red army is receiving the full cooperation of the Iranian Communists (members of the Tudeh party) in these patrols across the border."

Brock said the U. S. Army observer could not be named for security reasons but said he formerly was an O. S. S. agent during World War Two.

Brock quoted him as saying that the Russians are arming the Iranian Communists in the hope of an uprising and that "the Russians will then invoke the terms of an old Russo-Iranian treaty whereby the Red army is permitted to come to the aid of the Iranian government."

"In this way," Brock's report added, "the Russians plan to put the Tudeh party in power."

100 Injured As Red Bike Brigade Riots In Tehran

Tehran, Iran —(AP)— A big bicycle brigade of pro - Communist students demonstrating against the

Turn To Page 4 For More Of IRAN

"We Lead All The Rest"

FARM CORNER

By The Farm Editor

VEGETABLE FREEZING, CANNING SPURS BOOST IN PENNA. PLANTING

Harrisburg — Responding to the need for increased production of vegetables for canning and freezing, farmers of Pennsylvania have planted larger acreages than last year for sweet corn, green peas and snap beans, the State Department of Agriculture announces.

Federal-State production estimates given the Pennsylvania output of green peas for processing at 16,222 tons on a shelled basis, nearly 800 tons more than last year. Harvesting is nearing completion from 14,100 planted acres compared with 13,300 in 1950 and the 1940-49 average of 14,190 acres. Yield per acre this season is estimated at 2,300 pounds, only 20 pounds less than last year but 60 pounds above the average. National production this year is 15 per cent more than last year.

The Pennsylvania sweet corn crop for canning and freezing is being grown this season on 11,000

Turn To Page 4 For More Of FARM CORNER

CAR STRIKES BOY, 3, IN FRONT OF HOME

Three-year-old Harold Burkhart, son of Mr. and Mrs. Walter Burkhart, 412 High St., suffered a possible skull fracture and a fracture of the left collarbone when struck by a car in front of his home about 5:25 p.m. Friday, city police reported.

The boy was taken to St. Joseph's Hospital by the driver, John Keesey, 211 S. Pine St., York, and admitted for treatment. City police said Keesey is expected to file a report of the mishap with their department on Saturday (today).

Weather Calendar

COMPARATIVE TEMPERATURES

Station	High	Low
Water Works	81	55
Ephrata	81	55
Last Year (Ephrata)	79	62
Official High for Year May 17		92
Official Low for Year Feb. 9		6
Character of Day	Partly Cloudy	

WINDS
Direction—NNW Avg. Vel.—8 MPH

HUMIDITY
8 a. m.—43 11 a. m.—46 2 p. m.—38
5 p. m.—44 8 p. m.—52
Avg. Humidity—44

SUN
Rises—5:41 a. m. Sets—8:36 p. m.

MOON
Sets—10:48 p. m.

STARS
Morning—Mars, Jupiter.
Evening—Venus, Saturn.

NEARBY FORECASTS
(U. S. Weather Bureau)

Lower Potomac and Chesapeake Bay—Variable winds around 10 MPH Saturday. Fair weather with good visibility. New Jersey, Delaware, Maryland—Mostly sunny and a little warmer Saturday highest in middle 80s. Sunday some cloudiness warm and more humid.

EXTENDED FORECAST
(U. S. Weather Bureau)

Eastern Pennsylvania, Eastern New York, Maryland, Delaware, New Jersey and Virginia—Cool at the beginning of the period, turning warmer the first of next week. Temperature will average near to three degrees below normal. Showers likely about Tuesday. Total rainfall one-fourth inch or less.

Preliminary Plan Of Proposed $62,000,000 AF Depot In County

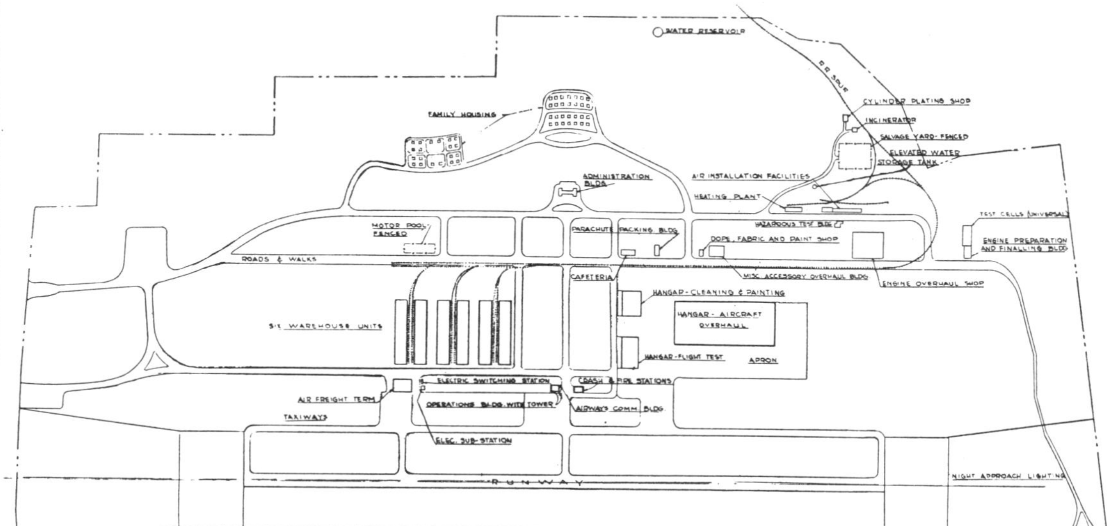

Here is a preliminary plan of the proposed new $62,000,000 Air Force aircraft and equipment maintenance depot to be constructed in Lancaster County, as presented Friday during an official briefing session for civic and industrial leaders of Central Pennsylvania, at Olmsted Air Force Base, Middletown. The plan provides for only one runway (foreground), but it will be 10,000 feet long. Officials say it will be capable of "handling all types of aircraft now in production and on the drawing boards." The vast base will have its own family housing unit, water reservoir and sewage disposal plant. Six large warehouses and an aircraft overhaul hangar sufficient to accommodate all modern types of planes also are shown on the plan. Sufficient area is included to provide for future expansion.

VA Maps Probe Of Charges Bad Drainage Hazards Home

Adverse conditions about which a young ex-serviceman and his wife have been complaining since the new Lafayette School was built adjacent to their home will be aired next week at a meeting attended by a Veterans' Administration representative and city officials, it was learned Friday.

The couple, Mr. and Mrs. Andrew G. Frankford, 1035 Fremont St., contend that their property, the purchase of which was financed through the VA, is generally devaluated. They claim their only available water supply is contaminated by muck draining off the school property and across an unfinished city street.

Further, they maintain, they find themselves literally marooned by deep water and mud which blocks the only paved approach to their property during heavy rainfall.

In a letter addressed to the president of a city bank which holds the mortage on the property, Loan Guaranty Officer M. J. Barnack of the Veterans' Administration Reginal Office at Wilkes-Barre proposed the meeting and urged:

"Since not only the rights of the veteran and the value of your (the bank's) security but also the rights of the U. S. Government have been seriously impared, we cannot overemphasize the importance of this conference."

Previously in the same letter Barnack had informed the bank:

". . . Mr. Ross E. Amos, Chief Appraiser of this office, will call on

Turn To Page 4 For More Of CONFERENCE

Invitations For Jap Pact Signing To Be Sent To 50

Washington —(AP)— The United States expects to issue invitations late this month to about 50 nations to attend a Japanese peace treaty signing conference in San Francisco opening Sep. 4.

Officials said that the invitations are expected to be sponsored jointly by the United States and Britain. Most of the countries which were and technically still are at war with Japan are expected to attend.

Announcement of the conference site and dates was made in San Francisco by Mayor Elmer E. Robinson who said that the sessions, lasting only about four days, will be held in the Opera House where the United Nations Charter was signed in 1945.

FORMALITY

The meeting will be purely formal because the plan is to iron out all peace treaty issues prior to the conference. In fact virtually all important issues have already been eliminated by agreement or

Turn To Page 4 For More Of TREATY

BOND POSTED FOR JAILED FREDERICK VANDERBILT FIELD

Order For Release Comes Too Late In Day To Free Millionaire

New York—(AP)—Grim-faced and flushed, millionaire Frederick Vanderbilt Field was jailed for contempt Friday, but ordered released on bond a short time later.

The order for his release came too late for the posting of bond Friday, however, and meant he would spend at least one night in jail.

Field chose imprisonment rather than expose the people who put up $80,000 bail for four runaway Communist leaders.

A Federal judge ordered him to jail for 90 days, or until he clears himself of contempt by revealing the long-secret backers of the gold mine of Communist bail money.

The immediate jailing of the 46-year-old "angel" of left-wing causes prevented him from attending an appeal later in the day before Appeals Judge Thomas W. Swan in New Haven, Conn.

After a two hour closed hearing, the government announced that Judge Swan ordered Field freed on $10,000 bail pending a formal appeal of the contempt sentence.

The $10,000 bond was described as temporary and may be changed after further consideration of the case.

Field for days has stubbornly re-

Turn To Page 4 For More Of COMMIES

10,000 - Foot Runway, Shops, Hangars Proposed For Depot

A detailed description of the proposed maintenance facility to be constructed in the Lancaster Area was incorporated into the voluminous brief presented Friday by Air Force officials.

The preliminary sketch of the Lancaster installation shows provisions for only one runway. It will be 10,000 feet long and capable of "handling all types of aircraft now in production and on the drawing boards."

Text of the Air Force brief on the proposed new maintenance facility to be constructed in the Lancaster area is as follows:

"The proposed Lancaster Air Force Base will provide a runway of a length and width suitable for all planned aircraft. This runway will be constructed in an east and west direction to provide landings and take-offs in accordance with the prevailing winds.

WOULD HANDLE ALL PLANES

"There will be the required overruns and approaches at the ends of the runways. This runway will be capable of handling all types of aircraft now in production and on the drawing boards.

"Included in the Maintenance facilities will be an aircraft overhaul hangar which will be able to accomodate all modern types of aircraft, including the B-36. This hangar will provide space for aircraft modification and repair and sheet metal repair. In conjunction with the aircraft overhaul hangar, there will be a cleaning and painting hangar, and a flight test hangar.

Turn To Page 4 For More Of LANCASTER

More Jet Engine Shops Proposed For Middletown

Olmsted Air Force Base, at Middletown, will be closed to flying if and when the huge aircraft maintenance depot in the Lancaster area materializes.

However, Olmsted would continue to operate as usual, only minus its aircraft and sheet metal facilities. And in the enlarged jet engine shop and its attendant facilities. These facts were contained in a brief presented Friday by Air Force officials.

The contemplated changes are designed to help strengthen Northeastern United States in line with the National Defense program.

WOULD BE CLOSED TO FLYING

Text of the Air Force brief insofar as contemplated changes for the Olmsted Air Force Base are concerned, follows:

"With the construction of Lancaster Air Force Base, Olmsted Air Force Base will be closed to flying and will continue to operate as usual less its aircraft and sheet metal facilities. Maintenance functions will be centered around the enlarged jet engine shop and its supporting units. A special purpose vehicle overhaul shop will be constructed. Storage of special purpose vehicles will occupy most of the present flying field and the remainder will be used for badly needed civilian parking. If possible a small liaison landing strip will be retained to accommodate administrative flights. Supply functions will continue to operate from existing facilities plus the planned supply and administration building and new warehouses. Supply will also

Turn To Page 4 For More Of MIDDLETOWN

SECTION NORTH WEST OF LITITZ MAY BE SITE

Project Would Augment Facilities Of Olmsted Field At Middletown

Plans for a new $62,000,000 aircraft and equipment maintenance depot in Lancaster County were unveiled publicly for the first time Friday by the Air Force.

While there was no official statement whatsoever about the probable location of the huge Air Force installation, some sources speculated the proposed base would be situated in a section northwest of Lititz.

The flat, open terrain of this section, as well as its accessibility to the Pennsylvania Turnpike and Reading Railroad right-of-way, were given by these sources in speculating on the likely location of the installation.

Air Force officials said the contemplated base in Lancaster would augment the facilities of Olmsted Air Force Base, Middletown, about 25 miles from here along Route 230.

Olmsted, described as "presently obsolescent for aircraft usage," would be closed to flying. Its present air strips would be utilized for warehouses and much-needed parking areas. The base would continue to operate as usual minus its aircraft and sheet metal facilities and with increased jet engine shops.

Friday's announcement does not mean the proposed changes have been authorized and all of the details completed. Instead, civic and industrial leaders of Central Pennsylvania merely were given a briefing on what the Air Force hopes to accomplish.

The Defense Department has asked Congress for authorization to spend 6,561,262,000 during the next two years for a vast military construction program in continental United States, possessions and abroad.

The proposed authorization would grant: $3,584,480,000 to the Air Force; $1,145,753,830 to the Navy, and $1,831,028,557 to the Army. Of the sum requested for the Air Force, $74,093,000 would be used to improve Olmsted's facilities and construct the new installation in Lancaster County.

Since $62,000,000 is earmarked for the Lancaster base, it is presumed the remainder of the $74,093,000 would go for changes at Olmsted Field.

The series of contemplated changes outlined Friday, the Air Force said, are designed to strengthen Northeastern United States in line with the National Defense program ordered by President Truman.

IMPORTANT STRATEGICALLY

Although small in size, Air Force officials made it clear that the Middletown Air Material Area is important strategically as well as economically.

They pointed out the area contains only 11.7 per cent of the nation's geographical area, yet boasts 42 per cent of the nation's population and more than 20 per cent of the Air Force's military aircraft.

Pointing up the extreme importance of this area in the nation's national defense picture, officials said there are more than 30 regular Air Force bases, 20 National Guard bases, and several Reserve bases

Turn To Page 4 For More Of AIRPORT

Proposed New Aircraft Base Here Heralded As 'Boom' To Community

Disclosure Friday that the Air Force contemplates constructing a $62,000,000 aircraft maintenance depot in the Lancaster area was heralded by a number of civic and community leaders as a "boom" for the community.

The officials were guests at a luncheon Friday at Olmsted Air Force Base, Middletown, when the Air Force took the wraps off its proposed $74,093,000 expansion program for the Northeast Air Materiel Area.

Lt. Col. Gale E. Snell, base adjutant, presented a detailed brief on the proposed changes which are designed to augment the over-expanded Olmsted facilities.

State Sen. Edward J. Kessler thought the project "would be a fine thing for the community." He added: "I am sorry to see more of our farmland used up, but we should do all we can to make our community more di-

Turn To Page 4 For More Of REACTION

Shortage Of Funds Curtails Work On Restoration Of Ephrata Shrine

Harrisburg — (AP) — The State Historical and Museum Commission said Friday that restoration work on the Ephrata Cloisters Historical Shrine has been halted due to the legislature's fiscal tieup.

"Work has been halted until funds become available," said Dr. Donald A. Cadzow, executive director of the commission.

He said the $40,000 appropriation made by the 1949 legislature for the Ephrata project has been used up and work closed down since June 1, the beginning of the 1951-53 biennium.

A bill boosting the appropriation to $75,000 is before the Senate, awaiting settlement of the current battle over whether to levy new taxes in Pennsylvania.

Buildings of the Cloisters, erected in the mid - eighteenth century, are being renovated in the exact manner in which they were constructed by a group of German Seventh Day Adventists.

The settlement, then in the wilderness of the province of Pennsylvania, was a Protestant monastery in which the medieval arts and crafts were practiced.

In restoring the buildings, tools similiar to those of the first settlers are being utilized.

SPECIAL TOOLS USED

The real harm in having the project halted, even though temporarily, Dr. Cadzow said, lies in the fact that men who have been taught to use these tools may be

Turn To Page 4 For More Of EPHRATA

GROUNDHOG HUNTER PAYS $25 FOR LOADED RIFLE IN HIS AUTO

Russell Frank Garber, twenty-eight, 11 Beach Lane, Middletown, paid $25 Friday on a charge of possessing a loaded rifle in an automobile in motion on a highway, according to State Game Protector John Haverstick, Lancaster. Garber settled on a field receipt, Haverstick said.

Garber, Haverstick said, was apprehended about 9:45 a. m. Friday in West Donegal Township by Deputy Game Protector Jacob E. Nagel, Jr., Elizabethtown R1, who was on patrol investigating complaints of illegal groundhog hunting.

Haverstick said that Garber had been hunting groundhogs. The game protector added that many complaints had been received about hunters failing to display hunting licenses in the middle of their backs. He said that display of the license is mandatory under the game laws which apply to groundhog hunting as much as they do to small game hunting in the Fall.

JAMES NORMAN HALL DIES AT TAHITI HOME

Papeete, Tahiti —(AP)— James Norman Hall, American author who was a famed teller of tales of the South Seas, died Thursday night of a heart attack at his home here. He was 64.

Hall, native of Colfax, Iowa, graduate of Grinnell College, became a resident of Tahiti in the South Seas in 1920.

Hall gained fame as the coauthor with the late Charles Bernard Nordhoff of a trilogy on the story of the British ship Bounty — "Mutiny on the Bounty" "Men Against the Sea," and "Pitcairn's Island."

Nordhoff and Hall became a popular writing team. Many of their stories were made into moving pictures.

Hall remained active as a writer up until shortly before his death. He contributed to a number of American periodicals.

His last published book with Nordhoff was "The High Barbaree," which came out in 1945. The two also wrote "The Hurricane," which was made into a movie.

NPA TO LIFT BAN ON SPARES FOR NEW CARS

Washington —(AP)— The National Production Administration announced Friday it will lift next week its ban against equipping new automobiles with a spare tire.

Manly Fleischmann, NPA Administrator, said in a statement that he has issued instructions for drafting of the order.

"This is being done because of an improvement in the rubber situation and a reduction in passenger car production," he said.

LANCASTER NEW ERA

Sports

Incredible Walcott Wins Title on Borrowed Time to Glorify Middle-Aged

.005 Points Separate First Four Teams in American Loop Race

By Ralph Roden
(Associated Press Sports Writer)

.005. That insignificant figure is the difference between first and fourth place in the sizzling American League pennant race today.

The Boston Red Sox lead the jam session by two percentage points. The Chicago White Sox are second, the New York Yankees third and the Cleveland Indians fourth.

Here's the situation in a nut shell:

	W	L	Pct	GB
Boston	52	35	.598	
Chicago	53	36	.596	
New York	50	34	.595	½
Cleveland	51	35	.593	½

The race tightened up considerably last night as both the White Sox and Red Sox lost while the Yanks and Indians won squeakers.

BOSTON DROPPED a 6-1 decision to the Detroit Tigers while the White Sox lost a 2-1 ten-inning battle to the Washington Senators. The Yanks edged the St. Louis Browns, 1-0, and the Indians nipped the Philadelphia Athletics, 1-0, in ten innings.

Meanwhile, the Brooklyn Dodgers retained their eight-game lead in the National League. The Dodgers defeated the St. Louis Cardinals 5-2, as the New York Giants trounced the Cincinnati Reds, 11-5, the Philadelphia Phils knocked off the Chicago Cubs, 4-3, in 11 innings and the Boston Braves humbled the Pittsburgh Pirates, 11-6.

MARLIN STUART, 32-year-old righthander, made his first start of the season and shackled the Red Sox on six hits before 45,653 fans at Detroit.

Stuart, called up late in May from Toledo, slipped his newly-developed slider past the Boston sluggers without trouble except for the sixth inning when singles by Lou Boudreau and Billy Goodman scored a run.

The Tigers hopped on Chuck Stobbs for five runs and the ball game in the fourth inning. Jerry Priddy, George Kell, Vic Wertz and Johnny Groth opened the inning with successive singles. One out later, Hoot Evers and Bob Swift singled and after Stuart forced Groth at the plate, Neil Berry clouted a two-run single to complete the rally.

CHICAGO WAS one out away from regaining first place. The White Sox led, 1-0, going into the ninth and Lou Kretlow retired the first two hitters. Ed Yost singled and Gil Coan whacked a double, his fourth hit of the game, to tie the score. The Senators, beaten ten straight times by Chicago, won out in the tenth on singles by Mickey Vernon, Sam Mele and Cass Michaels' run-scoring ground out.

Young Tom Morgan won a brilliant pitching duel from little Ned Garver, Brownie ace, at St. Louis. Morgan permitted three singles while Garver was tapped for six hits.

The Browns' argest crowd of the season, 15,242 fans, witnessed the well pitched game. The Yanks

—See BASEBALL—Page 10

IACC in Playoff Tilt

The Italian American softball team will continue its quest for a state championship tonight when it travels to York to finish a game with Hanover. Game time is 7:30 p.m.

The game, for District 3 title, was started last Sunday and halted by curfew after six innings with the IACC out in front, 9-5.

All players are asked to be at the clubhouse, N. Queen St. by 6:30 p.m.

Oldest Champ Traveled the Rockiest Road

by HARRY GRAYSON

First In Series

NEW YORK — (NEA) — Arnold Cream has done more for the middle-aged than Ezio Pinza, South Pacific and Satchel Paige.

At an admitted 37, and after 21 years, Cream—ring name Jersey Joe Walcott — is their heavyweight champion and that of the entire world. Some say he is 41. There is no birth certificate.

Ezzard Charles

There may have been more exciting fight stories than the one culminated by Old Man Walcott dropping the 30-year-old Ezzard Charles flat on his face in Pittsburgh, but none with more human interest.

Walcott, the oldest champion in history, has been on borrowed time since coming back in January of 1945 after having retired for the sixth time and being on the sidelines for three and a half years.

THE STORY of Walcott is the old heartbreak of boxing. There's never been a Cinderella story like it. Jersey Joe hit rock bottom so hard and long he almost dropped clear through. The blackest moment, he remembers, came one day in 1936.

"I broke my arm, couldn't work because of it," he recalls. "There was no relief money. I couldn't have gone any farther down, even if I pulled the stopper."

WALCOTT wasn't just talking when he spoke these words into the microphone from the Forbes Field battlepit after knocking out Charles in the seventh:

"I want to thank God for helping me to win. I always said that if God's on your side, you're bound to win sooner or later.

"I want to be a worthy champion, and try to help the youth of this country. I want to visit every church and Sunday school where they want me, and tell the young folks what it means to have God on your side."

This was not idle chatter. Camden county officials will tell you Jersey Joe has spent much time helping combat juvenile delinquency, speaking to groups of youngsters in schools, at playgrounds and meeting places.

PRAYER TO THE deeply-religious Walcott means sitting down and talking things over with God. Recalling how he felt before a highly-important meeting with Jimmy Bivins in Cleveland, Feb. 25, 1946, he says:

"Bivins' dressing room was next to mine. All the time before the fight, he had a record player going with loud jump numbers, and he was singing and jumping. The minutes before a fight are for prayer and for planning the fight, and here was a guy jigging around with jive."

Walcott doesn't smoke, and his favorite and strongest drink are the milk shakes he and his brother-in-law and pal, Joe Homes, get at a certain spot on New Jersey's Black Horse Pike. His wildest "play boy" habits are movies, blues records and a card game peculiar to Camden, known as "sixty-one" or "outhouse rummy."

WALCOTT BEGAN his ring career at 16 as a middleweight. Jack Blackburn, the one-time great lightweight, had him for a brief spell

Jersey Joe Walcott once was on relief, but his brood of six need worry no longer. Pop is the heavyweight champion at an admitted 37. Members of the Camden family are, left to right, Doris, 14; Ruth, 12; Carol 6, talking to her father on the telephone; Elva, 16; Vince, 11; Mrs. Walcott and Arnold, 17.

Quit Fighting Six Times to Go to Work

before being called away to develop Joe Louis.

Jersey Joe stricken with typhoid, was ill a full year. He married, and family financial worries left no time for training. He went into fights with no more preparation than a hair comb. He went as far as he could before keeling over from sheer exhaustion.

In June, 1941, Walcott hung up his gloves for what he believed was for good. There were five little Walcotts then, and he couldn't feed them on the peanuts he got for taking pastings.

BUT ALONG came James J. Johnston, one of the superior managers, and he convinced him that he could work in a defense plant and still fight. Joe's licese had run out during his retirement, and he applied for a new one. New Jersey Boxing Commissioner John Hall had seen Walcott box several times when Jersey Joe obviously was not in his best condition. He insisted that Walcott undergo a complete physical examination.

Johnston lost interest, however, and Walcott's only appearances from June 27, 1941, to Jan. 11, 1945, were two inconsequential matches in tiny Batesville, N. J.

Walcott applied for a post on the Pennsauken Township police force. He landed a job in the Camden shipyards. Some weeks, the pay was as high at $90.

Jersey Joe picked up a check for $49,782.28 with the heavyweight championship.

NEXT: Felix Bocchicchio and opportunity poke their heads through the hole in Jersey Joe Walcott's door.

Louis May Get First Crack at Walcott's Title

CAMDEN, N. J., July 21—(AP)—The only thing certain about the heavyweight boxing picture is that Jersey Joe Walcott is champion and that he has a very prosperous future.

Walcott is committed by contract to give Ezzard Charles a return shot at the title in New York.

BUT BIG QUESTION marks have suddenly appeared, fogging the heavyweight horizon. Will Walcott fight Charles next? Or will the new champion risk boxing's most coveted crown in the ring with the old Brown Bomber, Joe Louis? And then will Charles meet the winner of this match?

The answer might come from Jim Norris, president of the International Boxing Club that has exclusive rights to Walcott, Charles and Louis.

UP UNTIL yesterday, when Walcott was greeted by 100,000 wildly cheering neighbors here on his return from Pittsburgh where he lifted the title Wednesday, it appeared certain that the next big heavyweight fight would be a fourth Walcott-Charles meeting. Only the date and site were indefinite with New York, Pittsburgh, Cincinnati, Atlantic City, N. J., and Philadelphia mentioned as possible locations.

Then Felix Bocchicchio, Walcott's manager, let loose a statement that packed almost as much dynamite as the left hook that Walcott used to Kayo Charles. Bocchicchio said Joe Louis had asked for the first crack at Walcott's title.

Said Bocchicchio:

"I told Joe it was okay with me if it was okay with the International Boxing Club. Louis gave us two shots at the title. I think we owe it to him. Walcott will be glad to oblige Louis if Norris and IBC say okay."

LOUIS DENIED in Detroit that he had talked with anybody about a title fight but said, "I sure hope it's so." The Brown Bomber declared he was ready to fight Walcott at any time but that he really thought Charles deserved the first chance. "He's entitled to it. But, he does need a rest. He's been fighting too much," added Louis.

The only comment from the IBC

—See WALCOTT—Page 10

Roses Beaten as Official Protests

Cowdrick Charges Umps Delayed Tilt

Our Red Roses, having dropped a 10 to 3 decision in their last game at Harrisburg, get a chance to bolster their fourth place position in the Inter State League over the week-end when they go to Sunbury.

As it stands now, the locals are exactly six games ahead of the Giants and victories in the up-State city would just about clinch their first-division berth.

HOWEVER, THAT may be tough seeing as how the Giants, having been beaten by Allentown, are due to comeback. Manager Charley Fox's team, which last night dropped an 8 to 3 verdict to the Cards, has always been tough for the locals and only last week split a four game series here. On their own grounds, the Giants hold an edge over the Roses.

They meet in a single game tonight and then play a double-header tomorrow afternoon with members of the Red Rose Booster Club planning to be on hand in full force.

LAST NIGHT, Harrisburg had too many guns for lefty Joe Bernier, while Dave Freeman had too many curves for the Roses. Bernier was rapped for 12 hits in 6 2-3 innings with Joe Moresco finishing and giving up three blows in 1 2-3 frames.

On the otherhand, Freeman held the Roses to five hits in going the route.

Harrisburg scored twice in the first, twice in the fourth and routed Bernier with a six hit attack in the seventh. The Roses got one in the third and two in the seventh to pull up at 4 to 3 but then the Senators put on that seventh inning attack and it was all over.

Lancaster	ab	h	o	a	Harrisburg	ab	h	o	a
Wilkes cf	3	1	2	0	Burson ss	5	2	3	1
Walker lf	4	2	1	0	Fuller rf	4	1	3	0
Neal 2b	5	0	1	2	Cox cf	4	2	2	0
Ticco 1b	4	1	6	1	R'dazzo 1b	5	3	10	0
Louis 3b	5	0	1	0	Bowman 2b	3	0	0	2
K'check ss	4	1	4	2	Mattis 3b	4	2	1	1
Olivo rf	3	0	1	0	Qualben lf	5	1	5	0
Worley c	4	0	7	1	Jadwin c	4	1	3	1
Bernier p	0	0	1	2	Freeman p	4	3	0	3
Moresco p	0	0	0	0					
aPflasterer	1	0	0	0					
Totals	33	5	24	8	Totals	38	15	27	8

a-Flied out for Marisco in 9th.

LANCASTER	001 000 200—	3
HARRISBURG	200 200 60x—	10

R—Walker, Breiner 2, Fuller, Cox 2, Randazzo, Mattis 2, Qualben, Jadwin 2, Freeman. E—Randazzo, Bernier, Neal, Burson, Worley, Ticco 2. RBI—Walker, Burson, Fuller 2, Cox, Randazzo 2, Freeman 3. 2B—Walker, Randazzo, Qualben, Wilkes. 3B—Cox, Freeman. S—Bowman. Left—Lancaster 10; Harrisburg 10. BB—Bernier 3, Freeman 8, Maresco 1. SO—Bernier 4, Freeman 3. HO—Bernier 12 in 6 1-3 innings; Moresco 3 in 1 2-3. Loser—Bernier. U—Murphy and Emil. T—2:03. A—520.

Locals Get Chance to Bolster 4th Place

After the game business manager Bill Cowdrick said he was protesting to Prexy Gerry Nugent because the fray was held up while the umpires and Harrisburg officials argued in the dressing room. After Thursday's double-header, Harrisburg officials threatened to keep their team off the field unless umpire Tom Murphy was moved, and Cowdrick charged that they argued this point last night while the pitchers "cooled off."

IN OTHER games played last night, Hagerstown copped two from Salisbury, 2 to 0 and 7 to 2, while Wilmington took a pair from York, 12 to 1 and 7 to 2.

Midgets at a Glance

Midget-Midgets

LAST NIGHT'S RESULTS

CIO 17, Paradise Lions 2.

MONDAY'S GAME

Lititz Wrens vs. Slaymaker Lock Nine at F and M No. 2.

TUESDAY'S GAMES

Columbia Gold vs. Reamstown at Reamstown.

Millersville vs. Manheim Chix at Manheim.

Midget Division

LAST NIGHT'S RESULTS

Hager Blue Jays 14, Marietta 0.

TUESDAY'S GAME

Swamp Church vs. Lafayette at Lafayette.

OUR BOARDING HOUSE . . . . with Major Hoople

New Era Tourney

Hagers Win on No-Hitter, CIO First in Semi-Finals

By Bob Hutter and Steve O'Neill

A NO-HITTER in the Midget Division, and the opening of the second round of Midget-Midget play took the New Era Tourney spotlight last night.

Bobby Nonnemocher became the third hurler to rack up a no-hit, no-run performance as Hager's Blue Jays whitewashed Marietta VFW, 14-0.

The CIO Midget-Midgets became the first club to gain the semi-finals of the Tournament by stopping the Paradise Lions, 17-2. The city youngsters combined two-hit pitching with a 12-hit barrage.

THE REST of the teams take the week-end off, awaiting the continuance of play Monday evening.

Three games remain in the second round of the Midget-Midget Division, while the Swamp-Lafayette game, Tuesday will decide the last quarter-final Midget berth.

Monday evening's lone game pits two Midget-Midget squads against each other. It is:

Lititz Wrens vs. Slaymaker Lock Nine at F and M No. 2.

Then, Tuesday, three games will wind up second round play in each division. In addition to the Swamp-Lafayette contest, two games involving the smaller lads are on tap. Millersville and the Manheim Chix meet at Manheim, and Columbia Gold plays at Reamstown.

NONNEMOCHER had little difficulty in stopping the Marietta hitters. He did not allow a ball to be hit out of the infield and struck out nine batters, while facing only 17 players.

Four hitters reached first base. The Hager ace walked two, hit another, while the fourth runner reached first on an error. One Marietta player advanced to second in the fourth frame when manager Paul Reber's lads were handed a base on balls and the Blue Jays' lone error.

POWER PLUS pitching — that was the story in the CIO-Paradise contest in the Midget-Midget Division.

Twelve solid base hits, including two homers, two triples and a double were lashed out by Charlie Siegel's proteges in their triumph over Sam Wenger's lads.

But to top off the power hitting, Billy Vogel, CIO hurler, came through with one of his finest performances of the season, holding the visitors to just two hits, both singles.

CIO	ab	r	h	o	a	PARADISE	ab	r	h	o	a
Kiefer cf	3	1	1	0	0	Ebe'le 2b	3	0	0	0	0
Zwirn cf	0	1	0	0	0	Sta'er p	3	1	1	0	1
Kir'ner 3b	2	4	2	1	0	Shenk 1b	3	0	0	7	0
Frey c	3	2	2	9	2	Gra'm cf	2	0	0	0	0
San'llo c	1	0	0	2	0	Lo'cker c	2	1	1	3	0
Wolf ss	3	1	2	0	0	Gra'm rf	2	0	0	0	0
Wea'er ss	0	1	0	0	0	Ep'ade ss	2	0	0	1	1
Vogel p	4	1	1	0	1	Nichol lf	2	0	0	1	0
Mc'ney 1b	4	1	1	3	0	Gregg 3b	1	0	0	0	1
Hil'and 2b	1	2	1	0	1						
Mow'y lf	1	2	1	0	0						
Hain lf	0	0	0	0	0						
Grill rf	3	1	1	0	0						
Benn rf	0	0	0	0	0						
Totals	25	17	12	15	4	Totals	20	2	2	12	3

Paradise	100 10	2
CIO	257 3x	17

MARIETTA	ab	r	h	o	a	HAGER'S	ab	r	h	o	a
Rice 3b	1	0	0	0	0	Spe'ng cf	3	1	1	0	0
Blymier 2b	1	0	0	1	0	Wat'rs lf	1	4	1	0	0
Kugle ss	2	0	0	2	2	Shank 1b	4	1	2	3	0
Sau'ers p	2	0	0	0	1	Go'ley ss	4	1	3	1	1
Waller rf	0	0	0	0	0	Wa'fel 3b	3	1	1	1	1
Ri'ards lf	2	0	0	0	0	Har'sh 2b	1	1	0	1	0
Blymier 1b	1	0	0	2	0	Chi'an c	3	1	0	9	1
Miller cf	2	0	0	0	0	Mu'er rf	2	2	1	0	0
Hinkle ss	2	0	0	1	0	No'cher p	3	2	2	0	0
Grove c	1	0	0	6	0						
Totals	14	0	0	12	3	Totals	24	14	11	15	3

Marietta	000 00	0
Hager's	174 2x	14

LAST NIGHT'S FIGHTS
(By The Associated Press)

HOLLYWOOD, Calif— Charley Riley, 129½, St. Louis, stopped Dave Gallardo, 128, Los Angeles, 7.

CHESTER, Pa. — Joe Brewer, 152, Philadelphia, outpointed Jimmy De Cerio, 150½, Norristown, Pa. 8.

Midget Notes

FOR a team that is playing under tremendous pressure, the Columbia Pioneers are certainly a cool lot. The Columbians are the defending champions in the Midget Division of the New Era Tournament, which has all their opponents gunning for them. But, to top that off, the kids are in the midst of what might easily be a record winning streak. They have won 43 straight at the last count, which was a couple days ago.

When Charlie Siegel's CIO midget-midget team lost to the York Boys Club All Stars the other night, Dougie Wolf's 16-game hitting streak was ended. Little Dougie snapped right back, though, and said he didn't care about the streak, the thing that hurt most was losing the ball game. And that's quite an attitude for an 11 year old boy.

Elizabethtown Moose midget team takes pre-game practice just like the Major Leaguers. Manager Frank (Scoop) Peters has his boys out early for batting practice and then follows up with infield and

outfield drills just like the big leaguers. Incidentally, Scoop hits that ball for practice just as hard as the pros and that is probably why the E-towners look so good on the defensive.

Kenny Zimmerman, E-Town's leftfielder, made a great catch of Bill Kreider's towering drive to left. It was the hardest hit ball of the game, but Ken went right to the end of left field and made a fine one-handed stab.

Conestoga's two Kreiders, Bill and Bert, Jr., are the same twins that have been playing in New Era Tournaments since they first started, and, the manager of the team is their father, Bert, Sr.

Putts and Pars

YOUNG Dick Weaver, the McCaskey High golfer, boasts quite a record as a caddie at Meadia Heights. When Bobby Howells played Glenn Horst in the finals for the Meadia men's championship this year Weaver was his caddie.

Over the past six years, Dick has been the caddie for the club champion in the final match.

Bill Haverstick and J. Hay Brown were the latest winners in the Straub Cup tourney at the Country Club. Both won by 5 and 4 scores.

Haverstick put together scores of 35 and 32 for a 67 to defeat Ed Yale. Brown defeated B. M. Zimmerman in his match.

There was a familiar face around the pro shop of the Country Club this week. "Petie" Huegel, who was assistant pro to Abe Thorne up until this Summer, has been home on leave from the air force.

"Petie" is stationed at Vance Field, near Enid, Oklahoma. He reports he's been playing quite a bit of golf and is shooting in the low 70's on an "easy" course.

The 36-hole medal President's Tourney is now in progress at the Country Club. C. J. Martin, Tom Cence, and L. L. Bently, each of who finished with 140 to tie for first last year, are defending. Play started Thursday and will end tomorrow.

Meadia Heights has a big day planned tomorrow. It's Golf Day.

There's the Stock Yard Trophy Tourney, Senior's tourney, and hole-in-one, driving, and putting contests climaxed by a big steak supper.

The annual Stock Yard's tourney consists of 18 holes medal handicap with a nine-hole event for the women. Defending champion is Chuck Grube, Jr.

The various contests will be staged for the men.

George R. Smith will defend his Senior's title in a nine-hole medal play tournament.

The steak supper will be held for the members participating in the Stock Yard affair.

Long-hitting Dick Brown turned in his best round at Meadia this week, shooting a 69. Dick was playing with Tom Shields, pro Art Thorne, Jr., and sports scribe Curley Crudden.

Brownie was out in 33 and came in with a 36 for his par-breaking score. The course record is 66.

Work has started to change the location of the 17th tee at the Conestoga Country Club . . Once it is completed, you'll have to hook your tee shot to reach the green . . The hole is on a plateau with the fairway guarded by trees on both sides and, of course, there's always the creek to cross first.

It won't pay you to bet on the outcome of the match, but a sure-fire bet is that the foursome of Doc Eby, Sonny McLane, Red Webster and Ted Abele will be first off at Conestoga tomorrow . . They go off before the pro shop opens at 8 a. m. . . and do it every Sunday, too.

Tomorrow's Card

BASEBALL

INTER STATE LEAGUE
Lancaster at Sunbury.

CITY-COUNTY LEAGUE
Lititz at Elizabethtown.
Marietta at Mountville.
Chestnut Hill at New Holland.

EASTERN COUNTY LEAGUE
Ephrata at Bowmansville.
Schoeneck at Reamstown.
Cornwall at Denver.

Baseball Standings

NATIONAL LEAGUE

Teams	W.	L.	Pct.	G.B.
Brooklyn	54	32	.628	
New York	47	41	.534	8
St. Louis	44	40	.524	9
Cincinnati	42	42	.500	11
Philadelphia	43	44	.494	11½
Boston	38	44	.463	14
Chicago	35	44	.443	15½
Pittsburgh	34	50	.405	19

AMERICAN LEAGUE

Teams	W.	L.	Pct.	G.B.
Boston	52	35	.598	
Chicago	53	36	.596	
New York	50	34	.595	½
Cleveland	51	35	.593	½
Detroit	39	44	.470	11
Washington	37	49	.430	14½
Philadelphia	36	53	.404	17
St. Louis	27	59	.314	24½

INTER STATE LEAGUE

Teams	W.	L.	Pct.	G.B.
Hagerstown	61	27	.693	
Allentown	53	32	.624	6½
Wilmington	50	34	.595	9
Lancaster	50	37	.575	10½
Sunbury	45	44	.506	16½
Harrisburg	39	49	.443	22
York	32	57	.360	29½
Salisbury	18	69	.207	42½

Yesterday's Results

NATIONAL LEAGUE
New York 11, Cincinnati 5.
Brooklyn 5 St. Louis 2.
Philadelphia 4, Chicago 3 (11 inns.)
Boston 11, Pittsburgh 6.

AMERICAN LEAGUE
New York 1, St. Louis 0.
Washington 2, Chicago 1.
Detroit 6, Boston 1.
Cleveland 1, Philadelphia 0 (10 inns.)

INTER STATE LEAGUE
Harrisburg 10, Lancaster 3.
Allentown 8, Sunbury 3.
Wilmington 12, York 1 (1st).
Wilmington 7, York 2 (2nd).
Hagerstown 2, Salisbury 0 (1st).
Hagerstown 7, Salisbury 2 (2nd).

INTERNATIONAL LEAGUE
Syracuse 2, Baltimore 0
Springfield 4, Rochester 3
Buffalo 6, Toronto 3
Ottawa 3, Montreal 2

AMERICAN ASSOCIATION
Indianapolis 4, Toledo 2
Louisville 10, Columbus 4
St. Paul 10, Kansas City 6
Milwaukee 12, Minneapolis 11

EASTERN LEAGUE
Elmira 5-3, Schenectady 1-0
Williamsport 6-3, Binghamton 3-9
Hartford 5-2, Wilkes-Barre 3-0
Scranton 1-8, Albany 0-3

Tonight's Games

INTER STATE LEAGUE
Lancaster at Sunbury.
Hagerstown at Wilmington.
York at Salisbury.
Allentown at Harrisburg.

Tomorrow's Games

NATIONAL LEAGUE
Pittsburgh at Boston (2)
St. Louis at Brooklyn
Cincinnati at New York (2)
Chicago at Philadelphia (2)

AMERICAN LEAGUE
Washington at Chicago (2)
New York at St. Louis (2)
Boston at Detroit
Philadelphia at Cleveland (2)

Major League Leaders

NATIONAL LEAGUE

Batting—(Based on 200 times at bat)—Musial, St. Louis, .371.
Runs—Hodges, Brooklyn, 75.
Runs batted in—Kiner, Pittsburgh and Snider, Brooklyn, 65.
Hits—Ashburn, Philadelphia, 128.
Doubles — Robinson, Brooklyn and Wyrostek, Cincinnati, 22.
Triples—Bell, Pittsburgh, 8.
Home runs—Hodges, Brooklyn, 28.
Stolen bases—Jethroe, Boston and Robinson, Brooklyn, 15.
Pitching—(Based on five decisions)—Roe, Brooklyn, 13-2, .867.
Strikeouts—Spahn, Boston, 85.

AMERICAN LEAGUE

Batting—Coan, Washington, .344.
Runs—Williams, Boston, 72.
Runs batted in—Williams, Boston, 81.
Hits—DiMaggio, Boston, 119.
Doubles—Noren, Washington, 27.
Triples—Minoso, Chicago, 12.
Home runs—Zernial, Philadelphia, 23.
Stolen bases—Busby, Chicago, 18.
Pitching—Kinder, Boston and Martin, Philadelphia, 6-1, .857.
Strikeouts — McDermott, Boston and Raschi, New York, 87.

Softball Results

SOUTHERN END CHURCH LEAGUE

Colemanville	250 120 12—	13	16	2
Willow Street	304 020 20—	11	17	7

Herr and Morrison; Ruof and W. Kreider.

MANOR MILLERSVILLE CHURCH LEAGUE

Grace EUB	103 221 0—	9	13	6
Methodist	101 402 0—	8	8	4

J. Falk and Thumma; Geisler and Hashinger.

Lutheran	101 000 3—	5	8	3
Reformed	300 007 0—	10	19	6

McLaughin and Broome; Greer and Kramer.

Stehmans	001 101 1—	3	4	5
Kready Ave.	540 200 0—	11	20	3

Kauffman, Good and Fry; M. Charles and Koforth.

Central Manor	102 001 0—	4	8	2
Wash. Boro	130 000 1—	5	6	3

Horner and Lease; Sherrick and R. McDonald.

All In a Nutshell

APPROXIMATELY 40 drivers are expected to compete in the five-event racing program to be run off this evening starting at 8:30 o'clock at the Lancaster Speedway . . . Glen Teal leads at the half-way point in the Milwaukee Open Golf Tournament with a 134 . . Dick Savitt and Herbie Flam won their matches to give the United States a 2-0 lead over Japan in the American Zone Davis Cup play . . Leo Durocher signed to manage the New York Giants again in 1952 . . The Cleveland Indians purchased Indianapolis of the American Association . . Peggy Kirk leads in the 108-hole Scarborough Round-Robin Golf Tourney in England . . Whitney Reed defeated National champion Art Larsen, 6-4, 6-4, in the Pennsylvania Grass Court Tennis championships . . The American Football League will not operate in 1951 because of manpower situation . . Ab Jenkins, 68, smashed 22 land speed records in his Mormon Me-

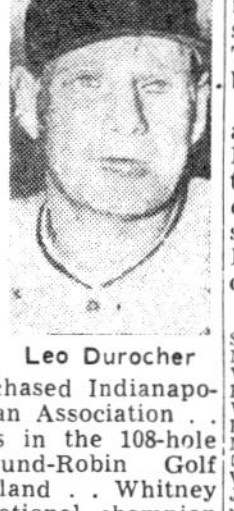

Leo Durocher

Rangers Edge Quarryville in Legion Playoff

The Amvet Rangers moved closer to the District 10 title in the Junior Legion League play-offs last night by turning back Quarryville 4-1, at the F and M field.

Both teams were City and County champions in their respective leagues. Another step in post-season rounds will be played on Monday, when Quarryville plays Elizabethtown at Quarryville.

THE RANGERS' ace hurler, Jerry Miller gave up only one hit and allowed one run in the top of the second inning. Cliff Tracey, also of the winners, led the batting with two hits at three trips to the plate.

The Amvet club sewed up the game in the bottom of the second with a pair of runs and threw in two more in the third for good measure. Their second inning splurge came on Bostic's double, Tracey's first single and a bingle by Good.

The Rangers' second two came at the expense of Q-Ville pitcher Fieler as he gave up a walk and two singles, one of which was Tracey's second of the evening. Miller struck out eight and walked four. F. Young was charged with the defeat.

Quarryville	ab	h	o	a	Amvets Rangers	ab	h	o	a
Shirk 2b ss	4	0	0	2	B'ubaker 2b	1	0	4	0
McC'dell cf	3	0	1	0	Evans lf	3	0	0	0
Work 3b	3	0	0	3	Fencil ss	2	1	2	3
Fieler 1b p	3	1	4	0	Bostic c	2	1	11	0
W'lace 2b ss	2	0	2	2	Tracey 1b	3	2	3	0
Reinhart lf	2	0	1	0	Schuler rf	3	1	1	0
Means c	1	0	5	0	Good cf	3	1	0	1
G. Young c	1	0	0	1	Smith 3b	3	0	0	1
W'gins 1b rf	1	0	3	0	Miller p	0	0	0	0
J. Y'ng p rf	2	0	0	0					
xGraybill	1	0	0	0					
xxPatterson	0	0	0	0					
Totals	28	1	18	7	Totals	22	8	21	8

x-Batted for T. Young in 7th.
xx-Ran for Graybill in 7th.

QUARRYVILLE	010 000 0—	1
AMVET RANGERS	022 000 x—	4

R—Fieler, Brubaker, Fencil, Bostic, Tracey. E—Fencil, Tracey, Wallace, Good. 2B—Bostic. BB — Miller 4, J. Young 1, Fieler 1. SO—Miller 8, Fieler 3. Loser—J. Young. U—Long and Planger.

Cards of Thanks

WE wish to express our sincere thanks and appreciation to our many friends who were so kind to us during our recent bereavement in the death of Jeremiah McKonly and also for the beautiful floral offerings.—The Family.

In Memoriam

Identified by The American shield are those honored heroes who gave the last full measure of loyalty and devotion

IN LOVING memory of my dear son, George R. Billger, who passed away one year ago today, August 9th, dearly loved and sadly missed by his mother.—Rebecca Troup.

F CEMETERIES

FOUR GRAVE LOT in Riverview Cemetery. Choice section. Sacrifice for quick sale. Phone 2-3558.

1 APARTMENTS

4 MODERN spacious rooms, all conveniences. Parking space. Apply 425 North Queen.

THREE-ROOM apartment, private bath. All utilities furnished. Phone Manheim 5-8691.

South Queen—4 rooms, bath, $60. HAINES, 24 S. Duke. Ph. 2-4629.

3 ROOM APARTMENT, employed couple preferred. Apply 452 North Mulberry.

NORTH DUKE STREET—3 rooms, bath, second floor. Phone 2-7018.

FOUR ROOMS, first floor. Oil heat, conveniences. Two adults. 11 East High, Maytown.

MODERN — 3 large rooms and bath, shower. Central. $75. Also furnished apartment, private entrance. Phone 2-4674, after 6 P. M. 2-1138.

44 E. VINE — Knotty pine living-bedroom comb., kitchen and bath. $50. Phone 2-6724, Broker.

SUITABLE for bachelor with kitchenette and bath. $40. Write Box 345, Lancaster Neswpapers.

BACHELOR APARTMENT — One room. Newly furnished. Tile bath and shower. $50. West End — 3 rooms bath. Immediate possession. Write Box 341, Lancaster Newspapers.

NORTH DUKE—2 rooms, kitchenette, bath. 2 rooms, bath, references. Inquire 33 West James.

IN THE COUNTRY—3 miles from city—4 rooms & bath—2nd floor—New—$78 50.
F. G. SHIRK CO.
5 N. Duke St. Ph. 2-0114

1 APARTMENTS

Mary St. 4 rms. B. 2nd floor. $70. Geo. W. Bard & Son, 423 W. James

MOVE IN and start living in this newly renovated four room and bath apartment on N. Mary Street. Very nicely furnished. $85. Employed couple preferred. Write Box 294, Lancaster Newspapers.

NORTH DUKE—3 rooms, kitchenette, bath. $65. Immediate possession. References. 33 W. James St.

DESIRABLE 3 rooms and bath apartment, recently remodeled. $60. Warren Henwood. 7628.

MODERN four room and tile bath. Use of Laundry, yard. $85 Including utilities. Phone 3-4247.

TWO BEDROOM apartment. West Orange St. $60. Adults. Write P. O. Box 686.

VERY NICE furnished four room apartment with bath and shower. Porch, garage, and electric range. Possession September 1st. Only middleaged working couple need apply. Rent $75. Phone 2-5419.

THREE ROOMS tile bath, near College. Inquire 336 W. Lemon St.

FURNISHED four rooms and bath. Surburbs. Phone Manheim 5-3184.

LINCOLN HWY WEST — Very attractive & modern. Five rooms & tile bath — 2nd floor.
Engle & Hambright, Inc.
46 E. Orange St. Ph. 8141

2 APARTMENTS WANTED

RELIABLE young couple with child, desire 3-4 room furnished apartment. Write Box 111 Lancaster Newspapers.

3 EMPLOYED ADULTS, desire four rooms, bath apartment. Reasonable. Phone 2-5258.

COUPLE DESIRE 2-3 rooms, private bath. Write Box 110, Lancaster Newspapers.

COUPLE DESIRES first or second floor, 4 rooms, bath. Central location. Phone 4-3669.

FOUR or five rooms, no children. Write Box 363, Lancaster Newspapers.

3 ROOMS AND BATH. Laundry. Reasonable. Write Box 347, Lancaster Newspapers.

VETERAN, wife and two children, urgently need 4 room apartment or small house by September 15. Call Landisville 4146.

COUPLE With two children desire first floor apartment or house for rent. Call 6993.

WANTED — 2-bedroom apartment. Good location. 3 adults. Call Lancaster 3-0210. Daytime.

URGENTLY needed two or three bed-room house or apartment Phone 3-7128.

EMPLOYED couple, no children, desire 3 rooms and bath. Reasonable. Phone Strasburg 4491.

FOUR ROOM apartment or small house, family of three. Reasonable. Phone 3-8348.

J LEGAL

AUDITOR'S REPORT
OF THE SCHOOL DISTRICT OF LANCASTER, PENNSYLVANIA
FOR THE SCHOOL YEAR ENDED JULY 2. 1951

The undersigned auditor, appointed by the Board of Directors of the School District of Lancaster, Pennsylvania, has completed his report of audit of the accounts of said District for the school year ended July 2, 1951; and, in accordance with the provisions of Section 2432 of Act No 14 approved March 10, 1949, as amended, gives notice that said report was filed on August 1, 1951 in the office of the Prothonotary of the Court of Common Pleas of Lancaster County and that said report will be confirmed absolutely unless an appeal is taken therefrom within thirty days after the filing thereof and that the following is a concise financial statement of the said District for the school year ended July 2, 1951.

RECEIPTS

Cash Balance on Hand and in Bank — July 3, 1950		$ 244,374.86
Property Tax — 1950		1,365,319.25
Delinquent Tax — Prior to 1950		15,600.23
State Appropriation — Teachers, Transportation, etc.		469,478.30
Tuition — Non Resident Pupils		26,271.68
Principal Amount of Investments Sold		502,945.59
Miscellaneous — Interest, Rentals, etc.		23,978.91
Total Receipts and Balance		$2,647,968.82

DISBURSEMENTS

Expenses of General Control		$ 43,397.51
Expenses of Instruction		1,274,457.25
Expenses of Auxiliary Agencies and Coordinate Activities		67,554.47
Expenses of Operation of School Plant		208,059.53
Expenses of Maintenance of School Plant		66,672.49
Expenses of Fixed Charges		69,501.44
Debt Service		253,535.61
Capital Outlay		634,291.82
Cash Balance on Hand and in Bank — July 2, 1951		30,498.70
Total Disbursements and Balance		$2,647,968.82

SINKING FUND REPORT

Balance in Fund at July 3, 1950		
Cash	$ 1,762.38	
Investments	603,384.00	605,146.38
Received from General Fund		11,000.00
Interest Income		15,549.37
Balance in Fund at July 2, 1951		
Cash	1,491.13	
Investments	630,204.62	631,695.75

ASSETS

School Buildings and Sites at Cost, Net of Depreciation of $3,359,675.70		$3,646,617.88
Textbooks and Equipment at Cost, Net of Depreciation of $266,977.19		296,373.62
Investments, other than those in Sinking Fund		557,917.40
Unpaid Taxes — Current Year 1950		16,873.00
Unpaid Taxes — Prior to 1950 (Liened)		48,986.36
Accounts Receivable		20,793.49
Cash Balance, exclusive of Cash in Sinking Fund		30,498.70
TOTAL ASSETS		$4,618,060.45

LIABILITIES

Bonded Indebtedness		
Sinking Fund 4½% due 4/1/52	$ 50,000.00	
Sinking Fund 4¼% due 8/1/52	350,000.00	
Sinking Fund 4¼% due 3/1/54	300,000.00	
Serial 4 % due 10/1/50-57	410,000.00	
Serial 2¼% due 12/1/50-55	239,000.00	
Serial 1½% due 5/1/51-70	1,330,000.00	
	2,679,000.00	
Less: Sinking Fund Balance consisting of Cash $1,491.13 and Investments $630,204.62	631,695.75	
Net Bonded Indebtedness at July 2, 1951		$2,047,304.25
Accounts Payable		182,175.00
TOTAL LIABILITIES		$2,229,479.25

Assessed Valuation of Taxable Real Estate $100,094,250.00
Number of Mills Levied — 14

Ralph E. Stine
Certified Public Accountant
Auditor

Dated at Lancaster, Pa.
August 1, 1951

4 AUTOMOBILES USED

1951 OLDSMOBILE Super "88", four door sedan. Private owner. Call Manheim 5-7916.

1950 Plymouth Special Deluxe Club Coupe, R. & H.
1949 Ford Custom 2 dr. R. & H. O.D.
HUNT MOTORS
EPHRATA'S FORD DEALER
1040 S. State St. Phone 3-2297

1936 Buick 7-Passenger, good tires. Check Motorcycle. Late 1948 model.
SAUDER CHEVROLET CO.
MANHEIM, PA. Phone 5-7381

BE SATISFIED
Buy one of our Clean Cars
1950 Ford Custom 2 dr Sedan
1949 Pontiac 2 dr. Sdn. R. & H.
1949 Ford Convertible Coupe
1946 Mercury Station Wagon. R&H
KELLER BROS AUTO CO
Authorized FORD Dealer
"We Appreciate Your Friendship"
LITITZ, PA Phone 6-2121

BEAUTIFUL Dark Green 1949 Hudson Super "6". 4 dr. sdn. Will trade. Rinehart Strasburg, Ph. 2411.

1937 PACKARD "6" 4 door sedan. Heater. Phone 9477.

REAL BUYS
YOU'LL ENJOY OWNING
1949 Dodge Wayfarer Sedan
1949 Plymouth 4 dr. Sedan
1949 Plymouth Suburban
1948 Plymouth 4 dr., 2 dr. Sedans and Club Coupe
These are all 1 owner cars in excellent condition.
Also a nice selection of good clean cars to select from.
KLINE MOTORS
DeSOTO and PLYMOUTH Dealer
LITITZ, PA. Phone 6-2352

1951 Chrysler New Yorker sedan
PAUL H. STERN
329 W. High, Manheim, Ph. 5-2193

1940 PACKARD Convertible, "6". Radio, heater. New Top. $200. Phone 2-1253.

1950 Buick Special 2 dr. Sedan
J. B. ZARTMAN
OPEN EVENINGS until 9:30
N. Broad St., LITITZ Ph. 6-0566

'48 STUDEBAKER
COMMANDER
LAND CRUISER
One Owner — Gray
Radio — Heater
H. LANDIS HILL, INC.
21 E. CLAY ST. PHONE 8156

1937 CHEVROLET Business Coupe
1938 PLYMOUTH Sedan
Both in excellent condition
H. H. MARTIN
Kissel Hill Ph. Lititz 6-2145

4 AUTOMOBILES USED

1950 OLDSMOBILE "98" four door sedan. $1850. Private parties only. Phone 4-3436 Columbia.

1951 MERCURY 4 dr. Sedan R&H, overdrive. 2800 miles. Like new, save $500. STOFFET 220 N. Ann.

1949 CHEVROLET Fleetline 4 dr. sedan. Loaded. Low mileage.
PAUL HAUCK
Route '222, Ephrata Ph. 3-5495

1941 Chevrolet Club coupe R-H $495
1938 Chevrolet 2 dr. sedan $195
Sturgis & Henry, mile west of Millersville Ph. 91-2301.

1949 OLDSMOBILE Rocket, 2 door Deluxe. Extras. Mearig's Texaco, Orange and Water Sts.

1949 PLYMOUTH Special deluxe 4 door, radio, heater. One owner. Phone 2-4370.

1950 FORD CONVERTIBLE Radio, heater, overdrive.... $1495
1950 DeSOTO CLUB COUPE One owner — beautiful.... $1675
1950 BUICK SEDANETTE Everything but music.........$1495
1950 DODGE SEDAN One Owner. Radio, heater......$1585
1949 DODGE CLUB COUPE Coronet model. Heater $1395
ALL FULLY EQUIPPED
GUARANTEED
LEON'S EXCHANGE
220-224 N. LIME ST.
Leon Lipman Carl Migdon

1949 DODGE Coronet Sedan, radio, heater, Gyromatic drive, $1565. Phone 3-3750.

1936 Plymouth 4-Door
JOHN M. ZIMMERMAN
1039 S. Duke St Call 2-4581

SPECIAL
'47 Chevrolet 4 dr. like new cond.
DOMBACH & NAGLE
21 N Charlotte St. Phone 2-3839

'48 KAISER Custom 4 dr. blue, air cond., good tires, one owner traded for a new Kaiser, consumers research claim Kaisers offer the greatest used car value. here is definite proof for $995. Community, 1005 E. King. 2-2488.

'49 FORD Custom 8. 2 dr. blue, spot and back-up lites, W. W. tires, new spare, perfect condition, R-H. If you're a Ford man this one should please you, only $1295. Community, 1005 E. King. 2-2488.

1950 Kaiser 4 dr. sedan, Heater
1949 Mercury 4 dr. sedan, R. & H.
1949 Vanguard Sedan
1947 Stud. Commander Convertible
COOPER'S GARAGE
KAISER - FRAZER Dealer
SALUNGA Ph. Landisville 3651

FOR REAL
HONEST-TO-GOODNESS
VALUES . . . SEE
WIGGINS
CHEVROLET CO.
HARRISBURG PIKE
PHONE 8257

4 AUTOMOBILES USED

'46 CHRYSLER Windsor 4 dr. blue, R-H, interior to match, perfect in every way, if you're a Chrysler man you'll like this one. Only $995. Community, 1005 E. King St. 2-2488.

1950 Chevrolet 4 door Sedan
1949 Mercury 2 door Sedan
1949 Chevrolet Club Coupe
1948 Chevrolet 2 door Sedan
1947 Chevrolet 2 door Sedan
1946 Cadillac 4 door Sedan
1941 Buick 4 door Sedan
SCHREIBER'S
Willys Sales & Service
SALUNGA Ph. Landisville 2711

YOU
CAN
ALWAYS
DEAL
AT
BRUBAKER'S
AT LOWEST PRICES!
YOUR CAR DOWN
18 MONTHS TO PAY
'51 Plym. Club.....$1795.
'51 DeSoto Clb.....$2295.
'50 Nash 4 dr.....$1495.
'49 Dodge Clb. $1595.
'49 DeSoto 4 dr...$1595.
'49 Plym. 4 dr.....$1295.
'49 Ford Clb.......$1295.
'49 DeSoto Clb. ... $1695.
'48 Plym. 4 dr. ....$1095.
'48 Plym. Clb. ....$1095.
'47 Plym. 2 dr. ....$ 945.
'47 Chev. 4 dr. ....$ 995.
'46 DeSoto 4 dr.....$1045.
'42 DeSoto Clb. ....$ 575.
'41 Dodge Clb. ....$ 495.
'40 Chrys. 4 dr.....$ 385.
'39 Dodge 2 dr.....$ 195.
'39 Pack. Conv.....$ 195.
'38 Chev. 2 dr.....$ 185.
'37 DeSoto 4 dr.....$ 125.
'36 Pont. 2 dr. ....$ 95.
BRUBAKER MOTORS
1020-60, Lititz Pike
Ph. 2-2119 — Trading 'til 9 o'clock

1949 Plymouth . . . $1325
Special Deluxe 4 door—one owner.
1947 Chrysler $1195
New Yorker 4 door—radio, heater.
1947 Buick $1050
Roadmaster 4 door, radio, heater
1947 Conv. $1195
Dodge, radio, heater. Cream puff.
1947 Mercury $995
Club Coupe — radio and heater.
ESHELMAN
MOTOR COMPANY
CHRYSLER—PLYMOUTH
W. Orange & Pine Sts.

1950 Olds. "88" 4 dr. Dark blue.
1948 Olds. "98" 4 dr. Grey.
1947 Olds. "68" Conv. Tan.
1937 Ford 2 dr. Sdn. Black.
1936 Olds 4 dr. Sedan. Black
SAUDER CHEVROLET CO.
NEW HOLLAND Ph. 4-2181
Open every Eve. except Sat. & Mon.

1951 Ford Victoria. equipped In paper
1951 Mercury, equipped; low mileage.
1950 Plymouth 4 door
1949 Mercury 2 door
1948 Chevrolet Fleetline
MARIS H. ESHLEMAN
555 New Holland Ave. Call 2-7132

1951 Chevrolet 2 door Deluxe. R. & H., W.W. Tires.
1950 Pontiac Chieftain Deluxe. 4 dr. R. & H., Hydramatic.
Donald H. Stauffer
Cor. Franklin and Clay Ph. 3-6822

SPENCE MOTORS
Ford Dealer—Quarryville
1950 Ford 4 dr., R. & H.
1950 Ford 2 dr., R. & H. Overdrive
1948 Packard 4 dr. R. & H. Clean.
1946 Buick Roadmaster, R. & H.
PHONE QUARRYVILLE 65

LINK'S
AUTO EXCHANGE
HARRISBURG PIKE Ph. 4-4030
18 MONTHS TO PAY
1950 Nash 2 dr. Sedan $1395
1949 DeSoto Club Coupe
1947 Pontiac Station Wagon
1946 Hudson 4 dr. Sedan $ 795

1941 PACKARD 4 door sedan. Radio, heater. Good rubber. Call 2-8808

ROLL YOUR OWN
It's smart to drive your own car —especially when you don't have to peel many leaves off the family Tobacco Plant to buy it.
1949 DeSoto 4 dr. Sedan, Htr.
1947 Chrysler 4 dr. Sedan, Htr.
1947 Plymouth 4 dr. Sedan Htr.
1940 Nash 4 dr. Sedan, Htr.
These are very clean, low mileage cars.
L. L. BOOK
DESOTO and PLYMOUTH Dealer
MANHEIM Phone 5-2257

1951 FORD Station Wagon, Never licensed. 1949 Ford Station Wagon, one owner, A-1 condition. Phone 3-3636. after 6 P. M.

2 BIG LOW PRICED
SPECIALS
1939 Plymouth Dlx. Sd.
$165.
1939 Buick Spc. Coupe
$275.
HARTMAN
PONTIAC, INC.
Home of Good Will Used Cars
425 W. King St. Phone 3-3826

"A1"
USED CARS
1950 FORD CRESTLINER
Looks new — runs new — carefully driven by local owner Has radio—heater—overdrive
1950 FORD TUDOR SEDAN
4 brand new tires—radio—heater. A local one owner car.
1949 FORD STATION WAGON
A wonderful work horse or pleasure car, that is in almost new condition. Priced right.
1949 OLDSMOBILE CONV.
Radio and Heater. Ready for the open road. Drive it.
1949 FORD CUSTOM TUDOR
Car has been well cared for. Has both radio and heater.
1946 PONTIAC "6' SEDAN
Excellent condition inside and out. Ideal family car.
WE SELL ONLY
GUARANTEED CARS
Visit Our Used Car Lot
COLUMBIA PIKE—WEST
PHONE 3-8083
GARDEN SPOT
MOTOR CO.
450 N. PRINCE ST.

'46 NASH Amb. 4 dr. 23 miles per gal. Perfect only $895. Good tires, radio, heater and over drive, runs like a rabbit. Community 1005 E. King. 2-2488.

4 AUTOMOBILES USED

1948 Chev. Aero Sdn. Fully equip.
WEAVER'S GARAGE
Bird-in-Hand Phone 3-9267

1951 Stud. Landcruiser Sd. low mi.
M. K. ENTERLINE
Cherry St., Elizabethtown Ph. 425

1950 Studebaker Champion Starlight Coupe, O.D., R. & H., $1495
1949 Plymouth Sd. R. & H. 1 owner
1948-1947 Willys Jeep
LEON HERSHEY
Kissel Hill Car Lot. Ph. Lititz 6-2357

1941 Oldsmobile Sedan, Hydramatic.
1941 Buick Sedan, Special. 1937 Plymouth Pick-up. Armand Paquin. 555 North St. Phone 2-9691.

WE GIVE THEM
ALL A RUN FOR
THEIR MONEY
That's Why They
Come to
QUEEN MOTORS
1951 Nash 2 door, R&H, overdrive
1951 Mercury 4-door, R&H
1951 Ford 2-door, radio, heater
1950 Buick 4 door, R&H, Dynaflow
1949 Buick Super 4-dr., R&H, dyna.
1949 Buick Conv., R&H, dynaflow
1949 Lincoln 4-dr., R&H, overdrive
1949 Pontiac Club Coupe, heater
1949 Plymouth Conv., radio, heater
1949 Mercury 2-door, R&H
1948 Pontiac Conv., radio, heater
1948 Chrysler 4-door, R&H
1948 Ford Club Coupe, R&H
1947 Chev. Fleetline 4-dr., R&H
1947 Nash 4-door, radio, heater
1947 Studebaker Clb. Cpe., R&H, OD
1946 Lincoln 4-dr., R&H, overdrive
1941 Mercury 4 door; radio, heater
1941 Plymouth 4-dr., radio, heater
1941 Chevrolet Clb. Cpe., heater
1940 Hudson 4-door, radio, heater
1939 Chrysler 4-door, radio, heater
1938 Ford 4-door, heater
1937 Chevrolet 2-dr., radio, heater
1937 Chevrolet Panel truck, heater
QUEEN MOTORS
950 N. QUEEN ST.

18 MONTHS
TO PAY
TODAY'S
SPOT SPECIAL
1948 PLYMOUTH
DELUXE SEDAN
Radio and Heater
$1125.
☆
1950 DODGE
CORONET SEDAN
Radio—Heater—Gyromatic
1949 DODGE
CORONET SEDAN
Radio and Heater
1949 FORD
2 DOOR CUSTOM
Heater and defroster
1949 FORD
CONVERTIBLE
Radio and Heater
1947 PLYMOUTH
4 DOOR SEDAN
Heater and defroster
OPEN 'TIL 9 P. M.
Many Others — Bank Financing
BOB HESS
DODGE — PLYMOUTH
Used Car Center
Harrisburg Pike Phone 2-5523

GOOD — SOUND
FAIRLY PRICED
1950 Packard Club Sedan — light gray. Ultramatic drive.
1950 Packard Sedan — black—10,500 miles. Ultramatic drive.
1950 Oldsmobile Club Sedan "76"
1947 Chrysler Sedan
1946 Nash Sedan
1946 Oldsmobile Coupe
35 Others—Many Cheaper Models
Packard-Lancaster Co.
426 N. Prince St.

IT
DOESN'T TAKE
THE F.B.I.
. . . to find out how superior our Used Cars are! Drive in today and double check any of the clean, powerful bargains on our lot. Do your own deciding. Be critical as you please. Greater values. Lower prices. Easy terms, if you wish. Look at these beauties:
'49 CADILLAC. . . .$2675
4 door "62" Sedan — One Owner. Hydramatic — Radio — Heater.
'50 PONTIAC. $2195
You'll never find better convertible weather than we are having this summer. And you never find a convertible in any better condition than this one. Has hydramatic — radio — heater and other extras.
'46 OLDS. $1045
"76" Hydramatic—Radio—Heater — Good tires—Beautiful black.
'47 STUDE. $950
Starlite Club Coupe—Radio—Heater.
'47 OLDS $1195
"78" Club Sedan — Hydramatic — Radio — Heater — like new white wall tires — Perfect in every respect.
And Many More . . .
All Values Galore!
Guaranteed Used Cars
50-50 guarantee
John S. GROFF, Inc.
Cadillac — Oldsmobile
625 E. Orange St. Phone 6271
Our Promise is Your Satisfaction!

4 AUTOMOBILES USED

1946 FORD Convertible. Excellent condition. Phone 4-2194.

1950 Chevrolet Fleetline 2 dr.
1949 Pontiac Chieftain 2 dr., Hydra.
1949 Chevrolet Styleline 4 dr.
1948 Packard "145" 4 dr.
1948 Nash 600 4 dr.
1947 Buick Super 4 dr.
1947 Pontiac "6" Club Coupe
1946 Ford Club Cpe. & Coach
1940 Packard "6" 4 dr. Sedan
1937 DeSoto 4 dr. Sedan
1934 Chevrolet 2 dr. Very clean.
18 MONTHS TO PAY
SEE LEPORE
Sinclair Station
Corner Duke and Liberty

TORT'S
CLEAN USED CARS
1949 Pontiac Chieftan, deluxe 2 door sedan, hydromatic, heater.
1949 Ford Custom Club Coupe. Radio and heater
1949 Buick Super Sedan. radio. heater dynaflow.
1949 Buick Roadmaster Sedan, clean, radio, heater
1949 Chevrolet Deluxe Coupe. Clean.
1947 Ford Coach. Like new.
1946 Oldsmobile "66" Club Cpe. Hyd.
1946 Chevrolet Sedan R&H.
1946 Plymouth Sedan. clean.
HENRY TORT
126-130 E. KING ST.
Phone 7912

OUR CARS BLOW THEIR OWN HORN
1951 DeSoto Custom Sportsman. Plenty of extras, still in paper. Save $300.
1950 Ford Custom 2 dr. Fully equipped from original owner. Like new. $1495.
1950 Cadillac "62" 4 door sedan Fully equipped. $3495.
1949 Cadillac "62" 4 door, fully equipped with electric windows. Low mileage. Original tires. $2645.
1948 Cadillac "62" 4 door sedan. 20,000 original miles $1995
1948 Buick Roadmaster 4 door Sedan. Fully equipped. $1295.
1947 Cadillac "62" Sedanette Fully equipped including Hydramatic. Very clean. Only $1595.
SHIRK'S
Manheim Pike & Dillersville Rd 8077

1951 Dodge Coronet 4 dr. Sedan. Gyromatic transmission. Radio. heat., seat covers.
1949 Plymouth Special Deluxe 4 dr. Sedan — Heater.
1949 Dodge Panel delivery. Looks like new. $950.
STEHMAN BROS.
SALUNGA Ph. Landisville 2911

MERVIN R. MURRY
1008 N. Prince St Ph. 2-7740

CREAM PUFF
1947 Chevrolet Fleetline Sd. R. & H. Clean. Very low mileage.
CLOISTER MOTORS, Ephrata 3-2492

'49 KAISER Custom 4 dr. original grey like new inside and out, 27,000 miles. W. W. tires, 21 miles per gal. Excellent value, traded on new Kaiser. $1495 Community, 1005 E. King. 2-2488.

1941 PLYMOUTH Station Wagon $450. Apply 620 West Marion St.

'48 CUSTOM 4 dr. black, fully equipped R-H, W. W. tires. fluid drive clean, shows good care. priced for quick sale at $1295. Community, 1005 E. King St. 2-2488.

Kaiser-Frazer Sales WITH service
FUHRMAN MOTORS Columbia Pa

1948 CROSLEY Station Wagon, New '50 motor. Good condition. Phone 3-3527.

The Big Lot with the
LITTLE PRICES
ON ALL CARS
18 MONTHS FINANCING
1951 Olds. "98" Deluxe 4 dr Sedan. Dark green. In paper....$2875
1951 Chevrolet Bel Air. 2-tone green. Loaded with extras. In paper. $2095
1951 Plymouth Cranbrook 4 door Sedan. Radio, heater. In paper. $1995
1951 Ford "8" Custom 2 door Sedan. Radio, heater $1895
1951 Chevrolet Styleline Deluxe 4 door sedan. Equipped $1795
1951 Chevrolet 4 door Sedan, radio, heater. Power Glide $1975
1950 Cadillac 52—4 door sedan fully equipped like new $3475
1950 Olds "88" 4 door Sedan Deluxe. fully equipped $1895
1950 Buick 4 dr. Sedan $1495
1950 DeSoto 4 dr. Sedan Custom. Radio. heater, white wall tires $1875
1949 Buick 2 dr. Sedan. Radio, heater, white wall tires $1495
1949 Ford 2 door Sedan, Radio, heater $1275
1949 DeSoto Custom 4 door Sedan. Fully equipped $1595
1949 Chevrolet 4 dr. Sdn. ... $1295
1949 Dodge 4 dr. Sedan . Radio and heater. Like new $1495
1949 Plymouth 2 dr. Sedan. Radio and heater $1295
1948 Chevrolet Club Coupe. Radio and heater. Very clean $1095
1948 Dodge 4 dr. Sedan. Dark green. Radio. heater. Very clean. $1175
1948 Chevrolet Convertible. New top. Radio and heater $1195
1947 DeSoto 2 door Sedan. Radio and heater $1095
1947 Chevrolet Fleetline 4 door sedan. Radio, heater. Very clean $1075
1946 Buick 2 door sedan, radio, heater. Motor overhauled. $1050
1946 Packard 4 dr. Sedan. Radio and heater .... $ 875
1946 Chevrolet 2 dr. Sdn .... $ 895
1946 DeSoto 4 dr. Sedan .. $ 975
1942 Studebaker 4 dr. Sedan Ready to go .... $ 295
1942 Packard Clipper 4 dr. sd. $ 495
1941 Hudson 4 door sedan. Very good condition .... $ 350
1941 Dodge Convertible. Radio and heater. Like new ...... $ 475
1940 LaSalle Club Coupe Radio and heater ....$ 495
1941 Buick 4 door Sedan ....$ 495
1939 Buick 4 dr. Sedan ......$ 150
1938 Dodge 4 dr. sedan ......$ 50
1937 Dodge 4 dr. Sedan ......$ 150
1937 Plymouth 2 door Sedan..$ 150
1937 Pontiac 4 door Sedan ..$ 175
1930 Ford Model "A" coupe
LANCASTER SALES CO.
ESTABLISHED 1937
Manheim Pike Ph. 4-0538
Famous for Spic-and-Span Cars

'47 BUICK convt. R-H, W. W. black, electric windows, looks and runs like new and priced for quick sale before cold weather sets in. $1195. Community, 1005 E. King. 2-2488.

'47 PONTIAC Station Wagon fully equipped, perfect condition, good tires, privately owned left at our lot for us to sell, owner must sell, bergain $1095. Community, 1005 E King St. 2-2488.

BUY & SELL. Edw. G. Reese. Kissell Hill, Lititz Pike, Lititz 6-8071.

1950 Chevrolet Sedan Delivery. Radio and Heater.
1949 Chev. Fleetline 4 dr., low miles
1948 Plymouth 2 dr. sedan, R. & H.
NEWCOMER MOTORS
MOUNT JOY, Pa. Phone 3-4821

1948 PONTIAC
"8" CONVERTIBLE
You'll never find better convertible weather than we are having this Summer. And you never find a convertible in any better condition than this one. The yellow finish is perfect and it has a new black top. Fully equipped with hydramatic, radio, heater, backup lites, turn signals, bumper ends and excellent tires.
Only $1350.
GUY R. GILGORE
Lititz and Oregon Pikes
PHONE 2-0477

4 AUTOMOBILES USED

BUICK DEALER
OFFERS GOOD VALUE
1950 Buick Super Riviera
1949 Ford Station Wagon
1947 Chrysler 4 dr. Sedan
MOHN BROS.
BUICK SALES AND SERVICE
939 N. Prince St. Dial 5125

1949 LINCOLN COSMOPOLITAN 4 door sedan, radio, heater, hydramatic. White side wall tires. Flashy two-tone paint job. Low mileage.
1950 Ford Custom V8 Tudor. Radio & Heater—maroon—one owner.
1950 Ford Custom V8 Tudor. Beautiful Gray—radio—heater.
1949 Ford Station Wagon. R & H.
1948 Studebaker Convertible — radio — heater — overdrive.
1947 Buick Conv R&H.
WOLF MOTOR CO.
1002 N. Prince St. Ph. 2-4187
102 W Liberty St. Ph. 3-9010

1949 Mercury Sdn. A bargain.$1495
1949 Ford Custom 4 dr. Clean.$1295
1946 Plymouth Spec. Dlxe Coach $ 795
STONER MOTOR CO.
FORD MERCURY SERVICE
45-50 S. Queen St. Call 2-9656

'50 Pontiac Chieftain "8" 4 door. R. & H.—Hydramatic.
'49 Chevrolet 4 dr. R.&H.
'50 Studebaker 2 dr.
'48 Studebaker Land Cruiser
'47 Pontiac Conv. New top $995.
47 Chevrolet 2 door R. & H.
'39 Studebaker Champ. 4 dr. R. & H.
'42 Olds 2 dr. Htr. Hydra.
'40 Olds 2 dr. Radio & Heater.
'47 Chevrolet Panel
Kachel Motor Co.
215 N Franklin St. Ph. 3-8948

1951 Lincoln Cosmopolitan 4 dr. Sedan. 6000 actual miles. New Car Guarantee.
1950 Mercury 4 dr. Sedan, R&H, Overdrive. Black
1950 Ford 4 dr Sdn., R&H, O.D.
1946 Studebaker 2 dr. Sdn., R&H
MELLINGER, INC.
NEW HOLLAND Phone 4-0651
Open Weekdays until 9 P. M.

18 MONTHS
FINANCING
LOW DOWN PAYMENT
LOW COST INSURANCE
LOW INTEREST RATE
USE YOUR CAR AS DOWN PAYMENT . . . IT MAY BE WORTH EVEN MORE
FREE APPRAISAL
CLOSE TO NEW CARS
1951 Nash Ambass. 4 dr. Hydramatic
1950 Buick Riviera Coupe
1950 Studebaker Champ 4 dr.
1949 Oldsmobile "98" 2 door
1949 Dodge Coronet Club Cpe.
1949 DeSoto Custom 4 door
1949 Plymouth Suburban
1948 Pontiac Station Wagon
1948 Chrysler Royal 4 door
1948 DeSoto Custom 4 door
1948 Ford Super 4 door
1946 Chevrolet 4 door—A1
1946 Nash Ambassador 4 dr.
☆
1948-47-46 Nash Amb. Clb. Cpe. R. & H.—overdrive. from $ 895
1948 Nash Ambassador 4 dr. $1275
1946 Olds. "76" 4 dr. R. H.. $ 995
1942 Stude. Champ. 4 dr. R&H $ 375
1941 Cadillac 2 dr. R. & H. A-1.
1941 Hudson 4 dr., heater .... $ 275
1941 Nash Ambas. 4 door....$ 495
HARRY R. BITZER
YOUR NASH DEALER
720 N. Prince St. Phone 2-4128
Open Sundays 10 A. M. to 5 P. M.

1950 Chevrolet Belair — very clean
1950 Ford Custom sedan
Many. Many Others.
J. G. BOOTH
7 N. MULBERRY ST.
816 S. PRINCE ST.

BUICK — CHEVROLET
LITITZ SPRINGS GARAGE
Broad & Marion, Lititz Ph. 6-2216

'47 FORD Super Deluxe club cpe., maroon, R-H, good tires like new, better than average and priced right. Only $1045. Community, 1005 E. King St.

1947 OLDSMOBILE 2 door, black. Excellent condition. Lititz 6-8646 evenings.

MILLER BROS.
GUARANTEED QUALITY
AUTOMOBILES
LEOLA Phone 6-2041
Just a Few of Our Selection
1951 Plymouth Convertible Coupe
1951 Chevrolet Belaire Coupe
1951 Pontiac "8" Catalina
1950 Ford Station Wagon
1950 Chevrolet Belaire Coupe
1950 Buick Spec. Del. Sedanette
1950 Pontiac Catalina
1950 Dodge 2 door Sedan
1950 Buick Special 4 door
1950 Ford Custom 2 door
1949 Chevrolet Deluxe 4 door
1949 Chevrolet Deluxe 2 door

1950 Chev. Belair, R&H, P.G., $1875
1950 DeSoto Sedan $1795
1949 Chevrolet Convertible $1395
1949 Studebaker Conv. OD. H..$1375
1946 Olds "76" Sedanette, R&H $1075
1940 Ford Station Wagon....$ 395
1938 Oldsmobile, R&H........$ 175
MICK & DICK
Manheim Pike

OLDSMOBILE
1949 Convertible "88" Rocket, Hydramatic, sidewall tires. Fully equipped, 21,000 miles. Excellent condition. Private party. Evelyn Brubaker. Mount Joy 3-5334.

'46 CHRYSLER Town and Country 6, hard top, here is just the car for that trip to the shore or mountain, all new heavy duty tires, completely refinished and fully equipped ready to go, cost over $3500. Guaranteed a big value for $1345. Community, 1005 E. King St. 2-2488.

D. L. NEFF
HUDSON Sales & Service.
LITITZ, PA Phone 6-7366
1947 Willys Station Wagon
1946 DeSoto Club Coupe.
Easy Bank Financing
50-50 Guarantee
STAUFFER'S
USED CARS
541 New Holland Ave.

60 cars to choose from. All makes and all models.
LANCASTER
LINCOLN-MERCURY CO
N Prince & McGovern. Ph 3-3681
Open Evenings

1949 FORD. Two door sedan. Radio, heater, and spotight. Hertzler's Garage, Clay.

'48 PLYMOUTH — 4 door — R. & H.
SANDERS Call 2-7605

4A AUTOMOBILES WANTED

Late Model Cars Wanted
IRVIN WOLF
Rear of Theatre Lititz
Ph. Lititz 6-2240 or Ephrata 3-2600

GET A BIG PRICE
Now's the time to sell your car while you can still get the high dollar. Bring it around to us where you'll get the most you can for your car.
LINCOLN CAR MART
LINCOLN Ph. Ephrata 3-2653

SOUTH CAROLINA BUYER
1006 N. Prince St. Ph. 2-7740

MIGDON 2-5280 2-7511

DeHAVEN 828 S. Prince Phone 2-5633

4A AUTOMOBILES WANTED

See North Carolina Dealer at Roth Esso Station Surprising Prices Harrisburg Pike & Dillerville Rd

LANCASTER SALES CO
Manheim Pike Phone 4-0538

5 TRUCKS AND TRAILERS

REO PICK-UP. Runs well. $65. RINEHART, Strasburg. Ph. 2411

1940 Dodge 1 ton truck
SAUDER CHEVROLET CO.
MANHEIM, PA. Phone 5-7381

1941 INTERNATIONAL K5. New Motor. Complete with bed. Perfect condition. Call 4-0166. New Holland.

1951 GMC Walk-in Delivery Truck
N. G. HERSHEY
Manheim Phone 5-3351

DAVID—Bradley 2 wheel cargo trailer, all steel body, 8' long. Complete with rack and tarpaulin, license holder, tail and stop lights. Ephrata Legion Park. See Mr. Rutt.

1951 Dodge ½ ton Pickup Deluxe Cab. Low mileage.
Showalter & Horning
NEW HOLLAND Phone 4-2184

TRUCK BARGAINS
1940 Chevrolet chassis and cab. U license
International model K7S7 tractor and 24-ft. trailer
Henry E. Martin & Sons
INTERNATIONAL DEALER
448 S. Prince Call 7413

1940 INTERNATIONAL 1 ton Stake body. A-1 condition. Union & Dorwart Sts.

One WB22 White Tractor ... $2200
One 260XW Brockway Tractor $2000
One T70C Autocar Tractor 90 engine ....$ 750
One EHT Mack Tractor $1200
Lancaster Motor
Truck Service
MACK TRUCK DISTRIBUTORS
459 Juliette Ave. Phone 6101

1946 FORD truck, Z tags, with racks; hauling 600 baskets tomatoes. $600. Phone Atglen 27-R-3, at Parksburg.

WB 28 Tractor with Auxiliary Transmission
White Indiana Service — Phone 6147

SCHOOL BUS
1951 Ford 48 Passenger
KELLER BROS.
Authorized FORD Dealer
"We Apppreciate Your Friendship"
LITITZ PA Phone 6-2121

1947 Ford ¾ T Panel
1941 Dodge 1½ T Stake "U" Tag
1938 International Panel
WOLF MOTOR CO
1002 N Prince St. Ph 2-4187

DEPENDABLE
USED TRUCKS
1951 Dodge 2T. Cab & Ch
1950 Ford ½T. Panel
1949 Dodge 1T. Express
1949 Reo 1T. Van body
1949 Stude. 1½T. Stake
1948 Dodge 2½T. Tractor
1948 Reo 2T. Cab & Chas
1947 Ford 1½T. Van body
1946 Chev. ½T. Panel
1946 Dodge Walk-in
1945 Dodge 1½T. Stake
1942 Ford ¾T. Walk-in
1941 Chev. ½T. Panel
1940 Ford 1T. Panel
1940 Chev. ½T. Panel
WORLD'S FAIREST GUARANTEE
Terms To Suit You
LOW BANK RATES
BOB HESS, INC.
DODGE "JOB RATED" TRUCKS
HARRISBURG PIKE
Phone 2-5523 or 6247

1946 Dodge, U license, good condition $775 Lancaster 3-0204.

1949 Ford 1½ ton Stake
1941 Dodge ½ ton Pickup
1940 Chevrolet ½ ton Panel
KELLER BROS.
Authorized FORD Dealer
"We Appreciate Your Friendship"
LITITZ, PA. Phone 6-2121

GOING OUT OF BUSINESS. Priced for quick sale, with low mileage. 1950 Reo W license; 1948 Chevrolet S license; 1947 G. M. C., T license; 1946 Reo U license. 452 Beaver St. Phone 8911.

WE ARE
OVERSTOCKED
in
1948 FORD
and
1948 DODGE
PANELS
NAME YOUR
OWN PRICE
No Reasonable Offer
Will Be Turned Down
WIGGINS
CHEVROLET CO.
HARRISBURG PIKE
PHONE 8257

1950 Chevrolet Cab over tractor "V" tag.
1950 Diamond T tractor "W" tag. Like new.
A. B. HOLLINGER & SON, INC.
Keller Ave. Phone 3-3633

Two-wheel trailer
KEN'S, Prince & Andrew 2-9393.

THREE TRUCKS for tomato hauling. Cheap. Phone 3-0082 Lancaster, or 2-1203.

1949 INTERNATIONAL Pickup
McCORMICK FARM EQUIP. STORE
Ephrata, Pa. Phone 3-2283

12' CATTLE truck body, good condition. Call Ephrata 3-0183.

Model "A" stake body truck.
N A Buhrman 205 N Christian

1947 Brockway Sleeper Clean
1946 CHEVROLET, chassis & cab van body
MARINE TRUCK &
EQUIPMENT SERVICE
G M C Dealer
Lincoln Highway East Ph 3-3674

REO TRUCKS are the
CHOICE of CHAMPIONS
J HARVEY SPAHR
Manheim, Pa Phone 5-2281

1935 DODGE panel body truck, excellent for farm use. Apply Ream's, 16 East King.

6 AUTO RADIATORS

B. & S RADIATOR REPAIR
212 N Christian St Phone 3-6491

BATTERY & BRAKE
16 E Walnut St Dial 6104

Auto Radiators Repaired. Cleaned
Vogt Radiator Co. 34 N Water

ALEX GERZ RADIATOR CO
435 N. Mulberry St Phone 2-6283

7 AUTO ACCESSORIES, SERVICE

4 WHITE SIDEWALL TIRES, size 700x15, and two almost new Goodyear tires, size 700x16. Will swap all six on four good tires 700x15, or sell outright. Manheim 5-8890.

BATTERY SERVICE
TIRES — BRAKES — IGNITION
Wheatland Auto Co., 136 S. Prince

7 AUTO ACCESSORIES, SERVICE

AUTO GLASS SERVICE
PITTSBURGH PLATE GLASS CO
N Prince & Walnut — Glass Corner

EXPERT REPAIR SERVICE
Hartman Pontiac 425 W King St

DELCO BATTERIES
ROAD SERVICE
BATTERY & BRAKE
16 E Walnut St Dial 6104

Quick Service at our
BODY and FENDER SHOP
EXPERT AUTO PAINTING
PACKARD-LANCASTER CO.
426 N Prince Phone 2-4171

TIRE RECAPPING
Goodyear All-Weather Tread
LEBZELTER'S
237 N Queen St. Ph. 5161

WHITE WALL
TIRES
ALL SIZES
WALTERS & FISHER
621 N Prince St Phone 2-1185

AUTO PAINTING — No waiting Give your car a "new look" Leo Weaver, 218 S. Christian 2-6498

8 BABY CHICKS & SUPPLIES

Sectional bolt-to-gether
BROODER HOUSE
Easily assembled — light weight —very sturdy. Size 12 ft.x20 ft.
SPECIAL $350
Sears Farm Store
212 N. Queen St.

READ OUR AD in this column appearing every Tuesday on our new
Musser Cross Chicks
MUSSER LEGHORN FARMS
Mount Joy Phone 3-4911

MARTIN'S NICHOLS CHICKS
Barred Cross & New Hampshires.
MARTIN'S HATCHERY, Route 30, 4 Mi. West of Lancaster. Ph. 2-2164.

DELAWARE PULLETS
MARCH 14c
Also Hatching Indian River Cross and New Hampshire Broiler Chicks each week.
Indian River Hatchery
LANDIS VALLEY Ph. Lanc. 6109

BABY CHICKS
MOORE FARMS. Call 2-1321

KERR CHICKERIES CO.
324 E Orange St Phone 2-4411

NICHOL CROSSES, Super N. H. Reds Barred & White Rocks 2 to 8 wk old Anthony Leghorns. Enos R BUCKWALTER, Lanc. 4. Ph. 5085

A. S. GROFF
21 S. QUEEN ST. CALL 5201
Day Old and
Started Chicks

HUBBARD'S
NEW HAMPSHIRES
Are noted for their High Egg Production and excellent Meat Qualities. Order yours today from
HUBBARD FARMS
MANHEIM PIKE Phone 2-2154

NEW HAMPSHIRES
J L. Harnish. Millersville 4876

DAY OLD GUINEAS & White Cornish White Rock Cross Chicks. Enos W Witmer. Phone 2-2100.

WHITE ROCKS
CONESTOGA POULTRY FARM
J G. Herr Landisville 3547

FLORIN FARMS Chicks
Mt. Joy 3-9891.

Special White Broiler Crosses. Horst's Hatchery. New Holland 4-9447.

TURKEY BROILERS
Day old and started Poults. Lowest prices.
EPHRATA HATCHERIES
R. 1 Ephrata Ph. Denver 7-4791

9 BOATS—ACCESSORIES

1951 Evinrude outboards $87.50 up. New boats $66.00 up F. O. B. Henwood Co. 324 E. King 8-6 P. M.

12' BOAT, with cover. Brand new. (Car top), $150. Apply 738 St. Joseph.

Used 16 H. P. Elto O. B. Motor. Snyder, 120 N. Franklin. Ph. 2-9472.

14' RUNABOUT Pen-Yan Boat with deck, used 4 years; trailer to haul same. 7½ Horse power Mercury motor, used 2 years. Boat "225. Trailer $75. Motor $175. Complete outfit $400. Phone Marietta 6-3384. Evenings.

7½ H.P. Scotatwater. Excellent condition. $125. Phone New Holland 4-7137.

5½ H.P. ELGIN outboard motor, excellent condition. $105. Phone 2-8519.

12' TROJAN and Trailer, 1951 Mercury Hurricane, 10 horsepower. 2-0048.

10 BUSINESS OPPORTUNITIES

WENTZEL
STANLEY M. HAS 'EM
401 W. Orange Ph. 4-0452 or 3-7215
OPEN UNTIL 8 P. M.

THRIVING MILK
BAR BUSINESS
IDEALLY LOCATED just outside a growing borough in a prosperous community on a busy hwy. Large macadam parking area. Established and steady growing business for life-time income. Just fine for husband and wife team.
$50,000.
Sale price includes large building—6 rm. conv. living quarters—milk bar restaurant equipment. All away below present replacement costs. Call us to see, and for further details. We'll listen to offers?

FOR SALE
MODERN
GROCERY STORE
LOCATED IN EAST YORK
Corner property, all good equipment. Clean stock. Reason for selling, owner leaving town.
IF INTERESTED CALL
York 4-9181
(NO TRIFLERS)

BEER DISTRIBUTOR BUSINESS for sale in city. Doing very nice business. $6,000 capital investment required. Will get original investment back during first year. Write Box 296 Lancaster Newspapers.

ONE OF OUR BETTER
ATLANTIC FRANCHISES
In Lancaster, will become available within the next month for a progressive SERVICE STATION OPERATOR.
Approximately $5000 in working capital requirel to finance the operation of this new modern station.
For further information call or write
The Atlantic Refining Co.
MANHEIM PIKE,
LANCASTER, PA.

RESTAURANT, beer and liquor license for sale. Make offer. Harry Cornwell, Florin, Pa.

GAS STATION for rent in city. Major oil company. Reasonable rent. Doing nice gallonage. $4800 capital for inventory. Good opportunity for live wire. Would be glad to have interview. Write Box 293, Lancaster Newspapers.

11 BICYCLES & MOTORCYCLES

1941 HARLEY Davidson, "74" Over head valve. Good condition. Reasonable. Phone Leola 6-3292.

1946 INDIAN CHIEF, buddy seat, spotlights, saddle bags, $285. John Royer, Hopeland, after 4 p. m.

1946 Chief A1. Call Donald Deen. Hensel 47.

1948 Harley Davidson "45" fully equipped — lots of chrome — light blue — saddle bags. Harry R. Bitzer, 720 N. Prince 2-4128

11 BICYCLES & MOTORCYCLES

WIZZER MOTOR BIKE; 24" wheels. Excellent condition. Must be seen to be appreciated. Phone 2-3718, after 5:30.

1947 HARLEY DAVIDSON, $375. 644 E. Madison St.

1948 CUSHMAN motor scooter. See at Shirk's Garage, Paradise. No phone calls.

48 HARLEY motorcycle, new battery, perfect 61 overhead, $250. worth of chrome, new tires, owner drafted into service, yours for $450. Community, 1005 E. King. 2-2488.

1949 HARLEY-DAVIDSON "74". Like New. With hydro-glide. Low mileage. Mac's Service Station, corner Front and Cedar Sts., Lititz.

Harley-Davidson Sales and Service New and used motorcycles. Terms.
Lancaster Harley-Davidson Co.
200 Hazel St Call 3-4031

FULL SIZE Girl's Elgin bicycle. Good condition. Phone 3-8507.

1948 HARLEY DAVIDSON "45". Phone 3-0397.

1948 Harley 740H $495
MICK & DICK
Manheim Pike

CUSHMAN Motor Scooters, sales and service. 218 Nevin St. Ph. 2-9272.

WORLD'S FINEST BICYCLES at no greater cost than many ordinary ones. Girls or boys.
SHENK BROS — 34 W KING ST.

New $44.95 Schwinn Bikes
SPECIAL $39.95—Terms.
Goodrich, Prince & Vine. 2-2196

12 COAL & FUEL

Buckwheat $11.00—Pea Coal $14.00
Nut Coal $17.50—Stove Coal $17.50
LANCASTER COAL CO.
Coal & Lumber 334 Mill St 3-9389

COAL & FUEL OIL. Zook Bros. Lanc. 3-0370 or Yard Lititz 6-0701.

FIREPLACE AND ALL KINDS OF stove wood for sale. 7834.

12A CAMERAS—SUPPLIES & PHOTOGRAPHERS

KODAK 16 mm Movie Camera with F1.9 lens, like brand new, Special $134.95. Shop in cool comfort. Complete camera supplies. DARMSTAETTERS 37 N. Queen

KODAK 35 with range finder and case. Used, bargain at $59.50 RICHARDS Photo Shop, 47 N. Prince

REVERE 16 M.M. magazine load—F 1:9 lens—This movie camera is just like brand new and can be had for only $130.
COE CAMERA SHOP, 148 N. Queen

KEYSTONE 16 MM. Movie Camera including lighting system, used 10 months. Kodascope 16 mm. Projector and screen, 50x50. Phone Landisville 4701.

Full line of Kodak Cameras
SHENK BROS —30 W King St

13 FOR SALE MISCELLANEOUS

Television and Radios will be found under Classification 30A. Cameras and Photographic Supplies are listed under Classification 12A.

50,000 BASKETS
½ bu. Peach. ⅝ bu. Tomato & Potato
LEAMAN SEED HOUSE
116 S. Queen St. Call 5484

TOBACCO SHED, must be torn down and moved. Make offer. Located at Rowenna. Geo. E. Hershey, Marietta R1.

40-GALLON domestic water storage tank and dome top coal heater, good condition, reasonable. Phone 2-7036.

RIPE AND READY
Now Picking Tri-O-Gem
HOME GROWN PEACHES
The Newer, better varieties. Selected for flavor, size and color. The choicest Peaches of the East. Come to our orchards at Lenover.
SAMUEL F. LANTZ
GOLDEN GARDENS
Phone Parkesburg 635-W

HOT AIR FURNACE, including pipe, good condition, reasonable. Phone Manheim 5-4221 after 4:30.

SAVABRUSH for hard paint brush HUHN'S Paint Store, 503 Manor

ENDURECOTE asbestos shingle coating—red or white $5.95 per gallon.
Capitol Insulation 42 N. Prince 7136

DUSTOP Air Filters, 16"x25"x1"
STEWART & FUSS, Ph. 3-0059

FOR SALE, Barber Chair and gas stove. Phone Leola 6-2242.

12 HOLE Ice Cream Cabinet. Good condition. Call 9783.

150 ACRES PEACHES
GOLDEN JUBILEE &
CUMBERLAND
MANCHESTER FRUIT FARM
Between Emigsville & Manchester on route 24 in York County
Paul A. Bear R. 1, Mt. Wolf
TROUT RUN FRUIT FARM
3 miles east of York on U. S. 30
Phone Manchester 3638

EAR CORN, delivered. $53 per ton. Jacob G. Rohrer. Quarryville 94-R-14.

ENCYCLOPEDIA Britannica, Jr. Winter coat and rain coat, size 12. never worn. Phone 4-1611.

30" TABLE-TOP Gas Range. 35 gallon Gas Heater. 2 inside solid wooden doors 32x81 and 34x81. Two inside wooden double doors 31½x89. Gas pipe like new ¾" and fittings. Phone 3-8407.

82 GALLON WATER TANK, extra heavy, Ruud Heater. Phone 4-1969.

Furniture tops Glass cut to size. Reisinger. 3-0391

LUMBER, rough. Air dried, 2x4's, 2x6's. 2x8's—ten to twenty feet long. A few girders. $80 per thousand. Call Manheim 5-3853, between five and six P. M.

ITHACA Pump Gun, 12 gauge, excellent condition. $70. Isaac Petersheim, Ronks R. 1.

WELSH Folding baby carriage. Phone 3-6173.

HAY-TIMOTHY, field baled.. No rain. $24. David Harrop, Glen Moore, Chester County. Phone 2-5497.

MODEL KITS
☆ Airplanes
☆ Boats
☆ Old Model Autos
Modeling building accessories, miniature motors, parts and tools for the hobbyist.
WIELAND'S
"WILDWOOD REFUGEES"
315 N. Queen St.

NOW PICKING
Golden Jubilee &
Jersey Land
Carman & Raritan Rose
Quality Crop — Moderate Prices
HERR'S FRUIT FARM
2 miles south of Mountville on road leading to Central Manor Camp Meeting Grounds.
Open Evenings
Phone Millersville 2686

HOT WATER HEATER, Weill McLain #5W-22, 8 years old, 700 Sq. Ft. radiation. Bucket-A-Day. 40 Gallon. Phone 2-5630.

LIMA BEANS — Hulled or unhulled. Sponsored by Missionary Project. Call Intercourse 55-R-21.

PLUMBING FIXTURES, water closets, lavatories and bathtubs. Good condition. Musselman's. Phone 2-2914.

USED: 12 cu. ft. Home Freezer, 18½ cu. ft. Home Freezer, G.E. Washer, good condition, Quality Electric Range. M. S. Sensenig, New Holland, Ph. 4-0691.

VACATION SPECIAL
Portable radios—various makes — special prices
HUSS
19 W. CHESTNUT ST.

TOBACCO BARN, 108'x36', $1,000. Paul Burdick, 5 miles south of Wrightsville, back of Long Level, 1½ miles northeast Prospect.

SEED RYE, Clarence Metzler, Landisville 6321.

WEATHER
(U. S. Weather Bureau)
Eastern Pennsylvania: Partly Cloudy And Cooler, Highest 55-60 Thursday. Friday Fair And A Little Warmer.

Intelligencer Journal.

The Leading Newspaper in the Garden Spot of America. Home Owned for Home Folks Since 1794

158th Year.—No. 112. | Lancaster City Zone Population, Official Figures of Audit Bureau of Circulations 112,897 | LANCASTER, PA., THURSDAY MORNING, OCTOBER 25, 1951. | CITY | THIRTY-TWO PAGES. | 30c PER WEEK—5c Per Copy

THE INTELL INDEX

ALLIED, ENEMY TRUCE TEAMS MEET

$2,500,000 Home Building Boom On In Lancaster And Suburbs

Spurt Laid To Fear Of New Restrictions On Building Materials

New home construction in Lancaster city and suburbs during the past eight weeks has developed into what local real estate men and contractors are calling a building boom, with the total cost of the new units conservatively estimated at more than two and one-half million dollars.

The building spurt began about six weeks ago when prospective home owners, apparently worried that the government would place new restrictions on materials, began pressing contractors to begin work on homes originally planned for next Spring, real estate men explained.

At the present time, the government prohibits the use of structural steel and limits the use of copper and iron in dwelling units contracted for after Oct. 1.

Much of the new construction is reported in the Grand View Heights section where 62 homes were completed or started since late August. Another 18 homes are being added to the School Lane Hills development while 12 are reported being built in the Bloomingdale development off the Lititz Pike, opposite the Overlook Country Club.

New construction in the city is mainly row houses with about 50 units being built, most of them in the Eighth Ward. At least a half-million dollars is being placed in new dwelling units in the city, real estate men estimate.

The current demand for homes has been for the better single houses and more than 70 per cent of the new houses in the city and suburbs will cost their owners from $20,000 to $28,000, realtors say.

Outside of the major residential developments, one contractor reported a steady demand for five room single houses costing from

Turn To Page 10 For More Of BOOM

The construction of new homes in the city and surrounding suburbs has developed into what local real estate men and contractors are calling a building boom. Much of the new construction is reported in the Grand View Heights section, where 62 homes were completed or started since last August. The top photo shows two new single homes being built on Louise Avenue, and the lower photo shows four homes under construction on Fountain Avenue. (Intell Photos)

"We Lead All The Rest"

FARM CORNER

By The Farm Editor

FARM CREDIT MEETING SLATED FOR MANHEIM TWP. SCHOOL NOV. 23

A general "farm credit" meeting of stockholders of two local agencies will be held in the Manheim Township High School, at Neffsville, on Friday, Nov. 23, the morning session scheduled to open at 10 o'clock.

This will be a combination annual meeting of the Lancaster Production Credit Association and the National Farm Loan Association of Lancaster County, both of which have members also in Lebanon and Dauphin Counties.

Election of directors and action on annual reports will feature the business sessions. A program of speaking and entertainment will be arranged.

RAIN SAVED TOBACCO CROP

One crop virtually saved by timely September rains was the cigar leaf tobacco grown in Lancaster and nearby counties, the State Department of Agriculture says.

In Clinton County and surrounding areas, where Type 53 tobacco is grown, the late plantings were hurt by drouth, although early planted crops were good.

September rains made substantial improvement in late planted

Turn To Page 28 For More Of FARM CORNER

Weather Calendar

COMPARATIVE TEMPERATURES

Station	High	Low
Water Works	70	47
Ephrata	68	56
Last Year (Ephrata)	55	47
Official High for Year Aug. 30		96
Official Low for Year Feb. 9		6
Character of Day		Cloudy

WINDS
Direction SE Avg. Velocity 11 MPH

HUMIDITY
8 a. m. 100% 11 a. m. 90%
2 p. m. 78% 5 p. m. 90% 8 p. m. 93%
Average Humidity 90%

SUN
Rises 6:24 a. m. Sets 5:12 p. m.

MOON
Rises 12:59 a. m. New Moon, Oct. 30

STARS
Morning—Venus, Mars, Saturn
Evening—Jupiter

NEARBY FORECASTS
(U. S. Weather Bureau)

Maryland—Mostly sunny and cooler, highest 60-65. Friday fair and a little warmer.

Delaware and New Jersey—Fair and cooler, highest 60-65. Friday fair and a little warmer.

Chesapeake Bay and Lower Potomac—Shifting winds becoming northwest 15 to 20 miles per hour Thursday morning and diminishing later in the day. Fair with good visibility, small craft warnings are displayed north half of Chesapeake Bay.

3 SLIGHTLY HURT IN 6 ACCIDENTS ON HIGHWAYS HERE

Fire Truck, Car Collide Near Bainbridge; Steers Flee Overturned Truck

Six motor vehicle accidents in the city and on county highways brought injuries to three persons Wednesday, but none of them hurt seriously enough to be hospitalized. Involved in separate mishaps were a fire truck and tractor-trailer carrying 25 steers.

A Marietta woman motorist was slightly injured at 1:40 p. m. Wednesday when her auto and the Bainbridge Fire Co. truck collided on Rt. 441, two miles west of Bainbridge. The truck was being used to haul water for nearby cisterns.

TREATED AT SCENE

Injured, according to Columbia State Policeman Walter Miller, was Catherine V. Petersen, forty-two, 108 Essex St. She suffered brush burns of the forehead and arms, body bruises and chest injuries and was treated at the scene by Dr. Michael Gratch, Bainbridge.

Police said the woman was travelling south on Rt. 441 and was attempting to pass the fire truck,

Turn To Page 10 For More Of ACCIDENTS

Truman Approves Pay Hike For Fed'l, Postal Employes

Washington — (AP) — President Truman Wednesday signed legislation increasing salaries of 1,100,000 federal "white collar" employes by $300 to $800 a year. He also signed another bill increasing salaries of most postal workers by at least $400 a year.

For most of the "white collar" workers, the pay boost will be 10 per cent. But those who make less than $3,000 a year will get $300 and those paid more than $8,000 will get $800.

The raises are retroactive to July 1.

These increases will add an estimated $420,000,000 annually to costs of the federal payroll. Getting the increases are the classified Civil Service workers in the government.

The separate, postal pay increase will add about $252,000,000 more to pay roll costs.

While rank-and-file postal workers get a raise of at least $400 a year, most postmasters, supervisors and inspectors will get an $800 annual boost.

These salary boosts also are retroactive to July 1.

The total payments under the retroactive features of the two bills will amount to $215,000,000.

The fact that Mr. Truman signed the measures before Nov. 1

Turn To Page 10 For More Of PAY RAISE

PO Workers Here To Get $30,000 Retroactive Pay

Lancaster city's more than 200 postal employes will receive an estimated $30,000 in retroactive pay and the annual post office payroll will be increased by more than $90,000 as the result of legislation signed Wednesday by President Truman.

The President's signature made effective pay increases ranging from $400 to $800 for postal workers.

Most of the city's postal employes will get the minimum $400 increase. This includes postal

Turn To Page 10 For More Of LOCAL

Mrs. Ogden Reid Says N. Y. Herald Trib Backs Ike As GOP Candidate

New York —(AP)— Mrs. Ogden Reid, president of the New York Herald Tribune, announced Wednesday night that the newspaper will support Gen. Dwight D. Eisenhower for the Republican Presidential nomination.

Mrs. Reid made the announcement to the Herald Tribune Forum audience after the forum ended and front page editorials endorsing Eisenhower appeared in both the New York and Paris editions of the paper. The paper identifies itself politically as Independent - Republican.

The editorial said the paper asked from Eisenhower "no word or promise at this time; it has received none."

However, it said, some people "see in the drawing to a close of his present assignment in Europe the occasion for a new call to effort and to service.

"And they believe that this call will not go unanswered."

For almost 20 years, the editorial said, "a Democratic administration has underscored the need for a new sense of purposefulness in the country, a fresh standard of integrity in government.

"During this long period in the opposition, Republicans have spoken with many voices. The time

Turn To Page 21 For More Of IKE

SIX LIVES LOST IN AUTO CRASHES IN NEARBY AREAS

Toll Is Three In York County, Two In Chester, One In Lebanon

Automobile accidents in nearby counties accounted for a total of six lives on Wednesday. Three died in York County, two in Chester County and one in Lebanon County.

Two youths were the fatal victims of an auto-bus crash in Lower Oxford Twp., Chester County, and three men were dead as the result of a truck collision north of York. A Lebanon County motorist was fatally injured when his car collided with a truck near Annville.

HIT BY BUS

The two youths were killed at 8:10 p. m. on Rt. 1, about four miles west of West Grove when their automobile was struck by a Trailways bus.

John Schofield, Oxford, deputy coroner, said the dead are: Robert Mullins, eighteen, Oxford R1, the operator of the car, broken neck; and Charles E. Johns, sixteen, Ox-

Turn To Page 10 For More Of FATALITIES

ARMSTRONG EXPECTS PLANT LAYOFFS TO REACH 210 BY NOV. 1

Current layoffs at the Armstrong Cork Company floor plant here are expected to reach the 210 mark by Nov. 1, officials announced Wednesday.

Meanwhile, officials also reported that a substantial portion of the plant will be closed down for three days next week for inventory.

Workers being laid off are employed in the rotary, calendar, print, molded, inlaid and other related departments.

Last week plant officials said 55 workers had been laid off and that a few more were scheduled to be laid off. The plant employs about 4,000 persons. No reason was given for the increase in anticipated layoffs reported previously.

FIREMEN RESPOND TO FALSE ALARM

City firemen responded to a false alarm sounded from Box 73 at Orange and Franklin Streets at 9:26 p. m. Wednesday.

Firemen said a young boy was reported seen walking away from the corner shortly after the alarm was sounded.

Late in September, two false alarms were sounded from Box 73 within three days. A seven-year-old city boy was nabbed by city police as he started to sound the alarm a third time.

EARLY WANT-AD DEADLINE

Due to the increased size of tonight's New Era—want-ads can be accepted for publication today up 'til 9:35 A. M. (instead of the usual 10:35 deadline.)

Want-Ads received after 9:35 A. M. today will be started in tomorrow's Intelligencer Journal.

READING CRIME FIGHTERS RAP CITY COUNCIL

Ministerial Group Assails "Generally Belligerent" Attitude Toward Betterment

Reading, Pa. —(AP)— The Ministerial Association Joint Committee on Crime Wednesday called the city council "generally belligerent x x x toward those interested in the betterment of the community."

Members of the crime committee were scheduled to appear before the council to report on gambling but instead sent a letter to the governing body.

FIVE RAIDS

The letter cited the raiding of five clubs last week by state liquor agents. "On the background of these activities there is no need to prove to council that violations of gambling laws exist in our city," the letter read in part.

The committee agreed last week to submit a report after charging that slot machines were again doing business in many locations.

There was practically no comment by members of council after the letter, signed by the Rev. James D. Matchette, chairman, and the Rev. Mervin A. Heller, secretary, was read.

"The full text of the letter follows: "On Wednesday last, October 17, members of the Joint Crime Committee of the Ministerial Association of Reading and The Greater Reading Council of Churches appeared before you with a communication relative to law enforcement. The communication came to you as a result of meetings with Chief of Police William P. Birney and Mayor John F. Davis. After having been referred by the chief of police to Mayor Davis, it

Turn To Page 10 For More Of READING

Gap Soldier Is Jailed On Charge Of Manslaughter

A twenty-one-year-old soldier stationed at Indiantown Gap was jailed Wednesday to face a single charge of involuntary manslaughter in court as the result of an accident three months ago in which two soldiers were killed.

Pvt. William J. Childers, Catlettsburg, Ky., was held in default of $500 bail following a hearing Wednesday before Justice of the Peace L. W. Musser, Manheim.

Fatally injured when a car operated by Childers rammed an embankment southwest of Manheim on July 25 were Sgt. Edward J. Robinson, forty, Trenton, N.J., and Sgt. Ernest J. Miller, forty, Bristol, Pa.

Mrs. Minnie Nafzinger, twenty-two, Annville R2, and Childers were

Turn To Page 21 For More Of SOLDIER

10 Delegates Renew Cease-Fire Parleys Stalled For 64 Days

Circus-Type Tent In Bean Field Homely Site Of Talk Renewal; Admiral Joy Said Afterwards That "Everybody Was Very Amicable"

Munsan, Korea (Thursday) —(AP)— Allied and Communist truce teams today met for the first time in 64 days in a new effort to end the 16-months-old Korean war.

They gathered in a circus-type tent put up in a bean field near the tiny, mud-hut village of Panmunjom, 31 miles northwest of Seoul. The new conference site lies in a no-man's-land between the opposing forces.

The 10 delegates sat down around the conference table at 11 a. m. (9 p. m., Wednesday, Lancaster Time), talked for 30 minutes and then recessed. At 11:55 a. m. they adjourned for the day but scheduled a meeting of subcommittees at 2 p. m.

The sub-committees were prepared to reopen discussions on a cease-fire line across Korea, the issue that had stalled the earlier truce talks for weeks.

"Everybody was very amicable," said Vice Adm. C. Turner Joy, the senior UN Command delegate at Panmunjom. "We have agreed to return to agenda item Number Two in sub-delegation meetings."

Hopes were bright that this time the negotiators would succeed in halting the see-saw struggle of two 500,000-man armies which have fought across the length and breadth of the Korean peninsula.

The war began June 25, 1950, when North Koreans invaded the

Turn To Page 10 For More Of CEASE-FIRE

INTERNAL REVENUE COLLECTOR PASSES UP HEARING DATE

Two More Agents Suspended In Growing List Of Irregularities

Washington—(AP)—Joseph P. Marcelle, former collector of internal revenue at Brooklyn, failed to keep a date with a House investigating committee Wednesday and was promptly subpoenaed to appear at 10 a. m. Thursday (today).

Adrian Dewind, committee counsel, said Marcelle accepted service of the summons in New York.

About the same time the Internal Revenue Bureau announced the suspension of two more agents in New York. Half an hour later, however, the Bureau said the announcement was "premature" and asked reporters to withdraw it. The announcement later was reinstated.

Marcelle, who submitted his resignation upon request Tuesday night, was scheduled to appear before a House ways and means subcommittee. The group is probing widespread charges of corruption in the Internal Revenue Service.

Chairman King (D-Calif) said that Marcelle, after first promising

Turn To Page 10 For More Of REVENUE

MELVIN BARR, GAP R1, IS WOUNDED IN KOREA

The Department of Defense announced Wednesday that Pfc. Melvin D. Barr, twenty-two, son of Mr. and Mrs. Harry M. Barr, Gap R1, was wounded in the hand Oct. 3, while fighting with U. S. forces in Korea.

Pfc. Barr

Pfc. Barr entered the Army on March 22 of this year. A brother, Pfc. John Barr, is now stationed at Camp Breckenridge, Ky. Melvin was employed by Sellers Hardware Store at Gap before he entered the service.

Fifty MIG Jets Jump Sabres In 10-Minute Fight

U. S. Eighth Army Headquarters, Korea. (Thursday)—(AP)—Fifty Russian-type MIG jets jumped 31 American Sabre jets on an early morning sweep into northwestern Korea today. Fifth Air Force headquarters said one enemy craft was damaged during the 10-minute battle.

It was the fifth straight day of jet combat over Korea. A flight of U. S. Superforts escorted by 60 Allied fighters Wednesday fought off swarms of Red jets all the way across Korea to the Sea of Japan.

The Sabre jets attacked today were flying escort for fighter-bombers assigned to knock out Red targets north of the battle line.

In a separate action today, two propeller-driven Corsairs and Ma-

Turn To Page 10 For More Of WAR

FBI Agents Crack 11th Embezzlement Case In Pittsburgh Area; 3 Persons Arrested

Pittsburgh —(AP)— FBI agents cracked their 11th big embezzlement in the Pittsburgh district Wednesday, arresting a bosomy redhead and two other credit union officers charged with taking $338,901 belonging to hundreds of department store clerks and other workers.

Some of the money went for good times and what one defendant called "a series of lost weekends."

Jailed for lack of bonds were 56-year-old Vice President Joseph B. Campbell of the Kaufmann Store Employes Federal Credit Union; Treasurer John J. Cain, 45; and the buxom redhead, Mrs. Nana Nicoll, 31, assistant treasurer and office manager.

"LOST WEEKENDS"

Cain is the only defendant to furnish a clue as to where the money went. He said he had been drinking heavily at the time and financed many "lost weekends." Campbell offered no explanation. The attractive divorcee said she got none of the money.

All three admitted in oral statements to Fred Hallford, FBI agent in charge of the Pittsburgh office, that they looted the Pittsburgh credit union by making fictitious loans. Hallford quoted Cain as saying the money was taken from late 1944 to early 1948.

The Pittsburgh FBI office, covering Western Pennsylvania and West Virginia, has broken one short of a dozen embezzlement cases in the past 14 months.

All but the latest have involved banks. Twelve persons have been

Turn To Page 21 For More Of EMBEZZLEMENT

"WAIT A MINUTE"—Pittsburgh—(AP Wirephoto)—Buxom red-haired Mrs. Nana Nicoll, 31, uses her finger to emphasize at a hearing Wednesday: "Wait a minute. I don't even know what is going on here." She was arrested by the FBI along with two others, including Joseph B. Campbell (left), on charges of taking $338,901 deposited by employees in Kaufmann's department store's federal credit union. Third man held is John J. Cain, 45, treasurer. Said Mrs. Nicoll, "I'll never be a bookkeeper again."

WEATHER
(U. S. Weather Bureau)

Eastern Pennsylvania—Cloudy With Occasional Rain Likely And Highest Temperatures In The Middle 50's Tuesday. Wednesday Mostly Cloudy And Mild, With Showers Likely.

Intelligencer Journal.

The Leading Newspaper in the Garden Spot of America. Home Owned for Home Folks Since 1794

158th Year.—No. 128. Lancaster City Zone Population. Official Figures of Audit Bureau of Circulations 112,897 LANCASTER, PA., TUESDAY MORNING, NOVEMBER 13, 1951. CITY TWENTY-TWO PAGES. 30c PER WEEK—5c Per Copy

THE INTELL INDEX

POLICE START PROBE IN POISONING

COUNTY HUNTER DROWNS IN RIVER

3 COMPANIONS ESCAPE DEATH AS BOAT SINKS

Edward L. Peters, 27, Conestoga R1, Victim Of Accident Near Falmouth

A county hunter, who had spent the day hunting on an island in the Susquehanna River, near Falmouth, drowned at 6:15 p. m. Monday as a boat carrying him and three others to shore, foundered.

Dead is Edward L. Peters, twenty-seven, Conestoga R1, whose body was recovered at 9:40 p. m. by searchers from the Middletown and Elizabethtown areas. Also assisting were State Police from the Harrisburg barracks.

His three companions, who escaped death are: Robert Powl, twenty-two, Drumore, operator of the boat; Peters' brother, Warren, twenty-nine, Conestoga R2, and Paul Trissler, fifty-seven, Conestoga, the drowned man's father-in-law.

Police said Peters, his brother and Trissler had spent the day hunting on the river island, located in the middle of the river above Falmouth. Also on the island was another party of Lancaster countians. Calvin Herr, Conestoga R1, Charles Daughton, Quarryville, and Willard Railing, Pequea R1.

The latter group had been first brought to shore Monday evening in the boat operated by Powl.

Powl, it was learned, then made a second trip to the island from the Elizabethtown landing, which is used by members of the Susquehanna Boating Club, to pick up the Peters brothers and Trissler.

While returning to the landing, Powl told authorities, the wooden boat began taking water over the sides. He said he attempted to prevent this by turning off the outboard motor and letting the boat drift. However, he said, as soon as he turned off the motor, water began pouring over the bow of the boat and it began to sink.

Edward L. Peters, the victim, who like all the rest of the party

Turn To Page 6 For More Of HUNTER

"We Lead All The Rest"
FARM CORNER
By The Farm Editor

Referendum On Tobacco To Be Explained Here

James E. Thigpen, director; and Claude Turner, of the Tobacco Branch, Production and Marketing Administration, U. S. Dept. of Agriculture, Washington, D.C., are scheduled to explain the pending tobacco referendum at a meeting in this city on Nov. 16.

This is a special session for members of the Lancaster County Tobacco Growers' Cooperative Association to be held in the 12th floor auditorium of the Griest Building, Penn Square, on Friday evening, opening at 8 o'clock.

Purpose of this special meeting is to give the membership an "unbiased presentation of the issues" involved in the referendum to be held throughout the county on Dec. 7, Harry E. Hershey, president, announced.

Pointing out that the outcome of the election will "definitely affect your income from your 1952 production of Type 41 tobacco," Hershey urged all members to attend in order to have the necessary in-

Turn To Page 18 For More Of FARM CORNER

Weather Calendar

COMPARATIVE TEMPERATURES

Station	High	Low
Water Works	58	23
Ephrata	56	29
Last Year (Ephrata)	48	26
Official High for Year Aug. 30		96
Official Low for Year Feb. 9		6
Character of Day	Partly Cloudy	

WINDS
Direction SE Avg. Velocity 5 MPH

HUMIDITY
8 a. m. 88% 11 a. m. 62% 2 p. m. 52%
5 p. m. 65% 8 p. m. 79%
Average Humidity 69%

SUN
Rises 6:46 a. m. Sets 4:50 p. m.

MOON
Last Quarter, Nov. 21

STARS
Morning—Venus, Mars, Saturn
Evening—Jupiter

NEARBY FORECASTS
(U. S. Weather Bureau)

Maryland — Cloudy with occasional rain Tuesday. Highest in upper 50's or low 60's. Wednesday considerable cloudiness and warmer, with scattered showers likely.

Lower Potomac and Chesapeake Bay—Southerly winds from 15 to 20 miles per hour Tuesday. Cloudy weather with occasional rain. Visibility fair.

Southern New Jersey and Delaware—Cloudy with some rain likely Tuesday. Highest temperature from 55 to 60 degrees. Wednesday considerable cloudiness and warmer with chance of showers.

Troop Train Late, Ephrata Folks Lose Chance For 28th Farewells

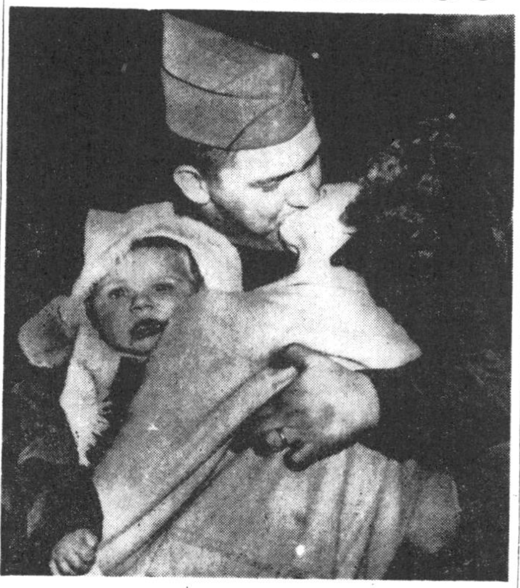

SQUEEZE PLAY—Norfolk, Va.—(AP Wirephoto)—Cynthia Martin, eleven-months-old, is caught in the middle as Sgt. Kenneth Martin, Lancaster, and his wife, Betty, say final goodbye shortly before the army transport carrying members of the 28th Division to Europe left Norfolk.

899th AAA (AW) Sails From Hampton Roads For Duty In Germany

(Special To The Intell)

Norfolk, Va.—At 4 p. m. Monday the last lines were cast off and the military transport "General Harry Taylor" headed east out of Hampton Roads bound for Bremerhaven, Germany.

Local contingents of Pennsylvania's 28th Division were on their way.

They left behind them on the dock many sorrowful relatives and friends — but none more so than a group of Ephrata residents who had come to bid Battery D, 899th AAA(AW), composed mainly of Ephrata men, farewell. For the Ephrata group was denied that last-minute chat, that farewell kiss or handclasp.

Battery D arrived on the last of the six trains which brought the troops from Camp Atterbury. The train was late.

Burdened with their equipment, the 60-or-so men of the Battery detrained. They waved to their relatives and friends. "We'll go aboard and stow our gear," they said, "and then come back down on the dock and say goodby. The ship doesn't saii for an hour yet."

But Battery D reckoned without military regulations. Once aboard the ship, they couldn't get off.

Typical of the disappointed parents was Harvey L. Ensinger, 118 Locust St., who had come to say goodby to his two sons, Sgt. Harvey, Jr., twenty, and Cpl. Clair, nineteen.

Between sobs, he told a reporter, "Our boys had been promised an hour with their friends and families before sailing. The last train was late, and our Ephrata boys can't get back off the ship."

With Mr. Ensinger were the boys' uncle and aunt, Mr. and Mrs. Jacob Ensinger, Harvey Jr.'s fiancee, Gloria Graybill, and Clair's sweetheart, Sidney Flemish, all of Ephrata. They had driven down together to see the boys off.

PRAISE RED CROSS

Mr. Ensinger had a good word for the Red Cross — whose representatives were giving out coffee and doughnuts to the embarking men.

"Just before the ship sailed a Red Cross worker took our pack-

Turn To Page 18 For More Of 28TH

GOODBYE DADDY—Norfolk, Va.—(AP Wirephoto)—Sgt. Kenneth Dudley, Columbia, falls out of ranks to say goodbye to his four-year-old son Kenneth, Jr., before boarding the army transport with the 28th Infantry Division bound for Europe where they will join Gen. Eisenhower's forces.

200,000 Watch As 28th Marches At Philadelphia

Philadelphia—(AP)—Hands to their helmets in rigid salute, eyes right to the reviewing stand before Independence Hall, the 28th Division bade a military farewell Monday to its native Pennsylvania.

For many men of the Keystone Division, it was a strange Armistice Day to mark the anniversary of the end of the first war in which the 28th fought overseas.

A solemn and silent throng, estimated at more than 200,000 persons, lined downtown streets on the mile-long parade route watching the men go by to the blare of bands and the steady "hip-ho-hip-hrup" of cadence-counting noncoms.

Here and there a woman or a girl or a youngster trotted along beside the marching troops to be

Turn To Page 6 For More Of PARADE

Mother Of Gen. Strickler Says Goodbye To 28th

Philadelphia — As always in such farewells as Monday when the 28th Division embarked for overseas duty there were tears and sighs.

But one pair of eyes — one mother among many saying goodbye to her "boy"—remained clear and steady.

"Yes, I am getting accustomed

Turn To Page 6 For More Of GEN. STRICKLER

General Strickler Leads Troops At Philadelphia

Philadelphia—(AP Wirephoto)—Maj. Gen. Daniel B. Strickler, commanding general of the 28th Infantry Division, followed by his four-man staff, leads 3,000 members of the division down Philadelphia's Parkway Monday before the units boarded a transport for Germany where they will join General Eisenhower's European forces.

Two Crack Trains Crash In Driving Snowstorm; 21 Dead

Evanston, Wyo. —(AP)— Two eastbound streamlined passenger trains crashed in a driving snowstorm Monday, piling up wreckage in a giant junk heap. Union Pacific authorities said 21 were known dead and six missing.

Eight were seriously hurt and hospitalized. Scores more — some sources estimated more than a hundred—were treated for minor injuries.

The smashup came in a rolling, hilly, snow-covered area about three miles west of this little Wyoming community some 80 miles northeast of Salt Lake City.

The Union Pacific's city of Los Angeles halted for a block signal. It was bashed in from the rear by the City of San Francisco.

The three-unit diesel power plant of the second train crushed five cars of the halted train. Cars of the second train left the tracks in a zigzag fashion, but remained upright.

Thomas E. Sharp, owner of radio station KFSD in San Diego, Calif., was riding in a compartment of the City of San Francisco. He said he was drinking coffee.

"The coffee flew out of my hand and the conducter flew into the room," Sharp said, explaining that the conductor had been standing in the aisle just outside.

The City of San Francisco's power units were intermingled with the five rear cars of the City of Los Angeles. Outline of the five

Turn To Page 18 For More Of TRAINS

MISSING BOY SOUGHT BY BERKS SEARCHERS

Reading—(AP)—A searching party led by State Police of the Reading barracks is scouring rural sections of Berks county Monday for any trace of a two-year-old boy missing since late Monday afternoon from his home near Tulpehocken Creek in Sinking Spring, west of Reading.

The missing youngster is Lester Weikel, Jr. Police grappled along the banks of the stream in fear that he may have fallen into the Tulpehocken.

Sixty neighbors, Boy Scouts of three troops and Spring Township police joined 14 troopers from the barracks in the hunt.

2 Local Persons Aboard Wrecked Train Are Safe

At least two local persons were aboard the wrecked "City of San Francisco", crack Union Pacific flyer involved in the Evanston, Wyo., collision Monday afternoon.

They are Dr. and Mrs. C. R. Farmer, 1022 Buchanan Ave. Relatives here said Monday night they had received a telegram from Evanston, telling of their safety.

Considerable anxiety had been felt for a time for the safety of the local man, who, with his wife, was returning home from San Francisco where he had attended the convention of the American College of Surgeons.

A number of other local physicians and surgeons also had been attending the convention but it was thought that most were not in the vicinity.

Dr. and Mrs. S. G. Pontius, Lancaster R5, were expected in Lancaster Tuesday (today) at 9 a. m. This schedule would place them 12

Turn To Page 6 For More Of DOCTORS

NEW CAR CATCHES FIRE, BUT UNDAMAGED

A new 1951 two door sedan, purchased Monday by Fred C. Resh, 229 N. Shippen St., city, was threatened by fire about 9:15 p. m. Monday on the Lincoln Highway, near Mellinger's Church.

Fire Chief George Hahn, of the Lafayette Fire Co., said the fire broke out in undercoating sprayed on the auto's exhaust pipe and muffler. Hahn said Resh had the fire extinguishe dbefore the arrival of firemen and there was no damage.

Husband Admits He Smuggled Poison To Wife In Co. Prison

D. A. Orders City Detectives To Investigate Mrs. Violet McEvoy's Death

City detectives at the request of District Attorney John M. Ranck have started an investigation into the death of Mrs. Violet G. McEvoy who died at 11 a. m. Monday at Lancaster General Hospital.

Mrs. McEvoy, forty-seven, 709 E. Fulton St., was taken to the hospital Saturday night after she told officials at the Lancaster County prison she had taken poison. She was being held at the prison pending transfer to the State Industrial Home for Women at Muncy, Pa.

An autopsy was performed Monday afternoon and Dr. Charles P. Stahr, deputy coroner, said it looked "definitely like a case of mercury bichloride poisoning." He pointed out, however, that the laboratory tests have not been completed.

Shortly after her death, her husband, John E., admitted smuggling mercury bichloride tablets to his wife in a can of crackers during a visit at the jail Saturday afternoon, according to Warden Walter N. Foust. Foust said McEvoy signed a statement saying his wife had asked him on previous visits to bring her the tablets for hygienic purposes.

HUSBAND QUESTIONED

Ranck said he had asked city detectives to investigate the case, so he could study all of the facts. McEvoy was questioned at police headquarters for two hours Monday evening and then released.

Detectives are studying Section 620 of the criminal code which makes it unlawful to convey liquors or drugs into prisons or mental hospitals. The section states in part that a person who sells, gives, or furnished to any convict in prison any kind of "spirituous or fermented liquor, drug, medicine, poison, opium, morphine, or any other kind of narcotics, without a written permit signed by the physician of such institution," is guilty of a felony and "upon conviction shall be sentenced to pay a fine not exceeding $2,000 or undergo imprisonment not exceeding five years."

Warden Foust said McEvoy told him his wife was formerly a hair

Turn To Page 18 For More Of PROBE

Principals

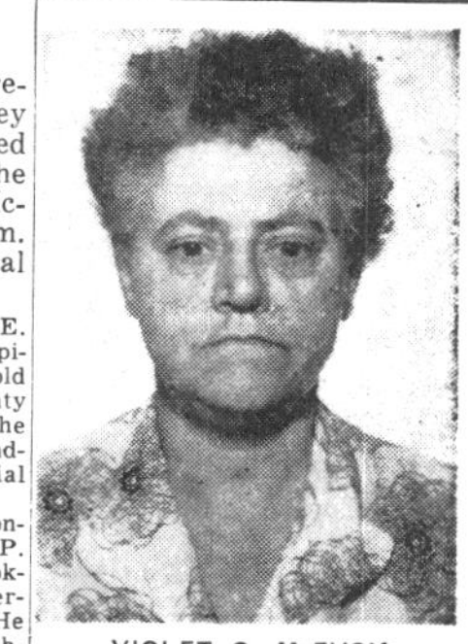

VIOLET G. McEVOY

JOHN E. McEVOY

SHOWERS EXPECTED IN COUNTY TODAY

Occasional showers are expected in Lancaster County Tuesday (today), adding to the more than four and one-half inches of rain which has fallen on this area in the past twelve days.

Monday was another ideal day with afternoon temperatures in the mid-fifties. The high at the Ephrata Weather Station was 56 degrees and a night-time low of 29 was recorded.

There was a lazy breeze from the northwest most of Monday and a bright sun shown through the few threatening clouds.

The forecast calls for temperatures to remain in the fifties Tuesday and Wednesday and rain is seen for both days.

Tax Men Looking Into Returns Of Reading Persons

Philadelphia —(AP)— Agents from the Rackets Division of the Internal Revenue Bureau here have been sent into the Reading area to check tax returns of persons connected with gambling, a bureau spokesman disclosed Monday.

The spokesman said that the agents "have been given a list containing the names of everyone in that (Reading) area who were mentioned in the Senate crime investigation."

Senator Herbert R. O'Conor (D-Md) and his Senate crime investigating committee made an extensive probe of gambling in the Reading-Berks County area several months ago.

The spokesman said the federal agents also were instructed to investigate everyone connected in any way with slot machines.

"We understand that things quieted down up that way for a

Turn To Page 18 For More Of READING

Zeamer Holds 23-Vote Plurality As Official Count Of Ballots Ends

Woodrow A. Zeamer, of Columbia, held a 23-vote plurality over A. E. McCollough Jr., for the Democratic County Commissioner post Monday as the official count of civilian votes cast in last Tuesday's election was completed.

The official vote in the county's 146 districts:

Zeamer, 11,057.
McCollough, 11,034.

It was the closest contest since 1947 when George H. Carpenter defeated Fred W. Wagner, of Columbia by 14 votes for one of the two Democratic County Commissioner nominations.

FINAL COUNT FRIDAY

The final vote in the Zeamer-McCollough race will not be known until Frinay, however. At that time ballots sent to Lancaster County residents in the armed forces will be counted.

That vote tabulation cannot change the outcome of the race, since only 19 military ballots were requested. To date, the Lancaster County Election board said, only 10

Turn To Page 18 For More Of VOTE COUNT

HIGH SPOTS IN LANCASTER SPORTS IN 1951

BY PETE BUSSER

The local sports year of 1951 was no more noteworthy than former years and yet it wasn't without its thrills and dramatic moments. New champions were crowned. Old champions went down fighting.

Each month had its highlights. From winter sports through spring and summer and then back, once more, to the indoor events. All fans had their particular sport. And each sport had its share of glory in the limelight. Each was a dramatic, thrilling moment in the local sports year 1951.

JANUARY

Ed Kemmler opened the local 951 sports year as he won the 2th annual Lancaster City and unty Table Tennis tourney held t the YMCA. Jere Schlemm Jr., aptured the junior singles title.

Sid Gordon, star baseball player for the Boston Braves, was the principal speaker at the annual Father and Pal banquet of Lancaster Lodge No. 228, B'nai B'rith.

Sid Gordon

The Oblenders team won the Class A championship of the City and County Women's Bowling Association. Members of the am were Emma Kepner, Mararet Slote, Earla Zerbe, Edith liller and Lena McConnell.

Becky Flemish captured the lass A All-Events women's bowlg title with a composite score of 520. Becky then teamed with label Gerhart to win the doubles tle.

A Lancaster Catholic High chool basketball team that had von 12 straight games had its reak snapped by Columbia High, 9-44.

FEBRUARY

Another consecutive victory reak was snapped early in Febuary when East Lampeter High chool's basketball team defeatd New Holland High, 46-44, to end e Huskies 34 victory string in unty League competition.

And still another all-conquering am was halted as Landisville, the Lanco League, sporting a reak of 19 straight triumphs, as stopped by Marietta, 91-64.

Basketball titles started to be ecided with Millersville Junior igh claiming the first championhip as they topped East Lampetr Jr. High, 31-27, to win the ounty Jr. High cage title.

Frank Chambers with 22 points led East Lampeter High School to the championship of the County High cage league as they defeated Ephrata, 50-48.

The District 3, PIAA swim tie was won by York High while Vest York High captured the disict wrestling honors.

MARCH

George Doherty of Millersville was named the outstanding wrestler in the meet as Millersville captured the State Teachers College wrestling championship.

Marietta won the Lancaster County Basketball League's flag with a 70-60 triumph over Landisville while St. John's E & R repeated as Church League champions.

Jerry Shervanik, Glenn Flegal, John Meys, Bob Brown, George Doherty and Bob King, all of Millersville, and Howard Beane of F&M, won matches as Millersville wrestled its way to the Middle Atlantic AAU wrestling championship with 47 points. The F&M Varsity Club tallied 20 points.

The highlight of the local basketball season was the Mount Joy High School-Fredonia High School game at Lebanon for the first Class C PIAA championship. Fredonia won the state title with a 49-43 triumph over the Rams.

Ducky Welsh

Ducky Welsh tallied 33 points to set a new individual high as Lancaster Catholic's cage team defeated John Bapst of Bangor, Me., 78-32, in the Eastern States Catholic basketball tourney held at Newport, R.I.

APRIL

Ball, bat and glove took over the local sports scene as scholastic, collegiate and independent baseball teams pried the lid off the outdoor season.

The Federated Sportsmen's Clubs of Lancaster County named John H. Gantz, Mount Joy R2 as the Outstanding Farmer-Sportsman in Lancaster County for 1950.

Larry Chapman of E-town High turned in the first local no-hit, no-run game of the season as the Bears defeated East Donegal, 6-0. Six days later his teammate, Nelson Chittum hurled a perfect game as E-town again topped East Donegal, 7-0.

Lancaster's entry in the Interstate League, the Red Roses, dropped their opening game to Hagerstown, 6-5.

McCaskey had a seven-game win streak snapped when York edged Coach Cliff Hartman's squad, 4-1.

Keith Kelley, fastballing Roses' righthander, came through with a no-hit, no-run Interstate loop game when he blanked Wilmington, 10-0.

MAY

Nels Chittum hurled his second consecutive perfect game as he blanked East Hempfield, 5-0, in a County High baseball league contest. Three days later the fourth no-hit, no-run game in the county high loop this year was recorded by Mt. Joy's Jerry Shupp as he shut out East Donegal, 6-0.

Early in May, Franklin and Marshall's track team captured its fourth straight "Little Three" track meet as they recorded 68 points to 43½ for Gettysburg and 42½ for Dickinson.

The Roses, in first place in the Interstate League May 6, were knocked into second place on May 8 but Johnny Walker's 10th inning homer gave them a 3-2 victory over Hagerstown and put them into first place once more.

Ben Brown, Mt. Joy High, won the singles championship of the Inter-County Scholastic tennis league while his teammates George McCue and Bill Beaston won the doubles title.

George McCue

H. H. "Billy" Haverstick carded a 64 at the Lancaster Country Club for a new course record.

The Roses had their win streak snapped at eight games May 16 as Sunbury trounced the local club, 4-0. Included in the eight victories were four straight extra-inning triumphs. On May 21, Sunbury knocked the Roses out of first place.

Lefty Dick Barr pitched Manor High School to the championship of the County High League as he struck out 18 batters, gave up no hits and shutout Mt. Joy, 5-0, in a seven-inning game.

Jimmy Foxx

Don Mulhatten tossed a no-hit, no run game in the City Legion League as Post 34 defeated the Optimist nine, 10-0.

JUNE

Jimmy Foxx, former star first baseman for the A's and Red Sox and a member of baseball's Hall of Fame was guest speaker at the Second Guessers early June meeting.

Bernie Reese succeeded Jimmy Cain as head football and baseball coach at Manheim Central High School.

Ben Brown successfully defended his Lanco Closed Tennis singles title for junior boys as he defeated Al Kegerise. The doubles championship went to the unseeded duo of Paul Hoh and John Y. May as they upset the top-seeded team of Brown and Bill Beaston.

Ben Brown

Dick Barr, star pitcher on Manor High's championship baseball team signed a contract to play ball in the Detroit Tigers' organization.

The 17th annual pro-amateur golf tourney at the Lancaster Country Club ended with a deadlock for first place. Walter Hall, Hershey pro, and his partner, Lynn Creason finished with a four-under-par 66 as did the duo of Johnny Weitzel and Herman Goetze of the Colonial Country Club at Harrisburg.

Bobby Hackett retained the Lanco Amateur golf title with a 79-78—157 over 36 holes at Meadia Heights.

July

Charley Neal, Bob Louis, Mike Korcheck, Ken Worley and Bill Peters represented the Lancaster Roses on the East team of the Interstate League that defeated the West All-Stars, 10-9 at Hagerstown.

Johnny Szajna pitched the first no-hit, no-run game in the Eastern County league this year as he hurled Schoeneck to a 12-0 victory over Ephrata.

Dave MacNicoll succeeded Bernie Rider as head grid coach at Lititz High.

Dave MacNicoll

Frank Zink successfully defended his Lancaster County Closed tennis title as he defeated Bobby Zink. Frank Zink and Gene Crider then won the doubles championship as they turned back Elwood Snyder and Bob Zink.

Bobby Howells captured the Meadia Heights golf club championship with a 3 and 2 victory over Glenn Horst.

Bobby Howells

Ronnie Owen, Larry Chapman and Paul Herr were selected to represent this area in the Legion's All-Star baseball game in Philadelphia. Owen and Chapman were named to the East's All-Star squad and for his mound work during the game, Owen was voted runnerup as the most valuable player.

The Rangers won their fifth straight District 10 Legion championship as they defeated Elizabethtown, 4-1, behind the pitching of Jerry Miller and hitting of Dick Fencel.

Ernie Nichols, Roses' righthander, hurled a seven-inning no-hit, game against Salisbury and won, 6-2.

August

Local Baseball headed down the home stretch in August as Bill Gable, Quarryville pitcher in the City-County League, struck out 17 Marietta batters as Quarryville won, 12-6.

Seventh-seeded Ray Stauffer of Harrisburg won the Red Rose tennis championship as he defeated the defender, Paul Hildebrand of Reading. Louise Fowler, Covington, Ga., won the women's singles title; Frank Zink and Gene Crider won the men's doubles title; Fowler and Evelyn Cowan won the women's doubles event while Gene Crider and Nancy Paden won the mixed doubles.

Gene Kruis succeeded Kenny Karl as athletic director and head football and basketball coach at Catholic High.

Gene Kruis

The Ephrata Lions defeated the Columbia Pioneers, 6-4, for the county's midget baseball title while the Manheim Chix whipped the Columbia Gold team, 5-3, for the midget-midget title.

Bill Donley of New Holland won the batting title of the City-County league with a mark of .427. His teammate, Bing Miller, won pitching honors with a record of 11-0.

Mickey Draude won the Conestoga Country Club's golf championship while Paul Dombach grabbed the links title at Overlook.

Art Byxbee won the golf championship at the Lancaster Country Club as he defeated Dan Rhoads. Billy Haverstick and Lynn Creason won the Central Penn partner best ball tourney held at Orwigsburg.

Billy Haverstick

Ronnie Berger Schoeneck, captured the batting title in the Eastern County League with a mark of .430. Denver's Bob Garman captured mound honors with seven wins and two losses.

Frank Kiester won the Inter-County Tennis League's singles championship as he defeated Ray Stauffer, 6-2, 7-5.

September

September opened with baseball playoffs in the spotlight as the Roses finished their Interstate League campaign in fifth place with 71 wins and 67 losses.

Hershey won the team title of the Inter-County tennis league with the Lancaster White team in second place.

Scholastic football opened with Catholic scoring a 9-0 victory over Columbia and Ephrata dropping a 27-0 decision to Muhlenberg Twp.

Denver won the 1951 championship of the Eastern County Baseball League as they swept a best-of-three series from Cornwall. Quarryville captured City-County League honors as they took a best-of-five series from Lititz, 3-2. Baseball came to a close with East Petersburg, behind the two-hit hurling of George McCue, winning the championship of the Central City-County League as they defeated Strasburg and took the final series, 2-1.

Dave Griffith, Ephrata's fine back, scored four touchdowns and passed for two more as the Mounts outscored Columbia, 45-21.

F & M's 10-game victory streak was halted by Lebanon Valley, 25-6.

Interest in baseball staged a revival as Jimmy Dykes, A's manager, spoke before an audience in a local theater.

Wally Witmer scored five touchdowns and paced F & M to a 52-7 triumph over Johns Hopkins.

October

Highlight of F & M's Homecoming early in October was the presence of Al Holman at Williamson Field as the Dips topped Dickinson, 27-6. Holman was head grid coach at F & M from 1931 to 1941.

Basketball put in a bid for attention as George Eshleman announced he had taken over the franchise of the Lancaster Roses in the Eastern Pro League. Hugh Sherrard was the former owner.

Howard Miller won the Second Annual Clarence C. Smith Memorial bowling trophy with a five-game total of 1031.

Manor High won the championship of the Lanco Scholastic soccer league as they gained a scoreless tie with East Hempfield to give them a loop mark of six wins, no losses and two ties. Carl Yoder, ex-McCaskey ace, drove home four goals as he paced the F & M soccer team to an 8-1 victory over an undefeated Gettysburg College team.

November

November opened with football championships awaiting many local teams. John Reynolds claimed the first title as they finished the finest season in the school's history with six win and one defeat to gain the Central Penn Jr. High title.

Hard rains caused the postponement of many games Nov. 2 but it wasn't enough to stop Solanco and West York from slipping and sliding in a contest played at Quarryville and won by the Yorkers, 33-0. Only half the field was used as the otherhalf was under water.

The Lancaster City and County Oldtime Boxers and Sportsmen had their day as more than 400 persons attended their annual banquet.

Ephrata High displaced Palmyra as Conference of Roses' champion.

The All-Lancaster team won the championship of the Lanco Midget grid league as they defeated the Bears, 55-14, to post their seventh victory against one loss.

William D. "Bill" Cowdrick, business manager of the Lancaster Red Roses baseball club for 10 years died after a long illness. His place in the Roses' front office was taken by Frank Spair.

George Darrah, sparkplub backfield ace of John Reynolds title team, was named the city's outstanding junior high school football player. Roy Garland, center on MSTC's football team was named to the All-State teachers first team.

Ten thousand fans watched Gettysburg, paced by Berky Ward, whip F & M, 40-20, in the annual Turkey Day classic at Williamson Field.

Basketball surged to the front as Elizabethtown College whipped Kings, 86-39, while F & M dropped an 81-60 verdict to Delaware.

Dave Griffith, Ephrata's great back, was named the county's outstanding scholastic football player for 1951.

December

For the second straight year, the F & M soccer team lost its bid for the Middle Atlantic title as they dropped a 4-1 decision to Lehigh.

Gus Lovett hit for 32 points as F & M defeated Swarthmore, 79-58.

The Lancaster Roses, under the managership of George Eshleman, had their 1951-52 debut spoiled by Reading, 60-56.

Eddie Kirchner was named the Outstanding Lineman at Catholic High and along with quarterback Dick Fencel was named to the Central Penn Catholic All-Star team.

F & M's high scoring cage team set a new school offensive record as they routed Ursinus, 103-41.

Olympics Or Bust: They Seek Places On U. S. Team

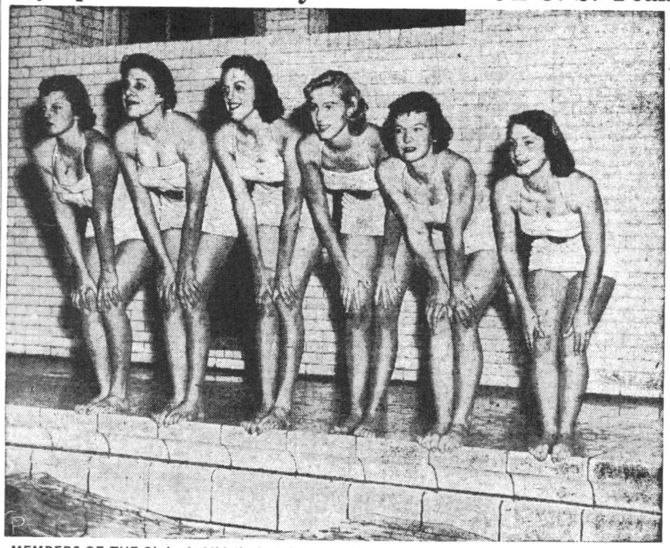

MEMBERS OF THE Ohrbach Athletic Association of New York, these comely lasses are working out regularly in the Brooklyn Tech pool, preparing for the 1952 Olympics. From left they are Marily Clark, Gloria Rosky, Natalie Swanson, Margaret Landers, Ingebord Giger and Mary Lou Mason.

F & M Tops Pitt To Take First Place In Y Senior Loop

F & M took over the top spot in the YMCA Senior basketball league yesterday as they scored a 66-61 victory over Pitt. It was the fourth triumph for F & M in five starts.

In other game, Penn outscored Navy, 55-42 and Notre Dame staged a 28-point last period rally to edge Citadel, 69-60.

LEAGUE STANDINGS

Teams	W.	L.	Pct.
F & M	4	1	.800
Citadel	3	2	.600
Pitt	3	2	.600
Penn	2	3	.400
Notre Dame	2	3	.400
Navy	1	4	.200

Jimmy Todd with 20 points and Jack Maurer with 18 led F & M to their victory. Pitt held a 29-23 lead at halftime but F & M came driving back in the third quarter to tally 24 points and take a lead they held to the end.

F & M	G	Fl	Tl	Pitt	G	Fl	Tl
Horner	3	1	7	Brubaker	6	7	19
Whiskeyman	1	0	2	Johnson	2	1	5
Maurer	8	2	18	Graybill	0	0	0
Todd	6	8	20	Wagner	5	1	11
Harnish	3	1	7	Wittel	2	3	7
J. Stetter	5	0	10	Kraybill	5	1	11
N. Stetter	1	0	2	Stoudt	4	0	8
Totals	27	12	66	Totals	24	13	61

Score by periods:
PITT .... 16 13 12 20—61
F & M .... 12 11 24 19—66
Referee: Keays

Penn	G	Fl	Tl	Navy	G	Fl	Tl
Steffy	4	2	10	Helt	2	0	4
Kendig	4	1	9	Eckman	8	4	20
Shenk	6	0	12	Schiding	0	1	1
Boose	7	0	14	Ellinger	3	1	7
Diego	5	0	10	McComsey	2	0	4
				Chaknos	3	0	6
Totals	26	3	55	Totals	18	6	42

Score by periods:
PENN .... 10 18 18 9—55
NAVY .... 13 6 10 13—42

Citadel	G	Fl	Tl	Notre Dame	G	Fl	Tl
Stetter	3	0	6	Melsom	8	3	19
Reardon	3	2	8	Haddad	2	1	5
Kraft	2	1	5	Gochenauer	6	4	16
Conley	9	8	26	Moran	5	2	12
Brosius	6	3	15	McCurdy	4	1	9
				Dicely	4	0	8
Totals	23	14	60	Totals	29	11	69

Score by periods:
CITADEL .... 13 16 17 14—60
NOTRE DAME .... 7 13 21 28—69

The Sunday News Brings You
LAST-MINUTE NEWS!
Local and World Events

SUNDAY NEWS

Read Complete Fiction Story
Sunday News Magazine
Last Page—Pink Section

LANCASTER, PA., SUNDAY, JANUARY 13, 1952

Gamblers Lose

32 Arrests, 32 Convictions In Year Is County's Record

Payoff To U. S. Is Last Straw For Many

Just can't pick up a dishonest dollar these days.

That's the nation-wide (and Lancaster-wide) lament of bookies, numbers writers, lottery ticket peddlers and gamblers in general since the government's recent action which requires them to "register" by buying a "gambler's tax" stamp, and turn over a percentage of their gross "handle" to the Federal Treasury.

No Sale Nere

In Lancaster, where no one has purchased such a stamp to date, the move increased the already heavy pressure exerted on the fraternity by city and state police crackdown campaigns.

According to figures released this week, covering first payments by Eastern Pennsylvania gamblers since the new law, the Internal Revenue Department was made richer by $1,960.87. Not a cent of Lancaster money was included in this amount, which represents payments squaring accounts for November, but nearby points are represented.

The amount—ten per cent of the total reported handle in wagers—came from gamblers in Lebanon, $749.16; Oxford, $200.76; Middletown, $43; Reading, $63.82, and Phoenixville, $765.83.

Why no tax stamp has been applied for in Lancaster is obvious, since doing so is to advertise that one is "in business." And it was already tough to handle a bet here. It's just as tough to place a bet, as any player who doesn't have an old contact will find if he should get a "hot" horse today and wish to put a couple of bucks on the nose.

32 Arrests, Convictions

A string of some 32 arrests and convictions of persons arrested on gambling charges or on charges growing out of gambling in the county throughout 1951 shows just how safe it is for a gambler to operate here.

Gamblers paid approximately $4,000 to the county in fines upon conviction, and nine of them went to jail for a total of 26 months, their terms ranging from 30 days to nine months, police records show.

With the new law, local gamblers were either forced out of business entirely by the prospect of facing a federal count in addition to a local one if picked up (since none complied with the federal law) or drastically restricted their operations, conducting them more furtively than ever.

Few will deny that gamblers still operate here. Getting evidence enough to arrest them and expect a conviction in court, however, is another story, one which police are busy "writing."

Not Many Left

Those who may be left undoubtedly consider themselves pretty shrewd operators. Whether they would be better off financially if they should turn to honest employment only time will tell.

Just how "shrewd" one has to be to get away with it is pointed up in the recent case of a gambler acknowledged by police to be one of the most experienced, careful bookmakers to operate here.

Even keeping his records in cipher based on Hebrew script failed to save him and his partner when their "pony ran out of the money." Local police forwarded the evidence to the FBI in Washington, where crack cryptogrammatists made child's-play of his code.

At the trial the jury was treated to what amounted to a first-grade reading class with six-foot blow-ups of samples of the coded records. Faced with the evidence, he pleaded guilty and was sentenced to nine months and fined $300 and costs as a repeater. In addition, $600 taken from him at the time of his arrest was kept by the county.

His partner, who had previously entered a guilty plea, got off with only two months and a similar fine and costs.

Customer Always Wrong

Incidentally (horse players please note), running records kept by the pair and confiscated by police showed their customers almost constantly in the red. Those who were winners were "small ones" and strictly the exception.

The player may find some consolation in the fact that he is not the only loser. Whether this "shrewd" operator came out on top financially in his operations here is extremely doubtful, particularly when one considers his loss of nine months (in jail) and the $900 "damages" through fine and confiscation—not to mention costs of court and fees for legal assistance.

Getting on his trail was a simple matter for police, they said. As a past offender he was naturally watched when he started arriving in town on a train from Philadelphia daily, returning the same way in the evening. But checking on his activities away from the train station was another matter.

He would enter a car which he kept parked at the station and begin a circuitous trip through town, one which didn't give the faintest inkling of his destination here. Detectives attempting to follow at a cautious distance consistently found themselves snarled in traffic, losing their quarry in the process.

Waited Along Trail

Police, finally finding that he usually drove through the 8th Ward after leaving the station, began anticipating his route and lying in wait. This way they would be on hand to take up the trail anew when he came along, thus learning a few more blocks of his general route almost daily.

It finally curved to the east end of the city, police relate, where one day their patience paid off. They closed in on a garage he had entered and confirmed their suspicions with the evidence they found there. The arrests followed.

This man was spotted and put under police observation mostly because of his past record. Other gamblers have come to grief through less obvious leads furnished police.

An anonymous telephone call led police to a numbers writer who, upon his arrest, told officers he had quit the business because his wife threatened to "turn him in." This didn't keep him from drawing a 30-day sentence and a fine.

Two-Bit Payoff

In still another numbers case, the young niece of a gambler who said she got from twenty-five to fifty cents for keeping his accounts "when his wife (who usually did it) was mad at him" put police on his trail.

In still another instance, a larceny suspect was found to have several lottery tickets in his possession when searched by police. Finding himself "on the spot," he gave police the name of his supplier. The supplier's arrest and conviction quickly followed.

To protect informants and police techniques, police usually omit details of "how we got wise to this guy" and dismiss the subject with a curt:

"We acted on information received."

Tip-Offs Secret

Hidden behind that statement may be the angry wife of a constant loser (possibly fresh from a family argument), a worried mother, the sucker himself, a close "friend" of the gambler or any conceivable source—often one that even the "smartest" operator would never dream of.

Barring moral considerations and considering only how the cards are stacked against gamblers here might prompt one to ask why they still operate. It would seem that, as is true of the consistent player-though-loser, they have "the bug."

In view of the record, chances are that the bug is going to bite them where it hurts eventually, even if they have refused to share their handle with the government. And it will be a double bite when it comes, in view of the fact that the government doesn't like to be ignored.

ENOUGH TO DISCOURAGE A GUY — The rough time Lancaster police were giving gamblers even before the Federal Government stepped in and decreed that they shall not operate without tax stamp and without kicking back part of their handle to Uncle Sam is illustrated above. The combination of police pressure and the increased risk, in ignoring the U. S. A., has driven most out of business and others deep under cover. At left Detectives Matt (left) and Farkas examine evidence taken in lottery raid. Lottery pay-off sheet (center) notifies customers of TEMPORARY delay in service due to new law. At right, stove in which bookie attempted to destroy evidence as raiders crashed in is shown. Detective Cogley managed to salvage betting slips, some charred, at lower left.

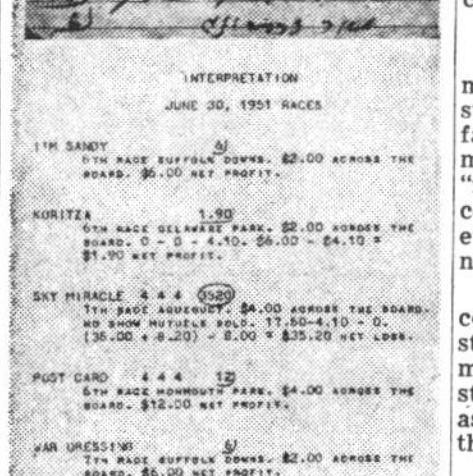

TANGLED EVIDENCE — F.B.I. quickly crackd cipher, based on Hebrew, used for record keeping by cagey bookie convicted here. Picture (above) is from photostat made of records sample. Interpretation of code is below.

TOOLS OF THE TRADE—Equipment used by bookie, and used by police as evidence to convict him in court, is examined by Detective Capt. Kirchner. Bookmakers and other gamblers in Eastern Pennsylvania have paid the Federal Government nearly $2,000 under the new gambling law, it was reported this week. None of the money came from Lancaster, where no gambler has registered.

Looking Ahead

Strike Of Steel Men Not Likely Is Outlook Now

BY THE WORLD STAFF OF THE ASSOCIATED PRESS

WASHINGTON—At the moment there seems little danger of a steel strike.

Phillip Murray's CIO Steelworkers Union has postponed its threatened walkout at least until Feb. 21. But chances of a walkout even then are slim the way things look right now.

The Feb. 21 deadline is evidently a union device to egg the Wage Stabilization Board (WSB) into speeding its recommendations for settling the dispute. If the board has come out with its findings by that date, time will be needed for industry-union negotiations on the basis of the recommendations.

Even if the board doesn't make the deadline, it seems hardly likely the union will strike, knowing the board would be bound to announce its findings in a few days anyway.

The union's basic decision is to let the WSB decide the case. It seems unlikely the union would cancel out that decision simply because the board might be late in reporting.

Finally, the union is not even threatening to strike after Feb. 21. It merely has voted that if no industry-labor agreement is completed by that time the union's policy committee will meet to decide what to do.

The union could renew the strike threat, but a better guess at this time is that a further strike delay would be voted.

The main danger of a strike would come if either the union or industry should reject the board's findings. It's believed more likely, however, that the board will go pretty well down the middle and that both sides will accept.

Beyond all this, President Truman has made it abundantly clear that the country cannot stand a steel strike now. So the White House is standing ready to stop a walkout with a Taft-Hartley Law injunction.

INCOME TAXES — Many taxpayers may not realize that federal income taxes will be higher next year even if Congress doesn't increase tax rates again.

When the tax-boosting law was passed last fall the increase in rates became effective Nov. 1.

So the tax increase on 1951 incomes, to be reported on returns due this March 15, applies only to November and December, or one sixth of the year.

The full increase in rates will apply to all 1952 and 1953 income. (The present law expires after that.) For a married person with no dependents and a net income of $5,000, the tax on 1951 income is $775. On 1952 income it will be $844.

RAINBOW — Look for some red faces when high military brass is called up by the House Armed Services Procurement Subcommittee. The committee is going to ask why the services can't get together and pay the same price for items they all use.

Sample question: Why do they require barracks bags and blankets in different colors (Air Force blue, Army olive drab, Marine Corps forest green, Navy white)?

TURKEY AND NATO — Look for Turkey and Greece to be assigned full military roles in the North Atlantic Treaty Organization (NATO) after they become members.

Official informants say the U. S., Britain and other original NATO countries at first thought of Turkey as participating in the proposed Middle East Command but not in Gen. Dwight D. Eisenhower's Western European Defense Command.

The Turks wanted none of that kind of deal. Now, informants say, the plan is to take Turkey into the Western European outfit with the idea that it will also be the key country in the Middle East Command whenever that is organized.

NEW POLAR AIR ROUTE — COPENHAGEN, Denmark — Scandinavian Airlines planes will probably be flying from Scandinavia to the U. S. Pacific Coast via the North Pole by late 1952.

Viggo J. Rasmussen, Danish director of the line said it had advanced plans for an express route across the Polar Sea and Greenland. The planes, Douglas DC-6Bs, will probably touch down on the Thule, Greenland, airbase if permission can be obtained from the military authorities.

Driver Dies, Truck Dragged 150 Feet

GROVE CITY, Pa., Jan. 12 (AP)—John Bulsone, 76, of Grove City R4, was killed today in a truck-train collision at the Mill Street crossing.

Bulsone's half-ton pickup truck collided with a Bessemer and Lake Erie passenger train. The train dragged the truck 150 feet.

Brazil Expects To Make Own Steel In Bigger Plant

RIO DE JANEIRO, Jan. 12 (AP)—Brazil plans to make all the steel she needs within a few years.

If she can do this, she can save a lot of foreign exchange or can use it for other goods and service

Also, her expanding economy will not have to depend upon what other steel producing countries may have available for export.

Major expansion will be at the Volta Redonda steel mill, built with U.S. help, which has been operating since 1946.

Volta Redonda now produces about 420,000 tons of steel a year. One phase of expansion, now unde way, is expected to bring it to 700,000 tons in several more months.

President Getulio Vargas has approved a second expansion of the mill, owned by Companhia Siderurgica Nacional, a joint government-private capital enterprise. D-tailed technical studies, including the financing, have been started.

The aim is, by around 1954, to expand Volta Redonda to its full capacity of one million tons a year. This is about what the country now uses—40 per cent of it imported.

"Of course," says Volta Redonda's assistant director, Euvald Simas Pereira, "the country's consumption will be larger by then, but so will the production of other plants."

The present expansion is being carried on with a loan of 25 million dollars granted about a year ago by the U. S. Export-Import Bank and an increase in the company's capital of an equivalent amount.

Morgenthau Sees Self - Sufficiency In Israel By '58

NEW YORK, Jan. 12 (AP)—Henry Morgenthau Jr., returned today from a honeymoon trip abroad with his bride of five weeks and predicted the state of Israel will reach "self-sufficiency" by 1958.

Morgenthau, who is chairman of the board of governors of Israel's 500-million-dollar bond issue, said he will make his first report to the board at a meeting tomorrow morning.

The former U. S. Secretary of the Treasury said he was "gratified" at the Israeli development of public works, local industry and the port of Haifa, he predicted the nation would attain "self-sufficiency" about five years after immigration stops, which he estimated should be next year.

WGAL-TV
CHANNEL 4 • LANCASTER

SUNDAY, JANUARY 27, 1952

11:45 AM—Sunday Serenade
12:00 Noon—Ranger Joe
12:15 PM—Filmette
12:30—Talent Time
1:00—I Love Lucy
1:30—Education in Action—F & M
2:00—Crime Syndicated
2:30—Beat the Clock
3:00—TBA
3:30—Hall of Fame: "The Story of Roger Williams"
4:00—Meet the Press: Averell Harriman, Guest
4:30—Juvenile Jury
5:00—Zoo Parade
5:30—Those Endearing Young Charms
6:00—Sanctuary Time
6:30—Groucho Marx: "You Bet Your Life"
7:00—The Royal Showcase: Vivian Blaine
7:30—Young Mr. Bobbin
8:00—Comedy Hour: Danny Thomas
9:00—TV Playhouse: "Segment"
10:00—Red Skelton
10:30—This Is Show Business
11:00—Toast of the Town
12:00—News—Sports Final
12:10 AM—Resume

MONDAY, JANUARY 28, 1952

6:45 AM— Test Pattern
7:00—Today—Dave Garroway
9:00—The Big Picture
9:30—Record Room (Wanted Persons)
10:00—Morning News
10:15—Arthur Godfrey Morning Show
10:30—It's in The Bag
11:00—Ernie Kovacs
11:15—Name the Brand
11:30—Strike It Rich
12:00—Noontime Musicale
12:15 PM—Love of Life
12:30—News of the World
12:40—Regional News
12:45—Search For Tomorrow
1:00—From the Kitchen Door
1:30—Mr. Wizard
2:00—Garry Moore
2:30—First 100 Years
2:45—Today With Kay
3:00—The Big Payoff
3:30—Ralph Edwards
4:00—Kate Smith Hour
5:00—Hawkins Falls
5:15—Gabby Hayes
5:30—Howdy Doody
6:00—Covered Wagon Theatre
6:30—Dave Brandt Sports Desk
6:40—Weatherman
6:45—World News
6:55—Regional News
7:00—Kukla, Fran & Ollie
7:15—In The Public Interest
7:30—Those Two
7:45—Camel News Caravan
8:00—What's My Name? Jerry Mahoney-Paul Winchell
8:30—Voice of Firestone: Eugene Conley, Guest Soloist
9:00—Lights Out—"The Third Door"
9:30—Robert Montgomery Presents: "Eva? Caroline?"
10:30—Stump Your Neighbor with Harold Miller
11:00—Foreign Intrigue
11:30—Racket Squad
12:00—News—Sports Final
12:10—Wanted Persons
12:15—Resume—Sign Off

TUESDAY, JANUARY 29, 1952

6:45 AM—Test Pattern
7:00—Today—Dave Garroway
9:00—Survival
9:30—Record Room
10:00—Morning News
10:15—Arthur Godfrey Morning Show
10:30—It's in The Bag
11:00—Ernie Kovacs
11:15—Name the Brand
11:30—Strike It Rich
12:00—Noontime Musicale
12:15 PM—Love of Life
12:30—News of the World
12:40—Regional News
12:45—Search For Tomorrow
1:00—From the Kitchen Door
1:30—Steve Allen
1:45—Music on Film
2:00—Garry Moore
2:30—First 100 Years
2:45—Today with Kay
3:00—The Big Pay Off
3:30—Bill Goodwin Show
4:00—Kate Smith Hour
5:00—Hawkins Falls
5:15—Gabby Hayes
5:30—Howdy Doody
6:00—Covered Wagon Theatre
6:30—Dave Brandt Sports Desk
6:40—Weatherman
6:45—World News
6:55—Regional News
7:00—Cisco Kid: "Freightline Feud"
7:30—Dinah Shore
7:45—Camel News Caravan
8:00—Texaco Star Theatre: Milton Berle
9:00—Fireside Theatre: "...light Song"
9:30—... Theatre: "Yesterday's ...e"
10:00—...ginal Amateur Hour
10:45—TBA
11:00—Ken Murray Show
12:00 Mid.—News—Sports Final
12:10 AM—Resume

WEDNESDAY, JANUARY 30, 1952

6:45 AM—Test Pattern
7:00—Today—Dave Garroway
9:00—Armed Forces Film
9:30—Record Room (Wanted Persons)
10:00—Morning News
10:15—Arthur Godfrey Morning Show
10:30—It's in The Bag
11:00—Ernie Kovacs
11:15—Name the Brand
11:30—Strike It Rich
12:00 Noon—The TV Farmer
12:15 PM—Love of Life
12:30—News of the World
12:40—Regional News
12:45—Search for Tomorrow
1:00—From the Kitchen Door
1:30—U. S. Marine Swearing-In Ceremonies
1:45—Teleshopper
2:00—Garry Moore
2:30—First 100 Years
2:45—Today with Kay
3:00—The Big Payoff
3:30—Bert Parks
4:00—Kate Smith Hour
5:00—Hawkins Falls
5:15—Gabby Hayes
5:30—Howdy Doody
6:00—Covered Wagon Theatre
6:30—Dave Brandt Sports Desk
6:40—Weatherman
6:45—World News
6:55—Regional News
7:00—Kukla, Fran & Ollie
7:15—York March of Dimes
7:30—Those Two
7:45—Camels News Caravan
8:00—Arthur Godfrey & His Friends
9:00—TV Theatre: "Miss O'Brien Entertains"
10:00—Blue Ribbon Bouts: Henry vs. Satterfield
10:45—Slants on Sports
11:00—Wrestling
12:00—News—Sports Final
12:10 AM—Wanted Persons
12:15—Resume

THURSDAY, JANUARY 31, 1952

6:45 AM—Test Pattern
7:00—Today—Dave Garroway
9:00—Pentagon—Washington
9:30—Record Room
10:00—Morning News
10:15—Arthur Godfrey Morning Show
10:30—It's in The Bag
11:00—Ernie Kovacs
11:15—Name the Brand
11:30—Strike It Rich
12:00 Noon—Noontime Musicale
12:15 PM—Love of Life
12:30—News of the World
12:40—Regional News
12:45—Search for Tomorrow
1:00—From the Kitchen Door
1:30—Steve Allen
1:45—Music on Film
2:00—Garry Moore
2:30—First 100 Years
2:45—Today with Kay
3:00—The Big Payoff
3:30—Bill Goodwin Show
4:00—Kate Smith Hour
5:00—Hawkins Falls
5:15—Gabby Hayes
5:30—Howdy Doody
6:00—Covered Wagon Theatre
6:30—Dave Brandt Sports Desk
6:40—Weatherman
6:45—World News
6:55—Regional News
7:00—Alan Young Show
7:30—Dinah Shore Show
7:45—Camel News Caravan
8:00—Stop The Music
9:00—Dragnet
9:30—Ford Festival
10:00—Martin Kane, Private Eye
10:30—Red Kain Comments on the News
10:45—Music on Film
11:00—Wrestling from Hollywood
12:00 Mid.—News—Sports Final
12:10 AM—Resume

FRIDAY, FEBRUARY 1, 1952

6:45 AM—Test Pattern
7:00—Today—Dave Garroway
9:00—Assembly VI
9:30—Record Room
10:00—Morning News
10:30—It's in The Bag
11:00—Ernie Kovacs
11:15—Name the Brand
11:30—Strike It Rich
12:00 Noon—Noontime Musicale
12:15 PM—Love of Life
12:30—News of the World
12:40—Regional News
12:45—Search for Tomorrow
1:00—From the Kitchen Door
1:30—Bride and Groom
1:45—Music on Film
2:00—Garry Moore
2:30—First 100 Years
2:45—Today with Kay
3:00—The Big Payoff
3:30—Bert Parks
4:00—Kate Smith Hour
5:00—Hawkins Falls
5:15—Gabby Hayes
5:30—Howdy Doody
6:00—Covered Wagon Theatre
6:30—Dave Brandt Sports Desk
6:40—Weatherman
6:45—World News
6:55—Regional News
7:00—Kukla, Fran & Ollie
7:15—Lanc. County Dental Health Week
7:30—Those Two
7:45—Camel News Caravan
8:00—RCA Victor Show: Ezio Pinza
8:30—We the People
9:00—The Big Story: "Case of the Trademark Killer"
9:30—Aldrich Family
10:00—Boxing: Wilson-Wallace
10:45—Greatest Fights: Louis-Godoy
11:00—Electric Theatre
11:30—Story Theatre
12:00 Mid.—News—Sports Final
12:10 AM—Resume

SATURDAY, FEBRUARY 2, 1952

8:00 AM—Musical Moments
8:15—Covered Wagon Theatre
9:15—Land of Story Books
9:30—Movies for Kids
10:00—Wild Bill Hickok
10:30—TBA
11:00—Lancaster Co. Dental Health Week
11:30—Kate Smith
12:00—Big Top
1:00—Highway Safety
1:15—Filmette
1:20—Stage One-Twenty
2:00—Colgate-Army Basketball
4:00—Mr. District Attorney
4:30—Gunther's Premium Playhouse
6:00—Stu Erwin: "Trouble With Father"
6:30—Dave Brandt Sports Desk
6:45—Filmette
6:55—Tomorrow's Sunday News
7:00—Crusade in the Pacific
7:30—One Man's Family
8:00—All Star Revue: Olsen and Johnson
9:00—Your Show of Shows
10:30—Your Hit Parade
11:00—Wrestling
12:00 Mid—News—Sports Final
12:10 AM—Resume

—Adv.

Gen. Soule, 51, Dies; Served In Korea

WASHINGTON, Jan. 26 (AP)—Maj. Gen. Robert H. Soule, former commander of the 3rd Infantry Division in Korea, died here today.

The 51-year-old inspector of infantry for Army field forces at Fort Monroe, Va., collapsed at the home of Maj. Gen. and Mrs. Willard G. Wyman. The general and Mrs. Soule were visiting the Wymans.

Soule commanded the famed "Rock of the Marne" Division in Korea for more than a year.

Nationwide Rites Planned To Stir Spiritual Forces

PHILADELPHIA, Jan. 26 (AP)—The American Legion initiates its nationwide movement to inspire a spiritual reawakening of the American people with a ceremony here at the chapel of the Four Chaplains on Feb. 3.

A service commemorating the ninth anniversary of the date when the four — Catholic, Jewish and Protestant chaplains surrendered their life belts to enlisted men and went down praying together aboard the torpedoed U.S. Transport Dorchester, will be conducted in the memorial chapel.

Similar services will be sponsored by the Legion in churches and synagogues all over the nation to inaugurate the American Legion's program urging regular church attendance. Daily prayer and Scripture reading and emphasizing religious training of children.

SUNDAY NEWS BROADCASTS
Local News - Saturdays at 6:15 and 11:10 WGAL
See Sunday News Preview Saturdays at 6:45 on TV

WGAL
NBC • 1490 Kc. • Mutual
WGAL • FM • 101.3 Mc.

SUNDAY, JANUARY 27, 1952.

7:00 AM—Sign-On
7:01—United Press Headlines
7:05—Sunday Musicale
7:40—News & Weather Report
7:45—Guest Star
8:00—Gospel Tide Hour: United Brethren Church
8:30—Jack Arthur Show
9:00—United Press News: Dolly Madison
9:30—The Eternal Light
10:00—Radio Bible Class
10:30—St. Joseph's Workshop
11:00—Calvary Independent Church
12:00—Concert Miniature
12:15 PM—News at Noon
12:25—Local News: Sunday News
12:30—Here's To Veterans
12:45—Frank & Earnest
1:00—Critic At Mike
1:15—Mike 95
1:30—The Lutheran Hour
2:00—The Catholic Hour
2:30—American Forum of the Air
3:00—The Head & The Heart
3:30—Earl Godwin's Washington
3:45—John Cameron Swazey
4:00—The Falcon
4:30—Martin Kane
5:00—Whitehall 1212
5:30—Forward America: G.E. Appliance
6:00—United Press News: Kranich
6:15—Bobby Benson
6:20—Sunday Melodies
6:30—The Big Show
8:00—Phil Harris & Alice Faye
8:30—Theater Guild of the Air
*9:30—THE $64 QUESTION
10:00—Tin Pan Alley
10:30—Eileen Christie & Co.
11:00—United Press News
11:10—Local News: Intell
11:15—Starlight Serenade
11:30—The Bob Snyder Show
12:00—News
12:05 AM—Rock A Bye Dudley
12:30—News & Sign-Off

★ JACK PAAR EMCEES

—Adv.

WLAN
ABC • 1390 kc ★ FM • 96.9 mc

SUNDAY, JAN. 27

7:00 AM—News Headlines & Weather
7:05—Comic Weekly Man
7:30—The Calvary Hour
8:00—Old Fashioned Revival Hour
9:00—Pentecostal Echoes
9:30—Voice of Prophecy
10:00—Mt. Calvary Church (E-Town)
11:00—First Methodist Church, Lancaster
12:00—News—ABC
12:15 PM—Everyday Health
12:30—Piano Playhouse
1:00—Christian Business Men
1:15—Dick & Ruth Neiman
1:30—Date With A Disc
2:00—Music You Want
2:30—Concert of Europe
3:00—This Week Around the World
3:30—Billy Graham — "Hour of Decision"
4:00—CBS Symphony
5:00—Boston Blackie (G.E.)
5:30—Greatest Story Ever Told (Goodyear)
6:00—Drew Pearson Show
6:15—Monday Morning Headlines
6:30—Allan Jones Show
7:00—Sammy Kaye's Sunday Serenade
7:30—Tribute To Jerome Kern
8:00—Stop The Music
9:00—Walter Winchell
9:15—Marlene Dietrich in "Cafe Istanbul"
9:45—The Three Suns
10:00—Paul Harvey — News
10:15—Communism In Europe — Vincent Tortora
10:30—George Sokolsky—News
10:45—Dr. Gino's Musicale
11:00—News
11:15—Thoughts in Passing
11:30—Orchestra from ABC
12:00—News
12:05 AM—Music by Ralph Flanagan
12:30—News
12:35—Sign Off

—Adv.

NETWORK KEY STATIONS

Morning

9:00—WNBC, World News, WOR News, H. Hennessy; WCBS, Trinity Choir; WJZ, Dr. D. Barnhouse
9:15—WNBC, Sunday Comics; WOR, Magic of Believing; WCBS, World News
9:30—WOR, Radio Chapel; WJZ, Voice of Prophecy; WCBS, E. Power Biggs, Organist
9:45—WNBC, Male Quartet
10:00—WNBC, National Radio Pulpit; WJZ, Message of Israel; WCBS, Church of the Air; WOR, News, H Gladstone
10:15—WOR, Health Clinic
10:30—WNBC, Children's Hour; WJZ, Dillard University Choir; WCBS, Church of the Air; WOR, Lorraine Sherwood
10:45—WOR, Your Hymnal
11:00—WOR, News, H Gladstone; WCBS, Salt Lake City Tabernacle; WJZ, Kelvin Keech
11:15—WOR, Brunch with Dorothy and Dick; WJZ, Frank and Ernest
11:30—WNBC, News, C McCarthy; WJZ, Christian in Action; WCBS, News, Invitation to Learning
11:45—WNBC, Jane Pickens

Afternoon

12:00—WOR, Henry Gladstone; WCBS, People's Platform; WNBC, This Is My Favorite; WJZ, Concert of Europe
12:15—WOR, Dinah, Perry, Frank
12:30—WNBC, The Eternal Light; WOR, News, M. Elliott; WJZ, Piano Playhouse; WCBS, Howard K Smith
12:45—WOR, Pet Show; WCBS, Bill Costello, News
1:00—WCBS, String Srenade; WJZ, Dr. W Ward Ayer; WNBC, Critic at Large; WOR, Festival of Recorded Opera
1:15—WNBC, Mike 95
1:30—WNBC, The Endless Frontier; WJZ, National Vespers; WCBS, Herbert Hoover, Talk
2:00—WNBC, Catholic Hour; WJZ, Marines in Review; WCBS, The Symphonette
2:30—WCBS, New York Symphony; WJZ, Christian Science; WNBC, American Forum
2:45—WJZ, Ted Malone
3:00—WNBC, The Head and the Heart, Drama; WJZ, The Baptist Hour
3:30—WNBC, Earl Godwin, News; WJZ, Dr. Billy Graham, Sermon; WOR, News, McCutchen
3:45—WNBC, J Cameron Swayze; WOR, Fun in Stamps
4:00—WNBC, The Falcon, With Les Damon; WJZ, Old Fashioned Revival Hour; WCBS, Edwin C. Hill; WOR, Bobby Benson, Western
4:30—WNBC, Martin Kane, Private Eye; WOR, Under Arrest; WCBS, Its Always Sunday, Drama
5:00—WNBC, Whitehall 1212, Drama; WOR, The Shadow; WJZ, Sunday Serendae; WCBS, Arthur Godfrey
5:30—WOR, Detective Mysteries; WCBS, Hearthstone of the Death Squad; WJZ, Greatest Story Ever Told; WNBC, The Silent Men

Evening

6:00—WNBC, Texas Rangers; WOR, Gabby Hayes Show; WCBS, My Friend Irma; WJZ, Drew Pearson
6:15—WJZ, Monday Headlines
6:30—WCBS, Our Miss Brooks; WJZ, Vancouver Symphony; WOR, Nick Carter, Drama; WNBC, The Big Show
7:00—WOR, Peter Salem; WCBS, Jack Benny
7:30—WOR, Melvin Elliott, News; WCBS, Amos and Andy; WJZ, The Great Adventure, Drama
7:45—WOR, Magic of Believing
8:00—WJZ, Stop the Music; WCBS, Edgar Bergan; WNBC, Phil Harris and Alice Faye; WOR, Official Detective, Drama;
8:30—WNBC, Theater Guild; WCBS, Broadway Playhouse; WOR, Magazine Theatre, Drama
9:00—WJZ, Walter Winchell; WCBS, Meet Corliss Archer, Comedy; WOR, Opera Concert
9:15—WJZ, Cafe Istanbul
9:30—WCBS, Meet Millie; WNBC, $64 Question; WOR, John J. Anthony Hour
10:00—WNBC, Tin Pan Valley, Musical; WCBS, News, The People Act; WJZ, News, Paul Harvey; WOR, Out of the Thunder, Drama
10:15—WJZ, Gloria Parker
10:30—WNBC, Eileen Christy and Company; WJZ, George E. Sokolsky; WCBS, The Choraliers; WOR, Health Clinic
10:45—WJZ, Dr. Gino; WOR, March of Dimes
11:00—WNBC, News; WOR, News, M. Elliott; WCBS, News, Hugh Holder; WJZ, Late News
11:15—WNBC, Clifton Utley, News; WCBS, Think Out Loud; WJZ, Passing Thoughts; WOR, Youth on the March
11:30—WNBC, Viewpoints U.S.A.; WJZ, Dr. Billy Graham, Sermon; WCBS, Joe Reichman Orch.
11:45—WOR, Ira Brant Trio

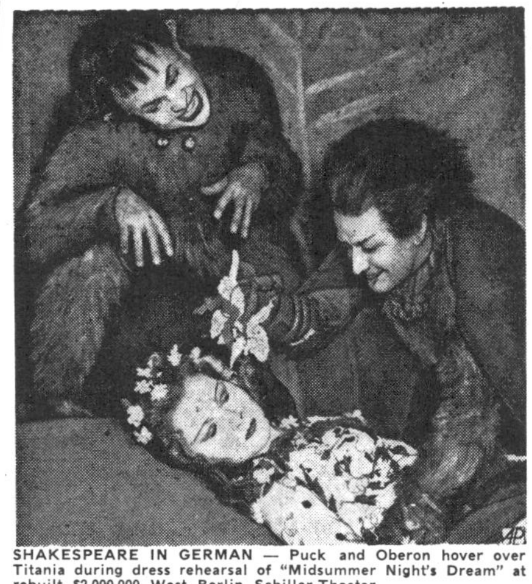

SHAKESPEARE IN GERMAN — Puck and Oberon hover over Titania during dress rehearsal of "Midsummer Night's Dream" at rebuilt $2,000,000 West Berlin Schiller-Theater.

Adele Addison, Negro Soprano, Newest U. S. Star

By W. G. ROGERS
Associated Press Arts Editor

NEW YORK, Jan. 26 (AP)—From an obscure Sunday-school platform to the stage of this city's famed Town Hall, from potted palms and lillies at Easter and Christmas to floral tributes from thrilled New Yorkers—that's the story of Adele Addison.

Perhaps you don't know the name of this young Negro soprano. Perhaps you haven't heard her on records, or on the air, or at Tanglewood, or in opera, or as soloist with the Boston symphony, or at her debut here last week when critics praised her "truly beautiful voice of pearly lustre," a voice "intrinsically pure and lovely."

If you haven't heard it, it's as sure as anything can be in the world of music that you will. But even this early in her career, her story is worth telling because it has an important lesson for millions of young Americans who year after year become an engineer instead of a general, a baseball player instead of an explorer, a hat designer instead of a singer.

Nowadays old friends rush up to the vivacious, pretty Miss Addison and exclaim: "I always knew you were going to be a singer!"

She is a singer; they couldn't be righter. But if they always knew it when she, in short dresses, was singing "Away in a Manger" in a Baptist church in Springfield, Mass., they were smarter than she was.

It began in Mt. Calvary Baptist Church Sunday School, she says, where she was invited to sing oftener than others because, since she could memorize, she could be counted on at least to get through a Sunday solo. It continued in junior high, where she had operetta roles. And there a teacher, suspecting an unusual talent, invited outside judges to listen to her: one of them started then to give her voice lessons, still gives them to her.

She went to a classical high school to learn the languages she needed either for medicine or as school mistress. But a second perceptive teacher entrusted her with more solos with the glee club, and at graduation encouraged her to go on studying.

Before she knew it, she was launched on her first year (1942) at the Westminster Choir College in Princeton and it began to look as though she couldn't help singing and earning a living too. This season she will make about 30 appearances in Canada and this country.

Video Clotheshorses Cope With Problem Of Newest Look

NEW YORK, Jan. 26 (AP)—If you are a woman in television, you've got to be a clotheshorse. The public, it seems, demands it.

"Television is so intimate," explains Faye Emerson "the performers come into the living room. The audience is as conscious of your clothes as they are of any guest's. They remember what you wear—and they start writing in when you repeat too often on a dress."

Perfect Showcase

Fortunately for the bank accounts of the feminine television headliners, the garment industry has discovered that TV is a wonderfully effective show case for its wares and stands ready and anxious to extend a helping hand.

It was not always that way. It was only a short time ago that performers were beset by the problem of begging, borrowing and buying different dresses for each appearance. Studio lights were hot, makeup ran and clothes took a frequently fatal beating. Most designers and dressmakers were reluctant to risk their best models.

Boosts Dress Sales

Those who did, however, soon noticed the impact of televized clothes on a rapidly expanding audience. Store buyers took to making morning - after - the - show telephone calls requesting "a dozen Maggi McNellises," or telegraphing the network for the designer of a Faye Emerson gown. The public took to writing in wholesale lots begging Eloise McElhone for more information about her darling black crepe.

This is very pleasant, but it still hasn't erased all the problems of dressing for television.

In the old days, for example, white was Faye Emerson's favorite color. It has been practically eliminated from her wardrobe now because white, except when used very sparingly in carefully planned spots, creates something called halation, or flaring of light.

Miss McNellis once specialized in black and navy blue dresses. Today she's strictly a pastel girl, because black and blue, combined with her very dark hair drains color from her face and replaces it with shadows.

Betty Furness, a blonde, has best results with dark colors, and is scared to fool around with yellow, pink, beige and powder blue.

"Sometimes they turn out looking like flesh—and then you're in awful trouble," she said. "The letters start coming."

HAVE BIG WARDROBES

All the women headliners have big suit collections—most of them have 10 or more. The average number of afternoon and cocktail hour dresses runs around a score. Each has a couple of dozen evening gowns. All this doesn't represent a working wardrobe, for most of their clothes are always in temporary retirement.

CD Civil Defense Hits Its Stride

AS Lancaster County marks mid-point of National Defense Week, the local emphasis continues to be on building up Civil Defense units as well as supporting the armed forces. With flags flying to honor the effort, CD officials can count some 4,000 Lancastrians enrolled in various phases of the elaborate program, plus some 15,500 volunteer firemen. The County CD Director, Col. J. Hale Steinman, has called for still more volunteers to man the many posts which must be filled for complete functioning of the organization. In World War II there were about 26,000 countians assisting in civil defense. Photos on this page represent a round-up of recent activities of a few of the many CD groups in Lancaster County.

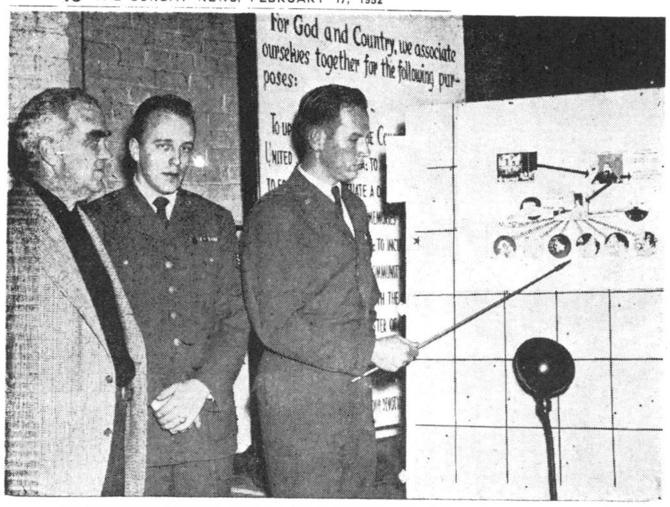

POINTERS FROM THE AIR FORCE—Training for plane-spotters was given by AF personnel, and inspections of the county's 15 posts have been scheduled Feb. 25-27. At instruction session, above, are Leon S. Duckworth, county air observer chief; Sgt. Thomas J. Cleary and Lt. Allen C. Kulp.

SKY-SCANNERS making practice run on spotting "enemy" planes from top of Griest Building are Mrs. Charles Y. Tanger and Robert Miller.

TOOLING UP—Rescue Division of Civil Defense is being equipped with portable kits containing emergency material displayed above by (l-r) Legionnaires Samuel B. Sheetz, George Ward, John A. Linton, Herbert Gansman and H. L. Lichty.

AIR RAID SHELTER SIGNS are scheduled to be erected in midtown Lancaster this week, marking 16 buildings inspected and chosen for the purpose (see air view below at right). Walter Milley paints arrow.

RADIO CONTROL of simulated evacuees streaming from a bombed Philadelphia is demonstrated by "hams" Walter Goodman and Art Jenkins with mobile unit.

TAKE COVER HERE—Buildings selected as public bomb shelters are: 1. Griest Bldg., 2. Fulton Bank, 3. McCrory's, 4. Sears Roebuck, 5. Court House, 6. Lancaster Newspapers, 7. Kirk Johnson, 8. H. L. Green, 9. CTC, 10. American Seed, 11. Arcade Market, 12. Municipal Bldg., 13. Legion Home, 14. Armory, 15. Herr & Co., 16. Pittsburgh Glass.

LADIES aid CD volunteer police, too. Among 28 signing up with Police Captain W. B. Hershner and administrator K. L. Shirk are Mrs. Marie Smithson, Mrs. Gloria Matroni and Mrs. Leah Meister.

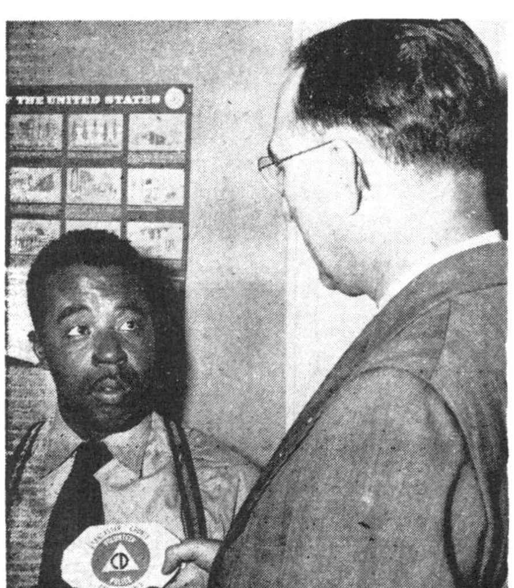

ARMBANDS for volunteer police—a familiar feature of World War II—are being distributed again. Here Fred F. Wilson, a commissioned member of the corps, received insigne from Police Commissioner Fred G. McCartney.

KEY POINTS in the city-area CD set-up are mapped at Civil Defense headquarters, with different symbols marking various facilities. They range from message centers to an emergency morgue for which the Central Market has been designated. Inclusive CD plan for county covers such operations as security, communications, transportation, engineering, wardens, medical, emergency welfare and evacuation. Tuesday night a "red" alert will be given here, with the new E. Pa. regional director on hand. Reports will be given.

ALERT CALL from State CD office rings in at Lancaster control center on second floor of Manufacturers' Building. Col. J. K. Borneman, who has been succeeded as administrative officer by Max Stierstorfer, stands by as Gil Lyons takes call.

Lancaster Platoon's
Boot Camp

35 "BOOTS" of the Lancaster Platoon wind up their strenuous training at the U. S. Marine Corps' Parris Island camp this week. They'll start their first leave as full-fledged Marines on Friday. Official Marine Corps photos on this page show some members of the group, recruited as a Lancaster County unit, during various phases of their training. Finished with "boot camp," they'll now be split up and assigned to many different types of service.

NOT AS EASY as one-two-three is exercising with rifle while calling out the numbers, as shown here by Quentin R. Aukamp, Willow Street R1, and Paul Wiker Jr., 12 Green St., Lancaster.

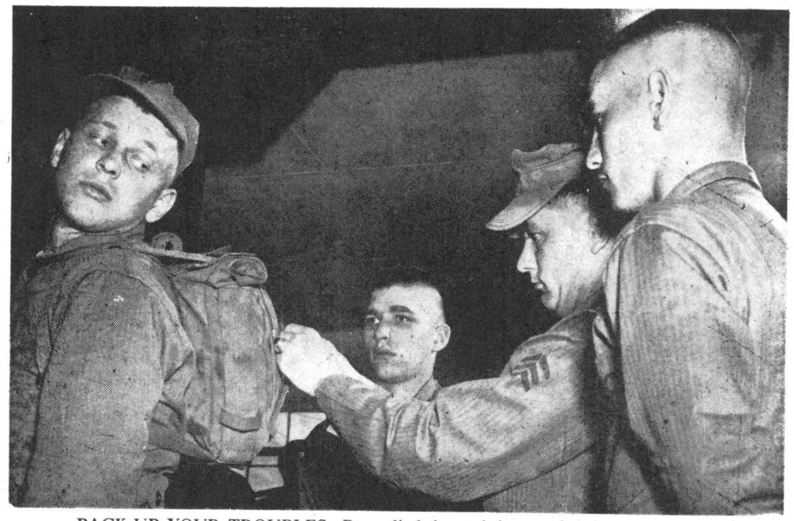

PACK UP YOUR TROUBLES—Boots find the pack is one of their most important items of equipment. Here proper adjustment is shown by Sgt. W. J. Migues to Pvts. Francis E. Wettig, Manheim; Allen G. Trimble, New Providence R1; and Henry E. Trimble, 457 Pershing Ave., Lancaster.

A MARINE'S BEST FRIEND is still his rifle, and proper care of the weapon is one of the first lessons. Rifle of Pvt. Raymond W. Scott, 561 Burrowes Ave., is inspected by drill instructor. Next in line, nearest camera, is Pvt. Jean B. Broillet, formerly employed by D. S. Warfel.

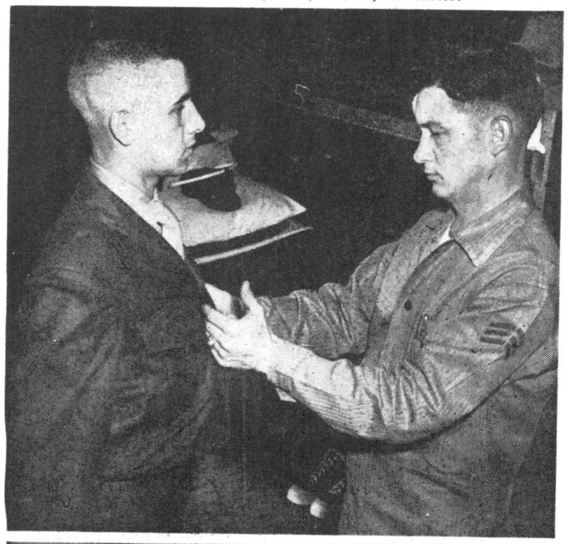

PERFECT FIT—Every Marine's uniform is tailored for him individually. At left, sergeant checks fit of jacket on Pvt. Robert H. Krushinsky, 452 Poplar St.

AT HOME ON THE RANGE—A Marine recruit spends three weeks on the Parris Island rifle range learning the fundamentals of good marksmanship. Taking a lesson in adjusting the sling for various firing positions are Pvts. Gerald E. Zepp, 128 Beaver St., Lancaster; Lloyd E. Hurley, Quarryville R1; Francis E. Wettig, 334 S. Charlotte St., Manheim; and brothers Kenneth and Vincent S. Findley, Manheim R2. Instructor, at left, is Pfc. H. L. Taylor, Greer, S. C.

HOT CHOW and plenty of it at noontime is a prime requisite for the boots. Working out on well-loaded trays at table in foreground are Pvts. Charles Groff, Lancaster R5, left; and William L. Myers, 536 N. Mary St., Lancaster, right. Much of training is done in fatigue uniform.

HOME-TOWN PINUPS are favorites, and here Pvt. Lloyd Bowers, 135 Chester St., Lancaster, gets a smile out of Pvt. Herbert Carvell's admiration of photo of his wife, who lives at 218 Noble St., Lititz.

MARINES ON THE MARCH—Doing a left oblique into the camera while marching on the main drill field at Parris Island are, left to right in front rank, Pvts. Harry L. Lehman, 253 N. Second St., Columbia; Jere L. Todd, 715 N. Cherry St., Lancaster; and Donald E. Reisinger, E. Front St., Marietta.

GAS MASK DRILL—Part of boot training covers the use of chemical agents in warfare and protection against them by troops in the field. Here S/Sgt. Henry J. Gamache instructs Pvts. Wayne R. Williams, Lancaster R5; Arthur L. Kerst, 137 N. Pine St., Lancaster; and Jere L. Todd, Lancaster.

MAIL CALL—Evening brings letters from home and one of the brightest spots of the day to the recruits. Here three members of the Lancaster Platoon grin over their mail. They are (l-r) Pvts. Paul Walker, 112 Green St.; John Argire, 407 W. King St.; and Gerald Zepp, 122 Beaver St., all of Lancaster.

Only one of every 300,000 letters mailed in the United States is lost before delivery.

Moroccan Tribesmen Clash With Police

MEKNES, Morocco, April 5 (AP)—Armed Moroccan tribesmen from the Atlas Mountains foothills clashed today with French police and soldiers outside a local court at Mrirt. Five Moroccans were killed.

Mrirt is about 75 miles south of Meknes in the interior of French Morocco. The tribesmen came from the hills to protest the trial before a local kaid's (leader's) court of several persons accused of agitating against the authorities.

Woman, 50, Killed In Head-On Crash

GREENVILLE, Pa., April 5 (AP) — Two autos collided head-on about three miles east of here today, killing a woman and injuring five other persons.

Mrs. Arthur B. Good, 50, of Clarks Mills, Mercer County, died in Greenville Hospital some 45 minutes after the crash.

"GREATEST SHOW ON EARTH" FILMED—Starting Thursday at the King Theater, Lancaster, will be Cecil B. DeMille's mighty Technicolor production, "The Greatest Show on Earth," a Paramount picture about the lives and loves of the men and women of the great circus. Scene above is climax of the contest in recklessness between two aerialists played by Betty Hutton and Cornel Wilde.

4 N. Y. Acts Booked At Ephrata Legion

The Ephrata Legion has booked for tonight's floor show at 6 and 10:30 p.m. the following acts from New York City: Al and Connie Fanton, "Youthful Dance Stars," who just returned from a triumph tour of England; Jack Parker and Doll, "Juggling Jewels"; Shelly Keller, Master of Ceremonies, with a package of jokes; Ron and Mary Norman, "Novelty Surprise."

FATAL MID-TOWN CRASH

AMBRIDGE, Pa., April 5 (AP) — Frank Zorman, 67, was killed by an auto today at a downtown intersection. Police said the driver of the car was John C. Kronstain.

The Sunday News Brings You
LAST-MINUTE NEWS!
Local and World Events

SUNDAY NEWS

Read Complete Fiction Story
Sunday News Magazine
Last Page—Pink Section

LANCASTER, PA., SUNDAY, APRIL 13, 1952

Blood Typing Program

Community's Teamwork In Manheim Gets Results

Borough Is Among First Towns In Nation To Push Blood Plan

When a community sets its collective minds to something, better stand by for action!

If anyone should doubt the truth of this, he might consider the case of Manheim Borough's community-wide blood typing program, which recently hit its peak and has just been extended.

Manheim is one of the first communities in the country to launch such a wide-range blood typing program and achieve success. It is the only community in Lancaster County to do so.

Since the campaign began seven weeks ago nearly 2,500 persons of the borough and immediate vicinity have availed themselves of the service. That's nearly half the borough's population and represents a response which "far exceeded the expectations" of the program's sponsors, according to Paul Evans, chairman of the drive.

Initiated and underwritten by the Manheim Veterans of Foreign Wars, Post 5956, the program first gained the backing of all community doctors. Other community organizations joined in, donating their time and services and rounding out a well-oiled machine to get the task done.

Launched with a broad publicity campaign and a thorough-house-to-house canvassing job, the blood typing program rolled into rapid motion, accelerated by offers of free transportation to the typing center, free baby sitters while having the job done, and, of course, the fact that the service itself was free of charge.

Through these collective efforts the borough is now probably the best prepared of any community in the country to cope with an emergency which would result in a large number of casualties, according to the program sponsors.

They say they have been able to learn of only two other places in the United States where such a program was successfully carried out. In neither of these places—Allentown, Pa., and Jackson County, Michigan—was information on the result of the program immediately available.

Master records, containing the name and blood type of every person who took part in the program, will be prepared for publication (probably in booklet form) and ultimate distribution to every doctor in Manheim and every hospital in Lancaster County, according to chairman Evans.

MAY DISTRIBUTE MORE

If possible, he added, the booklets will also be distributed to every practicing physician in the county.

The booklets would provide a doctor with ready reference to a person's blood type in the event the person should meet with accident or for some reason need a transfusion. In this way they would supplement individual cards, containing the same information, which are issued to those having their blood typed.

Further, these records would serve as a guide to potential donors having the "right" type of blood, although no one who has his blood typed under the program is obliged in any way to become a donor, Evans stressed.

An obvious advantage of a doctor readily learning a patient's blood type and who may have the same type (and therefore be a potential donor) is the time it would save in an emergency, Evans points out. The time saved could be a matter of life and death to the patient.

The latter would be particularly true of the more rare types, where hundreds of persons must be processed in order to obtain only a handful of donors.

One Manheim doctor reported a recent case where type AB Rh-negative blood was required and suitable donors were not immediately available nor was there sufficient blood of this type in the blood banks. Only 22 of the nearly 2,500 persons listed on Manheim's blood-type index during the current drive have this type of blood.

Even that number having this rare type is considered high in relation to the number of persons tested, it was explained.

Evans says the program has been extended to afford an opportunity to those who failed to have their blood typed during the main drive to do so.

Under the extended program a person who wishes his blood typed may contact any Manheim doctor and arrange to have it done—still free of charge, he added. The information would be added to the master list. Anyone who already knows his blood type due to a test taken outside of the current program is welcome to have the information entered on the master list, Evans added.

Information gained during the blood typing program is invaluable, comments still another Manheim doctor, adding that "we dare not forget that it is not forthcoming without effort, and that over a period of time." This typing effort would be rather futile if tried after an emergency, he continues, and a great amount of confusion and loss of life could result if large amounts of blood were required and would not be immediately forthcoming.

Backs Doctor's View

A review of the effort put forth by various groups in Manheim to make the program a success backs up the doctor's remarks concerning the energy which must be expended.

The VFW, which is paying all costs, hired Lancaster General Hospital technicians to do the actual typing work. Manheim doctors donated their time and sat in at the fire hall blood typing headquarters to certify cards.

In rapid succession other organizations threw their weight behind the project—the Fire Company, the Woman's Club, the auxiliary to the VFW, the Lion's Club, the Junior Chamber of Commerce, the Boy Scouts and the Girl Scouts.

Car pools were formed to provide transportation to and from the fire hall, where the typing center was set up; Girl Scouts turned baby-sitters for persons wishing to leave children home while having their blood typed; hand bills were distributed and individual homes canvassed.

In brief, everything was designed to make the path to the blood typing center as direct and convenient as possible. That a community can produce results with thorough planning—and an emphasis on teamwork—is evident in the results achieved in Manheim.

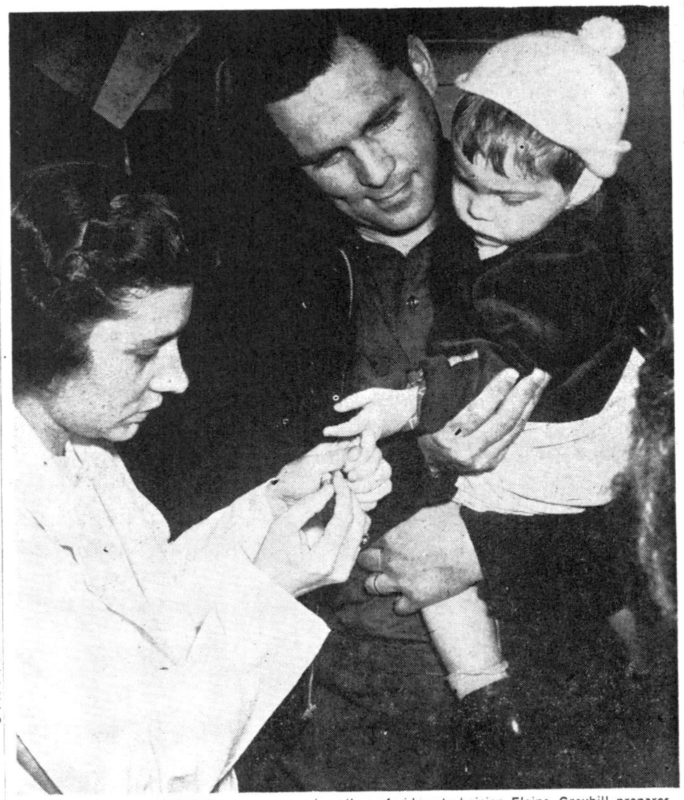

YOUNG MANHEIM CITIZEN seems more curious than afraid as technician Elaine Graybill prepares to "tap" his fingertip for blood sample. He's Stephen Vogel, 16-month-old son of Mr. and Mrs. Nevin Vogel. That's his dad holding him. Youngest to be blood typed during the main drive in Manheim was a two-week-old child. Oldest was an 80-year-old man. The town was one of the first in the country to launch such an extensive drive, is the first in Lancaster County to do so.

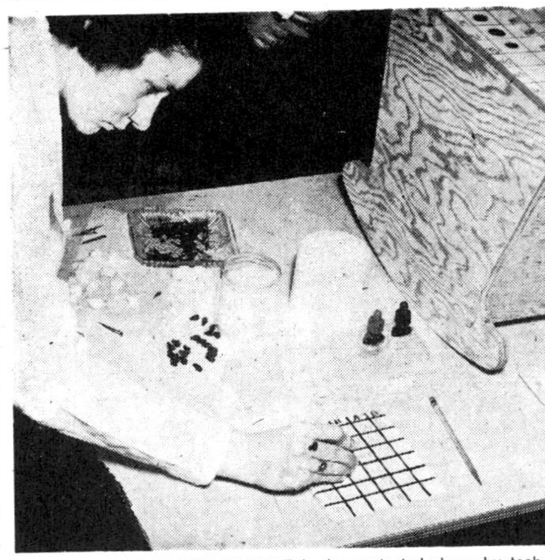

ANALYSIS OF BLOOD SAMPLE is demonstrated above by technician Graybill, shown with apparatus used in blood typing program. Here she places blood sample on porcelain index plate, applies chemical in phase of typing process.

FREE BABY-SITTERS were provided to enable people with young children to go to the blood typing center at the fire hall with a minimum of inconvenience. Here Girl Scout Lorraine Ridinger cares for Charles Musser (left) and his younger brother, Michael, as Mrs. Dean Musser, the boys' mother, leaves to have her blood typed.

7 TRAINS HALTED BY ENGINE FIRE

Servicemen And Holiday Travelers Stranded For While At Herkimer, N. Y.

HERKIMER, N.Y., April 12 (AP)—Fire in a Diesel locomotive today delayed a westbound New York Central train loaded with servicemen and Easter-holiday travelers, and six other trains also were held up.

Firemen confined the flames to the locomotive, which was valued at $250,000 by a railroad spokesman. The extent of damage was not determined.

No one was injured.

About 25 soldiers, sailors, Marines and airmen got off the train—the Southshore Express—and set out to hitch-hike. Other passengers waited for a relief engine to haul the 17-car train to Utica. Six other trains were delayed for over an hour on track 1.

The fire broke out a mile west of the Herkimer depot.

The two-unit locomotive was detached from the train while firemen extinguished the flames.

Looking Ahead

Stassen Backers Curtail Campaign In Economy Move

BY THE WORLD STAFF OF THE ASSOCIATED PRESS

WASHINGTON — Supporters of Harold E. Stassen for the Republican presidential nomination are beginning to curtail their publicity set-ups for "economy reasons."

The Stassen headquarters in the Willard Hotel here is closing out next week. It also is reported the campaign office at the McAlpin Hotel in New York City is closing. The headquarters at the Penn Sheraton Hotel in Philadelphia will carry on.

Stassen's financial backers and others were counting heavily from the start on his making a good showing in the Wisconsin primary. But after he ran third to Taft and Warren there they reportedly were told they could not count on so much campaign money as they had hoped.

Workers here are reported ready to work "harder than ever" for the former Minnesota governor despite his primary setbacks.

SOLDIER VOTE

WASHINGTON - (AP) - The Defense Department has sent the White House a draft of legislation which would permit servicemen to vote in next November's election on a ballot printed and distributed by the federal government.

Sen. Green (D-RI) who fought successfully to allow such balloting in 1944, is expected to introduce the bill. It's strictly a guess whether Congress will pass it in the press of other business.

The Defense Department drafted the legislation at the request of the White House.

ALL KINDS OF PLANES

WASHINGTON - (AP) - The Defense Department has ordered an inquiry into whether too many types of military aircraft are being developed.

In the procurement program for the fiscal year beginning next July the Air Force is ordering 39 types, the Navy 27.

NON-PARTISAN

WASHINGTON - (AP) - Showcases in the House of Representatives stationery store display two elephant statuettes, only one donkey.

But, to even things up, it contains six plaques of Robert E. Lee and only two figures of Abraham Lincoln.

AVIATION BRIEFS

WASHINGTON - (AP) - Alarmed at foreign developments on jet-propelled aircraft and missiles, the Navy plans to spend nearly 38 million on pilotless "drone" target planes next fiscal year . . .

Rising costs make the "K-1" bombing system used on the B-36 and B-47 cost more than did a complete World War II B-17 . . .

TOPSY-TURVY

WASHINGTON - (AP) - Nils Lennartson, public information director for Secretary of Commerce Sawyer, was a public relations employe for U.S. Steel until 1948.

Now that the government has taken over the steel industry, Lennartson technically heads the whole industry's public relations.

CAPITAL BRIEFS

WASHINGTON - (AP)- Patients in veterans hospitals hit a record 101,000 in March . . . A congressional resolution directing the President to set aside a day of prayer each year has been sent to President Truman for his signature . . . Jack Kroll, director of the CIO Political Action Committee, says the CIO will not commit itself on a presidential candidate until after the conventions.

SOUTH AFRICA

CAPETOWN, South Africa (AP)—Prime Minister Daniel F. Malan has called his Cabinet to meet tomorrow to deal with the mounting constitutional crisis over race segregation laws.

Malan announced his government intends to place before Parliament as soon as possible a bill barring the courts from knocking out any more of the racial segregation laws his party favors. Parliament meets Tuesday.

The Supreme Court recently threw out a Malan government law restricting the voting rights of Cape coloreds (persons of mixed blood). Opposition leaders predict a bitter fight of explosive possibilities.

NEW TRADE TALKS

BUENOS AIRES (AP)—Britain and Argentina will begin new trade talks soon.

Europe At Eastertime Colored With Fear, Joy

LONDON, April 12 (AP)—Europe at Easter. . .

Gaily painted eggs and festive cakes. . .

Hatred, venom and fear. . .

Christianity strong and militant . . . and Christianity struggling for survival.

In old, weary Europe, rent by a ceaseless clash of ideologies, divided by an Iron Curtain, how is the church faring at this Eastertide in its struggle?

Church On Increase

Church officials give this picture: in Poland, Austria, Denmark, East and West Germany, Italy, Switzerland, Greece and Spain, church attendance is climbing steadily. Attendance remains high in Norway, Sweden and France.

Behind the Iron Curtain, the battle is a fierce one. In satellite nations, Communist governments are trying to force the idea of the "national church" upon millions of the devout. And in the Soviet Union itself, the continued operation of one church—the Russian Orthodox—is only at the sufferance of a dictatorial government.

Reds Are Cautious

Yugoslavia occupies a strange twilight position. Its Communist regime, cast out of the Moscow fold, moves warily under the critical eyes of the West. It has avoided any open declaration of hostility against religion as such, but has taken stern steps to remove church influence in public affairs. Church doors are open, as they are in other Communist-ruled countries; but, as in other Communist countries, church attendance is frowned upon.

The Russian Orthodox Church occupies perhaps the oddest of all positions in an unreal world. There is still much attendance at church on the part of the older people and on the part of the youngsters they bring up in the faith. The in-betweens — those indoctrinated in communism's official atheism—are the ones who stay away, mostly in the hope of worldly reward.

But it often suits Moscow's purposes to use the Orthodox Church as an arm of state policy, just as the czars did, and for his reason the Orthodox Church gives the appearance of flourishing.

Russian tradition calls for a tremendous celebration at Eastertide, and resurgent Russian nationalism today is such that the traditional celebrations are tolerated, even there are religious overtones. Therefore, many Russian housewives today are again painting hens' eggs in brilliant colors and preparing the little cakes they will take through the streets for the priests' blessings.

White Easter For World Of Fashion

By DOROTHY ROE
AP Fashion Editor

NEW YORK, April 12 (AP) — It's a white Easter for fashionable paraders across America.

White hats and veils, white gloves and accessories will be the order of the day, an advance survey of top designers and the nation's best-dressed women indicates.

In New York, gray is the favorite suit color, with navy taking first place across the country, and black and white a close runner-up on all fronts, says the New York Dress Institute.

Flower hats are next in importance to white. Bright red is a close contender. Hats for the most part are small and closely fitted to the head in profile, bonnet or pillbox silhouettes. The severe sailor is not so much in favor this year as usually.

NO DUST BAG TO EMPTY
IT'S QUIET NO ROAR
Only $1.25 A WEEK!
Small Down Payment!

WEATHER
(U. S. Weather Bureau)
Eastern Pennsylvania: Fair And Cooler With Highest 66 To 74 Degrees Today. Lowest Temperature Tonight 40 To 48 Degrees. Tomorrow Fair And Little Change In Temperature.

Intelligencer Journal.

The Leading Newspaper in the Garden Spot of America. Home Owned for Home Folks Since 1794

THE INTELL INDEX

158th Year.—No. 278. Lancaster Metropolitan Area Population Official United States Census Figures 234,717 LANCASTER, PA., WEDNESDAY MORNING, MAY 7, 1952. CITY TWENTY-FOUR PAGES. 30c PER WEEK—5c Per Copy

RUSSELL WINS VICTORY IN FLORIDA

14-Year-Old Boy Held In Slaying Of Classmate

60 Shad Trucked Around Dams In Start Of Program To Restock River

"SHAD TAXI" ARRIVES AT DESTINATION—Horace Pyle, Chester County Fish Warden (in water), carries a shad from the tank truck which transported them from Perry Point, Md., to Peach Bottom yesterday and prepares to release the fish as the experiment to revive the State's fishing industry got underway. The two men on the tail gate of the truck had just completed tagging the fish before passing it on to Pyle. Left to right are John Ogden, District Supervisor, Southeast Division, State Fish Commission; Dr. Gordon L. Trembley, chief aquatic biologist for the Fish Commission; Charles Walburg, U. S. Fish and Wildlife Service, and Warren Hammer, State Fish Commission, on tail gate of truck, and Ambrose Critchfield, Fish Commission employe, standing atop the tank truck. (Intell Photo)

TAFT BACKERS LEAD IN OHIO PRIMARY VOTE

Senator Stakes Out Ballot Claim For Big Share Of Delegates

COLUMBUS, O., May 6 (AP)—Sen. Robert A. Taft staked out a primary ballot claim tonight to the lion's share of Ohio's 56 GOP presidential delegates and Sen. Estes Kefauver bid strongly for a substantial part of 54 Democratic nominating votes.

On the basis of early returns from possibly record primary balloting, Taft candidates were leading in contests for 32 delegate places and had won eight others unopposed.

These eight delegates, with others he and Gen. Dwight D. Eisenhower picked up earlier in the day in Missouri, put Taft back into the lead in Chicago convention delegates as tabulated by The Associated Press.

284 TO 281

Taft's total now was 284 to Eisenhower's 281, on the basis of pledged, instructed, favorable and conceded delegates. Taft, however, claims about 80 more delegates than his total.

Former Gov. Harold E. Stassen of Minnesota, whose delegate candidates have indicated they would go to Gen. Dwight D. Eisenhower as second choice, led in no reported race in the early tally. Some contests yet to be heard from were in areas where Stassen won nine delegates in the 1948 primary.

KEFAUVER MEN

Kefauver's candidates were showing their heels to delegates running for a party organization slate pledged to former Sen. Robert J. Bulkley in contests involving 19 Chicago Democratic convention votes.

Bulkley's men led in races for two convention votes and already had been assured of 22 full-vote delegates in districts where they were unopposed. Kefauver had one delegate unopposed and was contesting for 30 others, with some district races unreported.

With no presidential popularity

Turn To Page 6 For More Of OHIO

Kenneth Teacher Is Victim Of Tragedy Near State Capital

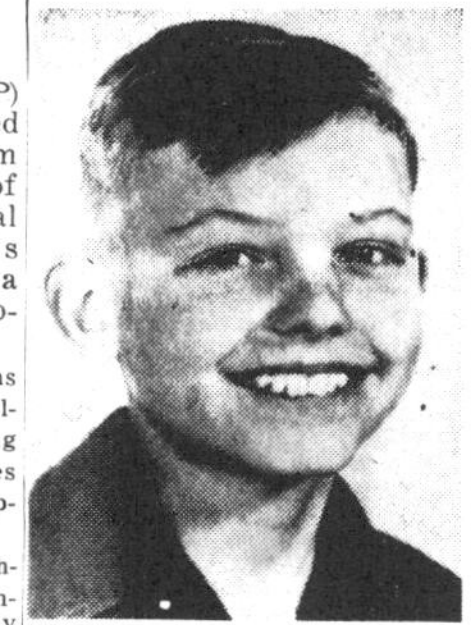

KENNETH TEACHER JR.

Charges Will Be Filed Against John Sarver; Boy Makes Statement

HARRISBURG, May 6 (AP)—A 14-year-old boy was held today in the fatal shooting and stabbing of a classmate in a clump of woods near the city line.

District Attorney Huette F. Dowling said charges will be filed Thursday against the youth, John Sarver II, on the basis of a statement he made to police. He declined to give the nature of the charges.

The Sarver youth, he said, admitted to "accidentally" shooting Kenneth E. Teacher Jr., 13, and then stabbing him with a machete "partly to conceal the (bullet) wound and partly to hide the crime."

Dowling said young Teacher apparently was alive when the machete was used on him "sawing fashion" near Paxtang Parkway where the boys had been target shooting last night.

Coroner Thomas J. Fritchey said in his autopsy report that 19 inches of intestine was pulled — "apparently by hand" — from the body of the Teacher boy.

Death could have been caused by either the bullet or the three-inch disemboweling knife wound, Fritchey said.

Young Sarver, a bespectacled blonde, was impassive as he spent most of the day in Dauphin County Courthouse with his father, John Sarver, Jr., a food company representative who lives in suburban Wilson Park.

Mr. and Mrs. Kenneth Teacher, parents of the dead youth, were distraught at their Thornwood Apartments home near John Harris High School.

The Sarver boy was removed to the Dauphin County Children's Detention Home to await filing of the charges. Dowling said an out-of-

Turn To Page 6 For More Of BOY

SEN. KEFAUVER LOSES BITTER DIXIE BATTLE

Decision Not Apparent Until Midnight; Georgian Still Has Uncounted Reserves

MIAMI, Fla., May 7 (Wednesday) (AP)— Georgia's Senator Russell won a bitterly-fought victory yesterday over Senator Kefauver of Tennessee to capture the first Democratic presidential preference primary to be held in Florida in 20 years.

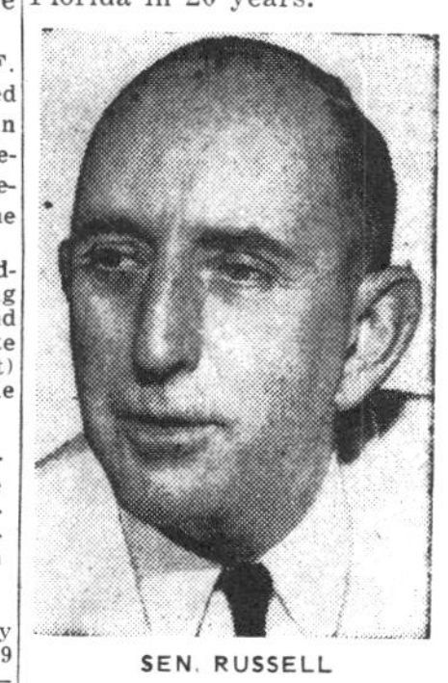

SEN. RUSSELL

The decision wasn't apparent until near midnight when Kefauver was running out of strongpoints while Russell still had a heavy reserve of precincts in the rural areas which contributed his greatest support.

The vote from 1073 out of 1682 precincts:

Russell 228,860
Kefauver 220,457

Russell clung to a slim lead from the time the returns began pouring in, but Kefauver got a flood of votes in Dade (Miami), Pinellas (St. Petersburg), and Volusia (Daytona Beach) counties which kept him

Turn To Page 6 For More Of FLORIDA

WILSON SAYS PAY RAISE IN STEEL WILL HIT DEFENSE

Former Mobilizer Sees Increase Of Five To Six Billion Dollars

WASHINGTON, May 6 (AP) — Former Defense mobilizer Charles E. Wilson told Congress today that if the government-recommended pay raise for steel workers spreads through industry it will drive defense costs in the next year up by five to six billion dollars.

The former General Electric executive, who quit the mobilization post in the dispute over steel, made the estimate in a volunteer statement as a witness before the House Labor Committee in its investigation of the Wage Stabilization Board and its handling of the steel crisis.

After committeemen had about exhausted their stock of questions, Wilson said he had not been asked but he wanted to volunteer the suggestion that if the 26-cent hourly package recommended by the WSB for the CIO steelworkers is allowed to stand, Congress had better hike military appropriations.

If it "Goes across industry," Wilson estimated, the resulting in-

Turn To Page 6 For More Of STEEL

"We Lead All The Rest" FARM CORNER

By The Farm Editor

DAIRY EDUCATIONAL DISPLAY NOW HERE

Dairy farmers, distributors, and others interested in the milk industry are invited to visit an educational exhibit which will be located at 632 Second st., this city, and continue today, Thursday and Friday, open from 9 a. m. to 3 p. m. daily.

Production of clean milk, with emphasis of sediment controls, will be the theme of the display, which will include different types of milk strainers, various types of milk cans, filter disk dispensers, and display of used filter disks showing sources of extraneous matter in milk. There will be a general collection of milk equipment — ancient, more recent, and

Turn To Page 14 For More Of FARM CORNER

Weather Calendar

COMPARATIVE TEMPERATURES

Station	High	Low
Water Works	85	44
Ephrata	84	47
Last Year (Ephrata)	70	42
Official High for Year May 6		84
Official Low for Year Jan. 30		7
Character of Day		Partly Cloudy

WINDS
Direction WNW Av. Velocity 18 MPH

HUMIDITY
8 a. m. 71% 11 a. m. 74% 2 p. m. 62%
5 p. m. 43% 8 p. m. 29%
Average Humidity 56%

SUN
Rises 5:57 a. m. Sets 8:04 p. m.

MOON
Sets 4:21 a. m. Full Moon, May 9

STARS
Morning—Mercury, Venus, Jupiter
Evening—Mars, Saturn

NEARBY FORECAST
(U. S. Weather Bureau)

Lower Potomac and Chesapeake Bay — Winds mostly northwest 15 to 25 miles an hour today. Fair weather, good visibility.

Maryland—Mostly sunny and cooler, highest low or middle 70's today. Lowest tonight 45 to 50. Tomorrow some cloudiness, little change in temperature.

Delaware and Southern New Jersey — Mostly sunny with the highest 68 to 70 today. Lowest tonight 42 to 48. Tomorrow fair and little change in temperature.

EXTENDED FORECAST
(U. S. Weather Bureau)

Extended forecast for the period from today through Sunday:

Eastern Pennsylvania, Eastern New York and Mid-Atlantic States—Temperature will average near normal in the north and a few degrees above normal in south portion; cooler today and warmer over the week-end; showers about Friday and in the north portion Sunday.

Plans Call For Placing 2,500 Fish In Susquehanna Above Dam

By HAROLD J. EAGER
Intell Sports Editor

Chased from its natural spawning grounds in the Susquehanna River some 40 years ago by 20th century technology, the fish that once provided Lancaster County with a huge industry, was brought back to these waters yesterday by the same 20th century technology.

It marks the start of a new chapter in the story of the shad, a chapter that may mark the beginning of another bright era in the history of the fish, or a chapter that may go down as just another failure in the attempt to induce the shad to buck the man-made barriers that drove him from these waters.

It is an operation for which the state has earmarked the sum of $10,000 through special legislation. Gordon L. Trembly, chief aquatic biologist of the State Fish Commission, said he understands that $3,200 of this money was set aside for the purchase of fish. He would not hazard an estimate, however, as to what the cost of the project would be or if the sum set aside would be sufficient.

The first step in yesterday's historic experiment was to bring 60 adult white shad, including both roe and buck, by truck from the headwaters of the Chesapeake Bay upstream to Peach Bottom.

Turn To Page 16 For More Of SHAD

115

Days In Which To Register For The Nov. 4 PRESIDENTIAL ELECTION

ANGLERS CAN KEEP SHAD, GET 50 CENTS

Not only will Lancaster county anglers be permitted to keep any shad they catch in the Susquehanna this year, but they can make a half a buck on the deal.

All the U. S. Fish and Wildlife service requests is that anglers catching shad remove the little red tag from the shad's dorsal fin and mail it to the U. S. Fish and Wildlife Service laboratory at Beaufort, N. C., stating where the fish was caught and the date. The government will pay fifty cents for each tag returned.

MERCURY SETS NEW YEAR'S HIGH OF 84; COOLER HERE TODAY

The mercury rose to 84 degrees here yesterday—a new high for the year—topping by one degree the previous 1952 high set on April 20.

A bright sun helped push the temperature upward, after playing hide and seek with rain clouds all day Monday.

Downtown stores and offices had a taste of real summer weather, with a few of the Penn Square bards predicting the sidewalk warm enough to fry eggs.

In the county, however, brisk breezes moved across the open fields taking the sting out of the sun's rays.

22 MORE VOTERS REGISTER HERE

Voter registration for the Nov. 4 Presidential election took another spurt yesterday as 22 persons added their names to the registration lists.

Twelve others filed changes of address to qualify themselves to cast a ballot.

Of the new registrations, 15 were Republicans, 6 were Democrats and one registered as an independent.

The Registration Office in the courthouse will be open from 8:30 a. m. to 5 p. m. today to receive new registration and changes of address.

Shortage Turns Once Lowly Spud Into Vegetable 'Prince'

The lowly spud has come into his own. He is now the prince of vegetables.

Two years ago the U.S. Department of Agriculture couldn't give potatoes away for hog food. No one wanted them.

Today it's hard to find a hundred-pound bag of U.S. No. 1 potatoes at any price — OPS notwithstanding.

The potato shortage in these parts has reached such proportions that at least one restaurant — who caters to the "meat and potato" type of customer — has served notice that French fries will come off the menu within a day unless a few bags of old potatoes are located.

The supply of old potatoes — cooks say you can't make French fries from new spuds — is exhausted. And the supply of new potatoes, mostly from Florida, are in extreme short supply.

In addition to being in short supply, the new potatoes available here aren't much bigger than marbles.

Many reasons are advanced for the peculiar conditions existing in the potato market. Each group concerned with potatoes, the grow-

Turn To Page 6 For More Of POTATOES

REPORT PROGRESS IN DEVELOPMENT OF PARKING AREAS

Progress was reported yesterday in the development of several potential off-street parking areas in downtown Lancaster City.

"Development of a number of parking areas looks encouraging," a spokesman for the sub-committee on off-street parking of the Chamber of Commerce reported following a meeting in the Griest building.

The sub-committee of the General Parking and Traffic Committee of the C of C is attempting to develop the potential off-street parking areas in line with a plan of action adopted early this year.

Six sub-committees have been assigned to specific areas in which they are investigating proposed sites for parking lots. Indications at yesterday's meeting pointed to at least one off-street lot being developed in every area.

The committee spokesman asserted that in some areas "definite action seems likely in two or three lots." Locations of these proposed lots were not given pending final approval by owners.

It is the job of the six sub-committees to interest present owners and operators of parking lots in expanding their facilities, and to interest businessmen in investing in suitable sites.

A survey of potential parking areas in the downtown shopping district disclosed there are 2,189 off-street parking spaces which could be added, bringing the city's

Turn To Page 6 For More Of PARKING

CHILDREN'S SAVINGS DISAPPEAR AT SCHOOL

The week's savings of children at the Burrowes East End School in Lancaster Township—about $30—disappeared yesterday noon from a desk at the school.

State Police, who were investigating, said yesterday was banking day at the school when the children bring their pennies, nickels and dimes to be deposited in a savings account. It is part of their training in thrift.

The money was to have been taken to the bank in the afternoon but was found missing after the noon hour, police said.

POLICE GO ON 'TOUR' TO FIND TOT'S HOME

Lester Moyer, 2, was returned to his home by city police last night after he was found wandering in the 700 block of E. Frederick Street by James Henderson, 1411 N. West End Ave. at 7:35 p.m.

Henderson turned him over to police. When no one called for him, they took him for a ride in the nieghborhood where he was found. He was finally recognized by a neighbor and turned over to Mrs. Miriam Haddox, 532 Hamilton St., who is caring for him, police said.

Ridgway Discloses Enemy Rejection Of POW Proposal

TOKYO, Wednesday, May 7 (AP)—Gen. Matthew B. Ridgway disclosed today the Communists have rejected an Allied offer to trade the 12,000 U. N. prisoners in their hands for the 70,000 Allied-held Reds who have agreed to return to Communist control.

Ridgway ripped the veil of secrecy from the high-level truce talks at Panmunjom and revealed the details of the U.N. Command's overall solution to the deadlocked armistice negotiations.

In a sharply worded statement Ridgway said, "The responsibility for peace in Korea now rests on the Communists."

INTERVIEW OFFER

If the Reds agreed to the U.N. proposal for trade of war prisoners, Ridgway said, after an armistice the U. N. would be willing "to permit any suitable international body or joint Red Cross teams, together with observers from both sides, to interview the persons held by the U. N. Command who have indicated they would forcibly oppose repatriation."

The Allied supreme commander said the U.N. would then return to the Reds any prisoners which an impartial, neutral survey showed were willing to go back.

Ridgway said the Reds have rejected this "fair, equitable solution."

OTHER ISSUES

On the other two issues blocking a truce, Ridgway said the U.N. Command had offered to drop its demand for a ban on airfield reconstruction if the Communists would abandon their nomination of Russia as a "neutral" nation to help police the armistice.

Ridgway said both sides agreed at Tuesday's secret session to release details of the Allied offer.

Olds Retires As Chairman Of U.S. Steel; Fairless Successor

BENJAMIN FAIRLESS

NEW YORK, May 6 (AP)—Irving S. Olds retired today as chairman of United States Steel Corp. and Benjamin F. Fairless was named to succeed him.

Fairless also will continue as president of the steel industry giant, becoming the first man in the corporation's 50-year history to hold both posts. He also was named chief executive officer.

Retirement of Olds, who has been chairman since he succeeded the late Edward R. Stettinius on June 4, 1940, was announced after a meeting of U. S Steel directors.

RETIREMENT AGE

The directors' announcement noted that Olds, who is 65, had reached the corporation's retirement age. He will continue as a director and a member of the Finance Committee.

Olds plans to resume active practice of law with the New York

Turn To Page 14 For More Of OLDS

Clarence Watson Signs Professional Baseball Contract With Red Sox

Young Manheim Twp. Pitcher Assigned To Class A Albany Club

By HAROLD J. EAGER
Intell Sports Editor

Clarence J. Watson, one of the brightest young pitching prospects ever developed in Lancaster county, yesterday signed a contract with the Boston Red Sox of the American Baseball League.

Informed sources said the Lancaster youngster received a substantial bonus for signing with the Boston club, but there was no indication as to just how much that bonus might be.

A son of Mr. and Mrs. M. H. Watson, 942 Salisbury Ct., Grand View Heights, the twenty-one-year-old righthander was signed in Malone, N.Y., by Neal Mahoney, Red Sox scout.

He was assigned immediately to Boston's Albany, N.Y., farm club in the Class A Eastern League. The fact that he was placed in Class A baseball, veteran baseball observers said, is an indication of how highly the Red Sox regard the young pitcher. Normally, an inexperienced youngster is placed initially either with a Class D of Class C club.

Yesterday's signing took place in Malone due to the fact that Watson has been playing summer baseball in a non-professional league there for the past six weeks.

At least four different major league clubs, it was reported, had been bidding for Watson's services in recent weeks as the result of impressive pitching at Malone. Since arriving there, he had pitched two one-hit games.

By signing a contract, Watson gives up his collegiate baseball career.

For the past two years he had been a mainstay of the Villanova College nine. During this past Spring he won five games while losing only two for the Wildcats. He had a 4-3 record in 1951.

But though he will no longer be eligible for collegiate athletics, Jack informed his parents by phone yesterday that he does intend to complete his college education. He will be a senior at Villanova this Autumn.

The Manheim Township youngster has been watched with deep interest by major league scouts ever since he was a freshman in Manheim Township High School.

A varsity pitcher for all four of his years at Manheim Township, Watson compiled what is probably the most outstanding pitching record ever owned by a Lancaster county high school hurler.

He pitched for Coach Paul Wenrich's Blue Streaks in the 1946, '47, '48 and '49 seasons.

During those four seasons of high school baseball, he compiled a record of 24 victories and only one defeat. Two of his wins were no-hit games.

In 1946, as a freshman, he won four and lost none. The next year he won seven and lost none, capping the season by pitching Manheim Township to a 2-0 win over Elizabethtown for the County High League title. He had a 7-1 record for 1948. Quarryville beat him 2-1 that season for the only loss of his high school career. He had a record of six wins and no losses for his senior year and may have done better but three weeks before the league season closed he was forced to the bench with an injured arm.

Watson also was quite a pitcher in Junior Legion League competition during those same years. He was selected the outstanding individual player in the annual Pennsylvania All-Star Junior Legion game in Philadelphia in July of 1947.

Baseball, however, wasn't Clarence's only sport in high school. He was a topnotch quarterback on the football team but he forsook football to concentrate on baseball when he entered Villanova.

During the summers of 1950 and 1951, Clarence played baseball with Augusta, Maine, in the Maine Summer League, a fast non-pro circuit filled with topflight collegiate players.

THE METAMORPHOSIS OF A PLAYER'S NAME

Clarence Watson, by any other name, is still the same Clarence Watson, the baseball pitcher from Manheim Township.

Back in his student days at Manheim Township High his teammates tagged him with the nickname "Beaky." Then he went on to Villanova College and he became "Jack" Watson.

His stint as a player in the Maine Summer League his mates decided Clarence wasn't a name for a baseball player. They tagged him with his middle name. "Johnny." So from now on it's probably going to be "Johnny" Watson.

CLARENCE J. WATSON

BRAVES ROUT CUBS IN SIX-RUN FIFTH FOR 10-3 VICTORY

CHICAGO, July 15 (AP)—The Boston Braves blended two singles with five walks, a sacrifice and two of three errors by shortstop Roy Smalley to fashion a six-run fifth inning in routing the Chicago Cubs, 10-3, for their fifth straight victory today.

Boston	AB	H	O	A	Chicago	AB	H	O	A
Jethroe,cf	4	0	6	0	Addis, cf	5	3	1	0
Logan, ss	4	1	5	2	Miksis, 2b	5	1	1	2
Tor'son,1b	5	0	7	2	H'r'nski,rf	5	1	1	0
Gordon, lf	4	0	0	0	Sauer, lf	5	3	2	0
Cooper, c	5	2	4	0	Atwell, c	2	1	5	0
M'th'ws,3b	3	0	1	2	Pramesa,c	1	1	3	0
Dittmer,2b	3	2	2	4	Fondy, 1b	4	1	10	3
Daniels,rf	4	2	1	0	Serena, 3b	4	2	0	3
Wilson, p	5	1	1	1	Smalley,ss	4	1	1	2
					Lown, p	2	1	1	1
					Ram'dell,p	0	0	0	0
					Kelly, p	1	0	1	1
					aJackson	1	0	0	0
					Manville,p	0	0	1	0
Totals	37	8	27	11	Totals	39	15	27	12

a—Struck out for Kelly in 8th.

Boston	010 260 100	—10
Chicago	110 000 100	— 3

R—Jethroe, Gordon 2, Cooper 2, Mathews 2, Dittmer 2, Daniels, Addis, Hermanski, Smalley. E—Smalley 3. RBI—Sauer 2, Daniels 2, Addis, Cooper 2, Dittmer, Jethroe, Logan. 2B—Sauer, Hermanski, Serena. HR—Cooper. S—Logan. DP—Dittmer, Logan and Torgeson; Wilson, Logan and Torgeson; Mathews, Dittmer and Torgeson. LB—Boston 9, Chicago 10. BB—Off Lown 6, Ramsdell 2, Wilson 1. SO—Lown 4, Kelly 2, Wilson 4, Manville 1. HO—Lown 4 in 4 2-3, Ramsdell 0 in 0 (pitched to three batters in 5th), Kelly 3 in 3 1-3, Manville 1 in 1. Wild Pitch—Kelly, Wilson. WP—Wilson (8-7). LP—Lown (3-6). U—Dascolf, Secory, Warneke and Goetz. T—2:29. A—6,694.

Form Still Prevails In Closed Tennis Tourney

Earle Frey Ousts Harold Mull In Day's Lone Upset

One upset featured yesterday's action in the Lancaster County Closed Tennis Tournament third round action as Earle Frey defeated Harold Mull, 7-5, and 6-4, to move into the quarter-finals.

Other third round activity in the men's singles division found the favorites advancing with relative ease. Top-seeded Gene Crider defeated Bill Donecker, 6-2, 6-2. Elwood Snyder, Harold Fellenbaum and Jim Kilgour, other seeded stars, also moved into the quarter-final round.

The women's singles competition and the men's doubles event got off in fine style with eight matches played in the ladies' event and four first round doubles matches for men finished.

All the girls' singles matches were decided in straight sets although Mary Anne Schofield seeded number two in the division, Mt. Joy, was extended before whipping Barbara Miller in a long second set that was finally decided in Miss Schoefield's favor at 8-6.

CHAMP WINS EASILY

Nancy Paden gave away only two games in defeating Elsieanna Henry, 6-1, 6-1, in another girls' test.

In the doubles, the events were also decided in straight sets. Elwood Snyder, who moved into the quarter-finals in the men's singles on the strength of his victory over Clarence McCue, teamed up with Glenn Miller to defeat Harold Martin and Charles Kepner, 6-4, 6-3.

Today's action calls for competition in all events, with activity beginning at 4:30 p. m. with Mary Ann Schofield playing Joanne Brown and Ruth Carothers meeting Sally Lied.

TENNIS TOURNEY SUMMARIES

YESTERDAY'S RESULTS

MEN'S SINGLES
(Third Round)

Earl Frey def. Harold Mull, 7-5, 6-4.
Elwood Snyder def. Clarence McCue, 6-4, 6-4.
Harold Fellenbaum, Mt. Joy, def. Bill Newkirk, 6-4, 6-2.
Gene Crider def. Bill Donecker, Ephrata, 6-2, 6-2.
Jim Kilgour def. Ralph Paden, 6-1, 6-0.

WOMEN'S SINGLES
(First Round)

Mary Ann Schofield, Mt. Joy, def. Barbara Miller, 6-2, 8-6.
Joanne Brown, Mt. Joy, def. Pat Evans, 6-0, 6-1.
Ruth Carothers def. Jeanne Thomas, 6-1, 6-0.
Sally Lied def. Dorie Freiley, 6-3, 6-3.
Nancy Paden def. Elsieanna Henry, 6-1, 6-1.
Marilyn Newcomer, Mt. Joy, def. Adele Kegerreis, 6-1, 6-3.
Sylvia Mentzer, Ephrata, def. Poanne Kramer, Mt. Joy, 6-4, 6-4.
Polly Schmidt def. Dorris Mull, Ephrata, 6-2, 6-2.

MEN'S DOUBLES
(First Round)

Joe Grosh and Gary MacFarren def. Mike Bair and J. Shertzer, 7-5, 6-0.
Earl Koth and Dick Blakinger def. Bill Donecker and Mel Royer, 6-4, 6-4.
Elwood Snyder and Glenn Miller def. Harold Martin and Chase Kepner, 6-4, 6-3.
Enck and Schiffer defeated George Brown and Jim Spangler, 6-3, 6-3.

TODAY'S SCHEDULE

MEN'S SINGLES
(Quarter-Finals)

5:30 p.m. Glenn Miller vs. Earle Frey.
Gene Crider vs. Dick Divit.
6:30 p.m. Jim Kilgour vs. Jim Meminger.

MEN'S DOUBLES

6:30 p.m. Frey and Gould vs. Mull and Fenninger.
Snyder and Miller vs. Enck and Schiffer.
Newkirk and Steinman vs. Byerly and Divit.
7:00 p.m. Crider and Kilgour vs. Brown and Kegerreis.
McCue and Meminger vs. Graham and Foster.
7:15 p.m. Grosh and MacFarren vs. winner of Crider-Kilgour and Brown-Kegerreis match.

WOMEN'S SINGLES
(Second Round)

4:30 p.m. Mary Ann Schofield vs. Joanne Brown.
Ruth Carothers vs. Sally Lied.
5:30 p.m. Nancy Paden vs. Marilyn Newcomer.
Sylvia Mentzler vs. Polly Schmidt

SPORTS Pages 16, 17, 18, 19

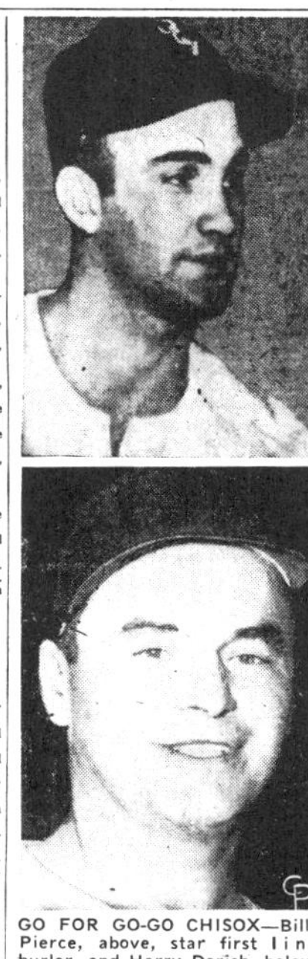

GO FOR GO-GO CHISOX—Billy Pierce, above, star first line hurler, and Harry Dorish, below, relief specialist, are two big reasons for the contending position of the Chicago White Sox in the American League race.

Maxim, Gavilan Taken To Task For Ducking No. 1 Contenders

NEW YORK, July 15 (AP)—Robert K. Christenberry, chairman of the New York State Athletic Commission which governs boxing here, today took to task world boxing champions Joey Maxim and Kid Gavilan.

Christenberry charged that both Maxim, world light heavyweight ruler, and Gavilan, world welterweight titleholder, have repeatedly ducked the No. 1 contenders in their respective divisions.

"It perturbed me no end when I learned that Jack Solomons, British promoter, tried to line up a London title bout between Joey Maxim and Randy Turpin," Christenberry said.

SIDES WITH MOORE

"Archie Moore of St. Louis has been by-passed too long by Maxim. He is the legitimate light heavyweight contender and not Turpin. I have a letter and a challenge check for $2,500 from Moore, who has complained that he couldn't get a crack at the title.

"I hate to see Moore become another Harry Wills case and I hate to see him not get his chance at the title when he becomes too old to fight."

Moore, who has been meeting heavyweights for years although he often fights around 175 pounds, is 36. He recently beat Clarence Henry in Baltimore. His only defeat in 18 bouts in the last two years came last December against Harold Johnson in Milwaukee. Moore had beaten Johnson in 1949 in Philadelphia.

"I feel more perturbed about Gavilan not giving Billy Graham a return bout," Christenberry continued. "Gavilan recently stopped Gil Turner, a legitimate defense by the way, but he again by-passed Graham, the No. 1 contender.

"I have a $2,000 check from Graham as a challenge to Gavilan and it was filed before Turner's challenge.

"Those of us who are responsible to the public should see that those fighters who deserve a crack at championships get that chance.

Idaho, after 50 years of exploration, was almost completely abandoned by white people because of hostile Indians.

Intelligencer Journal

LANCASTER, PA., DAILY INTELLIGENCER JOURNAL, SATURDAY MORNING, JULY 26, 1952.

Wide Anti-Foreign Unrest Shuts U. S. Clubs In Iran

Embassy Begins To Index Names And Addresses Of American Residents

TEHRAN, Iran, July 25 (AP) — Seething, anti-foreign unrest led American clubs in Iran to close their doors today. The U. S. Embassy began indexing addresses and phone numbers of American residents.

A new demonstration developed against the British on this first Moslem Sabbath since Premier Ahmed Qavam fell and Dr. Mohammed Mossadegh, the Nationalist chieftain, regained the government's reins.

"Death to Churchill," shouted a Moslem religious group of 300 near the police-guarded British Embassy. "Down with Britain."

SIGNS REPLACED

They ripped away street markers of Churchill Street, which has borne the British Prime Minister's name since the wartime Big Three conference at Tehran, and replaced them with signs reading Mossadegh Street.

Mossadegh, who usually does no official work on the Moslem Sabbath, summoned British Charge d' Affaires George Middleton to his big yellow brick home and talked with him two hours.

Middleton said the talk was friendly. He declined to disclose the subject but said speculation that it concerned the British-Iranian oil nationalization dispute was "not far wrong." Mossadegh won a legal point Tuesday in the ruling by the International Court of Justice that the court lacked jurisdiction to judge Britain's suit for compensation and damages.

Maj. Gen. Wayne Zimmerman, head of the U. S. Army mission in Iran, ordered the officers' and non-commissioned officers' clubs to close. A newly-opened American Club, available to all U. S. nationals in Tehran, also was shut down.

It is believed the orders are intended to keep American cars, or cars with diplomatic license plates, from congregating so heavily at one spot as to irritate and offer a mass target for anti-American crowds.

Similarly, American personnel were instructed to limit any party they give at their homes to no more than a dozen persons.

LABELED 'ROUTINE'

The U. S. Embassy described its collection of data on Americans here as a "regular, routine check-up." But the work was obviously prompted by the demonstrations.

Though anti-American feeling has flared among Iranians, who figure the United States supported both Qavam and the British side of the oil dispute, it has not yet taken a violent form.

A U. S. Army sergeant was injured slightly by a flying stone when he got out of a taxicab in the midst of a street outburst yesterday, but that is believed to have been an accident.

Despite the anti-British chanting today, the Moslem crowd appeared in a gay, holiday mood and did not attack the embassy. Among those in the embassy compound were reported to be two British nurses who took refuge there after a crowd attacked the Princess Asraf Pahlevi hospital and nursing school Wednesday.

Time Out For A Sandwich

While the various delegations battled on the convention floor in Chicago, Sen. Estes Kefauver's wife, Nancy, and his father, Robert Cook Kefauver, shared a sandwich at a snack bar. Judging by their smiles they were unworried by the Stevenson steamroller.

Murray Orders Steel Union Workers Back To Jobs, Ending Walkout

Great Strike Officially Ended With Action By CIO President; Settlement Hailed As "Mighty Victory" For Labor; Tieup Lasted 54 Days

WASHINGTON, July 25 (AP)—The great steel strike officially ended today as CIO President Philip Murray ordered his 650,000 union workers back on the job and hailed the settlement as a "mighty victory" for labor.

The end came at 4 p.m., EST, on the 54th day of the walkout that cost the steel workers 350 million dollars in lost wages, threatened to wreck the nation's economy and gravely jeopardized the defense program.

Even with the back - to - work movement set to begin almost immediately, the effects of the strike, the longest in the industry's history, will be felt for months.

4 TO 6 WEEKS

Industry experts said it will take at least four to six weeks before enough steel pours from the 380 strike-idled mills to satisfy current needs.

Defense officials planned to announce rules Monday for dividing up the first trickle of production, with emphasis on tonnage for military needs.

Some defense plants, notably including a factory producing artillery shells, had been closed because of lack of steel and others had been reduced to skeleton supplies.

The end of the costly strike came when Murray's 175-man Wage-Policy Committee officially approved an agreement reached at the White House yesterday seven hours after President Truman, in blunt terms, demanded an immediate settlement of the dispute.

The policy committee said the agreement "marks a great new forward stride in the efforts of the steelworkers . . . to achieve a decent life for themselves and their families."

Actually, the agreement represented substantial concessions by both sides. The union lost out on its No. 1 demand for a tight union shop and settled for a modified version which provides loopholes for new employes to withdraw from the union and for old employes who are not union members now to remain non-union.

As for the steel companies, they granted wage benefits totalling 21 cents an hour, retroactive to last March 1, and won from the government the right to raise their prices an average of $5.65 a ton. Some companies had suggested as much as $12 a ton more to absorb the cost of the wage increase.

TO BEGIN BARGINING

COATESVILLE, Pa., July 25 (AP)—The Lukens Steel Co., at Coatesville, Pa., will reopen collective bargaining with representatives of the CIO-United Steelworkers Union tomorrow morning as an aftermath to the announced settlement of the nation-wide steel strike.

Lukens is one of the nine basic steel plants in the Philadelphia area.

The Lukens management issued a formal statement signed by Charles Lukens Huston, Jr., president of the company, announcing "local differences may be resolved promptly. Lukens Steel stands ready to resume operations as soon as an appropriate new agreement has been made with the union."

At the Bethlehem Steel Plant at Bethlehem, Pa., a special crew of 54 entered the plant, under union agreement, at noon today to prepare the plant for resumption, though pickets were still operating.

Joins Parade For Brother

Mrs. Ernest Ives, sister of Gov. Adlai Stevenson of Illinois, joins cheering demonstrators parading for her brother on the floor of the Democratic national convention at Chicago, after his name was placed in nomination for the presidency. With her is Rep. Charles B. Deane, of Rockingham, N. C.

LANC. TWP. GETS APPROVAL FOR 1ST CLASS VOTE

Petition To Place Issue On Ballot Is Granted By Court

The movement of two second class townships toward first class status gained momentum yesterday.

The Lancaster County Court gave formal approval to Lancaster Twp. to vote on whether it wants to become a first class township.

PETITIONS OUT

At the same time petitions were circulating in Manheim Twp. for the signatures of at least five per cent of that township's voters. When these petitions are completed spokesmen for Manheim Twp. will also go before the court and ask that the first class township question be put on the ballot there.

The Lancaster County Court yesterday gave authorization to Lancaster Twp. on the basis of the petition signed by at least five per cent of the township voters.

The petition, having 521 signers, more than the five per cent, was presented by Attorney F. Lyman Windolph, representing the township supervisors and the township school board.

TOOK EXTRA STEP

Manheim Twp. announced the first class referendum plans before Lancaster Twp. did. The reason Manheim Twp. is behind is because it went through another step. Manheim Twp. took a special population census, which Lancaster Twp. did not.

Officials of Lancaster Twp. held that, since they have a smaller area, it was not as hard to prove they had at least 300 persons to the square mile.

Following the court action yesterday morning, Windolph said that is the last step in Lancaster Twp. When the township voters go to the polls to vote in the presidential election, they will also have a chance to say if they want to switch from second to first class township status.

LINKED TO MERGER

The Lancaster Twp. supervisors and school board circulated the petition in the last month. Five per cent of the registered voters would have been 180. Sponsors said they got the rest for good measure.

The first class township movements in both townships were linked with a recent merger drive by the city.

Under first class status, all the residents of the townships, plus all persons in the city, must vote before any part can be annexed. Under the present second class status, a property owner next to the city may file a petition himself for merger.

Evelyn Ay, Ephrata, Wins Miss Penna. AMVET Crown

MISS EVELYN AY

Miss Evelyn Ay nineteen-year-old daughter of Mr. and Mrs. Richard Ay, 123 Park Ave., Ephrata, last night won the Miss Pennsylvania AMVET title at a beauty contest in the Abraham Lincoln Hotel in Reading.

Miss Ay was chosen from among eight other contestants at the eighth annual Governor's ball. She represented the Ephrata AMVET post.

The Ephrata girl was selected as runner-up in the beauty contest at Stumpf Field last Saturday when the Lancaster Red Roses selected their queen for the Inter-State League beauty title.

Miss Ay, a University of Pennsylvania student, is currently attending Albright College where she is a first year student in medical technology.

The blonde, blue-eyed queen is five feet six and weighs 125.

WINS DEFENSE BOND

Her victory last night won her a United States defense bond and clothing prizes.

Contestants in the competition represented AMVET posts throughout the Eastern and Midwestern part of the state.

HAMILTON REPORTS $506,709 NET LOSS FOR 6-MO. PERIOD

Contrasting Profit Of $201,289 For Same Period In '51 Noted By Watch Co.

Operations at the Hamilton Watch Company for the first half of this year show a net loss of $506,709, company officials reported yesterday.

In comparison, the company's operations during the first half of 1951 resulted in a profit of $201,289.

Net loss for the second quarter of 1952 was listed as $175,944. The company said that was not as severe as the first three months of this year, when it lost $330,765.

All losses are estimated after tax carry-back credits, the company said.

LUCKEY HAS STATEMENT

George P. Luckey, company president, said:

"While it is yet too early to make any definite prediction concerning the remainder of the year, it is noteworthy that June operations produced a small profit—the first since December, 1951.

"We enter our principal selling season in the fall," Luckey added, "with inventories well adjusted to current volume.

"Advance reports from retail jewelers indicate increased interest in Hamilton watches under the new line policy of direct selling, which becomes effective Aug. 1."

The company listed defense sales for the first six months of 1952 at $1,700,000. Luckey said continued progress in tooling and rate of production "will increase such volume substantially."

Special Training Program Set Up For Sales Staff

Hamilton Watch Company's sales staff is meeting this week and next for special training in direct selling to retail jewelers. Starting Aug. 1, Hamilton drops its established policy of selling watches through wholesalers.

Monday, Tuesday and Wednesday of this week new additions to the field force were assigned territories, thoroughly indoctrinated with procedures and familiarized with the Hamilton watch line.

Thursday the company's veteran salesmen gathered to attend the opening session of the complete field and office sales personnel.

Lowell F. Halligan, Vice President in Charge of Sales, keynoted yesterday morning's conference with a review of Hamilton's sixty year's of successful operation.

U.S. Will Still Aid Denmark Despite Her Deal With USSR

WASHINGTON, July 25 (AP)—President Truman ordered aid to Denmark continued despite Denmark's delivery of a 13,000-ton oil tanker to Russia on July 7.

The President said he had decided that stopping military and economic assistance to that country would "clearly be detrimental to the security of the United States."

WEAKENS NATO

He said it would mean "weakening defenses of NATO, contributing to the strength of the Soviet Union, fostering the political and propaganda objectives of the Communist bloc, and defeating the purposes of the Battle Act."

The Battle Act—named for Rep. Battle (D-Ala)—provides that any country which knowingly permits export of strategic materials to the Communist bloc becomes ineligible for further U. S. mutual security assistance.

EXCEPTIONS

However, the legislation authorizes the President, on the recommendation of the Mutual Security Agency (MSA) to make exceptions when this action is considered in the interest of American security.

In the case of Denmark, 11 government agencies—including MSA—recommended the action taken by Truman.

Truman made known his decision in identical letters to chairmen of the Senate and House Committees on Appropriations, Armed Services, and Foreign Relations.

Mentzer Elected Commander Of Legion Dist. 10

Charles Mentzer, New Holland, was elected commander of Lancaster County Council, District 10, American Legion, at a meeting of the Council last night in the Ephrata Legion Home, with Cloister Post 429, as hosts. He succeeds Ambrose S. Plummer, Elizabethtown.

Council also named its members for the state committees which will function at the state convention in Philadelphia, Aug. 5-9.

They are: Henry B. Brandt, credentials; Richard A. Snyder, legislative; Frank Walter, internal organization; James L. Shaeffer, constitutional amendments; and William Fishburn, resolutions.

PLAN HERR SUPPORT

District 10 also made plans to support a former county council commander, Robert W. Herr, Quarryville, for State Commander.

It was announced that the district membership was now at 7,840.

The group voted to present a trophy to District 10 Junior Legion baseball champions, St. Joseph's will represent the city league and Ephrata and Manheim, the county.

MOUNT JOY BUILDING ISSUE BACK IN COURT

Efforts of Steven K. Estock, Mount Joy builder, to complete his home, subject of a lengthy borough and court battle, was back in court again yesterday.

After a series of actions Estock finally a few weeks ago appealed to the Lancaster County Court from the order of the Mount Joy Borough Board of Adjustment.

Yesterday the Board of Adjustment and the borough asked the court to throw out the appeal. They maintain in part that Estock waited too long before filing his appeal.

CAR GOES OVER BANK AT MYLIN'S CORNER

A car operated by Viola Stewart, 328 Green St., failed to negotiate a right turn at Mylin's Corner, in West Lampeter Twp., went over a five-foot embankment and ended up in a wheat field at 2:30 p.m. yesterday, according to Police Chief Frank Horner.

Horner said the car, going north on Route 72, attempted to turn right onto Route 222. Damage to the car was estimated at $100.

The driver was prosecuted for reckless driving before Willow Street Justice of the Peace M. G. Pyfer.

E-TOWN MAN HELD

Lawrence C. Murphy, 815 S. Spruce St., Elizabethtown, was arrested by Constable E. K. Coble on a bench warrant for non-support from Delaware County last night. He was held at the city police station.

WORK COMPLETED ON CHESTNUT ST.

Chestnut Street between Duke and Prince Streets which has been closed to traffic since July 16 was opened yesterday.

The two blocks were closed in order that the street could be resurfaced.

The Conestoga Transportation Co. announced that the buses rerouted because of the work would return to their normal route.

MILD CONDITIONS HERE MAY BE MARRED TODAY BY HIGHER MERCURY

Lancaster's pleasant summer weather of yesterday may be marred today with higher temperatures and some cloudiness.

A high of 85 degrees was recorded yesterday at the Ephrata Weather Bureau, compared with 84 degrees a year ago. The low was 58 degrees, compared with 67 a year ago.

Not only the temperature, but also a lower humidity added to make yesterday one of the most comfortable summer days in weeks. The humidity was recorded at 51 per cent at 8 p. m. last night.

The mercury is expected to reach a high of 86 to 91 degrees today with a possibility of scattered thundershowers.

PEDESTRIAN SAYS HE WAS HIT-RUN VICTIM

Elton L. Herbert, of 521 N. Queen St., told police he was struck by a hit-and-run driver as he was standing on the corner of Queen and Chestnut Streets at 3:22 p.m. yesterday. He was treated for brushburns of the forehead at Lancaster General Hospital.

Herbert said he was struck by a car turning right off Chestnut Street as he was standing on the northeast corner, according to police. Police are investigating the accident.

Harriman, Dever Started Bandwagon For Stevenson

CONVENTION HALL, Chicago, July 25 (AP)—Averell Harriman of New York and Gov. Paul Dever of Massachusetts threw their more than 150 votes to Illinois Gov. Adlai Stevenson to start a bandwagon rolling for Stevenson at this Democratic National Convention tonight.

On the second ballot, Harriman had 121 votes, 84½ of them from New York.

Dever received 30½ votes on the same ballot.

PLATFORM SUPPORT

Dever said Stevenson told him he would be happy to support the party's platform.

It was reported on the floor that Kefauver was about to withdraw from the contest.

Arkansas previously for Russell, tossed 20½ of its 22 to Stevenson.

Harriman issued this statement:

"I am deeply grateful for the support given me and the principles for which I stand both before and during this convention, by my friends in the Democratic party.

"I came to this convention to fight for my nomination and for a liberal, progressive, platform true to the highest traditions of Franklin Delano Roosevelt and the fighting policies of President Harry S. Truman. I am proud that this convention has adopted such a platform. At this time in the deliberations of this convention, I withdraw as a candidate and urge my supporters to cast their votes for my old friend, Gov. Adlai E. Stevenson of Illinois. I have asked my own alternate, sitting in the New York delegation, to do so.

NO OTHER MOTIVE

"I want to make it perfectly clear that I am governed by no other motivation than that the Democratic party unite behind the fine liberal candidate who will lead our party to victory in November."

Dever told the convention:

"Mr. Chairman, my fellow delegates. Of course, I have been flattered by the persistent support accorded by my friends to my candidacy for President of the United States.

"This afternoon I have talked with the governor of Illinois. He informs me that he will happily accept the nomination of this party for the highest temporal office in the world.

READ PLATFORM

"He has read its platform. He believes in it. For that reason I am asking those who have supported me to cease in that support.

"I personally shall vote for that American I feel to be the best equipped to lead this nation in the four years which lie ahead of us. I shall vote for Gov. Adlai Stevenson."

Only 50-50 Chance Seen For Recovery Of Brien M'Mahon

NORWALK, Conn., July 25 (AP)—While other members of the family were at the bedside in Washington of U. S. Sen. Brien McMahon, his brother, Dr. John McMahon, said here late today he believed the senator still had a "fifty-fifty" chance of recovery.

Earlier in the day the physician had told newsmen that the senator had taken a "turn for the worse."

The senator, operated on in Washington several weeks ago for what was announced as a sacroiliac (lower back) condition, had hoped to head the Connecticut delegation to the Democratic convention here last night his colleague, U. S. Sen. William Benton, put his name in nomination for the presidency.

NAMES WITHDRAWN

Moments later however Benton withdrew McMahon's name in accordance with the latter's bedside wishes, while the convention gave him a hearty ovation.

The precise nature of McMahon's illness has been in dispute. The senator's family has insisted throughout that he was suffering from a sacroiliac condition. Others close to the senator have said it was of a more serious nature. His office in Washington said today it was understood he was "resting comfortably" and recovering slowly.

Efforts to reach another brother, Dr. William H. McMahon, who went to Washington yesterday to visit the ailing senator, were unavailable in the capital as were those to learn more about his condition from other members of the family who went from Norwalk.

CITIZENSHIP DAY

WASHINGTON, July 25 (AP)—President Truman today set aside Sept. 17 as citizenship day to commemorate the signing of the Constitution on that day in 1787 and the attainment of citizenship by naturalization.

ARMSTRONG OFFERS 5-CENT HOURLY HIKE

A five-cent hourly wage increase was offered to Local 285, United Rubber Workers (CIO), yesterday by management of the Armstrong Cork Co.

The increase would be the same as that granted recently to the International Association of Machinists, agent for 500 Armstrong machinists. The union took the offer under study.

The increase would be effective at once, subject to WSB approval, the company said. Other provisions of the offer would be: extension of contract to Nov. 1, 1954, with a wage reopener a year earlier; more liberal holiday pay; two weeks vacation after three instead of five years; and increased night work differential from nine to 10 cents.

SERTOMANS HEAR TALK ON CLUB IMPORTANCE

Importance of service clubs to the American way of life was cited yesterday by Richard C. Murray, executive secretary of Sertoma International, as he addressed the Sertoma Club of Lancaster.

During the luncheon meeting at the Stevens House, Murray listed the achievements of Sertoma International and its affiliated clubs in the United States and Canada.

Charles M. Ruth, of Harrisburg, governor of the Fourth District, also attended the session and introduced the international officer. The main headquarters of Sertoma is located in Kansas City, Mo.

BACK FROM CONVENTION

Mr. and Mrs. Charles D. Mease and Fred Y. Oren recently returned from the state convention of Prothonotaries and Clerks of Quarter Sessions in Wellsboro.

Mease is prothonotary of Lancaster County and Oren in deputy prothonotary.

Six Of Farouk's Top Aides Resign After Army Coup

CAIRO, Egypt, July 25 (AP)—Gen. Mohamed Naguib Bey's Army-backed governmental house-cleaning reached to King Farouk's own palace today. Six of the monarch's top aides resigned.

At the same time, Egypt's new strong man moved anew to crush opposition to the lightning military coup by which he installed the anti-corruption government of Premier Aly Maher Pasha.

Maher (Pasha's new Cabinet took over today, pledged to try to end the crisis which has swept this Middle East country for six months. The Cabinet hopes to end the corruption Maher Pasha said brought the crisis about and to settle Egypt's dispute with Britain over the Suez Canal and the Sudan.

OFFICIALS JAILED

In jail on orders of Gen. Naguib are five high-ranking police officials, accused of "conspiring to arouse trouble and undermine public security."

Also reported under arrest was Maj. Gen. Sirry Amer Bey, commander of Egypt's Frontier Corps. The report said he was caught trying to flee across the border.

Other unconfirmed reports said several top officials in the Ministry of Interior, which controls the nation's police force, also were under arrest.

DISPATCH MISSING

(A part of the dispatch carrying this report was missing and may have been held up by military censorship. But monitors in Beirut, Lebanon, quoted the Egyptian state radio as announcing the arrest of two generals in the Internal Security Department—Gen. Abdul Munsef Mohamed, the assistant director, and Gen. Mohamed Imam Ibrahim, head of a special section—and the governor of Cairo, Gen. Ahmed Talaat. The jobs of all three of these men would come under the Ministry of Interior. The account quoted a communique from Gen. Naguib saying an attempted mutiny in the police and Army had thus been quelled.)

The new Premier, still in Alexandria after he and his Cabinet were sworn in there last night at the King's summer palace, announced the resignation of the palace aides. He also said Farouk had officially appointed Naguib as the Army's commander in chief—a post the general already had seized in the coup early Wednesday—and had promoted him from his former rank of major general to that of lieutenant general.

Hostage Police Officers Nab Suspect During Wild Chase

MIAMI, Fla., July 25 (AP)—George Arthur Heroux, 22, one of the FBI's 10 most wanted criminals, was captured today after a wild chase in which he used two officers as hostages.

The capture and release of the hostages followed a bullet-punctuated chase which ended as the policemen swerved their car into a tree, stunning Heroux.

Heroux was sought on charges of robbing the South Side Bank in Kansas City, Mo., of an undisclosed amount of money last Nov. 10, and of making off with $62,000 in currency from the Johnson County National Bank in Prairie Village, Kan., last Nov. 23

DRIVEN AWAY

Police Chief Barron Shields and Patrolman Robert Dubray of suburban El Portal were forced at gunpoint to drive Heroux away from a house where the officers began an investigation.

Chief Shields said he remained in his car when Dubray went to the house to inquire about a disturbance. He found Heroux and Mrs. Peter Bennett, the landlady arguing about rent.

Dubray reported that as he rejoined the chief, Heroux dashed up with a pistol and shouted "I want to get out of town fast. Do what I tell you or I'll kill you."

RADIO ALARM

He forced the officer to get in beside the chief and he made the chief drive off. A radio alarm soon warned all police cars.

Watching his chance, the officer swerved his car off the road and into a tree, stunning Heroux. Both the chief and Dubray jumped on the man and had him in custody when pursuing detectives pulled alongside.

The officers were hostages for about 45 minutes.

Shields said he and Dubray were disarmed at the start and had guns pointed at them for the entire time of the chase.

Neither officer was hurt in the deliberate crash into the tree.

Students Hail Driving Courses In Hershey Panel

HERSHEY, Pa., July 25 (AP)—Driver training courses in high schools were hailed here today as a "life-saver" by a panel of four high school students from widely-separated communities in Pennsylvania.

The students, all licensed drivers themselves, said their courses were very helpful in creating the proper attitudes for safe driving.

Participating in the panel sponsored by the Pennsylvania Automotive Association were Mary Speare, Reynoldsville; Grace Steffen, Wilkinsburg; James Clarke, Lansdowne, and William Hudson, Chambersburg.

PEDESTRIANS BLAMED

Earlier, the safety committee of the association was told that a majority of pedestrians killed in accidents on the state's highways seem to be victims of their own shortcomings.

"In other words, pedestrians are running or walking to their own death," said T. Elmer Transeau, State Highway Safety Director.

The association, attended by new car dealers from all over the state, endorsed a program of advancement of driver safety, including these three points:

1. Alert the public to the need for more pedestrian responsibility.
2. Support a proposed amendment to the state motor vehicle code to make the pedestrian assume his "rightful" responsibility.
3. Back appropriate local ordinances calling for proper control of pedestrian traffic.

Used His Head

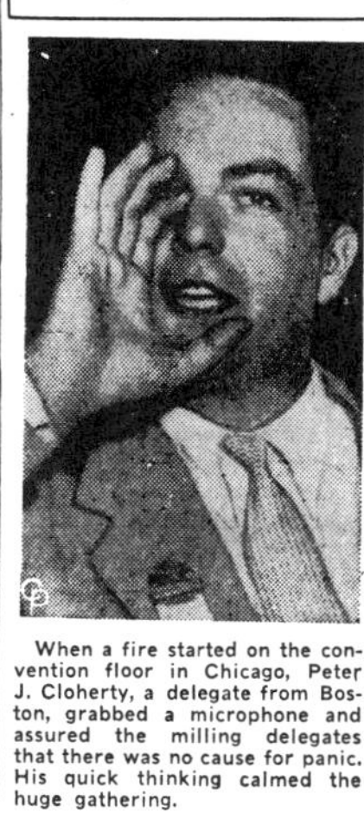

When a fire started on the convention floor in Chicago, Peter J. Cloherty, a delegate from Boston, grabbed a microphone and assured the milling delegates that there was no cause for panic. His quick thinking calmed the huge gathering.

TROOPER WHO KILLED EX-CITY MAN ACTED 'IN LINE OF DUTY'

Coroner W. E. Andrew of Stroudsburg, ruled yesterday that State Trooper Peter Walsh shot and killed Raymond C. Noss, formerly of Lancaster, "in the line of duty."

Noss was fatally wounded Thursday five miles east of Stroudsburg as he got out of a car that had been reported stolen a short time earlier.

Noss at one time lived at 222 W. Vine St., with his wife Mary, from whom he was later estranged. He was employed at Armstrong Cork Co. as a floor plant production worker from April 18 this year to June 17.

UNOFFICIAL LOW BIDS REVEALED FOR AREA HIGHWAY PROJECTS

HARRISBURG, July 25 (AP)—The State Highways Department today opened these unofficial low bids on road construction projects:

Lancaster County—Construction of two concrete bridges over Richard Run and bituminous surfacing of 1.80 miles along Route 340 in Salisbury Township, Raub and Jim Maser, Inc., Brownstown, $178,301.

Lebanon County — Bituminous surfacing of 1.01 miles of highway in Richland and Mill Creek Twps., Ralph V. Daniels, and Troutman Brothers, Camp Hill, $57,347.

WEATHER
(U. S. Weather Bureau)

Eastern Pennsylvania — Rather Cloudy Today With High Of 78-84 With A Chance Of Scattered Showers. Tomorrow Partly Cloudy And Rather Warm.

Intelligencer Journal.

The Leading Newspaper in the Garden Spot of America. Home Owned for Home Folks Since 1794

159th Year.—No. 45. Lancaster Metropolitan Area Population Official United States Census Figures 234,717 LANCASTER, PA., THURSDAY MORNING, AUGUST 7, 1952. CITY TWENTY-FOUR PAGES. 30c PER WEEK—5c Per Copy

THE INTELL INDEX

CLOUDBURST FLOODS STREETS, CELLARS

District Attorney Warns "Cowboy" Drivers

Teen-Agers Told To Abide By Laws Or Lose Licenses

Beyer Also Promises That Offenders Will Be Petitioned Into Juvenile Court; Makes Announcement After Conference With Probation Officer

Teen-age "cowboy" drivers were handed an ultimatum yesterday.

Either they drive safely and abide by the State Motor Vehicle Code, or their operators' licenses will be revoked and they will be petitioned into Juvenile Court.

The crack-down resulted from many reports throughout the county of racing on highways, "jack-rabbiting" and other "stunt driving" by teen-agers seeking a thrill.

The drive of vital import got underway yesterday in a conference between District Attorney John W. Beyer and County Probation Officer Edgar R. Barnes.

MAP PLAN OF ACTION

The two met to map plans for action to halt "cowboying" juveniles on city and county streets and highways.

Beyer emphasized that it's not only in one borough but in several throughout the county that the problem must be faced.

Barnes, who through his work comes in close contact with juveniles and juvenile delinquents, added that "we are naturally both very concerned about it."

He was referring to a wave of complaints from over the county concerning young drivers plowing recklessly over the highways. Complaints reached a new crescendo this week on the heels of last Friday night's death of a teenager, passenger in an automobile being operated by another teenager, who was allegedly "stunt driving" when the fatal accident occurred.

Beyer said that the Court will

Turn To Page 4 For More Of COWBOYS

ARMS PRODUCTION POSSIBLY HELD UP YEAR BY STRIKE

Parts Of Secret Report To Pres. Truman Is Made Public

WASHINGTON, Aug. 6 (AP) — Portions of a secret report to President Truman, made public today, said it may take an entire year to offset the impact of the steel strike on military production.

The swift rise in output of critical munitions—a 50 per cent jump from February to May — was stalled in June when the 54-day strike began, the report said.

Acting Defense Mobilizer John R. Steelman released the excerpts, after deleting secret data.

Ammunition output, it was said, may not get back on schedule until early next year.

BRIGHT SPOTS

Some bright spots were highlighted, however. These included reports that:

1. The new T48 medium tank, due to replace the Army's M47, now is rolling off the assembly lines.

2. Total war plane output continued to increase, both in numbers and weight, despite the steel shutdown.

3. Serious losses of perishable foods was avoided. The strike settlement came "just in time" to avoid waste of fruits and vegetables although some local losses are still anticipated.

However, the report was an unhappy one, for the most part, in terms of preparedness progress. Steelman said 299 plants working on military contracts had been either closed or slowed down by July 25, when the strike nded.

"The effects of the steel stoppage will be felt heavily for the

Turn To Page 4 For More Of MUNITIONS

EIGHT MEN DEAD IN ACCIDENT ON CARRIER

WASHINGTON, Aug. 7 (AP)—Eight men were killed and an undetermined number wounded in an accident aboard the U. S. carrier Boxer, the Navy reported early Thursday.

A naval officer said the tragedy occurred about 50 miles off the Korean coast but was not due to enemy action.

Details of the accident were not disclosed immediately, although it was reported unofficially to be due to an explosion aboard the 27,000-ton carrier. Date of the accident was not given.

Damage to the ship itself was comparatively small, the officer said. The vessel is scheduled to stay in the Korean area and not return to base for temporary repairs.

"We Lead All The Rest"

FARM CORNER

By The Farm Editor

25 Countians To Defend 4 Titles In 4-H Club Contests

Twenty-five Lancaster County 4-H Club members have been chosen to defend four state championships and compete for honors in five other contests at 4-H Club Week which opens Monday at the Pennsylvania State College.

The 25 farm youngsters have won places on nine teams representing the county, and an additional 15 girls will make the trip to the Centre County campus as delegates from 4-H Home Economics Clubs.

The contingent includes James Martin of New Holland R2, who was named State 4-H Champion last year by scoring 388.4 points out of a possible 400 as a member of the swine judging team.

Martin will make the trip this year as a member of the poultry judging team with Mary Mentzer, New Holland R2, and Floyd Kreider, Manheim R1.

The dairy demonstration this year will be seeking its third straight state championship. Its members are Richard Hess, Stras-

Turn To Page 4 For More Of FARM CORNER

Weather Calendar

COMPARATIVE TEMPERATURES

Station	High	Low
Water Works	83	70
Ephrata	85	73
Last Year (Ephrata)	82	48
Official High for Year June 26		100
Official Low for Year Jan. 30		7
Character of Day		Partly Cloudy

WINDS

Direction ESE Avg. Velocity 3 MPH

HUMIDITY

8 a. m. 90% 11 a. m. 80% 2 p. m. 80%
5 p. m. 90% 8 p. m. 100%
Average Humidity 88%

SUN

Rises 6:07 a. m. Sets 8:11 p. m.

MOON

Rises 9:17 p. m. Last Quarter, Aug. 12

STARS

Morning—Jupiter
Evening—Venus, Mars, Saturn

NEARBY FORECASTS
(U. S. Weather Bureau)

Maryland—Rather cloudy, warm and humid today with scattered showers and thunderstorms likely. Tomorrow some cloudiness and warm with scattered showers likely near the coast.

Delaware and Southern New Jersey — Rather cloudy, warm and numid today with scattered showers and thunder showers. Tomorrow partly cloudy with some chance of scattered showers.

Lower Potomac and Chesapeake Bay—Winds mostly southerly, 10 to 15 miles an hour, rather cloudy today with some risk of scattered thundersqualls. Visibility fair to good.

This 'High' Old Car Went Where Others Feared To Tread

Yesterday's heavy rains gave the owners of late model cars headaches which escaped the operators of outdated vehicles. For instance, the high, old-model auto shown here was able to navigate flooded North Queen Street, between Liberty Street and McGovern Avenue, while the high waters proved too formidible for the newer, lower-constructed cars. This was one of many spots in the city which was virtually inundated by yesterday's sudden downpour. At the right of the photo here is Business Press Inc., building where the cellar was flooded. Trailers at the left are completely surrounded by water. (Intell Photo)

FATHER GIERINGER APPOINTED RECTOR OF OHIO COLLEGE

St. Anthony's Pastor Given Post At Pontifical College Josephinum

By direct appointment of Pope Pius XII, through the Apostolic Delegate to the United States, the Rev. Paul A. Gieringer, pastor of St. Anthony of Padua Catholic Church here since 1947, has been named Rector of the Pontifical College Josephinum, at Worthington, O., effective immediately.

REV. PAUL A. GIERINGER

Announcement of the appointment was made in Washington, D.C., late yesterday, by the Most Rev. Amleto G. Cicognani, the Apostolic Delegate, to whom it was forwarded from Rome by the Sacred Congregation for Seminaries and Universities, by authority of

Turn To Page 20 For More Of FATHER GIERINGER

Penn State College To Buy Landisville Research Lab

The Southeastern Pennsylvania Field Research Laboratory at Landisville will be sold this month to the Pennsylvania State College which has been operating the research farm under a 20-year lease since last summer.

The transaction involves 27 acres of land lying between the old and new Harrisburg Pikes, a brick dwelling which serves as an office, a large barn, tobacco shed, and several smaller structures.

OWNED BY FARM LEADERS

A non-profit corporation formed by six area farm leaders purchased the property in May of last year, investing $32,500. The corporation then leased the facilities to Penn State so that an all-crop experimental station could be established in Lancaster County.

This all-crop station was opened officially this spring when equipment from the former Tobacco Research Laboratory at Roseville was moved to Landisville. Actual work at the Landisville site, however, began last year when winter grains were planted.

A. G. Bucher, secretary of the corporation, said yesterday that certificates of indebtedness issued at the time of purchase have been recalled as of Sept. 1. They will be redeemed at face value of $100 plus interest for one year.

MEMBERS OF GROUP

Levi H. Brubaker, Marietta Pike, is president of the group which spearheaded efforts to find a permanent location for extensive research in all crops in Lancaster County. Other members are Bucher; Floyd S. Bucher, former county agent; J. Collins McSparran, Drumore, new secretary of the Pennsylvania State Grange; Alvin

Turn To Page 6 For More Of PENN STATE

LISTS STILL GROWING AS 101 MORE REGISTER

Voter registration continued at a lively pace yesterday as 101 persons enrolled to vote at the Nov. 4 presidential election.

An additional 34 persons qualified to cast a ballot by changing their voting address to conform to their present place of residence.

The new registrations by parties: Republican, 68; Democratic 24, and others, 9.

32

Days In Which To Register For The Nov. 4 PRESIDENTIAL ELECTION

Registration Office In Court House

Open Today 8:30 A.M. to 5 P.M.

Nine Hungarian Olympic Athletes Hide In Helsinki

STOCKHOLM, Sweden, Aug. 6 (AP) — Nine Hungarian Olympic athletes have refused to return to their Communist-ruled homeland and have taken refuge in Western legations at Helsinki, Finland, the Stockholm newspaper Dagens Nyheter reported tonight.

It said the nine dropped out of sight one by one over last week end in a smartly executive maneuver designed to avoid drawing attention to their flight.

Their disappearance was discovered yesterday when Hungary's team leader tried to get his squad together for a post-Olympic tour of Finland, the paper said.

TOUR CALLED OFF

Fearing more desertions, the report from Helsinki said, the Communist coaches called off the tour and chartered two airplanes which flew the rest of Hungary's crack Olympic squad back behind the Iron Curtain today.

The missing team members were not identified immediately.

Hungary's Olympic team finished third in the unofficial team standings, immediately behind the United States and Russia.

ROMANIANS TOO

The reported defection of the nine athletes from Red Hungary followed by a day the disappearance of the Romanian team after he expressed unwillingness to return to his Communist-run homeland.

The Romanian, Panai Calcas,

Turn To Page 4 For More Of HUNGARIANS

COUNTY SCHOOL BUS INSPECTION AUG. 27

State police announced yesterday arrangements have been made with Arthur P. Mylin, superintendent of county schools, for the annual inspection of all buses used to transport Lancaster County school children.

The vehicles will be inspected Aug. 27 between 8 a.m. and noon at these places:

Quarryville — Intersection of Route 222 and the Buck Road.

Mount Joy — Marietta Street at the southern borough limits.

Ephrata — Mountain Springs Hotel on Route 332.

Lancaster — The Lancaster State Police barracks, Lincoln Highway East.

SAWYER STUDYING DROUGHT IMPACT VIA FIELD POLL

Sharp Increases In Produce Prices, Setbacks In Rural Trade Seen

WASHINGTON, Aug. 6 (AP) — Fearful of the impact of the drought on business activity and employment, Secretary of Commerce Sawyer has taken a poll of his field offices which shows:

No serious slump in any area, but some sharp increases in produce prices; scattered setbacks to rural trade; some decrease in the hiring of harvesters and, in a few areas, a threat to factory production if dry weather persists.

The drought has business men as well as farmers scanning the skies for rain clouds. Sawyer has ordered a repeat survey next Monday, with field men reporting by wire.

Most of them informed him that crop damages — estimated at around a billion dollars — so far has not been reflected in curtailed buying or hiring in agriculture centers.

Concern was felt, however, that sales of farm implements ulti-

Turn To Page 4 For More Of DROUGHT

COUNTIAN GETS $8,000 FOR 'PIKE DAMAGE

A Rapho Twp. man has been awarded $8,000 by a board of viewers for land taken from his 116-acre farm for the construction of the Eastern Extension of the Pennsylvania Turnpike.

Aaron A. Witmeyer had asked the court to appoint viewers to assess his land damages after he and the Pennsylvania Turnpike Commission could not agree on the amount due him for his loss.

Twenty-four-and-a-half acres of his farm were taken for the pike, and in addition a quarter of an acre was taken for an easement to re-locate a township road.

Viewers, who filed their report yesterday, were George S. Bleistein, Peter W. Reinhard and Thomas M. Trout, all of Berks County.

Near Inch Of Rain Falls Here Within 90-Minute Period

Northern Section Of City Hit Hardest By Sudden Downpour

A cloudburst loosed nearly an inch of rain upon the Lancaster area within 90 minutes yesterday, flooding cellars of homes and business places and popping sewer covers at several places in the city and stalling traffic.

Weather observers said the rainfall from 4:30 p. m. until 6 p. m. measured .71 of an inch, but residents of the northern area of the city said the intensity of the downpour seemed even greater.

It was in this area that several cellars were flooded when sewers were incapable of carrying off the downpour.

SEWER COVERS "POP"

In addition to flooding some cellars, the torrents of water, coursing through sewers, actually popped three sewer covers in various parts of the city.

At Charlotte and Orange Streets a cover was popped off and a geyser sprayed about five feet into the air. Covers also were blown off by the force of the water at Water and Lemon Streets and Duke and Clay Streets.

Police replaced the three covers. The storm also broke down two large limbs in the city, one in the 400 block of E. Chestnut Street and another in the 600 block of W. Vine Street.

Water-filled intersections in the northern area stalled an estimated 25 automobiles during the storm, giving tow truck operators more then enough business for the 90 minute period.

MORE RAIN FORECAST

Meanwhile the weatherman predicted more scattered showers for today.

Usually busy city thoroughfares were virtually impassable for the storm's duration as the seweage system proved unable to cope with the rushing waters.

North Queen Street, between Liberty Street and McGovern Avenue was flooded with at least 26 inches of water, miring several vehicles. McGovern Avenue between Prince and Queen was flooded as was Prince Street at Clay.

The Lemon Street crossing of the

Turn To Page 4 For More Of CLOUDBURST

CATTLE HERE FOR SHOW ARE VICTIMS OF RAIN

One hundred thirty of the area's best dairy cows were looking for a dry place to lie down last night.

And the staff of the Southeastern Pennsylvania Artificial Breeding Cooperative worked furiously into the late hours to rescue the prized cattle from the elements.

The cows, all entered the Co-op's cattle show today, were delivered to the Harrisburg Pike center during the drenching rainfall yesterday afternoon and evening. Water, draining from the highway and surrounding high areas, turned the Co-op's grounds into a quagmire.

All available barn space was utilized and straw was used on the wet grounds under the canvas shelters which had been erected earlier to house the animals.

DELUGE UNCOVERS ANOTHER "BUG" IN NORTHERN BY-PASS

Drainage Conduit Causes Flooding Of Homes In Green Terrace

Another "bug" in the Northern by-pass construction was disclosed during yesterday's cloudburst, when the cellars of four Green Terrace homes were flooded with stench-filled water poured into them by a drainage conduit of the construction project.

The conduit, designed to carry excess water off fields to the north of the proposed road, actually acted as a spouting that directed the water onto the lawns of homes, running into outside ceptic tank openings, backing the contents of the tanks into the cellars through the inside cellar drains.

Prior to construction of the by-pass roadbed there was a natural watershed, flowing southwest, in the fields to the northeast of Green Terrace.

NATURAL DRAINAGE BARRED

These fields, however, were filled in for construction of the bypass

Turn To Page 6 For More Of GREEN TERRACE

Knee-Deep In Water At Green Terrace

Eden Fire Chief Elmer D. Lipp shows depth which water reached in the basement of the home of David R. Spence, 971 Green Terrace, Homeland, after last night's sudden downpour. Several homes in the area had basements flooded by water backed up from by-pass which passes the rear of the area. Chief Lipp brought an Eden Fire Company pump to get water from the basements. (Intell Photo)

Pa. Draft Boards Not Considering Calling Fathers, Official Says

State Selective Service headquarters had nerve-calming news yesterday for Lancaster County fathers nineteen through twenty-six years.

To heads of families who may have become jittery over a hint dropped in Washington this week by Maj. Gen. Lewis B. Hershey, national draft director, that it may be necessary to draft some fathers to maintain the armed forces at current strength, came this memorandum from Harrisburg:

"Pennsylvania draft boards have a backlog of some 6,500 qualified men to use up before even CONSIDERING the induction of fathers."

CREDIT FOR 28TH

Lt. Col. Frank J. Graf, deputy state director, said "We're in better shape than many of the states because of the credit we received for the induction of the 28th Division back in 1950."

Pennsylvania has a quota of 1,398 men for the August call and 763 for September. However, Graf said he expects the call for the rest of the year to be larger.

Lancaster County's three boards have total calls for 41 men.

The deputy state director explained that local boards are now examining men in the twenty-two and twenty-one-year age groups. That would leave a pool of thousands of nineteen and twenty-year-olds still untapped.

Little Liz - - -

A man shouldn't trust his wife with the car until she learns to drive into the garage without shutting her eyes.

LANCASTER NEW ERA

The Weather
(U. S. Weather Bureau Forecast)
Fair and Cooler Tonight, Fair and Cool Tomorrow
Temperature Today: High 78; Low 65
Temperature Yesterday: High 79; Low 62

76th Year—No. 23,341 | Lancaster Metropolitan Area Population Official United States Census Figures 234,717 | LANCASTER, PA., FRIDAY, AUGUST 22, 1952 | CITY EDITION | 22 PAGES | 30c PER WEEK—5c Per Copy

UN Bombs Reds All Across Korea

10 BOARDS TO MAP POLICY ON AMISH PUPILS

Seek to Get 14-Year-Olds In School; Gov. Fine May See Directors

That knotty question of getting the Amish to send their 14-year-olds to school was revived today, with three developments:

1. An unprecedented meeting of 10 school boards in the Amish section was called for next Tuesday night. A spokesman said "uniform enforcement measures" will be discussed.

2. The Governor's office at Harrisburg promised to grant a long-standing request for Gov. John S. Fine to see officials of the affected schools in Harrisburg either next week or the first week of September.

3. Several districts were reported delaying the start of their new terms until the Amish problem is settled.

Not Open To Public

The school board huddle was called for the Western School in Earl Twp., on Route 23 west of New Holland. A spokesman said it will not be open to the public.

The spokesmen, who asked not to be named right now, put it this way:

"We have decided that there has got to be common policy on the matter. If the Amish persist in keeping their children out, there will have to be enforcement measures.

"But we want all the boards to have a common policy. We don't want one board criticizing what another one is doing."

34 Jailed In 1950

The spokesman declined to say it in so many words but his announcement was seen a warning that possibly Amish parents will be fined again like they were in 1950. When they refused to pay the fines, 34 of them were jailed.

"We must act," said the spokesman. "The State Department of Public Instruction has notified us that our state appropriations will be withheld this year if we don't enforce the law."

Among the districts invited to the meeting, although it was not known if all would attend, were: Earl, W. Earl, E. Earl, Leacock, Caernarvon, Brecknock, Paradise, Salisbury, and Bart Twps.

100 Illegally Absent

All have had attendance problems, involving 14-year-olds. It is estimated that some 100 14-year-olds in these districts have been illegally absent. They include Amish and members of other Plain Sects too.

The Amish take the position that it violates their religion to send their youngsters to high school after they reach age 14.

The high court of the state last winter upheld the right of the State to enforce the law against the Amish.

Following which S. H. Good, of New Holland, a member of the

—See AMISH—Page 11

Week-end Will Be Fair and Cool Here

A fair cool weeke-nd with no rain—that's what the weatherman says is in store here.

And to get it off to a good start, today was clear and moderate, with a 2 p.m. temperature of 78. The Bureau says tonight will be fair and cool and no warm-up is due until Monday. No rain is foreseen until Tuesday or Wednesday.

Today's weather brought a distinct change from the clammy heat of yesterday. Scattered evening showers preceded the arrival of cooler air.

But Texas was still in trouble, with the mercury heading for the 100-degree mark in parts of the state for the 21st consecutive day. Five more deaths were reported in Texas yesterday.

Court House Is 100 Years Old Tomorrow

New Era Photos

Symbols of justice: left—"Miss Justice" atop the Court House dome; center—the ancient bell that tolls the hours and opening of each Court session looks out on First Presbyterian church steeple; right—the familiar clocks in the dome. Two pictures of Miss Justice were taken with New Era's telephoto lens.

The stately old County Court House, seat of justice and repository of deeds and decisions (and many proverbial closeted skeletons) will observe its centennial tomorrow.

But be at peace, no one is going to rattle the skeletons in celebration.

Truth is, like those of most centenarians, the observance will be a quiet one. There will be no program and business will go on as usual.

That's not to minimize the significance of the citadel, however. Court House functions and services have reached into the lives of hundreds of thousands and over the years have shaped the entire courses of those of many more.

Over the century — despite the fact that one veteran reporter always referred to it as "the mausoleum" — the Court House has been a backdrop against which have been cast in bold relief, all types of humankind's frailties and faits accomplis; vices and virtues; crimes and compassion; cruelty and commiseration.

It's been the stage of pathos and drama, suffering and frustration, with not infrequent interludes of

—See COURT HOUSE—Page 11

STOCKYARD INN ROBBED OF $120.35

$650 Cash, $425 Diamond Are Stolen in Columbia

A burglar broke into the bar room of the Stock Yard Inn, 1147 Lititz Ave., early today and stole $120.35 from a cash register, according to Manheim Twp. Police Chief John M. Kauffman.

In three other robberies, an uncut diamond valued at $425 and $650 in cash were stolen from a Columbia jeweler's home, and intruders took $24 in cash from two city homes.

Door Was Unlocked

The robbery at the Stock Yard Inn was discovered by Harold Morrison, Paradise, the bartender, when he opened the place for business at 7 a. m. today.

Chief Kauffman said entrance to the Inn was gained through an unlocked door on the east side. The intruder used a steel bar used to sharpen knives in the hotel kitchen to force the door between the dining room and bar room.

Taken from Bedroom

The diamond and $650 cash was taken from the home of Mr. and Mrs. James W. Pinkerton, 1011 Walnut St., Columbia, between 2 a.m. and 7 a.m. today, according to Columbia borough police. Entrance was believed gained through an unlocked door. The diamond and $625 of the cash were in a wallet in a second floor bedroom.

Nicholas Mazur, who lives in a second floor room at 510 N. Duke St., told city police that during his absence yesterday afternoon the room was looted of a total of $10.

R. W. Painter, 340 Beaver St., said someone stole $14 from the top of an electric refrigerator on the first floor of his home between 5:15 a.m. and 5:45 a.m. today. Painter told city police he had gotten up at 5 a.m. to go fishing, and had placed the $14 atop the refrigerator while he went to a nearby restaurant to telephone his fishing companions.

Registration Office Plans Night Hours Sept. 8 to 13

The registration office at the courthouse will keep night hours during the last week of the current voter registration period, under tentative plans.

That would be Sept. 8 to 13. The books close Sept. 13 until after the November election.

The night hours would be for the purpose of making it easier for daytime workers to register. Normally, the office closes at 5 p. m.

Officials said exact details of the night hours program are not worked out yet. It was held probable the office will be open until 9 or 10 p. m.

6,000 Cards Mailed

In another registration development, it was announced that the Lancaster County Democratic Committee is finishing the job of mailing 6,000 remind-you-to-register postal cards to city residents.

David R. Eaby, Democratic chairman, said the mailing list came from comparing names in the city directory with the voting list from the registration office and mailing to those not shown on the list.

Most people said the Democrats had a good idea there. But some

—See REGISTRATION—Page 11

Traveling Registrars List Sites for 2 Days

Traveling registrars will sit at the following county places during the next two days:

Tomorrow — Nathan Schaeffer school building, Manheim Twp.; Wayne Weidman property, Brickerville; and Freeland Groff property, Quarryville.

Monday—high school building at Smoketown; Central high school building, Little Britain Twp.; and Penryn fire hall in Penn Twp.

BOOK SALESMAN JAILED FOR YEAR

Accused of Cheating 8 Physicians of $113.80

Hiram Harry Griffith, 65, Nanticoke, a free-lance medical book salesman who was accused of cheating eight city physicians of $113.80 by false pretense, was jailed for one year by Judge Joseph B. Wissler in court this morning.

Griffith pleaded "no defense."

City Detective S. K. Cliff testified that Griffith was taken into custody after complaints were received June 3 that he had taken orders accompanied by checks from local doctors for medical publications which were never delivered.

Used Fictitious Name

When apprehended at a local hotel, Griffiths was found to be registered under a fictitious name and gave a fictitious East Orange, N. J. address, Cliff told the Court. Investigation later disclosed that the firm Griffiths said he represented was non-existant. Also that he had cashed the eight checks amounting to $113.80 and spent all but $22 of the money before he was arrested.

District Attorney John W. Beyer pointed out to the Court that Griffith was arrested under similar circumstance at Carlisle in 1934 and served a term in the Cumberland County prison.

Counsel for Griffith said his client intended to fulfill the orders, but was unable to obtain the publications from the distributor. He admitted there was false pretense on the part of his client, but

—See COURT—Page 11

IKE, NIXON WILL BACK M'CARTHY

But Won't Necessarily Support Senator's Views

WASHINGTON (AP)—Sen. Richard M. Nixon of California said today both he and Gen. Dwight D. Eisenhower will support Sen. Joseph McCarthy of Wisconsin—if he is renominated—without necessarily endorsing McCarthy's views.

Nixon, the GOP vice presidential nominee, told a reporter he and Eisenhower, the presidential candidate, will back all Republican Senate and House nominees in an effort to gain GOP control of Congress in November.

But Nixon added:

"I want to make it clear that in supporting any particular candidate neither I nor Gen. Eisenhower will endorse the views or the methods of Republican candidates which happen to be different from our own.

"We recognize that in both the Republican and Democratic parties there is and should be room for individuals who have differing views on key issues."

Have Views on "McCarthyism"

Nixon said both he and Eisenhower had stated their views on

—See NIXON—Page 11

HOSPITAL'S NEW ENTRANCE READY

General Will Use It First Time Tomorrow

The new main entrance to the Lancaster General Hospital on N. Duke St. will go into official use tomorrow morning.

The present Lime St. entrance will be closed tomorrow, and sealed off so that alterations may proceed in the old building.

To avoid inconvenience for the hundreds of visitors who use the main entrance daily, moving of the business offices, reception desk, switchboard, admissions and general offices will be started tonight to the area of the N. Duke St. lobby.

Ambulance Entrance

The Lime St. entrance, when alterations are completed, will house the emergency ward. The ambulance driveway has been excavated to the north of this wing, on Lime St.

Changes to be made in the old building include enlargement of the pharmacy, establishment of a central sterilizing department, moving of linen supply, and renovation of operating rooms, the X-ray department and service pantries.

The new building is expected to be opened for patients shortly, officials said. Plans call for transfer of some patients from the old building to the new while the alterations are in progress.

Woman, 45, Dies On Marketing Trip

Mrs. Emma Wiebush Palmer, 45, of 48 S. Lime St., was stricken fatally while returning home from market at 11:50 a. m. today.

She collapsed while walking on Church St., between Duke and Rockland Sts., according to city police who conveyed her to the General Hospital. Dr. Miles Harriger, an interne, pronounced her dead on arrival at the hospital.

Dr. Charles P. Stahr, deputy coroner, said death resulted from a coronary occlusion. Police notified her husband, Richard F. Palmer, who was working at the Hamilton Watch Co. One son, Richard, nine, also survives.

Fall-Winter Store Hours Start on Sept. 2

The Retailers' Committee of the Lancaster Chamber of Commerce has recommended that stores return to their fall and winter closing schedules on Tuesday, Sept. 2.

That would mean opening at 9:30 a.m. and closing at 5:30 p.m.

Labor Day usually marks the final Monday closing. Most stores close each Monday during July and August. Daylight Saving will end Sept. 28.

Extra-Wide Aisle in Parking Lot for Ladies

YONKERS, N. Y. (AP) — The Otis Elevator Company opened a new 180-car parking lot for its employes today.

Close to the gate it has a "ladies row." it has an extra-wide aisle.

German-Made Products Back

Christmas Goods Arriving, Stores See Colorful Season

Don't look at the calendar now, but Christmas goods are pouring into the warehouses of many Lancaster stores.

If you know the right people and peek behind the warehouse doors you really can get an eye-full of the spangles and tinsel that will lure the Christmas dollars this coming Yule season.

German Products Back

For one thing, German-made products are back in quantity for the first time in many a year. German Christmas tree decorations will be available in new styles and gay colors. World War II just about brought an end to the making of toys and decorations in Germany.

Germany, too, has entered the cheap tool market and the first of the shipment have actually been delivered in Lancaster and soon will be on the counters. The cheap tools from German factories are already on sale in some Pennsylvania cities.

Also Japanese Goods

But Germany won't have any strangle hold on the Christmas market. American-made goods will predominate and Japan will have a big hand in filling the counters with holiday goods.

It all adds up to the fact that it will be a knock down and drag out tussle for yuletide business and the merchants are preparing for a colorful season.

The price tags are not in place yet, but generally, merchants say they don't anticipate any great change in the price levels as compared with last holiday season.

Today's New Era

U.S. TAX COSTS EVERYONE $10 WEEKLY IN PA.

$5 Billion State Levy, $65 Billion for Nation Set Records

New Era Washington Bureau

WASHINGTON—The federal tax bill for Pennsylvanians averaged out to $10 a week for each man, woman, and child during the 12 months ended June 30.

That breaks down into $1.40 a day, six cents an hour, and one cent every 10 minutes for each person in the state.

The figures come from a new report of the Bureau of Internal Revenue.

Record Breaking Total

The report showed that a record breaking total of more than $5 billion was paid by Pennsylvanians in taxes and social security contributions during the last fiscal year.

For the nation as a whole, that same figure came to a record shattering $65 billion dollars.

The Pennsylvania collections topped by about one and one quarter billions the previous record tax take from this state. That was $3.8 billions during the 1950-51 fiscal year.

Officials said the worst was yet to come. Not all increased levies were in full force for the 12-month period. Collections in the current fiscal year will almost certainly be higher.

Stiff Corporation Increase

Pennsylvania corporations felt a stiff increase, the report showed. Their corporate tax payments came to $1,821,000,000 against the previous year's $1,101,000,000.

Individuals in Pennsylvania paid $2,622,000,000 income taxes. That was up 30 per cent over the $2,068,000,000 collected in 1950-51.

The income taxes included $1,818,000,000 in the form of withholding taxes from Pennsylvania wages and salaries.

Miscellaneous internal revenue collections for Pennsylvania included federal excise taxes on everything from liquor to auto tires. They amounted to $680,250,000, compared with $709,920,000 last year.

This was seen showing a drop in consumer purchasing power.

The U.S. figure was about 14½ billion dollars more than in the previous 12 months. In addition, federal agencies other than the revenue bureau took in $2,364,500,000 for fiscal 1952.

$75 Billion Estimated

In the 1953 fiscal year, which started July 1, President Truman has estimated collections will total about 75 billion dollars.

These gross figures do not include billions of dollars refunded

—See TAXES—Page 11

LITITZ MAN IS HIT ON DESTROYER

Lt. Maguire on Ship Shelled Off Korea

Lt. Francis William Maguire, of Lititz, was seriously wounded when the U. S. destroyer minesweeper Thompson was hit Wednesday off northeast Korea, the Navy announced yesterday at Washington.

The ship was hit off Songjin by the same Communist shore guns that struck the vessel a year ago.

Lt. Maguire

Lt. Maguire's wife, Mrs. Mary E. Maguire, who resides at 424 Laurel Ave., Lititz, and is an employe of the New Era in Lancaster, first learned of his injury yesterday when the news came over the Associated Press teletype.

Details Due In Few Days

A Defense Department telegram meanwhile was received at her home by her mother, Mrs. Frank Sinz. Confirmation was secured through the office of Congressman Paul B. Dague in Washington. The Navy said further details should be available in a day or two.

Lt. Maguire, formerly of New York City, is a veteran of World

—See CASUALTY—Page 11

Ritnour Plane Broke Up in Air Before Crash

WASHINGTON (AP)—A beechcraft plane which crashed July 7 at Wellington, Va., while enroute from Lancaster, Pa., killing four persons, began to disintegrate while in the air, a Civil Aeronautics Board report disclosed today.

CAB investigator Richard C. Hughes said in a report that several residents in the area heard the plane and when they looked up they saw parts leaving it in the air. Lightning was flashing nearby, but Hughes expressed no opinion whether it was responsible.

"Questioning of witnesses failed to produce anyone who had seen the aircraft prior to the breaking up, which pointed to the possibility that the disintegration began while the plane was in the overcast." Hughes said.

Pilot, 3 Others, Die

The dead included the pilot, George H. Ritnour of Lancaster, and all three passengers, John D. Eshelman and Molly B. Eshelman of Sanford, N. C., and John H. Musser of Sullivan's Island, S. C.

(Ritnour was manager of the Lancaster Municipal Airport. Eshelman and Musser were southern representatives of John W. Eshelman and Sons, local feed company. Ritnour was flying them back to their homes.)

Hughes said the pilot apparently intended to make the flight from Lancaster, Pa., to Sanford without any intermediate stops and to fly under contact conditions.

No Radio Contacts

No flight plan was filed, nor were any known radio contacts made by the flight after take-off, he said.

"Residents of the area heard the engine of the plane which was reported as being unusually loud. Upon looking up at the source of the noise the aircraft was observed with parts leaving it in the air. Some parts descended into an open field, while the fuselage continued

—See PLANE—Page 11

YEAR MORE DUTY FOR STRICKLER

Army Keeps General on Active Status

GOEPPINGEN, Germany (AP) — Maj. Gen. Daniel B. Strickler, commander of the 28th Infantry Division and former lieutenant governor of Pennsylvania, said today he has received orders from the Army Department "to remain on active duty at least one more year."

Strickler gave up his state office when he was recalled to active military service in August, 1950, after the outbreak of the Korean War. The 28th Division, Pennsylvania's National Guard, was federalized a month later.

Strickler brought the Keystone Division to Germany last year in the buildup of American forces on the Iron Curtain front. About 4,000 troops, the last Pennsylvania National Guardsmen in the outfit, were returned to the United States this year for release.

Tells It To Chaplain

Strickler disclosed his army orders in answering a question by the Rev. Dr. Stewart M. Robinson, chairman of the General Commission on Chaplains, touring troop centers in Germany.

Dr. Robinson, pastor of the Second Presbyterian Church of Elizabeth, N. J., said mutual friends had asked about the general's prospects of returning to civilian life in the near future.

"Since there is a necessity for a strong American force in Europe, and the Department of the Army desires my services, I am happy to continue to lead the division with which I have been so long associated," Strickler said.

FIVE WONSAN WAREHOUSES DEMOLISHED

2 MIGs Hit, Allied Planes Raid Near Manchuria; Foe Repulsed on Land

SEOUL, Korea (AP)—U. N. fighter-bombers today smashed Communist targets all across the Korean peninsula.

U. S. Sabre jets damaged two Russian-built MIG15 jets.

On the ground, Allied soldiers repulsed two light Red assaults.

Twelve B26 bombers staged a daylight raid on a Communist supply area at Anak, on the Haeju peninsula, near the 38th parallel in Western Korea.

5 Warehouses Razed

On the East Coast, Allied planes demolished five large warehouse buildings near Wonsan, the Air Force said.

Fighter bombers slashed at Red battle lines.

The Air Force said U. S. Sabre jets damaged two Russian-built MIGs during the afternoon. The aerial duel between two Sabres and two MIGs from a formation of 16 was on a sweep that took the American planes within 30 miles of the bombed-out Suiho power plant on the Manchurian border.

The new claims brought to 28 the number of Red jets damaged during August—in addition to 26 shot down and two others probably destroyed.

Six U. S. Sabre jets scrapped with elements of a flight of 10 Russian built MIGs near Sinuiju, in Northwest Korea, but failed to score.

The Air Force said U. N. pilots destroyed 11 Red-occupied buildings, 15 gun positions, 49 bunkers and four mortars, and inflicted 20 troop casualties.

U.N. Beats Back Assault

U. N. infantrymen early today beat back a 16-man Chinese assault on Bunker Hill, in the west. On the Central Front, U.N. soldiers hurled back a probing Red platoon in a 40-minute battle near Capital Hill.

The U. S. Navy said Communist shore guns Wednesday hit the American destroyer - minesweeper Thompson off Northeastern Korea. Four crewmen were reported killed and nine wounded.

Searchers today recovered the bodies of three more of the 30 American infantrymen presumed drowned in a flash flood during training last Monday. So far, bodies of 15 members of the 45th Division unit have been found.

Driver Exonerated In Death of Boy, 7

John D. Meisenberger, 43, of 810 Fremont St., was exonerated today in the highway death of George Michael Miller, 7, of Columbia R1.

The boy died yesterday in Columbia Hospital of injuries suffered Wednesday evening when he darted into the path of Meisenberger's car in front of his home.

Following a conference with State Policeman Edward Hermesky, Dr. I. L. Moyer, Columbia deputy coroner, announced: "We find no evidence of negligence to warrant the holding of an inquest and hereby exonerate the driver."

Free Hunting, Fishing Licenses for Vets End

No more free hunting and fishing licenses will be issued to servicemen, the county treasurer's office announced today.

The practice was stopped as of July 31 under instructions from the State, officials said.

They also announced that the 1952 hunting and fishing licenses are now on sale at the N. Duke St. office. The old licenses expired Aug. 31. A hunting license costs $3.15 and a fishing license $2.10.

'Notorious Way of Life'

Moscow Calls N. Y. Crime So Bad Streets Are Not Safe

WASHINGTON (AP)— Radio Moscow has let loose a fresh blast at U. S. morality.

It picked on New York City this time and said crime has reached such a pass there that "it has become extremely dangerous for people to appear alone in the streets."

This terror, Moscow added, is not confined to the streets of New York, but also to its subways.

Jersey City Also Attacked

The State Department told reporters about the broadcast, which was picked up by American government monitors. Jersey City and Baltimore also have come under attack.

The Russian radio cited a series of articles by the World-Telegram and Sun — it called it a "reactionary paper" — as an illustration of what it called "the notorious American way of life."

It said all its material for the broadcast came from these stories.

Said the broadcast:

"No one except the very bold or people in groups will risk walking in the evening in the city's parks.

Cite Subway Crimes

"The same paper reports that a number of the city's subway stations have become places of robbery and other crimes when a number of passengers congregate there. Thus, to travel on the subway is no longer safe."

Radio Moscow gave as its reason for an upsurge in New York crime the claim that people have been "driven to desperation" by the high cost of living.

"Naturally the paper says nothing about other types of criminals, such as those who openly and before the eyes of the courts and the police engage with impunity in robbing the treasury, in bribery, and other such remunerative affairs."

A Title Changed Hands

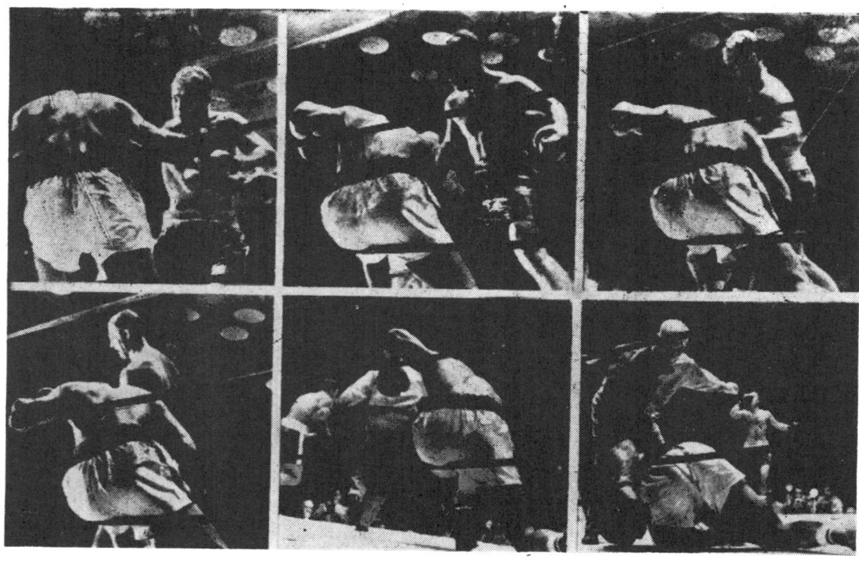

AP Wirephoto

Here is the sequence camera's record of the 13th round knockout that transferred Jersey Joe Walcott's heavyweight championship to 28-year-old Rocky Marciano at Philadelphia last night. It starts with Walcott reeling from an explosive right and sagging into the ropes as Marciano swings back with a left. Marciano then turns away and is guided to a neutral corner by Referee Charles Daggert, who completes the count as Marciano watches.

Marciano's Recklessness Doomed Walcott With One Punch in 13th

by GEORGE KIRCHNER

PHILADELPHIA—Youthful recklessness outwitted age and experience inside the boxing ring last night, and so today a new heavyweight is resting on fistiana's No. 1 throne.

Twenty-eight-year-old Rocky Marciano, his face and head badly battered and bleeding so profusely that he could barely see, defied the fates and walked straight into the 38-year-old Jersey Joe Walcott, lashed out with a terrific right and knocked the Camden, N. J. titleholder stiff in 43 seconds of the 13th round of their scheduled 15-rounder.

THAT'S THE way the bushy-haired Brockton, Mass. slugger ascended the throne in this bloody battle, and today he's eager to carry on. His manager, Al Weill said that "we'll honor our return contract with Walcott, but this time it will be under our terms. We're the champions now."

But as it shaped up today, it is not likely that Jersey Joe will ask for more. He took a terrific beating from his younger opponent and it took quite a spell to bring him out of it. Whether it was this reaction or whether it was because of his age that influenced his decision is questionable. But one thing sure is that Felix Bocchiccio, his manager, said immediately afterwards that his fighter was through.

In his own right, Walcott first hinted that he'd like to go on, but later said "I'll do just as Felix wants me to do.." When the crowd of reporters were filing from the dressing room, Bocchicchio was still insisting that Jersey Joe's fighting days were over.

BE THAT AS it may, the old Pappy guy went out winning more friends in defeat than he gained when he beat Ezzard Charles in the first defense of his title in this same Municipal Stadium ring.

And he went down as a gallant champion, putting out with his every last punch, taking everything the younger Marciano had to offer in the middle rounds and then bouncing back . . (as he has so often in his career) . . to steal the show and thunder away from his opponent.

AFTER IT was all over, Walcott said he thought he was ahead at the time he was hit by this lightning-like right. Both judges, as well as referee Charley Daggart agreed with him, for all three had scorecards giving Joe an edge of at least two rounds.

"I thought I was ahead by at least two rounds," Joe commented as he began donning his clothes. "In fact, I thought I had him when I knocked nim down in the first. I hit him with a pretty good left hook to do that and I thought I had enough to beat him. He's a rough, tough puncher and he can hurt you with one punch."

NO BETTER proof of this can be found than in the sudden (almost amazing) ending, for it took Marciano only one blow to belt the old-timer into fistic oblivion and become the new heavyweight king. And it'll be a long time before those fans who saw it will stop talking about this terrific right hand blow.

It came with less than 40 seconds of the 13th round having gone by. Marciano, having taken a pretty good pounding from the seemingly-rejuvenated Walcott in the previous round came out to stalk his cagey rival. Few figured he would dare to do much more than stalk. You could have got 100 to 1 that he'd cast caution to the winds

ESPECIALLY NOT when he saw Walcott, as cagey a fighter as has ever worn the heavyweight throne, backed to the ropes. The customers figured Joe was doing this purposely; that he wanted Marciano to come to him so that he could sting him again with his lightning left jab, just as he had countless times before.

But Rocky apparently didn't care what Walcott's plans were. He had made up his mind that he was going to shoot for the works in this one time and so when he saw Joe go to the ropes, he was quick to follow.

WALCOTT HAD no sooner touched his back to the strands than he dropped his guard for only a brief instant. But that was all Rocky needed. With the speed that surprised even his most loyal followers, the Brockton slugger whipped out with a dynamic right.

It caught Joe squarely on the chin and you knew without looking a second time that it was all over. The champ dropped like a bag of sand to the floor, but not fast enough to escape being hit a second time. Marciano, trained to follow up every punch, had started hooking with his left. He tried to stop it, but Walcott felt the sting as he went down.

Later on Rocky explained how it happened.

"When I walked in there," he said, "I faked a left hand, aiming it in a downward direction and I think I fooled him with it. Anyway, the next thing I saw was an opening, so I lashed out with my right. Believe me, I put everything I had into the punch. It caught him flush on the chin and by that time I was following with another left. When I saw him sagging towards the canvas I tried to stop, but I guess I wasn't quite quick enough."

THE NEW champion was jubilant, but it'll take some days before he'll want to do much appearing in the public eye. Walcott's sharp hooks and jabs wreaked considerable damage on Rock's eyes and nose and he bore a deep gash on the top of his head.

As a matter of fact, his manager Weill said that after the seventh round . . (the cuts came in the sixth) . . his fighter told him that he couldn't see. And that this situation remained so for four rounds.

"He talked about seeing something on Walcott's shoulder," Weill said, but when we looked there was nothing there. That convinced us that he was having eye trouble."

LIKE HIS rival, Marciano also thought he was ahead at the time of the ending. He offered no alibi for being knocked down in the first round, but left you under the impression that his description of Jersey Joe as "a real tough fighter" was good enough to explain the KD.

He didn't have to say anything about being in a tough scrap. That was evident to all inside the stadium. Walcott had surprised him by jolting him with a sharp left to floor him in the first and the old pappy guy was cute enough, strong enough, agile enough and boxed enough to give his younger foe all he could handle.

AFTER WINNING that first round

—See FIGHT—Page 21

The Officials' Scorecard

	1	2	3	4	5	6	7	8	9	10	11	12	
Referee Daggert	W	M	W	M	M	M	W	W	W	E	W	W	Walcott 7-4, one even
Judge Tomasco	W	W	M	W	M	M	W	W	M	M	W	W	Walcott 7-5.
Judge Clayton	W	W	M	M	M	W	W	W	M	W	W	W	Walcott 8-4.

Facts and Figures

PHILADELPHIA (AP)—Financial facts and figures of last night's heavyweight title fight:

Paid attendance—40,379.
Gross receipts—$504,645.
Federal tax—$100,929.
State tax—$40,373.
City tax—$18,167.
Net receipts—$345,177.
Walcott's share—(40 per cent) $138,070.
Marciano's share—(20 per cent) $69,035.
Theater TV receipts (estimated)—$125,000.
Walcott's TV share (estimated)—$50,000.
Marciano's TV share (estimated) $25,000.
Walcott's total purse (estimated)—$188,070.
Marciano's total purse (estimated)—$94,035.

Champ's Mother, Sisters Prayed During Contest

BROCKTON, Mass. (AP)—While Rocky Marciano's friends and neighbors continued celebrating his knockout victory over Jersey Joe Walcott, the devoted mother of the new Heavyweight Champion, Mrs. Lena Marchegiano, today patiently awaited his triumphal homecoming.

During all the time Marciano was in action against Walcott, the former's mother, surrounded by her sisters and neighbors, had prayed aloud that the oldest of her three sons would gain victory and escape harm.

In the living room of the modest Marchegiano home, a Boston newspaperman was getting a blow-by-blow account of the bout by telephone from his office. But never did the mother interrupt her prayers to listen to the happenings in Philadelphia.

WHEN THE END came, the reporter broke the news to the mother in this fashion:

"You're the mother of a new champion."

At first Mrs. Marchegiano appeared stunned by the good news. It was several minutes before she regained enough composure to reply: "He has always been my champion."

Then she lifted the prayer book she had been reading and said humbly: "I owe it all to this."

Although extremely proud of her boy's fistic success, the mother never has seen him fight, nor watched or listened to radio or television accounts of his bouts.

Shoot at Sportsfarm

Will Hemming and his son, Will, took first place in a Father, Son and Daughter Shoot held Sunday at the Lancaster County Sportsmen's Association Sportsfarm. They had a score of 561.

Next Sunday, Sept. 28, the Lancaster Junior Rifle Club will hold its annual Trophy Day Shoot at the same place.

14 Stitches Needed to Close Champs' Wounds

PHILADELPHIA (AP)—It took 14 stitches to patch up Rocky Marciano, the new World's Heavyweight Champion, after he won the title last night from Jersey Joe Walcott.

Dr. Vincent Nardiello, a member of the New York State Athletic Commission and Marciano's physician, said he had to take eight stitches to close a gash on the top of the champ's head.

Another six stitches were required to sew up a cut on the bridge of Marciano's nose.

3,600 Missed Bout As TV Blacked Out

NEW YORK (AP)— Thousands of fight fans across the nation watched Rocky Marciano win the Heavyweight Boxing Championship from Jersey Joe Walcott on large television screens in theaters.

However, about 3,600 people in the New York Academy of Music missed the picture when operations difficulties blanked out the screen. Many paid $4.80 for loge seats, the other $3.60, but the management permitted them to hear a description of the bout after announcing they would get a refund on their tickets.

Approximately 50 theaters in some 31 cities, with Philadelphia and the New England area blacked out, carried the fight on large screens on a closed TV circuit.

There was no home television or radio broadcast, and promoters declined to comment before the bout.

However, it was reported the International Boxing Club figured to get about $125,000 from the theaters. Walcott is to get about 40 per cent Marciano, 20 per cent of this, it was understood. For each seat, the IBC was to get $1.

At the small Guild Newsreel Theater in Radio City, tickets for 450 seats were sold out at $4.80 each two weeks ago.

IN THE DRESSING ROOMS

Rocky Is a Humble Champ

By Ralph Bernstein

PHILADELPHIA (AP)—Rocky Marciano was a humble boy in his dressing room last night after winning the heavyweight boxing championship.

His first remark, after hilarious well wishers quieted down enough for the Rock to be heard, was a tribute to the vanquished Jersey Joe Walcott.

"He's a helluva fighter, a good tough guy."

WALCOTT REPAID the compliment in kind. He quit the ring.

Jersey Joe wants no more of the rough, tough Brockton, Mass., bully boy, who doesn't mind getting hit with everything but the kitchen sink while waiting to land just one punch.

Marciano's reticence may have been due to his physical condition. The Rock looked like anything but a champion as he entered the dressing room. He had a bad cut on his scalp, a big mouse under his left eye and a jagged gash at the end of his right eyebrow.

He was sick at the stomach and tired. Winning this title had been no tea party for the 28-year-old slugger.

HE MANAGED to tell reporters that he won with a smashing right hand to the jaw.

"Yes, I hit him with a left as he was going down, but it was the right that did the trick," said Rocky.

Marciano said the first round punch that sent him to the floor for the first time in his career was the hardest he ever took. He classed it with punches Carmen Vingo hit him with some time ago.

On the other side of the Stadium the scene was different. A heart broken Jersey Joe sat with head in hands. One of his brothers came in and broke into tears as he wrapped his arms around Walcott's sweaty body.

The 38-year-old Camden veteran found his defeat hard to believe. He had never given defeat a thought. Now he was through with boxing for good.

FELIX BOCCHICCHIO, manager of the ex-champ, told the press that as far as he was concerned, Jersey Joe was retired.

"He looked pathetic against the ropes and I don't want him to get hurt. He still has all his faculties and has money in the bank. Joe has made over a million dollars in the ring. He's retiring. Joe has been a great champ and that's the way we want people to remember him," said Bocchicchio.

WALCOTT SAID that if retirement was Felix's decision, that was okay with him.

Both Boccnicchio and Walcott agreed that this was one of the greatest fights Jersey Joe ever put up. Bocchicchio ranked it with the first Joe Louis-Walcott bout, the one most of the boxing world thought Walcott won. The ring officials decided otherwise.

The wise old Jerseyite was ahead on most cards, including the two judges and the referee, when the explosive ending came last night.

The reporters finally ran out of questions, just as Jersey Joe finally ran out of gas at the amazing boxing age of 38.

McCaskey Wins 1st Soccer Tilt

Jim Neely's McCaskey High School soccer team opened its season yesterday by downing East Lampeter High, 4-2 in a game played on the local field.

The game was the initial tilt of the year for each squad.

McCaskey will see action again today travelling to Manor for a game slated for 4 p. m.

Score by periods:

McCaskey	0	1	2	1—4
E. Lampeter ..	0	1	1	0—2

McCaskey Scoring: Good, Myers, Fry, Getz

E. Lampeter Scoring: Shaeffer (2)

Local Fisherman Lands Rare Fish

One of the rarest of fishes was caught recently by a Lancaster angler while fishing off Cape May.

Gerald Offenbaker, 911 N. Duke St. was successful in hooking and bringing to net a rare specimen reported to be a rabbit fish. The strange looking creature weighed 7½ pounds and measured 23½ inches.

Offenbaker in comany with Chet Garreth, Jack Stockton, Howard Deverter and Sunny Hohenadel were fishing from the Sea Cloud skippered by Capt. Edward Bates out of Port Norris, N.J., when the fish struck at his hook baited with a clam.

Skipper Bates stated that in thirty years at sea with fishing parties, he had seen only three rabbit fish and this was the second caught on rod and line.

The rabbit fish, considered edible, has the same appearance as any other fish except for the construction of head and face that bears a striking resemblance to a rabbit. This is particularly true of the mouth of the fish from which, it seems, the fish derived its name.

TACKLE WAS SWIMMER

SAN JOSE, Calif. (AP)— George Porter, double duty tackle at San Jose State, was a star swimmer at Burlingame, Calif., High.

WEATHER
(U. S. Weather Bureau)
Eastern Pennsylvania — Sunny And Somewhat Warmer With High 82 To 86 Today. Tomorrow Fair And Continued Warm.

Intelligencer Journal.

The Leading Newspaper in the Garden Spot of America, Home Owned for Home Folks Since 1794

159th Year.—No. 90. Lancaster Metropolitan Area Population Official United States Census Figures 234,717 LANCASTER, PA., MONDAY MORNING, SEPTEMBER 29, 1952. CITY EIGHTEEN PAGES. 30c PER WEEK—5c Per Copy

THE INTELL INDEX

BARD REVEALS ADLAI HAS ROOTS HERE

Stevenson Makes Public Income For Decade

ADLAI SHOWS 1942 TO 1951 TAX RETURNS

Gross Income For Period Over Half Million; Paid $212,000 Taxes

SPRINGFIELD, Ill., Sept. 28 (AP)—Gov. Adlai E. Stevenson tonight made public federal income tax returns showing he had a gross income of slightly more than half a million dollars during the 10 years 1942 through 1951.

He paid taxes totaling nearly $212,000.

In precise figures, the Democratic presidential nominee's gross income for the period was $500,052.84 and his taxes came to $211,980.42.

That left his net income for the period at $288,066.42.

UNPRECEDENTED

Stevenson's disclosure of his tax record was an unprecedented move for a presidential candidate.

He declared yesterday that he feels "every candidate for high public office should, as a matter of course make a full disclosure of his personal financial condition over a period of years."

At his headquarters, some of the nominee's aides said privately they felt his action would touch off a public demand that Stevenson's Republican opposition follow his lead and make their returns public too.

The returns revealed that during 1949 through 1951, when he was governor of Illinois he received gross income totaling $151,110.26. In addition to his state salary of $35,209.68.

DIVIDENDS

Most of the income outside of Stevenson's salary as governor came from dividends received on investments in corporations. The dividends for the period from 1949 through 1951 totaled $131,600.78.

Stevenson's 1951 return listed

Turn To Page 4 For More Of STEVENSON

"We Lead All The Rest"
FARM CORNER
By WILLIAM R. SCHULTZ

15 TO REPRESENT COUNTY 4-H'ERS AT DISTRICT DAIRY SHOW

Fifteen members of 4-H Clubs in Lancaster County have been selected to represent this area Wednesday in the Southeast District 4-H Dairy Show to be held at the Reading Fairgrounds.

The club members and their project animals were chosen on the basis of their showing at dairy roundups held in conjunction with the Southern Lancaster County and West Lampeter Community fiars.

Five members of the Holstein Club will show six animals of that breed at Reading. J. Mowery Frey Jr., Lancaster R7, will compete with a junior calf and a three-year old cow; Phyliss Rutt, Ephrata R1, with a senior calf; Robert Welk, Strasburg R1, a two-year-old heifer; Barbara Ann Kenner, Manheim R3, a junior calf, and Norma Welk, Strasburg R1, a junior yearling.

The 4-H Ayrshire Club will have four members showing six animals. Abram G. Flory, Manheim R3, will enter his two-year-old heifer and senior yearling in the Reading show; Melvin Good, Lititz R3, will compete with a senior calf and junior yearling; Norman Kreider, Columbia R1, will enter a senior calf, and Florence Mae Flory, Manheim R3, a senior yearling.

Faye Bushong, Columbia R2, whose two-year-old heifer won grand championships in the Guernsey competition at both community fairs, will compete at Reading with that animal. Five other members of the Guernsey Club with entries at

Turn To Page 11 For More Of FARM CORNER

Weather Calendar

COMPARATIVE TEMPERATURES

Station	High	Low
Water Works	77	41
Ephrata	79	43
Last Year (Ephrata)	72	50
Official High for Year, June 26		100
Official Low for Year, Jan. 30		7
Character of Day		Clear

WINDS
Direction—WSW Avg. Velocity—5 MPH

HUMIDITY
8 a. m. 90% 11 a. m. 76% 2 p. m. 67%
5 p. m. 81% 8 p. m. 87%
Average Humidity 80%

SUN
Rises—5:58 a. m. Sets—5:50 p. m.

MOON
Sets—1:02 a. m. Full Moon, Oct. 3

STARS
Morning—Jupiter
Evening—Venus, Mars, Saturn

NEARBY FORECASTS
(U. S. Weather Bureau)
Southern New Jersey, Delaware and Maryland. Sunny and somewhat warmer with high 80 to 85 in the interior and 75 to 80 on the coast today. Tomorrow fair and warm.
Lower Potomac and Chesapeake Bay: Southerly winds, 10 to 15 miles per hour, over the north portion today. Fair weather and good visibility.

Sailor Critically Injured In Crash Near Landisville

Robert Maina, 19, Canadigna, N. Y., Placed In Iron Lung After Emergency Operation; Auto Crashes Into Another Stalled Car 3 Miles East Of Borough

A nineteen-year-old sailor was critically injured early today in an auto collision on Route 230, about three miles east of Landisville.

He was identified by State Police as Robert Maina, of Canadigna, N. Y. Officials at the Lancaster General Hospital said he was suffering a severe laceration of the neck and that his condition was grave.

He underwent an emergency operation in the hospital's receiving ward, then was given blood plasma and placed in an iron lung in a desperate effort to safe his life.

2 OTHERS HURT

Two other sailors in the same auto with Maina, were also injured. They are: Shinton L. Knight, twenty-one, of Buffalo, N. Y., lacerated right leg; and Donald Gosper, eighteen, of Canadigna, lacerated scalp. Both were treated at the Lancaster General Hospital.

According to State Policemen Fred Urban and Vernon Meily, who are investigating, the auto was operated by Knight and was traveling east on Rt. 230 when it crashed into the rear of a car driven by Brynton T. Ennos, twenty-two, of Oil City, Pa., also a sailor.

Ennos, police said, told them he was also traveling east at the time and his car started to slow down, apparently because it was running out of gasoline.

Just before the car came to full stop, he told the policemen, he was hit from the rear by Knight's car.

Police said Maina, riding in the front seat of the Knight car, was thrown through the windshield by the impact.

Ennos was headed for Bainbridge

Turn To Page 4 For More Of ACCIDENTS

Issues Denial

NEWBOLD MORRIS

MORRIS EPISODE CALLED BUNGLING INQUIRY ATTEMPT

House Probers Said Housecleaner Picked Because He Might Be Pressured

WASHINGTON, Sept. 28 (AP)—The Newbold Morris episode was described by House investigators today as "an awkward, bungling attempt" by the Truman administration to investigate itself. "It failed ingloriously," the congressman said.

Morris was named last Feb. 1 to head a government house-cleaning drive. On April 3 he was swept out of office in a dispute with the then attorney general J. Howard McGrath, which also cost McGrath his Cabinet post.

The House probers, a judiciary subcommittee headed by Rep. Chelf (D-Ky), said today that Morris wasn't the right man for the job and that there is some ground for believing he was deliberately picked because he might be susceptible to pressure.

McGRATH ACTION

And it said there is serious doubt that McGrath, who named Morris as his special assistant, acted in good faith in inviting him to start his task by investigating the Justice Department.

In New York City,, Morris commented:

"I was given a completely free hand in my investigation and there were no strings attached and the only conditions were laid down by

Turn To Page 4 For More Of MORRIS

Sparkman Sees No Vote Impact In Nixon Furor

WASHINGTON, Sept. 28 (AP)—Sen. John J. Sparkman said tonight he didn't believe the furor over the expense fund of Sen. Richard M Nixon, his Republican opponent for vice president, will "have any great impact on the election one way or another."

Questioned in a radio interview, the Democratic vice presidential nominee said he didn't want to pass judgment on either Nixon's $18,000 fund or the one Gov. Adlai Stevenson, the Democratic presidential candidate, has said he used to get good men in his Illinois administration.

Earlier, interviewed on a television program, 'Youth Wants to Know,'' Sparkman said, "I personally would not" accept such a fund as Nixon had.

NEVER HAD A FUND

The Alabaman told his radio interviewers he had never had a fund of any kind, not even a campaign fund. He said that since he had been in Congress he had managed to save some money every year. He was first elected to the house in 1936, re-elected to subsequent Congresses and sent to the Senate in 1946.

"I've made it a point all my life to put some of my money into savings," Sparkman said. 'I've

Turn To Page 11 For More Of SPARKMAN

5 BRECKNOCK TWP. SCHOOLS CLOSED BECAUSE OF POLIO

County Death Toll Now 5; Two More Victims Are Critical

An outbreak of deadly bulbar polio, in Lancaster county has resulted in the closing of five Brecknock Township schools it was announced yesterday.

Thus far five persons have died since the first of the year of polio infections and two more persons were said to be in critical condition in Lancaster General Hospital's unit last night.

The fifth death was that of Walter Matz, forty-three, Bowmansville, which occurred at 3:15 p. m. Saturday at Lancaster General Hospital.

Reported in grave condition, and confined to an iron lung was George Zell, thirty, Terre Hill. He was admitted to the hospital earlier yesterday. Meanwhile the condition of Nelson Blessing, five, son of Mr. and Mrs. George S. Blessing, Brunnerville, remained critical last night.

BELIEVE BOTH BULBAR

Zell, hospital authorities said, is suffering bulbar polio and the child is believed to have the same type

Turn To Page 11 For More Of POLIO

Eisenhower Mum On Making Income Tax Returns Public

NEW YORK, Sept. 28 (AP)—Gen. Dwight D. Eisenhower kept mum today on whether he would match Gov. Adlai E. Stevenson in making public his income tax returns for the past decade.

Headquarters of the Republican presidential candidate said he was spending a day of rest and would have no statement on income taxes or any other topic today.

An aide to Stevenson, the Democratic presidential nominee, said the Illinois governor was preparing to reveal his returns to "clear the air once and for all."

RELAXING

Eisenhower spent much of the day relaxing from his recent 12-state campaign tour and preparing for the next one, which will cover 24 states and 8,000 miles, starting Tuesday.

He attended services at the Protestant St. Paul's Chapel at Columbia University in the morning. He romped with his grandchildren in the afternoon and devoted the evening to forthcoming campaign speeches.

While neither Eisenhower nor his headquarters had any comment on income taxes, members of his staff were carefully studying Stevenson's list of contributors and recipients of an Illinois campaign fund released by Stevenson on Saturday.

AMMUNITION

The study was aimed at determining whether it contained campaign ammunition for the Republicans.

Stevenson, in saying he intended

Turn To Page 4 For More Of EISENHOWER

GOP NAT'L COMMITTEE APPEALS FOR FUNDS

WASHINGTON, Sept. 28 (AP)—The Republican National Committee appealed today for more money.

In a telegram to all members of the committee, Chairman Arthur E. Summerfield suggested that local committees consider door-to-door canvassing.

"We find ourselves caught up in two problems," he said. "First, the overwhelming public demand for Eisenhower and Nixon radio-TV appearances, campaign literature, banners, etc., comprises an ever-increasing burden upon our finances.

"Second, the cost of television, a brand new item in national campaigns, makes the financial squeeze even tighter."

COUNTY PAYS TRIBUTE TO BORO OF QUARRYVILLE

Lancaster County pays tribute to the bustling borough of Quarryville in this morning's Intelligencer Journal.

A full page layout, including stories of the history of the town in the southern end of the county and of its industry, is included in this issue of the Intell. It will be found on Page 5.

'Peeker' At Bible School In City Escapes Students

A prowler broke away from several students at the Lancaster School of the Bible, 325 W. Chestnut St., Saturday night and escaped over a wall after he was discovered looking in the windows of the girls dormitory.

City police reported that several of the men students found him trying to open one of the doors. When they asked him what he wanted he said he was "looking for a place to sleep." Before they could stop him, he jumped over a wall between the Bible School and Stevens Elementary School and was last seen running towards Chestnut and Charlotte Streets, students reported.

Before he was found standing at the door, he had been seen by several of the students looking in the windows, it was reported.

He was described as about 28, 5 feet 7, weighing about 160, and wearing a green jacket, with tan trousers.

TWO OTHER COMPLAINTS

City police also investigated two other prowler complaints. At 11:04 p. m. Mrs. Edna Flyte, 446 W. Chestnut St., reported that some-

Turn To Page 4 For More Of PROWLER

STEVENSON TO APPEAR HERE LATE IN OCT.

GOP Leaders Asking Nixon To Include City During Pa. Tour

Gov. Adlai Stevenson, the Democratic presidential candidate, is scheduled to appear in Lancaster late in October and local Republican leaders are requesting that the three-day tour of Pennsylvania next week by Sen. Richard Nixon, GOP candidate for vice president include a stop here.

Those were the week-end developments in the growing battle by both parties to garner the 32 electoral votes of Pennsylvania in the Nov. 4 election.

Gen. Dwight D. Eisenhower's headquarters already has announced that the GOP presidential nominee, who already has spoken in Philadelphia, will stop at six places in Pennsylvania, including Lancaster, on Oct. 16.

TRUMAN ALSO COMING IN

And yesterday at Pittsburgh, President Harry S. Truman, disclosed he plans to return to the Keystone State the last week before the election to help try to swing this key state to Stevenson. There is a possibility that Lancaster will be included on the itinerary.

Wilson Wyatt, campaign manager for Stevenson, said the two-day whistle stop tour through Pennsylvania will take place sometime after Oct. 22 with major addresses planned for Philadelphia and Pittsburgh.

Although dates and schedules still remain unsettled, campaign headquarters at Springfield, Ill., said that Stevenson plans to carry his candidacy through Scranton, Wilkes - Barre, Lancaster, Harrisburg, Altoona and Johnstown.

One plan calls for him to enter the state Oct. 24 and 25. An alternative proposal for invading Pennsylvania sets the dates for Oct. 29 and 30. A final decision is scheduled to be made within two weeks.

Sen. Nixon will make a three-day tour of Pennsylvania Oct. 8 through 10, delivering major speeches at Pittsburgh Oct. 8,

Turn To Page 4 For More Of CAMPAIGN

Group Named To Study Penn State Loyalty Process

STATE COLLEGE, Pa., Sept. 28 (AP)—A special faculty committee was named today to study loyalty review procedures at the Pennsylvania State College which resulted in the dismissal of one faculty member.

The committee of seven professors will make a complete investigation of the procedures established by the college under the State Loyalty Oath law and would be in a position to recommend specific changes.

It also would have the power to recommend to President Milton S. Eisenhower a rehearing in the case of Wendell Scott MacRae.

MacRae, former publications production manager for the college's Department of Public Information, was dismissed Aug. 28 following the refusal of the college loyalty review board to certify him as "not subversive." As required by state law.

The special committee was nam-

Turn To Page 4 For More Of LOYALTY

Great Grandfather Was Lancaster County Resident

Jesse W. Fell, great-grandfather of Gov. Adlai E. Stevenson, who once taught in Lancaster County schools. He is the man who historians say is responsible for the Lincoln-Douglas debates, and who is credited with inspiring the Great Emancipator to try for the presidency.

Jesse W. Fell Played Important Role In Lincoln's Career

By CHARLES W. FITZKEE

Former Federal Court Judge Guy K. Bard, Democratic nominee for U.S. Senator, revealed to Pennsylvania voters over the week-end that Gov. Adlai Stevenson not only comes, "like Lincoln, out of Springfield, Ill.," but "he is also the direct descendant of a Lancaster County man who was a founder of the Republican party and one of the first to suggest to Lincoln that he become a candidate for president."

Judge Bard, a native and resident of Lancaster County, made his revelation, the most fascinating to be brought before the electorate thus far in the presidential campaign, at a rally held Saturday night at the Ephrata Fair.

"Stevensons' maternal great-grandfather was Jesse W. Fell, who grew up in Fulton and Little Britain Twps.," he told one of the largest crowds ever to gather at Ephrata to hear a candidate speak.

WAS A SCHOOL TEACHER

"His father was a hat-maker who also did farming, and his mother was a minister of the Society of Friends. Jesse Fell taught for a time in the public schools at Eastland, Little Britain Twp. Then he moved west, studied law, and located at Bloomington, Ill., where he became a man of distinction and influence," he continued.

"Many Lincoln biographers attribute to Jesse Fell the inspiration and inception of the agitation which resulted in Lincoln's nomination," the Lancaster County jurist said.

"It was at Fell's solicitation, according to Lincoln biographers John G. Nicolay and John Hay, that Lincoln wrote the 'briefest of all autobiographies' Fell, who was an intimate personal and political friend of Lincoln, had it lithographed and spread broadcast throughout the country. The original, in Lincoln's handwriting, is now in the Library of Congress at Washington."

Gov. Stevenson's paternal grandfather, Adlai E. Stevenson, Judge Bard pointed out, "was a Democrat, and was vice president under Grover Cleveland. His maternal great-grandfather, Jesse W. Fell, born and reared in Lancaster County, was one of the founders of the Republican party.

"These deep roots in both political parties undoubtedly explain the political support given by the Democrats and Republicans alike in Illinois to Gov. Stevenson.

"It is apparent that the same

Turn To Page 4 For More Of BARD

Jesse Fell's Role In History Uncovered By County Woman

By JANE N. MAGEE

Lancaster County's role in the nation's political picture has always been that of a great one, but one of its most fascinating links with the nation's history was almost buried in the sands of time.

That link was the story of Jesse W. Fell, a young school teacher who went out of Lancaster County and into Illinois—the man who was later credited with inspiring Abraham Lincoln to try for the presidency—the man who still later would become the great-grandfather of Adlai E. Stevenson.

Recently that link was uncovered and put into its proper space in the chain which so closely binds Lancaster County with the history of this country.

PAPER REVEALS STORY

The Fell story was uncovered again after many years by Mrs. E. M. Hufford, Ephrata R2, into whose hands came some Lancaster newspapers of 1909. One of these relates the story of Jesse W. Fell, once of Little Britain and Fulton Twps., and his persuasion of Lincoln to chance the presidency.

How interested those Southern Lancaster Countians of more than a century ago would have been had they been able to foresee the strange—but great—role that Jesse W. Fell, one time a teacher in the Eastland School, Little Britain Twp., and in a Colerain Twp. School, would play in the history of the United States—even the history of the world—for over a century and a half.

But who then could know that young Fell, the teacher, would one day be among the first to

Turn To Page 4 For More Of FELL

Democratic Candidates Make Whirlwind Tour Of County

Statewide and local candidates, led by former Judge Guy K. Bard, nominee for U. S. Senator, toured Lancaster County Saturday with stops at Columbia, Marietta and Quarryville, and a night rally at the Ephrata Fair. The caravan, members, shown in front of the Columbia Municipal Building are, front row left to right, State Sen. George M. Leader, York County, for state treasurer; Judge Bard, Philip Ragan, for Congress; Edward G. Wilson, for the State Senate; rear row, left to right, County Commissioner Woodrow A. Zeamer; A. H. Fritz, Quarryville, state committeeman and former county chairman; Lee Work, and Samuel Nuss, Lititz, for the General Assembly; David R. Eaby, Democratic County chairman, and Philip J. Price, Columbia, for the General Assembly.

Little Liz - - -
Too many people looking for work quit looking as soon as they find a job.

LANCASTER NEW ERA

The Weather
(U. S. Weather Bureau Forecast)
Fair Tonight
Cloudy, Cooler Tomorrow
Temperature Today: High 63; Low 30
Temperature Yesterday: High 57; Low 23

76th Year—No. 23,397 | Lancaster Metropolitan Area Population Official United States Census Figures 234,717 | LANCASTER, PA., MONDAY, OCTOBER 27, 1952 | CITY EDITION | 28 PAGES | 30c PER WEEK—5c Per Copy

12,000 Greet Ike Here; Opposes U.N. Troops on Korean Front Line

FOES OF FIRST CLASS TWPS. PUSH DRIVES

Manheim and Lancaster Groups Outline Reasons For Voting 'No'

Foes of the first class township movements in Manheim and Lancaster Twps. are pushing their drives.

Both the Manheim Twp. Taxpayers Association and the Lancaster Twp. Citizens Committee held meetings yesterday and then issued statements.

The Manheim Twp. statement said it was pointed out at its meeting that "about 85 per cent of the industrial property in Manheim Twp. has already petitioned to move into the city.

"This means that our township has now become almost entirely a residential community, in which it is assumed the city may not be interested (for annexation)," O. L. Williams and Paul C. Dellinger, co-chairmen of their group, said in a statement.

Stuck With Higher Costs

Myron W. Jones, co-chairman of the Lancaster Twp. committee, said, among other things, that "the present officials of our second class township cannot guarantee anything because they may not stay in office. Once a first class township, you can never go back. You are stuck with these higher costs forever."

Jones said the statement, which w s mailed to homes in Lancaster Twp. today, was prepared by his group's legal committee, composed of John W. Beyer, chairman, Owen P. Bricker, Walter F. Kaufman, and S. Richard Harr.

Manheim Twp. Statement

Since the Manheim Twp. meeting, to which interested citizens were invited, was closed, Williams and Dellinger said their statement was a summary of what went on.

That session was held at the Lincoln-Mercury garage, N. Prince St. and McGovern Ave. Williams said Bernard J. Myers Jr. was chairman of the meeting and a report was given by Glenn C. Abel.

Text of the statement on the Manheim Twp. meeting:

"The meeting opened with a statement by the chairman, O. L. Williams, as to the general purpose of the meeting, which was to point out the increased costs that will accrue if the first class town-

—See TOWNSHIPS—Page 24

Hopeland Baby Girl 39th Polio Patient

The illness of Rebecca Farlow, 11 months, daughter of Mr. and Mrs. Richard W. Farlow, Hopeland, was diagnosed definitely as polio today at the polio unit of the Lancaster General Hospital.

The child was admitted last night. Her case is the 39th of polio in the county thus far this year.

Mrs. Patricia Houser, wife of Dean C. Houser, 932 Union St., was discharged from the unit yesterday. Mrs. Houser, who gave birth to a baby girl while at the hospital, was admitted Sept. 4.

Vandals in Car Shoot Out Several Street Lights

State Police were called to Silver Springs last night when vandals in an automobile shot out several streets lights and drove away.

City police also investigated a vandalism complaint of boys damaging radio aerials on parked cars in the vicinity of Shippen St. and Howard Ave.

Crowd estimated at 12,000 hears Dwight D. Eisenhower (arrow) at Pennsylvania Railroad station. (Other pictures on pages 2 and 6.) New Era Photo

H. H. SNAVELY DIES, AGED 81

Ex-County Treasurer Widely-Known Farmer

Harry H. Snavely, eighty-one, widely known farmer and a former county treasurer, died yesterday at 11:45 p.m. at his home at West Willow R1, West Lampeter Twp. He had been ill several weeks.

Noted for his progressive attitude, Snavely was a leader in the introduction of practices for the improvement of farms and farming. He was one of the first men in the state to win the designation of "Master Farmer."

Active in Conservation

Last August he received a conservation award for his interest and achievement in soil and water conservation. He was a past president of the Lancaster County Soil Conservation District.

He was a man of homely philosophy and good humor. One of the events he enjoyed most was the party honoring him on his 80th birthday, held in June, 1951. The party, arranged by his nephew and wife, Mr. and Mrs. Snavely Garber, who reside on the farm.

400 at Birthday Party

A 60-pound cake was a big feature of the party, attended by about 400 guests on the double barn floor. Snavely joked with the guests and swapped stories happily.

Snavely started to make his mark as a farmer from the time he began to operate his Willow Street farm in 1898. He laid out his first

—See SNAVELY—Page 24

HARRY H. SNAVELY

DRIVER NABBED 4 TIMES IN YEAR

J. C. Trostle Jr. Cited as Habitual Offender

Jacob C. Trostle Jr., 242 W. Orange St., cited by city police as a habitual traffic law offender, was given a hearing before Inspector Charles H. Stormfeltz in Speeders' Court today. He faces a suspension of one year.

Lt. David Strayer, of the Police Traffic Bureau, testified Trostle was arrested four times since Sept. 30, 1951 on motor code violations.

Three times he was charged with reckless driving and on two of these occasions, Trostle had been drinking, police records showed.

Police Cite Recklessness

The police stated: "Trostle's reckless operation of motor cars is not only a direct violation of the State vehicle code but is a hazard to the life and limb of our citizens."

Other motor code violations against Trostle include ignoring an officer's signal to halt by city police and a stop sign violation at Oxford brought by state police.

John W. Buyers, Paradise R1, clocked at 75 miles per hour by state police on Route 115, Chestnut Hill Twp., Monroe County, on May 12 failed to appear for a hearing. He faces the loss of his driving privileges for 90 days.

LEWIS ORDERS MINERS TO PITS

Follows White House Meeting With Truman

WASHINGTON, (AP) — John L. Lewis today ordered striking soft coal miners to go back to work at once.

The chief of the United Mine Workers messaged all union district officers that it was his opinion work should be resumed pending government reconsideration of whether the miners may have a $1.90 a day pay increase which the industry has agreed to. The Wage Stabilization Board (WSB) trimmed the rise to $1.50, holding that a higher boost would violate the government's anti-inflation program.

Direct Appeal To Lewis

President Truman had appealed directly to Lewis to get the miners back to work.

Truman invited Lewis to the White House last night and made the request. Lewis promised cooperation. Immediately after this conference, the President left on his final political campaign tour.

Associates of Lewis have made it plain that he expects the full pay raise will be approved in a day or two.

It seemed perfectly clear, however, that Lewis expected the government to reverse its Wage Board's stand, and okay the full $1.90 pay raise.

General Leaves Without Hat But Gets It Back

Gen. Eisenhower doffed his brown felt hat before he went on the speakers' stand here today.

He left it with someone by the side of the stand. Then he walked off without it.

The lack of a hat was noticed when the general went to get back on the train. W. Hensel Brown, one of the reception committee, yelled up for someone to bring down the general's hat. And that they did. So the hat got to the train before it pulled away.

Heifer Killed by Auto As it Darts from Field

A heifer belonging to Walter F. Eberly, Quarryville R3, was killed as it darted from a cornfield into the path of an auto driven by Norman K. Hackman, Lancaster R6, on Route 372, between Quarryville and Green Tree, at 5 p. m. yesterday.

Today's New Era

'Mamie Is a Honey!'

Ike's Wife Looks Fresh and Vibrant After Long Tour

Presented Big Bouquet of Red Roses by GOP Women; Warm Personality Wins Many Friends

By Jean M. Bollinger

"Mamie is a honey!"

That was the exclamation heard on all sides at the PRR station, on the platforms and through the crowds as Mrs. Eisenhower smiled and beamed at the throngs who greeted her here today.

She proved, also, that "she's the most obliging person," when she even tore off some of the roses in her bouquets and handed them over to youngsters who pleaded for them.

A 'Good Campaign

General Eisenhower's wife has long had the reputation of being a "good campaigner," and the impression she left on the Lancaster crowd today adds to her glory in that respect.

From the moment she came out on the rear platform of the special train, until the train moved off down the tracks, Mamie smiled on all her well-wishers. The only time she looked serious was on the grandstand, as she listened to the general's speech. All through the address she listened attentively to every word he said—and her eyes never left his face.

This was Mrs. Eisenhower's second visit to Lancaster with the General. The first visit was March 1950 when the General spoke at Franklin and Marshall College. And today, the local women who also had seen her previously, said: "She's always the same — that personality just glows!"

Mamie Appears Vibrant

The women of the reception committee and the large number of members of the Women's Republican Club and its Junior Group who were on hand to greet Mrs. Eisenhower expressed surprise that she could look so fresh and vibrant after all these weeks of the whistle-stop tour.

"She's so full of life," the local women marvelled, as Mamie alighted from the train and hurried up the steps at the station.

And then all the women looked her over—from top to toe. The ensemble she wore for her visit here

—See MAMIE—Page 2

Citizens for Eisenhower Being Organized Here

Plans are under way to form a Citizens for Eisenhower Committee in Lancaster.

Named co-chairmen are Mrs. J Hay Brown and Mrs. Keith Powlison.

A meeting was held this afternoon at Mrs. Brown's home. Speaking was Mrs. Gertrude Nauman, a member of the National Citizens for Eisenhower, Harrisburg.

Ike Greets 3 Twice Removed Cousins Here

By Herbert B. Krone

Three "twice removed" cousins captured some of the spotlight when Gen. Eisenhower made his whistle-stop visit to Lancaster this morning.

The grandmother of the three Lancaster residents and the mother of the general were sisters.

The three who point with pride to their kinship with the GOP candidate are: Meredith C. Lentz, 1303 Cheves Place, and his sisters, Mrs. Fred Koser, Landisville and Mrs. Robert Gold, Lancaster R1.

Lentz said he has communicated with the general a number of times by mail and felt pretty certain he would recall the relationship.

The general had walked only about 50 feet under the train shed when Lentz and his two sisters stepped forward and introduced themselves. The general smiled broadly and in his address told the audience that he was happy to find "thrice removed cousins in Lancaster."

There the two families had a difference of opinion. Lentz and his sisters say they are but "twice removed" — the general said they

—See COUSINS—Page 6

Lensman on Ike Train in Tilt with Police Here

Police started to handcuff Frank Jurkowski, photographer with Gen. Dwight D. Eisenhower's party today as he tried to shoot a picture from the roof of the station here.

Jurkowski is with International News Photos and had climbed to the roof to take a shot of the crowd and the general as Eisenhower made a speech.

Gov. Sherman Adams, Eisenhower campaign manager, interceded and cooled off the officers.

Both railroad and state police were involved in the incident.

GOP Candidate Calls for U. S. Government That Serves 'Not As a Boss, But As a Helper'

By Jerry Conn

Gen. Dwight D. Eisenhower brought his campaign for President to Lancaster today.

A crowd which police set at 12,000 gave him an uproarious welcome in the parking lot of the Pennsylvania Railroad Station.

Ike flashed that famous grin of his, held up his fingers in the V sign for victory, and then got down to business.

The GOP standardbearer declared that the United Nations troops do not belong in the front lines in Korea.

"The South Koreans deserve, and want to, defend themselves," Eisenhower declared. "It is our job to make them ready."

Eisenhower said a program he would initiate to train the South Koreans to defend themselves would be part of helping people all over the world to defend themselves against Communism.

"The United States," he said, "cannot build a Roman wall around the world.

Wants Friendly Government

Eisenhower also described his philosophy of government at home.

"The national government must be a friendly government," he declared.

"It must serve, not as a boss, but as a helper."

Salutes Lancaster County

And Ike took time out to salute Lancaster County.

Pointing out that the Eisenhower tribe stems from the Pennsylvania Dutch, he said "any Eisenhower feels like he is coming home when he comes to this heartland of the Pennsylvania Dutch."

The crowd was delighted with this reference to home and cheered lustily.

Speaks Overtime

Members of the official party said Eisenhower must have become so engrossed in his speech that he went overtime. He spoke about 20 minutes.

He was scheduled to leave Lancaster at 10:35 a. m. but his 20-car "Look Forward Neighbor" special didn't steam out of the station until 11 o'clock.

Flanking the general as he spoke was his smiling wife Mamie. Also state dignitaries including Sen. James H. Duff and Gov. John S. Fine.

The estimate of crowd size came from State Police Lt. Reese Davis of the Lancaster barracks.

Introduced By Diehm

Eisenhower was introduced by State Sen. G. Graybill Diehm. Diehm said he was "the leading serviceman of the world and the next president of the United States."

The crowd chanted "We Want Ike." Eisenhower, dressed in a brown suit with a brown flowered tie, signalled V for victory some more and then held up his hand. The crowd went silent.

"My fellow Americans," he began, "there are many reasons why I have especially felt gratified in coming to Lancaster this morning. "Let me thank you for taking out this hour of a busy day to come here so I could meet you face to face.

Outlines 'Few Thoughts'

"I would like you to listen to a few thoughts I have in my mind about this political campaign."

Eisenhower then said he wsa honored to be on the same platform with Governor Fine, Senator Duff, Sen. Martin, and to have been introduced by Senator Diehm.

"The Eisenhower tribe," said the General, "has always been on the move. It travelled through Germany, Switzerland, and Holland and finally came to Lancaster and Lebanon Counties.

He drew a laugh when he declared:

Greeted by Third Cousins

"It was very cheering and warming when two goodlooking ladies came up and met at the train and said they were my third cousins."

But the General said he didn't come here to reminisce.

"I came here to talk about the great decision that will be made a week from tomorrow. I, for one, am glad it is no longer off than that."

The crowd laughed.

Deep Religious Faith

"Our ancestors," went on the General, "had their roots in deeply felt religious faith that insisted that man is made in the image of God.

On that faith, he said, is founded the concept of the rights of the individual on which American democracy is based.

In some countries, he said, dictatorships, or a small oligarchy, took over to solve the problems that needed solving.

Cooperation Of Individuals

But free governments, he said, solve the problems through cooperation of individuals.

"When we talk about the fear of regimentation," Eisenhower said, "we are not talking about an academic subject. The struggle has been going on since man walked upright."

Present Regime Reactionary

Talk about reactionaries, he said, and you find it is the present

—See IKE—Page 6

2 Michaelis Kin There As Ike Sends Greetings

Gen. Dwight D. Eisenhower added greetings to the family of his former aide, Brig. Gen. John H. Michaelis, of Lancaster, after concluding his formal speech this morning.

"Before I leave," he told the audience, "will someone please take my greetings to the family of Gen. John Michaelis? They're old friends of mine."

He was not aware, in the hustle and bustle of arrival, that the General's mother, Mrs. O. E. Michaelis, and sister, Miss Louise Michaelis, were near the platform.

Despite the headlong rush from the platform after his speech, Mrs. Eisenhower held up the whole party while she stopped to chat with Mrs. Michaelis and Miss Michaelis.

Mementos for Crowd

Lucky Ones Get Handshake Others Roses, Autographs

By Gerald S. Lestz

A cheering, applauding Lancaster County crowd estimated at 12,000—bigger than the audience which heard Dwight D. Eisenhower earlier in the morning at Philadelphia—turned out to sound off for the GOP standard bearer here today.

Oldsters and youngsters, farmers and babes in arms, jammed the parking space of the PRR station, overflowing into surrounding streets and fields, some standing more than a block away to hear Ike's words carried through amplifiers.

People were at the station as early as 8 a.m., two hours and 20 minutes in advance of the special train's scheduled arrival. More than a dozen policemen were on duty at key points to direct foot and auto traffic.

Officials with the train, looking out over the sea of faces, commented that it was a better turnout than at Philadelphia, where Eisenhower spoke indoors at 8 a. m.

Crowd Orderly Till Speech Ends

The crowd remained orderly until Eisenhower's speech had been concluded and the official party was leaving the platform. Then they broke through the ropes and past the policemen and surrounded the presidential candidate, his wife, and his daughter-in-law.

Hands stretched forth with papers for Ike to autograph. People closed in to touch the General and to shake hands with him.

Richard Eby, this city, holding his five-month-old daughter Candace Maurene, was one of those lucky enough to get a handclasp. He shouted his success back to his wife, who stood on the sidelines.

As the party proceeded down the ramp to the waiting train, police held back some of the enthusiastic well-wishers, but a number got through anyway.

"We're two minutes late," commented one of the train officials, looking worriedly at his wrist watch.

Mamie Stays On Platform

Eisenhower stepped up to the platform, then went inside the rear car. But Mamie and her daughter-

—See CROWDS—Page 6

6 Key States—1

Texas' 24 Electoral Votes In Doubt 1st Time Since '28

There are six big states which have, among them, more than one-third of all the electoral votes in the country. Every one of the "big six" is a red-hot battleground. Today's story on Texas is the first in a series presenting the picture in these states.

By Dave Cheavens

AUSTIN, Tex. (AP)— Two and a half million Texas voters may hold the key to the White House door for either Gen. Dwight D. Eisenhower or Gov. Adlai Stevenson.

Texas' 24 electoral votes — sixth biggest block in the nation — are in doubt for the first time since 1928 and the second time this century.

Democratic rebellion that splintered off segments of the once-solid Texas party in 1944 and 1948 split it wide open his year.

For the first time in history, a Democratic governor of Texas has joined the Republicans in backing their presidential candidate. Gov. Allan Shivers' simmering displeasure with New Deal and Fair Deal policies boiled over when Gov. Adlai Stevenson said he could not agree with Texas claims to submerged offshore lands and their potential — and disputed — oil wealth.

Unprecedented In Texas

The revolt brought an open alliance between Shivers, his established state party machinery and a militant Republican organization making its first serious effort in a quarter of a century to win the Texas electoral vote. Nothing like it had ever happened in historically-Democratic Texas.

The outcome is so uncertain that both parties sent their presidential candidates criss-crossing the state.

HE HASN'T LEARNED TO FALL UP, YET—Tay-Ru, Viennese juggler who is performing with a circus troop in Paris, has mastered the art of juggling while doing a precarious hand-stand, but he hasn't learned to fall upward, yet. The safety net above him is for protection of high-wire aerialists.

Santa Claus Parade Man Is Busier Than St. Nick

WINDSOR, Ont., Nov. 15 (AP)—Ben Matlock and his dozen employes are busier these days than Santa Clause and his helpers.

Unblessed by the magic which enables Santa to cover the world in a single night, Matlock has to get his Christmas show on the road in early November in order to span Southeastern Ontario alone by Dec. 25.

Matlock produces Santa Claus parades which make a circuit of a score of Canadian cities each Christmas season. And if maybe you think that isn't a lot of work, well—

Readies Candy Train

There's frosting-like decorations to be spun on the candy train, furnishings to put in Santa's home on the road, trimmings to be hung on Cinderella's carriage—even little Martian men to create to ride the rocket ship.

Of the 15 story-book floats, the one old St. Nick himself rides in is a 50-foot combination truck and trailer. Santa— frequently in the person of Matlock himself—rides in a huge sleigh behind eight husky reindeer.

Others are a rocket ship, a toonerville train, and floats for Jack the Giant Killer, Humpty Dumpty and other nursery rhyme characters.

Imagination Helps

Matlock builds his exhibits of wooden frames, wire mesh, gobs of papier mache— and imagination. He first sketches the figures in colors, then draws up working plans and finally pitches in with his workers to make them.

In the business five years now, he says he has learned to save a lot of work by using real children instead of papier mache dummies for most of his story book characters.

M'Caskey Won Grid Title the Hard Way

On Wings of Prayer

McCaskey Kids Asked Help from Above in Last Minutes of Game

by GEORGE KIRCHNER

GLORIOUS FINISH . . . McCaskey High School's gallant football team fiinished off its most glorious season yesterday afternoon on the wings of a prayer.

Approximately 10,000 fans jammed Small Field in York to watch Boyd Sponaugle's Red and Black eleven conquer York, 13 to 6, and achieve its first Central Penn Football Conference championship, but only the players, themselves, knew that the prayer which they had uttered as a group just before the finish of this thrilling ball game had been answered.

EVERYONE inside the field saw the Red and Black youngsters go into a huddle with less than two minutes remaining. It was a tense and exciting moment for the spectators, but twice as crucial for the players. McCaskey was protecting a 13 to 6 lead; York had the ball on its own 35 yard line and while 65 tough yards separated the Bearcats from the touchdown they needed, everyone knew that these could be traversed quickly . . . especially if York's great passer, Ellsworth Kissinger were to start clicking.

Doubtless, there were many in the Lancaster stands who had flashes of memory that took them back to the Tornado's 21 to 21 tie with Reading, and they must have remembered how the Red Knights uncorked a dazzling aerial attack to come from behind and tie.

Would York duplicate this feat?

There's a pretty good chance that this upsetting thought might have creeped into the minds of some of the players who were putting up such a gallant fight for the Red and Black.

THAT'S conjecture, but the one thing all the fans know is that when York called for time, the McCaskey kids went into a huddle all of their own. This is hardly a new procedure in football, but you could see from the stands that this wasn't the usual kind of a huddle. Not the kind where each fellow grips the other fellow's hand and they vow to do their best.

Somehow there seemed to be something almost solemn about this and the minute you spotted young George Darrah down on his knees you knew then that something unusual was taking place out there in the mud of Small Field.

AFTER the game was over and some of the shouting had died down in the McCaskey dressing room, co-captain Bernie Gross was asked to explain.

"What did you say in that last huddle?" the McCaskey leader was asked.

Without flinching, Gross replied:

"We said the Lord's Prayer, just as we have been doing all season."

AND so while 10,000 people sat almost too excited and tense to even breathe, these 11 kids from McCaskey High put their heads together and in all seriousness sought Divine aid.

"That was nothing new today," young Gross, who was playing his last game for the Red and Black, continued. "All season whenever things got tough we would take time out to pray. I don't know who started it; I don't even know who suggested it today. All I know is that this seemed like our toughest spot and so we just went into the huddle and prayed."

SOME people may have their own ideas about this, but those kids believe . . . and they should know . . . their prayer was answered. That was the strength they displayed in those last couple of minutes when the struggle was at its peak and the chips were really down.

Factually, the customers left the field appreciating that the Red and Black team, which had carried on so nobly to score its two touchdowns, was just about invincible when the Yorkers made their last desperate and determined bid.

AND that's how this thrilling game came to its glorious conclusion. Non . . . (not even the partisan Yorkers) . . . could deny but what the Lancaster lads deserved their victory and the championship that went with it.

They had, through sheer courage, fine playing and an undying spirit, come out on top in spite of the handicap of being outweighed and outmanned. Coach Eddie Waleski had two platoons to throw at McCaskey's group of 16 players, yet the fresh replacements could not wear down these gritty kids.

They had scored early in the game and then had muffed at least five or six chances . . . (one when they were only inches away) . . . but instead of folding under such bad breaks, they bounced back and won out in the third quarter.

IT was a brilliant catch by their end, Don Shelton, who snared the ball right from out of the hands of a York defender, that paid off. It was Darrah's accurate passing that enbaled Shelton to make the catch and once he had his hands on the ball, the McCaskey end, who is definitely a candidate for All-State honors, shook himself loose and went into the end zone for what was to prove to be the winning touchdown.

But this happened in the third quarter and York still had plenty of time to rebound. With Kissinger heralded as the Conference's leading passer, you knew that anything could happen. But not against this McCaskey team. These kids simply dug in their cleats and fought it out and when they felt the need of further assistance, they turned in the right direction.

And so they were able to bring this great season to a close in such a glorious fashion . . . truly on the wings of a prayer.

THEY deserve your highest commendation, for not only did they prove themselves champion football players, but . . . (and to many this is much more important) . . . they proved to be God-fearing, God-loving young Americans.

The city, as a whole, may well be proud of each of them and we're happy to lead in the salute which they and their coaches so richly deserve.

Here are the Boys Who Carried McCaskey to Football Title

New Era Photo

GAME STATISTICS

	McCaskey	York
First Downs	11	9
Rushing by	10	7
Passing	1	2
Penalty	0	0
Net yards rushing	190	159
Net yards forwards	64	36
Forwards Attempted	8	12
Forwards completed	3	4
Intercepted by	2	0
Punts number	2	3
Punts average	37	*21
Fumbles by	4	2
Ball lost, fumbles	3	2
Penalties	2	3
Yds. lost penalties	10	15

*Includes blocked kick.

Fans Parade Downtown to Hail Champs

Hail the champions . . . That's what Lancaster did last night as thousands of well-wishers turned out to honor the McCaskey football team upon its return from York, where it had defeated York 13-6 to capture the Central Penn Conference championship.

A spontaneous parade "dreamed up" by the Lancaster Junior Chamber of Commerce attracted large throngs of people along the city's streets last evening.

FROM THE moment the Red and Black gridders left the field at York they were heroes to all of Lancaster, but when they arrived at the city lines on Columbia Ave., they were really treated as such.

A police motor escort stopped the buses hauling the local gridders and the band just as it entered the city. Head coach Boyd Sponaugle and the Tornado co-captains Bernie Gross and Don Harman were hustled into a waiting convertible, as were Cliff Hartman, Jim Zwally, B. B. Herr, Don Witmer, and J. J. Neely, into other cars.

From the corner of Race and Columbia Aves., the parade started its trek through the city streets toward the school.

Led by the snappy McCaskey band, the parade moved east on King St. to the Square, north on Queen to Chestnut, where it proceeded out to Franklin and then to the school.

Here's How the Victory Was Attained

FIRST QUARTER

McCaskey's Tony Diamontoni's kickoff was taken by Banks who carried to the 30. Kissinger's pass was almost intercepted by Brown, but fell incomplete. Moore gained four, but Brown intercepted Kissinger's pass on the next play and romped from York's 41 to the eight. Diamontoni's pass fell incomplete, but Brown slashed to the three and on the next play bucked over his own right tackle for the first TD. Brown's placement was wide. McDonald took the kickoff for York on the eight and carried to the 41. Pfaltzgraff gained one and Banks two, but Banks was dropped for a five-yard loss on the next play. Zeager's punt was hauled down by Darrah as a free catch on the McCaskey 28. Darrah got four to the 32, and after Diamontoni's pass fell incomplete, Brown gained five to the 37. Darrah's punt rolled dead on the 26. Way broke through the Tornado defense for 54-yards before Darrah hauled him down on the 20. Moore moved to the 14, Erney to the 12, Moore again to the nine, Way to the seven, Banks to the five and Moore sliced over his own left tackle on a reverse for the score. Kissinger's kick was also wide. Diamontoni took Brown's kickoff on the ten and got to the 36 where he fumbled and it was recovered by York's Watkins. Moore lost one, but Way raced to the 26 for a first as the period ended.

SECOND QUARTER

N. Brown dropped Kissinger's pass in the end zone. Way gained five, but York lost the same on an offsides penalty on the next play. Moore scampered to the 15, Banks to the 13, before a Kissinger pass failed to connect. Moore then moved to the 10 and Kissinger hit Brown on the seven, but McCaskey took over. Brownie moved to the 10, and then romped 56-yards to the York 34. Darrah moved to the 32, and Gross to the 24. Diamontoni lost a yard, but Brown made five to the 20. A pass failed and Brown made it a first on the 13. Darrah was hit back on the 15 and McCaskey lost five more for being offsides. Darrah's pass eluded Saunders in the end zone, but Diamontoni hit Gross on the five and the latter had to leave the game temporarily after receiving a cut over the eye on the play. Brown gave McCaskey a first on the one and an offsides against York moved to the ½. A pitchout to Brown lost five, a mixup in the backfield two more and a pass fell incomplete. Fryberger's try for an 18-yard field goal hit the upright and York took over on the 20. Way gained five, a Kissinger pass missed and Moore was stopped cold. Then Shelton blocked Zeager's attempted punt and McCaskey took over on the 25. Diamontoni was hit trying to pass back on the 35, and his next aerial fell incomplete as the half ended with the score deadlocked 6-6.

THIRD QUARTER

Diamontoni carried the kickoff from his own six to the 36. Brown gained seven and Gross picked up six more to the 48. Brown lost one, but moved to York's 44 on the next play and then added four more to the 40. Gross was stopped cold, but Darrah got two. York was penalized five for offsides and Brown followed with runs of three and eight to the 22. Darrah's pass was grabbed by Saunders on the four. Brown lost six to the 11, and then a pitchout eluded Brown and was recovered by York's Graybill. Banks gained four, but Moore fumbled on the next play and Martin recovered for Lancaster on the 22. An offsides penalty moved the ball to the 17, and Gross carried to the 10. Darrah hit the line twice to the six, but Brown was dropped on the seven. Fryberger's second attempted field goal from the 17 was wide and York took over on the 20. Pfaltzgraff fumbled and Martin recovered on the 18. Diamontoni was hit back on the 31 trying to pass: But on the next play Darrah flipped one to Shelton who grabbed it on the eight, fought off Staub, and raced over for the score. Fryberger booted the extra point and McCaskey was out in front 13-6. McDonald carried the kickoff to the 30, Banks moved to the 35 and Way to the 36 as the period ended.

FOURTH QUARTER

Kissinger lost one and Zeager punted to Darrah on the McCaskey 28 and he returned to the 36. Brown went to the 38, but an offsides lost the Tornado five. Darrah erased that in a hurry with a romp to the York 47. Darrah again carried to the 43, and Brown broke loose for 37 yards to the six before Way bumped him out of bounds. Danley recovered Gross' fumble on the four. Banks moved to the seven and Moore to the 22. Kissinger's pass missed and Banks gained one. Kissinger hit Zeager on the 36, Staub gained to the 42, Erney to the 46, Kissinger to the 48 and Erney to the 50. Kissinger's flat pass was broken up by Darrah and his next attempt was intercepted by Harman on the McCaskey 46, and he moved back to York's 47. Brown went for two, Darrah for five and Brown for two more. Playing safe, Darrah punted and Shelton downed the ball on the three. Three sneaks by Kissinger gave York a first on the 17. A pass, Kissinger to Fleming was good to the 33. Another aerial fell incomplete and he hit Moore on the 38 as the game ended. McCaskey 13, York 6.

Mayor Gives Way to Principal In Being 1st to Hail Victors

THE MCCASKEY dressing room was a bedlam five minutes after the game ended . . . There was so much shouting that one guy couldn't be heard above another and everything that was said was lost to posterity.

Mayor Kendig C. Bare came in to congratulate the coaches and the players, but gave way this time to his father-in-law, Dr. B. B. Herr, the supervising principal at McCaskey. . . .

The boys had promised their principal that they would win this one for him and he was as happy about it as any kid on the squad.

Coaches Boyd Sponaugle, Cliff Hartman and Eddie Haller came in for their share of congratulations and all the spectators who could gain admittance helped the players whoop it up.

The only fellow who remained cool and collected was Dr. George Gerlach, the team's physician, and while all the shouting and back-slapping was going on around him, the doctor, with no assistance, calmly applied two sutures to a nasty cut which Bernie Gross suffered over his right eye.

The injury, doc said, came in the early minutes of the game, but the plucky young Gross insisted on going on. However, once the game was over, the doc lost little time reaching for his needle. Young Gross hardly blinked as the stitches were applied and the doc, despite all the handicaps, turned in a quick and neat job.

Someone got the idea that instead of removing their T shirts in the ordinary manner, it would be more fun to tear them off. And the idea spread like wildfire. So much so that the dressing room was soon littered with pieces of torn shirts.

Then the subject of eating came up. Coach Sponaugle had told the boys that there'd be no eating after breakfast, and you can appreciate what their appetites were like after such a stiff struggle.

Assistant Principal Don Witmer soon settled this question by informing them that arrangements had been made to serve them a turkey dinner at the Hotel Locust in Columbia.

Someone asked Don what would have happened had the decision been in reverse, but the assistant principal artfully dodged an answer.

When Don (Inch) Shelton caught that pass and ran for the winning touchdown, he was earning his second steak dinner. He had earned the first by blocking a York punt and the second came on the TD. Who must pay? Why coach Sponaugle, of course. He made the promise.

For a time it looked like fate was turning away from the locals. Twice Bob Fryberger tried placement kicks, but both times he missed. His first, from a tough angle, struck the goal posts, but instead of bouncing over, as they generally do, this one bounced back. In his second, he was on the 17 yard line, which left him with a 27 yard boot, a test even for the pros.

And when McCaskey missed out when it was only inches away in the second quarter, you got the uneasy feeling that maybe this wasn't just the day.

But it all turned out in our favor and the boys came bound-

—See NOTES—Page 40

All of City Hails Team for Thrilling 13-6 Win over York

by BOB HUTTER

ALL of Lancaster is today praising McCaskey's Red Tornado and well it should, because the Red and Black gridders are the champions of the Central Penn Football Conference.

Yesterday afternoon before a crowd of 10,000 (7,446 paid) at York's Small Field, the Red Tornado defeated the York Bearcats 13-6 to achieve this goal which has never before been won in the modern history of Lancaster High.

The championship, which the boys won yesterday, is the first time in at least 23 years that a Red and Black team has gained sole possession of a title.

AND THEY DID IT the hard way from the first game to the last. This year's McCaskey team was sized up by coach Boyd Sponaugle prior to the start of the season as a squad that showed plenty of spirit and desire to play football, but was lacking in weight to be considered a strong contender.

In fact, Boyd had said that he thought the boys would have accomplished a great feat if they split even in their ten games. But here was a squad that became instilled with the Sponaugle mastery and determination and just wouldn't say quit.

TODAY AS THEY take time to celebrate their accomplishments, something which they didn't bother to do during the season, they boast an overall season's record of seven wins, one tie and two setbacks—and are champs.

To point to this fellow or that boy and say that because of him this goal was reached would be impossible, for here was a group of boys that played as a team and because of that are today celebrating as a team.

If it is possible for one Lancastrian to be happier than another the nod would have to go to coach Sponaugle. He was so overwhelmed by what his boys had accomplished yesterday that he was almost speechless.

"I can't believe it," are the words that rolled from his mouth once he reached the McCaskey dressing room where all pandemonium had broken loose. "These kids are the greatest bunch of fighters I have ever seen. I told them when the season first started that I wanted only boys who wanted to play football and as everyone can see that's the kind that made up our squad. Every boy, including the reserves wanted to play and when you want something hard enough, it always seems to be reachable. These fellows sought this title and they won it, I think that tells the whole story."

WHILE THE genial McCaskey mentor passes on all the praises to his players it is quite evident that he and his assistant Cliff Hartman are more than due for their share of the glory. For it was the masterful planning of the coaches that set the stage for the Red and Black gridders to almost stop cold the passing of the brilliant Ellie Kissinger and the highly touted York running attack.

As one local follower of the Tornado was heard saying after the game, "If a play works once for the opposition they may as well scrap it because Sponaugle will come up with a plan to stop it before it works again." And that's typical of the manner in which the McCaskeys performed yesterday as well, as all season.

Shelton, Ill, But Insisted On Playing Against York

Don Shelton, McCaskey's top candidate for All-State honors, scored the winning touchdown, blocked a kick, tossed several fine blocks and played well even though he was suffering with a severe sore throat.

The Tornado ace started feeling "grippy" Wednesday evening. He insisted he was going to play and asked Dr. George Gerlach, team physician to do something about curing him in a hurry.

Doc started early Wednesday evening to administer penicillin, and the treatments continued right up to game time.

THEY WERE fooled once by the Yorkers, but try as they may, coach Eddie Waleski's charges couldn't muster up enough force to get another attack going. You could tell almost from the minute the locals stepped on the gridiron to start warming up for the game that they had designs on upsetting the Bearcats, who were picked by some to end this hotly contest race with a victory that might be as great as three touchdowns.

Larry Brown gave Kissinger his first hint that there would be no passing done against the Tornado, in the second minute of play, he grabbed an aerial on York's 41, got a good block from Don Shelton, and romped to the eight. Then when a McCaskey pass didn't work Brownie took charge. A criss-cross play which sent the fleet-footed Tornado slicing from his lefthalf post over his own right tackle was put to use and in two trys Larry covered the eight yards and McCaskey had its first score.

YORK GAVE indications that it wasn't to be counted out a few minutes later when it marched 74-yards in seven plays and tied the score at 6-6. But as far as the Sponauglemen were concerned that was it for York. The Bearcats had their brief fing of prosperity but that was it, for McCaskey held the upper hand the rest of the way.

In fact, from the early minutes of the second period on all the play was done in the York end. Only when the Bearcats kicked off to start the second half and punted a little later did McCaskey find itself having to work out of its own territory.

A CHECK BACK shows that be-

—See McCASKEY—Page 40

The Sunday News Brings You
LAST-MINUTE NEWS!
Local and World Events

SUNDAY NEWS

Read Complete Fiction Story
Sunday News Magazine
Last Page—Pink Section

LANCASTER, PA., SUNDAY, DECEMBER 14, 1952

Over $3,700,000 In New Churches Built Or Started Here In 1952

Wave Of Religious Construction Gives Lancaster County \$1¾ Million Worth Of Completed Structures, \$1½ Million More Underway; Boom To Continue

One of the greatest church-building years in history has given Lancaster County $3,700,000 worth of new church structures either completed or started in construction during 1952.

Completed new church plants total \$1¾ million. Buildings started during the year represent well over \$1½ million more. In addition, before 1953 is many months old, another three-quarters of a million dollars in church construction will be under way.

ST. JAMES' Episcopal Church is building a $175,000 addition to its parish house. Steel and brickwork are shown in view from rear of new city structure. (Sunday News Photos)

SACRED HEART'S new sanctuary, first Catholic church to be built in Lancaster City in the past 25 years, is the largest such project now underway locally, costing $425,000.

New spires pushing into the sky here represent part of a nation-wide wave of church-building which is unparalleled. "There never has been anything like it," comments a spokesman for the Bureau of Church Building and Architecture of the National Council of Churches.

In the nation as a whole, an estimated billion dollars worth of new Protestant churches are in the process of being planned in architects' offices. All three major faiths have taken part in the surge. Catholic expansion has been especially notable in the midwest and far-west areas, according to Msgr. Thomas J. McCarthy of the National Catholic Welfare Conference. Dr. Emil Lehman, assistant executive director of United Synagogues of America, told the Associated Press that "More and more building is going on all over the country."

2 Costliest Projects

Costliest of the local projects are Sacred Heart Catholic Church, which is well along on its $425,000 sanctuary, and Trinity Lutheran Church's $450,000 parish house which is to be started in spring.

But thousands of Lancaster Countians will be attending their Christmas services this year in brand new churches. Even more will worship in new Sunday School rooms.

"The growing demand for church education buildings is the greatest problem of our local congregations," says the Rev. David E. Maugans, of the United Churches of Lancaster County.

That fact is reflected in the great number of church-school projects built, begun or planned here.

In City Area

On the list of new construction finished during 1952 are such major structures as these in the Lancaster City area: Calvary Independent Church in Grand View, $300,000 (First Baptist moved into the former Calvary building and spent $48,000 on it); Grace Evangelical Congregational church school, $210,000; Otterbein EUB's annex, $135,000; Bethel Mennonite, Manor Ridge, $40,000; and St. Matthew Lutheran parsonage, $21,000.

Through hundreds of thousands of dollars have been spent in countless renovation and redecoration projects throughout the county, this Sunday News survey includes none of that — only some of the major construction work which represents actual enlargement of church plant.

In the county there were at least a dozen construction porjects completed during the year, including two complete new sanctuaries in Ephrata, Trinity Lutheran, $325,000, and Church of the Nazarene, $50,000. Still in process in Ephrata is the First EUB Church on which $143,000 had been expended up to Aug. 1.

Dedication Today

One of the new county structures, a church school annex erected by Metzler's Mennonite Church near Akron, will be dedicated today. Its cost was about $25,000.

In Manheim, Salem EUB church-school was completed at a cost of $145,000, and the Brethren in Christ added a $13,000 annex to the front of the church. At Bareville the Conestoga Church of the Brethren occupied a new church costing some $100,000.

At Florin Glossbrenner EUB finished a church-school and parsonage, half of a projected plan, at a cost of $76,000, and Cross-roads Church of the Brethren built a new structure.

Columbia's new Salome EUB Church cost $200,000. Highville EUB completed a new building, as did the New Providence Church of God. Mt. Pleasant Mennonite Sun-Church cost $200,000. Highville EUB completed a new building, as did the New Providence Church of God. Mt. Pleasant Mennonite Sunday School cost $40,000, and Georgetown Methodist built a parsonage costing about $15,000.

Many More Started

Just as impressive as the list of new structures dedicated and put into use during the past year is the number on which construction was begun. To start with those in the city area:

Except for finishing touches, the new First Church of Christ, Scientist, is ready for its dedication. Costing about $175,000, the structure represents one-third of the eventual church plan.

Steelwork is rising on the new sanctuary for St. Peter's E&R Church, to cost $210,000. Educational buildings for Covenant EUB and St. James' Episcopal are underway, costing respectively $189,960 and $175,000. Bethany Presbyterian's $60,000 project and the $58,000 annex of Community Methodist of Grand View Heights are well along.

Out in the county districts many more churches have work in progress, ranging from those which have just broken ground to others about ready for dedication services. Included are:

An addition to the Columbia First Church of God, costing $55,000, to be dedicated Jan. 11; Brownstown Ebenezer EC, $60,000; St. Stephens E&R, New Holland, $75,000 parish hall; Middle Octoraro Presbyterian Sunday School, $45,000.

New Sanctuary

Mellinger's Lutheran, near Schoeneck, is building a new church costing $100,000. The $20,000 parsonage of St. John's E&R at Denver is to be completed in June. Additions are underway also at Cedar Grove Presbyterian and Fairview Church of God.

Scores of other churches in the county are working on expansion plans which range from those no farther along than a "building fund" to others for which contracts are soon to be let.

Among those expected to get underway shortly are the following in the city area:

St. Luke's E&R, $40,000 church-school, due to start in spring; Redeemer Lutheran, $85,000 program including Sunday School wing, approved by congregation; Emmanuel Lutheran, first of three educational units, costing $75,000, fund all pledged or promised, and construction to start in spring.

Will Ask Bids

At Columbia, the First English Lutheran Church expects to let contracts within a few months for a complete new church plant costing about $75,000. Ruhl's EUB near Manheim expects to complete a new parsonage by next September. Christ Lutheran, Elizabethtown, has a $50,000 building plan. Willow Street E&R has scheduled a Sunday School building for 1953.

A beginning on its $350,000 building program is expected in 1954 by the Elizabethtown Church of the Brethren. Lancaster Church of the Brethren has an 8-to-10-year fund-raising drive before it begins its $250,000 building on Fordney Road.

Degel Israel congregation has a fund drive underway for a new synagogue.

At Lititz, the Church of the Brethren expects to be ready to put up a new educational building within 5 or 6 years, and St. Paul's Lutheran Church is raising $100,000 for a similar project, having already purchased a house across the street for Sunday School overflow classes.

Investment Soars

Many more such projects could be listed. However, those above are symptomatic of the period of church expansion in which churches find themselves, both locally and nationally. According to the National Production Authority, money invested in new religious construction rose steadily from $76 million in 1946, the first postwar year, to $452 million in 1951. This year's totals are still incomplete.

Inclusion of rooms for special purposes, such as recreation and leisure and baby-sitting, is a modern trend. Also, more of the structures are being built on simple, functional lines — especially the educational plants.

Nationally, Catholics have been opening 150 to 200 new churches a year ever since the war; Methodists have been adding two new churches a day; in five years Presbyterians have spent an estimated $60 million on $1,662 new church structures; and the trend applies all along the line.

Looking Ahead

Nixon May Seek Solon Pay Boost, Outside-Aid Code

BY THE WORLD STAFF OF THE ASSOCIATED PRESS

WASHINGTON — Vice President-elect Nixon, still burning over the way Democrats made a campaign issue of the $18,000 fund some of his California constituents raised to help out with his senatorial duties, plans to urge the new Republican Congress to either give itself more money or give official status to such outside funds.

He will be backed in this by Gen. Eisenhower.

Authority for this is a man high in the Republican party, well placed to keep track of the new administration's planning.

Coupled with the proposal is one for a code of ethics for Congress members and government officials.

Amid the uproar over the Nixon fund came disclosure that many other legislators had received such assistance. All insisted that the money came with no strings attached. Eisenhower said Nixon was "clean as a hound's tooth" in accepting aid from his own constituents.

Nixon and other members contended that their congressional income was insufficient to cover their expenses.

For the past few years senators and representatives have received $12,500 a year salary, plus a $2,500-a-year tax-exempt personal expense allowance.

The Republican informant says Nixon believes Congress should "either give its members enough money to run their offices efficiently or give official status to outside aid like the Nixon fund, with a requirement for public disclosure of the donors and how much they contribute."

(Under the Constitution Congress may not vote its members more money effective in the term in which the action is taken.)

QUARTERS ALLOWANCE

WASHINGTON (AP) — A Senate Armed Services Committee informant says there's no chance Congress will allow the law providing "quarters allowance" for dependents of enlisted men and non-commissioned officers to lapse.

The Pentagon is reported preparing an urgent request to Congress to beat the April 30 expiration date to avoid hardships.

DORMANT OPS

WASHINGTON (AP)—The Office of Price Stabilization, in line with recommendations of the DiSalle report, will simply mark time for the most part until the Republicans take over Jan. 20.

The agency will not be completely inactive, but price actions probably will be confined chiefly to minor fields.

Michael V. DiSalle, former price administrator, was recalled early this month to study controls and recommend a course. He said clearly that at least until Jan. 20 there should be no major decontrol, suspension or policy change.

HAPPY WITH DURKIN

WASHINGTON (AP)—From top to bottom, the Labor Department's 7,000 employes heaved a sigh of relief when Gen. Eisenhower picked Martin P. Durkin as his secretary of labor.

Democrat Durkin, who has resigned as head of the AFL Plumbers Union as a preliminary to taking office, is well known in the department's corridors and in the offices of most top officials.

He may reorganize the department—and undoubtedly will bring in some new people to top spots—but there's no fear he will shake it up to the limits allowed by civil service.

NEW ITALIAN LINER

GENOA, Italy (AP) — Italy's new 30,000-ton high speed trans-Atlantic liner, the Andrea Doria, will leave here Jan. 14 on her first regular trip to New York. In her final trial runs she recorded speeds up to 26.44 knots. She is expected to make the southern route crossing in eight days, compared with present runs of 9 to 11 days.

YULE EXCHANGE

OSLO, Norway (AP) — The traditional exchange of Christmas gifts between members of the U. S. Air Force in North Africa and the Norwegian air base of Gardermoen will take place at Gardermoen on Thursday. A plane from Wheelus Field in Tripoli will carry 80 cases of oranges to Norway and take back 700 Christmas trees for American families in North Africa.

German Military Type Still Survives In Eastern Zone

By TOM REEDY

BERLIN, Dec. 13 (AP) — Systems come and systems go, but the German officer goes on and on forever.

Spare, buck-toothed and dynamic, Vincenz Mueller is the new chief of staff of the Russian zone's growing Red Army.

Pleased Them All

Mueller, the professional soldier, has vaulted from the Kaisers through the Nazis to the Communists with remarkable ease. He is the one man in Germany today who has pleased royalty, nationalists, Nazis and Moscow Reds with equal success.

Today Gen. Mueller is the top operating boss of the East German Army and Navy and its eventual air force. Politicians are above him, of course, but no other soldier is. Other Nazi generals are dead, in jail or in disgrace, but not Mueller. How he managed this is a masterpiece of political nimbleness learned through many years of standing on the brink of intrigue.

The Russians think Mueller's allegiance lies with them. For the moment they undoubtedly are right, but a rundown of his life makes it clear Mueller is a man who knows how the wind is blowing and he blows with it.

Great Confusion

Wrapped up in his 5-foot-8 frame, and his high intellectual forehead, enhanced by horn-rimmed glasses and a piercing glare, is a magnificent assortment of lifetime confusions.

Mueller's Catholic background and his current fealty to the Communist state is a paradox in itself. Born in Bavaria 58 years ago, young Vincenz grew up in a Bavarian monastery. Even today he has an austere, monastic outlook on most things.

At voting age, he became an officer in the Kaiser's World War I army with a bent toward engineering. After the collapse of the empire, Mueller managed to wrangle a spot on the general staff of the Reichswehr, the organization of 100,000 men which Field Marshal Von Seeckt secretly built into the solid nucleus for Hitler's rampaging armies two decades later.

Faith In Comeback

Under Von Seeckt, Mueller was exposed to the philosophy of the German officer's eventual "comeback" and he must have learned it well. The stormy 1930s found Mueller serving as adjutant for Gen. Kurt von Schleicher, whose efforts to organize the government met with disaster. The Hitler purge, which cost Schleicher his life, slid past young Maj. Mueller as though he wasn't there.

Instead of being branded by association with Schleicher, Mueller actually won his way into Nazi circles. By the time the second world war broke, he had risen to chief of staff of the 17th Army. Under the fuehrer's system, this would have been impossible unless Mueller had proven his loyalty to the Hitler regime.

Disaster struck the little general, now a three-star, when he took the German Eighth Army deep into the Soviet Union in 1942 and Stalingrad turned the tide in the Russians' favor.

Nazi generals and officers fell to the Soviet scythe. But Mueller bounced again. He quickly joked forces with the Kremlin's "Free German Committee" headed by the exiled Communist politicians Wilhelm Pieck, Walter Ulbricht and Wilhelm Zaisser. Mueller satisfied all that he had been converted to communism and he was released to the Soviet zone of Germany to carry the banner soon after the war ended.

He's An Organizer

Mueller's first task for the Reds was to organize the National Democratic party, consisting of former Nazis who professed a new-found allegiance to Moscow. As the political secretay and deputy chairman, he was and is the real boss of this outfit.

The little general extended his work two years ago with a trip to West Germany in which he tried to drum up the support of former officers in the West for the Eastern "peace campaign." The drive fell flat but Mueller at least convinced his Red bosses that he was reliable. Out of that came his elevation to high councils in the organization of the East German armed forces and eventually his selection as chief of staff.

The choice of Mueller was almost inevitable. He is the one trained, who seems to have completely adopted the Russian concept.

Seen Playing Game

Some Germans think Mueller is playing for bigger game than even his present high post. They believe he is counting on the day, if it comes, when the Socialist unity (Communist) party may lose favor with the Kremlin and he can promote his own NDP to the top hole. That would make him the real boss of the East Zone. People who know him say Mueller can be, and probably is, just that ambitious.

If the Pieck-Ulbricht team ever suspects that, however, the little general may stub his toe for the first time. The way the Reds do things, that would be the last time too.

The Sunday News Brings You
LAST-MINUTE NEWS!
Local and World Events

SUNDAY NEWS

Read Complete Fiction Story
Sunday News Magazine
Last Page—Pink Section

LANCASTER, PA., SUNDAY, JANUARY 4, 1953

More Parking Space Opening Up For '53, But It's Still Problem

4 Major Midtown Lancaster Projects To Add 200 Off-Street Spaces, All Within 3 Blocks of Penn Square

Lancaster City is carrying its downtown parking headache into the new year, but at least a partial remedy is in sight.

The relief is seen in four major but individual projects which will add 200 or more new off-street parking spaces within a three-block radius of Penn Square. Present indications are that all four projects will be completed before the city hails another new year.

One of the announced projects is conversion of the city-owned Southern Market House into a parking garage. Tentative layouts show the building could hold at least 65 cars without constructing additional stories.

The conversion will be made "early this year," Mayor Kendig C. Bare told the Sunday News this past week. Asked if he could name a specific month for the conversion, the mayor pointed out that "That's what we have been trying to do for two years." The building was purchased by the city in 1950 for that purpose.

To Demolish Buildings

Another 65 cars will be accommodated in a parking lot to be located on Chestnut St., opposite the postoffice, according to plans made known this past week by Col. J. Hale Steinman and John F. Steinman, who represent owners of the properties involved. Demolition of buildings located on the site is scheduled to begin shortly after May 1.

Less than two blocks from this site, another parking lot for some 45 cars is scheduled for completion this year. The lot will be located on Orange St. with frontage on both Prince and Water Sts. The Atlantic Refining Company plans to build the lot when it replaces the company service station, presently located on part of the land, with a new one.

No date has been set for the project to begin, a spokesman at the company's regional office in Reading told the Sunday News, but original plans call for completion in 1953.

It was further learned that the Atlantic company stepped up its building program for the location by at least a year when informed of Lancaster's need for additional off-street parking space in the central area. First announcement of the project was made through the off-street parking committee of the Lancaster Chamber of Commerce following a door-to-door survey.

Some of the buildings on the location, including a corner fruit market, have already been vacated. An apartment building at the rear of the gasoline service station is still tenanted, however. Plans call for demolition of the buildings.

Plan 24-Car Lot

Most immediate relief is seen in a 24-car lot scheduled for completion within 30 to 60 days. It will be located in the first block of Beaver St., at the rear of 38 S. Queen St., and adjacent to a present parking lot of about the same size, it was revealed.

Results of a C-of-C survey, published in Oct. 1951, showed 2,233 off-street parking spaces available in the central area, but only 1,554 of them open to the public for short-time parking. Some spaces are for strictly private or customer-only use, while others were limited to all-day or all-night parking.

Last year saw less than 50 new off-street parking spaces made available downtown, a spot survey shows. Construction was begun on another lot for about 20 cars, however. It is located in the 200 block of N. Water St., at the rear of the fire-gutted old Maennerchor building.

A 10-car lot located on Howard Ave., well outside the Penn Square area and not included in the above estimate, was built last year and is now reportedly doing a fair business. The owner complained to the city of no customers shortly after opening the lot to "help ease the parking problem," but has since withdrawn his complaint.

Another outlying parking lot, but one which is certain to see much use, opened officially only yesterday at Lancaster General Hospital. Located near the hospital main entrance on Duke St., it has a capacity of about 100 cars. It is open free of charge to all persons having business in the hospital, is certain to relieve much of the parking congestion on Lime, Duke and Frederick Sts., which have previously borne much of the hospital visitor traffic.

In addition to downtown parking lots and garages, Lancaster presently has 908 street curb spaces for the short-time parker which are controlled by parking meters, according to Robert M. Chryst, city traffic engineer. Of these, 23 are set for 12-minute limits (at Penn Square and in front of the postoffice); 78 for 30 minutes; 397 for one hour, and 410 for two hours, he explained.

Present thinking of the city on conversion of the Southern Market House for parking calls for leasing the property to a private operator, according to Mayor Bare. The city neither intends to go into the parking business nor to delegate such power to an authority, he indicated. In this way the city would retain close control over the operation and at the same time limit the city's liability, he explained.

Major hold-up on the conversion has been the preparation of the Central Market House for the switch-over. Southern Market House stand-holders will be invited to do business in the latter market when the conversion gets underway. At present, Southern Market stand-holders have only short-term leases with the city. Many of them have objected strongly to the planned change.

Plan Extra Days

Under the plan, Central Market will keep its regular Tuesday and Friday hours. Stand-holders from the closed Southern Market would take over Central Market on Saturdays, and possibly on Wednesdays.

How to arrange for common use of stall equipment in Central Market is yet to be ironed out. Many of the installations, such as meat display cases, are of a permanent nature and privately owned, which gives rise to the possibility that the city may see fit to provide common stalls for all market merchants. The city has drawn up new plans for the market for a stall distribution study, the mayor said.

A new lighting system has been installed at Central and the heating plant modernized in preparation for the switch-over. Commissioner John E. Spidle, director of parks and public property, said that in addition to these improvements, inside painting is planned.

Generally, the Southern Market building will hold more cars if the operator hires attendants. If customers are left to park their own cars, all indications are they would take up more room than necessary and thereby cut down the number of cars which could be accomodating. Mayor Bare says that the idea of installing parking meters in the market has been ruled out.

More Cars, Trucks

In spite of these obstacles, the parking picture in Lancaster seems bright this year. This in face of the fact that the number of cars and trucks is on the increase. Latest figures show 25,626 vehicles registered in the city alone in 1951, and all predictions are that the number will continue to spiral. There were only 18,197 vehicles registered here in 1940.

Traffic Engineer Chryst says he hopes a planned survey of Lancaster traffic to be made jointly with state engineers will turn up some answers. The state has given no indication as to when it will be able to send men to help with the survey, however, he adds.

He says he has followed closely developments of the parking ban in Philadelphia, the push-button parking system in use in the State of Washington, multi-story and underground parking garages employing ramps, and the Park-and-Shop system used in Allentown — all with an eye to adapting them to Lancaster's traffic problems.

Merchants Cooperate

The Park-and-Shop plan, in which merchants cooperate to provide cheap, nearby parking for patrons, was brought into sharp focus here during the Chamber of Commerce's intensive study of the city's problems. The Chamber even acquired the right to use the patented name, but not enough support for the plan was mustered here.

Another hot city traffic issue which went "down the drain," at least temporarily, was a proposal to make N. Prince St. a one-way traffic artery south. It was beaten down by well-organized opposition.

Now, one spokesman close to the city's commerce says, the operators of businesses on N. Prince St., are 100 per cent for such a move and he would like to see it revived.

Whether this plan is again brought up for consideration, only time will tell, but it appears certain that Lancaster's traffic problems will be brought increasingly into focus as the year wears on.

PUSH-BUTTON system lifts cars for "pigeon-hole" parking.

SOME SNAGS REMAIN, but Lancastrians should be able to park in city-owned Southern Market House (above) before the year is out. Mayor Kendig C. Bare said his closest estimate as to when the market will be converted for public parking is "early this year." The market was purchased by the city for that purpose two years ago. It can accommodate some 65 cars on its ground floor, with the possibility of adding space by building upward, as shown in inset above. This open-air multi-story garage is located in Philadelphia.

SELF-CONTAINED PARKING for shoppers is being built into many new shopping centers, like this one in suburban New York. Lancaster opened less than 50 new off-street parking spaces in 1951, plans some 200 this year. System shown above has been studied here.

Sandburg Wants Poetry Warmer; Definite Action

Associated Press Arts Editor

NEW YORK, Jan. 3 (AP) — "I'd like to see more love of people expressed in modern poetry," says Carl Sandburg.

He stopped here a short time before going to Chicago and Galesburg, Ill., for gala celebations of his 75th birthday next Tuesday.

"All this metaphysical junk that gets printed today!" The very idea of it brings a scornful glance to the bright eye of this most unmetaphysical poet, author of "Chicago Poems" and "Corn huskers," who eloquently apostrophized the "Hog Butcher for the World," and who sang "I am the people—the mob—the crowd—the mass."

New Book Out

His birthday will be observed, too, with the publication of another book, "Always the Young Strangers," the memoirs of his rich Midwest childhood.

"For years I carried this book around in my head," he says. "I've talked off most of it to friends." To him it reads, as it will to others, "kind of like a first book; I've had the same feeling as with 'Chicago Poems.' "

That volume appeared in 1915. And in those years and after, it is true, as he recalls, that "we had arguments, we had fights," but there was "a camaraderie, a fraternization" that he misses now.

However much of the world has changed, he looks pretty much as he used to when he and his guitar were acquiring a reputation with a repertoire of folk songs and Sandburg songs on college campuses. Thousands must have seen and heard the troubadour then, and he still travels some.

His face, the hard keen face of a fighter, is furrowed, to be sure, and his hair is snow white. It curls down on both sides across his forehead, framing it, and almost touches the still dark eyebrows.

When I saw him at his publishers he wore a dark blue shirt, a lighter blue-striped tie and glasses. He had a wine-red scarf wrapped a couple of times around his neck, which had been stiff, and he was smoking pieces of cigars.

It isn't that he is economical like his father who, he remembers, used to make a cigar last from one payday to the next. He figures he gets less nicotine if he cuts one up in several pieces and lights up one at a time.

He has been poet and novelist, newsman on a regular beat and on assignments, reviewer, author of children's stories, biographer and autobiographer, hobo, guitarist, lecturer.

He's getting to be a collector of gold medals: from the American Academy of Arts and Letters last year and from the Poetry Society of America this month. When it is pointed out that there are not many honors available to writers which haven't been conferred on him, he answers;

"All I really want is to be alive, and in health, to stay out of jail, to eat and sleep, and to get what I write printed."

I think he'd also like to see a slightly different cast to contemporary writing. He likes a book to "leave you loving people," gives as an example Olive Schreiner's "The Story of an African Farm," claims "Tom Wolfe had the thing so lacking now."

"A clean, clear-cut statement is out of order in a book now," he charges. "This marks the removal of the poet from the people. And just now in the world battle with totalitarianism it is not nice to find that the poets are not speaking plainly for democracy."

Crippled Children's Society Meets Mon.

Herbert J. Borchert will speak on "Who's Handicapped?" at the annual meeting of the Lancaster County Society for Crippled Children and Adults tomorrow at noon at the Hotel Brunswick.

Borchert, now in the feed milling business at Hegin, Pa., is former executive director of the Montana Society for Crippled Children.

Walter C. Miller, president of the Lancaster County Society, will conduct the meeting. Board members and officers will be elected, and annual reports presented.

DOG LICENSES ON SALE

The County Treasurers office in the courthouse annex announced yesterday that 1953 dog licenses are on sale.

The deadline to get them is Jan. 15.

Looking Ahead

U. S. Import Curb Law May Bring Counter Measures

BY THE WORLD STAFF OF THE ASSOCIATED PRESS

WASHINGTON—Look for nations affected by the new U. S. restrictions on imports of dried milk products under a legal requirement called thoroughly objectionable by President Truman to strike back with curbs on U. S. farm products.

The Agriculture Department set quotas this past week on imports of dried milk, cream and buttermilk for the first nine months of this year. The action was taken, however, under the Defense Production Act, which expires June 30. Whether this law will be renewed under the Eisenhower administration remains to be seen.

Although the amount involved is comparatively small — such imports amounted to only about eight million dollars' worth the first nine months of 1952—it is feared that foreign reaction will be much the same as that which followed the imposition of cheese quotas in 1951.

The Netherlands restricted imports of American wheat after the cheese deal, and Denmark, Canada, Australia and New Zealand have protested.

One official, basing his guess on the hullabaloo over cheese, commented: "We expect a roar out of all proportion to the real economic harm done."

One fear is that many foreign governments, not those of the dried milk countries alone, will take the new quota as an indication of broader U. S. policy.

EWING'S PLANS

WASHINGTON (AP)—Word from Security Administrator Oscar Ewing, now on a speech tour of the Far East, is that he will return by Jan. 15 to make an accounting of expenses of the trip as asked by Comptroller General Lindsay C. Warren.

Ewing has said his resignation will go to President-elect Eisenhower on Jan. 20, when he is to be succeeded by Mrs. Oveta Culp Hobby. After that, Ewing has told friends, he intends to work on a book—a biography of President James K. Polk.

He says he does not plan to resume the New York law practice he left to enter government.

TOKYO TAKE-OFFS

WASHINGTON (AP)—Officials of Japan Air Lines Company have arrived in this country to buy planes with which they hope to open a Japan-Hawaii-San Francisco route in March or April.

Japan's first postwar International aviation venture, it will use the American planes — and American pilots — until they can be replaced by Japanese craft and men.

The airline officials say they also hope to get going soon on Japan-London and Japan-South America services.

SEA FOOD

WASHINGTON (AP)—The United Nations Educational, Scientific and Cultural Organization (UNESCO) plans to begin studies this year or next to see if the world's food supply can be increased from the sea.

Tamon Maeda, chief Japanese delegate to UNESCO, said on a visit here he believes his own nation, The Philippines, New Zealand and other "ocean countries" would benefit from the studies.

FAR EAST FUTURE

WASHINGTON (AP)—U. S. business executives and government officials will meet here Jan. 14-15 to consider America's policy toward Japan, which those arranging the conference say "will determine in large measure the future of the Far East and possibly of the entire free world."

The international affairs division of the graduate school of Johns Hopkins University, Baltimore, is sponsoring the conference.

WANT HOLY LAND TOURISTS

JERUSALEM, Jordan Section (AP)—Jordan wants to build a big tourist business in her section of the Holy Land. The government has set aside $150,000 to restore historic sites, improve roads and erect new buildings. The government also has asked the U. S. State Department for technical assistance in preparing publicity.

Picture Story of High Points in Sports Dinner Here

Ken Kreider presents Carl Yoder with award. Senator Duff watches. Bobby Shantz with award. Leon Duckworth accepts. New Era Photos

Over 450 Fans Attend Banquet Here Honoring National, Local Sports Figures

by John Finnegan

Over 450 fans last night sat in on one of the finest sports affairs ever held in this city.

The occasion was the Seventh Annual Sportswriters and Broadcasters fete at the Hotel Brunswick, highlighted by the appearance of the most imposing array of celebrities ever to appear here at one time.

To say the affair was a huge success would be an understatement. For from the time toastmaster George Kirchner presented Mayor Kendig C. Bare for the welcoming address until Senator James H. Duff capped the proceedings with a stirring talk some three hours later, the audience was kept in various stages of high good humor or held spellbound by the distinguished guests.

HIGHLIGHT OF the banquet, from a local standpoint, was the naming of Leon S. Duckworth as the recipient of the annual award presented by the 'Scribes and 'Casters for outstanding contributions to sports.

The selection was kept a top secret until Harold J. Eager, Intell sports editor, made the presentation. The choice proved to be a popular one among all those present. The big, affable "Ducky", familiar to nearly all Lancaster sportsmen, merited the award in the opinion of the Association members for his unselfish and tireless efforts in nearly all fields of sports endeavor for the past 30 years.

Sharing the spotlight with Duckworth was young Carl Yoder, F and M's All-American soccer star who was honored for his outstanding performances during the past season. Ken Kreider of WGAL made the presentation.

ALSO HONORED by the association were two of the famous sports personalities present. Dave Brandt, sports director of WGAL-TV presented little Bobby Shantz of the Philadelphia A's with an award honoring him as Pennsylvania's outstanding baseball player.

Another award went to Jim Trimble, Pro Football Coach of the Year, and Philadelphia Eagles mentor, and was presented by John Rineman, sports director of WLAN.

As the toastmaster called upon those present to take a bow or deliver a talk to the gathering, there may have been a suspicion that he was picking names at random from Who's Who.

Senator Duff, Whitey Kurowski, new manager of the Roses and ex-Cardinal star, Jim Trimble, of the Philadelphia Eagles, the Pro Football Coach of the Year, Ken Loeffler, coach of LaSalle's National Invitation Basketball Champions of 1951-52; Charley (Red) Ruffing, one of the all-time New York Yankee greats; Bobby Shantz, the pint sized Philadelphia A's portside mound sensation; Kenny Raffensberger, ace left of the Cincinnati Reds; and Carl Voss, referee-in-chief of the National and American Hockey Leagues, were some of the celebrities.

THEN THERE were Cy Perkins, Phil's coach and former backstopping great for the A's; Billy Darnell, popular wrestling star, Moe Henderson, coach of the Hershey Bears; Mike McNally, head of the Cleveland Indian farm system; Gerald P. Nugent, president of the Inter State League; Ed Hogan, Phila. Eagles publicity director; and Ed Pollock, sports editor of the Philadelphia Evening Bulletin.

Also on the speakers platform was Lancaster's Yoder, who made a big hit and impressed everyone present with his modesty in accepting his award. Yoder credited his teammates and coaches for his achievements.

Lena Blackburn, former Roses manager, Carl N. Netscher, the association president, who was also presented with a surprise award for his efforts in behalf of the banquet and Mayor Bare completed the personalities on the speaker's platform.

THE FANS were kept in a hilarious mood throughout the greater portion of the evening by the individual efforts of the majority of those mentioned. To name anyone as outstanding would be next to impossible. Whitey Kurowski, proved to be an adept after dinner speaker, and had the gathering rolling in the aisles with some amusing baseball anecdotes. Jim Trimble and Ken Loeffler pitched in with their share of the jokes, as did Gerald Nugent and Senator Duff.

It was interesting to note the presence of two famous "Big Reds" on the platform, Ruffing and Duff.

RUFFING WON the crowd over immediately with his easy going, matter of fact presentation, which sparkled with humor. But while the gum chewing former Yankee great wowed the crowd with his stories, the other "Big Red", Senator Duff, sobered the gathering with an ominous warning that "the period in which we are living is without a doubt the most critical in our history," and pointed out the terrifying proportions of the atomic bomb.

It seemed a fitting close to the banquet that the Senator should inject this note, for it seemed as if the entire sports loving audience then realized just how great this Country of ours is, with it's Shantzes, Ruffings, and Trimbles.

Big Game Tonight
Teachers-E-Town Clash

It's Millersville State Teachers vs. Elizabethtown College in the local collegiate basketball game of the week tonight at E-town at 8:30.

This game has always created local interest because it pits two interesting clubs against each other in a healthy tiff, crowded with tradition and spirit.

Over the past three campaigns, Max Bishop's Marauders have slipped into a 5-1 lead in the series.

THIS YEAR finds Millersville with a 5-4 over-all record, against E-town's 3-5 mark. Millersville has won from Lincoln, East Stroudsburg, Shippensburg, Kutztown and Lock Haven, while losses have been to St. Joseph's, LaSalle, Villanova and West Chester STC.

Joe Dodd's Blue Jays have won from Lincoln, Lycoming and King's, while losses have been to Lebanon Valley, West Chester STC, Gettysburg, Juniata, and Indiantown Gap.

THE ONLY yardstick for measurement on the two clubs can be taken off the Lincoln and West Chester games. Both clubs played these two opponents. Millersville beat Lincoln, 72-44, while E-town bumped the same outfit, 58-52. Both lost to West Chester STC, Elizabethtown by a 65-48 count, while Millersville dropped an 85-79 overtime fray to the Golden Rams.

Football Cards Seek 8th Coach

CHICAGO (AP) — The Chicago Cardinals were on the prowl for a new head football coach today—again.

After one year of service, Joe Kuharich was dismissed yesterday by general director Walter Wolfner.

Kuharich, hired in 1952 after guiding the University of San Francisco through an undefeated 1951 campaign, compiled a 4-8 record for the Cards. They ended the season in a tie for last place in the Eastern Division of the National Football League.

THE CARDINALS, striving to reach championship status, have been directed by seven head coaches in four years.

The firing of Kuharich stemmed from Wolfner's insistence that he release two of his assistants, Bill Daddio and Mike Nixon. Kuharich said he wouldn't stay if they had to go.

Indians Sign 4, 20 Now in Fold

CLEVELAND (AP)—The Indians put away the signed contracts of pitcher Bob Hooper and outfielders Jim Friedley, Herbie Adams and Al Smith today. Now they have 20 players in the fold, with 25 to go.

Hooper is the pitcher got last season in a trade from the Athletics for Dick Rozek, and Adams is a former Chicago White Soxer.

Friedley started with the Indians last season, then was sent to Indianapolis.

SPORTS

Roses Contact Piedmont League as Inter State Survival Grows Dimmer

by Bob Hutter

THE existence of the Inter State Baseball League doesn't look too bright for the coming season, but Frank Spair, general manager of the Red Roses, apparently isn't going to let any stones unturned in his fight to keep organized baseball in Lancaster.

Following the session of League officials yesterday, which left the question of whether or not there will be an Inter State League still unanswered, Spair announced that he had been in contact, with officials of the Piedmont League, also a Class B circuit.

"I haven't made any definite application for entry," Spair said, "but I have been working on the possibility of joining that league should our Inter State League fail to exist."

ONLY YESTERDAY it was learned that York and Hagerstown, also members of the Inter State League, had made the same move in "feeling out" the Piedmont League.

At present the Piedmont circuit is comprised of six teams, but from all reports is in favor of increasing the loop to eight teams.

But before local baseball fans become all excited about joining another league there is still a slight chance of the Inter State loop continuing.

THE SAME problem which confronted president Gerald Nugent and the loop officials several months ago still faces the group . . . that of lining up a sixth team.

Five members of the circuit said yesterday they were ready to go, including Lancaster, York, Hagerstown, Sunbury and Salisbury.

Several cities were represented in yesterday's session, all of which are interested in becoming the sixth member of the league. But none of the three interested groups were at the moment ready to operate.

JOHNSTOWN SEEMS to be the most logical choice and in order to give the representatives from the Pennsylvania city more time to work out their problems, yesterday's meeting was adjourned until Monday, when the group will meet in York.

Johnstown was represented at the meeting by Leon Abravanel and Robert Markel and it was primarily at their request that yesterday's session was adjourned.

THEY TOLD Nugent they wanted more time to discuss the situation and work on the possibility of lining up a working agreement with a Major League team. The Big League tie-up appears at the moment to be the big obstacle confronting the Johnstown group.

Nugent admitted that the league has just about given up hopes on Eddie Kirschner. It was Kirschner who was given the Wilmington franchise last autumn and transferred it to Hazleton.

Earlier this week Kirschner informed Nugent he was considering moving the franchise to Allentown since there were indications the Hazleton ball park would not be available for the entire 1953 season.

Kirschner wasn't present at yesterday's meeting but Nugent said Kirschner told him by phone that he was going to meet in New York this week with William Walsingham, vice president of the St. Louis Cardinals, to discuss rental of the Allentown park. The Cards own the park there.

Nugent, however, made it plain that the league wasn't counting on Kirschner anymore.

Representatives from Cambridge and Frederick, Md., were also present yesterday but Nugent said neither club could be considered as ready or available for entry in the league this season.

WEATHER
(U. S. Weather Bureau)
Eastern Pennsylvania — Some Cloudiness And A Little Warmer Saturday With High In The Upper 40's. Sunday Considerable Cloudiness And Somewhat Colder In The Afternoon.

Intelligencer Journal.

The Leading Newspaper in the Garden Spot of America. Home Owned for Home Folks Since 1794

THE INTELL INDEX

159th Year.—No. 208. | Official United States Census Figures Lancaster Metropolitan Area Population 234,717 | LANCASTER, PA., SATURDAY MORNING, FEBRUARY 14, 1953. | CITY | EIGHTEEN PAGES. | 30c PER WEEK—5c Per Copy

ARMED BANDIT STICKS-UP DRUG STORE

Fine Censorship Order Begins To Take Effect

NEWSMEN IN CAPITAL RAP RESTRICTIONS

AP Newsman Denied Access To Material For School Health Story

HARRISBURG, Feb. 13 (AP) — The Pennsylvania Legislative Correspondents Association today called for an end of restraints at all levels of government "in the free flow of public information."

It asked Gov. John S. Fine and the Legislature to provide ready access to news to which the public is entitled.

The association, oldest of its kind in the nation, took the action at a special meeting called to discuss Fine's order that all except "purely routine" news releases on state government activities must first be cleared by his office.

"It is evident that state officials in general now construe the Governor's order as a form of censorship," the association said in a resolution.

VOLUME REDUCED

The resolution was adopted as the volume of departmental news releases was reduced to a trickle. The Governor's news clearance order also resulted in an Associated Press newsman being denied immediate access to school health examination statistics.

Fine, woh originally said the order was issued to insure conformity with administration policy, later contended that no censorship was involved. He said it was intended to prevent underlings from pinning the administration label on "pet legislation."

The legislative writers, representing all three news services and most of the metropolitan newspapers in Pennsylvania, joined a growing list of organizations which have questioned the Fine order.

Others include the Pennsylvania Newspapers Publishers Association, Pennsylvania Society

Turn To Page 5 For More Of CENSORSHIP

"We Lead All The Rest"
FARM CORNER
By WILLIAM R. SCHULTZ

40 P.C. Of County Farmers Seeking Federal ACP Aid

Four out of every 10 Lancaster County farms have made application for federal funds or materials to carry out approved conservation practices during the coming year.

Cash payments and materials totaling $140,818 will be distributed to 8,120 Garden Spot farm owners who have enrolled in the 1953 Agricultural Conservation Program, Landis G. Becker, Production and Marketing Administration chairman here said yesterday.

Seventy per cent of this amount will go to farmers carrying out "limited" conservation practices, Becker explained. These include such practices as applying limestone, phosphate materials, potash, or establishing ladino pastures, and seeding ryegrass as a winter cover crop.

The remaining 30 per cent of the

Turn To Page 5 For More Of FARM CORNER

Weather Calendar

COMPARATIVE TEMPERATURES

Station	High	Low
Water Works	43	32
Ephrata	44	31
Last Year (Ephrata)	38	19
Official High for Year Jan. 24		63
Official Low for Year Feb. 2		13
Character of Day		Partly Cloudy

WINDS
Direction WNW — Avg. Velocity 20 mph

HUMIDITY
8 a. m. 68% 11 a. m. 63% 2 p. m. 67%
5 p. m. 71% 8 p. m. 73%
Average Humidity 68%

SUN
Rises 6:59 a. m. — Sets 5:38 p. m.

MOON
Rises, 6:40 p. m.

STARS
Morning—Saturn
Evening—Venus, Mars, Jupiter

NEARBY FORECASTS
(U. S. Weather Bureau)

Maryland—Mostly sunny and somewhat warmer Saturday. High 48 to 52. Sunday increasing cloudiness, probably followed by rain at night.

Southern New Jersey and Delaware — Mostly sunny and a little warmer Saturday. High 46 to 50. Sunday increasing cloudiness and turning a little cooler in the afternoon.

Lower Potomac and Chesapeake Bay — Southwesterly winds 15 to 25 miles per hour Saturday. Fair weather and good visibility.

EXTENDED FORECAST
(U. S. Weather Bureau)

For the period, Saturday through Wednesday, for Eastern Pennsylvania, New Jersey, Delaware, Maryland — Temperatures will average three to five degrees above normal. Rising temperatures Saturday and Sunday; colder Monday and warmer again toward the end of the period. Rain likely Sunday and again about Wednesday.

'Sir Valentine' Crowned At Manheim Twp. High

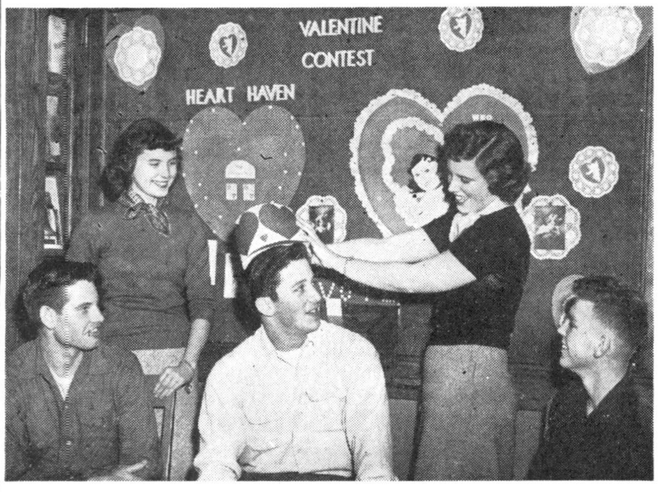

Manheim Township High School's "Sir Valentine," in the person of Scott Bomberger, (center), is crowned by his "campaign manager," Shirley Reynolds, as the Valentine contest held at the school for the benefit of Heart Haven ended yesterday afternoon. At left, seated, is Chris Kunzler, and at right, seated, is Bill McCoy, the two runners-up in the contest. At left, standing, is Emma Sigafoos, president of the Senior Library Service Club, who made the decorations for the contest, shown in the background.

SCOTT BOMBERGER "SIR VALENTINE" AT MANHEIM TWP.

School's Unique Contest Netted $92.69 For Lancaster's Heart Haven

Scott Bomberger, seventeen, a member of the senior class at Manheim Township High School, was chosen "Sir Valentine" by his schoolmates yesterday in a unique project to raise funds for Heart Haven. The contest netted $92.69.

Bomberger, is the son of Dr. and Mrs. Paul E. Bomberger, 1262 Lititz Pike.

TWO RUNNERS-UP

Two runners-up also were named: Chris Kunzler, seventeen, a member of the junior class, son of Mr. and Mrs. Christ C. Kunzler, Bareville R1, and Bill McCoy, fourteen, a freshman, son of Mr. and Mrs. Merton W. McCoy, Bareville R1.

Students balloted during the past two days for their candidate for "Sir Valentine" by placing a coin — usually a penny — in a large heart-shaped envelope posted on the Library bulletin board. They could vote as many times as they wanted, provided they paid every time. Soon the envelope became so bulging that an ordinary bucket was called into play, and was three quarters full of pen-

Turn To Page 5 For More Of VALENTINE

ADLAI HOPES TO GO TO KOREA IN MARCH

NEW YORK, Feb. 13 (AP)—Adlai E. Stevenson, the defeated Democratic candidate for president, announced tonight he hopes to visit Korea in March.

He leaves March 2 on air and sea voyage around the world.

"I am traveling as a private citizen for my own self-education," Stevenson said in a statement issued by the Democratic National Committee.

High Court Voids Columbia Athletic Field Land Sale

The State Supreme Court ruled yesterday that the school district of Columbia borough could not sell a part of a tract of land given to the school district to be used for the youth of the community.

Justice Allen M. Stearne in an opinion delivered at Philadelphia upheld the order of the Lancaster County Orphans' Court which set aside the sale of part of Glatfelter Memorial Field. The board had approved sale of the land for $20,000 to the Columbia Malleable Castings Co., which has a plant adjoining the athletic field.

"The school district, under a mistaken view that it owned the land, agreed to sell a portion of the land. This is a community project and not a public school auxiliary," the Supreme Court ruled.

"If the school district is unable or unwilling to administer further the trust as it has been created it should resign or be removed and a new trustee appointed in its place and stead. If, however, it should subsequently appear that the community itself is unwilling or unable to meet the necessary expenses and charges of maintenance and administration, and in consequence the purposes of the trust cannot be carried out, then at an appropriate time and upon adequate proof, the whole project may be sold."

The field was deeded in trust to

Turn To Page 5 For More Of OPINION

RHODA LIPINS LEAVES LEBANON HOSPITAL

Rhoda Lipins, ten-year-old Brooklyn, N. Y., girl orphaned Wednesday night when an automobile crash killed her parents and another couple in an accident on the Pennsylvania Turnpike, near Lebanon, was discharged from the Good Samaritan Hospital, Lebanon, yesterday.

Relatives drove her to Lancaster, where she was placed on a train for New York.

Rhoda left the hospital not knowing that her parents had been killed. When she asked for them, attendants said, she was told that they were injured in the accident also.

GOP Moves To Beat Morse In Ore.; Solon Hits Businessmen's Survey

WASHINGTON, Feb. 13 (AP)—Sen. Morse (Ind-Ore) told the Senate today liberals must stop talking about a "honeymoon" with the Eisenhower administration.

He declared the "issue has been joined" already, describing it as "a fight between liberals that seek to protect the American people and reactionaries who seek to exploit the American people for the selfish interests of a few."

Paraphrasing Winston Churchill's famous wartime stand, Morse said the fight must be conducted "in the streets, in the alleyways and on the housetops" if the liberals are to succeed.

55 APPOINTMENTS

He explained his comments were inspired by the appointment of 55 business executives to make a survey of the operations of the Mutual Security Agency abroad. The

Turn To Page 5 For More Of GOP

SALEM, Ore., Feb. 13 (AP)—A bill designed to force Sen. Wayne Morse to run as a Republican when he comes up for re-election in 1956, was introduced in the Oregon Legislature today.

Republican party leaders are known to feel that they can beat Morse in a Republican primary, but might have trouble unseating him if he runs as an independent. He bolted the Republican party last fall and since has identified himself as an independent.

SOME DOUBT

There was some question whether the bill was constitutional. But it went before the Legislature with the names of 25 of the 60 representatives and nine of the 30 senators as co-sponsors with State Sen. John P. Hounsell, Republican, its author.

The bill says that a person elect-

Turn To Page 5 For More Of MORSE

DULLES SAYS U.S. NOT MAKING BLOCKADE PLAN

Reportedly Tells Solons He Will Consult Congress Allies On Moves

WASHINGTON, Feb. 13 (AP) — Secretary of State Dulles reportedly promised senators today that the Eisenhower administration will consult Congress and U. S. Allies before undertaking any drastic new moves in the Far East.

A curtain of secrecy around Dulles' testimony, imposed at his request, developed quick holes as members of a Senate foreign relations subcommittee gave newsmen their impressions of what he said.

Committee members said Dulles informed them the administration is not planning any action now toward a blockade of Red China.

TO HEAR VAN FLEET

Across the Capitol, Chairman Short (R-Mo) of the House Armed Services Committee announced that Gen. James A. Van Fleet, retiring commander of the U. S. Eighth Army in Korea, will testify March 4 on his views on the Korean War.

Short said he hopes the public will be able to hear at least part of Van Fleet's testimony "because the public has a right to know."

Van Fleet stirred widespread interest earlier this week with a statement that an all-out Allied offensive in Korea now could defeat the Communists.

Congress members said Van Fleet's prediction is contrary to what they have been told by the Pentagon high command.

FOR UNIFIED ACTION

Informants who heard Dulles testify said they understood the secretary of state plans to keep American Allies fully informed and to consult them in the hope of gaining unified action in any further moves in the critical Far East

Turn To Page 5 For More Of DULLES

Manheim Twp. Commissioners Set 1953 Budget At $61,550

A proposed 1953 budget, calling for expenditures totaling $61,550, was introduced last evening at a meeting of the Manheim Township Commissioners.

The budget document is the first for the township since it changed its form of government from that of a second class township to a township of the first class.

TAX RATE UNCHANGED

Retention of the township's present three and one-half mill tax on real estate is the basis for the proposed 1953 budget. Estimated assessed evaluation of the township is $11,060,000. However, this figure is expected to be slightly higher, George H. Goll, township secretary, said.

CHANGE MEETING NIGHT

Meeting night of the Manheim Township Commissioners last evening was changed from the first Friday evening of the month to the second Wednesday of each month.

That means the commissioners will hold their next regular meeting Wednesday, March 11.

In addition, the Commissioners announced that the township zoning office now will be open every Wednesday evening instead of Friday. The change, insofar as the zoning office is concerned, starts next Wednesday, it was announced.

The Commissioners, in deciding to change their meeting night, said under the present setup many of the monthly bills are not received in time for action on the regular meeting night.

Following a 20-day waiting period, while the budget is open to public inspection ,the document will be formally adopted by the Commissioners.

RECEIPTS OF $66,231.21

Estimated receipts listed in the 1953 budget total $66,263.21—$5,383.32 less than the $71,646.53 taken in during 1952 by the township. The total estimated expenditure

Turn To Page 5 For More Of MANHEIM TWP.

FIRE SCARE

City firemen were summoned to the home of Warren Anderson, 1 Quade Court, when an oil burner flared up at 5:45 p. m. yesterday. Fire Chief Harry Miller reported there was no damage.

6 Children Alone In Home When Fire Breaks Out

Six children, ranging in age from two to nine years, escaped injury when fire broke out in their White Owl Alley home as they were alone last night.

Fire Chief Harry E. Miller said an observing neighbor saw smoke coming from the upstairs of the home of Mr. and Mrs. John Green, 518 White Owl Alley, and called firemen.

Firemen said a fire had broken out in a pile of rags and paper in a second floor front bedroom about 11:40 p. m. yesterday.

It is believed one of the children was playing with matches. The children, John Jr., nine, Patsy, seven, Joseph, six, Richard, five, Barry, four, and Terry, aged two, told police their parents were working at the time.

All of them were downstairs when police and firemen arrived, but Chief Miller and Battalion Chief Edward Koerkle said they learned Barry and Richard had both been upstairs previously.

There was only slight damage,

Turn To Page 5 For More Of FIRE

ALARMING DROP HERE IN VALENTINE MAIL

It may be the weather, or it may be the times, for the volume of Valentine's Day greetings dispatched via the postal service fell alarmingly below expectations yesterday.

Postal officials last night estimated that 84,000 of the February 14 messages of love and friendship passed through their hands up to midnight.

The total is far behind last year's record 125,000, and this morning's collections are expected to yield only a thousand or two more.

Downtown merchants either sized up the trend in advance, or more people are taking to delivering the cupid and heart-bedecked cards in person, for store counters were well cleared, offering little choice for late shoppers last evening.

Whips Out Gun In Payment For Vial Of Cold Tablets

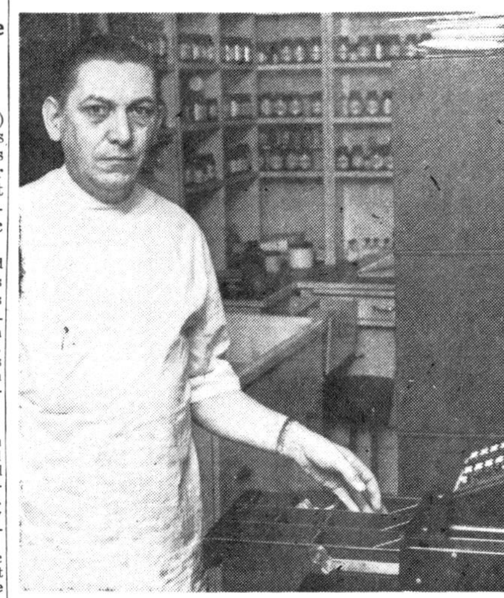

CASH REGISTER EMPTY—John H. Henkel stands at the empty cash register in the Henkle and McAllister Drug Store, Lime and Chestnut Streets, shortly after he was held up by a man and robbed of $210 at 8 p. m. yesterday. (Intell Photo)

Henkel And McAllister Pharmacy Report Between $210 And $225 Taken

A lone gunman armed with a nickel-plated revolver escaped with between $210 and $225 in a daring hold-up at the Henkel and McAllister Pharmacy, Chestnut and Lime Sts., early last night.

Within two hours after the gunman had forced John H. Henkel, forty-two, 631 W. Chestnut St., to empty the cash register of a heavy Friday night's receipts, swift-moving detectives had rounded up three suspects.

However, Henkel said none of them was the person who had committed the robbery.

The money, he told police, was in small denominations, probably two twenty dollar bills, four tens, about 20 ones, and maybe 22 to 25 five dollar bills. The bandit didn't bother with the change.

POLICE COMB CITY

Detectives S. K. Cliff and Al Farkas early today were combing city clubs and taprooms in an effort to locate the suspect.

Henkel, they said, gave them a good description of the man. He identified him as about five feet five inches tall, weighs about 150 pounds, and had straight black, well-groomed hair, parted near or in the middle.

He was wearing a tan and brown tweed overcoat and a suit and wore tan leather gloves. Also, Henkel told Detective Cliff, he believed the bandit had a scar just above the upper lip on the right side of his face.

Detectives immediately began checking their rouges gallery and statistics file on known robbers.

The hold-up occurred about 8:30 p. m. yesterday. At 8:35 p.m. four police cruisers were converging on the spot but were unable to find any trace of the man in the immediate vicinity.

Henkel told police he had been "real busy" up until just before 8:30 p.m. yesterday. He was alone in the store and the gunman walked in and asked for APC tablets, used for the relief of headaches and colds, and which do not require a prescription.

The pharmacist said he got the pale green tablets, put them into a vial and set them on the counter in front of the man. The gunman asked him the price of the tablets, and Henkel said he replied they were "twenty-five cents."

DRAWS REVOLVER

Detective Cliff said the gunman had placed a pair of tan leather gloves on the counter, and after Henkel told him the price, put on the left glove, made a movement to unbutton his topcoat as if to get his wallet, and drew the revolver from his belt.

Henkel told police the weapon was tucked in the front of his belt and was rather small. Police said they believe it to be a .32 caliber revolver.

The gunman, Henkel said, ordered him to "empty the cash register out," as he thrust the gun toward his stomach.

Henkel said he complied immediately, and handed the wad of money across the counter to the

Turn To Page 5 For More Of HOLDUP

3rd Class Cities Pledged To Promote Continued Progress

Directors of the League of Third Class Cities in Pennsylvania yesterday issued a statement of policy in which they pledged 'our best efforts toward establishing conditions that will promote the continued progress of our cities."

The statement, released following a meeting at Harrisburg, pointed out that the policy group of the League feels that "local municipal problems best can be solved by a reduction, rather than by an increase in restrictions and requirements imposed on local government by the State Legislature.

"The success of such a local government program will be a great contribution toward the continued progress and prosperity of Pennsylvania."

Mayor Kendig C. Bare, new president of the League, presided over the session.

HANDS OFF POLICY

Walter E. Greenwood, executive director of the League, told newsmen following the meeting that our policy will be to "take no stand on programs which have to be voted on by the people."

The veteran League official stated that "we are not denying the people the right to determine their own government."

Previously, the League was reported opposed to any legislation setting up an optional city manager program in Third Class cities of the Commonwealth.

.Greenwood said the League's board of directors also agreed that policy would be: to sell city property by auction as well as bids; to propose legislation allowing city employes to build city streets the same as the State Highways Department; to ask legislation to provide a reserve fund for city-owned

Turn To Page 5 For More Of LEAGUE

BART TWP. FARM REPORTED SITE FOR MIGRANT LABOR CAMP

An unidentified farm in the Nickel Mines section of Bart Township was reported being considered as the site for a migrant farm labor distribution camp proposed for this area.

Spokesmen for the Farm Service Corp., which plans to build the camp for Puerto Rican farm workers coming into Pennsylvania, said last night that farms in four counties are still being studied.

Roy Wenger, of Cambridge, who is to manage the camp, said sites in Lancaster, Chester, Lebanon and Berks are still under consideration. He would not identify the Lancaster County site.

Meanwhile, the Farm Service Corp. and residents of the Beartown area completed a settlement ending the possibility that a Beartown farm would be used. Christian Kilmer, who owns the Beartown farms, received $500 under terms of the settlement; Styer and Evans, a New Holland real estate firm, was reimbursed for expenses totaling $85, and a $765 deposit on the Kilmer farm was returned to the corporation.

C Of C Will Elect 6 New Directors, List Nominees

Twelve members of the Lancaster Chamber of Commerce yesterday were nominated for the six-directorships to be filled by April 1.

The nominations were made during a meeting of the present Chamber board of directors. A C of C spokesman pointed out that according to the by-laws, any member in good standing may submit nominations until 4 p.m. next Wednesday.

THOSE NAMED

Nominations made yesterday — twice the number to be elected — follow:

Mark W. Anspach, Sears, Roebuck and Co.; Ernest L. Bertram, Bertram Rubber Co.; William P. Brinton, Keystone Pretzel Bakery; Samuel P. Ellenberg, Dun and Bradstreet, Inc.; Benjamin L. Herr, Funeral Home, Lampeter; Andrew S. Morgan, Lancaster County Gas Division, United Gas Improvement Co.; Melvin J. Powderly, Lancaster Newspapers, Inc.; J. Frank Powl, New Holland Ma-

Turn To Page 5 For More Of C OF C

Ohio Beef Challenges New Zealand Meat In State-Wide Price War

MARION, O., Feb. 13 (AP)—Ohio-grown beef challenged New Zealand meat today in a state-wide price war.

Ohio beef sold for 39 cents a pound in Marion and Columbus, about the same price New Zealand frozen beef brought in other markets in Columbus, Oberlin and Cleveland.

In at least one case, lower prices for domestic meat meant no loss to the sellers. Merle Wise, who began his sale of cut-rate Ohio meat yesterday at 39-59 cents, said:

"This New Zealand beef sorta made us mad. Waldock's (a meat packer) at Sandusky and a small wholesaler here and I sorta combined on this deal. Each of us is shaving his profit so no one will lose money."

LOSING A LITTLE

But, in Columbus, O., the manager of Eavey Super Market, where similar prices for domestic choice beef prevailed, admitted his organization may be losing a little money to meet New Zealand com-

Turn To Page 5 For More Of BEEF

Lancaster County Grapplers Ready For State PIAA Championships

Three Southeastern Regional champions, representing a trio of Lancaster County High Schools, will seek state PIAA championships this Saturday in the final mat trials of the year at State College. Jere Hemperly, left, McCaskey's 112-pounder, will be making his second appearance in the finals. He won the District and Southeastern Regional titles in the 95-pound division last year but lost out in the finals. This year he was champion again in the districts and regionals, but at 112-pounds. Sam Menefee, center, will carry Manheim Twp. hopes into the State trials with his sights set on the 145-pound division crown. At right is Carl Longenecker, 133-pounder from Manheim Central. The boys' coaches, McCaskey Coach Jerry Brooks, Manheim Township's Nelson Gibble, and Manheim Central's Sherwood Hollobaugh, have spent the week working the boys with wrestlers from Millersville, Stevens Trade, and Franklin and Marshall. Hemperly and Menefee are in good physical condition for the championship tests but Longenecker was out of school all day Wednesday with a bad cold and may be slightly weakened by the effects of his ailment. (Intell Sports Photos)

Browns Seen Headed For Baltimore

Mayor Confirms Reports That Transfer Negotiations Have Been In Progress For "Some Weeks"

BALTIMORE, March 12 (AP)—The first concrete word that a shift of the St. Louis Browns is in the making came out today when Mayor Thomas D'Alesandro admitted that negotiations to bring the American League team here have been going on for "some weeks."

There has been talk for almost a month that the Browns would be shifted somewhere but officials have denied the stories, and only last week one high official tabbed the subject a "dead issue."

As it turned out, however, the issue still is very much alive.

"I can't confirm or deny the announcement that Baltimore is returning to big league baseball through the transfer of the St. Louis Browns here," said D'Alesandro. "However, I have been participating in negotiations for some weeks along with Thomas Biddison, city solicitor, and James Anderson, president of the board of parks and recreation, to bring the Browns here.

HARRIDGE AWARE OF PENDING TRANSFER

SARASOTA, Fla., March 12 (AP)—President Will Harridge of the American League said tonight negotiations have been going on for the transfer of the St. Louis Browns to Baltimore but "I don't think they are anywhere near the closing stage."

At the same time Arthur Ehlers, general manager of the Philadelphia Athletics confirmed that a meeting of the American League has been scheduled for Clearwater, Fla., for next Monday. He said he wouldn't care to comment on the reported franchise transfer.

Bill Veeck, president of the Browns, was reported travelling in Florida and could not be reached for comment.

However, another high baseball official in a position to know how far negotiations have progressed said, "You are on the right track," when the Associated Press asked him to confirm the story. He asked that his name not be used.

In St. Louis, the Globe-Democrat said:

"Whether the transfer would take effect at once, in time for the Browns to open the American League season in Baltimore next month, or would not be consummated until 1954, could not be determined.

"There were indications in St. Louis, however, that the Browns were planning to go ahead with operations here (in St. Louis) in 1953."

Word of the negotiations leaked out late today when a man high in baseball's inner circle told the Associated Press that the switch from St. Louis to Baltimore was probable and that it might be made by next Monday.

TODAY'S LOCAL SPORTS LINEUP

BASKETBALL
INDUSTRIAL LEAGUE
Penn Boiler vs. Haddad, 7 p. m.
IBEW vs. Assn. Deaf, 8:30 p. m.
(Both games at Nathan Schaeffer).

WRESTLING
F & M in Eastern Intercollegiates at Princeton.

NCAA Tourney Moves Into High Gear Today With Four Regional Basketball Playoffs

NEW YORK, March 12 (AP)—With the preliminary skirminishing out of the way, the NCAA basketball tournament gets going in earnest tomorrow night with four regional tournaments at widely-scattered centers.

Nine teams who won their way to conference championships start all over again, on the route to a title, with seven at-large teams also scrapping for the crown they seldom win. Only twice in 14 years have teams from outside the conferences won the title.

The conference kingpins are favored to win it again this year, since teams high up in the latest Associated Press Poll of the top 10 are pegged in each of the four regionals. The regional winners will meet in the finals at Kansas City next Tuesday and Wednesday, March 17-18.

Kansas' defending champions, currently rated fifth in the nation, appear to have the most difficult road to the finals. This is so even though they have the shortest distance, geographically speaking, from their regional tourney at Manhattan, Kas.

The big seven champions, with a 16-5 season record, meet Oklahoma City (18-4), a strong independent team ranked 10th in the country. In the first round. Then they must face the winner of the game between Oklahoma A & M, 22-6 champions of the Missouri Valley, and Texas Christian's southwest conference champions.

Indiana, voted best in the country, is the favorite in the Chicago get-together, while Washington, No. 2, is outstanding in the Corvallis, Ore. regional and Louisiana State, No. 7, has the best record in the Raleigh, N. C., tournament.

Indiana (19-3) goes against De Paul (18-7), which edged Miami of Ohio, 74-72, in a preliminary round game Tuesday night. The other Chicago game matches Notre Dame (18-4) against Penn's Ivy league champions.

The far west tournament has two All-America players, 6-7 Bob Houbregs of Washington and 5-7 Johnny O'Brien, who scored 42 points as Seattle whipped Idaho State, 88-77, in a preliminary round game Tuesday.

The other far west game has Wyoming (20-8), champions of the Mountain States (skyline) conference, against Santa Clara (19-6) which won the far west regional tourney last year.

MOOSE BOWLING TOURNEY OPENS THIS SATURDAY

The Moose Bowling Leagues announced that they would start their annual tournament this weekend with competition scheduled to run a total of four week-ends.

Singles and doubles are slated to be run off this coming Saturday and Sunday and next Saturday and Sunday.

The five-man team event is listed for Sat. and Sun., March 28 and 29 with the finals on Sat., April 4.

Any member of the Moose is eligible to compete in this tourney. Entrants can sign up for this event at the Moose Home or by contacting tournament manager Karl E. Geesey.

SPORTS Pages 36, 37, 38, 39

IT'S EASY to find out for yourself why so many folks like you are switching to Calvert. Just pick the smoother, mellower whiskey in this simple test:
1. SNIFF ½-oz. samples of Calvert and any other whiskey. Compare their aroma—without knowing which is which.
2. TASTE Calvert and the other brand to judge them for smoothness mellowness — freedom from harshness.
3. CHOOSE the whiskey that tastes better to you. We feel sure that you'll pick finer, smoother-tasting Calvert. But you be the judge. Fair enough?
GET A TRIAL BOTTLE TODAY!
$2.81 PINT Code No. 189
$4.45 4/5 Qt. Code No. 188
A
B

Little Liz - - -
Women always run through a wolf's mind. They wouldn't be safe if they walked.

LANCASTER NEW ERA

The Weather
(U. S. Weather Bureau Forecast)
Fair and Cool Tonight;
Tomorrow Cloudy and Mild.
Temperature Today: High 49; Low 38
Temperature Yesterday: High 50; Low 40

76th Year—No. 23,516 | Lancaster Metropolitan Area Population Official United States Census Figures 234,717 | LANCASTER, PA., TUESDAY, MARCH 17, 1953 | CITY EDITION | 28 PAGES | 30c PER WEEK—5c Per Copy

1,000 GI's Unhurt in Test A-Blast

Bare and Monaghan Are Unopposed for Mayor Nominations

Incumbent Still Not Saying If He Will Run; Files Petition 20 Minutes Before Yesterday's Deadline; Democrats File Complete City Slate

It looks like Bare versus Monaghan for mayor of Lancaster next November.

Kendig C. Bare, 205 Race Ave., stands unopposed for the Republican nomination for his second term. He still has not said he definitely would run, although he filed his petition before the 5 p. m. deadline yesterday.

Thomas J. Monaghan, 839 Highland Ave., filed his petition with the rest of the Democratic slate yesterday afternoon. Monaghan, an investment agent, is USO chairman, and active in church and civic affairs. He also is unopposed.

KENDIG C. BARE
For Mayor, Republican

THOMAS J. MONAGHAN
For Mayor, Democrat

Democrats Fill Slate

The last two candidates to be picked by the Democrats were Mahlon McKonly, 430 E. Orange St., beverage distributor, for city treasurer, and William E. Weisgerber, retired member of the Franklin and Marshall College faculty, for city controller. Weisgerber lives at 615 N. President Ave.

Those two weren't picked until late yesterday afternoon. The other Democrats were announced earlier in the day.

20 Minutes Before Deadline

Twenty minutes before the 5 p. m. filing deadline yesterday, Bare and Commissioner John E. Spidle came to the courthouse together and filed their nomination petitions.

It was noted that they filed both the petitions circulated for them by the Republican organization and also by a group of independent Republicans.

Asked by a reporter if that meant he was running, Bare hesitated and seemed at loss for an answer.

Is this perhaps a necessary formality? the reporter asked. Bare quickly replied "that's it," adding:

Promises Clarification

"I shall have a clarification of my position within 24 hours."

This morning, the mayor said: "Commissioner Spidle and I have a certain program we support and for which we are working.

"In fairness to the public and to ourselves, we will try to find out within a few days what the other people stand for and what they are prepared to do."

Wants Talk With Templeton

Asked if that meant he wanted to talk to Daniel S. Templeton, the other Republican candidate for City Council, Bare said "I certainly would like to sit down and talk with Dan."

In contrast with Bare and Spidle, the rest of the Republican candidates, including Templeton,

—See POLITICS—Page 6

Dr. Berberian Would Not Accept Salary

Dr. Harry S. Berberian, one of the Democratic organization candidates for City Council, said today "I think the people and not the politicians" should decide the issue of merging the two city-owned markets.

"If I am elected, I will not accept a cent of salary," he said. "I am not a politician and am not interested in politics. We should get businessmen, not politicians, at the head of our city government. We should quit voting for jobseekers, people who are seeking an easy buck. If we can get a man like the head of General Motors into federal government, we should be able to do likewise, on a smaller scale, in municipal government."

DEMOCRAT WILL RUN FOR WARDEN

Zeamer Backs Candidate Despite Mrs. Horting

The local Democrats are running their first candidates in years for prison warden and prison inspectors. Therein lies a story:

First, the sponsor of the candidates was County Commissioner Woodrow A. Zeamer — over the vigorous objections of Mrs. Ruth Grigg Horting, acting Democratic county chairman.

Second, when Zeamer brought the warden candidate in to file his petition, it was discovered he was not a registered voter. So he had to register first and then became a candidate.

How It Happened

Here is what happened:

Before the Democratic slate was filed yesterday afternoon, a reporter asked Mrs. Horting about reports that the Democrats were going to file a slate of prison officials.

"We won't if I have anything to do with it," said Mrs. Horting, who has replaced David R. Eaby, county chairman who is ill.

She went on to explain that, under the Democratic Earle administration, a law was passed mak-

—See DEMOCRAT—Page 6

CITY IS ASKED ABOUT WATER FOR BAUSMAN

Goberman Says He Is Paying for Lines Built By Suburban Co.

Representatives of property owners in the Bausman-Millersville pike area today asked City Council what they must do to obtain city water.

The city, according to members of the Committee, said it will do these two things:

It will take up at caucus next Monday morning the question of whether the city has sufficient water to supply consumers in the area the committee represents.

If the Bureau of Water says it can supply the water then Council will tell the group in detail what procedure to follow to file application for city water.

The conference this morning, held behind closed doors, followed the announcement by the Lancaster Suburban Water Co., a private concern, that it will extend its service into the Bausman area. The plan was made known last week by a representative of the Suburban Co. when he appeared at a public meeting held in Bausman.

Allen N. Goberman today announced that he is paying for the line being built by Suburban and that it will be his property, to supply a development with a number of homes which he plans to start near Millersville.

Goberman, who is president of a building concern, had this to say:

Will Cost $60,000

"There is no water line out there now. I am personally paying for the water line. I am running approximately 10,000 feet of line to my development grounds, at an approximate cost of $60,000.

"The eight-inch line being laid from Atkins and Davis Aves. will belong to me personally. Residents of Bausman approached the Lancaster Suburban Water Co. and ask-

—See WATER—Page 6

Wife Upheld In Divorce Appeal

Need Not Be Congenial with Husband's Kin

PHILADELPHIA (AP) — The all-male Pennsylvania superior court ruled today that a wife "at her peril is not bound to establish a congenial relationship with her husband's relatives."

The court's ruling came in a decision in the appeal of Lillian L. Coon, North Plainfield, N. J., from a divorce decree granted her husband in Lancaster County court. The appellate court reversed the decree.

Assigned To Lancaster

The court led up to the statement in this way:

Louis B. Coon, formerly of W. Chestnut St., Lancaster, married Lillian in 1920 and left their home in North Plainfield, N. J., in 1949 when his employer, Sperry Gyroscope Co. assigned him to the Lancaster, Pa., plant.

In July, 1950, Coon filed for a divorce on grounds of cruel and barbarous treatment and indignities. The decree was granted on grounds of indignities.

The court noted today that in 1946 Coon was assigned by Sperry to a plant in Long Island and maintained a room there, spending his week-ends at home. But the court added "even while home he never spent his time with the family, instead playing golf with an enthusiastic foursome.

Coon complained in his divorce suit, the court added, that his wife was "out of step with his mother" and "incompatible with his aunt."

"A wife at her peril is not bound to establish a congenial relationship with her husband's relatives," the court commented.

S. Queen St. Fire House Will Be Remodelled

The city has plans for extensive alterations to fire engine house No. 2 at 416 S. Queen St.

The plans call for replacing the old "hinge" doors with overhead doors that open automatically. Also to tear out the complete front and replace it, making one instead of two small doors. Inside, the house will be painted and otherwise fixed up.

The city controller has asked bids on the project. They will be opened Monday, April 13.

Today's New Era

Lenten Guidepost -- 24

40 Acres of Children

By Leah E. Young
of Courtland, Virginia

"In this good country you can dream as big as you wish, and the Lord willing, makes these dreams come true." I said this 43 years ago when my husband, John, and I stood looking at the rough farmhouse that was to be our home here in Virginia.

John is a good man and shared my faith and hopes. We wanted a big family, with education and careers for all.

What better place could the son of a Negro slave and his wife find, to make those dreams come true, than this wonderful 40-acre farm?

Leah E. Young

As the years went by we began to pay for the farmhouse. John farmed well; I raised ducks, turkeys, geese and pigeons . . . corned fresh herring and canned all the food I could lay my hands on. We always had plenty to eat.

A Prayer At Planting

Nothing is more exciting than growing your own food. Every spring, when the earth was soft, rich and brown as we started planting, I would get down on my knees in thankfulness.

"Bless these little seeds, Lord," I would say. "There are so many to feed."

Because the nearest church was far away, and our family was growing fast, it became increasingly difficult to make the long

—See LENTEN—Page 4

Awesome violence of today's atomic explosion is shown in this photo taken seven miles from blast site in Atomic Proving Grounds, Nev. Picture was made with a 28-inch lens. Vertical streamers, left, caused by rockets. AP Wirephoto

U. S. AID FOR BIG FAMILIES URGED

Priest Proposes Monthly Payments to Mothers

PHILADELPHIA (AP) —A Jesuit priest urged today that a federal aid system be set up to provide for outside financial assistance to "the parents of larger families" in the U. S.

The proposal came from the Rev. Francis J. Corley, S. J., of the Institute of Social Order at St. Louis University and editor of the monthly magazine "Social Order."

In an address to the National Catholic Family Life Conference, Father Corley declared "it is imperative we stop ignoring the personal and social harm that results every day from the serious imbalances between wages and needs."

He advocated monthly payments of $12 for the third child in every family, $10 for the fourth child and $8 for the fifth and each succeeding child.

Point To Liquor Revenues

Father Corley asserted that "a nation which can afford to spend 9.2 billion dollars a year on alcoholic beverages can certainly raise 1.75 billion a year for improved care of its children."

"The parents of larger families make an immeasurable precious contribution to the well-being of future America," the priest contended. "It is disgraceful that we reward their contribution only by laying upon them the tremendous burden of building the nation's future alone."

Live Irish Shamrock On Mayor Bare's Desk

Live shamrock from the Emerald Isle adorned the desk of Mayor Kendig C. Bare today to mark St. Patrick's Day.

The shamrock was flown into the United States by one of the airline companies. Mayor Bare also sported a traditional green neck tie.

Bulletin

MIG Attacks B-50 Near Siberia

Washingtonn (AP)—United States reconnaisance bomber fought off a Russian-made MIG-15 jet fighter off the east coast of Kamchatka Sunday.

The Air Force, announcing the incident, said today it took place about five miles east of the Siberian peninsula in the North Pacific Ocean.

The U. S. plane, a B-50, was on a "routine weather reconnoisance flight from an Alaskan air base."

Two Russian type MIG-15's intercepted the American aircraft but only one attacked.

The U. S. plane "returned fire but there appeared to be no damage to either craft."

Grunewald Pleads Guilty

Washington (AP)—Henry W. Grunewald, Washington "mystery man" and wire puller, pleaded guilty today to a single count of contempt of Congress.

Grunewald, known as "The Dutchman," withdrew his previous plea of innocence to a 31-count indictment, and entered a plea of guilty to the first count.

TV Viewers Here Struck By 'Horror' of Explosion

Television viewers here were given a close-up view of an atomic blast today as a grim reminder of the need for civil defense.

The pooled telecast of the blast itself, over the ABC, CBS and NBC networks, was one phase of a three-part educational demonstration by the Atomic Energy Commission and Civil Defense authorities.

Fascination and fear were the two most frequently marked reactions from viewers in the WGAL-TV area, where the blast was seen on Channel 8.

Watch In Silence

At one hotel, diners who were having breakfast left their tables to come to the lobby and watch the grim "show" from Yucca Flat, Nev. They watched in silence, then returned to their eggs and coffee.

"I think everybody should have watched it," said one housewife. She added that watching the servicemen stationed near the blast site gave a "fearful sensation — you didn't know what would happen to those boys."

"Just horror," was the terse comment of another woman who was asked her reaction.

Picture Is Clearer

Technically, the view of today's A-bomb test was superior to that of a similar telecast from Yucca Flat a year ago, according to WGAL-TV engineers. Viewers also said today's picture was clearer than that of Sunday, when a tele-

—See TV—Page 2

Manor High Is 'Worst' In County, Group Claims

Manor-Millersville High School is the "worst in the county" says the Manor Twp. Citizens' Committee, and then it goes on to explain why.

The statement is made in material prepared by the committee for distribution to residents of the area. The committee is backing a slate of Republican candidates running for office in opposition to the GOP organization ticket.

Meeting This Evening

The committee is explaining its stand to residents at a series of organizaion meetings. First of these will be the session of the Millersville Home and School Association, this evening at 8 o'clock at the Millersville Junior High School.

The original part of the high school was built in 1879, the committee states, and when the addition was erected in 1921, the school was designed to hold 250 students. It now has 483.

Of these students, 130 walk to classes each day in the Millersville fire hall two blocks away, "because there's no room for them in the school itself."

Other comments on the high school follow:

"The state standard is 22 students per classroom. We have 40.25 per classroom in our jam-packed school.

"Our basketball team can't use its own gym — it's too small. We have to use the college gym.

"The auditorium holds only half the students. It serves as the school's only study hall — holding as many as 150 students at a time.

Eat Between Lockers

"At mealtimes, our children eat in the basement, at tables wedged in between lockers filled with sweaty sneakers and gym clothes. The room has just two

—See SCHOOLS—Page 2

More Than 2 Colors Used 1st Time In Ad

Today for the first time a full page appears in this newspaper printed in more than two colors.

Two primary colors, red and blue, were used to produce the attractive cover page of today's Spring Fashion Section.

This color page was printed on one of the eight units of the new Hoe Color Convertible press installed by the Lancaster Newspapers during 1952.

Previously, advertisements have appeared in black and only one additional color.

Efforts are being continued in the Production Departments of this newspaper to make possible a wide variety of newspaper color printing and to improve the product.

F & M ELEVEN TO PLAY LAFAYETTE

Game Will Be Staged Here on Oct. 31

By George Kirchner
New Era Sports Editor

Franklin and Marshall College will play Lafayette in football here next fall, it was announced today by J. Shober Barr, director of athletics.

The date for the game is Oct. 31 with the Leopards replacing American International College on the Dips' eight-game program. AIC, which was played in Springfield, Mass., last year, was dropped after F and M returned with a 40 to 38 victory, but a badly-battered football team.

NYU Drops Football

Arrangements with Lafayette were able to be made only because New York University, which was scheduled to have played the Leopards on Oct. 31, dropped football.

Barr said that while the two schools signed only a one-year pact, both were confident that they could arrange their schedules so that their teams would meet again in 1954. If such arrangement can be made, it is planned then to sign a two-year home-and-home pact which would carry on through 1955.

Met Last In 1937

F and M and Lafayette met last in football in 1937. The Leopards edged the Diplomats 14 to 0. However, in a game before that in 1934 F and M defeated Lafayette by the same count, 14-0. Although the two schools have met only eight times, one of F and M's first football games away back in 1890 was played with Leopards and the locals won it 18-10. In the series F and M has won two to Lafayette's six.

F and M opens its eight game schedule on Oct. 3 with Johns Hopkins here and meets Dickinson, Drexel, Albright, Lafayette, Ursinus, Muhlenberg and Gettysburg on successive Saturdays. The home games include: Johns Hopkins, Dickinson, Lafayette and Muhlenberg.

SHOCK FELT FROM UTAH TO PASADENA

St. Patrick's Day Blast Among Smallest of A-Bomb Tests

By Bill Becker

ATOM BOMB SITE, Nev. (AP)—America's most daring atomic troops took a battering today but came unscathed through a low level nuclear blast that jolted communities as far distant as 300 miles.

Shortly after the rumbling explosion, the two battalion combat teams moved through a heavy pall of dust in their scheduled maneuver. Gen. John R. Hodge and other observers in foxholes only two miles from blast center reported no injury to troops or the 20 newsmen up front for the first time.

The Civil Defense test home only 3,500 feet from ground zero apparently was demolished, Harold L. Goodwin, FCDA test director, said after a helicopter inspection. Only one wall was standing, he said.

Civil Defense Workers Watch

In open-mouthed awe, Civil Defense observers from all parts of the country watched the explosion blow skyward.

The 1,000 troops and 20 newsmen —closer to atom fire than any human has been since Hiroshima and Nagasaki — escaped injury and the soldiers moved in within an hour to capture their atomized objective as planned.

Gov. John Fine of Pennsylvania keynoted the feelings of observers as he called it "A challenge to all humanity."

"Prepare To Fall"

Goodwin said "we have been acting largely on theory up to now, but now we know. If we fail to prepare now, it means we are going to prepare to fall."

From Elton C. Fay, AP correspondent in the front line, came this description of how it felt:

"You are shaken by an ungodly power. The dust obscures sight. The pressure wave surged overhead. Rocks hiss through the air, missiles as deadly as bullets. You are not particularly frightened. You are just awed."

Set On Schedule

The device, of a type hitherto untested, was set off promptly on schedule at 5:20 a. m. (8:20 a. m. EST .

As correspondents, after waiting the required four seconds, looked up the horizon was lighted with a boiling purple fireball. Gathering huge pieces of the desert floor as it rose, it seemed to leave behind it a silent vacuum.

Then came the sound, one thunderous wave.

Sharp Shock

The shock of the blast was sharp and bounced over the mountains ringing the test site to crack down as far away as Pasadena, Calif., Cedar City, Utah, and points in between, it was announced here. In Las Vegas, nearest sizable city, 75 miles away, it flared a brilliant white, over nearly half the horizon, then turned yellow before finally fading away into pink. But it

—See BLAST—Page 2

Springlike Weather Back, Mercury Is 49

On-again, off-again springlike weather was on again today, as the official entry of the season approached.

Spring will arrive at 5:01 p. m. Friday, marking the vernal equinox and entrance of the sun into Aries. Meanwhile today was rather sunny and the 2 p. m. temperature was 49.

Tonight will be fair and cool, said the forecast, and tomorrow will be quite cloudy and continued mild. Temperatures will average slightly above normal through Sunday, according to the extended prediction. Rain is expected Thursday and Sunday.

Traffic Posers

This is the second in a series of traffic posers prepared in cooperation with traffic authorities. This one was suggested by City Police. It is interesting to note that the right answers are based on common sense, decency and courtesy.

Car "A" and car "B" are both traveling west on W. Chestnut St. at 12 miles an hour. Car "C" has sounded horn indicating his wish to pass. Should car "A":

(1) Accelerate and move to right?
(2) Maintain present position?
(3) Sound horn in response?
(4) Swerve to right to force car "B" to speed up?

THE RIGHT ANSWER IS (1).

Section 1004 of the Pennsylvania Motor Code states: "Upon all highways of sufficient width, except upon one-way streets, the driver of a vehicle shall drive the same upon the right half of the highway, and shall drive a slow-moving vehicle as closely as possible to the right-hand edge or curb of such highway ..."

RECORD ROOM — Except for occasional programs, Hangout dances are tuned to recordings. Above, James Bear at mike announces a number while Joseph Cooper prepares to spin the platter. About three orchestra dances are held yearly. Proceeds of one dance per month go to some worthy charity. Seven have benefitted — including Community Chest, of which YWCA is a member.

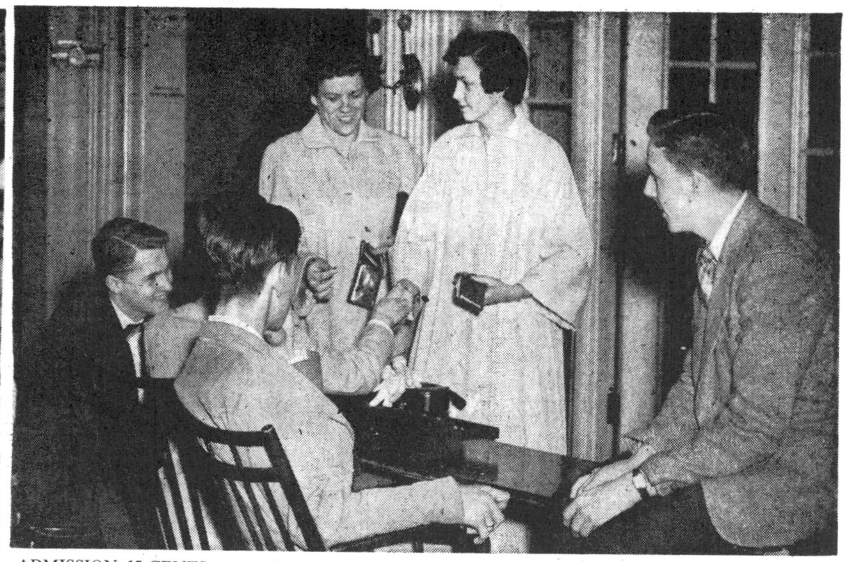

ADMISSION, 15 CENTS —No strain on the teen-ager's budget is the 15-cent admission price to Hangout dances. Girls arriving at YWCA for affair are shown above at registration desk.

'Hangout' Is 10 Years Old

END OF LENTEN SEASON heralds social revival for teen-agers especially, as the YWCA's Saturday night Hangout prepares to celebrate its 10th anniversary. Started in 1943 to fill a wartime need, Hangout has continued ever since. Now it plans an expanded and more varied summer program of three nights per week in cooperation with other YW groups. As Lancaster's only informal Saturday co-ed recreation available to the 15-to-18 set, Hangout has attracted a membership of 1,000 young people, with average attendance between 200 and 300. Though admission costs only 15 cents, Hangout has contributed $197 to seven worthy charities since last October, when council voted proceeds of one dance per month for the purpose.

DIG THAT CRAZY RHYTHM—Hangout provides only Saturday program of its type regularly available to teen-agers of city and county. Teen-age Dept. of YWCA is sponsor, and adviser is always present with two adult couples as chaperones.

MAY I? — Informality keys Hangout Saturday nights. Here Alvin Yoffee, right, cuts in on Joseph Cooper for dance with Louise Bush.

TAKE A POWDER—Powder room at YW is busy place at intermission. Seated are Joan Benedick and Polly Hammon.

RULING BODY—Hangout Council of 18 from McCaskey, Manheim Twp. and East Lampeter Highs meets monthly to plan program. Shown (l-r): Phyllis Cox, Richard Ayer, Audrey Cope, Jim Baer, Diane Gibble, Dick Gaintner, president Molly Smith, adviser Carolyn Dunn, Jim Campbell, Charmaine Wiker, Joe Cooper and Joyce Wireback.

TWO STRAWS and one coke make things chummy for James Campbell and Gerry Case. For nondancers there are other amusements, including ping-pong, pool, chess, checkers and similar games.

SHALL WE DANCE? — Mike Cummings asks Phyllis Hollinger for this number at Hangout affair. Dances are held every Saturday during winter, 8:30 to 11 p. m., unless there are conflicting dates for teen-agers.

WEATHER
(U. S. Weather Bureau)
Eastern Pennsylvania — Generally Fair Today, With High 48 To 56. Tomorrow Increasing Cloudiness And Cooler With Some Rain Likely At Night.

Intelligencer Journal.

The Leading Newspaper in the Garden Spot of America. Home Owned for Home Folks Since 1794

159th Year.—No. 261. Official United States Census Figures Lancaster Metropolitan Area Population 234,717 LANCASTER, PA., FRIDAY MORNING, APRIL 17, 1953. CITY FORTY-SIX PAGES 30c PER WEEK—5c Per Copy

UN READY TO RESUME TRUCE TALKS

Bingo Won't Be Tolerated Here After May 10

DA, OPERATORS IN AGREEMENT ON DECISION

Beyer Has Statement After Meeting; AMVETS Close Immediately

Bingo, the numbers game that has been played at countless fairs and social gatherings and in many private and public clubs and parks here for many years, will not be tolerated anywhere in Lancaster city and county after May 10.

That was the word that came out of a hour-long meeting called by District Attorney John W. Beyer and attended by 16 operators of the game yesterday afternoon.

The closed meeting was called following a renewal of state-wide attention on the gambling game, egal in Pennsylvania, and subsequent complaints to the district attorney's office concerning the bingo games in Lancaster County.

All those present yesterday agreed on the May 10 deadline, it was stated following the meeting.

STATEMENT ISSUED

In a statement issued at the session's conclusion, it was explained that all operators present "informally agreed to devote their efforts to furthering the legislature in clarifying the legal situation which is involved."

(There are presently three bills involving bingo pending before the State Legislature—each to legalize the game under certain restrictions.)

Beyer emphasized that all organizations operating bingo games here will be expected to comply with the deadline.

Attending the meeting, according to the statement, were the invited representatives of organizations conducting bingo games in the city and county as well as representatives serving other organizations who asked permission to sit in on the session.

"We discussed the problem of the complaints and the proportions to

Turn To Page 34 For More Of BINGO

"We Lead All The Rest"
FARM CORNER
By WILLIAM R. SCHULTZ

INDEMNITY PAY FOR BRUCELLOSIS MAY BE HALTED

Suspension Order Said Being Prepared Now In Harrisburg

The Bureau of Animal Industry at Harrisburg was reported yesterday preparing an order which would suspend federal indemnity payments for cattle reacting to brucellosis tests.

Hints of the move came when district agents of the Bureau were instructed not to accept applications for brucellosis testing unless herd owners agree to waive the federal share of indemnity payments.

The suspension is believed temporary, and an explanation is expected today with an official announcement of the action.

Dr. Guy M. Graybill, head of the brucellosis division, refused comment last evening until Agriculture Secretary Miles Horst issues an announcement.

Federal appropriations provide about one-half the funds used to

Turn To Page 34 For More Of FARM CORNER

Weather Calendar

COMPARATIVE TEMPERATURES

Station	High	Low
Water Works	58	42
Ephrata	57	42
Last Year (Ephrata)	66	38
Official High for Year Feb. 21		70
Official Low for Year Feb. 2		13
Character of Day		Partly Cloudy

WINDS
Direction W Avg. Velocity 16 mph

HUMIDITY
8 a. m. 92% 11 a. m. 69% 2 p. m. 45%
5 p. m. 54% 8 p. m. 55%
Average Humidity 63%

SUN
Rises 5:24 a. m. Sets 6:44 p. m.

MOON
Sets 11:36 p.m. First Quarter, April 20

STARS
Morning—Mercury, Venus
Evening—Jupiter, Saturn

NEARBY FORECASTS
(U. S. Weather Bureau)
Southern New Jersey and Delaware — Fair today, with high 54 to 58. Tomorrow increasing cloudiness and cool.
Maryland — Fair today with high 54 to 58. Tomorrow increasing cloudiness and cool, with showers by night.
Lower Potomac and Chesapeake Bay—Winds mostly westerly 15 to 20 mph. Fair today, with good visibility.

Firemen Fight Factory Blaze

Chicago firemen are shown here battling a blaze that followed an explosion in a five-story brick building housing a manufacturing firm on Chicago's North Side. A mile-square area was rocked by the blast.

Democrats Must Nominate Over 3/4 By Write-Ins

Over three-fourths of the Democratic candidates to be nominated for offices in the county's 19 boroughs must be chosen by write-in votes May 19, a check of the Municipal primary ballot revealed yesterday.

By actual count, there are 173 offices in the boroughs for which the Democrats do not have candidates. In some instances, the boroughs are so overwhelmingly Republican that the Democrats don't even attempt to file nominating petitions.

However, political observers said that the number of vacancies this year is larger than in the 1951 Municipal primary.

By comparison, Republicans will nominate only 24 candidates in the boroughs through write-in votes.

On the other hand, the Democrats have no nomination contests for borough offices at the May 19 primary. Republican voters will be called upon to resolve 12 such contests.

The Democrats have a complete ticket in the field in Columbia, a party stronghold, and nearly complete tickets at Quarryville and Adamstown.

In a number of boroughs, including Akron, Christiana, Lititz, Mountville, Terre Hill and Washington Boro the Democrats do not have a single candidate on the ballot.

The number of offices in the various boroughs where Democrats will be nominated by write-in votes are:

Adamstown, five; Akron, nine; Christiana, 15; Denver, eight; East Petersburg, 12; Elizabethtown, 12; Ephrata, 11; Lititz, 14; Manheim, 16; Marietta, 9; Millersville, 8; Mount Joy, 8; Mountville, 10; Quarryville, one; Strasburg, 12; Terre Hill, 10, and Washington Boro, 13.

TRUCK OVERWEIGHT

City police last night prosecuted Raymond Alloway, York R4, for operating an overweight truck. Alloway's tractor-trailer was 12,490 pounds in excess of the maximum weight allowed, police said. Also prosecuted last night for driving too fast for conditions was Paul S. Shenk, Washington Boro R1.

MORSE TAKES U. S. PRESS TO TASK ON OBJECTIVITY

Oregon Solon Says People Losing Confidence In Accuracy Of Newspapers

WASHINGTON, April 16 (AP)—Sen. Morse (Ind-Ore) told the Senate today "the people are losing confidence in the objectivity and accuracy of the American press."

He said large segments of the press are following "a distorted, slanted line" in their news columns. And he suggested that the American Society of Newspaper Editors, meeting here this week, "had better ponder it well."

Morse said particular study of news coverage of congressional debates on Hell's Canyon Dam project in Idaho would be merited.

ENDORSES PROJECT

Morse had taken the floor for a 10,000-word speech endorsing the proposed Hell's Canyon project. He

Turn To Page 34 For More Of MORSE

LICENSE SUSPENDED 45 DAYS BY PLCB

HARRISBURG, April 16 (AP)—The State Liquor Control Board today suspended the license of Clarence P. Schlossman, Mountville, for 45 days, effective May 7.

Reasons listed for the suspension included: sales to intoxicated persons; licensee intoxicated while in charge of licensed establishment; licensee's employees intoxicated while on duty on licensed premises and disorderly operation.

Stratojet Goes 130 Mi. Faster Than Sound With Aid Of Wind

WASHINGTON, April 16 (AP)—The world's fastest known bomber, the B47 Stratojet, has flown 794 miles an hour — 130 miles an hour faster than the speed of sound. But it had the aid of high winds.

The Defense Department permitted Boeing Airplane Company, manufacturer of the B47, today to make the first disclosure of a supersonic flight by a bomber.

An experimental fighter type rocket plane, the Navy's Skyrocket, has flown 1,238 miles an hour. Air Force jet fighters in Korea often have exceeded the speed of sound in steep dives.

IN LEVEL FLIGHT

But the six-engine, swept-wing B47 attained its supersonic speed in level flight, and kept at 794 miles an hour for 30 minutes.

It did so while flying eastward from Albuquerque, N. M., toward Wichita, Kan., at an altitude of 40,000 feet, by hooking onto a jet stream—one of the recently-discovered mysterious "rivers" of high winds in the upper skies. The B47 was designed for the "600 miles an hour class."

Boeing said the B47, known as No. 2137, has just completed a 1,000-hour shakedown program, simulating combat conditions. The Air Force had asked for the trials in an effort to evaluate techniques and equipment.

121 FLIGHTS

The program included 121 flights, averaging 8½ hours—and more

Turn To Page 15 For More Of BOMBER

TWO FIRES IN CHICAGO KILL AT LEAST 20

16 Still Missing; Police Estimate Toll May Reach Up To 30

CHICAGO, April 16 (AP)—An explosion-sparked fire which flashed through a factory and a nursery fire started by a child today killed at least 20 persons. The factory fire turned some workers into human torches.

Police Capt. Robert Ryan said the factory toll might "reach at least 30." Fifteen hours after the blaze, 16 persons still were listed as missing.

A spokesman for the factory said some of the missing may have gone to their homes or elsewhere.

WITHIN MINUTES

The twin-blazes—separated by two miles but occurring within minutes of one another—injured at least 41 persons, 37 at the factory and four at the nursery in an apartment building.

Scorching flames turned the Haber Company factory about two miles northwest of The Loop into an inferno, spreading panic among workers in upper floors of the four-story building. Some leaped from windows. Others fled from lower exits, their clothes ablaze.

Sixteen bodies were taken from the old factory to the morgue. Capt. Ryan said two more bodies had been spotted in the water-filled basement but had not been recovered.

LONG NIGHT AHEAD

Ryan said rescuers faced a long

Turn To Page 15 For More Of FIRES

Eisenhower Hit By Slight Attack Of Food Poisoning

AUGUSTA, Ga., April 16 (AP)—President Eisenhower was stricken today with a "slight attack of food poisoning" but an aide said there was no cause for alarm.

The President went to bed shortly after he returned to Augusta tonight after a 12-hour trip which took him to Washington for a major foreign policy speech and to Salisbury, N. C., for the 200th anniversary celebration of that state's Rowan County.

James C. Hagerty, Eisenhower's press secretary, told newsmen in Salisbury late in the day that the President had been suffering from a "slight attack of food poisoning" all day.

SLIGHT FEVER

The President also had a slight fever all day, Hagerty added.

Shortly after Eisenhower returned to Augusta by plane tonight, Hagerty said in reply to questions that there was no cause for alarm.

Hagerty said neither Dr. Howard Snyder, the President's physi-

Turn To Page 34 For More Of ILLNESS

Three City PTA's Act On Teacher Salary Question

Parent Teacher Associations of the Wharton and George Washington schools went on record at meetings last night urging that a revised teacher salary schedule be adopted by the City School Board.

At a third PTA, that of the Wickersham School, the group passed a motion that the school board give further consideration to the teachers' request for increases, but not necessarily adopt the entire schedule as asked.

The Lancaster Teachers' Association is campaigning to have the revised schedule be made a part of the 1953-54 city school budget. The board at its last meeting tentatively adopted a budget which made no provision for any teacher salary increases other than legislative-mandated increments.

Two members of the association's salary committee, spoke at PTA meetings last night. Charles R. Eshleman Jr., of the McCaskey Faculty, spoke at the

Turn To Page 15 For More Of PTA

1953 HAS PRODUCED 41 DAYS WITH RAIN IN LANCASTER AREA

The weatherman put in a bid for generally fair weather today — probably so he could haul his tattered umbrella to the repair shop for rehabilitation.

Early yesterday's showers gave April 16 the distinction of being the 41st rainy day of 1953—a mark that has seen Lancaster County dodging precipitation practically every other day.

It was the 10th day of rain for April, and the .14 of an inch that it produced raised the month's total to 2.63—or a little more than half an inch less than the normal for the entire month.

April, in fact, was almost up to March in total days (11) but lagging in total precipitation (5.37). January still stands second to March in the 1953 moisture derby with a 13-day total of 4.04 inches, almost an inch above normal. February produced a sub-normal mark of 2.73 in its six wet days.

FOP Lodge Here Praises Bill For Promotion Tests

Official of Red Rose Lodge, 16, Fraternal Order of Police, said last night they favored legislation now before the State Senate, which would require police promotions in third class cities to be made on a competitive examination basis.

However, Kenneth I. Witmer, president of the lodge said the membership adopted no resolution to that effect, although they were definitely in favor of the proposed bill.

NO BEARING HERE

The reason no resolution was made, Witmer said, was that members of the local lodge felt the proposal does not have any direct bearing on the City Police Department.

"We feel that in Third Class cities where police departments are controlled lock, stock and barrel by politics, that the bill will be well received."

But, he added, the local lodge didn't feel "any appreciable difference would be felt here."

He said the membership discussed the bill at their meeting in the Police Station last night and the general consensus was that "it is a good piece of legislation."

Mayor K. C. Bare and City Solicitor B. M. Zimmerman had previously voiced opposition to the bill which already has been given an okay by the State House of Representatives.

President Challenges Russians To Prove Peace Move Sincerity

Global Disarmament, Steps To Ease Tension Suggested In Speech

WASHINGTON, April 16 (AP)— President Eisenhower today challenged Soviet Russia's new regime to prove its peace overtures are sincere by agreeing to global disarmament and by taking concrete steps to ease the tensions that threaten World War III.

"The first great step along this way must be the conclusion of an honorable armistice in Korea," the President said in a speech widely heralded as America's answer to the Soviet peace offensive.

Key Quotes Page 19

Once the path of peace has been clearly charted, once the fears of East-West strife have abated, Eisenhower proposed setting up a multi-billion dollar fund from the savings of disarmament to wage a "new kind of war"—an all-out global war against "the brute forces of poverty and need."

WORLD AID FUND

For this purpose, Eisenhower suggested that a "substantial percentage" of the savings achieved by calling off the arms race should go into a fund for "world aid and reconstruction."

Some 400 of the nation's leading editors volleyed applause as Eisenhower addressed the American Society of Newspaper Editors in his first full-dress speech on for-

Turn To Page 34 For More Of EISENHOWER

PEACE CHALLENGE — President Eisenhower challenges Russia's new leaders to prove their will for peace by ending the Korean war, lifting the iron curtain from satellite countries and joining a world disarmament pact that would outlaw atomic weapons. The President made his challenge in a speech in Washington before the American Society of Newspaper Editors.

Pravda Says Eisenhower Failed To Prove His Point

MOSCOW, Friday, April 17 (AP)—Pravda declared today that President Eisenhower failed in his peace program to prove with facts that Russian policy is to blame for present world tension.

The Communist party newspaper ran a 300-word story on Eisenhower's speech to the American Society of Newspaper Editors in Washington yesterday. It included a complete outline of his five-point disarmament proposal.

Pravda's story, attributed to the Soviet news agency Tass, said Eisenhower blamed present world tension on Russian policy, "though no facts were given to prove this."

CHINA QUESTION

Tass said Eisenhower had "completely by-passed" the "question of China and the restoration of her national rights, as well as such a question as the restoration of German unity in accordance with the Potsdam agreement.

Tass said:

"President Eisenhower pointed out that at present the question of the 'chances for establishing a

Turn To Page 34 For More Of PRAVDA

PEACE ADDRESS WINS APPLAUSE OF CONGRESSMEN

Some Say President Has Seized Initiative In Cold War

WASHINGTON, April 16 (AP) — President Eisenhower's global peace challenge to the Russians was applauded generally by members of both parties in Congress today.

Several lawmakers spoke of Eisenhower having "seized the initiative" in the cold war. There were a few scattered dissents.

Sen. Welker (R-Idaho) rated it with Theodore Roosevelt's speech about speaking softly but carrying a big stick.

"The Russians now must move in one direction or the other," Welker commented.

PEACE WITH HONOR

Sen. Knowland of California, chairman of the Senate Republican Policy Committee, told his colleagues the speech was a demonstration that the free world intends to remain strong and united until a "peace with honor" is assured.

He said it served notice that there will be "no more Munichs" or sacrifices of the rights of small nations.

Senate Democratic Leader Lyndon B. Johnson of Texas commented:

"The President is calling upon the Russians to demonstrate their good faith by hard deeds and not just by soft words. He is also warning them that the free nations

Turn To Page 34 For More Of REACTION

VOLUNTEER POLICE IN CD ORGANIZATION MEETING APRIL 27

Sheriff Abe Lane, director of the Security Division of the Lancaster County civil defense organization, yesterday announced plans for a joint meeting of city and county volunteer police personnel on Monday, April 27.

The important session, Sheriff Lane said, will be held in the auditorium of the YMCA, starting at 7:30 p.m.

The law enforcement official urged all commissioned volunteer policemen and women in the city and county to attend, as well as persons who attended the recent training sessions but who have not yet received their commissions.

A speaker will be present from the State Police Training Barracks at Hershey to discuss riot control, Sheriff Lane said.

Marine's Heart Was On Queen St. As He Left Battlefield On Easter

CPL. JAMES R. BURIE

The thoughts of a Lancaster Marine, who had just left one of the bloodiest battlefields of the Korean War, were on the fashion parade on N. Queen Street on Easter Sunday.

The information that Cpl. James R. Burie, 539 W. Vine St., was thinking of his home town was contained in a letter the Marine sent to Edward G. Wilson, local business man, who publishes "World Travelers of Lancaster County, a news letter and directory sent free to all service personnel.

Corporal Burie, who enlisted in the Marine Corps in 1951 for combat duty, wrote in his heart-warming letter:

"Your newsletter arrived Easter Sunday and I just can't say how

Turn To Page 15 For More Of MARINE

REDS ASKED TO GET DOWN TO BUSINESS

Suggest Swiss Handle PWs Who Don't Want To Go Home

MUNSAN, Korea, Friday, April 17 (AP)— The U. N. Command today said it was ready to resume the Korean armistice talks if the Reds will get promptly down to business on the last key issue — handling of Red prisoners who don't want to go home.

A letter turned over to the Communists at Panmunjom today:

1. Suggested Switzerland as the neutral nation to take custody of such prisoners—in Korea.

2. Went further than the latest Red offer by proposing a 60-day time limit after which the neutral state would arrange the "peaceful disposition" of those who still refused to go home.

EARLY START

3. Offered to send lower level liaison officers to Panmunjom as early as tomorrow "to discuss matters incidental to reopening plenary sessions of the armistice delegations. . . ."

While today's move was made toward a possible truce in the nearly three-year-old war, the first of the Allied sick and wounded to be exchanged were waiting at Kaesong, just six dusty miles from freedom.

The letter handed over at Panmunjom today was from Lt. Gen. William K. Harrison Jr., senior Allied armistice negotiator, to Lt. Gen. Nam Il, senior Red delegate.

Nam earlier had asked the Allies to resume the full-scale armistice talks.

50,000 TO RESIST

Nearly 50,000 of the 132,000 prisoners held by U. N. forces have said they would resist repatriation. When the Allies broke off the truce talks last Oct. 8, the Reds

Turn To Page 34 For More Of PRISONERS

200 CHINA REDS ARE DRIVEN OFF PORK CHOP HILL

Americans Regain Height, Smash Flank Attack Near Main Line

SEOUL, Friday, April 17 (AP)—American soldiers drove 200 Chinese soldiers off Pork Chop Ridge today and smashed a nearby flank attack on the approaches to the main Allied line in Western Korea.

A frontline officer said the U. S. troops restored their positions on Pork Chop at 8:30 a. m. This was the first indication that the Chinese assault which was launched after dark Thursday had forced the Americans off at least a section of the ridge.

The attacking Chinese streamed down Old Baldy, a key strongpoint wrested from the Allies a month ago. They surged against Pork Chop Ridge, swarmed into the trenches and clashed in savage hand-to-hand combat with the Americans.

HURLED BACK

A second Chinese force of 200 troops split off and assaulted West View, an Allied outpost hill just east of Old Baldy. A U. S. First Corps spokesman said American

Turn To Page 15 For More Of WAR

George Kell Hitting At .415 Clip To Lead American League Race

—4 For 4—

Meet Philadelphia's "Fearsome Foursome"

Roberts, Simmons, Shantz And Kellner Win Four In Same Day

ROBIN ROBERTS

CURT SIMMONS

BOBBY SHANTZ

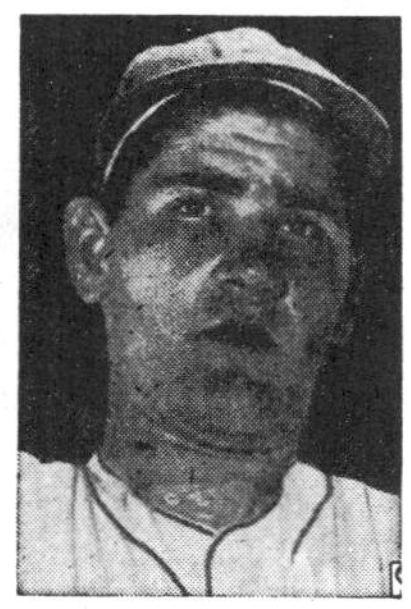

ALEX KELLNER

PHILADELPHIA, May 4 (AP)—For the baseball fan interested in pitching artistry, now is a good time to take a look at the "fearsome foursome" of Philadelphia's two major league clubs.

At this early stage of the 1953 season the Philadelphia Phillies and Athletics are flirting with pennant ambitions because the two top men on each staff have just about handcuffed opposition batters in their starts to date.

Like yesterday, when managers Steve O'Neill and Jimmy Dykes started the foursome and walked off with four complete games, four victories. O'Neill's Phillies climbed into a tie for the National League lead. The A's jumped to third place in the American League.

Robin Roberts boosted his season record to four wins, lone loss, by overpowering the Chicago Cubs, 5-1. The lefty in the National Leaguers' tandem, Curt Simmons, shut out the Cubs, 2-0, in the second game to match Roberts' 4-1 record.

In Chicago, lefty Bobby Shantz kept shooting for a second successive most valuable player award in the American League with a 4-2 win to make his 1953 log 3-2. Then Alex Kellner also a southpaw, managed a 10-6 victory, his fourth against one loss.

The last time both Philadelphia clubs swept doubleheaders on a Sunday was July 30, 1950.

Glancing back to the start of the season, you'll find the New York Giants beat Roberts on opening day and he hasn't been stopped since. He's gone the route in each of his five outings and leads the league in strikeouts with 26. Yesterday he fanned six and walked two while keeping the Cubs to six singles.

Simmons also walked two and struck out five as he shut out the Cubs, with five singles. Second to Roberts in strikeouts with 25, Simmons has lost only to the Cardinals, 1-0, in 11 innings.

Burly Kellner is the surprise of the four to date. Alex brushed the New York Yankees off without a run in 18 innings. Then the Cleveland Indians edged Kellner, 2-1, his lone defeat. Yesterday, the A's hitting was enough to offset 10 singles and one double for six White Sox runs. Kellner yielded five walks and struck out four, the first time this year he's walked more than he fanned.

Shantz, as usual, had his control in passing only one while whiffing four. He gave up eight hits, including a home run and double to former A's first baseman, Ferris Fain. Bobby, only losses so far have been to New York, 4-1 and 5-2. Last year he was 4-3 against the champs.

Shuk Has 3 Winners At Pimlico Opening; 11,585 Bet $800,000

BALTIMORE, Md., May 4 (AP) — Jockey Nick Shuk, Maryland's hottest rider, gained his third winner on Pimlico's opening day program when he drove Mrs. Samuel M. Pistorio's Brazen Brat to a popular win over Sweet Vermouth.

Pimlico, which will have a 21-day meeting climaxed by the $100,000 Preakness, was host to a crowd of 11,585 fans today who bet approximately $800,000 on the program.

Brazen Brat, a 5-year-old mare, was $3.60 for $2 favorite in the six furlongs Rogers Purse and was running her first race in the colors of Mrs. Pistorio. She had previously been owned by R. Bruce Livie's Bobanet Stable and was purchased only today by Mrs. Pistorio.

Beaten by a nose in her last two starts at Bowie, Brazen Brat was gaining her first win of the 1953 season and turned the six furlongs over a fast track in a snappy 1:11 3-5.

Lord Admirality finished third in the allowance feature, two lengths behind Sweet Vermouth and a nose in front of Jack the Great.

Shuk, who wound up the Bowie meeting Saturday with 43 winners, showed that he has lost none of his touch at this track. In addition to winning with Brazen Brat, he was astride the third and fourth race winners—Mrs. Fred Killian's Bon Lynn ($11.60) and Life Policy ($4.80), owned by the estate of C. B. Bohn.

GARDEN STATE ENTRIES

1ST — $3,500, 2 y.o., 5 f.:—Tops 115, Tiger Cat 118, Peddie 118, Roman Mirage 118, Blue Scamp 118, Hot Pilot 118, Martyr 111, Good Tune 118, Woodlands 118, Canaria 118, Zero Lad 118, Mielaison 118, Iron Heels 118, Rags 118, Ticonderoga 118, Farjac 118.

2ND — $3,000, clmg., 3 y.o., 6 f.:—Malzinia 114, Helot 118, Gay Drummer 115, Wolf Cry 115, Director Belle 115, Cognac 115, Jimminy Joy C 105, Mr. Minority 115, Jersey Devil 115, Panting 115, Challenge Jane 119, T-Formation 115, Chan 108, Our Topper 110, Dazzling Miss 110, Barbara Belle 110.

3RD — $4,000, 3 y.o., 6 f.:—Peleliu 109, China Doll 107, Where Are We 110, Rawar 119, Elained 109, Wiser Yet 107, Twilight Song 110, Mystery Flight 103, War Lass 114, Pearl Diver 103, Admiration 108, First Star 107.

4TH — $3,500 clmg., 4 y.o. & up, 6 f.:—Warmed Over 112, Gambler 115, Star Z 115, Passing Parade 115, Estuary 104, Our Town 113, Milldale 115, For Rent 120.

5TH — $3,500, clmg., 4 y.o. & up, 1 1/16 mi.: — Bases Loaded 112, Rusty 114, Dollargofast 114, Grey Arrow 114, Jay Window 113, Sun Roamer 114, Point Fortune 114, Bob F. 112, Highquillo 112.

6TH — $6,000, 3 y.o., 1 1/16 mi.:—Heuso 116, By Zeus 114, Better Goods 118, New Dream 116, Scimitar 118, Joe Jones 113, Sakr-El-Bahr 108, Bassanio 108, Dandola 114.

7TH — $5,000, 4 y.o. & up, 6 f.:—War Phar 125, Do Report 122, Brush Burn 122, Recover 104, Wonderful You 104, Pacific Ocean 109.

8TH — $4,500 clmg., 4 y.o. & up, 1 1/16 mi.:—Thasian Hero 114, a-Lone Shadow 106, Ardoch 119, Rock Span 111, c-Hierarch 119, a-Tape Reader 118, c-The Eagle 119, Bertrandville 112, Bigdome 108, Pine Ville 111. a—Prisjoe Stable and Potato Chip Farm. c—Carolyn K. Stable entry.

PIMLICO ENTRIES

1ST — $2,500 clmg., 4 y.o. & up, 6 f.:—Satartia 118, Surprising 116, Johns Ex 113, Blue Fedora 113, Nicodem 121, Detective 118, Caveswood 114, Poe's Poem 111, King's Tip 119, Sandvar 116, Foggy Night 116, Dainger Girl 113, Double Nip 118, Miss Judex 108, Slush 119, Bo Mowlee 118.

2ND — $3,000 clmg., 3 y.o. & up, 1 1/16 mi.:—Sparkling Rock 112, Monacoan 116, Tampero 117, Bakers Raider 117, Peaceful Scot 117, Albion 112, Lina 2d 114, Revenger 113, Toy Fox 120, Hackensak 117, Inchobar 115, Nora's Bonnet 107, Attention Sir 120, Eagle Speed 117, Temm 115, Flaming Lady 116.

3RD — $3,000 clmg., 2 y.o., 5 f.:—Bountiful Miss 115, Yellow Fly 115, Rough Spin 115, Jacklyn 115, Libby's First 115, Mid Admiral 115, John Nick 113, Sir Ivanhoe 118, Nell Jay 115, a-Assistance 115, Light Lewis 118, Sir Dude 118, a-Dotty Byrne 115, Chowgarh 110, Black Widow 115, Spring Rain 118. a—Firman-Nydrie Stable entry.

4TH — $2,500 clmg., 4 y.o. & up, 6 f.:—Mary Agnes 113, Psychic Dream 110, Mad Marie 113, Ritbred 111, Fern Gold 112, No Disgrace 115, Heddy B. 107.

5TH — $2,800 clmg., 4 y.o., 6 f.:—Intheswim 108, War Colleen 117, Little Herman 117, Silver Spot 111, Peat Smoke 113, Quick Imperial 119, Miss Bobbie 108, Ed-Ells Gal 117, Plentiful 106.

6TH — $3,800, 3 y.o., 1 1/16 mi.:—Buck N Gee 121, Mr. Skip 118, Famous 121, White Cliff 121, Anns Love 121, Cover Off 111, Sally Catbird 116.

7TH — $4,000, 4 y.o. & up, 1 1/16 mi.:—Gloriette 109, Sonic 114, Again 2nd 114, G. R. Petersen 118, Potpourri 116.

8TH — $3,000, 4 y.o. & up, 1 1/16 mi.:—Dead Duck 116, Whirling Dough 120, Fifty-Five 117, Roedna 111, Fugitive 123, Gala Morn 119, Work Done 119, Inanabout 112.

PIMLICO RESULTS

1ST — $3,000, 2 y.o., 5 f.:—
Militant Miss (Barrow) $11.80 $7.20 $3.60
Waited (Hartack) 26.80 8.00
Quick Imp (Shuk) 2.40
Time—1:01 2/5. Scratched—Moon Dash, Tod Manley, Bobsled, Assistance.

2ND — $2,500, 4 y.o. & up, 6 f.:—
Dance Light (Barlow) $51.40 $19.40 $8.80
Christmas Morn (Edwards) . 9.00 4.60
Cross Bones (Shuk) 3.00
Time—1:14 1/5. Scratched — Caveswood, Running Short, Dainger Girl, Mother's Cheer.

DAILY DOUBLE — Militant Miss and Dance Light Paid $204.10.

3RD — $2,500, 4 y.o. & up, 1 1/8 mi.:—
a-Bon Lynn (Shuk) ... $11.60 $4.80 $3.40
In the Market (Lasswell) .. 5.60 4.40
Luscious Fruit (Caffarella) 5.60
Time—1:55 2/5. Scratched — Peaceful Scot, Fiery, False Front, Daylight Time, Martha Paula, Flaming Lady.

4TH — $3,000, 2 y.o., 5 f.:—
Life Policy (Shuk) $4.80 $3.80 $2.60
Ridgewell Boy (Cardoza) ... 15.00 5.80
Andy Johnson (Hewitt) 3.00
Time—1:01 2/5. Scratched—Sir Dude, Red Cardinal, Above, Daddy Darling.

5TH — $2,800, 3 y.o., 6 f.:—
Newberry (Hewitt) $12.00 $7.40 $5.40
Primoridal (Tryon) 16.80 8.60
So Mild (Hartack) 4.00
Time—1:14 3/5. Scratched—Miss Bobbie, My Ag, Brudon.

6TH — $3,800, 3 y.o., 6 f.:—
Eternal Sir (Monteiro) .. $8.20 $3.60 $2.80
Spring Grove (Hewitt) 2.80 2.20
Abracadabra (Nash) 3.20
Time—1:12 4/5. Scratched—Cover Off, Sir Stake.

7TH — $4,500, 4 y.o. & up, 6 f.:—
Brazen Brat (Shuk) .. $3.60 $2.40 $2.20
Sweet Vermouth (Lynch) 3.80 2.80
Lord Admiralty (Burr) 3.80
Time—1:11 3/5. Scratched — Gloriette.

8TH — $3,000, clmg., 4 y.o. & up, 1 1/16 mi.:—
Little Captain (Vasil) $14.00 $7.40 $6.80
Donna Boorse (Cardoza) ... 7.80 6.60
Reunion (Passmore) 6.80
Time—1:47 3/5. Scratched—Side Saddle, Happy Bull, Reveille, Sir Lopez, Recluse, Sunnyman, Jack Fizz.

Redlegs Whip Giants, 9-5, After 12-4 Loss In Opener

NEW YORK, May 4 (AP) — Gus Bell and Ted Kluszewski collected 10 hits and drove in 12 runs between them as the cellar dwelling Cincinnati Redlegs snapped an eight-game losing streak today, dividing a double header with the New York Giants.

A slim gathering of 7,248 saw Cincinnati capture the second game, 9-5, after the Giants had won the opener, 12-4.

Bell's three-run homer off Larry Jansen went to waste in the opener, but the slugging outfielder came through with a grand slam belt and three singles to drive home five runs in the nightcap. Kluszewski matched Bell's five-hit total and batted in four runs. His four - bagger with two mates aboard off loser Jim Hearn in the opening inning of the nightcap gave the Redlegs an early 3-0 lead.

(First Game)

Cincinnati	AB	H	O	A
Bridges,2b	5	2	2	1
Hatton, 3b	5	0	2	0
Marsh'll,rf	3	1	2	0
aPost, rf	0	0	0	0
Klus'ski,1b	4	3	6	1
Gr'ngr's,lf	3	0	3	0
Bell, cf	4	1	2	0
McMil'n,ss	4	0	4	2
Landrith,c	4	0	3	0
Raf'b'g'r,p	1	0	0	1
bFoiles	1	0	0	0
Nevel, p	0	0	0	1
cMarquis	1	1	0	0
Smith, p	0	0	0	1
King, p	0	0	0	1
dBork'ski	1	1	0	0
Totals	36	9	24	8

New York	AB	H	O	A
Will'ms,2b	4	2	1	5
Dark, ss	4	2	1	2
Th'ms'n,cf	5	1	3	0
Irvin, lf	4	2	3	0
Th'pson,lf	0	0	0	0
L'kman,1b	4	2	11	0
Spencer,3b	5	3	1	1
Mueller,rf	5	2	1	0
Yvars, c	5	1	6	0
Jansen, p	3	3	0	1
Wilhelm,p	1	1	0	0
Totals	41	19	27	9

a—Ran for Marshall in 8th.
b—Grounded out for Raffensberger in 5th
c—Singled for Nevel in 7th.
d—Singled for King in 9th.

Cincinnati .... 000 100 300 —4
New York .... 022 100 07x—12

R—Bridges, Kluszewski, Greengrass, Bell, Williams, Dark 2, Thomson, Irvin 3, Lockman, Spencer, Jansen, Wilhelm. E—Bell, Greengrass. RBI—Irvin 2, Jansen, Spencer 5, Dark, Kluszewski, Bell 3, Thomson, Lockman. 2B—Wilhelm. 3B—Irvin, Spencer. HR—Irvin, Bell, Spencer. S—Williams. DP—King, McMillan and Kluszewski. Left—Cincinnati 7, New York 9. BB—Raffensberger 1, King 2, Jansen 1, Wilhelm 1. SO—Raffensberger 1, Jansen 3, Wilhelm 2. HO—Raffensberger 9 in 4; Nevel 3 in 2; Smith 3 in 1 1-3; King 4 in 2-3; Jansen 5 in 6 (none out in 7th); Wilhelm 4 in 3. R-ER—Raffensberger 5-5, Nevel 0-0, Smith 2-2, King 5-5, Jansen 4-4, Wilhelm 0-0. W—Jansen (2-2). L—Raffensberger (0-3). U—Donatelli, Gorman, Conlan, Warneke. T—2:29.

(Second Game)

Cincinnati	AB	H	O	A
Marquis,cf	4	2	4	0
Hatton, 3b	3	1	2	1
Bell, rf	5	4	2	1
Klus'ski,1b	4	2	8	1
Gr'ngr's,cf	5	1	2	0
Bridges,2b	3	2	3	5
McMil'n,ss	5	1	2	2
Seminick,c	5	0	3	0
Church, p	4	2	0	1
Podb'lan,p	0	0	1	0
Totals	38	15	27	11

New York	AB	H	O	A
Will'ms,2b	4	1	4	3
Dark, ss	4	0	2	4
Th'ms'n,cf	4	3	2	0
Irvin, lf	4	2	2	1
L'kman,1b	4	1	9	1
Spencer,3b	4	1	1	1
Mueller,rf	4	0	2	0
Yvars, c	3	1	5	0
aGilbert	1	0	0	0
Hearn, p	1	1	0	0
Lanier, p	1	0	0	0
bWilson	1	0	0	0
Koslo, p	0	0	0	0
Corwin, p	0	0	0	0
Totals	35	10	27	10

a—Grounded out for Yvars in 9th.
b—Grounded for Lanier in 8th.

Cincinnati .... 300 010 401—9
New York .... 000 000 320—5

R—Marquis 2, Hatton 2, Bell 2, Kluszewski 2, Church, Williams, Thomson 2, Irvin, Lockman. E—None. RBI—Kluszewski 3, Bell 5, Irvin, Lockman, Thomson 2, Mueller, McMillan. 3B—Irvin. HR—Kluszewski, Bell, Thomson. SB—Greengrass. S—Hatton 2, Marquis. DP—Hatton, Bridges and Kluszewski; Williams, Dark and Lockman; Williams and Lockman. Left—Cincinnati 8, New York 3. BB—Hearn 2, Corwin 1. SO—Church 2, Podbielan 1, Hearn 1, Lanier 2. HO—Church 10 in 7 2-3; Podbielan 0 in 1 1-4; Hearn 7 in 4 1-3; Lanier 6 in 3 2-3; Koslo 2 in 1 1-3; Corwin 0 in 2-3. R-ER—Church 3-5, Podbielan 0-0, Hearn 4-4, Lanier 4-4, Koslo 1-1, Corwin 0-0. W—Church (1-1). L—Hearn (1-3). U—Gorman, Conlan, Warneke and Donatelli. T—2:09. A—7,248.

MANOR "9" TOPS M'CASKEY, 6 - 4

Lloyd Bortzfield proved just as effective at the plate as he was on the mound yesterday as he batted and pitched Manor to a 6-4 exhibition victory over the Central Pennsy league-leading McCaskey nine.

Bortzfield went the route for the club which holds down a runner-up post in Section 2 of the County league and was touched for four hits.

He was instrumental in the scoring in both big innings for Manor. In the second inning he tripled to drive in one run, and scored himself on Rylee's single. In the fourth, another three-run frame, the Manor star opened the scoring with a homer with the bases empty.

Ron Etter started for McCaskey and gave way to Montgomery in the sixth inning. Etter absorbed the loss.

Score by innings:

McCaskey	011	020	0—4	4	4
Manor	030	300	x—6	5	0

Etter, Montgomery (6) and Wiker, Harmon; Bortzfield and Herr.

HONEY BROOK WINS

Honey Brook came up with a three-run rally in the sixth inning yesterday to defeat Paradise, 9-7, in an exhibition game on the winner's diamond.

Paradise	004	110	0—7	2	2
Honey Brook	231	003	x—9	8	4

Wenger and Benner; Lowe, Holland and Leisey.

TIGERS BLAST 4 YANKEE HURLERS FOR 10 TO 8 WIN

DETROIT, May 4 (AP)—The last-place Detroit Tigers, getting a big and unexpected boost from relief pitcher Art Houtteman, slammed the Yankee hurlers for 18 hits and a 10-8 victory today that knocked the New Yorkers out of undisputed possession of first place in the American League.

Pounding Yankee ace Vic Raschi and three reliefers, the Tigers dropped New York into a first-place tie with Cleveland and set up a battle for the league lead tomorrow night when the two teams meet in a game at Cleveland.

Houtteman, the big right-hander, came on in the eighth inning and, amid boos from the crowd of 7,405, cut off a four-run rally by the Yankees. With the tying run on first, he got the last out of the inning and then retired the side in order in the ninth, striking out Mickey Mantle to end it.

New York	AB	H	O	A
Rizzuto,ss	3	1	2	4
dCerv	1	0	0	0
Brid'w'r,ss	0	0	0	0
Mize, 1b	4	1	9	1
Woodl'g,lf	4	0	0	0
Mantle, cf	4	2	2	0
Bauer, rf	4	1	3	0
M'D'ald,3b	4	1	2	1
Berra, c	4	0	2	0
Martin, 2b	3	2	4	4
bNoren	1	1	0	0
Carey, 3b	0	0	0	1
Raschi, p	2	0	0	3
Miller, p	0	0	0	1
aBollweg	1	1	0	0
M'Don'd.p	0	0	0	0
cRenna	1	1	0	0
Black'ell,p	0	0	0	0
Totals	36	11	24	15

Detroit	AB	H	O	A
Hatfield,3b	5	3	0	4
Kuenn, ss	4	1	0	3
Sullivan,lf	5	2	2	0
Nieman,rf	5	3	4	0
Dropo, 1b	5	2	12	2
Lund, cf	4	3	2	1
Batts, c	4	2	4	1
Priddy, 2b	3	1	1	1
Newh's'r,p	1	1	1	1
Marlowe,p	1	0	1	0
Madison, p	2	0	0	0
Hout'm'n,p	0	0	0	0
Totals	39	18	27	13

a—Singled for Miller in 7th.
b—Hit a home run for Martin in 8th.
c—Singled for McDonald in 8th.
d—Flied out for Rizzuto in 8th.

New York .... 000 102 140— 8
Detroit .... 010 114 21x—10

R—Rizzuto, Mize, Woodling, Mantle, Bauer, McDougald, Martin, Noren, Hatfield, Kuenn, Nieman 2, Dropo 2, Lund 2, Batts, Madison. E—Madison. RBI—Mantle, Mize, Bollweg, McDougald, Noren 3, Lund 2, Sullivan 2, Batts 4, Hatfield, Kuenn. 2B—Mantle, Martin, Hatfield, Lund 2, Sullivan. 3B—Nieman, Sullivan. HR—Mize, Noren. S—Rizzuto, Kuenn. DP—Raschi, Rizzuto and Mize; Martin and Mize. Left—New York 5, Detroit 7. BB—Miller 1, Newhouser 1, Marlowe 2. SO—Raschi 1, Blackwell 1, Newhouser 1, Madison 1, Houtteman 1. HO—Raschi 10 in 5 (none out in 6th), Miller 2 in 1; McDonald 4 in 1, Blackwell 2 in 1, Newhouser 3 in 4; Marlowe 2 in 1 1-3, Madison 6 in 2 1-3, Houtteman 0 in 1 1-3. R-ER—Raschi 5-5, Miller 2-2, McDonald 2-2, Blackwell 1-1, Newhouser 1-1, Marlowe 2-2, Madison 5-1, Houtteman 0-0. WP—Madison. W—Madison (2-0). L—Raschi (1-2). U—Soar, Rommel, Berry and McKinley. T—2:43. A—7,045.

LITITZ HIGH NET TEAM WINS 10TH

Lititz High School, beaten only once this season by the Inter-County Scholastic champions, Mount Joy, scored its tenth tennis victory yesterday as they whipped Wyomissing, 6-1, at Lititz.

It was the second meeting of the two clubs this year. In an earlier engagement, the Lititz netmen squeezed in with a 4-3 win.

Wyomissing's only victory yesterday was in the number one singles match when Dick Rickenbach defeated Joe Grosh, 6-1, 6-3. Morris Fredericks also found a rugged competitor in Bob Dries and was extended to three sets before getting the win. The last set finally went to Fredericks, 10-8.

The summaries:

LITITZ 6, WYOMISSING 1
SINGLES
Rickenbach (W) defeated Grosh (L) 6-1, 6-3.
MacFarran (L) defeated Meinig (W) 6-1, 6-0.
Fredericks (L) defeated Dries (W) 6-3, 3-6, 10-8.
Stout (L) defeated Muhlenberg (W) 6-1, 6-0.
Runk (L) defeated Sutton (W) 6-1, 6-1.
DOUBLES
Stout and Fredericks (L) defeated Dries and Muhlenberg (W) 6-1, 6-1.
Runk and Davidson (L) defeated Rickenbach and Meinig (W) 6-1, 6-3.

SETS NEW WORLD'S WEIGHTLIFTING MARK

PITTSBURGH, May 4 (AP)—Alex Bilin, representing the Pittsburgh Boy's Club, lifted 287½ pounds in the two-hand military-press weight lifting competition of the Allegheny Mountain Association's Amateur Athletic Union Saturday night and officials said it set a new world's record.

The former record of 286 pounds was set by a Russian, officials said.

M'CASKEY HAS TWO TEAMS IN ACTION TODAY

McCaskey High School sends its league-leading baseball team into Central Pennsy League action today and its track team to Hanover for the Hanover Relays in the feature attractions on another heavy Tuesday sports card.

Two collegiate contenders, Millersville and Franklin and Marshall, serve up some local entertainment in diamond drills and the huge County High baseball league offers another eight-game program.

McCaskey's nine is currently tied with Hershey and John Harris for the league lead with a record of six wins and two losses. Their opponents today will be the seventh place Steelton team (2-6), and the game will be played at Steelton.

Millersville, rained out of its initial test with Shepherd, will try to get in this home tussle with the West Virginia college at Millersville today. The Marauders carry a 4 and 2 record this season.

F&M, with a record of four wins and four losses, takes on the always-tough Lebanon Valley nine at F&M today in an effort to move into the winning side of the ledger.

McCaskey's track team, beaten last Friday for the first time in dual meet competition since 1951, will send its representatives to Hanover in search of glory in these annual trials.

In the County High league, Mount Joy, unbeaten in four Section 1 starts in the County high league, looks for win number five against the fifth-place Marietta team.

Solanco and Manor feature Section 2 action with the runner-up berth at stake in the meeting of these two clubs at Solanco and in Section 3, the lead is up for grabs with the two current pacers, Manheim Central and East Lampeter, battling for the top rung.

Section 4, with a single game dividing the first and last place clubs, has Cocalico (3-2) host to Salisbury (2-3) and Upper Leacock (3-2) at Warwick (2-3).

CAPTAINS TENNIS TEAM

Nancy J. Eckman, daughter of Mr. and Mrs. John A. Eckman, 1026 Woods Ave., has been elected captain of tennis of the Women's Athletic Association at Springfield College, Springfield, Mass., for next year. She is a sophomore majoring in physical education.

TODAY'S LOCAL SPORTS LINEUP

BASEBALL
COLLEGIATE
Shepherd at Millersville STC.
Lebanon Valley at F & M.
CENTRAL PENNSY LEAGUE
McCaskey at Steelton.
COUNTY HIGH LEAGUE
Section 1
Marietta at Mount Joy.
Elizabethtown at East Donegal.
Section 2
Manor at Solanco.
Manheim Twp. at Columbia.
Section 3
New Holland at West Lampeter.
Manheim Central at East Lampeter.
Section 4
Upper Leacock at Warwick.
Salisbury at Cocalico.
CENTRAL CITY-COUNTY LEAGUE
Bird-in-Hand at Mountville.
Manheim at East Petersburg.
TRACK
McCaskey in Hanover Relays.
SOFTBALL
INDUSTRIAL LEAGUE
Hubley vs. Hagers at DeWalt.
CTC vs. Armstrong at Lehigh.
YMCA SOFTBALL LEAGUE
St. Paul's ME vs. Church of Christ at F & M.
United Brethren vs. Church of God, at Edward Hand.

ANGLER'S ALMANAC

MAY

Su	Mo	Tu	We	Th	Fr	Sa
					1	2
3	4	5	6	7	8	9
10	11	12	13	14	15	16
17	18	19	20	21	22	23
24	25	26	27	28	29	30
31						

SUSQUEHANNA OUTLOOK

(Monday, May 4)

COLUMBIA—Catties biting. River clear.

SAFE HARBOR — River clear, about normal. Not many anglers. Good cattie catches.

PEQUEA — River clear. No reports.

HOLTWOOD — No reports. River still high, cloudy.

FISHING CREEK — River high and clear. No reports.

PEACH BOTTOM — River clear. Catching catties.

CONOWINGO — Catching catties. River fairly clear.

DEER CREEK SCHWEERS LANDING—Catching hickory shad, perch, catties. River normal, rising slightly.

SEEKS MIDGET GAMES

Jay Cassidy, manager of a midget-midget baseball team, made up of youngsters between the ages of ten and twelve, is seeking games with youngsters in this age bracket. For information, call 3-6320.

GEORGE KELL

KISSINGER DOES IT AGAIN; LANDS 12-POUND CATTIE

The "old pro" did it again. Frank Kissinger, the man who only reports in with the big ones, took a 28½ inch cattie home yesterday after a battle with the 12 pound, seven ounce fish in Lake Clark, his second big cattie catch of the year.

Several weeks ago, he landed a seven and one-half pound catfish at Creswell.

Kissinger said he caught yesterday's prize in open water, on a herring. The man, who gives away more than he takes home, says "this one he's going to eat."

Kissinger's fishing prowess was further complimented yesterday when his fish was ruled out of the annual Columbia contest. Seems his luck is just too good to be true and the other anglers want no parts of a contest which includes an entry by Frank Kissinger.

MOUNT JOY GIRLS NET TEAM TRIUMPHS

The Mount Joy girls tennis team, following the pattern set by the boys team, racked up their third straight win of the season, and protected their unscored-upon mark as they defeated Lititz, 7-0.

The girls have not suffered a defeat in two years of interscholastic competition.

MOUNT JOY 7, LITITZ 0
SINGLES
Schofield (MJ) def. Whitmeyer, 6-0, 6-2.
Markley (MJ) def. Sensenig, 6-0, 6-0.
Thome (MJ) def. Meiskey, 6-1, 6-0.
Schroll (MJ) def. Reist, 6-3, 6-1.
Braught (MJ) def. Adams, 6-2, 7-5.
DOUBLES
Schofield and Rutt (MJ) def. Whitmeyer and Meiskey, 6-0, 6-3.
Thome and Barninger (MJ) def. Sensenig and Longenecker, 6-3, 6-1.

NAT'L LEAGUE PACK PACED BY WYROSTEK

NEW YORK, May 4 (AP)—George Kell, a sparkplug in the surprising early season showing of the fourth-place Boston Red Sox, has taken over as the American League's leading hitter.

The 30-year-old third baseman, who led the junior circuit in batting in 1949, has collected 27 hits in 65 at bats for a .415 mark. Kell had 12-for-27 (.444) last week and picked up 20 points as he shot past Gene Woodling of the New York Yankees.

In the National League, Johnny Wyrostek of the Philadelphia Phillies, although he was unable to maintain last week's .500 pace, still is the pace-setter, at .451. Records includes games played Sunday.

WOODLING HITTING .408

Woodling, sidelined with an eye inflamation last week, dropped to second in the American League at .408. The Yankees flychaser had only three hits in 13 at bats.

Dave Philley of the Philadelphia Athletics and Cleveland's Al Rosen are tied for third at .380. Philley had seven safeties in 24 trips and Rosen eight-for-22.

In fifth place comes Pete Suder of Philadelphia, .366 followed by Tom Umphlett, Boston, .333, Mickey Mantle, New York, .317, Cleveland's Ray Boone, .308, Ferris Fain, Chicago, .300 and Harry Simpson, Cleveland and Milt Bolling, Boston, .298 each.

Cincinnati's Jim Greengrass zoomed into second place in the National League with .405. The rookie outfielder had 10-for-20 last week.

Duke Snider of the Brooklyn Dodgers and Hank Sauer of Chicago are deadlocked for third with .371.

Next come Milwaukee's Bill Bruton with .368, Carlos Bernier, Pittsburgh, .367, Jackie Robinson of Brooklyn, .365, Red Schoendienst, St. Louis, .345, Connie Ryan, Philadelphia, .339 and Cal Abrams, Pittsburgh, Richie Ashburn, Philadelphia and Bobby Adams, Cincinnati with .333 each.

HOME RUN LEADERS

Five players share the American League lead in home runs with four apiece. They are Mantle, Vic Wertz and Dick Kryhoski of St. Louis, Gus Zernial, Philadelphia and Dick Gernert of Boston. The veteran Bob Elliott of St. Louis is the pace-setter in runs batted in with 18.

In the National League, Eddie Mathews of Milwaukee, with six, is the home run leader and Brooklyn's Roy Campanella is tops in runs batted in with 22.

Milwaukee's Max Surkont heads the National League pitchers while Mel Parnell, Boston, Early Wynn, Cleveland and Marlin Stuart, St. Louis are tied for American League honors. Each has won three games and lost none.

SPORTS Pages 19, 20

Eddie Olson Voted Most Valuable In AHL

NEW YORK—Eddie Olson, United States born veteran leftwing of the Cleveland Barons, has been selected as the most valuable League for 1952-53, by the sportswriters and sportscasters of the seven league cities. Olson, a native of Hancock, Michigan, who was the first American born player to ever lead the American Hockey League in scoring during a season, polled a total of 24 points out of a possible 35.

In adding the latest honors to his season collection, Olson increases his league bonus money to $900.00, having previously been voted the leftwing berth on the first all star team, which gave him $300.00, and he received another $300 for his feat in leading the circuit's point scorers. In addition to the $300.00 for his most valuable award, Olson will receive the Leslie Cunningham Trophy, presented annually by the St. Louis Flyers Booster Club.

Olson was a fine choice for most valuable honors, and the selecting committees could not have made a better decision. His leading point total of 86, comprised of 32 goals and 54 assists, was one of the most important factors in Cleveland winning the regular season championship. In the playoffs he gathered in 8 points more on a goal and seven assists to aid his team in the winning of the Calder Cup playoff title.

His value to his team, the basic point for recognition for the award, went much further than his scoring feats however. At one time or another throughout the season, Eddie played all positions on the team except goaltender.

Olson's teammate, all star goaltender Johnny Bower, was the runnerup for most valuable selection, with 12 points out of a possible 35. Olson had four first place votes, one second and one third, with one city not considering him.

How the cities voted:

City	1	2	3
Buffalo	Bower	Eddolls	Olson
Cleveland	Olson	Bower	Juzda
Hershey	Olson	Solinger	Henry
Pittsburgh	Marshall	Olson	Sollinger
Providence	Olson	Bower	Williams
St. Louis	Olson	Fielder	Burnett
Syracuse	Burnett	Mathers	Bower

Rain Halts Parades, May Clear Tomorrow

Little Liz - - -
There is nothing like an ache-by-ache account of your ills to give people a pain in the neck.

LANCASTER NEW ERA

The Weather
(U. S. Weather Bureau Forecast)
Cloudy Tonight, Tomorrow; Warmer Tomorrow.
Temp. Today: High 58; Low 50
Temp. Yesterday: High 68; Low 42

77th Year—No. 23,580 | Lancaster Metropolitan Area Population Official United States Census Figures 234,717 | LANCASTER, PA., SATURDAY, MAY 30, 1953 | NOON EDITION | 16 PAGES | 30c PER WEEK—5c Per Copy

Train Hits 17 Autos on Water St.

RAIN HALTS PARADES IN CITY, COUNTY

GAR Program Is Halted First Time in Memory; May Be Clear Tomorrow

Driving rain today flooded out local Memorial Day parades and exercises, and put a general heavy damper on the many activities which had been planned for the holiday.

It was the first time in the memory of local descendants of Civil War veterans, who sponsor the day's events, that rain had caused calling off of the city parade and exercises. County events were postponed.

A small hearty band, however, paid a brief tribute to the GAR in a wreath-laying ceremony at Penn Square during the peak of the downpour.

Cloudy-Warmer Tomorrow

End of the rain was not in sight at noon, but forecasters said it would taper off and possibly cease this evening. Tomorrow is to be partly cloudy and warmer.

The rain came as a complete surprise, since fair weather had been forecast for just about every spot in the East. But the experts said this is what happened:

A long ridge of high pressure extending north-south across Pennsylvania broke down during the night into two high pressure centers, allowing a "tongue" of warm moist air to enter from New York.

The "tongue" was limited to the area extending from the northern Great Lakes across western New York, across the northern part of Pennsylvania to Philadelphia and New York City.

Washington, D. C., had fair weather today. Pittsburgh was partially clear. Harrisburg, which also had rain and thundershowers, was on the western edge of the wet blanket. The rain did not arrive in the New York area until about 9:30 a. m.

Started About 6:15 A. M.

The steady rain did not start here until about 6:15 a. m. A few showers had fallen during the night. Some thunder was heard this morning.

There was a strong chance that today's rain might make this the second wettest May in the annals of weather records here. Tops for all times is the 8.37 inches of May, 1867. Second high, until this year, was May, 1949, with 6.82 inches.

May Set May Record

Up until today, the total for this May was 5.99 inches at the Ephrata Weather Station. All that was needed to beat the 1949 figure was .83 inch, and that appeared easily possible at mid-morning.

Safe Harbor had .31 inch through the night until 10:30 a. m.

Here is a run-down on the status

—See WEATHER—Page 8

Manor-Mt. Joy Game Postponed Second Time

The Manor-Mount Joy county high school baseball league championship game, postponed last night because of light failure, was postponed again today because of rain.

No new date has been set. The game was about to enter the third inning last night at Stumpf Field, with Manor leading 1-0, when the arc lights blinked out and officials decided to postpone it until 2 p. m. today.

Wreath Is Placed At Monument During Driving Rain

New Era Photo

John Long, eight, son of the Rev. Alfred L. Long, places wreath in rain at Soldiers and Sailors monument in Penn Square. Also present for the ceremonies are: Mrs. Anna Long, Howard Schnee, the Rev. Mr. Long, Mrs. Mame Smith and George Long. George F. K. Erisman, venerable Union Fire Co. member, stood under an umbrella to watch a few feet away.

WAR CONTRACT AT ARMSTRONG

New $861,341 Project For Shell Containers

A new $861,341 ammunition container contract for the Armstrong Cork Co. was announced today.

The contract was announced by the Philadelphia Ordnance District. No details were given.

The Ordnance District also announced a new $432,500 shell contract for Lehigh Foundries at Easton. Lehigh has a local branch on Fountain Ave., which already is making 60 millimeter mortar shells.

Several Contracts Now

Armstrong already has several contracts to make shell containers. One was awarded in April, 1952, and the other last January. In addition, Armstrong is preparing to start production of a new type of 20 millimeter armor-piercing shell for the Navy.

The shell containers are made in the tube department of the floor plant where containers for Armstrong products are also made. The metal tops are fabricated at the closure plant and then the whole container is put together at the floor plant.

Value of the previous contracts was not listed.

SUES MOTHER-IN-LAW

CHATTANOOGA, Tenn. (AP)— Mr. Lamb has sued Mrs. Wolfe. Walter Lamb asked $25,000 damages yesterday in a petition against his mother-in-law, Mrs. Blanche Wolfe. Lamb charged Mrs. Wolfe with "alienation of his wife's affections."

Ike Will Place Wreath on Tomb of Unknown Soldier

By The Associated Press

The United States, mindful of prolonged and dreary fighting still going on in Korea, honors in Memorial Day ceremonies today those who fought and died in past battles.

Big cities and small towns stage parades and memorial services while families of those still fighting pray their men will be home for more thankful exercises another year.

Ike Will Place Wreath

In Arlington National Cemetery President Eisenhower is to place a wreath at the tomb of the unknown soldier.

The President then plans to attend Arlington National Cemetery memorial exercises but will not make a speech.

Similar solemn services were the theme for the day in cemeteries throughout the land.

There were signs that past bitterness of war is being forgotten.

Individual Confederate flags fluttered over Confederate graves for the first time at Rock Island Arsenal in Illinois. These Confederate soldiers buried on Northern soil had died while held as prisoners.

Honor German POW Dead

In Battle Creek, Mich., German flags were placed over 26 graves of Germans who died as prisoners of war at Fort Custer during World War II. The flags were obtained from the West German government by the Gen. George A. Custer American Legion Post. In answering the post's appeal for German flags, Chancellor Adenauer said his government was "deeply moved by your intention to remember German soldies' graves."

Jet Ace Is Honored

Living war heroes shared Memorial Day honors.

In Miami, Fla., the world's second leading MIG killer, 28-year-old Capt. Manuel J. Fernandez Jr., was in for a warm welcome from his home town. The program included a parade, reception and the traditional presentation of the keys to the city.

Ball for Queen Keeps Her Out Until 4 a. m.

Coronation Oddities

Prince Charles Will Wear White Silk Shirt, Shorts

LONDON (AP)—Odd things happen when Coronation fever strikes this capital of eight million.

These are some of them:

Buckingham Palace solemnly announced that four-year-old Prince Charles will not dress up when he goes to see his mother crowned in Westminster Abbey Tuesday. He will just wear a white silk shirt and white silk shorts, an official said.

For lesser men, life was less simple.

Getting Fitted

A sleek Rolls Royce with the five stars of a field marshal was parked for an hour outside London's biggest clothes rental firm — the owner was apparently inside getting outfitted.

London bookmakers once more have the cockneys baffled. A banner outside their Victoria Club headquarters read, "Vivat Regina." Experts say that is Latin for "Long Live the Queen," but it didn't mean much to the bettors.

Albert Shardlow has a television set. His wife, Leonora has another. But neither will watch the Coronation telecast. The Shardlows went before a bankruptcy court yesterday and said the TV sets were their only assets. The court ordered them disconnected.

The Daily Mirror and Daily Sketch, rival London tabloids, have been using gold ink for their titles these days. Now the Daily Mail says anyone who wants it can have the entire mail printed in gold on June 3. The price will be 18 pence (21 cents), compared to three and a half pence (1.75 cents) for the same paper in black ink. June 3 is the day after coronation.

Toast The Queen

Passengers and crew of a British Overseas Airways plane will toast the Queen at noon on Coronation Day. When the sovereign's well-wishers raise their glasses, the plane, bound from Frankfurt to Rome, will be 19,000 feet over the Alps.

The Dean of Westminster, Dr. A. C. Don, has suggested that the

—See ODDITIES—Page 8

Elizabeth's Husband Greets Visiting Royal Guests

LONDON (AP) — Queen Elizabeth II, bubbling with joy, danced late at a pre-coronation ball and didn't get home until four o'clock (London time) this morning.

Only 100 persons were still waiting outside Buckingham Palace in the cold dawn light to cheer the youthful monarch as she returned from the dance at stately old Hampton Court Palace — the same place where her ancestor, King Henry VIII, held his revels 400 years ago.

There had been 20,000 wildly cheering Britons gathered about as the Queen left for the ball with her husband, the Duke of Edinburgh, and Princess Margaret.

The Queen brought her young sister home with her. Margaret, who didn't have a date, popped into the palace for a minute and then drove on to her own residence. Clarence House.

No Engagements Today

With the strenuous routine of Coronation just three days off, the Queen made no engagements for today and planned to rest and take things easy. Palace sources said she and the Duke might run down to Windsor for a breath of air, but would otherwise stay quietly at home.

The ball was given for Elizabeth by the Brigade of Guards. Radiant in pink and white chiffon with a diamond tiara and necklace, she opened the festivities by dancing with the commander of the household brigade, Maj. Gen. Julian Gascoigne.

The party got under way after one of those mishaps that so often plague people giving a wingding for the boss — the lights went out just as the Queen arrived.

She had barely entered the 438-year-old red brick tudor structure through the Anne Boleyn gate when the King's staircase, where she was to be received, was plunged into darkness.

The formal ceremony was hur-

—See CORONATION—Page 8

Recording of Auto Races May Rouse Driver in Coma

PHOENIX, Ariz. (AP)—An hour-long tape recording of the Indianapolis Speedway race is to be made today in hopes that the roar of speeding cars may rouse an injured driver from a five-month-long coma.

The tape recording is to be played at the bedside of Bobby Ball of Phoenix, former Indianapolis driver who was injured in a midget auto race at Gardena, Calif., Jan. 4 and has been unconscious ever since.

Dr. John Eisenbeiss, Ball's physician, gave tentative approval to the unusual treatment on the thought that the familiar roar of the track may provide enough stimulus to restore Ball to consciousness.

BRITISH COURTESY

GIBRALTAR (AP) — All British warships and naval establishments at this British base lowered their colors to half-mast today in honor of America's Memorial Day.

Today's New Era

Inquest Bares Death 'Game' by Teenage Drivers

NORRISTOWN, Pa. (AP) — A probe into the auto death of 14-year-old Mary Jane Linsenbigler has uncovered a game called "points" in which teen-age drivers try to outdo one another in breaking traffic laws.

Contestants are credited with points for the number of traffic stoplights they pass, for exceeding the speed limit and other violations.

The young motorists keep their own score "on the honor system."

Dorothy Cohan, fifteen, testified that Mary Jane was killed during a game of "points" the night of May 20. She and Mary Jane, the girl testified, were passengers in a car which struck a utility pole and overturned near Valley Forge.

Maureen Connolly Wins French Tennis Title

PARIS (AP) — Maureen Connolly, the U. S. Wimbledon Tennis Queen, today won the French championship in her first shot at the title by defeating Doris Hart of Coral Gables, Fla., 6-2, 6-4.

A near capacity crowd of 11,000 in Roland Garros Stadium saw the 18-year-old blonde from San Diego, Calif., gain sweet revenge for her recent loss to Miss Hart in the Italian championships at Rome recently.

ALLIED GUNS, PLANES RIP SEIZED HILLS

Chinese Cling to Fallen Outposts; Losses High; U.N. Main Line Intact

SEOUL (AP) — Chinese Communists clung grimly to three battered outposts near Panmunjom today as Allied big guns and warplanes poured tons of explosives and blazing napalm on the smoking, shell-torn hills.

The Reds wrested outposts Vegas, Carson and Elko from U. S. and Turkish infantrymen in a division-strength assault which opened Thursday night along a five-mile front only 30 miles north of Seoul.

Fighting continued on the East-Central front where the Reds seized several outposts Wednesday night in a 6,500-man attack along a 20-mile front defended by South Korean infantrymen.

Losses Are Heavy

There have been no official casualty reports from either battle yet, but losses on both sides were believed high.

Turkish officers estimated the Chinese lost 3,000 killed and wounded in the 28-hour battle for the low hills which guard the invasion route to Seoul and the main Allied defense line.

Lt. Gen. Maxwell D. Taylor, Eighth Army commander, said Communist capture of the three outposts did not threaten the U. N. main line. He said the Red attacks so far were local engagements rather than a general offensive.

British troops of the Duke of Wellington Regiment hurled back two Red battalions of about 1,500 men, which attacked the Hook, another strategic outpost about 12 miles east of Panmunjom.

Officers of the 25th Division said Americans and Turks pulled off Elko and Vegas so quickly the Reds plastered the hills with mortar and artillery for four hours after the evacuation was complete.

Left Nothing of Value

The Allied troops brought their dead and wounded down the hill and left "nothing of value," a spokesman said.

Maj. Gen. Bruce C. Clark, commander of the U. S. First Corps, sent a message to Division headquarters praising the troops' "valiant achievements."

"Please pass on to the officers and men who bore the brunt of the vicious Chinese assaults of the past 36 hours, especially to the Turkish brigade, 14th Infantry Regiment, 35th Infantry Regiment the Marine Corps, tankers and the Army tankers, my appreciation for a job well done," Clark said.

Drop 500,000 Pounds Of Bombs

Fifth Air Force fighter-bombers and twin-engine B-26 bombers

—See WAR—Page 8

LEFT-TURN BAN ON MONDAY

Signs to Be Posted at Prince and Chestnut

Banning of left turns at Prince and Chestnut Sts. is due to go into effect Monday.

If weather permits, signs will be posted Monday at the intersection prohibiting all left turns, according to Capt. Ray E. Charles, of the Traffic Bureau. If it is raining Monday, he said, the signs will be posted on the first clear day, and the ban will go into effect when the signs go up.

The move is being taken as another step toward clearing away causes for congestion in the mid-city area.

Curbs To Be Painted

Curbs at a number of busy intersections will be painted yellow for a distance of about 65 feet from the intersection, to indicate no parking, thereby giving motorists a clearer view as they approach the cross streets.

First of the curbs to be painted under this plan were those on the east and west sides of N. Queen St., south of Frederick, which were completed yesterday.

Holiday Death Toll Rises Slowly In Early Hours

By The Associated Press

The death toll from violent accidents rose slowly in the first hours of Memorial Day as millions of motorists prepared to head for the highways on the first holiday of the spring season.

Traffic accidents, as expected, took the biggest toll, with 22 persons killed in motor mishaps since 6 p. m. (local time) Friday. One person drowned and four others lost their lives in mishaps of miscellaneous causes.

The National Safety Council has estimated 240 persons will be killed in traffic mishaps in the 54 hours between 6 p. m. Friday and Sunday midnight.

There were 363 persons killed in traffic accidents in the three-day 1952 Memorial Day holiday. Drownings totaled 85 and 62 died from miscellaneous causes for a total of 510, one of the biggest death tolls for the Memorial Day holiday.

WILEY ASSAILS CRITICS OF U.N.

Takes Indirect Slap at Taft on Korean Issue

WASHINGTON (AP)— In an indirect thrust at Senate Republican Leader Taft of Ohio, Sen. Wiley (R-Wis) today condemned those "who would divide us from our Allies and who are blind to the consequences of the act."

Wiley, chairman of the Senate Foreign Relations Committee, did not mention Taft's name in an address prepared for Memorial Day services in Arlington Cemetery. Nevertheless, it was the first strong criticism from Taft's Senate GOP colleagues of the views the Republican leader voiced this week in a speech read for him in Cincinnati.

Taking direct issue with Taft's proposal that the U. S. "abandon any idea of working with the United Nations in the (Far) East" Wiley pleaded for preservation of the U. N. "as the instrument for working out the ills of a sick world."

Ask Ike To Clarify Issue

Two Democrats, Sens. Hill (Ala) and Ellender (La), meanwhile, called on President Eisenhower to clarify his administration's stand on a closely related issue — a proposal to cut off U. S. fund payments to the U. N. if it seats Communist China.

Eisenhower is reported to have discussed at a cabinet meeting

—See WYLIE—Page 8

Phila. Man Dies While Walking on N. Queen St.

A Philadelphia man collapsed in the first block of N. Queen St. today and was rushed by police cruiser to General Hospital where he was pronounced dead on arrival at 7:50 a. m. Death was attributed to a heart attack.

The dead man was tentatively identified as Joseph D. Breslin Sr. Cards on his person indicated a Philadelphia address of 5325 Upland St. He was about 51 years of age.

Police revealed also that the man had had a heart attack last evening when a little before 8 o'clock he collapsed in a restaurant on Manor St. A police cruiser that time too conveyed him to St. Joseph's Hospital. The cruiser picked him up again at the hospital and conveyed him to the Earle Hotel. Police later learned, however, he had previously checked out of the hotel, so his whereabouts between 10 o'clock last evening and 7:30 this morning are unknown.

JUMPS RAILS, WHIPS CARS INTO HOMES

Train Also Injures Man Reported Lying in Center of Street

A 13-car freight train was moving south on Water St. at 12:45 a. m. today and a rear car jumped the track.

These were the results:

Swinging crazily to the right, the car hit 17 parked cars in two blocks of Water St., damaging all of them and wrecking most of them.

Many of the cars were total wrecks, with sides torn off, roofs pushed in, and rear ends collapsed.

Buildings Damaged

Some of the autos were pushed into nearby buildings. Fire escapes were broken. Outside water spigots were torn off.

"It looked like an auto graveyard for two blocks," said Fire Chief Harry Miller. Firemen were called out to guard against spilled gasoline from the broken auto tanks.

Damage was seen running into the many thousands.

The train kept on going. The crewmen were in the front of the train and were unaware what was going on.

Man On Tracks Hit

At Water and Conestoga Sts., Melvin Schlossman, thirty-eight, of Shantytown, was lying on the tracks. Police said he apparently had been drinking.

The front of the train struck Schlossman, pushing him off the track. Police rushed him to St. Joseph's Hospital, where he was admitted in what appeared to be a serious condition.

However, later this morning, hospital attaches said he was found to be in a less serious condition, suffering mostly from brush burns of the back. He also had cuts on the head and feet.

Between Walnut, Chestnut

Because of the Memorial Day holiday, investigators were slow in getting into action. Sgt. J. R. Frantz, of the Pennsylvania Railroad police, said the rear car jumped a switch on Water, about mid-way between Walnut and Chestnut.

Frantz said there was evidence the bar which holds the switch in place had been tampered with.

Parking Meters Ripped

Four city parking meters were ripped out on the west side of Water, between Chestnut and Orange. They were said to be damaged beyond repair.

The noise was described as terrific as the loose freight car went down the street, lashing out like the tail of a snake and sending the parked automobiles sprawling.

Neighbors along the way were awakened and rushed outdoors.

The caboose was next to the en-

—See TRAIN—Page 8

Harvey B. Lutz, Retired Attorney, Dead at 80

Harvey Breneman Lutz, retired local attorney, died today at 1:15 a. m. in the Masonic Hospital, Elizabethtown. He was eighty.

Born in Blainsport, a son of the late Joseph K. and Frances Breneman Lutz, he practiced law in this city for many years. He was a member of the Lutheran Church and Lancaster Lodge 476, F and AM.

Surviving are a daughter, Kathryn, wife of Theodore Storb, city; and two grandchildren.

Employe Recreation Now Includes the Whole Family

It used to be that Pop went out with the plant bowling team and left Mom and the kids home to twiddle their thumbs.

But the trend now is away from that. The men and women from the assembly line hold bridge tournaments, picnics, roller skating parties, and even a pinochile game now and then. And the family comes along.

"The trend in employe recreation programs is toward including the whole family. Industrial programs don't want to break up families."

Authority for that statement is Albert H. Spinner, the newly-elected president of the National Industrial Recreation Association, a nation-wide organization with some 300 company members across the country, with thousands of recreation-minded employes.

Tribute to Armstrong

Spinner also is director of employe activities at the Armstrong Cork Co. and he considers his selection for the top post a tribute to Armstrong's own employe activities program.

Spinner was elected at a meeting of 350 industrial recreation directors at Cleveland last week.

But back to the philosophy of the new prexy of the recreation directors.

'Varsity' Days Over

"I believe that the days of the varsity team program in industries is also past," says Spinner.

"I mean where there was emphasis on a winning soccer team, or a winning baseball team, or a winning basketball team in competition among different industries.

"Now we take it for granted that every industry employe who wants

—See EMPLOYES—Page 12

WEIGHING-IN—At Crispus Attucks Center, three-month-old Sydney Bridgett goes on the scales while his mother, Mrs. Sydney Bridgett, watches smilingly and Miss Dolores Plank, Visiting Nurse, moves the weights. Both Center and VNA are Red Feather agencies, and plan open-house programs during coming week.

20 Ways To Say—

"Thanks!"

THANK YOU WEEK starts tomorrow, with many of Lancaster's 20 Red Feather agencies opening their doors to show appreciation for public support given the Community Chest in 1953. Anything from table tennis at the Salvation Army, to movies at the Crippled Children & Adults Society, to square dancing at the YWCA, may be enjoyed and observed all this week. Purpose of this first Thank You Week is to inform Lancastrians of the number of agencies participating in, and dependent upon, Community Chest contributions, and to show what each is doing because of public support. Sunday News photos show partial preview of week's activities.

PLAYTIME finds Lancaster Day Nursery yard well-equipped to give small-fry a workout. Soon scene will be multiplied many times as Recreation Association opens summer playground program. Other Red Feather agencies, not represented in photos on page, include Family & Children's Service, Boys' Club, Salvation Army, YWCA, Society for Crippled Children & Adults, Guidance Clinic, Rossmere Sanatorium, Shelter Home, Social Service Exchange and USO.

SAY "AHHHH" — Varied reactions by other youngsters awaiting turn for dental look-see are caught by camera as Susan Plotnick opens wide for Visiting Nurse, Mrs. Elizabeth Jacobs. Programs scheduled at center every day but Saturday.

COOK-OUT COMING UP—Girl Scouts' "Thank You" will be a demonstration cook-out in the patio of Community Chest Building, 129 E. Orange St., Tuesday 2 to 5 p. m. Girls of Troop 95, shown in practice session, will show how it's done. With them are Mrs. Paul Strubhar (left), assistant leader, and Miss Kay Yoder (right), leader.

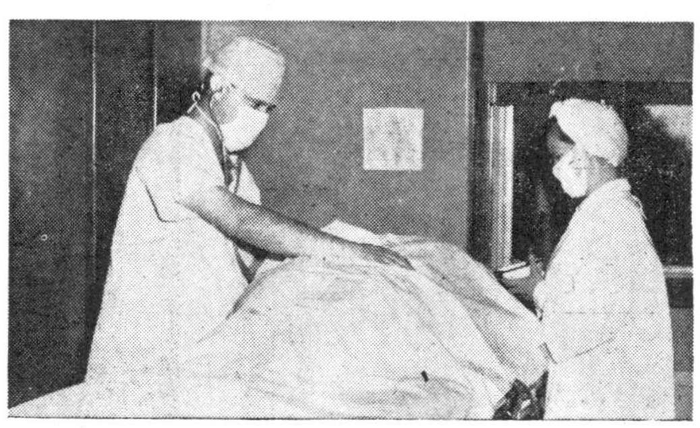

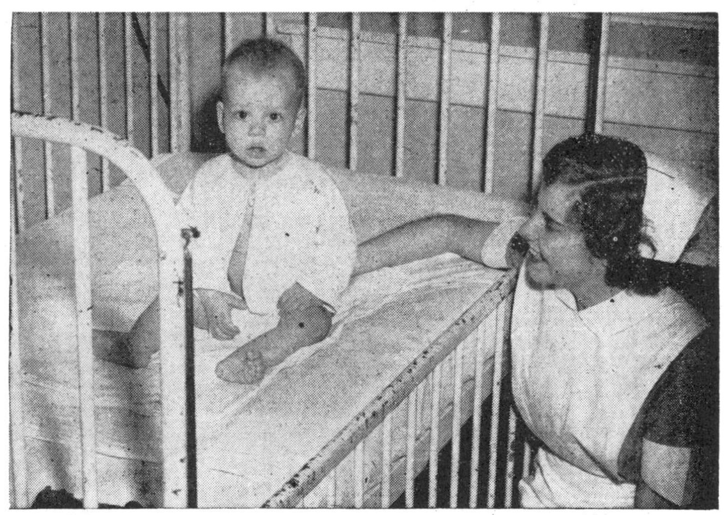

←OSTEOPATHIC HOSPITAL will open doors to visitors for official "Thank You" next Sunday 2-5 p. m. Typical maternity ward scene at left shows actual patient being cared for by Dr. Henry Steffy and Mrs. Phyllis Graybill. Hospital is one of 20 participating Red Feather agencies.

40,000 LANCASTRIANS said "yes" to Community Chest this year, and now 20 agencies answer "thank you." It's expressed for St. Joseph's Hospital by eight-month-old John C. Chancly, with prompting from nurse Joan Hinkle in Children's Ward. Open House is next Sunday 2-4 p. m.

WELL IN HAND—That's how the situation remains at Lancaster Blind Association, open to visitors tomorrow 2-4 p. m. They'll see blind workers at jobs like this. Supervisors is Mrs. Ella Mae Bailey; seated (l-r): Miss Grace Tangert, Mrs. Kitty Keller, Jerry McClarigan.

KNOTTY PROBLEMS are solved by Boy Scout Cub Pack 180, Den 4, in meeting at 553 Spruce St. Den Mother is Mrs. Harry Hosan, with group at right. Den meeting will be held for public Friday 4-6 p. m. in patio at 129 E. Orange St. Also, next Saturday afternoon, Boy Scouts will have open house at Camp Chiquetan, and Girl Scouts at Furnace Hills. With many public assists, Community Chest is holding expenses for entire week's programs to less than $50.

CHILD HAD CONVULSIONS

Ada Mae Gebhard, three, 440 S. Christian St., was conveyed from her home last night by city police to the General Hospital, where she was admitted. Police said she went into convulsions. Hospital attendants said she may be suffering with measles.

S. Queen St. Fire House Improvements Started

Repairs and improvements are being made to Engine House No. 2, S. Queen St. as part of a long-range program to improve the city fire stations.

Automatic doors will be installed and the building painted. Equipment has been transferred to Engine House No. 3 until the repairs are completed.

2 TEAMS NAMED FOR 4-H WEEK

Selected for Poultry, Dairy Demonstration

Dairy and poultry demonstration teams to represent Lancaster County during the 29th annual 4-H Club Week at State College in August have been announced by Clarence E .Craver, assistant county agent.

Selected for the dairy demonstration team are Miss Shirley Rutt, daughter of Mr. and Mrs. George Rutt, Stevens R1, and Robert Rohrer, son of Mr. and Mrs. Raymond Rohrer, Lancaster R7.

The state championship in this event was won last year by Richard Hess, Strasburg R1, and Kenneth Kreider, Quarryville R1.

John Neff, son of Mr. and Mrs. J. Robert Neff, Lancaster R7, and J. Mowery Frey Jr., Lancaster R7 have been selected for the poultry demonstration team.

NewLampeter-Strasburg Teachers Are Named

Two new teachers were elected and one teacher was transferred at a recent meeting of the Lampeter-Strasburg School District.

Succeeding Miss Jean Hays who resigned as instrumental music teacher is John A. McKenzie, Harrisburg. Elected to teach at Oak Hill was Mrs. Ethel R. VanNatta, Strasburg. She succeeds Mrs. Lois Shreiner who has accepted a position in the Lancaster City School District. Mrs. Esther Herr has been transferred from the Lampeter grade school to Willow Street. Vacancies still existing in the district are: grades 1-2 at Strasburg; art, physical education, library and grades 1-2 at Lampeter.

William Musser was elected solicitor by the board, and the First National Bank of Strasburg was named depository.

TREATED FOR BURNS

Albert Becker, thirty, 24 Old Dorwart St., suffered burns of the arms, right hand and face while burning trash in a furnace at the Salvation Army building yesterday. He was treated at the General Hospital.

SIDE GLANCES - - - By Galbraith

GAS
Galbraith
6-23

"You get lots of bent fenders, don't you, Mrs. Jones? Must be more bad drivers in this town than I thought!"

Lex Barker Raps Critics Of His Conduct Abroad

By Jimmie Fidler

HOLLYWOOD — I have just mulled through an interview that Lex Barker gave in London, answering the critics who have publicly disagreed with Lex and Lana Turner traveling all over Europe together.

I might add that I have been one of the critics.

Lex Barker

In his statement to the press, Barker declared that inasmuch as he and Miss Turner are adults, no one has any right to censure them for being traveling companions. I wonder if Lex includes his parents and his minister among those "who have no right to censure?"

Most people will not agree in the mitest with the actor's reasoning. To begin with, Barker and Miss Turner are not merely adults. They are public figures (and what figures, as of this moment!)

Lana has long been a popular idol of teen-age girls. Her every move is followed avidly by millions of youngsters who like nothing better than to emulate a glamorous movie queen. My own youthful daughter is a Lana Turner admirer — or rather, she was until I told her a couple of things about ladylike behavior.

As for Barker, he, as the latest and probably the second most popular star of the "Tarzan" pictures (no actor has ever approached Johnny Weissmuller's popularity as the ape man), carries a tremendous responsibility to boys. His influence is almost equal to that of the cowboy stars. If Lex will be honest with himself, I am sure he will admit that he would not want his own children, if ever he has any, to pattern their lives after the current Turner-Barker farce.

Responsibility Cited

Screen stars who occupy the spotlight—and particularly those who wield influence over the very young — should go out of their way to avoid even the appearance of evil-doing. Whether or not they are actually doing evil is not the point; They should avoid even the appearance. If a star (and Lex and Lana are not the only screen notables who should take this to heart) is unwilling to accept this responsibility, he has no right to be a public idol.

The motion picture industry, lax as always, about the morals of their contract players, will probably do nothing in the present case. That is one reason the industry is flat on its back. Even powerful Rome fell when its people flaunted God.

The Gall Of It!

Santa Anita has never had a horse race as hot as that now on between two Hollywood producers, each of whom wants to be the first to reach the screen with a three-dimension movie starring either Jane Russell or Marie Wilson.

The reason is obvious. If not, let me explain to you that the film industry, or parts of it, now plans to use 3-D to sensationalize feminine pulchritude, as well as to scare audiences out of their wits. And Hollywood has the gall to call this a great advancement in the world of entertainment!

TEEN ROAD-E-O HERE SATURDAY

Contestants to Compete For Scholarships

Youthful auto drives will compete for $1,950 in scholarship prizes here Saturday in the Pennsylvania State Teen-Age Road-e-o of 1953 at McCaskey High School.

G. William Stoler III, Lancaster, who is State chairman of the affair, reported today that contestants have already been entered by 33 cities and boroughs. Saturday's winner will compete in the national contest sponsored by the State Junior Chambers of Commerce in conjunction with the United States Jaycees and the Liberty Mutual Insurance Co.

A $1,000 scholarship will be first prize in the national contest, with additional scholarships of $500, $250 and two of $100.

Two Tests And Quiz

Each contestant here Saturday will be given a pre-established driving test, a road test in traffic, and a written quiz. Registration will be held Friday at the Stevens House from 3 to 10 p. m.

Members of the JCC and their wives will be hosts to contestants and their chaperones at a "coke party" Friday night. Awards will be presented Saturday at 6:30 p. m., at a banquet in the Stevens House.

Judges will be Otto F. Messner, secretary of the State Department of Revenue; Col. C. M. Wilhelm, State Police commissioner; and Commissioner Fred G. McCartney, Lancaster City Police Force.

Order of Bullfrogs Plans Outing Sunday

The Ancient Order of Croaking Bullfrogs of Quarryville will hold their annual outing Sunday at the Roy Collins farm, two miles south of Quarryville, off Rt. 222.

In case of rain the event will be held July 5. Lester Murphy is chairman for the outing. Each member is to bring a guest. A special program has been arranged.

A regular meeting of the group will be held in Quarryville, on June 30, at 8:30 p. m., it was announced by Wesley Hammon, master croaker. Plans will be discussed for the purchase of ground for a new home.

K of C Auxiliary Plans Final Program Tonight

A Ladies' Night program will feature the final summer meeting of the Auxiliary to the Knights of Columbus, Council 867, at 8 p. m. today in the K of C Home, 22 S. Prince St.

Mrs. Paul Grimm will present vocal selections for the program preceding the buffet luncheon. Prospective members are also invited to attend.

Mrs. James Gabriel, chairman, is assisted by Mrs. Walter Siderio, Mrs. Joseph Lombardo, Mrs. Joseph LaMonaca, Mrs. Stella Trenta, Mrs. James Shaeffer, Mrs. John Cantwell, Mrs. Norman Hohenwarter and Mrs. Robert Riley.

94th Division to Hold Reunion in New York

The fourth annual reunion of the 94th Infantry Division of the U. S. Army will be held in New York City July 24, 25, and 26.

During World War II the 94th was active in the front lines in Europe, including the famous Battle of the Bulge.

Screen-Stage Star

ACROSS

1 Star of stage and screen, Henry ——
6 He —— in various roles
11 Sea eagles
12 Claw
13 Most rational
14 Prayer
16 British money of account
17 Retains
19 Mine shaft hut
20 Exposes to moisture
22 Short-napped fabric
23 Summits
24 He is —— at his profession
26 Wave top
27 Sphere
29 New Guinea port
30 Scottish sheepfold
31 Feminine appellation
32 Diminish
35 Fence steps
39 Cooking utensils
40 Separate column
43 Paradise
44 Abstract being
45 Pertaining to the sun
47 Consume
48 He has appeared on several of Broadway's ——
50 Pompous show
52 Russian storehouse
53 Puff up
54 Pauses
55 Hinder

DOWN

1 Dreaded
2 Decorated
3 Compass point
4 Writing table
5 Flower
6 Ceases
7 Paving substances
8 Fourth Arabian caliph
9 Masculine appellation
10 Pries
13 Rail bird
15 Bird's home
18 Babylonian deity
21 Pastimes
23 Thirty (Fr.)
25 Large plant
26 Containers
28 Exist
29 Musical note
32 Mimics
33 Mock
34 Handled
36 Form a notion
37 Conductor
38 Grafted (her.)
40 Misplaces
41 Morindin dye
42 Bound with tape
45 Clan
46 Chest rattle
49 Aeriform fuel
51 Rodent

Answer to Previous Puzzle

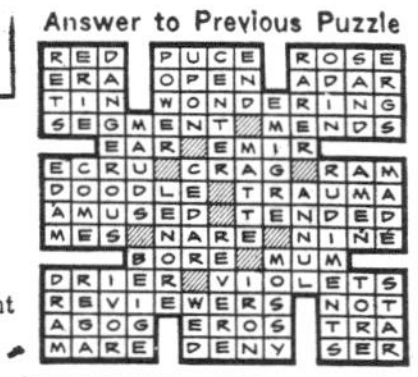

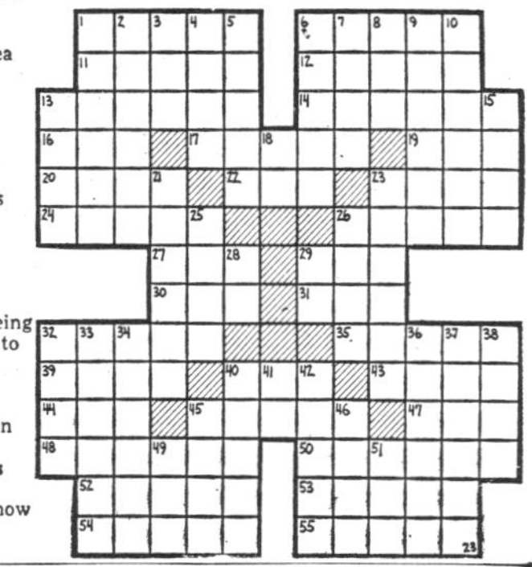

TURNS IN FALSE ALARM

An eight-year-old girl was picked up by city police for turning in a false alarm from Box 63, Duke and Church Sts., at 9:02 p. m. yesterday. She was released to her parents and Sgt. John Ehleiter will continue the investigation.

The Beast From 20,000 Fathoms

3-DIMENSION
THRILLS THAT CAN ALMOST TOUCH YOU!
"IT CAME FROM OUTER SPACE"
A fearsome SPACE SHIP hurtles at you from another world!
A HELICOPTER'S churning blades whirl inches from your head!
XENOMORPHS STALK AMONG YOU...WITH THE POWER TO LOOK LIKE MEN...OR CHANGE TO OBJECTS OF AWESOME TERROR!
A terrifying AVALANCHE smothers you with tons of crushing fury!

FOAM RUBBER cushioned insoles and arch supports

The Sunday News Brings You
LAST-MINUTE NEWS!
Local and World Events

SUNDAY NEWS

Read Complete Fiction Story
Sunday News Magazine
Page 14 of Pink Section

LANCASTER, PA., SUNDAY, JULY 26, 1953

'ALUMINUM-SKINNED' plant of Alcoa, as seen from intersection of Bypass and Fruitville Pike, will look like this when finished in October. Parking area at far left is completed; bus port will be added though no public transportation has been definitely arranged. Two-story office section will blend with one-story factory portion of same height. Long, low lines were designed to fit in with countryside.

Alcoa Plant To Be Completed By October; Full Production In '55

Half-Million Pounds Of Aluminum Rivets, Nails, Bolts, Etc., To Be Shipped Every Month From Factory Here

Lancaster's new $3,000,000 Alcoa plant, when it reaches full production about two years from now, will be shipping more than half a million pounds of screw-machine products every month. Completion of the plant is scheduled for October, and most of the machinery is to be installed by next March.

Those figures, revealed for the first time today by Aluminum Company of America officials, include such impressive monthly production totals as 200 million rivets, 60 million fasteners, 40 million nails.

STEELWORK for plant has been completed, in current view corresponding with architect's sketch at top of page, and block-laying is under-way. Final stage will be application of aluminum panels to exterior. (Sunday News Photo)

Details of the "aluminum-skinned" fabricating plant—how it will look, what it will make, how it's progressing—are contained in a "report to Lancaster" prepared for Sunday News by Alcoa. It reveals that a number of newly-developed machines will boost the output of the factor—second largest in Lancaster on a one-floor basis.

The plant is rising steadily around completed steelwork on an 84-acre plot angled into the southwest intersection of the Rt. 230 bypass and Fruitville Pike.

Payroll $2,500,000

Looking ahead to full production during the summer of 1955, when 450 people will be employed with an annual payroll of $2½ millions Alcoa points out that its Lancaster products will be small but numerous. They will include screw-machine items such as nuts, bolts, screws, rivets, nails and washers; and such miscellaneous standard items as pipe plugs, U-bolts, studs and stud bolts, binding posts and binding screws, pipe and tube fittings and house numerals. In addition, special products will be made at Alcoa's new plant to fit customer's specifications.

Lots of hardware of this sort will go into the building of the plant. In addition to quantities of aluminum nails, nuts and bolts in the actual construction, there will be a gleaming facing of aluminum panels all over the structure, aluminum reflectors on the lamps, aluminum desks and chairs in the offices.

Big feature of the whole Lancaster project is the modern new central plant building. This structure is to be 24 feet high—in keeping with the low, level contour of the region—and its external walls covered with trapezodial aluminum panels. Groundwork for the new building was begun May 23.

With the exception of specially constructed areas, such as passageways, the floor of the main plant will be of concrete. Some 4,000 cubic yards of concrete will be required—equal to a standard highway nearly two miles long.

5½-Acre Floor Space

Two hundred thousand square feet of floor space—roughly 5½ acres—will be made available for machinery, chemical treating sections and storage spaces. And the design of this new plant will permit expansion on three of its four sides to an area of 400,000 square feet—practically double its initial size.

While immediate expansion is not expected, the anticipation of an ever-expanding market for aluminum screw-machine products warranted the planning of an expandable building.

While immediate expansion is not expected, the anticipation of an ever-expanding market for aluminum screw-machine products warranted the planning of an expandable building.

The competition for screw machine products is great. Some 1500 companies now manufacture such products from various metals —with five such companies presently located right in Lancaster. Two hundred companies also make rivets. The new Lancaster Works will be the only Alcoa plant turning out a full line of such products.

Aluminum Panel Siding

On June 22, erection of some 1,000 tons of structural steel framework was begun on the site. To this framework will be added a concrete block wall and over 55,000 square feet of aluminum panel siding.

Each of these aluminum panels will be open-ribbed, 18 inches wide, and ranging in length from 11 feet, 3 inches on the bottom row, to 14 feet, 1 inch on the upper row. Each panel will be .04 of an inch thick with three ribs approximately 4 inches wide and 1½ inches deep—with a special pattern finish.

The panels will need no painting and no cleaning. They will neither corrode nor rust and maintenance problems will be practically non-existent.

Once the framework of the building is erected, the cement block wall will be put in place. The wall consists of blocks one foot thick for a height of four feet around the building. From that height on up, concrete blocks 8 inches thick will be laid. The difference in thickness is to allow for the interior installation of a sound-proofing wall, four inches thick, consisting of perforated trapezoidal panels backed up with fiberglass. This will prevent the noise and vibrations of machines and presses from escaping outside.

Within the plant too there is to be sound-proofing—between the rivet section and others.

To Shoot Pins Into Wall

Fastened to the concrete wall outside the building will be aluminum bars 1 inch wide, ¼ inch thick and ten feet long. Each of these bars will be held to the wall with two pins, 1⅝ inches long, literally "fired" through the bars and into the wall by a powder-charged gun. The bars will be arranged end to end in two horizontal lines ringing the building.

In front of the plant, facing the Fruitville Pike, will be the Lancaster work office building. Attached to the plant, this will be a two story affair 25 feet high. It will also be aluminum paneled, though with some changes in architectural design.

The showfront of Alcoa's midstate plant, this office building will be 300 feet long and 44 feet wide. Its furniture will be of grey aluminum with varied-colored upholstery.

Waste Products No Problem

Several hundred feet to the rear of the plant will be a waste treatment plant to handle all dyes, oily wastes, acid and caustic waste. It will be a two story building, with a basement, thirty feet high, 23 feet long and 21 feet wide. All waste material from the manufacturing plant will be drawn off through pipes to this building.

Some of the machinery for the main plant will come from Edgewater, N.J., where it is presently

Page 22—ALCOA

Land, Housing, Trained Labor, Facilities, Pointed To Lancaster

When the Aluminum Company of America announced last Dec. 3 that it would build a plant in Lancaster, it marked the culmination of a long search and a program of planning which is still in progress.

Alcoa's Lancaster installation developed from the company's realization that it needed a separate plant, properly situated and large enough to handle the growing demand for aluminum screw-machine products. Along with the need to make room for planned expansion of other facilities at Alcoa's Edgewater, N. J., operations, this started the company scouting around for a site. In excess of 50 acres of land was required.

Lancaster was picked as the site for a number of reasons:

1. It has enough land of the proper type.
2. It has desirable housing locations for both native Lancaster people and for the new citizens who will come to this area from other Alcoa locations.
3. It has an excellent reservoir of the type of people Alcoa desires for employes.
4. It has good transportation facilities for importing raw materials and shipping finished products.
5. It is in a good position to serve market areas.

Alcoa found what it wanted in Lancaster — along the Fruitville Pike near the Bypass — and since the first of this year has gradually been taking its place in the community as an integral part of Lancaster's growing industrial scenery.

From 3 Owners

About half the 84 acres purchased by the company were secured from Manor Realty, a subsidiary of the Pennsylvania Railroad. Another 32 acres of land were bought from Elmer L. Esbenshade of Lancaster, and ten acres were purchased from Harry Hess, a local farmer.

Grading and excavating of the tract officially got underway March 18, when the new Works Manager, Robert Chestnut, turned the first spadeful of earth at ground-breaking ceremonies. Participating in the ceremonies were Daniel Rhoads, president of the Manufacturers Association of Lancaster; president James J. Rudisill and members of the Industrial Development Committee of the Lancaster Chamber of Commerce.

The initial work crew on the grading and excavation numbered about ten men who removed some 70,000 cubic yards of earth. With the aid of special pneumatic drills mounted on wagons an additional 10,000 cubic yards of rock were blasted loose. This preliminary work was somewhat held back by an abnormal amount of rain during the grading period.

All work at the site is being performed under the supervision of Alcoa's own engineering forces, which will coordinate the various contractors involved in the work. The largest single contract for the work was awarded the Mellon-Stuart Company of Pittsburgh. It covers all concrete construction, masonry, exterior walls and partitions, storm, sanitary and industrial waste sewers, underground water and gas lines, plumbing and brick paving of certain interior floor sections.

4 Main Units

The main features of the whole project are two training buildings, the main industrial plant and an office building.

As the construction program gets into full swing, upwards of 200 men will be engaged in the laying of foundations, erection of structural steel, construction of underground facilities, and all the main jobs which go into the building of a modern industrial plant.

Once the grading and excavation work was well underway, two training buildings began taking shape on the site late in April. Each of the two buildings — 12 feet high at the eaves — is 100 feet long and 40 feet wide, with a floor space of 4,000 square feet apiece.

The training buildings each has a classroom for instruction in the use of gauges and testing equipment, blueprint reading, mathematics and related courses. Over 40 pieces of shop equipment such as automatic screw-machines, nail headers, rivet headers, thread rollers, lathes and presses will be used in the training.

Will be Warehouses

These buildings will be used for training purposes for some time after production gets underway in the main plant. Eventually, they will be used as warehouses.

The actual training program for technical employes got underway June 29. The program is designed to train a selected group to set up and operate automatic screw, nail and rivet machines. A limited number of tool room mechanics and repairmen, will also be trained.

Director of training is Edmond Cotton, formerly of the Edgewater, N.J. operations, who will be assisted by a staff of seven.

First to enroll in the training program are three Lancaster County men: Bernard Vollenweider of Ephrata, who will study the operation of automatic screw machines; Harry Deisley of Lancaster, who will work on fastener machines, and Edgar Hess of Peach Bottom, who will study rivet department operations.

Since the hiring of these men, three others have joined the training squad and additional trainees will be hired as full-time employes at a rate of about five per week over a three-month period. Approximately 70 will be given technical training for six months in fundamentals in the use and operation of the various machines. Upon completion of this basic course, they will receive continued instruction for higher skills.

Looking Ahead World Wide

Rhee Expected To Try Forcing U.N. Into Renewed War

TOKYO—UN authorities fear that South Korea will attempt almost any kind of action—if a truce is nailed down—to force the UN to renew the fighting. Allied officials are equally determined that nothing must stand in the way of a successful truce. Get tough policy? Yes, such a policy is expected from America if South Korean political leaders continue their way.

Many UN officials have lost patience with President Syngman Rhee and his foreign minister, Pyun Yung Tai. They consider the South Koreans have acted in bad faith on the armistice issue.

Pyun

Another development you may look for: transport by boat of Indian troops on the Truce Commission directly to the between-lines "demilitarized zone" to guard anti-Communist captives. By this method the Indians actually will never touch foot on South Korean soil.

LONDON — Government Row feels the meeting of the Supreme Soviet (Parliament) has been postponed because the purge of Russian Deputy Premier L. P. Beria is not yet complete; there may be further "tidying up" to meet the stresses and strains within the Kremlin hierarchy before next month's meeting.

Britain will go into any meeting of four-power foreign minister with a major plan to turn such a session into an immediate top-level conference if the Russians show themselves really co-operative.

The British Foreign Office privately thinks the chances of getting Edgar Sanders freed from his 13-year sentence in Hungary are slightly better than they were a month ago. A government statement is possible this week.

In view of the international situation and possibility of having to recall parliament, the British House of Commons will be adjourned instead of prorogued next week, and the speaker given power to interrupt the long summer vacation.

WASHINGTON — GOP leaders expect to reap rich dividends next year from President Eisenhower's unique "get-acquainted-with-Congress" program.

Ike has been host at breakfast, luncheon or dinner to every Senator and Representative. They have been White House guests in small groups. There has been ample opportunity for exercise of the President's well-known, man-to-man charm.

Republican strategists believe the intimate gatherings will mean votes when the chips are down in 1954 — a Congressional election year.

They feel Ike's popularity is so great that the voters will want to assure him continued control of Congress by returning to office legislators who can say convincingly that they are his loyal friends.

Democrats admit privately that the President has made marked progress in his efforts to end GOP factional strife.

The Republican top brass is not perturbed by the lack of any impressive legislative record in the session now grinding to a close. The sights are set on next year.

PARIS — In the next few weeks Allied diplomats say the Russians will concentrate on trying to defeat a September re-election of West German Chancellor Konrad Adenauer.

These key men say that the Communists will follow the usual line of asking that the "free election" problem in Germany by settled by East (Communist) Germans and West Germans rather than through Big Four talks. This line is regarded as a subterfuge; many Westerners believe that the Russians never will face the real issue but will try to rally all force against Adenauer. The latter — bitterly opposed by the Socialists — really holds a key to Allied, and especially American policy. Officials say that if Adenauer is defeated it would be the death of the proposed European Army Treaty and would call for a major American policy change.

WEATHER
(U. S. Weather Bureau)
Eastern Pennsylvania—Mostly Sunny, With High In Low 80's Today. Wednesday Fair And Slightly Warmer.

Intelligencer Journal.

The Leading Newspaper in the Garden Spot of America. Home Owned for Home Folks Since 1794

160th Year.—No. 48. Official United States Census Figures Lancaster Metropolitan Area Population 234,717 LANCASTER, PA., TUESDAY MORNING, AUGUST 11, 1953. CITY TWENTY-TWO PAGES 30c PER WEEK—5c Per Copy

THE INTELL INDEX

NEW NAME ENTERS BENEDICT PROBE

City Urged To Take River For New Water Supply

First Part Of Survey Of City Water System

Because of its importance, the Intelligencer Journal will present, in daily installments, the complete report of Gannett Fleming Corddry & Carpenter, Inc., the engineering firm retained by the City of Lancaster to make a survey of the city's water system.

The first installment of "Report on Increasing Present Water Supply" follows:

Letter Of Transmittal

Aug. 4, 1953

Kendig C. Bare, Mayor
City of Lancaster
City Hall
Lancaster, Pennsylvania

Dear Sir:

Pursuant to our agreement, we take pleasure in submitting herewith our Report on Increasing the Water Supply of Lancaster.

Our findings and recommendations summarized below are discussed at greater length in the report.

Findings

1. We find the Water Department is serving at present a population of over 73,000 people, plus a large industrial demand.

2. With normal growth, the population served in twenty years should be about 84,500 and in forty years about 95,000.

3. The annual increase in your water requirements since 1934, when the present filter plant went into operation, has been 56 percent as compared with a population increase of 19 percent.

4. The present (1952) maximum monthly demand averages 12.3 million gallons per day with peak days approaching 15 million gallons.

5. We estimate that in 40 years future requirements will reach a monthly average of at least 21 mil-

Turn To Page 5 For More Of TEXT

Long Range $7,411,000 Program Recommended In Engineering Survey

A four-step improvement and addition program sufficient to take care of Lancaster City's water needs for the next 40 years, at an estimated cost of $7,411,000, was recommended yesterday to City Council.

The long-term program is contained in a voluminous survey prepared by Gannett, Fleming, Corddry and Carpenter, Inc., Harrisburg engineering firm, at a cost to the city of about $6,000. The survey got under way early in February.

A survey of sanitary and storm sewer systems here also is being made by the Harrisburg firm. This survey, also expected to be presented soon, will cost the city about $5,000.

Here are the details of the four-point proposal, which includes using the Susquehanna River as a new source of raw water, as submitted to Council yesterday:

"(1) Improve the present filter plant by adding new clarifiers and aerators, new lift pumps and other minor improvements.

"(2) Construct a new 500,000 gallon elevated tank in the east end of the city.

"(3) Construct a large storage reservoir with ultimate capacity of 30 million gallons, west of Rohrerstown at an elevation that would give service to the city by gravity through a new 42-inch pipeline.

"(4) Initiate the Susquehanna River project by the construction of an intake, pumping station, filter plant, pipeline to the Rohrerstown reservoir, and other facilities needed in this project."

COST BROKEN DOWN

Estimated cost of the four-step program is:

Part 1 — Filter plant improvements, $427,000.

Part 2 — 500,000 gallon elevated storage tank, $138,000.

Part 3 — 30 million gallon storage reservoir with connecting pipeline to city, $2,169,000.

Part 4 — Susquehanna River development with pipeline to new reservoir, $4,677,000.

Total cost of four-part program, $7,411,000.

This program, the report emphasizes, "does not provide for any immediate additional source of supply which would be required if there should be a drought equal

Turn To Page 6 For More Of WATER

COUNTY SCHOOL BUS INSPECTION AUG. 26

Dr. Arthur P. Mylin, superintendent of the Lancaster County School Board, and Corporal Philip S. Gerhard, Lancaster State Police, completed arrangements yesterday for the annual inspection of all county school buses. Gerhard said that the buses will be inspected on Wednesday, Aug. 26.

Dr. Mylin, he said, will send letters to all the local school boards notifying them where to take their vehicles for the check.

Inspection stations will be set up at the Lancaster State Police Barracks, in Mount Joy, Columbia, Ephrata, Gap and Quarryville.

FARM CORNER

"We Lead All The Rest"
By WILLIAM R. SCHULTZ

FARMERS, AIDED BY RAIN, NOW FACE NEW PEST

Tomatoes, Potatoes Given 'Lift,' But Grasshoppers Causing Heavy Damage

Lancaster County farmers yesterday heralded the weekend rains as life saving to their 1953 crop of tobacco and late potatoes, and then turned to fighting another pest reported taking a heavy toll in tobacco and tomatoes.

Sunday's slow, steady rain, and yesterday's scattered showers ended, at least temporarily, the threat of severe damage to the tobacco.

But with the tobacco harvest expected to be well underway in a week to 10 days, growers feel at least a full inch of rain is still needed for near normal yields.

The new pest is the grasshopper and it is causing heavy damage in to hay fields. Associate County tobacco and tomato fields adjacent Agent Harry S. Sloat said last

Turn To Page 6 For More Of FARM CORNER

Weather Calendar

COMPARATIVE TEMPERATURES

Station	High	Low
Water Works	78	60
Ephrata	78	58
Last Year (Ephrata)	86	69
Official High for Year, July 18		97
Official Low for Year, Feb. 2		13

Character of Day, Partly Cloudy

WINDS
Direction—SW Avg. Velocity—12 MPH

HUMIDITY
8 a. m. 85% 11 a. m. 75% 2 p. m. 73%
5 p. m. 68% 8 p. m. 70%
Average Humidity 74%

SUN
Rises—6:11 a. m. Sets—8:07 p. m.

MOON
Moon rises 5:17 p. m.

STARS
Morning—Mercury, Venus, Mars, Jupiter
Evening—Saturn

NEARBY FORECASTS
(U. S. Weather Bureau)

Maryland and Virginia—Some cloudiness but mostly sunny, with high in middle 80's today. Wednesday fair with little change in temperature.

Delaware and Southern New Jersey—Mostly sunny, with high in low 80's today. Wednesday fair with little change in temperature.

Lower Potomac and Chesapeake Bay—Gentle to moderate southwesterly winds today. Fair weather. Visibility good except fair to poor in early morning with haze and ground fog.

Hoover Observes Birthday

SAN FRANCISCO, Aug. 10—Former President Herbert Hoover quietly observes his 79th birthday in his suite at the Mark Hopkins Hotel here today. Mr. Hoover said he planned no special celebration, just a quiet dinner with friends. The former president has been assigned by President Eisenhower to head the new Commission on Reorganization of the Executive Branch of the Federal Government. (AP Wirephoto)

3 Red-Softened Americans May Be In 1st Flight Home

HONOLULU, Aug. 10 (AP)—Three Americans softened to communism may be aboard the first planeload of liberated prisoners of war flying home today.

A partial news blackout and contradictory statements by military spokesmen here indicated a possible repeat performance of a "mystery flight" in last spring's sick and wounded prisoner exchange. Then a group of freed captives suspected of having swallowed Red indoctrination was flown under wraps to hospitals in the United States.

PWS ABOARD SHIP

INCHON, Korea, Tuesday, Aug. 11 (AP)—A group of quiet, happy Americans got settled today aboard the ship that will bring them home from bleak months of Communist captivity in Korea.

Three hundred twenty-eight liberated prisoners, the vanguard of more than 3,000 walked quietly aboard the U.S. military transport Gen. Nelson M. Walker. It was scheduled to leave Inchon harbor late Tuesday on the 2-week trip to San Francisco.

There was little shouting or excitement as the men approached the Gen. Walker in a landing craft and filed aboard. About the only time they demonstrated was to oblige photographers and cameramen by waving hands, caps and handkerchiefs.

The first report from Tokyo said 17 disabled Americans left Haneda Airport Monday night, but no destination or arrival time in the United States was announced.

MIGHT BE MORE

Then a military spokesman here who later attempted to retract his words indicated more freed prisoners might be aboard.

He had said that the plane's manifest showed 21 passengers, in-

Turn To Page 6 For More Of PRISONERS

Reds Free More Prisoners In 7th Day Of Exchange

PANMUNJOM, Tuesday, Aug. 11 (AP)—Americans freed from long months and years of Communist captivity were homeward bound today while the traffic down Freedom Road moved again in the seventh day of prisoner exchange.

One hundred Americans and 300 other Allied prisoners were in today's liberation quota. The exchange began promptly at 9 a.m. (7 p.m., EST, Monday). The first American arrivals appeared healthy.

The Communists reported they would return 400 Allied prisoners tomorrow, lowest number since the exchange began last week. The 400 will include 75 Americans, 52 British, 25 Turks and 250 South Koreans of whom 125 were classed as sick and wounded.

South Koreans returned today appeared to be wearing newly issued uniforms. The Americans and Turks were fabled blue uniforms.

The Turks, more demonstrative than the British or Americans, rolled into Panmunjom singing and shouting. They littered the road with caps, shirts and shreds of prison garb.

Several British in one truck were survivors of the "Glorious Gloucesters," the Commonwealth Division outfit which held off human wave attacks north of Seoul early in 1951 before it was engulfed.

The Communists had said there would be no sick and wounded prisoners in today's group. There were no ambulances in the first contingent passing through Panmunjom.

CHOKED WITH EMOTION

The Americans jumped from the high tailgates of the Russian-built trucks and responded to roll call alertly: "Yes sir." But some were choked with emotion as they reached freedom.

Cpl. Lahman L. Bower of Berkley, Mich., was the first American returned today. He was with the U. S. 2nd Division when he was captured. Bower was held in a Red camp at Pyoktong.

A number of Communist Red Cross workers observed today's exchange. With them were Red Cross representatives from Allied na-

Turn To Page 6 For More Of SWITCH

Mrs. R. G. Gassert 2nd Ephratan To Receive 'Handy-Homers' Award

Another Ephrata woman has received a two-dollar award from the editors of "The Handy Homers", daily panel which appears in the Intelligencer Journal, for a suggestion on how to make over an old radio cabinet into a bookcase.

She is Mrs. Raymond G. Gassert, Ephrata R3, whose suggestion is featured in the panel today with a thank-you line. Mrs. Gassert thus becomes the second county resident to have her suggestion illustrated in "The Handy Homers."

Mrs. Russel Mentzer, 42 S. Maple St., Ephrata, who submitted a suggestion in the name of her daughter, Dona Lee Mentzer, was the first. Her suggestion appeared on June 30.

Mrs. Gassert

Oddly enough, Mrs. Gassert and Mrs. Mentzer are friends, although each sent in suggestions to the editors of the panel without knowing that the other had done the same. In fact, the two winners' husbands are cousins.

Mrs. Gassert's winning suggestion shows how easy it is to remove the works from the cabinet of an old radio and add shelves for books.

Although she herself hasn't actually tried remodeling the old radio in her attic, she has seriously considered doing so often. And she has seen it done by one of her friends, she says.

Mrs. Gassert, who has two active youngsters, finds it really pays to come up with a household hint that will make less work for her, once in a while. She has many such suggestions on the tip of her tongue and says she sent several others to the editors of the panel at the time she sent her winning one.

OTHER IDEAS

Among them were the following which she has found to be quite effective: sewing a pocket on a shower curtain to hold soap and washcloth, and using bobby pins

Turn To Page 6 For More Of AWARD

ENEMY MUST RETURN ALL PWS--DULLES

Even Those Convicted Of So-Called Crimes; We Will Hold Back

WASHINGTON, Aug. 10 (AP) — Secretary of State Dulles said tonight on returning from Korea the Communists must return all American war prisoners, even those convicted of so-called crimes.

He told reporters at the Washington Airport the United Nations Command "wouldn't return" Chinese and North Korean Communist prisoners convicted of crimes "until we know the attitude of the Communists toward ours."

Dulles had conferred with President Eisenhower in Denver earlier today on plans for American retaliatory steps against the Communists in Korea if they refuse to release all U. S. prisoners of war.

NEWS CONFERENCE

At a news conference in Denver he said the United States would adopt "reciprocal measures" if the Communists failed to return some American prisoners in their hands.

Dulles, accompanied by Henry Cabot Lodge, ambassador to the United Nations, and Assistant Secretaries of State Walter Robertson and Carl McCardle, arrived by plane at 5:04 p.m. EST.

Asked specifically if he believed terms must return all United Nations prisoners, including those convicted of crimes, Dulles replied, "Yes."

He said the United Nations Command holds "a very substantial number" of Communist prisoners

Turn To Page 6 For More Of DULLES

Martin Defends New 'Toughness' In U. S. Policy

WASHINGTON, Aug. 10 (AP) — House Speaker Martin (R-Mass) said tonight President Eisenhower demonstrated a new "toughness" in American foreign policy when he ordered the U. S. 7th Fleet to stop protecting Red China against possible attack from Formosa.

The result, he said, has been "an amazing chain of events" that led to a truce in the 3-year-old Korean War and found reflection in the current strife behind the Soviet Iron Curtain.

Martin also declared that since the Eisenhower administration took office last Jan. 20, "record after record has been broken" in the realm of national prosperity—more jobs, higher wages, bigger savings deposits.

"AN APPRAISAL"

Martin set forth his claims of Republican prowess in a televised film entitled "The 83rd Congress—An Appraisal," sponsored by the

Turn To Page 6 For More Of MARTIN

LITITZ RIFLEMAN WOUNDED IN KOREA JUST BEFORE TRUCE

A Lititz rifleman, serving with the U. S. 7th Division, was wounded in action in Korea on July 24, just two days prior to the signing of the armistice it was announced yesterday.

The casualty is Pfc. William E. Kline, seventeen, son of Mrs. Sarah Smith, 430 N. Cedar St., Lititz.

PFC. KLING

The Defense Department informed Mrs. Smith that her son had been "slightly wounded by artillery fire." She also received mail from her son, written from a Taegu, Korea, hospital.

In his letters he said he is "feeling much better and getting wonderful treatment." But he is disappointed that he will have to spend his eighteenth birthday, Wednesday, in bed.

Pfc. Kling entered the service Nov. 20, 1952, and has been in Korea since May 16. He was attached to the 31st Regiment of the 7th Infantry Division.

CITY GIRL SERIOUSLY INJURED BY AUTO

Five-year-old Pamela White, daughter of Mr. and Mrs. Robert White, 319 Coral St., was hospitalized suffering serious injuries after she was struck by a car in front of her home yesterday evening.

The little girl, doctors said, is suffering a frontal skull fracture, possible back injuries and a laceration of the left side of her forehead. She was admitted to St. Joseph's Hospital and her condition last night was said to be "fair."

City police, who investigated, said that the little girl darted from behind a parked car into the path of an auto driven by Paul E. Haleman, 418 Pearl St. Haleman took her to the hospital.

Cpl. Haggerty, Of State Police, 'Talked' To Him About Case, Good Says

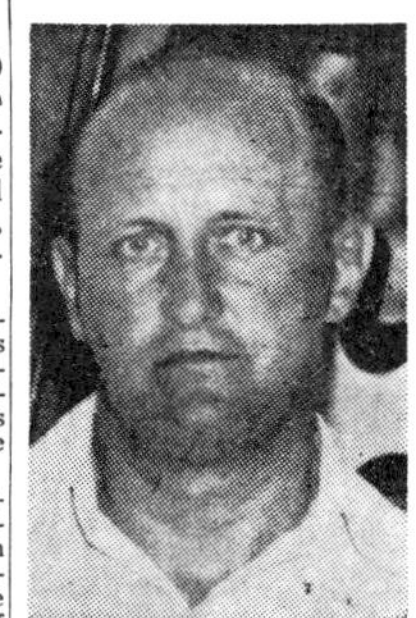

MICHAEL A. GOOD

CPL. J. J. HAGGERTY

Mt. Joy Officer Claims He Had Decided To Lessen Charge Before

A report that Cpl. James J. Haggerty of the Pennsylvania State Police, "talked" to Mount Joy Police Officer Michael R. Good before the latter lessened the drunken driving charge against Lawrence A. "Whitey" Benedict was confirmed last evening by District Attorney John W. Beyer.

The fact that Cpl. Haggerty "had talked to him (Good)," Beyer told the Intelligencer Journal, is included in a report on the case involving the Lancaster contractor which was handed to him early yesterday afternoon by William C. Storb, first assistant district attorney.

Storb — assigned to the case by Beyer on Aug. 6 with a "free hand to decide any question of law or procedure" — refused any comment as he handed his findings over to the district attorney.

When contacted at his home last evening, however, Storb confirmed a report that he had talked to Cpl. Haggerty and Lt. Reese L. Davis, commanding officer of Troop B, Squadron Four, Pennsylvania State Police, with headquarters at the Lancaster Barracks, yesterday morning on the Benedict case. Storb refused further comment, referring the reporter to the district attorney.

In confirming the report that Cpl. Haggerty had "talked" to Good, District Attorney Beyer said that "Officer Good came in yesterday morning and made an additional statement to Mr. Storb, in which he admitted Haggerty had talked to him, but said specifically that he had made up his mind before he saw Haggerty that he was going to change the charge against Benedict."

District Attorney Beyer said he expects to issue a formal statement today on the basis of Storb's report.

Policeman Good, in a signed statement issued to County Detective Harry E. Myers Friday night, changed his previous story and admitted that he had suggested that the drunken driving charge against Benedict be lessened to a charge of reckless driving. It was while Good was in Storb's office yesterday morning making an additional statement that Cpl. Haggerty and Lt. Davis appeared.

Good left the office temporarily, it was learned, while Storb talked with the two State Policemen.

SHRUGS SHOULDERS

Located in North Queen Street restaurant last evening, Haggerty merely held out his open hands and shrugged his shoulders when asked if he had talked to Good about the Benedict case, or if he had been in to see Storb on the matter.

It was a different story with Lt. Davis, however. Reached at his home in Reading, Haggerty's commanding officer confirmed the report that he and Haggerty had seen Storb on the Benedict case. When asked for additional comment he replied:

"I've made a report to my immediate superior officer. He will have to make any comment from here on in."

Lt. Davis' superior officer is Maj. William F. Hoffman, commanding officer Squadron Number Four, at Philadelphia.

Maj. Hoffman said last evening he had not received any report on this matter from Lt. Davis as yet. "However, if the facts are as you state," Maj. Hoffman said, "I naturally will order an investigation to ascertain what took place. Chances are I'll have a report from Lt.

Turn To Page 6 For More Of HAGGERTY

McCarthy Says Red Member Has Access To Our Secrets

WASHINGTON, Aug. 10 (AP)—Sen. McCarthy (R-Wis) said tonight new evidence has come to light indicating that a member of the Communist party now has access to secret data of the Atomic Energy Commission, the military and the Central Intelligence Agency.

McCarthy made the statement to newsmen after questioning four witnesses for two hours at a closed-door session of his Senate investigations subcommittee. He refused to name the witnesses.

There was a report from authoritative sources that the alleged Communist works for the Government Printing Office. But there was no confirmation of the report elsewhere. The huge printing plant handles a wide variety of material from various government agencies.

Sen. Dirksen (R-Ill), who attended the hearing, said the subcommittee had run across "the beginning of a trail" which might lead to sensational disclosures.

"It very definitely involves the national security," Dirksen said, "if the facts are as they were developed today."

A reporter asked Dirksen: "Does this involve Communists presently in the government?"

Dirksen: "Yes, if the case is made."

McCarthy and Dirksen declined to say where the alleged Communist with access to atomic data works in the government — whether in the Defense Department, the AEC, the CIA, or in some other agency.

NO FURTHER DETAILS

McCarthy also refused to give any further details on the new evidence he said the witnesses had

Turn To Page 6 For More Of McCARTHY

DEMOCRATS TO FILL WEISGERBER SLATE VACANCY THURSDAY

A meeting of the Lancaster County Democratic Executive Committee to fill the vacancy on the city ticket caused by the death of William E. Weisgerber, nominee for city controller, has been set for noon Thursday at the Hotel Brunswick.

The meeting of the executive committee was called by David R. Eaby, chairman of the Democratic county committee.

The committee also is expected to fill vacancies on township and borough slates where candidates nominated by write-ins failed to accept nominations.

Another subject scheduled for discussion at the luncheon meeting is the naming of a county campaign manager for the November municipal election.

NECKTIES, ICE CREAM ON STATE SALES TAX LIST

Items Included In Tentative Listing Of Levy Beginning September 1

HARRISBURG, Aug. 10 (AP)—You will probably have to pay Pennsylvania's new one per cent sales tax on that quart of ice cream you take home to the children and the birthday necktie you buy for Cousin Wilbur.

Those items were included in a tentative list of taxable items compiled by the State Revenue Department today in preparation for the Sept. 1 starting date of the new levy. It's part of a massive sheaf of regulations being prepared by the department.

By the end of the week, the department hopes to have its permanent regulations ready for distribution to some 40,000 retailers. Conferences with retailers, manufacturers and contractors have been going on since last week.

Sales under 11 cents are exempt from the sales tax.

Broadly, the tax law, as written by the Legislature, exempts food and clothing but there are many borderline cases such as

Turn To Page 18 For More Of SALES TAX

8 MORE NABBED FOR IGNORING TURN BAN

City police nabbed eight motorists last night for violating the "No Left Turn" ban at Prince and Chestnut Streets.

Prosecuted under the recently established city ordinance were:

Arthur T. Fukty, 132 S. Poplar St., Elizabethtown; Jay C. Hippey, 30 Hager St.; Robert L. Haldeman, Mount Joy R1; Elizabeth Diersen, 517 W. Walnut St.; Harold Myers, 208 Stevens St.; Elmer B. Schrell, Lancaster R1; Joseph E. Clinton, 1125 Jamaica Rd.; Paul H. Krantz, Willow Street R1; Albert D. Myers, 27 W. Frederick St., Raymond B. Leaman, Willow St. R1; and Richard B. Keller, 216 E. Lemon St.

Identity Of Suspect In Gaspe Murders Reported Established

MONTREAL, Tuesday, Aug. 11 (AP)—The Montreal Gazette says today in a front page story that police are believed to have established the identity of a man wanted for the Wanton murder of three U. S. bear hunters in Gaspe.

The Gazette says no arrest has been made but quoted a police official close to the province-wide investigation as saying:

"We're keeping an eye on the suspect and can pick him up anytime, probably in a day or two.

"But we are fitting the pieces together and trying to get a bit more evidence before reopening the inquest into the murders."

MANHUNT SHIFTS

According to the Gazette, the investigator said the giant manhunt, centered in the Montreal area for the last 10 days, now had shifted back to the Gaspe and Quebec districts.

The biggest break in the case reportedly came four days ago when police raided a home in North Montreal and found a German Luger pistol they believe was used in the killings.

The remains of the victims—Eugene H. Lindsey, 45, and his son, Richard, 17, both of Hollidaysburg, Pa., and Fred Claar, 20, of East Freedom, Pa.—were found several weeks ago in the bush on the Gaspe Peninsula, where they had gone to hunt bear early in June.

Recovery of the alleged mur-

Turn To Page 6 For More Of HUNTERS

Little Liz . . .

Some folks seem to have mastered the art of getting credit for the hard work others have done.

LANCASTER NEW ERA

The Weather
(U. S. Weather Bureau Forecast)
Fair, Cool Tonight;
Warm Tomorrow
Temp. Today: High 78; Low 56
Temp. Yesterday: High 78; Low 52

77th Year—No. 23,649 | Lancaster Metropolitan Area Population Official United States Census Figures 234,717 | LANCASTER, PA., FRIDAY, AUGUST 21, 1953 | CITY EDITION | 22 PAGES | 30c PER WEEK—5c Per Copy

Fire Razes Maple Grove Ballroom

Wheatland Fire Chief Richard Wise, Lloyd Keller, caretaker, and Miles Messerman, fireman (left to right), look over the ruins of the Maple Grove dance hall. Picture made looking toward Lincoln Highway with entrance to hall at left.

New Era Photo

FAMILY FLEES AS 60 MEN FIGHT FLAMES

Damage Set at $75,000; Out of Control an Hour; Use Water from Pool

A flash fire which raged out of control for nearly an hour destroyed the sprawling frame ballroom in Maple Grove amusement park, just west of the city, early today.

The caretaker, his wife and two small children asleep in a small frame house just south of the ballroom, were routed by firemen and escaped injury.

Damage, according to Nicholas Sacoolas, 601 W. Orange St., owner and operator of the park, will exceed $75,000. The building is covered by only a small amount of insurance, Sacoolas said.

60 Firemen Fight Blaze

Seven county fire companies with about 60 men fought the blaze.

Six hoselines were laid to pump water from the nearby swimming pool into the burning building. Tongues of flame leaped high into the early morning sky and could be seen for many miles.

Nothing To Salvage

The building with its kitchen equipment, vending machines and supplies was left a twisted mass of charred ruins. There was nothing left to salvage. Heat was so intense that glass bottles in the supply room were melted.

Cause of the fire has not been determined, according to Chief Richard Wise, of the Wheatland Fire Co.

However, it was known that yesterday the ball room floor was cleaned and waxed. The brooms and mops used in the cleaning and the remaining waxes and cleaning materials were stored in a closet in the south end of the building. That closet was enveloped in flames and about consumed when the first firemen entered the building.

Spontaneous Combustion

This led to the theory that the fire may have been started by spontaneous combustion.

The ballroom was not used last night and the final inspection was made by Lloyd Keller, the caretaker, about 1:15 a. m. today. He returned home from another job at that time and after inspecting the place went to the little frame building at the southwest corner of the ballroom property and went to bed.

Keller said he and his wife, and their children, Harriet, eighteen-months-old, and Dianna, three, were asleep when a fireman pounded on the door and told them to get out in a hurry.

The Keller cottage is just three feet from the ballroom but firemen kept it doused with water and saved the little structure and its contents.

Chief Richard Wise, of the Wheatland Fire Co., one of the

—See MAPLE GROVE—Page 6

AUTOIST DIES, FATHER HURT IN CAR UPSET

2 Drumore R1 Men Are Thrown Out, Car Lands On Son's Head

Harry Aldus Wright, thirty-one, Drumore R1, was injured fatally when his automobile ran off Route 222 and upset, three miles north of the Maryland line at 7 p. m. yesterday.

He died of head injuries in the General Hospital at 4:40 a. m. today.

The victim's father, Aldus Wright, fifty-five, same address, was a passenger in the car and suffered brush burns of the back and a lacerated forehead. He was treated at the hospital.

Men Operated Farm

Wright and his wife, the former Eva Gore, lived with his parents. He and his father operated a farm near Fishing Creek.

According to state policeman Fred Urban, the father and son were returning home when the accident occurred.

Police said the younger Wright was driving a 1937 model car and apparently applied his brakes after coming over the crest of a hill. Police believe the brakes grabbed, causing the car to skid off the left side of the road and upset on the grass. The car continued 65 feet after rolling over, Urban said.

Both Are Thrown Out

Both occupants were thrown out and the car landed on the son's head, police said. He died of a crushed skull, according to Dr. Charles P. Stahr, deputy coroner.

Both men were taken to the hospital in the Quarryville ambulance.

It was the 18th highway death in the county this year, three less than during a corresponding period last year when 21 deaths were reported.

Born in Lancaster County, he was the son of Aldus G. and Minnie Miles Wright, Drumore. He attended the Methodist Church.

His wife, Eva Gore Wright, his parents and a sister, Mrs. Gordon Lineberry, Oxford, survive.

Grunewald, Friend Found Overcome By Escaping Gas

JERSEY CITY, N. J. (AP) —A man police identified as Henry Grunewald of Washington, D. C., was found overcome by gas fumes with a woman in an apartment early today.

Police Lt. Michael Mannion said papers in the man's wallet gave his address as 4100 Cathedral Ave., Washington. This is the address of Henry (The Dutchman) Grunewald, who figured prominently in a congressional inquiry into influence peddling.

Police said Grunewald, sixty-three, and Mrs. Ann Anderson, forty-six, were found overcome by gas fumes from two open jets of a kitchen stove, on which food had been cooking.

Both were reported in good condition at Jersey City Medical Center today. The wife of Grunewald (The Dutchman) was enroute there to see the hospitalized man.

Today's New Era

Cool Nights, Warm Days Expected to Continue Here

August's four-day spell of cool nights and fair warm days is expected to extend through the week-end and well into next week, according to the Weather Bureau.

Tonight is to be clear and cool, with a low between 48 and 55, and tomorrow is to be sunny and continued moderately warm, with a high between 78 and 82. The extended forecast says temperatures will be near normal through Wednesday, with the possibility of showers at mid-week.

Low temperature last night was 52, at the Ephrata Weather Station.

GROVE AWARDED TUITION REFUND

City School Board Ordered to Pay $183

The Court ruled today that Arthur S. Grove, 720 Third St., is a resident of the city and as such is entitled to a refund with interest from the Lancaster School District for tuition paid for his children who attended city schools.

The decision was handed down by Judge Joseph B. Wissler. It refunds to Grove $176.48 with interest or a total of $183.24.

Also Former Teacher

Grove is a former teacher of industrial arts in the Reynolds Junior High School. He resigned in August. At that time Wallace L. Robinson, president of the School Board, said his resignation eliminated the need of a hearing. Charges were not made public but the Board said they had nothing to do with Grove's action to recover the tuition paid for his children.

In his suit, Grove contended that his children resided at the city address and went to Pequea on holidays and over the weekend to visit their mother, former postmistress at that place. The Board contended the children's legal address was with their mother and therefore it was necessary for them to pay out-of-town tuition for attending city schools.

Registered In City

Grove testified he is registered to vote in Lancaster city. His automobile operator's license bears a Pequea address but one motor vehicle is registered at a Lancaster address.

He said he spends from Sunday to Thursday nights in Lancaster but frequently goes to Pequea to visit his wife. He said he spends about a third of his time in Pequea during the summer where he rents and repairs boats.

The case was heard without a jury and left to the Court for a decision.

Man at Penn Dairies Hurt In 14-Foot Fall

Jackson Ulmer, twenty-eight, 38 Church St., an employe of Penn Dairies, Inc., was injured when he fell between 12 and 14 feet at work this morning.

Police conveyed him to the General Hospital at 11:30 a. m. and he was admitted suffering a possible fractured skull and concussion.

Police learned Ulmer was climbing a ladder with a can of cream in his one hand. His other hand slipped from the ladder rung and he fell to the bottom of a pit striking his head on the concrete floor.

Autoist Who Hit Child Dies of Heart Attack

SAN DIEGO, Calif. (AP) —An automobile driver died yesterday after his car hit a child.

The coroner's report said Lester P. Bleicher, forty-two, of nearby Harrison Canyon, was backing out of his yard and accidentally ran into Phillip Turner, six. He was taking the boy to a hospital when he was stricken with a fatal heart attack. The coroner said the child was only bruised.

Private Car Sales Taxed Under New 1% State Levy

Most Casual Sales Exempt; Jobbers Must Tax All Retail Sales Unless Items Are Resold

HARRISBURG (AP)—The State Sales Tax Bureau said today manufacturers, wholesalers and jobbers must collect the new one per cent sales tax on all retail sales they make after Sept. 1.

But their transactions with retailers or others are exempt from the levy if the items will be resold.

Regulations Defined

The ruling was made as part of regulations dealing with isolated or casual sales which the bureau defined as:

1. Infrequent sales of non-recurring nature made by a person not engaged in the business of selling tangible personal property.

2. Sales of articles of tangible personal property acquired for use or consumption by a seller and not sold in the regular course of business engaged in by such seller.

But in any event the isolated sale of a motor vehicle, such as a person buying an automobile from a friend not in the automobile business, is subject to the tax.

Examples Of Exemptions

The bureau gave these examples of casual sales which are exempt from the tax:

1. A grocer selling his cash register or store fixtures or an insurance company selling its typewriters.

2. Sale of an entire business by

—See SALES TAX—Page 6

YOUTH, 18, IS PUT ON PROBATION

Beyer in Court for First Time Since 'Fix' Probe

Clyde Heisey Kemmerly, eighteen, Columbia R1, who was involved with five juveniles in the theft of storm sewer plates from Elizabethtown borough and from the Ironville Rd., pleaded guilty to larceny charges in court this morning.

Judge Wissler suspended the jail sentence and placed Kemmerly on probation for one year on terms that restitution be made and that the youth pay the county $25 and costs. The youth was a first offender.

Beyer Handles Case

District Attorney John W. Beyer, who was back in court today after being absent last week, handled the case.

It was Beyer's first appearance in Court since the "fix" investigation following the arrest of Lawrence A. Benedict, on drunken driving charges.

State policeman William J. Devlin testified that Kemmerly was involved with the juveniles in the theft of the storm plates and the stripping of parked vehicles of auto parts.

Myers Also on Probation

Albert Charles Myers, nineteen, Columbia R1, pleaded guilty to re-

—See COURT—Page 6

Wife, 35, Must Support 3 Children of Mate, 82

Thelma Fulton, thirty-five, Paradise R1, was ordered in court today to pay $10 per week to her husband, John G. Fulton, eighty-two, Paradise R1, for the support of their three children, ages 12, 14, and 16.

The couple separated some time ago and the husband is unable to work, the court was told.

$25,000 BARN FIRE AT STRASBURG

Man, Son Save 16 Head of Cattle

Fire of undetermined origin leveled a large barn and adjoining milkhouse on the farm of John A. Fisher, off Miller St., Strasburg, early this morning.

Strasburg Fire Chief Charles S. Aulthouse estimated the damage at $25,000.

Firemen were called to the scene at 3:45 a. m. after Fisher's son, Aaron, discovered the blaze. The father and son led about 16 head of livestock from the barn.

Crops Were In Barn

Chief Aulthouse said baled hay and other seasonal crops were in the barn. When the Strasburg firemen left the scene at 8 a. m., the hay was still burning. One hose line was left behind to protect against a further outbreak of flames.

The frame structure of the 65 by 90 foot barn was destroyed, leaving only the high stone foundation. Also ruined was a freezer and milking equipment in the milk-house.

200 Ft. Of Hose Used

Firemen laid about 2,000 feet of hose from a hydrant on Miller St. Besides the Strasburg company, fire units from Paradise, Gordonville and Lampeter were at the scene. The Lampeter and Paradise companies stood by in case sparks ignited frame homes along Miller St. The main farm house, a brick structure, was not damaged.

Although there was some farm machinery in the barn, the bulk of the equipment is kept in another building that was not touched, Chief Aulthouse said.

Despite the early hour, many spectators were attracted to the blaze.

Ex-County Pair's Baby Is Drowned

Word was received here today of the accidental death by drowning of the 19-months old son of a former New Holland couple.

Chester Wynn Byler, son of Chester and Miriam Smoker Byler, was drowned yesterday in Scottdale, Ariz., where the family now resides.

In addition to the parents and two brothers, Gerald and James, at home; the child is survived by the maternal grandparents, Mr. and Mrs. Daniel M. Smoker, Christiana; and the paternal grandparents, Mr. and Mrs. Daniel Byler, Mifflintown.

TV Stars Will Soothe N. Y. Subway Riders

NEW YORK (AP)— In the near future, the City Transit Authority says, dulcet voices of TV stars will reassure rush-hour subway crowds via public address systems.

The city's millions of riders will hear messages like this: "Folks, please don't crowd or push. After all there will be another train along in a matter of minutes" . . . or, "In just a moment you're going to get on the subway. Remember, you're riding on the biggest railroad in the world."

Shah Makes a Triumphant Return to Iran After Revolt

Mossadegh, 3 Henchmen Under Heavy Guard After Surrender to Zahedi's Forces

ROME (AP)—Triumphantly smiling Mohammed Reza Pahlevi, Shah of Iran, flew homeward today for a royal welcome in the explosive country he fled five days ago.

Awaiting him in his land of carpets, caviar and oil were a new premier loyal to the monarchy, jubilant crowds cheering their 33-year-old ruler and a pajama-clad prisoner under heavy guard—shaky old ex-Premier Mohammed Mossadegh.

Rome's Iranian colony and legation, which turned its back on the Shah's arrival as a fugitive Monday with 20-year-old Queen Soraya, came out in force to cheer his departure by plane early today.

Heads for Baghdad

In a chartered Royal Dutch (KLM) airliner, the Shah and a party of officials and newsmen headed for Baghdad, capital of his own country's next-door neighbor, Iraq.

The young monarch planned to lunch early this afternoon with Iraq's King Faisal, then perhaps fly on to Tehran later today.

Queen Soraya, exhausted and upset by the week's excitement, remained in Rome to rest up.

Also left behind was the Shah's strong-willed twin sister, Princess Ashraf. Mossadegh had exiled her

—See SHAH—Page 6

FRENCH ORDERED BACK TO WORK

Non-Red Unions Make Pact With Laniel

PARIS (AP)— Non-Communist unions ordered thousands of workers back to their jobs today — the first break in the wave of strikes that has strangled France for 16 days.

But the back-to-work trek was slow. Unions were meeting all over France to discsss the terms of settlement.

The Socialist Workers' Force (FO) and the Christian Labor Federation (CFTC) reached agreement with Premier Joseph Laniel's government early today for postal, telegraph and telephone workers to end their strike. Other government workers were expected to join the back-to-work movement.

Furthermore, a 48-hour strike of metal workers called by non-Communist unions began today. Thousands of workers were reported idle at steel mills and other factories in the nation.

The government was reported to have promised the postal, telephone and telegraph strikers:

1. To call into session before Sept. 30 a commission to consider a general upward revision of French wages.

2. To take no sanctions against strikers.

3. To consult the unions before putting into effect Laniel's proposed economy decrees upping retirement age limits and cutting other benefits.

Decrees Caused Strike

These decrees were the original cause of the strike. The strikers later added demands for wage increases and bonuses.

But observers warned that plenty of trouble may still lie ahead for Laniel.

Arrival of 1st PW Ship To Be Telecast Sunday

SAN FRANCISCO (AP)— Arrival here Sunday of the first ship carrying freed American prisoners of war from Korea will be telecast.

A one-hour telecast from the Ft. Mason Pier will be relayed over the NBC national network starting at 9 a. m. (11 a. m. EST). KRON-TV said the telecast would include interviews with men willing to be questioned.

Wiggins Building To Be Made Into Shopping Center

The H. H. Wiggins building on N. Queen St. will be remodeled into an arcade-type shopping center.

A permit for $30,000 for the work was issued today by the city building iinspector's office to John H. Wickersham, contractor.

Plans call for two new and larger display windows at the N. Queen St. entrance. A total of 13 stores, three of the open front variety and 10 closed shops, will be built along both sides of an eight-foot, six-inch aisle that will run along the center of the building. Work on the alterations will begin Monday.

Second Local POW Is Freed; Mom Starts Baking Christmas Cookies for 'Baby' She Hasn't Seen in 5 Yrs.

Cpl. Albert L. Sourbeer Jr., whose release from a Red prison camp was announced yesterday, hasn't been home for five years.

His parents, Mr. and Mrs. Albert L. Sourbeer, 514 Howard Ave., remember him as the seventeen-year-old baby of the family. When he finally returns home in the near future, he'll be almost 23.

'Still My Baby'

"I wonder if he's changed much," Mrs. Sourbeer mused between telephone calls this morning. "But, it doesn't matter," she continued, "he's still my baby."

Mrs. Sourbeer was busy all morning receiving callers and answering the telephone. Her husband went to work at 5 a. m. as usual. He said he's saving all his vacation time until his son returns.

This afternoon Mrs. Sourbeer tried to ward off well-wishers long enough to bake some Christmas cookies. "Albert loves Christmas

—See POW—Page 6

Mrs. Albert L. Sourbeer, center, is congratulated by Howard Ave. neighbors, Mrs. Ralph Harpel, of 513, left, and Mrs. Blanch Boas, of 511.

New Era Photo

Philadelphia Keeps Swamp As Feeding Place for Birds

PHILADELPHIA (AP) — Several million birds, including most everything on the wing from coots to crows, don't know it but one of their favorite feeding places is being saved, thanks to everyone from bird watchers to bankers.

The dining spot is the Tinicum Marshes, an area of 168 acres of low-lying land within the extreme southern limits of the city of Philadelphia.

There the year around, sometimes heading North and sometimes South, come herons, hawks, gadwalls, gallinules, coots, coocoos, ducks by the millions and short-eared owls. Many other species fill the trees and shrubbery around the area with their songs.

Swamp Never Set Aside

But the swamp, never set aside as a wild life preserve, was selected some six months ago by the Army engineers and the American Dredging Co. as the most likely spot to dump silt to be removed from the Schuylkill River as part of a river clean-up program.

Several hundred members of the Delaware Valley Ornithological Club protested quietly but insistently that such a proposal was not to be heard of.

They sent out letters to citizens whom they thought would be interested, too, in seeing the Tinicum Swamp turned into an official sanctuary.

Company Aids Project

The Gulf Oil Corp., owner of the land, was visited.

The company agreed to deed the marsh site to the city of Philadelphia for a sanctuary. An ordinance to that effect has been introduced and the City Council's Committee on Public Property and Public Works yesterday reported favorably a bill providing another dumping ground for the silt.

A spur line of a railroad runs across the new site, but that obstacle, too, has been removed: Allston Jenkins, president of the Ornithological Club, said the president of a "large central-city bank" whom he declined to identify, has agreed to underwrite the cost of track relocation, estimated to cost $60,000.

Ephrata Girl Crowned 'Miss America Of 1954'

The Weather
(U. S. Weather Bureau)
Eastern Pennsylvania — Partly Cloudy, Windy, Cooler Today, Highest Near 70 South Portion. Tomorrow Fair And Cool.

SUNDAY NEWS

3 A. M. Edition—Latest News by Associated Press and International News Service. Complete Local News and pictures by Wirephoto.

VOL. 31—NO. 1 LANCASTER, PA., SUNDAY, SEPTEMBER 13, 1953 52 PAGES—10 CENTS

Khrushchev Named No. 2 Man In Soviet Gov't

One-Time Boss Over Ukraine To Head Party

Now Ranks Next To Malenkov; Stalin Used Same Post To Seize Power

LONDON, Sept. 12 (AP)—Nikita S. Khrushchev, 59, a stocky one-time boss of the Ukraine, has been elected first secretary of the central committee of the Soviet Communist party, the Moscow radio announced tonight.

This gives him control over vast party machinery and makes him the second most important man in Russia. He ranks right after Premier Georgi M. Malenkov, the chief of the party's presidium.

Joseph Stalin used a similar post as secretary general of the central committee to make himself dictator of the Soviet Union.

Without the title, Khrushchev actually has headed a five-man secretariat of the central committee since last March. At that time Malenkov, who had taken over as successor to Stalin, resigned the central committee secretaryship to concentrate full attention on the premiership.

Laventi P. Beria was regarded as the No. 2 man under Malenkov until he was arrested last June, accused of being a traitor, and dismissed as internal affairs minister. Foreign Minister V. M. Molotov is the third man in the Soviet hierarchy.

The title of first secretary is a new one.

Stalin held the title of secretary general of the central committee and actual ruling power for many years before he made himself premier.

A stocky, round-faced, blunt-spoken Ukrainian, Khrushcher was first named one of the secretaries of the central committee of the Communist party of the Soviet Union in December, 1949.

He then left Kiev, moved to Moscow and gave up his jobs in the Ukrainian party. He took over the leadership of the important Moscow party organization, keeping at the same time his job as a secretary of the central committee.

Another of the secretaries of the

Page 10—BOSS

No. 2 Red

KHRUSHCHEV

Clergy Denies 'Red' Charges

WASHINGTON, Sept. 12 (AP)—Newly-unveiled Congressional testimony of a "highly successful" plot to plant hundreds of Reds among the U. S. clergy has brought a flow of denials from ministers named as Communist agents, dupes and pawns.

Not all of the clergymen were reached for comment on the testimony, taken at secret hearings in New York last July and made public yesterday by the House Un-American Activities Committee.

Says He's No 'Red Dean'

But Harry F. Ward, described in the hearing transcript as "the Red Dean of the Communist party in the religious field," said in New York:

"I am not and never have been a member of any political party."

Ward, former professor at Union Theological Seminary, accused the committee of arousing resentment by its actions "from all persons concerned with maintaining the freedom of speech, press, assembly and the exercise of religion set down in the Bill of Rights."

The "Red Dean" description of Ward was made by Manning Johnson of New York, one of three witnesses who said they were former Communists who had seen successful examples of Red infiltration of the clergy.

Johnson was a member of the national Negro commission of the Communist party national committee for about five years ending in 1940. The two other witnesses were Benjamin Gitlow and Joseph Zack Kornfeder, both also from New York.

Johnson said the scheme to switch from frontal assaults to boring from within against religion was "successful beyond even Com-

Page 10—CLERGY

LEWIS STONE DIES

HOLLYWOOD, Sept. 12 (AP) — Veteran stage and screen actor Lewis Stone, 77, died of a heart attack tonight.

US Sales Tax Will Not Pass, Reed Asserts

Bluntly Warns GOP Against New Levys, Any Failure To Lower Present Ones

WASHINGTON, Sept. 12 (AP)—In a blunt warning to the Eisenhower administration, Republican Rep. Daniel A. Reed of New York vowed today that Congress will not pass a national sales tax.

The 76-year-old chairman of the tax writing House Ways and Means Committee also served notice of battle against other efforts to raise taxes, or to postpone scheduled tax reductions.

Reed's statement left little doubt that unless the administration changes its course, he is ready to renew his intra-party fight with President Eisenhower on tax policy—one of the most spectacular scraps of the last session of Congress.

Sees Winning Support

Next time, Reed said, the winning margin of lawmakers will be on his side.

The tax chairman was overrun by administration supporters in the last session when he tried to end the excess profits tax on July 1, and to give individuals a 10 per cent income tax cut at the same time. Both actions were delayed until Jan. 1, as urged by Eisenhower.

But there has been increasing talk that the administration might recommend a national sales tax as a substitute for these or other scheduled losses in revenue, in order to achieve one of Eisenhower's prime goals: a balanced budget.

Secretary of the Treasury Humphrey has said only that a sales tax is being considered along with many other tax proposals.

Reed apparently is out to head off any move for more taxes.

"A general sales tax will not be approved by the Congress in the coming session," his statement said. "I base this prediction on reports coming to me from members of the Ways and Means Committee and other members of the House who are in their home districts."

The administration already has asked Congress to cancel a scheduled two billion dollar cut in cor-

Page 10—TAX

Mitchell Invites Party Talks On 'Loyalty Pledge'

CHICAGO, Sep. 12 (AP)— Stephen A. Mitchell, Democratic national chairman, said today he will welcome full discussion of the "loyalty pledge" issue at next week's party rally in the hope that debate will point the way to settlement of differences.

Southern objection to the pledge is expected to be spelled out anew at the sessions.

Mitchell was asked about the "controversy" at a news conference.

"I'm doing all I can to encourage discussion," he replied. "I think any problem, or point of difference, will move toward solution if the people concerned think about it and talk about it."

Crowning The New Queen

ATLANTIC CITY, N. J., Sept. 12—MISS AMERICA IS CROWNED—Miss America of 1954 —Miss Pennsylvania—in the person of Evelyn Margaret Ay, of Ephrata, a 20-year-old blonde, receives her crown from the past year's Miss America, Neva Jane Langley. (AP Wirephoto)

Miss Ay Takes Title, Awards Worth $50,000

ATLANTIC CITY, N. J., Sept. 12 (AP)—A statuesque ash blonde—Evelyn Margaret Ay of Ephrata, Pa. —won the title of Miss America of 1954 tonight.

The 20-year-old Miss Pennsylvania had won a bathing suit preliminary earlier in the week.

One of the tallest girls in the contest at 5 feet, 8, she weighs 132 pounds, has a 37-inch bust, 24-inch waist 36-inch hips.

Miss Pennsylvania rose on an elevator as her name was announced. She wore a long, red, velvet robe over her white evening gown.

The 51 other contestants threw confetti as she moved toward the center of the stage to receive the crown from last year's winner, Neva Jane Langley, of Macon, Ga.

"It's hard to express an emotion that's so deeply set," the new Miss America said in receiving the crown.

She walked down the 100-foot ramp in huge Convention Hall and bowed to the applauding audience of 15,000.

ATLANTIC CITY, N. J., Sept. 12 A statuesque ash blonde—Evelyn Margaret Ay of Ephrata, Pa.—won the title of Miss America of 1954 tonight.

The 20-year-old Miss Pennsylvania had won a bathing suit preliminary earlier in the week.

One of the tallest girls in the contest at 5 feet, 8, she weighs 132 pounds, has a 37-inch bust, 24-inch waist and 36-inch hips.

Miss Pennsylvania rose on an elevator as her name was announced. She wore a long, red, velvet robe over her white evening gown.

The 51 other contestants threw confetti as she moved toward the center of the stage to receive the crown from last year's winner, Neva Jane Langley of Macon, Ga.

"It's hard to express an emotion that's so deeply set," the new Miss America said in receiving the crown.

She walked down the 100-foot ramp in huge Convention Hall and bowed to the applauding audience of 15,000.

Across the front of her gown she wore a white, satin banner with gold letters, proclaiming her "Miss America of 1954."

Miss South Dakota, Delores Jerde of Spearfish, was awarded a $1,000 scholarship as the most talented contestant not in the finals. She had won a talent preliminary Thursday night with a piano rendition of Rhapsody in C Major by Dohnamyi.

For her victory in the weeklong pageant, green-eyed Miss Ay receives $50,000 in prizes, including a $5,000 scholarship, personal appearance fees, an automobile and a special wardrobe.

The other runnersup in the contest and the scholarships they receive are: Miss New York City, Joan Cecilia Kaible, $3,000.

Miss Virginia, Anne Lee Ceglis, of Norfolk, $2,500.

Miss Alabama, Virginia McDavid of Birmingham, $2,000.

Page 10—GIRL

Envoys Meet On Cold War

WASHINGTON, Sept. 12 (INS)—The State Department disclosed today that American diplomats to Iron Curtain countries will meet in Vienna Sept. 22-24 to discuss recent developments in the cold war.

The department announced that the U.S. representatives will confer with Assistant Secretary of State for European Affairs Livingstone B. Merchant.

Merchant will meet in the Austrial capital with the U.S. ambassadors to the Soviet Union, Czechoslovakia, Hungary, Romania, and Austria. Cicil B. Lyon, who represents the Berlin division of the Office of the U.S. High Commissioner for Germany, also will attend.

The department gave no agenda, and called attention to the fact that such regional diplomatic get-togethers are held periodically. But there was no doubt that effects of the recent German elections, and unrest in the Communist satellite states will come under analysis.

Before going to Vienna, Merchant will attend a meeting next Friday and Saturday in Luxembourg with the U.S. Ambassadors to the countries comprising the European coal and steel community.

Hurricane Blows Out Over Ocean

WASHINGTON, Sept. 12 (AP)—The Weather Bureau said tonight that hurricane Dolly, which swept up from the Bahamas off the Atlantic Coast, is blowing itself out some 570 miles northeast of Bermuda.

A final advisory on the season's fourth hurricane, named Dolly for the fourth letter of the alphabet, said:

"It is moving toward the northeast at about 35 miles per hour. Strongest winds are estimated at 65 to 70 miles per hour in squalls . . . and gales extending outward for 200 miles."

The 5 p.m. (EST) advisory said Dolly, born Wednesday, should continue moving rapidly toward the northeast the next 12 hours as it fades away, although its area of gales probably will expand.

Big Welcome Looms For Miss America

Lancaster will stage a bang-up welcome-home for Miss America, probably sometime this coming week. Plans include a parade and ceremonies at Musser Park, to which Governor Fine and Mayor Bare will be invited.

Harry B. Mosemann, of the Lancaster Amvets, said early this morning that he was going ahead with plans which he had cancelled earlier at Miss Ay's request, before she won the title.

Mosemann telephoned Miss Ay's hotel in Atlantic City just after midnight to find out just when she may be expected to return home, but was told by the telephone operator that she would be in conference with committees of the Miss America contest until at least 4 a.m.

The operator also said that the committee had decided to send a traveling secretary with Miss Ay wherever she goes, for the first time in the history of the contest. Mosemann said he'd keep trying to set a definite date for the welcome.

"The telephone operator was just as enthusiastic as we are here in Lancaster," Mosemann said. She told him how Miss Ay, when questioned about what she'd do with her winnings in furthering her career, said she would like to go to some country such as India where the people are starving, and help as much as possible. She is studying at the University of Pennsylvania to be a medical technician.

Mosemann recalled that Miss Ay was Miss National Amvet last year, and gave an example of her willingness to serve at that time. He said that she paid a visit to the Veterans Administration hospital at Lebanon Christmas morning and personally handed out yule stockings to 1,500 patients.

Ephrata Proud

"Ephrata is very proud of her" was the statement made by Burgess David E. Good for the people of Miss Ay's home community at midnight last night.

"When we get our hands on her

Page 10—LOCAL

Plush Wedding For Kennedy

NEWPORT, R. I., Sept. 12 (AP)—In one of Newport's plushiest weddings in years, beautiful Jacqueline Lee Bouvier became the bride of U. S. Senator John F. Kennedy of Massachusetts today at St. Mary's Catholic church.

Leaders of society, politics, business and the arts crowded every inch of the old brownstone church. Outside a crowd estimated by police as between 3,000 and 4,000 jammed narrow Spring street for blocks.

Many crowded the lawns of the church to catch a glimpse of the lovely brunette society girl, who was a Washington newspaper photographer, when she met her husband on an assignment.

Archbishop Richard J. Cushing

Page 10—KENNEDY

Dodgers Clinch League Pennant

NEW YORK, Sept. 12 (AP)—The Broklyn Dodgers clinched their second straight National League pennant and the 10th in the history of the club today with a 5-2 victory over Milwaukee at Milwaukee.

GOP Hopes To Boost Funds At Ike Party

HARRISBURG, Sept. 12 (AP)—Pennsylvania Republicans set out today to bolster their 1954 gubernatorial campaign chest with a $100 a plate birthday party for President Eisenhower at nearby Hershey Oct. 13. They hope to raise $600,000.

The big drawing card for the unique, money-raising event will be the President and his wife. Mr. Eisenhower, however, doesn't plan a formal speech.

Philip T. Sharples, State GOP finance chairman, said the party, on the eve of the President's 63rd birthday, is expected to net $600,000. The expense has been budgeted at $150,000.

Sharples estimated 20,000 Republicans will be at Hershey for the gala, circus-like event.

The Ringling Brothers-Barnum & Bailey 'big top" circus tent will be erected in a field to handle the buffet supper for the $100 a plate participants. Sharples said they will number 6,200 to 6,400—the seating capacity of the indoor Hershey Sports Arena where the actual party will be held.

The huge circus tent is a sixth of a mile around the outside.

The overflow will be seated outdoors in the adjacent Hershey Stadium.

The stadium, said Sharples, also will be utilized by Republicans who can't afford the $100 a plate accommodations at the arena.

"People there can bring their own box lunches," he said. "They'll have an opportunity to see the President and Mrs. Eisenhower, too."

He said the President and his wife will drive a horse-drawn Pennsylvania Dutch buggy into the arena after taking a turn or two around the stadium track.

Three big Philadelphia cater-

Page 10—GOP

Truman And Adlai Meet In Chicago

CHICAGO, Sept. 12 (INS)—Former President Harry S. Truman and Adlai E. Stevenson exchanged cordial greetings tonight in their first face-to-face meeting since last November when Stevenson was defeated by President Eisenhower in the race for the White House.

The two Democratic leaders met with a warm handshake three hours after Truman arrived in Chicago for next week's gigantic party rally.

7 Youths Charged After Disturbance

Seven youths were arrested by city police last night for allegedly creating a disturbance in the Fulton Theater.

They were charged with disorderly conduct by Donald Bonstein, manager of the theater. Two juveniles posted bail for hearing in juvenile court.

Others charged were: John S. Hill, seventeen, 515 Woodward St.; Charles L. Gray, twenty-three, 427½ North St.; Charles F. Stewart, twenty, 324 Green St.; Gregory M. Johnson, nineteen, 410 Howard Ave.; Herbert W. Frazier, nineteen, 336 North St. They all later pleaded guilty and paid the costs before Alderman Hubert Miller.

Rhee Waging Spy Cleanup

SEOUL, Sunday, Sept. 13 (AP)-President Syngman Rhee is waging a sweeping post-war cleanup campaign in a move he vows will rid the Republic of Korea Government of corruption and suspected subversives.

Political and youth organizations were included in the reshuffle.

In addition Rhee ordered the South Korean Army counter-intelligence Corps to investigate and arrest Koreans suspected of engaging in Communist espionage or anti-government activities.

The Korean CIC recently arrested a well known South Korean newsman on charges of spying. Chung Kook Eun, editor in chief for the South Korean daily "Unhap Shinmoon" has been undergoing severe interrogations since he was taken into custody Aug. 31.

Three high ranking officers of the South Korean army, including the former chief of ROK army intelligence bureau, Brig. Gen. Kim Chong Pyung, are now being tried by the high military court at Taegu on charges of violating the national defense law.

The national police have arrested their former Assistant Director Kim Eang Bong on charges of plotting against the government. Police alleged Kim had former an "unauthorized" group with more than 1,300 members in an attempt to "overthrow the government."

Demand Reds Return Son Of Gen. Van Fleet

PANMUNJOM, Sunday, Sept. 13 (AP)—Nine Reds who changed their minds twice head north today—beyond the bamboo curtain which still shields the mystery of what happened to more than 900 Americans, including the flier son of Gen. James A. Van Fleet.

The Pentagon in Washington caused a surprise by announcing that Air Force Capt. James A. Van Fleet, Jr., a B26 pilot, is among at least 917 Americans for whom the U. N. Command is demanding an accounting from the Reds.

Hitherto there had been no public indication that the son of the former U. S. 8th Army commander might have survived a B26 bomber strike near Sunchon, in northwest Korea, last Apr. 5, 1952.

9 Reds Go Back

The nine North Koreans going back to communism today are the first dispositions among more than 23,000 Reds who renounced Red rule after being captured during the Korean war. The nine changed their minds again after being brought to U. N. stockades in the demilitarized zone.

The neutral nations repatriation commission promptly heard their verbal applications and decided unanimously to hand over the nine to the Communists today.

In contrast, a long period of dickering and investigation is probably ahead in determining the fate of the 917 Americans, with no guarantee how many of them may still be alive.

The junior Van Fleet's name was on a Pentagon list made public Saturday, U. S. time, after notification of next of kin. It contained 309 Air Force names and brought to 917 the total announced in Washington.

Successor Named To Perle Mesta

DENVER, Sept. 12 (AP) — President Eisenhower today appointed Wiley T. Buchanan Jr., Washington, D. C. investment executive, as Minister to Luxembourg, succeeding Mrs. Perle Mesta.

The recess appointment is subject to Senate confirmation when Congress reconvenes.

Cool Nights Begin On Wednesday, Seer Predicts

Today there will be light wind becoming VERY UNSETTLED, Monday SHOWERS, Tuesday partly cloudy, Wednesday partly cloudy and the beginning of COOL NIGHTS, Thursday pleasant, Friday PLEASANT becoming unsettled, Saturday pleasant and light wind, Sunday COOL AND PLEASANT the night bright and pleasant for its the harvest moon. Oct. 20 and Nov. 8 are ideal WEDDING DAYS. (S.H.M.)

TEMPERATURES

	High	Low
Ephrata Weather Station	76	59
Ephrata 1952	93	59
Lancaster Water Works	76	55
Ephrata precipitation	.14 inches rain	
Lancaster precipitation	.10 inches rain	

Eastern Pennsylvania — Partly cloudy, windy and cooler Sunday, highest in the 60's in the north portion and near 70 in the south portion. Cooler Sunday night. Monday fair and cool.

Maryland, Delaware and Southern New Jersey — Some cloudiness, windy and cooler Sunday, highest in the 70's. Fair and cooler Sunday night. Monday fair and cool.

Lower Potomac and Chesapeake Bay — Shifting winds becoming northwest 20 to 25 miles per hour Sunday. Scattered thundersqualls mostly over south half tonight with fair to good visibility. Fair weather with excellent visibility Sunday.

Grand Jury Acts To Remove D. A.

SANTA FE N. M., Sept. 12 (AP)—A special Santa Fe County grand jury tonight filed proceedings to remove Dist. Atty. Bertrand Prince from office and urged the removal of State Comptroller Edward Hartmen.

The grand jury formally accused Prince of corruption in office and of trying to get a witness to perjure herself.

Hartman was accused of being "remiss, negligent and derelic in his duty" in connection with two audits by his office.

Sunday News Was 'Born' 30 Yrs. Ago

In the upper left portion of today's Sunday News you'll see printed an unpretentious milestone: "Vol. 31—No. 1."

It means that the Sunday News has completed 30 years of publication. Vol. 1, No. 1 hit the street on Sunday morning, Sept. 16, 1923.

In that first edition the Sunday News pledged to bring its readers all the local, state, national and world news, "without fear or favor." Since 1923 there have been great advances in the swift gathering and printing of the news, but that policy has held.

It has contributed to the constant growth of the Sunday News, as reflected in the most recent circulation figures. In August, net paid circulation of the Sunday News averaged 65,849 every Sunday—a gain of 3,133 copies above the same period last year.

News Index

Lititz Child In Polio Unit Here

Janice, five-year-old daughter of Mr. and Mrs. Glenn Knight, 111 E Lincoln Ave., Lititz, was admitted to the polio unit of Lancaster General Hospital yesterday morning.

Dr. Arthur S. Griswold, Lititz, the family physician, said last night the little girl had been ill about two days and was suffering from a mild form of the disease. He listed her condition as "fair."

12-Woman Safety Corp Unit Planned

(SEE STORY ON PAGE 17)

The city hopes to have a total of 12 Women's Safety Corps members on duty at dangerous school intersections by the first of the year, Mayor Kendig C. Bare said yesterday. This would more than double the originally - planned strength of the special school patrol now being formed.

Initially the corps will be made up of only five women, the mayor said. He indicated, however, that a call will be made at a later date for additional applicants as "we hope to add seven more by the first of the year."

Nine applicants for the five posts took competitive written examinations last week and those who scored passing marks are scheduled to be given physical examinations next Sunday, according to Mrs. Jeanette Pontz, acting secretary to the Police Civil Service Board. Final selection of the five will not be made until after the physical exams.

In view of this, Police Commissioner Fred G. McCartney said "we probably won't be able to get

Page 10—SCHOOLS

Suspect Identified in 'Pike Truck Slayings

Little Liz - - -

The hand is quicker than the eye, and there are plenty of black eyes to prove it.

LANCASTER NEW ERA

The Weather
(U. S. Weather Bureau Forecast)
Clear, Cold, Frost Tonight; Fair, Warmer Tomorrow.
Temp. Today High 58; Low 36
Temp. Yesterday High 57; Low 41

77th Year—No. 23,690 | Lancaster Metropolitan Area Population Official United States Census Figures 234,717 | LANCASTER, PA., THURSDAY, OCTOBER 8, 1953 | CITY EDITION | 48 PAGES | 30c PER WEEK—5c Per Copy

New Major Industry Coming Here

Pawn Shop Tip Starts Hunt for Cleveland Man

To Test Gun Given Stepfather of Woman Held in Custody

CLEVELAND (AP) — Homicide Capt. David E. Kerr said today Cleveland police have issued a two-state alarm to pick up a 25-year-old man for questioning in the recent Pennsylvania Turnpike shootings.

Kerr identified the man as John Wesley Wable, a former Cleveland factory worker. He emphasized no charges have been filed against Wable, but said a girl linked him with a wrist watch taken from one of the victims.

Kerr said the pickup alarm went to Ohio and Pennsylvania police and added that Wable "may be armed and dangerous."

Driving Light Blue Car

The man was last seen driving a light blue 1952 car with Pennsylvania license plates bearing the number, 8157E, and also has been issued Ohio plates, Capt. Kerr said.

The girl who was questioned, a 22-year-old blonde, was a friend of Wable, Kerr said. She was released after questioning. Kerr said a .765 German-made revolver was turned over to police by the girl's stepfather. The gun was similar to the one used in the Turnpike shootings, Kerr said.

The police official quoted the stepfather as saying Wable gave him the gun for safe-keeping several weeks ago.

Detectives George Gackowski and Louis Jalovec held the girl for questioning after recovering in a pawn shop a watch taken from the wrist of John K. Shepard, who was shot and seriously wounded July 31 near Lisbon, Ohio.

Detectives said the blonde was the girl friend of a youth they seek in connection with the killing last July of two truck drivers on the turnpike and the wounding of Shepard.

About 24 Years Old

The girl denied knowing his whereabouts, but detectives described the man as about 24 years old, six feet tall, and weighing about 155 pounds.

Shepard's watch was found at David's Loan Co. after police had sent a circular to all pawn shops in Cleveland describing the watch, giving its serial number, and

—See TURNPIKE—Page 10

Kidnap-Slayer Suspects Go to Jail

AP Wirephoto

Carl Austin Hall (right) and Mrs. Bonnie Heady at lockup gate in St. Louis city jail last night. Police official shown is not identified.

Dust Fire at Plastics Plant

Dust in a mechanical collector caught fire in the Lafayette St. plant of the Alphone Knoedler and Co., 651 High St., plastic products manufacturers, shortly before 2:30 p.m. today.

The dust collector stands at about the second floor level of the building. The burning dust and shavings sent out great clouds of smoke that could be seen over most of the city. Eugene Rhinier, plant manager, said no person was hurt.

Employes remained at their posts while Fire Companies 1 and 2 and Truck B extinguished the flames. There was no immediate estimate of damages.

Italy to Control Zone in Trieste

British, U. S. Troops Will Leave City Soon

WASHINGTON (AP)— The United States and Britain jointly announced today they will turn over their occupation zone in the Trieste area to the Italian government for administration "at the earliest practicable date."

This decision was disclosed as a step to halt the "recent deterioration in the relations between Italy and Yugoslavia." Both countries claim the entire free territory of Trieste.

American and British troops have occupied Zone A, including the city and port of Trieste, for nearly eight years. At present some 4,000 American and 3,000 British troops garrison the area. Yugoslavia occupies the remainder of the area, known as Zone B.

Troops Will Depart

The British and American troops will be withdrawn, the announcement said.

"It is the firm belief of the two governments that this step will contribute to stabilization of a situation which has disturbed the Italo-Yugoslav relations during recent years," the State Department said.

"They trust that it will provide the basis for friendly and fruitful cooperation between Italy and Yugoslavia, which is as important to the security of Western Europe as it is to the two countries concerned."

A State Department spokesman said the American-British decision has been communicated to both the Italian and Yugoslav governments.

Army Shows Atom Gun, New 58-Ton Tank Rescuer

ABERDEEN, Md. (AP)—The Army took the wraps off some of its hitherto secret equipment today in a display at the Aberdeen Proving Ground, but a number of atomic age guns and gadgets were conspicuously absent.

Ordnance items on view ranged from the latest in protective body armor to the new 280 millimeter atomic cannon, set up to fire a conventional shell.

But, abiding by the terms of an order issued last spring by Secretary of Defense Wilson, the Army made no effort to display such items as the new Nike antiaircraft guided missile, the "Ontos" carrier for antiaircraft weapons or the new T43 heavy tank. The Wilson order prohibited for reasons of security and economy any "public demonstrations of important new weapons and equipment."

Atomic Cannon Displayed

The 280 millimeter cannon which fired its first atomic round in Nevada last spring was out in the clear for public demonstration.

The Army, which has emphasized the mobility of the huge, 85-ton gun, scheduled bridge crossings today to prove that it can be moved virtually anywhere in a battle zone.

Also unaffected by the order was the 75 millimeter "Skyscraper" antiaircraft gun, with radar controls to detect and "lock onto" approaching enemy planes.

New Tank Retriever

Unveiled for the first time were a 58-ton tank retriever capable of hauling the Army's heaviest vehicles off the battlefield under fire; a 15-ton tractor which can travel 50 miles an hour and has a towing capacity of 75 tons; and a new twin 40-millimeter gun mounted on the chassis of the walker bulldog tank.

Most of the other new weapons had been displayed before includ-

—See WEAPONS—Page 10

They're 'Deeply Concerned'

Welsh Group Asks Queen's Mate to Quit Sunday Polo

OSWESTRY, England (AP)— A message telling of the "deep regret" of 13,000 good people in Wales that the Duke of Edinburgh plays polo on Sundays reached a Presbyterian conference at this Shropshire community today.

The Presbyterians of South Pembrokeshire would want the Queen's husband to be told of their "deep concern at the spiritual consequences." The message read:

Philip

"The South Pembroke Presbytery asks for representations to be made to the Duke of Edinburgh through the appropriate channels expressing its deep regret at his participation in sporting events on the Lord's Day.

Express Deep Concern

"The Presbytery is sincerely grateful for the cheerful and natural graciousness with which His Royal Highness undertakes his many and arduous duties.

"It is therefore extremely loath to criticize any actions in his leisure time, but feels bound to express its deep concern at the spiritual consequences in our national life which must result from participation in Sunday sport by one who is so prominent in our nation."

The duke who plays cricket and polo on weekdays, too, and also pilots a plane, has been recipient of raps on the knuckles before.

A month ago the Rev. Edward Pulford, rector of the village of Longhope, called on his parishioners to pray for the duke so "he may be brought to see the inadvisability of his attitude." The rector suggested a "fatherly word" from the Archibishop of Canterbury might influence the duke.

Was Rebuked Previously

Scottish clergymen previously rebuked Prince Philip for Sunday polo.

The duke fell off his horse during a polo match on a Sunday in July in Ambersham. He remounted and finished the match. Among the spectators was Queen Elizabeth II.

New Burrowes School Started

$315,000 Building Ready Next July

The Ground breaking ceremony for the new $315,000 Burrowes Elementary School, Orange St. and Ranck Ave., was held this morning with members of the Lancaster Twp. School District Authority, school board and officials on hand.

Joseph C. Moss, chairman of the school authority, broke the ground.

One-Floor Building

Construction work on the one-floor school began immediately. William Huber, architect, estimated that the building should be finished by July, 1954, in plenty of time for the fall term of school. Diller Plank is the general contractor.

The building, which will be shaped like an L, will have nine classrooms, one of which will be a kindergarten room. There will also be a health room, an office, kitchen and all-purpose room.

Officials Attend

Attending today's ceremony, besides Moss, Plank and Huber, were the following members of the Lancaster Twp. School District Authority; Alan R. McGarvey, secretary; Fred P. Bromer, treasurer, and Arthur F. Huber and J. B. MacKenzie Jr. The Lancaster Twp. School Board was represented by the following members: Clayton F. Erisman, president; J. Laurence Strickler, vice president; H. D. Stehman, secretary, and Richard H. Shopf, George E. Robey and R. B. Bechtold.

Fred S. Engle, supervising principal of the Lancaster Twp. Schools, was also present.

2 Vie for Nobel Writing Prize

Churchill, Hemingway Strongest Contenders

Churchill

Hemingway

STOCKHOLM, Sweden (AP)— Prime Minister Winston Churchill and American Novelist Ernest Hemingway are considered the strongest candidates for the Nobel Prize for literature this year, literary sources in Stockholm said today.

In a surprise move, the Swedish Academy announced today that the winner will be picked a week from now instead of, as usual, late in November. The 1953 Nobel Prize amounts to 175,292 Swedish crowns ($33,840).

Literary experts here said Churchill has been among the top candidates for the Nobel Prize for many years. Since publication of the first two volumes of his World War I memoirs "The Gathering Storm" and "Their Finest Hour," he has had many staunch supporters in the academy, which awards the prizes.

The British Prime Minister would be the first statesman ever to receive the world's highest award for literature. He would be the second historian to win the Nobel Prize. The first was the German Theodor Mommsen, who won the prize in 1902 for his monumental history of Rome.

Hint Captured Pair Only Guilty In Kidnap-Death

FBI Keeps Silent on Hunt for 2nd Man; Where Is $300,000?

KANSAS CITY (AP)—The possibility an ex-convict and his girl friend, both under arrest, carried out the kidnap-slaying of 6-year-old Bobby Greenlease by themselves grew today as the FBI kept a close-lipped silence in the hunt for a second ex-convict.

Carl Austin Hall, thirty-four, and his friend, Mrs. Bonnie Brown Heady, both have admitted participating in the kidnaping but say they didn't kill the child of wealthy 71-year-old Robert C. Greenlease, pioneer automobile dealer and distributor here.

A widespread search is on for Thomas John Marsh, thirty-seven, who like Hall has served time in the Missouri state prison. Marsh was named by Hall as the killer and accomplice in the kidnaping.

At St. Louis where Hall and Mrs. Heady are held police board president I. A. Long said police there weren't certain there was a third party."

Where Is The $300,000?

This turn of events brought this question:

What has happened to the $300,000 ransom money still unfound. Only about $292,000 of the $600,000 paid by Greenlease in vain to try to get his boy was found in suitcases in the possession of Hall.

There were indications FBI agents at many points were cooperating with local authorities in the lookout for Marsh but no nation-wide search had been issued by it, so far as could be learned.

All the FBI here would say is that there has been no federal complaint issued against March. The U. S. District Attorney's office said it had no comment at this stage beyond saying it was in the middle of the investigating.

G-Men Examine Backyard

Meanwhile at St. Joseph, Mo., 55 miles north of here, FBI men were reported minutely examining the yard and home of one of the abductors held in St. Louis, 41-year-old Mrs. Bonnie Brown Heady.

Twenty FBI agents were reported even sifting garbage taken from the home in the last two weeks.

The child's body was dug yesterday from a shallow grave in Mrs. Heady's backyard after she and her boy friend, 34-year-old Carl Austin Hall, were arrested at St. Louis for the kidnaping. The arrests followed payment of a record $600,000 ransom by the boy's wealthy parents.

Several key points in the case were shrouded with uncertainty today.

Where Is The $300,000?

What had happened to the $300,000 of ransom money missing? Hall told St. Louis he planned the ransom payment alone after March killed the boy a few hours after the kidnaping Sept. 28 and disappeared.

There was speculation here that Marsh himself may have been killed. But the hunt continued at least on a state level.

The FBI simply wasn't talking. All it would say was that no federal warrant had been issued.

Axe Is Found

But their agents were reported to have an axe at the Heady home. It was covered with a sub-

—See KIDNAPING—Page 10

State Checks Arrive For 7 School Districts

State subsidy checks started to arrive today for seven county school districts in the Amish areas.

The money was due last March but was frozen by the state because the districts were not then enforcing the compulsory attendance law.

Through the efforts of Sens. Diehm and Kessler, the money was released about 10 days ago. For the seven townships, it totals some $118,000.

BLAST KILLS WELDER

WILKES-BARRE, Pa. (AP) —An empty gasoline carrier exploded at nearby Hanover township yesterday killing a welder and seriously injuring another man.

Today's New Era

General Hosp. Asks Court To Name Two Arbitrators

Want Men to Help Settle Dispute over Construction Differences with Wickersham Firm

The Lancaster General Hospital is asking the county court to appoint two arbitrators to help settle differences it has with the Wickersham Engineering and Construction, Inc., over the building of the new $2 million Duke St. hospital building.

The request is made under the State Arbitration Act of 1927, according to Robert Ruppin, attorney, who is representing the hospital in association with Paul A. Mueller.

Ruppin said this is one of the first, if not the first, times local court action was brought under the 1927 law.

What Hospital Asks

What the hospital is asking, according to Ruppin, is this:

That the court name a neutral arbitrator and also an arbitrator to replace one designated by Wickersham. These two would join a third arbitrator picked by the hospital to settle the arguments over certain items in construction.

Ruppin said the reason the hospital wants the court to act is the fact that its own arbitrator and one originally designated by Wickersham failed to agree on the third, and neutral, man.

Ruppin said that, following provisions of the Architect's Code, the hospital's representative submitted a list of six names as suggested neutral parties but the Wickersham man refused to accept any of them, and also refused to make any suggestions of his own.

List Of Neutral Arbitrators

The list of suggested neutral arbitrators included, according to the court appeal:

Frank Chesterman, immediate past president of the Bell Telephone Co. of Pennsylvania; chairman of Governor Fine's committee on economies in the state government; director of a number of Philadelphia business concerns and chairman of the Philadelphia Parking Authority;

Ralph Kelly, immediate past president of Baldwin Locomotive Co.; past vice president Westinghouse Co.; director of Bell Telephone Co., the Philadelphia Co., Franklin Institute; past president Philadelphia Chamber of Commerce; chairman Hospital Planning Agency of Philadelphia since 1948;

Judge Herbert F. Goodrich, Dean U. of P. Law School, 1929-1940, Judge U. S. Court of Appeals since 1940;

Judge Vincent A. Carroll, Judge Common Pleas Court, Philadel-

—See HOSPITAL—Page 10

City Brethren to Sell Old Church

Plan $225,000 Edifice On Fordney Road

The Charlotte Street Church of the Brethren will be sold and a new church building erected on Fordney Rd. opposite Clearview Ave., it was announced today.

The congregation plans to sell its entire property on N. Charlotte St. between Lemon and Walnut Sts., and build on the three-acre plot it has owned for four years.

No definite plans for the new building have been made, but church officials estimate it will cost approximately $225,000. Plans for a new building have been under discussion since October 1949 when the congregation purchased the three-acre tract on. Fordney Rd. for $10,000 from the estate of Thomas P. Fordney.

Plan Parking Area

The site of the new church is one block from Esbenshade Rd. where the Calvary Independent Church erected its new building last year.

The Brethren membership, at a special congregational meeting last night, gave final approval to a resolution presented by the Trustee Board. The Board, by a majority vote of the congregation, was granted permission to negotiate with outside interested parties for the sale of the existing church facilities at 341-343 N. Charlotte St.

Will Sell All Buildings

The property includes the church building which is 50 by 87 feet; the

—See CHURCH—Page 10

Twin Brothers Born on Different Days at Ephrata

Twin sons, their first children, were born to Mr. and Mrs. Norman H. Shirk, East Earl, on two different days in Ephrata Community Hospital.

The older boy was born at 11:45 p. m. yesterday; the second at 12:20 a. m. today, 35 minutes later. Mother and infants are reported "doing fine," by hospital officials. It is the first time on record that twins have been born in the hospital on different days.

45 Terrorists Killed By Guards in Kenya

NAIROBI, Kenya (AP)—Forty-five Mau Mau terrorists were killed and 20 captured today in one of the biggest strikes since the emergency started.

A force of Kikuyu guards, police and troops attacked part of a big anti-White terrorist gang south of Nyeri and killed seven. The Kikuyu guards operating on their own then killed 31 and captured 20. The combined forces later killed seven more terrorists.

HOME BUILDING DROPS

PHILADELPHIA (AP)— A home building executive says home construction in the Philadelphia and southern New Jersey areas has fallen off more than 25 per cent in recent months.

1st Killing Frost, Low Here Is 29°

Coldest Night Since That of April 20

Temperatures dropped to 29 degrees here last night as the first killing frost of the season blanketed most of the county at daybreak.

The first killing frost of the season occurred on the same date as the first killing frost of 1952. However, a year ago the low temperature was 34 degrees.

Last night was the coldest night of the season. The previous low for the season was 36 degrees recorded on Sept. 24. It was the first time since April 20 that the mercury dropped to 29 degrees in the Lancaster area.

The mercury rose steadily throughout the morning and at noon the temperature was 54 degrees.

More Frost Tonight

The Weather Bureau forecast more frost tonight, fair weather and rising temperatures tomorrow afternoon. Warmer weather is forecast for the week-end. High temperature yesterday was 57 degrees.

Vegetation was blackened last night and roof tops had the appearance of being covered with a light snowfall. Tobacco has been housed and there was no crop damage from the cold snap.

Philipsburg in Centre county was the coldest spot in Pennsylvania last night, the mercury dropping to 23 degrees.

Philadelphia's low was 40, with the suburbs reporting temperatures of three to five degrees lower.

Plant Will Be On By-Pass at Old Phila. Pike

'Well Known' Metal Firm to Employ 250 At First, More Later

A major new industry is coming to Lancaster.

It will build its plant on the north side of the Old Philadelphia Pike at its intersection with the new by-pass.

The land, 28 acres of it, has been purchased from Walter M. and Miriam E. Landis.

"Well Known" Firm

The purchase was made by the "Lampeter Investment Co.," an organization expressly set up to make the purchase without revealing the name of the firm at the present time.

An official announcement today said a "well-known industrial corporation" is involved and the investment company will rent or sell the property to the corporation — the name of which is to be made public in 60 to 90 days.

Employ 250 Persons

The announcement said further that the new plant will employ 250 persons. There was speculation that is an extremely conservative estimate and that, ultimately, the plant will employ many more than that number.

The official announcement said:

"The purchase by the Lampeter Investment Corporation of 28 acres of land located on the Old Philadelphia Pike at the intersection of the Lancaster by-pass, is announced today by Paul A. Mueller, prominent local attorney and one of the incorporators of the corporation.

"The tract, which extends from the Pike to the right of way of the Pennsylvania Railroad, was previously the property of Walter M. and Miriam E. Landis.

One-Story Building

"Mr. Mueller stated that the Corporation would proceed immediately with the erection of a modern one-story industrial building suitable for a metal working plant, including machine shop operations. Present plans call for an initial unit of about 80,000 square feet.

"He said that it is probable that the plant will ultimately provide local employment for approximately 250 shop workers and clericals.

"It is understood that the Lampeter Investment Corporation will not itself engage in manufacturing operations, but intends to rent, or sell, the property to a well-known industrial corporation.

"Pending settlement of details, however, Mr. Mueller said that he was not free to disclose the identity of the prospective user. He stated, however, that barring unforeseen difficulties, this information would be made public within 60 to 90 days.

Contractors Bids Submitted

"A well has already been drilled on the property and several contractors have submitted bids for the erection of the building. It is anticipated that a construction contract will be signed shortly and that actual work will commence within 30 days.

"The plant is scheduled to be complete about March 1, 1954, if no major delays are experienced, and recruiting of necessary personnel will probably start about January 1, 1954."

EAST GERMAN CLASHES

BERLIN (AP) — Angry crowds clashed with Communist police in at least two Russian zone cities on the state holiday marking the fourth anniversary of the East German republic yesterday, according to the West Berlin newspaper Der Tag.

Report on Casablanca – No. 3

Military Learns Private Firms Build Bases Quicker

(Third of a Series)
By Robert C. Ruark

CASABLANCA, French Morocco—The change-over in the construction of our big atom-bomber bases in Morocco has taught, or should have taught, the government a salubrious lesson in how to go about the construction of our fortifications in foreign countries.

Ruark

One of the lessons is that after the military makes up its mind where to put a base, the net result can be achieved cheaper and more speedily if the professional civilian contractors are allowed to tackle the problem on a professional, civilian basis.

I mentioned yesterday that the day after Atlas Construction, here at Nouasseur, went off the old government cost-plus basis onto a straight contract, nearly 50 per cent of the personnal was found surplus—unneeded. The Congressional Record is crammed with instances of broth-spoiling by the Air Force and the Corps of Engineers, in intramural battles.

Must Adjust Contract

The new set up at Nouasseur—which might get our bases in Morocco complete and really ready for use by this New Year's—is that the military is now FORCED to define the program before Atlas will touch it, under terms of the contract. If changes are to be made, a new contract, or at least an adjustment of contract, must be made by the military to Atlas.

This, since Atlas is now on a straight fee basis, causes considerably less dilly-dallying and mind-changing, less bickering and backing and filling. Less dirt gets moved back and forth and more permanent construction results. And the pros—the civilians—with specifications firmly in fist, are allowed to go ahead and build the damned thing with all the hoary

—See RUARK—Page 10

WEATHER
(U. S. Weather Bureau)
Eastern Pennsylvania — Fair, With Highest 65-70 Today. Tomorrow Mostly Cloudy, Not As Warm, With Showers Likely.

Intelligencer Journal.

The Leading Newspaper in the Garden Spot of America. Home Owned for Home Folks Since 1794

160th Year.—No. 135. | Official United States Census Figures Lancaster Metropolitan Area Population 234,717 | LANCASTER, PA., FRIDAY MORNING, NOVEMBER 20, 1953. | CITY | FIFTY-TWO PAGES | 30c PER WEEK—5c Per Copy

THE INTELL INDEX

Lanc. Catholic Wins Football Championship

HEAD INJURY KILLED CATTLE BUYER

Kidnap-Slayers Will Go To Deaths Together

H-BURG CATH. DEFEATED BY 13 TO 7 SCORE

Crusaders' Ground Game, Razzle-Dazzle Decisive Factors In Battle

By PETE BUSSER
Intell Sports Writer

HARRISBURG, Nov. 19 — Lancaster Catholic High School, playing its last game of the season, won the championship of the Central Penn Catholic Football Conference here tonight as they gained a 13-7 victory over Harrisburg Catholic High at McDevitt Field before an estimated 4,000 fans.

Bobby Souders and Bob Kirchner tallied the touchdowns for Coach Gene Kruis' champions. The first came after 2:57 minutes of play and followed a bit of skullduggery on the part of Kruis. The second came in the second stanza after a sustained drive of 67 yards.

Harrisburg, conference winners the past two years, scored early in the third quarter on a sleeper pass play that was good for 63 yards.

STICK TO GROUND

Lancaster relied mostly on a powerful ground game. They battered the Harrisburg forward wall for 14 first downs, six coming in their second period scoring surge. Harrisburg notched four first downs.

It was the ninth victory in 10 starts for Lancaster and their fourth in league play. The Crusaders were unbeaten in the league. Harrisburg now sports a record of 5-3-2. In loop play they stand second with 2-1. They still have a game to play with Mt. Carmel Catholic.

Lancaster took the opening

Turn To Page 43 For More Of FOOTBALL

Swirling Fog Makes Travel Hazardous, 2nd Night In Row

Dense Blanket Cuts Visibility At Some Spots; Colder Weather Not Expected Until Saturday; Acrid 'Smog' Plagues Philadelphians

A swirling, touch-and-go fog made the going perilous for county motorists for the second day running last night and early today.

The dense mist, while quite as murky as that of the night before, reportedly was moving from place to place without setting up permanent housekeeping in too many locations.

A flurry of minor motor vehicle mishaps was attributed to the spotty visibility.

The speed of acold front moving in from the West, which is expected to draw off a hazy, eye-stinging curtain of smog that has plagued Pennsyvania most of the week, was variously estimated yesterday.

An early U. S. Weather Bureau report held out a promise of an end to the condition by this morning. But last night's late forecast predicted a continuation of the mild cycle through today with a high between 65 and 70. Tomorrow is expected to be mostly cloudy and not as warm, with a possibility of showers.

Around the city, the Grand View Heights section again experienced a consistently thick fog. The driver of a CTC bus lost his bearings in the midst of a run late last evening and improvised a route, providing some passengers with practically door-to-door service.

Local fans returning from the Lancaster Catholic - Harrisburg Catholic football game in the state capital reported clear sailing as far as Mount Joy, then

Turn To Page 14 For More Of FOG

FIRST BIG STORM OF SEASON HITS IN ROCKIES AREA

Foot And Half Of Snow; New Blast Is Reported

DENVER, Nov. 19 (AP)—A Canadian and Pacific cold air mass rolled out of the Rocky Mountains and into the Middle West today, leaving up to a foot and a half of snow in the mountain area. It was the season's first major storm.

At the same time, the Weather Bureau said a new storm might hit Colorado by Saturday or Sunday if it continues at present pace.

The sub-freezing blasts of last night and today took the mercury to a low of 1 degree below zero at Thermopolis, Wyo.

Clearing skies and slightly warmer temperatures, however, were reported throughout the western part of the state. Only eastern Colorado and southeastern Wyoming were still getting light snow late today.

PASSES OPEN

The state highway patrols reported all major passes were open.

Eastern Colorado farmers praised the new moisture as desperately needed for their winter wheat.

The new snow reached a depth of 17 inches on Coal Bank Hill, north of Durango, Colo., on the mountainous "million dollar highway," U.S. 550. Sixteen inches were measured on Wolf Creek Pass in southwestern Colorado and up to 12 inches on Monarch and Red Mountain Passes. Other Colorado passes recorded 6 to 10 inches of new snow.

The only loss of life reported was that resulting from a C47 transport plane crash in Albuquerque yesterday, when one man died and seven were injured. The plane, taking off from Kirtland Air Force Base, cracked up in blinding snow.

1,256 INDUCTION QUOTA FOR JAN.

Pennsylvania was assigned a quota of 1,256 men for induction in January, the second lowest call in 10 months, it was announced yesterday.

The quota is 10 higher than the 1,246 assigned the state for induction next month.

Henry M. Gross, state Selective Service director, said draftees will be drawn from the twenty-year-old class as far as possible or else from the oldest of the nineteen-year group.

JUDGE SETS DEC. 18 DATE OF EXECUTION

Greenlease, Father Of Victim Says "Too Good For Them"

KANSAS CITY, Nov. 19 (AP) — The kidnap-slayers of Bobby Greenlease were sentenced to death today and will go to the gas chamber together for their ruthless crime.

Federal Judge Albert Reeves set their execution date for Dec. 18, exactly one week before Christmas. Officers of the court said Carl Austin Hall, 34, and Bonnie Brown Heady, 41, would be taken into the gas chamber at the same time.

SHOULDERS SILENT

ST. LOUIS, Nov. 19 (AP)—Louis Shoulders, the former police lieutenant who broke the Greenlease kidnaping case, declined to comment today when notified the kidnap-killers have been sentenced to die for the crime.

"I have absolutely no comment to make on the Greenlease case any more," Shoulders said.

Shoulders won national attention for his arrest of Carl Austin Hall, the killer of Bobby Greenlease, at an apartment-hotel here Oct. 6. Shoulders later resigned from the police force, saying his reputation had been destroyed by an inquiry into the missing $300,000 in ransom money and handling of the arrest.

"It's too good for them but it is the best the law provides," said grim jawed Robert C. Greenlease Sr., multimillionaire father of the slain 6-year-old boy.

SENTENCE PRONOUNCED

Within minutes after a Federal District Court jury recommended

Turn To Page 14 For More Of KIDNAP

Hall And Mrs. Heady After Hearing Sentences

KANSAS CITY, Nov. 19 — Kidnap-slayers Carl Austin Hall and Mrs. Bonnie Brown Heady are shown leaving the U. S. Courthouse here today after hearing U. S. District Judge Albert L. Reeves sentence them to die in Missouri's gas chamber. (AP Wirephoto)

AFTER VERDICT — KANSAS CITY, Nov. 19 — A faint smile crosses the face of Mrs. Bonnie Brown Heady as she leaves the U. S. Courthouse here today after being sentenced to death for the kidnap-slaying of six-year-old Bobby Greenlease. (AP Wirephoto)

FOUL PLAY IS SUSPECTED IN MT. JOY DEATH

John A. Ortt, Parkesburg R2, Found Dead In Borough; Skull Fractured

A growing suspicion of foul play in the death of John A. Ortt, about fifty-five, Parkesburg R2 cattle buyer, was advanced yesterday when a pathologist's examination revealed he died of a fractured skull.

Dr. David E. Schlosser, Mount Joy deputy coroner, said last night that the post mortem examination conducted by Dr. Ward M. O'Donnel, pathologist at Lancaster General Hospital, showed Ortt's death definitely was not due to carbon monoxide poisoning as first assumed.

Instead, Dr. Schlosser said, he died of a skull fracture and resulting brain hemorrhage. The deputy coroner said the injury could have been suffered in a fall or due to foul play.

Ortt's body was found in his automobile about 7:35 a. m. yesterday, parked on Columbia Ave., Mount Joy, a block west of Main Street.

GAS NOT A FACTOR

An autopsy performed yesterday afternoon revealed the skull fracture which Dr. Schlosser said was due to an injury to the right temple area of the victim. The only other mark on the body was a bruise of the left knee. An analysis of the blood for carbon monoxide, Dr. Schlosser said, showed a very mild content of the deadly gas, not enough to cause death.

A police investigation was launched by Mount Joy Borough Patrolman Michael R. Good and Cpl. Leonard A. Mazakas of the State Police. However, the officers said last night they had no theories on how Ortt died.

Cpl. Mazakas said he and Good were in touch with Ortt's wife in Parkesburg yesterday, but at that time they didn't know death was due to a skull fracture. They said they were working under the impression Ortt may have been accidentally overcome by the fumes from the vehicle or died of natural causes.

Police said they learned Ortt

Turn To Page 14 For More Of BODY

Canada Gets 2nd Request On Questioning Ex-Russian

WASHINGTON, Nov. 19 (AP)—The State Department relayed to the Canadian government today a second request that senators investigating the Harry Dexter White case be allowed to question a former code clerk of the Russian Embassy in Ottawa.

And the Senate Internal Security Subcommittee showed every indication of pushing ahead with its inquiry into Communists in government in the face of the President Eisenhower's expressed hope the issue will be dead by the time of next year's election.

How long the investigation may go on is uncertain. But Chairman Jenner (R-Ind) said the subcommittee is concerned with the government's internal security and "our objective is to go right ahead with the kind of work we have been doing."

REQUEST REJECTED

Canada rejected one request earlier this month that the subcommittee be allowed to question the one-time Soviet code expert, Igor Gouzenko, who split with the Reds after World War II and disclosed details of a Russian atomic spy ring in Canada that reached into the United States. The Dominion government said Gouzenko had revealed all the information in his possession.

Senate investigators aren't convinced of that, and would like to go to Canada to see whether Gouzenko can give them any new leads or additional details of cases they already have investigated.

In Ottawa, Foreign Secretary L. B. Pearson told a questioner in the House of Commons his government was unlikely to change its position unless the new

Turn To Page 26 For More Of WHITE

Mitchell Says 1954 Issue Eisenhower's Performance

KANSAS CITY, Kan., Nov. 19 (AP)—Democratic National Chairman Stephen A. Mitchell said tonight the chief campaign issue in 1954 will not be communism but the performance of the Eisenhower administration.

In a speech prepared for delivery at a Kansas Democratic rally Mitchell declared:

"There is not and cannot be a valid issue between the Democratic and Republican parties on communism, because all Americans are on the same side of that question."

The Democratic chairman earlier today conferred with former President Harry S. Truman. At a news conference afterward Mitchell declined to comment on FBI Director J. Edgar Hoove's testimony that he had advised the Truman administration against keeping the late Harry Dexter White on his government job.

Atty. Gen. Brownell has charged White was retained and promoted despite FBI reports to the White House that he was a Soviet spy.

Mitchell declined to say wheth-

Turn To Page 14 For More Of MITCHELL

They See Not

Air Observer Posts Here In Need Of 'Eyes'

The Ground Observation Corps—an organization of volunteer aircraft spotters under supervision of the Air Force—has the vision of a blind man in Pennsylvania.

Official reports of the Air Force's Air Defense Command reveal that the eastern area of Pennsylvania has a requirement of 289 posts.

Of this requirement, only six—two per cent—of the posts are operated on a 24-hour basis daily. Fifty others are manned a portion of the time. Therefore, only 14 per cent of the required posts in this critical target area are fully or partially manned.

ONLY ONE IN COUNTY

In Lancaster County, where the Air Force has decided 17 spotter posts are needed, only one is manned on a 24-hour basis. This is the Neffsville post.

Leon Duckworth, chief of the county's GOC, said last evening that five other posts are partially manned. They are located at: Lancaster City, in the Griest building; Elizabethtown; Kirkwood; Akron and Marietta.

Thus, only six of the county's

Turn To Page 14 For More Of OBSERVERS

STATE POLICE SAY:

Quick, positive braking means locked wheels and locked wheels slide. Sudden application of the brakes and consequent sliding of tires is a costly practice on a dry road, but, the National Automobile Club warns, when the roadway is wet and slippery, it may end in disaster.

"We Lead All The Rest"

FARM CORNER

By William R. Schultz

2nd Wave Of Tobacco Buying Seen Developing Slowly

First offers to buy 1953 Lancaster County cigar leaf tobacco on a pull-off basis were reported yesterday as a second wave of buying appeared to be developing slowly.

One firm made its first offer for this year's crop—P. Lorillard Co., Inc., reported offering 16 to 18 cents a pound for stemming grades.

Three firms, inactive since late October, reentered the picture with offers in the 30-32 cent range for wrappers, ten cents for fillers.

They were R. D. Owens, A. Kenneth Mann Jr., and Richard C. Swope, the latter representing John Berger and Son Co., an Ohio firm.

LEVY FIRM STILL ACTIVE

Morris Levy and Sons, meanwhile, continued in the market paying from 30 to 35 cents, and ten.

Reports from the field also had Owens offering 15 to 18 cents for stemming stock.

Lorillard spokesmen confirmed that their buyers had been instructed to purchase in the 16 to 18 cent range.

The reentrance of three firms was viewed last night as a clue to Levy's success in moving crops Wednesday.

One packer explained the 30-32 cent offer was more than a test. "We expect to be able to buy at these prices," he said. "The 32-cent tobacco we want now is not the 38-cent tobacco we bought last month."

Bloch Bros. Tobacco Co., a large buyer of stemming grades, had made no move to challenge Lorillard late last night. With a larger percentage of late and stunted tobacco this year, it is expected lit-

Turn To Page 14 For More Of FARM CORNER

Weather Calendar

COMPARATIVE TEMPERATURES

Stations	High	Low
Water Works	58	29
Ephrata	57	28
Last Year (Ephrata)	52	43
Official High for Year Sept. 12		102
Official Low for Year Feb. 2		13
Character of Day		Clear

WIINDS

Direction WSW — Avg. Velocity 3 mph

HUMIDITY

8 a.m. 100% 11 a.m. 86% 2 p.m. 69%
5 p.m. 86% 8 p.m. 100%
Average Humidity 88%

SUN

Rises 6:54 a.m. — Sets 4:45 p.m.

MOON

Last Quarter, Nov. 28

STARS

Morning—Venus, Mars, Jupiter, Saturn

NEARBY FORECASTS
(U. S. Weather Bureau)

Delaware and Southern New Jersey — Mostly sunny, but some cloudiness today with highest 65-70. Tomorrow mostly cloudy, not as warm, with chance of showers.

Maryland — Fair with highest 68-74 today. Tomorrow mostly cloudy not as warm, with chance of showers.

Lower Potomac and Chesapeake Bay—South or southeast winds 10-15 mph today. Fair weather, visibility improving by noon today.

THANKSGIVING DAY DINNERS OFFERED TO 100 SERVICEMEN

Invitations have been extended to 100 servicemen and women to have Thanksgiving dinners in local homes, it was announced yesterday by Thomas J. Monaghan, USO chairman in charge of the project.

The deadline for extending the invitations is Saturday, Monaghan reminded. Persons wishing to entertain service personnel are asked to notify the YWCA.

The Jewish Community Center will be open from noon until 8 p. m. Thanksgiving Day with USO hostesses on duty for a USO-sponsored program for the servicemen and girls while they are awaiting their hosts to call for them, and while they are awaiting transportation back to the Bainbridge Naval Training Station.

Observance Of Lincoln's Address At Gettysburg Has County Flavor

Ninety years after President Abraham Lincoln delivered "a few remarks" that were later to be immortalized as the Gettysburg Address, some 300 persons yesterday paraded to the National Monument that marks the site of the famous utterance in the National Cemetery of Gettysburg to commemorate the historic address.

Maryland Gov. Theodore R. McKeldin, principal speaker at the Dedication Day exercises, praised the Civil War leader as a great man who "spoke from his heart"—one who "looked forward soberly to the responsibilities of the future" instead of back on the glories of the past.

The ceremony at Gettysburg had a distinctly Lancaster County flavor.

MANHEIM MAN EMCEE

Miles H. Keiffer, of Manheim, president of the Lincoln Fellowship of Pennsylvania, which arranged the program, served as master of ceremonies, while Dr. Herbert H. Beck, of Lancaster, lay one of the memorial wreaths. The other wreath was placed at the monument by Benton Gilbert, in behalf of the Sons of Union Veterans.

Governor McKeldin's address was based on Lincoln's words: "We cannot dedicate . . . we cannot consecrate . . . we cannot hallow this ground—it is for us the living, rather, to be dedicated here to the unfinished work."

The unfinished work to which America today is dedicated, he

Turn To Page 14 For More Of GETTYSBURG

2 More Parents Found Guilty In Stormy Absentee Hearing

Two Clay Twp. Mennonite fathers were adjudged guilty of violating the compulsory school attendance laws at a stormy hearing before Alderman J. Edward Wetzel yesterday afternoon, and released on their own recognizance until 10 a. m. Saturday pending an appeal.

Found guilty by the Alderman were Warren Seibel, Ephrata R1, a fourth offender, and John Rutt, Ephrata R1, a first offender.

The alderman directed Rutt to pay a $2 fine or undergo imprisonment for three days, and Seibel was fined $5 or five days in jail. He said he would give the men and their attorney, Daniel H. Shertzer, until Saturday to decide whether to appeal to the courts.

Shertzer and the alderman tangled verbally several times during the hearing which lasted 40 minutes. At the very outset Shertzer objected to what he termed a "private hearing," because friends and relatives of the defendants were not allowed into the office but stood in

Turn To Page 14 For More Of HEARING

LEB. CO. AMISH FATHER PAYS SCHOOL LAW FINE

A Lebanon County Amish farmer, the first to be prosecuted in that county during the current school term for failure to send his fourteen-year-old son to school, pleaded guilty yesterday and paid a $2 fine and costs.

The defendant was John Lantz, Lebanon R2, charged by Henry Wenger, supervising principal of the Northern Lebanon County School District, with failure to keep his son, John, in school.

Lantz was scheduled to be given a hearing last evening before Justice of the Peace John Demler, Jonestown R2, Union Twp., but appeared before Demler yesterday afternoon and paid his $2 fine and costs as a first offender.

Also appearing before Demler yesterday afternoon was Theodore Miller, Lebanon R3, accused of not sending his daughter, Barbara, to school regularly. Miller was found guilty and paid a $2 fine and costs.

City Budget Talks Again Today With 2 Big Items Hanging Fire

Lancaster City Council gathers around the conference table at 10 a. m. today for another discussion on the tentative budget for next year.

Although members of Council, thus far, have managed to remain silent on budget developments, it is generally well known around the Municipal Building that they still must settle two important items:

How much of a pay raise to give city employes and next year's tax rate on real estate.

As the council nears the end of the trail on its budget preparations it seems quite apparent, in view of the current "tight" municipal budget document, that a pay raise for city employes will necessitate an in crease in the tax rate.

TAX RATE 9 1-2 MILLS

Lancaster City's present tax rate is 9 1-2 mills—the third smallest tax rate of the 47 Third Class cities in the Commonwealth of Pennsylvania.

Only York, with a seven mill tax rate, and Allentown, with a nine mill rate, rank below the Red Rose City in this department.

Here, according to figures released yestreday by the Department of Internal Affairs, Harrisburg, is a comparison of 1952 tax

Turn To Page 14 For More Of BUDGET

Cousin Of City Resident Victim In Altoona Slaying

The Weather
(U. S. Weather Bureau)
Eastern Pennsylvania — Rather Cloudy. Mild Today And Tomorrow. Highest Today In The 60s.

SUNDAY NEWS

3 A. M. Edition—Latest News by Associated Press and International News Service. Complete Local News and pictures by Wirephoto.

VOL. 31—NO. 11 | LANCASTER, PA., SUNDAY, NOVEMBER 22, 1953 | 54 PAGES—10 CENTS

Woman, 67, Dies After Auto Strikes Culvert

Slain Altoona Man Planned Holiday Here

Murder Victim Is Teacher, 33, Relative Of Mrs. Robert L. Harner

An Altoona High School instructor who planned to spend his Thanksgiving holiday here with his aunt, Mrs. Robert L. Harner, of 752 S. Lime St., last evening was reported murdered.

A frequent visitor to Lancaster, thirty-three-year-old Bertram M. Isenberg, was shot in the head by a youthful soldier who had deserted his post several weeks ago at Fort Monroe, Va.

State Police reported that Charles N. Dermenzin of Duncansville, near Altoona, in Blair County, admitted in a verbal statement that he shot Isenberg Friday evening. No motive was given.

Gave Slayer A Lift

It appears, said State Police Sgt. Richard D. Grey, that Isenberg gave Dermenzin a lift in his auto, then was forced to drive to a lonely mountain road where he was shot and dragged from the auto. Dermenzin, twenty, buried Isenberg's body under leaves along the lonely stretch of mountain road.

Then, as the soldier attempted to drive Isenberg's auto away, he apparently wrecked it, police said. They found, Isenberg's body near his wrecked car.

News of the murder stunned the Harner family. They received a letter today, postmarked 4:20 p. m. Friday, from the victim in which he explained he would arrive in Lancaster to spend the Thanksgiving weekend

Page 17—ALTOONA

$240 Pay Boost Said Certain For Police, Firemen

A minimum pay raise of $240 appears assured next year for members of the City Police and Fire Departments.

City Council, it was learned yesterday, has not decided definitely on the size of pay increases for 1954 but is thinking in terms of at least $240 for policemen and firemen.

Increase For Others

Other non-elected city employes are in line for a raise. Because they are not on call 24 hours a day, they appear destined to receive a smaller pay boost which will be figured on an hourly basis and not a flat figure.

Council is not expected to reach a final decision on wages for next year until after it meets with representatives of policemen and firemen at 10 a. m. tomorrow. However, informed sources indicate that Council informally has agreed that members of these two departments should receive at least a $240 yearly boost.

Consider Tax Boost

Any sizeable increase in salaries is expected to bring about an increase in the existing 9½ mill tax rate on real estate. Although there has been no official comment following recent budget meetings, indications are that Council is thinking in terms of a one mill tax increase.

The tentative budget for 1954 must be introduced by Dec. 1.

Before municipal budget talks got under way delegations from the police and fire departments submitted formal requests for 15 per

Page 17—PAY

Ike's Brother Warns Of Reds In S. America

WASHINGTON, Nov. 21 (INS)—Dr. Milton Eisenhower stated flatly today that "One American nation has succumbed to Communist infiltration" and warned that the Reds are active in undermining other republics in the Western Hemisphere.

The President's brother made the statements in a report to the chief executive on "United States-Latin American relations." The 25,000-word report was based on Eisenhower's trip through South America last Summer and subsequent consultations with U. S. officials.

Eisenhower, president of Pennsylvania State University, did not mention Guatemala by name as the country which has succumbed to infiltration, but there was no doubt he referred to that nation.

The educator said that while many persons may not think Latin America is in the line of attack in the current world struggle "success by the Communists in these nations could quickly change all the maps which strategists use

Page 17—EISENHOWER

Rebuff Ike On Age Benefits

WASHINGTON, Nov. 21 (AP)—Rep. Daniel A. Reed (R-NY) said after a White House conference today that he still favors allowing increased social security taxes to go into effect in January, despite administration recommendations to the contrary.

He did not say what the present White House attitude is.

Reed, Rep. Carl T. Curtis (R-Neb) and Secretary of the Treasury Humphrey reviewed the whole social security program with President Eisenhower at a one-hour conference.

Rep. Reed is chairman of the House Ways and Means Committee and Rep. Curtis heads a subcommittee studying the social security program.

The committee last spring divided on the question of allowing

Page 17—REBUFF

Penn St. Name Change Noted In New Stamp Bill

U. S. Senator Edward Martin (R-Pa.), who last April introduced a bill to authorize issuance of a postage stamp commemorating the 100th anniversary of "Pennsylvania State College," last night told the Sunday News he will change the bill to read "Pennsylvania State University."

Penn State, whose president is Dr. Milton Eisenhower, broth-

Page 17—STATE

4 Operators Of Speedway Plead Guilty

Hugh W. Sherrard, 504 S. Prince St., one of four operators of the Lincoln Speedway, Inc., at Abbottstown, Adams County, has pleaded guilty to conspiring to violate Sunday laws and maintaining a public nuisance.

The four men entered the pleas in Adams County Court, Gettysburg. Sherrard is also operator of the Lancaster Speedway, Willow Street R1.

The above charges are the counts on which a grand jury returned true bills. A third count, maintaining a public nuisance through the week, was segregated from the original charge of maintaining a public nuisance on Sunday, by agreement of counsel and the office of District Attorney Daniel E. Teeter.

3 Others Plead

The other speedway directors are John J. Smith, Hanover; Hillen V. Rife, New Oxford R2; and Earl J. Haverstick, Abbottstown. All four will be sentenced next week on the charges to which they entered guilty pleas.

The auto speedway case was the last proceeding listed for the November term of court. It was pointed out, however, that because of the length of the trial list, which may extend beyond the Thanksgiving holiday, the remaining charge will not be pressed for this term of court, especially since the track is not operated during the winter months.

McCaskey Grid Fans Stampede Through City After Upset Victory

HERE THEY COME—McCaskey High School's band, shown above, headed a large victory parade through downtown Lancaster yesterday afternoon after the Red and Black team pulled a major upset by defeating its arch rival, York, by a 14 to 13 score. Yesterday's victory parade grew larger as it moved through city streets as students and alumni, many of them unaware of the outcome of the game, joined the celebration as they heard of the upset.

YEA McCASKEY!—That cheer echoed through downtown streets yesterday afternoon as jubilant rooters of McCaskey High School, shown in photo above, paraded in recognition of their team's thrilling defeat of a previously undefeated York eleven which already had won the Central Pennsylvania League football championship.

Tornado Beats York 14-13 To Salvage Season

An overjoyed McCaskey High School student body — which had little reason to shout and celebrate all year—late yesterday afternoon noisily paraded through downtown Lancaster in celebration of the Tornadoes' defeat of its arch rival, York.

Contest Thriller From First Play

The McCaskey-York football game yesterday was a thriller from start to finish.

And it was one of those games in which an electrifying-air of tension and expectancy was in evidence among the crowd of 5,000 fans almost from the opening whistle.

As the two clubs battled from quarter to quarter, that tension and expectancy mounted until it was at fever heat. Finally, when it was at an end and the victory belonged to McCaskey, the fans, to the last man and woman, let out one collective sigh of relief.

This, they agreed, one and all, was one of THE great ball games of this season.

The followers of the Red and Black really had something to shout about, for yesterday's 14 to 13 victory by an inspired McCaskey eleven ruined a perfect gridiron campaign for the visiting Central Pennsylvania League champions.

Prior to yesterday afternoon's tussle with McCaskey, which went into the game a decided underdog, York had racked up nine consecutive victories. McCaskey, on the other hand, had an unimpressive four-and-four record including only one league triumph, over William Penn.

Once the final whistle had sounded it didn't take the McCaskey rooters long to rally behind the classy Red and Black

Page 17—FOOTBALL

Mary S. Fry Fatally Hurt On Co. Road

Retired Teacher Was Driving Alone Near Reamstown, Had Flowers For Friends

A one-car accident to which there were apparently no witnesses resulted in injuries fatal to Miss Mary S. Fry, 67, Stevens R1, yesterday.

Miss Fry died in Ephrata Community Hospital at 1:35 p. m. The car she had been driving crashed into a culvert on the Ephrata-Reamstown road shortly before noon, officials estimated. She was Lancaster County's 33rd highway fatality of the year.

Earl Greenly, Ephrata, the first person at the scene, called an ambulance, which conveyed Miss Fry to the Ephrata Community Hospital. Dr. I. G. Wagner, Ephrata, deputy coroner, issued a certificate of accidental death due to a cerebral hemorrhage caused by a fractured skull. She also suffered a fracture of the upper leg, several broken ribs and a crushed chest.

Miss Fry

Driving Alone

Miss Fry was traveling alone at the time of the crash, cause of which is still undetermined. She had gone to Ephrata to pick up flowers for delivery to Mr. and Mrs. Ivan Weitzel, Ephrata R3,

Page 17—ACCIDENTS

Foul Play Is Ruled Out In Ortt's Death

State Police last night ruled out the possibility of foul play in the death of John A. Ortt, 55, Sadsburyville, Parkesburg R2. Ortt was found dead in his parked car in Mount Joy Thursday morning.

Ortt, a cattle dealer, was on his way from Belleville, Mifflin Co., to his Chester County home, having left a sale barn in Belleville at approximately 9 p.m. His movements from that time until his body was found in his automobile, parked on Columbia Ave., in the borough, have not been established by State Police, who say they checked every possible place he might have stopped and have found no one who saw him at any time.

Police said that although his wallet has not been found and there is no logical reason why his car should have been parked off Route 230, the most direct road to his home from Belleville, they theorize that he became sickened from carbon monoxide fumes and received the fatal injury in a fall. They found no indication of foul play at the hands of a passer-by or a hitchhiker, they said.

Dr. David Schlosser, Mount Joy deputy coroner, said death resulted from an intra-cranial hemorrhage caused by a skull fracture. Police said the fracture was apparently caused by a fall. Dr. Ward M. O'Donnel, pathologist at Lancaster General Hospital who performed the autopsy, said that Ortt's skull was ex-

Page 17—DEATH

CHS Gridders Are Honored

Approximately twenty members of the Lancaster Catholic High School football squad and their girlfriends were entertained last night by the Knights of Columbus at their headquarters, 22 S. Prince St.

The party was held as a testimony to the team's outstanding football record this fall of nine wins and only one defeat.

Squad chairman James Slager showed that his prowess is not confined to the gridiron when he presented his contribution to the refreshments — a huge layer-cake which he baked himself.

Host Committee

The host organization committee consisted of Michael Heider, Mrs. Tony Mariani and Mrs. Thomas Dougherty.

Refreshments consisted of milk and soft drinks, ice cream, banana splits and cake—donated by the Knights of Columbus wives and squad mothers.

Following the refreshments, a record dance was held at the K of C home.

City Detective Frank Matt, a member of the Knights, served as chairman of the finance committee for the party.

3 Twps. Plan Truant Crackdown Dec. 1

School boards of three Lancaster County Townships—Upper Leacock, Earl, and Leacock—have decided to begin prosecuting parents Dec. 1 if their 14-year-old children are not in school by that date.

In preparation for pupils who might return to school, one of the boards has agreed to supplement teachers' pay for each returned pupil, while the other two boards have discussed adjusting pay for teachers who might have pupils returned to classes.

In Earl township, teachers will be paid a certain amount per month, above the regular salary, for each pupil who is returned to school after being taken out by the parents.

Upper leacock school board members have agreed to do the same thing, and in East Earl township the problem was discussed by the board members because of requests from the teachers but no decision has been reached.

Called Added Burden

Spokesmen for the school boards stated that it is an added burden on the teachers to have to admit pupils in the middle of the semester because of the work the pupils have missed.

In Upper . Leacock, the school boards stated that it is an added burden on the teachers to have to admit pupils in the middle of the semester because of the work the pupils have missed.

In Upper Leacock, the school board passed a resolution Friday night stating that prosecutions would be made. The approved resolution said:

"Be it resolved that parents of 14-year-old elementary students who have completed eighth grade and who are not now in school shall be notified that the compulsory attendance provision of the School Code will be enforced if they are not in school by Dec. 1."

Members of the board will visit schools tomorrow to obtain information on absent pupils. On Tuesday they will visit parents of the absent pupils and explain to them what is required.

Lester R. Kurtz, president of the board, said that the board will hold parents responsible for the conduct of children while in school. A problem of discipline could arise if the

Page 17—TRUANTS

President Ike's Gettysburg Farm No 'White House'

WASHINGTON, Nov. 21 (AP)—President Eisenhower's farm home near Gettysburg, Pa., will be visited by the chief executive next summer, but is not slated to become the official "Summer White House."

That was the reply today of presidential press secretary James Hagerty to questions about the Eisenhower plans. Hagerty indicated that President and Mrs. Eisenhower also will spend some time at Denver, Colo., where Mrs. Eisenhower's mother lives.

There has been considerable speculation recently that some remodeling at the Eisenhower farm indicated it was being readied for use as the Summer White House.

The Weather

(U. S. Weather Bureau)

Maryland, Delaware and Southern New Jersey: Rather cloudy and continued mild Sunday and Monday. Highest in the 60s Sunday.

Eastern Pennsylvania: Rather coludy and mild Sunday and Monday. Highest Sunday in the 60s.

Lower Potomac and Chesapeake: Southeast winds 12 to 18 MPH Sunday. Rather cloudy weather. Visibility improving to good by noon Sunday.

TEMPERATURES

	High	Low
Lancaster Water Works	63	33
Precipitation — .02 Inches Rain		

Saturday Football Scores

Iowa 14, Notre Dame 14 (tie).
Harvard 13, Yale 0.
Dartmouth 34, Princeton 12.
Columbia 27, Rutgers 13.
Penn State 17, Pitt 0.
Villanova 14, Syracuse 13.
Delaware 34, Bucknell 13.
Georgia Tech 13, Duke 10.
Maryland 21, Alabama 0.
Michigan State 21, Marquette 15.
UCLA 13, USC 0.
Baylor 27, SMU 21.
Oklahoma 30, Nebraska 7.
Wisconsin 21, Minnesota 21
California 21, Stanford 21 (tie).
Rice 19, TCU 6.

Complete stories on these and other all games will be found on Sports Pages 29, 30, 31, 32 and 33.

Sees No Halt To Red Probes

WASHINGTON, Nov. 21 (AP)—Sen. Wiley (R-Wis) said today that despite adverse reaction abroad congressional investigations of alleged Communist infiltration into the government "are not going to be stopped by anything."

But Sen. Mansfield (D-Mont) predicted that if the Republicans try to roll out for political effect a series of exposes similar to the Harry Dexter White case they may keep Congress in such an uproar that vital legislation will be lost.

Wiley, who heads the Senate Foreign Relations Committee, said in a statement that many strong anti-Communist leaders abroad "are obviously deeply skeptical, to say the least, of our congressional investigations."

He said this is being exploited

Page 17—SEES

Exposed After 40 Years

'Piltdown Man' Clever Hoax, Not A Relic Of Early Man

LONDON, Nov. 21 (AP)—Three sleuthing British scientists declared today the skull of the fabulous "Piltdown man", accepted for 40 years by many of the world's top anthropologists as a relic of man's earliest history, is a phony.

They branded the relic the product of a "most elaborate and carefully prepared hoax," partly faked from ape bones.

'Discovered' In 1911

Charles Dawson, an attorney and amateur antiquarian, discovered part of the skull in a southern England gravel pit in 1911. In the next two years he produced from the same pit a jawbone and a tooth which some anthropologists said established the skull's age as at least 100,000 and perhaps 600,000 years old.

Dawson died in 1916 and a monument to his discovery now stands in the Sussex fields near the gravel pit where he found fame.

Dr. K. P. Oakley of the British Museum and two Oxford University professors, Dr. J. E. Weiner and Dr. W. E. le Gros Clark, reported in today's "Bulletin of the British Museum" that up-to-the-chemical tests have proved the jawbone and tooth to be deliberate fakes.

No Apes In Sussex

Both jaw and tooth, they said, came from a modern ape. Since apes don't live in Sussex that means they must have been planted.

The tooth, the investigators said, had been artificially pared down to disguise its original shape and the jaw had been stained.

The cranium itself is a genuine fossil, the scientists said, but they put its age at 50,000 years, less than half the previous widely held minimum.

They urged that experts taken in by the fraud should not be too hurt about it.

"The faking is so extraordinarily skillful and the perpetration of the hoax appears to have been so unscrupulous and inexplicable as to find no parallel in the history of paleontological discovery," they said.

'Words and Deeds' Help Island Win Its Identity

One of the Susquehanna's oldest arguments has been settled Many mapmakers have labeled the camelback island just below Fishing Creek as "Mount Jackson." Now a deed to the island, dated 1726, has been found, not only naming it Mt. Johnson, but giving a good reason for the name. As the world's only sanctuary for bald eagles, it has special interest for all Americans. Story on Page 23.

News Index

Cloudy, Mild Forecast Here

Cloudy, mild weather, with a possibility of local showers, is the weatherman's way of saying "more of the same to you" for Lancaster county today.

One consolation last night was that by midnight the fog had not as yet closed in to blanket the area.

The unseasonably warm weather—yesterday's high was 63 at the Lancaster water works — has caused this unusual situation: a layer of warm air has formed a ceiling over colder air at ground level; the upper layer acts as a lid, keeping any fumes and smoke from dispersing. This gave rise to such comments as some local residents made yesterday that the air had a disagreeable "taste." This was probably the same kind of "taste" that was so severe in the New York City and Philadelphia areas where the acrid condition made many persons ill.

Rocket Plane Sets New Speed, 1327 mph

LOS ANGELES, Nov. 21 (AP)—The Douglas Skyrocket shot to a sensational new speed mark yesterday: 1,327 miles an hour, twice the speed of sound.

Test pilot Scott Crossfield told reporters today he corkscrewed the research ship at top speed, testing her strength and power to maneuver.

"I rolled her around 360 degrees twice—and that was about all the maneuvers we had time for," he said.

11 Minute Flight

The flight, high above the Southern California desert, lasted 11 minutes from the time the tiny Skyrocket dropped from a B29 mother plane, at 12:01 p.m., until it glided down onto the dry lake that is Edwards Air Force Base.

The swept - wing plane was launched at about 32,000 feet, and climbed to an altitude "in excess of 60,000."

Crossfield said it burned up its three tons of fuel—liquid oxygen and alcohol—in three minutes, at the rate of about 200 gallons a minute.

The remainder of the flight, back to Edwards, was an eight-minute glide.

"It showed Mach 2 (twice the speed of sound) or better on the machometer for 5 or 10 seconds," Crossfield said.

Doubles Sound Speed

The National Advisory Committee for Aeronautics (NACA), which is using the plane for high-altitude, high-speed research, said the actual top speed was Mach 2.01, or slightly more than twice the speed of sound.

The speed of sound varies from 760 miles an hour at "standard temperature"—68 degrees above zero Fahrenheit—to 660 miles an hour at 67 degrees below zero.

Crossfield said he was so nervous before and during the flight that he felt as though had "the flu and a stomach ache" together.

He added that yesterday's mark was achieved in almost level flight. At first he climbed the Skyrocket at an angle of 30 degrees, then at 45 degrees, and then "nosed over to reach level alti-

Page 17—ROCKET

Completed Bypass Seen From Air

FIVE MILLION DOLLARS WORTH of traffic relief for Lancaster city is scheduled for full operation as of Tuesday. Grand opening of the Harrisburg Pike bypass (Rt. 230) will swing non-stop cars and trucks north of the city along a dual highway 11.2 miles long. Original 4.37-mile section of bypass was started in August 1950. New 6.75-mile extension has been under construction since November 1951. Total cost of complete bypass, linking Lincoln Highway on the east to Harrisburg Pike on the west, has been set at $5,009,995. Next step is expected to be link with Lincoln Highway (Rt. 30) somewhere west of city.

(Sunday News Air Photos By George King.)

BARRIER (indicated by arrow) is scheduled to be pulled away Tuesday as the Rt. 230 Bypass opens its full length for travel. Complex pattern in air view shows end of present portion and beginning of new, with interchanges which are expected to carry most of the bypass traffic to and from Lancaster city.

MEN AT WORK with surveyors' rods and tapes complete detail work on bypass extension as air camera watches. Note divider strip which separates east and west traffic same as on original road.

INS AND OUTS of traffic will be handled by this double-twist interchange which carries New Holland Pike over bypass at Country Club Heights. Portion labeled with "West" arrow held construction buildings of contractor, C. W. Good Inc. Only few small structures remain, at one exit.

ROADLESS OVERPASS between Homeland (foreground) and portion of Manheim Township beyond bypass, has been supplied with approaches, but no connecting streets. Bridge is a few hundred yards from Esbenshade Road, dead-ended by bypass, and no explanation.

RIVER AND 'LAKE' provided engineering problems for state highways department. Conestoga River was bridged short distance above city waterworks, and close to New Holland Pike interchange, which is visible near top of photo. Pond is on property of Eshelman experimental farm. Note how private roads are kept from bypass, making it first local "limited access" highway.

INDUSTRIAL SITES along bypass extension have been subject of official conferences. Such attractions as highway arteries combined with rail facilities are offered by wide area opened up for development by new road. New Holland railroad branch joins main line at point labeled "PRR."

THE END of the bypass to the east of the city presents a dramatic view from the air. Routes to be taken by traffic bound east and west are indicated. In immediate right foreground are highways department headquarters, with State Police Troop B barracks adjoining.

6 Lancaster Gridders on All Catholic League Team

by John Finnegan

LANCASTER Catholic High School, 1953 champions of the Central Pennsylvania Catholic League, received additional honors today when six members of its varsity squad were named to the league's All-Star eleven.

Led by Herb Moriarity, sensational Crusader center, who polled 24 votes out of a possible 25, the team is rounded out by four men from Harrisburg and one from York.

In addition to Moriarity, other Lancaster stars chosen include Ken Shank, brilliant end, who polled 22 votes, Bob Souders and Clyde Butz, backfield standouts, Lou Staffeiri, stellar tackle and Jim Schlager, bruising guard.

ROUNDING OUT the first eleven are Edward Furjanic, Harrisburg, end, John Vokes, Harrisburg, tackle, Joseph Martin, Harrisburg, guard, Richard Bowman, York, back, and Robert Piccolo, Harrisburg, back.

All are seniors with the exception of Furjanic, who is a sophomore and Staffeiri, a junior.

In addition to the six Lancastrians named to the mythical starting squad, another, Norm Bell, Shank's teammate at end, was named to a second string berth.

George Fay, tackle, John Trago, guard, and Bob Kirchner and Jim McCarty, backfield aces, received honorable mention.

The All-Star team was chosen at a meeting of the League's coaches at Harrisburg. Head coaches who participated in the voting included: Tony Cernugel, Harrisburg, John Sinkovitz, York, John McMahon, Delone, Joseph Apichella, Mt. Carmel and Gene Kruis, Lancaster.

Here's how the coaches rated the players chosen:

HERB MORIARITY JIM SCHLAGER CLYDE BUTZ KEN SHANK BOB SOUDERS LOU STAFFEIRI

KENNETH SHANK, end, Lancaster—"Without a doubt the best all around end we have had in many years. He has no equal defensively and can be counted on to carry out his assignment offensively"—Gene Kruis, Lancaster.

"One of the better downfield blockers seen this year, a solid defensive end."—John Sinkovitz, York.

"One of the hardest ends to get around that we have faced this year."—John McMahon, Delone.

EDWARD FURJANIC, end, Harrisburg—"Was one of our surprise finds of the year. Average pass receiver, best asset was his blocking."—Tony Cernugel, Harrisburg.

"He was the main reason our pitchouts didn't go against Harrisburg. We respected him very much."—Kruis.

"His crashing type defense was outstanding, was 5th man in our backfield."—Sinkovitz.

JOHN VOKES, tackle, Harrisburg—"Mainstay in our line both offensively and defensively. Has terrific speed for a big man."—Cernugel.

"Man who made his team's pitchouts go against us with his fine blocking."—John McMahon, Delone.

"A block of granite on defense, and a good hard charging blocker."—Joseph Apichella, Mt. Carmel.

LOUIS STAFFIERI, tackle, Lancaster—"A real competitor, he was the key to our offensive and defensive line. He is the best tackle I have ever coached."—Kruis.

"One of the best tackles in league, a player the quarterback could use to pick up yards anywhere on the field. He could blast them out of the way."—Cernugel.

"Most consistent offensive and defensive player I have seen all year."—Sinkovitz.

JOSEPH MARTIN, guard, Harrisburg—"Excellent middle man in an old defense (5-7-9) terrific spirit and hustle."—Cernugel.

"Did fine job on closing up middle of line against our offense."—McMahon.

JAMES SCHLAGER, guard, Lancaster—"The most underrated lineman on our squad, excellent blocker, hard to move on defense. He has been terrific for three consecutive years."—Kruis.

"The stone wall our boys complained about when trying to go through the middle of the Lancatser line."—Sinkovitz.

"Type of player any coach would welcome on a football squad."—Cernugel.

HERBERT MORIARITY, center, Lancaster—"A player's player and a coach's dream. A football player in every sense of the word. The main reason only one TD was scored through our varsity line this year. Great leader and a 48 minute performer."—Kruis.

"His defensive generalship was his most potent weapon, his ability to diagnose plays was the main headache to his opponents."—Sinkovitz.

"One of the roughest ,toughest linemen we had to face all year."—McMahon.

RICHARD BOWMAN, back, York—"Finest college prospect I have seen in high school ball this fall. His main asset is being able to play defense as well as offense."—Sinkovitz.

"A throwback to the old single wing triple threat, can run, pass and kick equally well."—Apichella.

ROBERT SOUDERS, back, Lancaster—"He is the finest and most versatile halfback we have had in the four years I have been here. A very fast, shifty, and hard running back. A great pass receiver. Also best defensive back on our squad."—Kruis.

"A fine halfback who possesses all the qualities of a great football player."—Cernugel.

"The kind of halfback that a coach enjoys working with because of his desire and his terrific competitive spirit."—McMahon.

CLYDE BUTZ, back, Lancaster—"A great leader, team player and field general. He was responsible for the success of our offensive attack this year. Our fastest back and hardest worker, he played to win."—Kruis.

"Best quarterback in the Conference. Could do everything, excellent defensive player."—Cernugel.

"Definitely a great asset both offensively and defensively for any team."—Sinkovitz.

ROBERT PICCOLO, back, Harrisburg—"Best back we had on our squad, he could run inside and outside. Loves football more than anything. Easy to coach and a great team player."—Cernugel.

"His bursting speed was his greatest asset, his broken field running was as deceptive as any other back in league."—Sinkovitz.

Second Team

Ends: Norman Bell, Lancaster; Francis Bach, Mt. Carmel.

Tackles: George Weitzel, Harrisburg; Robert Kerchner, York.

Guards: William Whare, York; Gerald Shrader, Delone.

Center: John O'Brien, Delone.

Backs: Albert DiEsposti, Harrisburg; Thomas Devers, Mt. Carmel; Donald Chrismer, Delone; Larry Fuller, Harrisburg.

Honorable Mention

Ends: Balistere, Harrisburg; Moore, York; Napoli, Harrisburg; Bevenour, Delone.

Tackles: George Foy, Lancaster; Tuleya, York; Chango, Mt. Carmel; Yohe, Harrisburg.

Guards: Swatski, Mt. Carmel; John Trago, Lancaster; Frye, Harrisburg; Hoerner, York.

Centers: Brown, Harrisburg; Bottini, Harrisburg; Lytle, York.

Backs: Robert Kirchner, Lancaster; Keffer, York; Redding, Delone; Sallinger, Harrisburg; James McCarty, Lancaster; Gorman, Harrisburg; Zambito, York; Greenholt, Delone and Kane, Mt. Carmel.

Catholic League's First Team

FIRST TEAM—Highest possible number of votes—25

		Height	Weight	Class	Votes
ENDS:	Kenneth Shank, Lancaster	6	165	Sr.	22
	Edward Furjanic, Harrisburg	6-1	160	So.	11
TACKLES:	John Vokes, Harrisburg	6-1	212	Sr.	20
	Louis Staffieri, Lancaster	6-1	205	Jr.	15
GUARDS:	Joseph Martin, Harrisburg	5-10	155	Sr.	20
	James Schlager, Lancaster	5-8	184	Sr.	15
CENTER:	Herbert Moriarity, Lancaster	5-9	190	Sr.	24
BACKS:	Richard Bowman, York	5-11	175	Sr.	22
	Robert Souders, Lancaster	6	150	Sr.	17
	Clyde Butz, Lancaster	6	168	Sr.	16
	Robert Piccolo, Harrisburg	5-9	150	Sr.	16

SPORTS

OUR BOARDING HOUSE . . . . . . with Major Hoople

MEL PARNELL

CARL ERSKINE

Erskine and Parnell Move Up in Pitching

NEW YORK (AP)—Brooklyn's Carl Erskine and Mel Parnell of the Boston Red Sox, two of Major League baseball's 20-game winners last season, moved well up among the lifetime pitching leaders as a result of their fine performances.

Erskine, who finished with a 20-6 record for the Dodgers, shows an overall slate of 71 victories and 34 setbacks (.676) for his six years in the National League. He ranks second to the Giants' Sal Maglie's .699 (72-31), figures compiled by the Associated Press showed today.

PARNELL NOW is second in the American League to the Yankees' Vic Raschi. Mel, with 21 and 8 during the last campaign, has 111 wins and 59 defeats for .653 while Raschi (13-6 last year) shows a gaundy .706, with 120 triumphs and only 50 losses.

Robin Roberts of the Philadelphia Phillies, who racked up 23 wins, is third in the National League with 114-73 (.610). He's followed by Preacher Roe, Brooklyn with 124-80 (.608), Al Brazle, St. Louis 92-60 (.605) and Jim Hearn, New York 72-48 (.600). Milwaukee's Warren Spahn, another 20-game victor, is seventh with 145 and 98 for .597.

In the American League, Mike Garcia of Cleveland ranks behind Raschi and Parnell with an 85-49 lifetime mark for .635. Next comes Bobby Feller with 249 victories (the most in either league) and 151 defeats (.623) and Bob Lemon, also of the Indians, with 140-85 for .622.

AMERICAN LEAGUE

Pitcher and Club	Won	4Lost	Pct.
Raschi, New York	120	50	.706
Parnell, Boston	111	59	.653
Garcia, Cleveland	85	49	.635
Feller, Cleveland	249	151	.623
Lemon, Cleveland	140	85	.622
Reynolds, New York	169	103	.621
Lopat, New York	147	96	.605
Shea, Washington	52	35	.598
Kinder, Boston	84	57	.596
x-Brecheen, Baltimore	133	92	.591
McDermott, Boston	48	34	.585
Dobson, Chicago	137	103	.571
x-Branca, Detroit	84	65	.564
Shantz, Philadelphia	61	48	.560
Trucks, Chicago	128	101	.559

x-Includes National League record.

NATIONAL LEAGUE

Maglie, New York	72	31	.699
Erskine, Brooklyn	71	34	.676
Roberts, Philadelphia	114	73	.610
Roe, Brooklyn	124	80	.608
Brazle, St. Louis	92	60	.605
Hearn, New York	72	48	.600
Spahn, Milwaukee	145	98	.597
Jansen, New York	118	84	.584
Konstanty, Phila.	55	41	.573
Staley, St. Louis	82	63	.566
King, Cincinnati	32	25	.561
Meyer, Brooklyn	75	59	.560
Pollet, Chicago	116	98	.542
Bickford, Milwaukee	66	56	.541
Simmons, Phila.	59	52	.532

The Scoreboard

by Harry Grayson

NEW YORK (NEA) — Walter Emmons Alston is a humble man, which is not the least reason why he is the new manager of the Brooklyn club.

Walter Alston first attracted the attention of the Dodgers' brass when he made no effort to screen his own mistakes.

Walter Alston

Managers in a baseball chain mail a box score and a report of the day's game or games nightly. The errors are there for the director of the farm clubs, the general manager and the president to see. They didn't see the game. The pilot could trace trouble to numerous things.

But honest and fearless Walt Alston would note: "Better charge this one off to me. I didn't get my hands up fast enough, so he went home when he should have been held up." "I let Pitcher Doakes stay in when I should have had him out of there." "I had Smith hit-and-run when he should have hit straightaway."

If Alston ever sends in a Ralph Branca as a relief pitcher in the ninth inning of a play-off game, he won't blame it on one of his coaches.

ALSTON WILL, by the way, coach at third base, where the

—See GRAYSON—Page 10

Fights Last Night

By The Associated Press

PHILADELPHIA — Johnny Bernardo, 165, Philadelphia, stopped Linwood "Porky" Sanders, 165, Philadelphia, 8.

PARIS—Percy Bassett, 129½, Philadelphia, outpointed Louis Carrara, 134, France, 10.

Browns Aim at Grid Title

Win Tomorrow Will Clinch East's Crown

Eagles Play Giants, But Seem Doomed To Finish Second

NEW YORK (AP)—The rampaging Cleveland Browns, with a victory streak of nine games, can wrap up their eighth straight National Football League divisional championship tomorrow.

And the man who thinks they can't lick the Chicago Cardinals would be the object of quizzical looks, indeed, if he spoke out. The hapless Cards have exactly one tie to show for their season's work, along with eight losses.

OTTO GRAHAM and Co. have licked the Cards seven times in a row, and this is no time to stop.

The Philadelphia Eagles, with a winning streak of six games, are in the unfortunate position of being the second best team in the Eastern Conference behind the Browns. They play the New York Giants, a good defensive outfit. But the Eagles have perhaps the most crushing offense in the league and most observers think they'll win much as they please.

Another Eastern Division game pits the Washington Redskins against the Pittsburgh Steelers. The Steelers' failure to compile a better than 4-5 record has been one of the mysteries of the loop. They still are strong on paper, but with Jim Finks injured, they'll be badly handicapped.

THE DETROIT Lions' 34-15 victory over Green Bay Thanksgiving Day all but cemented the Western Division title for them. The Los Angeles Rams and the San Francisco 49ers still are in the running, but time is running out on them.

The Rams play the Chicago Bears in Chicago while the 49ers tackle the Baltimore Colts. Both the Rams and the 49ers will be heavily favored.

Knockdown in 4th Round

AP Wirephoto

This is the first of two knockdowns Lulu Perez suffered in the fourth round at the hands of Dave Gallardo during their 10-rounder at Madison Square Garden last night. Gallardo won the unanimous decision.

Ding-Dong Hockey Battle

Hornets Regain 3rd, Bears Fight Tonight to Hold 2nd

The ding-dong battle in the American Hockey League continues over the weekend and Moe Henderson's Hershey Bears, holding down second place, find themselves with a tough assignment ahead.

The Chocolateers must tackle the Providence Reds in a pair of games with the first tonight in Hershey and the second tomorrow night in Providence.

THE REDS are sure to come storming into Chocolate-town anxious to regain their third position which they lost last night when Pittsburgh handed Syracuse a 6 to 1 defeat. By virtue of the win, the Hornets boosted their season's total to 21 points and stepped over the Reds, who have 20. Hershey is in second place with 22 points, so it follows that the Henderson-coached team must produce or slip down.

A full card is on tap for the League tonight with the leading Buffalo Bisons playing at Cleveland while Syracuse returns its visit to Pittsburgh and the Reds keep the Hershey fans excited.

TOMORROW night Hershey begins its long road trip by playing at Providence, while in the other League game Cleveland goes to Buffalo. The way things stand right now there's apt to be considerable shuffling in the standings between now and tomorrow night.

STANDINGS OF TEAMS

Team	W	L	T	Pts.
Buffalo	13	5	2	28
Hershey	10	10	2	22
Pittsburgh	9	9	3	21
Providence	10	11	0	20
Cleveland	9	10	0	18
Syracuse	8	14	1	17

LAST NIGHT'S RESULTS

Pittsburgh 6, Syracuse 1

TONIGHT'S GAMES

Providence at Hershey
Buffalo at Cleveland
Pittsburgh at Syracuse

TOMORROW'S GAMES

Hershey at Providence
Cleveland at Buffalo

Fight Tonight

TOLEDO (AP)—Johnny Cunningham and Carmen Basilio, two welterweight upset artists, match punches tonight in a 10-round nationally televised bout.

The scrap in Civic Auditorium will be carried over the ABC network, beginning at 9 p.m. (EST), with the Toledo area blacked out.

Alley Babble

BOB SNEATH hit his best form of the season as he fired a blistering 247-207—610 to pace the Home League, but got plenty of competition from Andy Gridina's 203-223—604, Harlen Gilgore's 221-220—603, Hank Sears' 228, Frank Severino's 225, Ben Zangari's 223, Amy Kline's, 221, Harry Stoe's 215, Wilmer Gingrich's 214 and Steve Goba's 213.

The Commercial League saw Frank Smithgall's 228—578, Paul Schaffstall's 200-201—569, Lou Layendecker's 554, Claude Herr's 559, Charles Burd's 221 and Barney McGaw's 214.

In the RCA American loop it was Clayton Bartlett's 217-183—572 that grabbed top honors, followed by Jim Scott's 244-161—561, Eli Schaefer's 198-181—544 and Gus Splinter's 222—518.

Merle Hoover's 190-225—576 was tops in the Press League, with William Sultzbach's 188-193—557, Robert Mann's 223—546, Raymond Peifer's 181-178—528, William Worley's 192—528, Richard Rhen's 221—524 and Ernie Kuenzli's 194-177—524 following.

Setting the pace in the Columbia Ladies Merchants circuit was Evelyn Myers' 168-157—474, and Beatrice Hoover's 175.

Violet Banner's 395, Sally Worst's 361 and Sassie Gray's 327 were outstanding in the Garden Spot Ladies Duck Pin loop.

Dottie Reppert's 169—466, Betty Enterline's 179—453, Jane Buch's 177—423, Elsie Stehman's 177—422, Betty Shire's 161—424, Ann Weidman's 165—421 and Delores Becker's 165—419 topped the Manheim Women's Farm League, but it was highlighted by Gracie Eshleman's making the 3-8-10 split and Mary Henry making the 3-7 split.

The Keystone Duck Pin circuit saw Helen Heeps' 132—370, Betty Myers' 145—348, and Alma Fulmer's 125—310.

Bob Stauffer came up with a fine 234 single to highlight the action in the Mr. and Mrs. League. Stauffer's 533 triple was second best though, as Hub Smith fired a 190-185—542. Also recorded were Chet Groff's 180—509, Hack Witman's 162—481 and Mary Smith's 178—480.

Gallardo Ends Perez' Win Streak

NEW YORK (AP)—Davey Gallardo had a win over Lulu Purez, a Jan. 1 date with the same fighter, and a laugh over the "Broadway Wise Guys" today.

The scrappy, 23-year-old Los Angeles featherweight set up the package last night by swarming all over the 20-year-old Brooklynite to score an upset, unanimous ten round decision in Madison Square Garden. He floored Perez twice in the fourth round.

As a result of the form reversal, the two will meet in a rubber match in the Garden New Year's night. The winner will get a Garden crack at Willie Pep, the former Featherweight Champion, in mid-February.

ONLY ABOUT two months ago Perez scored a TKO win over Gallardo in eight rounds and entered last night's bout a 17 to 5 favorite to repeat. But Davey never gave the 20-year-old Perez a chance to get started as he swarmed all over him from the opening bell.

The decision was unanimous. Judge Jack Gordon scored it 8-2, Judge Arthur Susskind, 6-4, and referee Al Berl, 5-4-1.

Gallardo lost his first fight with Perez when he suffered two deep cuts over his left eye which required 15 stitches. But before losing, he discovered that Lulu was a sucker for a right and couldn't do much when he was forced back.

The 23-year old Californian set the pattern for the fight at the opening bell when he tore after dancing Lulu and forced him on the defensive. He punched away at close quarters and nullified Perez' long range power.

IN THE fourth, he drove Lulu against the ropes and as Perez sagged, Davey pummeled him over the lower strand of the ropes, punching as his stricken foe fell over.

As soon as the referee finished giving Lulu the mandatory eight count, Gallardo stormed after Perez again and sent him through the ropes in the same manner.

Again after the eight count, Gallardo charged after Perez. He bulled him to the ropes and almost pushed him through to draw a warning from the referee. If Gallardo had scored a third knockdown in the round he would have won on a technical kayo under New York's three knockdowns in one round rule.

Mize Seeks Job

NEW YORK (AP)—For the first time since he started his major league career almost two decades ago, Johnny Mize, one of the greatest sluggers in baseball with 359 home runs, was job-hunting today.

The 40-year-old first baseman of the New York Yankees decided yesterday he had come to the end of the road as a player and asked the Yanks to make him a free agent so he could seek a manager's job at the Minor League meetings starting in Atlanta Monday.

Tonight's Sports

BASKETBALL

COLLEGIATE

Millersville STC at St. Joe.
Lebanon Valley vs. Gettysburg at York.

CHURCH LEAGUE

Ross St. vs. Hellenic, 6:30 p.m.
Broad St. vs. St. Luke's, 7:30 p.m.
St. John's vs. Ch. of God, 8:30 p.m.
Pearl St. vs. First Presbyterian, 7 p.m.
St. Paul's vs. Faith, 8 p.m.

HOCKEY

AMERICAN LEAGUE

Providence at Hershey.

Teachers in Philadelphia

Millersville Five Ready For Cage Opener Tonight

Max Bishop's Millersville State Teachers 1953-54 basketball edition opens its season tonight against St. Joseph's College at the St. Joe Field House, City Line and 54th Street in Philadelphia at 8:30 p.m.

The Marauders will start with Co-captains Charley Podlesny and Wally Evans, Billy Werkiser, Dave Fitzgibbons and Don Weining. In reserve will be Johnny Parker, George Ortlip, Joe Labatch, Bob Wentzel and Dick Erisman.

Podlesny, Evans, Fitzgibbons and Werkiser are veterans from last season, while Weining, a sophomore, was a squad member last year.

THE MARAUDERS are in good shape for the opener. They've had scrimmages against Lebanon Valley (twice), Delaware, Muhlenberg and F&M to-date and their offense has been clicking. In meeting St. Joe, they face a Philly foes that has always been among the top combos in Eastern Collegiate basketball. Last year the Philly Hawks defeated Millersville, 65-44. This marks the second meeting of the two in the history of the two institutions.

In scrimmages thus far, Bishop has used his entire ten-man squad, alternating them around until he has found a suitable combination. He intends to do the same against the Hawks. Eight of his ten squadmen are over six feet tall which gives him a new angle to work on since Marauder teams of the past haven't packed as much height as this one. His two little men, Podlesny and Werkiser, are the sparkplugs of the outfit with plenty of speed and shooting ability.

THE MSTC Junior Varsity will play the St. Joe freshmen in the preliminary at 6:45. On this Marauder club will be Don Wilson, Dick Shepps, Earl Wiggins, Johnny Smailer and Bob Wentzel with Jimmy Forjan, Marino DeFilippo, Harry Hill, Vern Achenbach, Bob Lehr and Bobby McCabe in reserve.

Views of Sports

by Red Smith

PHILADELPHIA—Obedient to annual custom, scores of college football coaches are gathered here this weekend, padding through the midtown streets and gazing about with dazed and grateful eyes as realization dawns that somehow they have survived another season.

They come each year to enjoy the coachly anguish of their colleagues in the Penn-Cornell and Army-Navy games, and on the Friday night between these exercises they disport themselves in the Racquet Club. Unless you have attended one of these parties, you cannot imagine how remarkably coaches resemble people when they put on dinner jackets and walk on their hind legs like performing bears.

AMONG THOSE present are three who have earned citations of exceptional merit. One, whose season ended with three victories in nine games, ought to be chosen coach-of-the-year by acclamation. A second should be saluted for extraordinary achievement in picking up the pieces of a ruined dynasty. There ought to be some sort of architect's award for the building project engineered by the third.

They are, from left to right, George Munger of Pennsylvania,

—See SMITH—Page 10

Last Night's Scores

HOCKEY

AMERICAN LEAGUE

Pittsburgh 6, Syracuse 1.

BASKETBALL

NBA

Milwaukee 55, Philadelphia 51.

New Police-Fire Hq. Coming Up

LANCASTER'S WORST CASE of "arrested development" will be remedied this year when an 80-year-old police station and a 55-year-old firehouse are replaced with a new Public Safety building to be erected at a cost of $522,700 at the corner of Duke and Chestnut Streets. Tearing down of No. 5 firehouse to make room for the new structure will start in two weeks. No decision has been made on the fate of the antiquated police station, but it will be vacated by the department. New building will combine headquarters of police and fire bureaus and civil defense.

WHISTLE STOP—Old police station (at lower end of arrow) is jammed into the middle of a block with no room to expand; it will move into new building which will be erected at opposite end of arrow, now occupied in part by Firehouse No. 5 on North Duke Street. Construction will start after firehouse has been torn away.

CROWDED CORNER—Even the office of Police Commissioner Fred G. McCartney in the old building is little bigger than a glorified telephone booth, measuring 12 by 13 feet. Commissioner stands beside "trophy case" of weapons taken from criminals. Modern intercom system contrasts with antiquity of building, erected in 1874.

OCTOGENARIAN — Lancaster's out-at-elbows police station will mark the 80th anniversary of its dedication on Oct. 1. As long ago as 1897 a chief of police was calling for immediate major repairs.

ADDED ATTRACTIONS that weren't thought of in 1874 when police station was built have had to be crowded into the old building. Above, Sgt. Kenneth Witmer handles a couple of them — telephone switchboard with five trunk lines, and two-way radio in communication with prowl cars and fire department. AT RIGHT is another bit of equipment headed for the boneyard. It's the old alarm bell in No. 5 Firehouse, which dates clear back to the time the house was built, 1899. Tape at bottom is punched to indicate number of rings. Board will come down with the building, to be replaced by new police-fire headquarters.

NEW SITE of police-fire headquarters on North Duke Street will occupy area of present No. 5 Firehouse (photo to right) and part of old railroad cut beside it. In foreground are ruins of Ranck tobacco warehouse.

POLICE COURT room doubles as squadroom, assignment desk and recreation hall. Old railing between Sgt. Raymond Wiggins and Officer David J. Dommel effectually dates the structure.

"BLACK HOLE OF CALCUTTA" was for many years the affectionate nickname of basement confinement cells. Five single cells and one large cell are crowded in cellar with sign painting and paint storage rooms, not to mention furnace room and steam pipes and antique plumbing facilities. There are no cells for women.

TRAFFIC JAM—The Traffic Bureau is in a bit of a jam itself, having been squeezed into what used to be the entrance hall of the police station. Shown at old station's most familiar spot are Capt. Ray Charles, Lt. Dave Strayer and Officer William Wissler. Filing cabinets were built into wall to save a little space.

EVEN THE GARAGE is hopelessly crowded, with traffic signs and stencils stacked in among motorcycles, squad cars and repair space. This was site of unloading of "loot" from hundreds of gambling and liquor raids.

WEATHER
(U. S. Weather Bureau)
Eastern Pennsylvania — Showers, Probably Scattered Thunderstorms, Windy And Turning Much Colder This Afternoon And Night With Showers Changing To Snow Flurries In The Mountains. Tomorrow Cloudy, Much Colder. Some Snow Likely.

Intelligencer Journal.

The Leading Newspaper in the Garden Spot of America. Home Owned for Home Folks Since 1794

THE INTELL INDEX

160th Year.—No. 187. Official United States Census Figures Lancaster Metropolitan Area Population 234,717 LANCASTER, PA., THURSDAY MORNING, JANUARY 21, 1954. CITY TWENTY-TWO PAGES 30c PER WEEK—5c Per Copy

New Farmers Market Due For City May 1

24 MARINES DIE IN BOAT CRASH

Area Smothered By Heavy Blanket Of Fog

MARY, LEMON ST. BUILDING WILL BE SITE

Between 75 And 100 Stalls Planned For Former Garage

A new farmers market is scheduled to be put in operation in this city about May 1.

The market will be housed in a former garage on the northwest corner of Mary and Lemon Streets and will be equipped with between 75 and 100 stalls. It is tentatively planned to call it the "West End Farmers Market".

Details of the project were revealed yesterday by D. D. Shaub, who has purchased the building from Bob Hess Inc., local auto agency.

Shaub now operates a food market in the former auto show room which fronts on Lemon Street and is connected at the rear to the one-story brick garage. He will take possession of the property March 1.

PARKING LOT AT REAR

The garage itself is 51 feet wide and 149 feet in depth along Mary Street. There is a parking lot in the rear of the building, entered from Spruce Street, that can accomodate between 50 and 75 automobiles.

Outlining his plans for the market, Shaub said he intends to put in the stalls and rent them to farmers, fresh and smoked meat dealers, produce and fruit dealers and any other merchants who desire to sell at the market.

20 APPLICATIONS

He said he already has some 20 applications on hand for stalls. Special refrigeration equipment needed by meat dealers, he said, will have to be installed by the

Turn To Page 6 For More Of MARKET

Site Of New Farmers Market In City

Above is the site where a new farmers market is scheduled to be put into operation about May 1. The market, on the northwest corner of Mary and Lemon Streets, will be equipped with between 75 and 100 stalls, according to D. D. Shaub, who planned the project and now operates the food market in the front of the building. The farmers' market will be located in the one-story brick garage at the rear of the building. (Intell Photo No. 121541)

FARM CORNER

"We Lead All The Rest"
By WILLIAM R. SCHULTZ

Benson Places 1954 Corn Crop Under Control

WASHINGTON, Jan. 20 (AP) — Secretary of Agriculture Benson today ordered the 1954 corn crop placed under production controls.

The regulations call for a reduction of 17.4 per cent in plantings in the commercial corn-producing area.

The secretary said a planting allotment of 46,995,504 acres for the commercial area compared with 56.819.428 acres in the area last year. The acreage planted to corn in the entire country last year was 82,430,000.

(Lancaster County was designated a commercial area late last year when the secretary indicated that controls were a probability. The 17.4 per cent reduction, if followed by growers, will reduce the county's plantings below 100.000 acres for the first time in recent years.

(A survey concluded here last

Turn To Page 6 For More Of FARM CORNER

Weather Calendar

COMPARATIVE TEMPERATURES

Stations	High	Low
Water Works	38	30
Ephrata	48	30
Last Year (Ephrata)	48	34
Official High for Year Jan. 1		50
Official Low for Year Jan. 18		-1
Character of Day		Cloudy

WINDS
Direction E-WSW Avg. Velocity 9 mph

HUMIDITY
8 a.m. 100% 11 a.m. 100% 2 p.m. 100%
5 p.m. 100% 8 p.m. 100%
Average Humidity 100%

SUN
Rises 7:22 a.m. Sets 5:09 p.m.

MOON
Rises 8:04 p.m. Last Quarter, Jan. 26

STARS
Morning—Venus, Mars, Saturn
Evening—Jupiter

NEARBY FORECASTS
(U.S. Weather Bureau)

Maryland — Cloudy and windy with showers and scattered thunderstorms turning much colder by afternoon in west portions and evening in east portions today. Much colder tonight. Tomorrow cloudy and quite cold with some snow likely.

Delaware and Southern New Jersey — Cloudy, windy and mild with showers and probably scattered thunderstorms today, turning much colder by afternoon or evening. Much colder tonight. Tomorrow cloudy and quite cold with snow likely.

Lower Potomac and Chesapeake Bay—South to southwest winds 15-25 mph today, shifting to northwest 25-35 mph this afternoon. Cloudy, showers and scattered thunderstorms today. Visibility fair in the south and poor with fog in the north portion.

MEMBERSHIP IN PA. MILK BOARD FILLED BY FINE

Governor Names Phila. Attorney, Joseph Henderson To 3-Man Group

HARRISBURG, Jan. 20 (AP)—Gov. John S. Fine today completed membership of the three-man State Milk Control Commission with the appointment of Benjamin Harrison Welty, Waynesboro.

At the same time, the governor named Joseph Welles Henderson, Philadelphia attorney and acting president of Bucknell University, as a member of the Delaware River Port Authority.

Welty's appointment fills the long-standing vacancy left by the resignation of P. Stephen Stahlnecker to join the Public Utility Commission. Welty's salary will be $10,000 a year.

Both appointments are subject to confirmation by the State Senate in the 1955 session.

Welty, long prominent in dairy farm and milk organizational activities, will serve until the end of the next session of the Senate, or untiy May 1, 1955, whichever comes first.

He will assume his duties with the commission after a short vacation. Other members are Chairman Joab K. Mahood and

Turn To Page 6 For More Of MILK

AMISH HEARINGS SET FOR FRIDAY

Alderman J. Edward Wetzel yesterday set 7 p.m. Friday for hearings for two Bart Twp. Amishmen charged with violating the compulsory school attendance law.

Those hearings will be followed at 7:30 p.m. by hearings for two Paradise Twp. Amishmen charged with the same offense.

Wh-o-o-o-s-h

Q'ville Savants Ready To Crash Light Barrier Feb. 2

The eyes of the scientific world will be on Quarryville on Feb. 2 when the Slumbering Groundhog Lodge will endeavor to crash the light barrier with its Arctomantic Time Reverser.

The time reverser will carry several of the lodge's members back to pre-historic times when the Shadow came into being as the accurate omen from which to predict the weather.

The ultra-secret machine, which is being guarded around the clock by a super sensitive radar screen, will be powered by the Atomic Energy machine which last year shot two groundhogs to the moon.

To achieve their goal of crashing the light barrier, the time reverser will have to travel at better than 186,000 miles a second.

The lodge's scientific minds are confident that this will be done. Secret tests "have been most satisfactory," it was reported at the lodge's headquarters.

The proclamation calling upon the patriarchs, the supreme enlightened and the faithful of the lodge to the Groundhog Day ceremonies, said that "if we succeed in accomplishing this scientific miracle, which smacks sharply with the theory of relativity and which has been carefully calculated using the equation 2,99796 x the tenth power of 10 cm per second, everything has been calculated to practical infinity."

The proclamation also points out that the lodge's feat last year in shooting two groundhogs to the moon has resulted in the Hamilton Watch Company producing a space clock.

The lodge also announced that it will be forced to accept the resignation of President Eisenhower as an honorary member.

Last March the lodge was notified that the President was resigning from all organizations of

Turn To Page 6 For More Of GROUNDHOG

Ouch!

Groundhog On Feb. 2 Menu At Brickerville

There are storm signals flying in the northern end of the county and it might be well for the staunch defenders of the faith, the redoubtable gentlemen of Quarryville's Slumbering Groundhog Lodge down in the southern end to take heed.

People in the northern end, for instance, these days are asking if the Lodge's days of glory are not numbered.

On such occasions in years past the Lodge, in all its mighty splendor, would merely have had to cast a collective glance of scorn at any mere mortal who dared utter such heresy.

That glance would have blown him away as the winter wind removes a flake of snow.

MOUNTAIN OF TROUBLE

But now, as flakes of snow do make a snowball, so, too, has the molehill of heretics grown into a mountain of trouble.

It started innocuously enough a few years ago when some of the unbelievers — "Cannibals" the Lodge contemptuously called them — gathered in the hills of Brickerville on that hallowed night of nights, Feb. 2, to dine on groundhog.

There was only a small band at first who gathered round the fes-

Turn To Page 6 For More Of BANQUET

RICE NAMED AS POSSIBILITY IN GOVERNOR RACE

Democratic Gettysburg Apple Farmer, Packer Non-Committal On Candidacy

PHILADELPHIA, Jan. 20 (AP)—The name of John S. Rice, Gettysburg apple farmer and packer, was advanced today as a possible Democratic gubernatorial candidate.

The 55-year-old Rice, who made a previous unsuccessful bid for the post in 1946 against U.S. Sen. James H. Duff, said he "hasn't been approached."

Asked if he would be available for the nomination if it were offered, Rice said "I haven't given that much consideration and wouldn't want to comment on the topic at this time."

He refused to either flatly put himself in or take himself out of the race.

Meanwhile, Philadelphia Mayor Joseph S. Clark, Jr., said at his

Turn To Page 6 For More Of DEMOCRATS

SUPER 'SOUP,' RAIN ALL BUT HALTS TRAFFIC

But Dense Mist Seen Being Chased By Cold Front On Way Here

A fog that was far from kittenish slinked into Lancaster County early yesterday and sat down on its haunches for a full-fledged visit.

The dense mist, accompanied by perfunctory light rain, made motorists super-cautious, caused meetings to be postponed and served as a silent valedictory for a short-lived spell of mild weather.

COLD COMING

Overcoats and mufflers will again be the uniform of the day for area residents by late today, the Weather Bureau indicated, basing its prediction on a cold air mass headed this way behind the sea of cottony fog.

Until the cold front arrives, the weather outlook today is for showers and perhaps thunderstorms, whipped by a lively wind. Tomorrow is seen as cloudy and considerably colder, with some snow a likelihood.

The fog moved in early yesterday and stuck around far into the night. A considerable flurry of minor traffic collisions throughout the county were attributed to the murky stuff that billowed over thoroughfares. The fact that there were no serious mishaps was laid to the slow speeds at which drivers were forced to move.

Figuring in the fog was the smothering humidity of 100 per cent that combined with rising temperatures to lay the smoke screen.

The fog covered practically all of the eastern half of the state. York Countians termed it the worst in recent memory and estimated visibility at 20 feet most of the day. At Harrisburg, the state capitol dome could not be seen across the street despite a score of floodlights playing on it.

Lancaster's Municipal Airport was bottled up all day, a situation that extended to Philadelphia, New York and many other eastern air terminals. Bus schedules were appreciably knocked out of kilter but trains were reported generally on time.

MOTELS JAMMED

Mist-weary drivers with formidable distances to travel took refuge early last evening in motels and other hostelries, rather than continue and risk a collision. Motels surrounding the Lancaster-Lebanon

Turn To Page 6 For More Of FOG

Tax Collection Costs Here Just Over 2 Per Cent

A shade more than two cents of each tax dollar collected in 1951 by the county, the city, the boroughs, the townships and the school districts, went to pay the cost of collecting the tax.

An analysis of tax reports for that year shows that the cost of collecting the levies was $147,356, which was 2.06 per cent of the $7,274,165 collected.

The analysis also showed that while the amount of taxes levied is increasing from year to year, the cost, percentage wise of collecting them, has remained nearly constant over the past 23 years.

The 2.06 per cent of 1951 is the lowest since 1930 when $84,690 was spent to collect $4,435,365 in taxes. This figures out to a percentage of 2.02.

In 1940, when local levels of government collected only $3,983,787 in taxes, 2.08 per cent of that amount,

Turn To Page 6 For More Of TAXES

GROUP OF GERMAN CIVIC LEADERS TO VISIT LANCASTER

Will Study Life Here As Part Of Project To See America In Action

A group of German civic leaders will spend between two and three weeks in Lancaster within the near future as part of a State Department program designed to foster better understanding and closer relations between this nation and the other nations of the free world.

Mayor Kendig C. Bare, announcing Lancaster's selection yesterday as one of the cities included in this particular project, said the city was proud and honored to have been selected.

Officially known as the "Cooperative Action Team Exchange Program", groups of German civic leaders from selected German communities have been invited to this country to watch America in action.

Under a program, set up by the Governmental Affairs Institute, which works with the State Department on the project, the various groups will be given a week of general orientation to American life before being assigned to various cities. The cities will be compar-

Turn To Page 6 For More Of GERMAN

POW VESSEL RAMS SMALL LANDING SHIP

Troopship Loaded With Chinese Captives Was Bound For Formosa

INCHON, Korea, Thursday, Jan. 21 (AP)—A troopship loaded with Chinese prisoners of war bound for Formosa rammed into a small landing craft today and spilled 24 American Marine guards to icy death in Inchon's outer harbor.

It was one of the greatest naval disasters of the Korean War period, surpassed only by a turret explosion in the cruiser St. Paul and the mine-blasting of a mine-sweeper.

The Navy said 28 men were fished from the icy, choppy waters. They included 24 Marines, 2 American soldiers and 2 Koreans who were manning the landing craft.

ROLLED OVER

The Navy said the blunt, towering bow of the troopship crashed into the side of the smaller vessel and rolled it over on its side.

The Marines, carrying heavy combat gear, pitched into the chill waters. Their craft sank almost immediately.

The rescued men were rushed aboard the hospital ship Consolation. They were suffering from shock and exposure.

The Marines were fully armed and equipped, carrying heavy rifles and wearing heavy service boots. Navy and Marine officers feared the heavy weight may have dragged many to their deaths when they were pitched into the harbor.

Navy said it had little hope

Turn To Page 6 For More Of MARINES

Seaway Measure Wins Okay In Senate 51 To 33

WASHINGTON, Jan. 20 (AP) — Supporters of the St. Lawrence seaway, after 20 years of effort, tonight won Senate approval of legislation to authorize the United States to join with Canada in building the controversial project.

Passage of the bill, which the pro-seaway forces had been freely predicting since the beginning of debate a week ago, came on a roll call vote with 51 Senators voting yes and 33 no.

It was a bipartisan vote which

Turn To Page 6 For More Of SEAWAY

2-Hour Search Ends With Tot, 3, Found On Nearby Q-ville R3 Farm

A frantic search by a southern Lancaster County mother for her three-year-old son ended about 4:30 p. m. yesterday when the child was found about a half mile from home, just as the Quarryville Fire Co. was being alerted to join in the search.

The lost child was Clayton A. Lamparter Jr., three, son of Mr. and Mrs. Clayton Lamparter, Quarryville R3, who wandered away from home about 2:30 p.m. yesterday.

COMB AREA

Mrs. Lamparter, aided by a few neighbors, began combing the immediate fog-covered area around her home and, when she was unable to locate her son, she asked Henry R. Bushong, a neighbor, to notify the Quarryville firemen.

Bushong immediately summoned Fire Chief Henry Martin who was reportedly hesitant because firemen in that area are presently threatened with a $1,000 damage suit as the result of a search for another lost child on Christmas Day.

After Bushong told Martin that neither he or other property owners in the area would "do such a thing" to firemen, the fire chief was about ready to summon other volunteer firemen when the lost

Turn To Page 6 For More Of BABY

DRIVER OF DRIFTING BUS PROSECUTED

Max Cohen, 20 E. Orange St., was prosecuted yesterday for leaving a motor vehicle unattended with the motor running and the wheels turned toward the street.

The charge was brought against Cohen, a Conestoga Transportation Company bus driver, by city police following an accident at 9:50 p. m. Tuesday. Cohen had parked a bus in front of the CTC waiting room, 19 S. Queen St., when it drifted down the street and crashed into Locher's Cut Rate Drug Store, 40 S. Queen St., causing damage estimated in excess of $500, police said. The charge was brought before Alderman J. Edward Wetzel.

STATE POLICE SAY:

VACATION TIP: Your vacation lasts only two weeks—Death is Permanent.

Time, 3 P. M.; Place, By-Pass; Visibility, Almost Zero

Visibility was down to almost zero as heavy fog blanketed Lancaster county, along with the rest of the eastern part of the United States, yesterday. The photo of the northern by-pass, above, taken about 3 p. m. from the New Holland Pike bridge, shows vehicles with their headlights burning as they groped through the dense fog. (Intell Photo No. 121542)

Dress Rehearsal For Jr. League Follies

SOUTH SEA ISLAND MAGIC complete with a chorus of Hula dancers in grass skirts and leis with hibiscus flowers in their hair set the scene for the "Legend of the Islands." Rehearsing the native dance routine, left to right, are: Mrs. James D. Phafl, Mary Ella Eckman, Mrs. Charles V. Snyder Jr. and Mrs. Richard K. Dodge. (Sunday News Photo)

Over 100 Dancers, Singers, Actors To Present 23 Scenes

With a cast of over a hundred singers, dancers and actors needing costumes for twenty-three scenes plus five between-scene interludes, costumes for dress rehearsal become the first consideration during the last few days before the opening of the Junior League Follies on Thursday at 8:15 p. m. in McCaskey High School auditorium.

Over the week-end theater trunks by the dozen have been arriving at Junior League Rooms and the place is a beehive of activity as the Follies cast arrives to be assigned the right costume and fitters from the costume committee follow through with pins, needle and thread to assure the right fit in time for the opening curtain.

FROM THIS MOMENT ON

"From This Moment On", the opening chorus until "So Nice Having You", the grand finale, the wide variety of acts are sure to cover the varying tastes of patrons attending the two performances on Thursday and Friday.

For those partial to South Sea Island magic "The Legend of the Islands" featuring two sailors and the Hula Chorus is made to order but if reminiscing about the Roaring Twenties is preferred, there will be a "Backward Glance" with flappers dancing the Charleston, a bit of phony tension with some gangsters topped off by the "Mink Chorus".

GIRLS — GIRLS — GIRLS

Since girls are synonymous with Follies, one of the most glamorous scenes will be "Girls, Girls, Girls", featuring showgirls in the Ziegfield manner and Rockettes in the modern tempo.

With the yen for South American cruises growing every day, "Haitian Holiday" has been dreamed up to take you there on the double, where Katie from Haiti rules the island realm with her natives. Intruding on the native scene are the exploring Spaniards with a chorus of senoritas very gifted in the art of waltzing.

SILENT MOVIE QUEENS

The "Three Little Queens" will take the audience back to silent movie days when Mrs. Richard Hoober portrays Mary Pickford, Mrs. Leland W. Shick does a very reasonable facsimile of Pola Negri and Debby Mumma is a lovely Pearl White.

In planning the Follies program, Dr. Kinsey hasn't been forgotten and neither has the weather, whether "Clear Or Cloudy". Those with an interest in art will discover that "It Begins With Art" and although there is a 'Salute to Paris" the local scene hasn't been neglected with a chance for members of the audience to see themselves as others see them marketing, or shopping or relaxing.

WILL BENEFIT LIBRARY

Both performances of the Follies will benefit the Children's Wing of the new Public Library, as will the proceeds from the cabaret party which will be held at the Hotel Brunswick Friday night, beginning at 11 p.m. Some of the cast will come in costume and present skits from the Follies.

Tickets for the Follies are on sale to the public at the Troup Music House. The ticket sale will continue through next Friday. Tickets for the cabaret will be available at the door the night of the party.

MINK CHORUS will have all eyes front and center in the scene "Backward Glance." Portraying chorus girls in a Chicago Night club, dressed in satin but wishing it were mink, left to right are: Mrs. Ben E. Mann, Mrs. George K. Reynolds Jr., Mrs. Frank L. Snavely, Mrs. John L. Farmer, Mrs. Edward Rick Jr., Mrs. John H. Swanger Jr., Mrs. Bertram L. Davidson Jr. and Mrs. Willis H. Nolt Jr. (Sunday News Photo)

HAITIAN HOLIDAY presented against the tropical background of the West Indies includes a Spanish Waltz number and Mrs. Robert N. Reynolds as Katie from Haiti and her 'natives'; Dick Farmer, Dick Hopf and John Moyer. (Sunday News Photo)

Rockettes are assigned saucy short ballet dresses aglitter with sequin stars. Pert costumes featuring strapless bodices of crushed black velvet with layers of white tulle forming the skirts and bodice ruffles, are worn by precision dancers of the modern ballet. Front row, left to right, are: Mrs. Edward M. Sager, Mrs. David S. Watt, Mrs. J. Ross McCray; back row, Mrs. James R. Lewis, Mrs. Herbert K. Cooper Jr., and Mrs. Albert Charleton. (Sunday News Photo)

FARM WOMEN INSTALL

Mrs. Abner Musser was installed as president of Farm Women's Society 11 at a meeting in the Quarryville Fire Hall. Mrs. Emmett Herr was installed vice president; Mrs. Martin Stoner, secretary; Mrs. Harry McComsey, corresponding secretary; and Mrs. William Fredd, treasurer. Mrs. R. C. Edwards was the installing officer.

A. B. Sinkler Nat. Aide For YW Centennial

Arthur B. Sinkler, executive vice president of the Hamilton Watch Co., is a member of the national committee sponsoring the centennial observance and celebration of the founding of the Young Women's Christian Association in 1885.

Mrs. Dwight D. Eisenhower is honorary chairman of the committee, comprising leaders in the religious, professional and business life of the nation. Mrs. Laurence S. Rockefeller, a member of the national board of the YWCA of the U. S. A., is general chairman for the observance.

At the annual electors' dinner in the local YWCA Friday night, Mrs. George Griest, chairman of the centennial committee for the 100th anniversary celebration here, discussed plans for membership development and fund-raising in anticipation of the event.

Eight persons were elected to the board of directors for three-year terms from 1954 to 1957. They are Mrs. Louis L. Bentley, Mrs. David F. Chambers Jr., Mrs. Paul R. Diller, Mrs. Donald M. C. Englert, Mrs. Daun Nesbit, Mrs. W. Robert Powl, Mrs. Charles V. Snyder Jr. and Mrs. C. C. Vogt.

Elected to the nominating committee were Mrs. Harland D. Fague, Mrs. Robert V. Moss, Mrs. George W. Stoler, Mrs. Harold A. Barr, Miss Jane E. Hubbell, Mrs E. G. Sarkisian, Miss Catherine McGuire and Miss Nancy Herr.

Rotating off the board of directors after three-year terms were Mrs. Earl A. Bagenstose, Miss Frances Coventry, Miss Margaret Galbreath, Mrs. E. M. Hartman, Mrs. John H. Hollinger, Mrs. J. Nevin Schaeffer and Mrs. Ivan J. Stehman.

The reorganization meeting, at which new officers will be elected, will be held Thursday. Mrs. Schaeffer, who is completing her term of office as president, was presented with a gift.

Guest speaker at the meeting was Mrs. Theodore D. Walser, an accredited observer to the United Nations, who said that there is no question but that the U. N. is the only hope for world peace at the moment.

Women's Republican Club Will Sponsor Wed. Card Parties

Women's Republican Club of Lancaster County will hold the first in a series of public card parties Wednesday at 2 p. m. in the club's headquarters 36 W. Orange St.

First Ward Women's Republican Club will sponsor the parties which will be held every Wednesday afternoon during February. Mrs. E. Silas Overdeer, president of the First Ward Club, is serving as general chairman of the parties. She will be assisted Wednesday by Mrs. Harry W. Buckius, Mrs. John F. Cresswell, Mrs. W. E. Leyder and Miss Frances R. Zech.

The parties will continue into the spring.

COVENANT EUB SOCIETY

Mrs. Charles E. Workman will review John R. Scotford's book, "Within These Borders," at a meeting of the Women's Society of World Service of Covenant Evangelical United Brethren Church tomorrow at 7:30 p.m. in fellowship hall of the church, W. Orange and Mulberry Sts.

Mrs. John Cousler is in charge of the program. Devotions will be led by Mrs. Ethel Heinaman. Mrs. Merl Hoffer will be song leader and Gilbert Hoffer will be soloist. Mrs. Richard P. Smith and Mrs. Jacob K. Shaibley will serve as ushers.

Lutheran Mission Societies Re-Organize, Name Chairmen

Officers of the Women's Missionary Society of the Lancaster Conference, Central Pennsylvania Lutheran Synod met yesterday afternoon with 98 women representing 1259 members of women's missionary societies of forty Lutheran Churches in Lancaster County.

Presiding at the meeting held in St. John's Church was Mrs. Warren Heinly, president, assisted by Mrs. Harland Fague, vice-president; Mrs. Gilbert J. Martin, secretary; Mrs. Ruth C. Hoh, treasurer; and Miss Sarah Bitner, statistical secretary.

The officers met with the delegates to explain the new organizational set-up and to answer questions presented by congregaitonal officers regarding conference procedures.

Chairmen Introduced

New personnel, chosen by the officers were introduced and spoke briefly on Conference work.

New county chairmen of the education division are: Mrs. Roy Franz, Millersville, mission study; Mrs. J. Samuel Parrett, Elizabethtown, magazine; and Mrs. George Heiges, Manheim, education.

Promotion division has Mrs. Fague as chairman with Mrs. Jacob Kreider, Lititz, Deaconess; and Miss Ella King, Columbia RD 2, student.

In the special gifts division Mrs. Nathan Carvell, Rothsville, will be in charge of special aids; Mrs. Celo Leitzel, Reamstown, thank offering; Mrs. Charles Schlitzer, Columbia, life membership; Mrs. George High, New Holland, patron and protege. Mrs. Clay Rice, Neffsville, is associate editor.

Program committee for the Rally on May 1 at Muddy Creek Lutheran Church will be Mrs. Russell Derr, Adamstown; Mrs. Jacob Longacre, Lancaster; Mrs. Maxwell Walton, Leacock; Mrs. Victor Navikas, Lancaster; and Mrs. Wilbur Allison, Maytown.

Convention Committee

Committee members for the Convention to be held Nov. 17 in St. John's Lutheran Church, Columbia, are: Mrs. James Zwally, Mrs. Herbert Hohman, both of this city; Mrs. Harry Shreiner, Columbia; Mrs. Frank Eves, Akron, Mrs. William Mumma, Landisville; and Mrs. Robert Witman, Manheim RD 1.

Nominating committee members are: Mrs. Robert Hanna, Lititz; Mrs. James Harrison, Lancaster; Miss Beulah Stauffer, Lititz, Mrs. W. L. Koder, Mt. Joy; and Mrs. W. E. Waybright, Denver.

BOOTH—GEITER

Sylvia Louise Geiter, daughter of Mr, and Mrs. James Geiter, 44 S. Pearl St., and Ross Ernst Booth, son of Mr. and Mrs. Vearl Booth, East Petersburg, were married at 2 p.m. yesterday in the Church of Christ. Paul O. Weber, minister, officiated.

The bride is employed at H. L. Green's and the bridegroom is in the U. S. Air Force stationed at Sampson Air Base, N. Y.

Local Women Receive Awards At Regional Flower Show In Phila.

Mrs. Walter C. Weber, Lancaster R2, won two blue ribbons in the Eastern Region flower show which was held in Philadelphia from Jan. 18 to the 22.

One of the blue ribbon displays was a shadow box in the Williamsburg scene which was made of dried flowers in their natural color. The other prize was for a semi-miniature.

Mrs. John Clark Missiner won honorable mention with a wall plaque arrangement.

The next meeting of the Gardeners' Workshop will be held Feb. 15 at 1:30 p. m. in the home of Mrs. Weber.

NEW ENGLAND WOMEN

The Lancaster Colony of New England Women will meet on Tuesday at 1:30 for dessert at the home of Mrs. Robert B. Thompson Jr. 1234 Wheatland Ave.

WEATHER
(U. S. Weather Bureau)
Eastern Pennsylvania—Partly Cloudy With High 38-40 Today, Tomorrow Considerable Cloudiness And Colder With A Few Snow Flurries In The Mountains.

Intelligencer Journal.

The Leading Newspaper in the Garden Spot of America. Home Owned for Home Folks Since 1794

160th Year.—No. 204. Official United States Census Figures Lancaster Metropolitan Area Population 234,717 LANCASTER, PA., WEDNESDAY MORNING, FEBRUARY 10, 1954. CITY TWENTY-FOUR PAGES 30c PER WEEK—5c Per Copy

STATE TAKES ACTION TO ELIMINATE TRAFFIC HAZARD AT ENGLESIDE

NEW RULES MAY AID FISHING IN SUSQUEHANNA

State Suggests Earlier Walleye Season May Improve Sport In Lakes

MARVIN E. MILLER
Intell Sports Editor

An earlier fishing season on walleye pike in the Susquehanna river lakes is seen by Charles A. French, executive director of the Pennsylvania Fish Commission, as a possible solution to improving walleye fishing for sportsmen in the area.

Further, the director expressed the belief that the new 1954 regulations, removing sizes, seasons, and creel limits from practically all pan-fish will enable a greater harvest of these species, which in turn should improve the fishing for game fish in Pennsylvania.

This came to light by the release of correspondence on the fishing situation in the Susquehanna lakes between John R. Helter, 53 Front St., Lititz, vice-president of the Lancaster County Federation of Sportsmen's clubs, and Director French.

The executive director, writing in reply to an appeal from Helter that the Fish Commission make known whether it is concerned with the steady decline of fishing in the river, also left go with a glowing report of plans for giving river fishermen some good sport.

OUTLINES PROGRAM

It included proposed ideas the commission is considering and also work which has been completed toward that end.

Helter, active in sportsmen's circles here for the past eight years, had cited particularly the decline in walleye catches from the man-made lakes at Holtwood, Safe Harbor and Conowingo.

He also noted that with the smaller walleye catches, local fishermen found bass and perch catches on the downgrade as well.

About the only fishing that has improved locally, he wrote French, is the catfish but he said even that has reached the stage where a 17 or 18 inch cattie is con-

Turn To Page 17 For More Of FISHING

Federal Funds May Be Used To Equip New Defense Hq.

See Possibility Equipment In CD Room In New Police-Fire Building Will Be Financed By Federal Matching Fund

The wisdom and generosity of city officials in providing space for Lancaster County Civil Defense headquarters may have paved the way for complete federal financing of the cost of equipping the headquarters.

That was revealed last night when a group of Civil Defense officials met in their present headquarters on the second floor of the Manufacturers Association building at 28 E. Orange St.

LAYOUT PLANS

The meeting was called to discuss plans for laying out and equipping the 60 by 80 foot room which will be designated to Civil Defense on the top floor of the new city police and fire headquarters building.

Max Stierstorfer, administrative assistant to Col. J. Hale Steinman, the county director of Civil Defense, informed the group that federal matching funds are available up to 50 percent for such a project.

The cost of the space provided by the city in the new headquarters, it was pointed out, can be figured as the matching amount of money that might possibly be obtained.

Estimated costs of equipping the new headquarters were discussed last night preparatory to making a formal request to State Civil Defense headquarters for matching funds

No action was immediately taken, however.

HQ. BREAKDOWN

As outlined during the meeting the new headquarters would contain a main control and meeting room, message room, waiting room and other partitioned office spaces.

In addition to Stierstorfer, the meeting was attended by Col. Frank M. Gavan, executive director; Capt. John M. Groff, special aide; Harry L. Wigham, communications chief; H. C. Kreisle, sirens officer; David Wagenseller, deputy controller; and Mrs. Nadene R. Rhoades, secretary.

WORK ON CITY'S POLICE STATION MAY START MAR. 1

Contractors Find Old Fire House Wall Part Of Legion Building

Barring unforeseen obstacles, and given a break from the weather, actual construction of the city's new $522,700 police and fire headquarters building on the northwest corner of Duke and Chestnut Streets may be underway by March 1.

A spokesman for Rice and Weidman, Inc., general contractors for the building, said yesterday that demolition of the 93-year-old North Duke Street firehouse, which is being razed to make way for the new structure, is expected to be completed within two weeks.

Demolition work on the firehouse started this week and is progressing rapidly.

Meanwhile, it was also learned that the destruction of the fire house is going to create a repair job for officials of American Legion Post 34, which owns the building adjoining the fire house.

The north wall of the firehouse has also served as the wall for the adjoining Legion property.

A portion of this wall will be torn down in the process of demolition. This, city officials said yesterday, will have to be rebuilt by the Legion.

The greater part of this wall, however will be utilized as the north wall of the new building, which will, like the firehouse, adjoin the Legion building.

ATTORNEYS GOING TO H-BURG TODAY; SEEK TRUCE FOR AMISH

Attorneys representing the Amish in an appeal of a compulsory school attendance law violation, announced yesterday that they will confer at Harrisburg today with representatives of the State Department of Public Instruction.

The attorneys, W. Hensel Brown and Charles W. Eaby, will be accompanied to Harrisburg by State Sen. Edward J. Kessler, who has been working to find a solution to the school problem.

The attorneys hope that one result of the conference will be Department of Public Instruction approval of a truce in the prosecution of the Amish until the courts can rule on the appeal.

The appeal is being made in the case of Samuel L. Smoker, Gordonville R1, who has been prosecuted seven times for failing to send his fourteen-year-old son to school.

Underpass Which State Proposes To Eliminate

This is the railroad underpass the State Highways Department proposes to eliminate. Described in the past by S. Edward Gable, president of the Lancaster Auto Club, as one of the worst traffic hazards in Lancaster county, the underpass is located on the New Danville pike, only a few feet from South Prince Street at Engleside. The Highways Department is asking to extend the New Danville Pike north, at a point just beyond the underpass shown above, to connect with Fairview Avenue, west of Prince Street.

SENTIMENT FOR DILWORTH SEEN BY DEMOCRATS

Policy Committee Puts Off Decision On Party's Candidate To Feb. 19

HARRISBURG, Feb. 9 — There was strong sentiment among Democratic leaders here today for Richardson Dilworth as the party's candidate for governor.

The Democratic policy committee, however, put off until another meeting here Feb. 19 a final decision on the endorsement of a candidate. The Philadelphia district attorney, however, held the inside track.

Dilworth, who attended the meeting, refused to say definitely that he will be a candidate.

SERIOUS PROBLEMS

"I have serious problems," he said in alluding to a requirement that he would have to resign as district attorney to become the Democratic gubernatorial candidate.

The sentiment for Dilworth, who ran unsuccessfully as the Democratic gubernatorial candidate in 1950, was not confined to Philadelphia. From many counties, especially those in the western and northern parts of the state, leaders said Dilworth was the man.

Considered as other serious contenders for the nomination were State Sen. John H. Dent, Democratic floor leader, of Westmoreland County, and Allegheny County

Turn To Page 20 For More Of DEMOCRATS

BAINBRIDGE SAILOR IS KILLED BY AUTO

HAVRE DE GRACE, Md., Feb. 9 (AP)—James M. Green Jr., 23-year-old navy man whose address was listed as Mishawka, Ind., was killed today by a car on U.S. 40, about a half mile south of the Susquehanna river toll bridge.

State police said the youth, stationed at the nearby Bainbridge Naval Training Center, was walking north on the highway when hit.

The driver of the car, Stanley Stagman of Richmond Hill, N. Y., was named in a technical charge of manslaughter.

U.S. Weather Bureau Is Now $27 Million A Year Operation

WASHINGTON, Feb. 9 (AP)—The ultra-scientific Weather Bureau celebrated its 84th birthday today with forecasts as usual and a fond look back at Mr. Increase Lapham, the man who sent out the bureau's first report in 1870.

Lapham had no elaborate charts in his Chicago office. No radio, no television. He got his information from people who told him about the weather via magnetic telegraph.

Lapham guessed what the weather would soon be like and made a forecast. Signal flags on the Great Lakes relayed the information. So did the magnetic telegraph.

He was following orders from President Grant who signed the bill creating the bureau on Feb. 9, 1870. Rep. Halbert E. Paine, a Wisconsin Republican, wrote the bill.

In the first year of the bureau's operation, Congress shelled out $50,000 for its operations. This year the service is costing the taxpayers 27 millions.

The bureau was in the War Department at first, then agriculture and in 1940 it moved to Commerce.

SUCCESS AND FAILURE

As everyone who has ever planned a picnic knows, the bureau has had a history of success and failure.

Back in 1892, for instance, a bureau spokesman noted today, California raisin growers saved a million dollars because a rain forecast came through in time for them to cover their raisins.

Then there's the story which everybody in the Weather Bureau seems to know. It deals with Professor Cleveland Abbe, who used to be the bureau's chief forecaster.

One day Abbe finished studying his charts and maps and issued a forecast: "No rain until tomorrow." He told an assistant to put out the forecast.

"But, professor," the assistant protested, looking out the window, "it's raining now."

The professor studied the situation for a minute and then concluded: "It can't be! The charts don't show it."

Incidentally, the bureau got a bit of present for its 84th birthday in a decision in a federal court in St. Louis. The court ruled against six Kansas City firms which were trying to sue the government for damages because the Weather Bureau muffed a forecast in the 1951 floods.

"Good news," said a bureau spokesman. "I don't think anybody has ever won any of those suits."

WARMER WEATHER MELTS MOST OF SNOW

Yesterday's warmer weather dissipated most of the snowfall which had blanketed Lancaster County Monday and the weatherman said today's weather would be about the same.

The Ephrata weather station reported a high reading of 44 degrees yesterday with the low of 23.

According to the U. S. Weather Bureau, today will be partly cloudy with a high of 38 to 40 degrees. Tomorrow will be colder with considerable cloudiness.

Yesterday most pupils in Martic Twp. had a holiday because school buses couldn't get through the snow-clogged southern end roads. No other schools were closed.

Elsewhere throughout the nation, unseasonal temperatures in the 60s were reported from South Dakota south to Missouri, and east to the Carolinas. Lincoln, Neb., recorded a record 68 and Omaha a 63.

SHOPPING CENTER BID MAY SET UP NEW ZONE CLASS

City Commission To Study Proposed Project For 8th Ward

A brand new city zoning classification may result through a recent request of a local building contractor to create a shopping center in a new residential district in the Eighth Ward.

That was brought out yesterday afternoon when the City Planning Commission announced it would make a study of the proposal and draw up a tentative draft of a new zoning classification which would cover it.

ASKED LAST DECEMBER

The request for the shoppng center was originally made to city council last December by Benjamin R. Groff, builder and developer of the Rolridge housing area in the southwestern corner of the city.

At that time Groff said he plans the shopping center, first ever proposed for the city, in a tract bounded on the northeast by Hershey Avenue, on the southeast by Hager Street and on the southwest by an unnamed alley. It is a tract 250 feet by 398 feet and is in the center of the Rolridge development.

Groff told council he wants to build a grocery store, drug store, barber shop, beauty parlor, flower and gift shop, children's shop, electrical appliance shop and a gasoline station.

He said he would build the structures and rent them to private operators.

The area is presently zoned a

Turn To Page 6 For More Of ZONING

WATCH INDUSTRY SAID SHRUNKEN BY SWISS IMPORTS

Hamilton Spokesman Urges U. S. Boost Tariffs By 50 Per Cent

(Intell Washington Bureau)

WASHINGTON, Feb. 9 — A spokesman for the Hamilton Watch Company today charged that unfair Swiss competition has reduced the American watch manufacturing industry to a "shrunken and insecure" status and asked the U.S. Tariff Commission to boost tariffs on imported Swiss watches and movements by 50 percent.

J. Bradley Colburn, representing the Hamilton, Elgin, and Waltham watch companies, charged that tariff inequities allow the Swiss watch industry to control 80 per cent of the American market, as the Tariff Commission opened full-scale hearings on proposed tariff revisions.

Colburn told the commission that Swiss competition has weakened the domestic watch industry to the point where it is "physically incapable of fulfilling its required national defense functions."

The American Watch Association, claiming to represent 75 per cent of the American industry, counterattacked Colburn's state-

Turn To Page 6 For More Of HEARING

DRIVER PROSECUTED IN CRASH NEAR BUCK

Two persons were injured slightly in a two-car accident on Route 72, one mile south of The Buck, last night.

The driver of one car, Charles W. Lumpkins, Baltimore, was given an immediate hearing before Justice of the Peace Abner Musser and was fined $10 and costs for reckless driving, state police reported.

Police said that Lumpkins, driving south on Route 72, lost control of his vehicle, swerved off the highway and then headed over into the opposite lane. He collided with a car operated by Donald D. Mussawir, Bainbridge, Md.

A passenger in Lumpkin's car, John Mason, also of Baltimore, and a passenger in the Mussawir vehicle, Joseph Buza, Elizabeth, N.J., were taken to a physician in Quarryville for treatment of lacerations. Total damage to both cars, police said, was $900.

RELOCATION OF NEW DANVILLE PIKE PLANNED

Would Feed Traffic Into Fairview Ave.; On-The-Spot Inspection Tomorrow

The State Highways Department has taken the first step toward removal of the traffic hazard at the intersection of the New Danville Pike and South Prince Street at Engleside.

An application, it was learned yesterday, has been filed with the Public Utilities Commission asking permission to relocate the New Danville Pike and eliminate the Pennsylvania Railroad underpass just south of the intersection.

The underpass has been the factor causing the traffic hazard.

As a result of the Highways Department request, officials of the PUC, the Highways Department and the City will meet at 11 a.m. tomorrow for an on-the-spot discussion of the proposal.

The state, it was learned, is planning to relocate the New Danville Pike, from a point just south of the present underpass.

MEET FAIRVIEW AVE

It would build up the road to a level with the PRR tracks and extend it north in front of the Pennsylvania Power and Light Co. substation to meet with Fairview Avenue at a point west of Prince Street.

This would make the road parallel and to the west of the PRR tracks.

City Traffic Engineer Robert C. Chryst, who with City Engineer J. Haines Shertzer will attend the meeting tomorrow, said that since the proposal would feed New Danville Pike traffic into Fairview Avenue a system of traffic signals would undoubtedly be necessary.

Traffic, under this plan, could feed from the New Danville Pike

Turn To Page 6 For More Of HAZARD

BETTER FLIGHT CONNECTIONS SET UP BY ALLEGHENY

Airline Moves Eastbound Flight Back To 11 a.m. Here; More Time At Phila.

Allegheny Airlines has taken another big step designed to give Lancastrians top-flight east-west air service.

David L. Miller, vice-president in charge of traffic and sales for Allegheny, announced yesterday that the schedule on a flight now stopping at the Lancaster Municipal Airport has been revised to give local patrons improved service to New York and Boston.

The change, effective March 1, involves Allegheny's Flight 302, now leaving Lancaster daily at 3:53 p.m. for Wilmington and Philadelphia.

As of March 1 this Flight will leave Pittsburgh at 9 a.m. and leave Lancaster at 11 a.m.

This means, Miller pointed out, that local patrons will be able to make better connections in Philadelphia with the American Airlines for flights to La Guardia Field in New York and Boston.

2ND TIME IN MONTH

This is the second time within less than a month that Allegheny has taken steps to give Lancaster improved air service.

Officials of the airline announced on Jan. 25 that it has applied to the Civil Aeronautics Board in Washington for permission to furnish two daily flights in each direction between New York and Pittsburgh, with stops at Lancaster.

This plan, as requested by Allegheny, would give Lancastrians one morning flight to New York,

Turn To Page 6 For More Of ALLEGHENY

"We Lead All The Rest"

FARM CORNER

By William R. Schultz

Landisville Lab Barn Offered As Site For Rural Meetings

The use of a barn at the Southeastern Field Research Laboratory in Landisville was offered last night for possible conversion to a meeting place for Lancaster County agricultural organizations.

The proposal was the first to be made in the search for a central gathering place for rural meetings, and it was advanced during a special meeting called by the Lancaster County Senior Extension Club for discussion of the problem.

Only eight of the Garden Spot's more than 30 farm and farm home organizations were represented and the session ended with no decision other than to survey the absent groups on their needs.

The Landisville property is owned by the Pennsylvania State University and was the former home of the Southeastern Pennsylvania Artificial Breeding Cooperative.

Dr. Beckford Coon, director of the laboratory, said the ground floor of the barn is not in use and would be available for renovation and conversion to a large meeting room and possibly kitchen facilities.

WOULD SEAT 300

The structure measures about 50 by 70 feet and could seat 200 to 300 persons, Dr. Coon estimates. Conversion for meetings would require installing a ceiling, walls and a suitable floor, plus heating and sanitation facilities.

The proposal was held for future discussion by a larger, more rep-

Turn To Page 6 For More Of FARM CORNER

Weather Calendar

COMPARATIVE TEMPERATURES

Stations	High	Low
Water Works	41	23
Ephrata	44	23
Last Year (Ephrata)	48	32
Official High for Year Jan. 27		64
Official Low for Year Jan. 18		-1
Character of Day		Partly Cloudy

WINDS
Direction WSW Avg. Velocity 21 mph

HUMIDITY
8 a.m. 100% 11 a.m. 64% 2 p.m. 59%
5 p.m. 66% 8 p.m. 72%
Average Humidity 72%

SUN
Rises 7:04 a.m. Sets 5:33 p.m.

MOON
Sets 1:06 a.m. Full Moon, Feb. 17

STARS
Morning—Mars, Saturn
Evening—Mercury, Venus, Jupiter

NEARBY FORECASTS
(U.S. Weather Bureau)

Delaware and Southern New Jersey — Fair with highest 43-38 today, tomorrow fair and colder.

Maryland — Fair with highest 43-48 today, tomorrow partly cloudy and colder with a few snow flurries in the mountains.

Lower Potomac and Chesapeake Bay—Westerly winds 10-15 mph shifting to northwesterly at night, fair weather, good visibility.

EXTENDED FORECAST
(U.S. Weather Bureau)

Extended forecast for the period from today through Sunday:

Eastern Pennsylvania, Eastern New York and Mid-Atlantic States—Temperature will average about two degrees below normal, moderately cold during first part, followed by a little milder toward end of week. Light snow likely by tonight, mostly over northern sections and precipitation likely again around Sunday. Total precipitation melted one-quarter to one-half inch.

Community Aid To Be Sought For Research In History Making Project At Wheatland

A research project on Wheatland, home of President James Buchanan in which all members of the community will be urged to take part is being sparked by the Buchanan Foundation for the Preservation of Wheatland.

The project, which will undertake to record and coordinate all phases of Wheatland, historically and culturally, from the time it was built through its current restoration, was outlined last night by Charles F. Montgomery, executive secretary of Winterthur, the Dupont mansion near Wilmington, which is now a museum.

JR. LEAGUE SESSION

Montgomery spoke at a meeting of the Junior League last night in the St. James' Parish House, to which League husbands and all members of the Buchanan Foundation Board and Restoration committee were invited. The Junior League is custodian of Wheatland, having spearheaded the drive about 20 years ago to acquire the mansion for the community.

This will be the first time such a complete research will have been made of any historic shrine in the nation, and Winterthur's interest in it is to oversee and aid the project because of the importance of preserving historic shrines. The Wheatland project, Montgomery said, undoubtedly will become the pattern for similar exhaustive studies of other shrines.

The work will be done entirely by volunteers, and it was emphasized that everyone in the community who wants to help may do so. An individual is expected to be named in the near future to head up the project, and to receive the names of volunteers.

Montgomery advised that the project should carry out the interpretation of Wheatland in four areas.

First, guides should be able to tell the visitors what was hap-

Turn To Page 6 For More Of WHEATLAND

How's He Doing?

Editor's Note—How's he doing, the United States weatherman, that is? With the unforecast snowfall of Monday still a prime topic of conversation, the Intell continues with its daily comparison of the official forecast issued by the United States Weather bureau and the actual weather.

THE FORECAST
For Tuesday

Considerable cloudiness, windy, highest temperature 36-42.

THE FULFILLMENT
On Tuesday

Partly cloudy, winds averaging 21 mph, highest temperature 44.

Little Liz---

For every girl who goes to college to pursue learning there are a dozen who go to learn pursuing.

LANCASTER NEW ERA

The Weather
(U. S. Weather Bureau Forecast)
Not So Cold Tonight; Warmer Tomorrow
Temp. Today High 28; Low 6
Temp. Yesterday High 30; Low 16

77th Year—No. 23,798 | Lancaster Metropolitan Area Population Official United States Census Figures 234,717 | LANCASTER, PA., SATURDAY, FEBRUARY 13, 1954 | CITY EDITION | 16 PAGES | 30c PER WEEK—5c Per Copy

Dulles Charges Soviets Are Afraid To Leave Austria

Cops Storm U. S. Church in Rome, Chisel Off Name

Worshipers Forced To Leave; News Photographer Arrested

ROME (AP)—Italian police descended today upon Rome's Church of Christ, chiseled its name off a wall and took a news cameraman of the Associated Press into custody for photographing them.

They vainly ordered an AP correspondent away from the scene.

The word "Christ" in six-inch-high letters, was the first word removed in this action against the Protestant religious organization, which has American financial backing.

Appears After Services

The Roman police struck quickly after worshippers were forced to leave a Church of Christ in Leghorn late last night.

AP photographer Remo Nassi, an Italian citizen, was seized with his camera and hustled off in a police car despite protests. AP correspondent Allan Jacks, a U.S. citizen, was ordered to leave, but refused.

Later Nassi was released without charges and his camera was returned.

The police left as soon as the name had been entirely removed from the wall.

Direct Orders Issued

The sign was removed on direct orders of the Rome Questura, or police headquarters, which is under the Italian ministry of interior.

The new premier of predominately Roman Catholic Italy, Mario Scelba, is the minister of the interior as well as government chief.

The chief of the police party declined at first to give his name and identified himself as "Commendatore Pinko." This was an obvious jibe at Church of Christ preachers, who in the past frequently have been assailed by Italian critics as leftists. This they have always denied.

Officer Apologizes

Later the police officer apologized and identified himself as Commissario De Rusk, the precinct captain.

In 1950, when the cult's troubles with Italian authorities first began the Italian interior ministry was headed by Scelba. He then criticized the Church of Christ and other Protestant evangelical cults as "aiding Communism in Italy."

Just two days ago, the Vatican and the Italian government celebrated the 25th anniversary of the Lateran pacts. The pacts establish the Roman Catholic religion as the Italian state religion.

Constitution Cited

The new republican constitution says "all religious confessions are equal before the law."

Last month Dr. Cline Rex Paden of Brownfield and Lubbock, Tex., who first organized the Church of Christ in Italy, visited the United States to report on what he called "continued difficulties" of the evangelical church in Italy.

In the first collective letter of its kind, Italy's top Roman Catholic prelates warned Catholics Feb. 1 against what was described as Protestant propaganda. The letter, signed by the cardinal archbishops of eight major Italian cities and

—See CHURCH—Page 4

Mercury Is Due to Rise After Drop to 6° During Night

The mercury dropped to six above zero here early today, but the Weather Bureau said more moderate weather was on its way.

Tonight is to be cloudy and not as cold, with a low between 15 and 20. Tomorrow is to be mostly cloudy and warmer, with a high between 35 and 40. The cold spell put slush ice back into the Susquehanna River.

Low for the state overnight was 10 below at Pleasant Mount in Wayne County. Philipsburg had five below. While no snow was forecast for this area, west central counties were told light snow was expected this afternoon and tonight.

New England was the cold area today, with 21 below at Burlington, Vt., and 17 below at Houlton, Me.

Mennonite volunteer workers find time to chat while waiting for the baskets of ground meat to cool before it is placed into tin cans.

Working on the final step—labeling of the cans—are, from the right, Dorothy Martin and Reba Dagen, both of Conestoga R1, and Ida Hess, Holtwood R1.

New Era Photos

15 Men Safe in Oil Burner Blast

$1,200 Damage at Hostetter Body Shop

Damage in excess of $1,200 was reported when an oil burner exploded, blowing out the front of a large boiler in the basement of Hostetter's Body Shop, Ruby St. and Prangley Ave., at 8:35 a.m. today.

Albert H. Hostetter, proprietor, said 15 employes were working in the one-story cinder block building, but none of the workmen were in the area of the boiler room at the time of the blast.

Explosion Put Out Fire

City firemen were called and Fire Chief Harry Miller, Battalion Chief Edward Koerkle and Companies 1, 6 and Truck B responded but the services of the firemen were not needed. Miller reported the explosion apparently put out the flames in the fire box.

The impact ripped a metal door from the front of the boiler and hurled it across the boiler room. The blast also blew out the skylight, shattered windows and blew open every door in the one-story building, causing slight damage to door frames, window sash, etc.

Hostetter estimated damage to the heating plant, which had been installed in 1948, at $1,000 and said other damage to the building would reach "several hundred dollars."

Valentine Mail Volume May Exceed Last Year's

Mailmen struggled under huge stacks of Valentines today, last day for mailing of hearts and flowers greetings.

Postmaster Frank R. Hammond said it appeared that this year's Valentine mail would top that of last year's. Yesterday's total of all cancellations was 121,000, and Thursday's was 90,000. Mailings earlier in the week were also heavier than usual.

A complicating factor today was the examination given employes who wished to qualify for supervisory promotions. Of the 26 taking the examinations, 12 were carriers, and substitutes carried their routes.

Ex-Red Slain in N. Y., Was Trained in Russia

NEW YORK (AP)—A man found dying of stab wounds in Harlem has been identified as a former Communist who trained in Moscow but later turned against the party.

The victim, Charles White, 51, a Negro, had appeared as a witness in deportation hearings against Communists and was scheduled for new testimony. However, police maintain that his death had nothing to do with politics. White was found in a Harlem doorway Thursday morning and was taken to Harlem hospital, where he died later in the day.

Mennonites Pack 40,000 Cans of Meat for Relief

2,500 Cans a Day Turned Out by Volunteers at Portable Cannery Set Up in Terre Hill

Volunteers from churches in the Lancaster Mennonite Conference, with the help of a portable meat cannery set up in Terre Hill, are turning out close to 2,500 cans of meat a day which will be sent all over the world to aid in relief.

The project which has been in operation around this area for five or six years is new for Terre Hill. The cannery, owned by the South Central Conference of Menonites of the Kansas area, is operated in Terre Hill under the direction of the Mennonite Central Committee of Akron.

The work of cutting up, grinding, and canning the meat was started on Monday and will continue for four weeks. The goal for the four weeks is 40,000 cans of beef, pork, and fowl which will be sent to Germany, Jordan, and Korea.

35 To 40 Needed Daily

About 35 to 40 volunteers are needed each day. Workers from the Lancaster Mennonite Conference will be working for two weeks and will be followed by workers from other branches of the Mennonite Church and by the Amish.

The meat which is used is donated by members of the Mennonite Church or is bought with funds contributed by the members. The meat is butchered by Ezra Martin Co., Lancaster; Elmer Sensenig, New Holland; New Holland Meat Market, and Charles and Leon Martin, Union Grove.

After the meat is butchered it is taken to the portable cannery which is situated in an old tobacco packing house. Then the volunteers begin working.

The meat is quartered and taken off the bones and put through a grinder. The ground meat is then cooked for 20 minutes and put into tin cans.

Then it is pressure-cooked in the cans for one and a half hours after which the cans are immersed in cold water. The final step is to wash and label the cans.

Assembly-Line Project

All the work is done in an assembly-line manner. Each person has his own job to do and it is done in the least amount of time.

After the canning process is finished the cans are packed and sent to the Mennonite Central Committee in Europe and are then distributed to the people.

Arlo Voth, White Water, Kan., and Marvin Hertzler, Denbigh, Va., travel with the cannery to various parts of the United States. The expected goal this season is 180,000 cans which will be processed in Illinois, Ohio, Indiana, Virginia, and other parts of Pennsylvania.

Kiwanis Camp Will Open Again

Boys' Club to Use It As Summer Project

The old Kiwanis Camp site near Williamson Park will be used as a summer camp for the Boys' Club of Lancaster, under plans being formulated by the club's board of directors.

Members of a special camp committee headed by Paul Lyet inspected the property this morning, accompanied by Mayor Kendig C. Bare and city commissioner Daniel S. Templeton.

A report will be made at the board meeting Thursday.

Charles W. Mayser, club president, said that use of the site for a summer camp would provide wholesome recreational activities during the summer months for the 350 boys currently enrolled in the club.

Started In 1925

The old Kiwanis Camp was started in 1925. Mayser was camp director in 1925 and 1926. During the early 30's, a National Youth Administration camp was located nearby. Use of the site by the NYA ended in 1943, and the city now owns the property.

The club plans to equip the camp with complete mess and sleeping facilities, and operate the camp in July and part of August. City officials have promised full co-operation, Mayser said.

30 Will Explore Uncharted Cave

Group to Spend Week In Crystal Cave Depths

CRYSTAL CAVE, Ky. (AP)—Physical examination began today for members of a seven-day exploration expedition into the uncharted labyrinths and streams of Crystal Cave's lower level. The expedition will get under way tomorrow morning.

At that time, 25 men and 5 women are scheduled to enter the cave for what is perhaps the most extensive cave exploration ever attempted on this continent.

All have been in training for a month, but Dr. Halvard Wanger, expedition physician, said last night that despite this training some members might be "washed out" for actual exploration.

Explores Crawlway

Dr. Wanger made a preliminary exploration today through the crawlway which members must travel before gaining access to the cave proper.

Crystal Cave, in the hills of Southern Kentucky 10 miles south of Louisville, is inside the 51,000-acre Mammoth Cave National Park area.

An advance camp will be set up by explorers, a mile inside the cave's entrance.

14-Inch Passageway

But before reaching the advance camp site, the explorers must crawl through a 1,000-foot passage of limestone. At one point this passageway is only 14 inches in diameter.

Sponsored by the National Speleological Society, an organization for the study of caves, the explorers hope to chart areas now unknown, study and photograph formations, gather samples of dirt, look for strange insects or animal life and study reactions of human beings living together for seven days underground in a temperature of 49 degrees and 100 per cent humidity.

SLIGHT EPHRATA FIRE

A gasoline engine, used to pump fuel oil from a truck to home storage tanks, back-fired and caught fire at the West End Service Station, Ephrata, at 2:30 p. m. yesterday. The fire was extinguished by the owners before the Pioneer Fire Co., of Ephrata, arrived. There was no damage.

Streetcar, Auto Crash; 6 Killed

LOS ANGELES (AP)—Six persons were killed early today when their automobile and a steetcar collided.

The victims were all Negroes—three women and three men—and their identities were not immediately learned.

Police described the accident as one of the worst of its type in recent years in Los Angeles. Firemen had to work more than an hour to extricate the mangled bodies from the wreckage.

The force of the impact hurled the Los Angeles Transit Lines car off the tracks and nearly to the street curb. Sixteen passengers on the streetcar were shaken up but none was seriously injured. A woman passenger on the streetcar fainted.

Surprised by Mother

Marine Fleeing Cop Shot; Kissed Girl Good Night

PHILADELPHIA (AP)—An 18-year-old Marine Corps private, surprised as he kissed a girl friend good-night in the vestibule of her apartment home, was shot and seriously wounded in the back early today as he fled a pursuing policeman in North Philadelphia.

Pvt. Thomas Penza, on leave after finishing boot training at Parris Island, S. C., was reported in fair condition at the naval hospital.

Ran Along Street

Detective Matthew Miller said the Marine was shot by Patrolman Robert Wells, attracted by the crash of glass and screams, when Penza running along a street, and ducking between parked cars, ignored shouts and warning pistol shots fired into the air.

Miller said Penza had escorted Jacqueline Ellis, 17, to her home and was kissing her good-night when the girl's mother opened the front door of the first floor vestibule.

Miller said Penza scrambled to get out of the vestibule. There was a scuffle, and the glass in the door was smashed. Mrs. Ellis screamed.

Hit in Back

Penza rushed outside. Wells, attracted by the noise, gave chase. When Penza refused to stop Wells fired at him, the bullet striking him in the back and emerging from the neck.

Police Seek Ban On Driver, 19

Was Recent Patient At Philhaven Hospital

Samuel S. Holsinger, nineteen, Lititz R1, would be ruled off the highways under action initiated by Ephrata borough police, following a 12-mile chase Thursday night in which he was clocked at speeds over 70 miles an hour.

Police said they learned Holsinger was recently discharged from Philhaven Hospital, Mount Gretna, and termed him "a definite hazard to motorists and pedestrians."

Father To Cooperate

From an authoritative source, it was learned today that Holsinger's father has promised police his cooperation in the matter, that he has persuaded his son to surrender his license "for an indefinite period" and that arrangements are being made for the youth to receive medical aid.

On the father's promise that he personally would see to it that his son does not drive, Ephrata borough police are said to be holding up action on charges of speeding, reckless driving and failure to heed the signal of an officer, pending developments to have the youth undergo treatment.

25 Shots Fired

Nearly 25 shots were fired by police in an attempt to halt the car during the chase which started at Ephrata and ended near Downingtown. One of the shots fired by Policeman Howard Bord punctured a rear tire, forcing Holsinger to stop.

Holsinger, police said, attempted to grapple with them but was taken into custody. Police quoted Holsinger as saying he led the officers on a chase "just to prove I was as brave as you are."

Canadian Pilot Lands His Jet 900 Miles Off Course

ST. LOUIS (AP)—"I was surprised to say the least."

That was the comment of Royal Air Force flying officer N. L. Harrison when he landed his jet plane at St. Louis' municipal airport last night—900 miles off course on a routine training flight.

Harrison, of Toronto, said all his navigational aids had gone on the blink shortly after he and officer G. G. MacLeod of Montreal left Portage La Prairie, Manitoba, late yesterday afternoon for a flight to North Bay, Ontario, also about 900 miles.

Confederate Vet, 107, Is Fighting Pneumonia

AUSTIN, Tex. (AP)—Confederate veteran Tom Riddle, 107, fought old age and pneumonia today and doctors said his condition remained critical.

Dr. Herman Wing, medical director of the Texas Confederate home where Riddle has lived since 1950, said he was "waiting hopefully."

Riddle is being fed intravenously and is kept under an oxygen tent.

Oil Will Be Sought Under Gulf of Mexico

TAMPA, Fla. (AP)— A four-month study of the makeup of the floor of the Gulf of Mexico, including explorations for oil deposits, will be made by an expedition leaving Tampa Monday.

The former pleasure yacht Vema will carry 15 scientists and 12 crewmen. The project is being undertaken by Columbia University with the financial backing of several oil companies.

CHIANG ADVISER DIES

TAIPEH, Formosa (AP)— Elder Statesman Tsou-Lu, former chancellor of Sun Yat-Sen University in Canton and one of President Chiang Kai-Shek's advisers, died today following a cerebral hemorrhage. He was 69.

Thousands Lose Savings As $12 Million Deal Fails

Collapse of Japan's Biggest Postwar Money Scheme Catches Top Politicians, Buddhist Priests

TOKYO (AP)—The ceiling has fallen in on postwar Japan's biggest financial scheme and Japanese from politicians to Buddhist priests are picking the plaster out of their hair.

Three top political parties, including the Liberal Party of Prime Minister Shigeru Yoshida, are scurrying out from under the wreckage of the 12-million-dollar investment company, Hoazen Keizai Kai.

Government investigators said the company's wizard, Matsutomi Ito, 47, spread contributions lavishly among the three top parties so he could use big names as "advisers."

Caught Thousands

Collapse of the company, due largely to misfired speculations in the stock market, caught hundreds of thousands of housewives and laborers. Their small investments, baited by promises of 15 per cent interest, had helped build the company.

Also among those caught in the collapse was the abbot of a large Buddhist denomination. Company records show he collected contributions from his flock and gave them to Ito to invest.

Ito is in jail, charged with swindling. Newspapers call him Japan's "Ponzi," a reference to the Boston swindler who once collected millions from gullible Americans.

Investors knew he was speculating in stocks and real estate but looked upon him as a wizard. For a time, he had an amazing run of luck. He paid the promised 15 per cent interest.

A Korean who became a naturalized Japanese, Ito had struggled along as an insurance salesman after the war until he made a hit in the stock market with borrowed cash. Soon he was soliciting contributions.

He poured much of it into stocks but also diverted some to politicians' pockets and spent others on plush houses and women, investigators said.

Bottom Dropped In Cottens

A year ago, the bottom dropped out of cotton textiles. Ito lost heavily. He scrambled for new money. It followed the same route.

Even at that, investigators say, Ito might have weathered the storm had it not been for Japan's poor farm crop last year, the worst in 16 years. Farmers, short on cash, began badgering Ito for their invested money. Down went Ito's interest to 2 per cent. Then down went Ito's company.

Figl Rejects Red Plan for Its Freedom

By John M. Hightower

BERLIN (AP)—Secretary of State John Foster Dulles declared today Russia refuses to get out of Austria because it would mean withdrawing her troops from Hungary and Romania.

He implied that he thought Moscow had reason to fear the consequences of such a move.

Dulles ripped into Soviet Foreign Minister V. M. Molotov for his proposal to grant Austrian independence only with a proviso that Soviet and other occupation troops remain on Austrian soil until Germany is unified, which now appears in the far distant future. The secretary took up the cudgels for Austria after Vienna's Foreign Minister Leopold Figl, appearing before the Berlin Big Four conference, formally rejected the Soviet plan.

Idea Unacceptable

To accept Russia's idea, Dulles said, would be to expose the United States before the world as "morally and politically bankrupt."

Backing up the Austrians, he ripped into Russia's program with the charge that it contained "poisonous proposals" for an "Austria without freedom." He expressed "earnest hope" that Molotov would withdraw his demands so that a treaty may be concluded immediately.

Dulles said a plausible explanation of the Molotov proposal is that the Soviet Union fears to withdraw forces from Austria which, under peace treaties made several years ago with Hungary and Romania, would also require withdrawal of supporting Red army units from those two countries.

Is It Decent?

"Is it, however, really decent that little Austria should have to continue to be an occupied state so that the Soviet Union will have a pretext for continuing to occupy also Hungary and Romania? So cynical an attitude will surely shock the conscience of the world."

Figl led off today's session of the Big Four on Austria with his rejection of the Moscow plan.

Western sources said it was hard to imagine anything more "brutal and cynical" than the Austrian treaty demands which Molotov has put before the parley here, including a demand that Big Four troops remain in Austria even after the conclusion of an independence treaty.

Study Korean Parley

Meanwhile, Molotov was believed to be in touch with Moscow and probably the Chinese Communist government at Peiping on the Western proposal for calling of a Korean peace conference April 15 at Geneva, Switzerland.

Under the Western plan, the United States, Russia, Britain and France would send invitations to the conference, but Red China

—See BIG FOUR—Page 4

Slap on Her Face Is Fatal to Bride, Husband Is Held

DARLINGTON, England (AP)—Ernest Hayman, 21, slapped his young wife's face in a lovers' spat two weeks after their marriage. She died.

Yesterday, Hayman was led in tears from a coroner's court to stand trial on a charge of manslaughter.

"It was our first quarrel," he said.

"I just slapped her face lightly. She didn't fall or cry out. I left the room then and when I came back she was dead."

A pathologist told the court Marina Hayman died of a broken neck through jerking her head back suddenly.

2 Hurt as Cars Run Off Roads

Parked Auto Sent Rolling Over Bank

Two persons were injured when the auto in which they were riding ran off a rural road and crashed into a tree about a quarter-mile north of Columbia, at 1:50 a. m. today.

Treated at Columbia Hospital were Edwin Derr, twenty-seven, Maytown, dislocated left shoulder and lacerated forehead, and Joseph E. Hank Jr., twenty, 274 W. Walnut St., Marietta, lacerated forehead.

Will Prosecute Driver

Pete Wein, twenty-five, 240 E. Market St., Marietta, driver of the car, was unhurt. State policeman Paul Mikos estimated damage at $500 and said Wein will be prosecuted before Justice of the Peace Glenn W. Kauffman on reckless driving charges.

Daniel W. Weaver, thirty-eight, Pequea R1, while driving south on the New Danville pike, one mile south of the city, dozed off at the wheel at 3:45 a. m. today, according to state police.

Total Damage $1,000

Weaver's car veered to the left and struck a parked car owned by Violet Benedict, Lancaster R6, the impact rolling the parked vehicle over an embankment.

Police estimated damage to the parked car at $800 and $200 to Weaver's auto. Weaver, who was unhurt, will be prosecuted for failure to drive to the right of the center of the highway, police said.

Boy, 10, Impaled on Iron Fence, Severs Artery

PUEBLO, Colo. (AP)—A 10-year-old boy who toppled from a wall and impaled himself on an iron picket fence was recovering early today from shock and loss of blood.

Jack Slate, only son of widowed Mrs. Myrlin Slate, managed to free himself and crawled to the home of a neighbor yesterday.

Hospital officials said the fifth grader was given blood transfusions which restored his strength. A jagged leg wound and severed artery were expected to heal.

Atomic Energy Message Listed

Ike Will Outline Its Peacetime Use

THOMASVILLE, Ga. (AP)—President Eisenhower will send Congress a special message next week on peacetime use of atomic energy by private industry in the United States and on sharing of certain atomic information with America's allies.

The President's plans were announced here today as he was spending the weekend bird hunting as the guest of Secretary of the Treasury Humphrey.

In 2 Main Sections

James C. Hagerty, presidential press secretary, told newsmen the special message to Congress will be in two main sections.

One, said Hagerty, will outline suggested legislation "to encourage peacetime use of atomic energy in this country by private enterprise."

The second section, he added, will deal with proposals Eisenhower has made in the past—in his Jan. 7 State of the Union message, for example—for changes in the law to permit exchange of tactical information about atomic weapons with America's allies.

Will Deal With Effects

Such information would deal with the effects of atomic weapons, and not in any way with how to produce the weapons.

Eisenhower has said he has no intention of asking that the law be amended to permit giving allies data on how to build the atomic bomb.

GIFTS FOR POSTMAN

OKLAHOMA CITY, (AP)—Postman Jack Eldridge hit a mailman's jackpot yesterday.

As he delivered his mail, he found a present in nearly every box. Neighbors learned Eldridge and his wife were expecting their first child and decided to surprise their friendly postman.

Mercury Hits 46 Below In Adirondacks Area

UTICA, N. Y. (AP)—They say the mercury hit 46 below zero early today in the Adirondacks north of Utica.

That was at Forestport. Residents of the nearby village of Ohio reported -44, and Old Forge -35.

Those were unofficial readings, but, man, it's mighty cold.

Temperatures worked upward today after 36 hours of sub-freezing weather in much of the state.

To Wed After Easter

Peter Lawford, Daughter Of Ex-U.S. Envoy Engaged

PALM BEACH, Fla. (AP)—An April wedding is planned by Miss Patricia Kennedy, daughter of former U.S. Ambassador Joseph P. Kennedy of Boston, and film actor Peter Lawford of Los Angeles.

Lawford

The engagement was announced here yesterday by Mr. and Mrs. Kennedy.

Miss Kennedy is 26. Lawford, 29, is the son of the late Lt. Gen. Sir Sidney Lawford and Lady Lawford of London.

The wedding is set for the week after Easter but no definite date has been arranged.

It will be the second British marriage for children of the wealthy Kennedy. His late daughter, Kathleen, was the wife of Britain's Lord Hartington.

Last summer, Patricia's brother, U.S. Senator John F. Kennedy (D-Mass), considered one of the country's most eligible bachelors, married Jacqueline Bouvier in a brilliant Newport, R.I., ceremony.

To U. S. In 1947

Lawford came to this country in 1947.

His late father served as a captain in the Boer War, commanded the Royal Fusiliers and was a general in World War I.

Today's New Era

44 HOUSES FOR SALE - SUBURB

8 ROOM frame home, 2 car garage. Old shade, on 3 acres. Phone 3-0857.

4 MILES north of city; 2 family home, large lot, garage and shop. Call 6077.

MILLERSVILLE. New 3 bedroom home. Immediate possession. Phone Millersville 8729.

OPEN FOR INSPECTION
SATURDAY & SUNDAY 2 TO 5 P. M.
STERLING PLACE IN BLOOMINGDALE

Lovely 1½-story brick home (nearly complete). Large living room with fireplace, 3 bedrooms, modern, efficient kitchen with Hotpoint dishwasher and range, ceramic tile bath with tile floor. All on 1 floor. Large storage space on 2nd floor. Hardwood floors throughout. Baseboard hot water oil heat. Large finished recreation room in basement. Attached garage with laundry. Large lot. This beauty built by Wm. M. Murray and son is a steal at $21,800.

MURRY & BOOK
Oregon Pike at Landis Valley
R. D. 5 Ph. Lanc. 2-0364 or 9901

LITITZ PIKE

Situated on a beautifully landscaped lot, having 10 trees, wildflower garden and flagstone terrace. This 2 story single residence has on the first floor, wall-to-wall carpet, center hall, living room with fireplace and bookshelves, dining room, modern kitchen. Second floor has 3 large bedrooms and tiled bath plus storage space. Automatic H. W. heat. Garage.

Chas. F. Bowman & Co.
39 W. Orange—Realtor—Ph. 3-3221

NEW HOME, Schaum's Corner, into Brownstown. Immediate possession. Bus transportation. Inspect after 4 P. M. and Saturdays. E. S. Wenger.

AS USUAL THE BEST!

700 BLOCK RESERVOIR ST.

2½-story, semi-detached brick residence with living room, dining room, tile kitchen, three large bedrooms, bath, large basement; good heating plant; front porch; front and rear lawn. This home is in A-1 condition. Don't miss it at $11,900!

800 BLOCK N. PLUM ST.

2½-story brick residence with living room, dining room, fully equipped kitchen, five bedrooms and bath, large closets; hot water heat; front porch. A beauty and only $10,200!

POPLAR ST.

Corner brick property—large storeroom, living room, dining room, kitchen, five bedrooms and bath. Priced low for quick sale. $8750.

700 BLOCK MARIETTA AVE.

2½-story brick residence with living room, dining room and kitchen. Second floor has two bedrooms and dressing room, beautiful new tile bath. Third floor has two large bedrooms and storage rooms; venetian blinds; front porch; hot water heat, oil burner; nice rear lawn. A-1 condition throughout. A real bargain at $9500.

Owen B. Caldwell
Open 8 A. M. to 9 P. M.
744 Columbia Ave. Call 2-2183

54 CLASSIFIED DISPLAY

44 HOUSES FOR SALE - SUBURB

Hamilton Park—$13,800

Large living room with fireplace dining room, modern kitchen and tiled bath, three nice bedrooms, storage attic, automatic heating, screened porch, sewer and water.

Myron-Bill Jones
Mrs. Richard A. Angle, Associate
44 North Lime Street Dial 6253

New Homes $12,500 up. Lester B. Herr & Sons, Builders, 2-0516.

Grandview Hgts.

Just listed—single stone and brick with large living room, dining room and kitchen. Two extra large bedrooms, tile bath. Hot water heat, aluminum storm windows, drapes, beautifully decorated. Priced for a quick sale at only $16,900.

New Holland Pike

The most for the money you'll ever see. Stone ranch homes with three bedrooms, tile bath and powder room. Knotty pine den, large living room, dining room and kitchen. Two-car garage, hot water heat, completely decorated. Let us show you at $21,500.

E. L. YACKLY CO.
207 E. King St. Dial 4-3744
Open 8:30 to 5:30
EVENINGS 7 to 9

Paradise — 2½ story with beautiful l. r., d. r., and modern kitchen and laundry on first floor; 2nd floor has 3 bedrooms and fine bath; 3rd floor has finished room; garage, well of water and cistern. Price under $10,000.

Approx. one acre with 4 bedroom residence; barn, etc. Immediate possession $8500.

ISAAC HERSHEY, Realtor
37 W. Main . . Strasburg . . 5041

ADAMSTOWN. Single 1½ story, 4 bedroom home. Hot water oil heat, basement garage. Opposite school. $11,000. Call Adamstown 4811.

MANHEIM TOWNSHIP—Off Oregon Pike, overlooking the beautiful Conestoga River:—4 room bungalow, all conveniences. Will finance responsible party with small down payment. Phone Leola 6-2068.

JUST LISTED
Roseville Road, East. A fine well built brick home with slate roof on large lot. 3 nice bedrooms, hot water oil heat. Fireplace, attached garage. This house immaculate and in perfect condition. Price under $20,000. For appointment to see Call
FRANK J. STOTT REALTOR
Phone 3-7867

PARADISE, substantial dwelling. H. W. oil heat. Macadam drive, garages. Immediate possession. $10,000. V. D. Kling Agency, Intercourse, Ph. Intercourse 8-3441 or 8-3467 or Lanc. 2-7492.

Ephrata Heights Better homes for less. Choice of type brick. Akron Cape Bod Style, R. Douple. Ph. Denver 7-7311 or Eph. 3-2958.

EPHRATA—Single brick, near center of town, all conv., 4 bedrooms, garage, $10,500. Single, modern 2 bedroom home, built 5 yrs. Owner leaving town. Can't be duplicated for $9700. Don't wait. Contact M. Yeager, Broker. Ph. Ephrata 3-2062 or L. E. Abraham, Ph. Ephrata 3-1289.

MILLERSVILLE
E. COTTAGE AVE.,
JUST OFF WABANK ROAD
RANCH TYPE HOME

3 bedrooms, tile bath, large living room, kitchen-dinette; oil burner, hot water heating, garage in basement. Lot 75'x234'.

CALL LANCASTER 2-9227

1022 JANET AVENUE
GRAND VIEW HEIGHTS
Living room, dining room, kitchen, 2 bedrooms and bath. To be fully decorated and landscaped. $17,500. With 2 additional bedrooms and bathroom on second floor. $19,300. CREAMER, Builder Ph. 2-7023

A REAL BARGAIN
2 years old, 2 bedroom, expandable second floor. Large living room, with large tile kitchen and bath. Full cement basement, oil heat, double hardwood floors, lots of room for garden, 75'x325'. 4 blocks from bus line in setting of beautiful farm country. 4 miles from center of Lancaster. Can't go any lower, $10,900. Phone Millersville 8660.

Florin. Frame, 6 rms., bath, 2 car garage. Good location. Owner will sacrifice.
JONES & ZINK, INC.
119 S. Market St., E-town. Ph. 64

54 CLASSIFIED DISPLAY

44 HOUSES FOR SALE - SUBURB

MARIETTA
Six rooms and bath — $4200
WM. T. KLINE & SON
Columbia Ph. 4-2176

NEW HOLLAND
Nicely decorated 6 room home, garage, enormous yard, old shade, many extras, only $8750.
WILKINSON
154 N. Prince Ph. 2-6320 or 3-7501

MILLERSVILLE SECTION—4 large rooms, expandable, second floor. Tiled bath and kitchen. Lot, 75'x 300'. Built 2 years. Owner wants quick sale. New price $10,900.
NEAR HOLTWOOD — good for sportsmen or Holtwood employee. Year around 5 room house, furnace, electric range, (no bath). 35 acres with good stream. $6250.
ELIZABETHTOWN—new house, 4 large rooms, expandable second floor. Available May 1. $11,500.
"C" KIENZY. Ph. 4-2071 or 2-3639

CENTERVILLE

large brick ranch home—breezeway. One-car garage. 3 acres of ground. Excellent condition.

MURRAY
PAUL G. & SON
39 N. Duke — Realtors — Call 5273

1225 ELM AVE.

Brick—2½ stories, seven large rooms, fireplace, tile bath, hot water oil heat.

HAMILTON ROAD

A really wonderful home containing all the refinements for gracious, modern living.

J. HERBERT FEHL
INC.
124 E. KING ST. CALL 2-4118
Holidays and Eves.
Phone 5680

NEARING COMPLETION
Several very attractive ranch type homes:

Manor Ridge	$12,250
Smoketown Road	$12,500
Media Heights	$16,000
Marietta Pike	$14,500—$16,000
Millersville	$14,500—$15,300

UNDER CONSTRUCTION
Wheatland Hills—West $16,000
Widmyer-Prangley Co.
204 Fulton Bldg. Phone 3-3854

NORTH OF LITITZ
Very nice bungalow with 5 rooms and tile bath, plus utility room. Oil hot water radiant heat, summer-winter hookup. Garage. Outdoor fireplace and picture windows. Excellent condition.
Samuel D. Stein Agency
REALTORS
122 E. King St. Phone 4-6861
Evenings 4-4431

45 MORTGAGE MONEY

Money Avaliable for Long Term Farm Loans at 4½% Interest
PAUL G. MURRAY & SON
39 N. Duke St. Call 5273

WANTED—$4000 first mortage on new home. Write Box 138, Lancaster Newspapers.

UNLIMITED amount of money available at 4½% for long or short term farm mortgages.
OWEN B. CALDWELL
744 Columbia Ave. Call 2-2183

46 REALTY MISCELLANEOUS

COLUMBIA Real Estate—John H. Kline, Columbia 4-8531.

REAL ESTATE & INSURANCE
J. H. Ruhl, Manheim. Ph. 5-2283.

FLORIDA $5.00
. . . starts you on the road to Florida land ownership. Write for details (send no money).
GARAPIC, KAUSEK & LORBACH
Winter Park, Florida

Real Estate & Insurance
E. D. Ober, 2-3441.

REAL ESTATE & INSURANCE
C. H. Shuffelbottom, Jr.

REAL ESTATE & INSURANCE
BUTTS-MECUM, Inc.
24 E. Orange St. Call 8129

REAL ESTATE & INSURANCE
HYMAN MISHKIN, 303 E. KING

G. B. Hetrick, 53 N. Duke St.
Real Estate & Insurance. 2-4353

47 REAL ESTATE WANTED

WILL TRADE BIG HOUSE FOR SMALL ONE. DOUGLAS WATT, REALTOR. Ph. 4-2659.

CONFIDENTIAL — COURTEOUS SALES SERVICE THAT BRINGS RESULTS
* Nothing to Sign
* Nothing to Pay for Advertising
* Spot Cash
GEO. W. BARD & SON
423 W. James Ph. 4-2607 Eve. 2-3390

6-ROOM house, urgently needed, in or near Lancaster or Gordonville. Phone Intercourse 8-3167.

54 CLASSIFIED DISPLAY

47 REAL ESTATE WANTED

START PACKING

Here today — gone tomorrow— List with Caldwell and that's what happens. We have buyers for all priced homes. Just start packing and we will take care of the rest.

OPEN
MONDAY thru SATURDAY
8 A. M. to 9 P. M.
Owen B. Caldwell
744 Columbia Ave. Call 2-2183

WANTED TO RENT—House in county, within 12 mile radius. Conveniences. Phone 3-8379.

3 BEDROOM house near school. Maximum rent $55. Phone 4-5205.

GIVE ME 30 days and I'll sell your home or no obligation.
EDGE 35 E. Grant St. Phone 4-2104

VETERAN, wife, baby need small house or apartment. Will do part time work for rent. Write Box 139, Lancaster Newspapers.

BUILDING LAND wanted—20 to 100 acres—$1000 per acre. Write Box 112 Lancaster Newspapers.

WANTED to rent 3 bedroom house. Have 3 small children. Vicinity, East Petersburg. Reasonable rent. 2-6194.

47A AUCTIONEERS

State-Wide Sales Service.
DIFFENBACH & BACHMAN
Ph. Lanc. 3-4464 or Leola 6-3394.

LANDVATER LLOYD L. Columbia 4-4976

SHAUB PARKE S. LAMPETER 3-0414
AT YOUR SERVICE ANYTIME!

48 PUBLIC SALES

PUBLIC SALE—2½ Story Stone Home, Fri., April 9th at 7:00 P. M. 226 Highlawn Ave., Elizabethtown. Living room with stone fire place, dining room, den & powder room, 4 bedrooms with bath, recreation room with fire place. Modern kitchen has dish washer, automatic disposal, 2-car stone garage. Can view after 4:00 P. M. any day. CAN OFFER FINANCING. IMMEDIATE POSSESSION. WILL SACRIFICE. Terms by
PAUL MARTIN.

GOCKLEY'S 36TH ANNUAL SPRING SALE SAT., APRIL 10, 1954, starting promptly at 12:00 o'clock at Fritztown, Berks County, Pa. Two pony teams, Livestock —Tractors and horse drawn farm machinery. Dairy and poultry equipment. 40 tons corn—300 bu. barley. New locust posts. Bring anything you have to sell. We sell on commission. Come in to park your car.
ELMER E. AND
JACOB H. GOCKLEY.

49 ROOMS FOR RENT

BROAD, 120 North—2 furnished bedrooms second floor. Gentleman. 2-7138.

BUCHANAN AVENUE, 946. Room with use of shower.

CHESTNUT, West, 515—Furnished bedroom, running water. Gentleman. $6. weekly.

COLUMBIA Avenue, 1598. Furnished bedroom. Gentleman preferred. Mrs. Ziegler. 2-8807.

CONCORD, 237 NORTH. Furnished room. Gentleman only.

DUKE, NORTH—Furnished bedroom. Gentleman only. Phone 2-8560.

EAST END—Room, front, second floor. Employed man and wife or middleaged lady. 9554.

ELM STREET, 251—Off West Chestnut. Furnished bedroom. Phone 2-7146.

FRANKLIN, 708 NORTH. Furnished room. Next to bath. Phone 9726.

HIGH, 428. Single front bedroom. Next bath. Phone 3-6637.

JAMES, 36 EAST—Pleasant large front room, twin bids. 2 employed gentlemen preferred. 3-3517.

JAMES, 418 WEST—Nicely furnished room, own television.

JAMES, East. Nicely furnished bedroom. Young lady. Phone 3-7488.

KING, EAST—Room. Double or single. Off street parking. References. Phone 3-2105.

LANCASTER AVENUE, 430 — Furnished housekeeping room, second floor. Noon to 6.

LIME, 43 SOUTH—Newly renovated bedroom. Business man. Reference. 2-7579.

MANOR, 416. Furnished bedrooms. Twin beds.

MULBERRY, 320 NORTH — Nice warm, furnished bedroom. Gentleman.

NEW, 234 East—furnished rooms for rent. Call 3-4904.

PRINCE, 144 NORTH—Furnished bedroom. Gentleman. 8630.

QUEEN, 203, South. Furnished room, running water. Employed person.

QUEEN, 133 NORTH — Furnished rooms. Quiet atmosphere. Employed gentlemen.

RUBY, 115—Pleasant second floor furnished bedroom. Employed gentleman. 2-6141.

RUBY, 110—Furnished bedroom. Phone 4-4481.

STATE, 735. Furnished room and half bath. Knotty pine. Lady. 4-5083.

54 CLASSIFIED DISPLAY

49 ROOMS FOR RENT

$6 PER WEEK
ST. GEORGE HOTEL

ST. JOSEPH ST., 651 furnished room, suitable for married couple or gentlemen. 2-4393 (5-7 P. M.)

VINE, 29 WEST—Nicely furnished double second floor front bedroom.

VINE, 31 WEST—Furnished room. Gentlemen.

48 N. WEST END:—Furnished Room, private bath. Phone 2-7033.

WALNUT, 136 EAST — Furnished rooms; gentlemen only. Phone 5905.

FURNISHED, 2 rooms; second floor, balcony; employed lady. Phone 2-8932.

LARGE furnished room next to bath. Ladies. 316 East Orange.

2 ROOMS, furnished. Light housekeeping. Gentleman. Phone 3-8602.

PLEASANT large bedroom, residential section, new home near R.C.A. Girl preferred. Reasonable. 2-2592.

54 CLASSIFIED DISPLAY

National Brand
Coffee
50c lb.
Fresh Roasted
with each purchase of 10 gals. of gasoline
HALLER'S
The Gas Pump Building
Prince & James Sts.

49 ROOMS FOR RENT

CENTRAL. One or two rooms, light housekeeping. Unfurnished. Phone 2-5796.

TWO FURNISHED light housekeeping rooms. Prefer mother and baby. 3-6415.

52 TYPEWRITERS

Large selection of new and reconditioned Typewriters. 202 W. King St. Ph. 6417.
H. G. BANCROFT
Also at 44 N. Prince St.

53 WANTED TO BUY

FULL SIZE pool table. Good condition. Phone 2-7301.

WE BUY used bicycles and tricycles in any condition. Phone 2-0257.

USED FURNITURE bought and sold. Anything sold on commission. F. M. Potts, 420 Susquehanna Ave. Phone 3-4401.

54 CLASSIFIED DISPLAY

53 WANTED TO BUY

HIGH PRICES FOR
CAST SCRAP IRON
BRUBAKER MFG. CO., INC.
LANDISVILLE Phone 6111

GOOD FURNITURE — ANTIQUES Pianos, dishes, utensils, marble tops. MERTZ, 217 N. Pine. Ph. 2-7635.

Highest Prices Paid
Furniture Stoves Mattresses, Refrigerators TV Pianos, etc. Porter, First & Dorwart. 2-2117.

CASH - for Old Gold & Silver BOWMAN'S Duke & Chestnut Sts

Furniture, antiques, dishes, utensils. TED MERTZ. PH. 4-3612.

DIAMONDS WATCHES, RIFLES SHOTGUNS, TOOLS, CAMERAS, MUSICAL INSTRUMENTS LUGGAGE, REVOLVERS E. Selfon Pawnshop 221 W King St

ANTIQUES and modern furniture —glassware and pianos wanted Before you sell call Jim 2-6843

54 CLASSIFIED DISPLAY

SAMPLE HOMES
Open for Inspection
SUNDAY 2 TO 6 P. M.
(WEEK DAYS BY APPOINTMENT)

LANDISVILLE, Stanley Ave.
3 Bedroom Ranch Type Home. $12,750. 10% down for Veterans; 20% down for Non-Veterans. Financing can be arranged.

CRESTDALE, Lincoln Highway, West
3 Bedroom Ranch Type Home. Completely equipped and landscaped.

E. R. NOLL
GENERAL CONTRACTOR
Lancaster R. 3 Ph. Landisville 6211

$23,500 BUYS THIS FACTORY BUILDING

Modern building completed in 1950 with approximately 80x110 feet of reinforced concrete flooring, free of all posts —on Route 222—3½ miles from Lancaster, situated in Landis Valley.

Can be used for light manufacturing—storage, warehouse, etc.

For appointment to inspect contact your broker or apply to . . .

HARRY R. BITZER
720 N. Prince St. — Phone 2-4128

54 CLASSIFIED DISPLAY | 54 CLASSIFIED DISPLAY

FOR SALE—HOLLOWAY BEACH, MD.
4-room Cottage (unfinished), screened porch, attached garage. Reasonable. Phone Lititz 6-6955 weekdays after 4 P. M. All day Saturday and Sunday.

MAIL ORDER

ORDER NOW
ALL-PURPOSE SHARPENER
Sharpens All Your Knives and Tools and Cuts Glass
Reg. Price $2.00
Only $1.00
Postpaid

MONEY BACK GUARANTEE

Send $1.00 check, M. O., or cash and your Combination Tool will be mailed postpaid.
REGAL SALES CO. P. O. Box 8238 Pittsburgh 17, Pa.

School Lane Hills

Beautiful California design home. Ideally situated at Southwest corner of Wilson Drive and Marietta Avenue.

This house has entrance foyer, large living room with fireplace and screened porch. Dining room, powder room, modernized kitchen and small pantry. Attractive spiral staircase to second floor landing—large master bedroom with tile bath and four additional bedrooms and two tiled baths. A rear staircase. Excellent oil fired vapor heating system. Laundry, incinerator, 2 car garage. Very attractive grounds. Beautiful plantings. Lot 240x175. Realistically priced at $48,500.

Please Call for Appointment To See It.

John B. Kendig, Jr.
502 W. KING ST.
PHONE 5123

WEATHER
(U. S. Weather Bureau)
Lower Susquehanna — (Cumberland, Lebanon, Franklin, Adams, York And Lancaster Counties): Mostly Cloudy, Some Rain Southeast Portion Early Saturday. Highest 64-70. Sunday Fair And Somewhat Warmer.

Intelligencer Journal.

The Leading Newspaper in the Garden Spot of America. Home Owned for Home Folks Since 1794

160th Year.—No. 285. Official United States Census Figures Lancaster Metropolitan Area Population 234,717 LANCASTER, PA., SATURDAY MORNING, MAY 15, 1954. CITY TWENTY PAGES. 30c PER WEEK—5c Per Copy

SECRECY LID CLAMPED ON HEARING

FRENCH WOUNDED ARE EVACUATED

FIRST GROUP BROUGHT OUT OF FORTRESS

450 Expected To Be Air-lifted From Captured Dien Bien Phu

HANOI, Indochina, May 14 (AP)—The first of seriously wounded French Union soldiers were evacuated from captured Dien Bien Phu tonight, the French Command announced.

The initial group of the 450 who are expected to be brought out by agreement with the Communist-led Vietminh arrived by plane at Hanoi just before 11 p.m. They included eight men—French paratroopers, Algerians and Foreign Legionnaires.

The French command said the helicopter which flew to Dien Bien Phu to bring out the first load was "blocked in" by stormy weather for hours after landing, delaying the evacuation operation.

FRESH DEMANDS

The delay had caused rumors that the Vietminh was placing fresh political demands as its price for carrying out the evacuation agreement reached at Dien Bien Phu yesterday when a French doctor headed a mission to the former French fortress 175 miles west of Hanoi.

The French spokesman had denied knowledge of any such demands being made by the Vietminh, however.

(French informants in Paris had reported that the Vietminh was demanding neutralization of the Dien Bien Phu area in such a way as to give it freedom for movement of troops in and out of the area. Such a right would facilitate the movement of battle-hardened regulars from Dien Bien Phu to attack Hanoi.)

SWITCH TO DAKOTA

The first helicopter load was ferried to Luang Prabang, the royal capital of Laos, and then transferred to a Dakota (C47) transport for the ride to Hanoi.

A French spokesman said the helicopter was forced to remain in Dien Bien Phu all day after

Turn To Page 12 For More Of INDOCHINA

FARM CORNER

"We Lead All The Rest"
By WILLIAM R. SCHULTZ

York 'Crosses' Win Coatesville Chicken Contest

A York County entry of White Cross-New Hampshire crosses placed first yesterday at Coatesville in southern regional judging of the 1954 Pennsylvania Chicken-of-Tomorrow contest.

The winning entry of 15 birds was raised over the 11½ week feeding period by Donald Keller of Dillsburg R3.

The top entries from Coatesville will go to Hollidaysburg this morning for the state finals. All 115 entries in the southeastern region will be sold starting at 10 a.m., Monday, at Producers' Cooperative Exchange in Coatesville.

Lancaster County's top entry placed fifth in the region. It was a pen of 15 White Rock cocker-

Turn To Page 16 For More Of FARM CORNER

Weather Calendar

COMPARATIVE TEMPERATURES

Station	High	Low
Water Works	63	41
Ephrata	64	38
Last Year (Ephrata)	81	61
Official High for Year May 2	86	
Official Low for Year Jan. 18	-1	
Character of Day	Clear	

WINDS
Direction ENE Avg. Velocity 11 mph

HUMIDITY
8 a.m. 90% 11 a.m. 65% 2 p.m. 58% 5 p.m. 58% 8 p.m. 59%
Average Humidity 66%

SUN
Rises 5:50 am. Sets 8:12 p.m.

MOON
Sets 4:30 a.m. Sunday
Full Moon, May 17

STARS
Morning—Mars
Evening—Venus, Jupiter, Saturn

NEARBY FORECASTS
(U.S. Weather Bureau)

Maryland, Delaware and Southern New Jersey — Cloudy, with occasional rain tonight, ending early Saturday. Highest Saturday 60-68. Sunday fair and warmer.

Eastern Pennsylvania — Mostly cloudy, some rain southeast portion early Saturday. Highest 64-70. Sunday fair and somewhat warmer.

Lower Potomac and Chesapeake Bay—Winds mostly northeast 10-20 mph northern half, 15-25 mph south half, diminishing Saturday. Occasional rain early Saturday. Fair visibility. Small craft warnings are displayed.

EXTENDED FORECAST
(U.S. Weather Bureau)

Extended forecast for period Saturday through Tuesday:

Eastern Pennsylvania, Southern New York and Mid-Atlantic States—Temperatures will average 3-4 degrees above normal. Rising temperatures during the first two or three days, continuing warm. Some rain likely in central sections early Saturday and showers likely about Wednesday. Total rainfall, ¼ to ⅓ inch.

They're Cleaning-Up, Painting-Up And Fixing-Up Everywhere In Lancaster This Week

Mayor Kendig C. Bare, third from left, accepts six new sidewalk trash receptacles yesterday as a gift from local service clubs. The clubs presented the receptacles as their part in Clean-Up Week. With the mayor, left to right, are W. M. Diehm, Kiwanis; Harold E. Martin, Optimists; Mayor Bare; Albert B. Wohlsen Jr., chairman of the Service Clubs Group; J. W. Clark, Lancaster American Business Club; Earl J. Nadeau, Lions; and J. F. Garber Jr., Rotary. (Intell Photo)

Seven members of the Order of DeMolay do their part for the Clean-Up Week observance by scrubbing the Court House steps last evening. The city Fire Department gave the boys an assist by lending them the fire hose. The boys are John Brubaker, David Martin, George Clair, Ronald Hess, Herschel Leapman, Donald Angevine, and Farrell Brody. (Intell Photo)

Wilson Raps Diehm Letter On Dague's Voting Record

Edward G. Wilson, unopposed at Tuesday's primary for the Democratic nomination for Congressman from the 9th District, last night lambasted a campaign letter sent out by State Sen. G. Graybill Diehm to Republican voters.

The Diehm letter, a copy of which Wilson said he received, said: "It is especially important that all Republicans indicate their support of the Eisenhower administration by voting for Congressman Paul B. Dague and giving him their endorsement."

Dague is seeking renomination for his fifth term on the Republican ticket.

LETTER 'FANTASTIC'

"This letter is utterly fantastic," Wilson told a meeting of Democratic workers at Smoketown.

"What Mr. Diehm seems to have forgotten is the fact that Mr. Dague has consistently voted against the program of the Eisenhower administration."

He added:

"If Mr. Diehm wishes, I, as the Democratic candidate for Congress, will be happy to supply the brilliant record of Mr. Dague in opposition to the Eisenhower team.

"Someone has his signals crossed."

ULCA EVANGELIST LAUDS ACTIVITY OF LAYMEN IN CHURCH

Rev. Clifton M. Weihe Explains Scope Of Lutheran Preaching Mission Here

The chief business of the church is evangelism, the Rev. Clifton M. Weihe, associate director of evangelism of the United Lutheran Church in America, said in an interview here yesterday.

REV. CLIFTON M. WEIHE

He added that the arousal of the laity in the churches in recent years has indicated a willingness on the laymen's part to get down to that business.

The Rev. Mr. Weihe is in Lancaster to serve in an advisory capacity for the Lutheran Preaching Mission which will be conducted by 41 churches in city and county tomorrow through Friday.

He pointed out that in recent years, laymen have become concerned about why almost half of America is unchurched and why, of the total population, something like only 20 per cent is in church or Sunday school on a given Sunday.

Laymen are wondering, too, why they are letting the pastors do almost all of the "ministry" in

Turn To Page 9 For More Of LUTHERANS

Bulletin

Ephrata Youth Killed In Auto Mishap On Rt. 222

A young Ephrata man died in Ephrata Community Hospital shortly after his automobile was involved in an accident on Route 222, six miles north of Lancaster, about half an hour earlier.

The victim was identified by state police as Ray W. Steely, about twenty-two, of 312 Duke St., Ephrata. He was apparently alone in the car at the time of the accident.

Scene of the mishap was a curve on Route 222 between the Conestoga Motor Inn and the Indian River Hatchery.

Police said the auto, traveling toward Ephrata, left the road on the westbound lane and apparently continued on the berm for a distance of about 200 yards before crossing a ditch and coming to rest in a field.

The driver was evidently thrown through the windshield, police said. He was conveyed to Ephrata in the hospital ambulance.

How's He Doing?

EDITOR'S NOTE—You were wrong, Mr. Weatherman—you were wrong. It was sunny, not cloudy—it didn't rain—and it was a wee bit warmer than you expected.

THE FORECAST
For Friday

Mostly cloudy and cool with light rain likely during the day and night. High 56-62.

THE FULFILLMENT
On Friday

Cooler during the early morning, but clear, sunny and pleasantly warm during the day. High of 64.

The bushes and grass around the Soldiers and Sailors Monument in Penn Square received its annual trimming last evening by these six members of the Lancaster Boys Club, contributing their time as part of the Clean-Up Week program. In background left to right are Jack Rathkey, Ronald Axe, and Atkie Caldwell, working on the bushes. Clipping grass in foreground are, left to right, James Bowman, Skip Skiles, and Ralph Klessinger. (Intell Photo)

Many Groups Join In Campaign To Make Lancaster Spic And Span

Lancaster received six new sidewalk trash receptacles as a gift yesterday as part of local service clubs' efforts in connection with Clean-Up, Paint-Up, Fix-Up Week which ends today.

The bright new gray cans are stenciled: "Help Keep Your City Clean." The six are the first of 10 such receptacles to arrive. They'll be placed in downtown locations, city officials said.

Representatives of the contributing clubs made the presentation at 4 p.m. to Mayor Kendig C. Bare, outside the Municipal Building.

Making the presentation were W. M. Diehm, of Kiwanis Club; Harold E. Martin, Optimists; Albert B. Wohlsen Jr., chairman of the Service Clubs Group; J. W. Clark, Lancaster American Business Club; Earl J. Nadeau, Lancaster Lions, and J. F. Garber Jr., Rotary.

BOUGHT BASKETS IN '53

This is the second year the service clubs have purchased containers for the city. Last year they bought wire trash baskets.

Last night, at 6:30 six members of the Lancaster Boys Club contributed their time to the Clean-up drive, by trimming the bushes and grass inside the Soldiers and Sailors Monument in Penn Square.

Under the supervision of Sherman Hill, club director, and Joseph Cassidy, program director.

Turn To Page 9 For More Of CLEANUP

Navy Airman In Crash Officially Declared Dead

The Navy Department has notified Mrs. Mary S. Martin, 530 Reynolds Ave., that her missing husband, Airman Lester L. Martin, twenty-three, has been officially declared dead.

L. L. Martin

The telegram extinguished any hope that he had survived a plane crash off the northern coast of Canada.

Martin was aboard a Navy plane that disappeared April 16 on a routine ice patrol from Thule, Greenland, to Ellesmere Island, off the northern coast of Canada. The wrecked plane was sighted April 27.

Martin, the son of Mr. and Mrs.

Turn To Page 16 For More Of SAILOR

CHESTER COUNTIAN ARRESTED IN CITY AS NUMBERS MAN

A Coatesville R1 man, reported to have handled $500 weekly in numbers plays, was arrested yesterday afternoon by city detectives.

He was identified as Harold G. Skinner, forty-one.

Skinner was arrested at 3:30 p.m. yesterday in a Seventh Ward hotel by Capt. of Detectives John Kirchner and Detective Paul Cogley. Detectives Al Farkas and S. K. Cliff kept his car under surveillance while he was taken into custody.

Capt. Kirchner said the man had $132 in cash and three slips of number plays, totaling $400, in his possession when arrested.

Detectives estimated that he took in about $500 a week as a "pick-up man." He said he was working out of West Chester and denied knowledge of other numbers writers in this area. Skinner commented that business was better on weekends because many persons get paid on Fridays.

Capt. Kirchner said police have been watching him for about two weeks.

POSTS $500 BAIL

He was charged with setting up and maintaining a lottery by Detective Farkas, and posted $500 bail for a hearing before Alder-

Turn To Page 9 For More Of NUMBERS

IT LOOKED LIKE ALL OF CAPITAL MIGHT TESTIFY

But McClellan Says Eisenhower Will Not Be Called To Hearing

By ARTHUR EDSON

WASHINGTON, May 14 (AP)—Just when it looked as if everyone in Washington would wind up as a witness before the Army-McCarthy hearings, Sen. McClellan today came up with some reassuring words.

"I'll not ask," McClellan said, "the President of the United States to come (and testify). No."

So Dwight D. Eisenhower appears to be out as a witness. But the way things now stand, he may be the only one.

Today three of the senators who are sitting as a seven-man jury in the case became witnesses. And there was talk of calling Sherman Adams, the presidential adviser,

Turn To Page 9 For More Of EDSON

ALUMINUM WORKERS WIN NLRB POLLING AT ALCOA FACTORY

The International Union of Aluminum Workers (AFL) won easily yesterday in a runoff election at the Aluminum Co. of America plant here to determine a union bargaining agent for hourly employes.

The Aluminum Workers outpolled the rival United Steel Workers of America (CIO) by a vote of 109 to 66. Two votes were voided. Results were announced by Leonard C. Gilbert, National Labor Relations Board representative from Philadelphia.

The runoff was ordered by the NLRB after an April 30 election in which the Steel Workers received 84 votes and the Aluminum Workers 83 votes. Sixteen votes were cast for no union in the first election.

DEMOCRATS IN PROBE IRATE, PROTEST ACT

Edict Concerns Famous Meeting Which Prepared Way For Challenge

WASHINGTON, May 14 (AP)—The Eisenhower administration today clamped a secrecy lid on a now-famous meeting which helped prepare the way for the Army's challenge to Sen. McCarthy (R-Wis).

The "don't talk" edict brought swift protests from Democrats on the McCarthy-Army Investigations subcommittee. They demanded that top federal officials—up to but not including President Eisenhower—be called if necessary to find out whether the Army's actions were masterminded at the highest level of government.

The meeting in question was held Jan. 21 and was attended by Sherman Adams, the President's top assistant; and Atty. Gen. Brownell.

SPONSORSHIP SOLD

NEW YORK, May 14 (AP) — The Dumont network announced today that its affiliate station WTVI in St. Louis, Mo., has sold sponsorship of the afternoon telecast of the Army-McCarthy hearings to the St. Louis Post-Dispatch.

This was the first sale of the telecast of the hearings to a commercial sponsor. The price was not disclosed.

The subcommittee yesterday relaxed its ban againist commercials on the program.

Dumont and the ABC networks have been televising the proceedings "live" from the hearing room in Washington.

Army Counselor John G. Adams testified Wednesday that Sherman Adams advised him at this meeting, held in Brownell's office, to keep a written record of the Army's troubles with McCarthy's office over Pvt. G. David Schine. Later publication of this record led to the present blazing row.

MORE DETAILS

Today Democrats on the subcommittee pressed for more details of the meeting, and down over

Turn To Page 9 For More Of McCARTHY

President Hits Unworthy Scene In U. S. Capital

WASHINGTON, May 14 (AP) — President Eisenhower declared tonight the heart of America is sound "even if at times our attention is diverted by unworthy scenes in our national capital."

The President's remark in an informal speech touched off a rousing ovation at an Armed Forces Day dinner at the Statler Hotel.

Eisenhower did not elaborate on his statement about "unworthy scenes in our national capital." But his remarks apparently were interpreted by many in the audience as an allusion to the row between Sen. McCarthy (R-Wis) and Secretary of the Army Stevens.

At the same dinner Deputy Sec-

Turn To Page 9 For More Of EISENHOWER

New Feature Monday

"Mark Trail" Latest Addition To Intell's Family Of Comics

A factual, constructive and phenominally authentic comic strip on outdoor life in general will begin in the Intelligencer Journal Monday with the Intelligencer Journal's presentation of Ed Dodd's "Mark Trail."

ED DODD

An ardent and enthusiastic conservationist, Dodd has incorporated in his cartoon strip all the do's and don'ts of the outdoors, while at the same time building up almost unprecedented readership through successful mastership of the art of suspense.

Dodd's "Mark Trail" will run daily in the Intell along with the other comics which have grown to be favorites throughout the years.

LIFETIME INTEREST

Ironically, Dodd has only turned to cartoon professionally in recent years, although his association with animals, nature and the outdoors in general has always been a part of his daily life.

A native of Georgia, he has traveled and camped all over the United States, Norway, and other parts of Europe, and visited

Turn To Page 12 For More Of MARK TRAIL

Do You Agree?

A reasonable amount of fleas is good for a dog; it keeps him from brooding over being a dog.

—Edward Noyes Westcott, 1846-1898, American banker and novelist.

LANCASTER NEW ERA

Lancaster Metropolitan Area Population Official United States Census Figures 234,717

78th Year—No. 23,900 | CITY EDITION | LANCASTER, PA., MONDAY, JUNE 14, 1954 | 26 PAGES | 30c PER WEEK—5c Per Copy

Local Weather

Fair and warm tonight. Tomorrow partly cloudy, hot and humid with thundershowers by afternoon or evening. Low tonight 62-66. High tomorrow 90-94.

Details on Page 3

City At Standstill For C. D. Drills

A smoke bomb was set off in Penn Square.

"Victims" are attended by stretcher crews.

City firemen use a resuscitator on "victim."

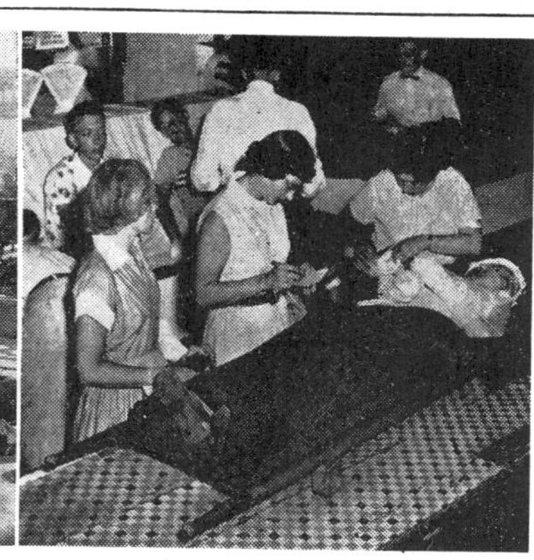

"Casualties" were treated in the Central market.

New Era Photos

Plane 'Crashes' In Penn Square During 'Raid'

Smoke 'Casualties' Add Realism; Few Violations Reported

Lancaster County stood still for 10 minutes this morning for the biggest full-scale air raid drill since the end of World War II.

The sirens wailed at 10 a.m. bringing all traffic and public activities to a stop in the city and most county towns. Pedestrians hustled to shelters.

The test, part of the international "Operations Alert," had two phases.

One was public participation. During the 10-minute period of the alert, the public was asked to stop all non-essential activities, and to take shelter. Few violations were reported.

2 'Incidents' Staged

The other phase was the staging of two "incidents" by the Lancaster County Civil Defense organization.

One of these was the theoretical crash of an enemy plane in Penn Square. The resulting "explosion and fire" resulted in several "casualties."

The other incident was an attempt to "sabotage" the Hamilton Watch Co. with an "atom bomb" smuggled in by truck.

On the whole, local CD officials were pleased with the test but noted that there still are rough spots that will be ironed out only through repeated practice and drills.

Smoke Adds Realism

Highlighting the Penn Square incident was the realism afforded by a smoke grenade set off in front of Watt and Shand's store, and also the efficiency with which CD emergency medical crews moved about treating the "injured."

CD officials generally were highly pleased with the test, both with the public participation and with the operations of the civil defense units.

Coordination Praised

Col. J. Hale Steinman, Lancaster County CD director, lauded the "excellent coordination of the medical and communication systems." He gave special praise to Dr. Edgar Meiser and his recently-formed emergency medical division.

Col. Steinman said he believes that a nation-wide test should be held about every three months for the benefit of both the public and CD personnel.

"Operation Alert" actually started long before 10 a. m. The CD headquarters at 28 E. Orange St. started activities about 8:30 a. m. The doors had been opened only a few minutes when the first calls came in from sector directors.

County Takes Part

Although the various county communities took part in the public participation phase of the test, they did not conduct individual local incidents as were held in the city.

Most of the county sectors, however, had their CD posts manned and reported that fact to local headquarters. Nineteen of the 21 sectors reported.

On the whole, the alert went off well in the county towns, although some difficulty was reported in hearing the "red" alert. By 9:30 a. m., reports had been received from Marietta, Lititz, Terre Hill, Manheim and several others.

Make Offers Of Aid

Although the county towns didn't hold incidents of their own, they did participate in the city's program with offers of aid. Some notified CD headquarters that they had doctors, nurses and ambulances available to help out in the city's "disaster."

The number of "dead" areas reported, sections where the sirens weren't heard, were fewer than in previous tests.

Complaints were received from Manheim Twp., the Fruitville Pike area, Linden, and Grandview Heights.

In the city, difficulty was reported in the Fountain Ave. and Hamilton Watch areas.

Minute Men On Job

A contingent of Minute Men took care of security provisions at head-

—See TEST—Page 10

Carr Says Army Talked of Schine Being 'Hostage'

Special Treatment Linked With Efforts To Halt Red Probe

WASHINGTON (AP) — Francis P. Carr testified today Army officials repeatedly linked talk of special Army treatment for Pvt. G. David Schine with efforts to stop Sen. McCarthy's investigation of Reds in the Army, then turned to speaking of Schine as a "hostage."

The chubby chief of staff for McCarthy's Investigations subcommittee named Secretary of the Army Stevens as having engaged in talk of preferential treatment for Schine.

But he said only Army Counselor John G. Adams, to his knowledge, spoke of Schine as a "hostage."

Adams, Stevens Disputed

Carr disputed much testimony given earlier in the McCarthy-Army hearings by Adams and by Stevens.

He said it was not true, as Adams charged, that Roy M. Cohn once threatened to "wreck the Army" and to see to it that Secretary Stevens was "through" if Schine were sent overseas.

Adams had testified that when he told Cohn Jan. 14 that Schine, a former subcommittee consultant, might face overseas duty, Cohn exploded with the threats.

Denies 'Wrecking' Statement

Carr, who said he was in the room at the time, swore that "Mr. Cohn did not make these statements."

"I don't recall him saying anything like that," Carr said.

He did recall, Carr said, that Cohn told Adams it seemed premature to be talking of Schine's going overseas since Schine had not completed his basic Army training.

No Threat At Ryan

Carr denied also that Cohn threatened he would "get" Maj. Gen. Cornelius E. Ryan, commander of Ft. Dix, N. J., for the "obscene way he had permitted" Schine to be treated while taking basic training at that post.

Carr, a rotund former FBI man, was called to the witness chair when the hearings subcommittee convened for its 33rd day. Sen. McCarthy had been the witness, with his cross-examination incomplete, when the hearings were recessed Friday.

'Catching Up On Sleep'

Chairman Mundt (R-SD) explained McCarthy was "catching up on his sleep" after a speech-making trip to the mid-west over the weekend.

McCarthy came in midway in the morning session of the hearings and took a seat and listened

—See HEARINGS—Page 10

Water Talks At Breaking Point

Townships Give Up Hope for Joint Authority and Consider Battle Over Rates

The long drawn out negotiations between the City Water Authority on the one hand and six suburban townships on the other hand appeared near the final breaking point today.

Official comment was lacking as both sides hesitated on pronouncing the final death knell to efforts for forming a joint water authority to finance the water improvement program.

Likened To Geneva

But privately spokesmen for both camps acknowledged "things are pretty well washed up." One spokesman likened the situation to the stalemated Geneva conference.

Specifically, the next step was to be a meeting of the township leaders to see if they wouldn't take another look at City Council's stand that it wants a free hand with extra water revenues under the expanded system.

Deadlocked In Profits

City Council has insisted it be permitted to spend water profits over and above expenses as it sees fit. The townships have been equally adamant that all such money be earmarked for water purposes only.

A township spokesman who asked not to be named said he doubted if any such meeting of township leaders will come about, that the townships are unable to give their blessing, as the city wants, to a leaseback authority under City Council's terms.

May Protest Increase

As a result of the situation, the possibility was held out that the townships will protest increased water rates when the city files its new schedule to amortize the water improvements program.

Some members of the authority, itself, were reported disappointed at City Council's insistence, as reported by Atty. William G. Johnstone, for a free hand with the excess water revenue.

Mercury in 90's 4th Day in Row

Hot Spell Due To Continue Tomorrow

Summery heat and humidity boiled up here again today with 90-degree temperatures for the fourth straight day, and the forecast said the heat spell will continue tomorrow.

It was "the good old summertime" in every way this weekend, as thousands jammed swim pools, public parks and every other outdoor recreation area. Yesterday's top temperature was 90.

With the mercury rising to 92 at 2 p.m. today, the Weather Bureau said tonight will be fair and warm, with a low between 62 and 66. Tomorrow is to be partly cloudy and not as humid, with thundershowers, and a high between 90 and 94.

Lancaster had thundershowers at 4 a. m. yesterday, but the rest of the day proved to be a scorcher. Considerable damage was caused by storms elsewhere in the state, in Wyoming County, Pocono Mountain areas reported numerous power failures. In Potter County, winds knocked down one house and moved another several inches off its foundation.

2 PILOTS KILLED

SEOUL (AP) — Two American pilots were killed yesterday when their F84 fighter-bombers collided about 10 miles southeast of Taegu. Their names were withheld.

'Bogus' Doctor's Trial Opens

State Agent Tells of Florin Man's Diagnosis

A state agent testified in Criminal Court here today that a "bogus" doctor diagnosed his ills correctly and then gave him medicine to cure them.

But he didn't take the medicine to see if it would work, testified Edward R. Williams, chief investigator for the bureau of professional licensing.

He was testifying in the case of E. Stanley Booth, fifty-one, who is known in the village of Florin, where he practiced, as "the doctor."

A small wiry man with a mustache, Booth followed proceedings calmly and with what seemed to be a professional manner. He is charged with practicing medicine without a state license.

'Store' Of Evidence

The floor in front of the jury of five women and seven men looked like a miniature drug store. All the evidence was piled there, including bottles of pills and other medicine, three cartons of medical books, instruments, and diplomas.

Williams, the first witness before Judge Schaeffer, testified he made an appointment and went to see Booth at his office on Market and Church Sts., Florin, last Nov. 16.

A woman dressed like a nurse took his blood pressure, which she said was alarmingly high, and checked his height and weight, testified the 69-year-old state agent. Then, Williams said, he went in to see Booth.

Booth, he said, pressed his forehead, and told him he had a sinus

—See COURT—Page 22

Pentagon Alarm System Fails In Air Raid Test

Ike Among Millions Taking Shelter In Nation-wide Exercise

By The Associated Press

Life skipped a beat today as millions of Americans and Canadians heeded wailing air raid sirens in the continent's first international civil defense exercise.

With grim, disciplined make-believe, young and old abruptly dropped their daily pursuits and, in city after city, sought shelter against the fury of mock atomic annihilation.

Early reports indicated that the public's brief participation, no more than 10 minutes in most cases, was successful.

But here and there a hitch developed. The alarm system didn't go off properly, so there was some confusion in the Pentagon, nerve center of America's military might, as to whether or not the test had started. Wardens passed the word.

President Eisenhower led the surge toward shelter. With the entire White House staff, he hurried to basement refuge areas.

54 Cities "Bombed"

The vast exercise assumed that widespread havoc was wrought by successful enemy bomb drops over 54 American and Canadian cities from Puerto Rico to Hawaii.

While the public's role was limited to taking shelter briefly, the exercise continued for hours and days for tens of thousands of civil defense corpsmen.

Officially, "Operation Alert" began 11 a.m. EDT. Federal civil defense authorities, however, left the public's time of participation up to local officials.

In Boston, New York and other Eastern cities, the sirens screamed at 10 a.m. several hours in advance of the presumed bomb drops.

For defense workers, millions perished in a flash of consuming fire, while hundreds of thousands of others lay maimed and in need of help.

New York City alone was presumed to be the target of three atomic weapons, one "Ground Zero" in the heart of midtown Manhattan, one in downtown Brooklyn and one in the Bronx. Each was supposed to be eight

—See CITIES—Page 10

AP Wirephoto

Eisenhower Goes to Air Raid Shelter

President Eisenhower makes his way to the White House air raid shelter in today's test, passing through a covered walk looking out on the rose garden. Flanking him are Wilton B. Persons, left, deputy assistant to the President and Sherman Adams, assistant to the President.

Attempt Made to Sneak A-Bomb Into Watch Plant

Found in Large Truck, Driver 'Arrested' in String of Incidents Showing Preparedness for Emergency

At 9:40 a. m. today a large van pulled up to the curb near the rear gate of the Hamilton Watch Co. on Wheatland Ave.

The driver got out, took the keys with him, lit a cigaret, and walked down the street.

At the order of Capt. William Schaeffer, of the plant guards, Charles Wagner, a guard, inspected the rear of the truck, found it contained a large wooden carton, covered by a tarpaulin. He lifted the box lid.

Runs to Guard Booth

"It's an A-bomb!" Wagner yelled to Capt. Schaeffer. Schaeffer ran to the guard booth and immediately put in a telephone call to local Civil Defense headquarters.

Wagner, having jumped out of the truck, started whistling at the driver, Robert Goodhart, who was sauntering down the street. He brought Goodhart back, and Karl Stammer, another plant guard, clapped him under arrest and held him in the guard house.

Adds Realistic Touch

That was the start of an incident which put a very realistic touch to Lancaster's part in the big Civil Defense test. The "A-bomb," which if it were real could have blown up the area for three miles around, set off a string of incidents designed to show how well this area is prepared for a genuine emergency.

Capt. Oscar Pennock, of Security, was sent by CD headquarters to the Hamilton plant. He was to have had another man with him, to question the truck driver and take him into custody, but there was a manpower shortage and he

—See HAMILTON—Page 10

425,000 In Pa. CD Air Alert

Smooth Functioning, Cooperation Reported

HARRISBURG (AP)— Pennsylvanians rushed for cover today as sirens sounded in the nation's greatest display of air raid preparedness since World War II.

Traffic everywhere ground to a halt as the "red alert" was sounded.

Civil defense headquarters in the state capitol was the focal center of activities. Employes there kept tabs on effectiveness of the mock atomic attack throughout the state. All other state workers were off because of the Flag Day holiday.

Excellent, Says Gerstell

Richard Gerstell, state civil defense director, described public participation throughout the Commonwealth as "excellent."

Gerstell and other Civil Defense officials at state headquarters in the state capitol building kept tabs on progress of the alert throughout the Commonwealth's 67 countries. Within an hour reports from 51 counties had been received.

Public participation as well as traffic control appears to have been excellent," Gerstell told a newsman.

'Courtesy Cars' Halted

In the capitol city, the only public transportation forced to halt was "courtesy cars" driven by employes of the Harrisburg Railways Co., whose bus drivers and maintenance workers are on strike.

The "red" alert followed by a half hour the "yellow" which signalled to the Commonwealth's 425,000 civil defense volunteers the approach of "enemy planes."

The alert was a "surprise" for no definite time other than "between 9 a. m. and 2 p. m." had been given out officially.

Officials Work In Raid Shelters

Government Aides Participate in Test

WASHINGTON (AP)—The government operated briefly from air raid shelters today as the nation's capital went through the motions of preparing to withstand an atomic attack.

President Eisenhower, with Mrs. Eisenhower and some 30 members of his staff, hurried to the White House underground shelter when the alert sounded, setting a pattern followed throughout the nation for a test alert involving 54 American and Canadian cities.

In his bomb shelter, the President watched a test of various emergency communications facilities, including telephone, teletype and radio. By teletype, the shelter was in touch with Western Union offices in Washington, Chicago, New York and Washington over facilities that could be used for any purpose.

Shelter Well Equipped

The shelter is equipped with working quarters and cots for sleeping, and is staffed by Secret Service men, Army personnel, doctors and nurses.

Although Congress continued its normal activities, executive agencies cooperated in the nation-wide civil defense test, and downtown traffic was halted.

At the Pentagon, nerve center of the nation's defenses, a partial failure of the alarm system left some of the Defense Department's 28,000 employes in doubt about when the drill started and stopped, but air raid wardens quickly passed the word and led workers to corridor shelter areas.

All the top military and civilian chiefs, headed by Secretary of efense Wilson, descended to the command post area in the subbasement of the Pentagon.

$4,000 Error Made in Tax Refund to Riveter

SANTA MONICA, Calif. (AP) — Mrs. Nettie G. Freeman, a $1.83 an hour riveter in an aircraft plant, is embarrassed with riches. She received a $4,181.42 check as a refund on her income tax. Mrs. Freeman figured the government owed her $148.80.

Mrs. Freeman doesn't intend to cash it, but the income tax office is open only during the hours she is at work.

Man and Wife In Hospital After Hammer Fight

A man and wife, both in their 60's were admitted to St. Joseph's Hospital this afternoon after attacking each other with a hammer.

Police said that Mrs. Daisy Clark, sixty-six, 251 W. Walnut St., called headquarters and said her husband had struck her on the head with a hammer and that she grabbed the hammer and hit him back.

When police reached the home they found the husband Walter Clark on the floor unconscious. Man and wife were taken to the hospital.

Solons Vote Hike In Butter Price

House Unit Wants To Up Party Support

WASHINGTON (AP) — The House Agriculture Committee today voted to raise the dairy support price from 75 to 80 per cent of parity between next Sept. 1 and April 1, 1955.

Agriculture Department sources said the effect would be to raise retail butter prices by about 3 cents a pound and cheese by 1½ to 2 cents.

Vote Is 22 To 6

By a 22 to 6 vote, the committee decided to write this mandatory 80 per cent price prop level for butter and other dairy products into the omnibus farm bill it will present to the House in a week or so.

The committee also approved a proposal by Rep. McIntire (R-Me) to broaden the criteria the secretary of agriculture must consider in arriving at the support level for two years beginning next April 1.

Parity is a price declared by law to be fair in relation to prices farmers must pay for products they buy.

62 Teams in Midget Baseball Tournament

Sixty-two teams, the largest field since 1949, will compete in The New Era's ninth annual Midget Baseball Tournament.

Thirty-three will participate in the Midget-Midget Division, which includes boys from seven to 12, while the Midget Division, 12 to 15, has a total of 29 entries.

Eight teams in the Midget-Midget Division represent the city, while 25 are from the county. In the Midget group, five are from the city and 24 from the county.

(Details on page 19.)

Challenged to Gun Fight

Duelist, 19, Waited 2 Days For Rival, 19, To Appear

ELGIN, Ill. (AP)—A 19-year-old boy waited in vain for two days for another youth to show up for a duel with .22 rifles was seized yesterday by a posse formed in the belief the duel was on.

The challenger, who South Elgin police chief Cliff Factly said took a few potshots at encircling officers, is William Frenchack. Factly said Frenchack gave up meekly when posse members closed in. He hadn't eaten or slept during his vigil.

Quarreled Over Girl

Police said Frenchack told of quarreling with Leroy Snow, 19, over two girls Thursday night and issuing a challenge for a duel with rifles at a gravel pit at South Elgin.

"You stand at one end and I'll stand at the other and only one will leave," Frenchack was quoted.

Frenchack went to the pit with rifle and ammunition Friday night.

Note Found On Car

Police got into the case when they found Frenchack's car near the gravel pit and read a note attached to the windshield advising Snow to fire three shots when he reached the pit and was ready to duel.

Snow? He told police he thought it was just a joke and went swimming instead.

Today's New Era

WEATHER
(U. S. Weather Bureau Forecast for Lancaster, Cumberland, York, Lebanon, Franklin and Adams Counties):
Fair And Warm Today. Moderate Tonight. Tomorrow Partly Cloudy And Continued Warm With Scattered Afternoon Thundershowers. High Today 90-95.

Intelligencer Journal.

The Leading Newspaper in the Garden Spot of America. Home Owned for Home Folks Since 1794

161st Year.—No. 29. Official United States Census Figures Lancaster Metropolitan Area Population 234,717 LANCASTER, PA., TUESDAY MORNING, JULY 20, 1954. CITY TWENTY-TWO PAGES. 30c PER WEEK—5c Per Copy

COHN REPORTED QUITTING M'CARTHY

Continued Heat Wilting County Farm Crops

Col. J. Hale Steinman Recipient Of Lancaster's Red Rose Award

City's Highest Honor Bestowed For Service As CD Head

Col. J. Hale Steinman was presented last night with the "Red Rose Award," the highest honor bestowed by the City of Lancaster, in recognition of his service as Lancaster County director of Civil Defense.

The award was presented by Mayor Kendig C. Bare during a surprise testimonial dinner attended by members of the staff of the county's Civil Defense organization at the Stevens House last night.

This was the seventh time the Red Rose Award has been made by the city. It was established in 1950 by Mayor Bare and is given "in grateful appreciation of outstanding service that has reflected credit upon and brought honor to the City of Lancaster."

TWICE HEADED CD

Co-publisher of Lancaster Newspapers, Inc., Colonel Steinman twice served as county director of Civil Defense. He organized what was then known as Civilian Defense for the county during World War II, heading that organization for more than two years.

When the Korean War again brought the need for another home front defense program, Colonel Steinman was again called on to head the county program and served as county director from January, 1951 until last July 1.

Mayor Bare, making the presentation to Colonel Steinman last night, said:

"I know that back in World War II Colonel Steinman was willing to undertake leadership of the Civilian Defense effort, which he handled very capably for two years until called to Washington on another assignment.

"In 1951 Colonel Steinman agreed to again undertake the assignment

Turn To Page 11 For More Of AWARD

Mayor Kendig C. Bare (left), presents Lancaster's highest honor, the "Red Rose Award" to Col. J. Hale Steinman (right) at a surprise testimonial dinner for the retiring Lancaster County director of Civil Defense. The dinner, held at the Stevens House last night, was given by members of the staff of the county's Civil Defense organization. From left to right are Mayor Bare, Col. F. M. Gavan, new county Civil Defense chief, Jack Anderson, state Civil Defense director for the eastern area, and Colonel Steinman. (Intell Photo)

MERCURY 95—SOAKING RAIN BIG NEED HERE

Thundershowers Tomorrow Seen Bringing Only Temporary Relief

Wilting heat again seared Lancaster County yesterday, shooting the mercury to 95 and striking a blow to struggling farm crops.

Across the nation the heat took the blame for the death of 248 persons and extensive damage to crops, cattle and poultry.

The temperature today is again expected to approach 95.

The county may be in for scattered thundershowers tomorrow, but they'll bring only momentary relief to city dwellers, and little aid, if any, to scorched farm crops.

Humidity here rose to an average 78 per cent, spelling out mugginess. The low yesterday was 66.

NEED SOAKING RAIN

But what's needed most — a long, soaking rain — is not foreseen. Snap showers don't send down enough rain to reach the roots of wilting corn, tobacco, or vegetables.

The Midwest has been hit even harder by the blowtorch weather. Crop, cattle and poultry losses mounted yesterday as the hot seige continued. In downstate Illinois, 9,000 dead chicks were counted in a three-day period, and in one county so many hogs had died that disposal of the carcasses became a problem.

The human death toll mounted by the hour. The heat wave was held responsible for 94 deaths in Missouri, 60 in Oklahoma, 40 in Kansas, 14 in Illinois and less than eight in each of 18 other states.

But Lancaster County farmers, although they are feeling the effects of the extended heat wave to write off any crops as lost to

Turn To Page 11 For More Of HEAT

Said Resigning Committee Due To Slanderous Probe

Brief, Lively Hearing Marks M'C Return To 'Red Hunt'

WASHINGTON, July 19 (AP)— Sen. McCarthy (R-Wis) went back to hunting Communists today, presiding at a brief but lively hearing during which:

1. Charles Wojchowski, who works at the Allis Chalmers plant in Boston, was ejected after making some references to "stool pigeons and informers."

2. Lawrence W. Parrish, an employe of the Bethlehem Steel Co. at Quincy Mass., was excused as a witness because the subpoena served on him was meant for another man with a similar name.

AMONG NINE

3. Two former undercover agents for the FBI ticked off the names of nine industrial workers, including Wojchowsky, who they said are Communists or had been members of the party in the past.

McCarthy repeated at the hearing that he has the names of 133 persons who are apparently Communists and who work in defense plants. He said he used the word "apparently" because some of them may be FBI agents.

It was the first time in four months that McCarthy has presided at a public session of his Senate Investigations subcommittee. He yielded the chair to Sen. Mundt (R-SD) during the McCarthy-Army hearings, in which he was involved as a principal.

UNDERCOVER MAN

Today's leadoff witness was James W. Glatis, who testified he worked his way into the inner circles of the Communist apparatus in the Boston area as an FBI agent. He said he took on the assignment because "I felt I would be doing a favor to my country" and because a Communist nephew had murdered his uncle in Greece during the civil war there.

After Glatis had referred briefly to Wojchowski being a fellow Red, McCarthy interrupted him to inquire if Wojchowski were present.

A short, stocky young man with a crew haircut arose and identified himself as Wojchowski. The senator asked him if he would like to be sworn as a witness so he could affirm or deny his Communist affiliations.

ASSERTS SELF

"I'd like to know what the charges are, who the accusers are," Wojchowski shouted. "I'd like to have time to prepare." He said a telegram practically convicting him had been sent to his employer and had just about cost him his job.

"I don't know who the stool pigeons and informers are," Wojchowski said.

McCarthy became incensed at this, saying: "You are not going to come here and call an FBI agent a stool pigeon!" He ordered Capitol police to remove Wojchowski from the hearing room, saying he would have a chance to come back later and testify. He is under subpoena.

Glatis also testified he knew Yates C. Holmes and Edward Garfield and had attended Communist party meetings with them. McCarthy said both men worked for Allis Chalmers and that they would appear before the subcommittee tomorrow.

WORKED WAY IN

The other undercover man was William Teto of Ashby, Mass. He testified that through "a carefully worked out plan of the FBI" he became a shop steward for the United Electrical Workers Union at the General Electric plant in Bos-

Turn To Page 11 For More Of HEARINGS

Usefulness Has Vanished, He Says; Senator Denies Getting Word

NEW YORK, July 19 (AP)— Roy Cohn, storm center of the Senate Permanent Investigations subcommittee, was reported today to have submitted his resignation as chief counsel.

Cohn, a New York lawyer, co-starred with Sen. Joseph R. McCarthy (R-Wis) in recent Washington hearings in which the Army accused them of bringing improper pressure in behalf of Army Pvt. G. David Schine, former subcommittee aide.

CAN'T BE REACHED

The Chicago Tribune and the New York Daily Mirror quoted Cohn as saying he had tendered his resignation. Cohn could not be reached for comment on the reports. His family here said he was out of town.

ROY COHN

The Tribune in a dispatch from Washington quoted Cohn as saying:

"I feel that my helpfulness to the subcommittee has been brought to the vanishing point. In any future investigation in which I appeared as chief counsel, all the slanders voiced against me would be repeated to minimize the evidence presented."

In Washington, McCarthy said:

"I have received no resignation. If one was sent, I hope it gets lost in the mails. I have urged that he not submit a resignation."

McCarthy said "several" staff members have offered to resign, but that "I have urged them not to" and that he expects them to stay on the job.

"RED VICTORY"

The Tribune quoted McCarthy as saying the departure of Cohn would be "one of the greatest victories ever scored by the Communist party of the United States."

The Tribune said that at a subcommittee meeting tomorrow Cohn faced possible ouster and that Senators Everett Dirksen (R-Ill) and Karl E. Mundt (R-SD) suggested a resignation would "ease the situation."

The New York Mirror said Cohn told it "three or four" other staff members will resign soon. The newspaper mentioned as possibilities Francis Carr, James N. Juliana, Donald Surine and Thomas Lavenia.

The Mirror said Cohn submitted his resignation during a weekend meeting with McCarthy, Mundt

Turn To Page 11 For More Of COHN

GOP CHIEFS NAME WM. H. WORRILOW TO HEAD FINANCES

Lebanon Steel Manufacturer Gets Campaign Post; Herbert Sorg Platform Chairman

William H. Worrilow Sr., Lebanon steel manufacturer, yesterday was appointed chairman of the Republican Finance Committee for the November election campaign.

The appointment was announced in Harrisburg by Miles Horst, state GOP chairman, who at the same time named Herbert L. Sorg, St. Marys, former speaker of the State House of Representatives, as chairman of the platform committee. The two appointments complete the party's pre-election organization.

Worrilow, president of the Lebanon Steel Foundry, was executive vice chairman of the Finance Committee in the 1950 and 1952 elections. He had been considered as one of half a dozen possible choices to succeed Philip T. Sharples, Philadelphia, who resigned shortly before the May primary.

An original Eisenhower delegate at the 1952 National Convention, Worrilow early this year had boomed Horst as a candidate for governor. Chief opposition to his selection to the Finance Committee post earlier had been on geographical location. Horst and Mrs. Sara Leffler, state vice chairman, are both residents of Lebanon County.

More recently it was felt that major Republican campaign contribu-

Turn To Page 11 For More Of GOP

43 Firms Already Lined Up For B-I-E Day Here In Fall

With 43 local industrial and business firms lined up for participation, next fall's Business-Industry-Education Day program sponsored by the Lancaster Chamber of Commerce has already set a record.

The date and plans for this year's program will be set on Thursday during a meeting at 4 p. m. in the auditorium of the city school administration building, 229 W Orange St.

A C of C spokesman, noting that the 43 industrial and business firms wh have indicated they will participate this year is a new high, pointed out that still others are expected to enter the program.

INSIGHTS INTO BUSINESS

Growing in popularity since it was started here in 1950, B-I-E Day is planned to give city and county teachers an insight into the workings of business and industry. It is estimated that some 700 teachers from city and county schools and colleges will participate this year.

During past years, and a similar precedure is expected to be followed this year, the teachers have been taken on tours through the various participating firms.

The idea for a program of this type was originated in Michigan in 1947 by Michigan State College. Lancaster's first program was started four years ago by the C of C and was the first conducted anywhere in Pennsylvania.

Here are the firms that have already reported that they will participate in the program:

PARTICIPANTS LISTED

Armstrong Cork Co., Bell Telephone Co., Brunswick Hotel, Burnham Corp., Business Press Inc., Conestoga National Bank, Conestoga Publishing Co., DeWalt Inc., J. C. Ehrlich Co., Farmers Bank and Trust Co., Food Fair Stores Inc., Gunzenhauser Bakery Inc.,

Turn To Page 11 For More Of FIRMS

WATER AUTHORITY ACTS TO STUDY OPERATIVE UNIT

4-Man Committee Named To Investigate Types Of Authorities

A four-man committee of members of the Lancaster Water Authority will make a thorough study of all aspects of its proposal on an operating authority for Lancaster's water facilities.

William G. Johnstone Jr., Authority solicitor, said the committee will include William E. Alexander, named Authority chairman last week; Albert S. Wohlsen, H. W. Prentis Jr. and himself.

This move is in line with an announcement by the Authority last week that it planned to discuss with City Council the possibility of organizing on an operating basis rather than as a lease-back authority.

As an operating authority, the seven-man group, named earlier this year by the city, would take over the city's water system, carry out the five and a half million dollar improvement and extension program and then, when the program is completed, continue to operate and maintain the water works.

MAY COMPROMISE

If a straight lease-back arrangement were organized, the Authority would only carry out the improvement and extension program and then turn the water works back to the city for operation and mainte-

Turn To Page 11 For More Of WATER

Climax Near At Geneva; Cease-Fire Optimism High

GENEVA, Tuesday, July 20 (AP)— The Geneva conference came to its climactic day today with indications that a cease-fire in the eight-year Indochina war would be signed before midnight.

A high Western source, not one of the optimists of this conference said the "best advice" was that French Premier Pierre Mendes-France would win his gamble and achieve an armistice by midnight — 6 p.m., EST—Tuesday, the deadline he had set for peace or his resignation.

'ARMISTICE SURE'

Pham Van Dong, foreign minister of the Communist-led Vietminh and once the stiffest of unbending Communist diplomats here, told correspondents an armistice was "absolutely sure."

The Moscow radio, in a broadcast, reported, "An agreement in principle has been reached on many of the documents containing main agreements for the restoration of peace."

Agreement had been reached, the radio said, on a temporary demarcation line for dividing Viet Nam, the holding of elections, and the withdrawal of foreign troops—three of the most troublesome points.

Western sources said France, Britain and the United States also were closer in agreement now than at any time since the conference started nearly three months ago.

AGREE TO PACT

For one thing, these sources said, the three Western Powers have agreed to form a Southeast Asia Treaty Organization to seal off that region from further Communist penetration.

Western informants said Britain,

Turn To Page 11 For More Of GENEVA

Mendes-France 'Peace' Deadline Expires Tonight

By HARVEY HUDSON

PARIS, July 19 (AP)—The contract between Premier Pierre Mendes-France and the French National Assembly runs out at midnight tomorrow.

Mendes-France promised to have a cease-fire for the Indochina war negotiated by that time or resign. At the same time, the deputies agreed to let Mendes-France work at Geneva without interruption or heckling from official debates.

DUE THURSDAY

The Premier will be back to report to the Assembly Thursday, win or lose at Geneva. He will tell

Turn To Page 11 For More Of MENDES-FRANCE

FLANDERS HOLDING OFF 'SHOWDOWN' VOTE ON M'CARTHY

Postpones Move For Senate Condemnation Of Probe Tactics To July 30

WASHINGTON, July 19 (AP)—Sen. Flanders (R-Vt) today postponed until July 30 his attempt to force a showdown Senate vote on his resolution to condemn the investigative tactics of Sen. McCarthy (R-Wis).

His decision not to introduce the censure motion tomorrow as planned, Flanders said, stemmed primarily from a desire that the vote "be as massive and bipartisan as possible." The proposal, he said, "represents an expression of conscience of the Senate."

In a statement, Flanders linked the postponement to three factors:

1. A request by Democratic Sen. McClellan, who is campaigning in Arkansas for re-election, that consideration be delayed until he can be present. Flanders said McClellan had suggested July 30 in a weekend conference with him here. The Arkansas primary will be held July 27.

2. To give other senators "an

Turn To Page 11 For More Of FLANDERS

FARM CORNER

"We Lead All The Rest"
By WILLIAM R. SCHULTZ

CARGILL TO TAKE SUPPORTED WHEAT TILL SEASON'S END

Announcement Ends Threats Of Storage Space Shortage In Pennsylvania

Threats of a shortage of storage space for Pennsylvania government loan wheat have been removed with an announcement that Cargill Inc. will accept price support wheat for the duration of the harvest season.

Landis G. Becker, chairman of the Lancaster County Agricultural Stabilization and Conservation Committee, said no limit has been placed on the amount of wheat to be accepted by Cargill for government storage.

The firm's facilities at Albany, N. Y., will be used to supplement Cargill's large storage tanks at Marietta, Becker explained.

Meanwhile, storage tanks operated by Nelson Weaver near Lititz and Quarryville were reported yesterday to have reach-

Turn To Page 18 For More Of FARM CORNER

25 ARE REGISTERED HERE OVER WEEKEND

Twenty-five residents of Lancaster County were qualified to vote in the fall elections over the weekend by registering or filing changes of address.

On Saturday, six Republicans, two Democrats and two independents enrolled at the Registration office at the courthouse. Seven others listed changes of address.

Yesterday, three Republicans and one Democrat registered and four removals were filed.

The Registration Office will be open today from 8:30 a. m. to 5 p. m.

STATE POLICE SAY:

"Safe speed is a speed determined by prevailing conditions—and only intelligent speed is safe speed.

OIL BURNER LIGHT CAUSES FIRE SCARE AT PRETZEL FIRM

The reflection from an oil burner at the Keystone Pretzel Bakery, 318 N. Concord St., caused a fire scare at 9:14 p. m. yesterday.

The burner is on the first floor of the bakery and someone passing by thought there was a fire inside, Battalion Chief Edward Koerkle said. Companies, one, four and truck B responded to a telephone call.

Firemen were also summoned to a home at 336 N. Franklin St., at 9:06 p. m. yesterday by an anonymous telephone call. They were unable to locate a blaze in the area, and residents at the address did not know who phoned firemen, they said.

Firemen extinguished a fire in the front seat of a car owned by Frank Brouch, 120 N. Queen Street, while it was parked in front of 519 Manor Street at 2:49 p. m. yesterday.

SUMMER ACTIVITIES GOOD CAMERA TARGETS

All sorts of summertime activities make excellent subject matter to enter in the Intelligencer Journal Snapshot Contest.

Don't forget, now that summer is here, to have your camera ready to snap those pictures. But remember, too, that the pictures you took last summer are also eligible for the contest this year. Any photo you've taken since July 1, 1953, can be entered.

But don't forget the rest of the seasons either. Corn shocks or burning leaves make good subject matter. Or the snow scenes you took last winter. All are good possibilities as money winners.

Send your pictures to:
Amateur Snapshot Contest Editor
Intelligencer Journal
8 West King Street
Lancaster, Pennsylvania.

PA. DRAFT QUOTA FOR SEPT, 1,555; HIGHEST SINCE JUNE, 1953

HARRISBURG, July 19 (AP)—State Selective Service Headquarters today announced a September draft quota of 1,555 for Pennsylvania, largest since June, 1953, when 2,244 men were called up.

The August call, announced some weeks ago, was 1,401.

Henry M. Gross, draft director, said all of the youths called by the September quota must be 20 years of age or older.

Weather Calendar

COMPARATIVE TEMPERATURES

Station	High	Low
Water Works	91	70
Ephrata	95	66
Last Year (Ephrata)	92	69
Official High for Year July 14		101
Official Low for Year Jan. 18		-1
Character of Day	Partly Cloudy	

WINDS
Direction NW Avg. Velocity 12 mph

HUMIDITY
8 a.m. 100% 11 a.m. 77% 2 p.m. 83% 5 p.m. 62% 8 p.m. 70%
Average Humidity 78%

SUN
Rises 5:51 a.m. Sets 8:29 p.m.

MOON
Rises 11:23 p.m. Wednesday
Last Quarter, July 22

STARS
Morning—Jupiter
Evening—Venus, Mars, Saturn

NEARBY FORECASTS
(U.S. Weather Bureau)

Eastern Pennsylvania—Fair today with high 84 to 88. Scattered showers likely tonight, ending early tomorrow and followed by mostly fair and warm tomorrow afternoon.

Maryland, Southern New Jersey and Delaware—Fair today with high 84 to 90. Chance of scattered showers tonight and tomorrow morning. Little change in temperature.

Lower Potomac and Chesapeake Bay—Winds mostly northerly or variable 10 to 15 miles per hour. Mostly fair today. Good visibility.

How's He Doing?

EDITOR'S NOTE—The weatherman tossed all possibilities into the pot to boil up yesterday's forecast—but many wrongs still do not make a right.

THE FORECAST
For Monday
Cloudy, warm and humid with scattered thundershowers. High 85-90.

THE FULFILLMENT
On Monday
Hot and humid, partly cloudy, traces of rain in early morning. High 95.

Auto Club Expects Many Guests At 50th Anniversary Picnic Thurs.

Many prominent out-of-town guests will attend the annual picnic of the Lancaster Automobile Club at Hershey Park on Thursday. The 1954 picnic, with a number of special events, is one of the features of the club's 50th anniversary being celebrated this year.

Russell E. Singer of Washington, D. C. executive vice president of the American Automobile Association, and several members of the national headquarters staff will represent the AAA.

Among state officials who have accepted an invitation are Otto F. Messner, secretary of revenue; E. L. Schmidt, secretary of highways, and Charles H. Buckius, chief engineer of the department; Col. C. M. Wilhelm, commissioner of the Pennsylvania State Police, and Ivan J. Stehman, chief of the Safety Department of the State Department of Public Instruction.

Senator G. Graybill Diehm and Assemblymen Norman Wood and Walter L. Bomberger are among the members of the Legislature who will attend.

The Pennsylvania Motor Federation, AAA, and a number of Pennsylvania's leading motor clubs will

Turn To Page 11 For More Of PICNIC

WEATHER
(U. S. Weather Bureau Forecast for Lancaster, Cumberland, York, Lebanon, Franklin and Adams Counties):
Some Cloudiness And Continued Hot Saturday And Sunday, With A Chance Of Late Afternoon Or Evening Thundershowers. High Saturday In Middle 90's.

Intelligencer Journal.

The Leading Newspaper in the Garden Spot of America. Home Owned for Home Folks Since 1794

161st Year.—No. 39. Official United States Census Figures Lancaster Metropolitan Area Population 234,717 LANCASTER, PA., SATURDAY MORNING, JULY 31, 1954. CITY EIGHTEEN PAGES. 30c PER WEEK—5c Per Copy

THE INTELL INDEX

E-Town College Plans Big Expansion Program

$200,000 FIRE GUTS CITY FACTORY

McCarthy Censure Battle Rages In Senate

500-STUDENT CAPACITY AIM OF CO. SCHOOL

10-Yr. Development Project Will Result In Number Of New Buildings

A 10-year development program, which will increase student capacity to 500, add a number of new buildings to the campus and result in alterations to some of the present structures, was announced yesterday by President A. C. Baugher of Elizabethtown.

Termed the largest expansion program ever undertaken by the college, owned and operated by the Church of the Brethren, its details will be more fully outlined this autumn.

CONVOCATION

Dr. Baugher said the plans, approved Thursday night by the 22-member board of trustee, will be enlarged upon during a Mid-Century Convocation to be held at Elizabethtown sometime prior to the Thanksgiving vacation period. The college will be host to all alumni and friends of the college during the convocation.

The Elizabethtown president, however, did outline generally the scope of the development program for the 10-year period.

Based on the anticipation of a need to make complete provisions for a student body of 500 men and women, additional residence halls will be constructed for both men and women students. Dining room

Turn To Page 4 For More Of E-TOWN

Appointed

Prof. K. Ezra Bucher, above, has been named director of the 10-year development program announced yesterday for Elizabethtown College.

E-TOWN COLLEGE BOARD CHAIRMAN RESIGNS POST

Dr. Rufus P. Bucher Cites Ill Health; A Trustee 40 Yrs.

The Rev. Dr. Rufus P. Bucher, Mechanic Grove, Quarryville RD, a member of the Board of Trustees of Elizabethtown College for 40 years and its chairman for 15 years, presented his resignation Thursday night at a meeting of the group.

In accepting the resignation, given because of ill health, the board elected Dr. Bucher as chairman emeritus, the first time such an honor has been bestowed on a retiring chairman. He will continue as a member of the board, Dr. A. C. Baugher, president of the college, said last night.

Dr. Bucher, a graduate of Eliz-

Turn To Page 4 For More Of BUCHER

FLANDERS IS ACCUSED AS TOOL OF REDS

Vermont Solon Battles For Censure Motion, Dirksen Makes Accusation

WASHINGTON, July 30 (AP)—The Senate erupted into a hot row tonight over a move to condemn Sen. McCarthy (R-Wis), with Sen. Flanders, (R-Vt) battling for censure and Sen. Dirksen (R-Ill) accusing Flanders of being an unknowing tool of Communists.

In an aura of electric tension, Flanders sparked the fight by formally presenting a resolution to put the Senate on record as condemning McCarthy's conduct as a senator and as chairman of the Red-hunting Senate investigations subcommittee.

Dirksen called Flanders an "honorable man" who could not have known "the Communist party got in bed with him."

SOLID PHALANX

He said the Communist party, the CIO, Americans for Democratic Action and an organization called the National Committee for an Effective Congress are marching in solid phalanx "crying for the blood of Joe McCarthy." All are arrayed, he said, against one "humble senator."

Maurice Rosenblatt, campaign director for the National Committee for an Effective Congress, quickly issued a statement saying Dirksen had thrown up a "smoke-screen."

"The only question before the Senate," Rosenblatt said, "is whether the taint of McCarthyism can be removed from our highest legislative body. His (Dirksen's) performance proves that the Flanders resolution is a must."

3 MAJOR CHARGES

Most of the Senate, and galleries crammed with onlookers, heard Flanders tick off three major charges against McCarthy:

He said the Wisconsin senator (1) shows "habitual contempt for people," (2) is responsible for action of former aides that compromise the honor of the nation, and (3) is in the same category as "Fifth Amendment Communists" because he has refused contemptuously to answer questions of a senate subcommittee about his integrity and financial dealings.

Then, for two and a half bitter hours, the Senate rang with angry debate.

Flanders presented his censure resolution—first of its kind in 25 years—declaring McCarthy's tactics tend to "bring the Senate into disrepute." And he told the Senate that McCarthy can no more be appeased than could Hitler or the

Turn To Page 4 For More Of McCARTHY

Flames Belch At Height Of Mid-City Fire

Flames and dense smoke pour from the upper floors of the Keiding Paper Products Co. building at Walnut and Shippen Streets last night at the height of th city's first general alarm blaze since the Overlook Bowling Alley disaster. The photo shows the east side and rear of the building where acrid smoke poured into a valley between high buildings frequently blotting the structure from view. (Intell Photo)

General Alarm As Flames Go Through Keiding Paper Co.

Explosion In Oven On 2nd Floor Of 4-Story Brick Building At 312 E. Walnut St., Believed Cause; No One Injured

A roaring fire, fed by tons of paper and belching flames 30 feet into the air at its height, ate through the Keiding Paper Products Co., 312 E. Walnut St., just east of Shippen Street, last night, inflicting upwards of $200,000 damage.

But city firemen, responding to their first general alarm blaze since the Overlook Bowling Alley disaster last year, succeeded in confining the hungry flames within the four-story brick building which was reduced to a hollow shell.

Fire Chief Harry E. Miller said last night the cause of the fire was not definitely known, but said it probably was traced to an oven, one of eight on the second floor of the building, in which paper products, mainly heavy paper flower pots, are made.

2 COMPANIES REMAIN

Engine companies Nos. 4 and 6 were still on the scene at 2:30 a. m. today but the blaze was said to be completely extinguished. Firemen, however, were remaining to wet down the ruins. It was expected they would be there for the greater part of the night.

All other apparatus returned to their houses about 1:45 a. m. today.

EXPLOSION IN OVEN

Chief Miller, and Oscar Campbell, 444 New Holland Ave., plant supervisor, said they learned from workmen, who narrowly escaped injury, that the fire began with a gasoline explosion in one of the ovens.

Campbell said last night damage to the loss of machinery and paper alone would amount to about $125,000. The cost of replacing the structure was estimated to be perhaps that much again, firemen said.

Campbell said the plant turned out about 6,000 paper mache flower pots daily. The home office is in Milwaukee, Wisc., and the building here is leased from Samuel Kline, Lancaster.

Origin of the fire was traced

Turn To Page 4 For More Of FIRE

WATER SITUATION WORSENS HERE AS DROUGHT REMAINS

Heat Wave Continues, Mercury Hits 99, No Relief In Sight

Lancaster County is faced today with worsening water shortages after the current heat wave again blistered the county yesterday, sending the mercury to 99, a new high for the 12-day swelter session.

Arid conditions, brought about by what apparently will be the driest July in at least 55 years, forced authorities to issue stiff warnings about rapidly disappearing water supplies. Meanwhile, Lancas-

Turn To Page 4 For More Of WEATHER

Bulletins

U. S. AIRLINER SAID DOWN IN NORTH SEA

ROTTERDAM, Netherlands Saturday, July 31 (AP)—Dirkswagers Shipping Agency today reported an American airliner is believed to have ditched in the North Sea with 72 persons aboard.

The agency distributed this message monitored from Scheveningen Radio:

"An American aircraft with four engines, a DC4 with 72 occupants, probably ditched into the sea on a line with Amsterdam and Dundee. Left Amsterdam at 11:08 p.m. GMT July 30 (6:08 p.m. EST)."

The broadcast said last radio contact with the plane was at 12:37 a.m. It asked all ships in the vicinity to keep a sharp lookout.

U. S. Air Force headquarters in London said it had received no word of any such plane missing.

SHIPS COLLIDE

POINTE AU PERE, Que., July 30 (AP)—The U. S. Navy cruiser Pittsburgh collided with the British freighter Slaney in the fog-shrouded St. Lawrence River tonight. First reports said two merchant seamen were injured.

PILOTS STRIKE

CHICAGO, July 30 (AP)—Union pilots struck against American Airlines at midnight tonight EST, the AFL Air Line Pilots Assn. said.

SEVEN REPUBLICANS REGISTER TO VOTE

Registrations nearly equalled removals yesterday at the Registration Office in the courthouse.

Seven Republicans enrolled on the voters list to become eligible to vote in the Nov. 2 election and eight other voters filed changes of address.

The Registration Office will be open today from 8:30 a. m. until noon.

"We Lead All The Rest"

FARM CORNER

By WILLIAM R. SCHULTZ

Few Tomatoes Available For Sale To Canners

Receiving stations for canning tomatoes will open Tuesday in Lancaster County under the cloud of what seems certain to be the lowest-yielding crop in the industry's history.

Canning company fieldman last night were pessimistic about 1954 prospects and reminded that even one or two inches of rain now would make little difference in the August crop. August is normally the month of heaviest pickings.

Tomato root systems have been driven down so deep in search of moisture, they explained, that nothing less than a sustained, soaking rain will benefit the crop.

Both the J. H. Heinz Co. and Campbell Soups Co. will open their receiving stations two days next week, and then move to an every

Turn To Page 4 For More Of FARM CORNER

COUNTY BOY, 6, IS POSSIBLE POLIO CASE

A six-year-old Lancaster R7, boy was admitted to Lancaster General Hospital yesterday as a possible polio patient.

If his ilness is diagnosed as polio, it will be the eighth case in Lancaster County this year.

Two other patients in the polio unit were reported in satisfactory condition last night. They are Ruth Miller, four, daughter of Mr. and Mrs. Oliver O. Miller, Sheridan R1, and Sue Jean Stoner, 10, San Carlos, Calif., who became ill while visiting her paternal grandmother, Mrs. Sue Stoner, 46 W. Frederick St.

U. S. Agrees To Build ROK Forces To Meet Red Threat

WASHINGTON, July 30 (AP)—The United States has agreed to build up South Korean defense forces to meet the threat of Communist expansion in North Korea, it was reported tonight.

While a joint statement by President Eisenhower and President Syngman Rhee issued at the White House made no mention of this, informed sources said the South Korean buildup would include jets, warships and a reserve Army force.

In a formal statement, Eisenhower and Rhee affirmed their determination to work together in close cooperation "to attain our common objectives" regarding Korea.

FRANK PROPOSAL

But there was no evidence Rhee had been able to achieve American backing for his frank proposal to launch a "counter attack" eventually against Communist China, whose armies helped consolidate Red rule in North Korea.

The details of the U. S. agreement to build South Korean forces came from a person who declined use of his name.

This source said no exact limit had yet been set on the size of the ground reserves which involves the rotation of seasoned troops into a militia while fresh soldiers are brought up for training.

The military buildup also will

Turn To Page 4 For More Of RHEE

MAN OVERCOME BY HEAT FALLS IN BRUSH FIRE

A seventy-year-old Lancaster R1 man was injured yesterday when he fell into a fire while burning brush off a field at River Drive and Valley Road, in Lancaster Twp., west of the city.

Enos M. Witmer, was admitted to St. Joseph's Hospital suffering from first and second degree burns of the arms and face. His condition was reported as satisfactory late last night.

Witmer, an employe of the School Lane Hills Co., Inc., was burning brush on their property about 5 p.m. when he collapsed. He later said it was from the heat. He said he "couldn't seem

Turn To Page 4 For More Of MAN

Dr. Hall Wires Acceptance Of Post As F & M President

Dr. William Webster Hall yesterday confirmed his selection as the next president of Franklin and Marshall College as first revealed by the Intelligencer Journal yesterday morning.

In a telegram yesterday to the committee named to select a new president, Dr. Hall stated he will accept the presidency. He now is president of Westminster College, Fulton, Mo.

His election to the post by the board of trustees appears almost a certainty as his is the only name which will be presented to the meeting Monday at 11 a. m. His selection must be made formally at that time.

MAY TAKE OVER NOV. 1

He will assume his duties here starting Nov. 1, it was reported.

Dr. Hall, who is fifty-one today, succeeds Dr. Theodore A. Distler, former F & M president, who resigned the position July 1 to become executive secretary of the American Association of Colleges with offices in Washington.

Dr. Hall was in Lancaster Wednesday for an interview and left with the promise he would make known his decision on the presidency before Monday.

It was following his interview that the Intell learned he had been offered the post.

Since Dr. Distler's resignation, the college has been run by an interim committee.

Dr. Hall has been president of

Turn To Page 4 For More Of F AND M

PARKED CAR STRUCK, DAMAGE IS $300

The parked auto of Robert Tilberg, 217 W. James St., was accidentally hit yesterday by one driven by George Krause, 466 S. Christian St., while Tilberg was watching a baseball game at Stumpf Field on the Fruitville Pike, Chief of Police John Kauffman, Manheim Twp. said.

Krause was driving north of the pike when he was crowded to the edge of the road opposite the baseball field by an unknown southbound auto, Chief Kauffman said, and struck Tilberg's waiting car. He was uninjured.

Approximately damage to both cars was about $300.

Boardwalk Burns At Steel Pier; Wilkes-Barre Has Costly Fire

ATLANTIC CITY, N. J., July 30 (AP)—Fire raced through a 200-foot section of the Atlantic City boardwalk tonight and was stopped as it nudged its way along the front of the famed half-mile-long Steel Pier.

Four stores fronting on the boardwalk were damaged by flames, water and smoke.

A huge General Motors exhibit at the entrace to the Steel Pier was scorched by the flames which broke out under the boardwalk at about 5:45 p.m.

SPREAD QUICKLY

The general alarm blaze spread quickly to a nearby Planter's Peanut store, where it fed on peanut shells and oils and continued a fiery march onto the pier.

All local fire apparatus was rushed to the scene as thousands

Turn To Page 4 For More Of SHORE

WILKES-BARRE, Pa., July 30 (AP)—A general alarm fire raged through a large lumber yard tonight causing an estimated million dollars damage before fire officials said they were confident of containing the blaze.

Fire Chief Ambrose Soricks who estimated the damage said his men had sufficiently wet down the area surrounding the Goff lumber company yard to virtually assure complete control of the blaze.

He said there was no longer any danger to gasoline storage tanks of the Atlantic Refining Company nor to freight yards adjoining the yard at South Street and Pennsylvania Avenue in the south side of Wilkes-Barre.

The flames gutted the main building of the lumber company

Turn To Page 4 For More Of WILKES-BARRE

3RD PERIOD OF INTELL PHOTO CONTEST ENDS AT MIDNIGHT TODAY

The third period of the Intelligencer Journal Snapshot Contest ends at midnight tonight, but don't put your camera away. The contest still has a long way to go—remember, there are still two more periods of three weeks each in which you may enter your favorite snapshot and possibly win an award. The fourth period officially opens tomorrow, August 1.

With hundreds of entries to scan, the judges will be busy for some time deciding which are the winning photographs. Names of the winners for the third period will be announced in the Intelligencer Journal of Monday, August 9.

There are many important things to remember when you enter a photo in the contest. If you fail to do some of them, there's a chance you may lose out on some of the prize money offered by the Intelligencer Journal. For a complete list of contest rules, see Page 9 of today's Intelligencer Journal.

And send your photos for the fourth period to:

Amateur Snapshot Contest Editor,
Intelligencer Journal,
8 West King Street,
Lancaster, Pennsylvania.

Weather Calendar

COMPARATIVE TEMPERATURES

Station	High	Low
Water Works	97	55
Ephrata	99	65
Last Year (Ephrata)	90	71
Official High for Year, July 14	101	
Official Low for Year, Jan. 18	-1	

Character of Day—Clear

WINDS

Direction—W Avg. Velocity—10 mph

HUMIDITY

8 a.m. 87% 11 a.m. 59% 2 p.m. 47%
5 p.m. 37% 8 p.m. 49%
Average Humidity 56%

SUN

Rises—6 a.m. Sets—8:20 p.m.

MOON

Sets 9:30 p.m. Sunday
First Quarter August 6

STARS

Morning—Mercury, Jupiter
Evening—Venus, Mars, Saturn

NEARBY FORECASTS
(U. S. Weather Bureau)

Eastern Pennsylvania—Some cloudiness and continued hot Saturday and Sunday, with a chance of late afternoon or evening thundershowers. High Saturday in middle 90's.

Southern New Jersey and Delaware—Saturday mostly sunny and continued hot, with chance of late afternoon or evening thundershowers. Highest 92-96 degrees. Sunday some cloudiness and continued warm with chance of showers by night.

Maryland—Mostly fair and hot, with chance of late afternoon or evening thundershowers Saturday and Sunday. High Saturday 95-100.

Lower Potomac and Chesapeake Bay—Southerly winds 10 to 15 miles per hour Saturday and Sunday. Briefly higher and possible late afternoon or evening thundershowers.

EXTENDED FORECAST

Extended forecast for period Saturday through Wednesday: Eastern Pennsylvania, Eastern New York and Mid-Atlantic States: Temperatures will average near normal and a few degrees above normal south portion. Warmer over weekend, followed by cooler Monday or Tuesday. Showers Monday and in north portion Sunday, will total ¼ to ½ inch.

STATE POLICE SAY:

Traffic laws will protect you—if you respect them. But two lives can be wrecked by disregard of a traffic law back of the wheel, or in the car ahead. Know and obey your traffic laws. Save a life — and you'll never regret it! Take a life—and you'll never forget it!

How's He Doing?

EDITOR'S NOTE — The weatherman, without saying so, actually forecast a drop in temperatures for yesterday. But instead the mercury soared to the highest mark of the current heat wave, and, of course, there was still no rain.

THE FORECAST
For Friday

Mostly cloudy and hot with scattered thundershowers. High 88-94.

THE FULFILLMENT

Partly cloudy and hotter with a high afternoon temperature of 99.

Do You Agree?

More than one cigar at a time is excessive smoking.

—Mark Twain, 1835-1910, pen name of Samuel Langhorne Clemens, American humorous writer and wit.

LANCASTER NEW ERA

Lancaster Metropolitan Area Population Official United States Census Figures 234,717

78th Year—No. 23,949 | CITY EDITION | LANCASTER, PA., WEDNESDAY, AUGUST 11, 1954 | 24 PAGES | 30c PER WEEK—5c Per Copy

Local Weather

U.S. Weather Bureau Forecast

Fair and cool tonight. Tomorrow partly cloudy with moderate temperature. Low tonight 56-60. High tomorrow 78-82.

Details on Page 3

Ike Opposes Breaking With Russia

4 Houses Must Be Moved for Manheim Pike

2 Located South of Manheim, 2 at North End of Boro

Relocation of Manheim Pike (Route 72) south of Manheim will necessitate moving or demolition of properties owned by R. W. Kreider and Robert R. Leese, it was learned today.

These two are in addition to two other houses, at the north end of the borough, which will have to make way for the road.

Kreider's property is an old double frame dwelling, now vacant, at 300 S. Main St., on the Eby St. intersection. A corner of the house is on the right-of-way, and Kreider said he stopped renting it out when he was told by the State Highway Department it was on the path of the new road.

Middle Of Roadbed

Leese's home is located south of Kauffman's Park, on the road between Route 72 and the Fruitville Pike. It is a one-story frame dwelling of modern construction, and is reported to be in the middle of the new roadbed.

While plans had not jelled completely today, there were indications that Kreider would raze his property, while the Leese home would be moved to a new location.

Preliminary work on construction was being done by workmen of Lee B. Marks, Lebanon R3, who has the contract for the work between Mechanicsville and the north end of Manheim.

$612,018 Total Value Of Job

Total value of all work currently being done on improving Route 72 is $612,018, nearly two-thirds of a million. Marks' contract is for $385,057. The other Route 72 project is for improvement between the north city by-pass and a point north of East Petersburg. This contract, for $226,961, was awarded to J. D. Eckman, Inc., Atglen, which has been at work for over a month.

2 Others To Be Moved

At the north end of the borough, two properties also will have to be demolished or moved. One is the property of Peter H. Snavely, garageman, at 191 N. Main St., and the other is owned by Mrs. Dorothy M. Way, at 204 N. Main St.

Snavely was said to have sold his property for use by a business concern, and to be considering moving across the street, but declined to comment on this today. The schedule was said to call for vacation of the property by Sept. 1.

Mrs. Way said her plans were not definite as yet. There is enough land at the rear of her home so that it could be moved back, she said.

Boy, 4, Hit by Car On North Market St.

Michael Fisher, four, 47 W. James St., suffered brush burns of both legs and a minor cut on the right ear when he darted into the path of an auto on N. Market St., between Frederick and James Sts., at 10:30 a. m. today.

He was treated at the General Hospital.

Mervin J. Umble, eighteen, Gap, driver of the car, said he had pulled from the Acme store parking lot and was headed south on Market St. when the accident occurred.

FIGHTERS WEIGH IN

NEW YORK (AP)—Archie Moore, world light heavyweight boxing champion, weighed 173 pounds today while Harold Johnson of Philadelphia, the contender, registered 172 1-2 at the weigh-in for their 15-round title fight tonight in Madison Square Garden.

Had Drug Since 1946

Kansas Farmer, Hit by Drought, Tries to Sell Opium

KANSAS CITY (AP)— U. S. narcotics agents said a one-armed Kansas farmer told them he tried to sell opium because the drought ruined his 160-acre pasture.

Officers who arrested Lawrence H. Bowman, 41, said they found a pound of opium worth $60,000 in his possession. Bowman, of Burlington, Kan., was being held in jail today in default of $2,500 bond. The agents said Bowman's alleged accomplice, Elwyn Earl Slane, 34, a printer, was arrested in Burlington with 30 grains of opium in his possession.

The agents quoted Bowman as telling this story:

In 1946 he smuggled opium into the United States from Japan, where he was stationed as a Marine. He kept the drug at home. He lost his right arm below the elbow in a threshing machine accident three years ago.

This summer his 80 head of Hereford cattle ran out of pasture and he had no money to buy feed, so he decided to sell the opium. Guided by information from Slane, the farmer came to Kansas City and tired to sell two ounces of opium to a man, who turned out to be a federal undercover agent.

Macks Consider Two Bids for A's

Private Parleys Held On Purchase Offers

PHILADELPHIA (AP)— Top brass of the Philadelphia Athletics huddled in secret today over at least two proposals to purchase the American League baseball club.

First off, they shifted the meeting site from the normal location in Connie Mack's tower office at Connie Mack Stadium to the downtown suite of a lawyer.

After an hour there — during which time the office staff would not even acknowledge an A's meeting was in progress — Connie, his son Earle and two attorneys emerged from the office.

Declined To Talk

They strode down the corridor, declining to talk to reporters. Outside, Connie got in his car and was driven away; Earle and the lawyers headed to another office.

The attorney in whose office the meeting was held, J. Channing Ellery, emerged to announce there had been a "temporary adjournment." He wouldn't say what was discussed, nor who was there.

Roy Mack, the elder of Connie's two sons who own the club with him, didn't come out of the office. Reporters waiting at the door guessed that he and two other directors of the club were holding another confab.

Macks Get 2 Offers

One of the two offers before the Mack family is from Chicago businessman Arnold Johnson who wants to take the club to Kansas City. The other is from a local

—See A's—Page 20

Ike May Vote in 1955 In Adams County, Pa.

WASHINGTON (AP) —Rep. Stauffer (R-Pa) said today President Eisenhower may be a registered voter in Adams County, Pa., next year.

Stauffer, whose congressional district includes Adams, Cumberland and York counties, said he was told by the President during a White House visit yesterday that Eisenhower hopes to have his Gettysburg farm home ready for occupancy soon and may be voting there next year. Gettysburg is in Adams county.

The President's voting residence now is New York City.

Goodness—Here or Hereafter?

Churches Seeking Accord On Hope for a Just World

(2nd In A Series)

By GEORGE W. CORNELL

EVANSTON, Ill. (AP)—One of humanity's oldest riddles—whether man's first duty is to the here or the hereafter—today poses a sharpened question for churches around the globe.

It is being preached on, studied, argued over, read about, analyzed and interpreted.

It is being discussed in Sunday schools and meetings and dealt with in scholarly papers and millions of words in the religious press.

Unity Would Help

"If the churches can speak on this with one mind, it is possible for them to bring guidance—and genuine hope—to a bewildered and menaced world," said Bishop J. Waskom Pickett, head of India's Methodist Church.

Couched in the phrase, "Christ—the hope of the world," the question is the theme of the two-week Assembly of the World Council of Churches, opening here Sunday.

"The theme has stirred a greater response than anything in the World Council's brief history," said the Rev. Robert S. Bilheimer, the council's associate general secretary.

At the heart of the question is whether Chri tians can hopefully fight for justice and goodness in this world, or whether those goals are deemed attainable only in a kingdom of God to come.

Hints In Scriptures

The scriptures abound with hints of the mystery:

"For now we see as through a glass darkly."

"But when that which is perfect is come, then that which is in part shall be done away."

"There are principles and standards for human society, rooted in God's everlasting will, for which men can work," said Dr. G. K.

—See CHURCHES—Page 6

John Declares He Left West Voluntarily

German Ex-Spy Chief Spikes Kidnap Story; Fears U. S. Plans War

BERLIN (AP) — Dr. Otto John declared today he went over voluntarily to the Communists in order to warn the world against what he called U.S. plans for a new war which would destroy Germany. He said he is now going to work for peace.

John told a news conference in the Soviet sector of Berlin he deserted as West Germany's security chief on July 20 to expose what he termed revival of Nazism in West Germany and to tell the "real truth" about the European Defense Community treaty.

Acting West German Chancellor Franz Bluecher called a special Cabinet meeting in Bonn to consider John's charges. The opposition Socialist party demanded a special session of Parliament to investigate what the Socialists called John's "treason to democracy." They asked also for the resignation of Interior Minister Gerhard Schroeder.

Seen 'Grotesque'

Bluecher interrupted the cabinet meeting to issue a special statement to newsmen assailing John's charges as "grotesque." He said John's accusations were "a repetition of the same propaganda line we have heard from the Communists a hundred times before."

In Washington, CIA Chief Allen Dulles' only comment was: "it's the straight Communist party line. It's sheer propaganda."

Appearing before more than 400 correspondents of the world press, John declared he went over to the Reds to join what he described as the only forum he could find to warn the world the United States is using Britain, France and the Bonn regime as "tools" for another war which would destroy Germany.

Officials Confer

In Bonn, Allied and West German officials plunged into special conferences to consider the impact of John's own statement he had voluntarily deserted to the East.

Chancellor Konrad Adenauer's government and the U.S. High

—See JOHN—Page 6

Trustee Asked For Fraim Lock

Creditors Oppose Move at Hearing

PHILADELPHIA (AP)—The E. T. Fraim Lock Co., of Lancaster, today asked the U. S. District Court to appoint an independent impartial trustee to operate the firm and attempt its reorganization.

Three attorneys for the firm's creditors opposed the petition. They told Federal Judge William H. Kirkpatrick that the request was submitted "in bad faith" and "the company does not have a chance to continue in business."

14 Employes on Payroll

John C. J. Wirth, of Lancaster, president of the company, told the judge that at the present time the firm has only 14 employes on its payroll, although it has facilities to employ about 80.

Attorney Carroll Wetzel, of Philadelphia, representing the Fraim Co. told Kirkpatrick that the company has a liability on paper of about $200,000. He indicated that an accounting statement showing the plant property and equipment to be worth about $63,000 was incorrect. He said that a recent appraisal showed that the plant and buildings had a minimum sale value of $159,000, while the machinery and equipment was worth more than $50,000.

Wetzel said that liquidation of the company as sought by creditors "will result in severe and unnecessary losses both to the company and its creditors and will cause further unemployment."

Not In Good Faith

B. M. Zimmerman, of Lancaster, representing the Irving Trust Co., of New York, which holds a $47,500 note, said that the present management is not acting in good faith in seeking a reorganization.

"We feel that the only course

—See FRAIM—Page 6

Today's New Era

Phone Lancaster 5251

New Era Photo

Elephants of the King Bros. circus halt on E. Chestnut St. during the parade this morning.

Mercury Stays In 70's Today

Low in 50's Due In This Area Tonight

Today's 2 p. m. temperature was 72, ten degrees below 2 p. m. yesterday, as Lancaster experienced a cool, clear day, with just the slightest hint of autumn.

The forecast said tonight is to continue fair and cool, with a low between 56 and 60. Tomorrow is to be partly cloudy and moderate, with a high between 78 and 82. Yesterday's weather included hail at Millersville and a sprinkle in the city, as well as a thunderstorm at Denver and showers at Ephrata.

Tobacco Yield Cut

As farmers went about their fieldwork with the crops which have been given a new burst of life by August rains, the U. S. Department of Agriculture said the county's tobacco yield may be the lowest since 1945, because of the June-July drought.

The total loss is expected to be 1.3 million pounds under the previous estimate, made 31 days ago. It puts the average expected yield at 1,400 pounds an acre on 26,000 acres, a drop of 50 pounds an acre from the July estimate.

The 1953 crop averaged 1,430 pounds an acre. In 1945, the crop averaged 1,300 pounds an acre. Total for the 1954 crop is now estimated at 36,400,000 pounds.

Full Recovery Impossible

The tobacco loss was part of the damage sustained by local farmers because of the drought. A federal-state survey showed that damage to corn, truck crops, pastures and hay seedings were well advanced in some instances and full recovery will be impossible.

Prospects for late maturing crops have been improved by the August rains, the State Agriculture Department said.

Field agents of the state emergency drought committee continued their survey here and in 20 other counties to determine what the prospects are for winter stores of feed.

Senate Adopts Immunity Bill

WASHINGTON (AP)—The Senate today passed and sent to the White House a bill to allow the granting of immunity from federal prosecution to witnesses whose testimony is desired in investigations of subversive activity.

By voice vote, after a three-minute explanation of its terms by Sen. McCarran (D-Nev), the Senate accepted a House-passed version of the measure.

Only Sen. Lehman (D-Lib-NY) voiced objections. He said he wanted the record to show that he was voting "no" on the bill—"not because I necessarily object to the bill but because of the way in which it was handled."

40 Quarts of Milk Stolen from Doorsteps

Marietta police today were investigating the theft of about 40 quarts of milk from doorsteps of borough homes.

Samuel Reynolds, employe of the Penn Dairies, told police that he delivered the milk at the usual time this morning. At daybreak the milk had vanished. Chief Leonard Tillman was in charge of the investigation.

FALSE FIRE ALARM

City firemen answered a false alarm turned in from Box 454 at the Webster Tobacco Co., 626 Columbia Ave., at 12:10 a.m. today. City detectives were seeking the identification of two boys seen running from the box shortly before the alarm sounded.

Thousands See First Circus Parade Here in 22 Years

Lancaster turned back the hands of time twenty-two years today as thousands of persons lined the streets to see the parade of the King Bros. Circus.

Police estimated that at least 10,000 persons were on the curbs of N. Duke and N. Queen St. to see the gold spangled spectacle.

It was estimated that more than 1,000 persons were jammed at Chestnut and Queen St. to see the parade turn north.

The matinee performance was a sell out. After the 4,000 seats were filled, other customers were given the choice of going home or sitting on the grass around the hippodrome track. Many stayed. Tonight's show is scheduled to start at 8 p. m.

Hundreds Join Parade

The three-quarters of a mile long parade moved over six miles of city streets as youngsters looked on in awed silence. Some of the parents were mere children when they saw the last circus parade on Lancaster streets and folks haven't changed — because hundreds fell in behind the last wagon and paraded right along to the circus grounds.

The parade was just like old times. There was the snorting steam calliope with live steam pouring from the brass pipes and making music the like of which few Lancaster youngsters had heard before.

Twelve elephants, linked trunk to tail and eight open cages of

—See CIRCUS—Page 3

4 Polio Patients Taken Out to See Parade

The parade provided a thrill for four youngsters in the polio unit of the General Hospital.

The four polio patients were taken outside the hospital on wheel chairs and placed on a truck. From their elevated position they saw the parade and smiled broadly at the clowns.

Several adult patients who could be moved on wheel chairs also were taken outside the hospital to see the parade. Nurses were close at hand but all admitted the parade was "just as good as medicine."

(Picture on Page 3)

Auto Chained to House 36 Hours

2 Agree on Damages, Car Released Today

The automobile of William R. Devlin, 977 E. King St., was released early this afternoon after being chained to the porch post at the home of Mr. and Mrs. Jay E. Fishel, 1527 Lincoln Highway East, for 36 hours.

Devlin's attorney said the adjustor for his client's insurance company and James Figari, owner of the property, reached an agreement on the payment of damage this morning.

Took Key To Parade

"But Mrs. Fishel, who had the key to unlock the chain, took her two-year-old son to see the circus parade and we had to wait until she returned before the car was released," the attorney said.

Mrs. Fishel returned at 1 p. m. and turned the key over to Figari, who removed the chain.

Figari chained the car to the porch post after it had careened from the Lincoln Highway East near Bridgeport, ripped through shrubbery, knocked down three mail boxes and then came to rest against the porch of the Fishel home at 1 a. m. yesterday.

The driver of the car left the scene on foot before state police arrived, but Devlin contacted police at 10 a. m. yesterday and said he had fallen asleep after having driven 300 miles. He told police his insurance company would take care of the damage, but Figari refused to release the car until full restitution was assured.

State police indicated no charges would be brought against Devlin.

Boy, 8, Is Bitten by Monkey at Circus

Lester Robinson, eight, son of Mr. and Mrs. B. Lester Robinson, 633 N. Pine St., was bitten on the right index finger when he became too friendly with a monkey in one of the cages at the King Bros. circus this afternoon.

He was treated at St. Joseph's Hospital, where he told attendants he stuck his finger through the bars of the monkey cage.

Hoover Willing To Aid Campaign

'Glad to Help' GOP In November Races

CEDAR RAPIDS, Iowa (AP) — Former President Hoover says he will be "glad to help in any way I can" in Republican political campaigning between now and the November elections.

He was completing a round of visits in his native Iowa today.

They began yesterday in his birthplace at the nearby village of West Branch, where more than 10,000 people gathered to honor him on his 80th birthday. After the "birthday party," he flew to Mason City and was scheduled to dedicate a school there and another in Cedar Rapids before flying to New York this afternoon.

Speculation Aroused

The nature of his speech at West Branch aroused considerable speculation as to whether it was an opening gun in the GOP political cannonading. He blasted the Democrats for presidential "misuse of power" in both domestic and foreign policies during the 20 years they were in office.

Before he left his hometown, a reporter asked him if he intends to make any campaign speeches this fall.

"I have no specific plans," he said, "but I'll be glad to help in any way I can."

Seemed In Good Health

Hoover's appearance, on his 80th birthday, deeply surprised people who had not seen him in some years. He was full of vigor. He marched through a warm sun, delivered a lengthy speech without a falter, rode dusty miles to dedicate schools in Iowa City and West Branch — and was still in a joking mood at the end of a long day.

The force with which he attacked the actions of the Democrats, and the applause he evoked, showed that he is still capable of taking part in a political affray.

10,200,000 IN AFL

NEW YORK (AP)—Membership of the AFL reached a record total of 10,200,000 in June, president George Meany said yesterday.

Sees Severance Of Relations as No Help to U. S.

Says West's Power Grows; Assails Talk Of a Preventive War

WASHINGTON (AP)—President Eisenhower said today the United States could not possibly serve its interests by severing diplomatic relations with Russia.

The President also told a news conference the free world is building up a structure which he believes will be impervious to any Communist assault.

As for waging a preventive war against the Communist world, as some people have urged, Eisenhower said there is no such thing as a preventive war—that it would be unthinkable for this country to undertake such a project.

Clark Speech Mentioned

Eisenhower's remarks came in connection with a request for comments on views expressed by Gen. Mark W. Clark.

Clark, retired former U. S. commander in the Far East, told the Senate Internal Security subcommittee yesterday that he favored breaking relations with Russia and reorganizing the United Nations to exclude the Soviet Union.

Eisenhower said he feels that, in general, many world tensions have eased in the last couple of years and the free world now has a better chance than before to obtain a solid peace.

Other Comments

The conference also touched on these other matters:

FARM—The President congratulated Senate leaders on pushing to approval a farm bill based on the administration's call for a shift from the present rigid price-support program to flexible supports. He said he wanted to make one thing very clear—that the administration victories reflected in the bills passed by the Senate and House were in no sense political victories.

Eisenhower called them steps toward a stable economy and therefore measures which will benefit everyone.

Report Being Prepared

THE ECONOMY — The White House is preparing a report on the American economy as of mid-year 1954 and the report shows a very hopeful picture, the President said. He added that the survey will be made public in a day or so.

In a related field, Eisenhower said he did not care to speculate at this time whether it will be possible to cut income taxes next year and balance the federal budget.

SPEECH ON CONGRESS — The Chief Executive disclosed he is at work on an address reviewing the accomplishments of Congress. He declined to shed any light on just when he will make the speech, and laughingly declined to say anything about such accomplishments until the session has been completed.

Will Entertain Cabinet

CABINET —The President announced he will be host Friday to the members of his Cabinet at his mountain lodge retreat at Camp David near Thurmont, Md., about 65 miles north of Washington. There will be a light lunch, the President said, a buffet supper in the evening and swimming for those who want a dip.

POLITICS—Eisenhower gave a resounding plug for former congressman Clifford Case, Republican candidate for the Senate from New Jersey. It came after a re-

—See IKE—Page 6

Ike Set to Halt Atomic Strikes

Says U. S. Can't Allow Cessation of Work

WASHINGTON (AP) — President Eisenhower said today he will use every legal means at his command to prevent strikes at the Oak Ridge, Tenn., and Paducah, Ky. atomic energy plants.

The President told a news conference this is one field in which the government cannot tolerate a cessation of work.

He made this comment when a newsman told him production workers at Paducah have voted to strike for higher pay tomorrow and that the situation at Oak Ridge is touch-and-go.

Will Use All Power

Eisenhower said he hadn't heard about the Oak Ridge situation. But he went on to say he is prepared to use all the power Congress has given him to prevent strikes at atomic installations.

He did not discuss specifically whether he will seek a no-strike injunction under the Taft-Hartley Act.

Legal Ground Work Laid

He could do this without delay at Oak Ridge, where a fact-finding board has laid the legal ground work by making a report as a result of a previous labor dispute.

Such a board report is a required preliminary to injunction action under the Taft-Hartley law.

Workers Vote To Strike

The 930 CIO workers at the Paducah atom bomb factory voted

—See ATOMIC—Page 6

DIDN'T KNOW IT WAS THERE

DETROIT (AP)—"It was so nice and clean I didn't know it was there," Edward Kubasiewicz said. He was explaining how he happened to walk right through a 20-by-70 inch plate glass window in a front door at police headquarters.

Kubasiewicz, on his way to get a driver's license, wasn't even scratched.

Manheim and Slaymaker Teams Win Midget Titles

A trip to Baltimore for a Major League baseball game, a cruise around the harbor, a tour of Fort McHenry and a Lancaster county roast turkey dinner today await the midget and midget-midget champions of Lancaster county.

The Manheim VFW team, 1953 champions, retained their midget title last night by beating the Elizabethtown Moose, 8 to 2.

The Slaymaker Lock nine, 1952 champs, beat the Paradise Lions, 7 to 2, for the midget-midget title.

On August 19, the New Era, sponsor of the tournament, will take the winners to Baltimore in chartered buses.

In addition, each member of the winning teams will receive heavy woolen jackets. The losers will receive satin jackets from the New Era.

A late-afternoon thunderstorm cut the size of the crowd at last night's Stumpf Field finals, but the stands were nearly filled.

Stories and pictures on Sports Page.

New Era Photo

Davey Yohn, two-year-old son of Mr. and Mrs. David Yohn Jr., Manheim R2, who serve as mascot and batboy for the Manheim VFW team.

SEATO Parley Gets Underway In Philippines

8 Nations Forging Alliance to Balk Red Drive in Asia

MANILA (AP)—Representatives of eight nations "that are ready to stand up and be counted in the struggle against aggression and tyranny" today began forging the links of economic and military chains they hope will halt Communist expansion in Southeast Asia.

In the sweltering heat of the Philippine Senate Hall, chief delegates of each government emphasized that their efforts were directed toward the preservation of peace.

After the colorful opening ceremonies, United States, Britain, France, the Philippines, Thailand, Australia, New Zealand and Pakistan began their closed door deliberations to iron out the few remaining kinks in a collective security alliance.

First Concrete Step

Thus was the first concrete step taken in Asia to unite anti-Communist nations of East and West against the threat of communism.

This much seemed probably: the conference nations will not muster a huge standing army patterned after the ill-fated European Defense Community.

U. S. Secretary of State John Foster Dulles told the conference, "for the free nations to attempt to maintain or support formidable land-based forces at every danger point throughout the world would be self-destructive."

That view seems likely to prevail, despite the pleas of Philippine Vice President Carlos Garcia for "a solemn covenant where member nations are pledged to act immediately in case of aggression, one for all and all for one."

Garcia was elected permanent chairman at Dulles' suggestion.

Young and vigorous Philippine President Ramon Magsaysay put his nation squarely on the record with these words:

"Ours is a nation whose love of peace and devotion to freedom have been tested on the crucible of suffering and sacrifice. In the past we have stood up to be counted; in the future we propose to do the same. For the present we regard with high hope this conference of like-minded states that are ready to stand up and be counted in the struggle against aggression and tyranny .... On the success of this conference may well depend the peace of Asia the next 10 years and the future of freedom in the world the next 1,000 years."

Dulles Declaration

Dulles declared the United States has no direct territorial interests in Southeast Asia, then said:

"We are united by a common danger, the danger that stems from international communism and its insatiable ambition . . . the danger manifests itself in many forms. One form is that of open armed aggression. We can greatly diminish that risk by making clear that an attack upon the treaty area would occasion a reaction so united so strong and so well placed that the aggressor would lose more than it could hope to gain."

The secretary rephrased his earlier advocacy of "massive retaliation at a time and place of our own choosing" with these words:

"So far as the United States is concerned, its responsibilities are so vast and so far flung that we believe we serve best by developing the deterrent of mobile striking power, plus strategically placed reserves."

New Era Photo

Brothers Show Little Remorse

Robert, nineteen, (left) and his brother, John L. Swift, eighteen, were boastful and showed little remorse as they left the County Prison this morning after confessing to local robberies.

Britain Seeks Talks Sept. 14

Wants Agreement To Rearm Germany

LONDON (AP)—Britain today proposed Sept. 14 for a nine-nation Allied foreign ministers conference in London to reach an agreement on rearming West Germany.

The countries approached are the six which signed the stillborn European Defense Community Treaty—France, West Germany, Italy, Belgium, Holland and Luxembourg—plus the United States and Canada.

It is the British hope that the talks will last four or five days—so that those foreign ministers who plan to do so can attend the opening of the 9th session of the U.N. General Assembly in New York Sept. 21.

The nine-power talks would be confined to the problem of finding an alternative to EDC. The United States, Britain, West Germany and Holland, among other countries, favor the admission of West Germany directly into the Atlantic Pact as a full member. Those countries suggest rearmament could take place within the 14-nation alliance under agreed safeguards against any possible revival of German aggression.

The United States, Britain and France as occupying powers also plan to negotiate with the Germans regarding a return of the sovereign independence Germany lost with the war in 1945.

Possibility of Arson Probed in Lititz Fire

The possibility of arson in a fire which destroyed a bank barn on the William Fry property, Lititz, early Saturday morning is being investigated by Paul Z. Knier, county fire marshal, and Robert M. Straham, state police marshal.

The fire caused damage estimated at $34,000. Firemen were summoned by an unidentified resident of Kissel Hill Road shortly after the fire was discovered at 3:15 a. m. The blaze broke out on the second floor of the building, in a section of the barn unused for some time.

Fry has an auto agency and garage on the property, tenanted by Donald Steffy, who lives in the farmhouse about 50 feet from the barn.

Jap Dusted by H-bomb Ash Pulls Out of Coma

TOKYO (AP)—A Japanese fisherman dusted by radioactive ash from a Bikini H-bomb test has pulled out of a coma and is recovering, doctors reported today.

Aikichi Kuboyama, one of 23 fishermen on the Lucky Dragon at the time of the hydrogen explosion last March, is now able to talk and eat, the doctors said.

3 Youths Admit Sticking UpStore

Arrests Also Solve 4 Local Car Thefts

Three teenage youths have confessed a $96 armed holdup at Lefever's grocery store near Safe Harbor Sunday a week ago, according to city and state police who apprehended them near Avondale Saturday night.

Police said the trio also solved four car thefts reported here since July 18 and admitted obtaining gasoline from two county service stations and driving away without paying the bills.

2 Are Brothers

They were identified as Robert Swift, nineteen, and his brother, John L. Swift, eighteen, both formerly of Sunnyside, Lancaster R7, who gave their address as 2031 N. Front St., Philadelphia, and Ernest McComsey, fourteen, of Avondale.

The Swift brothers have been charged with armed robbery and robbery with accomplice by Cpl. Mark Morgan, of the state police, before Alderman Wetzel. McComsey is being held for Juvenile Court action.

Additional complaints, including car theft charges by city police, were lodged against the trio, who will be questioned on other thefts.

One Marine Deserter

Robert Swift, police said, is wanted as a deserter from the U. S. Marine Corps, having left his unit near Camp Lejeune, N. C., without leave on Memorial Day.

In their statements to police, the trio said they stole an auto belonging to Phares C. Frey, 332 New Dorwart St., on Saturday, Aug. 28. While driving the stolen car to the Lancaster Speedway races that night, they said, they stopped at H. S. Flowers' service station at Elliott's Corner for gasoline and drove off without paying the bill.

Once 'Got Cold Feet'

The trio told police they planned a holdup for that Saturday night but "got cold feet" and called it off.

The next day, Sunday, they drove around the county looking over several places to stage a holdup. While driving around, they told police, they stopped at the service station of Fritz Kroeck, near Strasburg, obtained gasoline and again drove away without paying the bill.

They decided to rob Lefever's store, they said, when they observ-

—See YOUTHS—Page 14

Benjamin G. Hess Heads 7th Family Reunion

Descendants of the late Jonas and Emma Hess held the 7th annual reunion Saturday at Central Manor Camp grounds.

The following officers were elected: Benjamin G. Hess, Columbia R2, president; Amos M. Hess, Holtwood R1, vice president; Christian G. Hess, this city, historian; Mylin Hess, this city, secretary; Elvin S. Hess, Columbia R2, treasurer; Naomi Hess, Columbia R2, and Ida Hostetter, Leacock, children's game directors. Prizes were awarded to Naomi Marie Hess, youngest child; B. Frank Herr, traveling greatest distance; also Anna E. Hess and Ruth Hess, games.

Night-blooming Cereus Blossoms Reported

A night-blooming cereus displayed two blossoms, eight and ten inches across, last night at the home of Mrs. Alice Rote, 335 S. Prince St.

Two other cereus blooms last night were reported by Miriam and Ruth Sener, 233 N. Charlotte St.

The cereus, a species of cactus plant, blooms only once a year, and the blossoms die after opening for just one night.

HUSBAND ARRESTED

George Gibble, 470 Poplar St., charged with disorderly conduct and surety of the peace by his wife, Isabel, was arrested yesterday by city police. He will be given a hearing before Alderman Ober.

WOMAN BREAKS KNEE

Mrs. Bertha Howell, 1991 Park Plaza, suffered a fractured right knee in a fall yesterday. She was treated at the General Hospital.

Man Trapped by Tractor Instructs Rescuers in Work

MECHANICSBURG, Pa. (AP) — Robert Hollinger is alive today—thanks to his own bravery while facing the possibility of death for more than an hour.

Hollinger was pinned by the legs under an 18,000-pound tractor yesterday on his farm along Mechanicsburg RD3. Trapped and in constant pain from a broken leg, the 47-year-old farmer managed to give instructions to rescuers who worked for 70 minutes to free him.

The job was nerve wracking for the rescuers and the rescued. The huge tractor was precariously balanced and the least movement during the rescue operations could have topped the machine on Hollinger's chest. He suffered no other injuries.

Aircraft Show Finale Is Dedicated to Killed Pilot

DAYTON, Ohio (AP)—The 1954 National Aircraft Show winds up today on a note of tragedy with a program dedicated to the memory of a pilot whose plane exploded in a "ball of fire" as he tried yesterday for a new speed record.

Maj. John L. Armstrong, 32, died in a crash shortly after the Air Force announced that his name had gone into the record books with a new record of 649.302 m.p.h. over a 500-kilometer closed course.

Set Record Friday

The major, a Californian who lived at Fairborn, Ohio, set that record last Friday. It exceeded the old record of 607.1 m.p.h. set last May by Capt. Anders Westerlund of the Swedish Air Force.

He was making or preparing to make—Air Force authorities said they still were not certain which—a try for a new record in the General Electric trophy event when his F86H Sabrejet crashed 10 miles north of the aircraft show at Dayton's Cox Municipal Airport, Vandalia. The Air Force said Maj. Armstrong appeared early on the scene while another event was in progress and that he may have been making a preliminary run or may actually have been on the first lap of the event in whic hhe was the sole entrant.

He had taken off around a 100 kilometer (61 mile) closed course and had passed home pylon on the first lap.

The crash came about 27 seconds later. The cause was not determined.

D. A. Roussau, a Tipp City, Ohio funeral director, said, "he just flew to pieces and scattered all over the place."

The manner of the announcement and the successful try for the record in advance of the air show led observers to believe there might be a similar announcement today in the Thompson trophy event.

That is the last major event on the show program.

One Thompson Entry

Capt. Eugene P. Sonnenberg, 34, of the Air Proving Ground Command Eglin Air Force Base, Florida, is scheduled as the lone participant for the Thompson trophy. The old record for the event was set here last year by Brig. Gen. J. Stanley Holtener at 690.1 m.p.h. Gen. Holtener flew a North American F86D Sabrejet last year.

In the only other major event yesterday, 2nd Lt. William J. Knight of Mansfield, Ohio, and his radar observer, 2nd Lt. William K. Sellers of Tulsa, Okla., won the Allison trophy in a 10,000 altitude speed climb in 2 minutes 7 seconds.

Democrats Seen Centering Blow At GOP Slogan

'Peace, Progress and Prosperity' Targets of Labor Day Blasts

WASHINGTON (AP) — Democrats appear to be getting set for a frontal attack on the Republican's picked campaign slogan of "peace, progress and prosperity."

Labor Day weekend blasts at all three stanzas of the Republican refrain apparently signaled a chorus of Democratic dissent that could make foreign policy developments a major issue in the November election battle for control of Congress.

The Democratic National Committee supplied its candidates with some fresh ammunition on the international front with an assertion that Secretary of State Dulles is making foreign policy "politically palatable to the (GOP) Old Guard" with the result that "the drift toward general war goes forward remorselessly."

Kefauver Hits 'Progress'

Sen. Kefauver, a Democratic candidate for re-election in Tennessee, fired away at the "progress" theme with a statement contending that private utilities are getting Eisenhower administration help in a move to "break up the TVA" (Tennessee Valley Authority) system.

Organized labor's leaders hacked at the "prosperity" note, countering the contention of Secretary of Labor Mitchell that the administration is "currently making progress in providing more jobs for our people."

CIO President Walter Reuther declared that "in the light of our resources and our needs, our nation's unemployment is both un-American, uneconomic and unnecessary."

Lewis Cites 'Crumbs'

John L. Lewis, United Mine Workers president, accused the administration and Congress of "extending b e n e f i t s to organized wealth and offering crumbs to the lower income workers."

AFL President George Meany said the administration had done nothing to create jobs and stimulate purchasing power, adding that "only time will tell what a dangerous gamble this do-nothing policy will turn out to be."

President Dave Beck of the AFL Teamsters said the country is in a recession, but that he does not blame the administration.

In General Terms

Although the Republicans captioned one section of a campaign platform adopted at Cincinnati last week "progress and peace", they dealt with foreign policy only in general terms.

Observing that American troops are not fighting anywhere the GOP National Committee summed up this part of the platform with the statement "we are strengthening national defense against potential enemies from within and without, while exerting our continuing influence for world peace."

In an article to be published in the October Democratic Digest, the Democratic National Committee said that "the GOP right wing has been able to undermine the old bipartisan foreign policy and present to the world a false American image," and it added:

"It is substituting the visages of McCarthy, Knowland and Dirksen for the face of Eisenhower in the Republican portrait of America."

Sen. Knowland of California, the Republican Senate leader, has been booked by the GOP National Committee for extensive campaigning in behalf of that party's Senate candidates.

3 Boys 12 to 16 Admit $200 Theft

Three Conestoga R2 juveniles, aged 12 to 16, who were returned Saturday from Westfield, N. Y., as runaways, confessed to state police that they broke into the summer cottage of Samuel W. Lockard near Safe Harbor on three occasions and stole loot amounting to $200.

The last burglary occurred Sept. 1 and on the following day the three boys ran away from home when state policeman Edward Hermesky attempted to question them. The juveniles stole guns, ammunition, broke open a cigaret machine and stole cash and cigarets and also took some soft drinks. They were turned over to their parents, pending juvenile court action.

5 Drivers Prosecuted For Violations in City

Five motorists were prosecuted yesterday by city police before Alderman Ober.

Included were Philip A. Walker, 144 E. Chestnut St., ignoring a stop sign; Donald E. White, Quarryville R1, too fast for conditions; Donald C. Gainer, Conestoga, and Ronald E. Little, Ronks R1, reckless driving, and John R. Long, 409 Lafayette St., ignoring red traffic light.

Parking Meter Coins in 2 Boros Given Polio Fund

Parking meters are being used in Manheim and Columbia this weekend to collect contributions for the Emergency March of Dimes and Dollars.

The "meter campaigns" started yesterday and will end Tuesday morning. Columbia police have added a feature of their own—all parking fines collected over the weekend will also go to the polio fund.

Meanwhile Christian C. Rudy, chairman of the Lancaster County Chapter, National Foundation for Infantile Paralysis, announced that $38.50 has been raised for the polio fund recently by children's groups in the city and county.

Blaisdells Tell Of Hurricane

Father, Daughter See Cars Float by

Members of the family of George B. Blaisdell, 517 Hamilton Road, went through a number of unexpected experiences last week as hurricane "Carol" raged up the eastern coast.

Mr. and Mrs. Blaisdell and their younger daughter, Dorothy, came into Providence last Monday evening so that Miss Blaisdell could see the Pembroke campus. The evening was calm and clear.

Wind Lifts Up Car

Next morning Blaisdell and Dorothy drove to the campus, while Mrs. Blaisdell stayed at their hotel across town. The storm broke as the father and daughter were en route. Without knowing what was on the way, they drove over a bridge which was nearly submerged, and felt the wind lifting the rear of the car in the heavy rain.

The two arrived at the hospital which is part of the college and were told they would have to remain. Only emergency calls were being handled by the hospital switchboard, but the operator called Mrs. Blaisdell after several hours to tell her the father and daughter were safe. They had to stay until about 3:30 p. m.

Yachts, Boats Sunk

They saw cars which had been parked by vacationers, floating about like boats. A new sea food restaurant was swept completely from its foundation by what appeared to be a tidal wave. Yachts and other boats were wrecked and sunk.

Next day the three drove to Woods Hole, Mass., where the Blaisdells' older daughter, Margaret, had been taking summer study. The work there was closed a day early, since the rushing waters swept away much of the work they had been doing.

Many Roads Closed

Great trees were uprooted, and many roads were closed or clogged. Restaurants hurried to serve food that could not be iced because of the lack of electricity. Candles were at a premium. Broken glass was tossed from windows, adding to hazards. The Blaisdells returned here Friday evening.

Sea Anemone Robs Octopus of Fish, Then Kills Him

CLEVELAND, Ohio (AP) — Yesterday Cleveland's recently completed aquarium had an octopus and a sea anemone for tank mates. Today it has a sea anemone and three starfish.

The octopus and anemone, until Saturday, had kept to separate parts of the tank, the octopus looking like a pile of jelly, the anemone — about the same size as the octopus — like a stick with a feathery hat on top.

Saturday a fish intended for the octopus was trapped in the anemone's tentacles and consumed. The young octopus coasted over to investigate. The anemone, an old timer, flipped out a tentacle that delivers a poisoned sting.

The octopus died yesterday.

2 Soldiers Injured In Turnpike Crash

Two soldiers were injured in an accident on the Pennsylvania Turnpike in Lancaster county at 7:15 a.m. today.

Treated at Ephrata Community Hospital were Dennis L. Hobart, Ridgefield Park, N. J., for a back injury, and Robert J. Burnett, Rochester, N. Y., lacerated scalp and abrasions of the arms. They were discharged after treatment.

State turnpike police at Reading said the accident occurred about three miles east of the Reading interchange.

Evvy Is at Shore for Final Reign as Miss America

Evvy Ay's new hair-do, bangs and curls on the forehead, parted in the middle and gathered in the back brought a division of opinion among her Ephrata townsfolk today as the blonde Miss America 1954 returned to Atlantic City to start the final week of her reign.

Greets Arriving Queens

Queen Evvy was going through some of the same activities as she did a year ago, when she was Miss Pennsylvania and an aspirant for the crown. Her activities today consisted of greeting, as Miss America, the queens from the various states as they registered at Atlantic City.

All through this week she will also be talking to the contestants, at informal get-togethers, as the competition grows keener. There will also be a number of public appearances.

Evvy will wear a white ermine cape for the big night parade tomorrow at 7:30 p. m. She will reign over the three nights of preliminary competition, tomorrow, Thursday and Friday.

On Saturday night, ten girls will be competing in the finals, and Evvy will make her farewell speech and crown Miss America 1955. Then she'll attend the Miss America ball.

"I want to find out what it's like," she explains with a smile. "I don't remember the ball from last year."

Fiance To Be Escort

She hopes that her "favorite escort", who's Carl Sempier Jr., her fiance, will be able to be in Atlantic City from Thursday on. Her mother, Mrs. Richard Ay, will be able to attend some of the functions, but not all, since she is recuperating from a heart attack.

Her father and her brother, Ricky, will also be present. In the big outdoor parade, Ricky will pull her float, driving the car she gave him for high school graduation present.

New Era Photo

Julius La Rosa signs autographs at Ephrata.

Bishop to Bless New H. S. Wing

Catholics Will Hold Dedication Sunday

The Most Rev. George L. Leech, D.D., J.C.D., Bishop of Harrisburg, will bless the new wing of Lancaster Catholic High School during a dedication ceremony at 2:30 p.m. next Sunday.

Bishop Leech will also preside at the public Holy Hour of Reparation service which will be held at 3 p.m. at the football stadium of the school.

During the dedication the Bishop will be assisted by two chaplains. The Rev. George W. Rost, Harrisburg, a member of the Bishop's household, will be master of ceremonies. The brief program will be attended by local clergy, parents, friends and alumni of the school.

The school will formally open tomorrow morning with the celebration of the Mass of the Holy Ghost by the Rev. Robert C. Gribbin, newly-appointed principal. Tomorrow and Wednesday will be half-day sessions, with the first full session on Thursday.

E-town Man Heads District Moose

Walter Seiple, Elizabethtown, was elected president of the Eastern Division, Pennsylvania State Moose Association, at the group's 17th annual convention today at Harrisburg.

He succeeds George Rowe, Berwick. Other new officers are: Thomas Daugherty, Catasauqua, first vice president; Charles Leinhauser, Darby, second vice president; John Drucis, Mt. Carmel, third vice president; Alfred Eveland, Bloomsburg, prelate, and Wilmer Crow, Middletown, sergeant-at-arms.

The Hanover Lodge was awarded first prize for meritorious service at the convention, which started Saturday and concludes today. The Danville, Tower City and Chambersburg Lodges shared second place honors.

First Methodist Women Plan Dessert Meeting

The Women's Society of Christian Service of First Methodist Church will hold a dessert meeting tomorrow at 7 p.m. in the chapel, Duke and Walnut Sts.

A business meeting at 8 p.m. will be in charge of Mrs. Conley Bowers, new president. Mrs. Irvin Leiphart is chairman of the program which will include the showing of a film, "The City Story," in conjunction with the church-wide study of the year, "Crowded Ways."

Mrs. Walter Swarr and the committee on Christian Social Relation and Local Church Activities will be in charge of the dessert. Devotions will be conducted by Mrs. Russell Berkheimer. Members of all Women's Societies of the city Methodist Churches have been invited to attend.

Droodles

by ROGER PRICE

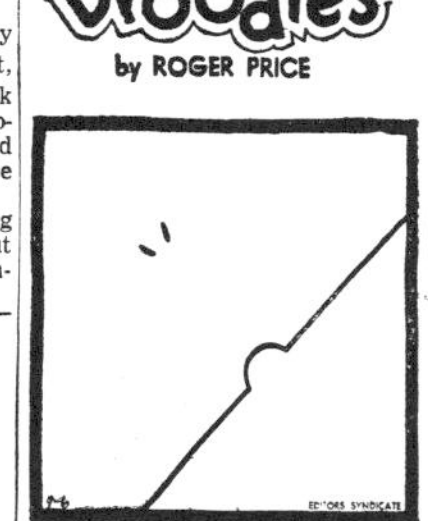

"MOSQUITO SHOWING GIRL FRIEND LATEST JOB"

I selected this as a Labor Day Droodle because Mosquitoes are always laboring. A Mosquito makes a one armed paper hanger look like a bum. If a Mosquito isn't rushing around collecting plasma he's busy recording "Buzz-buzzz-buzzzs" for the telephone company to use when you dial a busy number. And at night he has to work even harder, humming around your bedroom keeping you awake. And lots of times after he's flown to the ceiling, executed a perfect Immelmann turn and started to dive on you with all flaps up—you roll over and he winds up with a face full of innerspring mattress. Think how the Mosquito feels. Frustrated, that's how. So next time you see a Mosquito remember his problems and encourage him by giving him a friendly slap on the back.

Swooning Teenagers Mob Julius La Rosa at Ephrata

By Pat Nutter

A mob of swooning teenagers, reminiscent of the bobbysoxer fans of the early 40's, jammed Ephrata Legion Park last night to see Julius La Rosa in his first appearance here.

Fan clubs from as far away as Harrisburg were present to get a look at their idol. The singer was almost mobbed as he got out of his convertible behind the band stand, and as he started to sing a steady stream of flash bulbs went off in his face.

Crowd of 5,000

The crowd, which was estimated at close to 5,000, was the largest of the season.

La Rosa handled his fans with poise and kidded back when they shrieked questions. At one point he had to ask them to be a "little quieter so that the folks in the rear can hear too."

"The fans are wonderful. They have put me where I am and I love them," he told a New Era reported.

Mum on Godfrey and Dorothy

La Rosa repayed the fans for the big turnout by signing all autograph books handed to him estimated close to 1,000.

Although he was willing to talk about almost all phases of his life, he was reticent about discussing Aruthur Godfrey and Dorothy McGuire, the Godfrey entertainer he reportedly will wed.

About Godfrey and his abrupt dismissal from the show last October, La Rosa would say only, "I haven't seen Mr. Godfrey for a long time. We still have a speaking acquaintance."

Asked if he planned to marry in the near future, he said "I want to get married just like everyone else does, but I am not engaged now." On the subject of Miss McGuire, one of the singing McGuire Sisters appearing on the Godfrey show, La Rosa said "we don't talk about that any more."

What He's Been Doing

Since leaving the Godfrey Show the singer has been traveling from coast to coast—sometimes playing one-night stands and oftener appearing for a couple of weeks at various hotels, parks and fairs across the nation.

"Singing has brought me a lot of wonderful things. I've been able to buy a home for my parents near New York City, I have a couple of cars, a nice wardrobe—all the material things.

"More important to me though is the chance I've gotten to see the country and meet all types of interesting people. Lancaster County, with its rolling countryside and beautiful farms, seems like a page out of the past to me."

Radio and TV Work

La Rosa has road engagements booked for the remainder of the year. His ultimate goal is to do the type of radio and TV work that Perry Como does.

"Perry is my ideal person, not because of his singing, although that's good, but because he possesses the qualities I most admire in a man."

4 Men Travel With Him

The Brooklyn singer, who lives with his parents, usually gets home after every engagement, but "it's not as often as I'd like." He has one sister.

When he travels he is accompanied by four men, three of whom were boyhood friends from Brooklyn. Prior to his appearance here he was at the Indiana State Fair in Indianapolis. He left here for a week's appearance at the Vogue Terrace in Pittsburg.

City Man Says Success Hasn't Changed Julius

A city man who served in the U. S. Navy with Julius LaRosa during 1950-51 says that success hasn't changed the singer.

Paul Eberly, 916 Buchanan Ave., said that "Julius is the same down to earth guy he was when we were in the Navy together."

The city man was a clarinetist with the U. S. Navy Band in Washington, D. C., and LaRosa was a singer with the band. They got together for a short reunion at intermission time last night.

Firestone Union Votes on Pay Pact

AKRON, Ohio (AP)—Firestone Tire & Rubber Co. employes vote here today on an agreement to end a CIO United Rubber Workers strike which started Aug. 12.

The 10,000 Firestone workers here and about 15,500 in seven other cities are expected to give near unanimous approval to a proposed contract which provides average pay increases of 6½ cents hourly. Average hourly pay had been $2.10.

The new contract, which the union said "adjusts 89 inequities," was agreed upon in Cleveland late Saturday night after weeks of negotiations.

Fall Antique Show at York Opens in YMCA

York's annual fall antiques show opened today in the York YMCA auditorium, to continue daily through Thursday, 11 a. m. to 10:30 p. m.

The show is one of the oldest in the East, having been established in 1934. Thirty-five exhibitors are represented, including a number from Lancaster county, and several from Maryland, Delaware and New York. The display includes furniture, china, glassware, pottery, quilts, rugs, pewter, and prints.

World Coffee Surplus Expected Next Summer

WASHINGTON (AP)— The Agriculture Department says that starting about next summer world coffee production should move ahead of consumption — thus removing what has been considered a prime reason for high coffee prices in recent months.

But the department made no forecast yesterday as to whether the expected easing of the tight coffee supply would lead to a price drop.

2 DRIVERS PROSECUTED

Jerry R. Mayo, 921 N. Prince St., and Paul Rueger, 408 S. School Lane, charged with ignoring stop signs, were apprehended by Conestoga Twp. police over the weekend. They will be summoned for hearings before Justice of the Peace Herbert Murmeister.

Americans Trail British in Race Of Vintage Cars

HARROGATE, England (AP)—The clattering contest between 10 vintage American automobiles and 10 aged British cars started on another lap here today with the British enjoying a decided advantage.

The 1913 Lozier driven by Rod Lood of West Newton, Mass., broke a universal joint. No shop had one in stock, so Lood had to make a part. He has to finish it and drive to Boston in Lincolnshire, 111 miles away by 5:55 P. M. If he fails, the Americans go down 30 points.

The Americans are already four points down, due to time lost because of a steam leak developed by the 1906 Stanley Steamer being driven by Paul J. Tusek of Power Point, Ohio. The British had not lost a point as the contestants neared the half way mark in the 768-mile halfway from Edinburg to the South of England.

200 Attend USO Dance At Moose Hall Here

The weekly USO dance in Moose Hall Saturday night was attended by approximately 200 persons, according to Thomas J. Monaghan, chairman of the Youth Activities Committee, Knights of Columbus, which furnished chaperons for the dance.

A recruiting campaign for more junior hostesses is planned for the near future.

Seventy-two sailors, five WAVES and one soldier attended the USO-Inter-Faith Committee programs at the YWCA yesterday. Mrs. Everett M. Wilson was chairman, assisted by Mrs. A. H. Snyder, Miss Emily Ransing, Mrs. J. Russell Myers, Mrs. Harry Black, Mrs. Lottie Kilheffer, Mrs. Paul Herr, Mrs. C. J. Schreck, Mrs. Laura Sebelist and Elmer Dickson.

INCINERATOR FIRE SCARE

City firemen were called to the Shaub apartments, 401 W. James St., when smoke from a rear incinerator caused a fire scare at 5:55 p.m. Saturday. Engine Co. 4 and Assistant Fire Chief Frank Deen responded.

CARL KAUFFELD

Zoo Curator To Present Show At MSTC Location

Carl Kauffeld, curator of the reptile collection at New York's Staten Island Zoo, will present a demonstration program at Millersville State Teachers College on Wednesday, Oct. 6, at 1 p. m. in Lyte Auditorium.

Kauffeld spoke at MSTC during the summer session of the college, and his second appearance is being sponsored by the college entertainment committee, Miss Beatrice Datesman, chairman.

The program will be open to the public at no charge, Miss Datesman said.

'Dear Brutus' Is E-town Vehicle

The Elizabethtown All-College Players will present James Barrie's "Dear Brutus" on Oct. 22 at 8 p. m. in the college auditorium as part of the college's Mid-Century Convocation program.

The three-act tragic fantasy is being directed by Prof. Robert Newell, of the dept. of English. Cast in leading roles are Marigrace Bucher, Mount Joy, a junior; Jean Roland, Elizabethtown, an alumna; Samuel Williams, Clemson, S. C., a senior. Robert S. Young, administrative assistant to the president, is also cast in the play.

Other alumni appearing in the production are Mrs. Merle Black and Robert Trimble, both of Elizabethtown. Five students appearing in supporting roles are Barbara Theel, Glassboro, N. J.; Pauline Wolfe, Myerstown; Joe Cook, Milford, Del.; Jack Byers, Johnstown; and Janet Trimmer, New Holland.

Handicap Week Is Set By Mayor

This week has been officially proclaimed Employ the Physically Handicapped Week by Mayor Kendig C. Bare.

The Mayor's proclamation urged local officials, employers, civic organizations and citizens "to assist in every way possible to bring to the attention of our community that disabled veterans and other handicapped civilians are fully capable of performing efficiently, safely and reliably in thousand of different positions."

A local employ the handicapped committee sponsors a year-long program for placing handicapped persons in local industry. The local organization also will sponsor a poster and essay contest for school pupils, plans for which will be announced later.

Parking Lot In City Enlarged

Capacity of a public off-street parking lot on the east side of the first block of S. Beaver Street has been increased to 70 cars, it was announced yesterday.

The Lancaster Newspapers, Inc., owns the bulk of the land and leases a small portion from the Farmers Bank and Trust Co., trustee.

Enlargement of the lot was made possible through demolition of a warehouse building at 41 S. Beaver St.

Regrading and paving of the entire lot has now been completed. The lot is illuminated.

Flash On Sky Bares Fatal Auto Crash

BORDENTOWN, N.J., Oct. 2 (AP)—A state trooper saw a flash in the sky early today and upon investigating, came upon the wreckage of a car in which one Air Force man was killed and three others injured.

The flash was caused by the men's auto slamming into a high tension pole, parting a 26,000-volt line.

Dead was S-Sgt. Theodore Wright, 24, of Harrisonburg, Va. He was a passenger in the car driven by Sgt. Richard Bauman, 24, of Newark. Both were members of the Fifth Fighter Interceptor Squadron, McGuire Air Force Base.

Boy Scouts Name F. J. Chesterman

ROANOKE, Va., Oct. 2 (AP)—Francis J. Chesterman of Philadelphia, has been re-elected chairman of the executive committee of Region 3, Boy Scouts.

Twelve members were elected to three-year terms on the committee to succeed members, whose terms expired. They are:

Chesterman, Daniel W. Bell of Washington, D.C., Revelle W. Brown of Philadelphia, Dr. J. M. T. Finney Jr. of Baltimore, Elmer J. Halberg of Kittanning, Pa., Lyle G. Hall of Ridgway, Pa., James W. Hoyt of McKeesport, Pa., William Poole of Wilmington, Del., Albert S. Schmidt of Harrisburg, Pa., P. T. Sharples of Philadelphia, Fred A. Howard of Reading, Pa., and Sam A. Mooney of New Castle, Pa.

OCTOBER IS RESTAURANT HOSPITALITY MONTH

"A Restaurant Meal . . . . A Wonderful Deal!"

A Restaurant Meal Is A Wonderful Deal

By Your Lancaster Restaurant Reporter

Here it is Restaurant Hospitality Month again. That's one month I'm all in favor of—and with good reason. My assignment is to have a meal at each of the most popular restaurants of Lancatser City and County so that I can tell you about them. That's the kind of assignment reporters dream about.

My first stop was at the Stock-Yard Inn where Jim Fournaris, the manager, wins friends with a simple formula — good food.

I had fresh oysters and I recommend them to anyone who wants a luscious meal. With fresh vegetables, dessert, rolls and coffee they are a generous meal, as are all portions at the Stock Yard Inn.

Really though, I had a hard time deciding between oysters and sirloin steak. Sirloin steak served anywhere is great but at the Stock Yard Inn it's really distinctive. Like all the Inn's beef it's from prime show cattle.

The next day I visited The Rose Bowl, Lancaster's famous American-Italian restaurant. Being a spaghetti fan I ordered Spaghetti a la Rose Bowl. Try it. It embodies all the simplicity and succulence of the finest Italian cooking.

Always a nice feature at the Rose Bowl is the economical prices. Far less than a dollar you can eat a meal which brings visions of Rome. No wonder The Rose Bowl is attracting more and more people every year.

History and Steaks

Far a hearty meal in a historical atmosphere. I dined at the Revere Tavern in Paradise. A plaque placed there by the Lancaster County Historical Society interested me. It said. "This building prior to 1800 was one of many taverns along this highway. April 1854 to about 1865 it was owned by James Buchanan, fifteenth president of the United States. July 1841 to September 1854 it was the home of his brother and sister-in-law, the Reverand Edward Young and Eliza Foster Buchanan. She was the musicianly sister of Stephen Collins Foster whose immortal songs brought untold happiness into the world."

And may I say that the Porterhouse steaks and the crab cakes served nowadays at the Revere Tavern are doing their share to bring happiness into the world.

"Kumm Hop Die Pennsylwanisch Dietch Esse," The Willows invited me. Do you know what that means? Neither did I but luckily they sent along a translation: "Come Have the Pennsylvania Dutch Meal."

I didn't need a second invitation before driving five miles east of Lancaster on route 30 to this pleasant restaurant. For anyone who is tired after a day's work The Willows is the perfect place for relaxation. As soon as you enter, its charm seeps into you and soothes jangling nerves.

Of course, one of their wholesome Pennsylvania Dutch meals does its share in furthering that sense of well-being. I had Zuucker Gecured Sie Rick (smoked pork chop with cream gravy) and it was perfect. A lot of tourists dine at The Willows. It's no wonder our County is so famous if that's the kind of meals visitors receive here.

For a Special Place for Special Occasions the Stone Barn always fills my bill. That's another place with a delightful atmosphere. As the name says it's a stone barn but what a barn! It has the last word in everything necessary for the preparation and serving of delicious meals but at the same time it has lost none of its rustic beauty.

You can't just drop in at the Stone Barn because it's available only by reservation for private parties but I had the good luck to be a guest at a wedding reception there. The congenial owner, Leo Shopf, really goes all out for his guests. One of his specialties is barbecued chicken and it's superb. Other favorites there are charcoal broiled steak and baked ham.

Another delightful place is the Arcadia. It's on W. Orange St. in Lancaster and it comes to my mind whenever I'm looking for a friendly place to have a banquet. The food is wonderful but it's not the only main attraction of the Arcadia. Nor do I think its Old World charm is its chief delight. To me the nicest feature and the one that lures me back time and time again is the utter friendliness of the place.

The waitresses serve informally but you feel that they aim for your satisfaction. When I call the Arcadia to make reservations for a banquet and ask the manager what he can serve us, his answer is, "We'll serve anything you want—baked ham, turkey, roast beef, lobster tail, chicken. You name it and we'll serve it."

Restaurateur Leo Shopf reminds us that October is Restaurant Hospitality Month. Visit your favorite restaurant because, as the Lancaster County Restaurant Association says, "A Restaurant meal is a wonderful deal."

WEATHER
(U. S. Weather Bureau Forecast for Lancaster, Cumberland, Lebanon, York, Adams and Franklin Counties):

Partly Cloudy And Turning Colder, With A Few Scattered Showers Early Today. High Today 50-55. Fair And Colder Tonight, Sunday Fair And Cool.

Intelligencer Journal.

The Leading Newspaper in the Garden Spot of America. Home Owned for Home Folks Since 1794

161st Year.—No. 105.. Official United States Census Figures Lancaster Metropolitan Area Population 234,717 LANCASTER, PA., SATURDAY MORNING, OCTOBER 16, 1954. CITY TWENTY PAGES. 30c PER WEEK—5c Per Copy

HURRICANE RIPS LANCASTER COUNTY, DAMAGE WIDESPREAD, SEVERE

3 Die In State To Make Nation's Storm Toll 33

Called One Of Century's Most Erratic Storms By Bureau

NEW YORK, Oct. 15 (AP) — Hurricane Hazel, one of the century's most dangerously erratic storms, rocked New York with 100 mile per hour winds tonight. But it was a dying gesture on the part of the big storm.

"The worst is over," was the weatherman's cheering word as the barometer began to rise in mid-evening.

Far to the west of the city, the hurricane spent its waning strength against the immovable barrier of Pennsylvania's mountains. Then it died and its force was absorbed in part by a new storm center in southwestern New York.

Hazel's death toll stood at 33 in continental United States. It swept into the Carolinas from sea early today, battering its way into the Northeastern states after grazing Washington with unsurpassed fury.

Ashore and at sea millions cringed before its awesome might. Ships frantically changed course. Airplanes fled like game birds before a forest fire. Men pitted their puny strength in a frantic battle to blunt its destructiveness.

The storm gathered the momentum of an express train at times. Behind it thousands were left homeless.

Even in death, the hurricane was wickedly menacing as gales and dangerous tidal swells lingered on

Turn To Page 11 For More Of HOWLER

Shambles Of Unroofed Houses, Downed Trees In Hazel's Wake

By The Associated Press

Hurricane Hazel, a whirling monster even by hurricane standards, buzz-sawed its way across Pennsylvania tonight—dulling its powerhouse point against the mountains and plains of the Susquehanna River Valley but leaving at least three dead and a shambles of unroofed houses and overturned trees.

But even as the hurricane appeared wearing itself out, some after effects were building up — and reports of the widespread destruction were mounting.

There could be no doubt that the storm had hit Pennsylvania and hit it hard.

From every point in the hurricane's path — and the path stretched over the middle third of the state with the fringe punch extending border to border — came reports of sore hurts to life and property.

KNOWN DEAD

The known dead in the wake of the storm were:

Roy Barkley, 44, Listonburg, near Somerset, drowned in a rain swollen creek while trying to aid a stranded mother and her two children across a damaged bridge, the mother and her children later were taken across the repaired span safely.

Seven-year-old William Reese of Wyoming, killed when a tree blew on top of him at Kingston, near Wilkes-Barre. His mother, Mrs. Anna Reese, was injured critically.

Thomas J. Morgan, Harrisburg, bus driver, electrocuted when he got out of his crowded bus to investigate a live wire blown across the bus roof near Indiantown Gap.

All sailings from the port of Philadelphia were cancelled and Coast Guard crews were pressed into service along the water front.

All central city traffic police and highway patrolmen remained on duty through the night to unsnarl storm bound traffic and warn pedestrians off the streets.

Two reporting stations for the maritime exchange in this bustling

Turn To Page 11 For More Of STATE

Linemen Work On Poles As Gales Lash City

Working in 60-mile-per hour winds and lashing rain, Pennsylvania Power and Light Company men cut broken electrical wires which crackled along North Queen Street during yesterday's storm. Evidence of the high winds are the torn awnings on the second floor windows of B. F. Johnson grocery store at 634 N. Queen St. The wires crackled and sputtered along the block like fire crackers, threatening to set fire to autos parked along the curb, until workmen could reach the scene and cut power. This crew of PP&L workers are the same men who assisted in hurricane Edna several weeks ago in the Boston area. (Intell Photo)

Wind Velocity Here Reaches 85 MPH In Sporadic Gusts

A hurricane named Hazel — the first of her sorority ever to show face here — embraced Lancaster County early last evening and fled like a capricious flirt, leaving behind a deadly memory of her vicious whims.

She unmercifully whipped city and farm with gusts of her lashing breath that measured up to 85 miles per hour, and brought with her thundering torrents of pelting rain.

Other Stories, Pictures On Pages 2, 4, 6, 11, 15, 20

The damage was widespread and severe, and the full extent of this area's "biggest blow" will not be known until daylight illuminates the hurricane's path.

Property damage must be counted in the hundreds of thousands. The county lost between 500 and 600 of its precious trees, by conservative estimate. There were at least four major injuries received at area hospitals. And hope seemed dim for a lone duck hunter last seen in the choppy Susquehanna near Creswell.

Hazel moved fast out of sight, if not of memory. A Weather Bureau bulletin at 10:45 p. m. said:

"Hazel . . . is entering Lake Ontario en route to Canada. Goodbye Hazel."

As an epilogue to yesterday's elemental violence, the Weather Bureau decreed partly cloudy skies for today with temperatures turning colder. Today's high was forecast at 55 to 60 degrees.

Power facilities were undoubtedly the biggest single victim of Hurricane Hazel in Lancaster County. Disruption of electrical service was like a huge blanket over the county with only a few scattered pinpoints of light showing through.

The Pennsylvania Power and Light Co. called the hurricane's havoc the worst it has seen in this area in 30 years or more. Emergency crews were put on a stand-by basis as far west as Michigan and other crews were headed for active service here from all over the company's 28-county service area.

The State Department of Highways estimated that between 500 and 600 trees fell on roads for which it is responsible. Many of the trees toppled on automobiles and scores of the larger ones blocked traffic for periods ranging from a few minutes to several hours.

Many who have spent their lives in Lancaster County felt that the general destruction of the hurricane and the staggering amount of debris it scattered is probably unsurpassed in their memories.

Few escaped some degree of hardship caused by the violent gales.

Most homes were lacking electricity for varying lengths of time. Every hospital in the county was forced to depend on its emergency lighting system. Civil Defense personnel got real emergency training and performed their chores with dispatch. Fire and auxiliary police responded in strength and proved valuable aides to regular police and firemen.

LOW TOLL OF INJURIES

The unusually severe weather produced a surprisingly low toll on the county's population. By late last night hospitals had treated only four persons whose injuries could be termed "major."

There was, to be sure, a good sprinkling of minor mishaps—persons stumbling over fallen limbs, windows blowing shut in faces, emergency illumination making every household treacherous.

Area duck hunters had an unfortunate first day for their season.

One hunter, Lloyd Hostetter, of Conestoga R2, was believed lost in the Susquehanna near a river island north of Creswell.

Between 30 to 50 other hunters were reported marooned on river islands between Columbia and Washington Boro when the high winds ruled out returning to the mainland in small craft.

RAIN STARTED EARLY

Hurricane Hazel sent its first fleeting forerunners into the county between 7 and 8 a.m. yesterday in the form of light rain. The rain soon increased in intensity and introduced another—and more fearsome—phase of the eighth and most vicious hurricane of the 1954 season: powerful gusts of wind.

There was a succession of heavy showers all afternon and the wind became stronger as each hour passed.

Between 6 and 7 p.m.—some 12 hours after its gentle beginnings—the hurricane was at its peak in Lancaster County. Gusts up to 85 miles an hour were registered at Lancaster Municipal Airport at at 6:45 p.m. there was a steady velocity of about 60 miles per hour.

Lancaster had one and eighteen hundredths of an inch of precipitation up to 5 p. m. At the Ephrata Weather Station there was an official one and ten hundredths of an inch of rainfall up to 6 p. m., with an additional two hundredths of an inch falling in the evening.

Hurricane Hazel bored her way into the state almost due south of Harrisburg. She moved at increasing speed north and slightly westward, brutally grazing York, Lancaster, Harrisburg, Lebanon and Williamsport as she headed toward the New York border.

By 8 p. m. the heavy gusts had petered out and the local emergency appeared about over.

Public carriers threw schedules into the waste basket as the most violent of the winds approached. Rail travelers cooled their heels

Turn To Page 4 For More Of HURRICANE

"We Lead All The Rest"

FARM CORNER

By WILLIAM R. SCHULTZ

NEW PHASE OF 4-H CLUB STEER FEEDING PROGRAM PLANNED

A new phase of 4-H Club steer feeding work will be introduced in Lancaster County this year, County Agent M. M. Smith said yesterday.

The new project places emphasis on the commercial, rather than show, aspects of steer feeding and will require that club members place pens of five steers on feed.

These pens would be shown unhaltered at the Southeast District Show at Lancaster's Union Stock Yards in the fall of 1955.

Tentative plans are to sell the animals at the end of the annual district sale of show steers.

Smith said the new project ". . . will provide an opportunity for farm youth to feed out groups of steers for show and for market. This project will give practical experience that will come closer to

Turn To Page 15 For More Of FARM CORNER

CAPITAL REGISTERS GUSTS OF 95 MPH

WASHINGTON, Oct. 15 (AP) — A gust of 95 miles per hour, the highest wind on record here, was registered at the Washington National Airport weather station at 4:50 p.m. today as Hurricane Hazel moved toward the Washington area.

The previous record wind here was 92 miles per hour, recorded in 1942.

Weather Calendar

COMPARATIVE TEMPERATURES

Station	High	Low
Water Works	77	68
Ephrata	73	63
Last Year (Ephrata)	73	36
Official High for Year July 31		102
Official Low for Year Jan. 18		-1
Character of Day		Stormy

WINDS
Direction ESE
Avg. Velocity 55, Gusts to 70 mph

HUMIDITY
8 a.m. 100% 11 a.m. 100% 2 p.m. 100%
5 p.m. 100% 8 p.m 100%
Average Humidity 100%

SUN
Rises 6:15 am. Sets 5:24 p.m.

MOON
Rises 8:59 p.m. Last Quarter, Oct. 18

STARS
Morning—Jupiter
Evening—Venus, Mars, Saturn

NEARBY FORECASTS
(U.S. Weather Bureau)

Eastern Pennsylvania — Partly cloudy, rather windy and cooler, with a few showers in the mountains today. Highest 55-60. Cooler tonight. Sunday fair and not quite so cool in afternoon.

Maryland—Partly cloudy and cooler today. Highest 55 to 60 west and 60 to 64 east portion. Cooler at night. Sunday fair and a little warmer in the afternoon.

Southern New Jersey and Delaware — Partly cloudy and cooler today. Highest 58 to 63. Cooler tonight. Sunday fair, not quite so cool in afternoon.

Lower Potomac and Chesapeake Bay—West to north winds 20 to 30 miles per hour today. Weather partly cloudy. Good visibility.

EXTENDED FORECAST
(U.S. Weather Bureau)

For period today through Wednesday for Eastern Pennsylvania, Eastern New York and Mid-Atlantic States—Temperatures will average 2 to 5 degrees below normal. Quite cool over the week-end, warmer Monday and Tuesday, little change in temperature Wednesday. Heavy rains likely Tuesday or Wednesday.

PRUZZLE UNSOLVED; $150 NOW OFFERED

For the fifth consecutive week, fans failed to correctly solve Pruzzle, the Sunday News' prize crossword puzzle contest.

$150 is being offered this week for the correct solution to Pruzzle No. 6.

For the solution and explanation of the more difficult clues to last week's Pruzzle, please turn to page 12 in this morning's Intell Journal.

3 POLIO SUSPECT CASES DIAGNOSED; TOTAL REACHES 88

City Woman, County Baby And Girl Patients At Lancaster General

Three new cases of polio have been diagnosed at Lancaster General Hospital, it was reported yesterday. No new suspect cases were admitted.

Listed as positive cases now are Mrs. Richard Grim, twenty-nine, 640 Lehigh Ave.; Floyd Phillips, two-year-old son of Thomas J. Phillips, Christiana R1, and Miss Anna M. Kaylor, twenty, 29 W. Ferdinand St., Manheim.

The three new cases raise the number in the county for the year

Turn To Page 15 For More Of POLIO

Duck Hunter Is Missing; Farmer Blown From Steps

One man was missing and between 30 and 50 duck hunters were reported stranded on islands in the storm-churned Susquehanna River last night.

Missing is Lloyd G. Hostetter, Conestoga R2, who is believed to have met with an accident when he attempted to go to the aid of two duck hunters marooned on a small river island.

HEAR SHOTGUN BLASTS

Lending credence to the belief that Hostetter may have met with misfortune, was a report of a shotgun distress signal, a series of three blasts from a gun recognized in the hunting code as a means of signalling distress.

Reporting hearing the blasts was Preston Burkey, a deputy game warden patrolling the river area near Creswell. Earlier, Burkey said, he had seen Hostetter rowing his boat toward an island, about a third of the way across the river, where a brother Jacob, Willow Street and Aaron "Ernie" Stauf-

Turn To Page 15 For More Of DUCK HUNTERS

Yesterday's storm produced its share of bodily injury as well as property damage, but no deaths attributable to the storm were reported. One man was hurt when blown from the steps of his home.

Only four major injuries were reported by late last night and officials at the various hospitals indicated there were many minor injuries not reported to them because people didn't want to go outdoors.

E-TOWN FIREMAN HURT

One of the storm's early casualties was a member of the Elizabethtown Fire Co. who was hit on the head by a flying brick while helping put a tarpaulin on a dam-

Turn To Page 4 for More Of INJURIES

DAMAGE TO POWER LINES IN COUNTY WORST ON RECORD

Emergency Crews Called From Other Areas To Help Restore Service

Hurricane damage to power lines in Lancaster County was described as ". . . the worst in history" late last night as Pennsylvania Power and Light Co. officials labeled the Lancaster area the "hardest hit" in its 28-county system.

Emergency power repair crews from as far west as Michigan were placed on a stand-by basis as the storm raged through eastern Pennsylvania and PP&L of-

Turn To Page 15 For More Of PP AND L

How's He Doing?

EDITOR'S NOTE—The weatherman's gift for understatement was never so obvious as yesterday when Hurricane Hazel ripped and smashed her way out of the veil of obscurity he had attempted to weave around her with an innocently-worded forecast.

THE FORECAST
For Friday

Moderate to heavy rains with strong east or southeast winds. Partly cloudy with a few showers and northerly winds at night.

THE FULFILLMENT
On Friday

Driving all-day rains, followed by hurricane winds with gusts up to 85 miles per hour and evening showers.

"Early to Bed"

Want-Ad Deadline
6 P. M. Tonight

In order to publish the enlarged and colorful new Sunday News it is necessary to establish an early deadline for Want-Ads. All Want-Ads received before 6 P. M. today will start in tomorrow's Sunday News. The Want-Ad Department will be closed after 6 P. M. It will reopen Sunday 6 P. M. to 8:45 P. M. Call 5251 and ask for an Ad-Taker, your smiling Ad-Visor.

Eisenhower Blames Democrats For Sag In Farmer Buying Power

INDIANAPOLIS, Oct. 15 (AP)—President Eisenhower tonight blamed the Democrats for a 1951-52 sag in farmer buying power, and declared election of another Republican Congress in November would help build "a foundation of enduring prosperity" for American agriculture.

Addressing a cheering, capacity crowd in the 15,000-seat Butler University Fieldhouse, the President also sought again to erase any political advantage Democrats may have gained through Secretary of Defense Wilson's remarks about "kennel-dogs" and unemployment.

Without specific mention of those storm - stirring remarks, Eisenhower said:

"My heart truly goes out to every one of our citizens who wants to work and has no job, or who, in other ways, suffers these hardships. Efforts to eliminate distress

Turn To Page 4 For More Of EISENHOWER

WEATHER
(U. S. Weather Bureau Forecast for Lancaster, Cumberland, Lebanon, York, Adams and Franklin Counties):

Partly Cloudy And A Little Warmer Today, Clear And Cool Tonight. Tomorrow Partly Cloudy And Warmer. High Today 60-65.

Intelligencer DAILY Journal.

The Leading Newspaper in the Garden Spot of America. Home Owned for Home Folks Since 1794

161st Year.—No. 109. Official United States Census Figures Lancaster Metropolitan Area Population 234,717 LANCASTER, PA., THURSDAY MORNING, OCTOBER 21, 1954. CITY THIRTY-TWO PAGES 30c PER WEEK—5c Per Copy

TWO DIE IN AUTO ACCIDENTS HERE

County Polio Rate Highest In Pennsylvania

INCIDENCE HERE ONE FOR EVERY 2,607 PERSONS

Philadelphia Co. Has Greatest Number; New Victim Here

Lancaster County has the highest incidence of polio in relationship to its population of any county in Pennsylvania this year, according to figures of the State Health Department at Harrisburg.

At the time the figures were compiled there were 90 cases of the disease reported here. Latest census figures showed the county with a population of 234,717, indicating that one person out of every 2,607 has been stricken with the disease so far this year.

Three additional cases of polio have since been reported.

NEW CASE

Diagnosed as suffering from the disease yesterday at Lancaster General Hospital was Alma Eberly, twelve, daughter of Edwin Eberly, Reinholds R1. Her brother, Marlin, seventeen, was diagnosed Tuesday as suffering from the disease. Both were reported satisfactory last night.

A four-year-old girl, admitted as a suspect Tuesday, was discharged yesterday, while a twenty-two-year-old Drumore R1 man was admitted to the unit.

Pennsylvania's total of polio this year stands at 1,142 cases, compared to 1,109 for the same period last year.

Next to Lancaster, Bucks County rates second with one case for

Turn To Page 28 For More Of POLIO

"We Lead All The Rest"
FARM CORNER
By WILLIAM R. SCHULTZ

FEDERAL FUNDS INCREASED FOR CONSERVATION

1955 Allocations For County Farmers Doubled Over $65,000 Used This Year

Lancaster County's allocation for federal conservation payments in 1955 will be increased to $113,100—nearly double the amount paid to Garden Spot farmers this year.

The new budget is an increase from $105,000 allocated for the current Agricultural Conservation Program, and it compares with the estimated $65,000 actually used from this year's budget.

Miss Dorothy Y. Neel, ASC manager, said that $40,000 from the current budget had been reallocated to other counties when it became obvious it would not be used in this area.

The ACP program is the federal plan under which the government shares costs with farmers who carry out approved conservation practices on their farms.

ACP participation in Lancaster County dropped from 3,141 farmers in 1953 to around the 1,000 mark this year. Miss Neel explains that actual participation for 1954 will not be determined until all claims for payments have been filed.

The drop in participation this year was due largely to the new

Turn To Page 8 For More Of FARM CORNER

Weather Calendar

COMPARATIVE TEMPERATURES

Station	High	Low
Water Works	51	34
Ephrata	58	30
Last Year (Ephrata)	77	46
Official High for Year July 31		102
Official Low for Year Jan. 18		-1
Character of Day		Cloudy

WINDS
Direction NNW Avg. Velocity 10 mph

HUMIDITY
8 a.m. 82% 11 a.m. 66% 2 p.m. 80%
5 p.m. 86% 8 p.m. 80%
Average Humidity 79%

SUN
Rises 6:20 am. Sets 5:17 p.m.

MOON
Rises 2:26 a.m. Friday
New Moon, Oct. 26

STARS
Morning—Jupiter
Evening—Venus, Mars, Saturn

NEARBY FORECASTS
(U.S. Weather Bureau)

Lower Potomac and Chesapeake Bay—Winds mostly northwest 15-25 mph today diminishing by this afternoon or evening. Good visibility.

Maryland—Partly cloudy and somewhat warmer highest 58-64 today. Tomorrow fair and a little warmer.

Delaware and Southern New Jersey — Partly cloudy and somewhat warmer highest 60-64 today. Tomorrow fair and a little warmer.

Eastern Pennsylvania — Partly cloudy and somewhat warmer today and tomorrow. Highest today 55-62.

Western Powers Go Ahead On Giving Reich Sovereignty

Menacing Deadlock Over Saar Between France And Germany Tempers Optimism Expressed Earlier At Paris By Diplomats Facing 2 Problems

PARIS, Oct. 20 (AP)—The Big Three Western powers made progress tonight toward giving sovereignty back to West Germany, but faced a menacing deadlock between Germany and France over the Saar. Optimism expressed yesterday was tempered sharply.

The old French-German dispute over the future of the Saar was only one of two major problems facing the Western nations gathering here in increasing numbers to work out progressively the accords which they hope will make the West a solid bloc against Communist aggression.

Besides the Saar, there arose again the problem of how to control the amount of arms which West Germany will have, or will be able to make, once she becomes a nation allied in friendship with her former enemies of the West and free in almost every sense of the word.

MET FOR TWO HOURS

Ministers of the four powers met for two hours in the late afternoon to act on more than 100 pages of intricate text designed to make West Germany free, only not quite. The meeting was held at the Paris headquarters of the North Atlantic Treaty Organization.

"Solutions were proposed for the

Turn To Page 8 For More Of PARIS

SINKLER HAILS U.S. CRACKDOWN ON WATCH IMPORT

Hamilton President Says Move By President In National Interest

Hamilton Watch Co. president Arthur B. Sinkler declared yesterday that the Justice Department's anti-trust action against 18 American and six Swiss firms in the jeweled watch trade "highlights another issue in the struggle for existence by American watch companies."

"During the past 20 years," Sinkler said, "the domestic jeweled watch industry has been stifled by restrictive trade practices of the Swiss coupled with concessions in tariff on watches imported into the United States."

Sinkler said that the "coercive tactics of a world-wide Swiss cartel" have constituted a "serious threat to the continuation of free competition and the survival of a domestic industry that is essential to national defense."

The Hamilton president states:

"It is regrettable that an action by the Department of Justice is necessary to correct these restraints. . . (but) this forthright action of the Eisenhower administration. . . is certainly in the national interest."

Sinkler's statement referred to this week's action by the U. S. Attorney General against such firms as Bulova, Benrus, Gruen and Longines-Wittnauer for violating the Sherman Anti-Trust Act and the Wilson Tariff Act. The latter legislation forbids conspiracies involving imports and exports.

STATEMENT OF SINKLER

The complete statement follows:

"The anti-trust complaint of the Department of Justice naming as defendants most of the active participants in the Swiss watch cartel has again focused attention on the watch industry. The forthright action of President Eisenhower in recently withdrawing tariff concessions on watches given to the Swiss in 1936 was a first step in the direction of fair competition. The action of Attorney General Brownell yesterday highlights

Turn To Page 8 For More Of HAMILTON

President In Connecticut

Picture made through the transparent top of the Presidential car shows a serious-faced trio a President Eisenhower (left) arrives at Trinity College, Hartford, Conn., to receive an honorary degree. In the center is Dean Arthur R. Hughes of Trinity College, and at right is Gov. John Lodge of Connecticut.

County Home Storm Damage Not Covered By Insurance

The expense of replacing one roof and repairing another at the County home buildings must be borne by the taxpayers because the county carries no wind damage insurance it was revealed yesterday.

Woodrow A. Zeamer, minority county commissioner, said that several taxpayers had asked him to check the truth of the report that no extended insurance is carried on county-owned property.

He learned, he added, in conversations with State Sen. G. Graybill Diehm and Harry R. Metzler, Republicans, the other two members of the board of commissioners that such was the case.

Zeamer said he asked to see the insurance policies covering the county home and hospital but as yet they have not been made available for his inspection.

The roof of one wing at the county home was torn away and the roof on another part of the home was damaged by the hurricane which swept this section last Friday.

"I have no knowledge of the insurance coverage, the amount or the type of insurance on any of the county-owned buildings," Zeamer said. "I certainly recommend complete coverage."

The minority county commissioner declared that the condition "hints of poor management" and seems to me to be another example of false economy."

County employes are repairing the damage.

Sheppard's Attorney Blows Up On Hayes Angle Of Case

CLEVELAND, Oct. 20 (AP)—Defense Atty. William J. Corrigan blew up in court today at the murder trial of Dr. Samuel H. Sheppard. He roared at the top of his voice: "I know they're going to bring Susan Hayes into this courtroom.

"I know what evidence they have," shouted Corrigan as he waved toward the state's side of the counsel table. "I know how Susan Hayes has been blasted in the papers."

Then Corrigan angrily refused to question a prospective juror any further and allowed him to be seated as the sixth juror.

Mrs. Anna W. Foote, housewife and mother of five children, was accepted as the seventh juror just before the trial ended for the day. She was the third woman accepted.

MAY HAVE PANEL

Seating of the seventh juror before the overnight recess raised the possibility a full panel might be obtained before the end of the week. One was chosen Monday, two yesterday and four today.

Sheppard, 30-year-old osteopath, is on trial for his life. The state accuses him of beating his wife Marilyn, 31, to death last July 4. He denies the slaying. He said his

Turn To Page 8 For More Of SHEPPARD

On Way To Third Day Of Murder Trial

Dr. Samuel Sheppard (left), handcuffed to a deputy, is led from a jail elevator to the court room for the start of the third day of his murder trial in Cleveland.

Monaghan Hits Sales Tax As Burden To Vets

Thomas J. Monaghan, Democratic county campaign manager, yesterday told the party's newly-organized Veterans Committee that the veterans always become something "special" at election time but that "underneath all the assistance they receive there are stones tied around our necks that have us bearing a higher than proportionate cost of our government services."

W. Roger Simpson was named chairman of the committee, which will be expanded to include representatives of every community in the county.

Monaghan listed the state sales tax as the number one example that the veteran is socked with a high proportionate share of the cost of government.

NEW FAMILIES

"The veteran in most cases represents the newly-established family. His children are young. His need of items is greater because of the age and size of his family. He represents the group being hit hardest.

"If, as we all have to be, he is budget-conscious and his wife is making clothes for his children he has got to pay tax on the yard goods, buttons, and so forth. The bottle of cough medicine carries a tax. Sure, it doesn't, if it is prescribed by the doctor. But how many of us can run to the doctor every time our children have the

Turn To Page 28 For More Of MONAGHAN

MARYLAND WILL OPEN 12 MILES OF HIGHWAY

FREDERICK, Md., Oct. 20 (AP)—Maryland will open 12 miles of new dual highway tomorrow and erase one of the worst stretches on U.S. 40 in all its coast-to-coast length.

The new road is between Ridgeville, 33 miles west of Baltimore, and the Monocacy River, on the east edge of Frederick.

When the ribbons are cut, motorists will have a 55-mile-an-hour chute, without traffic lights and only a handful of side roads, all the way from the west edge of Baltimore to the east side of Frederick. There's no toll.

Ice Follies
Naked Truth: Can't Tell 'Em Sans Their All

Ten years from now — maybe sooner—they'll deny they ever had any part in it, but late last night several hundred exuberant members of the freshmen and sophomore classes at Franklin and Marshall College pranced about the campus sans pants, sans shirts—sans, in fact, everything but shoes.

It was a cool, cool evening, but that fact melted in the heat of the conflict between the embattled classes.

Starting out as the second event in a round of tests of strength on the campus, last night's frolic was billed as the "pants" fight. Last week a tug-of-war went to the frosh.

ACADEMIC MATTER

Technically, the question of whether the frosh would or wouldn't have to adhere to traditional frosh restrictions rode on the outcome of the pants fight.

Actually members of both sides conceded last night that it was purely academic, since the restrictions are scheduled to be dropped Saturday regardless of the outcome.

The tussle appeared, therefore to be merely an excuse for again opening the escape valve for youthful spirits that recently threatened a campus explosion of more serious proportions.

The frosh gathered early in the evening around a roaring wood fire in the rear of Hartman Hall.

But it wasn't until along about 11 p. m. that the sophs engaged them in combat.

In no time at all combatants

Turn To Page 28 For More Of F & M

PROGRESS ON PEACE MADE —EISENHOWER

President Says Administration Has Come Far In Long Fight

NEW YORK, Oct. 20 (AP) — President Eisenhower — in the face of Democratic criticism of the Republican regime's foreign policy—declared tonight his administration has "come far" in thwarting Communist aggression and toward winning lasting world peace.

The chief executive told a nationwide television and radio audience "the persistently aggressive design" of Russia and Red China "shows no evidence of genuine change."

But the "awesome" military might of America and the other free nations is "a deterrent to war," Eisenhower said at a dinner marking the 300th anniversary of Jewish life in America.

TO STAND READY

That might, the President told an applauding 1,800 diners at the Sheraton-Astor Hotel, will be kept ready "at all times, in today's uncertain world, . . . to deal effectively and flexibly" with any new Communist threat to the free world."

The White House billed the President's speech as "nonpolitical," but the address served to recall sharp criticism which former President Truman and Adlai Stevenson, the 1952 Democratic presi-

Turn To Page 8 For More Of EISENHOWER

MRS. HORTING SAYS DEMOCRATS WILL FULFILL PLEDGES

State Committee Officer Tells Manheim Rally Platform Will Be Enacted

Mrs. Ruth Grigg Horting, vice chairman of the Democratic State Committee, told a rally of Democratic workers at Manheim last night that the party's platform, pledge by pledge, will be enacted into law when the Democrats take over the state next year.

Mrs. Horting, who was a member of the Democratic platform committee and helped draft the document upon which State Sen. George M. Leader is running for governor, outlined some of the provisions in the platform.

She lashed out at the Republicans who, she said, "adopt a similar platform, year after year, and yet do nothing about it."

During the last Democratic administration, she pointed out, the Democratic party carried out every single pledge contained in both the 1934 and 1936 party platforms.

KEY TO VICTORY

Mrs. Horting, who recently returned from a 2,000-mile campaign trip which carried her into every part of the state, said the key to Democratic victory on Nov. 2, is to get the facts of the campaign and the party's platform before the voters and to get the voters to the polls.

The Democratic platform, she said, was written only after two days of public hearings at which any group could appear and present its recommendations and suggestions.

In contrast, she added, the Republican platform was written without any public hearings.

NOMINEES SPEAK

The Democratic nominees for the General Assembly from the county district also addressed the

Turn To Page 28 For More Of MANHEIM

EISENHOWER MAKES ISAIAH A 'PRIVATE'

NEW YORK, Oct. 20 (AP)—A lifetime of military service apparently has left its mark on President Eisenhower—tonight he inadvertantly gave the biblical Isaiah the rank of "private."

Near the end of his speech at the American Jewish tercentenary dinner, the President said:

"We know, with the 'private' Isaiah, that the work of righteousness shall be peace."

The prepared text of his speech, distributed to newsmen in advance, correctly identified Isaiah as "prophet," not "private."

Manheim Native Killed, Sister Hurt Critically

Lancaster County Highway Deaths Since Jan. 1, 1954
43
Same Date—1953—26

Nonagenarian Fatally Hurt At E-Town In Accident Earlier

A Lancaster County native, returning to Delaware after a family birthday party, was killed almost instantly in a two-car collision last night about three miles south of Manheim.

The victim is Miss Phylis Peifer, twenty-six, Kings College, Del., a daughter of Mr. and Mrs. Paul M. Peifer, 162 S. Grant St., Manheim. Dr. D. W. Martin, deputy coroner from Manheim, said the woman died almost instantly of a fractured skull and broken neck.

Her sister, Mrs. Marian Borch, twenty-three, also of Kings College, suffered a possible skull fracture, possible internal injuries, a severe head laceration and shock. She is in a critical condition at Lancaster General Hospital.

Mrs. Borch

The fatality was the fifth in the county since Tuesday and the 43rd so far this year. Mrs. Emma Fisher Braddock, formerly of Philadelphia, a ninety-one year-old guest at the Masonic Homes, Elizabethtown, was killed around noon yesterday while two sailors and a WAVE died in a bus-car collision at Penn Hill early Tuesday morning.

AT INTERSECTION

The accident occurred at the intersection of two township roads about three miles south of Manheim at 9:30 p.m., according to state policeman Nicholas Zulick. He said that one car driven by Mrs. Borch's husband, William, was heading south on a township road when he collided with an east-bound car operated by Gerald Ginder, seventeen, Manheim R1. The intersection is known as the Airydale School crossroads.

Borch, his wife and Miss Peifer were returning from a family gathering at the Peifer home in honor of Borch's twentieth birthday today.

As Borch's vehicle entered the crossroads, it was struck almost broadside by Ginder's car, police were told. The impact hurled both Miss Peifer and her sister out of the car. The victim was thrown under Ginder's vehicle and was killed almost instantly.

Police said that neither driver had a stop-sign, but that a stop sign had been erected ten days ago on the south entrance of road which Borch was traveling. They both told police they were travel-

Turn To Page 28 For More Of FATALITY

YOUNG GOP LISTS ITINERARY FOR 'CAMPAIGN CAR'

In Penn Square Tomorrow Night; Fifteen Directors Are Nominated

Fifteen directors to serve two-year terms were nominated last night at a meeting of the board of directors of the Young Republicans of Lancaster County at the Women's Republican Club headquarters, 36 W. Orange St.

The directors also announced the itinerary of their "campaign car" which has been arousing unusual interest in the current campaign.

The car will be at Elizabethtown tonight. Congressman Paul B. Dague, Republican candidate for re-election to his fifth term, will be the principal speaker at a rally to be held at 8 p. m. in the social room of the First National Bank.

At 7 p. m. Friday the campaign car and local candidates will be in the Griest Building quadrant of Penn Square. On Saturday the car will be at New Holland and next Monday the stop will be Terre Hill.

At that place a rally will be held at which the principal speaker will be Congressman Dague. On Friday evening, Oct. 29 the campaign car will tour Manheim and Lititz.

Directors nominated at the meeting, in charge of Edwin D. Eshleman, chairman, were:

Lancaster—Robert Chryst, Howard H. Bailey, Esther Holder, Gertrude May, Barbara Monyer, Verne Myrland, Bruce Ryder, Paul Stewart, D. Jane Stabley and Arthur Campbell.

Millersville—E. D. Eshleman.

Columbia—Wilson Bucher.

Elizabethtown — John Groff, Harold Greiner and Jamie Rowley.

Ephrata—S. Milo Herr.

Deadly Detour
Fifth Accident In 24 Days On Pequea Bridge

The fifth automobile accident in 24 days occurred at 5:30 p.m. yesterday on Route 222 on the Pequea Bridge, a mile and a half south of Elliott's Corner.

West Lampeter Police Chief Frank Horner pointed out that the bridge is too narrow for autos to pass and that three vehicles were waiting to cross the bridge. Route 222 is being used as a detour while Route 72 is temporarily closed.

The first car, operated by Mrs. Ruth L. Hurst, Hessdale, Pa., started across and skidded on the wet bridge. Her auto spun completely around.

The second car stopped suddenly to avoid hitting her and was struck in the rear by an auto operated by Mrs. Margaret E. Ross, Quarryville R2, according to Chief Horner. The second car was not damaged and the driver continued.

Chief Horner estimated damage to Mrs. Ross' auto at $300.

DAGUE TO ADDRESS CAMPAIGN GATHERING AT E-TOWN TONIGHT

Congressman Paul B. Dague, seeking re-election to his fifth term from the Lancaster-Chester County district on the Republican ticket, will address a campaign rally at Elizabethtown tonight.

The rally will be held at 8 p.m. in the social rooms of the First National Bank, Elizabethtown, and is under the sponsorship of the Elizabethtown Young Republican Club.

The party's candidates for the General Assembly, Norman Wood, Peach Bottom; Baker Royer, Ephrata; Edwin D. Eshleman, Millersville, and Paul G. Murray, Lancaster, also will attend.

Jamie Rowley, president of the club, will be in charge of the meeting. Congressman Dague will be presented by Richard L. Musser, chairman of the club's program committee.

How's He Doing?

EDITOR'S NOTE—Fair and cool you said, Mr. Weatherman. Come, please, and take a look at the pressing bill for our rain-dampened topcoat.

THE FORECAST For Wednesday	THE FULFILLMENT On Wednesday
Fair and cool, clear at night with scattered frost. High 60-65.	Continued cold with afternoon and evening showers. High 58.

WEATHER

(U. S. Weather Bureau Forecast for Lancaster, Cumberland, Lebanon, York, Adams and Franklin Counties):

Fair And Colder Today And Tonight. Tomorrow Some Cloudiness With Chance Of Light Rain. High Today 42-47.

Intelligencer Journal.

The Leading Newspaper in the Garden Spot of America. Home Owned for Home Folks Since 1794

161st Year.—No. 130. Official United States Census Figures Lancaster Metropolitan Area Population 234,717 LANCASTER, PA., MONDAY MORNING, NOVEMBER 15, 1954. CITY TWENTY-EIGHT PAGES. 30c PER WEEK—5c Per Copy

THE INTELL INDEX

GIRL DIES OF AUTO CRASH INJURIES

Opening Of New Library Building 'Milestone' In Continuing Effort

Dedication Ceremony Points Up Need For Sufficient Books

The new building for the Lancaster Free Public Library "marks a milestone in a campaign which has been carried on for many years, and which still will continue," F. Lyman Windolph, former president of the library board, said in the principal talk at dedication ceremonies yesterday.

"The objective of the campaign is to give Lancaster an adequate public library," Windolph said. "Today's dedication marks the erection of a fine and adequate library building.

"But there is no use to have a building without books. A library building without books in it would be just like a railroad station without any trains."

Windolph told the throng of nearly 1,000 persons that when they inspected the building after the dedication they would see for themselves that the book collection is grossly inadequate.

MUST JOIN HANDS

"We must all enlist for the duration. We must all join hands in order to see to it that Lancaster secures a fine and adequate library to house in the building that we are dedicating today."

Clifford J. Backstrand, president of the library board, presided at the dedication ceremonies, held on the library steps at 125 N. Duke St. Wallace L. Robinson was chairman of the dedication committee and the invocation was given by the Rev. Robert C. Batchelder, rector of nearby St. James' Episcopal Church.

Backstrand told the crowd that the library directors had long looked forward to the occasion, and expressed the hope that the public would have equal pride in the new building.

From the standpoint of permanency, the new building will be standing and serviceable 100 years from now, the board president said. Its basic structure can readily be altered by extending

Turn To Page 24 For More Of LIBRARY

Part of the crowd of 1,000 persons attending the dedication of the new Lancaster Free Public Library building on N. Duke Street yesterday afternoon are shown as Clifford J. Backstrand, president of the library board, opened the ceremonies on the steps of the building. Speaker was F. Lyman Windolph, a board member and president of the board for many years. Open house was held following the dedication. The library will be open "for business" today. (Intell Photo)

COMPROMISE ON CENSURE FADING OUT

McCarthy's Refusal To Retract Attacks Blamed, Debate Resumes Today

WASHINGTON, Nov. 14 (AP)—Efforts to compromise a censure resolution against Sen. McCarthy (R-Wis) appeared to be verging on collapse today in the face of McCarthy's refusal to retract his attacks on colleagues.

Although Republican leaders continued their attempts to work out a substitute for a resolution which would rebuke McCarthy on two points, one of them said the results were not encouraging.

The Senate starts its second week of debate tomorrow with Sen. Watkins (R-Utah), chairman of a six-man inquiry committee, planning to take the floor to answer McCarthy's charges the group served as the "unwitting handmaiden" of the Communists in recommending that he be censured.

TO QUIZ SOLON

Two hours before the senate meets McCarthy plans to question Watkins at a session of his investigations subcommittee. McCarthy contends the Watkins committee report absolved Brig. Gen. Ralph W. Zwicker of responsibility for the promotion and honorable discharge of an Army dentist whom McCarthy has called a Fifth Amendment Communist.

Watkins said he would be on hand. But as to who promoted the Army dentist, former Maj. Irving Peress, Watkins said "I'd like to know myself. I know Zwicker didn't."

Although Watkins said he was standing on his committee's principal censure recommendations—except for possible changes in the wording of its resolution to sofen one charge and strengthen another—Sen. Case (R-SD) said he would vote for a compromise "if I thought it provided a more constructive answer."

KNOWLAND HUDDLE

Case was reported to have huddled during the weekend with Sen. Knowland of California, the Republican leader, who has not committed himself on the censure resolution but apparently has been active in seeking some modifications.

Despite this activity, a Republican senator, who intends to vote to absolve McCarthy told a reporter he and others are having difficulty in finding any compromise language that might be acceptable to a Senate majority.

Morever, this senator, who asked to remain anonymous, said that McCarthy thus far has shown no indication he would go along with any compromise. The suspicion has been growing among McCarthy's friends that he would prefer to be censured and then carry his ideas to the country.

NOT CONVINCED

"We haven't been able to convince Joe that he ought to retract anything," this senator said. "But we think that if we can find

Turn To Page 24 For More Of McCARTHY

Fire Damages 3 City Homes; Family Flees

Fire damaged three homes in the city over the weekend. As a result of one blaze, Walter Keiser, forty-three, 806 E. Marion St., and his two children were forced to escape through a second floor window when their home filled with smoke.

In another fire, the homes of Henry O. Bennett, 313 Green St., and Russell L. Bair, 311 Green St., were damaged at an estimated loss of $1,500 at 10:50 a.m. yesterday.

Assistant Fire Chief Frank Deen said the fire was reportedly started by someone burning trash at the rear of the Bair residence. The wooden balcony of the home caught fire, the flames spreading to the balcony at the adjoining Bennett home.

FLEE TO SAFETY

Bennett said his wife, Ophelia, and his brother-in-law and sister, Mr. and Mrs. Thomas Reed, were all sleeping on the second floor. He said his sister was aroused first by the smoke and awakened the others. They fled to safety without

Turn To Page 4 For More Of FIRES

HOSIERY PLANT IS HIT BY FIRE; $5,500 DAMAGE

3 Companies Answer Alarm To Small Structure Near Farmersville

A small hosiery plant, located about half a mile north of Farmersville, was damaged when fire broke out in the one-story structure about 11:30 a. m. yesterday and resulted in a loss to the building and contents estimated at $5,500.

The 40x100 foot concrete block structure, located in Conestoga Valley between Farmersville and Brownstown, is owned by Amos Hoover, Ephrata R2, and is leased by Elwood Lees, 40 E. Walnut St., Ephrata. It is know as the Lees Hosiery Mill.

Lees told firemen he was working in his office when he noticed smoke coming from the ceiling. He said he tried to telephone the Akron Fire Co. but when he found the telephone out of order he had to send a neighbor, Bud Andes, to Akron to summon firemen.

Answering the alarm, in addition to the Akron firemen, were companies from Ephrata and Farmersville.

Because of the large amount of smoke, firemen were forced to break several windows to allow it to escape from the building. Akron Fire Chief Harry Frymyer reported that the blaze, believed caused by a short circuit in wiring, caused considerable damage to the ceiling while the heat, water and smoke damaged machinery and materials inside the shop.

Hoover estimated the building loss at $1,000 while Lees estimated his loss at $4,500. Lees and another man operate the hosiery mill and it was not determined last night how long it will be out of operation.

LIVED 4 DAYS AFTER MISHAP ON TWP. ROAD

Miss Dorothy Workman, 20, Victim Of Collision With Truck

Miss Dorothy Workman, twenty, New Holland R2, died at 5 p. m. yesterday at Lancaster General Hospital from injuries received when her convertible and a truck collided near New Holland Wednesday afternoon.

She resided with her foster parents, Mr. and Mrs. Ralph M. Miller.

Miss Workman never regained consciousness following the accident at 1:45 p.m. Wednesday at the intersection of Legislative Route 36013 and a township road, two miles south of New Holland.

Miss Workman

Her 1938 auto collided with a truck operated by Willie E. Beam Jr., Bareville R1, according to State Policeman Peter Andrusisian of the Ephrata substation.

Beam was driving a hay-laden truck owned by the Lancaster County Farm Bureau Cooperative Association, police said. He was on his way to make a delivery and was traveling west slowly on the legislative route, glancing at the mailboxes as he drove.

SAW NOTHING

He approached the intersection of the township road, he told police, and looked both ways, but did not see anything approaching.

As he started across the V-intersection, the auto operated by Miss Workman came over a crest on the township road and sideswiped the truck, police said.

The convertible then swerved to the other side of the road, crashed down a two-foot ditch and overturned twice. The young woman was pinned in the auto.

Police were not able to question the girl. They learned, however she was on her way to visit a friend when the accident occurred. She was employed at the New Holland Silk Mill.

ORDERS AUTOPSY

Dr. Charles P. Stahr, deputy coroner, has ordered an autopsy to determine the cause of her death. Following the autopsy, Trooper Andrusisian will consult with Dr. Stahr and District Attorney William C. Storb concerning the accident.

Born in this city, Miss Workman was the daughter of Harry S. Workman Jr., Columbia R2, and the late Ruth Rineer Workman. She was a member of Ronks Evangelical Church.

In addition to her father and foster parents, she is survived by a brother, Jack A. Workman, Colum-

Turn To Page 24 For More Of FATALITY

"We Lead All The Rest"

FARM CORNER

By WILLIAM R. SCHULTZ

STUDY LAUNCHED ON MARKETING OF COUNTY POTATOES

A special study of potato marketing and grading has been launched in Lancaster County by the Pennsylvania Bureau of Markets and the Pennsylvania State University.

Purpose of the work is to determine consumer acceptance of different types of packaging and grades, and to obtain information on farm costs in preparing special packs.

M. J. McMillen, of the Pennsylvania Department of Agriculture, will supervise the work in this area. The study will require an estimated six months to complete.

One of the questions the study hopes to answer is whether consumers will pay premium prices for "fancy" grades of potatoes and whether or not the labor costs of preparing these packs justifies the special work involved.

In addition, extensive informa-

Turn To Page 4 For More Of FARM CORNER

Weather Calendar

COMPARATIVE TEMPERATURES

Station	High	Low
Water Works (Saturday)	48	20
Water Works (Sunday)	61	24
Ephrata	64	32
Last Year (Ephrata)	37	24
Official High for Year July 31		102
Official Low for Year Jan. 18		-1
Character of Day		Clear

WINDS

Direction WSW Avg. Velocity 4 mph

HUMIDITY

8 a.m. 92% 11 a.m. 66% 2 p.m. 50%
5 p.m. 69% 8 p.m. 74%
Average Humidity 70%

SUN

Rises 6:48 a.m. Sets 4:48 p.m.

MOON

Rises 10:10 p.m. Last Quarter, Nov. 17

STARS

Morning—Mercury, Venus, Jupiter, Saturn
Evening—Mars

NEARBY FORECASTS
(U.S. Weather Bureau)

Lower Potomac and Chesapeake Bay—Northerly winds 10 to 20 mph today. Fair weather. Good visibility.

Maryland—Some cloudiness but mostly sunny and colder highest 45-50 west and 48-54 east portion today. Colder tonight. Tomorrow mostly cloudy and rather cool chance of occasional rain.

Delaware and Southern New Jersey — Some cloudiness but mostly sunny and colder, highest 46-52 today. Colder tonight. Tomorrow increasing cloudiness chance of occasional rain by afternoon or evening.

Eastern Pennsylvania — Partly cloudy and colder, highest 38-46 today. Colder tonight. Tomorrow increasing cloudiness and somewhat warmer chance of occasional rain by afternoon or night.

NORTH AFRICAN FRENCH CLASHES TAKE 31 LIVES

21 Killed In Tunisia, 10 Dead In Revolt In Algeria

TUNIS, Tunisia, Nov. 14 (AP)—At least 31 persons were killed in North Africa yesterday, 21 in the protectorate of Tunisia and 10 in the heaviest Algerian fighting since the rebellion broke out two weeks ago, French sources reported today.

Of the dead, 20 were Tunisian nationalist guerrillas who fell in a violent clash with French forces at Djebel Gárbou, in eastern Tunisia.

The biggest fight in Algeria came at Djebel Uchmoul, in the Aures Mountains of the southeast. A detachment of French parachutists lost two men and found five bodies of guerrillas on the battlefield.

TOOK DEAD, WOUNDED

It was thought the retreating Algerians took some dead and wounded with them.

In the Algiers region, two rebels of a force of 20 were killed in a fight near Tigzirt, and French troops lost one killed and one wounded.

The Tunisian fighting gave the French two prisoners and 23 weapons, the French said.

The Tunisian outlaws, or Fellaghas, are still active despite the offer of larger autonomy made to their country by French Premier Pierre Mendes-France four months ago.

Naguib Linked To Plot, Deposed As Egypt Boss

CAIRO, Egypt, Nov. 14 (AP)—Egypt's governing Revolutionary Council today deposed Maj. Gen. Mohamed Naguib as president and council chairman. It accused him of being implicated in a plot by the fanatic Moslem Brotherhood against the life of his rival, Premier Gamal Abdel Nasser.

The action against Naguib was taken after an early morning clash in suburban Heliopolis between police and a brotherhood mob in which two civilians were killed and two policemen seriously wounded.

Maj. Amin Shaker, a government spokesman, said Youssef Talaat, leader of the Brotherhood's secret order, was arrested and confessed Egypt's 53-year-old president had approved the assassination plot

Turn To Page 24 For More Of EGYPT

TWO WOMEN FOUND HACKED TO DEATH

ROCHESTER, N.Y., Nov. 14 (AP) — Two women were found hacked to death with an ax in the cellar of a two-family house nere tonight, police reported.

Detectives said they were questioning the husband of one of the women in connection with the deaths.

The victims were identified as Mrs. Millie Marcucci, 42, and her aunt, Mrs. Francesca Cotogno, about 76.

Police said Mrs. Marcucci's estranged husband Joseph, 27, was picked up about 20 minutes after the women's bodies were found and was being questioned in the case.

Navy Plane, Jet Search Aircraft Crash Into Sea

NORFOLK, Va., Nov. 14 (AP)—A two-engined Navy patrol plane with a crew of five aboard crashed into the Atlantic Ocean about 46 miles southeast of Cherry Point, N. C., tonight.

Three hours later, a Marine Corps Skyknight jet, instructed to search for the missing patrol craft while on a tactical mission from Cherry Point with two aboard, was reported missing in the same area and presumed down.

A spokesman at 5th Naval District headquarters here said the patrol plane radioed at 6:30 p.m. EST it would have to ditch.

SHIPS IN AREA

At that time two Navy destroyers — the Goodrich and the Turner — were in the area and im-

Turn To Page 24 For More Of PLANES

UNNECESSARY NOISE LAID TO MOTORIST

Donald M. Spencer, Cochranville R1, was charged yesterday by city police with making unnecessary noise.

Police said his auto was equipped with a straight pipe and no muffler.

Also prosecuted before Alderman J. Edward Wetzel were: Patrick H. J. Hall, 456 S. Shippen St., ignoring a stop sign; Jack E. Summers, 991 Clark St., too fast for conditions; Anna N. Lefever, Quarryville R2, failure to yield the right of way; Luther A. Eichelberger, 633 Lake St., too fast for conditions, and Arshaloys Mooradian, 668 W. Chestnut St., failure to yield the right of way to pedestrians.

How's He Doing?

EDITOR'S NOTE—About the only thing one can say about the weatherman's attempt yesterday was "he tried." Nothing more.

THE FORECAST
For Sunday

Cloudy, warmer with showers likely in the afternoon. High between 56 and 60.

THE FULFILLMENT
On Sunday

Some clouds, no showers. The high was 64 degrees.

STATEMENT DUE TODAY ON SCHICK MOVE TO COUNTY

Stamford Firm's Directors To Make Announcement After Special Meeting

STAMFORD, Conn., Nov. 14 (AP)—A company executive said yesterday an announcement would be made tomorrow on reports here that the Schick Electric Shaver Co. would move to Lancaster.

Cecil M. Arrowsmith, Schick's industrial relations director, said the announcement would come after a special meeting of the board of directors.

The Stamford Advocate, afternoon newspaper here, published the following story yesterday:

"Continuing reports here and in Lancaster, Pa., that the Schick Electric Shaver factory would be moved from Stamford to Lancaster would not be confirmed or denied by the company today.

SPECIAL MEETING

"However, Cecil M. Arrowsmith, industrial relations director, said that a special meeting of the Board of Directors would be held at the Stamford plant on Monday and that some announcement would be forthcoming after that meeting.

"The Schick officials have said for more than a year that the factory here was becoming too cramped but there was no indication that it would leave Stamford to get additional space.

"The company too has had considerable labor friction. It has an International Association of Machinists (AFL) contract.

SALES HIGH

"Currently, Schick's sales and profits are reported high and the stock is in the neighborhood of

Turn To Page 4 For More Of SCHICK

TRUCK INDUSTRY PAGES

Gov. John S. Fine has declared this week Truck Transportation Week in observance of the trucking industry's 51st year. On pages 13 to 21 of today's *Intelligencer Journal* you'll find news and pictures of the Lancaster City and County trucking industry.

Joe Backers To Start Drive For 10 Million More

NEW YORK, Nov. 14 (AP)—Supporters of Sen. Joseph R. McCarthy (R-Wis) tonight announced a nationwide drive for 10 million signatures on a petition backing McCarthy and "the fundamental principles he symbolizes."

George E. Stratemeyer, retired lieutenant general of the Air Force, launched the drive as chairman of a newly-formed organization called "Ten Million Americans Mobilizing for Justice."

The organization said it would seek to obtain the signatures dur-

Turn To Page 24 For More Of BACKERS

TEMPERATURES SEEN FALLING HERE TODAY

Falling temperatures are predicted for the county today, ending a spell of pleasant weather.

Compared with yesterday's high of 64 at the Ephrata Weather Station, the forecast sees the mercury rising to little more than the mid-forties today.

According to the late forecast, it will be fair today and tonight while skies will cloud tomorrow. Some light rain is expected tomorrow.

The mercury dipped to the freezing mark or below over the weekend to extend overnight cold snaps which started more than a week ago. Every morning for the past eight days, the thermometer at the Ephrata station has recorded freezing or below freezing conditions. Early Saturday, it was 21, while early yesterday a reading of 32 degrees was reported.

That Da Da Strain

South Rampart Street Parade Swingin' Round Kremlin Wall

LONDON, Nov. 14 (AP)—Moscow radio informed an Austrian listener today that hot Western jazz is being played in Russia and there are comrades who like it.

"Many of our Austrian listeners are interested in the jazz music of the Soviet Union," said a German language broadcast. "We recently received a letter from a listener in Vienna who asked whether or not there were Jazz fans in the Soviet Union," said the announcer, "and jazz orchestras that play in parks, theatres, culture places and parks, theatres, culture palaces and taurants and cafes.

WESTERN JAZZ TOO

"They perform not only Soviet jazz music but Western jazz as well."

It was only seven years ago that the Central Committee of the Communist party denounced jazz as decadent, savage and bad for youthful Russians. But the announcer today explained that Soviet jazz observes a precise and definite rhythm, possesses a pleasing harmony and has a melody that is clearly discernible.

Back before the party frowned on jazz there was a big orchestra leader named Sasha Svasman in Russia with a big nationwide success entitled "Svitsoo." It may not have been clearly discernible, but it sure did sound like "Sweet Sue."

Police Holding City Motorist In Hit-Run Mishap

A city motorist was apprehended by state police and is being held for investigation after a hit-run accident involving three cars occurred at 8:15 p. m. yesterday just north of the S. Duke Street bridge in Lancaster Twp.

Picked up at the Concordia Club, 132 N. Water St., in back of which his car was parked, was Charles Wood Jr., 450½ S. Shippen St. Police said Wood would not admit to operating the auto at the time of the crash.

State Policeman John Zabo said Wood's car is a red convertible, similar to the auto involved in the hit-run accident. He reported that Wood's car was damaged. Before being apprehended, Wood telephoned city police and informed them of the damage but did not state how it occurred.

Police said Ronald B. Mentzer, eighteen, of Lampeter, was travel-

Turn To Page 4 For More Of ACCIDENTS

JOE THE MOTORISTS FRIEND
Santa Delivers the Best to JOE
LIONEL TRAINS
ALL LIONEL TRAINS have real R.R. remote control knuckle couplers. All LIONEL rolling stock is detailed to blueprint perfection. And with famous LIONEL accessories you complete the picture of a big-time railroad in full operation. The whole array is colorful as only the real thing can be. See Joe's big display.
ELECTRIC TRAIN & TRESTLE SET
$15.95
HILL CLIMBING LOCOMOTIVE SPEEDS OVER AND UNDER ELEVATED TRESTLE
A most wanted outfit complete with trestles and twice as much track as found in ordinary sets. A truly sensational value that your boy has always dreamed about. Hurry to JOE's this week end for this sensational special.
ACT AT ONCE!
This sensational value will soon disappear from our counters, we cannot secure more shipments of this superb outfit from the factory any more this season.
COMPLETE WITH TRANSFORMER NOTHING ELSE TO BUY
The powerful transformer starts, stops and reverses your train. The outfit is complete with telegraph poles, a crossing signal exactly as pictured.
ELECTRIC
HAND CAR
RUNS ON ANY THREE-TRACK R. R.
This sensational accessory will add sparkle to your railroad, will run on either Lionel "O" Gauge, Lionel "027" or Marx track. Simply put it on the track and away she goes with the two industrious workmen pumping up and down. The snappiest thing you can add to your railroad system this year, and best of all it is at JOE'S sensationally low price.
$4.95
TOOL BOX
American Flyer
Come in and see for yourself all the popular American Flyer trains and accessories. They puff real smoke . . . They produce the "Choo-Choo" sounds of real locomotives, automatic coupling, air chime whistles and the many other wonderful features of railroading.
Amsco
Shu-Shine Bank for Kiddies
$1.98
NATIONALLY ADVERTISED
Your children will learn that good habits are fun when they use their own real Shinola Shoe Polish, dauber, polishing cloth and brush. Steel carrying case has a sturdy footrest . . . and built-in coin banks to teach thrift.
MEN'S & WOMEN'S RINK SKATES
★ With Metal Case
BOTH FOR ONLY $12.95
$2 DOWN
Here is an exceptional value from JOE'S. You get Men's or Women's Roller Rink Skates, the preferred kind with maple rink wheels . . . mounted on shoes of genuine leather . . . plus a handy metal skate case . . . handsome highly polished with metal latches and lock for your protection . . . has handy carrying handle.
KIDD-E-DOCTOR and NURSE, JR.
$1.98
Real Johnson and Johnson First Aid products, authentic-looking medical instruments - complete with carrying case.
TOOL CHEST
$1.98
A real BOY'S tool chest. NOT JUST A TOY. These chests are constructed and designed for real wood work. Consist of plane, hammer, braces, chisels and others including case.
FULL SIZE BICYCLE
$29.77
$5.00 DOWN
A full size bicycle for full grown boys and men . . . complete with new departure coaster brake, troxel saddle, standard make tires and bonderized, baked-on enamel finish . . . double bar frame . . . A sensational value!
ELECTRIC IRON
98¢
A safe electric iron for the little miss that will heat but will not burn.
IRONING BOARD
98¢
Folding ironing board just like mommy's made of sturdy wood construction.
DISH SET
98¢ UP
Complete place settings with cream pitcher and knives, forks and spoons. The little miss can now entertain in luxury. Your choice of plastic or aluminum.
FIX-ALL WRECKER
$1.39
Everything the young mechanic needs for endless hours of educational fun . . . has plastic wheels and tires that can be changed . . . spare tire storage locker, removable tow boom and bar . . . also tools as illustrated.
CHILD'S ROCKING CHAIR
$6.95
Upholstered in heavy quality textured material . . . ideal for small children to watch television . . . suitable for children age 2 to 10 years.
JOE THE MOTORISTS FRIEND
20 GREAT STORES
24 West King St.
Carlisle, 157 N. Hanover St.
Chambersburg, 59-63 N. Main St.
Cumberland, Md., 173 Balt. St.
Lewistown, 25 W. Market St.
Waynesboro, 6 N. Main St.
Gettysburg, 19 Chambersburg St.
Elizabethtown, 51 S. Market St.
Hanover, 100 Carlisle St.
Matinsburg, W. Va., 127 N. Queen St.
Baltimore, Md., 3117-19 Greenmount Ave.
Baltimore, Md., 415-19 S. Conkling St.
Baltimore, Md., 35 Shipping Pl., Dundalk
Winchester, Va., 101 N. Loudon St.
Front Royal, Va., 120 E. Main St.
Harrisonburg, Va., N. Court Sq.
Charlottesville, Va., 107 N. Main St.
Lebanon, 781 Cumberland St.
Harrisburg, 3rd & Broad Sts.
$6.98
CHAIR & TABLE SET
Table and Chair set just like Mommy's. Exceptionally sturdy table, with drop leaves, and chairs. Beautiful mahogany finish. . . . This cute little set will be at home in any room.
SIDEWALK BICYCLE
A tank type cycle complete with trainer wheels, chrome plated fully adjustable handle bars, truss rods, new type fenders complete with fender shields . . . A $25.00 value.
$4 DOWN
$19.88
OPEN TUESDAY and FRIDAY NIGHTS TILL 9:00

Merry Christmas

Holiday Greetings
A. B. ROTE & CO.
STRUCTURAL STEEL
241 N. PLUM ST.

Season's Greetings
A. J. CANTER
Cleaner Tailor
122 SOUTH QUEEN ST.
Lancaster Ph. 2-4428

Season's Greetings
Queen Roofing Co.
819 Highland Ave.
J. A. Norris

A Very Happy Christmas To All
from
J. C. NEUHAUSER & SON
996-998 E. Orange St.
Electric Motors, Repairing, Rewinding, Rebuilding

Merry Christmas
ANNA MYERS
Slenderizing and Sulphur Baths
445 E. KING ST. PH. 3-2245

Joyous Holidays
AMOS B. WITMER
Maytag Sales & Service
Cherry Hill Rd.
PARADISE, PA.

MERRY CHRISTMAS
HIGH WELDING CO.
Welding and Auto Springs
James and Water Sts.

BEST WISHES FOR CHRISTMAS
Armstrong Distributors
1039 N. Christian St.
Lancaster, Pa.

Holiday Greetings To All . . . from
DORWART
Lancaster's Only COMPLETE Sign Service
Phone 4-7620
James & Mulberry Sts.

Greetings to our friends and customers
EBERLY BUICK
Sales, Service
EPHRATA, PA.
Ephrata 3-2420

Holiday Greetings from
FALK BROS.
511 St. Joseph St.

We join with jolly Santa Claus in wishing you a Merry Christmas
PAUL C. MYERS
Well Driller
1824 Lincoln Hgwy. E. Ph. 2-8378

Good Wishes to All!
A. & J. DISTRIBUTING CO.
318 N. Marshall St.
Lancaster, Pa.

Hearty Season's Greetings
CARL B.
DROHAN
Builders' Supplies
MOUNT JOY — R. D. 2
Ph. 3-6401

THANK YOU . . . .

Is the most sincere expression we know of to convey to you our sincere appreciation for your friendliness and patronage during the past year.

May we extend to you our cordial greetings and good wishes for a Merry Christmas, and Happiness and Prosperity in the New Year.

Wissler Flower Shop and Greenhouses
144-46 N. Duke St. 963 E. Orange St.

Joy to you
from
CHARLES F. KRIMMEL
Formstone
417 W. Vine St. Ph. 2-3259

Noel
ORGANIC PLANT FOOD CO.
Grofftown Road near Water Works
Quality Fertilizers, Insecticides

Cheerio!
Yuletide Greetings from
Wade's Gift Shop
Friendly Year 'Round Service
MILLERSVILLE, PA.

Merry Christmas
SAUDER BROS.
Dearborn Farm Equipment and Ford Tractors
New Holland Ph. 4-8721

As the familiar carols fill the air, let us pause to give thanks for our many blessings.
ROOT'S
Landscape Service
MANHEIM
R. D. 1

Best Wishes to all for a Glorious Christmas Time!
H. B. GROFF, INC.
Quarryville, Pa.
Authorized Dealer for Massey-Harris, Ferguson & New Holland Farm Equipment

Season's Joy
We wish you all a Merry Christmas with good cheer abounding
ROY E. DUKE
Beer Distributor
127 Beaver St.
Lancaster, Pa.

Best Christmas Wishes!
Miles H. KEIFFER
"Everything Electrical"
MANHEIM, PA.
Phone 5-2241

Christmas Greetings
A. H. BURKET, JR.
Welding & General Maintenance
44 W. Liberty St.

Greetings
from
COOPER TOBACCO COMPANY, INC.
23 W. Chestnut St.

HAPPY HOLIDAY
to all
—from—
TERRE HILL SILO CO.
TERRE HILL, PA.
Phone Terre Hill 5-2221

Christmas Cheer
MISS BILLEE
Studio of Dancing
332 N. DUKE ST.

Noel - Noel - Noel
WARM GREETINGS
from
H. M. STAUFFER & SONS, Inc.
Your Coal and Fuel Oil Dealer
LANCASTER • LEOLA • RONKS • WITMER

GREETINGS
WEST WILLOW FARMERS ASS'N
Phone Lanc. 4-5019

AND YOUR INDEPENDENT NEIGHBORHOOD GROCER

A Joyous Yule and Best Wishes to All Our Friends and Customers
JAMES W. BELL
Hatter — Furrier
15 W. King St.

From that humble manger came a Light that was to shine on all mankind forever after.
D. M. Stoltzfus and Son, Inc.
Crushed Stone and Asphalt Paving
Talmage, Phone Leola 6-2601
Quarryville, Ph. Quarryville 6
Also Quarries at Cornwall and Cedar Hill

May the Yuletide Spirit be With You
Ruof's FLOWERS

BEST WISHES for a Merry Christmas
J. M. COLLINS
34 N. Market St., Lancaster, Pa.
• *AMOCO Service*
• *Parking*

Season's Greetings
John S. Groff

As the world grows still to mark the Holy Season, we speak our wishes of happiness for all.
GALEBACH'S
"The Friendly Store"
236 E. Fulton St.

Friendly GREETINGS to ALL
. . . wishing for all the joys of this — happiest of seasons!
BINKLEY & OBER, INC.
Crushed Stone & Vibrated Concrete Block
EAST PETERSBURG Ph. Lanc. 4-2628

Season's Greetings

We extend to all our friends and customers best wishes for a happy holiday.

ADLER'S
19 E. KING ST.

On that blessed night, the world was hushed with wonder, and hope arose anew for all mankind . . . Christ the Saviour was born. Today, we pray for His guidance, that we may find peace in our hearts and renewed faith in a world in which men everywhere shall live in good will and understanding with one another.

UGI
LANCASTER COUNTY GAS DIVISION
THE UNITED GAS IMPROVEMENT COMPANY

Our Good Wishes
that your holidays hold the best of everything for you and yours!
LEBZELTER'S
237-241 N. QUEEN ST.
LANCASTER

1954 News & Picture Highlights in Lancaster

Spectacular fire razes the clubhouse at Hiemenz golf course, off New Holland Pike at Country Club Heights, Oct. 19. Loss was estimated at $20,000 by Mr. and Mrs. H. John Hiemenz, operators of the course, who plan a new building.

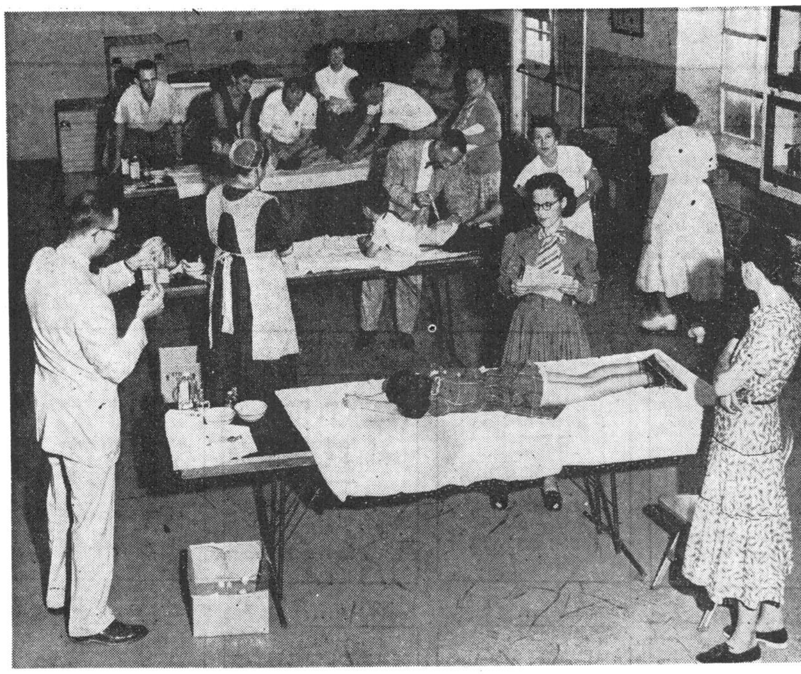

Schoeneck school children receive gamma globulin Oct. 2 in first mass inoculation for public school children at a central point, after a fellow pupil became ill with polio. At Elizabethtown, 900 pupils received GG through family physicians.

Local Review

(Continued From Page One)

pondered on how they might provide a water system for their residents, including the possibility of acquiring the Lancaster Suburban Water Co.

Refuse Disposal

An area authority—made up of the city and the six townships—tried to figure out a way for joint handling of garbage and rubbish. The city bought the historic Edward Hand farm as a proposed site, and at year's end landfill appeared to be getting the nod over incineration.

Lancaster Twp. was about ready to award a contract to build lines to supply water to Bausman. The Municipal Authority of East Hempfield Twp. was temporarily halted in its project to supply the Oyster Point and Rohrerstown areas with water.

Despite concerted efforts to hold down the deaths and injuries due to auto accidents, the bloody total spurted to 51. All-time high was the 59 of 1941.

The county took part in Safe Driving Day, Dec. 15, when a national endeavor was made for a substantial cut in accidents. Locally, there were nine accidents, no injuries, compared to seven accidents on Dec. 15, 1953.

Drought, Hurricane

Late spring and early summer brought searing drought to Lancaster County, wilting farm crops, forcing farmers to buy water which was hauled in by the truckload, bringing the specter of a crop loss up to $5 million.

August, however, brought providential rains to give new life to the parched soil. Crops made a recovery that farm experts called amazing, and by the end of 1954 the Garden Spot was telling of some of the best crops ever—in the year with the worst drought.

Never before had a hurricane caused considerable damage in Lancaster County, but the twister named Hazel, arriving on the evening of Oct. 15, left behind her a swath of wreckage which is still being cleared.

Thousands of dollars in property damage was caused by the big wind. Thousands of homes and business places were without electricity and telephone services. Trees were toppled by the hundreds. The results brought Lancaster County as close to a total disaster as any in memory.

"Hazel" is still a personality today. Children look at trees in woodlands, torn out by the roots, and say: "Hazel did that."

Queen Marries

Ephrata's Miss Evelyn Ay, green-eyed ash blonde who held the title of Miss America 1954, traveled some 80,000 miles by air to visit her loyal subjects, and then crowned a new Miss America at Atlantic City.

Miss Ay's final local public appearance was her most romantic—as she exchanged the vows of matrimony with Ensign Carl Sempier Jr., the fiance whose solitaire had been on her finger throughout her reign. Ensign and Mrs. Sempier are now living near Corpus Christi, Tex., where the bridegroom is taking Naval air training.

Republicans Hold

Lancaster County stayed firmly in the Republican column as Pennsylvania elected Democrat George M. Leader, of York County, to the governor's seat on Nov. 2. Cong. Paul B. Dague led the local GOP ticket as he was re-elected, and all other Republican candidates won.

But the county lead of the Republicans was down, and the city majority was closer than that by which Mayor Kendig C. Bare had won his mayoralty re-election the preceding year.

Near year's end, State Sen. Edward J. Kessler retired effective Dec. 31 from his post as labor relations director at Armstrong Cork Co., "to devote more time to public service."

With Mrs. Ruth Grigg Horting, of the city, named Secretary of Public Assistance in the Leader cabinet, Democrats eyed other state jobs now held by Republicans, and waited for the inauguration Jan. 18. Both parties looked to the primary election of next May.

Amish Puzzle

A knotty puzzler, centering on the Amish insistence that 14-year-olds be allowed to stay home to help on the farm, remained a complete enigma.

An injunction granted last spring halted prosecutions against Leacock Twp. Amish parents who kept their 14-year-olds home, pending disposition of a test case now in the State Superior Court. Boards of several other townships resumed prosecutions this fall. A few boards adopted a wait-and-see policy, but the pace of prosecutions has quickened since the opening of schools this fall.

110 Polio Cases

Polio cases totaled 110 here this year, first year when gamma globulin could be administered to large groups of persons who might have been exposed to the patients before diagnosis of the illness. The local rate was 75 per cent above the national rate.

Largest mass inoculation of gamma globulin took place at Elizabethtown, where 900 pupils got the shots. A total of 53,930 cubic centimeters of GG was administered in the county, provided free by the State Health Department, with a market retail value of $177,969.

Of the 110 men, women and children contracting polio, three died.

Trends

This was a year when the "do-it-yourself" movement reached a new high, extending even into children's toys and games at Christmas. It was a year when "split level" was added to "ranch style" as a popular term for new homes. It brought high prices for coffee, fancier sport shirts and vests for men, and the Dior's latest fashions, to which local woman gave the bird.

In the law courts, arbitration was used more frequently than in the past, for everything from auto damage cases to feed bill arguments to the differences between the Lancaster General Hospital and Wickersham Engineering and Construction, Inc. Home buyers were often able to get mortgage money with only the costs of settlement down, and the rest on installments.

Liberace Fans

Liberace won many local followers. High fidelity music listening—"hi fi" for short — won new advocates. Big dogs and cats of all sizes increased in numbers as local pets. More and more persons were getting a look at color television. "Lady policemen" — the women who protected school corners for the city and also helped with the downtown Christmas rush — were in great favor with the public.

Fewer and fewer autos here were black, and more and more were in the fancier pastel shades . . . Home entertainment was on the upsurge . . . While employment was quite high, overtime did not appear as plentiful as formerly. Families were growing in size, and three bedroom homes were far ahead of those with two bedrooms in the eyes of buyers.

Ladies, Bless 'Em

While stylists and curvaceous cuties like Marilyn Monroe squabbled over Christian Dior's "flat" flapper fashions, Lancaster women and girls showed only casual interest in accentuating or banishing their curves.

Instead they went completely overboard on a number of other fashion trends: rope beads, needle heels, separates (skirts and blouses, to the men), petticoats, and strubbly haircuts.

And while more and more teenagers appeared on the streets in blue jeans and leather jackets, when party-times arrived they donned a half-dozen frilly petticoats to join in the growing parade of billowing skirts.

Headlines

The year 1954 brought full measure of joy and sorrow, good news and bad, for the people of Lancaster County.

And city and county officially started their years with the taking of oaths of office. Mayor Kendig C. Bare, re-elected to start his second term, took his oath with City Commissioners John E. Spidle, re-elected, and Daniel S. Templeton, a new councilman. President Judge Oliver S. Schaeffer started his third 10-year term on the county bench.

Ground was broken for the new Monastery of the Immaculate Heart of Mary for the Dominican Sisters of the Perpetual Rosary on the Lititz Pike . . . The "dinky" diesel train between York and Lancaster made its last run . . . Dr. Orris H. Aurand, a Penn State professor, was elected superintendent of city schools to succeed Dr. Harvey E. Smith, who retired.

The Monument

Moving of the monument from Penn Square was again discussed. . . . A big water main broke in the 500 block of W. Orange St., flooding six city blocks . . . Jane Greiner's "Shorty" won the 1954 State Farm Show grand championship for steers . . . The "Hamboners," a rhythm quartet consisting of four teen-age boys, Warren Hyson, Charles Simms, Lewis Wilson and Joseph Jackson, won the Ted Mack TV amateur competition three times, went on to the national finals.

Arthur B. Dodge, honored as head of the Cork Institute for 20 years, received a silver bowl from H. W. Prentis Jr. in New York.

McCarthy Speaks

Sen. Joseph R. McCarthy, of Wisconsin, spoke before the annual banquet of the Manufacturers Association . . . . Most parking meter rates were doubled . . . . Unofficial southwest city bypass was foreseen as plans unfolded for removal of the Engleside bottleneck . . . City school board raised starging pay for teachers, and faced a number of suggestions for higher pay for all.

First church spire in West End was part of new Bethany Presbyterian building plans . . . the Child Development Center announced it would seek funds for a new building . . . Many benefitted from Social Security benefit increases . . . Mary Garden, almost mythical opera star, spoke here as guest of Lancaster Chapter, American Society for the Advancement of Management.

King and Prince intersection was called the city's most dangerous. . . Work was started on the new Public Safety building at Duke and Chestnut Sts . . . The horn comb factory of George Washington Crouse, 88, of Reinholds, only one of its kind in U.S., was demolished by fire.

Deaths by Fire

Fire deaths sparked a movement for an inhalator to be carried in city police ambulance, and the equipment was purchased . . . A public vote on fluoridation of the water supply, as a dental health aid, was proposed . . . The Lancaster Branch of the Pennsylvania Economy League said there was enough parking space now at McCaskey High School for concerts.

E. D. Eshleman, Millersville, was selected as Republican candidate to succeed Walter L. Bomberger of Manheim in the State Assembly, later won the post at the fall election . . . Arthur B. Sinkler, executive vice president, succeeded George P. Luckey as president of Hamilton Watch Co . . . Civic anger rose when a two-year-old girl burned to death in a boxcar home at Sunnyside.

New Building

Local households buzzed with discussion as the McCarthy-Stevens hearings were aired on TV. . . The Hamilton Club and the Lancaster Country Club started building programs . . . The state said it would provide a new bridge between Brownstown and Talmage. . . S. R. Fraim retired as head of the Fraim Lock Co. . . . Larry Flora, two, who got stuck in a sewer vent, was rescued by police using liquid soap, and his picture appeared in newspapers across the country.

Mary Sachs, women's apparel specialist, bought the Keiper-Long mansion on N. Duke St., for use as a fashion salon . . . Dr. Ward V. Evans, native of Rawlinsville, served on the board of three to consider charges against Dr. J. Robert Oppenheimer, atom scientist . . . Rebuilding began on the Manheim Pike . . . The Gap clock tower was all spic and span in its new location near Route 41.

Jane Pickens, former local songstress, made her comeback on TV . . . The Farmers Bank and Trust Co. let contracts for its new branch on New Holland Ave. . . Uncle Billy Adams, former slave, celebrated his 109th birthday . . . K. L. Shirk Jr. headed the State Junior Chamber of Commerce . . . Benrus sold its Hamilton Watch stock, under a federal court order . . . Alfred C. Alspach bought the Quarryville Sun from Howard Reynolds, who had been bringing the Sun up since '98.

Heroic Patrolman

Phyllis Boose, 12, Eichholtz safety patrolman, was seriously hurt trying to protect other pupils from a car which mounted a curb. . . . F&M collegians raided the Linden Hall dormitory at 2 a. m. . . . H. W. Prentis Jr. was made an officer of the Legion of Honor in France . . . Lancaster had its first drive-in church with modern religious movies . . . George W. Glatfelter started making his news for the year, throwing a picnic for all the kids in town, later appearing on a national TV show and ending 1954 with many gifts to customers.

A plane "crashed" in Penn Square during a Civil Defense test . . . New telephone numbers were on the way for all city area subscribers . . . WGAL-TV started using its new transmitter on Steinman Mountain across the Susquehanna from Marietta . . . Paul A. Mueller was elected vice president of the Pennsylvania State Bar Association, to become the next president . . . Clarence E. Pontz promised a plan for beautifying Long Park.

Color Wirephoto

The New Era printed its first color wirephoto, showing the Eisenhowers and Churchill . . . Countians got a good look at the full eclipse of the sun . . . St. Joseph's Hospital opened its new Atlee Memorial Wing, named in honor of Dr. John L. Atlee, noted local surgeon . . . Gov. John S. Fine and his sons picked cherries in the orchard of H. L. Shank . . . State Sen. G. Graybill Diehm was re-elected for his 13th consecutive term as GOP county chairman.

Col. Frank M. Gavan succeeded Col. J. Hale Steinman as county Civil Defense head . . . One person was killed in a crash at the Fruitville Pike intersection on the by-pass, starting a clamor for better safety measures which brought a ban on all left turns . . . The state fixed up a new sign which said "Village of Rhorerstown".

50th Anniversary

The Lancaster Auto Club marked its 50th anniversary, honoring Phyllis Boose and Dorothy Koehler, 12, Columbia Safety Patrol heroines . . . Donald Z. Esbenshade bought the Pequea Works, Inc., manufacturer of fishing tackle . . . Traffic lights went into use at Prince and Walnut Sts . . . A painter painted the wrong church at Churchtown . . . The Keller Bros. barn at Kissel Hill burned with $100,000 loss .

Dr. William Webster Hall was elected president of Franklin and Marshall College, succeeding Dr. Theodore A. Distler, who resigned to become executive secretary of the American Association of Colleges at Washington, D. C.

Curfews Return

The Conestoga Wagon rolled again, bringing added luster to a Lancaster County product of historic importance . . . The county court cracked down on morals offenders molesting children . . . Dr. H. M. J. Klein and Capt. John M. Groff lifted their voices on behalf of bringing the Baker Plan for civic development up to date, and City Council later allocated funds for the project.

Intercourse celebrated its 200th anniversary . . . O. L. Hampton, YMCA general secretary, and "Prof" A. W. Globisch, physical director, headed for retirement at year's end . . . The new Art Center of the Lancaster County Art Association opened . . . The city's assessed valuation was up $1 million, to $106.9 million.

Pvt. G. E. Wilson, former Mount Joy basketball star, was a hero in a Ft. Bragg plane crash. . . .Turnpike business brought a boom to northern areas of the county. . .Joselp R. Ranck, Leola, was named a brigadier general in the Army Quartermaster Corps . . . Chief Assawama, wooden Indian of the Indian River Poultry Farms, was kidnaped again and returned . . . City schools abolished "E" on elementary report cards.

Feagley Honored

Quarryville, where 85 per cent of the adults voted on Nov. 2, won the Legion voting plaque . . . Joseph C. Feagley was chosen as Lancaster's outstanding citizen for 1954 by Legion Post 34, for his leadership in construction of the Atlee wing for St. Joseph's Hospital . . . First Veterans' Day was held here, supplanting Armistice Day . . . The new Lancaster Free Public Library building was opened . . . Manheim Twp. women made a public move for a woman school director.

Lee Ann Meriwether, Miss America 1955, came here to open Bell Day for the Hearing Center . . . District Attorney William C. Storb warned property owners to read home repair contracts carefully before they signed . . . Mrs. Marvin Erb, Mt. Nebo, shot a 130-pound deer near her home . . . Miss Irene M. Lupold retired after 39 years as aide to three local Congressmen . . . Ira Bowman, bandleader, retired . . . A short "run" began on silver dollars of four dates in the 1880's, ending as soon as it was clear each cartwheel was worth only one dollar . . . Fulton National and East Petersburg State banks announced plans to consolidate.

Travelers on Route 72, the main highway to Baltimore, were able to use the improved Smithville underpass just before Christmas. With the opening of the final Pennsylvania link of Route 41, local residents had all modern highway between here and the New Jersey shore resorts and New York City, via the Delaware Memorial bridge and the Jersey Turnpike.

Electrical power lines battered by Hurricane Hazel are repaired by Pennsylvania Power and Light Co. workmen, Oct. 16. Working on Lincoln Highway East are Donald Sadler, Gettysburg R5, sawing off limb, and Donald Miller, 1024 Willow Street Pike, assisting.

Deaths

Two of Lancaster County's oldest residents, Mrs. Sarah Ann Swope, 105, of Linville Circle, and Martin Sweigart, 103, of Reamstown, died this year, leaving Uncle Billy Adams, ex-slave, now a patient at the Lancaster County Hospital, unchallenged for longevity at 109.

Death took many well known persons among them:

Frank L. Gunzenhauser, veteran baking firm executive.

Miss Laura A. Munson, seventy-four, retired city teacher.

W. R. Dry, sixty-six, city pharmacist.

Benjamin B. Wolf, eighty-three, clothing store founder.

George W. Leonard Jr., 81, ex-City Council member.

Alderman Hubert E. Miller, 66, of the 8th Ward.

Admiral C. H. McMorris, war hero, of Marietta.

Walter A. Heinitsh, 98, retired furniture merchant.

Roland H. Garver, 69, Ephrata ice cream manufacturer.

Constable Ivan Fry, 56, Brownstown.

Dr. U. I. Rosenthal, 82, former local rabbi.

Mrs. Kathryn Long Wagner, 85, oldest member of Lancaster Moravian Church.

Dr. Paul E. Bomberger, 59, prominent dentist.

William H. Kachel, 63, of burns received in Florida.

First Lt. John LeRoy Englert, 25, Ephrata, in training plane crash.

W. A. Turner, 96, Quarryville R1, homesteader in the old "wild west."

Charles M. Brubaker, 70, ex-Intercourse postmaster.

Chester Rhoads, 57, Buena Vista storekeeper.

Mrs. L. M. Austin, 65, active in veterans' auxiliaries.

Jacob F. Buck, 82, former Columbia police chief.

Dr. James Armstrong, 70, Columbia physician.

Frank C. Wagner, 66, retired insurance man.

Roy K. Geltz, 51, air park operator.

Stacy E. Peters, 69, former Stevens High School Principal.

C. Dudley Armstrong, 65, long a top official of Armstrong Cork Co.

Vaughn Voris, 59, former furniture merchant.

Mrs. Ella A. Lacy, 93, Lititz, oldest Linden Hall alumna.

Dr. David Galen McCaa, 72, former local radio pioneer.

Aaron W. Hess, ninety-one, retired banker and Hessdale grocer.

Dr. Harry W. Barnard, 80, veterinarian.

Miss Emma Sener, 90, "Miss Emma" to hundreds of former Sunday school pupils.

Charles Keath, 68, Lititz planing mill head.

Dr. Norman B. Laughton, 48, Manheim osteopath.

William E. Cogley, 77, prison clerk for many years.

I. C. Arnold, 94, oldest local bar member.

Frank C. Beckwith, 84, Hamilton Watch Co. board chairman.

Charles E. Vogt, 60, radiator expert.

E. Winslow Williams, 62, credit manager, U. S. Asbestos Division, Manheim.

Wilson R. Browne, 49, pictorial photographer and advertising agency head.

Albert Woodrig, 65, Wheatland Auto Co. president.

John Ruth, York, former local banker.

William C. Herwig, 49, realtor.

Charles Bond, 91, Manheim industrial pioneer.

Miss Effie Detwiler, 86, Columbia civic leader.

Joseph Martin, 67, druggist.

Isaac W. Martin, 92, Oreville home, Martin family historian.

Dr. Bernard Mishkin, 41, native of city, in Germany.

George K. Biemesderfer, 83, Hotel Brunswick secretary-treasurer.

Amos Stilwell, 81, driver of horse-drawn laundry wagons.

Charles Russell Frain, 53, New Holland engineer.

Carl A. Schlotzhauer, 68, portrait photographer.

Charles J. Trees, 79, baker.

William Scheid, 66, seed company founder.

C. Ralph Binkley, 48, Neffsville, business and civic leader.

Rev. Ellerslie A. Lebo, 51, pastor of St. Paul's Lutheran Church, Millersville.

Martin E. Musser, 78, attorney and "judge maker."

Ira H. Landis, 78, nurseryman and real estate developer.

William Klein, 70, Elizabethtown, founder of Klein Chocolate Co.

Mrs. Nellie Witmer, 86, one of oldest MSTC alumni.

Dr. C. N. Heller, 85, long associated with Franklin and Marshall College and Lancaster Theological Seminary.

Puzant Barsumian, 53, violinist and conductor.

Floyd A. VanDusen, 61, Watt and Shand advertising director.

Walter S. Mellinger, 75, attorney and candy manufacturer.

C. W. Stehman, 87, former city official.

Harrison S. Nolt, 66, farmer-banker.

Dr. E. Gerard Smith, 51, eye specialist.

Rev. William Henry Bollman, 59, pastor of First Evangelical and Reformed Church.

Charles H. Gable, 53, managing editor of Columbia News.

Earl W. Diffenbaugh, 62, insurance executive.

Leigh E. Wittell, 57, violinist, teacher and conductor.

Albert H. Shiffler, 99, retired city butcher.

George B. Marrow, 96, ice cream manufacuting pioneer.

Rev. John Harries, 60, former pastor of English Presbyterian Church, Marietta.

George D. Landis, 87, co-founder of Landis Valley Museum.

Dr. Francis Carroll Lowell, 71, physician and surgeon, and his brother, Howard Lowell, 73, attorney, a week apart.

Oscar P. Warfel, 72, Rohrerstown butcher.

David H. Huber, 94, Lancaster R7, farmer and bank director.

Make Your Home Attractive And Convenient

EGG CAUSES DEATH

DETROIT, Jan. 29 (AP)—An egg was blamed by police for the death today of a Detroiter.

Police said that apparently Frank Sepulski, 51, cooking his own breakfast, dropped a raw egg on the floor; it broke; he stepped on it and slipped, hitting his head on the floor.

Mirrors Give Illusion Of Size, Light To Homes

Want to make a small room grow?

One easy way to expand it, without knocking out a wall, is to use plate glass mirrors.

It's an optical illusion, of course, but mirrors can stretch a room in size, double the furnishings in number, and even increase light in intensity.

Here are some house-expanding ideas:

1. A narrow length of mirror on the window sill makes a shelf for potted plants which allows maximum sunlight for plant growth. Another mirror of equal size behind the shelf doubles the green, "outdoors" decorating effect of the plants.

2. A mirror secured to the closet ceiling will give a view of the top shelf and the hard-to-reach area near the wall. Mirrors will do a similar job above the kitchen cabinet shelves.

3. Mirrors about three feet square and mounted on wooden blocks can be placed at an angle on each side of a fireplace to reflect both heat and light into the room. They'll also make a small fireplace seem much larger.

4. Mirrors at slight angles on each side of an attic dormer window will reflect more daylight into the room, often turning a drab, useless attic into an active living area of the home.

5. A "mirror corner"—high, rectangular mirrors on each wall in a gloomy corner—will gather light from elsewhere in the room and dispel shadows. The addition of plate glass shelves for plants can turn the corner into the room's focal point.

Home fashions have never been more practical and at the same time more beautiful. The kitchen of Mr. and Mrs. Pryor Neuber, Lancaster R5, combines durability, convenience, functionalism and pleasing appearance. The knotty pine cabinets and walls have a dull finish because of their wax base varnish. The marble top of the utility table, center foreground makes for easy maintenance and handsome appearance. For informal meals Mr. and Mrs. Neuber find that their cozy breakfast nook is just the thing.

Today's Desk Is Fashion News

You have room for a desk in your home! Today's new desk fashions make this possible.

Some years ago, when a desk was a desk and nothing more, this may have been impractical. Space was too important to devote it to an item of furniture that might be used occasionally, and often looked too practical to be beautiful.

Today, however, desks are so well designed that they fit into any room, and may serve more than one purpose. Some have plastic coated top surfaces and can be used for dining or as additional servers.

Other desks are dainty reproductions of antique furniture. These, too, add beauty and function to your home.

If you have a student at home you will be particularly interested in the new Modern desks that have a compartment especially designed for a full-sized typewriter. This type of desk will be found as a part of a correlated group or as an individual unit.

For the career girl, the college girl, or the homemaker there is the vanity-desk. This item of furniture adds a note of practifal luxury to a room. The vanity-desk is available in any style, Modern or Traditional.

If you are currently using the family dining table for paying bills or for correspondence, be sure to look at the new desks being shown locally. They are definitely fashion merchandise and they will not go out of style.

Open Second Story Of Lincoln's Home

SPRINGFIELD, Ill., Jan. 29 (AP)—Six second-story rooms in the house where Abraham Lincoln lived from 1844 to 1861 will be opened to the public Feb. 12, the 146th anniversary of the Civil War president's birth.

Heretofore, visitors have had access only to the first floor. There were 425,000 visitors in 1954.

9000 Guards Going To Indiantown Gap

INDIANTOWN GAP, Pa., Jan. 29 (AP)—Officers of the Maryland and Virginia National Guard units met here today to make plans for summer training of some 9,000 guardsmen next summer.

Brig. Gen. William J. Verbeck, chief of the military district, met with Brig. Gen. William C. Purnell, Baltimore, assistant division commander of the 29th Guard Division, and Col. A. W. Ellis, Richmond, commander of the 176th Regimental Combat Team.

About 2,000 troops of the 176th will train at Indiantown Gap for two weeks beginning June 11.

More than 7,000 members of the 29th Maryland - Virginia National Guard division and the 231st Transportation Battalion will train at the post from July 23-Aug. 6.

Donegal Wins in Surprising Game

Unusual Tiff

by GEORGE KIRCHNER

New Era Sports Editor

OFF THE BACKBOARDS . . . It's a funny thing about these playoff games, they seldom, if ever, live up to expectations. Take, for example, last night's 29 to 26 victory which Donegal Township scored over Manheim Township before a screaming crowd of 2,300 at McCaskey High. The gathering was there expecting to see a wild-and-wooly scoring battle between two teams that had averaged close to 50 points all year.

Instead, they saw a game that came about as close as any to reminding the oldtimers of the days of yore. Guys like Hooks Mylin, who was in the audience, said later it carried them back to their high school days when a team that scored as many as 30 points was a sure-fire winner.

Yet in spite of the fact that it didn't measure up in the high-scoring sprees of today, the contest had its tense moments. For one thing, Donegal's comeback in the last four minutes added up to a thrill they'll talk about for a long time. At one stage, the Indians were eight points behind and appeared doomed. But they refused to let their opponents' tight zone puzzle them and kept pecking away until, finally, in the last 30 seconds, they snatched victory out of the fire.

Today all over the county, they're replaying the game with practically everyone handing as many bouquets to the vanquished as to the victors.

Coach Paul Wenrich and his crew came up with a style of ball that had the Indians baffled. Defensively, they jammed up the middle with a tight two-three zone that bottled up Donegal's tall Jay Metzler. Offensively, they played deliberate or possession basketball and for 30 of the 32 minutes, both styles clicked. If the Streaks made any mistakes at all it was when they stuck to their possession type when there were opportunities to score. But there's an old and logical reasoning that when you're ahead and have the ball, the other team can't score.

That's the way the Streaks played it right up to the finish and with but four minutes remaining, only the loyal Donegal rooters held hopes for their team. They seemed destined to drop their first game after 18 straight victories.

However, that's when the boys from the Mt. Joy area came to life. All evening . . . (excepting for one time when they had tied the count to 10 all) . . . they had been stymied. But now with the blue chips down and the clock running out, they made their bid. It was, in retrospect, a pretty terrific bid, for in less than four minutes they overcame a six point lead, tied it up and finally won out.

The game had a lot of unusual angles, not the least of which was the fact that while both teams were battling it out on the floor, Donegal was unable to make a single foul shot! The Indians had no less than 11 foul tries during the regular game, but not once did they click. Then with the game tucked away at 28 to 26 they got two more chances

just as the final gun sounded. People had surged on the floor when Johnny Hiestand stepped to the line to make the game complete. He missed his first try, but connected on the second, and that was the only foul shot made by the victors all night. Could be a record of some sort.

Speaking of records, the crowd, itself, established the first mark, for McCaskey's Jim Neely said after they had closed the doors that this was the biggest gathering ever crammed into McCaskey for a basketball game.

As it developed, it was also the most enthusiastic, for both sides gave out in full force and the spirit took you back to the days when Lancaster High was packing 'em in and whooping it up at the old Boys High school. For one night, at least, the oldtimers lived again.

In a battle fought as close to the vest as this one, there's bound to be disappointment for the losers, just as the victory becomes all the more glorious when a club comes from behind, as Donegal did. The Mount Joyers really whooped it up afterwards, showering their praise on each individual member, but the losers were far from forgotten. They had, everyone admitted, put up a terrific struggle and the kind that merited praise from all sides.

Coach Ken Depoe of the victors was immensely pleased with his club's comeback, but coach Wenrich was equally proud of his boys.

This is not the end for either side. Donegal must still get past the Lampeter-Strasburg-Paradise victor for the county title, while Township, although eliminated from the County High race, still has the District playoffs to face. The Streaks will compete in Class A in this race, while Donegal, no matter how it fares in Saturday night's championship game, will go after Class B honors in the PIAA's tournament. But right now, they'll be playing and re-playing last night's game, sharing their views with the 2,300 who were lucky enough to get inside the auditorium.

Over 2,300 enthusiastic fans jammed the McCaskey gym to see Donegal nose out Manheim Township, 29 to 26, last night, with the crowd, a portion of which can be seen here, being estimated as the largest ever to see a game at the local high school.

New Era Photos

Manheim Township's Dick Johns (22), and Donegal's Jay Metzler (15) battle three other unidentifed players for a loose ball. Ready to join the tussle is Jimmy Howry (11), of Township.

Last Second Goal Ruins Township's Controlled Play

by BILL FISHER

IT was incredible. And it almost defies description. Take two teams—Donegal and Manheim Township—two teams that had overwhelmed 35 opponents, averaged about 66 points a game, throw them together in a playoff, a game that has mushroomed into near hysteria, that had magnetized a record-breaking 2,300 into McCaskey Auditorium, everyone expecting an explosion of atomic intensity and what happens? It fizzled with a dull, dead thud, 29-26, Donegal.

But one thing sure. This was a real collector's item, a gem that will linger long in memories, that will be replayed until doomsday. It was utterly incredulous.

But—and the rest of this will probably be compounded with "but" and "if" and "perhaps"—it was planned that way. Manheim Township coach Paul Wenrich had planned and plotted it perfectly. He reasoned, logically enough, that Township had a better chance to beat Donegal by playing their (Township's) game. And his boys did just that.

Township played a slow, methodical, deliberate possession game. It almost worked. At various times the Streaks held a lead that varied from seven points in the first period, four in the second, eight in the third, and eight at the start of the last period. Only once, until the last three minutes, did Donegal pull even. The Indians did it 10-10 after Township had scored the first seven points of the game.

What Beat Them?

What, then, beat Township? Luck? or over-caution? or that something extra, that intangible of having it in the clutch? These are questions, not answers. Everyone to his own opinion. Perhaps a combination of all.

Throughout the game, until those final maddening moments, the question in back of everyone's mind was: "Is this that great Donegal team?" It was a question that begged for an answer. But there was none. Donegal did nothing, absolutely nothing, that would be expected of a championship team. The Indians played, if you'll pardon a crude but meaningful expression, a "lousy" game. Except for one thing. They won. And that is still what counts in any struggle for survival.

But you can't fault Manheim Township. They played their game to the hilt. Still and all, although Donegal played a poor game or, if you prefer, were outsmarted, Donegal won. When a team fumbles and fidgets and has a night when nothing seems to go right against a good team that is "on" its game and still has the stuff to win, well, that is the mark of a great team.

Township coach Paul Wenrich said afterward: "If I had it to do over again I would do it exactly the same way. Everything went as planned. We did everything but win."

Donegal Was Tight

Donegal coach Ken Depoe was at a loss for an explanation. He had suffered acute discomfort, died a thousand deaths on the bench and any satisfaction he got out of his team's winning came hard. He was asked over and over, "What happened?" The most oft-repeated answer was, "We were 'tight'. We never loosened up."

Donegal looked "tight." They were ragged. They missed shots (1 out of 12 foul shots, and that was the last one). They showed no semblance of the fire and dash that had characterized their games prior to last night.

Part of this is attributable to the play of Township. Wenrich devised a tight inside defense that jammed the middle and shackled Jay Metzler and Al Kugle. This left plenty of outside room, no more than 15 or 20 feet from the basket, but Donegal took a few outside shots, missed, then shied away from sets.

On offense, Wenrich stationed his big man, "Sonny" Warfel, in the corner — he moved into the pivot some in the second half, however—and concentrated the Township attack on stabs inside the shifting man-for-man Donegal defense.

Warfel and Metzler

The highly heralded scoring duel between Metzler and Warfel failed to come off. It failed because everything else that was expected to happen failed to happen. Metzler, who had averaged 26 points a game, scored 12. Warfel, who had averaged 23, scored 8.

When Donegal had the ball, Warfel guarded Metzler in the pivot. When Township had the ball, Kugle guarded Warfel and Metzler roamed beneath the basket.

It was, in the language that fits it perfectly, a crazy mixed-up ball game.

Shortly after the final period be-

—See BASKETBALL—Page 20

Section Three Playoff At Lititz Gym Tonight

The championship of Section 3 of the County High League will be at stake tonight when Lampeter-Strasburg and Paradise collide in a playoff at Lititz at 8 p.m.

Winner of tonight's game will meet Donegal, which squeaked by Manheim Twp., last night, for the Lancaster County High School Championship at McCaskey Saturday night at 8 p.m.

Solons Meet Tuesday on Pa. Race Bill

Senator Hopes to Get Issue Before Voters At Primary Election

HARRISBURG (AP) —Chairman G. Robert Watkins (R-Delaware) of the Senate Law and Order Committee said he will call a meeting next Tuesday to act on a bi-partisan horse-racing referendum bill.

Watkins said he hopes not only to get the bill out of committee but to make arrangements for holding the vote by the people in the May 17 primary election.

Should the measure win approval of the General Assembly and Gov. George M. Leader, voters would answer yes or no to this question:

"Do you favor horse racing with legal wagering within the commonwealth?"

Getting the bill out of committee would be the first step in the long legislative road to passage.

Long an Issue

Legalized horse-race betting long has been a controversial issue in the Pennsylvania Legislature. Sideline opposition has come from some church groups and reportedly from out-of-state racing interests.

Watkins estimated the Commonwealth could raise as much as 35 million dollars every two years through race tracks in the state.

Sound Out Voters

The purpose of the referendum bill, he emphasized, is merely to sound out the voters on whether they want legalized betting. Should the idea be approved later legislation would set up the machinery for bringing in the tracks.

Looking ahead, Watkins said major tracks could be built in the Philadelphia and Pittsburgh areas with smaller tracks possibly in the vicinity of Harrisburg, Scranton and the northwestern part of the state.

Up to Committee

Although Watkins already has said he believes the bill will win Committee approval, he said he is leaving it entirely in the hands of the Committee members.

The 16-member committee includes 10 Republicans and six Democrats with Sen. M. Harvey Taylor (R-Dauphin), president pro tempore, serving as an ex-officio member. Sen. Frank Kopriver Jr. (R-Allegheny) is vice-chairman.

Co-sponsors of the referendum bill with Watkins are Sens. Edward B. Watson (R-Bucks), John H. Dent (D-Westmoreland) and Anthony J. DiSilvestro (D-Phila).

Tag Team Match Tops Mat Bill Here Tonight

Promoter Dan Templeton Jr. presents his fourth pro wrestling show of the season at Maple Grove tonight with the Smith Brothers scheduled in a tag team feature against Kinji Shibuya & Brother Frank Jares over the one hour, two out of three falls route.

In a 45 minutes, one fall scuffle, Jack Wentzig meets Herb Larson. Wentzig defeated Larry Hamilton on the Feb. 16th card while Larson, who beat Steve Novak on the Jan. Jan. 19th card, will be showing for the second time here.

Andre Drapp meets Danno O'Shocker in a half hour opener at 8:30.

Gavilan Choice In Bout Tonight

Kid Is 2-1 Over Constance in TV Fight

MIAMI BEACH, Fla. (AP) — Kid Gavilan, former welterweight champion, was a 2-1 favorite to whip Hector Constance of Trinidad tonight in a 10-rounder.

Gavilan expects to weigh in at 152 pounds while Constance probably will weigh 148 at fight time.

CBS will telecast at 10 p.m., EST.

Trying Comeback

Gavilan is trying to stage a comeback after losing the title to Johnny Saxton in Philadelphia Oct. 20. He won a split decision over Ernie Durando Feb. 4 in New York but wasn't too impressive in that appearance.

Gavilan said after the fight with Durando, a welterweight, that he planned to fight only welterweights with the aim of getting a return shot at Saxton.

Never Been Kayoed

The Cuban Keed has never been knocked out in 118 fights and is expected to volley the Trinidad youngster with his usual assortment of hooks, jabs and his bolo punch.

Constance is a 24-year-old boxer who has engaged in only 38 fights, winning 24 and drawing in eight, with five defeats and one termed "no contest."

In previous fights in this country, Constance has beaten Chico Varona and Ralph (Tiger) jones and gained a draw with Johnny Brown twice.

Temple Grid Coach Here Next Monday

Al Kawal, head football coach at Temple University, will be the honored guest at a meeting of the Temple Alumni club of Lancaster, next Monday night at 8:30 o'clock at the Brunswick.

M'ville Girls Bow

The Gettysburg girls basketball team notched a 59-21 victory over the Millersville Teachers girls team in a game played last night at Gettysburg.

HOCKEY

INTERNATIONAL LEAGUE

Toledo 3, Fort Wayne 2 (overtime)
Grand Rapids 4, Cincinnati 1

The bird urbot lays 14,000,000 eggs.

FUNNY BUSINESS - - By Hershberger

"I'm so hoarse I can't yell 'Fore' loud enough!"

FDR held his first "Fireside Chat" in 1933.

Obituaries

Time and place of Service will be found under Funeral Invitations

(Continued from Page 3)

Edwin Bailey, 82, Dies Near Oxford

Edwin Haines Baily, eighty-two, Modern Acres, near Oxford, died yesterday morning at his home.

Born in Delavan, Ill., he was a son of the late Joseph C. and Priscilla Haines Baily and resided in Missouri and Kansas before coming to Lancaster County in 1902 where he began farming in Fulton Twp. He operated a southern Lancaster County farm until 1906 when he moved to Chester County. He and his wife, the former Mary H. Scott, were married in 1906 and she died in 1940.

A well-known dairy farmer, he was active in many organizations including the American Guernsey Cattle Club and the Friendly Farmers Club. He also was a 32nd degree Mason, a Spanish-American War veteran, a past director of the Mushroom Growers Association, a former member of the Oxford Rotary Club and a member of the Penn Hill Friends Meeting.

Surviving is a daughter and two sons: Edith, wife of Paul L. Haines, Westfield, N. J.; Joseph S., Oxford, and Dr. William H. Baily, Kennett Square.

Ten grandchildren and a sister, Miss Frances M. Baily, Oxford, also survive.

Elam G. Denlinger

Elam G. Denlinger, eighty-five, Strasburg, died at 4:30 p.m. Saturday at his home after a long illness. He was a son of the late Martin and Anna Groff Denlinger, East Lampeter Twp., and was employed as an ice man in Strasburg for 35 years. He was a resident of that community for 60 years. In addition to his wife, the former Lydia Groff, he is survived by a son and two daughters: Nettie, wife of Walter Sample; Mrs. Helen Hersh and Clyde B. Denlinger, all of Strasburg. One grandchild and a brother and sister also survive: Ida, wife of Reuben Buckwalter, Lancaster, and Martin G. Denlinger, Soudersburg.

John E. Yost

John E. Yost, eighty-three, Gap RD, died at 11:15 p.m. Saturday at his home. He was a son of the late John L. and Susanna Eash Yost and a member of the Millwood Mennonite Church. A farmer by occupation, he is survived by his wife, Kate E. Yost, and three sons and a daughter: Ray S., Kirkwood RD; R. John, Narvon RD; Sadie Mae, at home, and Harlan L., Silver Springs, Md. Fifteen grandchildren and these brothers and sisters also survive: Christian E. and Elizabeth E. Yost, both of Lancaster; Amos E., Bird-in-Hand, and Sue, wife of John Shenk, Lancaster RD.

Thomas S. Graybill Is Stricken, Dies

Thomas S. Graybill, seventy-eight, collapsed yesterday morning in the house where he roomed, 34 S. Lime St., and died a short time later.

Another roomer, Raymond Fuhrman, heard a noise in the bathroom and went to investigate. He found Graybill slumped over and summoned city police. They took him to Lancaster General Hospital, where he was pronounced dead on arrival at 7 a.m.

Dr. Charles P. Stahr, deputy coroner, said Graybill had suffered from a heart condition for some time and died of a cardiac occlusion.

Graybill was born in Drumore Twp., a son of the late Jacob and Elizabeth Fisher Graybill.

Surviving are his wife, Elizabeth K. Wile Graybill, Columbia, and three daughters and two sons: Anna Mae, wife of Albert G. Kuss, Lancaster, and Erna J., wife of Daniel Kiehl, and Miss Ruth Graybill, both of Columbia; Cyrus., Newtown R2, and Thomas A., Wrightsville.

Also surviving are 13 grandchildren; a great-grandson, and two brothers and a sister: John, Downingtown; Amos, Mountville, and Mrs. Sally Kirsey, Downingtown R2.

John Martin Gaul

John Martin Gaul, sixty-six, of 426 E. Strawberry St., died at 6 p. m. Saturday at his home after an illness of seven weeks.

He was a painter and conducted his own business in Lancaster until a year ago. He was the husband of the late Rachael E. Good Gaul.

Born in Strasburg, he was a son of the late John Martin and Mary Keen Gaul. He resided in the city the past 54 years, and was a member of Interdenominational Gospel Tabernacle of Lancaster, and the Fraternal Order of Eagles, Aerie 84.

Surviving are two daughters and two sons: Susanna, wife of George Heisler; Clara M., wife of Alfred Fisher; Theodore A., all of Lancaster, and Martin H.; also eight grandchildren and two great-grandchildren.

Mrs. Ballard E. Jones

Mrs. Pearl H. Jones, forty-two, wife of Ballard E. Jones, 437 Hodgson St., Oxford, died at 11:28 p. m. Friday in Lancaster Osteopathic Hospital, where she was admitted March 1 as a surgical patient.

She was born in Lincoln University, a daughter of Mrs. Margaret Jones, Oxford, and the late Harrison Jones and had lived in Oxford for 15 years. She was proprietor of a beauty shop.

Surviving, besides her husband, are four daughters: the Misses Priscilla, Lucille, Jane and Kathleen, all at home; her mother, Mrs. Margaret Ringgold Jones, Oxford; a sister, Mrs. Eva Stout, West Chester, and three brothers, Benjamin Rhodes, Coatesville; Lawrence Ringgold, West Chester, and Sherman Ringgold, Oxford.

Local Weather
(U. S. Weather Bureau)
Lancaster, York, Lebanon, Cumberland, Franklin, Adams Counties
Sunny And Warm Today, Fair, Moderate Tonight, Tomorrow Fair, Continued Warm. High Today 74-82.

SUNDAY NEWS

7 Sections, 80 Pages, Including Family Weekly

3 AM Edition
LATEST NEWS by Associated Press, INS, complete local news and pictures, plus AP Wirephotos 15c

32ND YEAR—NO. 32

LANCASTER, PA., SUNDAY, APRIL 17, 1955

City Fisherman Drowns As Boat Upsets In River

Truman Says Ike's Foreign Policy 'Fraud'

Stevenson Joins In Raking GOP Policies At Dinner For Rayburn

WASHINGTON, April 16 (AP)—Harry S. Truman accused the Eisenhower administration tonight of political fraud and trickery in the field of foreign policy.

From Adlai Stevenson came a call to Democrats to "stand for peace—which is the most urgent business of the 20th century, the hydrogen age."

The former President and the 1952 contender spoke at a huge, $100 a plate banquet honoring House Speaker Sam Rayburn—the beloved "Mr. Sam" of legions of Democrats.

Truman's speech was a raking attack on the administration. He accused it of bad management and blundering, as well as playing "political tricks with the grave and serious issues of both foreign and domestic policies."

For one thing, he lit into the administration for its announcement in 1953 that the 7th Fleet would no longer be used to "shield" Red China from Chiang Kai-shek's Nationalists.

Charges 'Fraud'

"The Republican administration must have known," Truman said, "that the picture of an unleashed Chiang Kai-shek invading China was a barefaced political fraud. But the idea behind all this was to attempt to discredit the sound policy of the Democratic administration which was carefully designed to limit the conflict in the Far East."

"And now the Republican administration is desperately trying not only to limit the conflict in Asia, but to get a permanent cease-fire there. I fervently hope they do. But the administration, by this unfortunate political maneuver in its State of the Union message, (in

Page 14—DEMOCRATS

Knowland Hits Adlai Speech

INDIANAPOLIS, April 16 (AP) — Sen. Knowland (R-Calif) said tonight that former President Truman's order neutralizing the Formosa Strait during the Korean War "made it possible for the Chinese Communists to move their troops to Manchuria and down to Korea."

Knowland, the Republican Senate leader, also said he was "amazed and shocked" at Adlai Stevenson's speech of last Monday night. Knowland said the 1952 Democratic presidential nominee "appears to be giving the green light to the loss of Quemoy and Matsu."

Stevenson's words, Knowland said, also "cast reflection upon the future of the island of Formosa itself."

In a speech before the Indiana Republican Editorial Assn., Knowland noted that "former President Truman is in Washington tonight where he is scheduled to join in the Democratic attack on President Eisenhower's administration."

"Perhaps he will explain," Knowland said, "why (former Secretary of State) Dean Acheson drew a defense line in the Pacific which placed Formosa and Korea outside our line of defense."

Veteran Democrat VIPs

WASHINGTON, April 16—Three top Democrats, who held government reins in the former administration, pose in happy three-way hand-shake at tonight's party honoring House Speaker Sam Rayburn. Left to right are Sen. Alben Barkley, former vice president; Speaker Rayburn; former president, Harry S. Truman. (AP Wirephoto)

Seven Burn Way Out Of Portland Lockup

PORTLAND, Ore., April 16 (INS) — Seven prisoners at the Rocky Butte jail in Portland escaped late today by burning their way to freedom with welding torches furnished by an outside confederate.

Working with machine like precision, the seven escapees quickly burned through the bars which covered the shower window of the jail. Heavy oxygen tanks were unloaded outside the fence which abuts the jail at the shower window. The torches, connected to a heavy hose, were passed to the inmates over the outside fence.

Sheriff Terry Shrunk said the outside confederates worked the valves on the tanks, while the escapees cut through the heavy iron bars over the window. The welding equipment later was abandoned at the scene of the break.

The prisoners, all of whom were serving terms for either robbery or petty larceny, were identified as Ernest D. Trujillo, 23, Lloyd Earg Eddy, 17, Edward S. Aldridge, 18, William S. Patrick, 24, Walter M. Chamberlain, 23, Victor V. Hanna, 28 and Leon S. Johnston.

Crazed Convicts Release Hostages

RUSK, Tex., April 16 (AP)—Eighty crazed inmates rioted today at the Rusk States Hospital and held a superintendent and two other persons hostage at knife-point for six hours before giving up.

At least 13 persons were injured.

The rioters, all Negroes, surrendered their hostages, gave up their knives, baseball bats, scissors and other weapons and returned to their rooms after a dramatic doorstep talk with Texas Ranger Capt. Bob Crowder.

Pruzzle 32 Worth $100

Ol' Pete shore was willing to give away his poke o' gold last week but no one accepted his offer by sending in the keyrect answer. Some of you folks were mighty close—one person stumbled over two letters; another missed by only three.

Pruzzle Pete

To make his treasure chest more tempting, Ol' Pete is going to add another twenty-five dollars this week.

So pardners, sharpen your pencils and your wits and see if you can't send in the solution to this Pruzzle No. 32.

Please turn to page 18 in today's Sunday News and see where you tripped in last week's pruzzle. That's where you'll find No. 32 so give it a whirl.

Accident Near City Hurts 3

Three persons were slightly injured at 8:50 p. m. yesterday in a two-car head-on crash on the Lincoln Highway at Maple Grove.

State Policeman Edward Schaeberle of the Columbia sub-station, who investigated, said that Ronald L. George, twenty, Pequea R1, operator of one car sustained a laceration on the back of the head.

Dr. Norman C. Crill, twenty-eight, 139 Millersville Rd., operator of the other vehicle, also sustained head lacerations and his wife, Mrs. Claire T. Crill, twenty-three, suffered injuries to the right wrist and knee. They were

Page 14—ACCIDENT

Lancaster Men Hurt In York County Crash

YORK, April 16—Two Lancaster County men were injured and damages estimated at $1,000 resulted when their car went out of control at Murphy's Hollow, one mile south of Wrightsville on the Long Level Road at 6:30 p. m. Saturday, State Police of the York substation reported.

Pfc. James E. Eberhart, who investigated the accident, said that a car operated by Harvey E. Zimmerman, 31, 1918 Manor Ridge Dr., Lancaster, went out of control and ran into guard rails along the east side of the road.

Police said Zimmerman told them he was forced off the highway by an oncoming vehicle. The force of the impact knocked out four guard fence posts and the rear window of the car, which was found about 50 feet from the scene.

A passenger in the Zimmerman car, Earl Heckel, 37, Ephrata R2, was thrown from the car to the highway and was knocked temporarily unconscious, police said.

Both men were rushed to the Columbia Hospital in the hospital's ambulance, where Heckel was admitted for observation after treatment of brush burns of the right arm, a laceration over the right eye and possible concussion. Zimmerman was discharged after treatment for body abrasions, police said.

First 30,000 Get Free Salk Shots

San Diego Leads Nation With Mass Shots For First, Second Grade School Children

SAN DIEGO, Calif., April 16 (INS)—Some 30,000 San Diego city and county school children bared their arms today to become the first of the nation's youngsters to be vaccinated this year with the Salk polio vaccine.

The first and second grade youngsters received their initial shots at 53 designated schools in the area.

It was the first mass polio vaccination since the historic announcement last Tuesday of the success of the vaccine.

The initial shipment of the vaccine sent to San Diego totaled 36,000 cubic centimeters, enough for one shot for 36,000 youngsters.

Vaccination teams from 175 members of the county medical society administered the shots. Some 350 nurses and 600 volunteers also aided in the mass immunization.

Children who had received parental permission and were eligible to receive the vaccine were given slips showing the time and place of the initial inoculations.

The second injection is to be given the same children within two or four weeks with the third or "booster" shot to be given by family doctors seven months hence.

Elsewhere in Southern California plans were being completed to inoculate tens of thousands of other first and second grade children on Monday. Some 275,000 youngsters were to receive their first vaccine on Monday.

In Northern California youngsters will not get the vaccine until next month.

The National Foundation for Infantile Paralysis had ruled that Southern California cities would have priority on the Salk vaccine because of the higher incidence of polio.

Wyeth Given Word To Ship Vaccine South

Orders for the shipment of Salk polio vaccine were received yesterday by the Wyeth Laboratories, Inc., Marietta, from the National Foundation for Infantile Paralysis.

First shipments of the vaccine will be made to the states of Maryland, Delaware and the District of Columbia. Other states included in the Wyeth area are: Pennsylvania, Delaware, Connecticut, Rhode Island and Maine. Dr. B. Scott Fritz, director of the laboratories, said that shipments to the remaining five states will begin as fast as the vaccine is approved by the National Institute of Health and shipment is directed by the polio foundation.

The director said that the inclusion of the southernmost states in the first shipment was in line with the foundation's announced policy of furnishing priority on the vaccine to the southern part of the U. S. Because of a longer warm season, the polio threat is greater in these sections. The field trials of last year were administered by the foundation in the same fashion. Dr. Fritz said that the vaccine is still in very short supply, but that he felt sure that his firm would be able to fulfill the requirements of two shots for each first and second grade pupil in the eight state area.

Dr. Jonas Salk, discoverer of the vaccine, has stated that two shots

Page 14—POLIO

Blackmailer's Bomb Rocks Dept. Store

PORTLAND, Ore., April 16 (AP)—Police today closed Portland's biggest department store, fearful that a blackmail bomb might rip into crowds of shoppers.

One bomb went off yesterday. Another was feared today because a $50,000 extortion demand was not paid. Aaron M. Frank, 64, president and general manager of Meier and Frank Co. whose department store occupies a 12-story, full block building, said he got a note yesterday afternoon demanding $50,0000.

N. Y. To Give Vaccine Free

NEW YORK, April 16 (INS)—The New York City Department of Health announced today that all persons under 20 years of age will receive free Salk polio vaccine inoculations.

Under the plan, announced after a three-hour emergency meeting, New York school children in the 5-to-9 age group will be given top priority and the first free shots.

The priority lineup is:

1. 5 to 9 years.
2. 1 to 4 years.
3. 10 to 14 years.
4. 15 to 19 years.
5. Pregnant women.

The priorities were based on the rate of occurrance of the disease in various age groups.

The health department, which would supply the vaccine to those on the priority list who are not eligible to receive free shots from the National Foundation for Infantile Paralysis, said its plan hinges on the availability of the vaccine.

The health department pointed out that pregnant women who are not able to obtain the vaccine through private channels probably will not receive free shots this year under the priority system.

Inoculations in New York City will begin April 25 with all children in the first and second grades of public, private and parochial schools, and all children in the third and fourth grades who participated in last year's field trials.

Man Goes Over Wall Of County Prison

Franklin Oscar Booher, 22, of Somerset, Pa., who was serving a one-to-two-year sentence for a New Year's Day burglary, escaped over the wall of Lancaster County Prison about 5 a. m. yesterday. He was recaptured about an hour later by city police, on the Oregon Pike, at Haskell Drive.

At 5:15 a.m. yesterday another trusted prisoner reported a 10-foot board leaning against the inside of the prison wall on the Orange St. side.

A check revealed that Booher, who had been let out of his cell to go to breakfast, had not reported at the kitchen and could not be found.

At 5:52 a.m. Warden Walter N. Foust, who had been summoned by the guards, asked city and state police to help in the hunt. At 6:08 — 16 minutes after they received the alarm — City Policemen Chester Corrigan and William Dull saw a man walking along the shoulder of the road. When they questioned him, he admitted his identity and offered no resistance. At 6:15 a.m. Booher was back in prison.

Warden Foust, who will prosecute Booher for breaking jail, said that he questioned the trusted prisoner, who was employed in the prison yard as a coal handler. He told the warden that some time ago, while whitewashing prison cells, he discovered the board in

Page 14—TRUSTY

Drowns

HARRY D. SCHWEERS JR.

Crash Victim, Kin In Double Funeral Tues.

Double funeral services will be held Tuesday for the victim of yesterday's highway accident and her brother-in-law, who had died earlier in the morning.

Miss Amelia Kauffman, 80, who was killed at 9:55 a. m. yesterday in an auto-truck crash on Route 30, two miles east of Columbia, and her brother-in-law, Harry C. Shookers, 91, Mountville, at whose home Miss Kauffman resided, will be buried from the Kraft Funeral Home, Columbia, Tuesday afternoon at two o'clock.

Reported in satisfactory condition last night at Lancaster General Hospital was Miss Mary Spiese, 3201 Atlantic Ave., Atlantic City, N. J., a friend of Miss Kauffman and a passenger in the car in which she was riding.

Retired Teacher

Mr. Shooker's daughter, Miss Amelia Shookers, 63, a retired Lancaster city school teacher, was treated at Columbia Hospital for lacerations and minor bruises and discharged later in the morning. Mrs. Patricia D. Russell, 28, Elizabethtown, another passenger in the car, was reported in satisfactory condition at Columbia Hospital last night. She also had minor lacerations.

State Policeman Donald Hollywood, who is investigating, said that the three women were passengers in a car driven by Clyde Kraft, Columbia funeral director, who was driving them to York to select a casket for Miss Shooker's father.

Aaron K. Rhoads, 53, High

Page 14—CRASH

Bee Blamed In 2-Truck Crash On City Street

It wasn't a bee in his bonnet that caused trouble for Nathan C. Krimmel, 16, 244 W. King St.; it was the bee in his truck, he told city police who investigated a two-truck accident on S. Prince St., between Seymour and Furnace Sts., at 4:07 p. m. yesterday.

He related that as he was driving north on S. Prince St., he was trying to get the bee out of the truck and noticed a car going west on Seymour St. that was trying to turn left onto Prince St. He said he eased to the left and struck a truck parked on the west side of Prince St. by George E. Bryson, 35, 724 S. Queen St.

Bryson was in a cafe at Seymour and Prince Sts. and heard the crash. A witness told police that the truck swerved all the way to the left side of the street and then ran along the curb for at least six car lengths.

Krimmel was prosecuted for reckless driving.

First Fatality Of Season At Shenk's Ferry

Harry D. Schweers Jr., 29, Is Victim; Father Escapes, Taken To Hospital

Harry D. Schweers Jr., 29, 22 Coral St., became the first drowning fatality of the season at 3:15 p. m. yesterday when a boat in which he was fishing with his father, Harry H. Schweers, 58, 712 S. Queen St., capsized at Shenk's Ferry midway between Safe Harbor and Pequea on the Susquehanna.

After the boat overturned and sank, the elder Schweers was able to swim some distance before being rescued by Eugene Campbell, 14 Hazel St. Artificial respiration was administered on the river bank by the rescue squad of the Columbia Hospital ambulance and the man was taken to the Columbia Hospital where his condition last night was listed as "satisfactory."

Stood Up In Boat

Witnesses to the accident told members of the State Police that the younger Schweers stood up in the boat prior to its overturning, and that he disappeared in about 15 feet of water, 30 feet from the shore. His body was recovered when fishermen in nearby boats began a sweep of the river. The body was taken from the water 45 minutes after the tragedy by E. L. Reynolds, 546 Beaver St., who snagged it with a fish-hook.

Boaters in the area at the time

Page 14—DROWNS

Save Boy, 2, Stuck In Well

AURORA, Colo., April 16 (INS)—A two-year-old boy was rescued alive tonight by a volunteer fireman, after being trapped four hours at the bottom of an 18-foot well in his backyard at Aurora.

The face of the boy — David Mark Counterman — was blood-smeared and bruised but physicians said he had no broken bones. He was taken by ambulance to Children's Hospital in Denver.

The boy fell down the 12-inch wide shaft while playing near the top of the well.

A power shovel dug a trench parallel to the well four feet wide and 14 feet deep. Then volunteer firemen using picks and shovels took over and dug down to the child, who had been encouraged by shouts from his father that "everything would be all right."

Military police from nearby Lowry Air Force Base joined policemen, firemen and other volunteer workers at the scene when the boy's plight was made public.

They worked by emergency flares and arc lights during the final phases of the rescue operation.

Special police details were required to hold back thousands of persons who gathered at the scene to witness the rescue.

Sunday News Today

Two Persons Get Bullets In Mail

Two Sunnyside residents complained to West Lampeter Police Chief Frank Horner yesterday that someone has been placing .25 caliber cartridges in their mail boxes.

They are H. F. Reedy and Amanda Alderfer, both of Lancaster R7. Chief Horner said they found the cartridges in their boxes on two separate occasions last week.

Weather

(U. S. Weather Bureau)

LOWER SUSQUEHANNA

Sunny and warmer today. Fair with moderate temperatures Sunday night. Monday fair and continued warm. Highest Sunday 74-82.

Lower Potomac and Chesapeake Bay — Winds mostly 10 to 20 miles per hour becoming southeast to south Sunday. Fair weather and good visibility.

Maryland — Some early morning cloudiness Sunday and cool breezes in the east portion. Fair and warmer in the afternoon with high 76 to 82 inland and 60's along the coast. Monday continued fair becoming warmer in the east.

Delaware — Some early morning cloudiness Sunday morning. High Sunday in the 60's. Monday fair and somewhat warmer.

Southeastern Pennsylvania and Southern New Jersey — Some cloudiness but mostly sunny and mild Sunday with high in the 60's except 55 to 60 along the New Jersey coast. Fair and mild Sunday night and Monday.

TEMPERATURES

	High	Low
Lancaster Water Works	71	49
Ephrata Weather Station	71	45
Ephrata 1954	55	40

Rt. 72 Span Takes Form In Manheim

NEW BRIDGE on Rt. 72 at south end of Manheim should be completed in from seven to eight weeks, a spokesman for the contractor said yesterday. Carpenters are shown (above) building forms for concrete deck. Background shows road leading to Lancaster torn up as part of rebuilding job which has seen road closed for several months. Work on eliminating a sharp "S" turn at the north end of the borough is also underway. The contractor said he doesn't expect the present detour to be lifted until some time after the bridge is complete. (Sunday News Photo.)

They Carry Local Hopes In 1955 Piedmont League

SPORTS

CARL WATSON, Pitcher · PAUL PETROSKEY, Catcher · BILL STUIFBERGEN, First Base · RON ESRANG, Second Base · REGGIE LEE, Shortstop · JIM MEYER, Third Base · JUNIOR REEDY, Left Field · BILL KERN, Center Field · DAVE SHEA, Right Field

Baseball

by GEORGE KIRCHNER

New Era Sports Editor

PLAY BALL! . . . Another baseball season is about to unfold in our town and for this you can find a lot of people who are thankful. Whether there are enough who will show their gratitude by patronizing the home club remains to be seen, but, at least, our town is still in organized ball and considering the number of cities . . . (some of them much larger than Lancaster) . . . which have been forced to drop out, this is to our credit.

What kind of a team will Kansas City provide to represent the town in the Piedmont League is another question that can not be answered at this moment. All we can do is hope that it'll be a better club than the team which finished tied for seventh—(or last, if you will)—last year. It could only be a notch worse, but it's better to hope that it might be considerably better.

NOT even Hank Biasatti, the young manager who will guide the team, can make a fair appraisal right now. He's been far too busy looking over his own candidates to pay even the slightest attention to the strength and weaknesses of the opposition. Furthermore, this is Hank's first year in Class "B" baseball, so he can't even hazard a guess on previous years.

"But," he hastens to add, "there's one thing I can tell you. This club that I brought north with me stacks up as a better all-around club than the one which Kemp Wicker had to start the season here last year."

THAT may not be saying too much, but it's, at least, a little encouraging, and the reason behind Biasatti's views, he explained, are two-fold . . . tighter defense and better batting power.

"It's hard to say how some of our hitters will do when the pitching gets tougher," the former A's first sacker opined, "but the way they belted the ball against

—See ROSES — Page 20

YESTERDAY'S RESULTS

AMERICAN ASSOCIATION

Denver 3, Indianapolis 1
Minneapolis 7, Toledo 2
Charleston 3, St. Paul 2
Only games scheduled

INTERNATIONAL LEAGUE

Montreal 10, Richmond 0
Toronto 5, Syracuse 1
Havana 6, Buffalo 0
Only games scheduled

EASTERN LEAGUE

Allentown 3, Elmira 2, 10 innings
Williamsport 4, Albany 3
Binghamton 5, Schenectady 0
Reading 5, Wilkes-Barre 3

RUNS FOR THE WEEK

NATIONAL LEAGUE

Team	M	T	W	T	F	S	S	Tls.
Chicago	x	x	1	2	..	..	..	3
New York	x	3	6	6	..	..	..	15
Philadelphia	x	x	x	3	..	..	..	3
Pittsburgh	x	x	4	2	..	..	..	6
Brooklyn	x	x	7	4	..	..	..	11
St. Louis	x	x	x	4	..	..	..	4
Milwaukee	x	2	9	2	..	..	..	13
Cincinnati	x	x	2	3	..	..	..	5

AMERICAN LEAGUE

Team	M	T	W	T	F	S	S	Tls.
New York	x	5	4	11	..	..	..	20
Detroit	x	3	11	4	..	..	..	18
Boston	x	7	2	3	..	..	..	12
Cleveland	x	3	6	x	..	..	..	9
Chicago	x	0	13	1	..	..	..	14
Washington	x	2	5	1	..	..	..	8
Kansas City	x	8	6	4	..	..	..	18
Baltimore	x	2	3	x	..	..	..	5

x-Did not play

Giuliano May Miss Roses' Opener

Tommy Giuliano, veteran second baseman, who finished last season's Piedmont League race with a .285 batting average, is not likely to be in the lineup when our Red Roses lift the curtain on the 1955 campaign with York at Stumpf Field tonight.

Game time is 8:45 o'clock, and, given a break in the weather, general manager Frank Spait says "we ought to pack the park."

Giuliano, who didn't join the Roses in spring camp until the last two weeks, is suffering with an aching shoulder and manager Hank Biasatti said this morning he doesn't believe the veteran will be able to start. However, Biasatti added he won't make a definite decision until nearer game time and if he has to change he'll substitute Ron Esrang, returning to baseball after a year's absence, in his place.

Others in Good Shape

But other than Giuliano, all the other Roses appear in good physical condition and anxious to get the season started. Manager Biasatti had his club out on the diamond yesterday and the boys engaged in a brisk two-hour workout, which the manager described as "just what they need for a final tune-up."

Carl Watson, a left-hander, who pitched for Biasatti when Hank managed Drummondville to the Class D Provincial League playoffs last season, has been nominated to do the chucking against the hard-hitting Yorkers. Watson's only comment last night was that "I'm ready." He's been working regularly in the spring games and it was as the result of his effectiveness in these exhibitions that he was named to start.

TOMMY GIULIANO

Biasatti said that Bill Stuifbergen, his long-ball hitter, will be at first with either Giuliano or Esrang at second; Reggie Lee of last year's team, at short and Jim Meyer, down from Williamsport, at third.

In the outfield, Junior Reedy of last season's squad, will patrol center with Bill Kern and Jack Haley, both of whom played for Biasatti at Drummondville, holding down the other outer posts.

Opening Night Ceremonies

All the pomp and ceremony of opening night will be carried out with Commissioner K. L. Shirk, who is about to retire from city duties, throwing out the first ball. Mayor Kendig C. Bare, who will be in the special box, turned the honor over to the retiring commissioner.

Spair introduced the team and manager to members of the press, radio, television, as well as other officials, at a buffet supper last night at the Arcadia. At the same time he announced that 51,250 tickets had been sold in advance, a new high for the Piedmont League and possibly a new high for minor league ball.

Mayor Welcomes Team

Mayor Bare extended official greetings and George Coe echoed the same sentiments from the Chamber of Commerce. Manager Biasatti responded and added "I hope we have a club that will prove so interesting that we'll double the advance ticket sale before the end of the season."

After tonight's single at Stumpf Field, the Roses go to York for a second opening there tomorrow night. After that they move to Sunbury for a single game on Sunday. They stay there for a tilt on Monday and then return to town to open a two-game series with Hagerstown next Tuesday.

In case tonight's opener is rained out — (and a decision won't be made until late this afternoon)—the Roses will have to wait until next Tuesday to open their campaign here.

HANK BIASATTI

Hopes High As Loop Opens 36th Year

By ED YOUNG

Associated Press Staff Writer

The Class B Piedmont League, a stubborn little circuit which has peddled its francises into three states in an unrelenting effort to make ends meet, launches its 36th baseball season tonight.

Undaunted by past financial reverses and optimistic that this will be the year that interest in minor league baseball revives, the eight-team loop opens its 140-game slate with the following lineup of games:

Norfolk at Portsmouth; Lynchburg at Newport News; Sunbury at Hagerstown; York at Lancaster.

Game times at all stops is 8 p.m. except Lancaster, where the late Friday night closing of stores has forced an 8:45 p.m. start. (All times local—Standard time in Portsmouth and Newport News, Daylight Time in Hagerstown and Lancaster).

Expect Big Crowds

Portsmouth, given good weather, expects to attract the heftiest opening night crowd—a gathering of 4,000. Newport News anticipates a turnout of 3,500 while a crowd of 2,500 is foreseen at Hagerstown and one of 2,000 at Lancaster.

Sunbury, Pa., the fourth new city admitted into the Piedmont in the past three years, won't make its home debut until Sunday. Neither will Lynchburg, an oldtime member of the league lodge. York and Lancaster will make their bows before the hometown folks tomorrow night.

Sunbury—which like Hagerstown, Lancaster and York is a former member of the defunct Class B Interstate League—replaces Colonial Heights-Petersburg, Va., in the Piedmont lineup. Like Ch-Petersburg, Sunbury will be a farm club of the Cincinnati Redlegs organization.

Probable pitchers for the openers tonight:

Norfolk at Portsmouth — Paul Doughty vs. Jim Barnhardt.

Lynchburg at Newport News—Chick McCombie vs. Bob Schassler.

Sunbury at Hagerstown — Bill Schneider vs. Al Bennett.

York at Lancaster—York pitcher unnamed. For Lancaster — Carl Watson.

Seeks 5th Title

Norfolk will be seeking an unprecedented fifth straight pennant this summer and from pre-season indications, the Tars will be hard to stop, eight straight upper-classification opponents, including the Kansas City Athletics, fell before the power-packed Tars in spring training exhibitions and manager Al Evans says he is "confident" his team will make a fight for the flag.

Evans, who'll do the Norfolk's catching, is a former major league receiver and succeeds Skeeter Scalzi as skipper of the champions.

Other new pilots this season are Ken Guettler, the old Piedmont League home run king, at Portsmouth; Hank Biasatti at Lancaster; George Kissell at Lynchburg; Johnny Welaj at Hagerstown, and Virgul Stallcup at Sunbury.

Holdover managers are George Scherger at Newport News and George Staller at York.

Besides Evans, playing managers will be Stalcup, a shortstop; Guettler, an outfielder; and Biasatti, a first baseman. The others will do their masterminding from the bench.

Norfolk, which copped the pennant last year with a typical late season sprint, looks ready to make its bid early this summer. The Tars have a seasoned club and one with lots of spit and polish, one that should be a contender all the way unless the other clubs come up with better than usual outfits.

Powerful Bait

CARBONDALE, Ill. (AP) — Tony Heine, operator of a sporting goods store, noticed an odd, fishy odor and investigated. A bottle of catfish bait had exploded.

Now he is telling his fisherman friends to be careful with the bottled bait, since it is powerful and definitely aromatic.

Pigeon Race Results

Bowman and Kinzer took the second pigeon race flown in concourse with several eastern cities this week flown from Manassas, Va. Red Rose club results follow:

	Yds. per min.
Bowman & Kinzer	1110.75
M. Abright	1096.05
S. Lockard	1073.26
E. Bigler	1072.18
R. Horne	1065.00
B. Weber	1056.40
R. Seitz	1049.52
H. Behmer	1032.30
L. Matroni	1020.59
J. Shreve	1000.92
R. Deibert	972.91
P.Grossglass	949.38
I. Weaver	919.49
R. Ault	860.47

1 Loft no report

Kid Pitcher Sparks Tigers' Early Drive

By ED WILKS

The Associated Press

Billy Hoeft, a lefty who has lost twice as many as he's won for Detroit in the past, told Manager Bucky Harris this spring that this is the season he becomes a winner. "Show me," said Harris.

So far, the kid's been showing him plenty. And since he started winning, the Tigers have been unbeatable, riding a five-game winning streak to within half a game of the American League lead.

It was Hoeft, a 22-year-old with three major league seasons behind him, who started the streak, shutting out the defending champion Cleveland Indians 3-0 on three hits last Saturday. And it was Hoeft again last night as the Tigers won No. 5, beating the Washington Senators 4-1.

Unearned Run

Hoeft whittled his earned run average down to 0.95, with Washington's lone tally unearned. He walked only one and struck out six.

Except for some shabby fielding and wild pitching by the Kansas City athletics last night, the Tigers would be in first place today with Cleveland instead of sharing second with the Indians. The A's failures allowed the New York Yankees an 11-4 triumph and with it the Bombers jumped back into the lead.

Chicago's White Sox tumbled out of first in a day game, losing to Boston and Ivan Delock, who spun a three-hitter for a 3-1 victory. Cleveland and Baltimore were idle.

Brooks Increase Lead

In the National, Brooklyn opened up a four-game spread over second place Milwaukee, coming from behind to beat the Chicago Cubs 4-2.

The Braves were beaten by Willie Jones' homer in the ninth last night at Philadelphia 3-2. Cincinnati broke up a six-game losing streak 3-2 at Pittsburgh under the lights and New York's Giants beat St. Louis 6-4 at the Polo Grounds.

The Yanks tagged five Kansas City pitchers for 13 hits — including a two-run homer by Mickey Mantle — but ran three runs across in the sixth without a single safety. Two hit batsmen, three walks and an error that prevented the third out accounted for the gifts.

Spoil His Shutout

Delock, a 25-year-old right-hander, didn't give the White Sox anything more potent than a single, but Chicago paired two of them with a walk to spoil his shutout

—See BASEBALL — Page 21

STS Looks Ahead On 50th Birthday

WITH 50 YEARS under its belt, Stevens Trade School is pausing only momentarily to look back. Visitors to the public "open house" Thursday, marking the school's golden anniversary, will find STS geared to looking ahead. They will find the state-supported school's administrators preoccupied with thoughts of increasing enrollment by 100 resident students next year, for instance. A final court decision is expected Friday on acquisition of the nearby Ann Street Home as an additional dormitory. When their tour guide takes them into the printing shop they will find two contrasting projects underway. One press is turning out a history of STS while another is going full speed ahead on the yearbook, looking forward to June graduation. Open house hours are 1:30 to 5 p. m. and 7 to 9 p. m.

(Sunday News Photos)

FACE-LIFTING is underway on main building at Stevens Trade School. Students are shown taking down old porch roof. Original project was to repair roof, but closer inspection indicated replacement would be necessary. Several designs for a new porch are under study.

COURT DECISION on sale of Ann Street Home to the state, for use as dormitory by STS, is expected Friday. STS superintendent John C. Stauffer (right) stands on steps of main entrance to home discussing plans with Samuel A. "Tiny" Wright of STS staff. Handy to the school, the building would become an annex—fitting into plans for increasing resident enrollment by 100 students. The home has been closed since War II.

3-YEAR PRINTING COURSE, presently restricted to the "letterpress" process, will soon be expanded to include "offset" lithography, according to Michael R. Fiorill (above), printing instructor. Fiorill here gives student Christ Elias tip on operating linotype (type-setting) machine.

HISTORY OF STS by James H. Hartzel, head of social science dept., and the school yearbook provide "live" projects for printing students. In photo at right, Mickey Shriver (left) and Charles Lavis operate press on which 260-page history is being printed. Students are doing all work except binding.

TIMELY ACTIVITY in bricklaying shop is building of outdoor fireplaces. Probably more than one "open house" visitor this Thursday will be thinking about building one in his own back yard, and will welcome the opportunity to pick up ideas. Kenneth Leptick is shown here with elaborate model.

FINISHING TOUCHES are being put on latest double unit in eventual 76-house development being built by students in learn-by-doing project, adjacent to Hickory Tree Heights. First six houses built and sold since 1953 are in background. Form at left marks spot where next two will be started.

GETTING READY for "open house," building trade students are spending some of their spare time making the buildings look their best. Painters here are Ralph Smith (left) and Earl Emerich.

WEATHER
(U. S. Weather Bureau Forecast for Lancaster, Cumberland, Lebanon, York, Adams and Franklin Counties):

Mostly Cloudy And Continued Warm And Humid With Showers And Scattered Thundershowers Today, Tonight And Tomorrow. High Today 75-80.

Intelligencer Journal.

The Leading Newspaper in the Garden Spot of America. Home Owned for Home Folks Since 1794

161st Year.—No. 291. Official United States Census Figures Lancaster Metropolitan Area Population 234,717 LANCASTER, PA., MONDAY MORNING, MAY 23, 1955. CITY TWENTY-FOUR PAGES. 30c PER WEEK—5c Per Copy

THE INTELL INDEX

PENTAGON REPORTED SHOCKED BY ADVANCES IN SOVIET AIR MIGHT

REDS ATTACK WEST'S TERMS ON BIG FOUR

Long Step Taken Toward Rejection Of Allied Conditions

By JOHN M. HIGHTOWER

WASHINGTON, May 22 (AP)—Russia took a long step today toward rejection of the terms and conditions set by the Western Powers for a top-level Big Four conference this summer.

An editorial in Pravda, bitterly attacking these terms as if they had been proposed by the United States alone, also suggested to experts here that the Soviet Union is trying to drive a wedge between the United States on the one hand and Britain and France on the other. The implication of the Soviet line is that it is only the American leaders who are being unreasonable.

Actually the terms for the meeting—that it should be short and confined to a definition of the problems and the methods to be used in solving them—were jointly proposed to the Russians in an American-British-French note two weeks ago.

MORE OUTSPOKEN

But since then President Eisenhower and Secretary of State Dulles have been more outspoken than their Paris and London Allies in emphasizing the strength and firmness of the Western stand. Apparently their assertions have annoyed the Soviets and also provided them with a convenient excuse for trying to change the nature and purposes of the meeting.

State Department officials said the Pravda editorial would have to be studied in detail. They would not be surprised if it was followed up by an official note from the Soviet government Monday or Tuesday along the same line, perhaps milder in tone.

Meanwhile the State Department had no formal comment. The initial reaction of U.S. officials was the Russians are not trying to get out of the Big Four meeting but probably are trying to twist it

Turn To Page 17 For More Of BIG 4

2 Senators Say U.S. Should Ask Soviet Pullback

Knowland, Capehart Urge Move Be Made At Big 4 Conference, Indiana Solon Says He Is Sure Dulles Will Make Request

WASHINGTON, May 22 (AP) — Sens. Knowland of California and Capehart of Indiana said today the United States should ask Russia to pull back within its prewar boundaries at the proposed Big Four conference.

The two Republicans offered the same proposal in different TV-radio interviews. Capehart said he was sure that's what the United States would ask of the Soviet Union.

Knowland, the GOP Senate leader, said the basis of negotiations with Russia should "depend on peace with honor rather than peace at any price."

LISTS CONCESSIONS

He suggested the Russians withdraw to their own frontier, give up control over Latvia, Estonia and Lithuania, get out of Poland and permit free elections there and allow free elections under U.N. supervision in Czechoslovakia, Hungary, Roumania and Bulgaria.

Knowland said Congress should be informed of the results of any Big Four conference immediately and the public should be advised within a year.

In answer to questions, the Californian said he would oppose any discussion of the Formosa question at the conference unless Nationalist China is represented.

NO APPEASEMENT

Capehart said he was confident President Eisenhower and Secretary of State Dulles "are not going in any way to appease the Russians, that they are going to stand up and talk and carry to that conference the viewpoint of the American people."

Capehart and Sen. Sparkman (D-Ala), both members of the Senate Foreign Relations Commit-

Turn To Page 17 For More Of SENATORS

ST. JOHN'S E&R CONGREGATION ELECTS PASTOR

Rev. Amos L. Seldomridge, County Native; To Succeed Rev. Noss

The Rev. Amos Leon Seldomridge, now pastor of Trinity Church, Saxton, Pa., was unanimously elected minister of St. John's Evangelical and Reformed Church here yesterday morning at a congregational meeting following morning services.

REV. A. L. SELDOMRIDGE

He succeeds the Rev. Christopher J. Noss, who left February 1 to assume a pastorate at Westminster, Md.

A native of Lancaster County and a son of Mrs. Roy F. Marks, New Holland, and the late Willis Hammond Seldomridge, the Rev. Seldomridge is a former Navy chaplain.

He was graduated from Franklin and Marshall College in 1941, from the Seminary of the Evangelical and Reformed Church here in 1944 and did graduate work at Union Theological Seminary, New York City, following his separation from the Navy in 1946.

His former churches were Jacobs

Turn To Page 17 For More Of ST. JOHNS

Principals At Dedication Of New Hospital Wing

Dr. Otterbein Dressler, professor of pathology at the Chicago College of Osteopathy and pathologist at the Detroit Osteopathic Hospital, delivers the main address during dedication ceremonies for the new wing of Lancaster Osteopathic Hospital yesterday afternoon. Others who participated in the dedication are, seated in front left to right, Fred Wiker, a founder, past president and presently a director; Miss Alma Trout, president of the Executive Council of the Guilds of the hospital, state guild president and member of the board; Henry H. Hanton, former board president and present secretary; Dr. Elwood W. Swift, chief of staff; Dr. Ned Swift, member of the founding group of the hospital; and Dr. George C. Wolf, medical director. In rear, left to right, are Martin C. Dellinger, chairman of the fund raising committee, who was presented with a certificate of merit; Alexander T. Stein, board president; the Rev. Wallace E. Fisher, who gave the invocation; Mrs. A. M. Winder, who received a certificate for merit for her father, George F. Hostetter, chairman of the building committee; and Rabbi William A. Sanderson, who gave the benediction. (Intell Photo)

RED STRENGTH FIGHT JOINED BY MAGAZINE

Officials Disagree On Whether Russia Is Ahead Or Behind

WASHINGTON, May 22 (AP)—Aviation Week said today that Russia has displayed over Moscow aircraft so advanced and so numerous it has shocked "even the top level and most knowledgeable military aviation leaders in the Pentagon."

The usually well-informed magazine thus joined the argument that has been raging the past week over how strong Soviet air power is. Most of the military and civilian officials who have expressed an opinion have agreed the Red air might is growing but they disagree widely on whether the Russians are ahead or behind the United States.

The Pentagon itself touched off the dispute by releasing intelligence reports which indicate Russia has increased her lead over the United States in numbers of supersonic jet fighters.

Aviation Week said every American should be shocked by the Soviet air growth and also by "what appears to be a deliberate deception practiced against them by some of the highest civilian officials in their government" in not disclosing what planes flew in the Russian air show in late April and early this month.

The magazine referred particularly to statements by Secretary of Defense Wilson that Russia is

Turn To Page 15 For More Of RUSSIA

COLUMBIAN HELD FOR DEATH OF WOMAN IN MD.

John J. Murray Expected To Be Released On Bail Today

John J. Murray, twenty-four, 132 S. Second St., Columbia, charged with criminal manslaughter in the death of a Cambridge, Md., woman, is expected to be released from jail today.

He is being held in default of $1,500 bail at the Dorchester Coun-

Turn To Page 15 For More Of COLUMBIAN

1,250 Tour Osteopathic Hospital After Ceremonies

A total of 1,250 persons toured the Lancaster Osteopathic Hospital yesterday following dedication of the new wing and the completely renovated older portion of the hospital at Orange Street and Cottage Avenue.

The dedication ceremonies were held on the steps at the front entrance, with an audience of about 800 seated in chairs on the lawn. It rained lightly, shortly after the start of the program, but not enough to hamper the festivities.

The principal speaker was Dr. Otterbein Dressler, Detroit, Mich., professor of pathology at the Chicago College of Osteopathy and presently pathologist at the Detroit Osteopathic Hospital. Alexander T. Stein, president of the board of directors, gave the address of welcome and dedication. The invocation was given by the Rev. Wallace E. Fisher, pastor of Trinity Lutheran Church, and the benediction by Rabbi William A. Sanderson, of Temple Shaarai Shomayim.

2 MEN HONORED

Framed certificates of merit were presented to Martin C. Dellinger, chairman of the fund raising committee, and George F. Hostetter, chairman of the building committee. Hostetter was unable to be present, so his citation was accepted for him by his daughter, Mrs. A. M. Winder. The certificates were in recognition of outstanding services to the fund raising committee in connection with financing and building the new wing.

In making the speech of dedication, Stein said that the growth

Turn To Page 15 For More Of OSTEOPATHIC

GOV'T AWAITING FRESH ADVICE ON RESUMING SHOTS

Take Cautious Attitude, Findings Of Experts To Be Studied

WASHINGTON, May 22 (AP) — Government health authorities maintained an attitude of caution today as they awaited fresh advice which could determine how soon the nation's antipolio vaccination campaign gets started again.

Specialists in the field confer tomorrow on the findings of a team of experts who have inspected the manufacturing and testing processes of vaccine producers.

Their conclusions possibly could result in still tighter safety standards for the vaccine already given to nearly six million youngsters. Any move in this direction would have a delaying effect on the drive to inoculate children of the most susceptible ages this year.

SLOWED AGAIN

The vaccination campaign, which has been on and off, slowed down again last week when the Public Health Service temporarily stopped clearing vaccine already produced.

Rep. Scott (R-Pa) told a TV-radio audience today the vaccine was released about two months

Turn To Page 15 For More Of VACCINE

5 Brooklyn Boys Are Charged In Dozen Holdups

NEW YORK, May 22 (AP)—A gang of five Brooklyn teen-agers were in jail today, charged with holding up at least 12 Brooklyn drug stores, gas stations and laundries in the last four months.

Police said they may be implicated in as many as 30 holdups. They put the total loot at $3,000 to $4,000, and said the boys "spent it on dames."

The arrest Saturday of a 15-year-old, whose name was withheld, led to the roundup of the gang. Police found a gun in the youth's closet at home. They said the 15-year-old "held the gun" in most of the stickups.

Late Saturday afternoon five

Turn To Page 15 For More Of GANG

9 Are Injured In Auto Crashes During Weekend

Nine persons were injured in a series of accidents reported on city and county highways over the weekend.

No one was seriously injured but a large amount of property damage resulted from the collisions. Police reported heavy traffic on the highways both Saturday and Sunday.

HELD AS HIT-RUN

John C. Krow, 230 N. Franklin St., this city, was charged with failure to leave identity at the scene of an accident by Columbia borough police after he allegedly hit a parked auto at Second and Walnut Sts., Columbia, at 2:30 a. m. Saturday. The parked car, police said, is owned by May Smith, 203 Walnut St., Columbia.

LANDISVILLE WOMAN HURT

Mrs. Harriet Swarr, Main St.,

Turn To Page 15 For More Of ACCIDENTS

"We Lead All The Rest"

FARM CORNER

By WILLIAM R. SCHULTZ

2-Day Grassland Show Set For Masonic Homes

Lancaster County will become the grassland farming center of southeastern Pennsylvania tomorrow with the opening the two-day Grassland Field Day program at the Masonic Homes Farm, in Elizabethtown.

This is the first grassland progarm of this scope to be offered in Lancaster County and the only event of its kind planned for the southeast this year.

An estimated 3,000 farmers from Lancaster and the five adjoining counties are expected on the two days. Duplicate programs will be offered during the hours 10 a. m. to 3 p. m. each day. State Secretary of Agriculture W. L. Henning will be guest speaker on both days.

Action demonstrations of farm machinery used in step of making and storing grass silage will be

Turn To Page 15 For More Of FARM CORNER

Hundreds Attend Enclosure Ceremony At New Monastery

Spattering raindrops that began to fall just as the ceremony was about to start, then held off until the very end, failed to deter hundreds of persons from attending the Solemn Blessing and Official Enclosure of Lancaster's new Monastery of the Immaculate Heart of Mary, for the Dominican Sisters of the Perpetual Rosary, carried out yesterday afternoon, with the Most Rev. Amleto G. Cicognani, Apostolic Delegate to the United States of America, officiating.

The colorful procession including more than half a hundred priests of the Harrisburg Diocese and 11 monsigniori, moved promptly from the old home of the Dominican Sisters, located several yards from the entrance to the new $450,000 property at 1834 Lititz Pike,

Turn To Page 17 For More Of MONASTERY

ONLY TRACES HERE OF MUCH-NEEDED RAIN; HUMIDITY IS HIGH

The best the weatherman could do yesterday for dry soil conditions was a mere sprinkling of rain in parts of the county.

What moisture there was in the air refused to condense. It took the form of a sticky, high, and uncomfortable humidity which averaged 84 per cent.

Scattered thundershowers today and tomorrow might help the severe farm conditions, the weatherman indicated. Accompanying the possibilities of rain will be the continued high humidity, however, and cloudiness.

The expected high today will be 75 to 80 degrees, compared with yesterday's high of 80 at the Ephrata Weather Station. The low there early yesterday was 53. Saturday, a hot sun sent the mercury to 84 degrees at Ephrata.

Sen. Russell Bows Out Of Democrat President Fight

WASHINGTON, May 22 (AP)—Sen. Richard B. Russell of Georgia, who has been a leading Southern contender in the past, said today he will not seek the Democratic presidential nomination next year.

Russell, who piled up a substantial bloc of votes at the Democratic national conventions in 1948 and 1952, said in an interview:

"Absolutely not. I will not be a candidate for the nomination this time."

The Georgia senator, who for years has served as unofficial leader of a powerful group of Southern Democratic senators, refused to speculate on other possibilities, including Adlai Stevenson, the party's 1952 nominee.

ACTIVE CAMPAIGNER

Russell was an active campaigner for the 1952 nomination and had a staff and headquarters at the Chicago convention.

Russell's decision to keep out of the next contest might shift some Southern sentiment toward Sens. Lyndon B. Johnson of Texas or Stuart Symington of Missouri, although national party leaders are working furiously to avoid any sectional splits.

Sen. Estes Kefauver of Tennessee, who made a strong bid for the 1952 nomination, appears to be a willing entry again this time. But many political observers doubt that Kefauver could pick up the Deep South support that has been loyal to Russell.

Weather Calendar

COMPARATIVE TEMPERATURES

Station	High	Low
Water Works (Saturday)	83	49
Water Works (Sunday)	80	52
Ephrata	80	53
Last Year (Ephrata)	70	44
Official High for Year May 5		88
Official Low for Year Feb. 3		-5
Character of Day		Cloudy

WINDS
Direction SE Avg. Velocity 7 mph

HUMIDITY
8 a.m. 90% 11 a.m. 87% 2 p.m. 79% 5 p.m. 87% 5 p.m. 79%
Average Humidity 84%

SUN
Rises 5:43 a.m. Sets 8:19 p.m.

MOON
Sets 10:36 p.m. First Quarter, May 28

STARS
Morning—Venus
Evening—Mars, Jupiter, Saturn

NEARBY FORECASTS
(U.S. Weather Bureau)

Southeastern Pennsylvania and Southern New Jersey — Mostly cloudy, warm and humid with showers and scattered thunderstorms today. High 75-82 except 68-73 vicinity of coast. Tomorrow considerable cloudiness and continued warm and humid with afternoon showers and thunderstorms mostly in the afternoon and evening.

Central and Northeastern Pennsylvania —Mostly cloudy and continued warm and humid with showers and scattered thundershowers today and tomorrow. High today in the 70's.

Lower Potomac and Chesapeake Bay—Southerly winds 10-20 mph today. Cloudy with showers and possibly a few scattered thunderstorms. Visibility fair to good.

Maryland and Delaware—Rather cloudy warm and humid with scattered showers and thunderstorms today and tomorrow mostly during the afternoon and evening hours. Highest today 78-84 except around 70 along the coast.

Apostolic Delegate Blesses Crowd

The Most Rev. Amleto G. Cicognani, Apostolic Delegate to the United States of America, is shown extending his blessing to a portion of the crowd of hundreds of persons who gathered yesterday afternoon to watch the colorful ceremonies of the Solemn Blessing and Official Enclosure of the new Monastery of the Immaculate Heart of Mary, for the Dominican Sisters of the Perpetual Rosary, along the Lititz Pike, just north of the city. Drawn up as a guard of honor, on either side of the entrance to the public chapel of the Monastery, the members of the Fourth Degree Assembly, Knights of Columbus, in full-dress uniform. Flanking the Apostolic Delegate are, left, the Rt. Rev. Msgr. Joseph J. Schweich, pastor of St. Joseph's Church, who served as deacon; and the Rt. Rev. Msgr. Charles J. Tighe, pastor of Assumption of the Blessed Virgin Mary Church, who was the sub-deacon. (Intell Photo)

Sports Roundup

Wynn Wins On One-Hitter; Roses Beaten

Cleveland called on Early Wynn to halt a two-game Indians' losing streak yesterday and the Tribe ace responded with a one-hitter as he blanked Detroit, 4-0.

His triumph didn't improve Cleveland matters too much, however, as the Yankees defeated Baltimore, 5-0 and 7-5.

In the national league the Dodgers were back at it again, whipping the Phillies, 8-3, with Erskine needing some relief in the ninth inning. The Giants picked up ground with 5-2 and 5-3 wins over Pittsburgh.

Five Lancaster Red Roses pitchers figured in a 14-hit Sunbury attack here yesterday in a Piedmont league fray which saw the Redlegs come out of it with a 17-2 triumph.

A state move to build a Curtiss-Wright plant in Northcentral Pennsylvania has drawn a wave of protest from the sportsmen and a hearing has been called on the matter.

These and other stories can be found today on Sports Pages 18, 19, and 20.

SPECIAL GAS SECTION

A Gas Section appears in today's *Intelligencer Journal*, pages 4 through 9.

Estimated 12,000 See Antique Auto Show Held For Child Center

An estimated 12,000 persons attended the third annual Antique Auto Show sponsored by the Lancaster Child Development Center Saturday and Sunday at the Lancaster Lincoln Mercury Co. showroom, North Prince and McGovern Ave.

Proceeds of more than $1,200 were realized for the Center through contributions and the sale of food and other items. Fifty automobiles, dating from 1899 to 1930, were exhibited by the Red Rose Antique Auto Club for the event.

Colorful antique auto aprons, auto models and costume jewelry were sold by the Auxiliary to the Child Development Center, while th Child Development Center PTA offered home-made pies, cakes and sandwiches for sale. More than 100 persons manned the various stands.

The show was open Saturday afternoon and all day yesterday. Among the ancient cars displayed were 12 not shown locally before. These included an 1899 English Bentley, a 1920 French Avions Voisin, a 1910 English Wolseley-Siddley; a 1902 Oldsmobile, a 1915 Brisco and two Knox cars with single headlights.

Chairmen for the event were Mahlon Patton, Antique Auto Club; Mrs. Olivia Stoner and Herbert Mearig, Child Development Center; Mrs. Durrell Hollinger, CDC Auxiliary; and Dr. Lewis Headrick, PTA.

WEATHER
(U. S. Weather Bureau Forecast For Lancaster, Cumberland, Lebanon, York, Adams And Franklin Counties):

Cloudy, Warm And Humid Today With Scattered Thundershowers Today And Tomorrow. High Both Days 85-90. Low Tonight In The 60s.

Intelligencer Journal.

The Leading Newspaper in the Garden Spot of America. Home Owned for Home Folks Since 1794

162nd Year.—No. 13. Official United States Census Figures Lancaster Metropolitan Area Population 234,717 LANCASTER, PA., FRIDAY MORNING, JULY 1, 1955. CITY FORTY-SIX PAGES. 30c PER WEEK—5c Per Copy

Steel Strike Apparently On, Talks Break Up

BIG WATER MAIN BREAKS IN CITY

Way Opened For Scrapping Dixon-Yates Plans

NO WORD OF AGREEMENT AFTER MEET

Negotiators Say Only That "We Are Continuing Our Meetings"

PITTSBURGH, Friday, July 1 (AP) — A nationwide strike of 600,000 men in the basic steel industry appeared to be on early today as top negotiators for the CIO United Steelworkers and pace-setting U. S. Steel Corp. broke up a five-hour meeting without word of agreement.

The negotiators said only, "We are continuing our meetings."

Picket lines appeared at steel mills across the country.

The union had made it clear it would not work without a contract and the rank and file wasted no time going into action.

NOT CLARIFIED

David J. McDonald, president of the CIO United Steelworkers, and John A. Stephens, vice president and chief negotiator for U.S. Steel Corp., declined to clarify the situation as they emerged from their long private negotiating huddle in a downtown hotel.

They said only that they had agreed on a single statement that "we are continuing our meetings."

However, they separated and Stephens walked with an attorney-adviser to U.S. Steel's office building while McDonald left for his hotel suite, saying:

"I've got to get some more

Turn To Page 12 For More Of STEEL

New Manager

ROBERT C. RESSLER

ROBERT C. RESSLER NAMED MANAGER OF BEARINGS CO.

Stockholders To Vote July 20 And 31 On Merger With Bower Co.

Robert C. Ressler, a life-long resident of Lancaster, has been appointed plant manager of the local Bearings Co. of America Division of the Federal-Mogul Corp. effective today.

His appointment was announced yesterday by J. W. Brady, Federal-Mogul vice president and general manager of the local plant.

B. F. Shaub and R. E. Morrison

Turn To Page 23 For More Of RESSLER

EISENHOWER ORDERS STUDY OF CONTRACT

Memphis Decision To Build Own Power Plant Sparks Action

WASHINGTON, June 30 (AP)—President Eisenhower opened the way tonight to scrap the Dixon-Yates contract, a private power project his administration had vigorously backed despite hot protests from public power advocates.

Eisenhower ordered a study to determine whether the contract should be canceled or continued in view of the announced decision of Memphis, Tenn., to build its own plant instead of taking Dixon-Yates power.

The president didn't say the contract would be abandoned. But one of his chief aides, Budget Director Rowland Hughes, said "one of the probable consequences" of the Memphis decision is that the Dixon-Yates plant won't be needed.

Hughes was ordered by Eisenhower to make the new study in conjunction with the Atomic Energy Commission and the Tennessee Valley Authority.

AT HEARING

Hughes appeared tonight at a hearing before a Senate Judiciary subcommittee on Dixon-Yates. Sen. Kefauver (D-Tenn), subcommittee chairman and bitter foe of Dixon-Yates, placed the White House announcement in the record.

Hughes commented:

"As you can see, we've got a

Turn To Page 12 For More Of DIXON-YATES

Thar She Blows And It's Water, Water Everywhere

Residents watch as water gushes from main which broke about 8 p. m. last night at Lehigh Avenue and Franklin Street. A six-foot stream of water shot up through the street when the main broke, sending between 750,000 and a million gallons of water streaming over the intersection. Water service to hundreds of residents was cut off by the break. Water department crews went to work immediately in an effort to repair the break. (Intell Photo)

ONE MILLION GALLONS FLOW OVER STREET

16-Inch Pipe Bursts Open At Lehigh Ave., Franklin Street

A 16-inch water main at Lehigh Ave. and Franklin St. split open about 8 p. m. yesterday, cutting off water service for scores of residents of the area, shooting up a six-foot stream of water, and sending between 750,000 and 1,000,000 gallons of water streaming from the intersection.

Service was restored to most residents of the area within two hours, but some families in a two block area in the neighborhood were still without water early this morning.

Crews immediately went to work pumping water from a large crater created in the center of the intersection last night. After the water was pumped out, they planned to excavate the hole in an effort to repair the broken main.

BLAME TRUCK TRAFFIC

Both Charles P. Abraham, superintendent of the Water Department, and City Commissioner Daniel S. Templeton, head of the Department of Public Safety, said they thought the break was caused by heavy truck traffic at the intersection.

Two crews were called out to first cut off the underground pipes supplying water to the main and then to start repairs. Valves were turned off at about 12 points.

This resulted in no water for the residents of homes served by these pipelines. But within two hours, water sources were restored to most, after workmen

Turn To Page 12 For More Of WATER

"We Lead All The Rest"

FARM CORNER

By WILLIAM R. SCHULTZ

No Shortage Of Wheat Storage Facilities Seen

Lancaster County farmers will harvest the 1955 crop of winter wheat without fear of a shortage of grain storage facilities.

The Pennsylvania ASC committee disclosed yesterday that 1,676,000 bushels of storage space has been allocated for wheat placed under federal price support loans.

The available facilities are believed adequate to meet demands on the program this year.

Meanwhile, the price support level for the 1955 crops of winter barley and winter oats were announced. Both are below the 1954 level.

Government loans will be available for barley at the rate of $1.05 a bushel for grain grading number two or better. This compares

Turn To Page 23 For More Of FARM CORNER

United Giving Said 'Must' For Fall's Community Drive

If the local community doesn't support the United Community Campaign in the fall, united giving will be set back for years, members of the campaign committee for the drive were told at their first meeting yesterday in the Armstrong Cork Co. offices.

The drive is a joint campaign of the Lancaster County Chapter, American Red Cross, and the newly enlarged Community Chest of Lancaster County with its 22 agencies. It is the result of months of work toward getting a more federated campaign in the Lancaster area.

Having a United Community Campaign will mean there will be no Red Cross drive next year, no YMCA budget canvass and no Bell Day for the benefit of the Hearing Conservation Center. The latter two campaigns have been eliminated because the YMCA and the Hearing Conservation Center this week were admitted as the 21st and 22nd member agencies of the Chest.

Martin C. Dellinger, who has been named general co-chairman of the campaign to serve with Daniel Rhoads, general chairman, stressed the importance of united giving and urged the full support of the people of city and county. Dellinger is president of the K-D Manufacturing Co.

Rhoads pointed out that it will be a big job to educate the public to the fact that the United Community Campaign is a larger drive — actually 23 drives in one— and that the goal will be consid-

Turn To Page 12 For More Of CAMPAIGN

CUPID SPARKS NEW MARRIAGE MARK IN COUNTY DURING JUNE

Cupid outdid himself in June in Lancaster County.

Mrs. Alice Frey, in charge of the marriage license bureau at the courthouse, announced yesterday that 245 marriage licenses were applied for last month, a new all-time record.

Last year 201 licenses were issued in June, which also set a record.

HOOVER IN PLEA FOR PROPOSALS OF COMMISSION

Former President Steps Out Of Public Life As 2-Year Task Ends

WASHINGTON, June 3 (AP) — Former President Herbert Hoover said today the budget can be balanced and taxes cut if Congress and the administration adopt the reorganization plans of the second Hoover Commission.

The 80-year-old chairman stepped out of public life, but not out of controversy, as the commission expired after a two-year exploration of government organization and policies.

He released, at a news conference, the hitherto secret report of the commission's task force on water and power. That report urged the sale, lease or transfer of all federally owned power plants along with "town sites and related buildings."

"MONUMENTAL WORK"

Although the 12-member Hoover Commission itself adopted milder recommendations to restrict gov-

Turn To Page 23 For More Of HOOVER

Real Estate Ratio In Market, Assessed Value At New Low

The ratio between the market value and the assessed value of real estate slipped to a new low in Lancaster County in 1954, the State Tax Equalization Board reported yesterday.

Figures for last year, released by the board at Harrisburg, showed that real estate in the county was assessed at only 24.6 per cent of the market value.

The market value was listed at a whopping $729,432,100 and the assessed value for tax purposes was only $179,496,492.

The gap between market and assessed value of real estate in Lancaster County has continued to widen since 1948 when the STEB made its first report.

The ratio between market and assessed valuation each year since the Legislature created the STEB to set the actual real estate valuations as a basis for determining state aid to school districts follows:

1948—27.41 per cent.
1949—27.23 per cent.
1950—26.46 per cent.
1951—25.40 per cent.
1952—24.79 per cent.

Turn To Page 12 For More Of TAXES

Girl Wanted In W. Va. Picked Up Here In Theft

An eighteen-year-old girl, arrested by city detectives yesterday for stealing from a dress shop, is wanted by federal authorities for escaping from the Federal Women's Penitentiary at Aldersen, W. Va., police learned.

She was identified as Awrana Lorane Longoria, of Vallejo, Calif.

Detectives started a search for her after they received a complaint from Mrs. Ruth Hippey, Lancaster R6, of the D and R Dress Shop, 140 S. Queen St. She said the girl tried on a dress and then asked if she could use the phone. When no one was looking, the girl left the store, wearing the dress and with $25 from the cash drawer, police said.

SPOTTED BY POLICE

At 1:30 p. m. Detective Frank Matt and Detective Sgt. David Rineer spotted her as she was getting into a taxicab at N. Queen and Orange Streets.

Police said she told a number of different stories, but finally admitted she had escaped from the prison. Capt. of Detectives John Kirchner phoned the prison and

Turn To Page 12 For More Of CONVICT

FURNITURE STORE WILL BE BUILT WEST OF CITY

Another major building project on the Lincoln Highway West, the second to be announced this week, was revealed yesterday when plans were announced for the construction of a modern furniture store.

The new business is planned by Oscar H. Gundel, of Conestoga, and is to be located on the south side of the Lincoln Highway, just west of Manor Ridge Drive.

Gundel, a native of Columbia, today starts his 11th year as a funeral director at Conestoga. He plans to continue this business.

70 BY 110 FEET

Tentative plans for the new store, Gundel announced, provide for a Colonial style one-story concrete block building measuring approximately 70 by 110 feet with a brick front and Colonial style entrance. It will also include a full length basement.

The building is to be constructed on a plot of ground measuring 180 feet wide by 175 feet deep with a 20-foot right of way from the edge of the highway.

LARGE PARKING AREA

Plans also call for macademizing the area around the store building to provide ample parking space for 50 to 75 cars.

Actual construction on the store is not expected to get underway

Turn To Page 12 For More Of STORE

Roses Dropped From First On Loss To Norfolk

The Piedmont league experienced another lead change last night as Lancaster bowed to Norfolk, 4-3, and stepped out of first while Newport News slipped back in on a 7-0 conquest of York.

Nellie Fox has regained the lead in the All-Star baseball poll and today's the deadline for balloting. Local votes must be on the Intelligencer Journal sports desk by noon today.

Tonight's Junior Legion baseball All-Star night and a pitching and hitting summary of the city and county All-Star squads have been compiled for this first annual game.

The ban of boxing in Pennsylvania will last until the final findings of the committee investigating the sports are released to the public.

These and other stories can be found today on Sports Pages 35, 36, 37, 38, 39, and 40.

BIG LEAGUE RESULTS

NATIONAL LEAGUE
Brooklyn 6, New York 5 (11 innings)
Milwaukee 7, Chicago 4

AMERICAN LEAGUE
Washington 3, Boston 2
Detroit 4, Chicago 3
(Only games scheduled)

Weather Calendar

COMPARATIVE TEMPERATURES

Station	High	Low
Water Works	86	57
Ephrata	89	56
Last Year (Ephrata)	89	55
Official High for Year June 17		90
Official Low for Year Feb. 3		-5
Character of Day ......Partly Cloudy		

WINDS
Direction SW Avg. Velocity 5 mph

HUMIDITY
8 a.m. 84% 11 a.m. 53% 2 p.m. 45%
5 p.m. 52% 8 p.m. 49%
Average Humidity 57%

SUN
Rises 5:38 a.m. Sets 8:37 p.m.

MOON
Sets 3:23 a.m. Saturday
Full Moon, July 5

STARS
Morning—Venus
Evening—Mars, Jupiter, Saturn

NEARBY FORECASTS
(U.S. Weather Bureau)

Central and Northeastern Pennsylvania — Continued rather cloudy, warm and humid with scattered afternoon and evening thundershowers today and tomorrow. High 85-90 both days.

Southeastern Pennsylvania and Southern New Jersey — Considerable cloudiness, hot and more humid today and tomorrow with scattered afternoon and evening thundershowers likely both days. High today 86-92.

Lower Potomac and Chesapeake Bay—Southwest winds increasing to 15-25 miles per hour today. Partly cloudy weather and good visibility except slight chance of scattered afternoon thundershowers.

Maryland — Partly cloudy and warm today with scattered afternoon or evening thundershowers in north and west portions. High 85-92. Tomorrow partly cloudy and warm with scattered afternoon and evening thundershowers.

Delaware — Partly cloudy and warm today, possibly scattered afternoon or evening showers or thunderstorms in the north portion. High 87-92. Tomorrow partly cloudy and warm with scattered afternoon and evening thundershowers.

Architect's Drawing Of Warner-Lambert Plant To Be Built At Lititz

This is an architect's drawing of the new $4 million Warner-Lambert Co. cosmetics plant to be built in Lititz. This view shows the portion of the plant facing east toward the borough. The plant will be L-shaped, according to details revealed earlier by Lawrence A. Flagler, vice president in charge of manufacturing. The portion in the center of the building, protruding toward the front, will be the office section. Behind it and to the right is the two-story manufacturing section, with actual manufacturing being done on the second floor and packaging on the first floor. The warehousing section is to the right. The company expects to break ground for the new plant sometime this month. (AP Wirephoto)

HOT, HUMID AGAIN TODAY, RAIN THREAT

Lancaster Countians were treated to hot, humid weather yesterday with more of the same in store for them today.

Yesterday's official high recorded at the Ephrata Weather Station was 89 degrees, just one degree lower than the high temperature recorded so far this year. The average humidity was 57 per cent.

However, according to the forecast, scattered afternoon and evening thundershowers today and tomorrow may provide some relief.

Public Bequests Of $30,790 Freed For Distribution Here

Public bequests of $30,790.30 were among funds totaling $219,474.47 ordered distributed in 13 estates in adjudications approved yesterday by Judge John L. Bowman in Orphans' Court.

Bequests of $17,841.36 were contained in the will of Mrs. Emma L. W. Johnston, late of Lancaster, who died April 9, 1945.

The sum of $3,960.34 was left to each of these organizations: Women's Society for Christian Service of the Philadelphia Conference of the Methodist Church; the Cookman Methodist Church, Columbia, as a memorial to her late husband, C. W. Johnson; Columbia Hospital as a memorial to her late husband, and the Lancaster County Chapter of the American Red Cross. In addition, she

Turn To Page 23 For More Of BEQUESTS

Wynn And Newcombe Likely All-Star Game Starters

Lopez Picks Nine-Man Hurling Staff In Effort To Stop Superior Nationals Punch

By JOE REICHLER

MILWAUKEE, July 11 (AP)—Early Wynn, Cleveland's powerful righthander, and Brooklyn's Don Newcombe, who also throws from the right side, appear to be the likely choices to obtain the starting assignments in the 22nd annual major league All-Star Game here next Tuesday.

Wynn

Newcombe

The odds-makers, probably respecting power over pitching, have installed the National League squad a slight 6-5 favorite to register its ninth victory since the classic originated in 1933. The Americans, who snapped a four-game losing streak last summer with an 11-9 victory in Cleveland, have won 13. There was no game in 1945.

A capacity crowd of close to 45,000 is expected to fill every available seat in County Stadium with all tickets sold weeks ago. The game, scheduled to start at 1:30 p.m. (CST), will be seen and heard via television and radio from coast to coast. Long range weather predictions are for high temperatures and higher humidity. No rain is forecast.

9 American Pitchers

American League Manager Al Lopez, in an effort to offset the superior punch of the Nationals, has selected a nine-man pitching squad headed by Wynn and rookie Herb Score of his own Indians, fireballer Bob Turley and southpaw Eddie Ford of the New York Yankees, righthander Dick Donovan and Lefty Billy Pierce of the Chicago White Sox, righthander Frank Sullivan of Boston, Jim Wilson of Baltimore and lefthander Billy Hoeft of Detroit.

Leo Durocher, National League pilot, will go with a streamlined staff of seven that includes righthanders Robin Roberts of Philadelphia, Gene Conley of Milwaukee and Sam Jones of Chicago as well as southpaws Joe Nuxhall of Cincinnati and Harvey Haddix and rookie Luis Arroyo of St. Louis.

First Game For Wynn

It probably will come as a surprise to most baseball followers that Wynn, just about the best pitcher in the American League today, has never pitched in an All-Star game before. In fact, the 35-year-old veteran, who boasts 196 lifetime triumphs, was selected on an All-Star squad only once previously, back in 1947. And that was only as an 11th-hour replacement for Bobby Feller, who was excused because of an injury.

Newcombe has never started before, although, he has appeared in three games — in 1949, 1950 and 1951. He was charged with the loss in '51. There is a possibility that Durocher may hand the opening assignment to Roberts who started four of the last five games. The Nationals won three of those although the Phillies' ace didn't figure in any of the decisions.

Speedball Pitchers

Although the working pitchers won't be named until Monday, it is almost certain the National League stars will see more speed than they've watched in a long time. Turley, Score, Sullivan, Hoeft, Pierce and Wynn currently rank No. 1 through No. 6 among the American League strikeout leaders.

Whether they can stop such fence busters as Duke Snider, Ted Kluszewski, Willie Mays, Eddie Mathews and Ernie Banks, each with more home runs than Mickey Mantle, the top American Leaguer, is anybody's guess. On paper, the senior circuit swatters far outrank their rivals by more than 100 home runs. The American League pitchers, however, have a decided edge in victories, shutouts and strikeouts.

Starting Lineups

MILWAUKEE, July 9 (AP)—Starting squads for the Major League All-Star game in Milwaukee, July 12:

NATIONALS	Pos.	AMERICANS
Kluszewski, Cincinnati	First Base	Vernon, Washington
Schoendienst, St. Louis	Second Base	Fox, Chicago
Mathews, Milwaukee	Third Base	Finigan, Kansas City
Banks, Chicago	Shortstop	Kuenn, Detroit
Ennis, Philadelphia	Left Field	Williams, Boston
Snider, Brooklyn	Center Field	Mantle, New York
Mueller, New York	Right Field	Kaline, Detroit
Burgess, Cincinnati, or Crandall, Milwaukee	Catcher	Berra, New York

Pitchers

Don Newcombe, Brooklyn (RH)	Early Wynn, Cleveland (RH)
Robin Roberts, Philadelphia (RH)	Bob Turley, New York (RH)
Gene Conley, Milwaukee (RH)	Dick Donovan, Chicago (RH)
Sam Jones, Chicago (RH)	Frank Sullivan, Boston (RH)
Harvey Haddix, St. Louis (LH)	Jim Wilson, Baltimore (RH)
Luis Arroyo, St. Louis (LH)	Herb Score, Cleveland (LH)
Joe Nuxhall, Cincinnati (LH)	Whitey Ford, New York (LH)
	Billy Pierce, Chicago (LH)
	Billy Hoeft, Detroit (LH)

NATIONAL LEAGUE ALTERNATES: Infielders Stan Musial, St. Louis; Gene Baker and Ransom Jackson, Chicago; Johnny Logan, Milwaukee, and Gil Hodges, Brooklyn; outfielders Willie Mays, New York; Hank Aaron, Milwaukee, and Frank Thomas, Pittsburgh; catcher, Stan Lopata, Philadelphia.

AMERICAN LEAGUE ALTERNATES: Infielders Bobby Avila and Al Rosen, Cleveland; Chico Carrasquel, Chicago, and Vic Power, Kansas City; outfielders Al Smith and Larry Doby, Cleveland, and Jackie Jensen, Boston; catcher Sherman Lollar, Chicago.

Voting Of Fans Shows How Mighty Have Fallen; Only Four Repeaters In Opening Lineups

With a couple of exceptions, the selections made by six and a half million fans and the two managers, was regarded as reasonably sound. The only grumbling in evidence was Durocher's failure to name center fielder Richie Ashburn of the Phillies, the National League batting leader; and Lopez' selection of six Indians after the fans had failed to pick a single member of the defending American League champions on the starting team.

Many Stars Bypassed

The voting of the fans demonstrated how far the mighty have fallen. Stan Musial was picked for the 12th time and Ted Williams for the 11th but such outstanding stars of former years as Jackie Robinson, Pee Wee Reese, Warren Spahn, Sal Maglie, Alvin Dark, Ralph Kiner, George Kell, Bob Lemon and Curt Simmons were bypassed.

Only four players — Kluszewski, Snider, Mantle and Yogi Berra — will be repeaters from last year's starting lineups, while a total of 23 players in all from the 1954 squads will be missing.

Roy Campanella, Brooklyn catcher, was the top vote getter in the fans' poll, but he had to bow out because of a knee injury. His place on the squad will be taken by Stan Lopata of Philadelphia, but who the starting catcher will be depends on the American League's starting pitcher. If Wynn goes as expected, the National League catcher will be Smoky Burgess of Cincinnati, a left-handed hitter. If a left-hander starts for the American League, however, Durocher will start Del Crandall, a right-handed swinger.

Starters picked for the first time are shortstop Ernie Banks of the Cubs and Detroit right fielder Al Kaline.

Banks — Snider — Mathews — Mueller — Ennis — Schoendienst — Kluszewski — Burgess ★ ★ Mantle — Berra — Kuenn — Fox — Vernon — Kaline — Williams — Finigan

Area Net Stars Compete In J-C Tourney Here Mon.

The cream of Pennsylvania's teenage tennis players are slated to compete in the second annual Jaycee State Tennis Tournament opening Monday at the Lancaster Tennis Club and running through Saturday.

Included among the nearly 100 entries are the Lancaster eligibles Ron Caulwell, Mel Grill and Ron Groff. Caulwell is subbing for the injured Dick Shertzer in the junior division while Grill and Groff will compete in the boys division.

All entries were either champions or runnersup in respective elimination tourneys throughout the state to determine representatives to the state affair here Monday. The winners and runnersup in turn will be eligible to compete in the National Jaycee tourney at San Antonio, Tex.

Heading the list of entries in the Junior division are Sam Hinkle, Hershey; Jack Beaston, Mount Joy; Harry Hoffman and Tony Liberman of Philadelphia and Bill Tobin, Haverford, the State boys Jaycee titleholder in 1954.

The list of boys competitors is headed by Ken Lehman, Hershey; Vern Oberholtzer, Mount Joy; Chick Hodge, Haverford; Cliff Keeven, Wayne; Dave Edwards, Wayne; Mike Drought, Abington; Nowell Lotshaw, Bethlehem, Bob Howe and John Custer.

Eligibles for junior play must be under 18 as of Jan. 1, 1955 while the boys division includes those 15 to 18.

English Tennis Title To Drobny

BIRMINGHAM, England, July 9 (AP)—Jaroslav Drobny won the Midland Counties Lawn Tennis Championships for the third time today, defeating Art Larsen of San Leandro, Calif., in a battle of left-handers 7-5, 4-6, 6-4.

Drobny, a self-exiled Czech with Egyptian citizenship who spends most of his time in England, paced himself well. He started out fast, bombarding Larsen with deadly ground strokes, then eased up. When Larsen put on the pressure and tied the set at 5-all, Drobny stepped up the pace and ran out the set.

Larsen found the range in the second set and his accuracy, coupled with several crucial errors by Drobny, gave him the set. He continued to play well in the early part of the third set, grabbing a 3-1 lead. But Drobny got straightened out again and took five of the next six games for the set and match.

OUTSIDER WINS

SALEM, N.H., July 9 (AP)—June Fete, a 30-1 outsider, pulled away over the final eighth of a mile for a surprise three and a half length victory today in the $7,500 White Mountain Handicap at Rockingham Park. June Fete returned $62.20, $21.60 and $10. Swift Steve paid $4.60 and $3.40 while Country Gossip returned $5.20.

Mountville Is Winner, Takes Lanco Lead

Mountville took a half game lead in its tight battle for first place in the City-County League as it plastered Marietta, 15-2, Saturday to break its deadlock with idle Strasburg.

Gene Kocher breezed to his seventh win on a six-hitter. His mates staked him to three runs in the first frame and before the battle was over, Mountville had lambasted Marietta pitching for 19 safeties.

LEAGUE STANDINGS

Teams	W	L	Pct.	G.B.
Mountville	11	2	.846	
Strasburg	10	2	.833	½
Lititz	8	6	.571	3½
New Holland	7	6	.538	4
Columbia	8	7	.533	4
Elizabethtown	4	9	.308	7
Marietta	3	10	.231	8
Bainbridge	2	11	.154	9

In another game, New Holland moved into the first division by percentage points over idle Columbia on an 18-9 decision over Bainbridge.

New Holland had an 11-1 edge after two innings.

Hal Ebersole and Mac McNaughton homered for Bainbridge. They were the first of the season for both men.

Marietta	ab	h	o	a	Mountville	ab	h	o	a
A. Kugle ss	4	1	2	3	J. Houck 3b	3	2	0	2
Sargent cf	3	0	1	0	C. Houck cf	6	2	4	0
R. McK'n lf	3	0	0	0	H. Houck lf	4	2	0	0
Coller rf	1	0	0	0	Copeland 1b	5	0	7	0
Bowles 1b	2	0	5	1	Fox c	4	2	3	0
Kriner 3b	2	0	1	0	Butz rf	4	3	3	0
Penwell 2b	2	1	4	1	Kreider ss	3	2	2	2
Boose c	3	1	7	0	Charles 2b	5	2	4	1
S'berger p	2	0	1	2	Kocher p	5	2	2	0
Seaman 3b	2	1	0	2	Henry lf	3	1	2	0
Grove p	1	0	0	1	Harz c	1	1	1	0
H. McK'n cf	1	0	1	0					
White rf	2	1	0	0					
Armold 1b	2	1	4	0					
Miller 2b	2	0	0	1					
Totals	32	6	27	11	Totals	43	19	27	5

MOUNTVILLE ...... 310 010 433—15
MARIETTA .... 000 000 200— 2

R—J. Houck 2, H. Houck, Copeland, Fox, Butz 3, Kreider 2, Charles 2, Kocher 2, Harz, White, Armold. E—White, Armold, Kriner, Penwell. 3B—H. Houck, Fox, Butz. 2B—C. Houck, Seaman. BB—Kocher 1, Shellenberger 4, Grove 2. SO—Kocher 3, Shellenberger 4, Grove 2. WP—Kocher (7-2). LP—Shellenberger (1-5).

New Holland	ab	h	o	a	Bainbridge	ab	h	o	a
Evans 2b	5	1	1	2	Mohr lf	3	1	3	0
Kurtz cf	3	0	0	0	Tierney ss p	3	1	2	3
Skiles cf	3	0	1	0	Ebersole 2b	5	2	2	2
Trolier ss	4	1	2	2	Burke cf p	5	1	0	1
Pauly rf p	4	1	6	0	Gingrich 1b	4	1	8	0
Mersky c	5	3	21	0	Campbell 3b	4	0	0	2
Hilliard lf	2	1	0	0	McN'ghton c	4	2	8	0
Witman lf	3	1	0	0	Dudley rf	4	1	0	0
F'houser 3b	4	0	0	0	Norris p cf	2	0	1	0
E'miller 1b	2	1	3	0	H'bery cf p	2	1	0	0
Shaub 1b	0	0	2	0					
Matroni p	3	1	0	0					
Baxter 3b	1	0	0	1					
Totals	39	10	27	5	Totals	36	10	24	8

BAINBRIDGE ...... 010 001 160— 9
NEW HOLLAND ... 740 001 60x—18

R—Tierney, Ebersole, Gingrich, Campbell, McNaughton 3, Dudley, Hockenberry, Evans 2, Skiles, Trolier 3, Pauly 3, Mersky 3 Hilliard, Witman, Frankhouser, Eidemiller, Matroni 2. E—Tierney, Gingrich, Campbell, Dudley 2, Evans. HR—Ebersole, McNaughton. 2B—Pauly. BB—Norris 4, Burke 3, Tierney 2, Hockenberry 1, Matroni 4, Frankhouser 5. SO—Burke 5, Pauly 1, Hockenberry 3, Matroni 10. WP—Matroni (2-0). LP—Norris (0-1). U—Witmer & Obetz.

Wins 8th Game

Eshelman Paces Petersburg Over Christiana 4-0

Don Eshleman picked up his eighth win against one loss on a five-hit, 4-0 victory for East Petersburg over Christiana Saturday that gave the Northern Division leading Petersburg nine a 1½ game lead over idle Mountville.

LEAGUE STANDINGS
(Northern Division)

Teams	W	L	Pct.	G.B.
E. Petersburg	15	5	.750	
Mountville	15	8	.652	1½
Artisans	13	7	.650	2
Ephrata	11	8	.579	3½
Manheim	12	9	.571	3½
Mount Joy	6	16	.273	10

(Southern Division)

Teams	W	L	Pct.	G.B.
Holtwood	13	7	.650	...
Quarryville	14	8	.636	...
Christiana	13	9	.591	1
Paradise	8	12	.400	5
Conestoga	3	17	.150	10
Gap	2	19	.095	11½

TODAY'S GAMES
Conestoga at Ephrata
Gap at Holtwood
Christiana at Manheim
Quarryville at Mountville
Paradise at East Petersburg

In the Southern Division, the first two teams, Holtwood and Quarryville in addition to Christiana, bowed to clubs from the northern sector of the loop.

Holtwood dropped a narrow 8-7 verdict to cellar dwelling Gap. Dick Shertz, working in relief of starter Hen Stauffer, blanked the Southern Division leaders from the fourth frame on.

Ephrata scored five in the fifth to back Ken Sweigart's stingy five hit twirling to defeat Quarryville, 5-2. His mates collected eight bingles off the offerings of Mel Rineer.

Bruce Wohnsiedler fanned 15 Artisan batters but it wasn't enough to prevent an 11-10 loss for Paradise in ten innings.

Al Eckert opened the tenth with a walk, the seventh off the left handed slants of Wohnsiedler, and romped the whole way home on a steal of second base and two errors.

Another Eckert, John, drove home three runs for East Petersburg in their shutout over Christiana. Singles by Risser and Ben Clinger followed by an error and Eckert's single accounted for three runs in the third.

George McCue, recently discharged from the service, rammed a triple in the sixth and scored on Eckert's double for the other Petersburg tally.

In the fifth game of the day, Mount Joy outscored Conestoga, 16-8.

Quarryville	ab	h	o	a	Ephrata	ab	h	o	a
Sample ss	4	0	0	7	Weachter 1b	3	0	11	0
F. Young 3b	3	0	1	1	H. W'ver 2b	4	2	4	3
D. Work cf c	4	1	1	0	P'becker rf	4	1	0	0
G. Y'ng c cf	4	1	3	0	Reich 3b	4	0	1	0
Eberly rf	4	1	2	0	Dull ss	4	1	5	5
McC'dell lf	3	0	2	0	Wolf cf	4	1	1	0
Deb'dine 1b	2	1	13	0	W'enroth lf	4	1	0	0
Myers 2b	3	0	2	4	Kurtz c	2	1	5	0
Rineer p	3	1	0	1	Sweigart p	3	1	0	3
Totals	30	5	24	13	Totals	32	8	27	11

QUARRYVILLE .... 011 000 000—2
EPHRATA .... 000 050 00x—5

R—G. Young, Rineer, Weachter, Dull, Wingenroth, Kurtz, Sweigart. E—Sample 2, F. Young, Myers. 2B—Work. BB—Rineer 2, Sweigart 2. SO—Sweigart 4. WP—Sweigart (6-4). LP—Rineer (1-3). U—Dennenberg & Erb.

Christiana	ab	h	o	a	East Petersburg	ab	h	o	a
Warden 3b	4	0	2	2	Lawder 2b	5	1	3	1
E. Steele ss	4	0	4	1	Risser 1b	5	2	7	0
Dyer lf	3	0	4	1	Clinger rf	4	1	0	0
Thomson cf	3	0	2	0	Germer 3b	4	1	3	1
H'berger rf	4	2	4	0	McCue cf	4	1	2	1
Barnett 1b	3	0	7	0	Eckert lf	4	2	1	0
Fieles c	3	1	3	2	C. Risser c	4	2	9	0
El. Steele 2b	3	1	0	3	Emich ss	4	0	1	6
Ladley p	3	1	1	0	Eshleman p	4	0	1	2
Totals	31	5	27	9	Totals	38	10	27	11

E. PETERSBURG ... 003 001 000—4
CHRISTIANA .... 000 000 000—0

R—Risser, Clinger, McCue 2. E—Lawder, Barnett, Fieles, El. Steele. 3B—McCue. 2B—Eckert. BB—Eshleman 1. SO—Eshleman 9, Ladley 4. WP—Eshleman (8-1). LP—Ladley (1-4).

Mount Joy	ab	h	o	a	Conestoga	ab	h	o	a
Derr 2b	4	1	7	1	Wittiger 3b	2	0	0	0
Krause lf	4	3	1	0	Kleinhaus 3b	1	0	0	0
Taylor ss	4	2	5	0	K'ffman lf	4	3	1	0
Wagner cf	5	3	1	0	Rankin rf	2	1	1	0
Rapp cf	0	0	0	0	D. B'an p rf	4	1	1	1
S'man 3b 1b	5	3	7	0	Ferrar ss	3	0	1	3
Heinaman c	5	1	8	2	Garvin ss	1	0	1	0
Geib 1b	0	0	1	0	Eckert cf	5	1	2	0
Weber 3b	3	2	1	1	Kneisley cf	0	0	1	0
Yordy rf	4	2	1	0	Dietrich 1b	5	1	5	0
Myers p	3	1	0	2	J. Warfel p	2	1	0	1
Keener p	2	1	0	1	C. Warfel p	3	0	0	0
					Erisman c	0	0	11	0
					Appel rf	1	0	0	0
Totals	39	19	27	7	Totals	33	8	24	5

CONESTOGA .... 211 031 000— 8
MOUNT JOY ...... 100 822 03x—16

R—Wittiger, Kauffman, D. Bachman 2, J. Warfel 3, C. Warfel, Derr, Krause 3, Taylor 2, Wagner 2, Shuman 2, Heinaman, Weber 2, Yordy 2, Myers. 3B—Wagner. 2B—Wagner, Yordy, Taylor, Shuman. BB—Myers 9, Keener 3. SO—Myers 5, Keener 2. WP—Myers (6-4). LP—J. Warfel (1-7). U—Ellwein & Bachman.

Gap	ab	h	o	a	Holtwood	ab	h	o	a
Patterson rf	5	2	0	0	Bortzfield rf	4	3	0	0
Bensinger 2b	3	1	4	2	J. H'etter 3b	4	2	1	3
Hilton lf	5	2	0	1	E'bach ss p	4	1	1	2
L. Coates cf	5	0	1	0	Huber lf	5	2	1	0
Norris ss	5	1	1	0	Eager cf	5	2	1	0
C. Coates c	4	0	6	1	L. H'etter c	3	1	8	1
Stauffer p	2	1	0	3	S'man p 2b	3	0	1	2
Shertz p	2	0	0	3	Dunkle 1b	3	1	9	0
Z'erman 1b	2	1	13	0	Trimble rf	3	1	2	6
Eavenson 3b	3	3	2	5	Binkley ss	1	0	0	0
Totals	36	11	27	15	Totals	35	13	24	14

HOLTWOOD .... 013 300 000—7
GAP .... 012 104 00x—8

R—Bortzfield, J. Hostetter 2, Eager, L. Hostetter, Shuman, Dunkel, Patterson, Bensinger 2, Norris, Stauffer, Zimmerman Eavenson 2. E—J. Hostetter 2, Eshbach 3, L. Hostetter, Bensinger 2, Zimmerman. 3B—Eavenson. BB—Shuman 3, Eshbach 1, Stauffer 5, Shertz 1. SO—Shuman 8, Stauffer 1, Shertz 4. WP—Shertz (1-1). LP—Shuman (5-3). U—Weitkamp & Kissinger.

Artisans	ab	h	o	a	Paradise	ab	h	o	a
Eckert cf	2	2	1	0	L'parter 3b	5	0	1	1
Fickes rf	4	1	0	0	Tompkins 2b	4	1	1	2
Souders ss	3	0	5	3	Bonawitz lf	5	2	0	0
Zangari 1b p	5	0	7	0	Born 1b	4	2	6	0
B'kman 2b	1	1	0	3	Sweigart cf	5	2	1	0
Hemperly c	4	2	13	1	Mellinger c	2	0	7	0
Harrison 3b	5	1	3	2	Irwin ss	4	0	0	2
Etter lf	1	0	0	0	Kliewer rf	4	0	1	0
Fry p	2	0	0	1	W'siedler p	4	1	1	2
Darrah ss	4	2	1	1	Wiker c	2	1	9	2
Harman lf	3	2	2	0					
Hyland 2b	1	0	2	0					
Glick 1b	2	0	1	0					
Totals	37	11	30	11	Totals	39	9x	27	9

x—None out when winning run scored.

PARADISE .... 100 040 104 0—10
ARTISANS .... 101 141 011 1—11

R—Lamparter, Tompkins 3, Bonawitz 2, Born, Sweigart 2, Wohnsiedler, Eckert 5, Fickes, Hemperly, Darrah 2, Harman 2. E—Lamparter 2, Tompkins 2 Born Kliewer, Sweigart 2, Wiker, Souders 2, Zangari 2. HR—Eckert, Harmon, Darrah. 3B—Tompkins. 2B—Bonawitz, Sweigart, Harrison, Brinkman, Born. BB—Frey 1, Zangari 4, Wohnsiedler 7. SO—Fry 3, Zangari 8, Wohnsiedler 15. WP—Zangari (6-2). LP—Wohnsiedler (2-6). U—Sneath & Wallick.

Farkas-Peek In Semi's At Schuylkill

ORWIGSBURG, Pa., July 9 (AP)—Four two-man teams of golfers emerged unscathed today as match play opened in the 7th annual Schuylkill Country Club's Best Ball of Partners Golf Tournament.

They are Al Farkas and Harold Peek of Media Heights; Bob Batdorf of Berkshire and Jim Rutter of Green Hill; Walter Naykut and Charles Falco of Wildwood, N.J.; and Oliver Lenhardt and Lin Passel of Plymouth.

They are the only ones left out of 16 teams teeing off in the championship flight today over the 7,100-yard, par 72 Schuylkill course.

Farkas and Peek downed the tourney medalists, Ed Gonsky of Wyoming Valley and Art Barny of Fox Hill 3 and 2 in the afternoon round.

Batdorf and Rutter defeated Ronnie Leo, Colonial, and John Boyanowski, Wyoming Valley, 4 and 3; Naykut and Falco defeated Andy Stofko and Ted Betley of Colonial 2 up; and Lenhardt and Passel defeated John Guenther, Schuylkill, and George Smith, Reading, 1 up.

Players tee off for the semi-finals and finals tomorrow.

In the morning round:

Gonsky and Barni defeated Roy Lovejoy and Albert Fingo, Plymouth, 4 and 3.

Farkes and Peek defeated Bob Taylor and Bill Allen, Colonial Heights, 2 and 1.

Leo and Boyanowski defeated Cy Powers and Joe Spisak, Lebanon, 1 up on the 23rd hole.

Batdorf and Rutter defeated Glenn Horst and Eugene Simmons, Media Heights, 3 and 2.

Naykut and Falko defeated Marvin Serber, Spring Haven, and Albert McQuiston, Chester Valley, 6 and 5.

Stofko and Betley defeated Art Garrison and John Horetsky, Hershey Park, 6 and 5.

Lenhardt and Passel defeated Frank Mihalek, Baltimore, and Paul Sieber, Schuylkill, 2 and 1.

Guenther and Smith defeated Frank Angelo and Austin McCarty, Bethlehem Steel, 3 and 2.

Penn Shell 1st In Hamburg Race

HAMBURG, Germany, July 9 (AP)—The University of Pennsylvania eight-oar rowing crew defeated one English and two German teams in the first day of Hamburg's big International Regatta.

The Penn-crew, which won at Henley, England, last week, crossed the finish line after 2,000 meters of stylish rowing in 6:54 minutes.

One and a half lengths behind, the Hansa boat of Hamburg came in second in 6:59.9 minutes, barely ahead of the Germania-Hamburger in 7:00. Four lengths behind the winning Americans were the British Royal Air Force crewmen in 7:17 minutes.

The Hansa crew took the lead at the start and held it up to 1,400 meters when Penn steadily pulled ahead and left the exhausted Germans behind without increasing their strokes.

City, County Legion Stars Play Tuesday

Picked stars from the six teams in the City Legion League and the 12 teams in the County Legion League will tangle Tuesday at Stumpf Field in a repeat performance of their recent all-star game won by the City nine. Game time is 5 p.m.

The players are asked to be at the ball park at 2:30 p.m. The game is a preliminary to the Piedmont League tilt between the Lancaster Roses and the Lynchburg Cardinals.

Major league scouts will be on hand to select players to participate in the annual Legion East-West game later in the season.

WEATHER
(U. S. Weather Bureau Forecast For Lancaster, Cumberland, Lebanon, York, Adams And Franklin Counties):
Mostly Cloudy And Warm, With Occasional Thunder Showers Today And Tonight. Tomorrow Partly Cloudy And A Little Cooler, With The Risk Of A Few Showers. High Today 85-90.

Intelligencer Journal.

The Leading Newspaper in the Garden Spot of America. Home Owned for Home Folks Since 1794

THE INTELL INDEX

162nd Year.—No. 26. Official United States Census Figures Lancaster Metropolitan Area Population 234,717 LANCASTER, PA., SATURDAY MORNING, JULY 16, 1955. CITY EIGHTEEN PAGES. 30c PER WEEK—5c Per Copy

HOPEFUL PRESIDENT OFF TO GENEVA

Leader Hails Schick Dedication As A "Great Day For Lancaster"

While guests and employes of Schick, Inc., stand at attention, the flag is raised in front of the new plant during dedication ceremonies yesterday. Two plant guards, Lloyd Rapp, Bainbridge, and Paul Whiteside, Witmer, were in charge of the flag-raising. The color guard was made up of Sgt. Charles Sonberger, representing the Army; Orbon Brown, CPO, Navy; Sgt. Herman C. Lohman, Marines; and Sgt. Edward J. McGurren, Air Force. (Intell Photo)

Community Joins In Exercises At New $2,400,000 Industrial Plant

With the raising of the American flag on the flagpole in front of the building at 12:50 p. m. yesterday, the new $2,400,000 Schick, Inc., plant at Greenfield Road and the Route 230 By-Pass was officially dedicated.

The raising of the flag by two company plant guards accompanied by a color guard to the Star Spangled Banner was one of several highlights in ceremonies yesterday officially dedicating the new plant. The affair was held outdoors in front of the building.

Principal speaker at yesterday's affair, attended by some 1,000 guests and company employes, was Gov. George M. Leader who hailed the event as "a great day for Lancaster, and for Pennsylvania."

Others who spoke at the ceremonies were Mayor Kendig C. Bare, Joseph B. Elliott, Schick president; Kenneth C. Gifford, Schick board chairman, and Mrs. Gifford.

Guests at the dedication included many of the leaders in industry, finance, business and government from Lancaster city and county. Also on hand were many prominent out-of-state guests.

Gov. Leader said the ceremonies were particularly meaningful to him since he has made economic development, and particularly industrial development, a major objective of his administration program. "It is my purpose to marshall all of the pertinent services and facilities of our state government, and bring them helpfully to bear on the task of expanding and stabilizing our industrial economy—to create new jobs, new business opportunities, new payrolls and new profits."

He said the story of Schick's

Turn To Page 9 For More Of SCHICK

Gov. George M. Leader speaks during dedication of the new Schick, Inc., plant on the Route 230 By-Pass yesterday. Others on platform are, left to right, Kenneth C. Gifford, chairman of the Schick board; Mrs. Gifford; Mayor Kendig C. Bare; and Joseph B. Elliott, president of the company. (Intell Photo)

HEAT WAVE BEGINS AGAIN IN COUNTY

Cooler Weather Forecast Tomorrow Seen Only Brief Respite

In what appears to be the makings of Lancaster County's second heat wave of the year, the temperature hit 90 yesterday.

It is expected to reach 92 again today, then cool off a bit for a Sunday breather.

Early next week, though, the U.S. Weather Bureau says, the heat will be on again.

An average humidity of 64 per cent aided in making yesterday sultry, resembling the all-too-recent 10-day heat spree.

Last night's late weather forecast called for a high between 88 and 92 for today. With a record of ignoring the weatherman's limitations and going far beyond them, the mercury may rise to even greater heights today.

SHOWERS FORECAST

Today is expected to be cloudy and occasional showers and thundershowers are predicted as usual.

Tonight, however, the weatherman says, will be clear and cooler.

This, he says, will last only until the first of next week. Then the forecaster has it, the temperature will start climbing once more.

Nationally, it was rainfall, not heat, that made news yesterday.

SHOWERS IN MIDWEST

Showers and thundershowers fell across a broad band of the eastern midcontinent from the Great Lakes to the Gulf of Mexico. Fort Wayne, Ind., reported 3.47 inches of rain in 24 hours.

Afternoon temperatures were mostly in the 80's from the southern Great Lakes southward. They were in the 90's and higher over the southern Palms and the interior valleys of Southern California.

Blythe, Calif., recorded a high of 107 and Yuma, Ariz., sweltered in 106 degree heat.

STATE POLICE SAY:

Will your vacation be a Peaceful Rest or a Rest in Peace. STAY ALIVE IN '55.

Sees Real Success If Kremlin's Words Not Idle Chatter

Heads For Potentially Historic Big 4 Meeting After Telling TV Audience Session Can Be Greatest Step Toward Peace

WASHINGTON, July 15 (AP)—President Eisenhower took off for the Big Four conference tonight, declaring there will be "no trouble" with the men in the Kremlin if they really mean their words of "conciliation and toleration and understanding."

The chief executive made the qualified forecast in a dramatic TV-radio address shortly before his plane, Columbine III, left the ground and headed eastward through the night for Eisenhower's potentially fateful meeting with the leaders of Russia, Britain and France.

HISTORY IN MAKING

In the broadcast he declared that if a 10-year-old spirit of mutual distrust can be lifted at Geneva, then "we will have taken the greatest step toward peace, toward future prosperity and tranquillity that has ever been taken in all the history of mankind."

The President, with his wife and son accompanying him, took off from Military Air Transport Service airport at 9:18 p.m. EDT.

All along the route from the White House to the airport, people leaned from automobiles and waved. At the White House gate a knot of bystanders had cheered as Eisenhower's limousine shot by—the ceiling dome light flicked on by the President, adding luster to his grin.

BECOMES JOVIAL

Eisenhower was in a jovial mood, contrasting with his grave manner in the broadcast. He shook hands heartily with the diplomats and with Vice President Nixon and Mrs. Nixon. He waved to the crowd. Mrs. Eisenhower beamed as did Maj. John Eisenhower.

The diplomats included the Soviet charge D'affaires, Sergei R. Striganov. His appearance came as a general surprise.

In his preflight broadcast Eisenhower promised he and Secretary of State Dulles would be firm in principle yet conciliatory in attitude at Geneva.

TOLERANT BEFORE

Eisenhower said Soviet Premier Bulganin "talked tolerance and understanding" at Moscow today. If that spirit really animates the Soviets at Geneva, he said, "there'll be no trouble between the Russian delegation and this country."

And, finally, the President asked all Americans to pray in their churches next Sabbath for success of the "At-the-summit" parley in relieving the world of that "terrible scourge"—war.

Eisenhower spoke from the White House broadcast room at 8:15 p.m. EDT, an hour and a quarter before he, his wife and his son were to enplane for Geneva.

Turn To Page 9 For More Of EISENHOWER

BULGANIN SAYS SOVIET GOING TO GENEVA FOR PEACE

Declares Others Preparing For War While Russia Seeks Ease In Tension

MOSCOW, July 15 (AP)—Soviet Premier Bulganin said today the Soviet Union is going to Geneva seeking peace—but it has noted war preparations by other states. He observed that the U.S.S.R. has "a very good army with all the necessary equipment" to safeguard its security.

Bulganin pledged the Soviet delegation to the summit talks to great efforts to "attain the lofty aims of the conference," and expressed hope the other powers would exert equal efforts. The Soviet aim, he said, will be to find a common ground for easing tension and strengthening confidence among states.

NOTES SUGGESTION

He read a statement, announced in advance as a general declaration on the summit conference opening Monday. He apparently took note of the recent suggestion

Turn To Page 9 For More Of BULGANIN

VOTERS UNABLE TO CHANGE POLITICS BEFORE ELECTION

The Lancaster County Registration Commission reminded residents yesterday that they cannot change their political affiliation until after the municipal election in November.

The reminder was issued said Wesley Shoenberger, clerk in charge of the office, because a number of voters have been appearing at the office in the courthouse to change politics.

The state election code prohibits a voter from switching parties between a primary and a November election.

Four persons enrolled to vote yesterday, two Democrats and two Republicans. Five others filed changes of address.

City Father Of 10 Children Wins $10,000 Jingle Contest

A sixty-one year old Lancaster man, father of 10 children, has won $10,000 first prize in a nation-wide jingle contest.

He is Frank Schaller, an engraver employed by Apple and Weber, jewelers.

Schaller, who lives at 535 Poplar St., was informed that he had won the $10,000 prize in the contest on Thursday.

He said last night he has no immediate plans for spending the money but pointed out "there's a lot you can do with $10,000."

Schaller was told about a month ago that he was "a potential winner" in the contest. A representative of General Electric, sponsor of the contest, interviewed him at that time.

Then on Thursday a telegram arrived, asking Schaller to telephone the representative in Philadelphia. He did, and was informed that he is first-place winner.

Schaller expects a representative to arrive next week — with the money.

FIRST WINNING ENTRY

Schaller, who is a notary public, said he has entered lots of contests but "this is the first time I have ever won anything."

He and his wife will celebrate

Turn To Page 9 For More Of PRIZE WINNER

"We Lead All The Rest"
FARM CORNER
By WILLIAM R. SCHULTZ

SPABC Reports 11% Increase In Bull Services

Artificial breeding of dairy animals continued its upward trend in southeastern Pennsylvania during the first half of this year with an 11 per cent increase in services by bulls at the Southeastern Pennsylvania Artificial Breeding Cooperative.

The report was given last evening by Earl Groff, president of the co-op, as more than 300 dairy farmers attended a twilight meet-

Turn To Page 9 For More Of FARM CORNER

Weather Calendar

COMPARATIVE TEMPERATURES

Station	High	Low
Water Works	90	66
Ephrata	92	53
Last Year (Ephrata)	94	63
Official High for Year July 5		97
Official Low for Year Feb. 3		-5
Character of Day		Clear

WINDS
Direction SSW Avg. Velocity 9 mph

HUMIDITY
8 a.m. 83% 11 a.m. 63% 2 p.m. 47%
5 p.m. 64% 8 p.m. 63%
Average Humidity 64%

SUN
Rises 5:47 a.m. Sets 8:32 p.m.

MOON
Rises 2:22 a.m. New Moon, July 19

STARS
Morning—Venus
Evening—Mars, Jupiter, Saturn

NEARBY FORECASTS
(U.S. Weather Bureau)
Southeastern Pennsylvania and South-

Turn To Page 9 For More Of WEATHER

Kenneth C. Gifford, chairman of the board of Schick, Inc., presents a silver tray in commemoration of the firm's 25th anniversary, to his wife, during dedication of the new Schick building yesterday. Mrs. Gifford was the wife of the late Col. Jacob Schick, who founded the company. Inscription on the plate paid tribute to her for "her deep devotion, her undying faith and her superb counsel without which this silver jubilee could not have been achieved." (Intell Photo)

—Sports Roundup—

Piedmont Plans For '56; Roses Beat Macs, 6-3

Directors of the Piedmont League expressed optimism over the circuit's future following a meeting at Hagerstown, Md., yesterday. Plans were made to finish the season with seven teams and also to operating in 1956 with eight clubs.

Lancaster's Roses got back on the winning track last night, thanks to a splendid relief job by Jerry LaBanz, as they topped Portsmouth, 6-3, at the Virginia city.

Veteran Jim Turnesa turned in a record 63 round to take the lead in the $35,000 Milwaukee Open yesterday while Bev Hanson assumed a first round lead in the Women's PGA tourney.

Turn to pages 11, 12 and 13 for details of these and other stories.

BIG LEAGUE RESULTS

NATIONAL LEAGUE
Brooklyn 12, St. Louis 3
New York 5, Chicago 3
Philadelphia 1, Milwaukee 0
Cincinnati 9, Pittsburgh 1

AMERICAN LEAGUE
New York 4, Cleveland 3
Chicago 5, Washington 4
Baltimore 8, Kansas City 5
Boston at Detroit, ppd., rain

President Ready For Journey To Big Four Parley

WASHINGTON, July 15—President and Mrs. Dwight Eisenhower, and their son, Army Major John Eisenhower, smile as they pose tonight in front of their plane seconds before they left for the Big Four conference at Geneva. The Eisenhowers left at 9:18 p. m., EDT, shortly after the President had made a dramatic plea by radio and television in a White House broadcast asking the prayers of the American people for success of the parley to end the "terrible scourge" of war. Major Eisenhower will act as an aide to the President at the conference. (AP Wirephoto)

Litiz Welcomes Warner-Lambert At Groundbreaking, Town Dinner

Groundbreaking ceremonies for the new $3,400,000 plant of the Lambert Pharmacal Co., in Lititz, and a dinner given by borough citizens for officials of the Warner-Lambert Pharmaceutical Co., were held yesterday. At left, Elmer H. Bobst, chairman of the board of Warner-Lambert, turns the first shovelful of earth during the groundbreaking in a pasture adjacent to Lincoln Avenue. Watching are, left to right, Paul F. Diehm, president of the Lititz Chamber of Commerce; Benjamin Forrest, Lititz burgess; Alfred E. Driscoll, former New Jersey governor, now president of Warner-Lambert, and Edward T. T. Williams, chairman of the executive committee of Warner-Lambert. Second picture shows a general view of the Lititz High School gymnasium during the "Welcome to Warner-Lambert" dinner given by the people of Lititz. Participants in the welcome dinner in the third picture are, left to right, Dr. Mahlon H. Yoder, who introduced Bobst; Driscoll; Bobst; Diehm; Dr. Byron K. Horne, toastmaster; Williams; Joseph C. Feagley, president of the Pennsylvania Chamber of Commerce, who brought greetings, and the Rev. Paul A. Miller, president of the Lititz Ministerial Assn., who gave the invocation. At far right, Bobst is presented with a plaque by the Pennsylvania Division of the American Cancer Society for his work in the fight against cancer. The presentation was made during the dinner by James M. Brittain, right, president of the state division of the ACS, and Dr. Roland A. Loeb, center, a director of the state division. (Intell Photos)

Intelligencer Journal.

The Leading Newspaper in the Garden Spot of America. Home Owned for Home Folks Since 1794

162nd Year.—No. 43. Official United States Census Figures Lancaster Metropolitan Area Population 234,717 LANCASTER, PA., FRIDAY MORNING, AUGUST 5, 1955. CITY THIRTY-SIX PAGES 30c PER WEEK—5c Per Copy

WEATHER

(U. S. Weather Bureau Forecast For Lancaster, Cumberland, Lebanon, York, Adams And Franklin Counties):

Partly Cloudy, Hot And Humid Today With Scattered Thundershowers, High 94-98. Tomorrow Considerable Cloudiness And Not Quite As Hot With Scattered Thundershowers.

GOP BEATS STATE INCOME TAX

ELMER BOBST 'COMES HOME' WITH BIG GIFT

Native Son Turns Sod For $3,400,000 Toiletries, Cosmetics Plant

An industrial tycoon yesterday returned to Lititz—a town which he had left penniless at the turn of the century—with a wonderful gift.

Elmer H. Bobst, chairman of the board of Warner-Lambert Pharmaceutical Co., came back to his home town to "repay, in a sense, for everything the town gave me as a child."

The gift was a $3,400,000 plant to be built for the Lambert Pharmical Co., a subsidiary of Warner-Lambert, adjacent to Lincoln Ave. at Lititz.

MORE THAN PAID

To many Lititz citizens and in the thinking of many county residents, Bobst had already more than "paid" his self-set obligation. His philanthropies to local institutions including Franklin and Marshall College and Lititz High School, are well known.

Bobst turned over the first shovelful of sod yesterday afternoon in groundbreaking ceremonies in a pasture where he had played baseball as a youth. More than 300 persons attended the ceremonies.

Principal speakers, in addition to Bobst, included Alfred E. Driscoll, former governor of New Jersey, now president of the Warner-Lambert Co.; Paul F. Diehm, president of the Lititz Chamber of Commerce, and Benjamin Forest burgess of Lititz.

The groundbreaking ceremonies were followed at 6:30 p. m. with a "Welcome to Warner-Lambert"

Turn To Page 6 For More Of PLANT

"We Lead All The Rest"

FARM CORNER

By WILLIAM R. SCHULTZ

EARLY PICKING LOWERING PRICES FOR GREEN WRAPS

Fresh Market Tomatoes Diverted to New Outlet As Seasons Overlap

The green wrap tomato market in Lancaster County has been driven down by a flood of fruit that in normal years would be allowed to ripen in the fields to be sold on the fresh market.

The situation is a source of concern to many persons in the field, who feel that what began as a new outlet for early tomatoes is beginning to have a serious effect on the entire tomato market.

Crux of the situation is the unprecedented siege of hot, dry weather that has plagued growers through the summer.

Where in a normal season the

Turn To Page 32 For More Of FARM CORNER

Weather Calendar

COMPARATIVE TEMPERATURES

Station	High	Low
Water Works	93	66
Ephrata	92	67
Last Year (Ephrata	86	58
Official High for Year, Aug. 2		103
Official Low for Year, Feb. 3		—5
Character of Day		Partly Cloudy

WINDS

Direction SW — Avg. Velocity 6 mph

HUMIDITY

8 a. m. 72% — 11 a. m. 59%

2 p. m. 54% — 5 p. m. 52% — 8 p. m. 66%

Average Humidity 61%

SUN

Rises 6:05 a. m. — Sets 8:14 p. m.

MOON

Rises: 8:56 p.m. — Last Quarter, Aug. 10.

STARS

Morning—Venus, Jupiter

Evening—Mars, Saturn

NEARBY FORECASTS

(U. S. Weather Bureau)

Southeastern Pennsylvania and Southern New Jersey: Partly cloudy, hot and humid today with widely scattered afternoon or evening thunderstorms. High 92-98 except along the immediate New Jersey coast. Tomorrow partly cloudy and a little cooler with scattered thunderstorms.

Central and Northeastern Pennsylvania: Partly cloudy today, hot and humid with a few widely scattered afternoon and evening thundershowers. High in the upper 80s in the central mountains to the upper 90s in the southeast. Tomorrow considerable cloudiness and not quite as hot with scattered thundershowers.

Lower Potomac and Chesapeake Bay: Winds mostly southwest 12-18 miles per hour. Mostly fair today except for chance of isolated evening thundershowers. Visibility mostly good.

Maryland and Delaware: Partly cloudy, hot and humid with scattered evening thundershowers today, high 93-98 except 88-93 along the coast. Fair tonight, little change in temperature. Tomorrow partly cloudy, continued warm with scattered thundershowers.

Teasing Showers Fail At Chasing Heat Or Drought

'Drizzle To Downpour' Rains Hit Scattered Sections Of County; More Rain, 100-Degree Temperature Forecast For Today

Rain, ranging from drizzle to downpour, came to Lancaster County last night, but it didn't wash away the heat wave which is expected to shoot the temperature to 100 degrees today.

More rain may be in store. The weatherman called for widely scattered showers and thundershowers again this afternoon and tonight.

After reaching a maximum of 92 yesterday, the Harrisburg weather bureau said it may go as high as 100 today. The year's high mark is 103.

No relief from the heat is in sight for the next few days, at least, the Harrisburg weatherman said last night.

Last night's storm, coming in a hit-or-miss fashion, cooled things off for a while.

The storm first struck about 7:30 p.m. at New Holland and for about half an hour treated the community to a heavy downpour of rain. Residents also reported a large amount of thunder and lightning.

Hensel, in the southern part of the county, experienced a heavy electrical storm which began about 9:40 p.m. and lasted for about 30 minutes. It also brought a gentle rain, the first

Turn To Page 6 For More Of WEATHER

Sports Roundup

American Loop Pennant Chase Really Tight

It's a crazy, mixed-up pennant chase in the American league today after crucial three game series ended with Cleveland and Boston defeating New York and Chicago, two games to one.

Chicago's loss yesterday left them barely in the lead as Cleveland climbed to within two percentage points with a 6-3 triumph over New York.

That Pennsylvania boxing ban, which was scheduled to be lifted Monday, Aug. 9, has been extended indefinitely by Governor Leader who claims the ban will stay until the new boxing code is approved for the state.

Meanwhile, Harold Johnson, who was implicated in the fight which brought about the 90-day ban, is appealing his six month suspension.

The Roses face Newport News tonight in the first of a three game series and the local club has been strengthened offensively and defensively by the return of Don Plarski, who was up there in the big time for a short period with the Kansas City Athletics.

These and other stories can be found today on Sports Pages 28, 29 and 30.

BIG LEAGUE RESULTS

AMERICAN LEAGUE

Cleveland 6, New York 3
Boston 7, Chicago 3
Baltimore 8, Kansas City 1
Washington 9, Detroit 6

NATIONAL LEAGUE

Brooklyn 11, Milwaukee 10
Chicago 11, Pittsburgh 10
Cincinnati 4, Philadelphia 3
St. Louis 3, New York 0

WARNING ISSUED BY MAYOR BARE ON WATER USE

Conservation Breaches Will Be Met With Stern Steps; Filtration Limit Cited

Mayor Kendig C. Bare, who earlier yesterday had asked the cooperation of all city water consumers in a number of conservation measures, last night warned that stern steps may be taken if cooperation is not forthcoming.

The city has asked that consumers immediately take steps to limit the use of water.

These steps include:

Suspension of car washing, limiting the sprinkling of lawns to the weekends and shutting down the city's playground wading pools except for weekends.

The car wash suspension, the mayor said, includes all commercial car washing operations. Most garage operators, it was indicated last night, have agreed to the move.

FILTRATION WOES

Yesterday's action, announced following a conference of city officials, was not taken because of a shortage of raw water in the Conestoga Creek. The move, the mayor explained, was made because demand on water during the current heat wave is exceeding the rated capacity of the city's filtration system.

These are the specific steps the city has taken and on which cooperation is being asked:

1. Immediate suspension of all

Turn To Page 32 For More Of CITY WATER

30 KILLED IN PLANE CRASH IN MISSOURI

American Airlines Craft Falls, One Wing Burned Off By Fire

FT. LEONARD WOOD, Mo., Aug. 4 (AP)—A flaming American Airlines plane, one wing sheared off by fire and seconds away from an Army airfield, crashed on this military reservation today, killing all 30 persons aboard.

Rescue workers, hampered for hours by intense heat from the wreckage and burning underbrush. finally recovered all the bodies.

Eyewitnesses at the reservation's housing area, where some 5,000 persons live, told how the stricken plane roared overhead, 200 to 500 feet above the ground.

"At first we thought the pilot would make it," Beverly Streeter, a Wac private from Asbury Park, N. J., said.

"Then we heard muffled explosions. Parts seemed to be dropping from the plane. We lost sight of it after that."

The bodies were taken to a temporary morgue, set up in an empty World War II barracks. Army ambulances shuttled back and forth over a freshly bulldozed path cut through the tangled wood. Less than one-third of the bodies could be readily identified; the rest were charred beyond immediate recognition.

The body of the plane struck in a ravine, shearing off a tree top.

Civil Aeronautics Authority investigators and American Airlines officials began an immediate investigation into the cause.

The 27 passengers and three crewmen included eight women,

Turn To Page 6 For More Of PLANE

BOY, 8, OF GAP R1, A POLIO SUSPECT

An eight-year-old Gap R1 boy was admitted to Lancaster General Hospital yesterday afternoon as a suspected polio case.

Hospital authorities last night said diagnosis of the case has not been completed.

The last previous polio case in Lancaster County was admitted to the hospital on July 25. Mary E. Fetter, eleven, daughter of Mrs. Helen Fetter, 432 S. Main St., Manheim, was diagnosed as suffering from a mild case of non-paralytic polio a week ago yesterday.

New Map Of Lancaster, Suburbs Shows Post-War Growth Of Area

A new map of the City of Lancaster and its environs up to a three-mile limit has been issued by the Lancaster New Era, the *Intelligencer Journal*, and the Sunday News.

It will be available to the public at small charge at the front counter of the Lancaster Newspapers building, 8 West King St.

This is the first completely new map of Lancaster since annexation caused the city's boundaries to assume a jagged outline, changing it from the four square shape it held for nearly 200 years.

However, when reprintings were made of the old map after the city began to change shape, a few alterations were made to the map. But none have been made since 1950.

Most of the work on the new map was done by Mrs. Mary Susan Schmuckle, staff artist of the advertising department of the Lancaster Newspapers. She was assisted in compiling information for the map by Henry E. Reemsnyder, superintendent of mails at the Lancaster Post Office, and J. Haines Shertzer, city engineer.

SIX MONTHS' WORK

It took Mrs. Schmuckle nearly six months to do the research for the map and to draw it. She drove over nearly every road which was to be included, plotting locations, curves and mileage, checking by tenths of miles. She visited all the new housing developments to check locations and names of streets.

Reemsyder provided lists of

Turn To Page 6 For More Of MAP

GOP Smiles After Tax Defeat

HARRISBURG, Aug. 4—State Sens. Rowland Mahany (R-Crawford), right, GOP floor leader, and M. Harvey Taylor, Senate president pro tem, are all smiles after the State Senate defeated the house-passed classified income tax, 26-33. The vote was along strictly party lines. (AP Wirephoto)

Eisenhower Hints Special Session Of Congress Looms

WASHINGTON, Aug. 4 (AP)—President Eisenhower said today he "has not by any manner of means dismissed the possibility" of recalling Congress for a special session.

In a news conference review of "successes and failures" of the session that closed Wednesday morning, Eisenhower lauded the lawmakers for a "bipartisan approach" and a "commendable" record in the field of foreign affairs.

But in the domestic field, he said, it failed to enact some bills "absolutely vital to our future."

ALWAYS POSSIBILITY

So, he said, in response to questions, "there is always the possibility" of a special session. But he also said, and repeated, that he has made no definite decision on summoning the legislators back to work later this year.

Of 13 measures the President listed as desirable a few weeks ago, he said Congress enacted only four—military reserves, housing, foreign aid appropriations, and a minimum wage boost.

He listed four others that Congress didn't pass as absolutely vital—school aid, health reinsurance, highway construction, and water resources.

On domestic legislation, he said,

Turn To Page 6 For More Of EISENHOWER

MRS. SAUDERS TAKEN TO COUNTY HOSPITAL

Mrs. Mary Sauders, Willow Street R1, charged with the slaying of William W. Glasgow May 4, was discharged yesterday from Lancaster General Hospital.

She was taken to the County Hospital. Mrs. Sauders has been ill since her arrest in May. She underwent surgery at the time and was later released from the hospital. Last month she was admitted again and her hearing on the murder charge set for July 6 was postponed. No new date has been set.

Youth Ducks Under Slow Train In Fleeing Police At Columbia

A young parolee wanted for questioning temporarily eluded the arm of the law yesterday by ducking beneath slow-moving freight in Columbia. He escaped under cover of the train at Union and Front Streets but was found an hour later along the tracks at Chickies Rock.

This time he surrendered meekly, telling his captor: "I'm tired."

Police said they wanted twenty-year-old Charles V. Thomas, Columbia R1, for questioning in connection with an automobile stolen in Wyomissing, Berks County. The car had been recovered Sunday by Columbia police on a routine patrol of Cedar Street.

RETURNED TO PRISON

Thomas, who police said had been released on parole six

Turn To Page 32 For More Of CHASE

CHARLES THOMAS

Leader Program DownedOn23-26 Hairline Ballot

Victorious GOP Schedules Another Roll Call Vote Today To Make Sure Democrats Cannot Revive Levy Again In 1955 Legislature

HARRISBURG, Aug. 4 (AP) — Senate Republicans voted to the man tonight to squelch Gov. Leader's proposal for a 411 million dollar classified income tax.

The roll call vote was 23-26 as the GOP exercised its hairline majority to snuff the life out of the governor's plan to balance his proposed $1,800,000,000 budget for the current biennium.

Almost immediately, Republicans scheduled another roll call vote for tomorrow to make certain Democrats can not revive the levy any more in the 1955 legislature.

Tempers flared as Democrats, in a last-ditch attempt to save the tax, described the Republican action as "a lynching party."

At one point, Sen. John H. Dent, Senate Democratic Floor Leader, sent a length of rope across the aisle to his Republican counterpart, Sen. Rowland B. Mahany, to help in what he termed the lynching.

Sen. M. Harvey Taylor (R-Dauphin),) Senate president pro tempore, took to the floor in his first major speech in 14 years in the Senate to accuse the governor of "a deliberate double cross."

The drama-packed session saw warning after warning by Lt. Gov. Roy E. Furman, Senate president, to Senators who resorted to personal attacks on other lawmakers in violation of the rules.

But the Republican majority remained united. The slow drone of the roll call came shortly after 8:30 p.m. It followed straight party lines. The only absentee was Sen. Miles R. Derk (D-Lycoming), recuperating from a heart attack.

Dent didn't resort to the usual parliamentary maneuver for seeking reconsideration of a defeated bill—changing two votes to be with the prevailing side.

FUTILE MOVE

He said it woud be "a futile and embarrassing" move in view of the declared intention of the Republicans to vote down any such reconsideration.

Dent sparkplugged the Democratic debate seeking Republican

Turn To Page 6 For More Of TAX

NEW RECORDS SET IN REAL ESTATE ACTIVITIES HERE

Dollar Value Of Mortgages, Deeds Recorded At New Highs

Activity in real estate in Lancater County is continuing at high levels this year with new records being set in the dollar value of mortgages and in the number of deeds recorded.

Frank L. Spence, recorder of deeds, reported yesterday that first seven months of the year totaled $28,231,377, a new all-time high.

The figure is $6,677,342 more than the $21,554,035 in mortgages recorded in the corresponding period of 1954, the previous record-high.

REASONS ADVANCED

The opening of scores of new residential developments in the county, the expansion of present developments and a spurt in the

Turn To Page 32 For More Of REAL ESTATE

Democrats Urge Registration To County's Women

An appeal to Lancaster County women of voting age to register to vote in the municipal election was issued yesterday by John E. Spicer Jr., Democratic county registration chairman.

"The failure of women to register and to vote badly distorts the political picture," said Spicer. "It gives the men an influence all out of proportion to their number and results in a lopsided over-masculine governmental set-up."

The registration chairman added that statistics show that in Lancaster County many women are not registered.

"Women and their special interests, as well as their vital concern with everything that affects their menfolk, should and

Turn To Page 6 For More Of DEMOCRATS

THE INTELL INDEX

The Tragic Parade of 1955

WEATHER

(U. S. Weather Bureau Forecast for Lancaster, Cumberland, Lebanon, York, Adams and Franklin Counties):

Mostly Sunny, Hot And Humid Today With High 90-95.

Intelligencer Journal.

The Leading Newspaper in the Garden Spot of America. Home Owned for Home Folks Since 1794

162nd Year.—No. 56. | Official United States Census Figures Lancaster Metropolitan Area Population 234,717 | LANCASTER, PA., SATURDAY MORNING, AUGUST 20, 1955. | CITY | TWENTY PAGES. | 30c PER WEEK—5c Per Copy

WORST FLOOD DISASTER HITS EAST

Police Query Steward In Waitress' Death

EARL DIEM IN CUSTODY OVERNIGHT

Autopsy Indicates Drowning In Death Of Mrs. Betty Reidenbach

Police, investigating the death of attractive Mrs. Betty R. Reidenbach, thirty-two, whose body was found late Thursday in the Conestoga creek, yesterday renewed their questioning of the steward at the Forty and Eight club—who is believed to have been the last person to have seen her alive.

The steward, Earl E. Diem, Lititz, was called in for questioning following announcement of the preliminary and unofficial results of the autopsy on the woman's body. Dr. Charles P. Stahr, deputy coroner, said the results indicated death was due to drowning.

Diem was questioned yesterday afternoon by Cpl. Mark Morgan, of the state police, and Manheim Twp. Police Chief John Kauffman, who are conducting the investigation. He was held overnight for more interrogation today.

Cpl. Morgan said authorities merely want to obtain more facts about the events prior to Mrs. Reidenbach's disappearance. Her

Turn To Page 12 For More Of DIEM

"We Lead All The Rest"

FARM CORNER

By WILLIAM R. SCHULTZ

USDA Divides N.J. For Milk Price Purposes

All of northern New Jersey and two adjacent shore counties comprise the marketing area for which any milk hearings will be considered by the U.S. Department of Agriculture.

The area includes Bergen, Essex, Hudson, Hunterdon, Middlesex, Monmouth, Morris, Ocean, Passaic, Somerset, Sussex, Union and Warren Counties, the USDA has announced.

The announcement was the result of a 4½-day public meeting held last month in Trenton to discuss which parts of New Jersey should be included in a proposed federal milk marketing area.

Trenton is not included in the marketing area.

Dr. C. W. Pierce, a professor at Pennsylvania State University, appeared at the public meeting on be-

Turn To Page 12 For More Of FARM CORNER

Crash Impact Hurls Man 20 Feet To Top Of House

FREAK ACCIDENT — Aldus Micken, seventy-six year old Willow Street man, receives help from an unidentified man after he was hurled through the top of his moving auto to the roof of this house along the Quarryville Pike south of Refton yesterday. Micken suffered painful injuries but his condition is described as satisfactory. The injured man was hurled through the cloth roof of his auto when it struck the north corner of the structure, owned by John L. Miller, Hessdale. Photograph by Robert Hurst, of Hessdale.

Aldus Micken, 76, Thrown Through Top Of Car To Roof Of Home At Hessdale; Injuries Not Serious; Auto Demolished

A 220-pound Willow Street man was hurled through the roof of his car 20 feet through the air to the top of a house in a freak accident on the Quarryville Pike at Hessdale shortly before 6 p. m. yesterday.

Aldus Micken, seventy-six, of Willow Street R1, suffered painful injuries but was described as satisfactory late last night at the Lancaster General Hospital.

The victim's injuries were listed as extensive lacerations and abrasions of the face, legs and arms and head injuries.

Micken was driving a 20-year-old automobile with canvas top and was hurled through the material by the impact of the collision.

State Police Officer Paul A. Bradigan said the dazed man gave him this account of the accident. He said he was driving south on Route 222, about two miles south of Refton, in his 1934 model sedan.

Micken said all he could re-

Turn To Page 14 For More Of ACCIDENT

CONOWINGO OFFICIAL SAYS REPAIRS AT DAM WON'T LOWER RIVER

Routine repairs to the Philadelphia Electric Co. hydroelectric dam at Conowingo, several miles below the Mason-Dixon Line will not lower the Susquehanna River level in lower Lancaster County, a spokesman at the dam said yesterday.

Last repairs were made at the dam about four years ago, the spokesman said, and it is due for another overhaul this September.

It will be about the same type of work as was done on the dam structure the last time, he reported.

The spokesman at the dam made the report to squelch the prevalent rumors in the lower part of the county.

MANHEIM TWP. SCHOOL WORK RE-BIDS LOWER

Earlier Rejections, Changes May Save $100,000 At Brecht, Schaeffer Schools

For the second time Manheim Twp. School Board opened bids last night for the new additions and renovations at the M. J. Brecht and Nathan C. Schaeffer schools.

The total of low bids last night showed, exclusive of alternatives, that the project will cost $488,237. However, the total is not definite since the board has yet to meet to study the bids and choose alternatives if they deem them necessary. The cost will probably be higher than that total.

Most of the contractors had representatives at last night's meeting, which was held in the high school, Neffsville.

BIDS TOO HIGH

Originally, a total of the base bids for general construction,

Turn To Page 2 For More Of MANHEIM TWP.

TRUCK KILLS 7-YR.-OLD GIRL AT KIRKWOOD

Victim's Parents Moving Here From Ohio This Weekend

A seven-year-old girl was killed almost instantly when she was struck by a truck at 6:15 p. m. yesterday in the square at Kirkwood. It was the third highway death in Lancaster County in two days.

The victim was Mary Ann Emerson, daughter of Mr. and Mrs. Frank Emerson, residents of Akron, Ohio, who are moving here this weekend. The tot had been living with her grandparents, Mr. and Mrs. Harry Gill, Kirkwood, for the past four weeks.

Her death raised the total number of vehicular fatalities in the county this year to 28. It equals the number during the corresponding period last year.

State Police Officer John Szabo said the child ran out of Harry Cramer's Grocery Store at the square and into the path of an unloaded dump truck operated by Henry Nelson Beyer, fifty-seven, Nottingham R1, Lancaster County.

The accident occurred on Route 472—an area where residents have battled futilely to have the State Highways Department put up some sort of traffic warnings.

Following last night's fatality, residents said they planned to circulate a petition to again ask the state for protection in the village.

Trooper Szabo said the girl was struck by the truck's grill, and then the vehicle stradled her. An investigation showed the wheels did not run over her, he said.

She was pronounced dead at

Turn To Page 2 For More Of FATALITY

Reserve Terms Of 6 Years Now Open To Youths

WASHINGTON, Aug. 19 (AP)—The Army announced today that enlistments will be accepted immediately for the new 6-year reserve training program.

The announcement also said the Army will be ready to take volunteers for the six months training plus 7½ years in active reserves phase of the new program in the "immediate future." Officials have said this means about Oct. 1.

Six-year enlistments directly into the reserves are open to youths of 17 and over who have not received a draft induction notice. Those accepted must serve two years on active duty, three years in the

Turn To Page 14 For More Of RESERVES

67 Die, Loss Possibly In Billions, State Is Reeling

TOLL MOUNTS

Pennsylvania Counts At Least 37 Dead As Waters Continue Rise

PHILADELPHIA, Aug. 19 (AP) — The most violent and destructive flood in Eastern Pennsylvania's recent history today left 37 persons dead and staggering damage for the living.

The death toll mounted when the Stroudsburg, Pa., Herald reported that at least 20 persons were known dead in the Monroe County area as flood waters all but isolated the hitherto robust resort center.

Gov. George Leader made a quick inspection trip to Stroudsburg and then flew back to Harrisburg where he wired President Eisenhower asking him to declare the region a disaster area and thus eligible for federal relief funds.

ANOTHER THREAT

Meanwhile, another flood threat grew, this time for communities along the roaring Delaware River. The flooding stream is expected to crest at Trenton, N. J., and Easton, Pa., during the early morning hours and then later in the day in Philadelphia.

The crest is expected to reach 38.1 feet at Easton, which would set a modern record and be just shy of the 38.6 set in 1902.

Elsewhere uncounted missing persons were still being sought along with washed-away homes,

Turn To Page 12 For More Of STATE

Weather Calendar

COMPARATIVE TEMPERATURES

Station	High	Low
Water Works	91	67
Ephrata	92	65
Last Year (Ephrata)	91	61
Official High for Year, July 23		103
Official Low for Year, Feb. 3		-5

Character of Day—Clear

SUN

Rises—6:19 a.m. Sets—7:55 p.m.

MOON

Sets—9:05 p.m. First Quarter, Aug. 25

STARS

Morning—Venus, Mars, Jupiter

Evening—Saturn

(U. S. Weather Bureau)

Southeastern Pennsylvania and Southern New Jersey—Mostly sunny and hot today and tomorrow. Highest in the 90s.

Central and Northeastern Pennsylvania—Fair hot and rather humid today and tomorrow. Highest 85-90 in mountains, 90-95 southeast of mountains.

Maryland—Sunny and hot and less humid today. High 90-95. Except middle of upper 80s higher mountains and coast. Tomorrow continued fair and hot.

Delaware—Sunny and hot and less humid today. High 90-95 except near 86 vicinity of the coast. Tomorrow continued fair and hot.

Lower Potomac and Chesapeake Bay—Gentle variable winds mostly west or northwest today. Weather fair with good visibility.

EXTENDED FORECAST

(U. S. Weather Bureau)

Extended forecast for period from today through Wednesday:

Eastern Pennsylvania, Eastern New York and Mid-Atlantic States:

Temperature will average 8 or 10 degrees above normal, becoming hot over weekend, cooler north portion late Tuesday or Wednesday. A few scattered thundershowers averaging generally ¼ inch or less, except possibly ½ to 1 inch near the coast.

New England Is Hit Hard

Nine States Dealt Near Knock-Out Blow By Rampaging Rivers, Largest Single Number Of Dead In Poconos Mts. With At Least 20 Deaths

By The Associated Press

The most devastating flood in Eastern U. S. history continued its relentless hammering today as the death toll climbed to 67 and property damage seemed headed for the billions of dollars figure.

Even as short-handed rescue workers and volunteers tried to patch up the remnants of totally devastated areas to the south, other communities in New England were feeling the full fury of the raging waters and the crisis there was heightening through the night.

The two points apparently hit the hardest are Stroudsburg, Pa., a resort center in the Pocono Mountains which counted at least 20 dead and scores missing and Waterbury, Conn., where at least 15 persons were reported dead.

POWERLESS CITY

Waterbury was a powerless city, laying helpless before the surging Naugatuck River which was moving at 50 m.p.h., sweeping away power lines and buildings. Fire Chief Francis T. Scully described the situation "as the worst disaster Waterbury has ever seen."

Stroudsburg was without drinking water and gas for heat and cooking. All bridges and main roads were washed out. But Horace Heller, editor of the Stroudsburg, Pa., Record reported the community was starting to assess the damage and make some headway in the mountainous task of rebuilding.

BURSTING DAMS

A chain of bursting dams sent the Blackstone and Mill rivers hurtling into Woonsocket, R. I., after 500 families were evacuated.

Officials in all areas said it would be many days before final figures on the dead, missing and damage are available.

Governors of Pennsylvania, Massachusetts and Connecticut proclaimed a state of emergency.

The latest reports put the biggest single number of dead in Waterbury, Conn., the brass manufacturing center. Mayor Richard Lee of New Haven quoted Waterbury Mayor Raymond Snyder as saying at least 15 persons lost their lives.

In Stroudsburg, Pa., a once-robust resort center in the Pocono Mountains, there were nine known dead and possibly 20 others missing. The community's principal roads and bridges were washed away or under three to four feet of water. The water supply for drinking purposes was cut off. The principal hospital in the area was isolated.

FOLLOWED DIANE

The storm developed Thursday after Hurricane Diane spent her fury in the Carolinas. In some

Turn To Page 12 For More Of FLOODS

Leader Requests Federal Aid In 'Disaster' Area

HARRISBURG, Aug. 19 (AP) — Gov. Leader tonight asked the federal government to declare flooded sections of eastern Pennsylvania as "major disaster areas."

Leader said he observed "devastating floods with attendant loss of life" during an air trip over the flooded sections.

He wired President Eisenhower:

"I therefore respectfully request that flood areas of eastern Pennsylvania be declared major disaster areas in accordance with provision of Public Law 875."

In the telegram, Leader said:

"Extremely heavy rains, principally in the Delaware, Lehigh

Turn To Page 14 For More Of LEADER

BOY, 11, IS INJURED AS BICYCLE HITS CAR

George Edward LeFevre, eleven, 1321 Quarry Lane, was admitted to St. Joseph's Hospital shortly after 7:45 p. m. yesterday after he struck the fender of an auto while riding his bicycle at Quarry Lane and Wilson Drive.

The boy, according to hospital authorities, is suffering a deep laceration of the right ear and possible concussion.

Columbia State Policeman Walter Miller said the car was being operated by A. Gertrude Herr, 653 N. Pine St., city, who was operating with a learner's permit. She was accompanied by a licensed driver, Alvin R. Hocke, 1803 Willow Street Pike.

Officer Miller said the car was traveling east on Quarry Lane and as the operator attempted a left turn onto Wilson Drive, the Lefevre boy ran into the right rear fender and was thrown from the bicycle.

Rampaging Delaware River Takes Lives, Destroys Property, Creates "Disaster Area"

The pictures above showing flood ravages in sections of Eastern Pennsylvania indicates graphically why Governor George M. Leader called on the federal government tonight to declare them "major disaster areas" and therefore eligible for federal aid. Picture at far left shows the Delaware River on a rampage at Mount Pocono, Pa. The west branch of the river south of Mount Pocono ripped through a plant at the water's edge slicing away a bank and tilting a water tower at a 45-degree angle. Top center of picture shows the washed out line of the Delaware and Lackawanna Railroad, crippled along most of its route. The second picture from left shows the Delaware at Easton spreading over the main highway between Easton and Phillipsburg, N. J. A two-part steel bridge across the Delaware at Stroudsburg was torn apart and washed downriver (third picture from left). The second section of the bridge was washed still further downstream. The photograph at far right shows a part of rescue operations that took place throughout the flooded area. An Air Force helicopter swings a man to safety from a flood-lashed house on the south side of Scranton. Another man, seen in a second floor window (arrow), awaits his turn as the helicopter swung back and forth to lift nearly a hundred persons trapped in their homes. (AP Wirephotos)

New Era Midgets Visit New York City

SPORTS

Lancaster County hospitality is widely-known and even more-so now . . . as a number of pigeons learned that the Paradise youngsters are quite generous with their food.

Kenny Kendig, Paradise midget-midget shortstop, has a chat with Giants pitcher Paul Giel.

Alvin Dark, Giants captain, accepts gift box of cheese from Tom Houder of Paradise, while Bertie Hershey, left, and Sam Wenger look on.

New Era Photos

Eating was one of the most constant and enjoyable parts of the big trip. Several members of Hager's Blue Jays are shown here with their plates "loaded."

New Era Photo

Members of the Hager Blue Jays, 1955 midget champions, enjoying the New York Giants-St. Louis Cardinals game at the Polo Grounds. The boys had choice seats in back of the Giants dugout as they watched the host Giants win the game, 4-1.

Look! Look! Look! Over Here! Over There!

Midgets Awed By "Big Town" Sights

by BOB HUTTER

"LOOK at the ships! Look at the airplanes! Look at that tall building! Look at that hit! Look what I got for only a nickel! Look at this and look at that, look here and look there!"

That's a sample of the fast tempo which yesterday engulfed the 30 youngsters, who as the result of their winning The New Era's tenth annual Midget and Midget-Midget championships, were taken by The New Era on an all-day trip to the fabulous "Big Town," New York City.

Day to Remember

It was a day that will long be remembered by the members of the Hager's Blue Jays, which captured the Midget Division title, and the 15 youngsters, who made up the Paradise Lions Midget-Midget championship squad. From the moment the champs boarded the two chartered buses at 7 o'clock in the morning until they set foot once again at home last night, they never got a chance to stop looking.

It was a day filled with thrills, new experiences and bewildering sites. Actually, the boys hardly had time to get the seats of our buses warm, before they reached the high pitch that made this trip one of the most enjoyable and interesting of all previous tours.

There's no doubt in anyone's mind that the ball game between the New York Giants and St. Louis Cardinals was the high point of the trip, but from all the reactions of the youngsters, there were other happenings that were almost on a par, if not equal, to the much-awaited trip to the Polo Grounds.

Plenty to Eat

For instance, only a few miles out of Lancaster the boys started quenching a new found thirst with all the ice-cold cokes they could drink, thanks to Brooks Riegle, manager of the local Coca Cola Bottling Works. A little later it was the candy donated by Bill Perry, local representative of Necco. Then, it was the box lunches, which added up to an "eating good time" going over to New York. However, it wasn't just the food and drinks that made the early morning ride a happy one, for the boys were awed first by the "jet" airplanes they saw parked, landing and taking off while passing the New Castle airport. Next came the Delaware Memorial Bridge, the size of which startled the youngsters, as well as the ships that were steaming up the Delaware River.

The Polo Grounds

Time passed quickly and before the champs realized it, they were speeding through the meadows outside of New York. A short ride over the George Washington Bridge and jaunt into Harlem placed the youngsters squarely at the gates of the Polo Grounds, home of the World Champion Giants.

Being the guests of Leo Durocher and the New York Ball Club, it was only natural that the cheers (and there were many) were loudest when the Cardinals were downed by a 4-1 margin.

From the ball game we "country boys" headed down Broadway and it was now that the tallest building in the world, the Empire State Building, loomed almost on top our buses. The first glimpse of the skyscraper came while still on the New Jersey turnpike, but the youngsters couldn't imagine its over-powering size until it appeared directly above them.

Along the Waterfront

The fascination of an automat was next in store for the starry-eyed youths, who quickly discovered that they could get plenty to eat and still have some nickles left for a "rainy day." With "tummies" full (yet), it was back in the buses again and a thrilling ride along the New York waterfront, where the champs saw some huge ocean-going liners, including the Christofero Columbus, one of the most modern ships sailing the blue today.

And, there was still more to come, for The New Era champion caravan then headed for the Holland Tunnel, a man-made underwater road, at which the youngsters marveled. It was all homeward bound from then on, but even this kept the boys on their toes, for while they had seen just about all the sights on the way over, they were all different now, because it was dark and the millions of lights that mark the roadways and cities on the way home kept them guessing right up to the last fleeting second of the trip that will help to make The New Era's 1955 Midget Baseball Tournament a memorable one.

Cheers, Cheese For The Giants

by BILL FISHER

LANCASTER County is known for many things. And what with the smash Broadway success of "Plain and Fancy" spreading characteristics of the plain County folk among the fancy folk of New York, Lancaster has become a by-word among metropolitan inhabitants.

"Plain and Fancy" notwithstanding, Lancaster County is now also known in New York — at least among the New York Giants baseball team—for still another thing: Cheese.

Yes, cheese.

One of the midget-midget players, Tommy Houder of Paradise, had a hankering to take the Giants something from home. He climbed aboard the bus yesterday morning with a cardboard carton addressed To: Leo Durocher and the Giants. From: The Paradise Midgets.

The carton contained five pounds of Lancaster County Swiss cheese; fresh off the Houder farm at Paradise.

Al Dark, captain of the Giants, accepted the gift from Houder and two of his buddies, Bertie Hershey and Kenny Kendig, in front of the Giants dugout before the game. Each of the kids was rewarded with a firm slap on the seat of the pants as Dark assured them that the cheese would be passed around in the Giants clubhouse. Be assured that the Giants are not "cheese champions" in the eyes of the Paradise boys.

And for more reasons than one. Another was Willie Mays who took time out to autograph a ball for Paradise pitcher Tommy Winters, and Paul Giel, the young bonus pitcher, who popped out of the dugout long enough to pose with a group of enchanted youngsters.

It was, in short, a day dedicated to baseball.

Unlike their doddering elders who go to a ball park for the simple satisfaction of watching a ball game, this gang of youthful exuberants made a regular production out of it. If you are a Dad and have ever taken your youngster to a big league game you have an idea what it was like. If not, use your imagination.

When it was all over at the Polo Grounds the Giants had thumped the Cards 4-1 on the strength of back-to-back homers by Wayne Terwilliger and Ray Katt. But the excitement started before the ball game.

"Look, Laraine Day!" exclaimed someone as we lined up to enter the press gate. And indeed it was; Mrs. Leo Durocher bustling along with a radiant smile "Pardon meing" her way through the mob.

"Gee, she passed right by me," said a delighted kid.

Inside the park we were ushered to choice grandstand seats about 20 rows behind the Giants dugout. Then it was all baseball and a souvenir search that would warm the most hardened huckster's heart.

Of course, everybody had to have a program, and before long ballpark appetites urged fulfillment. Soft drinks and hot dogs and popcicles and peanuts.

But the boys wanted tangible evidence of the trip, too. They bought New York Giant picture cards — a bit outdated as one youthful fanatic pointed out—because Sal Maglie was still pictured among the Giant heroes.

And they bought lapel pins with pictures of Willie Mays and Stan Musial hooked to red, white and blue ribbons emblazoned with miniature bats and gloves in their resplendent tarnishable gold. They bought ball point pens, too, shaped like baseball bats, and team pennants and autographed balls and miniature Louisville Slugger bats.

And one kid committed the unpardonable sin of buying a Dodger yearbook in the Polo Grounds.

"Well," he replied in complete youthful innocence, "the Dodgers are my favorite team."

Nothing transcends the allegiance of a 12-year-old baseball fan.

Biasatti and Oster Back on Active List

Manager Hank Biasatti and pitcher Bill Oster returned to the Roses active list today. Biasatti and Oster had been on the temporary inactive list but became active players today when the Piedmont's 27-player limit became effective for the remainder of the season.

Permutit Captures Industrial Loop's President's Cup

Permutit wound up its first year in the local Industrial Softball League in an impressive fashion as it scored an 8-2 decision over Trojan to capture the President's Cup series.

John (Cigar) Gibbs got off to a slow start for Permutit, being touched for two runs in the first inning, but from then on he was the complete master. The winning hurler allowed just six hits, while fanning four and walking none.

Some timely hitting by "Rebel" Potts and C. Long paved the way, but the Trojans made it easier by committing four costly errors. All of which didn't help Lloyd Neal, who handled the pitching chores for Trojan. Neal allowed ten hits and ran into trouble in the fourth, fifth and sixth innings.

Today's Chuckle

Life's necessities have increased to four—food, clothing, shelter, and endurance.

LANCASTER NEW ERA

Lancaster Metropolitan Area Population Official United States Census Figures 234,717

Local Weather

U.S. Weather Bureau Forecast

Fair tonight and tomorrow. Cool tonight with low 58-64. Cooler tomorrow. High 74-80.

Details on Page 3

79th Year—No. 24,279 | CITY EDITION | LANCASTER, PA., TUESDAY, SEPTEMBER 6, 1955 | 26 PAGES | 30c PER WEEK—5c Per Copy

$100,000 Fire in Ephrata Theater

New Era Photo

Fire-damaged interior of Roxy theater, Ephrata. At top are burned rafters and holes in roof. Fallen rafters lie in balcony and on main floor.

(Other fire pictures on Page 10)

Jewelry Store Also Wrecked; 2 MenOvercome

4 Driven from Beds; Police Are Probing Odd 'Circumstances'

Fire of undetermined origin caused damage estimated at $100,000 to an Ephrata movie theater and jewelry store early this morning.

The blaze wrecked the interior of the Roxy Theater, 36 E. Main St.

It also caused heavy smoke and water damage to the jewelry store, owned by Otis B. Billmyer, located in the same building.

Fire Chief Arthur Mellinger, of Ephrata's Pioneer Fire Co., estimated the damage to the building and contents at more than $100,000.

2 Overcome By Smoke

Billmyer, owner of the store, and Elmer Burkholder, a member of the Akron Fire Co., were overcome by smoke and were admitted to Ephrata Community Hospital for treatment. Their condition is fair, hospital officials said.

Driven from their apartments above the theater were Mr. and Mrs. Harry C. Dickersheid and their son and daughter-in-law, Mr. and Mrs. Wilbur Dickersheid. They were awakened by Ephrata policeman Lloyd Frymyer.

Another Fire 20 Feet Away

The fire which wrecked the theater broke out simultaneously with a smaller fire in a small storage building located about 20 feet to the rear of the theater building.

The Ephrata Fire Co. was answering an alarm sounded when the fire in the smaller building was spotted by John Hurst, president of the fire company and a milkman. Hurst spotted the smaller blaze while making his morning rounds.

As firemen arrived on the scene, shortly before 5 a. m., they spotted two shafts of flames shooting from the rear of the theater roof. They then summoned the Akron and Lincoln companies for assistance.

Unusual Circumstances

Because of the unusual circumstances surrounding the fire, Mellinger said, he has called in Paul Z. Knier, county fire marshal, and state police to aid in the investigation.

Most of the fire damage to the theater was on the stage, where the screen and other equipment were destroyed.

There was heavy damage on the balcony and roof. Some of the seats on the main floor of the theater were burned, and all were damaged badly by the smoke and water. Several rafters fell to the main floor.

Damage to the jewelry store was limited to smoke and water. Heavy smoke poured from the two apartments above the theater during most of the fire and a steady stream of water was pumped into them.

Mellinger estimated that hundreds of thousands of gallons of

—See FIRE—Page 10

City's Failure to Answer Ephrata Fire Call Is Probed

3 Radio Appeals for Aid Were Not Answered; Reading Called as Substitute

Failure of the Lancaster Fire Department to answer a radio message for aid sent by the Ephrata fire company early today is under investigation by City Fire Chief Harry Miller.

The call via fire radio was sent at about 4:55 a.m. by Fire Chief Arthur Mellinger, of Ephrata, directing fire fighting efforts at the blaze at a movie theater and jewelry store on E. Main St.

Mellinger was attempting to get the assistance of the Lancaster Fire Department's aerial ladder truck to fight the fire beneath the roof of the two-story building.

Then Called for Reading

Three times the Ephrata fire radio called the Lancaster Fire Department, but received no reply from the radio unit at the N. Queen St. firehouse, Mellinger said. He then sent a call to Reading.

The Reading Fire Department, a volunteer unit, was reached by telephone, and dispatched Washington Fire Co. No. 2 ladder truck. It arrived at the fire between 20 and 25 minutes after it was summoned, Mellinger said.

The distance from Reading to Ephrata is 19 miles; from Lancaster to Ephrata 13 miles.

Chief Miller said the man on duty at the Lancaster radio will not be on duty again for 48 hours, but that when he returns he will be asked to explain why the message was not received. Normally, he said, the man on radio duty, will relay such messages to the captain on duty.

He declined to say who was on duty at the time until the investigation is completed.

Radio Unit Working

The radio unit at Lancaster apparently was in working order this morning. Chief Miller conferred with Mellinger over the radio hookup later in the morning in an attempt to clear up the situation.

In his conversation with Mellinger, Chief Miller apologized for the failure to answer the call and promised that "disciplinary action will be carried out on the particular person responsible for not answering."

Firms Oppose Zoning Change On E. Ross St.

Ask Council to Deny Petition of Residents In Playground Area

Representatives of business firms in the E. Ross St. area protested to City Council today against granting a petition of residents there that the zoning be changed from C2 to C1.

The petition, signed by approximately 200 residents of the Sixth Ward, asks that the northeast side of E. Ross St. from Park Ave. to the New Holland Pike be changed from C2 to C1 with the hope of some day eliminating a truck terminal there.

(A C1 zone prohibits use of any building for trade or industry. C2 permits the truck terminal.)

Council, sitting as an appeal board, held a hearing on the petition Aug. 23, but no opposition was expressed at that time. The protestors said today that they did not know of the previous hearing and asked Council to hear their objections today.

Fulton St. Rezone Case

Opposition also cropped up today to another petition heard by Council Aug. 23. It is that of Bud Stauffer, operator of Stauffer Cigaret Sales and Service Co., asking that the northwest side of Fulton St. from Marshall to Franklin Sts. be re-zoned from R2 to C1 so he can build a sales and distribution center.

Frank B. Ganse, 239 N. Marshall St., presented a petition signed by 58 residents opposing the change as a danger to youngsters and property values. He said he was out of town when the public hearing was held.

No Action Taken

City Council took no actions today on the requested changes. Mayor Kendig C. Bare revealed during the hour-long hearing, however, that both the City Planning Commission and the Zoning Board of Appeals have recommended both changes be denied.

He stressed, however, that the boards acted only in an advisory capacity and that responsibility for the final decision rests with Council.

Business Firms Protesting

Most of this morning's discussion was taken up with the proposed zone change in the E. Ross St. area. Objecting to the change

—See COUNCIL—Page 10

Damp Moderate Weather Bears Slight Hint of Fall

Morning weather here today bore a tang of fall, but this afternoon was more like summer again, warm and damp.

Tonight and tomorrow are to be fair, the U. S. Weather Bureau said, with a low between 58 and 64 for the night, and cooler air due tomorrow, with a high between 74 and 80. The five-day forecast said temperatures would average near or a little below normal through Sunday, with rainfall averaging one-fourth inch or less and ending Saturday.

Today's 2 p. m. temperature was 82, and relative humidity was 69. A brief but heavy rainfall in the city area, near the end of Labor Day yesterday, totaled .24 inch at the City Water Works.

Red China Frees 9 U. S. Civilians At Geneva Talk

2 Others Can Leave If They Ask to, 3rd Free in 2 or 3 Months

GENEVA (AP) — Communist China notified the United States today that nine American civilians detained in China, including six women, were now free to return home.

Red Chinese Ambassador Wang Ping-nan told U. S. Ambassador U. Alexis Johnson at their 13th meeting that two other Americans could leave at once if they asked for exit permits and a third could leave within two or three months.

The two ambassadors have been meeting at intervals since Aug. 1, negotiating the release of 41 Americans imprisoned in China or denied exit permits.

First Result Of Talks

The announcement by Wang was the first positive result of the talks since they began.

There was no indication when the Chinese Reds would release the 29 Americans not mentioned on Wang's list, but the ambassadors agreed today to continue their secret talks on Saturday.

American delegation members were able to find only a partial identification for some of the Americans listed for release by Wang. A delegation spokesman said none had been imprisoned.

Listed For Departure

Listed for immediate departure were:

Miss Emma Angelina Barry, a young girl living in Shanghai with her mother, a white-Russian who was not an American citizen.

Ralph Sharples Boyd, Shanghai representative of the North American Syndicate, born in Washington, D. C., in 1891.

Mrs. Juanita Byrd Huang, a Southern Baptist missionary married to a Chinese citizen, born Mount Olive, Miss., in 1904.

Robert Howard Parker, a retired businessman born in Philadelphia, Pa., in 1873.

Howard Lischke Ricks, manager of Bills Motors Branch in Shanghai, born in Boscobel, Wis., in 1889.

Mrs. Howard Lischke Ricks, his wife, born in Shanghai in 1894.

Miss Eva Stella Dugay, known as Sister Theresa, a nun in the

—See CAPTIVES—Page 10

3 Polio Cases Bring Total to 14

31 Under Number at Same Time in 1954

Three new polio cases were reported today, raising the total for the year to 14, compared to 45 at this time last year.

The three new patients, all girls, and all suffering from mild cases, are:

Kathleen Worley, eight, daughter of Mr. and Mrs. William Worley, 628 Chestnut St., Columbia.

Vickie Sheaffer, two, daughter of Mr. and Mrs. Eugene Sheaffer, 220 Duke St., Ephrata.

Carol Weeks, eight, daughter of Mr. and Mrs. G. Kenneth Weeks, Mountville.

The Worley and Sheaffer girls were admitted to St. Joseph's Hospital Saturday, and diagnosis was made definite yesterday. The Weeks girl was admitted to the Lancaster General Hospital Sunday, and definite diagnosis was completed yesterday.

Too Early for Optimism

With current cases totaling about one-third of those at this time last year, Dr. Oscar Davis, county medical director, said it was too early to make final conclusions that this was a light polio year. He pointed out that September last year brought a sharp rise in the number of cases.

Nationally, the administration of the first mass shots of Salk vaccine was credited with having already been effective in lowering the incidence of polio.

Of the children contracting polio here this year, two were known to have received Salk shots in school this spring. The Weeks' girl was the second known to have had a Salk inoculation. The first was a boy who contracted polio last week.

Woman Bitten by CopperheadSnake

Mrs. James Patterson, of Holtwood, who was bitten on the left foot by a copperhead snake Sunday about 8 p.m., was reported in satisfactory condition today at St. Joseph's Hospital.

Mrs. Patterson was bitten by the snake as she walked up the steps leading to her home. Dr. W. A. Shuman gave her medical aid, and had her taken to the hospital. Her husband killed the snake, and said it measured 28 inches.

A number of copperheads were reported in the southern end of the county in the past week. Two were killed on the road between Colemanville and Pequea, near Camp May.

4 of 5 Parochial Schools Have Record Enrollments

Peak 240 Freshmen at Catholic High; City and Suburban Public Schools Open Tomorrow

The parochial schools in the city opened today with four of the five schools reporting record enrollments.

At Lancaster Catholic High School a record 240 freshmen met for orientation. The school officially opens tomorrow morning with Holy Mass.

McCaskey High School also held an orientation program for over 500 sophomores and new students today.

The city public schools open tomorrow as do schools in Manheim and Lancaster Townships, Lampeter-Strasburg School District, the Manor-Millersville area, and Lancaster Country Day School.

270 At St. Anne's

St. Anne's School opened with an enrollment of 270 pupils, largest in the school's history.

At St. Anthony's School a record group of over 400 children reported.

St. Joseph's School announced an enrollment of about 520 pupils, about ten higher than last year. The previous all-time high was 518 which was recorded a number of years ago.

Sacred Heart School reported a record 417 pupils returning to the classrooms, in comparison with about 392 pupils last year.

The fifth school, St. Mary's reported about 350 pupils, slightly lower than last year. However, last year's enrollment was the highest in the school's history.

Father Gribbin Speaks At Orientation Program

The 240 freshmen at Lancaster Catholic High School heard the Rev. Robert C. Gribbin, school principal, discuss the importance of a serious attitude toward school

—See SCHOOLS—Page 10

School Zone Speeder Prosecuted in City

Nelson L. Makle, 156 Pleasant Ave., Columbia, was charged with driving too fast in a school zone by city police before Alderman Newell.

He was allegedly clocked at 40 miles per hour on W. Orange St., from Charlotte St. to Marietta Ave., at 11:55 a.m. today, when pupils were being dismissed for the noon recess at Sacred Heart Parochial School, located on nearby Nevin St.

The speed limit for school zones is 15 miles per hour.

Farm Co-op Safe Robbed of $637

Acetylene Torch Used To Open Steel Door

Safe robbers used an acetylene torch to cut their way into a large vault safe in the office of the Lancaster County Farm Bureau Co-Op Association, Dillersville Pike, last night and escaped with $637.15 in cash.

The robbers used an acetylene torch, oxygen tank, crow bars, hatchets, chisels and other tools to open the safe. All were stolen from a building adjacent to the office, according to city Detectives Frank Matt and Paul Cogley.

Tried To Dig

Detectives said the robbers first tried to dig their way through the rear of the vault housing the safe, but gave up after hitting the reinforced concrete portion of the vault.

Then they went to work on the steel door of the safe, which police estimated weighs close to 1,000 pounds. After burning a hole, 14 inches wide and 12 inches long, in the area around the combination, they cut through to the inner-workings of the lock and opened the safe door.

Police said the burglars, who undoubtedly were professionals, stacked up tables from the office and salesroom to shield the glare of the acetylene torch from being seen on the outside of the building.

The burglary was discovered by two office employes, Elsie M. Metzler and Dorothy N. Neff, when they reported for work at 6:50 a.m. today. They notified Charles C. Burkins, the manager, who contacted police.

U.S. Auto Deaths Climb to 438 Over Weekend

Exceeds Prediction And Toll in 1954; 80 More Drown

By The Associated Press

A heavy toll of traffic accident deaths was made by American motorists during the three-day Labor Day weekend, exceeding advance predictions and the toll for the 1954 holiday.

Reports still trickling in today showed 438 persons died in traffic mishaps between 6 p.m. local time Friday and midnight Monday. An additional 80 persons drowned and 90 died in miscellaneous accidents for an overall total of 608.

This compared with a record high of 461 and record overall total of 658, both set in 1951. The 1954 traffic toll was 364.

The National Safety Council had predicted 400 would die over the holiday.

32 Hurt For Every Death

Council statistics show that 32 other persons are injured for every traffic death. Also, for every three persons killed, a fourth dies later of injuries.

This year's holiday toll also topped that of a non-holiday weekend tabulated last month for comparative purposes. An Associated Press survey of deaths during the Aug. 19-22 weekend showed 385 traffic deaths, 67 drownings and 85 violent deaths for miscellaneous causes.

The weekend took at least 27 lives in Pennsylvania, making it the third most tragic in the state this year. Over the Fourth of July 34 died, and 30 perished the second week-end of May.

Of the 27 Labor Day victims, 20 were killed on the highways, four drowned, two lost their lives in a plane crash in a field four miles south of Somerset, and one burned to death. In addition, seven Pennsylvanians were killed in accidents outside the state.

$15,000 Addition For Pa. Malleable

A one-story brick and cinder block building is to be erected for the Pennsylvania Malleable Iron Corp. to expand operations at its hardware division, 1285 Manheim Pike.

The building permit for the job, with cost estimated at $15,000, was issued today to Samuel E. Long, contractor, for the owner of the property, Elmer L. Esbenshade, by C. Edward Vatter, city building inspector.

Charles P. Speitel, president of Pennsylvania Malleable, said the new building would be between the two present buildings leased at the Manheim Pike site by the firm, which manufactures marine hardware and has its headquarters on S. Prince St.

Soap Gun Frees Gaspe's Killer

Surrenders After Being Loose for Hour

QUEBEC (AP)—Convicted murderer Wilbert Coffin bluffed his way out of jail with a gun made of soap early today. He tied up seven guards and locked the sergeant-at-arms in the boiler room.

But the 44-year-old Gaspe prospector, sentenced to hang Sept. 23, was persuaded by his lawyer to give himself up after only 1½ hours of freedom.

Takes Keys With Him

Brandishing the intricately carved soap gun, Coffin took all the keys of the jail with him when he left.

Lawyer Raymond Maher, who defended the prospector at his trial last year in Perce, Que., said Coffin hailed a taxi a few hundred feet from the jail and asked to be driven to the Quebec bridge, seven miles west of the heart of the city. As they neared the bridge Coffin told the taxi driver who he was.

"Then they began talking about the case," Maher said. "Coffin asked the driver if he knew where I lived."

The driver, Gaston LaBrecque, telephoned his office for Maher's address and then drove to the apartment in uppertown Quebec.

Coffin, convicted of murdering Richard Lindsey, 17-year-old Hollidaysburg, Pa., hunter, two years ago, made his way out of the grey stone prison at about 1 a.m. He arrived at Maher's home at 2:10 a.m.

Young Lindsey's bear-gnawed bones, along with those of his father Eugene, 47, and Albert Claar, 20, a friend, were found in Gaspe bushland after they set out on a hunting trip in June, 1953.

Hurricane Flora No Threat to U. S.

MIAMI, Fla. (AP) — Hurricane Flora, a well-behaved lady, was making a sweeping curve today that will keep it in the open Atlantic and away from the American mainland.

"This storm is not a threat to any part of the United States coast," the Miami Weather Bureau reported.

"Flora should get into an upper air current flowing from the south," forecaster Cecil Gentry said. "This should head it further north while it is still well away from the coast."

It was roughly a thousand miles from the nearest mainland point, Nantucket, and about 560 miles southeast of Bermuda.

Firm Short of Cash

500 Union Workers Lend $100,000 to the Company

CINCINNATI (AP)—More than 500 employes of the Hamilton Tailoring Co. are lending $100,000 to their employer.

Members of the CIO Amalgamated Clothing Workers voted the funds after the company became short of cash after recent acquisitions, a company official said.

The money was turned over to the tailoring concern by Jack Kroll, chairman of the Cincinnati Amalgamated Clothing Workers Board, who is better known nationally as director of the CIO Political Action Committee.

Deduct 10 per cent of Pay

Starting tomorrow, employes will have 10 per cent of their pay checks deducted as their share of the loan. The company will pay approximately $10,000 a month to the union until the debt is erased. The employes will receive debenture bonds, paying 3½ per cent interest, to cover their payroll deduction loans.

A company official said the union afforded a more attractive proposition than could have been obtained from a bank.

Hamilton Tailoring does a seven-million-dollar yearly business and claims to be the largest made-to-measure clothing organization in the world.

Made Loans Before

"I'm reluctant to talk about the loan because it may embarrass the company," Kroll said. "We've done this a goodly number of times here in Cincinnati and elsewhere."

Asked why the union would make a loan to management, Kroll answered:

"Our members work in the place. It's their jobs. The union functions to protect people's jobs. We feel we're a part of the industry."

Approve New Road Names In Eden-Bridgeport Area

New road names in the area east of the city, approved by township supervisors, were made known today by Postmaster Frank R. Hammond and Henry E. Reemsnyder, superintendent of mails.

These names have been approved for roads between Eden and Bridgeport, in East Lampeter Twp.:

Mill Cross Road — part of the old Eden-Bridgeport Road, leading south from Eden covered bridge to a dead end about one mile away at the Glass Road, meeting Pitney Road.

Pitney Road — new designation for Eden-Bridgeport Road from Bridgeport past intersection of Mill Cross Road, curving to meet Hempstead Road, which was formerly part of the Greenfield Road.

Hempstead Road — continuation of the Greenfield Road northeast of the city by-pass, dead ending at Willow Road.

Creek Hill Road — new name for old Rohrer's Mill Road.

Brook Farm Road—running parallel to Conestoga Creek, branching from Mill Cross Road.

Reemsnyder, who works with township officials in preparing road names, said that the Lancaster Twp. supervisors have approved the designation of the road leading north along the Conestoga on its west shore, between the Lincoln Highway and Ranck Road, as Conestoga Drive North.

Today's New Era

Phone Lancaster 5251

Police Rodeo 34 Years Old

FOUNDED IN 1921, the State Police Rodeo has become Pennsylvania's proudest "spectacular." This gigantic safety lesson plays to applauding thousands from one end of the Commonwealth to the other. Yesterday two full exhibitions were put on, at the Lebanon Veterans Hospital and for the Boy Scout roundup at Hershey. Other local appearances have included partial shows for the Lancaster Auto Club picnic at Hershey, Middletown Air Depot, and York's Labor Day field day. Behind the perfection of performance are long hours of rehearsal at Hershey barracks, as shown on this page, under the eye of Major Thomas F. Martin who has spent much of his 41 years of duty in the saddle.

SALUTE TO SAFETY, the Pennsylvania State Police Rodeo riders present arms to open the show. In full uniform with western style hats, the 85-man show staff presents a 2-hour program many times throughout the state. Above, preview performance was at Palmyra, in full uniform. Other photos taken during rehearsals at Hershey. (Sunday News Photos)

JUMPING THE "A"—"Skip," trained by Pvt. Guy Bell (standing at rear), hurtles through the human-figure "A" as part of the Rodeo show. The two husky troopers on the bottom of the pyramid are Privates Wayne Kerr (left) and Robert Caruso (right). On the top are Privates William Murtha and Andy Harchak. The crossbar of the "A" is Pvt. Stephen Pawlak.

FLAMING THRILLS keep spectators tense as nine horses and riders jump through the three hoops. Above, Pvt. A. Horvath jumps his horse through the fire hoop.

←

STIRRUP LAYDOWN, one of the many features of the trick riders, is performed at breakneck speed by Pvt. John Sabric, riding "Scholar."

PRAYING HORSE—Pvt. Russell Love shows just how serious the State Police and horses consider child safety. This is one of the eight dressage horses that sits like a dog, rolls on its back, and does many other tricks that a "smart" horse should know.

RIDING THE ARCH, Major Thomas F. Martin (center), led by the color bearers Sgt. Andrew Gecoloski (left) and Pvt. James Snee (right) prepare for the final salute to the audience. Capt. A. H. Kratzke (behind Major Martin) is partially blocked from view.

"WE LOVE THE UPPERCLASSMEN!"—That's the required chant for all Millersville State Teachers College freshmen who pass the "sacred" upperclassmen tree near the door to Lyle Hall dining room.

First-Class Fun

COLLEGE FRESHMEN all over the nation are learning the humility requisite to higher learning, with the aid of the traditional "frosh customs." First-year college students at Elizabethtown, Franklin and Marshall and Millersville are shown here as they jump through the sophomore-rigged hoops of ridiculous regulations. (Sunday News Photos)

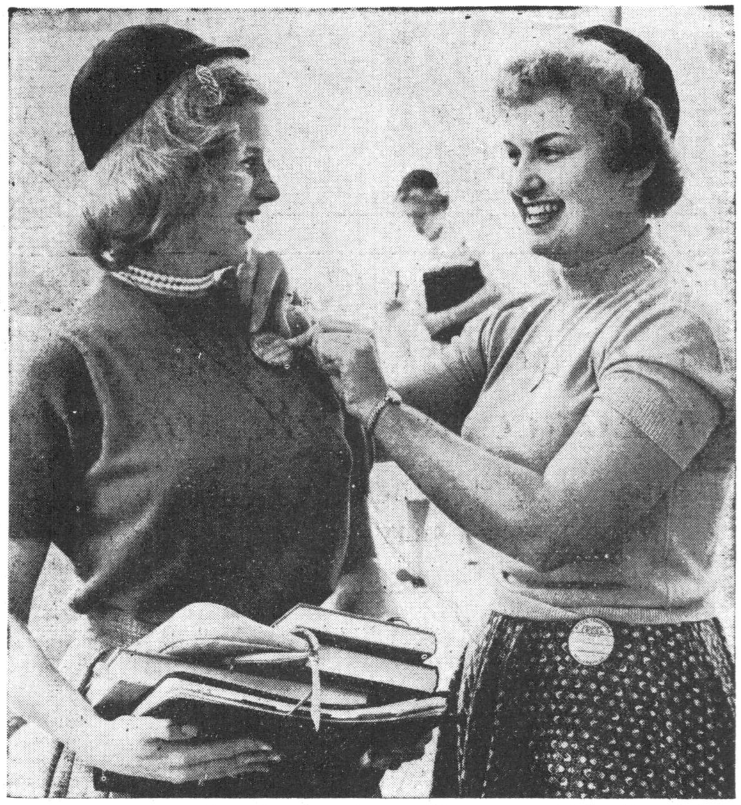

FROSH CUSTOMS require MSTC first-year students to wear "dinks" and identification buttons. Here Gail Hauck of Union, N. J. (right) adjusts badge for Jo Ellen Heberlein of Bryn Mawr.

"WE HAIL THEE, ALMA MATER!"—Reverent pause before the door of Old Main, with dink over heart and proper salutation, is compulsory for Franklin & Marshall College freshmen. Philadelphians (l-r) Dick Segal, Don Kane and Jay Federman comply.

BURYING THE BODY was part of MSTC's Freshman Week tomfoolery. Effigy which rebellious beginners hanged from upperclassmen tree lies sprawled on island in campus lake as oblivious students study, or something, on bench. End of restrictions depends upon football team's ability to win, which results in some very enthusiastic support on the part of the frosh cheering section.

'BACKWARD' STUDENTS—Coats and jackets worn in reverse, books carried in wastebaskets, rolled-up pants for men and dinks and name signs for all are among a long list of "customs" imposed on Elizabethtown College frosh. Shown above emerging from library are (l-r): Sara Cooper of Lancaster, Kenny Bowers of Landisville, Bill Pensyl of Portland, and Helen Louise Bucher of Mt. Joy.

CHEESECAKE of the male variety is provided at F&M by frosh Jay Demi of New Cumberland and John Remling of Scotch Plains, N. Y. Pants fight challenge will probably be issued to sophs tomorrow. Tribunal penalties on five violators have included lugging a bucket of stones and counting them when asked, and walking a five-foot plank which must be picked up and laid down every few steps.

SOPHOMORE WORD IS LAW—Elizabethtown College freshmen gather to hear the newest horrors dreamed up by their upperclass tormentors. Standing at left is Carlin Brightbill, of Cleona, chairman of the sophomore rules committee of the student senate. Among the regulations handed down were: no shaving for the boys, girls to wear their hair in five pigtails, everybody to wear coats and jackets backward and carry books in wastebskets or shopping bags, no jewelry to be worn, toothpicks to be supplied on demand, doors to be opened for upperclassmen, boys to wear ties and jackets at dinner and girls to have on stockings and heels.

Air Shots Show

$10,000,000 In New County Schools

COCALICO UNION High School at Denver, whose cost was about $1,-300,000, creates a striking pattern from the air with its fan-shaped parking area. More than 6,000 people attended open house at the school last Sunday.

SO BIG they can't be photographed adequately from ground level are Lancaster county's new high schools. Shown on this page are approximately $10,000,-000 in new school buildings, all either just occupied this fall or still under construction. Also, there are many new elementary schools, additions to present structures, and buildings planned to be started this term which add several millions to the total.

LANCASTER TOWNSHIP Junior High, erected at a cost of approximately $1,000,000, has spacious campus provided by athletic field.

COLUMBIA'S new $1,450,000 high school, delayed by shortage of structural steel, will occupy this site on Wissler's Hill, much of which has been re-graded for the project. Road at top right leads to Mt. Joy.

HEMPFIELD HIGH at Landisville, just completed this fall at a cost of approximately $1,344,000, will stage open house on Oct. 20, 21 and 22.

ELM TREE SCHOOL, built by Manheim Central District near Rt. 230 bypass to take care of children in southern Rapho Twp., is being used though grounds are still being completed (note tractor at lower right). It's typical of elementary schools in many sections of county.

LAMPETER-STRASBURG High School, erected at a cost of about $1,200,000, follows the generally popular pattern of one-and-two-story construction.

WARWICK UNION High School, a $2,000,000 structure, is being erected in the western section of Lititz adjoining the present athletic field.

PEQUEA VALLEY High, situated along historic Newport Road, cost about $1,350,000. [illegible] buses in rear, youngsters near flagpole.

WEATHER
(U. S. Weather Bureau Forecast for Lancaster, Cumberland, Lebanon, York, Adams and Franklin Counties):
Cool And Increasing Cloudiness Today, High 48-55, Occasional Rain Tonight, Low 45-50. Tomorrow Cloudy And Milder With Showers, Colder At Night.

Intelligencer Journal.

TELEPHONE 7-5251

The Leading Newspaper in the Garden Spot of America. Home Owned for Home Folks Since 1794

162nd Year.—No. 130. Official United States Census Figures Lancaster Metropolitan Area Population 234,717 LANCASTER, PA., TUESDAY MORNING, NOVEMBER 15, 1955. CITY TWENTY-SIX PAGES. 30c PER WEEK—5c Per Copy

WATER PROGRAM TO COST $7,700,000

HUGE SHOPPING CENTER LOOMS HERE

TRACT ALONG RT. 30 EAST IS SELECTED

Col. J. H. Wickersham Outlines Plans for Area That Covers 150 Acres

A multi-million dollar shopping center unlike anything yet planned for the Lancaster area is a distinct possibility in the near future—if there is enough local interest.

That was the word yesterday from Col. John H. Wickersham, Lancaster R4, head of John H. Wickersham Engineering and Construction Co.

Wickersham said yesterday he is thinking seriously of erecting a large-scale shopping center unlike anything now on the drawing boards for the Lancaster area.

OUTLINES HIS IDEA

His project, he said, would be on the order of City Line Center, in Philadelphia, or Suburban Square, Ardmore. It would include a large suburban department store, super food market and the other shops customarily found outside the larger cities.

But as yet, he admitted, it's still in his head. He said he hasn't started drawing up plans for the project on paper until he finds enough interest among local or national retail merchants to locate in the center. But he feels there is a definite need for such a development.

The shopping center, which would be developed over a period of years, would be located on the south side of Lincoln Highway East at the intersection with the Route 230 By-pass. The location would be a natural in terms of accessibility from all points of the county, he said.

Wickersham pointed out he has enough land to carry out his pro-

Turn To Page 8 For More Of CENTER

Bomber

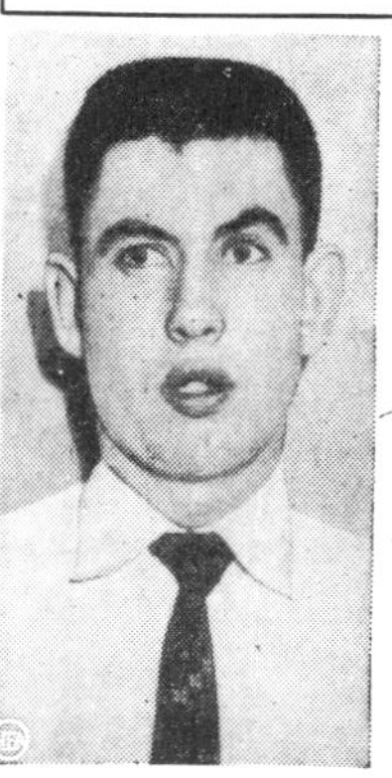

JOHN GILBERT GRAHAM

GRAHAM RELATES GRIM DETAILS OF AIRLINER BLAST

Tied 25 Sticks of Dynamite Together To Kill 44 Aboard Plane

DENVER, Nov. 14 (AP)—A young Denver construction and restaurant worker told tonight how he tied 25 sticks of dynamite together to make a bomb that exploded aboard a United Air Lines plane near Longmont, Colo., Nov. 1.

All 44 persons aboard, including the mother of the man, John Gilbert (Jack) Graham, were killed.

U. S. Atty. Donald E. Kelley said Graham, 23-year-old forger, had

Turn To Page 22 For More Of GRAHAM

LEADER SAID STUDYING NET INCOME TAX

2 Per Cent Levy May Be Keystone Of New State Package

HARRISBURG, Nov. 14 (AP) — Gov. Leader was reported today to be considering a 2 per cent tax on net income, as determined by federal deductions, as the keystone to a new tax package.

The levy would raise 350 million dollars between now and May 31, 1957.

The second part of the program, under discussion as the solution to the Commonwealth's long tax impasse, was reported to be either a 1 or 2 per cent levy on the business a Pennsylvania wholesaler does with a manufacturer. The yield on such a levy is still uncertain although the estimate ranges as high as 100 million dollars.

The two-part program would see abandonment of the governor's previous proposal, already passed by the House, to increase the 5 per cent corporate net income tax to 6 per cent.

STILL SPECULATIVE

An administration source who declined quotation by name, emphasized that the program was still in the speculative stage—that no definite decision has been made.

The income levy would be imposed, in effect, after such exemptions or deductions as those for dependents, interest payments, medical expenses, tax payments and unsual losses are allowed under federal income tax return on the baes of which federal taxes are computed as differentiated from the tax-on-tax proposal now before the House under Democratic sponsorship. The latter calls for a 7 per cent levy on the amount a Pennsylvanian pays in federal income taxes.

In another development, the House received four government reorganization plans from the governor.

They would strip from the Public Instruction Department the administration of a long list of state

Turn To Page 22 For More Of LEADER

MSTC Given Permission By State To Spend $250,000 For All-Purpose Athletic Field

FIRST PHASE—Workmen are shown as they applied the top layer of fine cinders to Millersville State Teachers College's new track that encircles the new football field, construction of which was recently finished at a cost of $27,750. Photo shows the track's 220-yard straightaway to the right of which will be erected permanent stands to seat 3,000 for football games, with dressing rooms, showers and storage space beneath them. (Intell Photo)

COMPLETION OF FOOTBALL FIELD MARKS 1ST STEP

Long-Range Program At College To Require 5 or 6 Years

By MARVIN MILLER
Intell Sports Editor

A long-range plan to provide Millersville State Teachers College with one of the finest athletic fields in Pennsylvania at a cost of approximately a quarter of a million dollars has been approved by the State Department of Property and Supplies and is in the blueprint stage, it was revealed yesterday.

Announcement of the planned project which will be carried out in eight separate phases of construction over a period of five or six years, was made by Paul W. McCloud of McCloud and Scatchard, landscape architects of Lititz, who have been retained by the State to lay out the field and have recommended an integrated order of construction of the facilities.

$254,983.15 ESTIMATE

The estimated cost of completion, including the building of a modern 4,000 person seating capacity football stadium, running track, baseball diamond, softball diamond, a soccer field, four tennis courts and two parking areas, is $54,983.15.

Approval of the athletic field

Turn To Page 18 For More Of MSTC

INTEREST RATE NOT INCLUDED IN ESTIMATE

City Authority Announces Figures After Meeting To Discuss Bond Issue

Lancaster's new water improvement and expansion program will cost approximately $7,700,000. The figure doesn't include any of the final interest charges on the bond issue that must be floated to cover the program.

The estimate was released yesterday by the City of Lancaster Authority following a two-and-a-half hour session with representatives of City Council, engineers, financial advisors and financial counsel.

The session was closed to the press. It was a special meeting at the office of the authority's solicitor, William G. Johnstone Jr.

The $7.7 million figure is higher than any of the estimated figures for the overall project discussed to date.

FORECAST BY INTELL

Last spring, the *Intelligencer Journal* forecast the cost of the program might run to seven million dollars because of suburban extensions and possible acquisition of the Belmont Water Co. The purchase of Belmont Water Co. has long since been dropped as a possibility by the authority.

Previous estimates on the project had ranged between six-and-a-half million and seven million dollars. Thus yesterdays announcement of 7.7 million dollars came as a surprise to most observers.

The original estimate of the project was first placed at five-and a half million dollars, but the figure was revised when the authority began considering extensions of city water into suburban areas.

W. E. Alexander, authority chairman, said the suburban extensions account for much of the added cost to the program.

A breakdown of the unofficial low bids submitted last week for

Turn To Page 8 For More Of WATER

It's Somebody's Baby Now!

By-Pass 'Bridge To Nowhere' Turned Over To Manheim Twp.

One of Lancaster County's ill-starred landmarks — "The Bridge to Nowhere" — is back in the news.

Several quite audible gasps of astonishment were heard at last night's meeting of the Manheim Twp. commissioners when they learned the state has turned the now infamous span over to the township for maintenance.

The almost unanimous reaction of the Commissioners was an "Oh, no."

Built in 1953 over the Route 230 by-pass at Homeland, the structure cost an estimated $80,000. The southern access to the bridge leads from Green Terrace. On the northern end of the span is only a field.

H. Richard Taylor read the letter from State Secretary of Highways Joseph J. Lawler informing them of their responsibilities. The letter said, in part, ". . . it was necessary to construct a local service road. . ." during the building of the bypass.

"This road was constructed by Authority of Section 3, of the Act of May 29, 1945, P. L. . .1108, and in accordance of that act, the maintenance of that road becomes the responsibility of your township."

The commissioners say they don't want it but as of last night were undecided what their course of action, if any, would be.

A three-man committee will study sites today for the erection of signs prohibiting trucks in the Grandview Heights area. The signs will be put up sometime this week. Although the truck ban ordinance is already in effect, it has not been enforced because of the lack of signs, Wayne Winters, commissioner, reported.

In another letter the Manheim Twp. commissioners were stymied, at least for the immediate future, in their efforts to have the Bel-

Turn To Page 8 For More Of MANHEIM-TWP.

Gettysburg Welcome Warm For Returning Eisenhowers

GETTYSBURG, Pa., Nov. 14 (AP)—President and Mrs. Eisenhower returned to Gettysburg today and a heart tingling home-coming welcome from "the people who are going to be our neighbors, God willing."

Thousands of them turned out in historic Lincoln Square, jamming the streets, perching on balconies and in windows, crowding onto roof tops.

Before the little, informal speeches could get under way, the high school band and what looked like most of Gettysburg's 7,200 citizens swung into "Happy birthday, dear Mamie."

BOUQUET OF ROSES

Burgess William G. Weaver told the chief executive and First Lady "how glad and happy we are that you have made Gettysburg your home." His daughter, Patricia, 13, handed Mrs. Eisenhower — 59 to-

Turn To Page 8 For More Of GETTYSBURG

UNSEASONAL WARMTH DUE TO END TODAY, HIGH OF 55 EXPECTED

It was fine while it lasted!

The unseasonal weather of the past two days was expected to depart last night and early today with a 20-degree drop in temperature from yesterday's 26-year record.

The Ephrata Weather Station recorded a high of 76 degrees, highest Nov. 14 reading since 1929. The mild temperatures were accompanied by alternately clear and partly cloudy skies.

But the Weather Bureau's forecast said today would be marked by increasing cloudiness and colder temperatures, with a chance of rain in the late afternoon or evening.

Columbia Speed Limit Dropped From 35 To 25

An ordinance lowering the speed limit on Columbia borough streets was unanimously passed by Borough Council last night.

The new ordinance changes the speed limit from 35 to 25 MPH on all borough streets except on Legislative Rts. 30 and 441 and Ninth Street to the Ironville Pike.

Council also recommended that the school zones be posted with 15 MPH speed signs as this is permitted by the State Highways Department for a distance of an eighth of a mile from each school building.

It was announced that the State Highways Department also agreed to paint crosswalks on the Lincoln Highway at the east and west entrances to the Columbia Malleable Castings Co. and to set up no

Turn To Page 8 For More Of COLUMBIA

"We Lead All The Rest"

FARM CORNER

By JOE WACHTMAN

Garden Spot Angus Quintet Tops Eastern National Show

For the third consecutive year a Lancaster County group of five Aberdeen-Angus steers yesterday was chosen best 4-H quintet at the Eastern National Livestock Exposition at Timonium, Md.

In addition, the Garden Spot's second entry of five Hereford steers placed fourth among 15 county groups competing. This was also a duplication of last year's judging.

In individual competition Lancaster County 4-H'ers rolled up a score of one first place, two seconds, a third, fifth, eighth, ninth, two tenths and a 13th place finish, with their ten baby beef entries.

Clyde Brubaker, Ephrata R1, also exhibited the champion Hampshire wether among 4-H Club animals in the sheep show.

The winning Angus group was composed of animals shown by Dorothy Stehman, Lancaster R3; Thelma Cassel, Manheim R1; Donald Hastings, Kirkwood; Betty Bowman, Ronks R1; and Donald Rutt, Peach Bottom.

For Miss Stehman it marked the second year in a row in which she was a member of the winning quintet. She also topped the county Angus group in individual placing by winning a second place ribbon.

Miss Cassel was third in the individual judging, Hastings ninth, and Miss Bowman 10th. All four competed in the middleweight class composed of 41 entries. Rutt was 13th in the heavyweight class made up of 37 animals.

The Lancaster County Hereford group of five was fourth among 15 quintets from states in the East.

Highest individual placing by a county contestant was the first place finish of Jane Greiner, Manheim R4, over a field of 35 in the lightweight class of Hereford judging.

Clyde Brubaker, Ephrata R1, was fifth in the same class. In middleweight Hereford competition Walter Augsburger, Reinholds R1,

Turn To Page 21 For More Of FARM CORNER

Weather Calendar

COMPARATIVE TEMPERATURES

Station	High	Low
Water Works	74	47
Ephrata	76	48
Last Year (Ephrata)	64	32
Official High for Year July 23		105
Official Low for Year Feb. 3		-5
Character of Day		Partly Cloudy

WINDS
Direction W Avg. Velocity 14 mph

HUMIDITY
8 a.m. 93% 11 a.m. 68% 2 p.m. 59%
5 p.m. 62% 8 p.m. 77%
Average Humidity 72%

SUN
Rises 6:48 a.m. Sets 4:49 p.m.

MOON
Sets 5:31 p.m. First Quarter, Nov. 22

STARS
Morning—Mars, Jupiter
Evening—Venus, Saturn

NEARBY FORECASTS
(U.S. Weather Bureau)

Southeastern Pennsylvania and Southern New Jersey — Increasing cloudiness and cool today followed by rain at night, highest in the 50's. Tomorrow cloudy with showers and little change in temperature.

Central and Northeastern Pennsylvania —Increasing cloudiness and cool today, high 45 north to 56 south portion. Occasional rain and cool tonight. Tomorrow showers and mild turning colder tomorrow night.

Lower Potomac and Chesapeake Bay—Northerly winds 15-20 miles per hour becoming northeast. Increasing cloudiness today with rain likely at night. Visibility mostly good.

Maryland — Increasing cloudiness today followed by occasional rain in the west portion in the afternoon and east portion at night. Showers, windy and mild tomorrow becoming colder late afternoon or at night.

Delaware — Increasing cloudiness today followed by occasional rain at night. Showers, windy and mild tomorrow becoming colder at night.

CITY AUTO CRASHES UP, INJURIES DOWN COMPARED WITH '54

The number of automobile accidents in the city for the first 10 months of this year continues to run ahead of the corresponding period a year ago, but the number of persons injured is lagging behind, Police Commissioner Fred G. McCartney revealed in his monthly police report.

There were 114 automobile accidents in the city during October, resulting in injury to 17 persons. This compares with October 1954 when there were 109 accidents with injuries to 29 persons.

For the 10 month period, there have been 905 accidents with injuries to 198 persons and two fatalities. Last year at the same time there were 791 accidents, three fatalties and 240 injuries.

8-COUNTY STUDY OF CONSERVATION NEEDS PROPOSED

Lower Susquehanna Watershed Problems Explored At Harrisburg Session

A committee of community leaders in eight counties, including Lancaster, will be named to study the "need for local watershed associations" in the Lower Susquehanna area.

This was the substance of a resolution adopted at a district-level conference on conservation conducted in Harrisburg last night by the Pennsylvania Chamber of Commerce.

The committee is to be named by Row W. Engle, president of the Harrisburg Chamber who presided at the conservation session in the Hotel Harrisburger.

The resolution also instructs the committee "to explore the proposition of forming a lower Susquehanna River watershed council to serve and coordinate the efforts of local

Turn To Page 8 For More Of WATERSHED

ASSESSMENT APPEALS TO BE HEARD TODAY

The Lancaster County Commissioners will sit today to hear appeals from 1956 real estate assessments in two boroughs and five townships.

The political subdivisions are Christiana and Strasburg boroughs, and Sadsbury, Salisbury, Paradise, Leacock and Strasburg townships.

The first of nine appeal days was held yesterday with no appeals being filed by property holders in Quarryville borough, and Fulton, Little Britain, Drumore, East Drumore, Colerain, Providence, Eden, Bart, Martic and Conestoga Twps.

City Loses New Bid For Taxes From Former Manheim Twp. Land

The Lancaster School Board yesterday lost another round in its legal battle to get school taxes from two Manheim Twp. properties annexed to the city in 1952.

The Commonwealth Court at Harrisburg denied an appeal from a State Council of Education ruling which gave Manheim Twp. the school taxes from the RCA plant property and the property of Elmer Espenshade.

Judge Walter R. Sohn, in denying the appeal, said the State Council of Education "is the sole and final authority to decide the propriety of an annexation of land for school purposes."

An estimated $45,000 in annual school taxes to Manheim Twp. is involved.

The case went to the Commonwealth Court as a test of the constitutionality of the powers of the state council to rule in annexation cases where voters may reside in one district for school tax purposes and in another for municipal purposes.

The appeal was filed on April 8, 1954 by Attorney Theodore L. Brubaker, solicitor of the Lancaster City School District.

TEST CASE

The test case, on a phase never before decided by the courts, attacked the action of the council in awarding to Manheim Twp. the school tax money from the two properties, while the municipal taxes on the properties went to the city.

In his appeal, Brubaker contended that a "no-man's" land was created by the decision, whereby residents of the tracts vote on one

Turn To Page 8 For More Of EDUCATION

BODIES OF TWO BROTHERS FOUND IN BURNED SHACK

ALLENTOWN, Pa., Nov. 14 (AP)—The bodies of two young brothers were found today in the ruins of a burned out wooden shack and police investigated the possibility of foul play.

The badly burned victims, William Stengele, 8, and his brother, David, 6, were identified by their Mother, Mrs. Adele Stengele, 26, from bits of clothing found in the ruins.

She told police the children apparently played truant from school and were not missed until they failed to return for lunch with their brother, Dale, 7.

SEARCH CONDUCTED

She learned of the tragedy while conducting an extensive search of the neighborhood.

Her husband, Roland, 27, a laborer at the Bethlehem Steel Corp. plant in nearby Bethlehem was at work. Police accompanied by a minister were sent to the plant to

Turn To Page 8 For More Of BODIES

BUTTON BUCK DARTS IN AUTOIST'S PATH, KILLED, CAR DAMAGED

A button buck was killed last night as it crossed the New Danville Pike, near the filtration plant, about 10:45.

The buck was run over by a car operated by James M. Witmer, Lancaster R6, resulting in extensive damage to the grill, headlight and fender of the auto. Another deer narrowly escaped injury as it, too, crossed the highway at the same time.

Game Protector John Haverstick reported the deer, which weighed 100 pounds, will be given to the Children's Aid Society, Neffsville, today.

President, Enroute To Farm, Waves To Gettysburg Crowds

GETTYSBURG, Pa., Nov. 14—President Eisenhower (right) waves from the hatch in the roof of his car as he leaves Gettysburg's town square today, on the way to his farm. Waving to the President are school children and others who jammed the square to welcome him and the First Lady back to their home. The President will continue his convalescence there. In background is the Lincoln Room where President Lincoln stayed after delivery of his famed Gettysburg Address. (AP Wirephoto)

Cleveland Slight Favorite Over Los Angeles Monday

Merry Christmas

SUNDAY NEWS Sports

Merry Christmas

1955 Lancaster County Sports In Review

From Donegal's Cage Winners To The Rise And Fall Of Baseball

Brilliant individual performances, thrilling team triumphs and the heartaches of passing friends combined to make the local sports year 1955 a very memorable one.

Names like Jay Metzler, Paul Ely, Billy Werkiser, Johnny Parker, Lefty Bob Nonnenmocher, Hank Biasatti, Don Martin, Jack Shertzer, Billy Haverstick, Bill Stuifbergen, Don Plarski, Joe Pahr, and Don Wert were steady headliners throughout the year.

Donegal's basketball champions long will be remembered. Millersville STC opened the year with a winning cage team and closed it the same way. McCaskey, too, had a court champion to add to its perennial tennis winnings. The baseball Roses had a wonderful year — on the playing field.

Miseries accompanied the local professional clubs, though. The Roses, both basketball and baseball, passed away. Their passing was not taken lightly. And there were others. Tom Floyd, Pete Flick and Harry Goodhart. They, too, were part of the scene. And there were others, both big and little. All contributed something to this passing year.

Champions All

ART BYXBEE

K. Simmons

G. Simmons

MICKEY DRAUDE

Gene Crider

June Honoman

JACK SHERTZER

JANUARY

McCaskey's cage team opened the year by losing to William Penn, 69-59, but a fellow named Paul Ely scored 32 points. More was to be heard from him as Coach Eddie Haller's Tornado went on to win the first half championship in the Central Penn League.

Ralph (Pete) Flick was honored by the Lancaster Sportswriters and Broadcasters Association for his contributions to local sports.

Donegal finished out the month unbeaten with 13 straight victories to its credit.

Johnny Russell scored 65 points for St. Luke's in a YMCA Church cage loop game. St. John's won 18 straight Church games before bowing to Ross St., 82-77.

Ely's 23 points helped McCaskey defeat Lebanon, 63-44, and gave the Tornado the first half championship in the Central Penn.

Millersville's tourney bound cagers notched their ninth straight win of the season and 21st consecutive in Teachers Conference play, stopping East Stroudsburg, 73-62.

Lampeter - Strasburg won six County High League games in a row before losing to Paradise, 48-42. Manheim Twp.'s Sunny Warfel tallied 43 points in a 92-50 win over Lititz that marked the Blue Streaks' seventh straight triumph.

FEBRUARY

St. Joseph College outscored Millersville, 64-55, to nip the Marauders' unbeaten skein at nine.

Donegal and Manheim Twp. clinched titles in Section 1 and 2 respectively. The Indians edged Columbia, 55-53, before 1,700 fans at Mt. Joy while the Streaks also won by two points, 57-55, over Ephrata. The triumphs marked the 15th straight for both teams.

Russell won the Church League scoring title with an average of 42.5 for 14 games. Monk Harrison, Church of Christ, was runnerup with 34.9 and had a high total of 828.

Lena McConnell rolled a high 549 to lead the Oblenders team to the Class A Lanco Women's Bowling Championship. Betty Gochenaur captured the All-Events title with a 530 single, 527 in doubles and 495 in team event for a 1,552 total.

Metzler's field goal with ten seconds to play gave Donegal a 29-26 playoff victory over Manheim Twp., before an audience of 2,300 fans at McCaskey. The crowd was believed to be the largest ever to see a basketball game in Lancaster County. The win was Donegal's 19th in a row while Manheim Twp. lost its first after 17 triumphs.

Ely set a new McCaskey scoring record of 41 points as McCaskey lost to John Harris, 71-70.

Donegal won the County High League championship on a 66-46 decision over Lampeter-Strasburg before 1,900 fans at McCaskey.

Millersville's cagers completed their regular season with a 17-2 record but dropped a 54-48 NAIA tourney game to Geneva.

Bill Fisher, Millersville STC, won the 157-lb. championship in the Teachers Conference wrestling tourney.

Lancaster Roses' cage fans got a look at the famed O'Brien twins, Johnny and Eddie, but the pro game was on its last legs here and it didn't return for the 1955-56 season.

MARCH

County High League teams were hooked up in PIAA playoffs that saw Donegal hike its victory streak to 25 before it dropped a 67-63 decision to Fountain Hill in the Class B playoffs. Lampeter-Strasburg and Paradise were eliminated early while Manheim Twp. moved along in Class A playoffs before Reading halted the Streaks, 74-45.

Reading was the Central Penn titleholder. It gained the pennant on a 70-64 victory over McCaskey. The Tornado did a complete about face in second half play finishing in the cellar. The title game was played before 5,000 fans at Hershey. It was the second game of a twin bill with Donegal defeating Eastern York County, 77-61, in a "B" playoff tilt.

Geneva took its best-of-three NAIA playoff series from Millersville, 78-67.

Metzler was County High League scoring champion with an average of 28.2 in eight games.

Elizabethtown College finished with a cage record of 14-9 while F & M posted a 6-11.

Local matmen, Rod Gibble, Manheim Central; Herb Witmer, Columbia; Ken LaBone, Manheim Twp.; Bill LaBone, Manheim Twp.; Walt Kottmyer, McCaskey and Dave Fritz, Columbia, gained individual titles in the District 3 wrestling tourney. Gibble, Bill LaBone and Kottmyer went on to Eastern championships.

Bill Wosnack of F & M won the 200-yard backstroke event in the Mid-Atlantic College swim championships.

St. John's defeated St. Luke's, 110-66, to add the YMCA Church League's playoff title to its regular season championship.

Billy Werkiser and Johnny Parker, Millersville, were named to the Teachers Conference All-Star first team. Werkiser set a school record for the season of 391 points.

The area college scoring crown went to Lebanon Valley's Howie Landa with a 24.5 average for 24 games on 173 field goals and 242 fouls for a total of 58. Werkiser was runnerup with 17.7.

George Shoemaker, Lancaster Merchants, won the Industrial League point crown with a 23.3 norm while the Lanco League crown went to Jack Keener, Rothsville, with 23.8.

APRIL

The John Porter Furniture team composed of Bill Binkle, Fred Draude, Will Gingrich, Dick Graeff and Andy Gridina won the

Page 28—NAMES

Won Run For The Roses

Hank Biasatti, field manager, and Frank Spair, business manager, led the Lancaster Red Roses to the Play-off championship of the Piedmont League in 1955. This great victory marked the first time that the Red Roses had won a title in organized baseball since 1945.

Athletes Who Excelled On The Lancaster Sports Scene In 1955

JOHN PARKER—Basketball

JAY METZLER—Basketball

WILL RISSER—Soccer

CLARA KILLAM—Field Hockey

TOM HEADRICK—Soccer

R. NONNENMOCHER — Baseball

DON MARTIN—Track

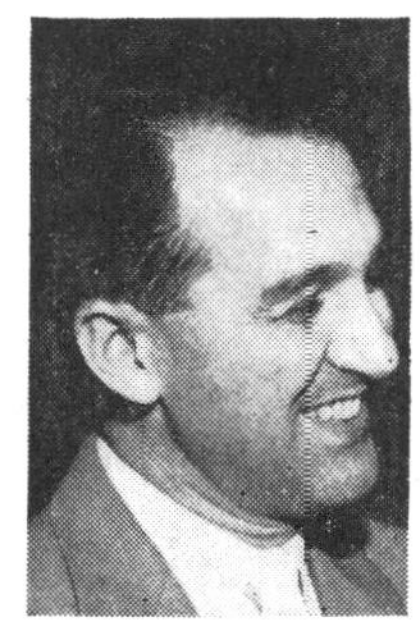

TONY TURCHETTA—Football

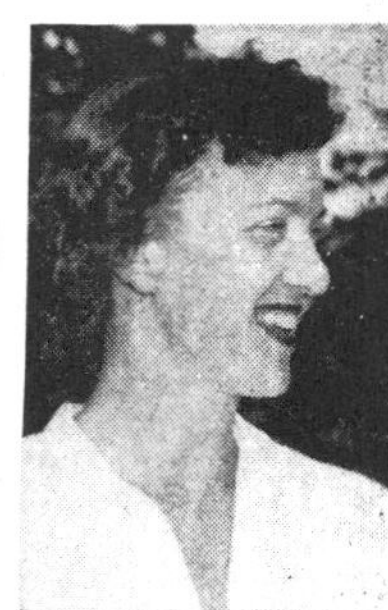

NANCY PADEN — Tennis

SALLY LIED—Tennis

BILL WERKISER—Basketball

BILLY HAVERSTICK—Golf

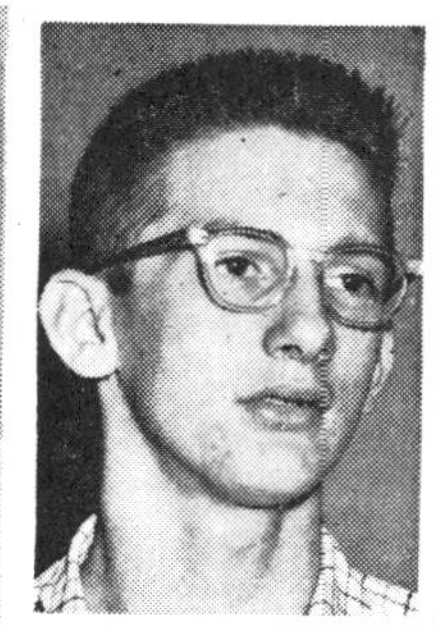

PAUL ELY—Basketball

DON WERT—Football

Injury-Beset Pro Rams May Pull Surprise

By BOB MYERS

LOS ANGELES, Dec. 24 (AP)—The machine - like Cleveland Browns, appearing in the title game for the sixth straight year, are favored to defeat the surprising Los Angeles Rams two days hence for the 1955 championship of the National Football League.

The Browns' margin of favoritism is slim, and few would be too surprised if the injury-beset Rams pulled another of a series of upsets Monday afternoon.

But harking back to one year ago, when the forces of Coach Paul Brown humiliated a great Detroit Lions team, 56-10, the cause looks bleak for the Rams and their coach, Sid Gillman, who already has achieved amazing success in his freshman year in professional football.

Attendance in Memorial Coliseum is expected to range from 60,000 up, provided the weather is satisfactory. The Rams have averaged 56,000 in their six home league games this season.

This annual struggle for the NFL crown will be televised nationally over the National Broadcasting Co. network, with the Los Angeles area blacked out.

Kickoff time is 1 p.m., Pacific Standard Time.

Herr Otto Graham, the field wizard of the Browns, led the club to nine victories, two losses and one tie in winning the Eastern Conference title.

Quarterback Norman Van Brocklin and his patchwork Rams won the Western Division title with an 8-3-1 record.

This will be Graham's second, and final, farewell to football. He retired after the 1954 wars but relented and returned at Brown's urging when the club got off to a poor start in the preleague season exhibitions.

Four times the Browns went down in that period, including a 38-21 loss to the Rams. Then No. 14 reappeared in the Cleveland quarterback spot and the club returned to its normal winning ways.

This is the third meeting for the championship between the two teams. Both rank as epics in a league abundant in storied contests.

Week's Top Bouts On TV

By International News Service

Thirty-three-year-old Willie Pep, freshly inspired by Sugar Ray Robinson's dramatic proof that old champions do come back, takes on a 22-year-old youngster making his first nationally-televised start in this week's feature fight.

The two-time featherweight titleholder continues his quest for a shot at the lightweight diadem when he meets aggressive Andy Arel of Massena, New York, in a scheduled ten-rounder Wednesday night at the Miami Beach Auditorium (ABC).

Chico Vejar of Stamford, Connecticut, the tenth-ranking welterweight contender, meets Paolo Melis of Italy in Monday night's feature at the St. Nicholas Arena (Dumont). No fight is scheduled for Friday.

East And West Elevens Accent "The Offense"

SAN FRANCISCO, Dec. 24 (AP)—What would you do, as a football coach, if you were handed two-dozen stars and told to have them ready to go against another hand-picked squad after nine days practice?

You'd accent the offense and let the defense take care of itself, the same way Woody Hayes of Ohio State and Jess Hill of Southern California are doing as they prepare their East and West squads for the 31st annual Shrine Game here next Saturday.

And, if past performances mean anything, you'd be right — the defense would work itself out.

Three of the last four Shrine classics have been decided by a single point, with the East winning each one. It was 13-12 last year, 21-20 two years earlier and 15-14 the year before that. Only in the 1953 game, which the West won, 31-7, did the pattern fail.

Hayes, whose version of the split T carried Ohio State to two straight Big 10 titles, will lean heavily in Saturday's game on the man who made it work — Howard (Hopalong) Cassady, the 178-pound two-time All-America halfback. The Buckeye bouncer, handicapped the first couple of practices by a heavy cold, has been pronounced ready to go.

But Hayes has indicated he won't rely exclusively on the pounding running game with which he pulverized Big 10 foes.

"Figure we may stick in a few pass patterns with this squad," he said after a workout at the University of Santa Clara. "(Stu) Holcomb knows a little bit about that sort of thing and we have a couple of pretty good passers on hand."

Holcomb, assisting Hayes with Rip Engle of Penn State, had one of the nation's best passers in Lenny Dawson at Purdue last fall. Holcomb gave up the Boilermaker coaching job to become athletic director at Northwestern.

"Pretty Good" Passers

The "pretty good" passers are Iowa's Gerry Reichow and Illinois' Em Lindbeck. Between them they completed 87 of 147 tosses for 1,307 yards in 1955. Reichow, the likely East starter at quarterback, wound up seventh nationally in total offense with 1,091 yards.

Head Coach Weeb Ewbank, Buddy Young, Of Colts, To Attend Local Sportswriters Dinner

Head coach Weeb Ewbank, of the Baltimore Colts, and one of his star halfbacks, Buddy Young, and one of the National Football League's all-time greats, will be among the nationally prominent sports figures who will be present at the tenth annual Lancaster Sportswriters and Broadcasters banquet at the Hotel Brunswick, Monday night January 23.

WEEB EWBANK

Ewbank, who will rate close-up as the NFL's coach of the year, because of his spectacular performance in piloting the Colts from out of nowhere into strong contention in the pro race, will be making his first appearence in Lancaster for any sporting event. Before assuming the top job at Baltimore, Ewbank was backfield coach for Paul Brown, at Cleveland, and is regarded in the trade as a formidable strategist.

Ewbank faced a job of developing three or four of the top rookies of the year during the past season including Alan (The Horse) Ameche, and Weeb is being lauded throughout the country for his splendid job.

Buddy Young is one of the great all-time greats of the NFL. An All-American at Illinois, he has been in the pro ranks for many years, but was still good enough during the past season to win a regular berth with the Colts. Young's vast experience in the pro league should make interesting material.

Don Kellett, president and general manager of the Colts, a former Boston Red Sox and Lancaster Red Roses shortstp, and prior to that an all-time great at Penn in football, baseball and basketball, who arranged for the appearence here of Ewbank and Young, also will attend the banquet if he gets back from the NFL meeting on the Coast in time. Don expressed the hope he could be present in order to renew the many acquaintenances he made here when he played baseball at Stumpf Field.

BUDDY YOUNG

8 Debutantes Introduced at Assembly's Christmas Cotillion

Three-generation groups were prominent at the Christmas Cotillion at the Lancaster Country Club. Here, Mrs. Rufus A. Fulton (left) and her mother, Mrs. John B. Canale, of Memphis, Tenn., chat with Mrs. Fulton's daughter, Miss Eunice Canale Fulton, one of the debutantes.

Miss Barbara Mann, in the group of young women introduced at the Lancaster Assembly party, pauses between dances to talk with her mother, Mrs. A. Kenneth Mann Jr., and her grandmother, Mrs. George S. Mann, of Millersville, in the foyer of the Lancaster Country Club.

Mrs. John L. Atlee Jr., (left), who was in the receiving line at the Cotillion and Mrs. John L. Atlee Sr. enjoy a conversation with Miss Ann Atlee, daughter of Dr. and Mrs. Atlee Jr., who was among the debutantes presented to the Lancaster Assembly last night.

New Era Photos

Mrs. Arnold Francis, of Orange, N. J., (left), among the guests at the debut of her granddaughter, Miss Jane L'Hommedieu, (center), is seen here with the debutante's mother, Mrs. F. Arnold L'Hommedieu in the midst of the debutante's array of flowers at the Cotillion.

Miss Carolyn Franklin, daughter of Mrs. Frederick S. Franklin Jr., and the late Mr. Franklin, admires the flowers she received at the Cotillion last night when she was in the group of debutantes.

New Era Photos

Miss Dorothy C. Hartman, daughter of Mr. and Mrs. Lewis E. Hartman, pauses at the lame-draped table holding her floral gifts at the Lancaster Assembly party where she made her debut last night.

Over 400 Attend Party Held at Country Club

THE SEASON'S most brilliant party—a Christmas Cotillion at which eight local debutantes were introduced—was held last night at the Lancaster Country Club, with over 400 attending.

The event was sponsored by the Lancaster Assembly.

The debutantes introduced were: Miss Ann Atlee, daughter of Dr. and Mrs. John L. Atlee Jr., 1315 Homestead Lane.

Miss Barbara Breneman, daughter of Mr. and Mrs. Joseph M. Breneman, Hamilton Road.

Miss Carolyn Franklin, daughter of Mrs. Frederick S. Franklin Jr., 1283 Wheatland Ave., and the late Mr. Franklin.

Miss Eunice Canale Fulton, daughter of Mr. and Mrs. Rufus A. Fulton, 155 River Drive.

Miss Dorothy C. Hartman, daughter of Mr. and Mrs. Lewis E. Hartman, 1305 Homestead Lane.

Miss Jane L'Hommedieu, daughter of Mr. and Mrs. F. Arnold L'Hommedieu, Lancaster R2.

Miss Barbara England Mann, daughter of Mr. and Mrs. A. Kenneth Mann Jr., 155 Wilson Drive; and

Miss Jane Watt, daughter of Mr. and Mrs. Charles G. Watt, 1025 Marietta Ave.

Several grandmothers of the debutantes were present at the Assembly. Miss Fulton's grandmother, Mrs. John B. Canale of Memphis, Tenn., and Miss L'Hommedieu's grandmother, Mrs. Arnold Francis of Orange, N. J., were among the out-of-town guests who attended. Also present were Miss Mann's grandmother, Mrs. George S. Mann, and Miss Atlee's grandmother, Mrs. John L. Atlee Sr.

RECEIVING the guests with the debutantes in the foyer of the club were the wives of the Assembly's Board of Directors: Mrs. S. C. Slaymaker, Mrs. Ben E. Mann, Mrs. J. Nevin Schroeder, Mrs. William H. Hager Jr., Mrs. S. R. Zimmerman Jr., Mrs. Arthur B. Sinkler, Mrs. J. Hale Steinman, and Mrs. John L. Atlee Jr. William Seawall stood at the head of the line and introduced the guests.

Following tradition, each of the debutantes danced the opening waltz with her father or a member of her family. The dance was led by Mr. Breneman and his daughter, Barbara. Miss Franklin danced with her brother, Fritz.

The girls were attired in full-length white ball gowns, long white gloves, and carried bouquets of flowers in pastel shades.

The gift corsages which they received from members of the Assembly and guests, were arranged on eight lame-draped tables along the left wall of the foyer. During the evening, the debutantes carried the various corsages while dancing.

MISS ATLEE wore a white taffeta gown designed with a strapless bodice and bouffant skirt trimmed with insets of shirring.

Her mother was attired in a gray silk faille gown, with a sheath skirt fashioned with back fullness.

Among the floral gifts which Miss Atlee received were a spray corsage of yellow orchids, and a fan-shaped corsage of white carnations.

MISS BRENEMAN was attired in a white satin and net gown, with sloping waistline accentuated by a huge tier of net which cascaded down the side of the bouffant skirt.

Mrs. Breneman wore black chiffon patterned with a skirt in soft folds trimmed with dull black sequins.

A bevy of pink ca[illegible]s and rose buds were among the debutante's corsages.

BANDS of silver and white hand embroidery trimmed the bouffant skirt of Miss Franklin's gown, designed with a strapless bodice.

Her mother wore a black taffeta sheath trimmed in black velvet.

One of the debutante's corsages was a circle of red roses centered with a cymbidium orchid.

THE STRAPLESS gown worn by Miss Fulton was of silk tulle and brocade embroidered in pearl and rhinestone leaves.

Mrs. Fulton wore a champagne brocade and satin sheath gown with matching stole.

Miss Fulton's flowers included a corsage of rose buds centered with large crushed carnations, and a similar bouquet of camellias centered with a large orchid.

MISS HARTMAN was attired in nylon tulle garnished with iridescent paillettes on the strapless bodice and bouffant skirt.

Her mother wore black satin fashioned with a bustle effect in back.

The over-all color scheme of Miss Hartman's flowers featured shades of pink, with a huge spray of pink rose buds included in the array.

UNUSUAL bac[illegible]atment highlighted the bouffant skirt of Miss L'Hommedieu's gown of white peau de soie. The fitted bodice was designed with shoulder straps.

Mrs. L'Hommedieu wore aqua peau de soie with back fullness accenting the sheath skirt.

The debutante's flowers included a huge spray of long-stemmed pink roses, and other bouquets in pink, white, and rose shades.

MISS MANN was attired in white tulle fashioned with a V-neck bodice of tulle ruffles adorned with rhinestones. The bouffant skirt was patterned in an apron effect of tulle ruffles.

Mrs. Mann wore rose silk taffeta with a pale pink stole.

Miss Mann's corsages featured a large assortment of orchids and rose buds in pastel shades.

WHITE TAFFETA embellished with rhinestones was worn by Miss Watt. The bodice was designed with narrow shoulder straps.

Mrs. Watt was attired in gray chiffon, with a tucked rhinestone yoke and full skirt.

A white satin muff with pink carnations was among Miss Watt's floral gifts.

Each of the debutantes had two escorts for the cotillion.

The foyer where the debutantes were introduced was draped with silver lame embellished with Southern smilax and twinkling pink and white star lights. The ballroom and adjoining porches were similarly decorated, and the orchestra played on a stage surrounded with frosted twigs and lights.

The over-all color theme of pink and white was carried out in the dining room, where a white Christmas tree trimmed with pink balls was featured. Four white lamp-posts filled with clusters of pink leaves and white Christmas balls stood at each end of the dining area.

Supper was served at midnight.

Among the dinner parties which preceded the Cotillion was one given by Miss Peggy Steinman, daughter of Mr. and Mrs. J. Hale Steinman, of Conestoga House, in the Hamilton Club, for Miss Atlee and Miss Fulton. The other six debutantes also were guests.

Miss Barbara Breneman, daughter of Mr. and Mrs. Joseph M. Breneman, selects a corsage from her gifts at the Christmas Cotillion where she made her debut last evening.

New Era Photos

Miss Jane Watt, debutante daughter of Mr. and Mrs. Charles G. Watt, returns to her table for another gift bouquet at the party at the Lancaster Country Club.

Fashion Tip:

From Paris come hats that will delight the traveling woman. Little head-huggers of jersey, they pack in a breeze into the handbag or pocketbook. They cover the ears and are worn low on the neck.

If you're short, take it easy on enveloping stoles and coats. Don't overwhelm yourself; you won't overwhelm others.

The new torso lengths call for a warning to the short-waisted. Moral: be sure it's for YOU, not just for fashion.

Evening bags are getting larger. The velvet clutch has grown. This is welcome news for every woman who's tried to stuff money, compact, lipstick, keys, mirror, cigarette case and lighter into a bag the size of a pillbox.

The turban appears in many guises this year. Some are warm and woolly, some are jersey and drapeable, some are golden and truly Oriental.

Auxiliary President Honored by Pope Pius

Mrs. Clara Renner, supreme president of the Auxiliary to the Knights of St. John, Columbus, Ohio, has been awarded the Pro Ecclesia et Pontifice medal by Pope Pius XII.

Mrs. Renner, who spoke at the Golden Jubilee celebration of the local auxiliary last July, will be invested Jan. 6 in St. Joseph's Cathedral, Columbus, Ohio, by the Most Rev. Michael Ready, Bishop of Columbus.

Dance to Be Held At Lititz Center

A New Year's Eve Frolic will be held in the Lititz Recreation Center from 9 p. m. to midnight New Year's Eve.

The dance is being sponsored by the Junior Board of Directors of the Recreation Center.

Weddings

Horisk—Chambers

The marriage of Mrs. Mary Chambers, Montgomery Valley Rd., Ardmore, daughter of Mr. and Mrs. John Meisenberger, West Lancaster, and H. C. Horisk, 11 Cedar Grove Rd., Whitemarsh Twp., were married Saturday at 11:30 a. m. in St. James' Evangelical and Reformed Church, Chatham Village, Philadelphia.

A reception was held on Christmas Day at the home of the bride's parents. Following a wedding trip to New York City, the couple will reside at 11 Cedar Grove Rd., Whitemarsh Twp.

The bride is a former x-ray and hydrotheraphy technician. The bridegroom is vice president of Berwyn Chemical Co., Bryn Mawr. He is also a professional hypnotist and appears before many groups in the Philadelphia area.

Graeter—Mummaw

The marriage of Miss Jean Mummaw, granddaughter of Mr. and Mrs. W. L. Reed, Gordonville, to Jack H. Graeter, son of Mrs. Lucreta Graeter, 350 S. Prince St., took place Dec. 23 in Elkton, Md., with the Rev. R. J. Sturgill officiating.

The bride is residing with her grandparents and the bridegroom is serving in the U. S. Navy.

HOLD FAMILY PARTY

The Killian family held a Christmas party last night at the home of Mr. and Mrs. Chester Petticoffer, 43 W. Farnum St. Twenty-one persons were present. A dinner was served and gifts were exchanged.

Engaged

BENDER—SCHLINKMAN

Announcement is made of the engagement of Mary Jane Schlinkman, daughter of Mr. and Mrs. Melvin Schlinkman, 473 Rockland St. to William Bender, Jr., son of Mr. and Mrs. William Bender, Leacock.

Miss Schlinkman is employed at the Village Restaurant. Mr. Bender is an employe of Forry's Construction, Lititz.

One family found that their baby's crankiness went away when they let him go back to bottles rather than cups. They decided they had weaned him too soon. Each baby is an individual, so don't feel that weaning when the neighbor's child is weaned is going to solve any of you problems with Baby.

Temple Christmas Dance Is Tonight

The 31st annual Christmas dance of the Lancaster County Alumni Association of Temple University will be held tonight from 10 to 2 o' clock in Hotel Brunswick.

More than 200 reservations have been made.

Christmas decorations and replicas of the Temple mascot, the owl, will be featured in the ballroom. The long tables on either side of the room will be centered with red and green candles.

Mrs. Arnold G. Clement is chairman and Aldoph C. Koehler is co-chairman.

A new taste is given to liver if it's soaked in a favorite barbecue sauce for 30 minutes before pan-frying or broiling.

In The World Of Sports In 1955

Dodgers, Podres, Nashua, Marciano Picked Off Most Of The Headlines

BY FRANK ECK
AP Newsfeatures Sports Editor

A baseball team that threatened to move to a city abandoned by the minor leagues, a 23-year-old pitcher, a 3-year-old horse and a fighter who knows only victory made off with most of the 1955 headlines in sports.

Frank Eck

The team, of course, is the Brooklyn Dodgers. For their fans, including those who prayed in front of television sets across the country, 1955 "was next year." The Dodgers won the National League pennant on the earliest date in history by 13½ games and then humbled the lordly New York Yankees in the seven-game World Series.

The pitcher is Johnny Podres, the southpaw with the herniated disc who limited the Yankees to two earned runs in 18 innings to become the World Series hero after completing only five games all season.

The horse is Nashua who with his 40-year-old jockey, stakeswise Eddie Arcaro, beat everything in sight, including the great Swaps, his conqueror in the Kentucky Derby.

The fighter is Rocky Marciano whose two dynamite-packed fists have given him 49 straight victories as a professional.

Fleck Beats Hogan

Golf brought temporary fame to unknown Jack Fleck of Davenport, Iowa when he conquered the great Ben Hogan in a playoff for the U. S. Open crown at San Francisco. It was Fleck's first golf victory of consequence and he is still looking for his second tournament win.

American tennis reached a new low. After Tony Trabert of Cincinnati and Doris Hart of Coral Gables, Fla., won National singles titles both turned professional.

WE WON IT! — Pitcher Johnny Podres jumps into Roy Campanella's arms and Don Hoak joins them as the Dodgers win their first World Series after seven failures.

College football featured two unbeaten giants in Oklahoma and Maryland, rivals in the Jan. 2 Orange Bowl in Miami. Two of the country's most-heralded backs were Ohio State's Howard Cassady and Texas Christian's Jim Swink, both All-Americas.

College basketball had an outstanding champion in the San Francisco Dons who capped a 28 out of 29 record with the NCAA title. The dominance of the pro Minneapolis Lakers ended as the Syracuse Nationals beat Fort Wayne in the National Basketball Assn. playoffs.

Horse racing fans all but forgot Native Dancer as Nashua pranced off with the horse of the year and 3-year-old honors.

Problem Children

The devastating Dodgers made a shambles of the National League race. Right from the start they proved the best, winning 22 of their first 24 games. Don Newcombe, a problem at the start, was suspended and fined but Manager Walter Alston's tactics with the giant Negro fireballer paid off. Newk won 20 games.

The Dodgers had as many problem children as sore-armed pitchers but sophomore pilot Alston led them to their first world championship, something they had battled for since 1916. Their victory in the World Series marked the first Series setback for the Yankees since 1942.

It was anybody's Series until Alston uncovered Podres in the third game. The miner's son from Witherbee, N.Y. out at various times during the season with back aches, arm miseries and a hairline rib fracture, hadn't pitched a complete game since his second straight shutout over Cincinnati in mid-June, yet his change-up beat the Yankees, 8-3. It was his 23rd birthday. Four days later he employed a fast ball to shut them out, 2-0. A great one-handed catch which left fielder Sandy Amoros turned into a double play saved the game.

The comeback of catcher Roy Campanella, who regained the No. 4 spot in the batting order, and the slugging of center fielder Duke Snider were big factors in their pennant drive. Snider led both leagues with 136 runs batted in.

There was talk that the Dodgers would move out of Ebbets Field to a bigger park. But where? President Walter O'Malley picked Jersey City for seven 1956 Dodger night games and the league approved.

Mays Hits 51 Homers

Willie Mays, who caught fire whenever the other team had Brooklyn uniforms, hit 51 homers for the New York Giants but the 1954 champions could do no better than finish third, 18½ games back. Their relief pitchers disappointed as did hurler Johnny Antonelli.

Robin Roberts of the Phillies joined Newcombe as the majors' only other 20-game winner. He won 23, lost 14. His teammate, speedy Richie Ashburn led the league in hitting with .338.

Four pilots lost their jobs. The Giants replaced Leo Durocher with Bill Rigney, the St. Louis Cardinals gave American Leaguer Fred Hutchinson the job of picking up where Eddie Stanky and then Harry Walker left off, and Bobby Bragan took Fred Haney's spot with the Pittsburgh Pirates.

In the American League, Casey Stengel led the Yankees to a 3 length victory over Cleveland, the Indians blowing the flag when they lost four straight to tail end Washington. It was Stengel's sixth pennant in seven years with the Yankees and the 21st for the club.

Kaline Is Top Hitter

Detroit's Al Kaline, a 20-year-old sophomore outfielder, led both leagues in hitting with .340 after hitting .379 the first half.

The Yankees were paced by Yogi Berra, the league's most valuable player for the third year, and Mickey Mantle's 37 homers, best in the circuit. A pair of southpaws, Whitey Ford and comebacker Tommy Byrne, with control and a slow curve, paced Yankee pitching.

Branch Rickey, the man who built winners in St. Louis and Brooklyn, fathered the farm system and the advent of the Negro in the big leagues, was asked to step down as Pittsburgh's general manager after the Pirates finished last the fourth straight time.

Near the year's end the first three major deals had Cleveland swapping Larry Doby for Chicago's Chico Carrasquel; Boston getting Bob Porterfield and Mickey Vernon from Washington in exchange for younger talent, and the Dodgers taking Randy Jackson from the Cubs for Don Hoak.

Nashua Earns $945,415

Nashua, winning 10 of 12 races and a record $752,550, sky rocketed his two years' earnings to $945,415, second only to Citation's $1,085,760. Arcaro missed his Sixth Derby but more than evened the score with Swaps and Willie Shoemaker with a pole to pole victory in a $100,000 match race at Chicago's Washington Park. Arcaro missed riding Nashua only in the Wood Memorial and for his nine wins aboard the big bay colt the Rockville Centre, N.Y. reinsman realized $67,745.

William Woodward, Nashua's owner, met a tragic end when his wife mistook him for a prowler and killed him with a shotgun blast in their home.

Willie Hartack rode 404 winners before a 10-day December suspension put him on the sidelines.

The best fighter continued as the most popular. Rocky Marciano, a shoemaker's son from Brockton, Mass., stopped England's Don Cockell in 54 seconds of the ninth round in San Francisco in May, and in September he flattened a game Archie Moore in 1:19 of the ninth before 61,574 paying $948,117 in Yankee Stadium. The world's heavyweight champion left his manager, Al Weill, speechless as he ran out of opponents.

Three new champions were crowned. Tony DeMarco knocked out Johnny Saxton for the welterweight title in April but suffered two knockouts at the hands of Carmen Basilio. Wallace (Bud) Smith beat Jimmy Carter for the lightweight crown in June and repeated in October.

While experts were picking Gene Littler to win the Open golf crown, Fleck came from nowhere to tie Hogan and beat him, 69-72, in the playoff. Littler was 15th. Julius Boros led the pros in money won with $63,121 by virtue of the half grand picked up in the Tam O'Shanter world tourney. Cary Middlecoff won $36,767 by taking six events but lost 4 and 3 to Doug Ford in the PGA final. Harvie Ward walked off with the U.S. Amateur while Australia's Peter Thomson, a non-winner during a two-year American tour, retained the British open crown. The British Amateur went to Lt. Joe Conrad of San Antonio, Tex.

Trabert captured the U.S. British and French crowns but failed in the Davis Cup competition and turned pro. Trabert also won the National indoor singles and doubles and the clay court crowns. Maureen Connolly announced her retirement and when Miss Hart quit the amateur ranks women's tennis was left without a leader.

Oklahoma gained top ranking in

HOWARD CASSADY

The Associated Press football poll as Bud Wilkinson's unbeaten Sooners made it 29 in a row and 53 straight in the Big 7 as they captured their eighth conference crown in a row. Michigan State, Maryland and UCLA were rated that way behind Oklahoma.

Army Conquers Navy

The usual number of upsets featured the fall sport with two of the major ones coming near the sea-

ROCKY MARCIANO

son's close. Ohio State beat Michigan, 17-0, to keep the Wolverines out of the Rose Bowl and Army turned back Navy, 14-6, after the Middies' All-America end Ron Beagle dropped a George Welsh pass 20 yards from pay dirt. It was the only bad play Beagle made all season as he and Welsh established new Navy passing records.

The milers again stole the foot racing spotlight with Wes Santee lowering the American record to 4:00.5. Santee, the ex-Kansas runner now a Marine lieutenant, also won the AAU indoor and outdoor mile crowns. Late in October the Missouri Valley AAU suspended him for accepting excessive expenses for three California meets. Three weeks later the suspension was lifted.

Gunnar Nielsen of Denmark set

made it four straight and Jenkins a world indoor record of 4:03.6 in the Millrose game but a week later Fred Dwyer beat him in the New York A.C. mile. It remained for three foreigners in one race in London to join Australia's John Landy and England's Roger Bannister as four-minute milers. Laszlo Tabori of Hungary was timed in 3:59 with England's Chris Chataway and Brian Hewson clocked in 3:59.8.

King Of Backstrokers

In swimming, Yoshio Oyakawa, former Ohio State star from Hawaii, captured four AAU backstroke titles. Ford Konno won three freestyle tests. Among the women, Shelley Mann, 17, from Arlington, Va., scored in two indoor freestyle championships and in the indoor medley. Mrs. Patricia McCormich of Los Angeles retained her four AAU diving titles.

In auto racing Bill Vukovich, seeking his third straight Indianapolis 500-mile victory, met death in a four-car crash. The race went to Bob Sweikert.

In crew Navy bowed to Penn after 31 straight and Cornell rowed off with the intercollegiate regatta.

In figure skating, Haynes Alan Jenkins, 22, from Colorado Springs won his third straight world crown while Tenley Albright, 19, from Newton, Mass., regained the women's title. In the nationals she

tallied for the third successive year.

Hockey Goes Limit

Detroit's Red Wings retained the Stanley Cup, beating Montreal, 3-1, in the seventh and deciding game of the National Hockey League playoffs.

Top weightlifter in the world meet at Munich was Paul Anderson, 22-year-old 340-pounder from Toccoa, Ga.

Don Campbell, 34, of England, streaked his jet-powered speedboat 239.5 miles per hour on Lake Mead, Nev., and Eddie Gerzine's 738 won the ABC singles bowling crown on the third day in Milwaukee.

Top dog in the 79th Westminster was Kippax Fearnought, a bulldog owned by Dr. John A. Saylor of Long Beach, Calif.

NASHUA

EDDIE ARCARO

SHELLEY MANN

WILLIE MAYS

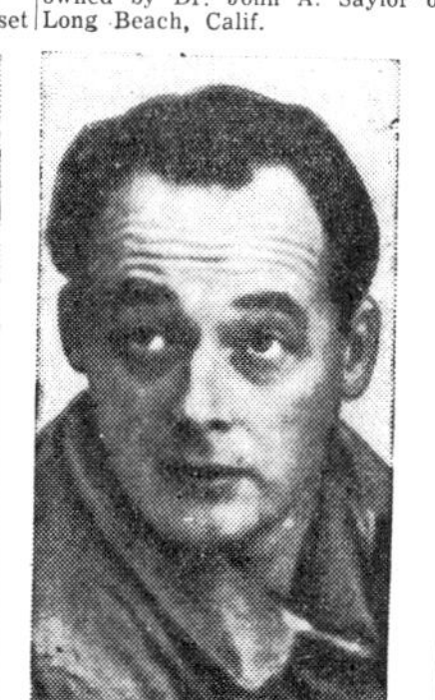

DON CAMPBELL

★★Cream Of The Crop In Their Fields★★

TENLEY ALBRIGHT

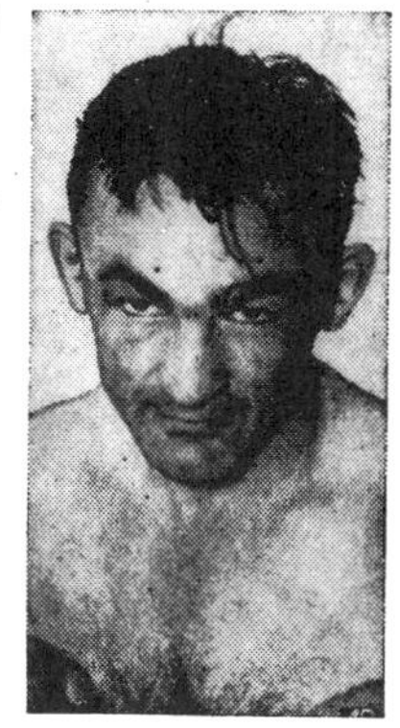

CARMEN BASILIO

PAT McCORMICK

the SUNDAY NEWS OBSERVER

By GEORGE CRUDDEN Sports Editor

THE year of 1955 in the realm of sports was distinguished by a local series of emotional shocks which had their affect on most fans.

There were some real highlights, of course, the Millersville State Teachers College basketball team and the Donegal basketball team, both of which won recognition beyond the confines of Lancaster County, and, finally, the Lancaster Red Roses, who returned to eminence in organized baseball, by winning the play-off title of the Piedmont League, the first organized baseball title to fall to this city since 1945.

There were many outstanding individual performances here in 1955 too.

But the removal from the local sports scene by death of such wonderful guys as Tom Floyd, Peter Flick, Harry Goodhart, Jake Weller and Joe McGeever, among others had a saddening effect on thousands of fans.

The folding of, professional basketball created a mild stir, but the unexpected announcement that organized baseball was dead here provided the main shock of 1955.

The coming year holds much promise, and the Sunday News wishes the best of everything to all the individuals and teams, veterans and newcomers alike, who will be back on the turf providing new and better sports thrills for the readers of this newspaper.

Happy New Year to all!

THAT grave concern is felt for the future of minor league baseball is indicated by this editorial from the Sporting News:

"A continuing mystery of the game is why otherwise practicable men can be so impracticable in the administration and conduct of baseball. Many executives, successful and resourceful in other lines of business, seem to lose all perspective when they become associated with the national pasttime.

"Instead of thinking problems through to logical conclusions, they often go off on a tangent and come up with weird ideas. Some would put Miami in the American Association to make that minor league stretch from Colorado to Florida; allow a city like San Francisco, touted as a likely major league member, to float in a financial morass; evade facing real issues by talking of television subsidies, bonus restrictions, option barriers and the like, all of which are subsidiary, after all, to cultivation of the grass roots from which the player talent must come, if it comes at all.

"However, luckily for the game, there emerges at times of crises someone with a constructive plan that serves as an inspiration to others and offers the prospect of providing material benefits that will spread to the profits of all.

"The progress the game has made has been due to those men who conceived the National League back in 1876; Ban Johnson, who restored respectability to the diamond sport in 1901; the minor league pioneers who organized the National Association in 1901; Judge K. M. Landis, who restored confidence in Organized Ball, and to other leaders who have guided the way in both the majors and minors.

"SOMETIMES, though, it has seemed that sight was lost of some of the fundamentals such as keeping the grass roots green. Without stability at the bottom, there can be no security at the top, as has been emphasized recently by the uncertainty in the lower minors. True, some strength has been breathed into them, through such realignment moves that brought into being the Southwestern League and placed other clubs in reinforced circuits in the same section. Except for shortsighted selfishness on the part of some leagues and clubs there would be more such developments in the minors.

"However, there is reason to be optimistic over the ability of the game to solve its problems as long as there is constructive thinking, willingness to accept progressive ideas and shed hidebound practices and a disposition to co-operate unselfishly with the other fellow. There have been many such high spots in the past and undoubtedly there will be again in the future."

S'LONG . . .

The Outdoor Angle

BY PETE BUSSER

MEASURES to conserve rockfish or striped bass in the Chesapeake Bay and its tributaries won't be cosnidered by the Maryland legislature until it convenes in 1957. In the meantime, various organizations down there and in Pennsylvania are working up preliminary reports.

The Maryland Rockfish Protective Association, the first of the conservation agencies, has circulated a questionnaire pertaining to this species of fish. From the answers it receives it hopes to be able to show something definite and concrete to the lawmakers to further their cause.

Pete Busser

If this organization or any other striped bass group can show that Maryland's economy won't suffer or that bettering sport fishing in the Bay area can add something to the economy then maybe conservation proposals may be turned into laws.

Through this questionaire, the Maryland Association hopes to be able to show definitely just what rod and line fishing means to Maryland.

The questions are:

1. How many fishing trips did you make on the bay this year?
2. Approximately how many hours on each trip?
3. Approximate cost per trip, bait, gear, lodging, gas, etc?
4. What kind of fish did you catch? How many? Approximate weight?
5. What area did you fish most? (Either Tolchester to the Bay Bridge or Tolchester north to the Susquehanna Dam.
6. What kind of gear did you use most? (Trolling, spinning, bottom rig).
7. What kind of bait was used? (Natural, live bait or artificial).
8. Do you think that rockfishing is as good now as it was five years ago?
9. What do you think would help the most to improve rockfishing?
10. Which of the following proposals do you favor the most? (1.) Make the rockfish a game fish. (2.) Close all tributaries to commercial haul seining. (3.) Stop all drift netting in the months of Jan., Feb., March and April.

All questionaires are to be submitted to Joseph F. Einwich, secretary of the Maryland Rockfish Protective Association at 3455 Mayfield Ave., Baltimore 13, Maryland. Maybe you didn't receive a questionnaire but if you have views on the subject it certainly wouldn't hurt to jot them down or pattern your ideas after the questions noted above and mail them to Einwich.

Under the present setup anglers can expect another poor year for rock in the Port Deposit-Havre de Grace sector. The arrival of the hug commercial nets last summer just about halted sport fishing and there is nothing to indicate that they won't reappear this summer with the same results—plenty of rock for the few commercialman and none for the rod and line majority.

King Tops In Y Foul Shooting

Andy King captured the foul throw tourney at the YMCA Saturday by dropping 27 of 30 attempts. Thirty boys participated in the tourney.

A Preview Of Sports In 1956

By BILL FISHER

You want to know who will win the World Series this year? Or the Olympics maybe? You won't find it here. But you will find a lot of other things, things like will call Frank Lane what and why and how Casey Stengel will win another pennant and what Russians will run down the steppes in world record time.

In short, everything that's going to happen this year in sports, and perhaps a thing or three that isn't. But if it doesn't it won't because we didn't say so.

So, hold tight, here goes:

JANUARY — Michigan State, Maryland, Pitt and TCU win the bowl games . . . Walter O'Malley says the Dodgers are so going to move to Jersey City . . . San Francisco continues unbeaten . . . Outlook dim in the Piedmont League . . . All's quiet with Frank Spair . . . Russians claim sure victory in Olympics . . . Jim Tatum rumored going to North Carolina.

FEBRUARY — Frisco's Bill Russell acclaimed greatest Russell since Jane . . . But Kansas fans chorus, 'Wait for Wilt the Stilt' . . . Players go south for Spring training . . . Ted Williams says he might retire . . . Lynwood Lingenfelter says Millersville could beat LVC any day . . . Nature Boy Buddy Rogers beats the Great Scott at Maple Grove . . . Yankees get Mickey McDermott in trade, give up no regulars in return.

MARCH — Ted Williams reports fish biting off Florida, says he may retire . . . Tony Trabert cleaning up on Jack Kramer's tennis tour . . . Kramer reports he's after Rosewall and Hoad . . . All's quiet with Frank Spair . . . Rogers beats Scott at the Grove . . . Frank Lane fumes at National League owners, says they won't trade with him . . . Jim Tatum rumored going to North Carolina . . . Jimmy Carter regains lightweight title . . . Another boxing investigation gets underway.

APRIL — Russian skier, Freezeyournoseoff, wins Olympic ski jump . . . Sports writers nickname him "Rudolf the Red Nose" . . . Don Bisplinghoff and Dow Fisterwald finish one-two in the Masters Tourney . . . Headline writers swoon . . . Frank Spair seen scouting around . . . Great Scott beats Rogers at the Grove . . . Frank Lane is looking for a trade . . . Mayo Smith is looking for a rightfielder . . . Jim Norris is looking for a place to hide.

MAY — Walter O'Malley is looking for Jersey City . . . Fans are looking for new faces at Maple Grove . . . Wes Santee claims he's all set to run a 4-minute mile . . . Baltimore lost in last place . . . Paul Richards asks for bonus rule change . . . Oriole fans give Richards the bird . . . Owners say TV is killing baseball.

JUNE — Casey Stengel says he isn't interested in making a trade . . . Yankees trade Don Richardson for Billy Pierce, even-up . . . Frank Lane is heard hollering in St. Louis . . . Johnny Saxton regains welterweight title . . . Boxing commissions begin another investigation . . . Jim Norris is out of town . . . Archie Moore clamouring for another shot at Marciano . . . Al Weil is out of town . . . So is Jim Tatum who is house hunting in Chapel Hill, N. C.

JULY — Dodgers and Giants play 22-inning night game the night before a triple-header . . . Players threaten to organize a union . . . Russians rumored loaded for Olympics . . . Wes Santee says he'll take care of that . . . Dick Showers says he'll take care of West Santee . . . Golfers decry Long Park course . . . What course? ask Park authorities . . . Rogers vs. Great Scott at the Grove . . . Paul Richards pays $64 million for a bonus baby.

AUGUST — Ted Williams leading American League with .468 average but insists he's thinking about retiring . . . Sam Snead, all set to win National Open, blows 1-inch putt on last green . . . Giants rumored headed for Minneapolis . . . Frank Spair rumored dickering to bring Giants to Lancaster . . . Looks like Dodgers and Yanks again as Pierce wins No. 20 . . . Russian runner, Worldrecordski, runs mile in 3 minutes flat . . . AAU moves to ban Russia from Olympics.

SEPTEMBER — Jim Tatum says he isn't interested in coaching job at North Carolina . . . Jim Norris says he isn't interested in anything . . . Frank Spair says he's interested in bringing baseball back to Lancaster . . . The Phillies flounder in sixth place . . . Our hitters didn't hit explains Mayo Smith . . . You're through replies Bob Carpenter . . . O'Malley reports Jersey City is a lousy baseball town . . . Otto Graham rumored coming out of retirement.

OCTOBER — Maryland coach Jim Tatum denies a rumor he is rumored looking for a job . . . Dodgers beat Yankees in World Series . . . Ted Williams says he's good for four more years yet . . . Penn wins a football game . . . So does McCaskey . . . Rogers beats Great Scott . . . Stengel says he will retire if George Weiss doesn't get him some pitching . . . U. S. runners beat Russians in Olympics.

NOVEMBER — Maryland finishes unbeaten . . . Jim Tatum says he's fed up with high pressure football, takes coaching job at Sewanee Teachers . . . Baseball players threaten to form a union . . . George Darrah being boomed for Little All-America . . . Frank Lane trades Walker Cooper for Bill Veeck . . . Oh no . . . Dodgers plan to play 10 games in Weehawken . . . Frank Spair offers Lancaster . . . Wilt the Stilt scores 86 points in Kansas debut . . . Coaches cry "hooped-up" ball.

DECEMBER — Frank Lane waivers Schoendinst to Yanks for Johnny Kucks . . . Great Scott beats Rogers . . . Grove fans beat each other . . . Frank Spair seen looking for a hustling ball club . . . Baseball players threaten to form a union . . . Boxers plan to form a union . . . Football players plan to form a union . . . Russians claim they invented union suits . . . Oops!

SUSIE HAD A LITTLE LAMB—Susie Lamparter, just eight years old, finds an Eastertime friend in a Hampshire lamb, just a week old, above. Susie lives at 120 College Ave., the lamb at Green Meadows Farm, Bareville R1.

FEATHERING THEIR NESTS for Easter with a good word in the Easter Bunny's ear are Kathy Lou Kieley, six, Ronks R1, center; and Michael and John Bachman, four and six, to left and right, of 462 New Dorwart St. Grandpa, John Werhel, raises bunnies.

It's Easter Time

It's a time for youngsters, both animal and human, as the festival of rebirth renews its ancient symbols. Sunday News photos show some of them, and their impact on a new and wondering generation.

EASTER EGGHEADS were a seasonal art-class project for thousands of school children this past week. Here Virginia Irwin, 725 W. Vine St., works on an original design in teacher Joan McComsey's 5th-grade room at Lafayette school.

WITH ALL THE FRILLS UPON IT — Top-hatted Glen Craley, above, gives Janet Snoke's bonnet that final fraction of an inch of inspired tilt at the fancy-dress pre-Easter party in Mrs. Harold Armstrong's second-grade classroom at John Henry Neff School. All they have to do now is hold it just that way until the big downtown Easter Parade.

TECHNICOLOR PEEPS delight Cheryl Weaver, 3½ years old, at her father's hatchery in Annville. The firm started the idea to create sale for surplus cockerel peeps.

EASTER GOOSE—As a fuzzy yellow gosling, Elmer the goose came to the home of Brandt Hughes, 1245 Pleasure Rd., just two years ago.

City's New 15 Million Gallon Reservoir Taking Shape

Concrete is now being poured for the floor of the City of Lancaster Authority's 15,000,000 gallon water reservoir near Oyster Point in East Hempfield Township. Excavation for the reservoir, which is 320 feet square and covers two acres, has been completed. The target date for finishing the job is this fall, according to construction engineers. When finished, the 20-foot high reservoir will be completely covered. It will have a concrete top, held by a "forest" of pillars. Ground around the huge reservoir will be graded, making it almost invisible to persons unaware of the location. Four hatches will permit access for cleaning. (Intell Photo)

WEATHER
(U. S. Weather Bureau Forecast for Lancaster, Cumberland, Lebanon, York, Adams and Franklin Counties):
Cloudy And Colder With Rain Today, Highest Temperature 50 - 55 Degrees. Windy Tonight. Tomorrow Clearing And Milder.

Intelligencer Journal.

TELEPHONE 7-5251

The Leading Newspaper in the Garden Spot of America. Home Owned for Home Folks Since 1794

THE INTELL INDEX

162nd Year.—No. 256. Official United States Census Figures Lancaster Metropolitan Area Population 234,717 LANCASTER, PA., WEDNESDAY MORNING, APRIL 11, 1956. CITY EDITION 24 PAGES. 30c PER WEEK—5c Per Copy

Stevenson Leads Illinois Popularity Contest

Lancaster To Be A Target During Nat'l CD Exercise

Week - Long "Operation Alert 1956" Will Be Held From July 20-26

Lancaster will be one of 10 Pennsylvania cities designated as targets in a nationwide simulated nuclear attack set for July 20-26.

"Operation Alert 1956," the code name for the test, will include an attack exercise in 76 U.S. cities. The attack will take up only a small period during the week, and government and Civil Defense agencies will devote the rest of the time to test emergency procedures which will not require any public participation.

C. Abram Snyder, director of the Lancaster County Civil Defense Council, notified sector directors and members of his staff last week that the test would be held and urged them to make preparations for exercises here. At that time, however, the Lancaster area had not been designated by the Office of Defense Mobilization as a "target" for simulated drills during the test.

OTHER TARGET AREAS

The other "target" areas in this state are Allentown - Bethlehem - Easton area, Erie, Pittsburgh, Wilkes-Barre, York, Johnstown and Philadelphia - Camden area.

Canada will participate in the simulated emergency, which will see President Eisenhower and key government personnel evacuating Washington for secret relocation sites.

The combination civil defense and government evacuation test will be similar to last year's exercise in which Eisenhower and

Turn To Page 4 For More Of CIVIL DEFENSE

Air Raid Siren System Enlarged, 'Blanket Coverage' Now Assured

Blasts from an augmented, and in some cases relocated, group of air raid sirens, will reach every portion of the city in the near future.

The blanket coverage will be created with the installation of seven new and more powerful sirens. When the project is completed, there will be 21 sirens in use in the city and one in the Bloomingdale section of Manheim Twp.

The new sirens will include four of 10 horsepower and three of five horsepower. At present there are 16 sirens installed, one of five horsepower and the remainder two horsepower.

In general, the more powerful sirens will be located near the center of the city, with the two horsepower units closer to the city line.

The city will ask for bids on the new units. Bids must be submitted by 10 a.m. Monday at the office of the city controller in the Municipal Building.

The federal government has approved expenditure of upwards of $3,580 on a matching basis, the city to pay half of the total cost.

Location of the sirens was

Turn To Page 4 For More Of SIRENS

MANHEIM TWP. TAX INCREASE UNDER FIRE

Democrats Claim Contradiction of Promises Made In 1952

The Manheim Twp. Democratic Club in a resolution adopted last night criticized the township commissioners and school directors for raising taxes "in direct contradiction to promises made by these bodies" before a referendum in 1952 which elevated the township from a second to a first class one.

The resolution was adopted at a meeting of the club held at the United Steel Workers of America office, 165 E. King St., at which Dan G. Diffenderfer, 9 E. Liberty St., was elected president. Diffenderfer succeeds George H. Carpenter, who served as head of the club since its founding.

"The residents of Manheim Twp. were emphatically assured that taxes would not be increased if we became a first class town-

Turn To Page 4 For More Of MANHEIM TWP.

Hammarskjold Opens On-The-Spot Talks In 'Powder Keg' Mideast

CAIRO, Egypt, April 10 (AP) — Dag Hammarskjold settled to on-the-spot talks tonight in his effort to still the Arab-Israeli violence disturbing the peace of the Middle East.

Amid reports of fresh incidents, the U.N. secretary general flew first to Tel Aviv and then to Cairo on the special peace mission he undertook by unanimous order of the Security Council.

Maj. Gen. E.L.M. Burns, the Canadian chief of the U.N. Truce Commission, met Hammarskjold on his arrival in Tel Aviv from Beirut, Lebanon, and accompanied him here.

Hammarskjold talked with Egyptian Foreign Minister Mahmoud Fawzi and arranged to meet premier Gamal Abdel Nasser tomorrow. A spokesman said the secretary general's plans are flexible, but he expects to remain here until Monday and then return to Israel for consultations with Premier David Ben-Gurion's government.

TALKS IN EGYPT

It was emphasized that the official talks are opening with Egypt, leader of the Arab bloc, though Hammarskjold and Burns had luncheon in Tel Aviv with three Israeli Foreign Office officials.

Turn To Page 20 For More Of DAG

DULLES REVIEWS MIDEAST PROBLEM FOR KEY SOLONS

Seen Paving Way For Possibility Of Using U. S. Troops In Disturbance

WASHINGTON, April 10 (AP) — Secretary of State Dulles paved the way today for a possible request that Congress give President Eisenhower blank check authority to use American troops in the Middle East if war dangers become acute there.

The secretary, keeping in close touch with Eisenhower, met for 1½ hours with 14 key members of Congress at the State Department. Eight were Republicans and six were Democrats.

He reviewed with them the tense Middle East situation made even more serious by new Arab-Israeli bloodshed. It was reported that he skirted—but did not directly raise—the question of asking Congress for a Formosa-type resolution.

MAJOR ADDRESS

The White House announced Eisenhower will make a major foreign policy address on April 21. It will be delivered in Washington before the American Society of Newspaper Editors and presumably will cover the Middle East crisis.

Focal point of Dulles' consultation with the congressional leaders was yesterday's White House statement that any aggressor in the Middle East will have to reckon with U. S. opposition.

The statement drew warm praise today from Britain and France, in strong contrast to the

Turn To Page 4 For More Of DULLES

Elected

REV. W. E. TREXLER

REV. W. E. TREXLER TO BE MODERATOR FOR E&R SYNOD

Pastor Of Lancaster's First Reformed Church Fills Newly Created Office

The Rev. Wilbur E. Trexler, pastor of First Reformed Church, 40 E. Orange St., has the unique distinction of being elected the first moderator of the Lancaster Synod of the Evangelical and Reformed Church.

The Rev. Mr. Trexler, who has been pastor of the local church since last July, was named to the office yesterday morning shortly after the 18th annual session of the synod got underway in the Myerstown Evangelical and Reformed Church, Myerstown.

The office of moderator in the E & R Church was created as a result of the planned merger of the E & R Church with the Congregational Christian Churches

Turn To Page 20 For More Of REV. TREXLER

LATE UPSURGE GIVES BOOST TO IKE TALLY

State's Former Governor Takes Big Advantage In Chicago Stronghold

CHICAGO, April 10 (AP)— Adlai E. Stevenson rolled up more votes than President Eisenhower tonight in the Illinois ballot count but a late upsurge downstate gave a big boost to the President's tally.

The two men were matched in the Illinois presidential preference primary, a popularity contest that was not binding on convention delegates.

Stevenson was given a decided advantage in Chicago, citadel of his Democratic party. But Eisenhower was far ahead outside of Chicago.

With returns passing the one-third mark from the downstate polling places, the President was pulling twice as many votes as Stevenson in that broad area. Downstate is where Illinois farmers vote, and the tallies were watched for an indication of reaction to the Eisenhower administration's farm policies.

But Stevenson had a midnight

Turn To Page 4 For More Of ELECTION

WHITES ATTACK NAT KING COLE IN BIRMINGHAM

BIRMINGHAM, Ala., April 10 (AP) —A group of white men attacked Negro singer and pianist Nat (King) Cole as he sang from the stage of Birmingham's Municipal Auditorium tonight. Cole was not injured.

Six men were taken into custody after the attack. Four were charged with inciting a riot. The other two were found in a car which contained two .22 rifles, a blackjack and a pair of brass knucks. They were questioned at length.

Cole, 37, was attacked in the first of two performances, which was for white patrons. Birmingham requires segregated audiences for such shows.

Cole gave a second performance for Negro patrons shortly after the attack.

Charged with inciting a riot are

Turn To Page 19 For More Of COLE

PAKASTANI HITS NEHRU IN SPEECH TO ROTARY HERE

Maj. Gen. M. Hayaud-Din, chief of the Pakistan Military Mission to the United States, last night in Lititz leveled an attack on "Pandit Nehru's so-called neutralism."

Speaking at a joint meeting of Lititz and Ephrata Rotary Clubs in the General Sutter Hotel, Gen. Hayaud-Din vowed that Pakistan "will stand only with those who fight communism."

"Nehru," he said, "calls himself a neutral when he says Red China should take over Formosa, that North Viet Nam should take over South Viet Nam, that North Korea should take over South Korea. But has he said anything about the liberation of the Soviet satellites or of Tibet?"

NOTES CONTRADICTION

In response to a question about the status of Kashmir from one of the more than 100 men and women in his audience, Gen. Hayaud-Din

Turn To Page 19 For More Of PAKISTAN

PRR SERVICE HERE DISRUPTED BY WRECK

Early morning Lancaster to Philadelphia service on the Pennsylvania Railroad's main line was extensively disrupted by a freight derailment in Philadelphia.

Westbound trains from Philadelphia stopped running completely for a time, while eastbound trains were routed to Trenton where passengers had to wait for shuttle service into the Quaker City.

Through trains from New York skirted the wreck scene, at Overbrook Station, joining the Main Line near Paoli.

Trains due here from Philadelphia were running from two to three hours late while those from Harrisburg were running on schedule but were detoured to Trenton.

Railroad spokesmen said traffic was expected to be back to normal by daylight.

Senate Hikes State Aid For Local Highways

HARRISBURG, April 10 (AP)—The Senate today approved an oft-amended plan to increase state aid for local roads from 18 million dollars a year to 30 millions.

Not a word of debate preceded the 47-0 vote. The administration-backed measure went back to the House for agreement on a series of Senate amendments. The House is expected to go slow on concurrence.

The most important change wrought by the Senate was increasing the ratio of distribution to give rural areas a better break than cities.

As passed by the House, 55 per cent of the money would be allocated on the basis of mileage and 45 per cent on population. The Senate revised that to 60-64, thereby cutting back proposed aid to cities.

Under the legislation, the formula would become permanent. In the past, the allocations were

Turn To Page 4 For More Of ASSEMBLY

POLICE ARREST TWO IN BOX FIRM THEFT

Two juveniles were arrested by Detective Frank Matt last night for burglarizing the Central Paper Box Co., 225 E. Grant St., over the weekend.

The boys, seventeen and fifteen, entered the building through the coal chute. The seventeen year old is a former employe of the company, Detective Matt said.

They got several dollars and a few candy bars in the burglary. The two were committed to the Rotary Home, pending disposition of the case by juvenile authorities.

First City Test Of Dairy Wells Shows Negative

The first quarterly test of wells at dairies distributing milk in Lancaster has shown them to be "all clear," Elmer B. Neff reported to the City board of Health last night.

Neff, an inspector for the board, stated that the wells were tested for bacterial count and all showed negative results.

The system of at least one laboratory test during each three-month period was instituted following the recent outbreak of paratyphoid. Water from the wells is sometimes used in machinery to cool milk following pasteurization, but does not come into contact directly with the milk.

Dr. E. W. Meiser, president of the board, said that at the time of the outbreak there were reports that over 50 per cent of the wells in the Lancaster area were contaminated. He indicated that he

Turn To Page 4 For More Of BOARD

"We Lead All The Rest"

FARM CORNER

By Joe Wachtman

Broiler Chicken Placements Rise To Record Level

Placements of broiler chicks in the 22 major producing states continue at a record pace while the downward trend of prices has been joined by a slight increase in feed costs, according to federal-state surveys.

The number of chicks placed, increasing steadily since last September, again established a new all-time record of 25,915,000 for the 22 states during the week ended March 31. The increase is only one per cent from the previous week but is 20 per cent above the corresponding week a year ago.

For Pennsylvania, the placements totaled 888,000, a gain of 63,000 in one week and only 10,000 fewer than the record set during the week of March 10.

The high state figure was

Turn To Page 19 For More Of FARM CORNER

UMBRELLA, TOPCOAT WEATHER EXPECTED

A dreary, drizzly day is predicted for this area today.

The Weather Bureau said in its late forecast last night that leaden skies should open occasionally, bringing rain which was predicted for yesterday but never came. Clearing and milder weather is seen for tomorrow.

The mercury will not rise much above the low fifties, the forecaster said, compared with yesterday's high of 58 degrees at the Ephrata Weather Station. The low there yesterday was 30 degrees.

Weather Calendar

COMPARATIVE TEMPERATURES

Station	High	Low
Water Works	61	26
Ephrata	58	30
Last Year (Ephrata)	79	42
Official High for Year, April 5		67
Official Low for Year, Feb. 22		12
Character of Day		Clear

WINDS

Direction ... Calm

HUMIDITY

8 a. m.—57% 11 a. m.—41%
2 p. m.—36% 5 p. m.—30%
8 p. m.—50% Avge. Humidity—43%

SUN

Rises—5:33 a. m. Sets—6:38 p. m.

MOON

Sets—7:38 p. m. First Quarter, April 17

STARS

Morning—Mars, Saturn
Evening—Venus, Jupiter

NEARBY FORECASTS
(U. S. Weather Bureau)

Southeastern Pennsylvania and Southern New Jersey—Cloudy, windy and cooler today with occasional rain. Rain tonight ending early tomorrow, clearing and milder. High today 45-50.

Central and Northeastern Pennsylvania—Cloudy and somewhat colder with occasional rain today and some wet snow in the mountain areas, high 45-50. Rain ending and becoming rather windy tonight. Tomorrow clearing and turning milder.

Lower Potomac and Chesapeake Bay—Small craft warnings displayed south portion of the bay. Increasing east to northeast winds reaching 20-25 miles per hour over the north portion and 25-35 miles per hour over south portion today. Cloudy with occasional rain and rather poor visibility.

Maryland—Cloudy, windy and a little cooler with rain today, high 45-50 west and in the 50s elsewhere. Tomorrow clearing and a little warmer.

Delaware—Cloudy, windy and a little cooler with rain today, high in the 50s. Tomorrow clearing and a little warmer.

EXTENDED FORECAST
(U. S. Weather Bureau)

Extended forecast for today through Sunday:

Eastern Pennsylvania, eastern New York and Middle Atlantic States:

Temperature will average 3 to 6 degrees below normal. Warmer Friday and in south portion tomorrow afternoon; cooler Saturday, warmer Sunday afternoon. Rain today, possibly mixed with snow in extreme north portion and rain again about Saturday. Total precipitation ½ to 1 inch south portion and ¼ to ¾ inch north portion.

Pakistan General Huddles With Rotarians

Maj. Gen. M. Hayaud-Din, right, chief of the Pakistan-Military Mission to the United States, talks with presidents of the Lititz and Ephrata Rotary Clubs prior to speaking at a joint meeting of the clubs last night in the General Sutter Hotel, Lititz. At left is Simon T. Fickinger, Lititz club president, and in the center is Wayne Heberlig, Ephrata club head. (Intell Photo)

Lancastrian's 'Ball In The Sky'

New Book Capsules Career Of Air Pioneer

By JOSEPH T. KINGSTON
(Intell Staff Writer)

An excellent condensation of the remarkable career of John Wise, the Lancastrian who, at the age of 38, was hailed at the "Father of American Ballooning," will be published Monday by Henry Holt and Co., Inc., New York.

The 190-page volume, titled "Ball In The Sky," is by Esther M. Douty and is published as one of the Holt Books for Young People series, for readers 11 years of age and older.

Miss Douty, a Washington, D.C. newspaperwoman, did some of her research on the subject of John Wise in the library of the Lancaster Newspapers, Inc., and also uitlized material available at the Lancaster County Historical Society and the Lancaster Free Public Library.

What emerged from all this is an intelligently written and most interesting study of the Lancaster youth who became America's pioneer scientific aeronaut and the discoverer of some of the most vital secrets of aerial navigation.

Employing semi-fictional narrative techniques, the author skilfully accomplishes the admittedly difficult task of interesting air-age youngsters in the crude experiments of the boy, John Wise, here in the Lancaster, Pa., of 130 years ago.

She has young John dropping his prized cat, "Tiger Tee," rigged to a home-made parachute, from the 195-foot steeple of Trinity Lutheran Church, and she has his first "fire balloon" — a toy device he sent aloft from his father's brick-yard in 1822 — setting fire to the "thatched" roof of a home on S. Duke Street.

Miss Douty follows John Wise through the local streets as he and a buddy watch the famous Marquis de Lafayette arrive here on September 27, 1825; to the Lancastrian School at Prince and Chestnut Sts., where Lafayette shakes his hand and learns that the 17-year-old youth hopes to "sail the air which lies high above the seven seas and flows over the four corners of the earth."

The author then quotes Lafayette as saying:

"Who knows, my son, perhaps you will . . . . do not mind the

Turn To Page 20 For More Of WISE

Inhabitants of Saint Martin, in the West Indies, although politically divided between France and The Netherlands, speak English.

Oldest members in point of service of Hager's Quarter Century club receive bonds from John C. Hager, right, treasurer. Left to right, Miriam Regennas, bedwear; Maude Frye, buyer children's dept.; Bertha Miller, women's apparel; and Ruth Good, infant's dept.

POLICE MOTTO

FREMONT, Ohio (AP)— Police Chief Myron Bork has this sign on his office wall: "A drunken driver needs a cop for a chaser."

300 Employes at Hager's 135th Anniversary Dinner

Employes of Hager and Bro., Inc. celebrated the store's 135th anniversary at a dinner held last night at Hotel Brunswick. About 300 persons attended.

The Hager store, founded in 1821, is the oldest department store in the United States operated continously on the same site under the same family name, management and ownership.

David Simon, a member of the firm of Michaels-Stern, of New York, a clothing manufacturing firm in business for 113 years, and dealing with Hager and Bro., Inc for the past 50 years, attended the dinner.

Another business guest from a 100-year old firm was John Herrmann, head of Herrmann Handkerchiefs, which celebrated its 105th anniversary last fall.

Another feature was the presence of several retired employes. They were: Miss Katherine Meiskey, Mrs. Mary Hohman, James Caithness and Ray Cramer.

Quarter Century Club

John C. Hager paid tribute to Hager's Quarter Century Club, whic consists of people employed by the store for 25 or more consecutive years. They were presented with Savings Bonds.

Quarter Century Club members are: Maude E. Frye, O. Ruth Good, Walter Frankford, Bertha P. Miller, Salinda B. Meiskey, Miriam M. Regannas, Ruth Hurst Dry, William H. Hager Jr., Fred W. Wells, Helen T. Neuhauser, Nathaniel E. Hager, John C. Hager 3rd, Lillian R. Ebersole, Rebecca N. Stauffer, Robert F. Warren, Mary Louise Sommer, Lucy B. Hardy, Mary Lefever, Ida B. Haeseler, Reda McQueney, Eleanor E. McEvoy, Margaret S. Haas, William S. Taggart, May Y. Burnside, Isaac K. Charles, Miriam G. Harner, Charles E. Keller.

To mark the anniversary, the store is holding a 10-day sale. And election contest, with the employees divided into two political parties will be held. Manager of the one party, "the Suggestive Sellers" is Redmond C. Hager; manager o fthe other party, "the Kourtesy Kids," is William H. Hager 3rd. George C. Werner, head official of the contest, explained the rules and described the prizes.

Outlines History

William H. Hager Jr., outlined the history of Hager's anniversary events and called for an outstanding effort to make the sale a success. Nathaniel E. Hager, advertising manager, spoke on mercandising and promotional plans for the sale and described the different kinds of "good service" needed to "put both political parties in the winning column."

Entertainment was provided by Prof. John B. Shenk, hypnotist, from Millersville State Teachers College. Colored pictures from last year's store party were shown by William H. Hager 3rd.

The Banquet and Entertainment Committee consisted of: Nathaniel E. Hager, chairman; William H. Hager 3rd, Mrs. M. Jane Dowd, Jack R. Hager, William S. Taggart, and Ray Frank. Sales Contest Committee members are: George C. Werner, Mrs. M. Jane Dowd, John C. Hager and Fred W. Wells.

New Holland Boatman Drowns In Susquehanna River

Intelligencer Journal
TELEPHONE 7-5251
The Leading Newspaper in the Garden Spot of America. Home Owned for Home Folks Since 1794
162nd Year.—No. 299 | Official United States Census Figures Lancaster Metropolitan Area Population 234,717 | LANCASTER, PA., THURSDAY MORNING, MAY 31, 1956 | CITY EDITION | 22 PAGES. | 30c PER WEEK—5c Per Copy

WEATHER
(U. S. Weather Bureau Forecast for Lancaster, Cumberland, Lebanon, York, Adams and Franklin Counties):
Cloudy, Warm And Humid Today With Highest In The 80s. Showers Ending Tonight. Thunderstorms Likely. Cooler Tomorrow, Cloudy And Less Humid.

RAY SENSENIG BODY MISSING AFTER SEARCH

Victim, 30, Working On Propeller; Wife, Son, 8, Witness Holiday Tragedy

A New Holland man fixing the propeller of his small boat lost footing and drowned in the Susquehanna River near Long Level at 1:15 p. m. yesterday.

Victim of the holiday tragedy was identified as Ray B. Sensenig, thirty, of 115 Earl Ave., New Holland. His body has not been recovered.

He disappeared beneath the surface after missing two life preservers thrown by his wife and while she scurried desperately for a third. His eight-year-old son also witnessed the drowning.

It was the first accidental drowning in the Susquehanna River in Lancaster County this year.

RAY B. SENSENIG

Sgt. V. E. Simpson, of the Columbia State Police, said Sensenig was reported standing in the rear of his 16-foot runabout when he lost footing and fell overboard—about 450 yards off the west shore.

Sensenig called to his wife, Elizabeth, for a life preserver and she tossed two into the water, each short of the goal, Simpson said. She was searching for a third when her husband disappeared.

Columbia State Police and Pennsylvania Fish Commission officers continued dragging until dark last evening and plan to continue the search this morning, assisted by Columbia Fire Police who have a barge outfitted for this purpose.

Thousands of persons were en-

Turn To Page 11 For More Of DROWNING

BABY'S BODY DISCOVERED IN CITY HOME

22-Yr.-Old Mother Tells Police Child Was Born Dead In January

The body of a new-born baby was discovered yesterday afternoon, hidden beneath the cellar steps of a city home and a twenty-two-year-old woman is being held by city police as a result.

Detective Frank P. Matt said the baby, a girl, was found at the home of James Brown, 365 S. Queen St. Held on an open charge, pending further investigation, is Mrs. Nancy Stetler, a roomer at the Brown home since February.

BORN IN JANUARY

Mrs. Stetler, according to Detective Matt, admitted that she gave birth to the baby in January.

She said the baby was born at the Lancaster YWCA in January and that she placed it in a shoe box, according to detectives.

They quoted her as saying that upon moving to the Queen Street address she wrapped it in newspapers, several bags, a tin box, and then in a carton wrapped in two pink towels. She hid it beneath the cellar steps.

Brown found the box yesterday when he started to investigate a "bad odor" in the cellar. Detectives said the fetus was beginning to decompose. Dr. Charles P. Stahr, deputy coroner, said it apparently died from strangulation because the umbilical cord had not been tied.

Police said Mrs. Stetler told them the baby was dead when it was born, that it did not move or breathe.

Detectives said Mrs. Stetler has been separated from her husband for three years and has two children. Detective Matt said she named the father of the baby but said he had no knowledge of the birth.

Mrs. Stetler was arrested by Detective Raymond Wiggins yesterday afternoon. She is being held at the police station. Detective Matt said he will consult with District Attorney William C. Storb today concerning the case.

The Fruits Of Victory

INDIANAPOLIS, Ind., May 30—Pat Flaherty, of Chicago, his face begrimed by the grueling 500-mile race, which he won today, gets a kiss in the winner's enclosure from actress Virginia Mayo. (AP Wirephoto)

Pat Flaherty Takes Indianapolis '500'; Accidents Mar Race

By WILL GRIMSLEY

INDIANAPOLIS, May 30 (AP)—Pat Flaherty, a red-haired Irishman from Chicago's tough roadster ranks, outgunned the veteran Sam Hanks in a stirring two man driving duel today to win the wreck-spattered 40th 500-mile Speedway race.

Flaherty, 29, barely avoiding a serious accident in the final 30 miles, drove his snub-nosed cream and rose machine across the finish line just 22 seconds ahead of the 41-year old Hanks from Burbank, Calif., making his 11th bid for America's premier auto racing prize.

The winning time was an average of 128.490 m.p.h., which fell well short of an anticipated record because of a series of accidents which kept the yellow caution flag flying for an hour and 11 minutes.

12 CARS WRECKED

Twelve cars were involved in smashups or accidents of a smaller nature all but one of the drivers walked away with no serious injuries. Two crewmen and two spectators suffered minor injuries.

Flaherty, the fastest qualifier with a record 145.596 mark in the 10 mile trials, himself barely escaped possible serious injuries when he sent his car careening around Dick Rathmann's machine which went into a spin on the northeast turn.

Following Hanks was Don Freeland, Redondo Beach, Calif., who made a strong finishing bid.

Johnnie Parsons, Van Nuys, Calif., who won a shortened race here in 1950, finished fourth, followed by Dick Rathmann, Trenton, N. J., fifth; Bob Sweikert, Indianapolis, the defending champion, sixth; Rodger Ward, Los Angeles, seventh; Bob Veith, Oakland, Calif., eighth, Jimmy Reece, Oklahoma City, ninth, and Cliff Griffith, Indianapolis, 10th.

The record for the 500 mile run around the 2½ mile brick and asphalt track is 130.840 set by the late Bill Vukovich, killed in a four car smashup last year. Sweikert won last year in 128.209.

TAKES LEAD AT 75

Flaherty who had suffered crackups in two of his previous attempts, shot into the lead at the 75 mile point and led virtually every lap thereafter. From the 200 mile mark, he never was headed.

Eleven times the yellow flag—calling for hold of positions and reduced speed — went up after crackups and accidents of a smaller nature. Old timers called it the most "caution time" ever used in the race.

Most seriously injured drivers were Jimmy Daywalt, Indianapolis and Tony Bettenhausen, Tinley Park, Ill., who crashed within seconds of each other.

Daywalt suffered burns and

Turn To Page 15 For More Of SPEEDWAY

$1,500,000 Shopping Center For Ephrata

U.S. ACCEPTS RUSSIAN BID TO AIR SHOW

President Approves Gen. Twining's Trip To Moscow For Aviation Day

WASHINGTON, May 30 (AP)—By personal decision of President Eisenhower, the nation's top air general will make an extraordinary journey to Russia to attend the Soviets' Aviation Day celebration June 24.

Gen. Nathan F. Twining, Air Force chief of staff, accepted the Soviet invitation today. Several other Air Force officers will accompany Twining on this rare high level visit, during which they will catch at least some glimpses of part of Russia's military might.

In directing Twining to accept, Eisenhower apparently overruled a military recommendation that the United States should hold off while trying to get the invitation broadened to include other members of the Joint Chiefs of Staff and a look at other Soviet forces in addition to the air force. Administration officials have been angling for such a wider invitation but so far in vain.

BOHLEN MESSAGE

It was learned that a message from Ambassador Charles E. Bohlen in Moscow, dispatched here over last weekend, helped to bring the discussion over the Soviet invitation to a head. The Bohlen message made clear that the United States was confronted with a firm invitation to send an Air Force delegation to Moscow and left little ground for belief that the Russians would be inclined to broaden the bid.

However, today's action gave rise to new talk of reciprocal action by the United States which might lead to further exchanges of military visits by the United States and Russia.

There was no comment from Sen. Knowland of California, Republican Senate leader, who has warned that if the exchanges

Turn To Page 11 For More Of TWINING

Baseball Scores

NATIONAL LEAGUE

Brooklyn 6-3, Philadelphia 5-12
New York 4-5, Pittsburgh 5-3
Milwaukee 9-11, Chicago 10-9
Cincinnati 6-6, St. Louis 3-5

AMERICAN LEAGUE

Detroit 11-5, Kansas City 3-1
Chicago 6-9, Cleveland 3-8
Baltimore 2-5, Boston 1-4
New York 4-12, Washington 3-5

(Details On Pages 15-17)

POPE UNDERGOES MEDICAL CHECK FOR WEAK VOICE

VATICAN CITY, May 30 (AP) — Pope Pius XII, suffered a slight weakening of his voice, underwent a general medical and cardiograph examination tonight.

Doctors said they found no physical disturbance, nor any infection of the pontiff's throat. The Pope has been tired by a heavy work load in May.

The condition of the 80-year-old head of the Roman Catholic Church was not considered serious, but he was urged to take a little more rest.

His audiences tomorrow will be restricted to a regular Thursday morning meeting with Msgr. Angelo Dell'Acqua, his prosecretary of state.

BLAMED ON HEAT

Some Vatican sources said the pontiff had felt the sudden onset of midsummer heat in Rome after a prolonged, unusually severe winter. The pontiff also was said to be disappointed with election results in Rome where Communists and Socialists won 29 of the City Council's 80 seats, largest number they ever held.

Major cause of the pontiff's indisposition, however, was said to be the enormous work load he carried throughout the month. He received about 200,000 people in daily audiences, gave 17 major speeches and spoke many times more to small groups of pilgrims.

TITO ON WAY TO RUSSIA

BELGRADE, Yugoslavia, May 30 (AP)—President Tito left tonight for Russia to discuss Yugoslav-Soviet relations.

W. T. Grant Chain, 4 Other Stores To Occupy Building

The W. T. Grant Company, chain department store operators, a syndicate drug store, shoe store, and two other retail units not yet classified, are combining to erect a $1,500,000 shopping center at Ephrata.

The announcement was made yesterday by A. G. Kurtz and Sons Inc., Ephrata, owners of the three-acre tract on which the shopping center will be located. Work on the project will begin immediately.

The one-story modern, shopping center will be under one roof and will have an area of 52,000 square feet. The Grant store will occupy 17,000 square feet of this space. The remainder will be equally divided between the four additional stores to occupy the site.

POOL OPERATION

The transaction was completed through a New York pool which buys, converts and leases desirable retail locations to members of the pool. Negotiations have been underway for several weeks and were completed yesterday.

The tract on which the shopping center is to be located, is at the intersection of South State Street and Route 222 on the southern limits of Ephrata. It was annexed to the borough several months ago, and is in the heart of a community business center established by Cloister Dairies in 1938, and which has grown steadily since.

Already under construction on the 20 acre triangle between the two thoroughfares, is an American Stores Company food store and an electrical appliance store by McCreary and Gamber, a local firm.

Three additional acres of land are under option in blank for a period of 90 days Kurtz reported. The name of the holder of the option was not disclosed by Kurtz, but sale of the area in part or whole is subject to the approval of the owners.

Part of the remainder of the tract, covering about two acres, is the site of the abandoned, water-filled Kurtz stone quarry which was pumped dry over a year ago by the Borough of Ephrata to determine if the flow of water into the quarry, which has a capacity of several million gallons, was sufficient to serve as an additional source of water to the borough.

Pumped out, the supply of water into the quarry was found to be insufficient, and since then the quarry has again been allowed to fill. It is expected that the quarry site will eventually be reclaimed.

BUSINESS SPACE NEEDED

Ephrata has been experiencing growing pains in its cramped mid-town shopping district for more than a decade, with retail locations at a premium.

J. J. Newberry Company, a chain department store two years ago purchased historic Mount Vernon Inn, and erected a $500,000 retail store that opened on March 1. The site was one of the last major business locations available in downtown Ephrata.

Located in the business area adjacent to the shopping center site are two auto agencies, two retail stores, Kurtz Concrete Inc., a farm implement and truck firm, two filling stations, dairy, lumber yard, used car lot, and water bottling plant.

HIGHWAY DEATHS PASS 'NORMAL,' NEAR FORECAST

By THE ASSOCIATED PRESS

Death on the nation's highways this Memorial Day passed the "normal" figure for a week day on Wednesday night and headed upward toward the 110 fatalities safety experts had forecast.

The normal figure for a non-holiday Wednesday at this time of year is 70.

But at 10:30 p.m., EST, with the toll still rising, 78 lives had been cut short by traffic accidents. In addition, there were 20 drownings and 27 deaths from miscellaneous holiday causes for an over-all total of 125.

There was some doubt that the highway toll of 110 forecast by the National Safety Council would be reached.

Earlier in the night, the council said in a guarded statement there might be a "good chance" the figure would be lower.

Ned H. Dearborn, president of the National Safety Council, pointed out that with only a few hours remaining of the 30 comprising the holiday period—from 6 p.m. (local time) Tuesday to midnight Wednesday—the traffic death total was well under the 110 fatalities forecast.

Last year the Memorial Day holiday fell on a weekend and 369 persons were killed in traffic accidents over the three-day period. Total accidental deaths that holiday numbered 596.

Since World War II there has been only one other one-day Memorial Day holiday. That was in 1951 and traffic deaths totaled 81.

THE INTELL INDEX

"We Lead All The Rest"

FARM CORNER

By Joe Wachtman

WEATHER CHANGE UPS FARM HOPES FOR 'CATCHING UP'

Holiday Rain Catches Hay Cuttings In Fields, Planting Advances Rapidly

Lancaster County farmers, whose crops have been delayed throughout the spring by killing frosts and other adverse weather conditions now can hope for a better break from the weatherman and a chance for the growing season to catch up to normal.

The generally favorable weather of this week has permitted a few farmers to begin first cutting of hay and early field planting of tobacco while others are completing the planting of corn.

The U. S. Weather Bureau promises above normal temperatures for eastern Pennsylvania through Saturday with possible rainfall of one-half to one inch through scattered showers. Many parts of the county will welcome the moisture on dry fields.

Yesterday's showers brought

Turn To Page 18 For More Of FARM CORNER

Weather Calendar

COMPARATIVE TEMPERATURES

Station	High	Low
Water Works	80	55
Ephrata	79	54
Last Year (Ephrata)	79	59
Official High for Year May 13	88	
Official Low for Year Feb. 22	12	

Character of Day—Partly Cloudy

WINDS
Direction SW Avg. Velocity 7 MPH.

HUMIDITY
8 a.m. 77% 11 a.m. 68% 2 p.m. 60% 5 p.m. 74% 8 p.m. 74%
Average Humidity 71%

SUN
Rises 5:38 a.m. Sets 8:26 p.m.

MOON
Rises: 12:58 a.m. Friday.
Last Quarter, June 1.

STARS
Morning—Mars
Evening—Venus, Jupiter, Saturn

WEATHER
(U. S. Weather Bureau)

Southeastern Pennsylvania and Southern New Jersey—Partly cloudy, warm and humid today with scattered thundershowers likely in the late afternoon or at night, high in the mid or upper 80s. Tomorrow generally fair and cooler.

Central and Northeastern Pennsylvania—Considerable cloudiness, warm and humid today, high in the 80s. Showers and thunderstorms today ending during the night. Squally winds likely with thunderstorms. Cooler by tomorrow morning. Tomorrow partly cloudy and less humid with rise in temperature.

Lower Potomac and Chesapeake Bay—Small craft warnings are displayed. Southwest winds 15-25 miles per hour today, occasionally 40 miles per hour or more in scattered thundersqualls this afternoon. Visibility mostly good.

Maryland and Delaware—Partly cloudy, warm and humid with scattered thundershowers this afternoon and night, high in the mid to upper 80s. Tomorrow fair and cooler. Small craft warnings are displayed.

Man Doggoned Mad, There's No Dog Agent

Amid reports of increasing depredations caused by stray dogs, one Lancaster County farmer said yesterday he intends to go directly to the State Department of Agriculture for action in the absence of a state dog law enforcement officer.

H. John Martin, of Ephrata R1, said he plans to call Harrisburg today after failing to get anyone here to examine the remains of the chickens and the dog which Martin shot as it slaughtered the birds in his chicken house.

At present, there is no dog law officer here. C. Allen Wiker left the post on April 16, and his successor, Veryl Weigel, will not start until June 15. Lancaster County's officer also serves Lebanon and Chester counties.

The enforcement officer is required to check on complaints of loss to marauding dogs, and to seek the owner of the animal. If the owner cannot be located, the victim is reimbursed by the State Department of Agriculture.

Martin said that the medium-sized canine got into his chicken house Sunday and, before he was stopped, he had killed 53 chickens, valued by the owner at about two dollars each.

Martin said he had called Wiker and Weigel, both of Columbia, but neither would handle the complaint.

Weigel said the Berks County dog law enforcement officer is serving this area temporarily. However, he said he does not know the Berks official's name.

All police agencies are supposed to have the name, he stated. However, a check indicated state police do not have the name.

Martin said yesterday that he was unable to learn the name

Turn To Page 11 For More Of DOGS

Changes Made In Procedure For County Assessors

Revisions in county real estate assessment procedure to more fully conform to the 1951 Assessment Law were announced yesterday by the Lancaster County Commissioners.

Richard L. Musser, chief clerk to the commissioners, said the new schedule would go into effect immediately.

The chief changes are in the time table for completing the assessments by the assessors and in appeal procedure.

All assessment work, including canvassing the district, for the 1957 assessment year must be completed by the assessor on Aug. 1 and their books returned to the County Commissioners office.

Presently, some assessors do not complete their work until October and November.

By Aug. 20, the commissioners will notify all property holders where changes in assessment have been made, Musser explained. Included with the notification will be a form of intention to appeal an assessment.

These intention to appeal forms, properly filled out, must be returned by the property holder to the county commissioners no later than Sept. 1, in the event the owner desires to appeal the new assessment.

Musser said that the only appeals that will be heard by the board are those cases in which the property owner filed an intention to appeal.

The next step in the procedure will be for the commissioners to notify property holders who filed intentions to appeal of the time and date on which their appeals will be heard.

Within five days after the hearing is held, the commissioners will notify the property holder whether or not the appeal has been granted and the amount of the assessment.

Driver Lands In Back Seat

Car Roars Through Gas Station At Lyndon, Leaves $4,000 Loss

A car roared out of control yesterday afternoon on Route 72 at Lyndon, crashed its way through a gasoline station leaving a trail of damage estimated at $4,000 and returned to the road, police reported.

The driver, Ammon E. Beck, twenty-eight, 528 S. Queen St., wound up with minor injuries in the back seat of the demolished vehicle.

Frank Horner, chief of West Lampeter Twp. police, said the car, going at a "very, very fast rate of speed," swept across the highway, knocked over a gas pump, swung around backwards, slammed through the station's office door, knocked out several window panes, rammed into a huge garage door and ricocheted back onto the highway.

Beck was taken to Lancaster General Hospital where he was admitted for observation of minor injuries.

No cars were on the highway at the time, the station driveway was clear when the car ran amuck, and two men in the garage managed to scramble to safety, Horner said.

He estimated damage to the station—owned by William McFalls—at $3,000 and to Beck's car at $1,000.

Beck said he lost control when he tried to apply his brakes as he drove north on the highway at about 4:50 p.m. Horner charged him with reckless driving before Justice of the Peace Myrtle Pyfer, Willow Street.

Memorial Rites Set Mood On Holiday, Traffic Light

Except for a short mid-afternoon downpour which sent picnickers scurrying yesterday afternoon, Memorial Day was celebrated quietly with the annual tributes to the war dead dominating the holiday.

Accidents which noramlly share headlines during the first holiday of the summer, were few, police reported. Traffic also was relatively light since the mid-week Memorial Day prevented long weekend trips to shore and other resorts.

Clear and comfortably cool weather marked the annual parade and services held at Penn Square and Lancaster Cemetery.

Moving in from the west shortly before 2 p. m., dark clouds dumped their rain in a hard, half-hour-long shower. But with the sun shining brightly again, most traces of the moisture were gone by 4 p.m.

Many residents of the city and suburbs spent the day at home and held back yard picnics. Others visited nearby parks.

POOLS DO WELL

Area swimming pools reported good, but not exceptional turnouts. It was noted that Memorial Day, which often is marked by bad weather, does not usually find too many swimmers at the local pools.

A large wreath was placed at the base of the Soldiers and Sailors Monument in Penn Square by Robert and John Long during brief ceremonies, under the direc-

Turn To Page 11 For More Of MEMORIAL DAY

STRAYERS GOING TO GLEN MILLS SCHOOL

Mr. and Mrs. David W. Strayer, who are resigning as superintendent and matron of the Rotary Home for Boys, have accepted positions at the Glen Mills School for Boys, it was announced yesterday.

The resignation of Mr. and Mrs. Strayer from the local home posts is effective June 9. They will take up their duties at Glen Mills on June 11.

Penn Square Scene Of Traditional Memorial Service

Mrs. Mame Smith, daughter of a Union Veteran, (right), in charge of the service at the Soldiers and Sailors Monument at Penn Square for her 37th year, is shown above with the sons of the Rev. and Mrs. Alfred L. Long, pastor of Christ Lutheran Church during yesterday's ceremony. The two boys, Robert (left) and John, placed the wreath in front of the monument after their father had given the invocation and a short talk.

Park the family car on one of the two lots and leave your cares behind. This was one of the first projects of the Lancaster Sertoma Club. The public has responded in vast numbers.

A NEW THRILL ON NEW SWINGS brought smiles to the faces of Judith Delray (left) and Beth Ann Reese. The Lancaster Sertoma Club installed $1,000 worth of new playground equipment in Long's Park during the last year.

NURSES ASSOCIATION of Lancaster County at Long Park is one of long list of outings held there. The Sertoma Club added 60 new picnic tables during the year.

Big Season For Long Park

Fun in Long Park will be more convenient for the more than 17,000 persons expected to use the added facilities during the average hot, sunny weekend this summer.

Now, for the fifth consecutive year, the Lancaster Sertoma club is again increasing the accommodations, aiding the Long Park commission in the upkeep of one of the two largest parks in and around Lancaster.

Buchmiller's, Reservoir, Williamson, Musser and Buchanan parks, too, are popular outing sites for Lancastrians. These views were photographed in Long Park.

CUB SCOUTS AND HOT DOGS go together naturally on a picnic. To provide cooking accommodations, 15 new charcoal grills like this one used by Pack 4, have been set up. Some are placed on the tees and greens of the former golf course.

The two original brick fireplaces in the park are still popular. Along with the 10 charcoal grills installed last year and the 15 this season, there are now 27 individual cooking sites.

Youngsters never seem to slow up—particularly around playground equipment. This merry-go-round was installed three years ago, during the Sertoma Club's second year in the Park project.

Keeping Long Park neat and clean to make the hours of relaxation and recreation pleasant is a job handled by the city maintenance crews. Long Park is operated by a park commission of which Mayor Kendig C. Bare is the chairman. Boys and man on shore are sweeping debris from lake surface.

New Era Photo

Part of first-day crowd at new Farnum pool.

200 Children Attend Opening of Farnum Wading Pool

Approximately 200 children attended the opening of the new wading pool at Farnum playground, Farnum and Strawberry Sts., yesterday.

The pool, constructed this spring, is the fifth to be added to the city's recreation system.

The other pools are located at Buchanan, Rockland and Green, Rodney and Sixth Ward.

Supervisors at the new pool are Stanley Wills and Eleanor Miller. The pool will be open from 1 to 4 p.m. Monday through Friday.

PROFIT NOT ENOUGH

Housing Project Can't Pay Taxes

• The four-year-old Hickory Tree Heights housing project has not produced enough income to permit it to pay school taxes, the Lancaster Housing Authority has told the City School Board.

The Authority's financial report was submitted at a board meeting last night. The board asked for the report because the Authority, though tax exempt, had agreed to pay taxes when able.

The tax bill for 1955-56 would come to $8,000. Tuition for the approximately 100 children living in the project and attending city schools is valued at around $20,000 by school officials.

The Authority statement said its surplus is $30,000, of which $17,000 has been set aside for contingencies.

$271,000 Income

The Authority listed an income of $271,000 from the housing project during the four year period. It paid out $98,000 in interest on the $715,000 bond issue, retired $80,000 worth of bonds, and the remainder of funds was used for repairs and improvements.

The district feels entitled to taxes because the city will assume ownership of the project in lieu of taxes 28 years after its inception.

New Teachers Elected

New teachers elected, and their salaries, are: Mrs. George F. Weiss, elementary, $3,800; Mrs. Helen Schafer Markham, elementary, $3,200; Mrs. Jacqueline Mull, elementary, $3,300; Mrs. Alma P. Duncan, half-time at Lafayette kindergarten, at annual rate of $4,200.

These resignations were accepted: Ronald B. Dellecker, instrumental music teacher at Reynolds, leaving for another position; Edwin B. McGehee, Hand, commercial, going to new post at Hempfield Joint High School; June P. Scouten, elementary, who will discontinue teaching; Beatrice M. Smith, elementary, going to Millersville State Teachers College.

Resignations also were approved for three teachers elected within the past four months but who have since changed their plans—William E. Schneider, Judy Goldhirsch Feldman, Helen M. Miller.

Vacancies Exist

Dr. O. H. Aurand, superintendent of schools, announced that several important teaching vacancies still exist.

It was reported that the district will pay off all temporary loans

—See HOUSINC Page 20

Burgess' Mother Off for Moscow

LONDON (AP) — The mother of runaway British diplomat Guy Burgess has gone to Moscow in the last two days to visit him, the Foreign Office announced tonight.

She applied to the Soviet Embassy in London for a visa and informed the British ambassador in Moscow of her plans three months ago, a spokesman said.

Donald Maclean—the other half of the renegade team of Burgess and Maclean—already has been joined in the Soviet Union by his wife and children.

Malcolm Stehman on Dean's List at PSU

Malcolm H. Stehman, son of Mr. and Mrs. Ivan J. Stehman, 2817 Marietta Ave., has been named to the Dean's List for the spring semester in the College of Agriculture at the Pennsylvania State University.

Stehman, who was enrolled in the wood utilization course, graduated last month.

8 Argentine Revolt Leaders Reach Caracas

CARACAS, Venezuela (AP)—Gen. Raul Tanco, a leader of the Peronista revolt which fizzled in Argentina a month ago, arrived here today, an exile. Seven other officers associated in the June 10 rebellion were with him.

Only two Argentines were on hand to greet the party. One identified himself as Rdolfo Martinez, "a personal friend" of exiled ex-dictator Juan D. Peron. The other was Jorge Miranda, a night club entertainer.

Tipsy Driver Hits Fire Hydrant

Brayton Roland Groff, twenty-three, Soudersburg, was arrested on drunken driving charges at 3 a.m. today by city police after his car collided with a fire hydrant in the 200 block of E. King St. Damage to the right front of the car was estimated at $200.

Groff was given a drunkometer test and later prosecuted by city policeman Alfonso Micciche.

PROVE WOMAN'S BIRTH

Letter Written on Shirt Cuffs Used as Evidence

LOS ANGELES (AP)—A pair of shirt cuffs mailed from San Francisco a few days after the earthquake and fire of April 18, 1906, probably will enable Mrs. Marion Howard Snell of nearby Panorama City to obtain a birth certificate.

Her attorney is using the shirt cuffs as evidence in his petition to Superior Court for a judicial determination that Mrs. Snell was born in San Francisco April 19, 1906. With such a decree she can obtain a birth certificate which she needs to get a passport for a trip to Europe.

Used As Postcards

Her father, the late Elbert J. Howard, mailed the shirt cuffs, like postcards, April 22, 1906, to his sisters, Mrs. James Rodgers of The Dalles, Ore., and Mrs. Dan Hawes, Sellwood, Ore.

In later years Howard got the cuffs back and often told how he used them because he could find nothing else on which to write.

'We Are Safe'

The message he wrote on the shirt cuffs said: "We are safe. The earthquake was dreadful. Also the fire. But we are safe and well. Edith (Mrs. Snell's mother) is in hospital. Baby girl was born in three hours after we got her there. Both doing well. We are camping in gov't tents. Eating gov't food and are under martial law."

PA. DUTCH IN U.S., CANADA PLAN EXCHANGE

KITCHENER, Ont. (AP) — Canadians and Americans of Pennsylvania-German extraction plan tentatively a series of trips across the border next summer in an effort to get to know each other better.

Stephen Jones, manager of the Kitchener Chamber of Commerce said yesterday that he plans to visit centers on the proposed route in Pennsylvania next month. These points include Williamsport, Harrisburg, Lancaster, Allentown and Scranton in Pennsylvania.

Jones said the tentative plans call for tours leaving from the United States to have a week's visit in the Kitchener area.

Steel Situation Still Unchanged

Joint Meeting to Be Resumed Monday

PITTSBURGH (AP)—Negotiators trying to break a deadlock in the 13-day-old nationwide steel strike met for 2½ hours today but United Steelworkers president David J. McDonald said "there's been no change in the situation."

Immediately after the joint meeting recessed, the industry negotiating team went into a private huddle with federal mediators who had been standing by.

Joseph F. Finnegan, director of the Federal Mediation and Conciliation Service, said the caucus was arranged at the request of industry negotiators.

Will Resume Monday

Union and company representatives said their meeting will resume Monday morning.

John A. Stephens, vice president of U.S. Steel Corp., and chief industry negotiator, had no comment.

Finnegan said mediators had no plans at present to caucus with the union unless such a session is requested. McDonald said he did not plan to make such a request.

McDonald reiterated his desire to negotiate an agreement that would end the strike and send his 650,000 basic steelworkers back to work. He added that as of now he could foresee no developments over the weekend.

Jailed for Auto Theft, Charged Twice More

Charges of driving an auto without the consent of the owner and tampering with a motor vehicle were lodged today against Eugene DeForest, this city, at the county jail. Prosecution was brought before Alderman Acker by James H. Yarnell, 326 Park Ave.

DeForest was jailed yesterday on auto theft charges brought by Lititz police chief Lloyd Hoffman.

DROODLES

by Roger Price

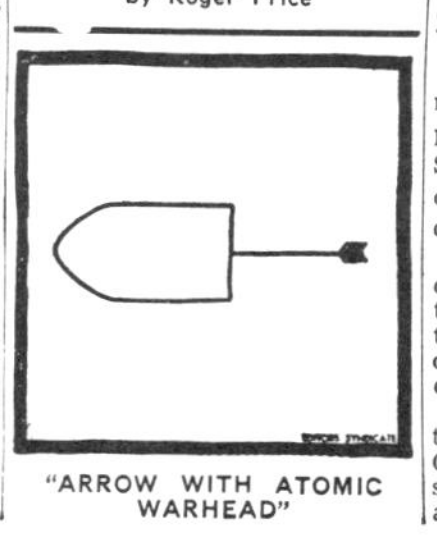

"ARROW WITH ATOMIC WARHEAD"

Return of Baby No Money Issue

Parents Say Kidnaper Now Fears Capture

WESTBURY, N.Y. (AP)—A Weinberger family spokesman said today the parents of the kidnaped baby now believe the kidnaper's fear of capture and not the amount of ransom is holding up the return of the baby.

David Holman, an uncle of Mrs. Beatrice Weinberger, mother of the missing 5 - week - old infant, made that comment when asked about reports that the Weinbergers had $25,000 ready to ransom the child.

Church Watch Off

Holman, a former Nassau County assistant district attorney, also revealed police no longer are watching St. Brigid's Roman Catholic Church here. It has been kept open 24 hours aday in hopes the kidnaper would leave the baby there.

A dim light burns outside the church at night but Holman said the kidnaper could run into the church with the child without risking identification.

"I don't think it's a case of money now," said Holman. "I'm afraid apprehension and fear on the part of the kidnaper will keep him hiding. If any contact is made now, it will be made indirectly."

Ninth Day

This is the ninth day since Peter was taken from his carriage on the rear patio of the home of his parents, Mr. and Mrs. Morris Weinberger.

Each time the telephone rings in their home they hope against hope that this time it will be the real kidnaper, with news of their baby and how they can get him back.

With deadly frequency, however, it is some misguided crackpot or sadistic joker who pretends he knows where the child is and cruelly raises the Weinbergers' hopes.

The FBI has been in the case officially for two days. Its operatives have maintained their traditional silence about their activities.

Blame York Blast On Carelessness

YORK, Pa. (AP) — Carelessness has been set by York fire officials as the cause of bottled gas explosions there Wednesday which injured 24 persons — hospitalizing half of them.

Gas escaped from a fire-damaged gas tank in the center of a crowd of about 50 spectators who came to the scene after two earlier explosions. Lewis Harbaugh and John Koch, assistant fire chiefs, said the gas was ignited and exploded when matches were lighted in the near vicinity.

All admitted to the hospital were reported in satisfactory condition suffering with burns and the effects of inhaling some and gas fumes.

F&M Professor Named to Special State Project

The State Department of Internal Affairs today announced appointment of Dr. Richard F. Schier, 213 Ruby St., a member of the F and M faculty, to a special project.

Dr. Schier is one of the men chosen to make a legal study of the courts' interpretations of state tax laws. Members of the study commission receive $18.24 per day.

The department announced also the appointment of Richard R. Conlin, 717 N. Franklin St., as a state geologist at an annual salary of $4,794.

FREE SWIMMING LESSONS BEGIN AT LOCAL POOLS

Free swimming lessons for children attending city playgrounds began this morning at Rocky Springs and Maple Grove pools.

Attendance, held down by rain, was lower than expected, according to Lancaster Recreation Association director Albert Reese. About 100 children registered at the first two of three half-hour sessions at Rocky Springs, and 60 were present for the first lesson at Maple Grove. About 300 children had signed up for the lessons.

The lessons, which were postponed from last Friday due to rain, are sponsored by the Lancaster Recreation Association, the Lancaster New Era, and the two swimming pools. They will continue each Friday morning for a period of five weeks.

Court Approves Merger by City

2 Lanc. Twp. Tracts Cover 12½ Acres

The court today gave final approval to the annexation by the city of two tracts of land, totaling 12½ acres, in Lancaster Twp.

Both tracts are located in the vicinity of Charles Rd.

One of the tracts, with 12.377 acres, is the property of Charles F. Hoffmeier and his wife, Gertrude, 1315 Wabank Rd. Part of the Hoffmeier tract, located on the west corner of Charles and Wabank Rds., previously was within city limits.

The other plot, with .258 acres, is owned by John H. Martin and his wife, Barbara W., 229 Lemon St., Elizabethtown. A dwelling on the plot to be annexed is tenanted by H. Grant Hurst and his wife Bertha D.

Home Builders' Group Chartered

The court today granted articles of incorporation for the Home Builders Association, a non-profit organization.

The association, with headquarters at 1801 Lititz Pike, lists its aims: "To associate home builders within the city and county, and to cooperate with all branches of the home building industry."

Officers are: Emanuel E. Murry, Lancaster R5, president; Benjamin R. Groff, 1712 Conestoga Ave., vice president; Elwood Snyder, 300 S. School Lane, secretary; Abram D. Mellinger, Lancaster R2, treasurer; Maurice H. Wenger, 152 Rose Dr.; Henry Weber, Lititz R2; Allan N. Goberman, 1200 N. School Lane; Harold Meyer, 211 Maxson Rd., and Edward C. Pontz, 102 Millersville Rd., directors. Murry, Groff, Snyder, Mellinger and Wenger are listed as incorporators.

WinsScholarshipto Cornell University

John S. Coppage Jr., son of Mr. and Mrs. John S. Coppage, 16 Elmwood Terrace, Lancaster, has won a John McMullen Regional Scholarship at Cornell University's College of Engineering.

Coppage, a graduate of Manheim Twp. High School, will enter the School of Chemical and Metallurgical Engineering in September.

6th Ward Citizens Plan Annual Festival Today

The Sixth Ward Citizens Association will hold its annual festival at the Sixth Ward playground today beginning at 5 p. m.

Ray Difley is general chairman. Rides, ponies and games will be featured, with music by the Bob Stetler trio. Rain date is Saturday.

MultinationArms Supply To Israel Is Considered

OTTAWA (AP)—Prime Minister Louis St. Laurent hinted today that multination supply of arms to Israel is under discussion.

He informed the House of Commons talks are being held "about the possibility of there being something that would not be exclusively a Canadian action" in supplying arms to Israel.

Reds Make Bid For New Europe Atomic Agency

Would Include U. S. Replace West's Six-Nation Organization

MOSCOW (AP) — The Kremlin today called for the establishment of an all-European organization—in which both the Soviet Union and the United States would take part—to control peaceful use of atomic energy.

A circular distributed to the American, British, French and other embassies proposed the organization as a substitute for Euratom, the six-nation agency which the nations of the Schuman coal-steel pool now are in the process of organizing. The six are France, West Germany, Italy, Belgium, the Netherlands and Luxembourg.

The Soviet statement charged Euratom would be a tool of the North Atlantic Treaty Organization. It asserted that West German participation in Euratom would deepen the division of Germany and in effect give the Germans the chance to manufacture atomic weapons.

Time Is 'Opportune'

The Soviet circular note said: "The Soviet government considers the moment opportune to convoke a conference of European countries to examine the problem of creating a regional organization for peaceful use of atomic energy.

"This organization could be created on an intergovernmental basis with the participation of all European states which express a desire to do so. The United States could also participate in this organization."

The Communist nations have their own atomic organization—the United Institute of Nuclear Research. It includes not only European states but Communist China, Outer Mongolia and North Viet Nam. The Soviet Union has contributed nuclear research

—See ATOMIC—Page 20

2d MSTC Session Opens on Monday

About 560 students completed the first summer session of Millersville State eachers College today.

Fifty-three courses were offered during the session, according to Dr. A. G. Breidenstine, dean of instruction.

he second session begins Monday, and will continue through August 24. Registration will open Monday morning with 42 courses offered. Over 500 students are expected to enroll.

City Hiking Club to See Show at Valley Forge

Members and friends of the Lancaster Hiking Club will attend the matinee show at the Valley Forge Round Stage in Valley Forge Park, tomorrow.

The group will meet at the statue in Buchanan Park at 12:15 p. m. Miss Elizabeth Hammond is chairman of the theater party.

Man Files Divorce Suit For Alleged Indignities

A divorce suit was filed at the Court House today by Thomas J. Balmer, forty-three, of 1609 Wiker Ave., against Irma Balmer, thirty-seven, 1010 Marshall Ave.

Balmer alleged indignities. They were married July 20, 1954.

POLICE FREE DOG CAUGHT IN ANIMAL TRAP

City police freed a dog caught in an animal trap in a field at the rear of the 700 block of New Holland Ave., yesterday.

The dog, a grey fox terrier, was treated for a bruised right hind leg by Dr. C. F. Batory, veterinarian, 1119 E. King St.

Game protectors are probing the legality of the four-inch pan type trap, which bore a name tag issued by Ray Schultz, of Washington Boro.

New Era Photo

Brenda Cole with inflatable globe.

Globe for "Ask Andy" Winner

Friday the Thirteenth is a lucky day for a fifteen-year-old city girl who today was awarded a Hammond's Inflatable International Globe for a question she submitted to "Ask Andy," New Era daily feature.

She is Brenda Cole, daughter of Mr. and Mrs. Martin F. Cole, 587 Pershing Ave.

Brenda won the prize, the first of its kind to be awarded here, for her question, "Can a Turtle Breathe Under Water?" The answer appears on page 15 of today's New Era.

Brenda's hobby is horses and she recently received her own colt.

A graduate of Edward Hand Junior High School, she will enter McCaskey High School this fall. This summer she is employed at a local restaurant.

Brenda has a sister, Linda, ten, and a brother, Jerry, 16.

ON SALE NEXT WEEK

'The Prophet and King' Is Stirring Biblical Novel

The Biblical saga of Saul is narrated in a new and challenging light in "The Prophet And The King," by Shirley Watkins, which will be published by Doubleday and Co., next week.

(Shirley Watkins is Mrs. John F. Steinman, of Drumore Farm, Pequea R1. The local publication date is next Tuesday; the national date is Thursday.)

The novel follows closely the lines of the Old Testament, but its author provides a character delineation of Saul which gives an absorbing answer to the "Why?" of the way the tragic events of his day took place.

You know the way the story must end, before you begin it, since the tale of the prophet Samuel and King Saul and young David has been recounted again and again through the centuries.

But you are intrigued to see the conflict develop, and as you read the story you live it. You are there, amidst the people of Israel and watching the principals as they act out their historic roles. You are carried forward until at last the story of Saul comes to its end, and once you have finished, you find you have been given much to ponder.

Highly Favorable Reviews

Listed as one of Doubleday's biggest novels of the season, "The Prophet And The King" has already received highly favorable reviews in book trade publications. It is a highly intelligent, artistically woven tapestry which strikes the imagination and leaves a lasting impression.

Mrs. Steinman puts the blame for the tortuous twisting of Saul's soul upon Samuel. In her deeply perceptive study, she traces the corrosion of Saul's mind, and how at last he is torn alternately between love and hate for David. She depicts Saul as a grand, great man, raised from obscurity to kinghood, assailed by doubt, and dying in defeat.

The principal figures are portrayed in full dimension, against a brilliant backdrop of Biblical ritual, customs and mores. Mrs. Steinman is a painstaking reporter, catching completely the spirit of the times. Her battle scenes are vivid, as carefully outlined as the dispatches of a modern war correspondent.

No Liberties by Author

One scene may seem at first glance to be unbelievable. This is the colloquy between Saul, who has been pursuing David to kill him, and David who has just refused to kill Saul as he slept. You may well ask whether two men, one the pursuer and the other the pursued, might take time out to commune. The answer is that it is in the Bible, and the author has has taken no liberties.

"The Prophet And The King" can be recommended for Biblical scholars as well as every reader. It in all likelihood will arouse discusion, for not all will agree with Mrs. Steinman's depiction of Saul and Samuel. But you cannot discuss it one way or another unless you read it. After that you can speak up, undoubtedly you will.

GERALD S. LESTZ

No Protests Filed On River Gas Line

Today was the last day to file objections against the proposed 30-inch gas line under the Susquehanna river from York to Lancaster county and the Army Corps District Engineers office, Baltimore, said no protests have been received.

The 2.6 miles of pipe are to be built below the Holtwood dam.

The Army Engineers said they did receive one inquiry from a sportsman who wanted to know whether construction operations would kill fish—especially if dynamite were used in blasting operations. The Engineers explained they had no jurisdiction over the fish problem.

The line would be built by the Transcontinental Gas Pipe Line, Corp., Houston, Texas, to transport gas from Texas and Louisiana to the New York area.

AP Wirephoto

2 Local Girls Compete for 'Miss Pennsylvania' Crown

Two local girls are competing this weekend with beauties from all over the state for the title of "Miss Pennsylvania."

Shown above by arrows are:

Miss Arlene Hubley, (left) 725 Centerville Rd., Silver Spring, "Miss Chiropractic." Miss Hubley is sponsored by the Penna. Licensed Chiropractic Assn. She was May Queen at E. Donegal Twp. High School in 1953, Poultry Queen in 1954 and Posture Queen of Pennsylvania in 1955.

Miss Cynthia Lee Brandt, (right) Maytown, "Miss Ephrata Fair." Miss Brandt is sponsored by the Ephrata Junior Chamber of Commerce and the Ephrata Fair. Assn. She represented Kutztown State Teachers College in the third annual National College Queen Contest last year, and was runnerup in Pennsylvania.

The "Miss Pennsylvania" contest opens today at Longwood Gardens, near Kennett Square. The winner will be announced tomorrow, and will compete for the title of "Miss America" in September in Atlantic City.

WEATHER
(U.S. Weather Bureau Forecast for Lancaster, Cumberland, Lebanon, York, Adams and Franklin Counties):
Cloudy, Warm And Humid Today With Showers Tonight Or Tomorrow. High Today 82-89. Mild Tonight. Warmer Tomorrow.

Intelligencer Journal.

DAILY

TELEPHONE 7-5251 The Leading Newspaper in the Garden Spot of America. Home Owned for Home Folks Since 1794

163rd Year.—No. 46. Official United States Census Figures Lancaster Metropolitan Area Population 234,717 LANCASTER, PA., THURSDAY MORNING, AUGUST 9, 1956. CITY EDITION 28 PAGES. 30c PER WEEK—5c Per Copy

THE INTELL INDEX

New fire house at Fremont and Prospect Streets will look like this sketch prepared for Henry Boettcher, architect. Of brick and cinder block construction, the fire house will face Fremont Street, with office-dormitory-kitchen wing in foreground and apparatus bay at rear. Ground Observer Corps post will be located atop apparatus bay and will be reached by separate entrance.

Eden Says Britain Can Never Accept Nasser's Seizure Of Suez Canal

Oil From Middle East Termed Life, Death Matter In Europe

LONDON, Aug. 8 (AP)—Prime Minister Eden told the world tonight that Britain never can accept Egyptian President Nasser's seizure of the Suez Canal.

He said Middle East oil that passes through the canal is a matter of life and death in Europe.

Eden first called on Queen Elizabeth II at Buckingham Palace with a situation report on the Suez crisis and then went before TV cameras and radio with his message. The radio carried his voice around the globe.

He said gravely:

"Through it—the canal—travels today about half the oil, without which the industry of this country, of Western Europe, of Scandinavia and many other countries could not be kept going. This is a matter of life and death to us all."

He said Nasser cannot be trusted to keep the canal open.

Of the 103-mile waterway, the Prime Minister said:

"The world's commerce depends on it. It is in fact the greatest international waterway in the world. What Colonel Nasser has just done is to seize it for his own ends. . . .

MERCY OF ONE MAN

"If Colonel Nasser's actions were to succeed, each one of us would be at the mercy of one man for the supplies on which we live. We could never accept that."

Emphasis in the Suez crisis shifted today to a peaceful settlement rather than deployment of force, despite authoritative reports that Egypt will boycott the 24-nation conference called by Britain, France and the United States to seek international control of the canal.

Nineteen nations, including hesitant India and Ceylon, have accepted invitations to the meeting to begin in London Aug. 16.

Britain's Foreign Office issued a statement giving assurance that "our intention is that the dispute on the Suez Canal should be peacefully settled." Nevertheless, Britain's greatest postwar military deployment in the Mediterranean continued in close coordination with similar French moves.

CURRENT TREND

Eden said, "The whole trend of the world today is against taking selfish action for purely national ends."

He charged President Nasser had taken over the Suez Canal Co.—an international enterprise—

Turn To Page 23 For More Of EDEN

ADLAI STAND TO COST HIM SOME BACKING

High Command Concedes Loss Of Vote, Dixie Democrats Bristle

CHICAGO, Aug. 8 (AP) — Dixie Democrats bristled today at Adlai E. Stevenson's more militant stand on civil rights, and the Stevenson high command conceded a loss of votes for the Democratic presidential nomination.

Supporters of Gov. Averell Harriman of New York, Stevenson's top rival for the nomination at next week's Democratic National Convention, tried to promote the idea that Stevenson had let him self in for a major setback—that the South was "running away" from the former Illinois governor.

Stevenson's top lieutenants said some votes have been lost, but only a few. They stuck to predictions their man will turn up with a quick victory in the presidential nominating derby.

And, so far, there are no signs of any real stampede away from Sevenson as a result of his pronouncement last night that Democrats, through their national convention and platform, should "express unequivocal approval" of the Supreme Court decision barring racial segregation in public schools.

Even with Stevenson taking that position, for a party declaration that would be highly unpalatable to most Southerners, there still appeared to be a good chance the bulk of Southern delegates would wind up in Stevenson's corner. At this point, there seems to be no other comfortable place they can go.

Harriman is the only other outstanding contender for the presidential nomination, and his views on civil rights and other issues long have made him unacceptable to the South.

EXPECTS TO WIN

Harriman said at Albany, N.Y., today, he is in the battle for the presidential nomination to the finish and expects to win.

Gov. A. B. (Happy) Chandler of Kentucky got into town today with 30 votes from his home state in his pocket and hopes of a Harriman - Stevenson deadlock that would let him slip in and grab the nomination.

Perhaps with an element of wishful thinking, Chandler told an interviewer Stevenson's new civil rights pronouncement "almost assures" a deadlock.

Stevenson himself picked up some expected but hitherto backstage support from Oscar L. Chapman, secretary of the interior under President Truman. Chapman has been friendly to Stevenson all along, but today he put it on the record with word to newsmen that:

"I have been telling my friends

Turn To Page 24 For More Of DEMOCRATS

SOVIETS PROMISE DECISION SOON ON SUEZ PARLEY

Shepilov Says Red Announcement Will Come Within 48 Hours

MOSCOW, Aug. 8 (AP) — Foreign Minister Dmitri Shepilov said today Moscow would announce within 48 hours whether the Soviet Union would attend the Aug. 16 international conference on the Suez Canal crisis. There was a strong indication the U.S.S.R. would accept.

Shepilov received British Ambassador Sir William Hayter and French Ambassador Maurice de Jean yesterday. Both men were reported to have had the impression Moscow would send representatives to the London conference—although with reservations.

The U.S.S.R. is understood to want the conference broadened to include more Arab and Communist nations in addition to the 26 countries invited.

Shepilov told reporters at an Indian embassy reception Moscow is studying the crisis with a view to define the Soviet position. Other highly placed Soviet sources said the Russians feel the position taken by Britain and France would create a real threat to world peace.

SOVIET GUEST

Egypt's President Gamel Abdel Nasser, who touched off the crisis by decreeing nationalization of the Suez Canal, had been scheduled to arrive in Moscow as a Soviet guest Aug. 16. But Soviet sources said that since the date conflicts with the international conference, Nasser most probably would postpone his trip.

This caused no surprise to Westerners here. A diplomatic source said he was convinced if Nsaser left Egypt now, he probably would find on his return he was no longer president. Moreover, the source added, the last thing Moscow would want at this critical moment would be Nasser making anti-Western speeches on Soviet soil.

Soviet circles did not rule out a Nasser trip later this year. Shepilov said "we still want to see President Nasser as our guest," but added it was up to Nasser to set the date.

CALM STUDY

Shepilov, asked for comment on the Suez crisis, would say only this:

"We are calmly studying and evaluating all factors which will make it possible to define our position on this question, with con-

Turn To Page 6 For More Of SOVIET

New City Fire House Plans To Be Offered For Final Approval

Plans for a new fire house at Fremont and Prospect Streets will be submitted to the City Council for final approval next week, Commissioner John E. Spidle, director of the Department of Parks and Public Property, announced yesterday.

The city expects to ask for bids on the new fire house in the near future.

Spidle said that other city councilmen have given tentative approval to the 98-foot-long by 48 feet-wide structure.

The building, which will include an apparatus bay, office, dormitory, kitchen, storage area, boiler room, and a Ground Observers Corps post atop the structure, was designed by Henry Boettcher, architect.

The site is the old Lafayette School grounds, and the fire house will be known as Fire Station Number Six. Part of the units now housed in the Public Safety Building will man the new station.

Commissioner J. Arthur Norris, director of the Department of Public Safety, has expressed the hope that the new station would be in operation before the end of the year.

The structure will face Fremont Street and will be set back 37 feet from the curb line of both Fremont and Prospect Streets. It will be of brick-faced cinder block construction.

The design conforms to the general residential character of the neighborhood and is similar to the new Lafayette School a few blocks away.

The apparatus bay, which includes provisions for drying hose and hose storage, will have electrically-operated doors at both ends, with 22½-foot-wide driveways from both Prospect and Fremont Streets.

The dormitory will be 40 by 15½ feet and the kitchen, nine by 15½ feet. An office, 20-by 17-feet will be in the front corner near the main entrance.

Inactive since the post atop the Griest Building was abandoned last year, the Lancaster unit of

Turn To Page 6 For More Of FIRE HOUSE

PAUL GARDNER

CAPT. JOHN M. GROFF

OLIVER J. SMITH JR.

3 Discussion Chairmen Named For Mayor's 'Look Ahead' Forum

Three discussion session chairmen for the three-day series on "Lancaster Looks Ahead" were named yesterday by Mayor Kendig C. Bare.

Capt. John M. Groff, 920 Buchanan Ave., was named general chairman. Oliver J. Smith Jr., 531 Burrowes Ave., will head the education panel, while Paul Gardner, Bausman, will be in charge of the commerce and retailing committee.

The discussions will be held Sept. 18, 19 and 20 at the Municipal Building, with three panels each day.

Other topics to be covered in the forum, devised by Mayor Bare to look forward 20 years in an effort to determine the needs of the next two decades, will include recreation, housing, health, industry, traffic, parking, highways and highways and transportation; positions, employment and people, and public and social services.

PANEL SETUP

John C. Stauffer, head of the Lancaster Recreation Assn., previously was named to head the recreation panel.

Each chairman will select three other panel members, each of whom will give a short talk on the subject. A question period will follow the sessions, to be held at 10 a.m., 2 p.m. and 8 p.m. each day.

Capt. Groff, the general chairman who will conduct the overall program, has been active in community affairs for many years.

Smith has been a city school director since 1951 and last year was elected president of the school board. Vice-president of Lancaster Press, Inc., he also has been active in the Exchange Club.

Gardner, former president of Dewalt, Inc., is a member of the Lancaster Area Incinerator Authority and president of the Lancaster Chamber of Commerce. He also has participated in Community Chest campaigns.

Young GOP Supports Nixon 2nd Term Bid

A resolution supporting Richard M. Nixon for a second term as vice president was passed unanimously by directors of the Young GOP of Lancaster County last night.

The resolution for the group to "redeclare its faith in Richard M. Nixon and urge his nomination as the Republican candidate for vice president" was proposed by W. W. Loose at the meeting at the Women's Republican Club, 36 W. Orange St.

The president of the group, Louis Weisman, said the resolution, which is to be forwarded to delegates from Lancaster County and to Leonard Hall, Hall, chairman of the Republican National Committee, was the first of its kind by Young GOPers outside of the New England States.

In declaring their support, the Young GOP said they were backing Nixon for his "extraordinary qualities of honor, courage, leadership and executive ability" and his "demonstrated and uncompromising loyalty to the country and to President Eisenhower."

They declared that Nixon's conduct in office has "increased manyfold his strength and appeal to young voters."

In addition to the resolution the group discussed tentative plans for the coming presidential campaign and set the date of their next meet-

Turn To Page 6 For More Of YOUNG GOP

Law Gives Car Dealers Right To Sue Makers

WASHINGTON, Aug. 8 (AP)—President Eisenhower today signed a hotly disputed bill giving dealers the right to sue automobile manufacturers on charges of coercive practice and bad faith cancellation of franchises.

Congress passed the bill amid conflicting arguments as to whether it would help or hurt private enterprise, and whether it would discourage or stimulate so-called "bootleg" sales of automobiles which allegedly permit the private buyer little or no redress if the car proves faulty.

The President, in signing the bill, said, "It constitutes only a partial solution to the problem. . . ."

UNWARRANTED INTRUSION

It might be considered an unwarranted intrusion by the federal government into an area traditionally reserved to private enterprise, and therefore "represents a new departure in the exercise of federal authority, a point which will undoubtedly come to the attention of the courts," the President added.

But, he said, he was approving the bill in view of the findings of Congress that the conditions in the automobile industry may be of a temporary nature. He directed government antitrust enforcement agencies to review conditions which brought about a demand for the legislation "to determine whether they continue to exist, to study alternative or different solutions to the problem, and to make recommendations for appropriate actions by the next Congress."

PALOMINO STALLION KILLS 4-YEAR-OLD

BEAVER, Utah, Aug. 8 (AP)— A palomino stallion bit and shook to death a 4-year-old girl who was petting him today.

Gloria Clark, her three young brothers and 7 - year - old David White crawled under the corral fence unnoticed. Gloria petted the palomino as her 10-year-old brother Tommy held her hand. The horse turned suddenly, took Gloria's neck between his teeth and tore her from Tommy's grip. The horse shook her several times, dropped her to the ground and ran.

A neighbor picked up Gloria and took her home where the family doctor pronounced her dead.

David White is a son of Howard C. White, keeper of the horse.

50 Firemen Fight Mail Car Blaze At Leaman Place

Fifty volunteer firemen early this morning were fighting a stubborn blaze in a steel railroad car on a Pennsylvania Railroad siding at Leaman Place.

The alarm, was sounded about 10:50 p.m. yesterday and the Paradise, Gordonville and Intercourse Fire Companies responded.

Firemen said the blaze broke out in third class mail which filled the inside of the box car.

An attempt was first made to extinguish the blaze as the railroad car was at the rear of Ressler's warehouse in Paradise. Later it was moved to a siding at the Supplee Willis Jones milk station, Leaman Place.

Water to fight the fire was being tapped from the Pequea Creek. Firemen also put to use a special PPL nozzle which is used to fight fires in the vicinity of high tension wires.

To get at the blaze it was necessary to chop holes through the roof of the car. Early this morning firemen had managed to get into the car and were hauling out packages of burning mail and extinguishing these fires outside the car.

The firemen expected it would take several hours before the fire would be brought under control.

It was learned that the fire was not interfering with other railroad traffic along the tracks in that area.

Baseball Scores

NATIONAL LEAGUE

Philadelphia 8, New York 3
Pittsburgh 8, Brooklyn 5
Cincinnati 8, Chicago 2
Milwaukee 10-1, St. Louis 1-2

AMERICAN LEAGUE

Detroit 8, Kansas City 7
New York 12, Washington 2
Boston 7, Baltimore 2
Chicago 7, Cleveland 6 (14 innings)

Details of games on Pages 18 and 19

"We Lead All The Rest"

FARM CORNER

By Joe Wachtman

H. H. Ranck Herd Tops DHIA Test Records For Year

A record number of cows produced near-record average quantities of both milk and butterfat under Red Rose Dairy Herd Improvement Assn. testing during the 1955-56 year, members learned last night at the annual banquet of the association.

Nearly 300 dairymen and their families jammed the facilities of the Lafayette Fire Hall to attend the event and hear the 17th annual report of the DHIA testing program.

Harry H. Ranck, Ronks R1, was honored as high herdsman of the year. His 24 registered Holsteins averaged 565.7 pounds of fat and 14,543 pounds of milk to lead all of the 253 herds containing more than five cows en-

Turn To Page 23 For More Of FARM CORNER

Hanover Boy, 9, Seriously Hurt By Auto In City

A nine-year-old boy dashing back to watch a ball game was struck and seriously injured by an automobile in the 700 block of Race Avenue last night.

Jeffery C. Stonesifer, son of Mr. and Mrs. Harry Stonesifer, of Hanover, was admitted in semi-conscious condition to Lancaster General Hospital.

His injuries were described as a possible brain concussion and cuts of the head and face.

The boy was injured about 7:45 p. m. in the 700 block of Race Avenue while visiting an aunt.

City police said the boy and his mother were visiting Mrs. Robert M. Knupp, 708 Race Ave. He had been watching a baseball game across the street from the house and ran home to ask if he could stay 15 minutes longer.

When he received permission he was so excited he dashed across the street without looking according to his mother.

He was struck by a car driven by Charles W. Shade, forty-one, 425 W. Marion St., city police said.

AF TO START USING '6-MONTH TRAINEES'

WASHINGTON, Aug. 8 (AP)—The Air Force announced today it will start using "six-month trainees" in its reserve program.

Until now the Air Force has been cool toward utilization of the youthful trainees, but the announcement said that in "re-evaluating" the reserve situation it had been decided a requirment existed for use of the men. The Air Force said the program will begin "soon," but administrative and training details have to be worked out.

Officials estimate that about 2,500 six-month trainees will be handled annually.

Weather Calendar

COMPARATIVE TEMPERATURES

Station	High	Low
Water Works	85	61
Ephrata	83	61
Last Year (Ephrata)	87	63
Official High for Year June 13		95
Official Low for Year Feb. 22		12

Character of Day—Partly Cloudy

WINDS
Direction WNW Avg. Velocity 6 MPH.

HUMIDITY
8 a.m. 90% 11 a.m. 74% 2 p.m. 62%
5 p.m. 63% 8 p.m. 63%
Average Humidity 70%

SUN
Rises 6:09 a.m. Sets 8:09 p.m.

MOON
Sets: 9:45 p.m.
First Quarter, Aug. 13.

STARS
Morning—Venus, Mars
Evening—Jupiter, Saturn

NEARBY FORECASTS
(U. S. Weather Bureau)

Southeastern Pennsylvania, Southern New Jersey—Fair and warm today, highest 85-90. Increasing cloudiness today with afternoon thundershowers.

Central Pennsylvania and Northeastern Pennsylvania—Increasing cloudiness warm and humid today with showers and scattered thunderstorms spreading over area from west tonight or tomorrow. Highest today 82-89. Mild tonight. A little warmer tomorrow.

Lower Potomac and Chesapeake Bay—Light variable winds mostly west 5-10 M.P.H. today. Fair weather. Good visibility.

Maryland—Sunny except for afternoon cloudiness in extreme west portion today and warm with high temperatures 84-88. Tomorrow warm with fair east and south portion and scattered afternoon thundershowers north and west portions.

Delaware—Sunny and warm today with high temperatures 84-88. Tomorrow fair and warm.

EXTENDED FORECAST
(U. S. Weather Bureau)

Extended forecast for the period from today through Monday:

Eastern Pennsylvania, Eastern New York and Mid-Atlantic States:

Temperature will averge 2 to 4 degrees below normal north and near or a little below normal south portion. A little warmer today and tomorrow, somewhat cooler over the weekend, warmer Monday. Showers and thunderstorms tomorrow and Saturday and probably over north portion Sunday or Monday. Total rainfall ¼ to ¾ inches south portion and an inch or more in north portion.

VIVA VISTA VISION

Argentina Plunged Into New 'Crisis' By Irate Film Fans' Strike For Wide Screen

BUENOS AIRES, Aug. 8 (AP)—The movies have gone flat and fans are hopping mad in Argentina's wackiest crisis — the wide-screen strike.

The issue has reached the highest levels of President Pedro Aramburu's provisional government. And no solution is in sight.

The trigger that touched off things in this ever-volatile Latin land was a government decree rolling back ceiling prices for cinemascope, superscope and vistavision movies from 9 pesos 40 centavos to 6 pesos 50 centavos (from approximately 35 to 20 cents).

Most foreign films shown here are imported from the United States and utilize some sort of super-duper "scope" effect. The government, battling inflation and trying to pacify the restive working class, declared the movie is a necessity, not a luxury, and figured 9 pesos 40 centavos was too high.

BEGAN LOOKOUT

Theater owners, protesting the rollback, started a lockout Monday.

Now if there is anything the Argentine likes, it's his movie.

Afternoon crowds, finding theater lobbies locked, rioted through this capital's downtown streets. One stone-throwing mob smashed virtually all the heavy glass entrance doors of the Gran Rex, one of Buenos Aires' plushest movies.

Yesterday the theater owners switched tactics.

They reopened, but all those previously billing wide screen movies substituted flat screen films, some so old they approached the nostalgic.

Vet Improved

FRANKLIN, Tex., Aug. 8 (AP) — Walter W. Williams, oldest surviving Civil War veteran, who has been ailing during the past week, felt well enough today to sit up in his rocking chair, chew a little tobacco, and complain of feeling hungry.

GESUNDHEIT

Wind Wafting Wheeze Weed

By ROGER CLINTON
Intell Staff Writer

A couple of mighty anti-social families will be coming to visit Lancaster in about a week.

Their names? Well, technically their last names are Ambrosiaceae and Amaranth. And these tongue-twisting names are nothing to be sneezed at.

As a matter of fact, they are scientific terms for ragweed and pig weed.

They, along with a few other weeds, are what sets a person to a wheezin' and a sneezin' in what's popularly known as the "Hay Fever" season.

According to Dr. Stephen D. Lockey, chief allergist at Lancaster General Hospital, the first grains of pollen of these weeds will start their annual airborne invasion of this area about Aug. 15 — six days from today.

And as the days progress, more and more grains of the weeds' pollen will fill the air. The height of the wheezin' and sneezin' season in the Lancaster area comes between Labor Day and Sept. 21 on the average, Dr. Lockey reports.

Actually, Dr. Lockey points out, this season coming up is not the true "Hay Fever" season. That

Turn To Page 24 For More Of HAY FEVER

'WeedySide' Of Life Is Illegal

The City has laws on its books to aid the allergic fraternity.

Property owners who, in the opinion of the City Board of Health, have unsavory clumps of weeds on their properties can be ordered to get out their mowers, sickles and weed killers and do away with the weeds.

If the property owners fail to remove the unhealthy conditions, the board can have the weeds cleaned away by other means. The law adds that the board can bill the property owners for the work.

WHISTLE STOP—Holding is one of the old tabus still close to the top of the list this year. Lancaster Catholic High players demonstrate offensive lineman grabbing opponent. Holding by either offensive or defensive side is worth 15-yard penalty.

A GOODLY CROWD WAS THERE—Many of the 1,000 spectators at the football clinic will be down on the field soon playing the new rules themselves. All Lancaster city and county scholastic and collegiate teams were represented, as well as Lebanon Catholic, Milton Hershey and Hershey High, Biglerville, Hanover and York high schools and some others.

It's Kick-off TIME!

–WITH NEW RULES

THIS IS A FORWARD PASS—New rule enables center to become an end and receive a pass. Here Ben Charles prepares to toss ball back to center who has just handed it to him. Center must be at end of line for this play, and must get ball on an actual pass, even if it's thrown this way. Official is George Bensinger.

***CHANGES** and new interpretations of football rules were explained to more than 1,000 coaches, players and spectators from Lancaster, York, Lebanon, Berks and Adams counties this past week at Lancaster Catholic H. S. It was the 6th annual rules clinic sponsored by the Lancaster County Chapter, PIAA Football Officials.*

NIX ON KICKS—It's strictly "signals off" for the boys on the sidelines this year. Such suggestions to the players as Coach Gene Kruis' "punt" gesture, staged for the benefit of the clinic audience and the entertainment of his LCHS team, would draw a penalty. Instructions may be relayed through a substitute.

ON THE AIR—Grant "Tick" Hurst of McCaskey High, at right, provides a running commentary via the public address system.

PRINCIPALS of the cast were members of the Lancaster County Chapter PIAA Football Officials. Shown are (seated, l-r): Ken McMillen, Al Weaver, Tick Hurst, George Bensinger and James Todd; (standing, l-r): Clair Young and Ants Souders.

ON YOUR GUARD—This year a guard is permitted to pull out of the line, take the ball from backfield man and run with it. Clue is requirement that he must face his own goal and step a yard back of line before receiving ball. Clair Young, at right, watches play.

Today's Chuckle

Advice to a discouraged bachelor: "If at first you don't succeed, try a little ardor."

LANCASTER NEW ERA

Metropolitan Lancaster Population 1954 (Est.) Penna. Dept. of Commerce 248,296

Local Weather

Lancaster U. S. Bureau

Fair and cooler tonight; tomorrow mostly fair with moderate temperature; low tonight about 48; high tomorrow near 72.

Complete Report on Page 3

80th Year—No. 24,605 | CITY EDITION | LANCASTER, PA., MONDAY, SEPTEMBER 24, 1956 | 26 PAGES | 30c PER WEEK—5c Per Copy

Sears Planning Store at Lititz Pike Shop Center

AP Wirephoto

Speed Boat Pilot Hit After Tumbling into Water

Gerald Waldman, Milwaukee, Wis., is shown just before he was struck by a boat (C-72) piloted by Elmo Belluomini, of Bakersfield, Calif., during the first race yesterday for Class A Hydroplanes at the Marine Stadium, Long Beach, Calif. Waldman's boat spun in path of Belluomini's boat and Waldman was knocked into the water and struck as Belluomini sped by, according to race officials. Waldman suffered serious arm and internal injuries.

3 DEAD, 42 MISSING

Hurricane Heads for Fla. Packing 100-Mi. Winds

NEW ORLEANS (AP) — Hurricane Flossy, packing 100 miles an hour winds, swept toward northwestern Florida today, leaving three men reported dead and 42 missing after it lashed near southeastern Louisiana.

The New Orleans Weather Bureau said in its 10 a.m. advisory the storm, sixth of the season, was centered about 80 miles southwest of Pensacola, Fla., and moving toward the east-northeast about 12 miles an hour.

"Movement is expected to continue toward the east-northeast at the same rate, bringing the center inland between Pensacola and Apalachicola, Fla., this afternoon or tonight," the advisory said.

Gulf Threat Over

The Red Cross in Biloxi said it appeared there was no further threat to Mississippi's Gulf Coast.

The hurricane had winds estimated at 100 m.p.h. near the center at 10 a.m. and gales extended outward 150 to 200 miles from the center.

The Weather Bureau reported a large squally area off the extreme northwestern Florida coast was causing winds to blow offshore and hold back the tide.

"This creates a dangerous situation," the Weather Bureau said, "since the hurricane winds will suddenly shift and may cause a rapid rise in the tide to about eight feet. This situation exists all the way from Pensacola to St. Marks."

Residents Evacuated

Residents of low - lying areas in the southern Alabama and northwestern Florida areas were moved to emergency shelters. Hundreds of persons in southern Louisiana began moving back to their homes.

The storm, which developed early Saturday, originally pointed toward the New Orleans area but took a northeasterly course early today.

Heavy rains fell along the Gulf Coast in advance of the storm. The Weather Bureau cautioned persons living in southern Alabama and Georgia and extreme northern Florida to watch for possible flood warnings.

2 Men Drown

Two men were assumed drowned below the mouth of the Mississippi River. Capt. V. J. Greene of the motor vessel Carport reported that Charles Ayres, 47, Brooklyn, N.Y., chief mate of the 300-foot vessel, fell overboard, and the second mate, John Ritter, jumped in after him and disappeared.

The Coast Guard searched for more than 40 men reported stranded on boats and oil riggs off southern Louisiana.

The Virginia D, a 60-foot tug sank in Mobile Bay, about 10 miles south of Mobile, early today but the four-man crew was rescued.

The coastal area at Grand Isle, La., was the first to feel the fury of the storm. Residents of the stringbean - shaped island fled their homes late yesterday. Some 200 stayed at the Coast Guard station and others scurried to the mainland as the island went 18 inches under water.

Set Up Disaster Forces

Emergency crews throughout the area went into high gear with the Coast Guard and National Guard setting up flood and disaster relief forces. Red Cross officials said 486 evacuees had reported to their New Orleans res-

—See HURRICANE—Page 8

Sec'y Wilson Is Operated on

Undergoes Prostate Gland Surgery

WASHINGTON (AP)—Secretary of Defense Charles E. Wilson underwent surgery today for a "benign prostatic condition," the Pentagon announced.

The operation was completed in an hour and 15 minutes at Walter Reed Army Hospital here. The Pentagon announcement said the 66-year-old defense chief was expected to be back at his office in about 20 days.

Decided Last Thursday

A spokesman said the decision to operate was reached late last Thursday, after Wilson's news conference. Earlier last week Wilson had gone through his annual routine physical examination, conducted by Air Force Col. Marshall E. Groover. Col. Groover reported to Wilson that his examination had disclosed a "urological condition" and recommended "surgery to correct a benign prostatic condition."

Earl Godwin, Radio Announcer, Dies at 75

WASHINGTON (AP) — Earl Godwin, 75, dean of Washington radio correspondents, died in his sleep early today at his summer home in Rehoboth Beach, Del.

Godwin had been a member of the staff of radio station WRC-NBC since 1936 and for years had a news program at 6:15 p.m. daily. Ill of a heart ailment, he had been unable to broadcast regularly since last May.

4 BOYS, 5 TO 8, ADMIT DRIVING ROAD SWEEPER

Four boys, five to eight years, picked up for questioning today by Manheim Twp. police, admitted being involved in the fire which damaged a road sweeper at the Brecht School Saturday night.

The boys told police there was a bonfire smouldering nearby and one of the group mounted the seat of the sweeper, pressed the starting button of the vehicle, which was in gear, and moved it forward so that the brush bristles caught fire.

Twp. police chief John Kauffman said the case would be referred to Richard Taylor, township commissioner in charge of roads, who estimated loss to the sweeper at $125.

Canada Ousts Red Diplomat

Sought Plans of New Jet Fighter

OTTAWA (AP) — Authorities announced today that a Soviet diplomat was ordered out of Canada and a Canadian civilian employe of the Royal Canadian Air Force dismissed because of Russian efforts to learn the secrets of Canada's new CF105 jet fighter plane.

The Foreign Affairs Department said G. F. Popov, second secretary of the Soviet embassy was ordered out of Canada July 12 and left a month later.

Made 'Clean Breast'

A Defense Department official said the Canadian civilian, a junior employe at suburban Rockcliffe Air Station was dismissed in June. The spokesman said the man—the department declined to name him—was asked to leave after he made "a clean breast of things."

The Foreign Affairs Department said in a brief statement:

"On July 12 the Soviet ambassador, Dmitri Chuvahin, was handed an aide-memoire stating that as Mr. G. F. Popov, second secretary at the Soviet embassy, had engaged in activities incompatible with his continued presence in Canada, he should be withdrawn. Mr. Popov left Canada Aug. 12."

LOSES INTEREST

Babe Zaharias' Condition Growing Visibly Weaker

GALVESTON, Tex. (AP) — Babe Didrikson Zaharias became "perceptibly weaker" the last 48 hours although she spent a restful night, hospital authorities reported today.

Yesterday, in what they called their "first realistic statement" about her fight against cancer, the authorities said the famed woman athlete's condition might become critical at any time.

'No Distinct Change'

The John Sealy Hospital bulletin issued this morning said:

"Mrs. Zaharias' condition remains the same. There is no fever and there has been no distinct change. She is perceptibly weaker than she was 48 hours ago, and she sleeps a greater proportion of the time. Babe is rational when awake, however. This morning she reports a particularly good night's rest."

Yesterday, in the lengthy review of her condition, the hospital said "Babe has continued to lose ground each week both as to weight and to strength."

Dr. G.A.W. Currie said the medical statement was issued because Mrs. Zaharias "has lost interest in newspapers." He said doctors at John Sealy Hospital avoided "giving discouraging reports to the press so long as Babe might read the reports and become unnecessarily depressed by them." A hospital spokesman said she does not listen to the radio in her room.

Mrs. Zaharias has been hospitalized since March 29. She was stricken with cancer in 1953. She has undergone three operations recently.

Horse Sits on Trainer, Breaks Man's Pelvis

TULSA, Okla (AP)—Officers said a 41-year-old aircraft plant worker here tried to teach his horse how to sit down yesterday, and was too successful.

Anrold Hall was seriously injured when the horse sat down on him. He was hospitalized with a broken pelvis.

Move to Declare City Man Dead

Petition Is First In Recent Years

Proceedings have been started at the courthouse to declare David H. Becker, formerly of 307 Green St., legally dead.

The petition is the first of its kind to be filed here in recent years, courthouse sources said.

According to law, a person who has been missing for seven years may be declared legally dead. Filing the petition were Becker's children: Robert Becker, twenty-three, New Providence R1, and Betty Becker, twenty-one, 113 S. Queen St., on behalf of themselves and their sister, Erla, eighteen, 109 S. Queen St.

$7,000 in Estate

Carl G. Herr, counsel for the Becker children, said the estate has funds totaling about $7,000. He said Becker has been missing since Dec. 20, 1946. In 1948, the local Orphans Court declared him legally missing, and the Conestoga National Bank was appointed trustee in his absence. When Becker resided here, he was employed at Raybestos-Manhattan, Inc., Manheim, Herr said.

Becker's wife, Laura Mae Becker, also has been missing from the area since the late 1940's, Herr said. The Orphans Court has set Oct. 25 for a hearing in the matter. If Becker does not appear at that time, he may be declared legally dead, it was reported, and his estate may be distributed.

Bus Overturns on N. J. Pike, 19 Hurt

HIGHTSTOWN, N. J. (AP)—An excursion bus with 39 persons aboard went out of control and overturned on the New Jersey Turnpike early today injuring 19.

Police said 17 passengers were treated at St. Francis Hospital, Trenton, and released. Two were hospitalized with lacerations.

Police quoted the driver of the vehicle as saying the bus would not respond to its controls. He said the vehicle ran off the road and rolled over on its side.

Man's Wrist Badly Cut When Tire Bursts

Two men injured at work today underwent emergency surgery at the General Hospital.

Omar B. Stoltzfus, twenty-three, Bareville R1, suffered a severe laceration of the left wrist when a tire burst as he was pumping it up with air. He was admitted to the hospital. John Glackin, sixty-four, 342 Maple Ave., suffered a traumatic amputation of the left index finger when caught in a machine at work.

Pa. Draft Call for November Is 1,423

HARRISBURG (AP)—State Selective Service headquarters today fixed at 1,423 the Pennsylvania draft call for November.

Director Henry F. Gross said all of the draftees must be at least 22 years of age and will go into the Army.

Today's New Era

Phone Lancaster 7-5251

Stevenson Sees Dangerous Drift In Foreign Policy

'Must Stop Bluffing Enemies, Misleading Our People,' He Says

TULSA, Okla. (AP)—Adlai E. Stevenson, hitting at the Eisenhower administration, said today "We cannot stop this dangerous drift in foreign affairs by pretending all is well while Communist influence is spreading everywhere."

In a campaign address prepared for delivery at a courthouse lawn rally here, the Democratic presidential nominee declared: "We must have a foreign policy that is firm, consistent and also comprehensible."

"We must stop bluffing our enemies, boasting to our friends and misleading our people here at home," he said.

Must Stop 'Pretending'

"We cannot stop this dangerous drift in foreign affairs by pretending that all is well while Communist influence is spreading everywhere, which North Africa is in rebellion, while the guns are loaded in the Formosa Strait, and when the Russians have a foothold in the Middle East for the first time, when the Suez life line of Western Europe is in peril for the first time, when Arab nationalism is rampant and communism its ostensible protector," he said.

"We must regain the moral leadership of the world."

He also hit at the Republicans on domestic policy. He noted that Vice President Nixon made a campaign address Saturday night in Colorado Springs, Colo., and Stevenson quoted him as saying there:

"We can look forward to a future in which poverty will be a forgotten word in the United States."

'A Hollow Echo'

Stevenson called that remark "a hollow echo" sounding back 28 years to the days of GOP President Hoover. He said the record of the 28 years between "Mr. Hoover's declaration of war on poverty" and Nixon's 1956 statement "is a record of consistent Republican opposition to every Democratic effort to end poverty in the United States."

"One of the central issues of this year's election," he said, "is

—See ADLAI—Page 8

Saw Doria, Then Changed Course

Stockholm Mate Tells Of Radar Plotting

NEW YORK (AP) — The third mate of the Swedish liner Stockholm testified today that he did not change course until he saw the lights of the Italian liner Andrea Doria less than two miles away.

The ships collided July 25 off Nantucket with a loss of about 50 lives, mostly on the Doria. The Doria sank.

Ernest Carstens—Johansen, 26, the third mate who was in charge of the Stockholm's bridge at the time, said he plotted the course of the Doria on radar when she was 10 miles off and again when she was 6 miles away.

Figured Clear Passage

Under cross-examination in a federal court pretrial inquiry relating to almost 40 million dollars worth of damage suits, the officer said he had calculated the Italian ship would pass his at a distance of six-tenths of a mile.

Under cross-examination by Eugene Underwood, attorney for the Italian line, he said he had not noted the exact time of the two plottings.

Underwood asked if the mate could calculate the speed of the approaching vessel without noting the time of the two plots by radar. "Not exactly, but I can see approximately if it is a slow or fast ship," said the mate.

Season's 8th Typhoon Heads Toward Formosa

MANILA (AP)—Typhoon Harriet, the season's eighth, swung northward away from the Philippines and toward Formosa today as it churned through the Pacific with 80-mile-an-hour center winds.

The Manila Weather Bureau said the typhoon was last located 400 miles east of the fishing port of Basco, in the rocky Batanes Islands off the northern coast of Luzon. It was moving northwest at about 12 miles an hour.

NO FUNDS FOR REPAIRS

Caramel Lawyer Favors Tax Sale

Counsel for the owners of the fire-swept ruins of the American Caramel Co. plant, Church St., said today the corporation is without assets and "perhaps the city could seize the property for unpaid taxes and sell it."

The statement was made by Aaron Dorfman, counsel for the 347 Church St., Corp. owners of the property.

In reply to a question by telephone, the attorney said:

Engineer Will Inspect Ruins

"The corporation is without assets either to clean up the ruins or make improvements. I suppose there is nothing left to do under the circumstances but to permit the city to take whatever action it considers best to collect the taxes."

The attorney made the announcement in a telephone conversation and close on the heels of statement by B. M. Zimmerman, city solicitor. The solicitor said the city was prepared to tell the corporation to clean up the ruins or face a sale of the property for unpaid taxes.

Prior to the fire, the corporation had plans for improving the property and leasing space to small industries and storage companies.

City Urged to Take What Action Is Best

The city employed Col. John H. Wickersham, engineer and builder, to inspect the ruins and determine whether they are a menace to the area. He will make a report soon.

It was learned Col. Wickersham and his engineers found the ruins in a dilapidated condition. The cellar is filled with stagnant water that is creating a stench, and a number of protests.

Somoza Takes Turn for Worse

Entire Left Side of Body Is Paralyzed

PANAMA (AP)—President Anastasio Somoza of Nicaragua, shot down Friday night, took a turn for the worse today in a Panama hospital.

A medical bulletin said he had developed paralysis of the entire left side of his body and that an emergency tracheotomy — opening a hole in the windpipe to facilitate breathing — had been performed.

The bulletin called the paralysis "an unexpected postoperative complication which has not been fully evaluated." Somoza underwent a 4-hour and 20-minute operation yesterday at Gorgas Hospital, in the Canal Zone.

Wholesale Arrests

In Nicaragua, wholesale arrests of opponents of the government have followed the attempted assassination.

About 200 persons, including two newspaper editors and a former president, were being questioned in a police search for possible accomplices of the assassin.

The Nicaragua strongman's son Luis, 34, took a firm hold on the country while Somoza underwent treatment at a U.S. hospital in the Panama Canal Zone for four gunshot wounds.

Luis Somoza and his younger brother Anastasio Jr., 32, were directing the search for the assassin's helpers. Luis acted as first vice president designate, an arrangement Congress was expected to approve at a meeting tomorrow.

There was no indication of the Somoza dynasty had been shaken by the attempt to kill its founder. Managua was as quiet last night as any Central American capital.

COOLER TONIGHT AND TOMORROW FAIR, MODERATE

Mixed-up weather continued here today, after summer ended on an autumnal note Saturday, and fall started on summer-like note yesterday.

The U. S. Weather Bureau said tonight would be fair and cooler, and tomorrow would be mostly fair and moderate. Low tonight is to be about 48, and high tomorrow near 72.

Yesterday's high was a balmy 84, with a thunderstorm last night following a heavier electrical storm Saturday night. Low last night was 60.

Lebanon Girl Diagnosed As Polio Patient Here

A Lebanon schoolgirl was definitely diagnosed as suffering from polio at the Lancaster General Hospital yesterday.

The patient is Suzanne Horney, twelve, daughter of Mr. and Mrs. John M. Horney, of 1105 Chestnut St., Lebanon, She was referred here for treatment from Lebanon.

Hospital authorities said her case was mild and non-paralytic, and her condition satisfactory. She had received two shots of Salk polio vaccine. She was admitted Tuesday, and diagnosis was completed yesterday.

Order New Election By N. Y. Dock Unions

WASHINGTON (AP) — The Nation Labor Relations Board today ordered a new bargaining election held within 30 days between rival New York waterfront longshoremen's unions.

Present contracts expire Sept. 30 and apparently there is no prospect of conducting the election before then.

2 Downtown Stores Slated To Be Closed

Sears Roebuck and Co. will erect a new store on a tract of nearly six acres at the Lancaster Shopping Center, between the Lititz and Oregon Pikes, it was announced today by Mark W. Anspach, local Sears manager.

Sears has purchased the southern end of the property which the shopping center bought from Walter M. Dunlap, and will build the store, Anspach said.

This will mean the closing of the Sears stores downtown, Anspach said. Sears has a retail store at 40 E. King St., and a farm store at 212 N. Queen St.

Expect to Open First

No time for start of construction was given today. Plans are now being developed, the manager said, and Sears expects to be the first store to open in the shopping center development.

The Sears building, he said, will be built so that it can be reached from other stores in the shopping center. The tract bought by Sears, he said, contains about 250,000 square feet, and has irregular boundaries on its northern edge. Since there are 43,560 square feet in an acre, this makes the Sears property 5.7 acres.

Total size of the property bought from Dunlap by the Lancaster Shopping Center, Inc., is 17 acres. This means the Sears property will take up about one-third of the entire shopping center area.

Sears has large stores in shopping centers at York and at Shillington, near Reading.

The local new Sears building is expected to be similar to those in the York and Reading suburban centers.

8th Chain Store

Announcement by Sears today brought to six the number of chain stores coming into the shop center.

The shopping center firm has already announced that leases were signed with W. T. Grant Co., Food Fair Stores Inc., S. S. Kresge Variety Stores, Endicott Johnson Shoe Co., and Mae-Moon, ladies apparel and accessory firm.

Also coming in on leases, it was confirmed today, are the Rea and Derrick drug chain, and G. W. Kinney shoe firm.

Food Fair Stores is a co-developer of the shopping center tract, having bought an interest in Lancaster Shopping Center, Inc., this spring. The shop center firm also owns a tract across the Lititz Pike purchased from Lowell O. Stengel.

Food Fair Plans Store

Food Fair plans a store on the former Dunlap tract, to occupy 30.000 square feet.

Previously announced plans of the Lancaster Shopping Center, Inc., called for construction to start in August. Originally this had been scheduled to start earlier. However, no construction work has been commenced to date.

The general plan for the shop center called for 30 modern stores with 150,000 square feet of display space and parking for 1,500 cars.

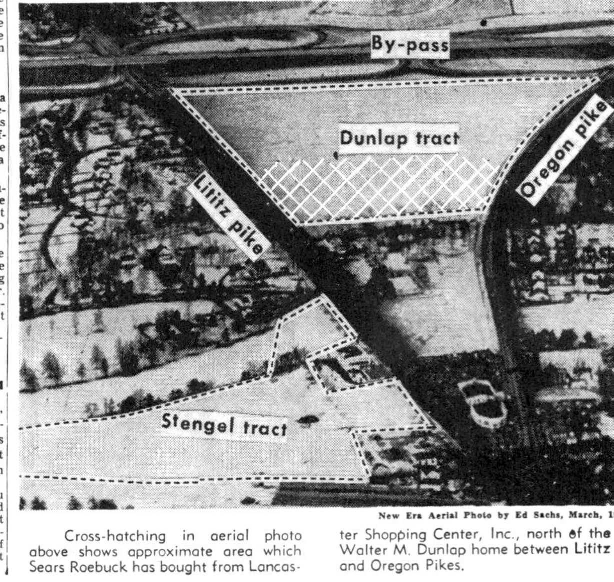

New Era Aerial Photo by Ed Sachs, March, 1956

Cross-hatching in aerial photo above shows approximate area which Sears Roebuck has bought from Lancaster Shopping Center, Inc., north of the Walter M. Dunlap home between Lititz and Oregon Pikes.

'56 Home Fashions Are Stylish And Practical

Value And Style Combined In '56 Home Furnishings

Greater values than ever before combined with high style design are the keynotes of the new furniture which is being introduced to homemakers all across the country.

More than ever, the designer's touch is evident in all price categories of home furnishings. Emphasis is being placed on the fine craftsmanship which makes styles long-lasting and not tiresome, as well as pleasing to the eye.

The international influence is still with us and likely to remain with us for quite some time. American designers borrow ideas from other lands and adapt them into styles which are suited to our particular way of life.

Italian Provincial styling, which made its entrance to the furniture field early in the year, has attained great popularity and is holding its own. Italian Provincial furniture in bedroom, dining room, or living room creates an impressive setting, yet its clean, simple lines prevent it from becoming overpowering. Some of the features of this styling have been used in modern and contemporary pieces, giving them a traditional feeling while maintaining an up-to-date look.

SCANDINAVIAN INFLUENCE

The Scandinavian influence in furniture design is as important as ever. It is seen in the sculptured look of many new pieces. Although this furniture is very simply designed, it brings with it a feeling of warmth.

Furniture inspired by Oriental design is becoming increasingly popular. Already well-accepted on the West Coast, it is slowly making its way across the country. Characterized by low pieces, it is particularly suited for the casual way of life.

One new grouping of correlated bedroom and dining room pieces combines Scandinavian and Oriental influences.

The collection is of lustrous walnut, in a spice-rich tone called mace. The grain of the wood is emphasized so that its natural beauty is fully apparent. The recurring theme of design in the collection is a parquet-type inlay of walnut resembling two slender elongated pyramids placed in an hourglass position. Some of the pieces in the group are also available with cane panels which effectively highlight the radiance of the walnut and add an Oriental touch with their interplay of light and shadow.

Another company has introduced a group of Danish imports. These chairs and tables feature grace without flimsiness. Their lightweight look disguises heavyweight comfort. Chairs are slim and are offered in a rich assortment of elegant fabric and fabric-backed vinyl coverings.

Seat cushions rest on a base of interlaced strands of tough, resilient rubber. Cushions are foram rubber and reversible, often having a contrasting pattern on each side.

A striking new collection makes use of a spacer unit for added interest. It sits on top of chest pieces and a hutch, cabinet, or another chest may be placed on top of it. The spacer unit is easily removed when a slight change of scenery is desired.

This softly sculptured contemporary furniture combines and stacks and moves easily from room to room. It is available in walnut with real silver trim.

Mrs. Nancy Howells, 2116 Clover Hill Road, reminds homemakers of the advantages and features of an automatic clothes dryer. Dryer shown above has whisper-quiet operation and holds 18 pounds of wet clothes. It is completely safe for any and all fabrics, regular wash and manmade fabrics. Two settings are available, one for regular drying and one for special drying. Safety thermostats maintain an ideal balance between imput of heat and billowing flow of air.

Texture Interest

Color and texture trends are the important things to watch in fabrics. For the past few years, fabrics which have "touch" interest have been popular, such as rough tweeds.

This popularity is continuing. Fabrics on new upholstered pieces are elegant; the weaves are flat but textured, and many types of fabric are used. It is felt, however, that this trend will gradually evolve into one of smooth, rich fabrics on upholstery. Evidence of this is already beginning to crop up.

Colors are either extremely bright or softly muted. Beige and brown are the top favorites, with gold and white also high on the list. Homemakers no longer fear these light colors since many fabrics are now protected by a special finish which makes them easy to keep clean.

Small prints are also popular, particularly on Early American pieces. Tweed is seen quite often.

Turquoise is the favorite accent color. Other shades of blue have also gained wide acceptance. On the way up the fashion ladder is red. It will add a touch of drama and high fashion to a room.

CLEAN OVEN

In the evening—after the oven has thoroughly cooled and won't be used again for several hours—place one tablespoon of household ammonia in a saucer which contains one cup of warm soapy water. The grease will wipe off easily in the morning.

Queen Elizabeth Is Getting Two Cygnets

OTTAWA, Oct. 6 (AP)—Queen Elizabeth II is getting two cygnets to add to the flock of Canadian-born trumpeter swans presented to her on her coronation in 1952. Captured in the Grande Prairie area of Alberta, the cygnets are being sent by plane to the Severn waterfowl trust in Gloucestershire, England.

Soviet Set To Spend $8 Million On Art

MOSCOW, Oct. 6 (AP)—The Soviet Culture Ministry has announced it will spend 35 million rubles—$8,750,000 at the official rate—each year to encourage production of works of art for museums and traveling exhibits. Government-operated shops will sell any pictures and statues the museums don't want.

Today's Chuckle

A change of lipstick now and then
Is relished by the best of men.

LANCASTER NEW ERA

Metropolitan Lancaster Population 1954 (Est.) Penna. Dept. of Commerce 248,296

Local Weather

Lancaster U. S. Bureau

Generally fair tonight and tomorrow, turning cooler tomorrow afternoon and night; low tonight about 48 in city, 44 in suburbs; high tomorrow near 58.

Complete Report on Page 3

80th Year—No. 24,617 | CITY EDITION | LANCASTER, PA., MONDAY, OCTOBER 8, 1956 | 28 PAGES | 30c PER WEEK—5c Per Copy

Larsen Pitches 1st No-Hitter In World Series

Hurls Perfect Game As Yanks Win, 2-0; Take Series Lead

BULLETIN

NEW YORK—Don Larsen pitched the first perfect no-hit game in World Series history today. The Yanks won 2-0.

NEW YORK—Don Larsen, big Yankee pitcher, set a World Series record when he retired the first 24 Brooklyn batsmen without yielding a hit or a walk in eight innings of the fifth game of the World Series.

The Yanks led 2-0 going into the last half of the eighth. The former record of retiring 22 straight men at the start of a game was set by Herb Pennock of the Yankees against Pittsburgh in 1927.

The Yanks collected their second run in the sixth with three hits after Sal Maglie had yielded only Mantle's homer in the first five frames.

First Two Fan

Larsen struck out the first two batsmen to face him, Gilliam and Reese both taking called third strikes. Snider went out on a fly to Bauer in right.

The Yankees also went down in order in the first. Bauer popped to Reese, Collins bunted and was thrown out by Robinson and Mantle flied to Amoros.

Some sparkling defensive play cut down Robinson at the start of the Dodgers' second. Carey deflected his hard smash and McDougald grabbed the ball and threw Robinson out on a close play at first. Hodges then struck out and Amoros popped to Martin.

Maglie retired the Yanks in order in the second, getting Berra and Slaughter on flies and striking out Martin.

Fourth Strike Out

Campanella became Larsen's fourth strikeout victim as the Dodgers again went out 1-2-3 in the top of the third.

Robinson threw out McDougald and Carey and Larsen both hoisted high fouls which Campanella caught near the plate in the Yanks half of the third.

Martin threw out Gilliam and Reese in the fourth then Snider, after hitting a long foul into the stands, was called out on strikes. Larsen's no-windup delivery, which he adopted in midseason, was proving very effective and not one Dodger had reached first base.

With two out in the last half of the fourth, Mantle drove a home run into the right field stands for the first hit and first run of the game. Snider made a diving catch of Berra's drive to center for the third out.

Mantle made a flashy one-hand running catch of Hodges' fly to center as the Dodgers went down in order for the fifth straight inning.

First Walk of Game

Slaughter drew the first walk of the game to open the Yankee fifth. Martin bunted to the hill and forced Slaughter at second. McDougald hit a hard liner to Reese, who held the ball after it popped into the air out of his glove and threw to first in time to double Martin.

Furillo and Campanella both went out on pop flies to Martin in short right in the sixth and then Maglie went out on strikes. That made six strikeouts for Larsen and 18 men retired in order.

Carey opened the Yanks half of the sixth by bouncing a single into center field for the second hit off Maglie. Larsen advanced him with a sacrifice. Carey scored easily when Bauer singled to left and Amoros fumbled the ball. Collins singled, sending Bauer to third. Mantle then grounded to Hodges, who stepped on first to retire him, then fired to Campanella, catching Bauer off third. Bauer was tagged in the rundown to complete a double play.

Four Days of Rest

Maglie, winner of the first game at Brooklyn last Wednesday, had four full days of rest for his ancient right arm. The opener was his first series triumph but his 13-5 performance in regular

—See SERIES—Page 23

DON LARSEN

Legislation to Halt Slums Will Be Sought Here

Real Estate Board Head Cites Influx, Asks Teeth in Law

John W. Butts, president of the Lancaster Real Estate Board, said today he will seek municipal legislation to halt the spread of city slums.

Butts said he will outline his plan to the Civic Improvement Division of the Community Council when it meets Oct. 17.

The plan, Butts explains, will call for the formation of a Citizens' Committee which in turn will call upon City Council for legislation which will enable the city to compel landlords to maintain set standards for property rented for human habitation.

Butts discussed his plan briefly at the Unitarian Forum held yesterday morning at the Church of Our Father, Unitarian. Today he enlarged upon the plan.

Urges Local Solution

A heavy influx of new families into Lancaster, Butts said, has added to the city's housing problem in the low income group.

"This is a problem," he said, "that must be solved by private enterprise — by our own people not with the aid of government funds. Let's not kid ourselves, every dollar we obtain from the federal government must be matched by one or more dollars of our own money."

The plan, he said, has been tried in a number of southern cities and in Chicago. He said the plan has been successful where tried.

Butts pointed out that the city has power to step in and "prop up" a property that is tumbling down. "But in most cases, there is where the power of the city ceases. We need legislation that will enable the city to deal directly with landlords who refuse to maintain decent housing standards."

He pointed out that "It is my opinion that the big majority of landlords try to do a good job in maintaining decent housing standards. But we need law with teeth to deal with those who won't cooperate."

It was known today that the plan already has been studied by Mayor Kendig C. Bare and members of Council who have been seeking a way to deal with living conditions in Sunnyside, along Barney Google Row and other blighted areas largely in the Seventh Ward.

5 Men, Woman Arrested in Raid

Five men and a woman were arrested when a detail of city police raided a third floor apartment at 34 W. King St., at 2:45 a. m. today.

Harold Henry Fisher, forty-eight, who occupied the apartment, was charged with maintaining and operating a disorderly house. He posted bail for a hearing before Alderman Hoover. Prosecution was brought by city policeman J. Frank Greenawalt.

James E. Hess, 631 Janet Ave.; Henry Burger Howell Jr., 22 E. Walnut St.; Walton Bricker, 733 S. Marshall St.; Lester Eugene Forry, Wrightsville R1, and Ruth Louise Kiehl, 444 N. Concord St., were charged with disorderly conduct. They pleaded guilty and paid costs before Alderman Hoover.

Police said they confiscated a quantity of beer, liquor and playing cards.

Egypt Offers Co-Op System To Run Canal

Ask New Talks to Reach Agreement; Soviets Back Plan

UNITED NATIONS, N. Y. (AP)—Egypt and Russia today rejected the British-French approach to the Suez dispute but called for U. N. negotiations to establish a cooperative arrangement for the operation of the canal.

Both told the U. N. Security Council that it is hopeless to seek a solution on the basis of the international control proposal backed by Britain and France.

Details of the proposed cooperative arrangement were not spelled out by Egyptian Foreign Minister Mahmoud Fawzi, but he said it would protect both the interests of the canal users and the sovereignty of Egypt.

Proposes Negotiation

The idea of a cooperative arrangement was set forth by Fawzi in a 7,000-word speech in which he proposed creation of a negotiating committee to seek a solution. The cooperative arrangement, he said, would be one of the objectives.

Soviet delegate Dmitri Shepilov quickly lined up behind Fawzi in favor of the establishment of a negotiating committee. He suggested that the committee might consist of either six or eight countries.

The body, he said, might include of the United States, Russia, Britvain, France, India and Egypt — or, if a larger body were desired, it might also include Yugoslavia and Iran or Indonesia and Sweden.

Shepilov called on British Foreign Secretary Selwyn Lloyd and French Foreign Minister Christian Pineau to withdraw the resolution which they placed before the 11-nation council last Friday.

He said any effort to have the council condemn Egypt for nationalizing the Suez "if fraught was the gravest consequences."

Lists Main Objectives

In expressing Egypt's willingness to create a negotiating committee, Fawzi outlined these main objectives:

"1. Establishing a system of cooperation between the Egyptian authority operating the Suez Canal and the users of the canal, taking into full consideration the sovereignty and the rights of Egypt and the interests of the users of the canal.

"2. Establishing a system for the tolls and charges which guarantees for the users of the canal a fair treatment free from exploitation.

"3. Providing for a reasonable percentage of the revenues to be alloted especially for improvements."

Soldier Killed On Turnpike

Two Others Injured in Wreck Near Reading

One soldier was killed and two others were injured in an accident on the Pennsylvania Turnpike, three miles east of the Reading interchange at 1:30 a.m. today.

Killed instantly was:

Gerald D. Blough, nineteen, Hollosopple, Somerset county, Pa.

The injured:

George C. Law, twenty-one, Box. 142, Hollsopple, injured head and leg. Admitted to the Ephrata Community Hospital.

John A. Grovichin, twenty, 353 W. 15th St., Cleveland, Ohio. Treated in the Ephrata hospital and discharged.

The three men were en route to Fort Dix apparently after spending leaves of absence at their homes.

Car Hits Tractor Trailer

Turnpike police said the passenger car driven by Law crashed against the rear end of a tractor trailer driven by Guy William Better, 2720 Chicago Drive, Granville, Mich. Both vehicles were headed east. Better was not hurt.

Dr. Ira G. Wagner, Ephrata, deputy coroner, said Blough suffered a broken neck.

The passenger car was demolished.

Civil Trial Opens Over Seized Hoxsey Pills

PITTSBURGH (AP) — A long delayed legal fight opened in U. S. District Court today over the government's contention to destroy pills seized at the controversial Hoxsey cancer clinic in Portage near Johnstown, Pa.

Selection of a jury to hear evidence in the 17-month-old civil case was expected to take most of the first day. The government seized several hundred thousand pills in a raid on March 25, 1955. U. S. officials say the pills were misbranded as effective in the treatment of cancer.

Burning Rags Cause Fire Scare at Store

Rags which had been placed beside the furnace ignited and caused a fire scare in the basement of the Army and Navy store, 53 W. King St., at 12:30 p.m. today.

Fire Chief Harry Miller, Assistant Chiefs Frank Deen and William Landis and Engine Co. 1 responded. There was no damage.

New Era Photo

Mrs. N. E. Snyder, 34 N. Shippen St., (left) gives her pledge to the campaign to Mrs. William Ramm, a volunteer worker.

Chest Drive in City Opens Today

1,700 Volunteers Aim For About $381,530

More than 1,700 volunteers began city solicitation for the United Community Campaign today.

The city goal has been set at about $381,530.

All divisions in both the city and county are now working on the campaign to reach the total goal of $840,431 by Oct. 26. County solicitation opened last week.

City Divisions Listed

The five city divisions opening their drives today include:

Large business, with a quota of $341,955, led by Donald H. Reynolds, chairman, and Edward A. Yale, co-chairman.

Small business, with a quota of $10,902, led by Thomas J. Monaghan, chairman, and John F. Briggs, co-chairman.

Clubs and organizations, with no quota set, led by Mrs. Harold E. Rochow, chairman, and Mrs. H. Clay Burkholder, co-chairman.

Public employes, with a quota of $15,336, led by Mrs. H. C. Kreisle, chairman, and Edwin D. Eshelman, co-chairman.

Residential, with a quota of $13,-337, led by Mrs. Robert R. Shoemaker, chairman, and Mrs. Grover C. Holder Jr., co-chairman.

Bridgeport Line Passes Tests

Water Meters to Be Available Tomorrow

The new water line to Bridgeport has passed leakage and sterilization tests, and will be turned over to the City of Lancaster Authority for operation immediately.

It was the first of five suburban Lancaster water lines to receive approval from the engineers.

Meters to Be Connected

Charles Sauer, line inspector for the Lancaster Water Bureau, said meters for residences which will be connected to the new main by private lines will be available tomorrow morning. More than 200 Bridgeport area residents have applied to connect to the main.

Meanwhile, Charles Rubert, resident engineer for Gannett, Fleming, Corddry and Carpenter, said "one small leak" is holding up the opening of the Eden-Country Club Heights line.

Boy Hit by Police Auto Taken Off Critical List

Clarence Wieder, ten, son of Mr. and Mrs. Harry Wieder, Lancaster R1, who was injured Friday morning when he was struck by a state police car while crossing Route 230 bypass to board a school bus, was taken off the critical list at the General Hospital today. His condition, which has improved slightly, is now listed as "serious."

State trooper Edward G. Bonk, driver of the car, said he was chasing a speeder at the time. The speeder was identified by Bonk as Joseph J. Carroll, Marietta, and speeding charges will be filed against Carroll before Justice of the Peace George A. Shenck, Landisville, sometime this week, police said.

MERCURY TO DIP 5 TO 7 DEGREES BELOW NORMAL

Temperatures are expected to average five to seven degrees below normal through Saturday, the U. S. Weather Bureau said today in its five-day forecast.

Today was sunny and mild. Tonight and tomorrow are to be fair, the forecast said, but a turn for the cooler is due tomorrow afternoon and night. Low tonight is to be about 48 in the city and 44 in the suburbs, and high tomorrow near 58. The mercury may drop into the 30's early Wednesday, producing scattered frost. Outlook for Wednesday is fair and cooler.

Suit on Alley Ownership Open

Jury Goes to Site at Old Northern Market

A suit to determine ownership of an alley on the north side of the old Northern Market House, Queen and Walnut Sts., went on trial in Common Pleas Court today.

The suit was brought by the Farmers Northern Market Co. and the Groff Realty, Inc. against the executors and trustees of the Fannie A. Mettfett estate and J. Richard Leaman, operator of a grocery store, which also borders the alley.

The Market Co. and Groff seek to have the alley declared private property. The Mettfett estate and Leaman are trying to show they have the right to use the alley.

Jury Taken to Site

Shortly before noon, members of the jury were taken to the site to make an inspection.

On hand to testify were members of the Lancaster County Historical Society including John W. W. Loose and Luther Heisey, officers of the society and men well-versed in local history.

Unique Surgery on Heart for Infant

HARRISBURG (AP) — Tiny Diana Holliday will go to Minnesota late this month for a unique heart operation her parents hope will save the 2½-year-old girl's life.

Blue-eyed, blonde-haired Diana, daughter of Mr. and Mrs. L. E. Holliday of nearby Middletown, was born with a double opening in the septum that divides the left and right sides of the heart.

Mrs. Holliday said Diana will be taken to the Mayo clinic Oct. 23 where doctors will attempt to plug the two holes. Without surgery, she added, Diana can be expected to live only five to six more years.

Today's New Era

Phone Lancaster 7-5251

Road Along River From Columbia To Marietta Dropped

SURVEY COMPLETED

Hearing Is Planned On West Bypass

The long-awaited engineering firm's report on a proposed route for the west city bypass has been received by the State Highways Department at Harrisburg, but the department is not making any announcements on what the report contains.

Receipt of the report was made known today by Theodore K. Rothermund, district engineer for the department. He said it has been reviewed in the district office, and sent on to the top offices of the department.

Officials Will Meet

Top officials of the department will call a meeting to be attended by representatives of the district and the U. S. Bureau of Public Roads, to discuss the report, Rothermund said. Meanwhile no announcement is being made on what routing the report recommends.

One thing is definite: Before any construction can begin, a public hearing must be held since this is a federal aid project, and from now on hearings will be held on all roads being built with help of federal money.

'Fast As Possible'

J. L. Stinson, district engineer for the U. S. Bureau of Public Roads, said at Harrisburg that the federal government wants to see the bypass link built "as fast as reasonably possible."

Stinson also said that the west bypass would be constructed as "probably more than one project", which was the first indication that all of the roadway would not be built at one time. The Route 230 bypass, with which the west bypass would connect, was built in two separate links.

At the public hearing, Stinson said, the state will give a full outline of what it proposes to do, and everyone interested will be given opportunity to speak.

Will Improve Road Over Chickies Hill

The state has dropped its plan to reroute the Columbia-Marietta Road along the Susquehanna River, and will improve the road over Chickies Hill.

A proposal previously considered, to take the road along the Pennsylvania Railroad tracks bordering the river, has been abandoned because right-of-way problems proved "insurmountable," according to Theodore K. Rothermund, district engineer.

Plan Public Hearing

Since this is a federal aid project, a public hearing will be held at which the state will show its plans, probably at Columbia, Rothermund said. Date for this hearing is to be announced in several days, he said.

The job is to be advertised for construction late in November, the engineer said.

Since the state has decided to use Chickies Hill for the route, after trying to find a way to eliminate it from the road, the plan calls for large cuts and fills on the hill.

Grade Will Be Reduced

The project will start within Columbia and extend to a point just within the Marietta borough limits, he said. While he did not outline the specific routing, he said that the new roadway would reduce the grade on the hill and eliminate curves.

A bridge at the foot of the hill toward Marietta will be widened, he said, and a curve there will be straightened.

Given High Priority

The Columbia-Marietta Road improvement has long been sought by residents of the area, because of the hazardous nature of the Chickies Hill portion. Philip J. Price, county highways superintendent, has pushed for work on the project, and the state has given it high priority among its plans for this county.

The Columbia-Marietta portion of Route 441, the River Road, would tie in with the stretch between Marietta and Middletown. The federal government is pushing for modernization of the Marietta-Middletown portion since it links the Marietta Air Force Depot with Olmsted Field.

OVER 'PIKE WORK

Pa. Sues Reading Co. for $9 Million

HARRISBURG (AP)—The Pennsylvania Turnpike Commission today sued a Reading engineering firm for $9,425,981 it said was paid illegally in construction of the northeastern extension of the super highway.

The huge counter suit was filed in Dauphin County Court in answer to a demand made last spring by Manu-Mine Research and Development Co. for 1½ million dollars the firm claimed it failed to receive for work done for the commission.

The Turnpike Commission in its counter suit said 7 million dollars was paid to Manu-Mine "for work which was totally unnecessary, which was improperly performed and which resulted in an unconscionable profit" to Manu-Mine.

Arthur A. Maguire, General Counsel for the Turnpike Commission charged in the suit that Manu-Mine and T. J. Evans, former commission chairman, formed a "unlawful, wicked and malicious conspiracy" to syphon off millions of dollars from the commission.

Grand Jury To Hear Case

The suit was another step in a series of moves by the Leader administration against operations of the commission under former Republican control. The Dauphn County Grand Jury already has fixed Oct. 22 for the opening of an investigation into what Gov. Leader has termed "one of the greatest public swindles of all time."

Evans and Manu-Mine have repeatedly denied any wrongdoing in their operations.

The new counter suit said contracts between the commission and Manu-Mine for flushing underground mine voids on the northeastern extension were illegal.

The contract, the suit said, were not approved by the State Highways Department as required by law and did not comply with the Pennsylvania Engineering code.

Charge Not Licensed

The suit contended that officers of the Manu-Mine firm headed by Charles W. Stickler, Evans' nephew, were not licensed as professional engineers.

The 35-page counter suit said that Manu-Mine's attempted 'to deceive and defraud" the Turnpike Commission on the work it was performing in supervising its own operations.

The suit said that Manu-Mine's agreement with the Turnpike Commission lacked legality on grounds that it was "A mere acceptance of whatever Manu-Mine proposed "without standard formality or protective features" common to the turnpike commission's normal contract procedure.

No bond was put up by Manu-Mine and no schedule of minimum wages was filed, the suit said.

Probers Told of Fake Telegrams

2 Deny Sending Wires On Social Security

WASHINGTON (AP) — Senate investigators received testimony today that faked telegrams opposing broadening of the social security program went to two Massachusetts senators last July.

John F. Lockwood, an investigator for the Special Senate Committee Investigating Lobbying, said he checked on 160 telegrams sent to Sens. Kennedy (D.) and Saltonstall (R.) and that some of them were sent without the knowledge or consent of persons whose names were signed to them.

2 Deny Sending Them

Two witnesses, Mrs. Grace M. Dahl, Alston, Mass., and Francis T. Burke, Salem, Mass., who have sold insurance for the Jack C. O'Conner Agency, Boston, testified they had not sent certain telegrams carrying their names.

Lockwood said the sales manager of the Boston insurance agency, Albert H. Stoddard, was the prime mover in the dispatch of 80 telegrams to Kennedy and 80 to Saltonstall.

He said most of the telegrams purportedly came from company agents throughout the state, but were sent from Boston and paid for by the O'Conner agency.

29 Persons Checked

The investigator said he checked 29 persons whose names were on the telegrams. He said 16 told him they had given their consent to the wires.

Of the remainder, Lockwood testified, seven said they did not send such telegrams or allow their names to be used for that purpose, while several others refused to make a statement or testify to the committee for fear of "reprisal."

Birdseye, Inventor Of Freeze, Dies

NEW YORK (AP)—Clarence Birdseye, 69, inventor of a quick-freeze food process that netted him a fortune, died last night in the Gramercy Park Hotel.

He developed the process on a $7 experiment based on an idea developed while working as a fur trader in Labrador. Six years ago he sold the process to General Foods for 22 million dollars.

Wash House Fire At Bowmansville

Fire which broke out in a terra cotta pipe chimney destroyed the roof of a wash house on the farm of Isaac Hoover, one-half mile south of Bowmansville, about 9 a.m. today.

The fire was discovered by Mrs. Hoover, who was heating water. She ran a quarter mile to a neighbor's home to report the fire.

The Bowmansville Fire Co. prevented the fire from spreading to the main farm house, which adjoins the 12 by 16 foot frame wash house. Chief Ralph Stover estimated damage at $300.

$105,000 Suit Against NFL to Be Reviewed

WASHINGTON (AP) — William Radovich, onetime football great at the University of Southern California, today was granted a Supreme Court review of his unsuccessful suit for $105,000 damages from the National Football League and others.

Radovich's suit charged attempts to monopolize interstate commerce in the business of professional football, in violation of the anti-trust laws. He contended the league and others by use of a reserve clause and a blacklist tied players to a particular club and prevented them from becoming free agents.

TO USE WELDED TRACK

PRR Plans to Eliminate 'Clickety Clack' of Wheels

PHILADELPHIA (AP)—The sometimes soothing, sometimes annoying "clickety clack" of the wheels on the railroad track may soon be a sound of the past.

The Pennsylvania Railroad is out to eliminate the noise. It is going to use a welded track instead of the standard bolted rail to do the trick.

Samuel R. Hursh, chief PRR engineer, announced that a stretch of welded or "continuous" rail will be put in operation this week near Johnstown, Pa.

Heavy Duty Area

"Seven miles of the rail 'without joint' will be placed in heavy duty, main line track in three areas of the railroad," Hursh said, "so we can determine in every da operation, under varying traffic and climatic conditions, the economic advantages of welded rail."

Hursh explained that rails joined in ribbon-like lengths by welding, instead of being bolted together with joint bars, stops the wheel click.

He said it is planned in the near future to install the new type rail on sections of the eastbound track of the Chicago-Pittsburgh main line at Van Vert, Ohio, and the northbound Washington-New York main line at North East, Md.

SHOT BY DODGER FAN

Off-Duty N. Y. Cop Killed In Row Over World Series

NEW YORK (AP)—An off-duty city detective was shot and killed outside a tavern today after an argument with another man over the World Series.

Dead was detective William F. Christman, 38, father of five children.

Police said they seized Robert Thompson, 25, shortly after the shooting.

Stops At Bar

Police gave this account of the shooting:

Christman dropped in at Carmichael's Bar and Grill near his home after he went off duty at midnight. The detective, a New York Yankee fan, was talking to the bartender about the series when Thompson broke into the discussion.

Thompson, a Brooklyn Dodger rooter, and Christman got into a heated argument.

Gets Rifle At Home

Thompson then left and went to his house nearby, picked up a .30 calibe rifle and returned to the bar.

The bar was closed when he got back, but he saw Christman stepping into a car. He walked up and fired, hitting the detective in the right side.

A passing motorist found the detective. Police, tipped off by the bartender, went to Thompson's house and seized him as he was preparing to go to bed.

"TRICK OR TREAT" Becomes "Share Our Surplus"

"POSTER GIRL" Sue Weidman, left, points to Church World Service poster dramatizing Trick or Treat drive which she and Davy Frey and Mary Ann Shelly, right, will aid on Tuesday evening.

A PENNY BUYS A POUND of food for the hungry overseas, to be taken from America's 9-billion-dollar surplus. Cost of shipping will come from Trick Or Treat drives such as the one in Lancaster City Tuesday, 6 to 8 p. m., when 100 young folks identified by "Share Our Surplus" armbands will canvass the city. Sunday News photos give preview of this new brand of Halloweening.

NEAT TRICK—This is the angle which most Lancastrians will get on the Trick or Treat campaign to send America's surplus foods to feed the millions of hungry and destitute overseas. Above, costumed Mary Ann Shelly wears official armband and holds out properly identified collection box.

←

FIRST RETURNS—A few SOS cannisters were distributed in stores around Lancaster city last week as an experiment for possible expansion next year. At left, Rocky Riedel, cowboy musician and student preacher, hands one of the cannisters to Eugene Riedel, of Lancaster City Christian Youth Council.

MAPPING THE MARCH—In an effort to have canvassers visit every house in the city Tuesday evening, Youth Movement officials block off map to assign a district to each team. Planners are (l-r) Eugene Riedel, publicity chairman for the drive; Lloyd Herr, treasurer of the Lancaster City Christian Youth Council; Marty Longenecker, action committee chairman; and Jack Messersmith, president.

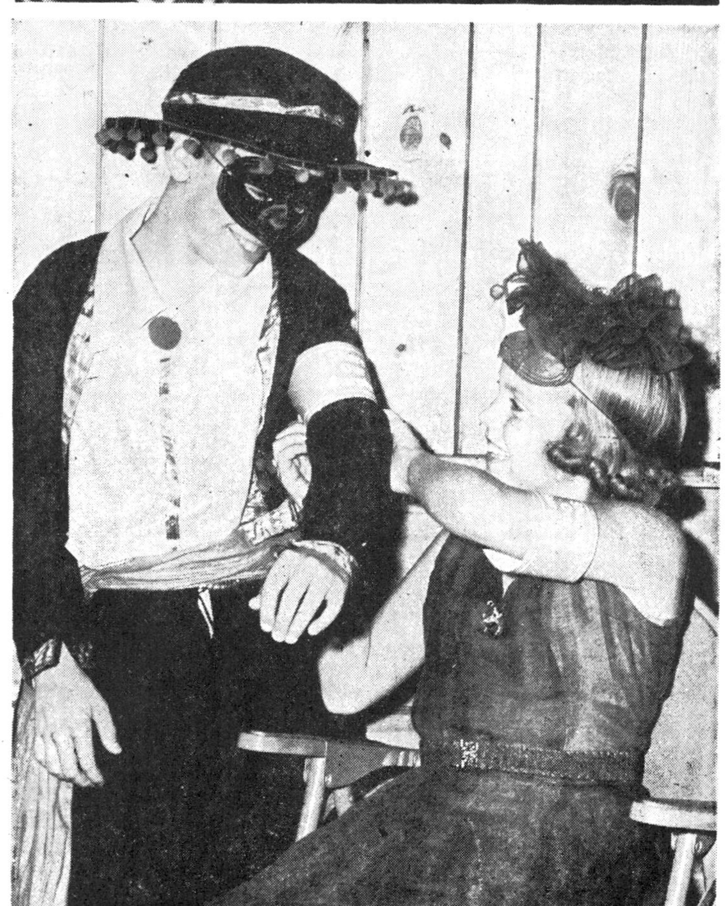

PREVIEW of Tuesday evening's citywide campaign for "SOS" is provided by costumed youngsters above. Davy Frey has official armband—bright red with white lettering reading "Share Our Surplus" — fastened on by Sue Weidman. They will join 100 other young folks from 10 city congregations in the drive.

1st United Nations Police Unit Lands in Suez

Today's Chuckle

Small boy to pal: "I'd go out and seek my fortune if I wasn't needed so badly at home as a dependent."

LANCASTER NEW ERA

Metropolitan Lancaster Population 1954 (Est.) Penna. Dept. of Commerce 248,296

Local Weather

Lancaster U. S. Bureau

Partly cloudy and mild tonight; tomorrow mostly cloudy and mild with risk of scattered showers; low tonight about 52; high tomorrow near 68.

Complete Report on Page 3

80th Year—No. 24,650 | CITY EDITION | LANCASTER, PA., THURSDAY, NOVEMBER 15, 1956 | 60 PAGES | 30c PER WEEK—5c Per Copy

$250,000 Loss In N. Queen St. Fire

92 Norwegian, Danish Troops Arrive in Suez

Land Near Ismailia; 100 More Expected To Arrive Tomorrow

LONDON (AP) — The first 92 men of the blue-helmeted U.N. police force landed near Ismailia in the Suez Canal zone today to keep Middle East peace.

The thin, lightly-armed force was rushed in 15 hours after Moscow reports had said Egyptian President Nasser had requested that Soviet volunteers be sent to Egypt immediately. The U.N. policemen, it was hoped, would forestall Egyptian reliance on Soviet help to eject British, French and Israeli forces.

After the arrival of the U.N. vanguard, an Egyptian Embassy spokesman in Moscow denied that a formal request for Soviet volunteers had been made. An Arab diplomatic source in Moscow said yesterday such a request had been made.

Want Prompt Withdrawal

The Egyptian Embassy spokesman said such a request would be made only if Israeli and French-British forces failed to withdraw from Egyptian territory promptly. He said he knew of no deadline.

The French and British have already said they would pull out when they decide the U.N. police force is adequate to take over peace preservation duties. But Israel has indicated determination to stay on in the Gaza Strip of Palestine.

An Arab "summit" conference of kings, presidents and high officials, meeting in Beirut, Lebanon, declared they would use force if Britain, France and Israel do not evacuate their troops "immediately and unconditionally."

The U.N. vanguard landed in Egypt on the orders of Secretary General Dag Hammarskjold who himself hastened to Italy en route to Cairo.

The first Swiss airliner loaded with 45 Danish troops touched down behind the Egyptian lines at Abu Suweir at 9:30 a.m. A second plane carrying 47 Norwegians landed at 10:02 a.m.

Abu Suweir is on the west side of the canal near Ismailia.

Supply Plane Follows

A third plane carrying equipment for the international police force landed 45 minutes later. The Swissair planes were chartered by the U.N. to move the police units and supplies to Egypt.

Word of the planes' arrival was radioed to the U.N. staging area at Capodichino, Italy, near Naples. Swissair officials said the aircraft were making a quick turnaround, but it appeared unlikely that a second contingent could be ferried to the canal zone today.

100 To Leave Tomorrow

Later a U.N. spokesman said a second group of about 100 men will leave the staging area tomorrow for Egypt. He said the second

—See TROOPS—Page 4

Interior of Kinney Shoe Store, 32 N. Queen St., this morning shows collapsed floor and debris left by fire last night. New Era Photo

Firemen Battle Kinney-Singer Blaze 5 Hours

Smoke Damage at 2 Adjoining Stores, And Printing Firm

A quarter of a million dollar fire which burned for nearly five hours last night damaged a commercial building and wiped out the stocks of two stores in the first block of N. Queen St.

Three business places on the second floor of the building and three in adjacent structures were damaged by smoke and water. The fire was confined to the one building.

Six firemen were hospitalized and 45 were treated for inhalation of toxic smoke.

Damage to the five-story, pre-Revolutionary War building at 32-34 N. Queen St. was estimated at between $80,000 and $100,000.

Two business places on the first floor suffered heaviest damages.

The G. R. Kinney Co., Inc., shoe store, stocked for Christmas trade, lost virtually all its stock. Robert C. Cardinal, the manager, estimated inventory loss at around $80,000.

The Lancaster office of the Singer Sewing Machine Co., lost most of its stock by fire,

Other fire pictures on pages 4 and 27.

water and smoke. William Walker, the manager, said he could not estimate damage. Firemen estimated it at around $35,000.

There was smoke damage to the Queen Beauty Salon and the dental office of Dr. Jacob Parman, dentist, on the second floor of the building.

Bell Records Salvaged

A Traffic Department office of the Bell Telephone Co. located about the center of the building at the second floor level was damaged by fire and smoke. One desk fell through to the basement when fire burned through the floor. Firemen early today salvaged all the company records, some of them from a desk that stood on the brink of a gaping hole in the floor.

Adjacent stores suffered smoke damage.

The Groff and Wolf Clothing store to the south was filled with smoke. A company official estimated smoke damage to stock at $10,000.

The Kay Jewelry Co., to the north, estimated its water and smoke damage at "around $8,000." Radio receivers and electrical appliances in the basement were damaged by water, store officials said.

At the rear of the building, the Commercial Printing Co. plant, located at Grant and Market Sts., has some undetermined smoke damage.

The fire was discovered at 7:42 p.m. and a telephone alarm brought three pieces of equipment. Alarms followed at 8:02, 8:15 and 8:22 bringing 87 firemen and most of the city's fire-fighting equipment.

Firemen were turned back many times by toxic smoke from burn-

—See FIRE—Page 27

Egypt Hedges On Volunteers

Asks Russia to Send Them If Troops Stay

UNITED NATIONS, N.Y., Nov. 15 (AP)—Has Egyptian President Nasser asked Russia to send so-called volunteers to Egypt?

An Arab diplomatic source in Moscow said yesterday Nasser had instructed his ambassador there to ask for the dispatch of volunteers immediately.

Today, an Egyptian Embassy spokesman in Moscow said his country would ask that Soviet volunteers be dispatched only if British, French and Israeli forces fail to get out of Egypt. He made no mention of a time limit, except to say that the withdrawal should be prompt.

A New York Times dispatch from Cairo last night said official Egyptian officials had made no comment on the report. Cairo newspapers and radio did not even mention the report, although they gave much space to a statement by President Eisenhower that the United States wuold oppose—probably through the United Nations—intervention by Communist volunteers.

In Bonn, the Syrian minister to West Germany said there were now no Soviet volunteers on Arab soil, and the question of volunteers for Egypt is "no longer of interest." He said the Arab countries now wished the U.N. to take matters in hand in the Middle East through its police force.

8 CHANGES SLATED

Expect Shakeup Of U.S. Diplomats

WASHINGTON (AP)—The Eisenhower administration is reported planning a major shakeup of ambassadors in at least eight countries during the next few months.

The reshuffle will send a new lineup of American envoys to the four most important Western European countries—Britain, France, Italy and West Germany.

In the Asiatic area, new ambassadors are to be appointed to India, the Philippines, Australia and New Zealand. Three of these posts are now vacant.

Nearly all the diplomatic changes have been planned for a long time, especially those involving the Western European posts. But they also come at a time when top State Department officials, including Secretary Dulles, are known to be dissatisfied with the caliber of some diplomatic reports immediately before the outbreak of Middle East hostilities.

Dulles is understood to have been particularly upset that Ambassadors Winthrop Aldrich in London and Douglas Dillon in Paris were unable to break through what is regarded as a deliberate blackout of news by the British and French foreign offices in the week before the invasion of Egypt.

Mrs. Luce To Quit

Both men were reported definitely resigning their present posts in keeping with previous plans. So is Ambassador Clare Boothe Luce, who has returned from Italy on one of her frequent visits to New York, after recovering from a serious illness. Mrs. Luce agreed to stay on until after last week's elections at White House urging.

Ambassador James Conant, former president of Harvard University, also is reported anxious to leave his post in West Germany.

To replace this foursome, the White House is reported urgently seeking top-flight businessmen who can also be counted upon to serve as effective diplomats during the critical weeks ahead.

Career diplomats will not be appointed to the jobs, regardless of their importance, officials said, because salaries and allowances do not cover the expense of running the embassies in the four capitals.

Ellsworth Bunker, retiring Red Cross president, is reported under serious consideration for the key job of ambassador to India, a spot that has been vacant six months. Former Ambassador John Sherman Cooper quit to make his successful race for Republican senator from Kentucky.

B36 Crashes, All 21 Survive

10-Engine Bomber Burns Near Denver

DENVER (AP)—A 10-engine B36 bomber crash-landed and burned in a stubble field north of Denver's municipal airfield today, but all 21 men aboard escaped death.

The giant craft is one of the type regarded by the U.S. Air Force as a top long-range weapon. Each costs an estimated 3½ million dollars to build.

The 21 men were taken to the hospital at Lowry Air Force Base, where the plane had taken off about 10 minutes before the crash.

Trapped Crewman Rescued

One crewman was trapped for nearly an hour in the nose of the plane before he was rescued by firemen from Lowry and Stapleton Airfield, the municipal airport.

By the time crash crews reached the scene all those aboard except this one man had scrambled free of the fiercely burning wreckage.

Soon after takeoff this morning, the pilot radioed he had run into trouble and would try to get back to Lowry. Then, realizing he did not have enough altitude, the pilot tried to make Stapleton but crash-landed a mile north of the north-south runway.

The plane skidded along on its belly, the fuselage broke into three sections and the wings were sheared off. Some of the crew were able to get out unaided and helped to remove injured comrades.

CAPT. RAYMOND E. CHARLES

Capt. Charles Will Retire

Traffic Bureau Head To Quit May 1, 1957

Capt. Raymond E. Charles, in charge of the city police traffic bureau since 1943, today submitted his resignation from the police force.

The resignation, submitted in writing to Mayor Kendig C. Bare, is to be effective May 1, 1957.

Actually, Capt. Charles is retiring. He was eligible to retire with a pension after 20 years' service in 1942, but he chose to remain at his post. Normally, when policemen stay on the job past their retirement terms, they may terminate their employment by submitting a resignation.

35 Years of Service

Capt. Charles, with 35 years of service, is one of the oldest policeman on the force in point of service. He is sixty-seven, and resides at 236 S. Ann St.

Police Commissioner Fred G. McCartney said a successor will be named at a later date. He said he learned of Capt. Charles' retirement plans yesterday. He said, "Capt. Charles has been an excellent police officer. His services

—See CHARLES—Page 27

Six Overcome At Fire Hospitalized

Two of six city firemen overcome by toxic smoke at the N. Queen St. fire last night were released from St. Joseph's Hospital this morning.

The pair, held overnight for observation, were Robert Stonesifer, thirty-one, 509 S. Lime St., and Donald Gohn, twenty-five, 632 Third St.

Meanwhile, one of four firemen admitted to General Hospital remained in fair condition this afternoon. He was Charles Benson, thirty-three, 654 Dauphin St.

The other three, all reported in satisfactory condition, are Lt. Harry Peters, thirty-five, of 206 Hershey Ave.; Jack Daily, thirty, 339 S. Broad St., and Thomas R. Toner Jr., 608 Fairview Ave.

Seventh Man Treated

A seventh man was treated in the Lancaster Osteopathic Hospital this morning for smoke poisoning.

He was Joseph Ryan, Buchanan Hotel. Ryan is the father of George Ryan, a city fireman, and usually answers alarms to help in case he is needed. He pitched in last night to help the firemen and at 4 a. m. became ill. Hospital authorities said it was a mild case of smoke poisoning.

Scores of Volunteers

Scores of volunteer firemen from suburban companies responded to a call for stand by help. The Southern Manheim Twp., Wheatland and Lafayette companies responded and took over the fire stations in the city that were left unguarded while the city department was in service.

The city police, General Hospital, St. Joseph's Hospital, Lafayette Fire Co. and Lancaster Osteopathic Hospital ambulances responded with physicians and nurses.

Directing fire aid operations at the scene of the fire was Dr. Harry S. Berberian, surgeon for the City Fire Department.

City Firm Buys By-Pass Farm

Harley-Davidson to Use Part of Tract

Sale of a 58-acre farm on the Route 230 by-pass, by the Christian K. Peifer estate to William Miller, owner of the Harley-Davidson Sales firm, 200 Hazel St., was announced today.

Miller plans to occupy some of the property for his business, and to sell off the rest of the land in parcels. Most of the land is in Manheim Twp., some of it zoned industrial, and the balance is in East Hempfield Twp.

5,300-Foot Frontage

The farm property has approximately 5,300 feet of frontage on various roads including both sides of the by-pass and the Flory's Mill Road, as well as on the roads leading to Shreiner's Crossing, East Petersburg and connecting the Harrisburg and Manheim Pikes.

Buildings now on the property include an old stone residence with eight rooms, bath and powder rooms and an unusual stairway; a tenant house; a stone summer house; a large bank barn and a tobacco shed. A stream runs through the property.

The sale was handled by the real estate firm of Leo I. Hain, Inc., which will act as selling agent for Miller. Price was not made public.

Sen. Kessler 'Good' After Eye Operation

State Sen. Edward J. Kessler, 16 Parkside Ave., is a patient at Lankenau Hospital, Philadelphia, where he underwent an eye operation Monday.

According to the doctor in attendance, Dr. Rod MacDonald, Sen. Kessler's condition is good, and he is improving very satisfactorily.

He will be confined to the hospital for several weeks.

REGIONAL PLANNING – 2

What Harrisburg Area Is Doing

Many Pennsylvania communities, heirs to 200 years of lack of guided development, are now beginning to do something about regulating future growth through regional planning commissions.

The job of straightening out the confusion produced in two centuries will not be accomplished overnight, but the sooner a start is made the better, says George G. Gordon, executive secretary of the Regional Planning Commission of Greater Harrisburg.

Harrisburg and its surrounding townships and boroughs are facing the same questions as the Lancaster area and others in the state—where major highways should be placed, how home developments should be set up, what to do about industrial growth, and problems such as water supply, sewage disposal and others which exist within municipalities or cut across their boundary lines.

The Greater Harrisburg Commission has 14 members, including Harrisburg City, Dauphin County, and townships and boroughs.

As an example of one step taken by the commission, Gordon points to a meeting held by its traffic, transportation and highway committee in October with representatives of the State Highways Department.

At this meeting, the Highways representatives gave the commission a view of its plans for the Harrisburg area for the next two or three years. The commission representatives were told the department plans work valued at $50,000,000 to $75,000,000 around Harrisburg in the next two or three years, and were shown a generalized hand-drawn sketch map of the proposed projects.

—See PLANNING—Page 4

Today's New Era

Phone Lancaster EX 7-5251

City Installing Yule Decorations Downtown

Downtown Christmas decorations are now being put in place on light standards by employes of the City Streets Department.

The decorations are paid for by the Retail Merchants Committee of the Lancaster Chamber of Commerce, through contributions of its members. The same as used last year, the decorations will be lighted for the first time Nov. 23, the evening after Thanksgiving.

Stores are also putting up decorations in the Christmas theme.

Weather Mild; Snow Out West

Weather stayed mild in Lancaster County today, while the western half of the nation got snow, strong winds and falling temperatures.

Tonight is to be partly cloudy and mild, with a low about 52, the U. S. Weather Bureau said. Tomorrow is to be mostly cloudy and mild with the risk of scattered showers, and a high near 68. Cold and rain is moving east more slowly than originally expected, the bureau said, but may arrive here by Saturday.

High yesterday was 68 downtown. The City Water Works had a low of 31 for the night, 14 degrees below the downtown reading of 45. Coldest weather in the nation extended from the West Coast into the Great Lakes region, with snow from Colorado and Wyoming into western Minnesota, measuring around four inches at many places.

Today Last for Mailing Packages Overseas

Today was the last day for mailing of Christmas parcels to military and authorized civilian personnel overseas.

Lancaster Postmaster Frank R. Hammond said no assurance could be given that overseas surface mail posted after today would reach its destination on time.

Deadline for air mail packages is Dec. 1.

SOME SINCE MIDNIGHT

1,000 Stand in Line for Elvis Presley's First Film

NEW YORK (AP) — About 1,000 persons were on line at the Paramount Theater today for the first showing of Elvis Presley's first film. Some had been waiting since midnight.

When the film began at 8:30 a.m., 1,800 persons—mostly teenagers but with a sprinkling of adults—had paid the 95-cent admission price.

Elvis Fails to Appear

There was some grumbling when the object of their affection failed to appear.

One of the early arrivals, a 15-year-old Brooklyn girl, grumbled: "Why wait on line here all night? I could see the picture at a local movie."

School officials, alert to the truancy prospects inherent in the situation, had five plainclothesmen of the Juvenile Aid Bureau on hand. They intercepted a dozen or so girls taking an unauthorized day off from classes.

Two middle-aged women huddled anxiously behind the box office. They refused to talk to reporters. Bystanders said they were the mothers of two girls, 12 and 14, who left Buffalo yesterday to come to see the film.

A family with different feelings about Presley were Mr. and Mrs. Edward O'Connor of Jersey City

—See ELVIS—Page 4

WEATHER
(U. S. Weather Bureau)
Cloudy And Cold Today, High 35 To 40. Risk Of Light Snow Tonight. Low Tonight 30 To 35.
(Details On Page 20)

Intelligencer Journal.

TELEPHONE EXpress 7-5251
The Leading Newspaper in the Garden Spot of America. Home Owned for Home Folks Since 1794

163rd Year.—No. 164. Metropolitan Lancaster Population 1954 (Est.) Penna. Dept. of Commerce 248,296 LANCASTER, PA., WEDNESDAY MORNING, DECEMBER 26, 1956. CITY EDITION 20 PAGES. 30c PER WEEK—5c Per Copy

AUTO ACCIDENTS KILL 2 COUNTIANS

Highway Slaughter Worst In U.S. History

2 ALL-TIME RECORDS ARE SHATTERED

Safety Council's Estimate Of 660 Traffic Deaths Is Also Shattered

By The Associated Press

The bloodiest yuletide America has ever known on the highways smashed two all-time records for any holiday weekend and the National Safety Council's prediction that 660 persons would die in traffic accidents.

Nor was the count complete.

By 1:30 a.m., EST, 680 had been killed on the streets and highways since 6 p.m. (local time) Friday. Another 47 died in fires during the 102-hour period, and 117 in a variety of accidents, for an over-all total of 844.

The books had not yet closed on accidents in the two Western time zones, and millions of motorists returning from Christmas trips still had an hour or so to add to the gory toll. In addition, the usual straggling reports of accidents within the accepted holiday period could raise the toll to near 700.

The books had closed on accidents only in the Eastern time zone, and the millions of motorists returning from Christmas trips still had one to three hours to add to the gory total in the other three zones. In addition, the usual straggling reports of accidents within the accepted holiday period could raise the total to near 700.

'DISAPPOINTMENT'

Ned H. Dearborn, president of the National Safety Council, called the fulfillment of the council's forecast a "bitter disappointment."

The old record already beaten was 609 traffic deaths, set in the three - day Christmas period of 1955. The old record for all accidental deaths in any holiday was 789, set in 1951's four-day Christmas weekend.

In the first 10 months of 1956 traffic deaths in the United States averaged 106 a day. An Associated Press survey during a nonholiday period, from 6 p.m. Friday to midnight Tuesday of the Dec. 14-18 weekend, showed 500 traffic deaths. The over-all accidental death toll for the period was 587, including 27 in fires and 60 in miscellaneous accidents.

Deaths by states this Christmas period with traffic, fire and miscellaneous accidents in that order:

Alabama 14 1 4; Arizona 5 1 2; Arkansas 11 1 3; California 64 2 5; Colorado 7 0 8; Connecticut 4 5 1; Delaware 1 0 2; Florida 19 0 4; Georgia 19 0 0; Idaho 2 0 1; Illinois 55 2 3; Indiana 15 1 4; Iowa

Turn To Page 7 For More Of DEATHS

This view from a catwalk in Studio A of the new Channel 8 Television Center emphasizes a maze of floodlights and spotlights. Reflectorized curtains pick up true colors for backgrounds in color telecasting.

Channel 8 Television Center Now Operating

WGAL-TV began full time operations yesterday at 6:45 a. m. from the new Channel 8 Television Center on Lincoln Highway West at the intersection of Abbeyville Road.

Inauguration of program service from the new facilities, said to be among the finest in the nation, was marked with special Christmas programs, including an hour-long program with the chancel choir of the First Methodist Church, Lancaster, and soloists.

To accomplish the move with no interruption in program service, an intricate schedule of moving was carried out last week when administrative, sales, production, art, photography and promotion departments were set up in the new quarters.

New studio and technical facilities were given final testing at the new building while the program staff and technical operators continued actual telecasting from 24 S. Queen St.

Monday night, after sign-off at the down-town studios, the last personnel moved into the new building to prepare for sign-on at 6:45 a.m. yesterday in one of the two major studios at the new Channel 8 Television Center.

Actually, the move will not be fully completed until technical equipment in the former studio is dismantled and installed in the second main studio at the new location. When this is accomplished, the station will hold formal opening ceremonies and open its doors to the public for pre-arranged tours.

Situated on the crest of a 25-acre tract adjacent to the Wheatland and Hamilton Park sections of Lancaster Twp., the red brick and Indiana limestone structure con-

Turn To Page 7 For More Of WGAL-TV

Hoad Beats Flam To Put Aussies In Tennis Lead

ADELAIDE, Australia, Dec. 26 (Wednesday) (AP)—Lew Hoad, the blond blaster from Down Under, got Australia off to a 1-0 lead in the Davis Cup challenge round today when he crushed Herbie Flam of Beverly Hills, Calif., 6-2, 6-3, 6-3.

Vic Seixas, the Philadelphia veteran, tangled with Ken Rosewall who took the American national championship home with him last fall, in the second match.

Hoad won the first three sets 6-2, 6-3, 6-3, and the match to give Australia a 1-0 lead in the best of five round.

Flam got off on the wrong foot when he dropped his first service. Both players were serving rushing the net and volleying. For Hoad this was the usual strategy, but for Flam, it was something unusual.

The 28-year-old ex-sailor usually stands in the backcourt and bounces the ball back at his opponent. He did not have enough speed on his first volley to cope with the muscular Hoad.

In the second game, Flam had Hoad down 0-30, but couldn't capitalize on his advantage. Again in the fifth game, Flam's

Turn To Page 7 For More Of TENNIS

$25 STOLEN FROM LABOR ASSN. CLUB

Burglars broke into the Lancaster Labor Assn. Club, 202 W. Liberty St., Monday night and escaped with $25 in cash.

Detective Raymond Wiggins said the money was taken from a steel filing cabinet in an office on the second floor. He said the handle was broken off the cabinet to gain entrance. Another box, containing $3 in change, was not disturbed. The burglary occurred between 6 p. m. Monday and 10:25 a. m. yesterday.

Entrance to the building was gained by climbing a fire escape and forcing open a door, the detective said.

"We Lead All The Rest"

FARM CORNER

By Joe Wachtman

State's Farm Crops Valued At $311 Million

Bumper yields far outweighed sharply lower plantings to produce farm crops valued at $311,915,000 for Pennsylvania farmers during the year, according to the State Department of Agriculture.

The figure is more than 21 million dollars or seven per cent higher than the $290,525,000 recorded during 1955.

Higher yields of corn, hay, tobacco and potatoes together with better prices for potatoes offset a continued decline in fruit as well as lower total acreage harvested by farmers of the state in the year just ending.

Value of the fruit production was estimated at $18,877,000 this year, a drop of 15 per cent from the $22,335,000 total of a year ago. All fruits but grapes shared in the decline in both production and value.

The corn crop, which established new production marks in southeastern and central areas, advanced in value by $14.426,000 to a total of 104 million dollars to lead the gains. The yield of 56 bushels of shelled corn per acre established an all-time state record while the total crop of 71,736,000 bushels was second only to the record 72,726,000 bushels of 1919.

Potatoes also established record yields per acre, with summer va-

Turn To Page 17 For More Of FARM CORNER

Fire, Water Heavily Damage Prince Street Planing Mill

Water from a sprinkler system set off by a roof fire caused thousands of dollars damage at the Frey & Son planing mill, 1000 N. Prince St., late Monday night.

Fire Chief Samuel L. Herr, of Southern Manheim Twp. Co., said the fire started in the roof. When firemen arrived, flames were shooting through the roof and a fire box at Prince and Liberty Streets was pulled, bringing out companies 4 and 6 and truck B from the city fire department at 11:50 p. m.

Chief Herr said the fire in the roof was immediately extinguished before it spread but the flames caused the sprinkler system to go off in the two-story building.

Before the sprinkler could be turned off the water soaked the office and planing mill and seeped through into the basement, causing extensive damage.

L. Ralph Frey and his son, Robert D. Frey, were not able to estimate the extent of the damage yesterday. Chief Herr said that included in the damage were several made-to-order wooden kitchens which were ready for delivery.

The fire chief said he was not able to determine what started the blaze but theorized that apiece of burning paper may have blown on the roof.

EGYPT BLOCKS UN PLAN FOR SUEZ PARLEY

Last-Minute Objections Throw Wrench In Settlement Conference

WASHINGTON, Dec. 25 (AP)—Egypt's last-minute objections are reported to have blocked a United Nations plan to begin talks on a permanent Suez Canal settlement before the end of this month.

President Nasser is understood to have assured American diplomats he is ready to resume Suez talks once the work of clearing the blocked waterway gets under way.

But just when such salvage operations to clear away sunken ships can begin is now unclear. The United Nations has ordered two of its top assistants to fly to Cairo to talk with Nasser about new conditions which are reported to have been imposed.

ISRAELI TIMETABLE

After agreeing to allow the job of clearing the canal to begin once British-French forces withdrew, Egypt is now reported insisting this task be delayed until Israeli troops pull out of the Sinai Peninsula. The Israeli government has set a withdrawal timetable which will require several weeks.

Top American officials had hoped Suez talks could begin in late December, in accordance with a plan developed by United Nations Secretary General Dag Hammarskjold. This plan was based on the expectation that British-French troops would be withdrawn and canal clearance operations under way by then.

Nasser, during several private meetings with American Ambassador Raymond Hare in Cairo, assured the State Department he was willing to resume such talks, which were broken off nearly two months ago when Israeli, British and French forces invaded Egypt.

Terre Hill Girl Breaks Leg On Christmas Gift

If Santa had brought new ice skates to Ann Louise Smith, six-year-old daughter of Mr. and Mrs. Harold K. Smith, 210 E. Main St., Terre Hill, the unseasonably mild weather yesterday could have saved her grief.

As it was, with reasonably pleasant weather. Ann Louise took her brand new roller skates on a "shake-down cruise" and was treated a short time later for a fracture of the right leg.

Attendants at Ephrata Community Hospital said the girl was released after she received treatment at 6:05 p.m. yesterday.

3 Phoned Threats Intensify N. Y. Police Hunt For Gotham's Elusive 'Mad Bomber'

NEW YORK, Dec. 25 (AP) — Three telephoned bomb threats were received by police within half an hour tonight in the midst of a newly intensified campaign to find New York's "Mad Bomber."

It was not clear whether the new bomb threats came from the unbalanced man who has plagued New York City's police with more than 30 homemade bombs in the last 16 years.

After a careful search of two movie theaters and a YMCA building turned up no bombs, police labeled the new threats the work of crackpots.

Only once before, as far as public records go, has the authentic "Mad Bomber" telephoned an advance warning. That was last May 2 at Radio City Music Hall when one of his bombs was found unexploded after a telephone call.

SCORES OF PHONY

Police get scores of phony bomb threats from crackpots in the course of a year. They investigate each one thoroughly and usually find no bomb.

But occasionally someone finds the pipelike black powder bombs of the phamtom bomber before they explode—or ehse they explode without warning in some public place.

He left his latest calling card yesterday at the big public library at 42nd St. and Fifth Ave.

The device was removed by a special police bomb squad.

The first telephoned threat tonight was received at Sloane House, a big YMCA building in midtown.

NOTHING FOUND

The caller told a telephone operator, "There's a bomb there." When questioned, he added, "In the Sloane House." Police searched the building thoroughly but could find nothing suspicious.

Less than half an hour later a male caller phoned the Beacon Theater at 74th St. and Broadway, and said: "Listen carefully, I'm not joking, there's a bomb in your theater."

A little later another threat was made at a theater in the Bronx. Police began careful searches of both theaters.

NEARLY $2,000,000 LOSS IN TEXAS BLAST

DALLAS, Dec. 25 (AP)—An explosion rocked a warehouse of the Yellow Transit Co. today, sending flame 200 feet into the sky and causing damage estimated at nearly two million dollars. No one was injured.

The blast was followed by a series of explosions from truck gasoline tanks and stored paint. Smoke from the flaming asphault roof of the rambling building was visible for miles.

Twenty - seven trailers loaded with merchandise were listed as a total loss.

Night watchman T. M. Terrell, 62, said he was drinking coffee in a dispatcher's office when he heard, "a big, loud explosion."

Stevens R1 Man Crushed, Mariettan Dies In Crash

MARK WEIDMAN

WILLIAM C. PENWELL

Father Of Two, 34, Victim While Acting As Good Samaritan

Tragedy on the highways struck twice at Lancaster County families over the holiday, killing a Stevens R1 father of two Christmas eve and a Marietta man early Christmas day.

The victims were identified as:

Mark Weidman, thirty-four, of Stevens R1, who died while playing the role of Good Samaritan, and

William Charles Penwell, twenty-five, 442 E. Front St., Marietta, killed in Dauphin County in an accident that also claimed the life of a companion from York.

Weidman died when he fell from the bumper of a stalled vehicle under the wheels of a neighbor's car pushing the disabled auto. He was the 55th to die in Lancaster County motor vehicle accidents this year. The count is six more than at this time last year and it is the largest since 1941 when 59 persons were killed.

Lancaster County Highway Deaths
SINCE JAN. 1, 1956
55
SAME DATE 1955—49

Penwell and George Joseph Lauer, twenty-eight, 3610 E. Market St., York, died when Lauer's auto left Route 441 and rammed a semi-trailer on a parking lot just south of the borough of Royalton.

Turn To Page 7 For More Of FATALITIES

Holidays Begin Wet, Close Dry And Brisk

Christmas 1956 is history.

It began in Lancaster County in a dense, wet mantle of fog last Friday and ended last night brisk and dry.

According to the weatherman, only hours separated the difference between a white Christmas and one that was not. The forecast calls for risk of snow tonight continuing into tomorrow. High temperature today will be about 40 degrees.

As the holiday came to a close, the big homeward rush was on. Traffic on county highways last night was reported extremely heavy.

Greyhound had to press spare buses into service to handle unprecedented passenger demands. But the buses were holding pretty close to schedule. The Pennsylvania Railroad reported similar conditions.

The holiday was over, but it was a memorable one in Lancaster County. It was marked by deeds of love, by joyous celebration and by tragedy.

The community united with Christian communities throughout the world in reaching out to soothe the hurt and help the helpless.

The anniversary of Christ's birth was celebrated in beautiful services in local churches of all denominations. The spirit of giving implicit in the holiday made itself felt beneath countless Christmas trees.

There were the traditional ingatherings of the clans and visits to homes of friends and neighbors.

ACCIDENTS KILL TWO

In two county homes, the joy of the season was marred by great sorrow. A Marietta man and a Brickerville father lost their lives in highway accidents.

Despite warnings and pleas to motorists, a record number of Americans met death on the nation's roads.

It was a far happier observance for three Hungarian youths who spent the holiday getting used to their new homes in the county.

Happier, too, for Mrs. John M. Martin, of New Holland, a victim of multiple sclersois, who was spending Christmas at home with her husband and children. Mrs. Martin, still confined to an iron lung, lay many months in St. Joseph's Hospital sure she would

Turn To Page 7 For More Of HOLIDAY

WHO WANTS ELVIS?

Lancaster Has One Of Its Own

Airman 2nd Class Bill Jenkins of Lancaster just strums his guitar now and again. Other times he sings and is much more mobile—a dead ringer of Elvis Presley. Airman Jenkins is "wowing" audiences around Finley radar base in eastern North Dakota.

FARGO, N.D., Dec. 25 — Give or take a few million dollars, there's not much difference between Bill Jenkins of Lancaster, Pa., and rock 'n' roll artist Elvis Presley.

Elvis' take this year is figured at several millions of dollars, but Jenkins pulled in something less than $2,000 — he works for the government as Airman 2nd class William Jenkins, age twenty.

Both strum a guitar now and again and both, to put it mildly, are "mobile" when singing a song. Toss in a pair of jumbo sideburns apiece and the girls seem to react in the same way — affirmative!

Jenkins began wowing the females around the Finley radar base in eastern North Dakota when he was transferred there from a similar base at Opheim, Mont., about a year ago.

Asked if he tries to imitate Elvis, Bill insists he's been performing that way ever since his father, J. Veryl Jenkins, of 52 Green St., Lancaster, a banjo player, gave him his first guitar when he was sixteen.

The Lancaster airman added singing to his act after entering service from McCaskey High School three years ago.

A brother, T-Sgt. John V. Jenkins Jr., is with the Air Force at Weldon, N.C. and a sister, Mrs. Charles Brubaker, lives at Lancaster.

Bill has teamed with Airman

Turn To Page 7 For More Of DOUBLE

City Expected To Make Budget Into Law Today

The 1957 budget ordinance is expected to be enacted into law this morning by the City Council without significant change in the measure, first introduced Nov. 27.

Indications are that the governing body has found no reason to revise upwards the pay raises to be given city employes.

The budget, while holding the 1957 tax rate to the 1956 level of 14 mills, provides pay increases of five per cent for police and firemen. They had requested at least twice that much, along with certain fringe benefits in the case of policemen.

Other city employes will get a three per cent raise. The budget calls for the setting aside of the equivalent of two per cent for the establishment of a "modest" pension system.

The uniformed forces have established retirement programs in operation.

The budget — a record $2,442, 123.81 — represents an increase of about five and one-

Turn To Page 7 For More Of BUDGET

$50,000 DAMAGE IN YORK COUNTY FIRE

YORK, Pa., Dec. 25 (AP)—A Christmas night fire burned out the interior of a large warehouse and caused an estimated $50,000 damage at Hungerford, about 20 miles south of York near the Maryland border.

William Free, president of the Hungerford Packing Co., made the damage estimate after about 100 firemen from four area companies brought the blaze under control. The fire threatened nearby homes and buildings for an hour and a half but none were damaged. No one was injured.

The state fire marshal's office was asked to investigate since the cause was undetermined. It was the third fire and second major blaze at the packing company in six months. Last June about $40,000 damage was done to the company's other large warehouse.

Only the concrete walls of the warehouse were left standing. Salt, sugar, empty cans and some packaged canned goods were destroyed by the flames.

Ike Leads List Of Headliners Of 1956 From Pennsylvania

Gen. Michaelis Is Among State Newsmakers

PHILADELPHIA, Dec. 29 (AP)—A man by the name of Eisenhower who once hailed from Texas, Kansas and New York and is now headquartering in Washington, officially became a citizen of Pennsylvania.

A sometime resident of Philadelphia and Hollywood became the first lady of a tiny principality, dreamy anachronism in the modern world. That, of course, was actress Grace Kelly metamorphosed into the Princess of Monaco.

They are just two of the more conspicuous examples of how Pennsylvania names, new and old, figured in the news of this year.

Down Gettysburg way the citizens of Adams and neighboring counties have for several years been rekoning their number one citizen is the President of the United States. In 1956 it was made official. Eisenhower became a registered voter of the state in the spring primary.

And on Nov. 6 Eisenhower carried his township, county and state, the first Pennsylvania citizen to be elected President in 100 years. James Buchanan, a Democrat, from the Lancaster region, was elected in 1856.

In politics, diplomacy, science, religion, journalism, organized labor; in literature, great music, and most of the lively arts; in research and humanitarian work, sons and daughters of Pennsylvania won headlines the world over.

Brig. Gen. John H. Michaelis, of Lancaster, combat veteran of World War II and Korea, and a one time aide to Gen. Eisenhower, returned to Washington and his new job as army chief of legislative liaison and was promoted to Major General.

George Kennan, former U.S. ambassador to Moscow, remained at a high place in the esteem of his fellow countrymen. He lives in Adams county.

PENNSYLVANIANS IN THE 1956 NEWS—These six Pennsylvania residents were among those who figured prominently in the news in 1956. From left, top row: President Eisenhower; Princess of Monaco, former Grace Kelly; former Philadelphia Mayor Joseph S. Clark, new U. S. Senator; bottom row, from left: Dr. Jonas Salk, discoverer of polio vaccine; Janet Blair, Altoona, TV star; and David J. McDonald, key man in labor picture. (AP Wirephoto)

Within the state, the shining figure in politics, after the President himself, was Pennsylvania's new senator, Democrat Joseph S. Clark, no stranger to headline prestige. His was the lone major Democratic victory in the state last November.

Long a dominant figure in Pennsylvania politics, James P. Finnegan managed, first, Adlai Stevenson's primary election campaign, and then the fall election drive itself.

Leader, A Newsmaker

As might be expected of any man at the top in Harrisburg, Gov. Leader was very much in the news all year. That he got a good deal of attention outside Pennsylvania was due chiefly to his status as one of the bright young men of the Democratic Party. At midterm, he is not quite the master of his house he used to be, owing to the Democrats' loss of majority voice in the Legislature. It's a cinch that Leader will continue to be top newsmaker.

Philadelphia Mayor Richardson Dilworth was seldom out of the limelight. Thomas D. McBride, 54-year-old chancellor of the Philadelphia Bar Assn., became the state's attorney general shortly before Christmas. One of the most widely known trial lawyers in the East, McBride throughout his career had been associated with the defense. Many found it strange to see the "great defender of civil rights," "the friend of the underdog" on the other side.

For his 21-year term on state

MAJ. GEN. MICHAELIS

supreme court, Chief Justice Horace Stern was honored as a great jurist.

The spotlight was focussed on two Pennsylvanians at the South Pole — Dr. Paul A. Siple, he comes from Erie, and Harold G. McRillis, of Sharpesville. These two and their colleagues are having a fresh look at Antartica in order to learn more about the weather.

State and nation paid new tribute to Dr. Jonas Salk, University of Pittsburgh scientist, for his development of the polio vaccine that bears his name. Dr. Isidor S. Ravdin, chief surgeon of the University of Pennsylvania Hospital, was one of the specialists who attended President Eisenhower during his operation for ileitis last June. The only reserve medical officer holding the rank of major general, Dr. Ravdin retired in October. The Army toasted him for his long and brilliant service. And in London, the Royal College of Surgeons made him an honorary fellow.

A key man in labor was David J. McDonald, president of the United Steelworkers. Another, although less publicized, was Thomas Kennedy, international vice president of the United Mine Workers of America. McDonald lives in Pittsburgh, Kennedy in Luzerne County.

Pennsylvania names ranking high in literary achievement included: Pearl Buck, founder of Welcome House in Bucks County; John O'Hara, who hails from Pottsville; James Michener, a Bucks County resident when not traipsing about the world; Rachel Carson, a native of Springdale, Allegheny County; Nora Waln, of Philadelphia.

Philadelphia-born Marian Anderson, one of the greatest singers, brought out her autobiography, "My Lord, What a Morning," described by many critics as an important and inspiring book.

Another native of Philadelphia, Dolores Wilson, a coloratura soprano, stepped in at the last moment on the night of Dec. 11 to sing the title role in "Lucia Di Lammermoor" at the Metropolitan Opera House in New York. Maria Callas, the star, had to bow out because of a shore throat. Miss Wilson came through admirably.

Top man of the top orchestra—any year—that could mean only Eugene Ormandy and the Philadelphia Orchestra.

Dr. Eugene Carson Blake of Philadelphia, president of the National Council of Churches, visited Communist Europe twice in 1956. His comments and those of the clergymen who went with him made the authority of his position especially newsworthy.

Entertainment, as a whole, was outdazzled by the unreal highjinks of the Grace Kelly-Prince Rainier wedding. Pennsylvania felt it had a vested interest in both the fandango of the engagement announcement and the actual wedding, as well as the subsequent activities of the royal couple. All the same, space remained for others from this state who have made the grade in the theater, movies, television, even bull-fighting.

Janet Blair, Altoona, became the new partner of comedian Sid Caesar on the TV. Ann B. Davis, Erie, was a continuing standout on the Bob Cummings TV show. Jack Palance, of the Hazleton region, found acting rewards in 1956.

Singer Shirley Jones, of Smithton, Westmoreland County, after a 1955 debut in a film version of "Oklahoma!", followed it up this year with an even greater success, "Carousel."

Bandsman Tommy Dorsey, who stemmed from Scranton, died during the year in his sleep at his Connecticut home.

Philadelphia playwright Joseph Kramm had another drama on view —"Build With One Hand." David Poleri, Philadelphia tenor, was praised for his performance in "Troilus and Cressida," at La Scala in Milan. Fred Waring and his Pennsylvanians were saluted on big television show in honor of the band's 40 years in show busikess. Band leader Russ Morgan, who is proud of being a Scranton-Nanticoke alumnus, had one of TV's better summer shows. Joey Bishop, Philadelphia comic, endeared himself to more and more people. Bette Ford, of McKeesport had the bull-fighting distinction. She fought bulls in Mexico and the Philippines and on a visit home in November said she'd like to display her skill at next year's Allegheny County Fair. Whether she'll get the chance is yet to be decided.

Adolph Hitler Is Dead – Legally As Of April 30, 1945

BERLIN, Dec. 29 (AP) — A West Berlin registrar's office has formally listed Adolf Hitler as legally dead.

Registration was a formality. The Berchtesgaden District Court officially pronounced Hitler dead last Oct. 25, fixing the date of his death as of April 30, 1945.

Firemen Wet Ruins In Phila.

PHILADELPHIA, Dec. 29 (INS)—Preliminary damage estimates soared to more than a million dollars today as firemen continued to wet down a gutted building in Philadelphia's central shopping district 24 hours after the nine-alarm blaze got underway.

The fire department said the figure would probably run much higher when all estimates on smoke and water damage are tallied.

The four-story building adjacent to the Gimbel Brothers Department Store housed a jewelers' cooperative, a hosiery store, shoe repair shop, clothing establishments, a credit firm and the Philadelphia Retail Merchants Association offices containing instalment buying records of 2,000,000 persons.

Firemen on duty today took precautions against the building walls toppling. Meanwhile, traffic in the busy central city area was still snarled for blocks around the fire scene which was roped off.

President's Reply To Bulganin Puts Arms In UN Talks

WASHINGTON, Dec. 29 (AP) — President Eisenhower was reported today to have prepared a letter to Soviet Premier Bulganin, saying that disarmament discussions belong in the United Nations.

Eisenhower's reply to a Nov. 17 letter from Bulganin was said to be ready for transmittal to Moscow. The letter has undergone a number of revisions, getting smaller each time. Now, it is understood to be quite brief.

Questions Dropped

Earlier versions were said to have included questions seeking more details on Bulganin's suggestion of a five-power meeeting on disarmament, including the Big Four and India. These questions are understood to have been dropped.

In the present version, Eisenhower is reported to say to Bulganin that disarmament talks for the present should be conducted at the U.N. The U.N. Disarmament Commission held one meeting recently and is expected to meet again shortly.

Meeting Not Needed

Eisenhower is said to have decided a five-power disarmament meeting would not be useful at this time unless—and here the door was held open—there was some assurance that progress could be made.

Officials were not sure when Eisenhower would send the letter to Moscow. They were agreed, however, it would be soon.

At the time of the Nov. 17 message from Bulganin, considerable interest was aroused by a Russian proposal for a system of mutual aerial inspection extending approximately 500 miles on each side of the Iron Curtain.

This proposal marked something of a reversal from Bulganin's rejection of Eisenhower's "open skies" inspection plan, proposed at the Geneva conference in 1955.

Togoland Would End Trusteeship

PARIS, Dec. 29 (AP) — The government of French Togoland decided today to ask the United Nations to abolish the U. N. Trusteeship under which that West African area has been run since December 1946.

Local autonomy was favored by a massive vote in a referendum held there Oct. 28.

The Trusteeship Committee of the U. N. General Assembly decided Dec. 5 to end a trusteeship over adjoining British Togoland next March 6.

Chevrolet Claims 1956 Production Title

DETROIT, Dec. 29 (INS)—Chevrolet Division of General Motors today claimed the 1956 production championship, declaring it outbuilt competitors by at least 300,000 units.

U. S. output alone was estimated at 1,621,270 cars and 353,401 trucks by Chevrolet General Manager Edward N. Cole.

The total, Cole said, would approximate 30 per cent of the industry and mark the 21st consecutive year Chevrolet has established production leadership.

ENROUTE TO CAIRO

CAIRO, Dec. 29 (AP)—V. K. Krishna Menon, India's roving diplomat, left Cairo today after a series of talks with President Nasser.

Chou-Pakistan Views Differ

DACCA, East Pakistan, Dec. 29 (AP)—Red China's Premier Chou En-Lai wound up a visit to Pakistan today by taking a boat ride with Prime Minister Husseyn Suhrawardy. The Pakistan leader had some harsh words to say about India's Prime Minister Nehru, whom Chou will see tomorrow in New Delhi.

Chou and Suhrawardy made a 12-mile river trip from Dacca to Narayanganj, an industrial town. They had separate talks with newsmen. Suhrawardy's remarks were pointedly pro-Western and anti-Nehru. Chou stressed that Pakistan - Chinese differences "do not prevent our friendship," and evaded questions about relations between Pakistan and India.

Suhrawardy told interviewers:

Can't Be Neutral

"I am on the side of the free democratic world because no small country, particularly when she is in danger, can afford to be neutral." He added that "Chou knows my mind perfectly . . ." and that he had arrived at a "fair understanding" with the Chinese leader.

Suhrawardy characterized Nehru's policies as "no neutraliams but pure, simple blackmail." He said "Nehru wants to get the maximum bargains both from the Western powers and the Communist bloc. He is neither honest with himself nor with others . . ."

Chou delivered an anti-Western anti-colonial speech at Dacca. He charged the colonial powers with trying to sow "antagonism and hatred" among African and Asian nations.

He voiced opposition to the setting of military blocs in the Asian-African region, saying they disrupted unity. Red China is among the objectors to SEATO, the Southeast Asia Defense Treaty Organization to which Pakistan belongs.

Today's Chuckle

If women's intuition is so wonderful, how come they ask so many questions?

LANCASTER NEW ERA

Metropolitan Lancaster Population 1954 (Est.) Penna. Dept. of Commerce 248,296

Local Weather

Lancaster U. S. Bureau

Increasing cloudiness and rather cold tonight; tomorrow mostly cloudy and warmer with rain likely by night; low tonight about 24 in city and 18 in suburbs; high tomorrow near 40.

Complete Report on Page 3

80th Year—No. 24,690 | CITY EDITION | LANCASTER, PA., THURSDAY, JANUARY 3, 1957 | 42 PAGES | 30c PER WEEK—5c Per Copy

U. S. Judge Bars Segregation on Miami's Buses

Rules State, City Laws Illegal, NAACP Says Ruling 'Far-Reaching'

MIAMI, Fla. (AP)—A U. S. District Court judge today ruled that Florida laws and Miami city ordinances requiring segregated seating on municipal buses are unconstitutional.

Judge Emett Choate made the oral ruling in refusing to dismiss a petition by Florida branches of the National Assn. for Advancement of Colored People requesting an end to segregated bus seating.

The judge refused to convene a three-judge court to hear arguments in the case. He said there was no substantial question of constitutional law in view of the recent U.S. Supreme Court decision banning segregated seating on buses in Montgomery, Ala.

The NAACP filed the suit Oct. 12, 1956, naming the Miami Transit Co., the city and the individual city commissioners.

Choate dismissed the transit company as a defendant, ruling it was a private enterprise and not an arm of the state. He gave the city 10 days to file an answer to his ruling.

Says It Can Be Extended

The judge's action touched only segregation on city transit buses, but G. E. Graves Jr. of Miami, attorney for the NAACP, said "It is apparent that the decision has a much more far-reaching effect than that. It can be extended to trains, suburban and interurban buses."

Dr. A. Joseph Reddick, pastor of Miami's St. James African Methodist Episcopal church, instituted the suit as president of the Florida NAACP.

He said it had no "direct link" with legal attacks on bus segregation in Montgomery and Tallahassee, Fla., but "came out of the Supreme Court decision in the Montgomery case."

Negroes Sit From Rear

Miami buses have signs asking Negro passengers to seat themselves from the rear.

Dr. Reddick noted that Miami Negroes have not been involved in a boycott and had not used any violence in their campaign against segregated seating.

"Our main concern has been to remove the statutes from the books," he said.

The bus company has contended since the case was filed that in requiring segregated seating it was merely following the laws of Florida and the ordinances of Miami and that it would continue to do so until the laws were changed.

SOUTH COLDER AS DEEP FREEZE MISSES COUNTY

It was colder down South than in Lancaster County last night, as this area escaped the deep freeze which had been predicted.

The U. S. Weather Bureau downtown recorded a low of 24; the City Water Works, 23, and Ephrata weather station, 20. Meanwhile Baltimore had 18; Washington, 21; Roanoke, Va., three; Richmond, 15; Greensboro, N. C., 12; Charleston, S. C., 19, and Augusta, Ga., 18.

Tonight is to be cloudier and continued cold here, with a low about 24 in the city and 18 in the suburbs, the bureau said. Tomorrow is to be mostly cloudy and warmer, with some rain likely by night, and a high near 40. Yesterday's high was 30. The cold has produced ice heavy enough for skating on ponds and small streams. The Susquehanna was frozen across at Safe Harbor this morning, for the first time this season. Usually the first freeze occurs about Dec. 4, officials said.

Arthur B. Sinkler, right, president of Hamilton Watch Co., and Dr. John A. Van Horn, director of research and development, examine world's first electric wrist watch, perfected by Hamilton.

H. W. PRENTIS JR.

Industry Will Honor Prentis

Secretary Weeks to Present Testimonial

H. W. Prentis Jr., chairman of the board of the Armstrong Cork Co., will be honored at a testimonial dinner during the 14th annual conference of the Lancaster County Manufacturers Association 6:30 p.m., Jan. 25, at Hotel Brunswick.

Sinclair Weeks, secretary of commerce of the United States, will present the testimonial and introduce Prentis.

A representative of the Manufacturers Association said today that the honor was being given Prentis "in recognition of his major contribution to industry, education and public affairs over a period of many years."

Joined Armstrong In 1907

Prentis, a native of St. Louis, Mo., joined the Armstrong Cork Co. in 1907. He was elected a vice president in 1926. In 1929, he was

—See PRENTIS—Page 10

Formosa Planes Drop Leaflets on Peiping

TAIPEI (AP)—Chinese Nationalist planes showered propaganda leaflets on Peiping during the night in the first "paper bomb" raid on the Chinese Communist capital.

Air force headquarters said all planes returned safely to Formosa despite some ground fire.

The mission involved a round trip of over 2,100 miles.

INTRODUCED BY HAMILTON

1st Electric Wrist WatchMadeHere

Hamilton Watch Co. ushered in a new era in timekeeping today with its introduction of the world's first electric wrist watch, perfected in Lancaster after ten years of research, development and testing.

No larger than a conventional wrist watch, the electric watch offers the highest accuracy and dependability ever achieved, and incorporates the first basic change in watch construction in almost five centuries, Arthur B. Sinkler, Hamilton president, said today.

Sinkler called the electric watch a "milestone in Hamilton's program of research and expansion," and predicted it would in time completely replace present-day automatic watches.

Available This Month

Unveiled at a New York press luncheon, the watch will be available to consumers sometime this month, in limited quantity. The first model, cased in 14 karat gold, retails for $175. A gold-filled model, at $89.50, will be available soon.

The radical structure of the electric watch completely eliminates the mainspring, an integral part of portable timekeeping devices since it was invented in 1480 by Peter Henlein of Nuremberg, Germany. The new watch is the only one in existence which runs without winding or without periodic agitation, Sinkler added.

Tiny Energizer Used

"The watch movement," he pointed out, "is so exquisitely engineered that a tiny Energizer the size of a small shirt button will run it for more than twelve months. In fact, Hamilton's electric watch would run for more than 20 years on energy that would operate a 100-Watt bulb for no longer than one minute."

Instruments used in America today are becoming more and more complex, Sinkler pointed out. As a result industry is beginning to demand greater miniaturization of all types to continue its technical advancement. This demand for smaller instruments makes it important to combine and miniaturize mechanical, electrical and electronic mechanisms, he said. Because of this a new technical revolution is in progress and Hamilton's electric watch with its miniaturized electric power plant and time-keeping assembly is a major step in opening the frontiers of this new era.

"The electric watch," he added, "also has profound implications for our national defense, with miniature timing devices so vital to modern weapons of war."

Chemical Energy

The electric watch operates on chemical energy stored in a tiny Energizer, according to Dr. John Van Horn, Hamilton's director of research and development. This energy is converted into electrical power as it releases a stream of electrons energy through interaction with permanent magnetic fields causes the balance wheel to oscillate. This oscillation is the mechanical energy which runs the watch.

Hamilton presently has more than 35 patents pending on this operation, he added.

"The over-all result is a precise miniature power plant built into

—See WATCH—Page 10

Reds Kill Fleeing Hungary Woman

VIENNA (AP) — Hungarian and Russian border guards opened fire last night on a group of refugees near the Austrian frontier and killed one of them, police said today.

The refugees finally were able to cross the border near the Austrian village of Andau, carrying with them the body of a 50-year-old woman shot to death almost within reach of freedom, police reported.

Of 158,183 refugees who arrived here since the start otfhe Hungarian revolution, 88,985 have left for other countries, officials said.

Democrats Get Sen. Control as Congress Opens

Prepare to Hear Ike Proposals for Standby Power in Middle East

BULLETIN

Washington (AP) — The House today ordered a Saturday session to hear President Eisenhower deliver a message on the Middle East crisis. It passed and sent to the Senate a resolution for a joint session that day.

WASHINGTON (AP) — Democrats took the controls of the new 85th Congress today—but only after a brief Senate scare—and started a session already confronted with a momentous foreign affairs issue.

President Eisenhower will go before a joint session tomorrow or Saturday to present this grave question — a request for advance approval to use U. S. troops against any Communist aggression in the Middle East.

The Democratic scare in the Senate arose from the silence of Sen.-elect Frank Lausche of Ohio, right up to the climactic moment, as to whether he would vote for the Democrats to organize the Senate. He did, and the Democrats prevailed on a 49-46 vote.

Ends GOP Hopes

Lausche's decision to stick with his party ended a short-lived renewal of Republican hopes that they might be able to seize control of the Senate from the Democrats despite the latter's numerical majority in the election returns.

The test came on the election of a Senate president pro tempore—the official who presides in the absence of the vice president.

The Democrats put up veteran Sen. Carl Hayden of Arizona as a replacement for the retired Sen. Walter George of Georgia.

The Republicans then sought to substitute the name of Sen. Styles Bridges of New Hampshire.

Lausche, when his name was called, voted against Bridges.

When the roll call was completed on that maneuver with the vote 49 - 46, the Republicans dropped the fight. They joined in electing Hayden by acclamation.

Stillness Over Chamber

The question of whether the Democrats might run into trouble in their efforts to organize hung

—See CONGRESS—Page 10

Asks 3.6 Billion Aid for Schools

Bill by Rep. Kelley Covers 6-Yr. Period

WASHINGTON (AP)—Rep Kelley (D-Pa) prepared a whopping $3,600,000,000 school construction bill for introduction in the House today.

The money, to be paid to state educational agencies on a grant basis, would be parceled out over six years, beginning July 1, 1957, at the rate of 600 million a year.

Kelley was author of the $1,600,000,000 school building measure which the House defeated last year by a 224-194 vote.

Aid On Primary List

The administration last year asked for a five-year plan granting a total of 1¼ billion to the states. This year, President Eisenhower has listed a school construction bill as one of the primary items in his legislative program but has given no figures.

Rep. McConnel (R-Pa), who pushed the administration measure in the house last year, said he will handle whatever the administration wants this year.

Powell Plans Change

A third figure in last year's tussle, Rep. Powell (D-NY), said he is ready to go again. Powell, a Negro, was author of an amendment to deny aid to school districts failing to comply with the desegregation decision of the Supreme Court. The House adopted the amendment 225-192 before it killed the whole bill.

Powell told reporters he will seek to have corresponding language put in this year's bill.

PO Studies 5-Ct. Rate on Letters

Dept. Preparing Plan For Improved Service

WASHINGTON (AP) — The Post Office Department said today it is "giving consideration" to a move to raise the postage rate on letters to five cents from three cents.

The department made the statement in response to inquiries about reports that Postmaster General Summerfield advanced the idea at a White House conference of Republican congressional leaders Monday. Any increase would require congressional approval.

Details Withheld

Summerfield, in the last two sessions of Congress, unsuccessfully urged making the letter rate four cents an ounce:

In the statement today the department asserted that it is currently "studying a revolutionary plan for a substantially improved mail service," but is not yet in a position to announce details.

Center Commission to Meet This Afternoon

The Lancaster County Community Center Commission was scheduled to meet late this afternoon at the office of Robert Chestnut, chairman, at the Alcoa plant.

No advance information was given on the nature of the meeting. The commission said in mid-December it would issue a report in the near future.

N. Y. Reds Plan Name Non-Party Action Assn.

NEW YORK (AP) — New York State leaders of the Communist party want to change its name and change it into a "Nonparty Political Action Assn.

The proposal was in the form of a majority report of the State Committee, approved 25 to 6 in a meeting on Dec. 8, and sent to party clubs yesterday along with a sharply dissenting report.

Gina Lollobrigida Says She's Expecting Child

ROME (AP)—Gina Lollobrigida is going to have a baby, she announced today.

"I must confirm that I am expecting a child," the film star said. "It has become too difficult to say 'no' all the time."

Maple Grove Field House Will Close As Sports Center

Edward H. Koerkle

New Era Photo

'Merchandise Mart' to Open Early This Year

Used 27 Years as Only Local Center For Athletic Events

The Maple Grove field house, Lancaster's only sports center for 27 years, will be closed next month.

The field house, nine acres of land and a roadway leading from the Columbia pike to the property has been leased to the Maple Grove Bargain Center, Inc., a new corporation.

It is understood that the field house will be converted into a merchandizing "mart" early this year.

The leased property is owned by the Lillie Coho estate.

Pool, Park Not Affected

The swimming pool, park and miniature golf course in the park are not involved. They are owned by other persons.

Daniel S. Templeton Sr., holder of the lease, said today that his present contract expires early next month and that he has been notified that it will not be renewed.

Templeton said he plans to run three more wrestling shows and then the lights will go out for the last night on roller skating and sports events in the only building of its type in the Lancaster area.

Backed by Mass. Group

The Maple Grove Bargain Center, Inc., is a new corporation. It is reported to be backed by Massachusetts financial interests who have maintained a close lipped policy on their plans for the future.

James P. Coho, attorney and representative of the Coho family interests, said today he is without details on future plans for the property. He confirmed, however, that the lease to Templeton has not been renewed.

It was learned that men back of the leasing of the property now operate a number of "Bargain Marts" in New England and other parts of the country.

Plan Huge Sales Floor

The plan, as it was understood in Lancaster today, is to convert the field house into a huge sales floor for the sale of many types of merchandise—a sales plan well known throughout parts of New England but fairly new in the Lancaster area.

One man described the "marts" as "the old-fashioned country store idea, expanded and brought up to date."

Templeton said he has no immediate plans for the future of a sports center but hopes to have an announcement within a week.

Maple Grove Field House was a headache to sports promoters. See George Kirchner's column on page 35.

'Playhouse 90'

ANNAPOLIS, Md. (AP) — Statehouse wags have coined a name for the 90-day session of the Maryland General Assembly which convened yesterday.

They're calling it "Playhouse 90."

BOY, 5, MAULED BY PACK OF SNARLING DOGS

VANCOUVER, B. C. (AP)—A 5-year-old Vancouver boy, frightened by a pack of snarling dogs, was hauled down and mauled by three of the animals yesterday when he panicked and ran.

Wayne Spankie suffered a severely bitten leg and lacerations on the face and arms. Hospital attendants said he would recover.

Three of the larger dogs leaped after him and pulled him to the ground.

One of the dogs fastened its teeth into one of Wayne's legs and pulled him screaming into a clump of bushes. A park caretaker beat off the dogs.

Koerkle to Be City Fire Chief

Will Succeed Chief Miller in September

Edward H. Koerkle, 18 S. Franklin St., will be named chief of the Lancaster Fire Department in September.

The announcement was made today by Commissiner J. Arthur Norris, director of public safety, who heads the city's fire fighting forces.

Koerkle, now assistant chief, will succeed Chief Harry E. Miller who plans to resign about Sept. 1 when he completes 50 years of service with the Lancaster Fire Department. Koerkle has been on the fire department about 35 years.

Selection of Koerkle as chief of the department will be one of the moves to be made this year in reorganizing the Fire Department.

Other Changes Planned

Other changes will include the retirement of Frank Deen, assistant chief, early in February when he becomes 80 years old. Deen is one of the oldest active fire fighters in the state and one of the last of the so-called old school firemen.

William Landis, made an assistant chief by City Council last week, is scheduled to remain in that capacity. Later in the year one of the present captains will be elevated to the rank of assist-

—See KOERKLE—Page 10

Reassessment Issue at Lititz

Saturday Meeting to Discuss New Figures

Lititz officials will meet with the county commissioners Saturday morning in an effort to gain backing for a speedy property reassessment in the borough.

Four councilmen — President Menno B. Rohrer, Dr. Byron Horne, Russell Templeton and Harry Ruley — Borough Manager David Bauer and Burgess Benjamin Forrest are to confer with the three commissioners in the commissioner's courthouse office at 9:30 a. m.

Bauer said today the borough, which wants to carry out its own reassessment to provide needed revenue in the next few years, will ask assurance from the commissioners that figures from the new reassessment would be used by the county in levying county taxes.

Wage Tax Considered

Earlier, Lititz council had announced it was considering levying a wage tax to provide needed additional revenue for this year but two days later Rohrer said the idea probably would be dropped.

Bauer also said Lititz is seeking between $15,000 and $20,000 in county funds to conduct the reassessment. Council said that is the approximate sum the county

—See REASSESSMENT—Page 10

Today's New Era

Phone Lancaster EX 7-5251

40,000 Road Deaths in 1956 Set U. S. Record

Traffic accidents killed more Americans in 1956 than ever before—and law officials throughout the nation are turning to get-tough policies to cut down the highway slaughter.

There was at least a 5 per cent rise over 1955. Safety experts estimate the total at more than 40,000.

The 1955 figure was 38,426. The previous high — 39,969 — was recorded in 1941.

Laws Rigidly Enforced

In states which had fewer traffic fatalities in 1956 than in 1955, credit generally is given to rigid enforcement of safety measures. In states where traffic deaths increased, similar crackdowns generally are planned.

A state-by-state survey by The Associated Press shows that these measures — —already in effect in some states and planned in others —include:

1. Increasing the number of police patrols on highways. This has top priority in most states.

2. New laws — or harsher enforcement of existing laws — calling for suspension of licenses and — or fines and imprisonment for motorists convicted of drunk driving, "chronic" negligence and speeding.

3. Tighter examinations for vehicle licenses and mandatory auto inspection programs.

4. Use of National Guard troops of sheriff's deputies to reinforce regular highway police during peak travel periods, such as holiday weekends.

5. Periodic roadblocks — with massed troopers stopping all cars and checking on licenses, intoxication and vehicle condition.

6. Expansion of the use of radar devices in catching speeders.

7. Establishing state speed limits where they are not already in force.

The survey came on the heels of the Christmas and New Year weekends when 1,115 persons were killed in the combined holiday periods—a new high.

Tennessee and Michigan are examples of states which took strong measures to reduce highway fatalities in 1956—are succeeded.

Tennessee effected a 16 per cent decrease from the preceding year—from 906 to 758—with strict enforcement policies. These included speedblocks, a concentration of radar-bearing squad cars in one area to check speeders, and roadblocks.

The Tennessee system of roadblocks was graphically illustrated over the New Year's weekend, when massed groups of troopers stopped 27,000 cars and made 708 arrests for intoxication, vehicle and license violations, and other traffic violations.

Gov. C. Mennen Williams, noting Michigan's decrease from 2,004 traffic deaths in 1955 to 1,725 in 1956, declared:

"The main weapons we have used are increased state police patrols; better control of driver licensing and suspension of licenses from dangerous drivers; use of National Guard troops to reinforce state police and sheriffs' road patrols, and widespread publicity."

ABANDON 2 OTHERS

'Copters Pluck 8 From Alpine Cliff

CHAMONIX, France (AP) — Daring helicopter pilots today snatched eight marooned Alpinists from the snowswept slopes of Mt. Blanc but gave up hope for two more frostbitten climbers marooned on Europe's highest peak for 12 days.

The rescue pilots had hoped to hover above the pair—Frenchman Jean Vincendon, 23, and Belgian Francois Henry, 24—and lower men to put them in baskets hanging from the aircraft, but this proved impossible.

May Be Dead

Both may already have died.

The rescue operation got under way at dawn with the first favorable helicopter flying weather in two weeks. The harried pilots got the eight men down within three hours.

The dangerous rescue operation was carried out 12,000 feet up the slopes of the 15,781-foot peak.

The two had set out two days before Christmas to scale Mt. Blanc despite adverse weather forecasts.

Two helicopters succeeded in making shuttle landings at the 12,000-foot level, where the eight rescue team was huddled in a climbers' shelter. But there was no landing spot near Vincendon and Henry, several hundred yards away.

Earlier Copter Crashed

The eight men had been trapped on the 15,781-foot mountain in earlier rescue attempts, four when their helicopter crashed near the two climbers. The other four had parachuted to the site.

Unable to move the helpless pair far because the hazardous weather conditions, the would-be rescuers bundled them into sleepnig bags in the wreckage and then made the perilous climb to the shelter.

All the rescued men were hospitalized, suffering from various degrees of frostbite. Some were in serious condition.

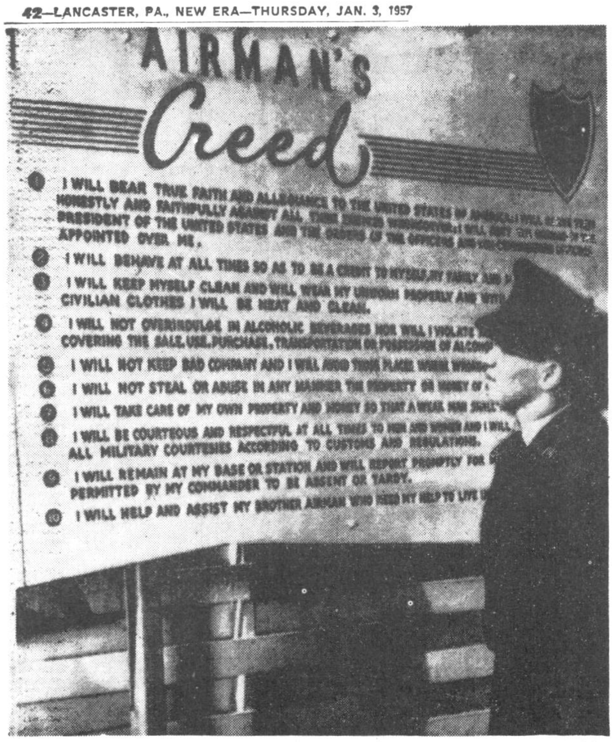

AP Wirephoto

Richard Hartman reads an Air Force poster at Lackland AFB, San Antonio, Tex.

Fire Kills 6 in Tarpaper Home Near Reading

Woman, 5 Children Die at Temple, 3 Escape; Stove Blamed

READING (AP)—A woman and five children burned to death today as flames roared through a one-story tarpaper covered dwelling at Temple, five miles north of Reading.

The victims were identified as:

Mrs. Esther Rothermel, 48, wife of Paul Rothermel in whose home the fire occurred:

Donna Rothermel, 4, and her brother, Eddie, 2, children of Mr. and Mrs. Marvin Rothermel of near Fleetwood, Pa. The children's father is a brother of Paul Rothermel.

Jimmy Brobst, 1, and his sister, Peggy, 3, children of Mr. and Mrs. James Brobst of Kutztown. Mrs. Brobst is a daughter of the older Rothermels.

Carol Ann Fromm, 4, daughter of Mr. and Mrs. Earl Fromm of Reading. Mrs. Fromm is a sister of Paul Rothermel.

All Children In Bed

Firemen said apparently the blaze was caused by a leaking oil stove in the living room of the house. All the children were in bed at the time but it was not learned whether Mrs. Esther Rothermel had arisen before the flames swept through the house.

Firemen said Paul Rothermel was believed away at the time. In all, the members of five related families had spend the night in the little home in the Berks County community of several thousand.

3 Manage To Flee

Three occupants of the house managed to escape. They were identified as Mrs. Gertrude Paine and her two children, Lois Mary, 3, and Thomas Jerome Paine, 1. Their relationship to the others was not learned.

Firemen and ambulances from surrounding towns rushed to the scene after the first alarm was sounded by a neighbor.

New Era Photo

Herr's Pond Skaters Enjoy First Real Cold Snap

Enjoying the crisp outdoors during the first real cold snap of the season yesterday afternoon by skating on Herr's Pond, Lincoln Highway West, are, from the left, Martha Zimmerman, Kurt Steinman, Judy Farmer, Paul Heine Jr., Robert Batchelder and Henry Smith.

DUE IN 2 WEEKS

Air Force to Discharge Runaway Columbian, 15

A fifteen-year-old Columbia boy who ran away from home early in December to join the Air Force is expected home in two weeks.

The boy is Richard Hartman, son of Mr. and Mrs. William Hartman, 841 Blunston St., Columbia.

Sends Civilian Clothes Home

Contacted this morning at Tidy Products Co., Columbia, where she works, Mrs. Hartman said she has learned the Air Force plans to discharge Richard and fly him home. She said Richard sent his civilian clothes home yesterday.

Mrs. Hartman said Richard will resume classes at Lancaster High School when he returns.

Richard, who is too young to meet Air Force age requirements, enlisted in the service under the name of his twenty-two-year-old brother, Charles. He was stationed at Lackland Air Force Base, near San Antonio, Tex.

Prior to his enlistment, Richard hitchhiked through Pittsburgh, Cleveland and West Virginia. After getting a taste of military life, he wrote home to ask for help in getting out of the service. His mother wrote Richard's commanding officer to ask for his discharge.

Mrs. Hartman said Richard left home because of "an impulse to go somewhere". She said he sent her a letter Friday saying that the Air Force is fine, but home is better.

"I think it's a good lesson for him," Mrs. Hartman concluded.

BILL KIRK

Kirk Leaves for Army Service

Former Roses' Hurler One of 7 Draftees

Bill Kirk, former pitcher for the Red Roses who got his start in the New Era Midget Tournament, left for two year's military service this morning.

Twenty-one-year-old Kirk, son of Mr. and Mrs. William A. Kirk, 334 N. Mary St., is one of seven men sent for induction by City Draft Board 85.

Leaving today are: Robert H. Ritter, twenty-two, 342 E. Orange St.; Harry W. Maser, twenty-two, 314 Locust St.; Jere J. Brooks, twenty-two, Willow Street R1; Christian H. Banzhof, twenty-two, 609 St. Joseph St.; Gerald L. Rote, twenty-two, Lititz; Dominic J. Roda, twenty-one, 234 W. James St.; and Kirk.

Hopes to Play at Knox

Kirk will be sent to Ft. Knox, Ky. He said Ft. Knox has a large athletic program, and he hopes to play baseball while he is stationed there. Kirk said he has a contract to report to the Montgomery, Ala., Kansas City Athletics' double A farm team after he is discharged from the Army.

Kirk is well known to local sports fans. He won the 1949 Lancaster Soap Box Derby, but lost in the first heat in the finals at Akron, O. Later, he was a star pitcher for McCaskey High School and for IBEW in the City Legion League.

Hurled Here in 1955

Kirk started in pro baseball in 1954, and pitched for the Red Roses during the stretch pennant drive in 1955. Last year, he compiled a 15-3 record with Columbia, in the Sally League, and El Paso, in the Southwestern League.

The draft board said one man failed to report for induction this morning after receiving several notices. He is Raymond Ellsworth Duncan, whose last known address is 332 S. Mill St.

Vandals Break School Panes

Club House Entered At Nathan Schaeffer

Vandalism at the Nathan Schaeffer school and Stumpf Field last night were reported to Manheim Twp. police.

Police were notified today that vandals broke into the school. Nine windows were broken, and a flagpole rope was cut. There was no damage inside the building, police said. A custodian discovered the broken windows at 6:30 a.m.

Club House Entered

Henry Garner, 1394 Orchard Lane, caretaker at Stumpf Field, reported today that youngsters have been breaking into the club house of the ball park.

Garner told police he caught one youngster in the club house yesterday. He turned the youth's name over to police. The intruders broke off locks of doors and gates of the park and club house, and broke light bulbs and plaster board inside.

CountianCharged As Drunk Driver

Harry Rogers, thirty-four, New Providence R1, was charged with drunken driving by city police following an accident early today on Church St., between Duke and Rockland Sts.

Police said Rogers' car, headed northeast on Church St., hit a parked car owned by Andrew Stoe, 320 Church St., causing slight damage.

Rogers was given a drunkometer test, which showed positive. He posted bail for a hearing before Alderman Hull.

Ship Sinks, 24 Saved

TORSHAVN, Faroe Islands (AP)—The 655-ton Icelandic trawler Godanes hit the rocks at Skaalfjord, Faroe Islands, today and sank after breaking in two. Twenty-four crewmen were rescued but the ship's master was missing.

17 Affected by Route Change

Properties Between Columbia, Marietta

Properties of 17 owners will be affected by the relocation of Route 441 between Columbia and Marietta, according to State Highways Department maps shown today.

Bids for the job are to be opened tomorrow at Harrisburg. Properties most considerably affected are those on Chickies Hill, where the relocation will be made. Some near Marietta, where the present route will be widened and improved, are affected on frontage.

Property owners involved will include, from Columbia toward the Marietta borough limits:

Elizabeth Greer, Daniel Good, Mrs. Raymond Eisenberger, Fred Houck, Mrs. John Simons, Wilson Simons, John H. Baker, Walter Drager, Dr. S. S. Simons, Charles Rich, Russell Armold, William Simons, William Young, Raymond Steel, Frank Ziegler, Robert Vanderslice and James Schlegelmilch.

Buildings to be removed are a frame shed on the property of Elizabeth Greer and a frame barn on the land of James Schlegelmilch.

Officials Hold Meeting

Highways officials held a meeting on the site this morning with representatives of utilities to outline the route and to discuss work the utilities will face with the relocation.

Taking part in the meeting were:

Philip J. Price, county superintendent for the State Highways Department; John Detz, assistant superintendent; Paul Shalkop, Harrisburg, who will be chief Highways inspector on the job; J. T. Shaub, Robert Keller and J. G. Sauter, of the Highways Department.

L. P. Bonfardin and W. H. Lindsay, Pennsylvania Railroad; George Morris and Harry Longenecker, UGI; Leon F. Hoffman, PP&L; Paul Bransby, Bell Telephone Co.; Thomas H. McCarty, Bell Telephone Co., and Lewis Garbacik, Marietta Gravity Water Co.

Businessmen Hear Talk On Near East at 'Y'

Dr. Frank C. Torrey discussed the troubles in the Near East and their effects on the world, at the luncheon meeting sponsored by the Christian Businessmen's Association today at the YMCA.

Benjamin R. Groff presided. Inductees honored were John Hendrix, Mount Joy; Paul Shirk, New Holland; Kenneth Brock, Marietta; Bruce Ranck, Leacock, and Frank Molz, Bausman.

BABY CUT IN FALL

Ruth Ann White, nine months, 20 Coral St., was treated at Columbia Hospital last night for a laceration of the right arm after she fell on a bottle. Ten sutures were required to close the wound.

Polio Shots Are Started At the Catholic Schools

More than 1,000 pupils in city parochial schools and several county public schools received shots of Salk anti-polio vaccine today as the mass inoculation program resumed after the holidays.

At Catholic High School, 600 shots were administered in the beginning of a week-long program of inoculations for parochial pupils. Parochial school officials estimated that over 2,000 children will have received the shots when the first round is completed at the high school and five elementary schools next Thursday.

Public School Schedule

Dr. O. H. Aurand, superintendent of city schools, announced the schedule of inoculations for city pupils today. The city program will begin on Jan. 7 and continue daily through Jan. 11 with over 6,000 pupils taking part in the program.

Because of the necessity for a lapse of seven months between the second and third shots, city pupils will not receive their third shot at the end of the current school year. Mrs. Gertrude Gress, director of school nurses, said that city pupils will probably receive their third shot during the first week of October in the 1957-58 school year.

The city program:

Jan. 7, Wickersham, Fulton, and Lafayette Schools. The second round of shots for these schools has been scheduled for Feb. 11.

Jan. 8, Higbee, Mifflin, Haupt, Ross, and Henry Schools. Second round scheduled for Feb. 12.

Jan. 9, Stevens, Eichholtz, Reigart, and Buehrle Schools. Second round scheduled Feb. 13.

Jan. 10, Hand Jr. High, Reynolds Junior High. Second round scheduled Feb. 14.

Jan. 11, McCaskey High School, and Wharton School. Second round scheduled Feb. 15.

Egypt Invasion Chief Must Retire

LONDON (AP) — The Daily Express said today Gen. Sir Charles Keightley, commander in chief of the British-French invasion forces in Egypt, is being "compulsorily retired" by the British government.

Keightley was not available for comment. A War Office spokesman declined to comment on the Express story.

The newspaper quoted Keightley, 55-year-old senior British army general, as saying: "I have a job to do at the War Office for a month and then they tell me I'm being retired."

Reception for New Members at Redeemer

The annual congregational meeting and reception for new members at Redeemer Lutheran Church, Sixth and Pearl Sts., will be held Jan. 16 in the church, with Mrs. Earl Bender as chairman.

Plans were announced last night at a meeting of the Ladies Aid Society of the church. The society made a donation of $350 to the church for debt reduction. The group also gave $20 for the cost of lighting the cross on the church exterior.

The society's next meeting will be held Feb. 6 in the church.

ANN GERACIMOS

Local Girl Wins Scholarship

Tops 6 Others in Rotary Competition

Ann Geracimos, daughter of Mrs. Katherine Geracimos, 14 Glen Moore Circle, has been awarded a Rotary Foundation Fellowship to study abroad for a year.

Miss Geracimos is the first candidate sponsored by the Rotary Club of Lancaster to win the scholarship. She won over six other applicants in the 268th Rotary District competition.

The fellowship provides funds for a year abroad at a school of the winner's choice. The funds include tuition, living and traveling expenses.

England or Scotland

A senior majoring in history at Wellesley College, Miss Geracimos intends to continue her history in either England or Scotland. She will leave at the end of the summer.

Miss Geracimos spent the summer of 1955 in Europe as a participant in the Experiment in International Living.

She is a member of the Wellesley yearbook staff, student representative for the alumnae magazine and participates in crew and swimming. A graduate of Manheim Twp. High School, she was valedictorian of her class.

Miss Geracimos is a former reporter for the Lancaster New Era.

Cafe Gambling Case Studied

City Owner Promises To End 'Book-Making'

HARRISBURG (AP)—Paul J. Severino, a Lancaster tavern owner, today promised the State Liquor Control Board that he would never again allow "book-making" in his establishment.

Severino made the statement at a hearing on charges of permitting gambling in the P and J Cafe, which he operates at 339 E. King St., Lancaster.

City Detective Paul R. Cogley told the commission that Severino was found guilty last September of bookmaking and permitting gambling in his establishment. The detective said he was given a year's probation, $300 fine and ordered to pay $124 costs.

Character Witnesses

"At least six very reputable people appeared at the trial as character witnesses for Severino," the detective said.

He explained that a Christopher Talarico had been arrested on bookmaking and common gambling charges along with Severino on July 21, 1954.

Talarico was found guilty and has appealed for a new trial. The detective said Talarico was taking horse bets at the P and J cafe. He said Severino, at the trial, admitted knowledge of Talarico's operations in his cafe.

The detective also said Severino admitted making baseball bets for his brother over a public telephone in the cafe.

The board took the case under study. A decision may not be handed down for several months.

Germany Drafts New Note to Reds

BONN, Germany (AP)—West Germany is drafting a new note to the Soviet Union with the aim of promoting direct negotiations on the German problem.

Foreign Office officials said a number of proposals are being considered by Chancellor Konrad Adenauer and his advisers. These include a possible demilitarized zone running through the heart of Europe, and a European security system based on a commitment by all members to refrain from the use of force.

Adenauer faces a general election in September in which his foreign policies will be a major issue.

Attempt to Break Into Young Funeral Home

An attempt to break into the Young Funeral Home, 317 E. Orange St. was made last night, according to city detectives.

Detective S. Kenneth Cliff said an attempt was made to pry open two rear doors and a rear window. The glass in the window was broken and the noise apparently scared off the intruders.

Mrs. George N. Young, who lives at the Orange St. address, said she heard glass breaking about 1 a.m., but saw no one. Robert Bomberger, an employe at the funeral home, discovered the attempted entry at 9:30 a.m.

Maisano Named Schick Field Sales Manager

John Maisano of 924 Pleasure Rd., Grandview Heights, has been named field sales manager by Schick Inc.

Detroit sales supervisor for the past two years, Maisano started with Schick in 1953 as a retail specialist in Providence, R. I. Later he was transferred to Dallas, Tex., as sales representative, and then went to Detroit.

A graduate of Providence College in Providence, Maisano is married and the father of a son.

Robert W. Thatcher Re-enlists in Air Force

Robert Walter Thatcher, 755 Stevens Ave., has re-enlisted in the U. S. Air Force. His name was erroneously reported as Charles Walter Thatcher yesterday.

HOME BUILDING HERE DOWN 18 P. C. IN 1956

Home building showed an 18 per cent drop in Lancaster County in 1956 as compared to 1955, according to figures assembled by Pennsylvania Power and Light Co.

The totals showed new homes to which electricity was supplied for the first time.

In 1955, the total in this county was 1,360. In 1956, it was 1,111, marking a decrease of 249 from the preceding year.

4 Charged for Ruining Lawns

Youths Face 12 Counts Of Malicious Mischief

Four youths from the eastern part of the county were charged with 12 counts of malicious mischief and one count of larceny each today, as the result of an escapade on the early morning of Dec. 26.

Frank Horner, West Lampeter Twp. police chief, filed the charges, alleging the youths damaged lawns along Route 222 and the Mylin's Corner-Elliot's Corner Rd., and stole a basket of apples from the Norman Huber fruit stand, Willow Street Pike.

One of the youths is David A. Benner, twenty, Ronks R1. The others are juveniles, ages fourteen, sixteen, and seventeen, Horner said.

Horner said the quartet deliberately ran the auto across a dozen lawns, casing more than $1,000 damage. They will receive hearings before Justice of the Peace Walter Dunlap. Horner said they are also being questioned in connection with other incidents of malicious mischief.

SHARF TO HEAD TECHNICAL UNIT OF COUNTY CD

Dr. John M. Sharf, 234 N. Charlotte St., has been appointed director of the Technical Division of the Lancaster County Civil Defense Council.

He succeeds Ralph W. Engstrom, Blossom Hill, who has resigned, after serving in the post for two years.

Dr. Sharf

The administrative change was announced today by David E. Wagenseller Jr., county CD director.

Dr. Sharf is a chemical engineer with the glass and closure products section of the Armstrong Cork Co. research and development center. He is a former deputy director in the technical division.

In 1955, Dr. Sharf attended atomic bomb tests at the Nevada Proving Grounds.

"I'M TRAPPED!"

Mother Calls in Fire, But Dies Trying to Save Baby

WALPOLE, Mass. (AP) — "My God, the house is on fire! I'm trapped!"

A few moments after shouting that frantic alarm into the telephone, Mrs. Doris Danehey, 30, and her only child, James, 4 months, perished last night in their bungalow.

Fire Chief Aaron Hill said Mrs. Danehey apparently passed up her only chance to escape by her attempt to save the baby.

Body Found Near Crib

The woman's body was found a few feet from the baby's crib. Michael Danehey, 32, a railroad trainman, was not at home when the fire broke out in his Walpole residence. He collapsed when he arrived home and was taken to a doctor's office.

'Screamed For Help'

Mrs. Isobel Schmidt of North Attleboro, a teelphone operator in the Walpole exchange, picked up Mrs. Danehey's message and relayed it to Phyllis Metzger, telphone supervisor, who said: "It was awful. I heard her cry and moan until she died. She screamed for help several times.

Fire officials said the blaze might have been caused by an exploding kitchen heater.

3 IN HOUSE SWORN IN

Clark Takes Oath As New Senator

WASHINGTON (AP)—Sen. Joseph S. Clark (D-Pa) and three new House members from Pennsylvania took the oath of office and today set up their new headquarters in the capital city.

Clark, former mayor of Philadelphia who defeated Sen. James H. Duff, has takne an apartment temporarily in northwest Washington. He and his wife expect to move into a house in the historic Georgetown section by Feb. 1. There the Clarks will have as neighbors former Secretary of State Dean Acheson, Sen. Symington (D-Mo) and other political and career government personalities.

Quigley To Be Aide

Clark's chief aide in Washington will be former Rep. James A. Quigley, Democrat from Camp Hill, Pa., who was defeated for re-election. Michael J. Byrne, who aided Clark as deputy mayor of Philadelphia, will head the Senator's Pennsylvania office in the federal building, Philadelphia.

New keystone state house members taking office today were Reps. S. Walter Stauffer (R), William S. Curtin (R) and Mrs. Kathryn Granahan (D).

Stauffer served in the 83rd Congress and was replaced in the last session by Quigley. This time he turned the tables on Quigley and once again represents the district in which President Eisenhower maintains his voting residence.

Curtin replaces Rep. Karl C. King, who was the only Pennsylvania Congressman to retire after the 84th session. Both are residents of Morrisville.

Mrs. Granahan, succeeding her late husband, is the lone woman in the Pennsylvania congressional delegation. She is from Philadelphia.

Joins Plan To Curb Debate

Clark took part yesterday in a conference with a Senate bloc that seeks to curb unlimited debate—the maneuver by which civil rights legislation has been stymied for years.

And Pennsylvania's new junior Senator also announced he would join in co-sponsoring with Sen. Douglas (D-Ill) legislation to provide federal aid for depressed industrial areas.

Clark said the bill is being prepared for early action. The plan provides for training unemployed men for new jobs and industries.

As an example, said Clark "coal miners out of work would be given training on new jobs and receive unemployment compensation at the same time."

Assigments Indicated

Clark found time yesterday to confer with senate Democratic leader Lyndon Johnson (Tex.) on committee assignments. Indications are Clark will be assigned to either banking and currency or labor and public welfare.

Clark has temporary quarters which he has set up in a section of the office of Sen. Mansfield (D-Mont). The former Philadelphia mayor will eventually occupy the quarters vacated by former Sen. Lehman (D-NY) when renovations to that office are completed.

Even as Clark prepared himself for his new duties in the Senate Office Building, the man he defeated, former Senator James Duff was clearing out the office he occupied here for six years.

Duff, expected to vacation in Florida for a time, plans upon his return to practice law in both Pittsburgh and Washington.

Mrs. Kathryn Granahan, Democrat of Philadelphia, only woman member of the Pennsylvania delegation.

John Bachman Head of Board

H. S. Stark President Of Chocolate Co.

John A. Bachman, Mount Joy, has been elected chairman of the board of directors of the Bachman Chocolate Manufacturing Co., Mount Joy, it was announced today.

Bachman served as company President since its founding in 1911. He is one of the pioneers of the Pennsylvania Manufacturing Confectioners Association.

Harry S. Stark, Mount Joy, was named president. Stark formerly served as vice president.

Other officers elected include: Richard M. Stark, Mount Joy, executive vice president and reelected secretary; Wilson C. Rich, Lancaster, vice president in charge of sales; Harry N. Nissly, Mount Joy, treasurer; Henry S. Kolp, Lancaster, treasurer, and Carl J. Houseal, Mount Joy, assistant secretary.

Chou Back in Peiping

HONG KONG (AP) — Communist Chinese Premier Chou En-lai returned to Peiping today after a tour of five South Asian countries, Radio Peiping reported.

DROODLES

By Roger Price

"TWO SKIERS DISCUSSING LATEST JUMP"

WEATHER
(U. S. Weather Bureau)
Cloudy With Rain And Moderate Temperatures Today And Tomorrow. High 38 To 42.
(Details On Page 38)

Intelligencer Journal.

TELEPHONE EXpress 7-5251

The Leading Newspaper in the Garden Spot of America. Home Owned for Home Folks Since 1794

163rd Year.—No. 172. Metropolitan Lancaster Population 1954 (Est.) Penna. Dept. of Commerce 248,296 LANCASTER, PA., FRIDAY MORNING, JANUARY 4, 1957. CITY EDITION 38 PAGES. 30c PER WEEK—5c Per Copy

COMMUNITY CENTER PLAN REVEALED

Outlay Of $1,500,000 Suggested By Commission

Site Donor Offers Access Road, More Land, Money To Move Power Line; 60-Day Deadline To Work Out Financing

A proposal to build a million and one-half dollar community center was submitted to city and county governing bodies yesterday by four of the five members of the Lancaster County Community Center Commission.

The proposal was contained in a six-part report on commission activities since it was formed last May.

The report contained no financial program, but it calls for solving this aspect of the problem within 60 days. It called on the city and county officials to "approve or respond otherwise" on the report within this period.

It is believed that the commission members will abandon the project if favorable action is not taken.

The report was signed by four members of the commission: Robert Chestnut, chairman; Robert Shoemaker, secretary; G. Theodore Storb and Elmer L. Esbenshade.

BRICKER NOT PRESENT

Owen P. Bricker, in recent weeks a vocal opponent of the site donated by Esbenshade, did not sign the report. He said last night that he was notified of a meeting called for yesterday afternoon on Wednesday night and was not able to attend because of prior engagements. He said he had received no copy of the report which was delivered to the city council and county commissioners yesterday afternoon.

TEXTS ON PAGE 15

The complete text of the letter and report filed by the Commission with city and county officials yesterday will be found starting on Page 15 of today's *Intelligencer Journal*.

Earlier Bricker said he would file a minority report if the major majority report does not "tell all the facts."

The six parts of the majority report were:

1. A letter to the officials outlining the proposed building.
2. A site report which, while not mentioning the Real Estate Board of Lancaster, Inc., by name, counters the realtors' objections of last June.
3. A synopsis of minutes of the commission's meetings from May through June.
4. A floor plan of the proposed 66,560 square-foot building.
5. A plot plan of the tract, enlarged by an additional five-acre tract, making a total of 23 acres, which Esbenshade will give if the program is approved.
6. A traffic flow map showing the access routes to the tract from all portions of the county.

The building floor plan—subject to revisions which an architect might feel necessary—shows a 328 by 200-foot building with an inclined floor area with a stage, a 120-by 200-foot flat floor area and a cluster of meeting rooms, offices and rest rooms and caterer's room.

THEATER FOR 1,600

The inclined floor area would be a theater with a capacity of 1,600 persons for the presentation of legitimate plays, professional or amateur; musical and similar programs.

The flat floor area—which could contain 3,500 folding seats—would be converted to either an exhibition (agricultural, automotive, flower, art, etc.) hall, indoor athletic arena or banquet area with about 1,500 capacity. A folding curtain wall would reduce the banquet area to half size if a relatively smaller group were holding a dinner.

While there would be no kitchen as such, there would be fa-

Turn To Page 22 For More Of CENTER

Record Shows No Disaccord On 'Gag Rule'

Owen P. Bricker's feud with his fellow members of the Lancaster County Community Center Commission took on a new dimension yesterday with the release of a synopsis of the commission's 19 meetings between May 12 and Dec. 14.

One of six parts of a report submitted by the four other commission members to the County Commissioners and the City Council, the synopsis is based on the minutes of the commission's meetings.

It showed that all members agreed that the meetings should be closed until the commission had reached some basic decision on the facilities for the proposed center.

Bricker has charged this agreement served as a "gag" rule. There is nothing in the synopsis to indicate that he objected to it prior to Dec. 7 when he challenged Mayor Kendig C. Bare to a debate on the suitability of the site at the Rt. 230-Bypass and Roseville Road.

The synopsis also traced the development of the commission's planning from the time it was formed until the project crystallized into the $1,500,000 program outlined in the majority's general report.

URGED ANOTHER LOCATION

It indicated that as early as June 15 Bricker recommended the Commission give consideration to another location. While not specified in the report, it is believed that this was the Maple Grove field house.

The commission later received a letter offering to sell an alternative site of nine acres — the same amount of land as at Maple Grove — on a half interest in an alternative site of nine acres — the same amount of land as at Maple Grove — with the other half to be donated by the owner.

While the substance of the let-

Turn To Page 22 For More Of MINUTES

City And County Officials Will Study Reports

Two of Lancaster County's three commissioners said yesterday they had no comment on the report of the Çivic Center Commission.

The no comment came from Commissioners Charles H. Pearce and Herbert R. Wagaman. Former State Sen. G. Graybill Diehm, the third member, was out of town.

A copy of the report and other notes of the city-county named commission members was received yesterday afternoon at the courthouse. Pearce and Wagaman said they had "glanced" at the "voluminous" papers presented and would study them in detail later.

Mayor Kendig C. Bare also had no comment. He indicated that the report will be circulated to all members of City Council for their perusal.

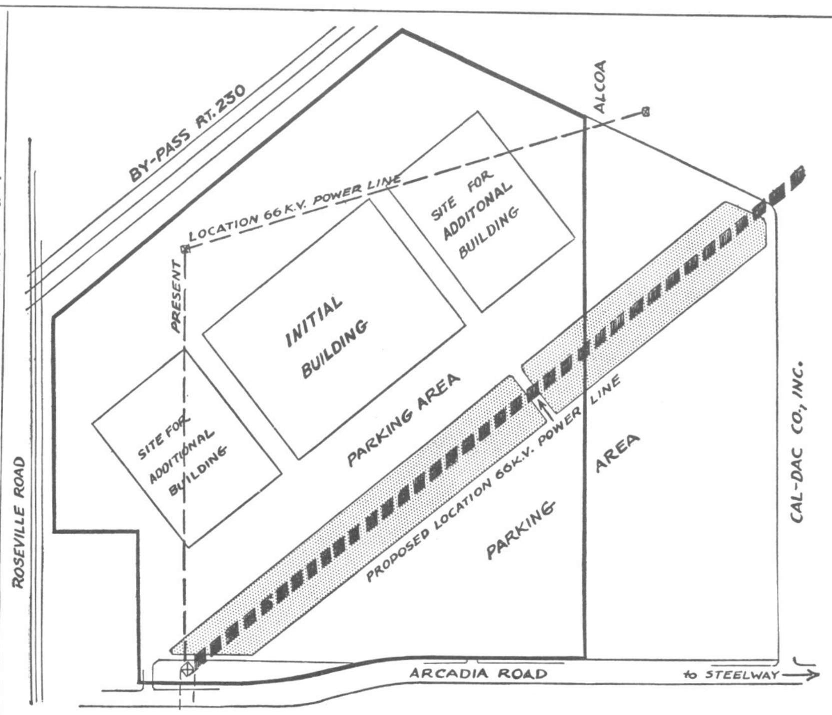

Location of Proposed Civic Center building is shown in this adaptation of plot plan submitted to the city and county yesterday by the Lancaster County Community Center Commission. The program calls for moving of present power line (dash lines) to new location (heavy dotted line) with grass plot separating parking areas. Original 18 acre tract is bordered by heavy black line. An additional five acres, offered by Elmer L. Esbenshade between original tract and Cal-Dac Co., Inc., land is at right. Diagram also shows possible locations for future buildings not included in report.

NEW CONGRESS OPENS, FACES BIG PROBLEMS

Foreboding Foreign Policy, Touchy Civil Rights Among Top Questions

WASHINGTON, Jan. 3 (AP) — A new Congress that faces foreboding foreign policy problems and a touchy civil rights issue opened for business today. Democrats took control after a dramatic moment of Senate uncertainty.

And behind a facade of the customary good will and harmony of opening day, touches of tension were apparent over the grave question of granting President Eisenhower's request for power to send American troops into action against any Communist aggression in the Mideast.

Out of the first round of activity of the 85th Congress came a decision that on Saturday the President will come to Capitol Hill in person to deliver a special message and urge his Middle Eastern policy on a joint session of Senate and House.

CLIMACTIC VOTE

First, the Senate is going to put in a solid seven hours tomorrow leading up to a climactic vote at 6 p.m. EST.

The result will determine how far a band of Northern and Western senators of both parties will get in rewriting the rules and curbing the filibuster—a device to convert lung power into legislative power which Southerners have used with deadly effect against civil rights legislation.

Even members of the coalition conceded it was a pretty futile fight. In the lineup against them were the rival party leaders of the Senate, Democrat Lyndon Johnson of Texas and Republican William Knowland of California.

Johnson and Knowland were tapped to keep their leadership posts at routine party caucuses during the morning.

HARMONY AND GAYETY

Then, promptly at noon, gavels cracked down in Senate and House and rapped the new Congress into session. It was all harmony and gayety as members took their oaths of office before applauding, packed galleries, or went out of their way to shake hands with political enemies as well as friends.

But inevitably and quickly, at

Turn To Page 22 For More Of CONGRESS

Ike To Make Plea For Mideast Authority To Congress Saturday

WASHINGTON, Jan. 3 —President Eisenhower will appear before Congress in person at 12:30 p. m. EST Saturday to present his plea for special authority to prevent Communist aggression in the Middle East.

What he wants—and what he appears likely to get—is approval of a resolution authorizing him to use American military forces if he should deem it necessary.

The administration has been pushing for quick action on the request for standby authority. The sense of urgency was underlined by the White House request for a joint session at which the President could present his arguments. Both Senate and House leaders were agreeable.

HIGHLY DANGEROUS

Eisenhower and Secretary of State Dulles already have talked with groups of senators and representatives. Dulles, for example, has described the situation in the Middle East as highly dangerous and said that Russia "may well move" to expand its influence there.

Russia has accused the United States of wanting to assume power over the area in the wake of the Israeli-Arab troubles and the British-French invasion of Egypt following Egypt's seizure of the Suez Canal.

The administration's Middle East resolution, besides asking standby authority for the President, calls for spending 400 million dollars in economic aid for the Middle East countries during the two years beginning next July 1.

LITTLE OPPOSITION

There has not been much outcry against either part of the proposal. However, it remained to be seen whether it would be adopted by anything like the margins given the "fight if we must" resolution Congress adopted in 1955 in the Red China-Formosa situation.

The Formosa resolution authorized the President to use U.S. armed forces and any measures he might find necessary to safeguard the Chinese Nationalist island from Communist attack. So far, Formosa has not been invaded.

The Senate approved the Formose resolution 85-3 and the House endorsed it 409-3.

Rep. Burdick (R-ND) challenged the constitutionality of the Middle East resolution in a statement today. He said that under it, Eisenhower could start a war without coming to Congress, whereas the Constitution reserves to Congress the authority to declare war.

Planning Unit Seeks To Save Historic Bldgs.

A proposal that a study be made of possible City Council legislation designed to preserve historic buildings was voiced at yesterday's meeting of the City Planning Commission.

James Todd Baldwin, a member of the commission suggested that the planning commission write to the State Bureau of Community Development to see if the city could pass ordinances giving the planning commission power to act.

He also suggested that the commission meet with the County Historical Society and the local unit of the American Institute of Architects on the problem.

Baldwin said the commission should determine if it is possible to place some regulation on the demolition or alteration of buildings older than a date which might be determined as significant in history.

In other action at the meeting, the commission approved a suggestion to push for improvement of conditions in the Conestoga

Turn To Page 22 For More Of PLANNING

Adlai Says Ike Trying To Save Mideast Snafu

WASHINGTON, Jan. 3 (AP)—Adlai Stevenson said today President Eisenhower, by seeking standby authority to use U.S. military forces in the Middle East, "is evidently trying frantically to fill the vacuum that his own policy helped create before Russia does."

Yet, by implciation, Stevenson supported the President's protective request to Congress. He said that he himself had called more than a year ago for a "declaration that the United States would oppose any changes in the Middle East by force and warned that Russian influence was spreading dangerously."

Stevenson, the defeated Democratic presidential nominee, also said in a statement that Eisenhower continually told the nation during the political campaign that the United States would not be involved in war but was now asking for "another military blank check" in the Middle East.

BANKRUPTCY

Stevenson added in his statement:

"If the result of the Suez disaster is to jolt us into recognition at last of the bankruptcy of our Middle East policy and the hypocristy of the Republican campaign, it may yet do some good."

"But another threat of military intervention, another enlargement of our already global military commitments, won't in itself stop

Turn To Page 22 For More Of ADLAI

Francis P. Sharpless, Insurance Executive· Civic Leader Dead At 62

Francis P. Sharpless, prominent Lancaster insurance executive, died at 10:05 p. m. yesterday at Lancaster General Hospital several hours after he was admitted. He had been suffering from a heart condition and was under the care of a physician for several years.

Sharpless, who resided at 585 N. School Lane, was sixty-two.

A native of West Chester, he had been a special agent here for the Provident Mutual Life Insurance Co. for many years. He also was active in civic affairs.

A graduate of Haverford College, class of 1916, he served 18 months in France from 1917 to 1919 with the American Friends Service Committee. Then from 1920 to 1924, he was resident manager of the Columbia Milling Co., Columbia, only to leave this post

Turn To Page 22 For More Of SHARPLESS

FRANCIS P. SHARPLESS

BREAK IN COLD SNAP PREDICTED TODAY

Moderate temperature readings are due here today, the weatherman said in his late forecast, which will break up the first cold spell of the new year.

According to the prediction, the mercury will peak somewhere between 38 and 42 degrees today, while the low tonight will be around 34 degrees. nItermittent rain is expected to accompany the rising mercury, the forecaster added.

The warming trend is expected to melt away the ice on numerous county ponds and creeks which ice skaters have been using to good advantage the past few days.

HOME BUILDERS ASSURED WATER LINES TO CURBS

Authority Extends Policy Followed During Expansion To Suburban Areas

The City of Lancaster Authority voted yesterday to continue its "free connection to property line" policy along its water mains where a new home is actually under construction.

The action establishes as future policy a practice carried out during the current extension of water lines to new suburban areas. The policy also provides that meters will be supplied future water users.

While the new system was under construction, the service lines were laid to the curbs of all properties containing homes, as well as to the curb line of vacant lots when owners requested the service.

Installation of connecting lines from the curb to the house, and coupling of the meter provided by the authority, will continue to be paid by the property owner.

Yesterday's move came after an

Turn To Page 22 For More Of WATER

Objections Of Real Estate Board Refuted In Report

The Esbenshade site "is a logical and highly desirable site upon which the proposed Community Center should be constructed," the commission's report submitted to the city and county governments concluded yesterday.

The report thus was in direct contradiction to objections of the Real Estate Board of Lancaster, Inc., which said on June 26 that:

1. The water table of the site at the Rt. 230 Bypass at Roseville Road is very high and that the installation of sanitary and storm sewers would be costly.

2. That no building could be erected on the land that would not rise above high tension wires, and the cost of moving

Turn To Page 22 For More Of OBJECTIONS

"*We Lead All The Rest*"

FARM CORNER

By Joe Wachtman

RONKS R1 YOUTH NAMED COUNTY'S FFA STAR FARMER

Solanco Vo Ag Instructor To Receive Honorary Keystone Farmer Degree

J. Richard Herr, Ronks R1, a senior vocational agricultural student at Lampeter-Strasburg High School, has been named Lancaster County Star Farmer of 1956-57 and will head a list of 11 Future Farmers of America from the county to be awarded the Keystone Farmer degree during Farm Show Week.

Owen

Herr

The Honorary Keystone degree will be awarded to Jackson H. Owen, vocational agriculture instructor at Solanco High School, at the same ceremony in the Forum at Harrisburg.

Five of the youths scheduled for the award are students or former students of Owen at Solanco while three are from Lampeter-Starsburg, two from Penn Manor and one from Manheim Central.

They are: Solanco—Robert Bucher, son of Mr. and Mrs. Paul Bucher, Peach Bottom; Clair Carter, son of Mr. and Mrs. Rosco Carter, Quarryville R3; Marion Findley, son of Mr. and Mrs. Edgar L Findley, Quarryville R3; Glenn A. Aument, son of Mr. and Mrs. Roy Aument, Quarryville R1; Calvin D. Keene, son of Mr. and

Turn To Page 34 For More Of FARM CORNER

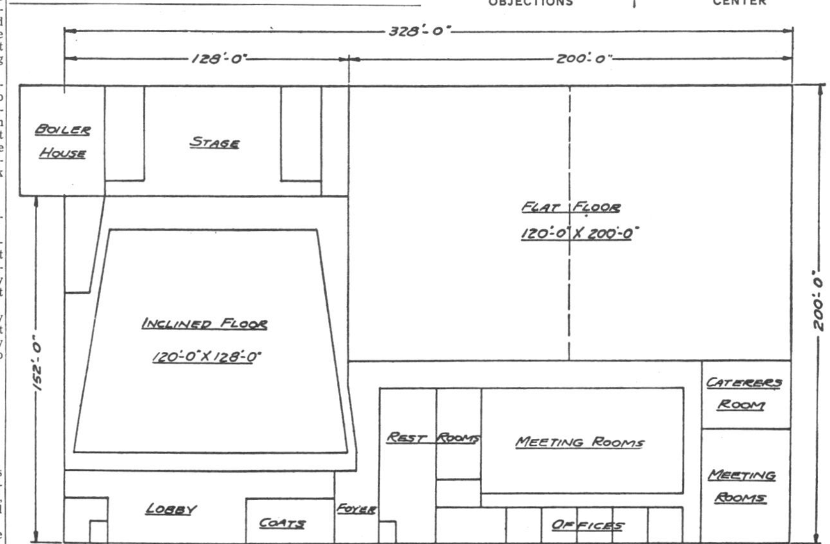

Floor Plan For Proposed Community Center

Floor plan for proposed Community Center included in the majority report of the center commission includes a theater, left, with inclined floor with a seating capacity of approximately 1,600 persons. The large flat floor auditorium would be used for exhibits and large meetings. It could be converted to a banquet hall with seating capacity for 1,500. Dotted line shows folding wall which could seal off half the room for smaller gatherings. Smaller meeting rooms and offices are in lower right. The 328 by 200-foot building would have an area of approximately 66,560 square feet.

Audrey Eshleman, who won the "Miss Ike Girl of Lancaster County" title last fall, as she left for the inauguration this morning.

New Era Photos

Three girls who got up at 4 to 5 a. m. to make the trip to Washington. Left to right, Phyllis Reddig, thirteen, Reamstown; Leslie Althouse, ten, Denver; Ann Schlegel, nine, Denver.

GROUP TOO SMALL

Buses Replace Inaugural Train

Nearly 275 Lancaster and Lebanon County residents left here for President Eisenhower's public inauguration early this morning—by chartered bus instead of the special train they expected.

George H. Van Zandt, 719 Highland Ave., chairman of a committee to arrange an inauguration train to leave Lancaster, said the train was canceled because too few people bought tickets.

Six Conestoga Transportation Co. buses took the group from the railroad station to York. There they boarded an inauguration train from Harrisburg for the rest of the trip to Washington.

People began arriving at the railroad station as early as 6 a. m. They still thought they were to take a train, and some moved to the rear of the station to be near stairs to the railroad tracks.

About 6:10 a. m., the trainmaster announced over the public address system that buses would replace the special inaugural train. The announcement brought grumbles and exclamations of surprise. Two women, who arrived just as the last bus was pulling out at 6:30 a. m., protested, "But we were told there is a train." They got on the bus.

More From Lebanon

A bus rolled in from Lebanon carrying approximately 35 persons from that area. Others drove their own cars from Lebanon and parked them near the station. All expected a train to be waiting. They were disgruntled when they were ushered on to another bus.

The change from train to bus meant extra traveling time for the inaugural sightseers. The special Lancaster train was to run to Columbia, and then down the Susquehanna River line to Washington, without going the extra distance west to York.

It meant a longer day for the group which will arrive back here early tomorrow morning. Many got up at 3 or 4 a. m. today to make the trip. Their sleepy faces showed it. Most brought along lunches and thermos jugs of coffee, though free buffet was to be provided on the train from York. Raincoats and umbrellas protected against an early morning drizzle.

A Few Left Over

When the six buses were filled, many were standing in the aisles, and there were a few persons left over. Van Zandt drove them to York in his car. The buses stopped at Columbia to pick up ten more passengers. The final total was estimated at 250 to 275.

Van Zandt said the new timetable runs like this: arrival in Washington, 10:30 a.m.; departure for York, 8:55 p.m.; arrival at York, 11:15 p.m. From York, the buses will again take over to bring the group to Lancaster.

Railroad officials said this morning that a quota of 300 passengers is required to hire a special train. Thus the inaugural group was 25 to 50 persons short. The officials said they arranged the buses as an alternate means of transportation, at no change in cost of the round-trip ticket. The ticket cost $4.80 for adults, with half-fare for children under twelve.

Egypt Sets Loss At $1.5 Billion

CAIRO (AP)—The Egyptian Middle East News Agency claimed today that Egypt's losses from British, French and Israel aggression amounted to nearly 1½ billion dollars.

"Egypt will claim reparations to this full amount and will not object to her claim being investigated by expert committees from abroad," the agency said.

The agency reported that the value of enemy property seized in Egypt amounts to only 490 million dollars.

4 Baghdad Pact Nations Back Ike

ANKARA (AP) — The four Moslem members of the anti-Communist Baghdad Pact today announced full support of the Eisenhower Doctrine on the Middle East.

Their support of Eisenhower's proposal to check Red aggression had been expected.

The four Baghdad Pact members — Turkey, Iraq, Iran and Pakistan — signed a communique after a two-day meeting. They also called for the United Nations to monitor Israel-Arab peace and advocated full freedom of navigation through the Suez Canal.

10% INCREASE

Record 2.9 Million Are Enrolled in U. S. Colleges

WASHINGTON (AP)—A record 2,947,000 students enrolled in U. S. colleges last fall, the government announced today.

Lawrence G. Dethick, Commissioner of Education, said total enrollments, already 10 per cent above last year's previous high, are expected to reach nearly 3¼ million with additional entries during the year.

The fall, enrollment survey of 1,852 institutions of higher education showed an increase for the fifth consecutive year in nearly all categories.

Some highlights of the report:

723,000 First-Time Students

The number enrolling for the first time in a college or university reached a record 723,000—7.1 per cent above the first-time enrollment in 1955 and 53.2 per cent more than in 1951.

Teachers colleges enrolled 13.5 per cent more than in 1955, technological schools 13.4 per cent more and theological schools 2.3 per cent more. However, theological schools showed a 5.5 per cent decrease in first-time enrollments, technical schools a 14.4 per cent increase.

The University of California led the field in total enrollments with 40,788 on all campuses, excl[illegible] e[illegible] [illegible]on work. The University of Minnesota was second with 33,303.

URGES LOSS OF PERMIT IF AUTO USED IN FELONY

PITTSBURGH (AP) — The State Legislature today was urged to enact a law permitting the courts to suspend or revoke drivers' licenses of persons using autos in the commission of felony.

Judge Henry Ellenbogen of Allegheny County Common Pleas Court also proposed that the legislation cover persons convicted of stealing autos.

Calling the modern automobile an important tool of today's criminal, Judge Ellenbogen pointed out that in the first six months of 1956 an estimated 134,320 autos were stolen ,an increase of 22.3 per cent over 1955.

Sees 3 to 5% Hike in Economy

Armstrong Economist Talks Before ABC

The year 1957 should bring about an increase of from three to five per cent in the nation's business economy, Albert G. Matamoros, associate economist at Armstrong Cork Co., said today.

Speaking before the Lancaster Chapter of the American Business Club in the Arcadia, Matamoros said that is the general forecast by economists and business experts. Three principal reasons for continued economical growth, he said, were expected additional governmental spending, more private business expansion and increased consumer spending.

Some Trouble Sources

However, Matamoros warned that, although the general picture is good, 'individual businesses may have their troubles. Chief trouble sources would be possible "serious inflationary consequences" from higher federal spending, the steadily declining corporate profit rate and consumer resistance to ever-rising prices. The so-called 'tight money" market will also continue to prevail, he said.

Thus, said Matamoros, the last few months of 1957 could bring about "the first real test the postwar economy has had." Also, he went on to say, the "test" might continue through 1958 and 1959.

Sales Executives Plan Annual Essay Contest

The Lancaster Sales Executive Club is holding its fourth annual essay contest for high school juniors and seniors on the subject "Selling as a Professional Career."

Entries must be submitted to chairman Jack Schleenbaker by March 1. First prize is a $50 bond to be awarded to the county-wide winner. A $25 bond goes to the second place essay. Top two essays in each participating school will get $10 and $5 certificates. Winners will be announced, and prizes awarded at a banquet April 17.

DROODLES

By Roger Price

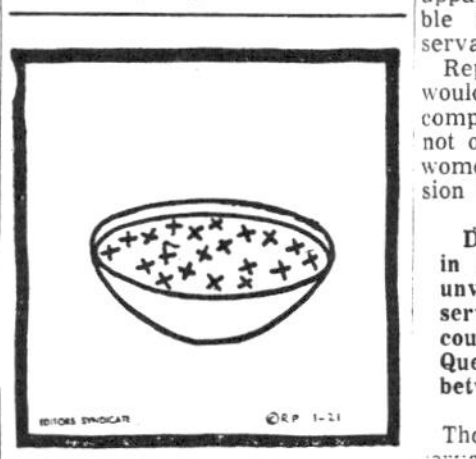

"ALPHABET SOUP FOR ILLITERATES"

11 Hurt in Crash Of Elverson Bus

Skids Into Auto on Icy Ramp, Hits Tree

PHILADELPHIA (AP) — A bus and an automobile collided today on an ice-covered ramp of the Schuylkill Expressway at West Conshohocken today, injuring 11 persons.

Nine of those injured were passengers aboard a bus operated by the Laguna Industries, Inc., of Elverson, Chester County. Also injured were the bus driver, Albert Silvestrini, 31, of Conshohocken, and John Kennedy, 50, of Phoenixville, a passenger in the car, operated by Gerald Synkckowski of Phoenixville.

Police quoted Silverstrini as saying a car going up the ramp in front of the bus started to slide back down the icy roadway. Silverstrini said he applied his brakes and the bus skidded into the path of Synkckowski's car, which was coming down the ramp, also in a skid.

Bus Careens Into Tree

The bus then careened off the highway and into a tree.

Four of the bus passengers were treated at Bryn Mawr Hospital which said they were in good condition.

The others were treated by a private physician. They included Mrs. Philomena Flamini, 64, (225 N. Poplar St.) and Mrs. Eleanor Lasorta, 35, (717 Walnut St.) both of Norristown.

Diana Churchill Leaves Husband

LONDON (AP)— Sir Winston Churchill's eldest daughter, Diana, has separated from her second husband, British Defense Minister Duncan Sandys.

"We have parted, but I cannot say yet exactly what we will do," Mrs. Sandys told a reporter yesterday.

She married Sandys in 1935 after divorcing her first husband, John Bailey. Mr. and Mrs. Sandys are parents of a son and two daughters.

PLEADS, PAYS COSTS

Harold K. Coble, 613 E. Orange St., charged with disorderly conduct by Shirley Mumma, 321 W. Walnut St., pleaded guilty and paid costs Saturday before Alderman Ober.

7 ORIGINAL BACH SCORES FOUND IN U. S.

BETHLEHEM (AP) — A Boston University Scholar has authenticated a rare musical find at Moravian churches and at Winston-Salem, N. C., of seven forgotten compositions by two members of the famous 18th Century Bach family.

The time-yellowed scores for five symphonies and two sonatas were found in archives by researchers of the Moravian Music Foundation. They are the work of Johan Ernst Bach and Johann Christoph Friedrich Bach.

Six of the compositions are by Johann Christoph Friedrich Bach. They are a symphony in D minor, symphony in E major, symphony in F major, symphony in B-flat major and two sonatas, one in A major and the other in F major. The seventh work, a symphony in B-flat major is by Johann Ernst Bach.

Court to Review Film Blacklist

23 Ask Millions For Being 'Barred'

WASHINGTON (AP) — The Supreme Court today granted a hearing to 23 movie actors and other film workers who sought millions of dollars in damages on a complaint that a Hollywood "blacklist" kept them out of work.

The 23 claimants said they were blacklisted by the film industry after they refused to testify in 1951 before the House Committee on Un-American Activities. Each asked damages of $2,250,000.

The suit was against major film companies, film distributing companies and members of the House Committee. California courts dismissed the litigation on the ground there was no showing of injury to any "legally protected interest" of the 23 because none had an employment contract. In appealing to the Supreme Court for a hearing the 23 contended they had been denied equal protection and due process of laws.

The 23 claimants included film players Gale Sondergard and Howard Da Silva.

Berber Warriors Hold Rabat Roads

RABAT, Morocco (AP) — From 2,000 to 3,000 armed Berber tribesmen, supporting a defiant provincial governor, were reported today in control of two main highways leading into the province from this capital.

Elements of the Moroccan army, supported by armored vehicles, were in the area, but no engagement has occurred, according to informants here.

The governor, Addi ou Bihi, was deposed earlier today by the palace in Rabat and replaced by Sultan Mohammed ben Youssef's top military aide. But the replacement, Maj. Ben Larbi, was unable to get to his post.

Shops Wrecked in Cypriot Fighting

NICOSIA, Cyprus (AP)— Turkish and Greek Cypriots fought for the second day today in Nicosia's streets.

Eleven shops and warehouses in the Greek sector were smoking ruins in the wake of torch and bomb attacks last night by bands of fanatical young Turks.

Two Greek Cypriot men were wounded in the new outbreak. Turkish auxiliary policemen opened fire to break up a clash on a street dividing the Greek and Turkish sectors.

Disabled Plane Lands Safely on Soapy Strip

TAMPA, Fla. (AP) — A private plane with four persons aboard circled Tampa International Airport for an hour and 49 minutes yesterday with a disabled nose wheel before being brought in smoothly on a runway made slick by concentrated soapsuds.

Robert Walker of Tampa kept the plane aloft until the soap could be brought in from MacDill Air Force Base and spread on the runway. Flying with Walker were his son, Jackie, 10; Graham Smith; and Smith's son Scott, 11.

Hubley Takes Over New Plant

Operations Will Start In About a Month

Hubley Manufacturing Co. today took possession of its new $1,500,000 plant along the Eden-Bridgeport Rd.

The Austin Co., which constructed the plant, signed the building over to the Hubley company, effective today.

Operations in the new quarters will begin in three weeks or a month, according to officials of the toy firm.

No production equipment has been moved into the new building. Plant maintenance men started today to prepare for the arrival of equipment.

Moving Starts This Week

Joseph M. Breneman, Hubley president, said actual moving will start this week on a department-by-department basis, he said, to minimize interruption of production.

The new one-story plant has 155,000 square feet of floor space including the boiler house.

Workmen today put finishing touches on painting of the office quarters, and the black paneled main lobby and reception room.

Operations in the plant will include plating, assembly and shipping. For the present time, die casting and painting of toys will be done at the old Hubley building, N. Plum St. and Elizabeth Ave. Manufacture of leather holsters for toy pistols will be done in the assembly department of the old building.

500 to Work There

Of the firm's 700 employes, about 500 will make the move to the new plant, and about 200 will remain at the Plum St. site, Breneman said.

Eventually, it is hoped, all plant operations will be transferred to the new quarters.

Construction of the new plant began last March on a 59-acre farm formerly owned by Henry K. and Mary Landis. The plant is located across the Eden-Bridgeport Rd. from the Easthome plant of Northome Furniture Co. in East Lampeter Twp.

$400,000 Fire At Bala-Cynwyd

Trevor Country Club Heavily Damaged

PHILADELPHIA (AP) —Fire today caused an estimated $400,000 damage to the Trevor Country Club in suburban Bala-Cynwyd.

The damage estimate was made by the assistant fire chief James W. Mullin, of Lower Merion Twp., who said the smoke, fire and water damage was extensive through the entire rambling frame structure.

The fire was first reported by a woman living nearby in Bala-Cynwyd. Cause of the blaze was not learned immediately.

The club, devoted to tennis and squash, has 387 members. It was founded 47 years ago.

Refuelers Could Cut Jets' Time

WASHINGTON (AP) — If jet tanker planes had been available, three B52 bombers could have clipped about six hours from the time it took them to circle the globe last week.

That is the estimate of Lt. Col. James H. Morris of San Antonio, Tex., who piloted one of the three heavy jet aircraft more than 24,000 miles in 45 hours and 19 minutes.

During their round-the-world journey, the B52s were refueled at intervals by KC97 tanker planes which are driven by conventional non-jet engines. To take on fuel from these tankers, the heavy jets must slow down and drop to 20,000 feet — the maximum altitude that can be reached by loaded KC97s. The B52s also lose time in climbing back to their normal cruising level, which on this flight was between 35,000 and 50,000 feet.

HONORED AT ACADEMY

Cadet Capt. John H. Clark II, son of Mr. and Mrs. John H. Clark, 1604 Wheatland Ave., was one of ten cadets and four teachers recently inducted into the Order of Anthony Wayne at Valley Forge Military Academy. Induction into the order is the highest honor given at the academy for efficiency and effort beyond the call of duty.

QUEEN TELLS HUSSEIN:

It's Me or the Harem—She Wins

CAIRO (AP)—Jordan's King Hussein is reported to have taken advantage of the Arab summit parley last week to patch up his troubles with his blonde Queen Dina.

The 22-year-old monarch got a promise of 35 million dollars from Egypt, Syria and Saudi Arabia.

On the domestic front he kissed and made up with Dina, who had been visiting her parents in Cairo since Sept. 13 amid rumors that the royal match would end in divorce.

The Cambridge-educated Dina, six years older than her husband, apparently had been having trouble adjusting to Hussein's conservative Moslem country.

Reportedly he promised her she would be his wife, queen and companion in the modern sense, not one of a number of the king's women tucked away in the seclusion of the harem.

Dina became the first queen in Jordan's history to appear unveiled in public. Then conservative forces around the court — reportedly including Queen Mother Zein — came between her and Hussein.

The Jordanian public is so conservative that fanatics occasionally have thrown acid in the faces of unveiled women on the streets of Amman.

Hussein also at times has slipped back into the playboy role of his single days. Dina was humiliated by reports he had been seen in public with other women.

King Hussein of Jordan and Queen Dina in recent photograph.

New Era Photo

Jesse Owens at local railroad station.

JUVENILE DELINQUENCY

'Kids Need to Be Wanted'--Owens

By Bill Fisher

"Sports is no cure-all, but it can go a long way to help fight juvenile delinquency," Jessie Owens declared today as he arrived in Lancaster to speak at the 11th annual Sportswriters and Broadcasters Banquet at Hotel Brunswick tonight.

Owens, four-event winner in the 1936 Olympics at Berlin and considered America's all-time track great, is now a member of the Illinois Youth Commission in Chicago.

"Kids need to be wanted," he said, "there are too many that don't have that feeling. Our job is to create it. It is a job for the parents, too, because it is a social problem. We go into the neighborhoods and to the parents and we try to get them interested as well as the kid."

Owens explained that the Youth Commission, a State organization created about a year and a half ago, deals with corrective and preventative delinquency.

"My job with the commission is preventive. We want to get to the kids, give them something to do and make them wanted so they don't become delinquents.

"We are not concerned with sports alone. Some kids don't like sports. Some are more interested in music or crafts. We try to develop a program that offers something for all the kids.

"One thing a lot of people seem to forget," he continued, "is that delinquency is also a parental responsibility. The parents must show some interest in the activities of their children. We go into the homes and talk to the parents and try to tighten the tie between the parents and the child."

Owens explained that his work with the commission was concerned chiefly with the "have-nots."

"It isn't the kids on the varsity or who are active in school affairs that we try to reach; they already have something to do. We try to reach the kid who has nothing to do but run around the neighborhood. We try to get the parents interested. We find a spare basement in the neighborhood and let the kids fix it up and plan programs to keep them busy.

"It's a big job. If we reach four out of ten kids then I'd say that's a pretty good average.

"Getting sports personalities to work within the program is a good way to get the kids interested. We have organized a group of athletes in the Chicago area who go out among the kids. Fellows like Gene Baker of the Chicago Cubs, Adolph Kieffer the swimmer and a lot of others. The kids are attracted by the names. Athletes can do a lot to help with the juvenile problem."

Owens has also spread goodwill for the United States throughout the Far East. Last year he toured India, Malay and the Philippines as an emissary for the government.

"Everyone over there is interested in sports. We went out into the schools and clubs and tried to spread the American Way. They loved every minute of it."

Publisher Faces Blackmail Charge

LAS VEGAS, Nev. (AP) — A warrant charging blackmail is on its way here today to be served on publisher Herman Greenspun.

The complaint charges Greenspun and private investigator Wilbur McNich with attempting to blackmail Dist. Judge John Sexton, who presided over a recent libel case in which Greenspun was ordered to pay $180,000 to Las Vegas Atty. George Franklin.

Greenspun said that his paper, the Las Vegas Sun, conducted an "investigation" of the judge. "The results of this investigation came before him in open court in the form of a motion."

CUBS HOLD PARTY

Members of Den 1, Cub Scout Pack 125, sponsored by the 6th Ward Citizens Association, held an ice skating party yesterday at Hershey. The group was accompanied by Mr. and Mrs. Elvin Boas and Mrs. Hilda Donnelly.

Japan on Way to Recognize China

HONG KONG (AP)—Peiping radio today said Japan's ambassador to Afghanistan told Red Chinese Premier Chou En-lai that Japan "already has de facto relations with (Communist) China."

De facto relations are relations in fact, as contrasted with de jure (in law) relations which result from mutual diplomatic recognition by governments. Japan recognizes the Chinese Nationalist government on Peiping.

The broadcast said Chou replied: "De facto relations are important and formal diplomatic relations will come as a last step."

AT READING MEETING

Three members of the Lancaster Toastmasters Club attended a meeting of Area 3, District 38, yesterday at Reading. They are: Richard Warren, Donald Cairns and Paul Steele. Cairnes was a member of a six-man panel.

DETECTIVE SAYS:

Doctor Gave Patient, 81, Vast Amount of Heroin

EASTBOURNE, England (AP) — One of Scotland Yard's ace detectives testified today that Dr. John Bodkin Adams admitted giving an 81-year-old patient a huge amount of heroin in the last two days of her life.

Detective Supt. Herbert Hannam said he confronted the portly society physician with the fact he had prescribed 75 tablets, each one-sixth of a grain, for Mrs. Edith Morrell the day before she died in 1950.

Scotland Yard maintains that Adams, inflamed by greed, pumped massive doses of narcotics into three patients and was responsible for their deaths.

Rolls-Royce Given Doctor

Five justices of the peace are holding the hearing in this Victorian seaside resort to determine if there is sufficient evidence to bring the 260-pound doctor to trial on a charge of murdering Mrs. Morrell, who left him a chest of antique silver. Her son later gave Adams a Rolls-Royce.

Hannam, the 38th witness called, conducted the long investigation which resulted in Adams' arrest. The inquiry involved thumbing through the wills of between 300 and 400 persons who had died in Eastbourne in the last 20 years.

Gifts In Lieu Of Fees

The detective said the doctor told him a lot of gifts he had received in patients' wills had been in lieu of fees. Adams said the chest of silver Mrs. Morrell left him was of no use to him since he was a bachelor.

Hannam also testified that Adams told him:

"I have one thing in life, and God knows I have vowed to Him I would, that is to relieve pain and try to let these dear people live as long as possible."

Today was Adams' 58th birthday. As he sat impassively in the courtroom, his attorney handed him a bundle of letters, including several birthday cards.

JERRY GEHMAN
"Neat guy"
LOIS MECUM
"Hate to see him"
VICKI WEISBURG
"Bad influence"
WOODY SPONAUGLE
"Not a good example"
"ELVIS"
LEE TODD
"He's alright"
DELORES FITTING
"He's wonderful!"

New Era Photos

'DON'T BE CRUEL'

Are Teen-Agers Cooling Towards Their Top 'Cat?'

By Jane Birney

What happened to the stampeding hordes, the screaming mobs of teen-agers "dedicated" to Elvis?"

Even the "Elvis" buttons are not so evident on the teen-agers' jackets anymore. Is the rage for Elvis Presley just a fad like so many of the fickle youngsters' heroes of previous years?

And is some one like Alan Freed—the disc jockey that had New York's teen-agers in a frenzy yesterday and today—going to knock Elvis from his pedestal?

A survey of teen tastes around the town shows up some surprising sidelights on the Presley craze.

SALES OF PRESLEY RECORDS in Lancaster—which for awhile were running as high as 700 a week—are showing a considerable drop.

Record shops which had trouble keeping Presley records in stock are now, in some cases, cutting down or canceling orders.

Other names, like Tab Hunter and Harry Belafonte, are now on the top, put there by the fickle fans who shift devoted allegiance from one idol to another with the ease of experienced drivers.

Perhaps Presley needs a new "gimmick" or maybe he ought to go to England where the British teen-agers are great rock 'n' roll fans.

In taking the "Presley Pulse" in Lancaster during the height of his popularity, it soon became obvious that Lancaster teen-agers, no exception to the general rule, were for the most part, ardent fans.

Local record stores were mobbed with fans particularly as each new record hit the market, and juke boxes and dance halls jumped with Presley rhythm.

"What do you think of Elvis?" was asked of his biggest group of fans, the teen-agers. The response was good, both pro and con. Seldom was heard, "I haven't thought much about him."

IN INTERVIEWING a group of Lancaster Twp. Junior High School "fans" at a local record shop where they spend several hours each week, the replies went something like this:

YOLANDI MENGALI — (beaming)—"He has a very good voice and is talented both as a singer and an actor."

MARIANNE ROWELL — "He's got a fair voice but he can't act."

JERE STAUFFER—"He's a pretty good singer."

JOHN BERGEN—(shrugging)—"Too much of a showoff."

YOLANDI—"I buy all his records, but I'm definitely not the screaming type."

MARIANNE—(agreeing)— "I can't stand girls who scream."

JERE—(enthusiastically)—"Boy, you sure can tell he's made a lot of money. Look at all those cars!" (As "Too Much" was playing in the background.)

It is interesting to note that the presidents of student councils of four schools are in agreement in disliking Elvis whereas the schools' newspaper editors are fans.

HERE ARE SOME of the reactions:

JUDY ANDERSON, president of Manheim Twp. High School Council, predicts that Elvis is just a fad and will not last. She rates Crosby and Sinatra much higher.

WOODY SPONAUGLE, McCaskey Council prexy, says, "He's hardly a good, clean-cut American boy."

RONALD SMITH of East Lampeter, feels that Elvis doesn't have the personality that a top star should have and thinks his appearance is "sloppy."

BONNIE BOWEN, editor of Reynolds Junior High School paper, and Jerry Gehman, sports editor, were interviewed together. Bonnie likes his voice but not the way he moves, whereas Jerry thinks his voice is good and his appearance is fine including his haircut.

DELORES FITTING, one of the editors at Edward Hand Junior High School, goes all out in saying, "I'm with him all the way. I like him better than any other singer." She and Lee Todd of Lancaster Twp. Junior High School, both like Elvis' devotion to his parents and think that this illustrates his real character.

LOIS MECUM, senior editor of Manheim Twp. High School paper, says that although she doesn't like to see him, she is very fond of his mussic which in her opinion has good rhythm and "is great to dance to." She doesn't think his voice is really a good one, but it has an "intimate quality which is appealing."

Are the Stephenson girls, Linda and Kim, students at Lancaster Country Day School, going to be proved wrong in their firm prediction that Elvis will last?

Both of these ardent supporters were interviewed on the telephone. With strains of "Love Me Tender" setting the mood, the girls enthusiastically discussed the singer. Said Linda, "He's been growing on me. I think his music is great." "People can't help liking him," added Kim. Both are convinced he will last as long as he keeps coming up with something new.

IT MAY BE that the cause for the slump is nothing new recently on his part. Someone should write him several new songs. Rock 'n' roll is by no means dead if that jam of 5,000 persons to see a movie and stage show at New York's Paramount Theater is a sign. It could be that the star, Freed, and new singers like Tom Sands will replace Presley.

Of course the Presley fan clubs—several of which are flourishing in the Lancaster area—are duty-bound to keep his name alive and his platters spinning until the last "Houn' Dog" yelps.

If Elvis is on the wane, maybe in ten years, he, like Frank Sinatra, will make a comeback with a more mature, sideburnless approach.

As the footlights dim, do we hear the dying strains of "Don't Be Cruel"?

IFCA Circle Will Serve Spaghetti

Lancaster Circle, International Federation of Catholic Alumnae, will serve its annual supper, open to the public, on March 2 from 5:30 to 7 p. m., in the cafeteria of Lancaster Catholic High School, Juliette Ave.

The menu will center on spaghetti and salads.

Tickets may be obtained from any of the members or at the door.

Proceeds will go to the Circle's charity fund.

Mrs. Frank A. Christoffel Jr. and Mrs. Robert M. Landis are general co-chairmen.

Mrs. Wallace T. Bucher is chairman of the salads, assisted by Mrs. William O. Frailey III and Mrs. Jack Metzger.

Decorations will be arranged by Mrs. James Wagner. Miss Ruth W. Sullivan will direct a large group of girls who will serve.

YWCA Plans New Course In Bridge

Two new courses will be added to the spring term of the YWCA Informal Education program, starting next week.

A six-weeks course on advanced bridge will begin March 4 at 8 p.m. Instructor for the course is John Fellenbaum.

Instruction will include advanced bidding techniques, opening leads, signals and discussions of card combinations. One hour of each class period will be spent in supervised play.

A "Poise through Speech" class will be conducted by Mrs. Nathaniel P. Lauriat. It will open March 5 at 7:30 p.m. and continue for six weeks.

The course will cover voice use and control, ways to be at ease in speaking to or presiding over groups, and the method of developing a good "public personality."

Mrs. Lauriat previously taught in the San Jose, Calif., Adult Education program, and conducted her own radio program of news and interviews, in Poughkeepsie, N. Y.

THE LAST POTTERY class of the season to be conducted by Richard A. Fleckenstein will start March 6 at 7:30 p.m.

The class in general pottery will be open to those with previous experience and to beginners.

Registration for classes must be made by Wednesday. All classes are open to both men and women.

ON DEAN'S LIST

Janet Burton Bell, daughter of Mr. and Mrs. Lyle W. Bell, 838 Fountain Ave., has been named to the dean's list at Mary Washington College of the University of Virginia, Fredericksburg, Va.

Susan Lockwood Is Engaged to William Fishbeck

SUSAN LOCKWOOD

Mr. and Mrs. Louis H. Lockwood, Rohrerstown, announce the engagement of their daughter, Susan Lockwood, to William A. Fishbeck, son of Mr. and Mrs. Fenton Fishbeck, Alma, Mich.

Miss Lockwood is a graduate of the University of Michigan and has done graduate work there and at Oxford University, England. She is a member of Pi Sigma Alpha, national honorary Political Science Society. At present, Miss Lockwood is resident director of one of the Women's Residence Halls at the University of Michigan.

Mr. Fishbeck received a Bachelor of Mechanical Engineering Degree from the General Motors' Institute and is now a senior in the University of Michigan School of Medicine.

A June wedding is planned.

New Era Photo

Women Build Scenery for Style Show

Three members of the Welcome Wagon Newcomers Club turn "carpenters" as they build the sets for the Children's Fashion Show on March 12. Mrs. Harry Collins, left, and Mrs. William Zerbey, center, put final touches on a cardboard well, while Mrs. Donald Brown paints the Mother Goose character of Humpty Dumpty on a paper wall.

All-Children Fashion Show On March 12

Sugar plums, candy canes, lollypops, and candy taffies — "sweets" enough to delight any child—will form the setting for an "all-children" fashion show to be presented March 12 at 8 p. m. in the Regency Room of Odd Fellows Hall, 213 W. Chestnut St.

The show will be sponsored by the Welcome Wagon Newcomers Club for the benefit of Lancaster Chapter, Muscular Dystrophy Association.

The entire show will be modeled by children of the club members. The models range in age from 18 months to eleven years and will include boys and girls.

Decorations will be centered about the "Mother Goose" theme. A well made of half of a packing barrel, with painted corrugated paper for the roof will be used with a stuffed cat to depict the "Mother Goose" character of "Pussy in the Well." A stone wall in the background painted on heavy paper will support a replica of Humpty-Dumpty.

Mobiles of sugar plums, candy taffies, lollypops, and candy canes of colored construction paper will be balanced on tree branches. Mrs. Donald Brown designed the set.

THE CHILDREN will walk through an archway of cardboard candy canes when they model the fashions.

Models are: Nancy Nickel, four, and her sister, Susan, two; Kim McNabb, five; Elyse Brown, six; Barbara Protafiewicz, seven, and her sister; Linda, five; Diana Protafiewicz, eight; Rosalynn Palmer, eight, and her sisters, Roberta, six, and Rhonda, five; Patricia Ann Brady, eighteen months.

Judith Ricker, eleven; Stephanie Grizzell, nine; Mary Jane Ready, four, Kathy Chiffriller, five; Harry Huber, five, and his sister, Beth, eight; James Wentling, four, and his brother, John, two-and-one-half; Cathleen Ann Collins, four, and her brother, Willard, six; Bradley James, two-and-one-half; David Gulya, five, and his brother, three; Dena Tamany, eight, and her sister, Bari, two-and-one-half.

H. B. Weaver Jr. Weds Miss Webster

Mr. and Mrs. Avery D. Webster, Baltimore, Md., announce the marriage of their daughter, Miss Barbara Beveridge Webster, to Herbert Bachman Weaver Jr., son of Mr. and Mrs. Herbert Bachman Weaver, 1305 Marietta Ave.

The wedding took place Thursday in St. Luke's Chapel, Washington, D. C., in the presence of the families.

ENGAGED

HUFFMAN—WIEBUSH

Mr. and Mrs. John Charles Wiebush, 550 St. Joseph St., announce the engagement of their daughter, Kathryn Mary Wiebush, to Burl Huffman, son of Mr. and Mrs. J. E. Huffman, Kirbyville, Texas.

Mr. Huffman, who is serving in the U.S. Navy, is stationed at the Bainbridge Naval Training Center. The wedding will take place April 6.

Prospective Student Nurses To Be Entertained at Tea

Junior and senior girls from city and county high schools, who are interested in nursing careers, will be entertained at a tea on March 3 from 2 to 4 p. m. at the Lancaster Osteopathic Hospital, 1100 E. Orange St.

The tea will be given by the Auxiliary to the staff of the hospital.

Parents of the girls also are invited. During the tea information will be given the guests on the seven scholarships available to student nurses.

The awards, all of which are for three-years' training at the Philadelphia Osteopathic Hospital, are given by the board of directors and the staff of the local hospital. Dr. Harold Finkel, chairman of the scholarship committee, will explain the awards and also will discuss the nurses' training program.

Following the tea the guests will be taken on a tour of the hospital.

Mrs. Charles Noll is general chairman of the event, assisted by Mrs. John Atkins Jr., Mrs. Herman Fishman, Mrs. Lewis Yunginger, Mrs. George Wolf, Mrs. Rudolph Rigano, Mrs. Harold Finkel, Mrs. Roscoe Thome, Mrs. Whitlaw Show and Mrs. Edgel Wiley.

Miss Rohrer Is Married to H. R. Barnes in Belgium

The marriage of Miss Dorothy G. Rohrer, daughter of Mr. and Mrs. Walter M. Rohrer, Paradise R1, to H. Richard Barnes, son of Prof. and Mrs. Horace R. Barnes, 1518 Clearview Ave., took place yesterday at 8 p. m. in the Missionary Church in Brussels, Belgium, with the Rev. George Winston officiating.

The bride and bridegroom are studying in Belgium preparatory to going to the Belgian Congo as missionaries in September.

MRS. H. RICHARD BARNES

The bride wore a gown of silk faille with a yoke of Belgian lace and a fingertip length veil attached to a cap of pleated silk trimmed with orange blossoms. She carried a bouquet of white carnations.

Her maid of honor was Miss Grace Dibble, of Church Hill, Tenn. She wore a red satin gown with matching hat and carried a bouquet of red and white carnations.

Arnie Sareski of Morden, Manitoba, Canada, served as best man. Ushers were Hans Scheuzger, Switzerland, and Donald Lundquist, Minneapolis, Minn. Edwin Holland, of Bedford, England, played the wedding music. Miss Winsome Schroeder, of Cambridge, South Africa, was vocal soloist.

After a reception in the home of friends in Brussels, the couple left on a trip to Switzerland.

THE BRIDE, a registered nurse, is taking courses in languages, tropical diseases and teaching. She was graduated from Paradise Twp. High School, the Philadelphia School of the Bible, West Suburban Hospital School of Nursing, Oak Park, Ill., and Wheaton College, Wheaton, Ill. She also took a course in obstetrics at Preston Maternity Hospital, Philadelphia.

The bridegroom is a graduate of Franklin and Marshall Academy and College, the Wharton School of the University of Pennsylvania, and Philadelphia Bible Institute. He is studying languages and the Colonial Course and will be working in a business capacity in the Belgian Congo.

Douglas Ayer Weds Today

The marriage of Miss Charlotte E. DeWese, daughter of Mr. and Mrs. Willis L. DeWese, 5821 Rambo Lane, Toledo, Ohio, to Douglas Bernard Ayer, son of Mr. and Mrs. Raymond B. Ayer, 27 Albright Circle, Madison, N. J., formerly of 328 Perry Ave., Lancaster, will take place today at 7:30 p. m. in Our Saviour Lutheran Church, Toledo, with the Rev. Richard L. Smith officiating.

Given in marriage by her father, the bride will be attended by Miss Lynne Rae Ayer, sister of the bridegroom, Madison, N. J., as maid of honor. Bridesmaids will be Mrs. John Miller and Miss Marilyn Shurtz, both of Toledo, Ohio; and Mrs. Dean Riggs, cousin of the bride, Avon Lake, Ohio.

The bride's gown of Chantilly lace over satin has a fitted bodice with Sabrina neckline trimmed with sequins and pearls. The skirt features a cascade of lace and pleated tulle ruffles in the front and a chapel train formed by a lace redingote edged in a pleated tulle ruffle. Her fingertip length veil of illusion is attached to a pillbox of lace trimmed with sequins and pearls. She will carry a white Bible, a childhood gift from her parents, with white carnations.

The attendants will wear ballerina length gowns of Arcady blue crystalette with scoop necklines and three-quarter length sleeves. They will wear matching head clips with face veils and carry bouquets of pink carnations.

Richard N. Ayer, Madison; N. J., will serve as best man for his brother. Ushers will be Milton K. Morgan Jr., Defiance, Ohio; Richard E. Royer, Angola, Ind.; and P. Niel Yocom, Urbana, Ill.

The bride is a secretary at the Juvenile Court in Toledo. The bridegroom was graduated from Pennsylvania State University, where he received a B.S. degree in chemistry. He is a member of Alpha Chi Sigma fraternity and is employed as a chemist with Gulf Oil Co. in Toledo.

WEDDINGS

Cunningham—Tomlinson

The marriage of Ruth H. Tomlinson, 409 E. Strawberry St., daughter of the late Mr. and Mrs. Elmer F. Bauer, to Howard J. Cunningham, son of Mr. and Mrs. Howard Cunningham, 738½ Marietta Ave., took place today at 11 a.m. in Memorial Presbyterian Church, with the Rev. Frederick S. Price officiating.

The attendants were Mrs. Jessie Miller and Carl Sirbak. A reception followed at the bride's home.

The couple will reside at 409 E. Strawberry St.

Tangert—Fiorentino

The marriage of Mary Catherine Fiorentino, foster daughter of Mrs. Theresa Madonna, 137 Howard Ave., to Howard Charles Tangert, son of Mr. and Mrs. Harry Tangert, 462 Rockland St., took place today at 3 p.m. in St. Mary's Catholic Church, with the Rt. Rev. Msgr. Charles J. Tighe officiating.

The couple will reside at 40 W. James St.

Arment—Ecker

The marriage of Jeannette Ecker, daughter of Mr. and Mrs. Lowell Ecker, Lititz R3, to William R. Arment Jr., son of Mr. and Mrs. William R. Arment Sr., Lancaster R3, took place Feb. 16 at 12:30 p. m. in Otterbein Evangelical United Brethren Church, with the Rev. D. LeRoy Fegley officiating.

Chilean to Speak Here on Tuesday

Carmen Orrego-Salas, wife of the composer Juan Orrego-Salas, of Santiago, Chile, will speak at the meeting of the Towne Club Tuesday at 1:30 p. m. at the YWCA.

The mother of four children, she teaches English to adult classes of men and, women at the Chilean North American Institute, and is on her second lecture tour of the United States.

Her subject will be "Women's Quest for Understanding and Peace."

Sleek-Line Swimsuits

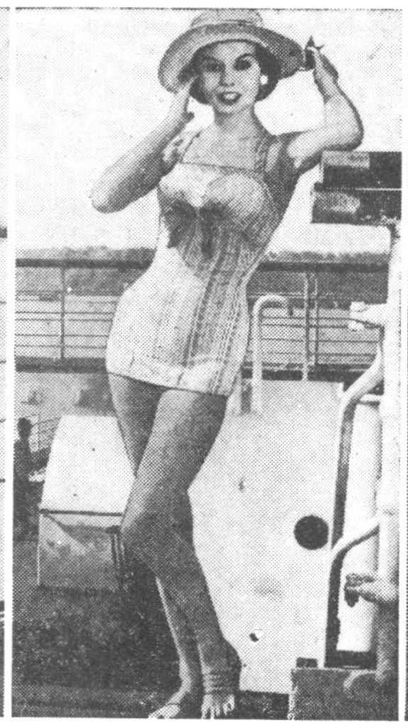
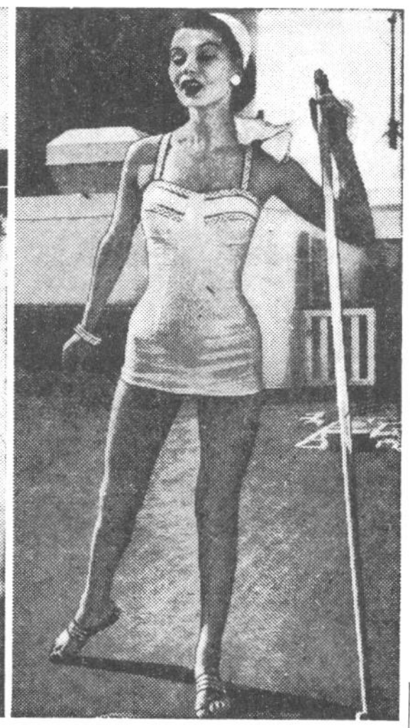

Swim suits to swim and sun in either now (on a winter vacation) or later (next summer) show the influence of daytime and evening fashions. Leaning on shiprail, this girl wears (left) cabana-striped swim sheath by Sprite in an elasticized wool knit. Neckline and shoulder straps are in a black boucle braid. The Empire line appears (center) in bamboo-striped swim sheath with bow to emphasize the Empire bustline. Waffle pique lastex suit (right) is in white, is edged with turquoise faille. The faille is embroidered in white. Sleek lines and figure control typify these new suits.

Lines suggest an evening gown in sheath of chromspun and elasticized cotton with Grecian draping.

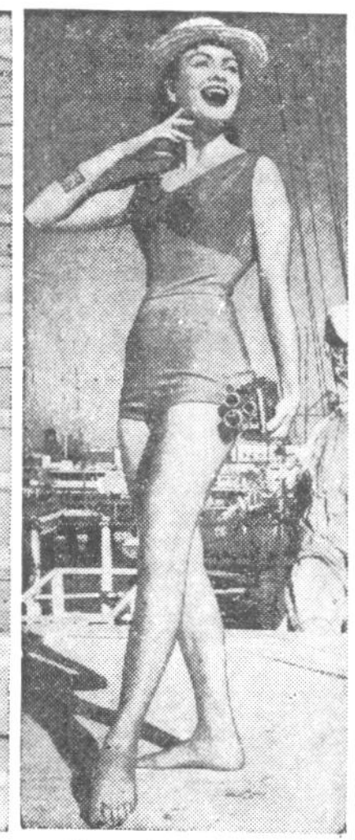

This dramatic draped swimsuit has jersey top combined with lastex to give suit a slim-torso look.

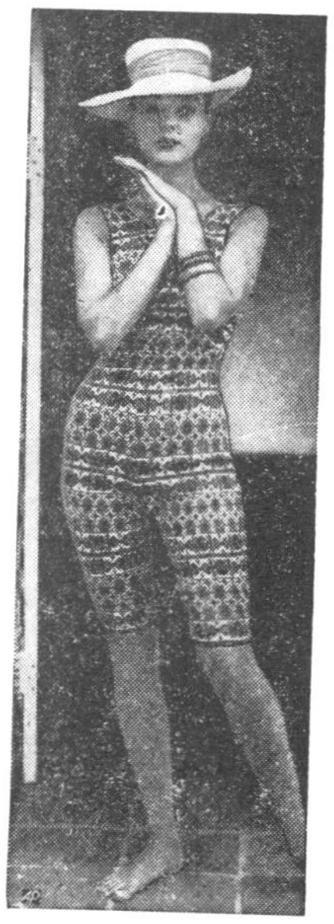

The French Look

French designer Hubert de Givenchy chooses a Corsican print for swim suits. Outfit at left has cap sleeves and print combined with elasticized cotton knit. Suit at right is long-legged, form-fitting sheath with high neck.

"Midas Touch" swimsuit is made of quick-drying taffeta lastex, with panels of golden lurex.

"Little Boy" swimsuit creation features a portrait neckline and cap sleeves.

WOMEN

FAMILY LIFE

Spanking Often Most Effective Punishment

By Garry Cleveland Myers, Ph.D.

Parents have been indoctrinated with the dictum, "Suit the punishment to the offense."

Dr. Myers

If a tot bites his playmates, for example, isolate him from them. If he breaks toys deliberately or through carelessness, take them away for awhile. Make sure he understands the relation between the punishment and the offense.

THIS THEORY reads well, but it often doesn't work. Usually, it's too slow and long-drawn out, too indecisive. The tot of two or five may fail to see what it's all about and find self-amusement while supposedly being punished.

Denied the companionship of children he has bitten, he loses the very thing he needs most — mingling with them, he has no chance to learn to play with them.

IN BOTH INSTANCES, he needs supervision to curb his aggressive ways. Be on hand to encourage him in wholesome fun with children and toys and to curb him effectively when he becomes aggressive or destructive. The moment he bites another child, spank or paddle him soundly.

Of course, if such an offense occurred in nursery school or kindergarten, requiring him to sit unamused away from the group for an appreciable period may work. At home, however, the situation is usually very different.

This also applies to the child who is careless or deliberately destructive with his toys. Restrain his too quick or too rough movements by gentle interception or positive suggestion.

SPEND LOTS OF TIME with him so that he will have fun using his playthings carefully. If he ignores your warning, or deliberately harms his playthings right before your eyes, give him a sound spanking. But see that he gets lots of play practice with toys.

Don't worry about making him understand the relation between his wrong act and the punishment for it. Just be sure he understands that doing what he knows he shouldn't is followed as soon as possible with quick, decisive discomfort.

AS YOU KNOW very well, he will tend to avoid doing what is sure to bring him immediate pain and to do only what promises pleasure.

(My bulletins, "Your Child and His Playmates" and "To Spank or Not To Spank," may be had by sending a self-addressed, U.S. stamped envelope to me in care of The New Era.)

Prayer Leaflets Are Distributed By Church Women

United Church Women of Lancaster will provide prayer leaflets and schedules of services for World Day of Prayer, to be observed Friday, to local persons unable to attend the services at Bethany Presbyterian and St. Paul's Evangelical and Reformed Churches.

The call to prayer leaflets, prepared to aid persons in conducting services in homes and institutions, will be distributed by a committee headed by Mrs. Harold Quickel and Mrs. B. H. Hogentogler.

The leaflets will be placed on trays in the Lancaster General Hospital, the Lancaster Osteopathic Hospital, Rossmere Sanatorium and the Lancaster County Prison.

In addition, three groups of women will conduct services Thursday; the day before the world-wide observance, at six homes: Town House Convalescent Home, Long Home, Diffenbach Home, Ann C. Witmer Home, Lancaster County Home and the Lutheran Home.

The committees include Mrs. Quickel, Mrs. Ralph Laushey and Mrs. William A. Bachman; Mrs. Leon Klaus, Mrs. Harold Pieffer and Mrs. Harry Hart; and Mrs. John Byers, Miss Bertha Hart and Mrs. Herbert Hubbell.

Braille programs of the service have been secured for the local Blind Association. Melvin Huber will be in charge of the blind observance.

100 Prospective Nurses Entertained

The Auxiliary to the staff of the Lancaster Osteopathic Hospital entertained approximately 100 junior and senior high school girls, interested in nursing careers, their parents, guidance counselors and school nurses, at a tea yesterday at the hospital.

Dr. Harold Finkel explained the scholarship awards, given by the hospital board of directors and staff for three years' training at the Philadelphia Osteopathic Hospital. The guests were taken on tours of the hospital by members of the staff.

Plan Jam Sessions For Jr High Pupils

A jam session will be featured at the regular "every-other-Monday" Y-R Hop for junior high school pupils beginning today at 6:30 p.m. in the Young Republican Club headquarters, 7 N. Duke St.

The Y-R Hops are sponsored by the Young Republicans of Lancaster. A brief meeting will be held to discuss future events.

Mr. and Mrs. Chester Weaver, Mrs. Gloria Werle and officials of the Young Republican Club will be chaperons. Special dances will be held and prizes awarded. Refreshments will be served.

ON DEAN'S LIST

Shirley A. Cashman, 140 College Ave., and Charles F. Eshleman, 722 Second St., both seniors at Gettysburg College, have been named to the Dean's List for the first semester.

AMY VANDERBILT

Cross Should Not Be Worn As Decoration

The cross is a symbol of Christian faith.

I do not like to see it cheapened by having it made into ordinary costume jewelry.

The cross should not be worn to decorate anything.

"DEAR MISS VANDERBILT: Is it improper for a Latter Day Saint to wear a cross around her neck?—M. G., Castledale, Utah."

No, the Mormons, who do not follow Christ, do not wear a cross.

Incidentally, it is poor taste for non-Christians to wear the cross as a mere decoration, just as it would be sensitive to Jews if Christians wore mezuzahs as mere good-luck charms.

Will Show Film

The Lancaster WCTU will show the film, "Far From Alone" at a public meeting Thursday at 2 p.m. in First Methodist Church, 300 N. Duke St.

FAVORITE

540

by Laura Wheeler

Your favorite pineapple design in a lovely oval doily, with a wide border of pineapples too! Easy, interesting crochet — handwork you'll be proud to display!

Pattern 540: Crochet directions for oval doily 16x27 inches, round doily 14 inches in No. 30 cotton.

Send TWENTY-FIVE CENTS in coins for each pattern — add 5 cents for each pattern for 1st-class mailing. Send to Lancaster New Era, 72 Needlecraft Dept., P. O. Box 161, Old Chelsea Station, New York 11, N. Y. Print plainly PATTERN NUMBER, your NAME, ADDRESS and ZONE.

Our gift to you—two wonderful patterns for yourself, your home—printed in our Laura Wheeler Needlecraft Book . . Plus dozens of other new designs to order—crochet, knitting, embroidery, iron-ons, novelties. Send 25 cents for your copy of this book NOW—with gift patterns printed in it!

Youth Council Plans Dinner

The Lancaster City Christian Youth Council will sponsor a Youth Night program May 3 in the YMCA, with the Rev. Richard H. Adams, president of the Lancaster Ministerial Association, as speaker.

Dinner at 6:30 p. m. will be followed by slides, "The Story of the United Churches." The Rev. Mr. Adams will speak at 8 p. m.

Women Baked All Night, Sold 6,000 Fasnachts

The women of St. Mary's Catholic Church sold 500 dozen fasnachts yesterday after the Masses, and had requests for several hundred dozen more.

The women baked all Saturday night, with the assistance of some men of the parish.

Proceeds will be used for general parish purposes. The sale was substituted for the annual parish supper, which could not be held because of renovations at the church.

ENGAGED

SMITH — FOULK

Mr. and Mrs. Clem R. Foulk, Paradise R1, announce the engagement of their daughter, Jeanne E. Foulk, to Ronald J. Smith, 632 East End Ave., son of Woodrow F. Smith, Renovo, and Mrs. Eileen Drumater, Covington, Pa.

Miss Foulk, a graduate of Paradise High School, is employed at The Willows. Mr. Smith attended Renovo High School and served in the U. S. Marine Corps. He is employed by Easthome Furniture Industries, Lancaster.

MULL—SMOKER

Mr. and Mrs. George Smoker, 717 Second St., announce the engagement of their daughter, Elizabeth C. Smoker, to A-2c Ronald E. Mull, son of Mr. and Mrs. Paul Mull, 435 N. George St., Millersville.

Miss Smoker is employed at Bell Telephone Co. Her fiance, who served two years in Tokyo, Japan, is stationed at Dover Air Force Base, Dover, Del.

ANDREWS—ERISMAN

The engagement of Miss Laberta Rae Erisman, daughter of Mr. and Mrs. Raymond G. Erisman, 533 S. Prince St., to Clifford J. Andrews, son of Mr. and Mrs. John Andrews, Lititz R3, has been announced by her parents.

Miss Erisman is a secretary for David F. Chambers Jr., attorney. Her fiance, who served four years in the Navy, is employed by DeWalt Inc.

BLOOM—ESHLEMAN

The engagement of Miss Miriam Eshleman, daughter of Mr. and Mrs. Jay Eshleman, Quarryville, to Richard L. Bloom, son of Mr. and Mrs. William L. Bloom, St. Petersburg, Fla., has been announced by her parents.

Miss Eshleman is a senior at Lancaster General Hospital School of Nursing. Her fiance teaches at Southern Lancaster County Area High School.

BARBARA E. ESHLEMAN

Miss Eshleman Is Engaged

Mr. and Mrs. David H. Shopf, 48 S. Duke St., announce the engagement of the latter's daughter, Barbara Elaine Eshleman, to J. Frederick Rieker III, son of Mr. and Mrs. Jacob F. Rieker, 37 E. Vine St.

Both are graduates of McCaskey High School. The bride-elect is a secretary for Knights Life Insurance Co. of America. Mr. Rieker is associated with his father in the wholesale meat business. He served three years in the U. S. Coast Guard.

A late August wedding is planned.

64 at USO Program

Sixty-four servicemen attended the Lancaster USO Center in the Malta Temple yesterday. The inter-faith program was directed by First Methodist Church. Mrs. Lester Flawd was chairman.

THESE WOMEN — By d'Alessia

"No, the job wouldn't DARE disagree with her . . . She didn't agree with IT!"

4-H Clubs Work For Community Betterment

Production Of Red Meat Set New Peak In '56

HARRISBURG — Red meat production in commercial slaughtering plants of Pennsylvania last year reached the highest of record since compilation of annual reports was started in 1948, the State Department of Agriculture announced following Federal-State surveys.

"Learn By Doing" Is 4-H Club Slogan

By Victor Plastow, Asst. County Agent

The 4-H Clubs are groups of young people, chiefly in rural and suburban areas, who carry on a wide variety of farming, homemaking, community service, and other projects.

They raise livestock and poultry, grow gardens and field crops, conserve the soil, sew, cook, preserve food, make things for the homes, and work for community betterment.

Any boy or girl between 10 and 21 years of age may join by agreeing to follow 4-H ideals and standards. The main requirement is a willingness to "learn by doing," which is the club motto. Character development and good citizenship are long range goals.

By 1956 there were about 90,000 4-H Clubs with more than 2,156,000 members in all 48 states, Alaska, Hawaii, and Puerto Rico. In the past half century, 4-H has helped to develop nearly 20,000,000 young citizens who have participated in its program.

The 4-H program is a part of the national education system of cooperative extension work, which the United States Dept. of Agriculture, the State land-grant colleges, and the counties share. The Federal Extension Service, United States Dept. of Agriculture, Washington, D. C., gives national leadership and the state extension services give state leadership to the program.

Two important groups helping to further the program are the National Committee on Boys and Girls Club Work, 59 East Van-Buren St., Chicago 5, Ill., and the National 4-H Club Foundation, Silver Spring, Md.

EDUCATIONAL OBJECTIVES

The term "4-H" refers to "head," "heart," "hands," and "health," which are emphasized in the club program, and which imply these educational objectives of members:

HEAD — To learn the value of science through applying the latest scientific knowledge to farming and homemaking projects.

HEART — To develop wholesome character and personality and the qualities of good citizenship, often through working together.

HANDS — To acquire useful skills in farming, homemaking, mechanics, and vocational trades.

HEALTH — To cultivate good health habits which lead to satisfying, happy living.

GUIDEPOSTS FOR 4-H'ERS

Ten guideposts are used by cooperative extension workers and volunteer leaders to aid 4-H members in analyzing their situations, needs, and interests. These point the way to building programs that will prepare the young people for better living physically, mentally, and spiritually:

1. Develop talents for greater usefulness.
2. Join with friends for work, fun, and fellowship.
3. Learn to live in a changing world.
4. Choose a way to earn a living.
5. Produce food and fiber for home and market.
6. Create better homes for better living.
7. Conserve natures resources for security and happiness.
8. Build health for a strong America.
9. Share responsibilities for community improvement.
10. Serve as citizens in maintaining world peace.

As in the democracy in which they live, 4-H'ers themselves largely run their clubs, elect their officers, help plan and hold their meetings, and select their projects. Each club drafts its own programs to suit its members and the localities in which they live.

Miss Joan Paes, Strasburg, R1, holds the champion Ayrshire female at the Southeast District Dairy Show held this past August. Miss Paes was on the State Dairy Judging Champion team also and had the highest over-all dairy score in the Lancaster County Ayrshire Club for 1956.

New Mexico's Palace of the Governors at Santa Fe, built in 1610, is the oldest government building in the United States.

In Short Hills, N. J., there is a charitable organization known as New Eyes for the Needy, Inc., which gathers discarded eyeglasses, old and silver frames, etc., to make new eyeglasses for needy people in this country and in medical missions abroad. New Eyes for the Needy is a volunteer, nonprofit group.

ATA Promising As Cure For Canada Thistle

Canada thistle, long one of the hardiest and most troublesome weed pests, is giving ground to a new and unusual chemical.

Application of amino triazole (ATA) to thistle foliage has given excellent control in recent trials by agronomists in Ohio, Indiana, Illinois and Oregon.

For as long as they can remember, farmers in many northern states have had no doubts as to the weed they consider the worst. Canada thistle has won their vote by a large majority. In fact, 43 states have declared the weed noxious.

The best answer is a "one-shot" treatment. Now, ATA may fill the bill.

Sprayed on thistles without cultivation, ATA will usually kill the tops, and if the tops are not killed, later growth is white — that is, without chlorophyll — for some time. If the tops are killed, sometimes the first sprouts from the roots come up with white leaves. Without chlorophyll, the plant soon dies.

HIT WHILE THEY'RE DOWN

Although weed specialists have had some hopeful results with the new chemical, they still aren't able to depend on a single applicaton to kill Canada thistle. A technique which has been both effective and economical with many herbicides is to "hit 'em while they're down," to plow or cultivate the weeds while they are weakened by an application of herbicide.

In Ohio this was tried with ATA on thistles, letting the weeds get a reasonable start — about 6 inches high — then spraying and waiting for at least 2 and preferably 3 weeks before plowing the weeds under. This controlled about 95 per cent of the thistles, permitting the growing of a practically clean corn crop following the late plowing. Results have been similar in Indiana and Illinois.

. . . Reprinted in part from "What's New In Crops & Soils."

Local authorities report that ATA is giving excellent control when used on poison ivy and poison oak — and there's no drift hazard.

HERE COMES PETER COTTON-TAIL, not hopping down the bunny trail, but nestling in the cellophane straw forming the base of an Easter nest bonnet worn by Mrs. Wallace Bucher, at left.

TRIO OF TRUMPED-UP TOPPERS is modeled here by (l-r) Mrs. Lloyd Ulrich, Mrs. Richard Powl and Mrs. Albert J. Long. Mrs. Ulrich, typically feminine, couldn't decide between two hats and wore both. Spring posies in profusion dot Mrs. Long's chapeau, and colored Easter eggs gained first prize for the prettiest hat for Mrs. Long.

EASTER Charade

Easter bonnets that owe nothing to New York or Parisian inspiration are being whipped up by Lancaster women's clubs as the annual springtime millinery euphoria spreads across the land. Needle and thread are least necessary in the operation. All designs depend on the originator's feeling for realism or access to a double-handful of anything lying around. These prize-winners were presented to many an "o-oh and a-ah and for-goodness-sakes" at a hat social by the Mothers Club at Sacred Heart parochial school.

CHICKEN-IN-THE BASKET is the title of the chapeau at right designed by Mrs. Richard Schulz. Two live chicks contained in a plastic humidifier won first place in the "most original" class.

WHIRLWIND IN A POPPY PATCH aptly describes the melange which Mrs. Clarence Mathiot titled, "Ecstasy." This brazen bonnet won Mrs. Mathiot first prize in the funniest hat division.

Come Rain Or Come Shine Trailer Built By Quarryville Sportsman Fills The Bill

By RED BRICKER

Any angler forced to leave a good site just when the fish are starting to bite to find living accommodations for the night, or to hurry home, can appreciate Paul W. Smith's new sportsmen's trailer design.

The Quarryville angler found himself in this situation too many times, especially on trips to Canada, so he sat down one night and started figuring out a new type of vacation travel kit.

He started with a regular trailer carriage and took it from there. His first thought was to design something that would include both boating and hunting facilities.

So the boat design came first and from his thoughts came the first "Kingfisher" the name he has bestowed on his trailer-boat unit.

The boat is a 14-foot aluminum craft and Smitty first worked out a system of installation on the roof of a trailer. Then he devised a means of getting his 175-pound boat to that roof-top rest.

His finished masterpiece includes a metal roller, mounted at the rear end of the roof over which the boat slides. A ladder gives him easy access to his boat-house and with a little experience two persons can easily roll the 14-foot boat on or off the roof.

Then, since no fisherman with a boat would be caught dead without a motor, he figured in a storage well for that important item in the rear end of the trailer.

IDEAL FOR TRIPS

And with this he had his problem solved. Now he has a compact home on wheels and a boat right with him at all times. He can take those trips to Canada, or to Fishing Creek which happens to be another favorite spot for the Quarryville angler, and he's ready for action.

Now he can just drive the trailer close to the water, remove the boat from the roof and he's ready for fishing.

If things are going well, and the fish are biting, he can hold his spot because home is just a few feet off shore — and he'll have all the comforts he needs.

For his interior, Smitty followed standard trailer designs but he laid them out to suit the fisherman. There's a comfortable bed aft with locker space below and a bed light for the angler who wants to read up or new ways or catching his prey.

And, if there's a lady along, and invariably they insist on plenty of clothing for all occasions, there is a large closet to accommodate a lot of wearing apparel.

For that same lady, if she wishes to take care of the cooking, Smitty has a compact unit. Butane gas supplies him with a heat source for a four-burner range and for a space heater — a welcome addition most nights along the waterfront.

And the butane gas also gives him illumination for the trailer if electricity is not available. If there are electrical outlets nearby the trailer is wired for use.

A sink, with cabinet space underneath, and an ice chest completes the cook shack. Water is supplied from a 32-gallon tank and a pump at the sink allows easy access to the water supply.

Built-in cabinets over the sink and range allow storage space for the dishes and other necessary utensils.

In the other end of the trailer is a dinette which converts into bunk space for two more anglers.

The entire interior of the first "Kingfisher is fir paneled. The inside dimensions are 16 feet by eight feet with a good six-six head room.

"I've been fishing 30 years, with about three trips to Canada a year," Smitty said. "That got me thinking about the idea. There are so many lakes where there is good fishing but no living accomodations and I started working out the complete vacation unit.

"I'm considering a few improvements," he added. "I could use this butane gas for a gas refrigerator. I think that might be better than an ice chest and a winch on the roof might make raising and lowering the boat an even easier project."

Smitty would have liked to find a closer building point but he had to send his designs to Baltimore for final development.

PATENT APPLIED FOR

However he sent those same designs to the U. S. Patent Office and his patent is applied for and under examination.

"I'm going to put the thing on the open market," Smitty added. "I'd like to find some dealer willing to take the franchise for this area and then we can start working out the price."

But right now Smitty is far more interested in getting some personal pleasure out of his new design. The trip to Canada isn't planned until late July but Fishing Creek just might draw the Smiths and their Kingfisher on the maiden run.

Paul W. Smith, Quarryville Sportsman turned designer demonstrates his idea for fishing comfort — a trailer AND a boat. Smith is showing how the boat is removed from its rack atop the trailer. The stern of the boat is resting on a steel roller which makes the job an easy one for two people. Built into the rear of the trailer, the door of the compartment to house the motor is open giving the assistant a platform to stand on while helping remove or replace the boat. A ladder at right gives the bow man easy access to the roof and a reinforced platform guarantees him steady footing. That boat is a 14-foot aluminum job and is strapped in place for hauling. (Intell Sports Photo)

MASON-DIXON TRACK DRAWS LOCAL LADS

Four drivers from Lancaster are slated to compete in the races at the Mason - Dixon Speedway, located near Oxford, tomorrow at 2 p.m.

This will be the second racing card for the new season. The Lancaster quartet is Walt Ragan, last week's winner, Jack Raezer, Bobby Cain and Joe Davis.

Tomorrow's program consists of three heat trials, a consolation event and the 35-lap feature.

BROWNS ASK WAIVERS ON GEO. RATTERMAN

CLEVELAND, April 12 (AP)—The Cleveland Browns of the National Football League today asked waivers on veteran quarterback George Ratterman, who was out with a leg injury most of last season.

The 30-year-old former Notre Dame star put in three seasons with the Buffalo Bills and two with the New York Yanks before joining the Browns in 1952. He was understudy for Otto Graham until Graham's retirement at the end of the 1955 season. Then the leg injury prevented him from taking over the quarterback assignment.

Coach Phil Brown said he didn't think Ratterman could make the team next year, and he asked for waivers "so George will have every opportunity to make a new connection."

Celtics Shook By Team Friction

BOSTON, April 12 (AP)—Squad friction, complaints about the officials and another outburst by Coach Red Auerbach shook the favored Boston Celtics today as they girded for their deciding National Basketball Assn. playoff game with the relaxed St. Louis Hawks.

Tied at three games apiece, the teams will meet for the world championship of pro basketball tomorrow afternoon (2:30 P. M., EST) in the seventh and final contest at Boston Garden.

The game will not be televised.

St. Louis recoiled from the brink of elimination last night to square the series when Cliff Hagan tipped in a missed shot by teammate Bob Pettit as the game ended. The score was 96-94.

That Hagan shot was a sore point on the Boston squad in the wake of the defeat.

"Nobody blocked Hagan out on the rebound after Pettit's shot," said Hagan's old Kentucky teammate, Frank Ramsey, who was on the Boston bench at the time. "The last thing we said was to be sure and block out everyone, but Hagan wasn't blocked," Ramsey said.

Rookie Tom Heinsohn was the Celtic assigned to cover Hagan.

"I was trying to help (Jim) Loscutoff cover Pettit," Heinsohn said. "Pettit got by Loscutoff and I ran over to help out."

"Loscutoff had Pettit covered," Ramsey countered. "Hagan should have been blocked out."

Block Shoot Today

The Southern Lancaster County Farmer - Sportsmen's Association will hold a block shooting match for hams today on the organization's grounds, starting from the scout house. The shoot will begin at 1 p.m., weather permitting.

Beck Profited From Fund for Friend's Widow

Today's Chuckle

The fellow told his boss he was entitled to a day off with pay. . . to make up for the coffee breaks he missed while he was on vacation.

LANCASTER NEW ERA

Metropolitan Lancaster Population 1954 (Est.) Penna. Dept. of Commerce 248,296

Local Weather

Lancaster U. S. Bureau

Partly cloudy with chance of scattered thundershower tonight; tomorrow partly cloudy with chance of scattered thundershowers; low tonight about 58; high tomorrow near 80.

Complete Report on Page 3

81st Year—No. 24,799 | CITY EDITION | LANCASTER, PA., FRIDAY, MAY 10, 1957 | 24 PAGES | 42c PER WEEK—7c Per Copy

ProbeTold Beck Split $11,585 With Banker

Also Hear Testimony He Pocketed Fees from Teamsters Investments

WASHINGTON (AP)—Senate Rackest investigators developed testimony today that Teamsters Boss Dave Beck and a mortgage banker split $11,585 derived from handling a fund raised by unions for the widow of Beck's "best and closest friend."

The Seattle mortgage banker, Donald Hedlund, said Beck handled the transaction for Mrs. Ray Leheney, widow of the man Hedlund said was Beck's best friend.

It was testified Beck handled the deal as trustee for "the Ray Leheney Memorial Fund," about $80,000 which had been collected from unions after Leheney's death. Leheney formerly was head of the union label department of the American Federation of Labor.

Hedlund's story was related to the Senate rackets investigating committee under questioning.

Got Brokerage Fee Share

It capped earlier testimony that Beck collected a one-third share

AP Wirephoto

DONALD HEDLUND
Tells of Beck Profits

of something over $20,000 in brokerage fees on the investment of union funds in the mortgage market.

Sen. McClellan (D-Ark), chairman of the committee, spoke of the payments to Beck as a "kickback."

There was testimony from Hedlund too of substantial profits to Beck from joint purchases of land later resold to a company in which Hedlund was interested.

But the banker denied the land deals were a "payoff," as suggested by committee counsel, for Beck's investing union funds through Hedlund's companies.

Fees Totaled $58,959

In a later summary of the testimony, committee counsel said it showed Beck received a share on profits or fees totalling $58,959.91 on mortgage purchases and sales, and the real estate deals.

Newsmen were told there was a violation of the law regulating trusteeship laws in collection of brokerage fees by Beck in connection with the investment of Teamster Union funds.

Hedlund testified that he, Beck, and teamsters union lawyer Si-

—See BECK—Page 5

Bulletin

16 Rescued in Navy Plane Crash

OAKLAND, Calif. (AP)—Sixteen Navy men aboard a huge Trade Wind flying boat were rescued today within a few minutes after the plane flopped into San Francisco Bay. All aboard were accounted for.

The flying boat, a successor to the famed Mars type plane, had just left Alameda Naval Air Station on a training flight. A witness said the 2 million dollar craft "flopped like a bird" as it fell into the shallow water.

'Solid South' Is Dead, Ike Tells GOP in Dixie

Urges Party Drive to Recapture Congress in Next Year's Elections

WASHINGTON (AP) — President Eisenhower said today there no longer is a "Solid South" controlled by the Democrats. He urged Dixie Republicans to launch a political offensive in the party's drive to recapture control of Congress next year.

Eisenhower said there have been "impressive increases" in GOP strength in the South during the last 20 years.

"The Republican party is, of course, in the South to stay," he said.

Telephones Message

Eisenhower sounded his call for renewed Republican activity in Dixie in a telephoned message to party workers attending a regional GOP rally at Louisville, Ky. Representatives from a dozen states were on hand for the session, the fourth of a series of such rallies being held around the country.

In the talk, Eisenhower also spoke out once more in defense of the administration's $71,800,000,000 spending budget.

"This budget is a budget for peace—for the defense of our nation and the free world," he said.

'Needed To Keep U.S. Safe'

Eisenhower added that the money he has requested from an economy-minded Congress is the amount required to keep our nation safe in the world."

On the political front, Eisenhower spoke first of "impressive increases" in GOP Dixie strength, and then said:

"There is no longer a 'Solid South' controlled by one political party.

"It's difficult to believe that in 1940 our party polled only 20 per cent of the vote in the Southern States in a presidential election. Since that time, each succeeding national election has seen an improvement in this ratio, and last year the Republican national ticket received 48 per cent of the votes in these 12 Southern States, and polled over 50 per cent in six of them.

"That is good news."

Eisenhower said, however, that "unfortunately we did not have candidates in 65 of the 114 congressional districts" in the 12 Southern and border states last year.

4 New City Grade Schools Proposed, Also Junior High In Buchanan Park

New Era Photo

Haupt School, Lime and Lemon Sts., built in 1880, oldest city school and one of the 11 which would be eliminated if city school board adopts plan for doing the "whole job" to revamp the system.

Dr. Aurand Also Would Abandon 11 'Oldest Schools'

Five new schools should be built to meet the fast growing educational needs of Lancaster, Dr. O. H. Aurand, city superintendent, said today.

Dr. Aurand proposed a plan which he said would meet elementary school needs for 50 years.

If the school board wants to do the "whole job" of modernizing the system, he said, the cost would not run beyond $8,000,000, which falls within the present borrowing capacity.

Drastic Realignment Urged

He urged drastic realignment, some of it at once, to meet problems causing by steady growth in school population, crowding, outmoded school buildings, and recent population shifts within the city.

Dr. Aurand's plan, and possible alternatives, were outlined in a special report to members of the school board.

To do the "whole job", his plan calls for:

Four new elementary schools, one in each quarter of the city, costing an estimated $5,400,000.

Retention of the three newest present elementary buildings, Washington, Lafayette and Wickersham, and elimination of all the other 11, most of which are over 50 years old.

Discarding Reynolds Junior High School's present site and building a new junior high, probably in Buchanan Park; and improvement of Hand Junior High.

That would sum up the "whole job." If the board were to decide against this approach, Dr. Aurand made other suggestions which would combine new construction with improvement of existing properties.

But, said Dr. Aurand, no matter what else is done or not done, steps must be taken at once to alleviate crowding in the southeastern quarter, served by Washington, and the southwestern, served by Lafayette. This should be done, he said, by adding new buildings.

"Need for a building in the Washington area is immediate," he asserted. "At Lafayette, it is not more than another year away."

If the four new elementary schools were erected, one for each quarter of the city, the building serving the northeast would be in the Wickersham area, and that for the northwest would be at a location not pinpointed in the report. The other two would be in the Washington and Lafayette areas.

Short-Term Solution

If the northeast and northwest do not receive new elementary schools, Dr. Aurand said, a short-term solution might be obtained by expansion of Ross and Wickersham buildings for the northeast, and modernization of Stevens and Fulton for the northwest.

Building the two new schools for the Washington and Lafayette areas, and modernizing others in the remaining two sectors, would eliminate all schools erected prior to the turn of the century. About 2,400 pupils would be relocated through this alternate.

The four elementary schools recommended under the "whole job" program would each eventually be able to house 1,000 pupils.

Schools To Be Abandoned

Old schools which would be abandoned under the "whole job" proposal, and the dates of their building, are:

Haupt, 1880; Eichholtz, 1888; Henry, 1888; Buehrle, 1895; Mifflin, 1895; Reigart, 1895; Wharton, 1895; Higbee, 1902; Stevens, 1904; Fulton, 1918; Ross, 1924.

Dates of erection of the other schools show the city has built three new elementary schools in

—See FOUR NEW—Page 2

Pa. Crackdown On Teen Drivers

State Police Drive Opens Tomorrow

HARRISBURG (AP) — State police tomorrow will begin a campaign to correct some of the driving habits of teen age motorists.

Col. Earl J. Henry, state police commission, said he ordered the "crackdown" with the endorsement of Gov. Leader.

"I feel it is proper that this stepped up effort should begin this Mothers' Day weekend," Leader said. "We want to do everything in our power to eliminate these family tragedies."

He called for "installing in some of our teen age drivers the sober realization of how much responsibility lies in their hands," Leader added.

Henry said patrols have been ordered to "regulate and control all careless operating actions of teen agers."

Capt. John Pezzent, Troop B commander here, said local troopers will "cooperate 100 per cent" in the statewide "crackdown on teen age violators."

British Labor Party Win 12 Town Councils

LONDON (AP)—Britain's socialist labor party had a clear-cut victory today in municipal elections in England and Wales.

The Laborites wrested control of 12 town councils from the Conservatives in the voting yesterday to give them their strongest grip ever on local governments. Socialists gained a net of 202 council sets in the 400 boroughs where elections were held yesterday.

Free Salk Shot For All Planned Here

A communitywide mass Salk vaccine inoculation, to provide one free anti-polio shot to any person desiring it, is planned here for next week.

Pending definite word on availability of vaccine, the program is now set up for next Thursday, Friday and Saturday.

The vaccine is to be made available by the Lancaster County Chapter, National Polio Foundation. The shots will be administered at a number of locations the public can visit.

Osteopathic Program

Osteopathic Hospital completed arrangements yesterday for having osteopathic physicians administer inoculations at the hospital and at Trinity Lutheran Church, between 9 a. m. and 6 p. m. Thursday through Saturday.

The Lancaster City and County Medical Society was in the process of working out its plans today. The Medical Society members expect to provide the shots at clinics to be set up at the city and county hospitals.

While vaccine has been provided free in programs for school children, this is the first time free inoculations are being set up for adults.

Polio Foundation officials said they hope to have word by Monday at the latest on whether the vaccine will be released on time for the start of the program Thursday.

Under the plan, any person who wishes to obtain one free Salk shot can do so through this program, whether it be his first, second or third. In most cases, it would be the first.

Record Of Date

Each person getting an inoculation will be given a slip stating the date the shot was provided. For most effective results, three inoculations, properly spaced as to time, are recommended.

The State Board of Health will furnish the needles and syringes needed for the inoculations.

South 'By-Pass' Opens Friday

Will Link Ann And S. Queen Sts.

A new half mile stretch of street designed to drain some traffic from the central section of the city will be opened next Friday morning.

The new street, a section of Chesapeake St. from S. Queen to Ann St. will form a type of downtown "by-pass."

Commissioner Daniel S. Templeton Sr., head of the Department of Streets, said there will be a ribbon-cutting ceremony at 10 a.m. after which the first automobile will be permitted to use the new street.

Traffic coming from the south will be able to leave S. Queen St. at Chesapeake St., go east across Duke St. to Ann and then turn north to the Lincoln highway, where it can go east. East bound traffic coming from the south must now go through the congested central section.

Street 25 Ft. Wide

The new street is 25 feet wide but is so designed that it may be widened in the future with little cost, officials said.

"We believe this new street is a partial answer to handling through traffic which originates from the south," Commissioner Templeton said.

The commissioner said the new street also provides a "short cut" for RCA employes who reside in the southern section of the city.

BE FRIENDS OF PEOPLE, POPE URGES POLICE

VATICAN CITY (AP) — Pope Pius XII today urged police "to extend a helping hand" and serve as "friends of citizens rather than enforcers of law."

He gave that advice to several hundred Rome policemen in an audience in the Vatican's Benediction Hall.

Praising their work, the Pope called the police the "eye, ear and heart of the city." He said they must above all "be courteous" and provide an example of Christian charity.

Employment Up 400,000 in April

WASHINGTON (AP) — The government said today the over-all job situation showed further seasonal improvement in April and total civilian employment reached 64,261,000.

This is a gain of about 400,000 for the month, about normal for this time of year when there is an increase in outdoor work.

Total unemployment dropped by 200,000 to a total of 2,690,000. The total civilian labor force during April was set at 66,951,000.

Today's New Era

Phone Lancaster EX 7-5251

U.S. Sub Saves 10 from AF Raft

Navy Crew Ditched Burning Patrol Plane

HONOLULU (AP)—The submarine Bream rescued 10 men from a raft early today after their Navy P2V patrol plane ditched in the Pacific 170 miles southwest of here.

The downed crewmen were "all uninjured and in good condition," the submarine radioed.

The Navy said the plane, on routine operations from nearby Barbers Point, went down after an engine caught fire.

No Time To Signal

The Navy said the plane's crew had no time to send a distress signal before the ditching.

Rescue officials praised the pilot for a "spectacular job" in bringing the burning plane down safely, and the crew for getting onto the raft.

Two rescue planes circled the raft and dropped flares to guide the submarine to the spot.

Hunger Strike of Refugees Spreads

VIENNA (AP) — Hunger strikes among Hungarian refugees in Austria, protesting their inability to get visas for the United States, spread to Vienna today.

Refugees in a Vienna camp announced they had cut down on their eating. A partial strike in a camp for 2,400 refugees near Salzburg went into its fourth day.

The Intergovernmental Committee for European Migration said there are 34,488 Hungarian refugees in Austria out of a total of 171,259 who had fled here since last October. About 5,000 returned to Hungary.

GARDENS FEEL EFFECTS OF LACK OF RAIN

The long continued lack of rainfall is beginning to have a parching effect on gardens, vegetable plantings and pastures, County Agent M. M. Smith said today.

"While no drought conditions exist," Smith said, "the farmers do need rain." U. S. Weather Bureau records show the last rainfall of any size was less than a third of an inch, on April 28. May thus far has produced only a sprinkle of rain, while providing a lot of sunshine.

The federal forecast said there was the chance of a scattered thundershower tonight, and that chances were better for scattered thundershowers tomorrow. Temperatures zoomed to 84 at 1:30 p.m. today, equalling the high of yesterday.

Charlie Barnet Takes 10th Bride

HOLLYWOOD (AP) — Bandleader Charlie Barnet has married for the 10th time. "We are ideally happy and deeply in love," says his new bride, actress-singer Joy Windsor.

She says she met Barnet two weeks ago and started singing with his band.

220,970 YULE CARDS WON BY CALIF. WOMAN

LONG BEACH, Calif. (AP) — Mrs. Claude L. McFaddin has won a long legal battle and collected the prize — 220,970 Christmas cards.

A truck delivered the cards — nearly two tons of them — to her home yesterday, ending a dispute that began after she purchased them in January 1955 from a dump for $25.

California Artists, Inc., a division of the H. S. Crocker lithography firm of San Francisco, instituted repossession proceedings, claiming it had sent the cards to the dump to be destroyed, since they were obsolete. A court valued the cards at $8,000, but Mrs. McFaddin thinks they may bring up to $45,000.

COURT ORDERS

10 P.M. Curfew On Boy, 18, For 3 Yrs.

Ronald Edward Rowland, eighteen, 304 N. Franklin St., who was shot by a companion with a zip-gun in February, pleaded guilty to burglary and larceny charges in court today.

Judge Johnstone, after hearing details of the shooting as well as the burglary from Detective Frank Matt, placed Rowland on "strict" probation for three years.

Terms of the probation included that Rowland make full restitution, pay costs and "be home by 10 o'clock every night."

Stole Cash and Tools

Detective Matt testified that Rowland, on the night of April 3, entered the Hoyt Wire Cloth Co., 10 Abraso St., and stole approximately $20 in cash and tools valued at $10.

As to the shooting, Matt said, Rowland was wounded in the early morning of Feb. 23 by a so-called "zip" gun in the hands of a companion, Charles Cater, twenty-one, 356 Howard Ave.

Matt said police had several versions of the shooting and that Cater, who is awaiting trial on charges of pointing a deadly weapon and violating the firearms act, claimed it was accidental. Rowland, who underwent surgery at the General Hospital to have th bullet removed from his neck, will testify against Cater, Matt told the Court.

The detective added that Rowland was "keeping bad company" and "staying out late at night," which he blamed for Rowland's latest trouble.

HEAVY INFESTATION

Caterpillars Peril Trees

Damage caused by tent caterpillars may run far higher than usual this spring because warm and rainless weather has caused a heavy infestation, authorities warned today.

The number of trees showing the large webs of the caterpillars is considerably greater than usual in this entire area of the state.

Unless they are checked, the small brownish caterpillars with black stripes can wreak permanent and severe damage to trees, according to County Agent M. M. Smith. Entire large limbs which are covered by the webs can be killed, Smith warned.

DDT Best Treatment

Spraying with a form of DDT is the best method to kill the caterpillars, Smith said. If 50 per cent DDT wettable powder is used, it should be mixed two pounds to 100 gallons of water. One quart of 25 per cent DDT in liquid form can also be used to 100 gallons of water.

Orchard operators usually keep ahead of the caterpillars, Smith said, and spray early. But homeowners are not always as aware of the damage that might be caused by the webs.

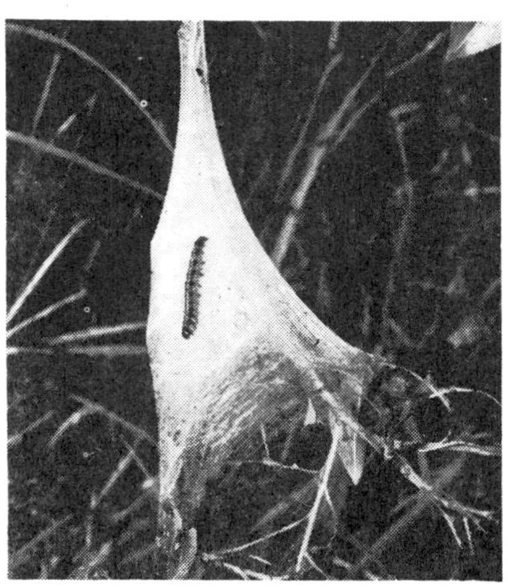

New Era Photo

Close-up of caterpillar "tent", with caterpillar at work.

AT QUENTIN SHOW—Eddie Keifer, 903 Landis Ave., Lancaster, is shown on his horse, "Chalk Talk" which he rode in the road hack class of the spring horse show which opened at the Quentin Riding Club last night. The show will be continued today. Eddie won 4th and 5th place ribbons at the Willow Street show in Lancaster county a few weeks ago and also took a second place ribbon recently at the Linglestown show. (Sunday News Photo)

Slash In Budget Would Slow Up Nike Defenses

WASHINGTON, May 18 (AP) — Congress has received word from the Army that an administration cut in budget requests will slow up completion of the Nike guided missle antiaircraft defense system by three or four years.

In closed door testimony made public today, Lt. Gen. Carter B. Magruder, deputy chief of staff for logistics, said the reduction of $1,600,000,000 in total funds sought by the Army would delay installation of universal ground control equipment at its 250 Nike batteries surrounding major cities and defense posts.

Cut To 40 Percent

Magruder appeared before a House appropriations subcommittee last month. He said the Army will now be limited to installing the equipment at only 40 per cent of its Nike units by mid-1960, instead of 60 per cent as first planned.

He said the goal of equipping all Nike battalions would be delayed three or four years. Gen. Magruder said the universal ground control equipment can handle both types of Nike missiles the Ajax and the Hercules.

Lt. Gen. James M. Gavin, chief of research and development, told the same House group there is a defense against Intercontinental Ballistic Missiles and the nation must get on with devising it.

"One of the most significant things . . . is that defense against a surface-to-surface missile, including the ICBM, is entirely feasible," Gavin said, adding:

It's Not Asolute

"One reads all the time about this weapon being an absolute weapon. We know that it is not at all. There is a defense against it. We must get on with getting such a defense for our country."

Along the same line, Maj. Gen. John P. Daley, director of special weapons in the Research and Development Office, said the Army believes development of surface-to-air missiles capable of destroying intercontinental weapons is entirely feasible.

ON RECORD

BIRTHS

Mr. and Mrs. Valentino Ruse, Stevens, a daughter, at 9:38 a. m. yesterday, at Ephrata Community Hospital.

Mr. and Mrs. Paul E. Shupp, 422 Washington Ave., Ephrata, a son, at Ephrata Community Hospital.

Mr. and Mrs. Daniel W. Mentzer, 330 N. Mulberry St., a son, at 3:30 p.m. yesterday, in Lancaster General Hospital.

Mr. and Mrs. Ralph M. Snyder, Mount Joy R2, a son, at 2:33 p.m. yesterday, in Lancaster General Hospital.

Mr. and Mrs. Lyndell M. Breault, 919½ N. Prince St., a son, at 11:43 a.m. yesterday, in Lancaster General Hospital.

Mr. and Mrs. Theodore Murr, Willow Street, a son, yesterday at 3:08 p.m., in St. Joseph's Hospital.

Mr. and Mrs. Eugene Ruf, 426 W. Lemon St., a daughter, at 11:44 a.m. yesterday, in St. Joseph's Hospital.

Lt. and Mrs. Peter Charles Aleexih, Bermuda, a daughter, May 12, in a Bermuda hospital. Mrs. Aleexih is the former Sally Ann Herr, Lancaster R2.

Mr. and Mrs. William R. Aller, Park House, Elizabethtown, a daughter, at 9:26 a.m. yesterday, in Lancaster Osteopathic Hospital.

Dr. and Mrs. Jay Adams, Columbus, Ohio, a son, Friday, in Columbus Osteopathic Hospital. Mrs. Adams is the former Joann Forney, daughter of Mr. and Mrs. Charles Forney, Lancaster R3.

Mr. and Mrs. William Chubb, 37 N. Market St., Elizabethtown, a daughter, at 8:21 a.m. yesterday, in Lancaster General Hospital.

Mr. and Mrs. Edwin N. High, Ephrata R3, a daughter, at 4:39 a.m. yesterday, in Ephrata Community Hospital.

Mr. and Mrs. Sherman J. Leed, 110 E. Chestnut St., Ephrata, a son, at 6:05 a.m. yesterday, in Ephrata Community Hospital.

Mr. and Mrs. Kenneth G. Rineer, Conestoga R1, a daughter, at 6:51 a.m. yesterday, in Lancaster Osteopathic Hospital.

Mr. and Mrs. John G. Hoffecker, Paradise R1, a son, at 12:22 p.m. yesterday, in Lancaster General Hospital.

Mr. and Mrs. Leon Shenk, Lititz R3, a daughter, at 2:52 a.m. yesterday, in St. Joseph's Hospital.

Mr. and Mrs. Eugene Vitale, 650 E. Mifflin St., a son, at 6:04 a.m. yesterday, in St. Joseph's Hospital.

Mr. and Mrs. Robert A. Fridy, 21 S. Broad St., Lititz, a son, at 6:23 p. m. yesterday, at Lancaster General Hospital.

Mr. and Mrs. Mervin H. Bare, Witmer, a daughter, at 3:29 p. m. yesterday, at Lancaster General Hospital.

Mr. and Mrs. Elmer S. Stoltzfus, Elverson R2, a son at 10:24 p. m. yesterday, in Ephrata Community Hospital.

Mr. and Mrs. Donald E. Mullady, 536 W. King St., a daughter, yesterday, at 5:36 p. m., in Lancaster General Hospital.

Mr. and Mrs. Woodrow Stetler, 2045 Lincoln Highway East, a son, at 5:52 p. m., yesterday, in Lancaster General Hospital.

Mr. and Mrs. Paul M. Schaeffer, 1369 Pleasure Rd., a son, at 9 p. m. yesterday, in St. Joseph's Hospital.

100 Horses Open Show At Quentin

BY MARGARET L. SMITH

The Quentin Riding Club's annual Spring Show opened last night with an entry list of at least 100 horses, a goodly number for the Spring Show, which used to be just a one-day event.

Twelve classes were run off last night, with nineteen more scheduled for today, starting at 1 p.m.—the second and final day.

Outstanding early in the evening was the open jumping class in which Allan Garner, Denver, took two horses over the course without a single fault between them. They included Rudolph, given first place, and Calypso, both owned by R. B. Snyder, Denver. Calypso, a palomino, is the former Frosty Morning, formerly owned by Ralph S. Kurtz, Denver. None of the other eight horses in the class were able to negotiate the course without a fault.

Later in the evening Garner repeated his double win in the Knock Down and Out, this time placing Calypso first with a perfect performance, and Rudolph second.

Jean Ramsey, eleven, daughter of Mr. and Mrs. William Ramsey, Landisville, captured the children's horsemanship class for riders 12 years of age and under, with Queenelle Minet, Lancaster in second place. There was stiff competition in the class, in which fourteen excellent junior riders competed.

Miss Janet Hippey, of Will-O-Brand Stables, Willow Street, began what looked like a winning streak by getting the blue ribbon in the amateur three-gaited saddle horse class with Star Saphhire, then coming out later and winning first in the amateur five-gaited class with Don't Tell.

Clark Wins Again

Loren Clark, Lititz R3, whose hobby is collecting blue ribbons in horse shows, added another to his collection last night in the Western class, with a new horse named Elvis. There were 12 competitors in the class, and Clark's son, Jerry, the only child rider in the event, placed fourth with his buckskin pony, Little Buck.

The judges are Walter L. Graham, Devon, saddle horses, and John J. Burkholder, Lancaster, hunters and jumpers. Lloyd Gerhart, Ephrata, is ringmaster, and William A. Hockley, Lebanon, is steward. E. R. Worrell, Lebanon, is announcer.

Winners in ten of last night's 12 classes were as follows:

Class 1, Road Hack, saddle horse: 1, Sir Prize, owned and ridden by Phyllis Ann Zuber, Millersville; 2, Country Boy, Edward C. Fry, Harrisburg; 3, Skyline, Betsy Long, Lebanon; 4, Sonny, Leo Kiefer, Jack Kiefer, rider, Lancaster; 5, Alla Susie Q, Stevenson Bysher, Flourtown; 6, Dusty, Irvin Aumen, Annville.

Class 2, Children's Horsemanship, 12 years and under: 1, Jean Ramsey, Landisville, riding Little Man; 2, Queenelle Minet, Lancaster, riding Bingo; 3, Ruby Zemo, Middletown, riding The Medic; 4, Kathryn Williams, Annville, riding Candy Cane; 5, Michael Savastio, Hershey, riding Captain Midnight; 6, Linda Long, Annville, riding Toots.

Class 3, Amateur Three Gaited: 1, Star Saphhire, Will-O-Brand Stables, Willow Street, Janet Hippey rider; 2, Sunday Afternoon, Queenelle Minet, owner-rider; 3, Colonial Sensation, William E. Speer, Burnham; 4, Gleam O' Goshen, Miss Mary Jane Ward, owner-rider; 5, Brandy Glen, Jack Kiefer, owner-rider; 6, My Gifted Rhapsody, Carolyn Greenaward, York, owner-rider.

Class 4, Open Jumping: 1, Rudolph, R. B. Snyder, Denver, owner, Allan Garner, rider; 2, Calypso, Snyder, owner, Garner, rider; 3, Patsy, Irvin Aumon, Annville, owner, Andy Kreider, rider; 4, Boume, R. V. Rill, Baltimore, owner, Buddy Conrad, rider; 5, Boumi, Rill, owner, Conrad, rider; 6, Calispo, J. V. Savastio, Hershey, owner, Johnny Frye, rider.

Class 5, Roadster: 1, On Time, Eddie Herr, York, owner-driver; 2, District Attorney, J. Marlin Burkholder, Greencastle, owner-driver; 3, Martha's Way, H. A. Saylor, York, owner, Guy Barrick, driver; 4, Miss Lancaster, W. B. Jackson, Manheim R1, owner-driver; 5, Madame B. A., Eddie Herr, owner, Rodney Kitzmiller, driver; 6, Lady Esther, Eddie Herr, owner, Miss Suzanne Person, driver.

Class 6, Western: 1, Elvis, Loren Clark, Lititz R3, owner-rider; 2, Little Lady, Bobby Loch, Allentown, owner-rider; 3, Miss Abilene, Dick Myers, Lancaster, owner-rider; 4, Little Buck, Jerry Clark, owner-rider; 5, Poco Sandy, Dawnee Stables, Donald Metz, rider; 6, Skip, John L. Glick, Bareville, owner-rider.

Class 7, Amateur Walking Horse: 1, Midnight Storm, J. Marlin Burkholder, owner-rider; Go Boy's Onyx, Norman Eshelman, Mechanicsburg, owner-rider; 3, Greystone Marianne, Greystone Stables, York, George Livingston Jr., rider; 4, Go Boy Blue, Faith Ribbons, Haverford, owner-rider; 5, Midnight Sunrise, Richard Stumpf, owner-rider; 6, Go Boy's Topper, Mr. and Mrs. Lawrence Leonard.

Class 8, Amateur five gaited: 1, Don't Tell, Will-O-Brand Stables, Janet Hippey, rider; 2, Scotland's Little Man, Mary Jacobs, owner, Walter Jacobs, rider; 3, She's A Daisy, Mr. and Mrs. Stuart H. Raub, Lititz R3, owners; Stuart H. Raub III, rider; 4, Eddie's Noble Prince, Ralph B. Bongart Jr., Columbia, owner-rider; 6, Copper Penny, Daniel Bixler, Harrisburg, owner-rider; 6, Red Rhapsody, Carolyn Greenawalt, York, owner-rider.

Class 9, Fine Harness Pony: 1, Mighty Mouse, J. Marlin Burkholder, owner, Peggy Moyer, driver.

Class 10, Knock Down and Out: 1, Calypso, R. B. Snyder, owner; Allen Garner, rider; 2, Rudolph, Snyder, owner; Garner, rider; 3, Calispo, J. V. Savastio, owner; Johnny Frye, rider; 4, Baume, R. V. Rill, owner; Buddy Conrad, rider; 5, High Tempest, Apalachian Stables, Marion Glassberger, rider; 6, Patsy Irvin Auman, owner, Andy Kreider, rider.

HONORED AT LEBANON VALLEY COLLEGE were these men who received honorary degrees at special convocation services held in the college church. They are (l-r): Walter E. Remmers, vice-president of the Union Carbide and Carbon Corp., who received the Doctor of Laws degree; I. Lynd Esch, president of Indiana Central College, Doctor of Humane Letters; Dr. Frederic K. Miller, president of LVC; Paul Price, director of Church School Administration of the Evangelical United Brethren Church, Doctor of Divinity; and Edward William Coble, Lancaster, chairman of the building committee, board of trustees of LVC, Doctor of Laws. (Sunday News Photo)

LVC Dedicates 3 New Buildings

ANNVILLE, May 18 — Four honorary degrees recognizing leaders in education, industry and religion were conferred by Lebanon Valley College during Dedication Day ceremonies today at the college.

The degrees were conferred during a convocation held in the college church to Edward William Coble, 344 N. West End Ave., Lancaster, Doctor of Laws; Dr. Paul Price, director of Church School Administration for the Evangelical United Brethren Church board of Christian Education in Dayton, Ohio, Doctor of Divinity; Dr. I. Lynd Esch, Indiana Central College president, and the convocation speaker, Doctor of Humane Letters, and Dr. Walter E. Remmers, vice-president of Union Carbide and Carbon Corp., Doctor of Laws.

Dr. George G. Struble, chairman of the college's English Department, had charge of the investiture service. The men were presented to Dr. Miller by Dr. Young, Dr. Maynard Sparks, college chaplain, Dr. Howard M. Kreitzer, dean of the college and Dr. Howard A. Neidig. Dr. Miller presided at the convocation. During the service two selections were sung by the LVC Glee Club under the direction of Dr. James M. Thurmond.

The guest speaker was I. Lynd Esch, Ph.D., LL.D., who used as his subject "We Dedicate Life." He congratulated the college for its progress, noting that "these splendid buildings are the tools to be used for the noble purpose of building life."

Buildings Dedicated

Following the convocation, services of dedication were held, with Dr. Miller and Dr. E. N. Funkhouser, of Hagerstown, Md., board of trustee president, in charge. Dr. Young led the service at the George Daniel Gossard Memorial Library, named for the late 10th president of the college.

The new science hall was dedicated to the memory of Dr. Andrew Bender and Dr. Samuel H. Derickson, former science department chairmen. Dr. E. Craig Brandenburg, executive secretary of Christian Education for the EUB conducted this service.

The final dedication took place at the Mary Capp Green Residence Hall and honored Mrs. Mary Capp Green, of Lebanon, a former dean of women at LVC, who was introduced as a special guest by Dr. Funkhouser.

Approximately 500 alumni and friends attended the convocation and dedication, which was followed by a dinner celebrating the college's initial development campaign. During the dinner, held in Lynch Memorial Hall, citations were given to nine outstanding supporters of the recent development campaign.

EARLY SPECTATORS line fence to watch drag races held at Garden Spot Airport yesterday by Red Rose Timing Assn. and sponsored by North Lancaster Kiwanis Club. Their ranks were swelled as racing continued into the night until an estimated 10,000 persons watched. (Sunday News Photo)

TWO SPORTS CARS are "waved off" by starter in early heat at Garden Spot Airport where first drag strip race in this area was held yesterday. An estimated 300 cars were entered in the races which lasted until midnight. (Sunday News Photo)

10,000 Watch Lancaster's First Drag-Strip Contest

Their tires screeching as they pushed against asphalt, two souped-up cars roared down the new runway at Garden Spot Airport, and flashed by eight cone-like markers a quarter of a mile from the start.

One car — the one which passed the markers first — returned to the head of the drag strip. The other, eliminated, drove off.

The first two cars had hardly cleared the track when a second team was waved off by the starter, and, shortly after 7 p.m., Lancaster's first hot rod drag-races were under way.

They continued until dusk fell, and even after under the glare of floodlight. Late in the evening, the crowd of onlookers—some from neighboring states — had swelled to nearly 10,000.

With more than 300 hot rods and sports cars from seven states entered, there were over 300 heats to run before the winners could be determined. Race officials did not expect to be able to announce any winners until early Sunday morning.

Various categories were established, depending on horsepower and the advertised weight of the automobiles.

The races were supervised by the Red Rose Timing Assn., using equipment of the Automobile Timing Assn. of America. They were sponsored by the North Lancaster Kiwanis Club, with the proceeds to be used for the club's work with children.

The turn-out of spectators, who lined both sides of the airport runway and sometimes were warned back when they encroached on the fast end, was unexpectedly large. Some stood on car tops and engine hoods, better to see the races.

Cars were parked all over the airport grounds, and many were halted along the Lincoln Highway West nearby.

Records Unofficial

An official of the ATAA said that because there had been insufficient time prior to check equipment, there would be no official records on the time of the races. Winners would be determined through elimination at each heat.

The official said normally two records are kept: one, the time for the quarter-mile distance starting from a dead halt, and the average speed over an additional one-fortieth mile. This would give a top speed after the vehicles were given a quarter mile to get rolling.

The cones contained electrical devices to simultaneously record the speeds of the two cars as they roared by.

Research Men Hear Paper By Dr. Bissinger

Dr. Barnard H. Bissinger, head of the mathematics department of Lebanon Valley College, contributed a paper at the fifth annual meeting of the Operations Research Society of America held at the University of Pennsylvania in Philadelphia.

Dr. Bissinger, whose home is in Annville, is a son of Mr. and Mrs. John B. Bissinger Jr., 85 Spencer Ave., Lancaster.

Subject of the paper Dr. Bissinger presented at the parley was "An Application of General Plant Account Theory to the Fitting of a Survivor Curve to a Physical Group Property Account Stub Life Table."

Besides being a member of the research society, Dr. Bissinger has been honored three times recently by being named to additional learned societies, including the National Council of Teachers of Mathematics, the Mathematical Society of India and the Societe Mathematique de France.

A graduate of Franklin and Marshall College, Class of 1938, Dr. Bissinger holds a master's degree from Syracuse University and a doctor's degree in mathematics and aeronautical engineering from Cornell University.

He is also a member of the London Mathematical Society, American Mathematical Society, Mathematical Assn. of America, and the Institute of Management Sciences.

DR. BARNARD H. BISSINGER

Woman Hit By Stones Tossed From Window

Mrs. Henry Young, 544 W. James St., reported to city detectives that while walking by a house at 526 W. James St. at 11 a. m. yesterday someone dropped some stones out of a third-floor window. She said she was struck on the head by the stones, but did not require medical aid. Police are investigating.

This is the property occupied by Mrs. Edna Hotchkiss, who reported yesterday to police that a brick had been thrown through her window Friday night.

60,000 Bibles Distributed Here Gideon Soc. Told

Sixty thousand Bibles have been distributed here by the Gideon Sociey of Lancaster County, it was revealed last night at the Society's annual banquet in the Hotel Brunswick.

Over the nation, the more than 100 diners were told. 30 million have been given out by the Gideons.

The group, including about 20 local clergymen, heard an address by Raymond Martsoff, of Shamokin, state vice president of the Gideons.

Other speakers were City Commissioner John F. S. Reese, director of accounts and finance; Aaron Denlinger, vice president of the local group, and C. Lester Gehr, its president.

Today, Gideons will hold their annual field day, with visits to many of the community's churches.

80 FROM RCA IN NEW YORK

Eighty employes of the Lancaster plant of RCA are seeing the sights in New York City this week-end. The group, loaded into two buses, left Lancaster yesterday for the excursion which will include a trip through the United Nations and sightseeing through the city.

Obituaries

Time and Place of Services will be Found Under Funeral Invitations Page 39, Column 2.

H. Reemsnyder Dies At Lunch In Cafeteria

Henry E. Reemsnyder, sixty-nine, 1595 Wilson Ave., superintendent of mails at the Lancaster Postoffice, collapsed and died while eating lunch yesterday at 12:20 p.m. at the YMCA cafeteria.

Reemsnyder

Reemsnyder had spent the morning with the family of Dr. J. R. Coder, chiropractor, 34 N. Lime St., and Mrs. J. R. Coder and their son George were with him at the table.

The East Lampeter ambulance was called, and Reemsnyder was taken to Lancaster Osteopathic Hospital. Dr. Guz Mazzola, interne, responded with the ambulance. Reemsnyder was pronounced dead on arrival.

Dr. C. P. Stahr, deputy coroner, said preliminary examination indicated a coronary death. The body was removed to the Fred F. Groff Funeral Home, 234 W. Orange St.

Reemsnyder was with the postal department 41½ years. He could have retired at age sixty, but stayed on with the hope of retiring at age seventy next March.

He did the bulk of the Postoffice work on compilation of street names, forming a directory list which was revised each year. He obtained the cooperation of supervisors of suburban townships in getting houses numbered and streets named, to facilitate mail deliveries.

He started his postal career Oct. 1, 1915, as a carrier. In 1921 he transferred to clerk duties, and in 1926 was made foreman of mails. He became assistant superintendent of mails in 1943, and in 1952 was named to the post of senior assistant superintendent of mails. He became superintendent in 1955.

Reemsnyder is survived by his wife, Helen A., a patient at a Harrisburg hospital; one son, Henry E., Jr., and a grandson.

HART INFANT

The infant daughter of Harold S. and Shirley Miller Hart, of 154 E. Walnut St., died yesterday morning in St. Joseph's Hospital.

Cake Contest Winner Named

Mrs. Warren Sickman, Conestoga, last night won the cake decorating contest, feature of the closing evening of the Home and Garden Show at the Guernsey Pavilion, Lincoln Highway East.

More than 1,500 persons attended during the day and evening. They brought the total attendance since Tuesday to an estimated 5,500.

Mrs. Sickman submitted a cake decorated with a coconut lamb. She received an electric frying pan as a prize.

The show was sponsored by the Lancaster Junior Chamber of Commerce, with Marvin K. Shearer and Harry K. Landis III as chairmen of the show committee.

The cake contest was sponsored by the Jane-Cees, made up of Jaycee wives.

Louise Kopp Dies Of Virus Illness

Miss Louise Mae Kopp, thirty-six, 2733 Lititz Road, died at 11:30 a.m. yesterday at her home after a short illness.

Attending physicians pronounced the death due to a virus infection which affected the heart.

Born in Neffsville, she was the daughter of Arthur F. and Elizabeth Kratzut Kopp. She was a member of St. Peter's Evangelical Lutheran Church, and active in the Sunday School.

Besides her parents she is survived by one sister, Arlene, wife of R. D. Templeton, Neffsville.

MRS. JOSEPH COSTARELLA

Mrs. Christine Costarella, seventy-eight, 214 E. Lemon St., died Friday at 11:30 p. m. in Martin's Convalescent Home, 643 E. Orange St., where she had been a guest for the past four years.

She was born in Pentidattilo-Reggio Calbira, Italy, a daughter of the late Salvo and Maria Muscianesi Costarella. She was a member of St. Anthony's Catholic Church.

She was the widow of Joseph Costarella.

Surviving are five daughters: Imara, wife of Frank Familiari, Italy; Frances, wife of James Congello, Lancaster; Mary, wife of John DeLaurentis, Lancaster; Justina, wife of Joseph Palumbo, Lancaster; and Jean, wife of Anthony W. Faranda, Lancaster; 19 grandchildren; and 12 great grandchildren.

MRS. GEORGE B. HAGENS

Mrs. Cora E. Hagens, seventy-four, 126 N. Mulberry St., died yesterday at 12:30 a.m. at her home following an illness of six weeks.

She was the widow of George B. Hagens. She was born in Fulton Twp., a daughter of the late John and Martha Jane Jackson Whirt.

She resided in Lancaster six years, having formerly resided in Camargo. She was a member of Mount Eden Lutheran Church.

Surviving are a son, John W., at home; two grandchildren; two brothers, Harry E., and Caley, and a sister, Florence, wife of Chester Smith, all of Lancaster.

MRS. ELAMUEL WOLFSKILL

Mrs. Sarah Binkley Wolfskill, eighty-eight, formerly of Reinholds, died at noon yesterday at the Maple Farms Home, Akron, after a lingering illness.

She was the widow of Elamuel Wolfskill and was a daughter of the late Benjamin and Susan B. Garner Binkley. She was a member of the Muddy Creek Church.

Surviving are a daughter, Cenia, wife of Charles Shupp, Denver RD, nine grandchildren and 18 great-grandchildren, and a sister, Susan, wife of Walker Stetler, Denver.

JOHN S. SNYDER

John S. Snyder, seventy-nine, Harristown, Paradise Twp., died Friday at 11:10 p. m. in the Aierstuck Nursing Home, Leola, after an illness of two years.

Born in Paradise Twp., a son of the late Samuel and Anna Slack Snyder, he was a retired farmer. He had been a member of the former Christ Episcopal Church, Intercourse, where he also served as a vestryman.

MELCHI INFANT

The infant daughter of Richard L. and Esther Flaharty Melchi, 539 N. Mary St., died Friday night at St. Joseph's Hospital.

Besides the parents she is survived by a sister, Sharan Anne, at home.

Perched in the hay loft, Frederic Miller, Henry Walter III and Tom McCloud provide rhythm accompaniment for the dancers.

Heading the waiting line at the "chuck wagon" are Mary Beth Carl and Sharon Gibbel.

Barn Dance

Rock 'n' Roll took a setback — temporarily at least — when Mary Catherine Walter of Lititz R3 decided to entertain at a square dance and barn party Wednesday evening. Encouraged by cool breezes, approximately 40 teenagers enthusiastically danced the traditional Paul Jones, Comin'-Through-the-Rye and Dig-for-the-Oyster, as seen in general photo above. Rock 'n' Roll reared its frenetic head once or twice, but in square-dance form. Between dances the guests consumed quantities of hamburgers, soft drinks and ice cream. Added attractions were old flatbed wagon, plenty of straw and a real barn. Mary Catherine is the daughter of Dr. and Mrs. Henry Walter Jr.

A wagon wheel (photo at left) provides a good leaning post at intermission time for Larry Gassert and Kathleen Twitmire.

Today with Women

Relaxing on an old buckboard farm wagon (photo at right) between dances are (l-r): Mary Catherine Walter, the hostess; Margaretta Light, Clay Burkholder and Peter Robinson.

WEATHER
(U. S. Weather Bureau)
Fair And Warmer Today, High 82-87. Partly Cloudy And More Humid Tomorrow With Scattered Thundershowers.
(Details On Page 20)

Intelligencer Journal.

TELEPHONE EXpress 7-5251

The Leading Newspaper in the Garden Spot of America. Home Owned for Home Folks Since 1794

164th Year.—No. 15. | Metropolitan Lancaster Population 1954 (Est.) Penna. Dept. of Commerce 248,296 | LANCASTER, PA., WEDNESDAY MORNING, JULY 3, 1957. | CITY EDITION | 20 PAGES. | 42c PER WEEK—7c Per Copy

$250,000 BLAZE AT LITITZ CHURCH

The roof of historic Lititz Moravian Church was a mass of flames when this aerial photo was taken about a half hour after the fire was discovered. The white church steeple stands out against the smoke and fire, the top still untouched by flames. On the church lawn at left the Lancaster City Fire Department's aerial truck has just arrived on the scene. The aerial ladder was used to play water onto the flaming roof. The church parsonage, at top, was heavily damaged by fire and water, but other nearby buildings were spared. (Intell Aerial Photo By Richard K. Reinhold)

Historic Moravian Bldg. Wrecked As Roof Burns

Spark From Painter's Blow Torch Believed Cause Of Early Afternoon Fire; Adjoining Structures, Priceless Mementoes Saved

A tiny spark from a painter's blow torch is believed to have touched off a quarter of a million dollar blaze that wrecked the historic Lititz Moravian Church early yesterday afternoon.

Ironically, the painting job was the final phase of a two-year, $80,000 program of interior and exterior renovation to the 170-year-old structure in the heart of Lititz.

Besides the church, the adjoining church parsonage was heavily damaged by fire and water. Priceless documents of the Moravian Church as well as the bulk of the other furnishings in the parsonage was saved, however.

The spectacular blaze that ate through the roof of the church broke out shortly before 1 p. m. It was fanned by a brisk breeze. Four hours later charred roof beams and the skeleton of the church steeple collapsed with a roar into the pure white interior of the building.

The church pastor, the Rt. Rev. Carl J. Helmich and his family are on a New England vacation and were unaware of the blaze late yesterday.

OTHER FIRE PICTURES PAGES 8, 20

Braving the scorching heat and heavy smoke, volunteers and firemen managed to carry out much of the parsonage's contents before damaging streams of water from hoses poured into the building.

One unidentified man carried out the church records — which date back as far as the middle 18th century.

Unofficial estimates set the damage as running into a "quarter of a million dollars."

However, a spokesman for the church's board of trustees, pointed out that the historical loss to the community will be "tremendous."

Lititz Moravian Church has become a heritage to the community as well as to Lancaster County. For generations it has been a popular site for tourists. And townspeople over the past two centuries gathered to worship there, especially at Christmas and Easter times.

These same townspeople stood stunned as the blaze raced through the church roof. The crowd numbered into the thousands as flames shot more than 50 feet into the air and a grayish pall of smoke was blown over the town.

The wind-whipped flames threatened a girl's dormitory on the Linden Hall Junior College campus. But Dr. Byron K. Horne, headmaster of the school, said a shift in the wind prevented the fire from spreading to the school itself.

HALL UNHARMED

Also located on the property with the church and school was "Fellowship Hall." This building, stood some 30 feet to the west of the church proper, but because of the westerly winds, was in no immediate danger. This building contains the church museum with its

Turn To Page 8 For More Of CHURCH

Senate Okays Big Defense Fund Measure

WASHINGTON, July 2 (AP) — Defense-minded senators slowed down the congressional economy wave tonight by passing a military money bill carrying more than 34½ billion dollars in new funds.

Passage was by a unanimous 74-0 vote.

The Senate total was $34,434,229,000,—$971,504,000 — more than the House voted on May 29.

This biggest annual money measure now goes back to the House which is expected to send it on to a Senate-House Compromise Committee later this week or early next week.

As the bulky defense bill left the Senate it included most of the defense funds finally asked by President Eisenhower. Less than a quarter billion dollars were missing. And these may be provided by supplemental appropriations or authority to transfer other unspent funds.

OPERATING FUNDS

The bill carries new annual operating funds for the fiscal year that began Monday.

The Senate voted $16,384,093,000 for the Air Force; $10,054,255,000 for the Navy and Marines; $7,397,156,000 for the Army; $682,375,000 for interservice activities; and $16,350,000 for the office of the

Turn To Page 8 For More Of SENATE

Fire Guts House Near Murrell, 12 Are Homeless

A family of 12 was left homeless yesterday when flames from a coal oil stove on which children in the family were doing some baking ignited the brick summer kitchen attached to the kitchen addition of the house.

The interior of the 14-room frame dwelling belonging to Eli S. Stauffer, Ephrata R3, was completely gutted and the west side of the kitchen wing was burned off from foundation to roof.

The property is tenanted by Amos B. Stauffer, son of the owner and is located a mile and a half south of Murrell, in Earl Twp.

Ephrata Fire Chief Arthur Mellinger was in charge, since Ephrata was first on the scene, about 3:40 p.m.

Robert Risser, Lincoln fire chief, said the owner set the building loss at $13,000 and the tenant's loss at $3,000, the latter representing furniture and personal property.

The tenant's wife, Florence, was treated at Ephrata Community Hospital for a scalp laceration, received when burning debris struck her on the head. She was treated and discharged.

Neighbors summoned firemen when they saw flames rising from

Turn To Page 8 For More Of FIRES

That Juke Box Wasn't Fooling

SAN MIGUEL, Calif., July (AP)— Mr. and Mrs. Paul Jones were joking about the tune blaring from their restaurant juke box: "The train came through the middle of the house."

Then it did — into their restaurant.

A Southern Pacific freight hit a truck at a crossing today. Fourteen gondola cars, loaded with sugar beets, were rocketing off the tracks, and one crashed into the restaurant.

Jones and two others were slightly injured.

Hundreds Killed By Quakes In Iran Area Near Baku Oil Base

TEHRAN, Iran, July 2 (AP) — Earthquakes spread death and destruction today over a wide area of northern Iran adjoining the big Soviet Baku oil production base on the Caspian Sea. Hundreds were killed.

The path of ruin—as known here—reached around and over the towering Elburz Mountain range on a 500-mile arc and swept through at least 120 Iranian towns and villages.

Every Iranian port and village on the Caspian was hit. What happened in nearby Soviet Asia was a mystery.

The arc of destruction—as pictured in official reports here—reached from Mianeh, near the Soviet border in Azerbaijan in the northwest, to Veramin, south of Tehran, and to Curgan, near the Soviet frontier on the northeast.

AT LEAST 200

The toll in Iran tonight was counted as: at least 200 persons killed. Many hundreds, perhaps thousands, injured. Immense property damage.

The disaster apparently centered at the base of the eternally snow-capped, 18,600-foot Mt. Demavend, and in its ring of resort villages.

The peak is a dead volcanic cone 45 miles northeast of Tehran. It is the highest of the Elburz range that slopes off toward the Caspian Sea and Soviet Asia.

The area is both a winter and summer playground that has been favored by the Shah on skiing and other outings. It is also known as an area prone to earthquakes.

VILLAGES RUINED

Reports said most villages around Mt. Demavand's great base were ruined by a quake lasting two minutes and three seconds.

A government report said the village of Navak, near Firizkuh, was destroyed and there was no definite word on the fate of its 310 people.

Tehran was shaken but no deaths were reported here. The building of the Ministry of Justice and the Central Railway Station were damaged slightly.

Rail communications were interrupted but resumed late in the day after repairs on the Tehran-Caspian Sea line and stations along the way.

The longest tremor in Tehran last 30 seconds.

50,000 SQ. MILES

The devastated area in Iran was estimated at nearly 50,000 square miles.

It extended from south of Tehran to the Russian border on the north and included all towns and villages along the Caspian Sea's southern edge.

The Soviet Union's big Bak uoil production works is on the Caspian Sea to the north. There was no word here of what happened beyond the Soviet border.

Redlegs Take Over Loop Lead

St. Louis rookie Von McDaniel eased the Braves out of first place with a 4-2 win yesterday and the Cincinnati Redlegs, 8-6 winners over Chicago in a 10-inning game, took over as league leaders.

NATIONAL LEAGUE
Cincinnati 8, Chicago 6 (10 innings)
St. Louis 4, Milwaukee 2
Brooklyn 6, New York 0
(Only games scheduled)

AMERICAN LEAGUE
New York 6, Baltimore 4 (11 innings)
Chicago 4, Detroit 2
Boston 2, Washington 1
(Only games scheduled)

(Details on Page 12)

Leader Scores Legislature In Television Talk

HARRISBURG, July 2 (AP) — Gov. Leader fired a broadside of criticism tonight at the Republican-controlled 1957 session of the General Assembly.

He said the five-and-a-half-month session had been "unproductive," "destructive" and had "missed great opportunities" for service to Pennsylvanians.

The Democratic chief executive detailed his complaints with the Legislature in a 30-minute television report carried by eight stations in the state.

The state Republican organization immediately asked the stations to grant equal time for a reply next Tuesday by George I. Bloom, the state chairman. Bloom said the time was requested "so we can expose Gov. Leader's demagoguery and answer him point by point."

A party spokeman said several of the stations had replied they would grant the equal time.

Leader mentioned politics directly just once in the talk. He said he had asked the Legislature at the start of the session "for agreement on a program that would be good for Pennsylvania."

"My duty was to seek accom-

Turn To Page 8 For More Of LEADER

535 MAY DIE ON HIGHWAYS ON 4TH

CHICAGO, July 2 (AP)—Traffic accidents may kill 535 Americans during the long Independence Day holiday, the National Safety Council said today.

The 102-hour period runs from 6 p. m. local time Wednesday to midnight Sunday.

That would be a new high for the Independence Day holiday. The record is 491, established during a four-day period in 1950.

"We Lead All The Rest"
FARM CORNER
By Joe Wachtman

Wheat Loan Rate Goes Up A Cent Per Bushel Here

Wheat loan rates for the 1957 crop will be one cent a bushel higher than a year ago for Lancaster County growers, the Agricultural Stabilization and Conservation Committee announced yesterday.

The national average support rate for 1957 crop wheat is unchanged at $2 a bushel, according to a separate announcement from the U.S. Department of Agriculture.

Opening prices for wheat placed under loan at grain warehouses will be $2.11 per bushel for No. 1 grade in Lancaster County until July 22. This price then goes up at intervals through the remainder of the year.

For farm stored wheat, farmers will receive $2.22 per bushel for No. 1 grade, $2.21 for No. 2 and $2.19 for No. 3 — a one-cent increase for each grade from 1956, according to Miss Dorothy Y. Neel, manager of the local ASC office.

Deductions from these prices include: light garlicky, 6 cents; garlicky, 15 cents; light smutty, 2 cents; smutty, 6 cents a bushel.

A year ago, the beginning of the wheat harvest saw open market prices only a few cents lower than the $2.10 a bushel rate then paid for wheat stored in elevators under government loan and the cash

Turn To Page 16 For More Of FARM CORNER

Anti-Flu Shots Being Developed

WASHINGTON, July 2 (AP)—The National Institutes of Health said today six American firms have developed an experimental vaccine to combat Asiatic flu.

A spokesman said the vaccine has been sent to various laboratories throughout the country for testing, but that there has been no application to NIH as yet for its clearance as a licensed vaccine.

If current experimental tests are successful, he said, the manufacturers presumably will apply for licensing.

Pitman-Moore Co. at Indianapolis said it has received a government contract for about half a million doses of the new vaccine.

Hibbard O. Ball, executive vice president, said the vaccine will be used for immunizations in the armed forces.

SAMPLES TESTED

Ball said samples of Pitman-Moore's pilot batch have been sent to the NIH for testing.

Eli Lilly & Co., another Indianapolis pharmaceutical firm, an-

Turn To Page 8 For More Of VACCINE

Assessor Will Get All Data From New Records System

EDITOR'S NOTE—This is the fourth in a series of articles on Lancaster County's real estate assessment equalization program, which will provide the answers to such questions as what the program means, why it is being done, and its effect upon the county's property owners.

By CHARLES W. FITZKEE

The uniform permanent records system which the county will set up as part of an assessment equalization system will provide all the detailed information required by the chief assessor to set a valuation upon each parcel of land and building.

The form and content matter of the records was decided upon — at the command of the legislature — by a committee of 10, composed of five members of the Pennsylvania Assn. of County Commissioners, four members of the General Assembly and the chairman of the Local Government Commission.

This permanent records system eventually will replace the "book method" used in Lancaster County. These assessment books, one for each district, supply only a fraction of the information which will be available under the permanent records system.

Basically, the present system of assessment in Lancaster County does not conform with the provisions of the Fourth to Eighth Class County Assessment Law.

The first of the permament records are tax maps. Under the Lancaster County program the tax maps will be constructed from information provided by aerial photographs and by the description of property contained in deeds.

All the maps will be on a scale large enough to indicate all property and lot lines, set forth dimensions or areas, indicate whether the land is improved, and identify the respective land parcels or lots by a system of numbers or symbols whereby the ownership

Turn To Page 8 For More Of ASSESSMENT

Few Scattered Thundershowers May Dampen Holiday Mood Here

The threat of "a few scattered showers and thunderstorms" hangs over Lancastrians planning the picnics, outings and fireworks displays that had come to be a part of the tradition of Independence Day.

The U.S. Weather Bureau at Harrisburg said last night temperatures will be warmer during the day and will turn cooler in the evening. Humidity is also expected to be higher for the holiday tomorrow.

Practically all business activity will be halted for the Fourth.

Stores, banks, offices, the Municipal Building and the Court House all will be closed. The Post Office also will be shuttered, with only special delivery mail to be delivered. Postmaster Frank R. Hammond said pick up of mail deposited in mail boxes will be made on a holiday schedule.

Although traffic is not expected to be as heavy as would be the case if this were a four-day weekend upcoming, state and local police are alerted for extra precautions.

City and state police officials also have warned that there will be a crack down on illegal fireworks.

Legal fireworks will cap several of the community programs ob-

Turn To Page 8 For More Of HOLIDAY

Firemen play water on Lititz Moravian Church during blaze that destroyed the 170-year-old building yesterday. The hoses play water from the Lancaster City Fire Department's aerial truck B, called to the scene to help fight the blaze. Four hours after the fire was discovered the charred beams of the roof and the steeple collapsed into the church interior. (Intell Photo)

BASEBALL'S "ALL-STARS" WHO WILL CLASH IN 24TH ANNUAL CLASSIC IN ST. LOUIS TUESDAY

NATIONAL LEAGUE — AMERICAN LEAGUE

Roy McMillen · Hank Aaron · Ed Bailey · Willie Mays · Frank Robinson · Don Hoak · John Temple · Stan Musial · Ted Williams · Mickey Mantle · Yogi Berra · Nellie Fox · Harvey Kueen · Al Kaline · George Kell · Vic Wertz

National League Favored

Thomas Hits Homer In 13th To Sink Giants

NEW YORK, July 6 (AP)—Frank Thomas whacked his ninth home run into the upper left field stands off New York Giants' pitcher Stu Miller today to boost Pittsburgh to a 13-inning 3-2 victory.

Minutes before, Thomas had been shaken up when he collided with shortstop Dick Groat going after a pop fly in the bottom of the 12th. It was the second homer in two games for Thomas, and it gave Pirate reliever Bob Purkey his eighth victory against seven losses.

Spencer Hits Two

Purkey started the 10th for the Bucs after Vern Law had held the Giants to seven hits in nine innings and gone out for a pinch-hitter. Two of the Giant hits off Law were home runs by Daryl Spencer in the second and seventh innings, his fifth and sixth.

Curt Barclay weakened only in the third inning in holding the Pirates to 2 runs and 7 hits during the first 12 innings.

Pittsburgh took a 2-0 lead in the third when second baseman Bill Mazeroski slammed a triple to right centerfield, scoring Dick Rand and Bill Virdon.

Fail To Score

Three singles in the Giant 11th failed to produce a game-winning run. Danny O'Connell singled to right and was out trying for a double. Willie Mays and Gail Harris followed with safeties, but Spencer flied to right to end the threat.

Defense was the dominant factor on both sides until Thomas ended the 3 hour, 15 minute errorless struggle. Only six walks were given up by the four pitchers, three by Barclay.

PITTSBURGH	ab	h	o	a	NEW YORK	ab	h	o	a
Virdon cf	6	1	7	0	Lockman lf 1b	6	0	8	1
Maz'ski 2b	6	1	2	6	O'Con'ell 3b	6	2	2	7
Fondy 1b	5	1	14	2	Mays cf	6	1	4	1
Thomas lf	5	1	0	0	Harris 1b	5	1	14	4
Groat ss	5	0	4	3	cVirgil lf	0	0	1	0
Baker 3b	6	0	1	2	fJablonski	1	0	0	0
Mejias rf	5	3	4	1	Spencer 2b	5	3	5	6
Rand c	2	2	5	1	Mueller rf	5	0	1	0
dFoiles c	0	0	0	0	Bressoud ss	5	3	1	6
Law p	3	0	2	0	Katt c	2	0	2	1
aSkinner	1	0	0	0	bThomson	1	0	0	0
Purkey p	0	0	0	1	Westrum c	1	0	0	0
					Barclay p	4	1	1	2
					eSauer	0	0	0	0
					Miller p	0	0	0	1
Totals	44	9	39	16	Totals	47	11	39	29

a—Grounded out for Law in 10th.
b—Grounded out for Katt in 10th.
c—Ran for Harris in 11th.
d—Ran for Rand in 12th.
e—Walked for Barclay in 12th.
f—Grounded out for Virgil in 13th.

Pittsburgh	002 000 000 000 1	— 3
New York	000 100 100 000 0	— 2

R—Virdon, Thomas, Rand, Spencer 2. E—None. RBI—Mazeroski 2, Spencer 2, Thomas. 3B—Mazeroski. HR—Spencer 2, Thomas. S—Rand 3. Dp—Spencer, Bressoud and Harris; Fondy (unassisted). Left—Pittsburgh 9, New York 8. BB—Law 1, Purkey 1, Barclay 3, Miller 1. SO—Law 2, Barclay 1. HO—Law 7 in 9, Purkey 4 in 4, Barclay 8 in 12, Miller 1 in 1. R-ER—Law 2-2, Purkey 0-0, Barclay 2-2, Miller 1-1. W—Purkey (8-7). L—Miller (3-5). U—Crawford, Venzon, Ballanfant, Jackowski. T—3:15. A—5,334.

WASHINGTON, July 6—GETS 1,000TH HIT—Mickey Mantle, New York Yankees slugging outfielder, poses in dressing room after getting his 1,000th major league hit in eighth inning of the Yanks-Senators night game here Friday night. Umpire John Stevens stopped the game, called for the ball, and gave it to Mantle as a souvenir. Yanks defeated Washington 5-3 in ten innings. (AP Wirephoto).

6-5 Choice To Win Star Tilt Tuesday

BY JACK HAND

ST. LOUIS, July 6 (AP) — The National League team with five Cincinnati Redlegs in the starting lineup is favored over the New York Yankee-dominated American League squad in the 24th All-Star Game to be played Tuesday at Busch Stadium.

In recent years, the National has whittled the American's series margin to 13-10 by winning six of the last seven games. Ironically, much of this has been at the expense of manager Casey Stengel whose Yanks usually humble the opposition in the World Series. As an All-Star manager, Casey has won only once, 1954, in six attempts.

Back in St. Louis for the first time since 1948 when the American League finished on top 5-2, the annual mid-season contest is sure to draw a capacity crowd of 31,000. The long range weather forecast calls for hot, humid weather with scattered thundershowers.

The game will be beamed on network (NBC) radio and television across the nation as part of the five-year contract by which baseball gets $3,250,000 per year for the All-Star and World Series rights. Sixty per cent of this amount goes to the player pension fund.

Game Time Varies

Game time is 1:30 p. m. (EST) with a series of alternatives in case of bad weather. If it should be rained out Tuesday afternoon it would be played Tuesday night. If not then, Wednesday morning or afternoon.

Because of the National's recent victory surge, the fact that it will be played in a National park and the "Stengel jinx" on the American, the National has been made a 6 to 5 man-to-man choice.

Manager Walter Alston of Brooklyn and Stengel, who got their jobs with pennant-winning performances in 1956, won't name their starting pitchers until Monday. The rest of the lineup already has been chosen by vote of the fans with heavy Cincinnati participation.

Frick Steps In

In fact, the Cincinnati vote was so heavy that all National starters, except Stan Musial, would have been Redlegs if Commissioner Ford Frick hadn't stepped in. Frick put Willie Mays of New York in center field and Hank Aaron of Milwaukee in right instead of Cincinnati's Gus Bell and Wally Post. He also arbitrarily named Musial for first base but it turned out "The Man" from St. Louis already had enough votes to offset the Cincinnati campaign for their George Crowe. It will be Musial's 14th All-Star game, a record.

Walter Alston · Casey Stengel
OPPOSING MANAGERS

Musial, Mays and Aaron will be surrounded by Redlegs with Johnny Temple on Second, Roy McMillan at short, Don Hoak at third, Frank Robinson in left and Ed Bailey catching. Bell also was picked to the squad by Alston whose 25-man roster includes six each from Cincinnati and Milwaukee, four from St. Louis, three from his own Dodgers, two each from the Phillies and Giants and one each from Chicago and Pittsburgh.

Warren Spahn · Billy Pierce
PROBABLE STARTING PITCHERS

Stengel had two Yanks in the starting lineup, catcher Yogi Berra and center fielder Mickey Mantle. He picked six more, including infielders Bobby Richardson, Gil McDougald and Bill Skowron, catcher Elston Howard and pitchers Bobby Shantz and Bob Grim. Closest to the Yanks' eight is Detroit with four, Baltimore, Cleveland and Chicago with three each, Boston with two and Kansas City and Washington one each.

Fox At Second

Vic Wertz of Cleveland is the American first baseman, Nellie Fox of Chicago at second, Harvey Kuenn of Detroit at short and George Kell at third. Ted Williams of Boston who will be playing his 12th game, will be in left and Al Kaline of Detroit in right. Stengel left himself only one lefthanded pinch hitter, Charley Maxwell of Detroit.

The pitching may be lefthanded on both sides with Alston expected to pick between Milwaukee's Warren Spahn, who has made the team nine times and pitched in five games, and New York's Johnny Antonelli. His other pitchers are lefthanded Curt Simmons of the Phils, and righthanders Lew Burdette of Milwaukee, Larry Jackson of St. Louis, Clem Labine of Brooklyn and Jack Sanford of the Phils.

Although the National starting lineup will include only two lefthanded batters — Musial and Bailey—Stengel may pitch either Chicago's Billy Pierce or his own Bobby Shantz. Both are lefthanders and Pierce has started three All-Star games, allowing only one run in nine innings. If Stengel decides to save his lefties until later in the game when lefthanded batters will be in action for the National, he might go with Early Wynn, the veteran Cleveland righthander. Stengel also has Don Mossi of Cleveland, a lefty, and Jim Bunning of Detroit, Billy Loes of Baltimore and his own Grim, all righthanders.

However Stengel indicated in Washington he might pitch a righthander. Stengel admitted a sentimental attachment for Pierce. "But I don't see how I can go against the odds with all those righthanders to face," he said.

Writers traveling with the Yankees thought Wynn was the best bet for the starting job although he was scheduled to pitch Sunday. Loes, a former Brooklyn Dodger, and Bunning were other starting possibilities. Loes was hit hard last night by Boston and Bunning pitched a complete game Friday night, beating Kansas City 8-4, with eight hits.

According to the rules, all starters, except pitchers, must remain in the game for at least three innings. The big stars, like Williams, Mantle and Musial probably will play the entire nine. Pitchers cannot pitch more than three innings unless the game goes into extra innings.

As recently as 1949, the American held a 12-4 margin in this lopsided rivalry. However, the American has won only once, 1954, in the last seven years.

Among the missing on the National side are such familiar names as Robin Roberts, Roy Campanella, Don Newcombe, Bob Friend, Ted Kluszewski and Duke Snider. Every American starter of 1956 is back except first baseman Mickey Vernon of Boston.

Bosox Jolt Orioles On Extra Base Hits

BOSTON, July 6 (AP)—The Boston Red Sox went for the long ball to rout Baltimore 11-2 today as big Frank Sullivan turned in his fifth consecutive victory.

Jackie Jensen's 11th home run—a solo blast to the center field seats—Billy Klaus' ninth with a mate aboard and a two-run triple by rookie Frank Malzone were the biggest blows.

Extra Base Hits

Seven of the 13 Sox hits went for extra bases while Sully, the 6-7 Californian, scattered 10 Oriole safeties.

The triumph was No. 8 for Sullivan and strengthened Boston's hold on third place in the American League race.

The home forces delighted a Fenway Park crowd of 13,390 by taking the lead in a two-run third inning for a 3-1 lead, then topping off a busy afternoon with five runs in the seventh that made it a runaway.

Break Deadlock

In the third, Jimmy Piersall tripled to the base of the center field barrier and scored when Mickey Vernon pushed a single to left. That broke a 1-1 deadlock. Jensen tagged a pop fly single to center for the other run of the inning.

Malzone's triple in the seventh was off Art Ceccarelli. Vernon and Jensen had drawn walks off 18-year-old bonus boy Jerry Walker in his major league baptism.

The Malzone drive caromed off the wall above the 379-foot mark in left center. The third baseman now has 56 runs batted in to put himself closer to the league head in that department.

Vernon doubled once and Sammy White twice for the other Sox extra base hits.

BALTIMORE	ab	h	o	a	BOSTON	ab	h	o	a
Gardner 2b	4	2	1	2	Piersall cf	3	3	2	0
Boyd 1b	5	3	6	0	Klaus ss	5	1	1	4
G'd'an 3b-ss	4	1	2	1	Williams lf	3	0	3	0
Fr'cona rf	3	0	2	0	dStephens lf	0	0	1	0
Triandos c	4	1	7	0	Vernon 1b	4	2	7	0
Nieman lf	4	2	3	0	Zauchin 1b	0	0	2	1
Pilarcik cf	3	0	1	0	Jensen rf	4	3	2	0
Busby cf	1	1	2	0	Malzone 3b	5	1	1	4
Miranda ss	2	0	0	1	Lepcio 2b	4	0	3	0
aKell 3b	2	0	0	0	White c	4	2	4	0
Brown p	2	0	0	1	Sullivan p	4	1	1	0
O'Dell p	0	0	0	0					
bZupo	1	0	0	0					
Walker p	0	0	0	0					
Ceccarelli p	0	0	0	1					
cDurham	1	0	0	0					
Totals	36	10	24	6	Totals	36	13	27	9

a—Flied out for Miranda in 7th.
b—Grounded out for O'Dell in 7th.
c—Grounded out for Ceccarelli in 9th.
d—Ran for Williams in 7th.

Baltimore	001 100 000	— 2
Boston	012 102 50x	—11

R—Gardner, Triandos, Piersall 2, Klaus, Williams, Vernon, Jensen 2, Malzone, Lepcio, White, Sullivan. E—Boyd. RBI—Jensen 2, Vernon, Piersall 2, Klaus 2, Malzone 2, White, (Sullivan scored on wild pitch in 7th), Boyd, Nieman. 2B—Gardner 2, Triandos, White 2, Vernon. 3B—Piersall, Malzone. HR—Jensen, Klaus. SF—Piersall. Left—Baltimore 9, Boston 8. BB—Brown 3, Walker 2, Ceccarelli 1, Sullivan 2. SO—Brown 4, O'Dell 2, Ceccarelli 1, Sullivan 3. HO—Brown 5 in 3 2-3, O'Dell 4 in 2 1-3, Walker 0 in 0 (faced 2 batters in 7th), Ceccarelli 4 in 2. R-ER—Brown 4-4, O'Dell 2-2, Walker 2-2, Ceccarelli 3-3, Sullivan 2-2. WP—Walker, Ceccarelli. W—Sullivan (8-5). L—Brown (2-4). U—Runge, Paparella, Hurley, Umont. T—2:33. A—13,390.

Golf Play Is Held At Conestoga C. C.

Golfers at the Conestoga Country Club competed yesterday in a Best Selected nine holes, one-half handicap, event.

The winners include: First Division, Rick Goeke 27, Sam Mellon 28, Jack Albright 28, Al Kirk 28; Second Division, Mel Miller 25, Russ Peters 25, Bill Nitrauer 27, Jan Guiles 27, Ted Stoe 27, Pete Gerber 27, and Jim MacKenzie 27; Third Division, Park Dunlap 25, N. Kalle 25, M. Detweiler 26, W. Gingher 26.

SOLANCO MIDGET MIDGET LEAGUE

North Section

	W	L	Pct.
Mountville	9	1	.900
St. Anthony	7	2	.777
Manheim Chix "A"	7	2	.777
New Danville	2	6	.250
Manheim Chix "B"	2	7	.222
Willow Street	1	8	.111

South Section

	W	L	Pct.
Strasburg	6	4	.600
Christiana	6	4	.600
Paradise	5	4	.555
Quarryville	5	4	.555
Holtwood	5	6	.454
Gap	1	8	.111

GAMES LAST WEEK

Quarryville 9, Paradise 0
Christiana 19, Gap 4
Strasburg 5, Willow Street 2
Paradise 8, Manheim Chix B 2
Quarryville 12, Gap 3
Strasburg 5, Holtwood 3
Mountville 12, Willow Street 4
Christiana 8, New Danville 1
Christiana 8, Willow Street 2

MANOR-MILLERSVILLE CHURCH SOFTBALL LEAGUE SCHEDULE

Teams	W	L	Pct.
Central Manor	11	1	.917
Grace E.U.B.	9	3	.750
Reformed	7	5	.583
Green Hill	7	6	.538
Conestoga E.C.	6	6	.500
Stehmans	6	7	.462
Lutheran	5	7	.417
Washington Boro	2	9	.181
Methodist	2	11	.154

Names, Numbers Of Star Players

ST. LOUIS, July 6 (AP)—Names and numbers of players and coaches in Tuesday's All-Star Baseball Game at Busch Stadium.

AMERICAN LEAGUE

Pitchers—Jim Bunning, Detroit, 14; Bob Grim, New York, 55; Billy Loes, Baltimore, 18; Don Mossi, Cleveland, 12; Billy Pierce, Chicago, 19; Bobby Shantz, New York, 30; Early Wynn, Cleveland, 24.

Infielders — Joe DeMaestri, Kansas City, 2; Nellie Fox, Chicago, 2; George Kell, Baltimore, 3; Harvey Kuenn, Detroit, 7; Frank Malzone, Boston, 11; Gil McDougald, New York, 12; Bobby Richardson, New York, 29; Bill Skowron, New York, 14; Vic Wertz, Cleveland, 23.

Outfielders — Al Kaline, Detroit, 6; Mickey Mantle, New York, 7; Charlie Maxwell, Detroit, 4; Minnie Minoso, Chicago, 9; Roy Sievers, Washington, 2; Ted Williams, Boston, 9.

Catchers—Yogi Berra, New York, 8; Elston Howard, New York, 32; Gus Triandos, Baltimore, 11.

Manager—Casey Stengel, New York, 37.

Coaches—Frank Crosetti, New York, 2; Jim Turner, New York, 31.

Batting Practice Pitchers—Alex Kellner, Kansas City, 20; Wally Burnette, Kansas City, 24.

Batting Practice Catcher—Ray Berres, Chicago, 37.

NATIONAL LEAGUE

Pitchers — Johnny Antonelli, New York, 43; Lew Burdette, Milwaukee, 33; Larry Jackson, St. Louis, 39; Clem Labine, Brooklyn, 41; Jack Sanford, Philadelphia, 39; Curt Simmons, Philadelphia, 28; Warren Spahn, Milwaukee, 21.

Infielders—Ernie Banks, Chicago, 14; Don Hoak, Cincinnati, 12; Gil Hodges, Brooklyn, 14; Johnny Logan, Milwaukee, 23; Eddie Mathews, Milwaukee, 41; Roy McMillan, Cincinnati, 11; Stan Musial, St. Louis, 6; Red Schoendienst, Milwaukee, 4; Johnny Temple, Cincinnati, 16.

Outfielders—Hank Aaron, Milwaukee, 44; Gus Bell, Cincinnati, 25; Gino Cimoli, Brooklyn, 9; Willie Mays, New York, 24; Wally Moon, St. Louis, 20; Frank Robinson, Cincinnati, 20.

Catchers—Ed Bailey, Cincinnati, 6; Hank Foiles, Pittsburgh, 20; Hal Smith, St. Louis, 18.

Manager — Walter Alston, Brooklyn, 24.

Coaches—Bobby Bragan, Pittsburgh, 2; Bob Scheffing, Chicago, 24.

Batting Practice Pitchers—Dick Littlefield, Chicago, 34; Herm Wehmeier, St. Louis, 37.

Batting Practice Catcher — Hobie Landrith, St. Louis, 16.

THE OBSERVER

★ ★ ★ ★ ★ ★

By GEORGE CRUDDEN — *Sports Editor*

IT IS DOUBTFUL any baseball fan is going to shed crocodile tears for the alleged plight of some of the owners of major league clubs, who have presented their profit and loss statements at the hearings conducted by the House Anti-Trust Subcommittee in Washington.

We doubt, also, that the Congressmen are impressed by the statement by baseball commissioner Ford Frick that bankruptcy could be the end result for some of the clubs if baseball is put under anti-trust laws.

The rush of some major league owners to the fore with statements showing big blobs of red ink do not impress anyone very much, we repeat, because the same week the Milwaukee Braves gave an 18-year old high school kid $119,000 in bonus money merely for signing a contract!

NOW, WE ARE inclined to believe, that some of the major league clubs, actually do run to red ink, even with all the loot the majors are grabbing, these days, for television and radio rights. But, if true, that it is a tough job these days making ends meet even with all of the additional revenue, then Commissioner Frick and his associates, or, better still, the Congressional investigating committee, ought to call in, quickly, the guy with the net, to cart away the boys who are handing out 100G's for kids who are not yet out of high school let alone ready for the big league pits.

FORD FRICK

We repeat, there may be one or two clubs, who have a hard time making it, but if these baseball mohufs are trying to make a case in point, Milwaukee used very bad timing when it put out $119,000 for a player who may never see a big league ball park. It's happened before.

And, don't forget, Milwaukee outbid Brooklyn which went to 98G's for the kid.

SO THEY'RE swimming in red ink, are they!

We noticed one profit and loss statement that had one item of "other expenses" that came to something like $198,000. We wonder if this included items such as throwing money around for untried bonus players.

If that is the case, then there isn't any wonder why some of these so-called business men can't make a profit in baseball.

They've milked all the income there is to milk, and they have a real sizeable chunk in the till from TV and radio before, the umpire even makes the first call to play baseball, but if the moguls insist on throwing it around like confetti that's their business.

We'll cry tomorrow!

HERE'S SOME of those deals similar to the one the Braves made last week:

Frank Baumann got $100,000 from the Red Sox and he's back in the minors with a dead arm; Paul Pettit got 100G's from the Pirates and became a minor league outfielder; Billy Joe Davidson got $60,000 from the Indians and never made it; and the Orioles gave a kid $40,000 or thereabouts and he's not even in the minors.

That's only a few of them. In fact, only a handful of the big bonus babies have made it. So remember this name: Bob Taylor. He's a catcher and he's the lad the Braves gave $119,000 for signing.

This bonus business is the most ridiculous thing that ever happened to baseball.

TED WILLIAMS fans are entitled to a slightly smug smile of satisfaction these days because their boy merely emerged from the all-star ballotting as the all-star vote getter. That is, everywhere but in provincial Zinzinnati where they hold popularity contests instead of legit all-star polls.

TED WILLIAMS

The Splendid Splinter may be a pain in the neck to the Boston sports-writers, but to the fans he's the real all-star.

Some of the writers were in full pursuit of big Ted, crying for his scalp from official quarters, no later than this Spring when he took off on both major political parties, the Marine Corps and again the press, and many anti-Williams people who have felt that Ted was fair game for their own personal blasts ever since he broke in, believed they had the big Red Socker nailed to the mast.

But that blew over quickly and the first chance the fans got to tell Ted how they felt about him they paid him a tremendous tribute by giving him more votes than any other player in either league. (Outside of Zinzinnati where sometime they are going to send the bat boy up as their official pitching choice).

Even in New York, Mickey Mantle's home town, Ted ran only a few votes behind.

It leads this department to believe that the fans don't give a darn about Ted's pop-offs which are played up out of all proportions by the anti-Williams press in Boston, so long as he propels the baseball out of the park with his classic swing.

S'LONG . . .

Archie Moore Given Week To Sign For Bout

GRAND RAPIDS, Mich., July 6 (AP)—President Floyd Stevens of the National Boxing Assn. (NBA) said today that unless Archie Moore has signed for the defense of his title by "one week from tonight we definitely will strip him of the lightheavyweight championship."

And, Stevens said, the NBA "might at any hour" after midnight tonight declare the championship vacant and order the title "put up for grabs in a four-way elimination tournament."

Stevens said Moore's manager, Charley Johnson, called from New York today to request an extension of tonight's midnight deadline for Moore to sign for a championship fight.

Johnson said he needed more time to work out television and radio arrangements, presumably for a defense against Tony Anthony of New York. But Stevens told newsmen he declined to extend the deadline, informing Johnson the NBA might strip Moore of the title "at any hour" and definitely would be if he hasn't signed by next Saturday midnight.

The NBA suspended Moore last month and ordered him to sign by tonight or be stripped of the title.

Stevens said if Moore doesn't sign an elimination will be ordered between Anthony, Harold Jackson, Yolande Pompey and Yvon Durelle, who drew recently with Anthony. Anthony knocked Chuck Spieser out of the No. 1 challenger slot.

Moore last defended his title June 5, 1956, knocking out Pompey in the 10th round in a London fight.

POLICE-OPTIMIST MIDGET LEAGUE

Teams	W	L	Pct.
Local 285	7	1	.875
I.B.E.W.	5	5	.500
Hagers	5	5	.500
Oblender's	2	7	.222

POLICE-OPTIMIST MIDGET-MIDGET LEAGUE

Teams	W	L	Pct.
K. of C	7	1	.875
Food Fair	7	2	.777
Hubley	6	2	.750
Hamilton	6	3	.666
Schick	6	4	.600
Local 285	2	7	.222
Slaymaker's	1	6	.142
Salvation Army	0	10	.000

WEATHER
(U. S. Weather Bureau)
Partly Cloudy And Mild Today With A High Near 80.
(Details Page 24)

Intelligencer Journal.

TELEPHONE EXpress 7-5251

The Leading Newspaper in the Garden Spot of America. Home Owned for Home Folks Since 1794

164th Year.—No. 56. | Metropolitan Lancaster Population (Estimate) Penna. Dept. of Commerce 248,296 | LANCASTER, PA., TUESDAY MORNING, AUGUST 20, 1957. | CITY EDITION | 24 PAGES. | 42c PER WEEK—7c Per Copy

THE INTELL INDEX

Manor Twp. Sewer Decision Up To People

While tobacco is being harvested in many areas of the county, this field barely shows any growth. It is located along Route 222 near Ephrata, where crops are hardest hit by lack of rain. The plants shown would normally be about four feet high but are now less than one foot tall. (Intell Photo)

Leader Sees Drought, Says Situation Grave, 'Worse Than I Feared'

Powder-dry fields and parched crops in Southeastern Pennsylvania have created a farm situation which Gov. George M. Leader calls ". . . grave, even more than I had feared."

The governor's comment came last evening after he inspected drought conditions in four counties and paused for 20 minutes in Lancaster County to discuss the situation here.

"I plan to cooperate promptly and do everything in my power to help these farm families," Leader said after viewing crops and fields he said were "as bad as anything I've seen in the state."

County Agent Max Smith told the governor that conditions in the northern end of Lancaster County are comparable to those of neighboring Berks, Chester, Bucks and Montgomery counties which the official party toured.

Hardest hit by the drought here are the townships of East and West Cocalico, Brecknock, Rapho, Warwick, Mount Joy and Elizabethtown and the areas near Manheim and the hills at Mastersonville, according to Smith.

The four counties which the governor and his aides toured have formally requested federal aid and the requests are expected to reach the U. S. Department of Agriculture disaster committee in Harrisburg sometime next week. Lancaster County has not requested aid.

"I am told the committee will promptly analyze the request and pass them on to me. As soon as they reach my desk, I will do everything in my power to get help to these farmers," Leader said.

He cautioned that Massachusetts, New Jersey, Maryland, Delaware and Connecticut have been refused federal help or granted only partial help.

The governor's party traveled by auto to various farms in the area, accompanied by local officials. With the Governor were William L. Henning, state agriculture secretary, and L. H. Bull, deputy secretary of the department.

Smith's report to the Governor

Turn To Page 19 For More Of DROUGHT

Levittown Crowd Hits 2 Targets With Missiles

LEVITTOWN, Pa., Aug. 19 (AP)—Stones were hurled tonight in an eruption of new violence after a Negro family moved into this all-white community of 15,000 homes.

A state trooper and a photographer were struck by missiles thrown by someone in a crowd of 250 persons held back by police about two blocks from the ranch home of William Myers, 34-year-old Negro.

"You have struck one of my men," state police Lt. J. M. Wicker announced over a loudspeaker.

GIVEN 10 MINUTES

"I will not tolerate this. I give you 10 minutes to get back to your homes."

His announcement was met by boos and jeers, but the crowd started to disperse. About 150 persons continued to mill about, however.

Then Wicker, a veteran trooper, ordered 22 of his men to line up with riot sticks across the normally quiet residential street and the crowd was pushed back another 20 yards.

A truck driver identified as Donald Walker, 34, was clouted on the shoulders for what Wicker said was cursing officers and resisting the push-back. He was taken to a justice of the peace to be arraigned.

Hit by stones, but not seriously hurt, were state police Sgt. George Gollub and reporter-photographer Gordon Parker of the Bristol (Pa), Courier.

"We're here to stay," Myers said as he carted personal belongings into the $12,150 home. Furnishing were moved in last week.

"We Lead All The Rest"

FARM CORNER

By Joe Wachtman

Steam Hobbyists Begin To Arrive At Kinzers Fete

Boilers are being fired and pumps primed on a myriad array of steam equipment while threshing machines powered by hand, treadmill, sweep, steam and gas are all but ready for the opening of the ninth annual reunion of the Rough and Tumble Engineers Historic Assn., Inc., at Kinzers Thursday through Saturday.

Thousands of visitors from at least one-third of the 48 states are expected to flock into the small Lancaster County community for the event, with a large number of early arrivals already on hand.

In fact, visitors from New York, Ohio and other distant points in the past have so outnumbered those from Lancaster that special evening programs have been planned this year to swell local attendance.

Hobbyists of any sort of mechanical bent are invited to display their handiwork or to bring duplicates for swapping at the trading post. A special ladies hobby show is also planned.

A teeter-totter of mastodonic scale will support two huge mechanical monsters under a full head of steam, delicately balancing and counterbalancing on opposite ends of the king-sized version of a child's see-saw.

Threshing, once known only as hard work, will be done purely for fun in several contests to test the

Turn To Page 19 For More Of FARM CORNER

Irvin Graybill Jr., Stevens R1, shows some of the stunted corn in his 30-acre planting. The corn is not expected to produce ears and is being cut for silage. (Intell Photo)

Hamilton Taking Look At Far Eastern Watch Market

Entry of Hamilton Watch Co. into the Far Eastern watch market, where sales of the local made timepieces have been negligible in the past was seen a possibility yesterday in a statement made by Arthur B. Sinkler, Hamilton president.

His statement came on the heels of a visit here by representatives of the Japanese watch industry. They made a courtesy call as the guests of Hamilton following a trip to Japan by Sinkler.

"The best possibility for Hamilton to profit from this growing Far Eastern market," Sinkler pointed out, "is to enter into some kind of marketing or technical agreement which would permit a joint effort between Hamilton and a Japanese firm in exploiting this market."

Sinkler added that one result of the visit by Japanese representatives has been an expression of "interest" in Hamilton and specific proposals to the company for future marketing projects and other cooperative ventures.

"These proposals are being carefully examined by Hamilton because no possible method of increasing the prosperity of the company can be overlooked," he said.

Sinkler added that "one proposal in particular is being seriously considered" but emphasized that it is being considered only in terms of safeguarding Hamilton's position in the American watch industry and its own domestic manufacturing facilities.

Watches and clocks now produced in Japan are mainly for domestic consumption and Sinkler pointed out that the Japanese were greatly impressed with the quality and precision production

Turn To Page 6 For More Of HAMILTON

FLAMINGO FLING

Another Gang Held In Ornament Thefts

There was mounting evidence last night that the pilfering of lawn ornaments is—maybe it would be better to say has been—a favorite nocturnal pastime of a certain group of Lancaster's younger set this summer.

Hand in glove with the evidence, however, was tangible proof that the law was taking a view of the operation that was as dark as the "midnight requisitions."

State Police announced last evening that four more youths have been arrested on larceny charges. This brings to 13 the total number of arrests for lawn ornament thefts within the past three days.

Nine youth were arrested Saturday. Police said the operations of the two groups were apparently separate actions.

The four youths arrested yesterday are alleged to have taken five ceramic flamingos from lawns of homes in the Conestoga Gardens area of Lancaster Twp. on the night of Aug. 10.

They were identified as Michael L. Rohm, eighteen, 20 Green St.; Russell W. Baker,

Turn To Page 6 For More Of FLAMINGOS

TYPHOON HEADS FOR COAST OF S. KOREA

TOKYO, Tuesday, Aug. 20 (AP)—Typhoon Agnes spared Okinawa and southern Japan from her full fury today and churned toward the west coast of South Korea.

The season's first big storm, with center winds of 140 miles an hour, sent hundreds of Japanese fishing boats scurrying for cover in the ports of Red China and Japan.

19 MILES FROM GROUND

Believe New Mark Set By County Balloonist

CROSBY, Minn., Aug. 19 (AP)—An Air Force doctor probing outer space in a huge plastic balloon was believed to have set an altitude mark of nearly 19 miles late today when ground observers estimated the bag hit 100,000 feet.

Dr. David G. Simons, Marietta, Pa. riding in a gondola suspended from the helium-filled bag, radioed that he was very comfortable and feeling fine after eight hours aloft. He said temperature in the aluminum gondola was 64 degees.

Col. J. W. McCurdy of the Air Force, ground observers for the project, said any substantiation of the record would have to await check of the balloon's instruments. He explained that estimates from the ground were subject to "wide error."

McCurdy said as the helium in the balloon contracted when the sun went down, the bag dropped to an estimated 80,000 feet where it was believed it would drift through the night. The balloon will again rise when the sun comes up, expanding the gas, he reported. He called the slump in altitude natural and expected. McCurdy said the big bag was hovering in the Detroit Lakes-Fergus Falls area of Minnesota and that its future route would be determined by what winds it encounters.

McCurdy said radar tracking disclosed the balloon had shifted somewhat from its direct westerly route and was spotted above Sisseton in extreme northeastern South Dakota about 10:30 p.m. He said it was pursuing a southwesterly course at about 80,000 foot altitude.

From a mine pit 450 feet deep on the Cuyuna iron range near here, the balloon had travelled about 100 miles west and slightly north to a point just southeast of Detroit Lakes. It had averaged about 100 miles west and slightly

Turn To Page 6 For More Of BALLOON

MEETING WILL BE CALLED TO SETTLE ISSUE

Supervisors Will Go With Majority After All Facts Are Heard

The Manor Township sewer proposal fight moved closer to a climax last night as the township supervisors, meeting with the sewer authority, decided to place the fate of the project before the public at a mass meeting.

This meeting will be designed to make sure that "everyone affected understands the nature and seriousness of the sewage problem in the northeast portion of Manor Township," the supervisors said.

"If, after such a meeting, a majority still opposes the proposed project, the matter will be postponed indefinitely."

HALT ENGINEERING WORK

Until the issue is resolved the supervisors halted "any additional engineering work for the time being."

The supervisors decision was announced at the two-hour long meeting, held in the office of F. Tucker Smith, authority chairman. About 20 persons, including a number of opponents, attended the session.

Since the authority announced its plans to construct a $915,000 sewage system and treatment plant, nearly 400 of the 600 plus property owners affected have asked to be omitted.

Smith said that he believes post cards returned to the supervisors by property owners receiving a brochure explaining the project showed that people were not "fully informed" about the proposal.

He said that of the 114 cards returned, 75 were "negative" and 39 "affirmative." However, Smith added, "some of the comments indicated that some did not understand what was being proposed." He also said that six persons had signed petitions both for and against the project.

OPPOSITION HEARD

Gordon Gochenhauer and J. Richard Seitz, two leading opponents of the project, voiced their opinion that the people in their group are not against sewers.

Gochenhauer said that extension of water mains must come first and a "more sensible approach is needed."

"We are against this particular method and this particular project," he said.

He said that in the York area township sewer authorities floated bonds to install lines tied into the city system. The city expanded its treatment facilities and added 10 per cent to its sewerage charges to the township authorities. The

Turn To Page 6 For More Of MANOR TWP.

Columbia Girl Molested By Sex Parolee

A Columbia policeman yesterday caught a paroled sex offender as he emerged from the bushes near the Pennsylvania Railroad with a ten-year-old Columbia girl.

The man, Irvin F. Miller, thirty-three of York, tried to pull the child back with him as Patrolman Jessel Hollingsworth approached. The child wriggled free and Miller fled.

The patrolman fired two warning shots during the chase but Miller continued to run. Hollingsworth caught him at a "dead end" near the PRR transfer.

The child was immediately taken to a doctor who examined her. He said the child "could have been raped."

The girl told Hollingsworth that Miller lured her from the Amvet playground to a place near the old PRR tunnel. There, she said, the man undressed her, took pictures of her, committed an act of sodomy and attempted to ravish her.

JAILED FOR HEARING

Miller was committed to Lancaster County Prison last night to await a hearing. York police said last night Miller was paroled a year and two months before his sentence would have expired.

While the York man allegedly was committing the sex offenses, his parole officer was in York hunting him.

Miller received a five to ten-year sentence for a morals offense against two York eleven-year-old girls. He was originally scheduled for release from the Eastern Penitentiary in 1959.

Police were notified of the incident when a nine-year-old companion told the first girl's parents of Miller's luring their daughter away for picture-taking. The parents phoned police.

Hollingsworth caught Miller.

Miller was charged with sodomy and attempted rape before Justice of the Peace M. L. Schaibley of Columbia.

Atom Test Delayed

ATOMIC TEST SITE, Nev., Aug. 19 (AP)—A second postponement of the 13th atomic test this year was announced today by the Atomic Energy Commission.

HAROLD E. GREINER

E-town Man To Be New Clerk To Commissioners

Harold E. Greiner, Elizabethtown, has been selected as chief clerk to the county commissioners, it was revealed yesterday.

Greiner, who was employed in the auditor general's office at Harrisburg, replaces Richard L. Musser, also of Elizabethtown, who is resigning from the post on Aug. 31, to enter private employment. Musser held the post for eight years.

The official announcement of Greiner's appointment is scheduled to be made today by former Sen. G. Graybill Diehm, chairman of the board of commissioners.

Greiner has been prominently identified with the activities of the Young GOP of Lancaster County. He served as executive secretary in 1956 and is a member of the board of directors. He also is president of Elizabethtown Regional Young GOP.

SYRIAN NEWS HITS STOCK MARKET HARD

NEW YORK, Aug. 19 (AP)— A sharp drop clipped an estimated $3,850,000,000 from the quoted value of all stocks listed on the New York Stock Exchange today.

News that Communist officers had seized control of Syria's army touched off a decline which gathered momentum throughout the day, leaving prices $1 to $7 a share lower at the close.

International oils, which could be directly effected by developments in the Middle East, suffered from heavy selling pressure. Steels, motors, nonferrous metals and chemicals were among other declining groups.

Democratic Atomic Plans Said Adopted

WASHINGTON, Aug. 20 (AP)—The major part of a Democratic program for government-constructed atomic power reactors was reported adopted today by a Senate-House conference committee.

The result was a defeat for the administration, which had tried to knock the reactor projects out of the 389 million dollar Atomic Authorization Act.

Republicans and Southern Democrats had allied in the House to eliminate most of the projects from the bill. But Senate Democrats held firm last Friday night to restore the projects and send the bill to conference.

ALMOST UNANIMOUS

Rep. Carl Durham (D-NC), chairman of the Senate-House Atomic Energy Committee, said the conference committee vote was "almost unanimous." He predicted it would be accepted by the House.

Senate action is expected to come first, probably tomorrow.

Conference committee Democrats agreed to two compromises that pared 37 million dollars from the bill. But most of the Democratic program, vigorously opposed by the Atomic Energy Commission, was approved.

Republicans have characterized their opposition to the projects as a private vs. public power fight. Democrats have called that claim a smokescreen.

One compromise agreed to eliminate 40 million dollars for construction of a natural uranium gas-cooled reactor at the AEC plant in Arco, Idaho.

Mohn Issued Charters For Seven Hoodlum-Led Unions

WASHINGTON, Aug. 19 (AP) — Vice President Einar O. Mohn of the Teamsters Union took full responsibility today for issuing charters to seven New York locals described by senators as hoodlum-led phonies.

But Mohn said the idea originated with James R. Hoffa, another teamster Vice President who has become a central figure in the Senate investigation of the union.

Mohn said he was unaware of the locals' racketeer leadership, and okayed the charters as a routine thing.

Chairman McClellan of the Senate Rackets Investigating Committee has charged that the seven locals were used by Hoffa, Teamster boss in the Midwest, in a way calculated to extend his influence to New York.

The locals' votes helped defeat

Turn To Page 6 For More Of PROBE

EINAR O. MOHN

Syrian Troubles Blamed On Ike's Doctrine By Official

DAMASCUS, Syria, Aug. 19 (AP)—Foreign Minister Salah Bitar today blamed the Eisenhower Doctrine for Syria's troubles with the United States.

"Syria has been the target of destructive activities aimed at making her accept the Eisenhower Doctrine," Bitar said in a statement to a news conference.

"It is already known that the main object of the conspiracy to overthrow the Syrian and Egyptian regimes is to set up governments that will change from liberal foreign policies and join the imperialistic line."

QUERIED ON BREAK

Asked whether Syria might consider breaking relations with the United States, Bitar replied: "This question depends on the United States and steps she wants to adopt in the future."

Bitar denied that any of 10 officers fired from the army at the weekend were arrested. He said the officers were dismissed "in the country's interests."

American-Syrian relations have been near the breaking point since Syria accused the United States of plotting to overthrow the regime.

Three U.S. Embassy officials were removed at Syria's request and the United States in turn withdrew its ambassador and ousted the Syrian ambassador in Washington. (Both were absent from their posts at the time and will not return).

U.S. Embassy officials termed the Syrian charges a "complete fabrication."

(The U.S. State Department now has publicly adopted a wait-and-see attitude on Syrian developments. The United States has committed 174 million dollars in economic aid under the Eisenhower Doctrine to Middle East nations that agreed to oppose Communist intrusion. Syria, which has the only legalized Communist party in the Arab sphere, rejected the offer.

Bitar denied that Syria is turning Communist and insisted the policy remains one based on nonalignment and positive neutrality.

Cars Of Guests At Card Party Given Shuffle

Six youths had a field day last night with the cars of persons attending a bridge party in the 1500 block of New Holland Ave.

They let the air out of tires of two cars, pushed another one half way out into the street, and drove a station-wagon into a field about 10:30 p.m.

All of the vehicles were parked on Pinehurst Road by persons attending the party at the home of Robert P. Crowell, 1493 New Holland Ave., according to Manheim Twp. police.

A neighbor heard the air being left out of the tires and went to see what was going on. She told police she saw six youths jump into a car and drive off.

Lancaster City's "Waistline" Spreads From 8 Miles To 35 In 10 Years Of Fattening-Up

LIKE HANGING ONTO A BUCKING BRONC, city officials must move fast to keep up with the territorial expansion of the city. The crazy city outline looked suitable for this caricature to Sunday News artist.

Town's No "Square" Now; "Peninsulas" Present Problems For Police, Firemen, Engineers

Trim in all her measurements, the 2-mile-square city of Lancaster shunned 218 years of advances toward a bulging waistline. But in the past ten years, her figure has spread grotesquely over the map.

The recent final approval of the annexation of 609 acres upheld by the State Supreme Court jutted the city outline eastward to include the Schick plant. This is just the most recent of four "crazy quilt" boundary patterns probing away from the city — appendages that must get all of the attention given the main body by the city government.

It's no small item for city officials to take up the business of sending the necessities of daily living into these urban peninsula extending into the townhips' expanses. Nevertheless, such services as fire protection, police protection, traffic engineering and the like are all included in becoming a part of the city.

One of the first men to be confronted with problems when annexations crop into the picture is J. Haines Shertzer, the city engineer. Tracing the outline—especially one as contorted as Lancaster's new boundary — is a lot more work than marking a line on a map.

He may not be the man who goes out on the job each time—though in many cases he is. Nevertheless, he is responsible for having each of the annexed areas surveyed. He must determine to the precise foot where the city limit is located. He must then accurately transcribe that into map form.

Even Leaves Islands

Take a look at Lancaster city today. The staggering city line winds around private dwellings, bisects roads, splits other roads down the middle and in some places even leaves isolated properties as township domain, smack-dab in the middle of a city area.

Ever since Lancaster was laid out as a political subdivision in 1729 and when it was incorporated as a borough in 1742 and as a city in 1818, the 2-mile-square boundary held fast. Since 1947 the square pattern has been blown to pieces.

For more than two centuries, it was only a little better than an eight-mile trek around the outside limits of the city—a trek surveyors for the city made occasionally, although not in one jaunt.

Today, with long twisty appendages of the city jutting out into Manheim Township, Lancaster Township and East and West Lampeter Townships, it means almost a 35-mile hike to walk around the city.

AN AID FOR THE POLICE is the city line painted on the road. City engineers plotted the boundary line across various roads entering the city. A patrolman in a cruiser has a quick visual indication whether a violation or accident occurred inside or outside the city limits.

NEW CITY MAPS for the use of police, fire and other city departments are prepared by the city engineers. The exact boundaries of the city are designated so that a fast reference is available. Here, Police Commissioner Fred G. McCartney (left) and Sgt. Donald Wireback discuss police protection in the new areas. This map is located in the police radio room. (Sunday News Photos)

Inside that sprawling boundary line, the area of the city is only one-sixteenth of a square acre short of being 7 square miles. Originally the city area was four square miles.

With the city spreading out in such odd shapes and cutting so many crazy corners, it isn't hard to imagine the difficulties involved in providing police protection.

Used To Be Simple

Comparatively, it was a simple matter setting up patrols and investigation procedures in the once-square city. Now, all of the new areas need the same services.

City Engineer Shertzer played an important role in alleviating the situation for Police Commissioner Fred G. McCartney. He provided the Police Dept.—and the fire department and traffic engineer — with detailed maps of the new city boundaries. What's more, he had the streets which cut through the boundary lines marked with code lines. These almost insignificant markings on the streets give the cruiser patrolmen a clearcut indication of where the city's jurisdiction starts and ends.

Patrols through the new far-flung areas present problems. Those new areas jutting into Lancaster and West Lampeter townships are virtually isolated, cut off from the city by the Conestoga creek. Imagine the problem involved if a cruiser is patrolling the newly annexed area in Conestoga Gardens and there is an emergency call across the creek in the part of Hilltop Acres development now in the city. They can't fly.

Then, too, in each of the annexed areas there are spots where the new boundary line twists back and forth around property lines of owners who chose not to become part of the city. These present problems when there are emergency investigations of accidents or reports of burglaries.

Must Be Solomons

There have been cases where an accident happened on the dividing line. The police must determine whether the accident happened in the city or in the township before the investigation can be conducted.

According to Commissioner McCartney, if there's an accident, city police will report immediately and take care of injured persons and direct traffic no matter which side of the line it occurs. However, the investigation of the accident will have to wait until it is determined exactly where the accident occurrred.

One particular teaser came up since the annexation of the area jutting into West Lampeter township. There was an accident on Eshelman Mill Road. The city police responded and the car involved was in both the city and the township (the middle of the road is the dividing line). It wasn't until after the actual point where the accident occurred was determined that it was decided that the township police should investigate the accident.

Smooth Out Difficulties

Road maintenance hits similar bumps. However, in the course of time, working arrangements usually are developed in such matters. Where a segment of the city cuts across a road and perhaps only several hundred feet are not township responsibility, it is a usual practice to have the township care for the road and the city reimburse the township for materials and labor. Such a setup is reciprocal for other roads where more is in the city.

Fire protection, too, must be considered for the new areas. Fire apparatus is sent to any fire in the city — new or old.

At present, there is little problem with traffic flow, according to Robert Chryst, city traffic engineer. The new districts are already set up to handle the traffic, but as the areas are further developed, new problems are bound to arise.

It would appear that in the course of time changes will become necessary.

Although Police Commissioner McCartney feels it won't be necessary, a precinct setup for the police may some day be suggested. He feels that a precinct or sub-station system might sometime have some merit, but prefers to rely on the present modern communications system between patrol cars and the headquarters to allow Lancaster to provide efficient police protection from the central headquarters.

Currently, the fire department is widespread. At present there is no indication whether future development in newly annexed areas will provide a demand for further equipment and housing.

Traffic Engineer Chryst sees the possibility of a new problem — one that was predicted as long ago as the Norton report on traffic in 1929.

It seems obvious to him that the area along Lampeter road across the creek from Conestoga Gardens and the areas of Hilltop Acres and Linville Circle will be more and more developed into a residential section. That being the case, Chryst feels that there will be a demand for bridges across the Conestoga to eliminate the two or three miles of extra travelling north or south to get to places in the southern part of the city, like the Posey Iron Works.

ENGINEERS establish new city lines after annexations. Here, Joseph Schmalhofer, assistant city engineer (center), directs the operation of the crew. Charles Rotsam (left) is working at the surveyor's instrument, while Dan Gohn and Carl Simmons are in the background. (Sunday News Photos)

The Book Review

CHARLIE. By Ben Hecht. Harper.

If you're a celebrity and want to be remembered after you're gone, the surest way is to pick an articulate writer as your best friend.

Charles MacArthur probably wouldn't give a hoot about being memorialized. But the fortunate circumstance of having made friends with Ben Hecht when both were reporters in the fabled heyday of Chicago newspapering ("We trotted, coach-dog fashion, at the heels of the human race, our tails a-wag") has provided MacArthur with a biographer who knew him intimately, writes with great feeling and extremely well.

It's unfortunate that Hecht felt the need on occasion to copy four-letter words off toilet walls, but even this doesn't detract more than briefly from a job of character painting in fascinating depth. Most of the time, he has the good sense to let the story tell itself.

Hecht had access to many of MacArthur's love letters to his wife, Helen Hayes. Theirs was a devoted romance from the day they met in 1924 until MacArthur died in 1956. There are scores of anecdotes from the 41 years that Hecht and MacArthur were friends. A parade of prominents fills the pages; intimate little stories of the famous and little people and little things that helped MacArthur find so much —if sometimes raucous—enjoyment in life.

Taking stock at one point in the book, Hecht says: "I've stopped pretending that I am writing a biography. What I am writing is obviously a letter about a friend who died. My communication may have in it chiefly the moonings of one left on empty battlements."—Pete Arthur

A DICTIONARY OF CONTEMPORARY AMERICAN USAGE. By Bergen Evans and Cornelia Evans. Random House.

There is no "ought" in writing or speech. Nothing is right or wrong abstractly, there is only the standard of use, or so these 600 pages of examples have been assembled to prove. In other words, language is merely a matter, the Evanses say, of keeping up with the Joneses.

By this easy method, you do not have to know anything, you only have to count. If more people in your neighborhood confuse "lie" and "lay" than not, then you should confuse them, otherwise the Evanses will call you a purist and accuse you of showing off. They approve of "who do you want" and "more unique, most unique;" they see nothing wrong in "ump ump tastes good like a cigarette should," and they split infinitives as quick as you bat an eye.

I am a purist, which by their definition is just anti-Evans — and to be sure it is all relative. But they throw away too much too fast. Cut off an accuracy here, add vagueness there, and language is no longer a useful tool.

You remember the farmer with the horse to sell? He admitted to the purchaser, "It don't look good." But the purchaser thought it looked fine. He came back later however to complain it was blind. "I told you," the farmer retorted. The Evanses pave the way to "look good" and so on to the sign language, which is back where we started. We should go in the other direction, not the easy Evans way but the hard way, we should refine the language instead of blunting it.

GUNNER WITH STONEWALL, Reminiscences of William Thomas Poague. McCowat-Mercer Press.

When the first fever of Civil War enthusiasm swept the South, William Thomas Poague, then a young lawyer in Lexington, Va., enlisted in the Rockbridge Artillery, one of the most famed batteries in the Confederate Army. Its commander was the Rev. William N. Pendleton and its initial equipment included four six-pounders dubbed by the soldiers Matthew, Mark, Luke and John "because they spoke a powerful language."

Poague was elected junior second lieutenant, and was promoted to captain in command of the battery, early in 1862. Attached to the renowned "Stonewall Brigade" originally led by Stonewall Jackson, Poague commanded the battery in Jackson's Shenandoah Valley campaign, the Seven Days Battle of 1862 in front of Richmond, Second Manassas, Antietam and Fredericksburg. Later he led an artillery battalion at Gettysburg, in the Wilderness and during the long, bloody months to Appomattox.

His service was distinguished and his memoirs, here resurrected by the personal energy of Monroe F. Cockrell, are equally so. With an introduction by Bell Irvin Wiley, Poague's reminiscences are one of the most eloquent of Civil War memoirs, all the more remarkable because they were so long unknown.

Poague wrote his story in four notebooks, for his children. He never had any idea that they would be published, a fact that enhances their informal charm.

Salted with shrewd observations of men and strategies, spiced with colorful anecdotes, unassuming, gentle, consistently interesting, "Gunner with Stonewall" is a tremendously important addition to the ever-growing library of Civil War literature.

OPERATION SEA LION. By Peter Fleming. Simon & Schuster.

One of the things we remember best about World War II, aside from our own experiences, was the threat of the invasion of England in 1940. We sympathized with Poland, with the French beaten on the continent and the British kicked off it at Dunkirk. But the English in their homes, if they were no dearer, were nearer, we could visualize bombs on London as we hadn't been able to on Warsaw, we knew the channel coast and not the Polish frontier. We heard Churchill's ringing phrases.

So this account of Fleming's may well mean more to us than many war books, for it tells how Hitler tried and failed to invade.

Fleming believes Hitler kept on hoping for too long that his loud talk would scare the British right out of the war.

The Fuehrer wanted the English off his neck while he attacked Russia, and the idea was revived. Curiously the English, though they worried about it in 1914, were late this time but when they started they made up for it with some practical moves, and eventually with a good job of out-thinking their foes. As for the Germans, they blew hot and cold, prepared inexpertly for a cross-channel drive which Fleming thinks would have failed in the fall, and diverted their bombers fatally from Britain's desperately needed defense installations to open raids on London.

With a few pertinent quotes, Fleming smartly calls attention to the "Alice in Wonderland" air which that grim, fearsome and triumphant summer sometimes had. It's a rousing account, and a fine reminder of a people summoned to a heroic stand by a dauntless leader.

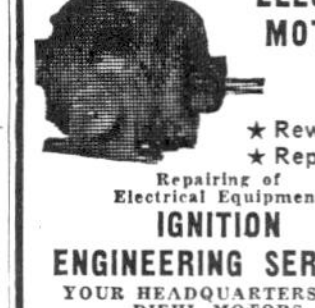

DOLLAR

Local Counterfeit Scheme "Most Daring, Dangerous, Colossal" Ever In U.S.A.

DOLLAR

LAST TRACES GONE — Two years ago the old tobacco warehouse (at right) at Grant and Christian Streets, headquarters for Lancaster's infamous counterfeiting ring of the 1890s, was torn away. Today (at left) the site is a parking lot. The building was last used by the gas company, and had the old police station as neighbor.

New Book Puts Lancaster Funny - Money Operation Of 60 Years Ago At Top Of List

Lancaster is proud of the many outstanding accomplishments of its citizens through the years, but there is one historic feat currently receiving nationwide attention which she would just as soon forget.

The "most daring, the most dangerous and the most colossal counterfeiting scheme in American history" was perpetrated 60 years ago by a pair of overzealous Lancastrians named William M. Jacobs and William L. Kendig.

The entire story is outlined in Murray T. Bloom's new book, "Money of Their Own," published by Scribner's. Bloom devotes the largest chapter in his book to the scheme, which forced the U. S. Treasury Department to call in an entire issue of currency, 26 million dollars worth of hundred-dollar bills.

Neither of the two masterminds was a Lancaster City native. Jacobs, born in Montgomery County, was a cigar manufacturer. Lancaster, the center of the Pennsylvania cigarmaking industry, attracted him in 1892.

2 Factories Burned

Earlier he had owned factories in Boyertown and East Greenville, both of which had been destroyed in "mysterious" fires. The losses in both of the blazes were most amptly covered by insurance.

Kendig's family moved to Lancaster about 1885 from Conestoga, where his father had been a conutry doctor. The father and his three sons purchased a tobacco-leaf wholesaling firm, which was also razed in a fire of slightly suspicious origin.

With so much in common it was inevitable that Jacobs and Kendig would eventually get together. Their first joint venture was a credit swindle they pulled off in 1893, purchasing merchandise from New York firms on credit, quickly reselling it at half price through a dummy firm in Philadelphia, and not paying the bills.

They next decided to try their larcenous skill in the field about which they knew the most: cigar manufacturing. With the help of two talented young Philadelphia engravers named Baldwin S. Bredell and Arthur Taylor, the duo began counterfeiting the Federal tax stamps required on cigars.

Aided by the cooperation of the local collector of internal revenue, Samuel B. Downey, who was slipped five hundred a month by J&K, the scheme went off without a hitch.

Stamps to $100 Bills

Bloom relates that in the fall of 1896 Jacobs decided that the conspirators should branch out even further. If revenue stamps could be successfully duplicated, why not hundred-dollar bills?

They decided to print 10 million dollars worth of the bills, depositing them in fifty key banks around the country. After a few weeks they would withdraw the money by check, invest it in securities, and distribute the proceeds to the members of the conspiracy.

Bredell and Taylor made the plates, while Jacobs and Kendig attempted to obtain paper upon which to print the money. However, impatient with the latter's slowness, the young engravers went ahead on their own and used "bleached" one dollar bills that they had split in half.

It was a too-lightly inked seal on one of the first batch run off by Bredell and Taylor that tripped them up. The job in general was so perfect that Treasury officials thought at first that something had gone wrong with their inking machinery.

However, William H. Moran, the sharp-eyed assistant to the secret service chief, noted that the paper seemed a trifle too thick. Bloom tells us that he put one of the notes in a pan of hot water and waited. In twenty minutes the rice paste holding together the two halves of the note face-to-face gave way, and a most ingenious counterfeit was discovered.

Called In Issue

Because of the expertness of the forgery, it was decided to call in all of the hundred-dollar certificates of that issue. Meanwhile, Secret Service men began methodically investigating the habits of all Philadelphia engravers. It was only a matter of time until they caught up with the high-living Taylor and Bredell, who led them to Kendig and Jacobs.

The arrest of the Lancaster pair came on April 19, 1899. The New Era of the next day proclaimed that "Lancaster's blank amazement at finding itself the lair of the most dangerous counterfeiters who ever plotted against the Treasury of the United States, and two of its most prominent men the leaders of these expert criminals, has been followed by the greatest excitement. Business was almost suspended in the city."

The detective - story chain of events included the hiring of a new Secret Service chief, specifically to crack the Lancaster case. The plot wound its way through a Philadelphia law office and a brazen attempt at bribery. It involved a newsboy who tossed a ball through the transom of the warehouse where the illegal operation was underway, to furnish an excuse for climbing inside and then letting in the federal agents. It saw the young engravers make a counterfeit plate and print bills while inside a penitentiary, in the hope of bargaining with the courts — a light sentence for their confession of the hiding place of the engraved plates. The details are in many places so incredible a mystery - story writer would hesitate to use them.

Kendig and Jacobs were sentenced to twelve years in jail and fined $5,000 apiece. However, they were pardoned by Theodore Roosevelt on July 1, 1905. The Intelligencer thought the pardon ill advised, calling the pair "the most dangerous thieves who were ever sent to the penitentiary."

Kendig returned to his wife's home at 416 N. Duke St., currently occupied by an apartment house. He lived in Lancaster until his death in 1954 at 89. Mrs. Kendig, the former Helen Bitner, received sufficient inheritance upon the death of their father to keep them both comfortably. They had no children.

Jacobs, who had lived at 315 E. Orange St., never returned to Lancaster. Shortly after he was imprisoned his wife sold their home and moved to Pottstown, where his brother, Irving, operated a cigar factory.

Jacobs worked for his brother for several years, moving to Norristown in 1918. He later became production manager for the Dill Company, manufacturing chemists. He died on July 30, 1934, at the age of seventy-one.

"Evidence" Gone

The site of the warehouse owned by Kendig at 212 N. Queen St. is now the Sears Roebuck Farm Store. The Jacobs cigar factory at the corner of Grant and Christian streets, occupied for a time by the Lancaster County Gas Division was torn down in November 1955 to make room for a new parking lot.

In his opening remarks on the case, Bloom blames the "logic of the age" for the immense scheme. He states that Jacobs "inhaled gradually, finally grew to appreciate the rich odor of decay" prevalent in the Pennsylvania of that era.

He says that in the rich and corrupt Pennsylvania of the 1890's, "crime was not the abhorrent, abnormal way of life, but the accepted manner of things. Only the nose-holders found themselves out of step."

Bloom calls Lancaster "an old city, redolent with history and the importance of social position." He insists that family and social position counted greatly in Lancaster in those days, and implies that it was a desire to "keep up with the Joneses" that started the pair on the road to dazzling success and then dismal failure.

Though the author blames the political morality of the Matt Quay era for the climate in which the Jacobs-Kendig frauds developed, he concludes that, in general, "counterfeiters counterfeit to make money." His rejection of Freudian psychology in the motivation of funny-money makers is refreshing.

There is some perverse satisfaction in finding a couple of local boys in the company of the world's best anything — even counterfeiters. Few of them have any resemblance to the general picture of the small-time malefactor. A New Jersey farmer, Emanual Ninger, was hailed as a great artist after his arrest for making beautiful copies of banknotes with just pen and ink and camel's-hair brush. He was a contemporary of Jacobs and Kendig, having been caught in 1896.

Then there was Artur Alvin Reis, who persuaded the printers of Portugal's paper money to run off a special issue of $15,000,000 worth for him. He set up his own banks to distribute it, and insisted he was not a counterfeiter but an "inflationist." Though the Bank of Portugal found itself the embarrassed owner of an extra three million dollars in usable currency, the political overtones were so violent that the episode led to the overthrow of the government and the setting up of the Salazar dictatorship.

Better Than Originals

The Yugoslavian Jose Beraha Zdravko made himself two million dollars by minting British sovereigns with more gold in them than the original. That was after World War II when people were seeking solid money as a hedge against inflation. England had gone off the gold standard and stopped making sovereigns, but those manufactured by Zdravko were in such great demand that they sold for much more than the worth of their gold content. And the man behind the scheme could not be convicted of counterfeiting legal tender because the sovereign wasn't legal tender any more.

Bloom points the moral that almost all counterfeiters get caught. One who didn't, however, is an unnamed Briton whose scheme for quick riches was similar to that with which Kendig and Jacobs started. He was a civil service employe who made his own revenue stamps to be affixed to telegrams in the London stock exchange in the 1870s. He retired at 40, and by the time the authorities caught up with him the statute of limitations had expired, though his profits had not.

There are many more, some just mentioned and others given the full treatment. Bloom concludes that the old-time counterfeiter of small means and grubby surroundings is being squeezed out by the big-time operation on a national scale—"Deliberate, illegal reproduction of another nation's currencies." It's been tried before with varying success. Bloom agrees with the military strategists who say that the H-bomb will be followed by a fleet of planes carrying a payload of counterfeit money to complete the demoralization.

On the other hand, perhaps inflation will make the counterfeiter obsolete because he simply can't compete with the speed of government presses.

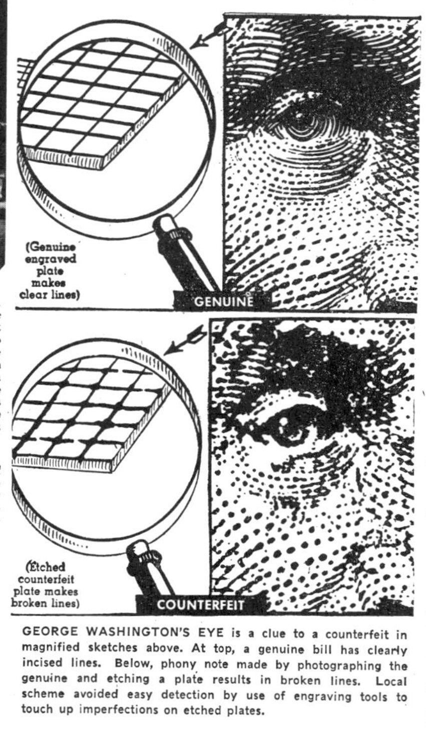

GEORGE WASHINGTON'S EYE is a clue to a counterfeit in magnified sketches above. At top, a genuine bill has clearly incised lines. Below, phony note made by photographing the genuine and etching a plate results in broken lines. Local scheme avoided easy detection by use of engraving tools to touch up imperfections on etched plates.

The Book Review

REMEMBER ME TO GOD. By Myron S. Kaufmann. Lippincott.

Adam and Bessie Amsterdam and their children, Richard, Harvard freshman, and his younger sister Dorothy, fill the many pages of this impressive first novel about a Jewish family in and around Boston in the opening years of the last war.

Adam is a special justice, to which he rose from butcher by hard study at night school. He is undistinguished, with only an elementary education, a man of great honesty and integrity. Bessie is conservative, with typical superficial suburban ambitions, and devout. Dorothy stutters, and has trouble finding a boy friend.

Richard is the central problem. A sensitive kid, possessing the drive we pretend to admire, he thinks about his problems: His Jewishness, his determination to succeed on Lampoon and get into the Hasty Pudding Club, his longing for a girl, with his affection now centered on Jeanie, of his own faith, and now on Wimsy. Richard is a creep, you are apt to suspect at first; you blush when he is brazen and forward, hate to believe success is won so unscrupulously, and don't understand how a boy so easily hurt himself can hurt others so easily.

There are stirring scenes — Dorothy with a Marine she picked up innocently, Adam chasing his stubborn son up the stairs of the dormitory. There is a mass of the most convincing detail, almost Dickensian in its abundance, caught by a tireless observer. The bumbling Richard who frankly acknowledges his own worst faults, the lovable Dorothy, the staunch father, the callow mixture of college boys and girls — these are the first fine, happy offerings of an astute and talented interpreter of American life.

Among the first ten contestants signed up to compete in the Miss Lancaster County contest are (l-r): Miss Gladys Geib (Lititz Lions Club); Miss Kay Musser (Ephrata Lions Club), and Miss Brenda Meyer, Brownstown (West Earl Lions Club).

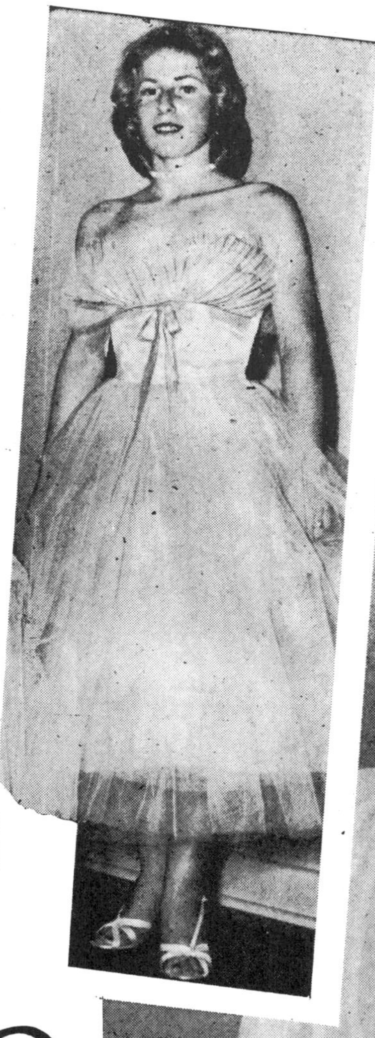

Left
Miss Bette Howry, Lancaster (The American Legion, Cloister Post 429, Ephrata).

Below
Miss Dorothy Fletcher (Marietta Junior Chamber of Commerce).

Miss America 1959?

THEY'RE COMPETING FOR COUNTY CROWN

Early contestants are preparing to compete for the title of Miss Lancaster County. They are sponsored by civic organizations. The winner will compete for Miss Pennsylvania of 1958, who will be eligible to compete for Miss America 1959. Miss Lancaster County will be selected Sept. 26 as part of the Ephrata Fair through the cooperation of the Ephrata Fair Association and the Ephrata Junior Chamber of Commerce.

Miss Gloria Ann Leakway (Mt. Joy Junior Chamber of Commerce) and Miss Lucille Hirneisen (Ephrata Kiwanis Club).

Miss Ann E. Aten (Lancaster Junior Chamber of Commerce); Miss Gladys Albright, Reamstown (East Cocalico Lions Club), and Miss Fae Ann Floyd (Manheim Junior Chamber of Commerce).

Today's Chuckle

John: "But couldn't you learn to love me, Anna?"
Anna: "I don't think I could, John."
John (reaching for his hat): "It is as I feared — you are too old to learn."

LANCASTER NEW ERA

Metropolitan Lancaster Population (Est.), Penna. Dept. of Commerce 248,296

Local Weather

Lancaster U. S. Bureau

Partly cloudy tonight and tomorrow. Warmer tomorrow afternoon. Low tonight near 48. High tomorrow in the low 70's.

Complete Report on Page 3

81st Year—No. 24,926 | METROPOLITAN EDITION | LANCASTER, PA., MONDAY, OCTOBER 7, 1957 | 30 PAGES | 42c PER WEEK—7c Per Copy

U.S. Gets 'Fix' on Soviet Satellite, Can Plot Path

May Be Able to Take Photos in 8 or 9 Days

WASHINGTON (AP)—U. S. Naval scientists said today they have a good "fix" on the Russian space satellite, and can plot its path ahead anywhere from 24 hours to a week.

A spokesman at the Naval Research Laboratory also said Navy scientists now know when they get the beeping signal from the satellite that their readings are precise to 1-10,000 of a second.

The latest information here is that the satellite is following what the spokesman called a "fairly circular orbit." The exact height has not been determined, he said, but it is a minimum of 400 miles high.

Smithsonian Institute Tracking

At Cambridge, Mass., Moonwatch officials said American astronomical observatories may get photographs of the Russian satellite within eight or nine days.

Dr. J. Allen Hynek, who is in charge of the optical tracking program of the Astrophysical Observatory of the Smithsonian Institution, said that radio tracking computations have by now "pretty well determined the orbit of the Russian satellite."

Dr. Hynek said the latest radio tracking computation showed that the satellite passed near Boston on a northwest southeast direction at "precisely 8 a.m. Eastern Daylight Time."

Foreigners Tour U. S. Lab

U.S. scientists, who hope the Russians will share any scientific knowledge gained through the satellite, gave a group of foreign scientists a tour of the Naval Laboratory.

The visitors, here for an international conference on rocket and satellite programs, included three Russians — A. A. Balgonravov, Sergei M. Poloskov and A. M. Kasatskin. U.S. reporters were not permitted to accompany the scientists on the tour.

U.S. scientists are tracking the Russian satellite with signals recorded at nine points in North and South America. The information received at these points is speed into Washington where it is fed into an electronic brain.

The receiving points, known as "minitrack stations" are located Lima, Peru; Antofagasta, Chile; Santiago, Chile, Antigua, British West Indies and San Diego, Calif.

Visible In Week Or 10 Days

With establishment of a fix on the Russian baby moon, Navy trackers said it should become visible in the continental United States "in about a week or 10 days."

A spokesman for Project Vanguad, the U.S. satellite program, said it is estimated that the Soviet satellite will begin at that time to make passages over he United States during predawn or evening twilight periods—the only times it would be visible.

He said the "extreme northwest portion of the country" would be the first to see it and that it would be in the evening.

Asked about reports the satellite already had been seen with the naked eye in Alaska, the spoke-

—See SATELLITE—Page 25

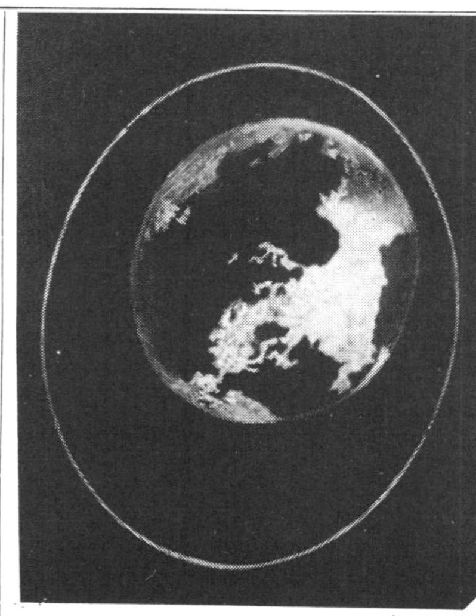

New Era Photo

Solid white line shows Russian satellite's orbit around earth in show at North Museum's planetarium. Satellite news was credited for capacity turnout at planetarium show yesterday.

Soviet Satellite Not Visible Here

Guesses Range Week — 162 Days Before Region Will Get Look

Scientists differed sharply today on when you'll be able to see the Russian "moon" that is circling the earth every 96.2 minutes.

In fact, some doubt that you'll be able to see it all without a telescope or binoculars.

Navy sicentists today said there isn't a chance of seeing Sputnik for at least a week or so, because it can only be seen when it passes over at dawn or dusk.

Dr. I. M. Levitt, director of the Fels Planetarium, Philadelphia, claims that Sputnik will be visible here in 162 days, and possibly a little sooner.

With Naked Eye

The Navy also said that the satellite "should be visible with the naked eye."

Not so, says Dr. Levitt. "At no time will it be visible with the naked eye," he said. "But you will be able to see it with a telescope if you know where to look."

But both agree that the satellite will only be seen in the light of dawn or dusk. When it passes over in full darkness or full daylight, there is no chance at all of seeing it.

In Australia, meanwhile, thousands throughout the state of Victoria reported seeing the man-made moon as it hurtled over the horizon as a pinpoint of light. They reported the sightings varied from 25 seconds to 2½ minutes.

After Midnight

Navy scientists released a time table showing the "moon's" next passage over the United States should be about 12:11 a.m. (EST) tomorrow.

The spokesman said Sputnik is moving across the U. S. in a southeasterly direction. It follows a fairly rigid course but, because the earth is turning beneath its path, moves westward about 1,500 miles with each circuit.

Dr. John M. Cavanaugh, curator of astronomy at the North Museum, said no attempt will be made to sight the satellite from the observatory at Franklin and Marshall College until more defi-

—See LOCAL—Page 2

Satellite News Inside

SOVIET REACTION——Pravda predicts revamp of U. S. foreign policy. Page 2.

U. S. PROGRAM—Not in competition with Reds, says Dr. John P. Hagen, director. Page 4.

FIRST U. S. SPOTTING—Three researchers at University of Alaska, spot satellite. Page 2.

ED CREAGH—Calls for U. S. to inform people on status of our satellite program. Page 14.

SPACE TRAVEL — A. F. "sends" man to simulated altitude of 95 miles in test chamber. Page 4

MILITARY VALUE — French air expert sees great military value in Red satellite. Page 2.

WHY U. S. FAILED?—Expert blames U. S. Army "stupidity." Page 2.

MYSTERY FOR WEST — Red satellite poses three questions for West. Page 2.

SOVIET ROCKET BOOSTER ALSO CIRCLING EARTH

LONDON (AP)—Russia disclosed tonight that the rocket which carried the "red moon" into outer space is also circling the earth.

A Soviet jet expert said yesterday the rocket which boosted the earth satellite 560 miles into the sky last Friday was 25 per cent more powerful than the rocket which carried the first Soviet intercontinental ballistics missile 3,500 to 5,000 miles during the summer. Maj. Gen. G. Pokrovsky said the rockets were similar.

Today's Moscow Radio announcement said: "It is not only the satellite which is being watched, but also the rocket that carried it onto the orbit. This rocket is also encircling the earth at approximately the same altitude as the satellite, but is separated from it by some 1,000 kilometers (about 620 miles). This distance will alter in the future."

Missile Flies 2,100 mph wth New U. S. Fuel

Large Scale Research Needed Before Mass Production Possible

CLEVELAND (AP) — A ramjet test missile burning one of the new high-energy fuels, a boron compound, has flown more than three times the speed of sound, or faster than 2,000 m.p.h.

This was disclosed today at the triennial inspection of the Lewis Flight Propulsion Laboratory of the National Advisory Committee for Aeronautics, the top government agency in basic air research.

NACA showed publicly for the first time a 2½ million dollar rocket engine research facility which was completed last August.

See Even Greater Gains

The agency said that the spectacular rocket developments of the past few years may be surpassed by even greater gains from the fuel research now under way.

Officials said the results have been encouraging, but some difficult problems remain. These include:

1. Danger to personnel. Boron compounds can be quite toxic.
2. Combustion deposits inside the engines, which cut down on performance.

NACA officials explained that while the petroleum fuels now burned in jet aircraft are relatively cheap, plentiful and safe, their energy content is too low to satisfy the needs of military planes and missiles.

The agency said in a report prepared for the triennial inspection that a theoretical study of a ramjet missile flying at 60,000 feet at a speed of 2,100 m.p.h. indicated that the use of boron could extend the range 40 per cent beyond that provided by conventional JP4 jet fuel.

Reds Fire New Type H-Bomb

LONDON (AP) — The Russians announced today they have successfully exploded a new type hydrogen bomb. The announcement said a "powerful hydrogen device of new design" was tested at a great altitude yesterday.

The emphasis the Soviet announcement put on the "new design" of the latest hydrogen bomb attracted especial attention here. And the speed with which the Russians disclosed the explosion — the next day — was significant. Usually they wait — or even keep the tests secret even after they are detected outside the Sovie Union.

U. S. Explodes Final H-Bomb in Test Series

ATOMIC TEST SITE, Nev. (AP)—The Atomic Energy Commission fired the 24th, and last, explosion of the 1957 test series at 5 a.m. (PST) today.

Code-named Morgan, the final shot in the Plumbbob series was detonated from a balloon tethered 500 feet above the Yucca Flat desert test area.

Satellite Spurs Aircraft Stocks

NEW YORK (AP)—Russia's man-made moon boosted aircrafts and other missile-making stocks early this afternoon but the Stock Market as a whole was lower:

The missile-related stocks were ahead from 1 to 3 points as Wall Street anticipated bigger spending as an answer to the Soviet success.

Martin Co. and General Dynamics were among the stocks which improved initial gains, surging ahead more than 3 points each. Douglas Aircraft trimmed an early 4-point gain to around 3. Boeing clipped a point from its initial rise of more than 3.

TRICKY BUSINESS

What Keeps Red Moon Up in Sky?

NEW YORK (AP)—What keeps a baby moon up in the sky?

Why did the Russians choose the height they did? And how did they get it up there?

The answers are not mysterious at all. Doing it is tricky.

To get a moon up, you lift it high into the air with a powerful multi-stage rocket. The rocket turns so that finally it is flying parallel to the earth's surface.

Rocket Fires Off, Kicking Moon Away

Then the final stage of the rocket fires off, kicking the moon away at tremendous speed.

If the moon travels at, say only 12,000 miles an hour, the earth's gravity quickly pulls it down to death.

But if the speed is 18,000 miles an hour, the earth's gravity counterbalances the moon's speed, pulling on it as the moon tries to fly off in a straight direction.

Flies in Circular or Elliptical Orbit

Result is the moon flies in a circular or elliptical orbit around the earth. If you can suddenly shut off gravity, the moon would take off into space.

There's so little air in space, that the moon is not slowed down much by friction. But there is enough air so that ultimately the moon begins to lose speed, and gravity says to it in effect, now come home and back to earth.

If the moon got going 25,000 miles an hour, it could thumb its nose at earth's gravity, and escape into space, never coming back.

Little Rock: The Past And What's To Come

(Nine Negro students are in school, but is Little Rock's problem solved? A Pulitzer prize winning reporter, who has been on the scene since the violence started, leans back for a long, objective look at what has happened and what's to come. This is the first of five articles.)

By RELMAN MORIN

LITTLE ROCK, Ark. (AP)—This is the eye of the hurricane, the dead center of the storm.

There is the same deceptive calm, the same oppressive feeling in the air, the sense of vast and destructive forces swirling toward disaster.

This is Little Rock.

A police car siren screams in the street. People who wouldn't have noticed it a month ago look up anxiously now. A riot starting?

"I've got a loaded shotgun beside my bed," says a man. If he hears a sound in the night, he will reach for it.

At night the telephoning starts, the threats and warnings.

"Who is this?" a click. The phone goes dead.

The calls come to parents. Segregationists would like to force a mass boycott of Central High School. "There's going to be trouble at school . . . better keep your daughter home." No name.

They come to the father of a boy who delivers the Arkansas Gazette, the Little Rock newspaper which opposes Gov. Orval Faubus. "If you don't want something to happen to your kid . . ." No name.

'There's a Slab For You'

They even come to legislators. A man's voice says to State Sen. Charles Yingling, "understand you're in favor of a cooling off period instead of closing the schools . . . there's a slab at the undertaker's where you'll be cooling off."

It's hardest on the parents.

Most are letting their children go to the high school — and worrying over what the die-hards may do in reprisal.

Some are keeping their boys and girls away — and worrying for a different reason. A woman, in tears, calls the segregationist Capitol Citizens Council. "My daughter wants to go back. She's falling behind in her studies. What shall I do?"

Soldiers inside a high school . . . fights and muttered threats there . . . business slowed to a standstill . . . feeling between neighbors so deep it may never be bridged . . . the atmosphere heavy with menace, dark and brooding.

Seeing Not Believing

Even seeing Little Rock today, you can't believe it.

Federal troops in a Southern city! Bayonets pointed at American men and women? Impossible. All that ended 90 years ago. It couldn't happen in this day and age.

But it has happened.

Force confronts raw force now.

Twice a day, the power of federal authority pushes through massive resentment to take nine Negro students to school, against the wishes of most of the people. Seventy per cent? Eighty? Who can say?

End Not in Sight

And no end is in sight in Little Rock. Nothing has been settled. A decision is postponed. But what happens when the troops are withdrawn?

Moderates can only hope. "Maybe people will get used to it . . ."

Segregationists say they are simply waiting. "We can't do much now. But you'll see . . ."

Little Rock is a nice place.

People say "howdy" to strangers. They are courteous in their cars, on the streets, in the stores.

They are proud of their city. It's a good looking city, clean and bright with tree-shaded streets. There is a church on every other corner, handsome buildings, good schools. People have two interesting and well-edited newspapers. It's a good community.

Yet, in other states and even in other nations today, Little Rock is an ugly symbol. It represents

—See LITTLE ROCK—Page 25

Faubus Says GIs Follow Girls in Dressing Room

Suggests That WACs Be Sent to School If Policy Is Unchanged

LITTLE ROCK, Ark. (AP) Gov. Orval Faubus today accused federal troops at integrated Central High School of following girl students into their dressing room.

In a letter to Maj. Gen. Edwin A. Walker, commander of all troops in the area, Faubus said:

"If you do not see fit to change this policy, and regard this type of action as necessary to carry out your mission of integrating Central High School, then may I suggest that you request of President certain number of members of the Women's Army Corps."

A spokesman for Gen. Walker said the governor's letter, although made public by Faubus, had not yet been received. The spokesman said there would be no comment until Gen. Walker had an opportunity to study the letter.

Faubus said the alleged invasion of privacy might be endurable on a temporary basis. But he wrote Walker:

"However, if federal troops are to remain as long as forcible integration of the school is necessary, then it is my opinion that you and your troops will be here for a long time."

Nine Negro students made a quiet entrance into Central today to continue their integrated education.

Thus started the third week with Central High under guard by U.S. Army soldiers and National Guardsmen called into federal service. Guardsmen were on patrol today.

50 Students Dispersed

About 50 white students lounged around the entrance before arrival of the Negroes. Principal J. W. Matthews appeared at the doorway and said something which newsmen could not hear. The white students dispersed.

In contrast to last week's 30 or more armed escorting troops, only a half dozen National Guardsmen walked beside the six Negro girls and three boys as they entered the school. There was no heckling. Several score white pupils looked on from school windows or at a distance on the campus.

Catch 4 Marietta Boys Looting Machine

Four Marietta boys, ten to fourteen, were picked up by Columbia borough police at 12:30 a.m. yesterday while in the act of looting a soft drink vending machine at the Pioneer gas station, 12th St. and Lancaster Ave., Columbia.

They were later turned over to Marietta police chief Leonard Tillman when they admitted robbing four Coke machines at Marietta.

Columbian Says Back Hurt in Eye Treatment

A Columbia man testified today he received back injuries during treatment for drooping eyelids, as trial opened in his damage suit against his physician and an acquaintance in Common Pleas court.

Chester M. Kline brought suit against Dr. John D. Denney, Columbia, and Ernest T. Rich, formerly of Columbia.

He said Rich gave him a treatment for drooping eyelids in Dr. Denney's office on Jan. 6, 1954. Kline said Rich is not a doctor. The treatment, Kline said, consisted of manipulating his head and twisting a knee in his back.

Tells of Meeting

Kline stated he met Rich in Dr. Denney's office some time before 1954. On Jan. 6, he took his wife to Dr. Denney for treatment of a broken arm. Rich was there and told Kline, "Say, you have drooping eyelids. You must have had a severe fall at some time." Rich offered to treat him for the drooping eyelids, Kline said.

Kline, Rich, Dr. Denney and Kline's wife all went into another room. Kline said he sat down. "Rich manipulated my head with quick movements for three or four minutes. Then he put an armlock on me and put his knee in the middle of my back and twisted."

Says Doctor Paid $15

Kline said Rich told him to relax, then repeated the action. "I jumped so far I carried him (Rich) with me," Kline said. He testified he had a sharp pain in the back. He paid Dr. Denney $15 for Rich's treatment, he said.

Most of the soreness disappeared in a week to ten days, Kline said, but enough continued to cause him to postpone a trip to Florida. When he did go to Florida, Kline said, he was un-

—See COURT—Page 4

MRS. MARY E. SAUDERS

Retrial Denied Mary E. Sauders

State Supreme Court Rules in Local Murder

The State Supreme Court at Pittsburgh today refused to grant a new trial to Mrs. Mary E. Sauders, convicted of first degree murder in the bludgeon slaying of William W. Glasgow, Willow Street R1.

Justice John C. Bell Jr., who wrote the opinion, said "Reviewing and analyzing the evidence—the evidence is sufficient in law to justify the jury's verdict of guilty of murder in the first degree."

Dissenting View

Justice Michael A. Musmanno filed a dissenting opinion, stating "They envelop the entire prosecution and conviction in clouds of uncertainty and indecision. Such a conviction cannot and should not stand. I dissent."

In appealing for a new trial, the defendant's counsel argued that Mrs. Sauders was convicted solely on circumstantial evidence.

When notified of the action of the State Supreme Court, District Attorney William C. Storb said Mrs. Sauders, who is still confined at the county prison, will probably be transferred to the State Industrial Home for Women at Muncy to serve the remainder of her sentence.

No Immediate Comment

Mrs. Sauders court-appointed attorneys, Jacques Geisenberger and Theodore Brubaker, said they were awaiting a copy of the opinion before making any comment.

The woman was accused of slaying Glasgow, a 70-year-old man with whom she lived, on May 3, 1955. Glasgow was employed as a handyman on the farm of the late Leroy Hilton, Willow Street R1.

Convicted in 1956

She was convicted in March, 1956, and was refused a new trial by Judge Wissler on Nov. 9, 1956. On Nov. 16, 1956, Mrs. Sauders was sentenced by Judge Wissler to an indeterminate term at Muncy.

The Court added that "she shall remain at that institution until she is discharged by law." The jury which convicted her had recommended life imprisonment.

GOP to Aim at Caramel Plant

City Group Pledges To Remove Hazard

Republican city candidates "will exert every effort until the American Caramel Co. factory is removed," Thomas P. McElwee, city council candidate told a meeting of Republican workers this morning.

"That building is a hazard to the health and safety of the community," he said. He spoke at the first of a series of daily meetings at party headquarters, 45 N. Duke St.

Building an "Eyesore"

Referring to the vacant caramel factory building as an "eyesore" which poses a difficult problem, McElwee promised, "We will use imagination, energy and enthusiasm to solve this unfortunate problem."

The problem requires working out the solution to questions raised by the federal government, McElwee noted. These questions arose as a result of a sheriff's sale of the property and federal tax liens lodged against it. A fire caused extensive damage after the sale.

"The complexities of the problem will be attacked on all fronts by all city council candidates," he said. The other four Republican candidates for City Hall positions were present at the meeting.

Starting tomorrow, the Republican headquarters will be manned daily. The general election is just four weeks from tomorrow. Miss Irene E. Lupold is in charge of headquarters.

Today's New Era

	Page
Comics	20-21
Editorials	14
Obituaries	3-22
Radio-TV	21
Sports	23-24-25
Theaters	4
Want Ads	25-26-27-28-29
Women	12-13

Phone Lancaster EX 7-5251

Shirley Dickel Is Given Year In Reformatory

No Clemency for Girl Who Tried to Run Down 5 Cops

Shirley Ann Dickel, seventeen, of 1929 Wabank Road, today was sentenced to serve one year in a Maryland women's reformatory on five separate convictions of trying to run down Baltimore policemen with her convertible.

Chief Judge Emory H. Niles, of Baltimore Youth Court, said "clemency was impossible in view of the offense. The girl is fortunate no fatalities or other injuries occurred."

Shirley Dickel

Miss Dickel last August led policemen on a ten-mile, 90 mile-per-hour chase through Baltimore, after she had been stopped for speeding outside of the city. During the chase she allegedly ran her car at four patrolmen and tried to force a motorcycle policeman into a truck.

Run Concurrently

Judge Niles imposed a one-year sentence for each of the five convictions, then said the sentences are to run concurrently.

Miss Dickel is to serve her term in the Reformatory for Women, Jessups, Md. She was convicted on the assault charges last week and still faces numerous traffic charges in Baltimore County.

Judge Niles noted he had received a psychiatric study on Miss Dickel, but did not comment on details of the report.

Was Running Away

Miss Dickel said she was running away from home to Miami, Fla., when stopped north of Baltimore. She said she had run away from home twice before. Witnesses testified at her trial that she jumped curbs and passed streetcars on the wrong side before she was stopped by a policeman's bullet in the shoulder.

50 MPH Winds, Rain Hit County

Northeaster Disrupts Power, Fells Trees

A northeaster brought rain and gusts of wind up to 50 miles per hour throughout Lancaster County yesterday.

Numerous power and telephone failures occurred as trees blew down across electrical lines. Some telephone failures lasted until this morning. Pennsylvania Power and Light Co. said about 3,000 customers were without power at one time.

A high voltage line blew down in Elizabethtown about 5:30 p.m. and power was off in half the town, about two and one half hours. Lancaster police were called eight times about minor power failures and damaged trees.

Warmer Tomorrow

The forecast calls for partly cloudy tonight and tomorrow. Low tonight is expected about 48 degrees. It is warm up tomorrow afternoon, with a high in the low 70's.

The storm began with a disturbance along the Atlantic Coast that surprised the Weather Bureau by moving inland instead of going out to sea as expected. Lancaster county was on the edge of the storm as it crossed Virginia. When it reached West Virginia, the storm met another low pressure area from Ohio and continued north over western Pennsylvania.

Tides three feet above normal came in along the Delaware River. Winds up to 74 m.p.h. blasted Chincoteague, Va. The worst of the storm here was late in the afternoon and early last night.

Power Off 2 Hours

A large plate glass window was broken by wind pressure at Raub Supply Co. W. James and Mulberry Sts. Power was off at the Ephrata American Legion for two hours.

Bell Telephone Co. said the worst damage came in rural areas. Phones in Millersville were transferred to emergency power.

Tennessee Gets First Sleet and Snow Storm

GATLINBURG, Tenn. (AP)—East Tennessee has had its first snow and freezing temperatures of the season.

New "Silly Dilly" Contest Starts

A sparkling new contest starts today in the color section of the want-ads. $25.00 weekly prize award will be given for the cleverest or funniest sentence composed of words in the Stop 'n Shop feature. It's another "Handy" brain storm, the bird that has all Lancaster "atwitter" with facinating contest games. Shopper's find the Armchair Shopping Center handy to select bargains in everything from hair-dos to automobiles. Turn now to Handy's Stop 'n Shop for fun and bargains for the whole family.

WEATHER
(U. S. Weather Bureau)

Partial Clearing Today With Little Temperature Change Today And Tomorrow. High 47-52. Low Tonight 34-38.

(Details On Page 28)

Intelligencer Journal.

The Leading Newspaper in the Garden Spot of America. Home Owned for Home Folks Since 1794

THE INTELL INDEX

Telephone EX 7-5251

164th Year.—No. 123. Metropolitan Lancaster Population (Estimate) Penna. Dept. of Commerce 249,799 LANCASTER, PA., WEDNESDAY MORNING, NOVEMBER 6, 1957. CITY EDITION 28 PAGES. 42c PER WEEK—7c Per Copy

DEMOCRATS WIN CITY

Meyner Named To Second Term In Garden State

Ike-Endorsed Wealthy Magazine Publisher, Malcolm Forbes, Goes Down To Defeat Before Smashing Reelection Triumph

NEWARK, N. J., Nov. 5 (AP) — Democratic Gov. Robert B. Meyner of New Jersey won a smashing reelection triumph tonight over a Republican who had an all-out endorsement from President Eisenhower.

Meyner led GOP State Sen. Malcolm S. Forbes 947,184 to 756,715 with 3,857 of the state's 4,219 districts reported.

The governor's victory enhanced his reputation as a strong-vote-getter in a normally Republican state. He swept to the front ranks of possible Democratic presidential nominees in 1960.

The Meyner win was a sharp blow to the Eisenhower administration. The President had appealed for a Forbes' victory as a shot in the arm for the GOP. The setback followed the recent Democratic victory in the special Senate election in Wisconsin.

ASSEMBLY SWEEP

Meyner capped his triumph with a stunning sweep of the State Assembly, controlled by the Republicans since 1937.

In conceding defeat, Forbes stated the campaign was fought out on state issues. But his campaign manager, Neil Duffy, saw "Sputnik, Muttnik and the stock market drop" as contributing factors to Meyner's reelection.

The governor, back at his home in Phillipsburg, was the center of a riotous celebration. Cars, fire engines and crowds jammed the streets of the small Delaware River town. He made a speech at the town's main intersection. Town fathers planned a school holiday tomorrow and a parade and demonstration in the high school stadium.

Meyner aimed much of his campaign at the Republican and independent voters who gave Eisenhower a huge 760,000 plurality in New Jersey in 1956. He succeeded almost completely, carry-

Turn To Page 15 For More Of MEYNER

Wagner Wins By 920,000 In New York

NEW YORK, Nov. 5 (AP) — Democratic Mayor Robert F. Wagner crushed Eisenhower-backed Republican Robert K. Christenberry tonight to win reelection by a plurality of almost 920,000 votes.

Complete returns gave Christenberry 587,440; Wagner 1,507,342.

The city ordinarily elects Democrats, and Wagner had been expected to win, but he said the margin of the triumph "exceeded my fondest expectations."

His opponent, a hotel executive, was making his first try for elective office.

Democratic Gov. Averell Harriman seized on Democratic victories here, upstate and New Jersey as an indication the voters are "disillusioned with the form of Republicanism you see in Washington under President Eisenhower and Vice President Nixon."

PEOPLE DISSATISFIED

The governor told Wagner's celebrating election workers at the Hotel Biltmore: "It shows that the people are dissatisfied with the disinterest of the administration of Eisenhower and Nixon and shows the respect they have for good government like Mayor Wagner's.

The mayor, son of the late New Deal senator who sponsored the Wagner Labor Relations Act, scored heavily in all sections of the city, including Harlem, where the vote is preponderantly Negro.

Harlem voted for the mayor by approximately 4 to 1. The Harlem voting had been watched with interest by politicians of both parties to see whether it reflected any reaction to efforts of Democratic Gov. Orval Faubus of Arkansas to block school integration in Little Rock.

Wagner had denounced the

Turn To Page 15 For More Of WAGNER

DENVER DEMOCRAT ELECTED BURGESS

William A. Keller, Denver barber and prominent northern end Democrat, yesterday was elected burgess of that borough.

He defeated Samuel H. Hornberger, Republican, by a vote of 371 to 296.

The Democrats also elected a school director, Paul S. Leed; school auditor, Phares G. Harting, and two councilmen, Paul S. Leed and Earl S. Shimp.

Thomas J. Monaghan and his attractive wife, Sylvia, display broad victory smiles last night in Democratic headquarters shortly after they had learned that they will be Lancaster city's next first couple. Monaghan was elected mayor in yesterday's Municipal Election. (Intell Photo)

Monaghan Leads Ticket To Victory

Budding Defeated By 1,236 Votes As Party Captures Every Office In First Sweep Over GOP Since 1933

By CHARLES W. FITZKEE

City voters in their greatest repudiation of the Republican party in a quarter century, yesterday swept to victory the complete Democratic city ticket, headed by Thomas J. Monaghan as mayor.

Complete unofficial returns from the city's 33 precincts gave Monaghan 10,389, and his Republican opponent, Attorney Harold W. Budding, 9,153.

Monaghan is only the third Democratic mayor in 60 years. His predecessors were James H. Ross, Lancaster merchant, swept into office in 1933, and the late Simon Shissler, who won in the election of 1898.

Monaghan, forty-three year old securities salesman and civic leader, carried with him to victory two city council candidates, a city controller, a city treasure, and three school director candidates.

Defeated for the mayoralty in 1953 by 591 votes, Monaghan yesterday rolled up an impressive 1,236 vote plurality over Budding.

Gov. George M. Leader was among the first to congratulate the new Democratic mayor. The governor called from the executive mansion at Harrisburg at 9:30 p.m. with his congratulatory message.

He also spoke to Mrs. Monaghan and Attorney David R. Eaby, Democratic county chairman.

Republican candidates were victorious in the county, but even there the Democrats made inroads on the usual top-heavy GOP plurality.

The complete unofficial results of the city council race, which gives the Democrats a three to two edge over the Republicans:

Christian Gottselig, D—10,133.
Joseph T. Fasnacht, D—10,204.
Eugene S. Rutherford, R—9,234.
Thomas P. McElwee, R—9,277.

In the contest for city treasurer, Walter E. Broome, D, trounced George L. Diehl, R, 10,196 to 9,235.

It was the same story in the race for city controller, with George W. Glatfelter, D, rolling up 10,115 votes to 9,305 by Wallace L. Robinson, R.

SCHOOL DIRECTOR VOTE

The vote in the school director race: John C. Truxal, D, 10,616; Dr. William A. Schaeffer, D, 10,426; David K. Shertzer, D, 10,227; Antonio Palumbo, R, 8,720; Glenna May Hazeltine, R, 9,093, and Albert J. Mathews, R, 9,170.

The outcome of the city voting was never in doubt. Monaghan edged into the lead from the first returns. His plurality increased steadily as usual staunch Republican districts failed to turn in their customary pluralities.

Monaghan carried 19 of the city's 33 precincts, many by unprecedented pluralities. In the sixth precinct the Eighth Ward he rolled up a lead of 496 votes.

Republican leaders, confident of victory, were stunned as the re-

Turn To Page 18 For More Of ELECTION

Mayor-Elect Set To Work On Platform

By NED WALL

Mayor-elect Thomas J. Monaghan said last night that the party's platform, endorsed by the public through the election of a Democratic City Council majority, will be advanced as rapidly as possible when the new officials take office on Jan. 6.

He called for cooperation of all segments of the community to "convert the platform into reality."

Monaghan praised the "numerous workers, friends, and voters who helped us achieve this victory."

Detailed Election Results Pages 18, 19, 20

"We will do everything possible with the mandate given us, to make Lancaster a better city," he said.

He said that he has been invited to attend budget preparation sessions of the present all-Republican council this afternoon. Under state law, the city's budget for next year will be prepared by the incumbent council.

The Democrats, in their campaign, pledged themselves to improve recreation and garbage collection and city equipment and services generally. Also pledged were support to the work of the Lancaster Redevelopment Authority and attention to the problems of Lancaster's "senior citizens."

The Democrats said they would protect the city's in-

Turn To Page 18 For More Of MAYOR

6th Precinct Cord Breaks

The cord that opens and closes a voting machine snapped yesterday at the polling place in the sixth precinct of the Eighth Ward.

What makes the event newsworthy is the fact that it was the first cord to snap on a voting machine since they were first installed 25 years ago.

George Huston, custodian of voting machines, quickly repaired the cord.

Victory Cries Ring In Hdqtrs. Of Democrats

By BARBARA LITTLE

Pandemonium broke loose shortly after 9 p.m. yesterday in the smoke-filled basement room of the Coho Building where Democratic headquarters had been a beehive of activity since the polls closed.

"We're in! We're in!" were the words that did it as the news of a Democratic victory in the city spread from the knot around the tabulating table to every person in the room almost instantaneously.

The shout went up and the room echoed with cheers. Thomas J. Monaghan — with one precinct out — had been elected mayor of the city of Lancaster and with him the entire City Democratic slate.

When Tom Monaghan arrived on the scene, the crowd rushed in to congratulate him — to pat him on the back, to shake his hand. These were the people who had helped him win, had guided his campaign; these were the people who had worked hard to win over their precincts; these were the people who had voted for him.

Monaghan, his now familiar grin spread across his face, climbed up on the table and told them,

Turn To Page 18 For More Of DEMOCRATS

2 More Union School Plans Get Approval

The voters of nine school districts yesterday approved the establishment of three more union school districts in Lancaster County.

These involved the districts of Washington Boro and Manor Twp.; the Hempfield Joint School District comprised of East and West Hempfield Twps. and Mountville borough, and the districts of East Donegal and a part of Mount Joy Twp. and Marietta and Mount Joy boroughs.

By an overwhelming vote, the voters of the Manor Twp. and Washington Boro school districts yesterday voted in favor of the formation of what will become the Manor Union District.

The total vote cast in both districts in favor of the union district was 878 votes as compared to 274 votes opposing the proposal.

In the three voting districts of Manor Twp. the vote was as fol-

Turn To Page 18 For More Of UNION

Lancaster Twp. To Stay 2nd Class, Voters Decide

The move to change the status of Lancaster Twp. from second to first class, lost yesterday by 101 votes.

Complete unofficial returns from the township's four districts showed 1,561 votes for the change and 1,662 against.

This is the second time that the electorate has rejected a proposal that the township go from a second to a first class one.

In 1952 the proposal was rejected by a vote of 2,702 to 1,096.

The move to have the township's status elevated was sponsored by the Lancaster Twp. Citizens' Assn. It was opposed by the Lancaster Twp. Citizens' Committee:

The vote by districts:

	Yes	No
First district	233	513
Second district	622	597
Third district	270	221
Fourth district	436	331
Total	1561	1662

BUTLER DEMOCRATIC FIRST SINCE 1917

BUTLER, Pa., Nov. 5 (AP)—Butler voters today elected a Democratic mayor for the first time since 1917.

Harry Pepper, a florist and the Democratic nominee for mayor, polled 2,889 v tes in 15 of the city's 17 precincts for an apparently safe lead over incumbent Mayor Walter Schweppe, a Republican. Schweppe had 2,545 votes.

A referendum authorizing a commission to report on the city manager form of government won approval by a more than three to one margin. The charter commission will make a report and recommendation which will be submitted to the voters next year.

Democrats Win Mayor Battles In Seven Cities

By THE ASSOCIATED PRESS

Democrats, re-electing mayors to unprecedented fourth terms in Pittsburgh and Scranton, turned out Republican administrations in five other Pennsylvania cities Tuesday, while the GOP retained a congressional seat at stake in a special election.

Pittsburgh's Mayor David L. Lawrence rolled up a 60,000 vote majority—his highest in four elections—while James T. Hanlon was a 3 to 2 repeat winner in Scranton.

Philadelphia, also a Democratic stronghold, gave nearly an 80,000 majority to District Attorney Victor H. Blanc—one of the worst lickings for the city's GOP in an off-year election.

With 23 mayoralty posts at stake, the Republicans lost at least

Turn To Page 15 For More Of STATE

Ike Makes Sudden Change In Thursday Speech Plans

WASHINGTON, Nov. 5 (AP) — Obviously spurred by Russia's feats in the earth satellite field, President Eisenhower tonight suddenly altered previous plans and decided to speak to the nation Thursday night on "Science and Security."

The White House said the speech — which falls on the 40th anniversary of the Russian Communist Revolution — will be "of major importance to the American people."

The topic, "Science and Security", was the same one chosen for a speech which previously had been announced for Nov. 13 at Oklahoma City.

Mrs. Anne Wheaton, associate presidential press secretary, said the subject of the speech Eisenhower will give at Oklahoma City will be changed.

She said Eisenhower wanted to reach a large audience immediately and this was the reason for the announcement tonight, which had not been heralded in advance. The Thursday night speech will be made from the President's office in the White House.

Any speech on "science and security" could be expected to be designed to allay anxiety and criticisms that have arisen over Russia's scientific achievements in recent weeks, notably the two man-made satellites now circling the earth.

It was not stated whether there is any significance in the date newly chosen for the Eisenhower speech. The Russians will be conducting big anniversary celebrations and the President's address could be calculated, for one thing, to vie for the attention of people in many lands.

Eisenhower said Oct. 22 that he planned a series of speeches. He then listed America's scientific position, national defense, econo-

Turn To Page 15 For More Of EISENHOWER

"We Lead All The Rest"

FARM CORNER

By Don Brandt

31 4-H Steers Picked To Show At Harrisburg

One hundred twenty-five baby beeves from the Red Rose 4-H Baby Beef Club took a walk in the rain yesterday at Lancaster Union Stock Yards and after the stroll, only 94 returned to stock yard pens for the Southeast District 4-H Baby Beef and Lamb Club Show.

The other 31 were returned to their farms to await the Pennsylvania Farm Show next January.

Winning the coveted chance for competition in the state event were the exhibitors of 14 Angus, 13 Herefords and 3 Shorthorns.

The steers which remained at the yard will go before the judges again today in competition with entries from the nine other counties in the district. Judging begins at 9 a.m. today, with the grand champion slated to be chosen this afternoon.

Lambs will be judged at 8 a.m. tomorrow, and all animals will be sold at auction tomorrow afternoon.

Choosing the state entries yesterday were Thomas King and Dwight Younkin, livestock exten-

Turn To Page 24 For More Of FARM CORNER

Intell To Conduct Yule Card Contest

The old folks and the young folks all get a lot of fun as well as religious inspiration out of the Christmas season, but this year the Intelligencer Journal is giving the children a chance for even more fun and prizes, too.

Any child under ten years old can enter the big Christmas Card Contest of the Intelligencer Journal and perhaps win one of eight prizes.

The contest which begins today will be run with two divisions, one for children under six and a second for children seven through 10 years of age.

The children must submit Christmas cards of their own design and construction to the office of the Intelligencer Journal by midnight, Monday, Dec. 2. The cards can be made with any art material.

The judges will consider originality and appropriate use of materials as well as attractiveness, neatness and workmanship in awarding the eight prizes in each division.

Complete details and contest rules will be found on Page 10.

Local Election Results At-A-Glance

Lancaster City
33 Districts Complete

Mayor	
Monaghan, Dem.	10,389
Budding, Rep.	9,153
Council	
Fasnacht, Dem.	10,204
Gottselig, Dem.	10,133
Rutherford, Rep.	9,234
McElwee, Rep.	9,277
City Treasurer	
Broome, Dem.	10,196
Diehl, Rep.	9,235
City Controller	
Glatfelter, Dem.	10,115
Robinson, Rep.	9,305
School Directors	
Truxal, Dem.	10,616
Schaeffer, Dem.	10,426
Shertzer, Dem.	10,227
Palumbo, Rep.	8,720
Hazeltine, Rep.	9,093
Mathews, Rep.	9,170
Recorder of Deeds	
Hensel, Dem.	10,132
Ackerman, Rep.	9,354
County Controller	
Dickel, Dem.	10,078
Brown, Rep.	9,324
Prison Keeper	
McGeehan, Dem.	10,066
Foust, Rep.	9,363
Prison Inspectors	
Nuss, Dem.	10,077
Zimmerman, Dem.	10,083
Groff, Dem.	10,124
Wenger, Dem.	10,110
Carter, Rep.	9,283
Sweigart, Rep.	9,300
LeFever, Rep.	9,258
Mease, Rep.	9,234
Amendment 1-A	
Yes	4,752
No	1,246
Amendment 1-B	
Yes	4,384
No	2,369

Lancaster County
(144 of 147 Districts, Including 33 City Districts)

Recorder of Deeds	
Hensel, Dem.	22,646
Ackerman, Rep.	34,363
County Controller	
Dickel, Dem.	22,494
Brown, Rep.	34,532
Prison Keeper	
McGeehan, Dem.	22,325
Foust, Rep.	34,699
Prison Inspectors	
Nuss, Dem.	22,173
Zimmerman, Dem.	22,426
Groff, Dem.	22,661
Wenger, Dem.	22,492
Carter, Rep.	34,212
Sweigart, Rep.	34,474
Lefever, Rep.	34,280
Mease, Rep.	33,933
Amendment 1-A	
Yes	19,816
No	6,005
Amendment 1-B	
Yes,	15,693
No	11,753

Teenagers Accent the Positive

Do come in at the time you, your date and your parents have agreed on before going out, says Kathy Witter (above), a Manheim Twp. High School junior. Kathy, daughter of James A. Witter, 1920 Sterling Place, thinks 11 p. m. is a good hour to come home after a movie date.

Accentuate the positive—this is the theme of a Teenage Code drawn up last month by a committee of approximately 75 Lancaster City and County high school pupils. The code emphasizes the "do's" rather than the "don'ts" of good social conduct. And—as the teens shown here prove—you can abide by the rules and have a good time. Rough drafts of the code have been sent to student bodies at all the high schools for further ideas and comments. The final draft will be compiled from these suggestions in January, and copies will be distributed to all area teens.

Do double-date frequently, particularly on first dates, is another tenet of the Teenage Code. Below, Lancaster Country Day School pupils enjoying an after-movie soda are (l-r): Sue Reigle, daughter of Mr. and Mrs. C. Brooks Reigle, Bareville R1; Ed Dinsmore Jr., son of Mr. and Mrs. Edmund F. Dinsmore, 2311 Wicklyn Rd., Margaretta Light, daughter of Mr. and Mrs. A. S. Light, 333 Race Ave., and Tom McEwan Jr., son of Mr. and Mrs. Thomas J. McEwan, 1401 Pleasure Rd.

Do call your parents if you must come home later than the agreed-upon time or if you have changed your plans as to where you are going, advises Patricia Emich, above. A junior at Hempfield High School, Patricia is the daughter of Mr. and Mrs. John H. Emich, East Petersburg.

Do budget and try to earn part of your allowance, says Louise Weaver (right), daughter of Mr. and Mrs. Leroy M. Weaver, 429 N. Pine St. Earning her allowance by doing household chores, and keeping a budget book, have helped the McCaskey High School senior learn about money.

Local Weather
(U. S. Weather Bureau)
Lancaster, York, Lebanon, Cumberland, Franklin, Adams Counties
Partly Cloudy, High 35-40, today. Mostly Cloudy And Colder Tomorrow With Some Snow. High Near 30.

SUNDAY NEWS

8 Sections — TV Week — Family Weekly — Full Color Comics

Metropolitan Edition
LATEST News—Associated Press
AP Photofax, Complete Local News and Pictures **15c**

35TH YEAR—NO. 17 LANCASTER, PA., SUNDAY, DECEMBER 29, 1957

CONESTOGA VALLEY High School, just off Old Philadelphia Pike near Witmer, shows progress on steelwork. Completion date is September 1958. (Sunday News Photos)

MANHEIM TOWNSHIP High School, at Neffsville, takes shape in progress toward completion estimate of June 1958.

Oil Coats Conestoga, Water Works Shut

River Water Pumped Into City System

Oil deposits in the Conestoga River yesterday forced the filter plant at the City Water Works to suspend operations.

J. Arthur Norris, commissioner for the Department of Public Safety, said the heavy accumulation of oil forced the plant to stop operations.

The department is relying on the new Oyster Point reservoir and Columbia pumping station, along with city standpipes and reservoirs to supply residents with water, he said.

The local plant is expected to resume filtering water this morning, Norris said, after the oil has passed downstream.

He said the oil, about 1,000 gallons, escaped from the American Paper Products Co. mill, Eden, sometime Friday.

It is the first time the Columbia station has supplied water to Lancaster since the new station was begun over a year ago.

Charles P. Abraham, water superintendent, termed the situation as "not serious" and said residents did not experience any lack of water after the local station stopped pumping.

The oil, he said, was discovered about 10 a.m. yesterday in the river but did not get into the clariflow basins until about 4 p.m.

Norris said the filter plant stopped operations immediately after the oil discovery. The filter beds were clean, however, he said.

Abraham said water pumping went on after the filtering stopped —using up some of the water in the tanks.

The station normally pumps between 15 and 16 million gallons of water during a 24-hour period, Norris said.

Abraham indicated that the water being pumped from Columbia will probably continue on a very limited scale throughout the night.

No Instruments

He said there was no way to check just how much water was being pumped inasmuch as the instruments are not set in the borough plant.

Abraham said operations are going along quite smoothly.

In the event the Columbia station was not in a position to pump water to Lancaster, the local station would probably have been forced to "skim" the top of the Conestoga River of oil in order to filter the water.

The oil, Norris said, was number six bunker oil — the type

Page 4—OIL

Miss DeMolay Of 1958

Miss Audrey Eshleman, Millersville, was crowned Miss DeMolay of 1958 last night at the 18th Christmas Dance of the Lancaster Chapter of DeMolay in the Moose Ball Room. She is shown above being crowned by the 1957 queen, Miss Veda Kay Sollenberger

Last night's crowning was the fourth for Audrey in 1957. Earlier in the year she was crowned queen of the Franklin and Marshall College Inter-Fraternity Ball; Pennsylvania Posture Queen; and Miss Artisan of 1957.

The theme of the dance was "Winter Melody." Decorations were white Christmas trees made of spun glass, twinkling lights, snowmen and Santa Clauses and all kinds of Christmas greens.

Decorations chairman was Elmer Lesher. Roy Barley was social chairman.

(Sunday News Photo)

H. S. Construction In Co. For '58 To Total $14,975,000

Six new high schools on which construction is already under way serve to underline the emphasis on education in Lancaster county in 1958. Total cost is $14,795,000. Two other high schools may be started during the coming year, and a number of smaller elementary buildings are being erected.

In a year when competition with Russia's education system will be of major concern, Lancaster will be bringing its school plant up close to the level of its needs.

In probable order of completion, the new high schools are:

Elizabethtown, fully occupied and requiring only completion of some interior features, including cafeteria, lobby, gym, offices; $2,500,000.

Penn Manor, due for completion June 1958; $3,335,000.

Conestoga Valley, due for completion September 1958; $1,830,000.

Manheim Twp., due for completion in 1959; $2,980,000.

Garden Spot, probably complete in 1959; $2,450,000.

Manheim Central, test borings made at site; $1,600,000.

Farther away but in the works are:

Ephrata Union, authority formed and land purchased.

Southern Lancaster County, 1,000-pupil high school in East Drumore Twp. recommended in survey.

When these eight buildings are occupied, every high school student in Lancaster county will be in a modern school.

In many cases old high schools are being converted to elementary use. This still leaves many grade-school pupils with no place to go, however, so a number of elementary buildings are going up. In most cases these are scattered in strategic locations through the various districts, and are much smaller than the high schools.

Continued school construction is also viewed as a solid backlog for the local economic situation.

Egypt Seeks Tighter Links To West: Dag

PARIS, Dec. 28 (AP)—Dag Hammarskjold met with French leaders today and is said to have convinced them he believes Egyptian President Nasser wants to tighten his links with the West.

The U.N. secretary general flew here at the request of Foreign Minister Christian Pineau direct from talks in Cairo with Nasser. France and Egypt have had no diplomatic relations since last year's British-French invasion of the Suez Canal zone.

There was no official disclosure of the conversations which Hammarskjold began with Pineau shortly after arriving last night. In the afternoon he saw Premier Felix Gaillard and Jacques Georges-Picot, director general of the Suez Canal Co.

French public opinion last year accused Hammarskjold of pro-Egyptian bias and a government spokesman stressed the importance of the cordial mood of today's reception.

It was reported reliably that

Page 4—EGYPT

Weather

(U. S. Weather Bureau)

LOWER SUSQUEHANNA

Partly cloudy, high 35-40 today. Monday mostly cloudy and colder with some snow. Highs near 30.

Middle Susquehanna, and the Poconos—Partly cloudy, with highs of 32 to 38 today. Monday mostly cloudy and colder, with some snow. Highs of 25 to 30.

Upper Susquehanna and North Central—Partly cloudy with a few snow flurries today. Highs of 30 to 35. Monday mostly cloudy and colder, with some snow, highs of 15 to 24.

South Central—Partly cloudy with chance of a few snow flurries in the higher elevations today. Highs of 30 to 35. Monday mostly cloudy and colder, with some snow. Highs of 18 to 26.

Regional Weather Page 4

TEMPERATURES

	High	Low
Ephrata Weather Station	44	27
Ephrata (1956)	44	32
Lancaster Water Works	45	26

Saturday Football

GATOR BOWL
Tennessee 3, Texas A&M 0

BLUE—GRAY GAME
Gray 21, Blue 20

EAST—WEST SHRINE
West 27, East 13

CHECK TREES, BALD 'MARM IS MISSING

LEBANON, Dec. 28—Guy Bord, 1111 Mifflin St., Lebanon, is eager to help the 19-year-old Atlanta, Ga., teacher in her search for peach leaves to relieve her sudden baldness!

But he doesn't know who she is! Atlanta doesn't know either! The Associated Press in Atlanta was contacted tonight and reported that the access to the name would have to be deferred until Monday, when the Atlanta city clerk office reopens.

Earlier tonight Bord called the Lancaster Sunday News office, Lancaster, to report that he had an ample supply of what the young lady was looking for to cure her baldness.

When the identity of the "victime" is divulged on Monday, Bord said he is ready to send as many peach leaves as the young lady needs. He has a total of two bags full of the "remedy."

Afro-Asians Assail Israel

CAIRO, Dec. 28 (AP)—Delegates to the African-Asian Conference shaped resolutions today to widen attacks on the West with Israel included as a new target.

The Palestine subcommittee of the nongovernmental, conference, drafted a resolution assailing Israel as "an American-British-French base" and demanding a concerted effort to get Palestinian refugees returned to their homeland.

The draft resolution must be approved by a parent, political committee before being voted on by the full conference of 400 delegates from 42 nations and dependent areas.

Nuclear Tests Attacked

Another committee, including a Soviet representative who came here as an invited observer, was working on a resolution to denounce nuclear bomb tests and foreign military bases.

The anti-Western line that has marked the conference all week persisted in all conference programs except for the dissenting voice of Sava Loizides, Greek Cypriot delegation leader.

He told a plenary session of the conference that the African and Asian governments loudly proclaim self-determination for peoples but failed to support the Greek Cyproit campaign for independence from Britain when the issue came before the U.N. recently.

Noting the 14 abstentions by African and Asian countries, Loizides told the conference "You see how divided were the Afro-Asian countries on the question of ending colonialism and the application of the principle of self-determination."

Car Hits Lebanon RR Crossing Gates

LEBANON, Dec. 28—Damage estimated by police at $200 occurred when a car driven by Harry W. Darkas, Lebanon R2, crashed into the Reading Railroad Company crossing gates at 12th and Railroad Sts. at 5:47 p.m.

Sgt. Paul V. Peiffer, of the city police, who is investigating, said the watchman told him Darkas didn't see that the gates were down.

Interlocked Treaties Are Dulles Aim

WASHINGTON, Dec. 29 (AP)—The United States has started trying to achieve greater "interdependence and interlocking" of its treaty-bound allies to tighten the fabric of free world defenses around the globe.

It has been a modest beginning. But State Department officials said today they have great expectations.

Secretary of State Dulles disclosed today he will personally head the U.S. observer delegation to the Jan. 27-30 meeting of the Baghdad Pact at Ankara, Turkey.

Ankara Emphasis

This decision apparently was aimed at dramatizing U. S. determination to draw the various free world alliances closer together. Presumably, Dulles would emphasize at Ankara the U. S. view that greater interdependence and interlocking among the treaties are necessary.

Dulles commented, as Russia launched a brother helps brother" economic aid program for 1958, that the West still "can look forward to the new year with confidence.

Dulles' year-end statement, drafted 10 days ago in Paris, was

Page 4—INTERLOCK

Youth Dashes Into Car's Path

A nineteen year-old city youth was injured shortly after 9 p.m. yesterday when he reportedly ran out in front of a car operated by Frank Fantz, 1366 Orchard St., on Route 30 east, in front of the County Home.

The victim, George Hartman, 900 E. King St., was conveyed to Lancaster General Hospital by city police. He underwent X-rays to determine the extent of his injuries. Attendants at the hospital said he would probably be discharged after treatment.

State trooper Stanley Springer took over the investigation of the accident.

3 Youths Hurt In Manheim Crash

Three youths were injured yesterday in an auto accident which occured at the intersection of Gramby and Main Sts. in Manheim at about 11 p.m.

The injured, who were treated at General Hospital, were: Robert Stanley, fifteen, 26 Carl St., lacerated forehead; Jack Lawson, sixteen, 418 S. Prince St., back injuries; and Ruth Kilhefner, seventeen, South Charolette St., Manheim.

All three were in a car operated by William B. Herr, eighteen, Lancaster R6, and were traveling west on Gramby. The other car, driven by Nevin K. Brubaker, nineteen, Manheim R1, was going south on Main St. Police said Herr passed a flashing red light and will be prosecuted.

BUT SHE PREFERS MOSQUITOES

Former Local Girl Has Missile Site As Neighbor

A former Manheim Twp. High School pupil who now lives near Cape Canaveral, Fla., has a missile lauching test site practically in her back yard — but science to her means mosquito bites.

She is Suzanne Brown, seventeen, who has devoted her science course at the Melbourne, Fla., High School to attempting to find a vaccine which will make humans immune to mosquito bites.

Susie, as she s known to her former classmates, is visiting over the holidays with her parents, Mr. and Mrs. Paul Brown, in the home of her grandparents, Mr. and Mrs. Frank S. Hatz, 7 Princeton Ave.

"We've been in Melbourne a little over two years," she said, "and it has really changed since we went there. There are a lot

Page 4—GIRL

SUZANNE BROWN

Kin Of Countians Safe From Blast Killing 11 Miners

News of the Virginia mine explosion was awaited tensely in two Lancaster County homes.

Relatives of two men who work for the Pocahontas Fuel Co. at Amonate, Va., telephoned The Sunday News yesterday inquiring about mine workers. None was listed either on the list of fatalities or on the list of rescued, indicating that they were not involved in the gas-produced explosion which took 11 lives.

Bruce Mahaffey of 204 W. Vine St., inquired about Earl Sluss, a foreman at Mine No. 31 (where blast occurred). He is a brother of Mrs. Mahaffey and is also married to Mr. Mahaffey's sister.

Thomas J. Nitz, of Willow Street R1, inquired about both his brother, Ralph Nitz, and his brother-in-law, Vern Counts. Both men work for the Pocahontas Fuel Co.

Eleven canvas-draped bodies were carried from the explosion-torn Pocahontas Fuel Co. mine at dawn today. A few hours later a 30-man team of federal, state, union, and mine company investigators began a probe in the disaster area — 500 feet below ground.

The gas-produced explosion early last night trapped 25 miners in two areas of the vast, subterranean chambers straddling the mountainous Virginia-West Virginia border. Rescue workers, with heavy oxygen tanks strapped to their backs, burrowed through fallen rock, dust and fumes to reach 14 survivors and lead them to safety near midnight.

To Be Laid Off

Pocahontas officials said all but three of the 11 victims had just 5½ hours left in the mine before they would have been laid off indefinitely. The company said it was cutting 70 per cent of its 534 employes from the payroll at midnight due to a shortage in coal orders.

Heading the investigative unit which moved into the mine at 11:15 a.m. today was Marling Amkemy, chief of the U.S. Bureau of Mines and top officials of the West Virginia Bureau of Mines, the United Mine Workers and the mine ownership.

Survivors testified that explosion of gases, found in all coal mining operations, sent the shock wave reverberating through the sprawling underground reaches of

Page 4—MINE

RUN OVER BY 3 RR TRAINS –BRUISED

GENOA, Italy, Dec. 28 (AP)—Mrs. Rosa Montobbio, 64, fainted last night and fell from a bridge to the railroad tracks 20 feet below.

Three trains roared over the unconscious woman crumpled between the rails before she was found and taken to a hospital for treatment of minor bruises.

Bier Of Slain Marine Given Honor Guard

Twenty-three-year-old Paul H. McClain will be buried Tuesday morning in the uniform of a Marine sergeant, but there will be no military rites at the funeral.

However, comrades from the U. S. Marine Corps will stand guard over the casket at the Fred F. Groff funeral home during a viewing scheduled from 7 to 9 p.m. Monday.

The father of the stab murder victim said yesterday, "We didn't want full military honors at the funeral; although he loved his uniform and the Corps, we just didn't think it was quite right."

The funeral will be held at 10:30 a.m. at the funeral home, and interment will follow at Greenwood Cemetery.

McClain's father, Frank X. McLain, 229 S. Ann St., said "I feel sorry for the kid that killed him, he's got to live with it the rest of his life."

McLain said he had very little bitterness toward sixteen-year-old Benjamin Harnish who wielded the knife which pierced his son's heart during an argument on a country road near New Holland early Friday morning.

Of his son, he said, "He was always the hard-luck one of the family, if there were any hurts or anything he got them, and he just grinned about them."

In the meantime, Harnish is spending his first week-end in the Lancaster County Prison, charged with murder.

Alone In Prison

Under constant surveillance, he is in a single cell completely isolated from the rest of the prisoners. A veil of secrecy has been thrown around his activities by Warden Walter N. Foust.

So strict is the isolation that only his attorney, John W. Beyer,

Page 4—LOCAL

SUNDAY NEWS Today

LAST MINUTE CHANGES in television programs listed in TV WEEK will be found today on page 18 of the Sunday News.

WOMEN today

Lancaster Intelligencer Journal

PAGE 16—FRIDAY, JANUARY 3, 1958

Fourteen Named In Best-Dressed Women's List

NEW YORK, Jan. 2—A race between younger women of elegance and the established leaders of world fashion, new arrivals and dramatic revivals in the top ranks, contributed excitement to the annual list of the world's best-dressed women, announced today by the Couture Group of the New York Dress Institute.

The list, compiled by the Dress Institute from written ballots distributed to 2000 international fashion experts, fashion editors, socialites and other celebrities, gives current honors for "distinguished taste in dress without ostentation or extravagance" to:

MRS. WILLIAM PALEY (New York)

THE DUCHESS OF WINDSOR (Paris and New York) and MRS. WINSTON GUEST (New York and Palm Beach) (tied for second place)

COUNTESS CONSUELO CRESPI (Rome)

QUEEN ELIZABETH II OF GREAT BRITAIN

AUDREY HEPBURN (Hollywood)

MRS. HENRY FORD II (Grosse Pointe, Mich. and New York)

VICOMTESSE JACQUELINE DE RIBES (Paris)

CLAUDETTE COLBERT (Hollywood) and MRS. WILLIAM R. HEARST, JR. (tied for eighth place)

THE COUNTESS OF QUINTANILLA (Madrid)

COUNTESS MONA VON BISMARCK (former Mrs. Harrison Williams, New York, Paris and Capri)

MRS. NORMAN K. WINSTON (New York and Paris)

MRS. THOMAS BANCROFT JR. (New York and Greenwich, Conn.)

In spite of the perennial honors paid to the Duchess of Windsor and Mrs. William Paley, this year's poll showed that very young women have erased the time-honored fasion cliche that "no woman can be well-dressed until she is past 35."

Flaxen-haired Mrs. Guest, wife of the noted sportsman and the former Lucy Cochran of Boston, is under 30, as are film star Audrey Hepburn, Mrs. Henry Ford II, American-born Countess Crespi, piquant and brunette Vicomtesse de Ribes and blonde Mrs. Thomas Bancroft Jr. Queen Elizabeth II, at 32, appears on the best-dressed list for the first time, while her sister Margaret Rose's name does not appear.

RETURN TO LIST

Claudette Colbert and Countess Mona von Bismarck returned to the list this year after several years' absence. When she was Mrs. Harrison Williams, Countess Bismarck was a fixture in the best-dressed ranks, appearing at or near the top of the list every year from 1933 until she went into semi-retirement in Europe. Since the death of her utilities-magnate husband and her subsequent marriage to Count Edward von Bismarck, she has returned to society in Paris and recently revisited New York.

Miss Colbert, now a hit on television as well as on the screen is the only familiar Hollywood name on the list this year, having edged out such famous "regulars" as Marlene Dietrich, Irene Dunne, and Rosalind Russell. Princess Grace of Monaco, who both as Grace Kelly of the films and as the bride of Prince Rainier III ranked high on previous lists, was missing this year.

Joan Crawford, Dinah Shore, Mrs. Gary Cooper, British ballerina Margot Fonteyn, Kay Kendall (Mrs. Rex Harrison), Dorothy Kilgallen, Merle Oberon, Elizabeth Taylor Todd and Loretta Young were among the entertainment world figures cited prominently in the balloting.

Politics and diplomacy made dressed ranks this year. Mrs. Eisenhower and Clare Boothe Luce, both of whom ranked high in former lists, again received many votes, but not enough to place them at the head of the list, the Dress Institute reported. Baroness Silvercruys, wife of the Belgian Ambassador to the United States; Mrs. Corrin Strong, wife of the Ambassador from Norway; the Countess of Motrico, wife of the Spanish Ambassador; Senora de Gonzalez, wife of the Venezuelan Ambassador and Mrs. David Bruce, wife of the U.S. Ambassador to West Germany all were mentioned by numerous Washington voters.

TWO NEWCOMERS

The two newcomers to the list this year are Mrs. Norman K. Winston, wife of the prominent builder of New York who was recently appointed U.S. Commissioner of Trade Fairs, and Mrs. Thomas Bancroft Jr. — young New York socialite and wife of the textile executive who is a grandson of the late William Woodward.

Here are four of the women named to the annual list of the world's best dressed women as announced by the Couture group of the New York Dress Institute. They are, top: Queen Elizabeth II and Mrs. William Paley; bottom: The Duchess of Windsor and Mrs. William R. Hearst Jr. (AP Wirephoto by Photofax)

Mrs. Stoler Hostess For Present Day Club

Twenty-two members attended the meeting of Present Day Club yesterday afternoon in the home of Mrs. George W. Stoler, 236 N. Duke St. Mrs. Meade Schaffner, sister of the hostess, was a guest. The paper on "Museums" was presented by Mrs. Howard L. Feather.

The next meeting will be held at 2:30 p.m. Thursday, Feb. 6, in the home of Mrs. H. Frank Eshleman, 1294 Wheatland Ave., when the paper on "Avocations" will be given by Mrs. George S. Mann.

Engagements

FRYE—SINGER

Mr. and Mrs. Russell Singer, New Holland, announce the engagement of their daughter, Ellen Singer, to Harold Frye Jr., son of Mr. and Mrs. Harold Frye, McKeansburg.

Miss Singer, a graduate of Garden Spot High School, New Holland, is attending Maryland Medical Secretarial School. Her fiance is employed by the J. S. Zulick Shoe Co., Orwigsburg.

LUDWIG—LONGENECKER

Mr. and Mrs. Walter S. Longenecker, York R3, announce the engagement of their daughter, Ruth E., to Paul E. Ludwig, son of Mr. and Mrs. Preston Ludwig, Red Lion R2.

Miss Longenecker is a senior at William Penn High School and is employed by the Lincoln Park Pharmacy, York.

Her fiance is a graduate of Red Lion High School and is a student at Pennsylyania State University.

Toastmistress Club To Be Represented At Regional Meeting

A meeting of the Northeast Regional Council, Toastmistress Clubs, will be held Saturday, Jan. 11, in the Hamilton Hotel, Washington, D. C.

Mrs. Paul Beck, vice president of Garden Spot Toastmistress Club 817, will be one of the speakers. Also attending from Lancaster will be Mrs. Samuel B. Tompkins, president, and Mrs. Warren Ammon.

The local club held a meeting last night in the N. Queen Street Branch of the Lancaster County National Bank. Mrs. Tompkins presided and members participated in a discussion on "Proper Parliamentary Procedure."

The club will have a dinner meeting at 6:30 p. m. Wednesday, Jan. 15, in Stock Yard Inn.

Coming Events

TODAY

Bucknell Alumni Club of Lancaster, reception for freshmen of the college, Conestoga Country Club, 7 p.m.

Marching Unit of Women of the Moose, Lancaster Chapter 767, Rock and Roll dance, Moose Hall, 8 to 11 p.m.

Head Of Conference ULCW Names 1958 Committees

Mrs. Harland D. Fague, president of the executive committee, United Lutheran Church Women of the Lancaster Conference, has named her various committees for the year 1958. They are as follows:

Membership committee — Mrs. Charles Weidman, Zion, Manheim, chairman; Mrs. Clarence Hagy, St. John's, Denver; Mrs. W. E. Waybright, St. John's, Denver; Mrs. Ralph Drukenbrod, Grace, Lancaster; Mrs. Eugene Browne, Zion, Leacock.

Education committee — Mrs. Herbert Hohman, Redeemer, Lancaster; Miss Mary Rowe, St. John's, Lancaster; Mrs. Francis Daehling, Zion, Lancaster; Mrs. Raymond Foellner, Zion, Manheim; Mrs. Robert Coble, Advent, Lancaster; Mrs. Christian Bretz, Christ, Elizabethtown; Miss Sarah Bitner, Emmanuel, Lancaster.

Christian Service — Mrs. William Bachman, St. Matthew, Lancaster, chairman; Miss Ella King, Concordia, Mountville; Mrs. Robert Hanna, St. Paul's, Lititz; Mrs. Richard Smith, Grace, Lancaster; Mrs. George Nickel, St. John's, Lancaster.

Offerings committee — Mrs. Albert Seitz, Trinity, Lancaster, chairman; Mrs. Ernest Hoh, Emmanuel, Lancaster; Mrs. Ernest Huston, St. Peter's, Neffsville; Mrs. Emery Witwer, Emmanuel, Lancaster; Mrs. Ray Newcomer, St. John's, Maytown.

Convention committee — Mrs. Ralph Gresh, Zion, Leacock, chairman; Mrs. Einar Palmgren, Trinity, Lancaster; Mrs. Wallace Fisher, Trinity, Lancaster; Mrs. Ray Evelan, Trinity, Lancaster; Mrs. Earl DeHart, St. Paul's, Bowmansville; Mrs. G. W. Schindehutte, Trinity, Ephrata; Mrs. Fague, St. Stephen's, Lancaster; Mrs. Drukenbrod, Grace, Lancaster; Mrs. Charles Schneider, Ascension, Lancaster.

Nominating committee — Mrs. Roy Frantz, Christ, Lancaster, chairman; Mrs. Gilbert Martin, St. John's, Lancaster; Mrs. James Weinhold, Muddy Creek, Denver; Mrs. E. Hoh, Emmanual, Lancaster; Mrs. Albert Reitz, Redeemer, Lancaster.

Reports and resolutions — Mrs. Hiram Sipes, St. Michael's, Strasburg, chairman; Mrs. Donald Gallion, St. Matthew, Lancaster; Mrs. Stacy Peters, St. John's, Lancaster.

Review of minutes — Mrs. George Heiges, Zion, Manheim, chairman; Mrs. Harvey C. Gibney, Trinity, Lancaster.

Budget — Mrs. Hoh, Emmanuel, Lancaster, chairman; Mrs. Drukenbrod, Grace, Lancaster; Mrs. Seitz, Trinity, Lancaster; Mrs. Raymond L. Fetter, Christ, Elizabethtown; Mrs. Fague, St. Stephens', Lancaster.

Members of the executive committee, in addition to Mrs. Fague, are Mrs. Drukenbrod, vice presiden; Mrs. Fetter, recording secreary; Mrs. Hoh, treasurer; Mrs. Waybright, statistical secretary; plus the chairmen of the education, Christian Service, education, and offerings committees.

K-C Auxiliary Plans Social For Tomorrow

The Auxiliary to the Knights of Columbus, Council 867, will sponsor an "Evening of Fun" tomorrow on the second floor of the council home.

The event is open to members, husbands and friends. A special prize will be awarded and refreshments will be served. Dancing will be to recorded music.

Hostesses will be officers and committee chairmen.

Lone Girl

DAYTON, Ohio (AP) — If ever a girl was a "loner," it's Janet Kraemer. Now one of the few full-fledged women chemical engineers in the country, she recently completed five years of being the lone female in classes at the University of Cincinnati.

Baking sheets that are open on at least three sides are the best sort of pan to use in making cookies. Because these pans allow even circulation of heat, the cookies will brown evenly and well.

Engagements

HAMILTON—RITZ

Mr. and Mrs. Ivan H. Ritz, 339 Nevin St., announce the engagement of their daughter, Beverly Ann Ritz, to J. Richard Hamilton, 506½ Church St., son of Mrs. Gladys Hamilton, Downingtown, and the late H. Frank Hamilton.

Miss Ritz is an intermediate student at the Philadelphia College of Osteopathy School of Nursing. Mr. Hamilton is employed in the engineering department of the Lancaster Branch of the New Holland Machine Co. Both are graduates of McCaskey High School.

ANDERSON—RINEER

Mrs. Pauline Rineer, Rothsville, has announced the engagement of her daughter, Chrystine, to A 2-c Odel C. Anderson, son of Mrs. Ruth Anderson, Waukon, Iowa.

Miss Rineer, a graduate of Warwick Union High School, is employed by the Walter Moyer Co., Inc. Airman Anderson is a graduate of Waukon High School and is serving in the U. S. Air Force at Westover Field, Conn.

SPEROS—GAST

Mr. and Mrs. James R. Gast, 231 E. Ross St., announce the engagement of their daughter, Ethel M., to Ernest Speros Jr., son of Mr. and Mrs. Ernest Speros, 524 N. Plum St.

Miss Gast is employed in the traffic department of the Bell Telephone Co. Mr. Speros is an employe of the K-D Mfg. Co. Both are graduates of McCaskey High School.

HAAS—TEZAK

Mr. and Mrs. Anthony Tezak, Royalton, announce the engagement of their daughter, Mary Lou, to George L. Haas, son of Mr. and Mrs. Charles Haas, Falmouth.

Miss Tezak is a senior at Middletown High School and Mr. Haas is a senior at Elizabethtown Area High School.

No date has been set for the wedding.

McKAIN—FAHRINGER

Mr. and Mrs. Claude R. Fahringer, 20 S. Mulberry St., Marietta, announce the engagement of their daughter, Ruth C., to Paris H. McKain, son of Mr. and Mrs. George L. McKain Jr., Marietta R1.

Donor Lunch Date Is Set By Sisterhood

The Sisterhood of Temple Sharai Shomayim will hold its annual Donor Luncheon at 12:30 p.m. Thursday, Feb. 20, in the Stevens House.

Mrs. Bennett Manus was named chairman at the Sisterhood luncheon meeting yesterday in Wise Memorial Hall of the temple.

Mrs. Robert M. Proller, president, is chairman of the congregational Purim Dinner to be held Sunday, March 2.

Rabbi Samson A. Shain reviewed the book, "Remember Me to God", by Myron S. Kauffman.

Thirty-five members attended and hostesses were Mrs. Morton Brodsky, Mrs. Leon Hurwitz, Mrs. Abe Giltman and Mrs. J. S. Allison.

The next luncheon meeting is planned for 12:30 p.m. Thursday, Feb. 6, in Wise Memorial Hall.

Willard Meeting

Mrs. James Gromling, 541 W. Walnut St., will be hostess for the meeting of Willard WCTU at 2 p.m. Monday. The discussion on "Highways to Total Abstinence" will be led by Mrs. P. G. Hiestand. A prayer service will be held at 1:45 p.m. preceding the regular meeting.

Congregational Meeting

First Reformed Church will hold its annual congregational meeting and social at 8 p.m. Wednesday in Harbaugh Hall. Elders, deacons and a trustee will be elected.

WE THE WOMEN

You Don't Need A Guide To Follow These Conversations

By RUTH MILLETT

Ruth Millett

CAN you guess whether it's Mama or Papa speaking?

"I'm not being hard on the boy. He simply has to learn to take responsibility."

"You expect too much of him. After all, he's only a child."

"What do you mean she has to have a new formal? What's the matter with the one she has?"

"After all, you can't expect her to wear the same dress to every dance. Besides, all her friends are getting new dresses for the Junior Prom."

"Quit worrying about that boy. He's old enough to take care of himself."

"You can go to bed if you want to, but I'm going to wait up for Junior."

"That boy friend of Dorothy's must think he lives here. Doesn't he have a home of his own?"

"Shssh. . . . Do you want him to hear you? You'll embarrass Dorothy to death!"

"A 14-year-old boy having to send a corsage to a girl for a high school dance! That's the silliest thing I ever heard of."

"Girls expect corsages. Of course, he has to send her one."

"That's the laziest kid I ever saw. All he does around this house is eat and sleep. When I was his age . . ."

"You forget he's a growing boy. Besides, I'll bet you were just as lazy as he is when you were his age."

You guessed it right every time. How could you have missed?

WEATHER
(U. S. Weather Bureau)
Cloudy with occasional light rain or snow today. High 34-40. Low tonight 27-32.
(Details On Page 20)

Intelligencer Journal.

The Leading Newspaper in the Garden Spot of America. Home Owned for Home Folks Since 1794

THE INTELL INDEX
Comic 6, 7
Editorial 10
Farm 16
Radio-TV 16
Sports 14, 15
Theater 16
Women Today 8, 9
Telephone EX 7-5251

164th Year.—No. 192. Metropolitan Lancaster Population (Estimate) Penna. Dept. of Commerce 249,799 — LANCASTER, PA., MONDAY MORNING, JANUARY 27, 1958. — CITY EDITION — 20 PAGES. 42c PER WEEK—7c Per Copy.

NEW CRISIS SEEN RISING IN CARACAS

Ruling Junta Meets In Extraordinary Session; Curfew Enforced

CARACAS, Venezuela, Jan. 26 (AP) — Venezuela's ruling junta met suddenly in an extraordinary session tonight. A new wave of tension swept through this capital city.

Fears were aroused that supporters of ousted Dictator Marcos Perez Jimenez might be on the verge of attempting a counter coup.

Armored cars took up patrol. All persons, even those with safe conduct passes, were warned to stay off the streets during curfew.

There were no immediate details on the reason for the junta session or the basis for the rumors of a possible counter move by Perez Jimenez followers.

A once powerful leftist political leader returned earlier today from exile and declared he was proclaiming a truce among the nation's political parties.

Jovito Villalba, one-time chief of the Union Republicana Democratia party, came back to Caracas from New York. He fled Venezuela after the 1952 presidential election. Villalba claimed victory in that election but Perez Jimenez seized control.

Villalba said Venezuela must now build a strong, expanding economy "so we don't have to depend only on petroleum or alms the United States might give us."

He said he had been in contact with other exiled political leaders and added:

PROCLAIMS TRUCE

"In their names and mine I proclaim truce among political parties. We will not break unity. We will support all progressive democratic expressions of the new junta."

Villalba said he believed the most important characteristics of the struggle that resulted in the ouster of Perez Jimenez was the fact that he "did not fall by a coup in the barracks but by the people combined with military youth."

NEW RT. 30 LIGHTS BEGIN OPERATING

New traffic signals along the Lincoln Highway West, at the intersections of the Millersville and Rohrerstown roads, were in operation yesterday.

The signals were installed by Hershey Lenhard, Lancaster city electrician, for East Hempfield and Manor Twps. following approval by the State Highways Department.

The lights remain on green for Lincoln Highway traffic and are activated by traffic entering the highway from either intersecting road.

DR. FUCHS REPORTS HE'S GONE 80 MILES

AUCKLAND, New Zealand, Jan. 26 (AP) — Dr. Vivian Fuchs, trekking from the South Pole to Scott Base on the second leg of his transantarctic journey, radioed today he has traveled 80 miles. He has 1,220 miles to go.

A dispatch to New Zealand from Scott Base reported the 12-man British party was traveling in a partial "white-out." The group left the pole Friday.

Navy Calls Off New Attempt To Fire 'Moon'

CAPE CANAVERAL, Fla., Jan. 26 (AP)—The Navy tonight called off for a few days at least another attempt to launch its Vanguard satellite vehicle.

It acted after a frustrating period of weather and mechanical difficulties extending over much of the past week.

Another launching may be attempted within a few days. However, the Navy may be unable to maintain the launching schedule which calls for a major effort in March unless its luck improves.

An informed source said launching preparations were suspended "to allow time for correction of mechanical faults which have developed over the weekend."

These preparations were known several times to have almost reached the firing stage.

MINUTES AWAY

It was learned that a launching was only minutes away Saturday evening at the time that Russia's Sputnik II came sailing over this part of Florida.

Persons on the beaches, watching the activity that could be seen at the closely guarded cape, plainly observed the Soviet satellite in two sweeps across the heavens, an hour and a half apart.

"That dead dog up there must be thumbing his nose at our Vanguard," one person remarked.

The close approach to a first full-scale launching of the three-stage rocket with a 3½-pound satellite in its nose left Vanguard workers and newsmen under considerable tension.

This was less true than the ill-fated Dec. 6 launching attempt, however, because the Navy had kept its plans a tight secret and the public generally did not become aware of the efforts under way.

By contrast last month the

Turn To Page 4 For More Of VANGUARD

ARTHUR B. EISENHOWER

Ike's Brother Arthur Dies In Kansas City

KANSAS CITY, Jan. 26 (AP)—Arthur B. Eisenhower, 71, older brother of President Eisenhower, died at his home late today.

He had been in ill health with a heart ailment for some time since his retirement from a post with a Kansas City bank.

Arthur Eisenhower was vice chairman of the board of the Commerce Trust Co. when he retired in 1956. He later suffered a heart attack.

During his banking career he gained a national reputation in flour and grain finances.

AIRLINES DIRECTOR

He formerly was a director of Trans World Airlines and the Coleman Co. of Wichita, and a number of other corporations.

Eisenhower joined the Commerce Trust Co. 53 years ago and in 1934 became its executive vice president and a director.

In Washington the presidential press secretary, James C. Hagerty, said President Eisenhower had been informed by the family of Arthur's death.

Hagerty said there would be no word from the White House tonight on whether the President would attend the funeral, nor would there be any statement from the President.

Dulles Lands In Turkey To Spur Allies

ANKARA, Turkey, Jan. 26 (AP)—John Foster Dulles flew into this frontier land alongside Soviet Russia today for a conference of the five-nation Baghdad Pact Alliance.

The American secretary of state has a key role in the four-day talks beginning tomorrow, even though he is attending the meeting of premiers and foreign ministers only in the capacity of observer. The United States is a member of several of the alliance's committees, but was not a signer of the pact itself.

Dulles' first appearance in the top Ministerial Council of the two-year-old alliance comes at a time when Soviet incursions have made the Middle East a major battlefield of the East-West cold war. Soviet offers of military and economic aid, which already have tempted several neutralist Arab lands, appear to be having a side effect of spurring Moslem members of the Baghdad Pact to seek spectacular parallel commitments from the West.

ON RUSSIA BORDER

The Baghdad Pact, which Dulles conceived originally girdles the southern rim of the Soviet Union and comprises Britain, Turkey, Iraq and Pakistan.

Dulles flew to Turkey from Tehran where talks during a 40-hour stopover had been designed to allay Iran's fears it is not getting sufficient help from its Western friends.

After being greeted by Turkish officials, Dulles read a statement to reporters and over the government-controlled radio Ankara praising Turkish concepts of collective defense and the Baghdad Pact goals.

He concluded: "The United States looks forward to a fruitful continuation of its association with the Baghdad Pact."

NOT FULL MEMBER

But during the Istanbul stopover, his assistant, Andrew Berding, told one questioner the United States still is unwilling to become a full member of the pact because it can better exercise its influence in the area by remaining outside the alliance.

Other statesmen here for the talks include Turkey's Premier Adnan Menderes, Iraq's strongman and ex-Premier Nuri Said, Iranian Premier Manouchehr Eghbal, Pakistan's Premier Firoz Khan Noon and Britain's Foreign Minister Selwyn Lloyd.

Menderes, who returned yesterday from a mysterious one-day mission to Baghdad, formally opens the conference tomorrow in the as yet unused wing of the new Turkish Grand National Assembly building in the center of Ankara. Even now tough Turkish troops are screening the flag-bedecked conference headquarters — troops packing pistols or fixed bayonets and reinforced by husky squads of plainclothes security men.

Keynote of the discussions will be "collective defense and economic cooperation," Lloyd told newsmen. The talks will be held in secret with each delegation briefing national correspondents within rearranged limitations.

U.S. BLDGS. HIT BY BOMBS IN TURKEY

ISTANBUL, Jan. 26 (AP) — One bomb blasted a warehouse of the U.S. embassy compound and another shattered a private bookshop near the U.S. Information Center in Ankara today.

The explosions occurred 11 hours before the opening of a four-day Baghdad Pact conference.

Secretary of State Dulles is in Ankara for the conference, but was not in the affected areas.

No injuries were reported.

An embassy spokesman said it was assumed the bombs were thrown from passing cars in both cases.

16-Block City Area Mapped For Redevelopment Work

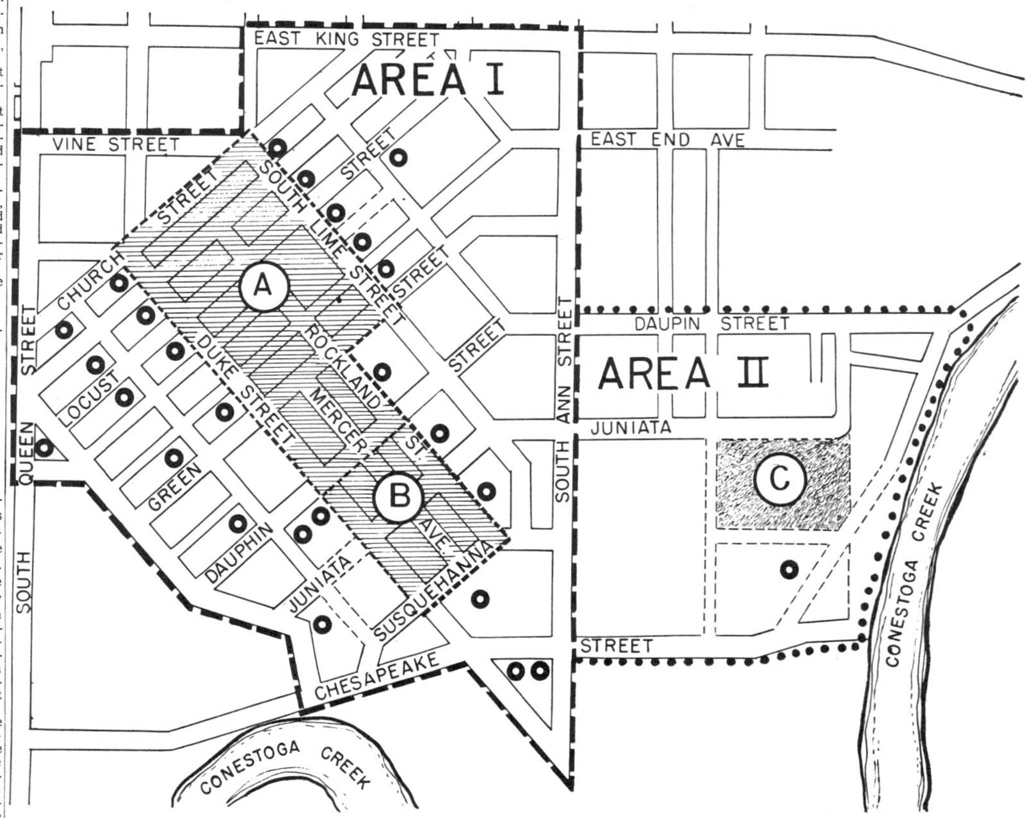

Tentative boundaries for proposed urban renewal project of Lancaster Redevelopment Authority is shown on this map showing portions of Seventh and Fifth Wards. Area I shows boundaries of project area proposed by authority. Alternate plan includes both Area I and Area II. Extension represented by Area II is designed to include school site (C) within project area. However, authority has asked the city School Board to include school in clearance area (shaded area) at location B. If project size is reduced, clearance area may be limited to all or part of section A. Black circles designate blocks within overall project area in which there are one or more blighted buildings which could be removed under the program. No attempt has been made to place the circles to indicate where on the blocks these buildings are located. Redevelopment Authority would plan redevelopment to not only increase property values within clearance area, but over entire project area as well. (Intell Map)

Susquehanna Up One Foot Above Flood Stage

Jammed with ice and swollen by heavy rains of the past week, the Susquehanna River had risen to a foot over flood stage yesterday afternoon but was holding fast at that point early today. The measurement at Columbia was 236 feet above sea level.

Scores of motorists thronged to the river yesterday afternoon to witness the ancient stream put on another of its "spectaculars."

OTHER STREAMS HIGH

Other streams in the county were also reported running bank full yesterday but there were no reports that any roads had been flooded out in the wake of Saturday's heavy rains.

The river had been ice-bound until the weekend when the ice broke, leaving wide channels of open water at Columbia and Washington Boro. However the ice jammed below Columbia, in the vicinity of the old dam, and below Washington Boro, in the Turkey Hill area, which caused some of the water to back up over the banks at Columbia.

York Co. Home Wrecked; Boy Dies In Blast

YORK, Jan. 26 — An explosion of undetermined origin rocked the nearby community of Loganville tonight, blowing up a three-story brick home and reportedly killing a fourteen-year-old boy.

It was the second explosion of its type in this area in as many days. Saturday evening a Pleasureville couple escaped serious injury when their house atop Pleasureville Hill blew up. Flames following the blast completed destruction of the building, occupied by Mr. and Mrs. Charles G. Krout.

Tonight's blast wrecked the home of Henry Elphick. The house was described as completely destroyed. A neighbor said the explosion had killed Elphick's son, Freddy, and seriously injured Mrs. Pauline Elphick, his mother. A third occupant, a son, Jack, appeared to have escaped harm.

Several other houses in the community of about 600 appeared to have been shaken. Damage seemed to amount to broken windows, for the most part.

Klan Leader Promises Rally — 'We'll Outnumber Indians'

MARION, S. C., Jan. 26 (AP)—The leader of the North Carolina Ku Klux Klan said today the KKK will hold another rally soon in Robeson County, N. C. and "this time there will be more Klansmen than Indians."

"The over-all picture will be a lot different," said the Rev. James Cole, South Carolina preacher who bills himself as the chief of the KKK in North Carolina.

"We don't expect to be broken up again," he said at his home here. "This time there will be more Klansmen than there will be Indians. I don't expect any trouble from the Indians."

WHOOPING INDIANS

The Klan's last meeting in Robeson County, near Maxton, on Jan. 17 was broken up by gunfire from angry Lumbee Indians. The Klansmen, outnumbered by hundreds of tribesmen, scattered like quail as whooping Indians fired hundreds of rounds of ammunition into the air and the ground.

At the Indian community of Pembroke near Maxton, Simeon Oxendine—son of Pembroke's Indian mayor, and leader of the Indian raid on the Klan—listened in silence to a report on Cole's statements.

"He said that, did he? Well, we'll just wait and see," Oxendine said.

GREATEST RALLY

"We definitely plan a meeting in Robeson in the Maxton area within the next month. It will be the greatest rally the Klan has had," Cole said.

"I expect there will be not less than 5,000 Klansmen there and probably more. Klansmen all over the South are pretty upset. I've had offers of 3,000 men from Texas and offers of men from Kentucky and South Carolina."

Consultants Outline Two Plans For Portions Of 3rd, 7th Wards

By NED WALL

Tentative boundaries for an urban renewal project area—including up to 16 square blocks for almost total clearance—have been set by the Lancaster Redevelopment Authority.

The proposed project area comprises approximately one-fourth of the Seventh Ward, but also includes nine blocks in the Third Ward.

A number of factors—including the total amount of funds from all sources to be made available for redevelopment, and Urban Renewal Administration review—could cause a considerable reduction in the clearance area, the area in which the greater portion of the funds will be used.

The boundaries are based on initial recommendations of the authority's consulting planning firm, Cooper, Alvere and Harkins, Philadelphia, as a result of its studies over the past four months.

This determination of tentative boundaries is only the first step in a lengthy process which, under normal conditions, means at least an 18-month interim period before actual clearance begins and residents of blighted buildings are required to leave their homes.

As shown in the accompanying map, the overall project boundaries are in two sections:

Area I, the area in which the authority desires to confine the project, is bounded by Ann Street on the east; Duke, Chesapeake and Strawberry Streets on the south; Queen Street on the west, and Vine, Lime and King Streets on the north.

Area II would include all of Area I, plus the blocks bounded by Dauphin Street on the north; the Conestoga Creek on the east; Chesapeake Street on the south, and Ann Street on the west.

The authority believes Area I would have a better chance of federal approval as an urban renewal area than Area I and Area II combined. However, the school board has announced plans to erect a new elementary school on Juniata Street (marked as C on map). Area II thus would include the proposed site.

But the authority has also asked the school board to consider placing the site within the proposed clearance area, where full federal participation would be more likely. Under the Urban Renewal Program, the federal government will provide up to two-thirds of the net cost of clearing blighted buildings, with local construction, including schools, counting as a local contribution subject to the financial grant.

MEET AT NOON TODAY

If the school were built at the board's proposed site on Dauphin Street, and the Urban Renewal Administration does not approve its inclusion in the renewal area, the authority could receive a partial grant. Thus, if 50 per cent of the children to attend the school were to come from the renewal area, then half the cost of the

Turn To Page 11 For More Of AUTHORITY

Retailers Call Meeting With City And CTC

Members of the Lancaster Chamber of Commerce Retailers' Committee will meet with officials of the City and the Conestoga Transportation Co. this morning in an effort to develop recommendations to stimulate downtown retail business.

George B. Coe, chairman of a special sub-committee appointed by the Retailers' Committee to obtain the recommendations, said the two main problems to be discussed at the meeting will be traffic and mass transportation.

Representing the CTC at the meeting, to be held at the Chamber offices, 45 E. Orange St., will be Thomas W. Meredith, executive vice-president of the company. Robert M. Chryst, city traffic engineer will be present and City Commissioner Joseph T. Fasnacht has been invited.

Coe said the retailers will try to exchange ideas and suggestions on the improvement of the business situation. He said the sub-committee's recommendations will be submitted to the Retailers' Committee at their next meeting.

Carole Carpenter Is Contest Winner

Carole Carpenter, Brownstown, is today's "Be My Valentine" contest winner. See last want-ad page for contest rules.

Official Admits Idaho Potatoes Used In Maine

LIMESTONE, Maine, Jan. 26 (AP)—The director of materiel at Loring Air Force Base said last night he wouldn't be surprised if Idaho potatoes were being shipped into the base, which is located in Aroostook County, the center of Maine's potato industry.

Lt. Col. James T. McNeely said, "There is no control over the buying of foodstuffs here. All potatoes, as well as other foods, are delivered by the Army Quartermaster Corps' regional office in Boston.

"I don't know for a fact that Idaho potatoes are delivered here," he added, "but I wouldn't be surprised to hear it."

Sen. Smith (R-Maine) protested yesterday that Idaho potatoes were being eaten at Loring and demanded an accounting from the Air Force.

IDAHO SPUDS COST MORE

A. K. Gardner, consultant for the Maine Potato Commission, said he told the nation's only lady senator that Idaho potatoes shipped to Maine cost $2.02 per hundredweight, plus three per cent tax, more than local spuds.

McNeely said that Frank W. Hussey, executive vice president of the Maine Potato Council, sent him a letter a week ago making the same protest.

"We Lead All The Rest" FARM CORNER

By Don Brandt

County's Field Crop Yields In '57 See $6 Million Loss

The release of the first U. S. Dept. of Agriculture estimates of 1957 farm production begins to draw the curtain on the discouraging results of farming in Lancaster County last year. In field crops alone, the poor weather lopped more than $6 million from the Garden Spot's share of the agricultural market compared to 1956.

Even more discouraging is the fact that the preliminary estimates on the drought's cost are based on Lancaster County's share of the 1956 production and average prices for most crops.

USDA is not yet able to assess how much more the county's portion of state farm production was affected by the drought.

The most serious slashes in Lancaster County farm earnings came in tobacco and corn. An indication that the facts may be even more costly than estimated by USDA is the picture in tobacco.

In 1956, Lancaster County raised 46,683,000 pounds of tobacco, with the state total at 51,000,000 pounds. USDA estimates that 1957 tobacco in Pennsylvania was cut to 41,160,000 pounds, reducing Lancaster County's share by more than nine million pounds.

Using the average price of 1956 tobacco, when the Garden Spot grossed more than $11 million, 1957 tobacco would be worth just over $9 million. But the harsh fact is that 1957 average prices for tobacco will probably be far less than the 24½ cents USDA used in the 1956 figures.

Even a "modest" cut in the average tobacco price could mean another $2 million reduction in the worth of last year's seedleaf production.

While corn losses cost another $2,700,000, the county's share of the corn silage market ironically increased by one-half million dollars.

The silage crop was not so

Turn To Page 16 For More Of FARM CORNER

WEATHER
(U. S. Weather Bureau)
Fair And Cold Today, Highest 26-30. Low Tonight 12-16. Light Snow Tomorrow.
(Details On Page 42)

Intelligencer Journal.

The Leading Newspaper in the Garden Spot of America. Home Owned for Home Folks Since 1794

THE INTELL INDEX

Telephone EX 7-5251

164th Year.—No. 207. Metropolitan Lancaster Population (Estimate) Penna. Dept. of Commerce 249,799 LANCASTER, PA., THURSDAY MORNING, FEBRUARY 13, 1958. CITY EDITION 42 PAGES. 42c PER WEEK—7c Per Copy

3 Homeless, City Fireman Overcome In Costly Blaze

RED HOT FLUE BLAMED FOR SMOKEY FIRE

Three persons were made homeless last night and a fireman required hospital treatment after a stubborn fire gutted the rear of a large frame house at 600 Fairview Ave., shortly after 9 p. m.

A telephoned alarm at 9:12 p.m. brought Engines 1, 2 and 6 and Truck B under Assistant Fire Chief William B. Landis to the scene. Flames were shooting from the second floor windows and portions of the roof at the rear of the house when firefighters arrived.

Firemen quickly brought the larger blazes under control but small smouldering fires throughout the second floor filled the house and surrounding area with a dense smoke.

WALL SET AFIRE

According to Fire Chief Edward Koerkle the fire was started in the rear apartment occupied by Walter G. Smeltz, when a flue pipe became overheated and ignited the wall. Smeltz was asleep in the apartment at the time.

He was awakened by the heat and ran to the home of a neighbor, Mrs. Ronald E. Sykes, 616 Fairview Ave., and she phoned the alarm to fire headquarters. The occupants of the front apartment of the house, Mr. and Mrs. Elmer T. Homsher, were not at home at the time.

Fireman Jacob Stoe of Truck B was overcome by smoke as he battled flames on the second floor of the house. Fellow firefighters helped him down a ladder and he was taken to Lancaster General Hospital in the police ambulance.

He was treated there for smoke inhalation and discharged. Firemen at the scene of the blaze had to face an additional hazard last night as the 20-degree temperature caused ice to form in the fire area, making it slippery underfoot for the firefighters.

Chief Koerkle said firemen were able to confine the blaze mostly to the rear of the building but said damage would total at least several thousand dollars. Firemen left the scene at about 11:40 p.m.

UNAWARE OF FIRE

Homsher returned to the house shortly before firemen left. He told Chief Landis that his wife was still visiting in Lampeter and did not yet know of the fire. He said he had a place for them to

Turn To Page 10 For More Of FIRE

Clothesline Counteracts Cancer Threat

CARDIFF, Wales, Feb. 12 (AP)—Twice a week Hassan Abdullah Burro walked into a dockside shop here and bough a brand new 54-foot length of clothesline.

The proprietor, finally overwhelmed by curosity, called in the constabulary. One policeman decided the direct approach was best and asked Burro what he did with all the rope.

'That's easy," said Burro, a little surprised, "I smoke it."

And the 64-year-old seaman from Aden, now working at a landlubber's job took the cop home and displayed his bubble pipe, one of those things that draw smoke through water.

"I smoke about 15 feet a day," Burro said, "and don't get cancer."

House Inquiry Files Returned By Sen. Morse

WASHINGTON, Feb. 12 (AP) — House investigators retrieved three heaps of secret files today from Sen. Morse (D-Ore), who said the documents show the Eisenhower administration is honeycombed with political immorality.

At the same time, the investigating group subpoenaed Dr. Bernard Schwartz, its ousted chief counsel, to testify tomorrow about his charge that a member of the Federal Communications Commission received a money payment in connection with the award of a TV license.

Schwartz turned what he called his "personal working files" on a six-month investigation over to Morse after Schwartz was fired Monday night by the House subcommittee on legislative oversight, which is looking into the FCC and five other regulatory agencies.

SEPARATE PROBE

In returning the files to the subcommittee, Morse c ll for a separate Senate investigation of alleged pressure on the agencies by White House and other high Republican figures. Morse's proposal got no immediate support, however, and the inquiry remained in the House group's hands.

Speaker Rayburn (D-Tex) said he wants the subcommittee to make a "real thorough investigation" and not just do "a lot of pinpricking."

Plainly smarting over charges by Schwartz and others that powerful interests turned the inquiry into a whitewash, Rayburn said

Turn To Page 10 For More Of INQUIRY

Snow In Florida

MIAMI, Fla., Feb. 12 (AP) — Snow blanketed Florida's capital city tonight and the Weather Bureau warned that winds up to 40 miles an hour would hit Miami by morning.

Signals Of 1 Explorer Radio Stop

WASHINGTON, Feb. 12 (AP)—The Defense Department said today signals from one of two radio transmitters in the American Explorer satellite apparently have stopped.

The transmitter, originally expected to function for from two to three weeks, was the more powerful of two encased in the 30-pound satellite.

The satellite was launched by the Army on the night of Jan. 31. If the batteries have gone dead, they lasted less than 12 days.

NO SIGNALS

The Naval Research Laboratory, which has charge of tracking the satellite, said, "Today's Explorer passes over the minitrack system have produced no signals on the 108.03 band." It said signals continue to come in strong from the second transmitter in the satellite. Predictions were that one would operate from two to three months.

The transmitter not heard from today operated with a power of 60 miliwatts, or 6-100 of one watt. This was the signal that was heard by amateur radio operators and the one which sent automatic reports of how the satellite was faring in its transit through space.

ORBITAL DATA

The second transmitter is still operating strongly on 108 megacycles with a power of 10 miliwatts. Signals from this less powerful transmitter, picked up by high - powered tracking stations, provide information about the orbital course followed by the satellite.

Ike Says March Should See End Of 'Downturn'

WASHINGTON, Feb. 12 (AP) — President Eisenhower, in an optimistic statement on the economic situation, said today that March should mark the beginning of the end of the downturn.

From other quarters, however, came predictions that the situation will get wrose before it gets better. Some economists expressed doubts that the upturn will come as quickly as the administration believes.

Eisenhower expressed concern over joblessness, which rose to 4½ million in January, and over the shorter work week in effect in some industries. He said he believed "we have had most of our bad news on the unemployment front."

NOT PROLONGED

"I am convinced that we are not facing a prolonged downswing in activity," he added. "Every indication is that March will see the start of a pickup in job opportunities."

The President issued what he called a fact paper showing what

Turn To Page 10 For More Of ECONOMIC

COLD FACTS

Sub-Freezing Weather Due Another Week

No break in the current cold snap is in sight until next week, says the weatherman.

Another 48 hours of sub-freezing temperatures are anticipated and the extended forecast calls for continued cold weather until Monday. Low yesterday was 19 degrees, the high 30.

And to make matters worse, there is a chance of snow for the weekend, beginning possibly tomorrow night.

The forecast calls for continued cold weather today and tomorrow, fair skies turning cloudy tomorrow, and a chance of some light snow tomorrow night.

Temperatures today and tomorrow will climb no higher than 26 to 30 degrees, says the forecast, and will dip down, to 12 to 16 tonight.

Temperatures should average six to eight degrees below normal through the weekend, with snow or rain Saturday or Sunday.

GOP Campaign Committees To Take Tex. Fund

WASHINGTON, Feb. 12 (AP)—The chairmen of the Senate and House Republican Campaign committees said today they will accept the $100,000 raised by a Houston, Tex., party dinner and spurned by the GOP National Committee.

Interviewed by telephone, Sen. Schoeppel (R - Kan) and Rep. Simpson (R-Pa) said Chairman Meade Alcorn's statement that the GOP National Committee will not accept funds from the dinner does not apply to their committees.

Alcorn's refusal was announced yesterday, with White House approval.

ACTION CONDEMNED

Schoeppel and Simpson joined in condemning the action of H. J. Porter, Texas GOP national committeeman, in appealing for contributions on the ground that Rep. Joseph W. Martin Jr., House minority leader, had helped obtain House passage of the natural gas bill in the past and was being counted on to rally support for it this year.

But Schoeppel and Simpson made it clear their indignation was not so great as to cause them—as it did Alcorn—to turn their backs on $100,000 in campaign contributions.

At Austin, Gov. Price Daniel of Texas told a news conference Porter should return the $100,000 to the contributors. Daniel, a Democrat, said Porter's "attempt to mix partisan politics and campaign funds with the natural gas bill" has hurt the pending legislation.

INCIDENT DEPLORED

"As governor of this state, I want the people of the nation to know that this incident is deplored by the great majority of our people," he said. "Neither Texas nor the merits of the gas bill should be judged by Mr. Porter's actions."

"I knew nothing about the Porter letter until I read portions of it in the papers," Schoeppel said when he was reached in Independence, Kan. "It was unfortunate and does not bespeak the attitude of the Republicans of Texas who contributed honestly to help elect Republican senators and congressmen.

"We are certainly not going to take the position, however, that any money forwarded to us by the Republican State Finance Committee of Texas will not be accepted."

9 ARRESTED IN SERIES OF 'GAS' THEFTS

Bainbridge Youths Accussed Of Stealing Hundreds Of Gallons

A lone police officer who kept a nightly vigil for a solid week, has rounded up a gang of youths accused of stealing hundreds of gallons of gasoline in the Bainbridge and Bossler Church areas since last August.

Apprehended by Benjamin D. Waltz, police chief for West Donegal and Conoy Twps., the group, with one exception, all reside in Bainbridge.

Three of them, Henry Halblieb, seventeen, Charles Sweigart, eighteen, and Dale Stump, twenty-two, all of Bainbridge, have been charged with larceny of gasoline. They posted bail for hearings before Justice of the Peace Lester B. Weidman, 1667 N. Market St., Elizabethtown.

The other six, one of whom lives in Lancaster, are sixteen years of age or under and are being petitioned into juvenile court.

Although Chief Waltz said he has gotten confessions out of the nine picked up, he believes there are other youths involved.

Monday night, Feb. 3, he related, he had posted himself on the farm of Leroy Rutt, in the Bossler Church area, where gasoline thefts had been reported. Within a short time an auto drove up and a youth started to pump gasoline from the pump.

When Waltz advanced on the youth, another shouted an alarm and both jumped into the auto and drove away.

FIRES 2 SHOTS

Waltz said the trunk lid of the car was open and he fired two shots from his .38 calibre pistol at a distance of from ten to 15 feet. One was a load of scatter shot. He said he believes he hit the car.

Waltz, however, said he doesn't think either of the nine youths he has rounded up were involved in this escapade.

One of the principal victims of the gang in custody, he reported, was W. E. Mohr, Bainbridge plumbing and heating contractor. Mohr's fleet of five trucks, the officer was told, were being drained of gasoline at numerous times since last August. Other victims included numerous farmers in the area.

The gang, Waltz said, admitted stealing between 150 and 200 gallons of gasoline. Waltz, however, says he would not be surprised if the total was in the "thousands." Halblieb, Sweigart and Stump each own an auto, he added.

Each night last week Waltz had posted himself at strategic spots near places where gasoline was being stolen and learned the identity of the gang one by one. This past Monday and Tuesday he started rounding them up and completed the job yesterday.

STOCKS POST SIXTH STRAIGHT DECLINE

NEW YORK, Feb. 12 (AP)— The stock market retreated today, posting its sixth straight decline, with much of the slump coming after President Eisenhower's economic statement.

Major issues lost a few cents to about $1 but finished above the lows for the day. Drug and tobacco stocks advanced against the general trend.

A ticket taker examines the credentials of County Detective Harry Meyers (right) as he entered the Fulton Art Theater last night to officially decide the status of the French Film, "And God Created Woman," which opened at the local theater. Myers headed a group of local official "reviewers" called in to determine whether the film is "obscene or objectional." (Intell Photo).

Bardot Might Go, But Fulton Show Was SRO

By NED WALL

A leggy, longhaired redhead with curves like those of the numerals comprising the 888 seating capacity of the Fulton Art Theater tiptoed on bare feet across the Prince Street movie house screen last night.

Whether Brigitte Bardot—star of the French film, "And God Created Woman" — will return tonight will be decided at a conference this morning in District Attorney William C. Storb's office. He is expected to receive a report of four police representaitves who viewed the film last night.

More than 1,000 persons were on hand last night in the wake of widespread publicity given the film following its banning in Philadelphia earlier this week. The Fulton had a capacty house for the first show — including the rarely used balcony — and about 200 were still around the box office when the doors opened at 10 p. m. for a second, unannounced showing.

County Detective Harry E. Meyers, who headed the inspection group, had no comment after the first performance. His group made no attempt to prevent the second showing.

Donald W. Bonstein, manager of the Fulton, said he had been informed by Meyers he would be notified of a decision by noon today. He said the management of the movie house has agreed to withdraw the film from further showing if the officials rule it objectionable.

BRIGITTE BARDOT

While the police gave no indication of their reaction, the full house at the first showing apparently enjoyed the film — which before the Philadelphia commotion had played in some 75 cities without drawing much attention.

The audience laughed at what were supposed to be emotional high points in the drama, probably because of ridiculous English dialogue dubbed into the sound track.

MANY COLLEGE STUDENTS

College students formed a relatively large segment of the crowd. But at least a half-dozen attorneys and a number of businessmen also attended. Almost half of the audience was women.

Those under 18 years of age were not permitted to enter.

The crowd showed up early and by 8 p.m. — a half-hour before the first show started — had formed a block-long line along Prince Street. Police were dispatched to the scene because of the number of people involved, but there were no incidents.

The film itself — flashed on a wide screen in color which showed Bardot and the Mediterranean near Toulon to perfection — deals with a young, loose-living, cha-cha loving girl who faces a return to an orphanage because of her inability to conform to the standards of her foster parents.

Bardot, who in France needs no designation other than "B.B.", much as "M.M." means Marilyn Monroe here, plays the girl who is saved through marriage to a

Turn To Page 10 For More Of FILM

Democrats Put Under Attack In GOP Oratory

By THE ASSOCIATED PRESS

Republicans in Lincoln Day speeches Wednesday night launched an attack on what one speaker called a Democratic attempt to "sell America short."

GOP orators also extolled the accomplishments and gains of the Eisenhower administration in the fields of economics, defense, science, foreign policy, agriculture, foreign trade and civil rights.

Three Cabinet officers were among the speakers who roamed the banquet circuit in search of votes to elect a Republican-controlled Congress in November.

BATTLE CRY

Secretary of Commerce Weeks sounded the most vehement battle cry in a speech prepared for a party rally in Brooklyn. He said the "Democratic gloom and doom brigade's whole program boils down to three words: 'Sell America short.' "

Brigitte Won't Play In H-burg

HARRISBURG, Feb. 12 (AP) —Dauphin County authorities went to the movies today. They saw Brigitte Bardot, French movie actress, in her controversial movie "And God Created Woman."

Dist. Atty. Huette F. Dowling decided the advertisement stating that the film shows "much more than American audiences are used to seeing of what 23-year-old girls are made of" was an understatement. He requested it be removed from the bill and Gerry Wollaston, representative of the Fabian Theaters, agreed.

Wollaston said a new film would replace the Mlle. Bardot movie tomorrow. "We aren't interested in showing movies objectionable to the authorities or the people," he added.

Dowling said the movie is "lewd and lascivious." People in Harrisburg "shouldn't be allowed to see a movie like that," he added.

ON THE LORD'S SIDE

Sunday School Locates 2 Missing Refugees In N.J.

A committee from the Akron Mennonite Sunday School proved recently that success can be had in any field if the Lord is on your side. They did something that the Communist secret police couldn't — they tracked down two Hungarian freedom fighters.

This story is not as sinister as it sounds, however, and it has a happy ending. It started last January 21 when the Mennonite Central Committee at Akron announced that two young Hungarians, here under their sponsorship, had disappeared.

The youths, Frank Banto, twenty - one and Paul Ritli, twenty, fled from Hungary and the Communists into Austria after participating in the 1956 revolt. They landed in an Austrian Mennonite refugee camp and came to America in July of last year.

They had taken up residence in New Holland and lived together in an apartment on Railroad St. On Christmas Day, 1957, the two youths disappeared. That's when the Sunday School Committee went into action.

A visit to the boys' room disclosed that they had left in a hurry. A Christmas dinner was on the table, only partly eaten. Unwashed dishes lay in the sink. The possibility of foul play might have been involved presented itself.

But then one of the investigators found something else. An address, apparently of a Hungarian, in Elizabeth, N. J. The address was carefully filed away in case it might be needed. It was.

After other leads on their whereabouts proved to be of no avail, one of the committee members decided to contact the Elizabeth, N. J. address. The reply was prompt. Yes, the two youths were in Elizabeth and in good health.

The reply explained that the boys had traveled to Elizabeth where they knew some of the many Hungarians who made their home in that city. They were under the wing of the members and pastor of the Magyar Presbyterian Church there and had obtained employment in a local factory.

YORK DA RESERVES DECISION ON FILM

YORK, Feb. 12 — York County District Attorney Frank B. Boyle and two members of his staff viewed a performance of "And God Created Woman" at a downtown movie house last night.

Boyle is scheduled to announce a ecision on the film tomor ow.

"We Lead All The Rest"

FARM CORNER

By Don Brandt

Extension Assn. Will Elect Five Committeemen

Five executive committeemen will be elected today by the Lancaster County Agricultural and Home Economics Extension Assn. The election will be part of the annual banquet meeting, to be held at 6:30 p.m. in First Presbyterian Church.

Featured on the program will be Dr. William M. Smith Jr., of Pennsylvania State University, who will speak on "Finding Strengths in Family Life." Harold McCulloch, assistant director of State Extension Service, will also make brief remarks.

J. Lloyd Rohrer, Lancaster R7, president of the executive committee, will be toastmaster. A member of the committee from the Southeast District, Rohrer is up for reelction.

Nominated with him for the district post are Donald S. Eby, Gordonville R1, and J. Arthur Rohrer, Paradise R1.

Other nominations include:

Northwest District — J. Homer Graybill, Manheim R3, incumbent; Victor M. Longenecker, Elizabethtown R3, and Harry S. Mumma, Landisville.

Northeast District — C. Warren

Turn To Page 38 For More Of FARM CORNER

WHAT'S WITH WATER?

Farm Irrigation Takes A Mighty Big Drink

(Editor's Note — This is the fourth in a series of articles on the water resources of the Conestoga Watershed. The material was presented at an open meeting of the Conestoga Valley Assn. when a panel of countians discussed the varying demands for water by Lancaster County interests.)

By DON BRANDT

Enough water to supply the maximum demand of Lancaster for 40 days was used last year by Lancaster County farmers in irrigation. More than 450 million gallons of water were pumped onto the 4,000 acres under irrigation in the county.

R. J. Hamilton III, president of Hamilton Equipment Co., Ephrata, used these figures to illustrate for the Conestoga Valley Assn. the amount of water taken from the Conestoga Watershed by agriculture.

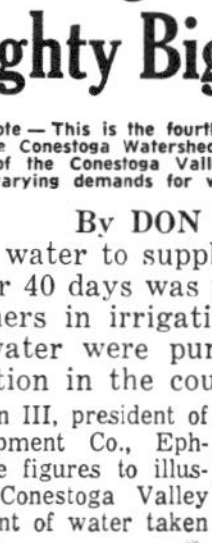

R. J. Hamilton

Storing that amount of water, he said, would require a lake 7,000 feet long, 1,000 feet wide and 10 feet deep. Almost all of that water, Hamilton added, came from streams.

The panelist explained the necessity for stream support of irrigation systems by describing the amount of water needed to irrigate one acre of land.

It takes 27,000 gallons of water to put one inch of water on one acre of land. To perform this job in one hour, the system must pump water at the rate of 450 gallons per minute.

A well must supply at least 250 gallons per minute, Hamilton said, to be practical for irrigation. Few wells in Lancaster County have that capacity.

Each acre of farm land requires an inch of water each

Turn To Page 10 For More Of WATER

Cold Greeting But Warm One

The trans-Antarctic expedition of Dr. Vivian Fuchs, British explorer, approaches a U. S. Navy greeting party two miles from South Pole, Jan. 20. Fuchs started his trip from the Weddel sea coast, 950 miles from the Pole. Picture was released by the Department of Defense yesterday,

(AP Wirephoto via Photofax)

WEATHER
(U. S. Weather Bureau)
Partly Cloudy, Windy And Cold With A Few Snow Flurries. Highways hazardous. High 12-20. Tomorrow Continued Cold.
(Details On Page 20)

Intelligencer Journal.

America. Home Owned for Home Folks Since 1794 The Leading Newspaper in the Garden Spot of

THE INTELL INDEX

Telephone EX 7-5251

164th Year.—No. 210. Metropolitan Lancaster Population (Estimate) Penna. Dept. of Commerce 249,799 LANCASTER, PA., MONDAY MORNING, FEBRUARY 17, 1958. FINAL EDITION 20 PAGES. 42c PER WEEK—7c Per Copy

WORST BLIZZARD IN 30 YEARS LEAVES CITY, COUNTY PARALYZED

Diggin' out. City street department equipment goes to work on E. King St. late last night as the city started digging out from under the weekend's 15 to 16 inch snowstorm. All available members of the street department were working in an attempt to open downtown streets. (Intell Photo)

Schools, Industries Shut Down In Wake Of Blizzard; Two Deaths

A howling snowstorm battered Lancaster into a state of helplessness yesterday and drifting snows today are likely to continue the paralysis.

The overnight snowfall buried Lancaster under 15 to 16 inches of snow, the deepest since 1947.

At least two deaths were attributed to the blizzard. Mrs. A. Marie Fritz, of Lancaster, collapsed while trudging through the snow to work at Lancaster General Hospital, and William L. Weaver was found dead in a field near Wakefield after working all night on a snow plow.

Not in 30 years has a snowfall so crippled the community.

Roads are all but useless. All schools, public, private and parochial will be shut down today. All but a few industries have told their workers to stay home.

Public transportation isn't moving. Cars and trucks lay buried under dunes of snow.

The howling wind which accompanied the blizzard is not expected to abate until sunset today at the earliest. Gusts up to 45 miles an hour were recorded last night and similar wind velocity is forecast for today.

And the coldest weather of the year is on tap, with a low of below zero predicted for tonight. The high today will be no more than 15 to 20 after an early morning low of 5 to 10.

Roads partially opened by hardworking Highway Department employes were drifting closed last night as the winds picked up force and pushed the fluffy snow around like so much dust.

Most rural areas were completely and hopelessly snowbound until sometime later today. And some urban and suburban areas were not much better off.

Driving is likely to be nightmarish again today with wind dumping back the snow that road crews so persistently push off the highways.

Stranded travelers sought refuge in hotels and motels. Railroad and long distance bus service was practically stalled. The Lancaster Airport was shut down.

All but a handful of Protestant churches cancelled their services yesterday. Catholic Masses were held but, as in the case of other churches which did conduct services, were lightly attended.

Only four bus lines operated in the city yesterday. But the Conestoga Transportation Co. hoped to have all its lines operating today.

How milk and bread would be delivered to homes was a question, but the bakeries and dairies are going to try.

Besides the school closings for the youngsters, only one benefit wrought by the storm could be determined. With cars buried and stalled, local streets and roads were practically free of accidents.

Most downtown stores would close today at any rate. But officials of those which normally open Monday had not decided what to do last night.

Highway crews were working on only the main arteries last night and are not likely to get to secondary roads even today.

The job of keeping just the major roads open was too much in some cases. About four out of five roads cleared Saturday night required work again yesterday, said Fred Wagner, county superintendent for the State Department of Highways.

Seventy-five per cent of the main roads had been cleared.

SEEKS HELP

Wagner is reaching out for all the help he can get for today. He has sent out an emergency call to nearby counties for heavy equipment. It is due to arrive today.

He is also hiring equipment and drivers from independent operators. His 180 workmen are weary. Some have worked 22 hours without a break.

And there is some danger that the equipment—about 80 pieces—will break down under the steady pounding.

The worst conditions are on Routes 72, 230 and 222, said Wagner. Four or five plows had to be dug out of drifts.

Wagner said the county was

Turn To Page 4 For More Of SNOW

City Starts Huge Snow Moving Job

Working in 12 degree temperatures, city street department crews began the mammoth task of removing tons of snow from the downtown area at 9 p. m. last night.

Schedule to work through the night, the department pressed into service all of its available equipment and hired upwards of 10 extra trucks to cart away the snow.

Christian Gottselig, commissioner of streets, said additional laborers are to be hired today to assist in snow removal.

Initial efforts on E. King Street between Shippen and Lime Streets were hampered by parked — and snowbound—cars which prevented a grader and snow loader from getting close to the curb.

The huge clean-up job — the biggest the city has faced in three decades—started after the department had been concentrating on keeping major streets plowed.

There was little prospect the removal task would be made easier by melting of snow as temperatures threatened to set record lows for this winter.

Mayor Thomas J. Monaghan said last night the city's men and equipment would be on the job "as long as necessary to clear the streets—there will be no ifs, ands or buts about it."

City Engineer J. Haines Shertzer said that ten trucks have been contracted for to assist in the snow removal. However, he added, some of the owners may be unable to get them in operation.

Local industry faced a similar problem in obtaining snow removal equipment to clear

Turn To Page 4 For More Of CITY

Who Wants To Go Where The Wild Geese Go?

Lancaster residents were unconvinced, but the geese aren't. They are heading north.

Clarence Nutto, Lampeter Road, reported 50 geese, flying quite low over the Conestoga River, yesterday about 3:30 p. m.

Nutto said the honkers were flying in groups of eight and, of all things, were heading north.

CD Will Assist Snow-Battered Northeast Pa.

By THE ASSOCIATED PRESS

Gov. Leader late Sunday ordered mobilization of key Civil Defense units and the State Highways Department in an "all-out" effort to relieve the critically distressed areas of northeastern Pennsylvania crippled by its worst snow storm in 50 years.

Rural Wayne County, in the extreme northeastern corner of the Commonwealth, was by far the worst hit.

The central and western parts were hit less harder.

An estimated 40 to 45 inches of snow fell in the county from early Saturday to late Sunday afternoon accompanied by howling winds up to 40 miles an hour which swept huge drifts of snow back on the highways faster than the harassed snow plow crews could clear them.

APPEAL TO LEADER

Late Sunday, State Rep. Arthur Wall of Honesdale appealed to the governor to declare a state of emergency. At that point even Route 6, main north south county artery, which had been kept open through the day, succumbed to the drifts which measured more than 25 feet in many places.

State Civil Defense director Richard Gerstell, called by Leader to direct the operations from

Turn To Page 4 For More Of PA. WEATHER

Biggest Snow Plow In County Is Broken Down

The State Highways Department suffered a blow last night when its largest piece of snow removal equipment, a Walters plow, broke several front axles.

The breakage, blamed on strain, occurred at 10:40 p. m. on Rt. 222, at Jenkins Corner, near the Maryland line. The plow had been working south and was on its way back when the axles broke.

Highway officials had been counting on the plow for snow removal today but indicated last night the break puts it out of action. The "V" type plow is capable of cutting a 16-foot wide path through drifts.

A grader was sent to the scene last night to bring the plow and crew back to the highway sheds.

Airman 'Back' From Seven-Day 'Moon Junket'

SAN ANTONIO, Tex., Feb. 16 (AP)—Airman Donald G. Farrell completed a seven-day make-believe trip to the moon and reported nothing seems impossible or boring about space travel.

His duties kept him too busy to get bored and he never was scared during the lonely test, the 23-year-old volunteer said after crawling from an experimental space cabin at Randolph Air Force Base.

"I realized all the time I was on the ground," he said, "but other than that it was a true simulated space flight."

Farrell said the only physical effects of his long confinement were a surprising loss of four pounds in weight and, "I'm a little tired."

He emerged at 9:35 a.m., one week to the minute after starting the experiment in a hermetically sealed steel chamber.

Throughout the seven days Farrell breathed the same repurefied

Turn To Page 4 For More Of SPACEMAN

"We Lead All The Rest"

FARM CORNER

By Don Brandt

Bred Gilt Sale To Auction 36 Gilts, 9 Boars

The first bred gilt sale sponsored by the Lancaster County Swine Producers Assn. will open at 1 p.m. Saturday, with a consignment of 36 gilts and nine fall boars from 15 swine breeders.

The event, to be held at the Paul Z. Martin Sales Barn, Blue Ball, was planned by Earl Fisher, East Earl R1, Arlie Anderson, Elizabethtown, and Harold B. Endslow, Marietta R1.

To be listed, a gilt had to meet one of these standards.

She is a purebred; she is a cross-bred sired by a registered boar; she is a cross-bred bred to a registered boar; if grade, she is sired by or bred to a registered boar of one of the common breeds of hogs.

All gilts must have been bred after Nov. 1, 1957. The fall boars will be purebreds, farrowed between Aug. 1 and Nov. 1, 1957.

Consignment to the sale was open to any breeder who pays the

Turn To Page 15 For More Of FARM CORNER

Pedestrians Spot Beauty Shop Fire

Smoke from a fire in the rear of the Lancaster Beauty Salon, 142 N. Queen St., caused extensive damage to the interior of the building yesterday afternoon.

Fire Chief Edward Koerkle said he could not determine the cause of the blaze.

The proprietor of the shop, Justin McCarthy, 141 E. Chestnut St., estimated damage amounted to "several thousand dollars."

The blaze was discovered shortly after 2:30 p.m. by two pedestrians, John Romanos, 136 Ruby St., and Joseph Maisano, 329 N. Charlotte St. They said they saw smoke coming from the rear of the building, so they investigated.

By the time firemen arrived, the entire three-story building was filled with smoke from the fire, which was centered in a small lounge in the rear of the shop.

Chief Koerkle said "five minutes more and we would have had our hands full."

CONTENTS DESTROYED

The contents of the room were destroyed and the flames were spreading to the second floor through the ceiling when firemen arrived. Destroyed were several pieces of furniture, including a sofa and lounge chairs. Koerkle said there was a record player in the lounge, and he theorized it might have short circuted causing the blaze.

McCarthy said he had stopped in the salon to make a telephone

Turn To Page 4 For More Of FIRE

Emergency Met In All Parts Of Garden Spot

In many instances yesterday volunteer fire company equipment was employed opening the path for ambulances or other vehicles used to transport patients to hospitals.

Such was the case at Terre Hill when Earl S. Smith, 137 W. Main St., was stricken ill and ordered to the Ephrata Community Hospital by his physician.

At first, about 4:30 p. m., the New Holland ambulance was called and started out on Rt. 73 to meet the Terre Hill Fire Co. However both turned back after getting only within three miles of each other.

Then, shortly before 6 p. m., Harry M. Mattis, a neighbor, offered the use of his four-wheeled drive jeep. Mattis started out with Smith as his passenger and the Terre Hill Fire Co. engine in the lead.

At Martindale they picked up the Martindale Fire Co. engine and a wrecker belonging to Jared Stauffer, Martindale. At Hinkletown, after making the trip through fields at some places, the caravan was met by State Police. Between Hinkletown and Ephrata, near the Bergstrasse Church, Smith was transferred to the Ephrata ambulance which completed the trip to the hospital.

A Maytown youth, believed stricken with appendicitis, made it to the Lancaster General Hospital late yesterday afternoon through the joint cooperation of the Maytown and Marietta firemen, and the Marietta ambulance crew.

The boy was Bobby Frank, son

Turn To Page 4 For More Of EMERGENCIES

Garbage Pickups On

Regular garbage collections were scheduled to be attempted this morning by the Grimm Disposal Service, holders of the city's garbage collection contract.

Commissioner John F. S. Rees said that Grimm informed him last night that his trucks would be out, although snow was piled as high as four feet along city sidewalks and curbs.

Storm Takes Lives Of Area Man, Woman

Two Lancaster County residents died in yesterday's heavy snowfall, apparently as a result of over-exertion while walking to and from work.

Dead are Mr. William L. Weaver, seventy-two, Peach Bottom, and Mrs. A. Marie Fritz, sixty-five, 433 S. West End Ave.

Weaver was stricken while walking from Wakefield to his home in Peach Bottom. He had gone to work with a State Highway's Dept. crew Saturday afternoon at 2 p.m. and worked all night on a snow plow. After getting off work at 11 a.m. yesterday and leaving the snow plow in Wakefield, he began to walk the half mile to his home.

His son Dennis F. Weaver, and Charles Grimsey, Wakefield constable, a neighbor, discovered his body lying in a field he had evidently cut across to shorten the distance to his home.

Mrs. Fritz died at 7 p.m. in Lancaster General Hospital after

Turn To Page 4 For More Of DEATHS

ONE EDITION

The customary three editions of the Intelligencer Journal are combined today in a final edition. Because of the severe weather conditions and hazardous highways, additional time was provided to aid delivery of the newspaper.

Man, Wife Marooned For Night In Stalled Truck

The right decision and a stroke of luck combined to save a county couple from a potential tragedy last night when the pickup truck in which they were riding became snowbound in an open field between Silver Springs and Mountville.

Phares Ray and his wife Ethel, who live on the Silver Springs-Mountville Rd., at Horizon Drive, were rescued from the truck at about 9 a.m. today after spending the night in the cab with the heater running.

The adventure began normally enough early yesterday evening when the Rays decided to have dinner at the Silver Springs Hotel. The snow didn't seem too bad at the time, Mrs. Ray said, and they didn't expect any difficulty.

MAKE RIGHT CHOICE

When they were ready to leave, however, they decided it might be a good idea to take their pickup truck instead of the family car since the truck had chains. This settled, they left for the hotel with their seventeen year-old son, Rodney.

After dinner Mr. and Mrs. Ray thought it best to start back home immediately and advised Rodney to accompany them. The boy, however, told them not to worry about him and went to see a girl friend at Florin. The Rays started home.

As they drove along the road

Turn To Page 4 For More Of COUPLE

NECK BROKEN

Youth Gravely Hurt Plunging Into Snow

A fifteen-year-old city boy was critically injured when he either fell or dove head first from the front porch of his home into a snow drift yesterday afternoon. The youngster suffered a broken neck.

Admitted to Lancaster General Hospital following the mishap was Thomas Lewis, son of Mr. and Mrs. Berton Lewis, 569 S. Duke St.

A hospital spokesman said the boy was in critical condition last night. He underwent surgery to relieve pressure on his spinal column, it was reported, and the boy was paralyzed from his neck down.

Mrs. Lewis said Thomas and his brother, Eugene, fourteen, and several other youngsters in the neighborhood were jumping from the front porch ' their home into a snowdrift about six feet deep. The bottom of the drift was about four feet from the top of the porch.

She said apparently Thomas lost his footing and either jumped or fell headfirst into the drift. He started to scream and his companions pulled him from the drift onto the sidewalk. Mrs. Lewis said he was crying and complained of his back hurting him when she ran out of the house to his aid.

She called the hospital ambulance. The accident occurred around 3 p.m. Mrs. Lewis said the boy landed in the snow headfirst, but she said he apparently hit only snow. There were no other objects buried in the drift.

Tracks of the Lancaster-Columbia branch of the Pennsylvania Railroad are completely covered after Saturday night's snowfall. Only the main line of the PRR remained open, but trains were running hours behind schedule. This view is from the Rohrerstown bridge looking toward Lancaster. (Intell Photo)

New Era Photo

Teenagers have a smoke and a coke last night, during a dance at the Malta Temple.

TOUR OF HANGOUTS

What's Good and Bad About Teenage Nightlife

City juvenile officer John E. Ehleiter toured Lancaster's teenage hangouts last night. He found hundreds of teenagers having a good time—and a few getting into serious trouble.

In a four-hour patrol of the city's eastern and southern parts, Ehleiter checked pool rooms, steak shops, a teenage dance and recreation clubs.

These were the trouble spots:

Two eighteen-year-old boys drinking beer in the 300 block of Church St., beside the empty caramel factory.

A sixteen-year-old girl and a boy about fifteen playing pool in an unlicensed pool room in Sunnyside.

These were the good things:

Eleven boys maintaining an athletic and social club in a garage in the 500 block of W. King St. The boys are called "The Diamonds," and have paid for most of their equipment themselves.

Two hundred fifty teenagers dancing to rock 'n roll in the Malta Temple. Most of the girls wore brightly-colored slacks and the boys wore shirts open at the collar. A few had black leather jackets.

More than one hundred boys playing ping pong, basketball, and working in the wood shop at the Boys' Club.

A girls' basketball game at Crispus Attucks Center.

Ehleiter concluded: "For the most part, the places Lancaster's teenagers go at night are 'good. They are supervised and nobody goes wrong. There are only a few bad spots; they're the ones I watch the most."

Will Do It Often

Yesterday was the first time Ehleiter patrolled the city at night. He's going to be doing it a lot from now on. It's the idea of Police Chief William B. Hershner, who thinks keeping in close contact with teenagers is one of the best ways to keep them out of trouble.

Ehleiter's job on these patrols will be to walk into a place, talk casually with the teenagers, make sure everything is all right, and leave. He'll be looking for one thing.

Will Act On Violations

"I want to find places that are making kids delinquent," said Ehleiter. "Places that aren't good for teenagers to go to. Many of these places are pool rooms, others are small restaurants and steak shops. It helps if the proprietors see me stop in. But I intend to close down the places that I find violating the law."

Ehleiter was accompanied last night by a New Era reporter and Anthony Guarna, assistant county probation and parole officer. This is a familiar routine to Guarna, he's been making nighttime tours for more than a year and one-half.

The Sunnyside Pool Room is one of the places Ehleiter says "aren't good for teenagers to go to." It is a dirty one-room shack with no toilet. There are three pinball machines, a tiny snack bar and a pool table.

Ehleiter and Guarna checked it twice. At 6:15 p.m., a girl and boy, both underage, were playing pool. No adult was around. At 9:20 p.m., the proprietor, John Wolfensberger, was there.

"I saw minors playing pool in here," Ehleiter told him.

"I didn't know it," Wolfensberger replied. "If I knew it, they wouldn't play."

"You'd better know it," Ehleiter said. "You'll be closed if this keeps up."

No Pool Room Permit

Then Ehleiter checked the pool room licenses. He found one for bowling, but none for pool. That was reported to licensing authorities today.

Ehleiter and Guarna drove around for a time, slowing the cruiser to look into a dozen places. A lot were closed.

On Church St., Guarna said suddenly, "Hold it." He'd seen two boys drinking beer. Ehleiter and Guarna ran from the car, stopped the boys, retrieved two half-empty bottles from a snow drift where the boys had quickly placed them. The boys are James D. Kiscaden, 630 W. Orange St., and David P. Singleton Jr., 586 N. Plum St. Both are eighteen.

Boys Held Overnight

They were held overnight in the police station for questioning. "Mainly we wanted to find out where they got the beer," Ehleiter said. "That's all the lead we needed." This morning Singleton was released. Kiscaden, a parolee, was still held pending a decision by Guarna.

The next stop was a two-car garage at the rear of 505 W. King St. For many months it has been a clubhouse for eleven boys, "The Diamonds." The boys sold Christmas cards to help buy furnishings, and some were donated by parents.

The garage contains a wood stove, a television set, a record player, two couches, some chairs and a movie projector. Walls are painted red or lined with red oilcloth.

When Ehleiter walked in, two boys were boxing on a linoleum square. Around the room was a barbell, punching bag and basketball hoop. Nothing was new but the boys were proud of all of it. "The parents of one boy let us start the club," said a sixteen-year-old, "after he got in trouble. Several of us were in trouble before the club. None of us have been since it was organized."

Girls are allowed in the club only for weekend dances.

Dance Is Good Example

One of the stops was a weekly dance at the Malta Temple sponsored by the Starlite Club. It was noisy but orderly. Many teenagers greeted Guarna and Ehleiter by their first names. The second-floor dance room was filled. Downstairs groups were watching a movie, playing cards and ping pong.

"Places like this dance, Crispus Attucks and the Boys' Club are fine," Ehleiter said at the end of his tour. "The trouble is the teenagers you want to go there usually don't go. 'I don't want to be a square,' they say.

"The only thing we can do is to keep checking them."

BLOW FOR LOVE: LICENSE FEE KEPT AT $2

LANSING, Mich. (AP)—Michigan lawmakers struck a blow for love and romance yesterday. By a 22-67 vote, the House killed a bill to raise the cost of a marriage license in Michigan from $2 to $5.

Rep. Adolph Blanchard of Bay City, who handled marriage license applications for 18 years as Bay City county clerk, said: "Five dollars is too much to ask for the privilege of getting married."

Rep. Chester Wozniak of Detroit asserted it was a matter of personal opinion. Married a little over a year, he said: "If I were to do it again, I wouldn't mind paying $5."

'Stock' Plan in Hospital Drive

About 16,000 Lancaster county residents will be asked to buy "shares" in their own security during the special gifts campaign of the Lancaster General Hospital capital fund drive.

The "stock plan" will be carried to the people by about 2,000 volunteer workers in the drive, it was announced by Richard Oblender, general chairman.

The people will be asked to give $10 monthly for a year. The $120 total is being called one share of the hospital drive.

Oblender, said a special pledge card has been designed similar to a time payment book. Persons pledging funds under the plan will receive a book to be mailed to the hospital each month with the $10 check.

The special gifts division has a goal of $250,000. The overall goal of the fund drive is $2,750,000 for construction and equipment for four additional floors atop the hospital.

Mrs. Frederick O. Schweizer and Albert B. Wohlsen, Jr. are chairmen of the special gifts group. Clarence C. Newcomer is chairman of the city division and Mrs. Ross E. Long and Mrs. Herbert K. Cooper, Jr. are co-chairmen of the county division.

9 Drink Wood Alcohol, Die

NEW YORK (AP)—Nine persons have died here this week from drinking wood alcohol.

Detectives have been assigned to locate the source of supply before more lives are claimed.

Four men and two women died after attending a Sunday night party in Harlem. Three men, not known to have attended the party, died yesterday.

600 at Union Lenten Service

Approximately 600 persons attended the first of the Downtown Churches Union Lenten Services last night at First Reformed Church, 40 E. Orange St.

The Rev. Wallace E. Fisher, pastor of Trinity Lutheran Church spoke on "Prayer." The Rev. Wilbur Trexler, host pastor, was liturgist.

Music was by the choirs of Trinity Church, directed by Donald F. Nixdorf.

Rev. Cathers To Speak

The Rev. W. Edgar Cathers Jr., pastor of First Methodist Church, will speak on "Bible Study" at next Wednesday's service. Liturgist will be the Rev. R. Ray Evelan, assistant pastor of Trinity Lutheran Church.

All services start at 7:45 p.m. Churches participating in the annual series are First Reformed, First Methodist, Trinity Lutheran, St. Paul's United Church of Christ and First Presbyterian.

Man-Wife Police Team Suspended after Brawl

PHILADELPHIA (AP) — Police Commissioner Thomas J. Gibbons yesterday suspended a husband and wife, both members of the police force, after a family quarrel during which pistol shots were fired.

Suspended pending further investigation were Benjamin H. Burgis, 31, and his wife, Germaine, 30. Police said three bullets were fired during the argument.

British Plane Hits Mountain, 34 Persons Die

Stewardess, Co-pilot Trudge in Knee-Deep Snow to Tell of Crash

BOLTON, England (AP)—A chartered British airliner with 42 persons aboard smashed against a snowcovered mountain today only five minutes from its destination. A policeman at the scene said 34 persons perished.

An injured stewardess, the only woman aboard, and the copilot struggled through knee-deep snow to a television relay station on top of the mountain and gasped out the first word of the disaster.

Rescue Teams On Way

Helicopters, snowplows and mountain rescue teams fought through a blizzard to the scene.

The twin-engine Bristol Wayfarer operated by Silver City Airways, was carrying automobile dealers from the Isle of Man in the Irish Sea on a one-day junket to Manchester, only 15 miles from here, to inspect a plant of the Exide Battery Co.

Wisecracking and jovial, the party of 39 businessmen boarded the plane for the 100-mile flight, waving goodby to wives and children. There was a crew of three aboard.

Plane Smashed To Bits

Thirty-five minutes later, with visibility cut by heavy clouds and the blizzard, the plane smashed to bits against Winter Hill, near the bleak moorlands of Lancashire and only 400 yards from a lonely TV tower manned by five engineers.

The snow was so deep that no vehicle could get within a mile of the wreckage.

Bulldozers and snowplows groaned through four-foot drifts, opening the way for ambulances, when the call for help went out from the TV station. Rescuers, lugging stretchers, blankets and medicines, struggled on foot the last distance.

Fined $250 for Annoying Negro

DOYLESTOWN, Pa. (AP)—Howard R. Bentcliffe, 45, was placed on probation for one year and fined $250 yesterday after pleading guilty to burning a cross and posting a warning when the first Negro family moved into the community of Levittown last August.

Bentcliffe, agreed yesterday to base his guilty plea on evidence taken at the trial last Jan. 30 in Bucks County court. At that time, Bentcliffe collapsed when he arose to present his own case, causing a mistrial.

The defendant is charged with posting and painting signs on the property of two families who were friendly to William E. Myers Jr. and his family. He is accused also of burning a cross on a third resident's lawn.

Around Lancaster

By the New Era Staff

Missing Puzzle Pieces

Some of the granite blocks in the 500-piece jig-saw puzzle on the Conestoga National Bank turned up missing this week. But the contractor assures they are on the way. The missing pieces in the new exterior are on the S. Queen St. side of the bank, where the scaffolding has been removed.

Raymond H. Aierstock, 310 S. Marshall St., contractor for the new face, explained that the Mount Airy granite pieces are being cut now at the quarries in the Carolinas. Each piece must be cut to exact specifications and fitted in place.

Aierstock said that if the stone arrives on time and the weather holds, the remodeling should be completed by the first week in April.

Mixup in Storm

An unidentified Lancaster resident spent several turbulent hours last week when he accidentally exchanged automobiles during the storm.

The missing automobile belonged to Jacques H. Geisenberger, local attorney. Both cars had the same color paint. In the storm they looked very much alike.

The man discovered his error and notified his attorney. A quick check revealed Geisenberger as the owner of the car.

The attorney chuckled at the mistake and drove the car left on the parking lot to the man's home and made a trade.

Leader Says Pa. Needs U. S. Aid for Jobless

Also Declares 10% Of Working Force in State Is Unemployed

WASHINGTON (AP) — Gov. George M. Leader of Pennsylvania said today that with 10 per cent of its working force unemployed the Commonwealth realizes its responsibilities to create jobs but that it can wave no "magic wand", to stop the national recession.

"We're not going to be able to buck it alone," said Leader. "We need help from Washington."

The governor made his remarks before a bipartisan meeting of Pennsylvania's Congressional delegation considering ways to combat rising unemployment in the state.

Most Of GOP Absent

Leader, whose invitation to attend the session was rejected by most of the state's Republican members of Congress, was accompanied by five of his cabinet members, who outlined various attempts to create jobs at the state level.

The governor himself announced that allocation of the state motor license fund subsidies to municipalities will be accelerated to give impetus to highway building and new employment opportunities.

The state administration's plans were heard by seven of the state's 17 GOP Congressmen and by the bulk of the Democratic delegation. Republicans attending included Reps. Scott, Curtin, Stauffer, Mumma, Bush, Saylor and Fulton.

Work On Dams Proposed

Rep. Walter, chairman of the Pennsylvania Democratic delegation, urged development of the Delaware River Valley through construction of proposed dams. The work, he said, should be undertaken as soon as possible so as to create jobs.

William L. Batt Jr., state secretary of labor and industry, said unemployment is spread throughout the Commonwealth and for that reason acceleration of public works to provide jobs must be accomplished on a statewide level.

Welfare secretary Harry Shapiro called for restoration of funds that have been cut from the federal aid program for hospital construction. He said Pennsylvania's hospitals are ready to go ahead with new construction this year if additional funds are provided.

Slum Clearance Urged

Commerce secretary William R. Davlin pointed out the opportunities for new jobs that would be created by a full-scale program of slum clearance and urban renewal.

Sen. Clark (D-Pa) announced that a housing bill designed to revive middle income housing construction this spring soon will be ready in the Senate.

3 Youths Held In 'Gas' Thefts

Two Bainbridge youths charged with larceny of gasoline have posted bail for court, and a third has been petitioned into juvenile court.

Posting bail before Justice of the Peace Lester B. Weidman, Elizabethtown, were Charles Sweigart, eighteen, and Dale Stump, twenty-two. Petitioned into juvenile court was Henry Halblieb, seventeen, also of Bainbridge.

The charges were brought by Benjamin D. Waltz, police chief for W. Donegal and Conoy Twps. The gasoline thefts occurred on the farms of Leroy Rutt, in the Bossler Church area, and W. E. Mohr.

Coin Machine Probe Planned

WASHINGTON (AP)—The Senate Rackets Investigating Committee is checking on allegations of widespread tie-ups among hoodlums, labor unions and operators in the coin machine business.

Counsel Robert F. Kennedy disclosed that Chicago, Cleveland and Detroit are among places under investigation. He said committee agents also are at work in Eastern cities which he did not name.

Hearings are planned in the spring.

Woman Questioned

The inquiry came to light when Mrs. Hyman (Myrtle) Larner of Miami Shores, Fla., was questioned by the committee about records of the Chicago Coin Machine Operators Assn.

Mrs. Larner said she had none of the records, but took the Fifth Amendment on many questions.

Kennedy said the study has been going on for five or six months. "We expect to get into some of the underworld figures of the country," he said.

City Plumbing Inspector Named

Landis J. Kofroth, sixty-two, 18 Chester St., has been named to succeed William E. Martin as city plumbing inspector effective March 17.

Mayor Thomas J. Monaghan said the appointment will be submitted to City Council for approval Tuesday. Kofroth, a plumber since his youth, was foreman for Riggs Distler Co. from 1942 to 1945.

AP Wirephoto

Wheel-less Flying Car by 1978?

DETROIT (AP)—A Detroit product designer predicted today that the car of 1978 will be a wheel-less vehicle, (above) propelled by ducted fans and moving about two feet above the surface.

The prediction was made by Carl Reynolds, a one-time Chrysler designer, attending the industrial designers institute conference here.

Reynolds, who played a major role in the design of automobile tail fins, said the car he foresees would be constructed of light metal to allow a small, lightweight engine to be used. This, he said, would make altitude maintenance and control much easier.

Reynolds said the car would be much larger than today's conventional car. The front end would be low to prevent lift at high speeds. The tail section would sweep back and a vertical and directional stabilizer would be used. The car would have ability to climb to an altitude of 100 feet.

"Upon limited access highways for inter-city travel," he added, "electronic devices, perhaps involving a guide beam or radiation system, will provide automatic steering and speed control."

About 100 leading product designers are attending the conference.

ANOTHER ICE CHUNK FALLS NEAR READING

READING (AP)—Mr. and Mrs. Edward Stork, of Shillington, have reported that a large chunk of ice apparently fell from the sky, nearly striking their car.

The couple reported they were driving on the Lancaster turnpike near Gouglersville yesterday when the ice fell.

Dr. Malcolm Reider, Reading research chemist, is analyzing the ice. He has been studying various ice specimens that have fallen from the sky in the area in the past year. It is believed the ice may have formed on commercial aircraft and fallen to earth.

4 in Assembly Running Again

Local Republican memebrs of the State Assembly will be candidates for reelection.

Primary petitions have been prepared for Paul G. Murray, representative of the city district in the State Assembly; and Norman Wood, Baker Royer and Edwin D. Eshleman, county representatives.

The petitions are expected to be circulated tomorrow.

Dague Petitions Prepared

At the same time, petitions have been prepared for Congressman Paul B. Dague, Downingtown, Republican representative of the Lancaster-Chester district, who will seek the Republican nomination for reelection, and for Maj. Gen. Daniel B. Strickler a candidate for the Republican gubernatorial nomination.

Three representatives on the State Republican committee also will seek reelection. They are: B. J. Myers, Richard M. Martin and Mrs. Helen G. Brown.

Strickler Workers Busy

Nomination petitions in behalf of Maj. Gen. Strickler have been distributed to every county in the state and today workers in his behalf were obtaining signatures which will qualify him for a place on the Primary election in May.

Senator Edward J. Kessler, of Lancaster, and Thomas A. Ehrgood, Lebanon, who represents the northern Lancaster and Lebanon district in the senate, are not up for election this year.

On the Democratis side, petitions are being circulated in behalf of Roy E. Furman who is a candidate for the Democratic gubernatorial nomination.

Regional Plan At Standstill

The Lancaster Regional Planning Commission will take up the question of what to do next, at its meeting Wednesday at 7:30 p. m. at the Municipal Building.

The commission has been waiting for action by the county commissioners or a proposal to establish a county-wide planning commission.

No decision on this request has been made. Instead, the commissioners appropriated $2,500 to cover the cost of a planning study by a volunteer committee. The group is to sound out sentiment about planning on any scale and file a report.

The planning commission will discuss whether to go ahead with its own program involving 10 member municipalities, or wait to see the outcome of the county study committee.

CAM JAMMERS TO MEET

The Lancaster Cam Jammers will meet at 2:30 p. m. Sunday at the club house in Conestoga to discuss reopening the Lincoln Highway West drag strip on April 5.

Son of Adenauer Tours Plant Here

Says W. Reich Economy Depends On Competition of Small Business

West Germany can't continue to have a healthy economy unless small businesses are given a chance to practice competition, the Rev. Paul Adenauer said here today.

Rev. Adenauer, son of the Chancellor of Germany, visited the plant of the Dodge Cork Co. as the guest of Arthur B. Dodge, president of the firm.

The visit was part of a seven-week investigation of small business practices in the U. S. being conducted by Rev. Adenauer, a Roman Catholic Priest, for his doctoral thesis from the Institute of Christian Social Sciences at Muenster, Germany.

Interested In Application

He said he was particularly interested in how American small business methods could be applied in Germany.

"The drift toward the cartels like Farben and Krupp began shortly after World War II," Rev. Adenauer said, "but now they've been stopped by legislation which took effect this year and which will encourage the competition of small business."

Speaking of his stern-visaged father, Rev. Adenauer said, "He isn't at all like he appears in his pictures. Instead of a cold dedicated politician, he's a warm and outgoing man whose greatest delight is in his 18 grandchildren.

"In spite of the fact that he's 82, his health is excellent and he just returned from a holiday in the south of France ready to tackle his job again."

Lauds Father's Hardiness

To illustrate the hardiness of his father, Rev. Adenauer described the recent January birthday party of the German Chancellor. "He began at nine in the morning, spent the day at official functions, and ended up after midnight at a family party," he said.

Rev. Adenauer, thirty-five, is making his headquarters at Georgetown University, Washington, D. C., during his U. S. stay.

Big Pa. Liquor Order Rejected

HARRISBURG (AP)—The auditor general's office today refused to approve $500,000 in liquor orders given by the State Liquor Control Board to obtain a special discount of $8,000.

Alfred T. Novello, deputy auditor general, said the department refused approval because the discount would not be passed on to the public in reduced prices.

"It is obvious that these purchases will have to be warehoused for long periods of time at heavy expense plus hidden administrative costs," Novello wrote the commission.

Ties Up Funds

"When we find that purchases will result only in tying up nearly half a million dollars in liquor control board funds for six months or more without earning anything, we must exercise discretion to disapprove the purchases," he added.

"Clearly excessive purchases which result in no benefit to the commonwealth, the consuming public and the taxpayers will not be approved," he added.

He said warehouse costs would exceed the $8,000 granted as discount to induce the purchase.

Fuchs Only 180 Miles From British Base

AUCKLAND, New Zealand (AP)—Dr. Vivian Fuchs has only 180 miles of easy territory to cover before reaching Scott base, the New Zealand Press Assn. correspondent there reported today. This expedition will be the first to cross the frozen continent by land when it reaches the British Commonwealth base.

New Era Photo

Arthur B. Dodge (left) greets Rev. Paul Adenauer.

Paratroopers Battle Rebels In Sumatra

Fighting Near Major Installations of U. S. Caltex Oil Fields

PAKANBARU (AP) — Central Sumatra government paratroopers landed in force today and locked in combat with rebel forces in this Central Sumatra heartland where the U. S. Caltex Oil Co. has major installations.

The Central Government launched its biggest land, air and sea offensive to wipe out the rebel movement which demands that an out-and-out anti - Communist government be set up in Jakarta.

Land On East Coast Too

Jakarta troops also landed at Dumai, on Sumatra's east coast, the one remaining Caltex oil port.

An Indonesian navy corvette took up a position off Padang, rebel port on the west coast, and gave all ships in the harbor until 10 a.m. Thursday to leave or face destruction.

The Jakarta forces at Dumai fought some skirmishes with rebel defenders. They apparently sought to drive inland to the Duri oil field, where a Caltex pipline to Dumai starts.

Prepare For Transports

The paratroopers landed on Pakanbaru's airfield and cleared it of obstructions in preparation for transport landings.

A rebel spokesman at Padang said the paratroopers landed at dawn and that by nightfall "we still have them encircled."

He said government troops had not reached the town of Pakbaru.

Djambek said government planes bombed and strafed the airfield before the paratroop landings. He cal ed the attack a "brutal deed, the same as those committed by Fascists and Communists."

He appealed to the people to fight the invaders.

"There is no other alternative but the defense of our soil," he said. "Kill them if you meet them."

Vow to Fight For Oil Fields

The rebels had vowed they would fight for the oil fields.

No Caltex evacuation was expected. Some wives and children of U.S. workers left several days ago after Caltex suspended operations. Remaining workers and their families had been ordered to concentrate near here, the headquarters of Caltex operations.

The feeling here was tense but there was no panic because both the rebels and the Central Government gave assurances on the safety of American lives and interests.

Government forces apparently were seeking to retake control of the Central Sumatra oil areas and bring oil royalties back into Jakarta hands. The rebels have been bartering the oil and collecting royalties for themselves.

Dumai is 100 miles north of here. A good road built by Caltex could take the Dumai invaders down toward Duri and Pakanbaru. The paratroopers began advancing up the road shortly after their landings.

Admit Rebel Victory

In Jakarta, the usually reliable newspaper Sulah Indonesia reported that the Central Government military commander in the North Celebes had conceded the rebels have captured the port city of Gorontalo.

The trading center of more than 15,000 persons was captured by forces of Lt. Col. D. J. Somba, who supports the rebel government in Central Sumatra.

CAR TAGS SENT ABROAD HIT BY PA. OFFICIAL

ATLANTIC CITY, N. J. (AP)—Royalty or no, auto license plates should go only to residents, says the director of Pennsylvania's Bureau of Highway Safety.

O. D. Shipley, attending a regional leadership conference of the President's Committee for Traffic Safety here, said Pennsylvania should stop sending licenses to former residents now living in foreign countries.

"We are even sending a Pennsylvania license to the princess of Monaco each year," Shipley complained. The princess is former movie actress Grace Kelly, whose parents still live in Philadelphia.

River Filter Unit Operating

The city's filter plant at Columbia was eased back into operation today after a two-week shutdown blamed on a "shot" of oil from the Susquehanna river.

The water will not be fed into the city system until it has been thoroughly tasted and tested and found to be "good drinkable water," said James J. Malone, acting city water superintendent.

Oil Still Picked Up

Malone said the oil still is being picked up from the river and that an oil slick was noted in the clarifier or sedimentation tank shortly before the test started at noon.

Chemical treatment at the plant has been juggled in an effort to find the right combination that will eliminate the oil and avoid the heavy medicinal taste that characterized the water two weeks ago.

Add Chlorine Later

A major change is that chlorine isn't being added until the final stage of treatment, and that activated carbon is being added to combat disagreeable odors and tastes, Malone said.

The last "bad" water was blamed on the chlorine reacting with phenolic oil. The revised treatment is designed to filter out the oil before the chlorine is added.

Malone said he expects to know by tomorrow morning whether the new setup is working properly.

"When we're satisfied it's good drinkable water, we'll send it through" to the reservoir at Oyster Point from where it will feed into the city mains, he said.

17 Bottles of Whisky Stolen

Burglars entered the Lancaster Labor Association Club No. 285, 202 W. Liberty St., early today and stole 17 bottles of whisky. No estimate was made of the loss.

Sixteen of the bottles were open and equipped with automatic shot pourers. One of the open bottles was full and the others only partly-filled. In addition, a full unopened bottle of whisky was taken.

After 2 A. M.

The burglary occurred between 2 a.m. when the club closed and 6:55 a.m., when Ronald Roberts, 740 S. Plum St., the day bartender, reported for work.

Detective David Rineer and Lt. Robert Swab, who are investigating, said entrance was gained by breaking a rear window. The thieves left with their loot through the front door. Nothing else was disturbed.

The whisky supply was kept on a rack under the bar.

Mack Denies Any Pressure In TV Case

Tells Probers Talks With Involved Miami Friends 'BotheredMe'

WASHINGTON (AP) — Former FCC Commissioner Richard A. Mack said today nobody put any pressure on him in a contested Miami television channel case — "they bothered me."

Mack, telling reporters he felt not too good, returned for questioning before a House subcommittee investigating alleged pressures and influences on the Federal Communications Commission.

Mack broke off his previous testimony before the committee almost two weeks ago and resigned from the FCC 10 days ago.

Several Contacted Him

Mack testified several people contacted him concerning the contest over TV Channel 10 in Miami.

"Nobody put any pressure on me," he said. "They talked to me, and I don't react to pressure."

Then Mack said, "Let me put it this way—they bothered me."

Asked what he meant by "bother," Mack said he had lived in Florida all his life, he had known some of the people involved in the Channel 10 case for years and they contacted him.

Can't Slam Door on Friend

When he used the term, "bothered," Mack said—"It's pretty hard to slam the door on a friend." He told the questioner, Rep. Harris (D-Ark), committee chairman, he thought Harris had had the same experience in legislation.

Harris said, "If I were you I think I'd go a little stronger."

And Rep. Mack (D - Ill) said "bothered" was "an understatement."

The committee dismissed Mack from its witness chair after about an hour and a half without asking him to name all those who had "bothered" him.

Contrast in Partings

The parting was a strange contrast to Mack's departure from the witness chair 10 days, helped by an aide. He left then under a tongue lashing from Harris who called Mack a "tool" of his friends and demanded he resign from the FCC.

This time, Harris thanked Mack for his cooperation and said "I wish you the best."

"I appreciate your courtesy," Mack said. "When you get down to Florida, come to see me."

When a reporter asked Mack if he had any immediate plans, he replied, "No, not now."

4 Youths Held for Boxcar Thefts

Four Washington Boro teenagers today were taken into custody by Columbia state police for burglarizing freight cars of about $100 in merchandise early last month.

Troopers said the boys, all of whom admitted the crime, will be held pending disposition of their case by juvenile authorities. One of the suspects is fifteen, the other three sixteen.

Some of the five cases of canned ham and lunchmeat and three cases of wine taken from Pennsylvania Railroad freight cars parked in Washington Boro were recovered, police said. State police worked with Sgt. Joseph Frantz of PRR police, who directed the investigation.

Ex-Reading Man Mate for Stassen

LOCK HAVEN (AP) — A Clinton County Republican leader said today Frank C. Hilton, formerly of Reading, will run for lieutenant governor in the May primary on a ticket headed by Harold E. Stassen for governor.

Sheriff George E. Hickoff, a member of the GOP state executive committee, said Hilton called him today and asked that he circulate nomination petitions on his behalf.

Hilton was formerly national commander of the Veterans of Foreign Wars and a late appointee as property and supplies secretary in the administration of former Gov. John S. Fine.

Conestoga Val. Opens Equipment Bids Apr. 8

Bids for furnishings and equipment for the new Conestoga Valley Joint High School will be opened by the joint board at 7:30 p. m. April 8.

At its meeting last night, the board announced bids will be sought for the items. Teachers will hold a joint meeting next Wednesday to acquaint themselves with operation of the three-municipality jointure.

7 Men Leave Here for Army

Seven local men left for the Army this morning. They took a bus from draft board 84 offices, 20 S. Duke St.

The men are:

Lee Roy K. Renier, nineteen, Quarryville R1; Howard W. Brackbill, twenty-two, Smoketown; Glenn F. Gainer, twenty-two, Holtwood R2; Chester T. Seig Jr., twenty-two, Pequea; John L. Baker, twenty-two, Lancaster R7; William L. Eby, twenty-two, Kinzer R1; Richard B. Blantz, twenty-two, Quarryville.

Around Lancaster

By the New Era Staff

Downtown Scene

Dr. George R. Huber, optometrist at 220 N. Duke St., is a handy man with the camera and caught this one-horse vehicle parked in front of his office.

The farmer tied his horse and buggy to the standard of a parking meter in front of Dr. Huber's office. The horse pushed a bit over the yellow line but it would take the wisdom of a Solomon to decide whether the vehicle was legally parked.

Cave Open Again

A cave in Lititz Springs Park, closed for many years, has been reopened as part of the program to fix up the park.

Elmer H. Bobst, chairman of the board of Warner Lambert Pharmaceuticals, Inc., asked that the cave be opened because he remembered it that way when he was a child in Lititz.

The 40-feet deep cave was closed to keep children out of it. The Lititz Springs Park Trustees now plan to erect a screen about ten feet back from the cave mouth.

They estimate it will cost $75 to remove a stone cover from the cave entrance, and erect the screen.

Bobst recently donated $100,000 to repair the park.

Reason For Pause

City Council was a bit startled yesterday when the Bureau of Police asked for money to buy a whip.

No, it wasn't an error. It turned out to be a radio aerial, the long whip-like type. Council granted the request.

Penn Manor OK's Dress Like This - -

Sport shirt, crewneck sweater, khaki pants.

New Era Photos

Straight skirts, blouses, cardigans and dress.

Immediate reaction of parents to Penn Manor High School's new student code of dress is "very favorable," Principal A. Landis Brackbill said today.

"I've received more than ten telephone calls from parents, and only two of them have been opposed to the code," Brackbill said.

Pictures above, posed by Penn Manor students, show examples of clothes given an okay by the code. The boys are Jim Kirk, left, and Jack McDonald. The girls, left to right, are Mary Lou McClellan, Joan Robb, Marlene Stekervetz and Joyce Perry.

Pictures at right were taken of teenagers around the city. They show clothing ruled out by Penn Manor.

- - But Not This

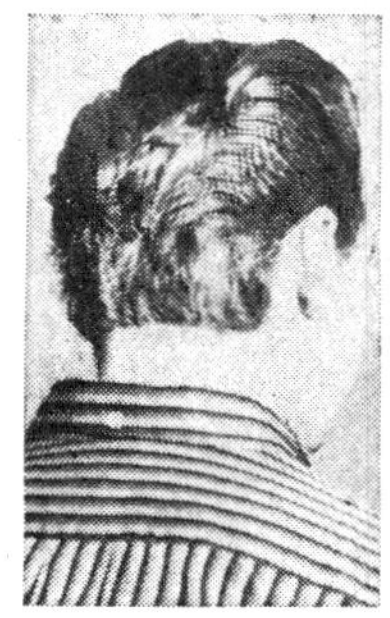

Duck tail haircut.

Tight sweater.

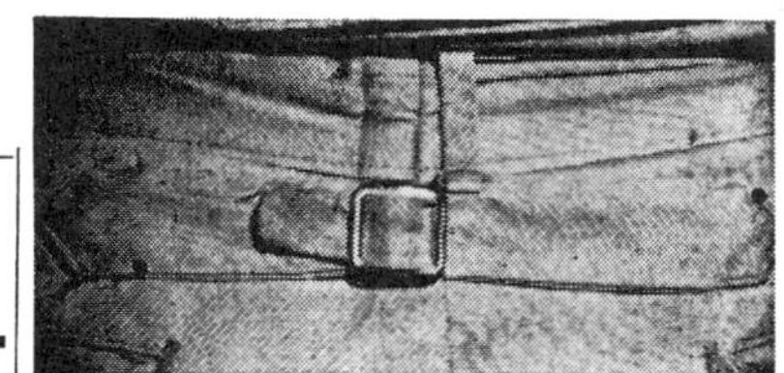

Ivy league buckle.

Motorcycle jacket, boots, tight levis.

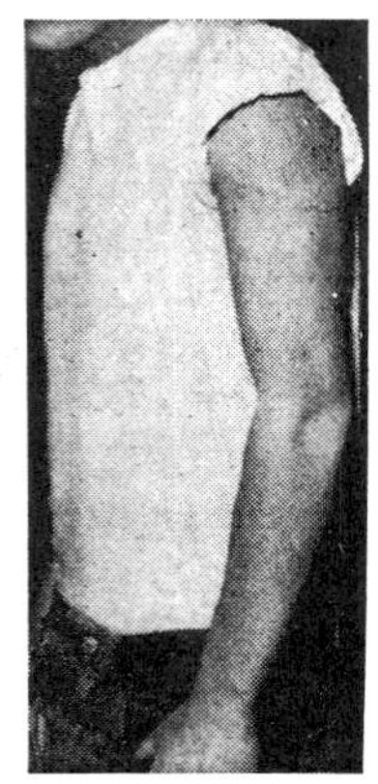

T-shirt, no belt.

Shoe cleats.

THIRD IN CLASS

DAR Bars German from Good Citizenship Award

MARLBORO, Mass. (AP)—Should a high school girl, born in Germany and still a German citizen, be eligible for a good citizenship award of the Daughters of the American Revolution?

Marlboro High School authorities say she should.

The DAR says she shouldn't.

The problem arose when Ilse Naujoks, Marlboro High senior, was nominated by the faculty and classmates for the award, given for dependability, service, leadership and patriotism.

DAR Disqualifies Her

The DAR's Massachusetts state regent, Mrs. Alfred E. Graham, notified the school committee last night that the award is made only to U. S. citizens and hence Miss Naujoks is disqualified.

High School Principal John F. Francis replied that in 17 years the school has submitted nominations "never once has U.S. citzenship been mentioned as a requirement."

Mrs. Graham said she did not make the ruling disqualifying Miss Naujoks. She said she submitted the question to the DAR's national officers.

Citizenship Award

"After all," she said, "it is a citizenship award."

Mrs. Graham said a similar case arose in Colorado and was decided the same way.

Francis said the girl had "begged off" from talking with newsmen about the controversy. He said he assumed she wanted to spare her parents unwanted publicity.

The girl is 18, daughter of Mr. and Mrs. Fritz Naujoks, who came to the United States six years ago. Francis said she ranks third in a class of 101, topped by two boys.

Probers atOdds On Kohler Case

WASHINGTON (AP) — Sen. Curtis (R-Neb) told the Senate Rackets Committee today "I'm not satisfied with the investigation taking place here" into violence in the Kohler Co. strike.

Chairman McClellan (D - Ark) told him "there is no disposition by the committee or any member of its staff not to get the truth" as to whether the company or the striking United Auto Workers Union was to blame for violent acts.

Can't Pin Responsibility

McClellan said local police in Wisconsin and detectives hired by the company when the violence was at its height in 1954 couldn't pin down who was responsible.

"The whole thing was reprehensible from my viewpoint," he said. "But I'm not going to take the blame for this committee's not being able to dig it up four years later."

In testimony later a UAW unionist said the Kohler Co. triggered a near riot in 1955 during which company officials have said they were threatened by a cursing mob.

Robert Treuer of Sheboygan, Wis., a public relations man for the UAW, told the Senate Rackets Committee he thinks the presence of Edmund Biever, manager of the struck Kohler Co. plant, "triggered this thing."

DRIVER PLEADS GUILTY

Walter Andrew Weaver, 359 S. Queen St., pleaded guilty to a charge of drunken driving. Sentencing was deferred until Friday.

Weaver was arrested Dec. 14 by city policeman Raymond Antonelli.

COMIC CONTEST ENDS MONDAY

There is still time left to enter the Lancaster Newspapers, Inc. contest "Name Your Favorite Comic."

Entries must be postmarked not later than Monday, March 17.

Just name your favorite comic in the New Era, Intelligencer Journal or Sunday News. Prizes are three table radios and six camera sets in each of three age categories. The age groups are 12 and under, 13 to 19 and 20 and over. Entries must show name, age, address, telephone number and name of newspaper in which comic strip appears.

RUSSIAN BALLET WILL TOUR U. S. CITIES IN 1959

MOSCOW (AP) — Impresario Sol Hurok signed an agreement today to bring the famous Bolshoi Theater Ballet to the United States for a tour. A number of details remain to be worked out.

The ballet agreed to visit the United States for what Hurok said would be a minimum eight-week engagement in April, 1959, opening at New York's Metropolitan Opera. A minimum of 150 performers will make the trip, one of the biggest tours of the Bolshoi's history.

There has been no agreement yet on which of the company's prima ballerinas will make the tour.

More Snow Fence Assured

The southern end of the county has been promised more snow fencing next winter, a spokesman for Fulton Grange said today.

Charles G. McSparran, Peach Bottom, reported the promise was made by Fred Wagner, superintendent of the local office of the State Highways Department. McSparran headed a grange committee which conferred with Wagner some two weeks ago and requested more fencing. Bad conditions which followed last month's severe snow storm were cited.

More Sent to North

According to McSparran, the southern sections had about half the amount of fencing supplied in the past. McSparran quoted Wagner as saying the reduction in fencing was made by the Highways Department because it felt the southern counties in the state needed less than those in the north.

However, McSparran said snow storms usually come down the river, hitting the rolling countryside hard and causing much drifting.

Results of the conference were aired at a grange meeting Monday night. McSparran also reported Wagner will pass on his committee's request to widen Route 72 between the Buck and Smithville from two to three lanes this summer.

Square Traffic StudyNext Wk.

A detailed study of Penn Square traffic will be made on Wednesday and Friday of next week, Robert M. Chryst, city traffic engineer, said today.

A team of between six and eight men will make the study between 8 a.m. and noon and 2 to 6 p.m.

They will record the number and type of vehicles that travel through the square, how the vehicles enter and leave the square, and the effect the monument has on traffic flow in the square.

Bus Stop Trial Later

The study was ordered by the City Traffic Bureau to help determine whether bus stops should be set up in the corners of the square. Another phase will be creation of trial bus stops in the corners. Date for this hasn't been set, Chryst said, but it will be done during the evening hours of slack traffic.

Next week's survey will be postponed to the following week in case of bad weather, Chryst said.

He said members of the team that will do the work will be briefed at a session Tuesday at 2 p.m.

H. S. Equipment Costs $111,881

Manheim Twp. School District has awarded $111,881.80 in contracts for part of the equipment in its new high school now under construction.

Equipment purchased included auditorium seats, chair-desks, cafeteria seats, and materials for home economics, science and library.

American Seating Co., Harrisburg, received contracts totaling $50,443.80; William M. Kishbaugh, Metalab Co., $24,890; C. G. Wall Associates, Upper Darby, $20,000; Remington-Rand, $14,455.90, and L. B. Herr and Son, $2,092.20.

Queen Awaiting Divorce Word

COLOGNE, Germany (AP)—Iran's Queen Soraya was reported awaiting word from Tehran that Shah Mohammed Reza Pahlevi has divorced her.

The Shah was reported concerned over lack of a male heir. Soraya, his wife of seven years, is childless.

She is said to have rejected a proposal that the Shah take a second wife who could present him with a son. This is permissible under Moslem law.

Mayor, Hershner Discuss Police Dept.

Mayor Thomas J. Monaghan conferred for 1 1-2 hours this morning with Police Chief William B. Hershner.

Monaghan said the entire department and its operation were discussed, but that no decision was reached on filling of vacancies created by recent promotions.

COULD BUILD HIGHWAY

Seven Miles of Concrete Going Into PP&L Plant

Enough concrete for seven and one-half miles of two-lane highway, or 20,000 cubic yards, will be used in building foundations of a huge power plant on Brunner Island, Pennsylvania Power and Light Co. said today.

PP&L announced Hughes Foulkrod Co., Philadelphia, has a contract to supply several hundred workers to build the foundations. PP&L will provide construction materials for the $50,000,000 plant, to be located in the Susquehanna River opposite Bainbridge.

PP&L declined to estimate how much the work will cost. It said construction of foundations for the main power plant, office building, transformers, switchyard, turbines, water intake and coal handling facilities will be completed in 1958 or early next year.

More than 1,500 tons of steel will be used, and almost one and one-half miles of water pipe, up to eight feet in diameter.

Hughes-Foulkrod will build a 240-foot bridge over a stream, and relocate and pave a dirt road. Dikes will be placed along the river bank near water intake pipes.

Preliminary work on the 766-acre plant site started several months ago. The 330,000 kilowatt plant, largest single unit in the PP&L system, is scheduled to be finished late in 1960.

Museum Curator Is Given New Job

Robert P. L. Frick, state field museum curator assigned to the Landis Valley Farm Museum, today got a new job.

He was appointed acting chief of the Pennsylvania Historical and Museum Commission's division of historic sites and properties. Frick will continue to direct Landis Valley, in addition to 17 other historical properties maintained by the commission.